O9-CFT-959

DATE DUE			
			PRINTED IN U.S.A.

FACTS BEHIND THE SONGS

Garland Reference Library
of the Humanities (Vol. 1300)

FACTS BEHIND THE SONGS

A Handbook of American Popular Music from the Nineties to the '90s

Marvin E. Paymer
General Editor

Garland Publishing, Inc.
New York & London
1993

Riverside Community College
Library
4800 Magnolia Avenue
Riverside, California 92506

REF ML 102 .P66 F2 1993

Facts behind the songs

Copyright © 1993 Marvin E. Paymer
All rights reserved

Library of Congress Cataloging-in-Publication Data

Facts behind the songs : a handbook of American popular music from the
    nineties to the '90s / Marvin E. Paymer, general editor.
       p. cm. — (Garland reference library of the humanities ; vol. 1300)
    Includes bibliographical references and index.
    ISBN 0-8240-5240-4 (alk. paper)
    1. Popular music—United States—Dictionaries. I. Paymer, Marvin E. II. Series.
ML102.P66F2 1993   93–24342
781.64'0973—dc20   CIP
                                      MN

Printed on acid-free, 250-year-life paper
Manufactured in the United States of America

For Caroline Sarsfield Lach

Can I help but rejoice
That a song such as ours
Came to be?*

*"WITH A SONG IN MY HEART"
(Richard Rogers, Lorenz Hart)
© 1929 (Renewed) WARNER BROS. INC. &
MARLIN ENTERPRISES
All Rights Reserved. Used by Permission.

Contents

Tables

Preface

Popular song surrounds us. We hear it, sometimes unwillingly, as background music at the dental office, in the shopping mall, at the supermarket, in the elevator, or when a telephone is on hold. So much a part of twentieth-century life has this music become that we seldom pay attention to it. Yet if we listen closely, we will hear the music, the songs.

This volume is about the songs themselves: where they come from, their subject matter, the characteristics of their lyrics and music, the influences that shaped them, how they were introduced and popularized. It is conceived as a one-volume source of information about popular song in the United States from the 1890s to the 1990s.

A bewildering number of changes have occurred during those one hundred years. The venue moved from Tin Pan Alley to Broadway, and then branched out to such diverse cities as Nashville, Detroit, Memphis, and Los Angeles. Dissemination progressed from sheet music to radio, recording, film, and television. The fox trot largely overcame the waltz, the guitar the piano, electronic instruments the "acoustic." Harmonies became bolder, rhythms more pervasive. There were invasions from abroad, most notably from Britain, Brazil, France, Cuba, and Mexico. Very often the performance became more important than the song itself. Increasingly, the performer wrote the song.

Facts Behind the Songs: A Handbook of American Popular Music From the Nineties to the '90s is intended as an encyclopedic overview of a fascinating, if often neglected, body of work: twentieth-century popular song. It is our intention not to be comprehensive, but rather to survey various aspects of songs and songwriting. A survey is by nature selective. In choosing the songs for this book, we have endeavored to include all significant standards, using the criteria of record sales; radio, television, and film performance; and public familiarity. A number of lesser-known songs are also included in order to illustrate various points of the text.

Inevitably, many songs are omitted, in particular songs of fleeting popularity, or songs that failed to cross over to the mainstream from such genres as Country and Western, Folk, Rhythm and Blues, Rock 'n' Roll, Rock, or Soul. Yet we believe the songs included in this volume are a representative sampling of the vast kaleidoscope of popular music in the United States, even though they amount to only a fraction of one percent of the estimated one million songs published between the years 1890 and 1990. For more complete lists of songs, the reader is referred to two comprehensive indices, *Popular Music, 1920–1979*, edited by Nat Shapiro and Bruce Pollock (1984), and *Popular Music, 1900–1919*, edited by Barbara Cohen-Stratyner (1986)—which together list about 20,600 songs—and to the approximately 10,000 songs listed in Roger Lax and Frederick Smith's *The Great Song Thesaurus* (1989).

Only true songs, pieces with words and music, are considered in *Facts Behind the Songs*, although ragtime and other purely instrumental genres are discussed as they pertain to popular song. Also included are pre-1890 songs that relate to the text, as well as songs of foreign origin, if they achieved popularity in the United States during the period in question. The punctuation of song titles, whether it is correct or not, corresponds to that of the published edition.

Throughout this volume, songs are dated most often according to their first publication or earliest copyright in the English language. However, this dating does not always coincide with that of the medium of introduction (play, film, recording) or type of award (Academy, BMI, Grammy), the date of which may be directly cited in the text. Dating in Tables 2 to 7 and Table 15 is of the songs themselves, In other tables, dates coincide with those of the award, film premiere, or first stage production in the English language, whether it occurred in Britain or the United States.

Short lists of songs appear in a number of these articles under the rubric "Additional Songs." Where appropriate, an entry may also include a bibliography. Tables, when they appear, are all-inclusive, containing new titles as well as songs already mentioned in the article. Cross-references are provided in boldface within an article, and as a "see also" topic at its end.

There are two main sections to the book. Part I consists of the articles, arranged alphabetically. Signed articles are by contributors; all unattributed material has been written by the General Editor. Part II is a catalogue of all songs mentioned in the articles, including the title, year of publication, lyricist, composer, and the articles in which the song is discussed. By referring to the two parts of the volume interchangeably, the reader should be able effortlessly to find the "facts behind the songs."

List of Illustrations

Acknowledgments

Over the four years that have elapsed from its inception to its indexing, a number of people have helped in the preparation of this book. Above all, the sharp eyes and unerring instincts of Hermine Williams have provided constant support. Every article bears the imprint of her careful scrutiny and many of her suggestions have been incorporated into the final text. In addition, she helped greatly in preparing the Catalogue of Songs. A large debt of gratitude is also owed Edith Borroff for suggesting articles for inclusion as well for affording advice growing out of her experience in the field of American popular music.

At Garland Publishing, Guy Marco offered invaluable suggestions as to the organization of the volume and even concerning the title itself. Marie Ellen Larcada has been a steady source of strength through all stages of the endeavor. Thanks also go to Helga McCue and Kevin Bradley for their perceptive recommendations in copyediting and production.

Many others, some of them contributors, helped in various ways. In the early stages of the project, Elliott Antokoletz provided names of possible contributors. William Askin afforded technological assistance and help in the preparation of the manuscript. From Jeffrey Cahn came a wealth of information about late twentieth-century popular performers as well as a remarkable collection of photographs from the Jeff Cahn Collection. Henry Kelly demonstrated the rise of exoticism in the performance of popular music. I am also grateful to Ehrick Long for continually updating his tables of awards and to Howard Rasher for his legal advice.

As always, special thanks go to my wife, Edye, and to my children, Steve, David, Madalene, and Jonathan (and their spouses), for steadfast encouragement throughout this endeavor.

Marvin E. Paymer
Sarasota, Florida

Editors and Contributors

Associate Editor
Hermine W. Williams
Hamilton College
Clinton, New York

Consulting Editor
Edith Borroff
State University of New York at Binghamton
Binghamton, New York

Contributors
William D. Askin
Stamford, Connecticut:
    Barbershop, Gay Nineties, Player Piano

Jeffrey Cahn
Granada Hills, California:
    Country and Western, Depression Years, Disco,
    Names, Rhythm and Blues, Rock 'n' Roll, Singing
    Groups, Soul, World War I, World War II

Barry Keith Grant
Brock University
St. Catherines, Ontario, Canada:
    Cover, Doo-wop, Film Music, Film Musicals, Min-
    strel Show, Motown, Protest Song, Scat Singing,
    Top Forty, Vocalese

Henry Kelly
Ossining, New York:
    Brazil, Reggae

Ehrick V. Long
Hunter College, City University of New York
New York, New York:
    Academy Awards, Awards, *Billboard*, BMI, Grammy
    Awards, Rap, Table 1: Academy Awards (Oscars)
    for Best Song, Table 4: BMI Awards, Table 10:
    Grammy Awards, Television

Loonis McLohon
Charlotte, North Carolina:
    Arrangement, Childhood, Crossover, Repeated
    Note, Torch Song

Allen Sigel
University of Buffalo
Buffalo, New York:
    Popular Song

Don Tyler
Central Florida Community College
Ocala, Florida:
    Hit Song, Roaring Twenties, Swing, *Your Hit Parade*

Otto Werner
Colorado State University
Fort Collins, Colorado:
    Africa, Recording

Hermine W. Williams
Hamilton College
Clinton, New York:
    Freedom Song, Gospel, Opera, Religion, Women
    as Songwriters

Classified Guide to the Articles

1. Origin
Adaptation, Borrowing, Brill Building, Broadway, Classics, Collaboration, Composer-Lyricists, Composers, Film Music, Film Musicals, Harlem, Lead Sheet, Lyricists, Musical Comedy, Musical Plays, Nashville, New York City, Opera, Operetta, Performer-Songwriters, Revues, Sheet Music, Tin Pan Alley, Vaudeville, Women as Songwriters.

2. Foreign Influence
Africa, Argentina, Austria, Belgium, Brazil, Britain, Canada, Cuba, Czechoslovakia, Denmark, Foreign Influence, Foreign Language, France, Germany, Greece, Gypsy Music, Hungary, Ireland, Italy, Latin America, Mexico, Russia.

3. Domestic Influence
Bebop, Bluegrass, Blues, Cakewalk, Coon Song, Country and Western, Dixieland, Folk Song, Gospel, Jazz, Minstrel Show, Motown, Ragtime, Rhythm and Blues, Rockabilly, Soul, Swing, Zydeco.

4. Dissemination
Academy Awards, Arrangement, ASCAP, Awards, Barbershop, Big Bands, *Billboard*, BMI, Brass, Cabaret, Copyright, Cover, Crossover, Disc Jockey, Grammy Awards, Guitar, Hit Song, Instrumentation, Jukebox, Muzak, Percussion, Piano, Player Piano, Radio, Recording, Singers, Singing Groups, Song Pluggers, Strings, Television, Top Forty, Woodwinds, *Your Hit Parade*

4. Historical Survey
Depression Years, Gay Nineties, Golden Age, Landmarks of Stage and Screen, Popular Song, Roaring Twenties, World War I, World War II

6. Genre
Art Song, Ballad, Beguine, Bolero, Boogaloo, Boogie-woogie, Bossa nova, Calypso, Catalogue Song, Cha cha cha, Charleston, Conga, Dance Crazes, Doo-wop, Fox Trot, Freedom Song, Funk, Guaracha, Heavy Metal, Inspiration, Mambo, March, Merengue, Novelty Song, Occasional Song, One-step, Peabody, Polka, Pop, Protest Song, Punk Rock, Rap, Reggae, Rock, Rock 'n' Roll, Rumba, Salsa, Samba, Show Tune, Standard, Tango, Torch Song, Two-step

7. Song Subject
Age, Anatomy, Angels, Baby, Beauty, Beginning, Birds, Birth, Boating, Boy, Cardinal Points, Childhood, Christmas, Circus, Cities, Closeness, Clothing, Colors, Comparatives, Crying, Dancing, Day, Days of the Week, Depth, Doll, Dreams, Endearment, Ending, Enduring Love, Falling in Love, Farewells, Fathers, Feeling, Fire, Flowers, Food and Drink, Fools, Forgetting, Forgiveness, Friendship, Girl, Greetings, Happiness, Heaven, Height, Holidays, Home, Humor, Imagination, Jewelry, Kissing, Lady, Life, Loneliness, Love, Lovers, Luck, Madness, Magic, Man, Marriage, Meeting, Memory, Mind, Money, Months, Moods, Moon, Mothers, Mountains, Names, Nations, Night, Nonsense, Ocean, Patriotism, People, Places, Questions, Rainbow, Religion, Rivers, Romance, Seasons, Seeing, Sentiment, Sky, Sleep, Smiling, Stars, States, Streets, Subjects, Sun, Superlatives, Sweetness, Talking, Telephones, Tenderness, Thinking, Time, Time of Day, Togetherness, Trains, Travel, Trees, Waiting, Walking, Waterfront, Weather, Wishing, Woman, Wonder, World, Writing

8. Style of Music and Lyrics

AABA, Accompaniment, Alliteration, Arpeggio, Bass Line, Blue Note, Break, Broken Chord, Cadence, Call and Response, Chorus, Chromaticism, Circle of Fifths, Coda, Contractions, Countermelody, Counterpoint, Dialect, Dummy Lyrics, Dynamics, Enharmonic Equivalence, Fade-out, Form, Harmonic Rhythm, Harmony, Improvisation, Interval, Key, Length, Lyrics, Melody, Meter, Modality, Mode, Modulation, Octave, Patter, Pedal Point, Pickup, Quotation, Range, Repeated Note, Rhyme, Rhythm, Riff, Scale, Scat Singing, Sequence, Slang, Society Tempo, Syncopation, Tempo, Texture, Tonality, Triplet, Vamp, Verse, Vocalese, Waltz

Part I

The Articles

a

AABA

"AABA" denotes a formal plan that dominated the **choruses** of popular song from the 1920s through the 1950s, and continued in use to a lesser extent thereafter. Usually in a **length** of thirty-two bars, the plan designates four sections: a primary theme (A), a repetition of that theme (A), the introduction of new thematic material (B), and a recapitulation of the first idea (A).

This **form**, with its fine balance between repetition and contrast, lends itself well to popular song. Derived from the much-older ternary or song form (ABA), it is the B section—the **release**, or bridge—that supplies the contrast. Representative examples of songs in AABA form from each decade are "Five Foot Two, Eyes of Blue; Has Anybody Seen My Girl?" (1925), "As Time Goes By" (1931), "Almost Like Being in Love" (1947), "Satin Doll" (1958), "Yesterday" (1965), "What I Did for Love" (1975), and "Memory" (1981).

Very often the second A-section is slightly changed to accommodate the **modulation** to the release, giving the plan AA'BA, found in such songs as "Somebody Loves Me" (1924) and "'S Wonderful" (1927). Changes can also occur in the last A-section, giving the plan AABA'; examples are "Moonlight in Vermont" (1944) and "Cabaret" (1966), both of which have **codas**.

Needless to say, many other varieties of form—and even apparent formlessness—exist in popular song. A slightly earlier favorite could be schematized as ABAC, where the primary theme (A) is followed by a second idea (B), then a return to the first theme (A), and a new idea (C); examples are "Mary's a Grand Old Name" (1905), "My Melancholy Baby" (1912), and "April Showers" (1921).

The emergence of **country and western, folk, rock 'n' roll,** and **rock** in mid-century saw a reaction against the thirty-two-bar song in AABA form. Formal ideas often reverted to the strophic song and narrative ballad of the 1890s. For example, the form of the 1960 song "A Taste of Honey" can be schematized as ABABAB. Pete Seeger's "Where Have All the Flowers Gone?" (1961) merely repeats verses, giving a formal plan of AAA.

Sometimes AABA form is expanded by recapitulating the release and A-section. An example is the 1981 song "Memory," from *Cats*, with a formal plan of AABABA—with the last two repeats moving to a higher **key**. The 1976 song "Theme from Mahogany (Do You Know Where You're Going To?)," is even more expansive, repeating the release and two statements of the A-section in a succession of keys, giving the plan AABABAA.

But songs in simple AABA form, the favored form of **Tin Pan Alley** and the **Golden Age,** continued to be written into the 1990s.

ACADEMY AWARDS

The Academy of Motion Picture Arts and Sciences presented its first awards to honors to the 1927–28 film season. Since that time, its **awards,** called "Oscars," have been given annually in more than twenty areas of achievement. Inasmuch as most early films were silent, there were no music awards until the advent of sound in the late 1920s and its subsequent development during the 1930s. Songs from films were not awarded Oscars until 1934, when "The Continental," from *The Gay Divorcée,* was so honored (see Table 1). Since that time many songs have received the award: both outstanding ones, like "Over the Rainbow" (1939) and "White Christmas" (1942), and lesser-known songs, such as "Chim Chim Cher-ee" (1964) and "Theme from *Shaft*" (1971).

Ehrick V. Long

TABLE 1

Academy Awards (Oscars) for Best Song

Year	Song Title	*Lyricist/Composer	Film
1934	The Continental	Herb Magidson/Con Conrad	The Gay Divorcée
1935	Lullaby of Broadway	Al Dubin/Harry Warren	Gold Diggers of 1935
1936	The Way You Look Tonight	Dorothy Fields/Jerome Kern	Swing Time
1937	Sweet Leilani	Harry Owens	Waikiki Wedding
1938	Thanks for the Memory	Leo Robin/Ralph Rainger	The Big Broadcast of 1938
1939	Over the Rainbow	E. Y. Harburg/Harold Arlen	The Wizard of Oz
1940	When You Wish Upon a Star	Ned Washington/Leigh Harline	Pinocchio
1941	The Last Time I Saw Paris	Oscar Hammerstein II/Jerome Kern	Lady Be Good
1942	White Christmas	Irving Berlin	Holiday Inn
1943	You'll Never Know	Mack Gordon/Harry Warren	Hello, Frisco, Hello
1944	Swinging on a Star	Johnny Burke/James Van Heusen	Going My Way
1945	It Might as Well Be Spring	Oscar Hammerstein II/Richard Rodgers	State Fair
1946	On the Atchison, Topeka and the Santa Fe	Johnny Mercer/Harry Warren	The Harvey Girls
1947	Zip-A-Dee-Doo-Dah	Ray Gilbert/Allie Wrubel	Song of the South
1948	Buttons and Bows	Ray Evans, Jay Livingston	The Paleface
1949	Baby, Its Cold Outside	Frank Loesser	Neptune's Daughter
1950	Mona Lisa	Ray Evans, Jay Livingston	Captain Carey, USA
1951	In the Cool, Cool, Cool of the Evening	Johnny Mercer/Hoagy Carmichael	Here Comes the Groom
1952	High Noon (Do Not Forsake Me)	Ned Washington/Dimitri Tiomkin	High Noon
1953	Secret Love	Paul Francis Webster/Sammy Fain	Calamity Jane
1954	Three Coins in the Fountain	Sammy Cahn/Jule Styne	Three Coins in the Fountain
1955	Love is a Many-Splendored Thing	Paul Francis Webster/Sammy Fain	Love is a Many-Splendored Thing
1956	Whatever Will Be, Will Be (Que Sera)	Jay Livingston, Ray Evans	The Man Who Knew Too Much
1957	All the Way	Sammy Cahn/James Van Heusen	The Joker Is Wild
1958	Gigi	Alan Jay Lerner/Frederick Loewe	Gigi
1959	High Hopes	Sammy Cahn/James Van Heusen	A Hole in the Head
1960	Never on Sunday	Manos Hadjidakis, Billy Towne/Manos Hadjidakis	Never on a Sunday
1961	Moon River	Johnny Mercer/Henry Mancini	Breakfast at Tiffany's
1962	Days of Wine and Roses	Johnny Mercer/Henry Mancini	Days of Wine and Roses
1963	Call Me Irresponsible	Sammy Cahn/James Van Heusen	Papa's Delicate Condition
1964	Chim Chim Cher-ee	Richard M. Sherman, Robert B. Sherman	Mary Poppins
1965	The Shadow of Your Smile	Paul Francis Webster/Johnny Mandel	The Sandpiper
1966	Born Free	Don Black/John Barry	Born Free
1967	Talk to the Animals	Leslie Bricusse	Doctor Dolittle
1968	The Windmills of Your Mind	Alan Bergman, Marilyn Bergman/Michel Legrand	The Thomas Crown Affair
1969	Raindrops Keep Fallin' On My Head	Hal David/Burt Bacharach	Butch Cassidy and the Sundance Kid
1970	For All We Know	Robb Roger, James Griffin/Fred Karlin	Lovers and Other Strangers
1971	"Theme from Shaft"	Isaac Hayes	Shaft
1972	The Morning After	Joel Hirschorn, Al Kasha	The Poseidon Adventure
1973	The Way We Were	Alan Bergman, Marilyn Bergman/Marvin Hamlisch	The Way We Were
1974	We May Never Love Like This Again	Joel Hirschorn, Al Kasha	The Towering Inferno
1975	I'm Easy	Keith Carradine	Nashville
1976	"Evergreen (Love Theme from A Star is Born)"	Paul Williams/Barbra Streisand	A Star is Born
1977	You Light Up My Life	Joseph Brooks	You Light Up My Life
1978	Last Dance	Paul Jabara	Thank God It's Friday
1979	It Goes Like It Goes	Norman Gimbel/David Shire	Norma Rae

Year	Song	Writer(s)	Film
1980	Fame	Dean Pitchford/Michael Gore	*Fame*
1981	Arthur's Theme (Best That You Can Do)	Carole Bayer Sager, Christopher Cross, Peter Allen, Burt Bacharach	*Arthur*
1982	Up Where We Belong	Will Jennings/Jack Nitzsche, Buffy Sainte-Marie	*An Officer and a Gentleman*
1983	Flashdance . . . What a Feeling	Keith Forsey, Irene Cara/Giorgio Moroder	*Flashdance*
1984	I Just Called to Say I Love You	Stevie Wonder	*The Woman in Red*
1985	Say You, Say Me	Lionel Richie, Jr.	*White Knights*
1986	Take My Breath Away	Tom Whitlock/Giorgio Moroder	*Top Gun*
1987	(I've Had) The Time of My Life	Frankie Previte/Donald Markowitz, John DeNicola	*Dirty Dancing*
1988	Let the River Run	Carly Simon	*Working Girls*
1989	Under the Sea	Howard Ashman/Alan Menken	*The Little Mermaid*
1990	Sooner or Later I Always Get My Man	Stephen Sondheim	*Dick Tracy*
1991	Beauty and the Beast	Howard Ashman/Alan Menken	*Beauty and the Beast*

Ehrick V. Long

*Writers credited solely with lyrics or music are set down in that order and separated by a slash: eg., Oscar Hammerstein II/Jerome Kern. The presence of a comma indicates that the writers are jointly credited for the music, the lyrics, or the song.

Bibliography

Kaplan, Mike, ed. *"Variety" Major U.S. Showbusiness Awards.* 1982.

Osborne, Robert. *60 Years of the Oscar: The Official History of the Academy Awards.* 1989.

See also: **Awards; Film Musicals**

ACCOMPANIMENT

Accompaniment has two contexts in popular song: method of performance and **texture**. In performance it implies the presence of a principal part, usually assigned to one or more vocalists. In popular music, accompaniment is almost always instrumentally conceived: executed by either a soloist (usually on piano or guitar), an ensemble (a trio or other small group), or an orchestra. The relationship between accompaniment and principal part can vary from one of subservience to one of equality and, in music like **rap**, to instances where the accompaniment is actually more important than the "principal part."

In texture, accompaniment can vary from homophony to heterophony, or even to polyphony. Very often, as with jazz soloists or small groups, it is improvised, usually within strict parameters. With larger aggregations, such as the big bands, **improvisation** gives way to **arrangement**, which may involve changing length or structure, or to orchestration, which implies a change of medium. Most sheet music is written with relatively simple arrangements for piano, which include basic harmonies cued in for piano and guitar. Sometimes a mere **lead sheet** suffices, in which case—as in Baroque music—the realization is left to the accompanying performer(s).

In some music, however, such as the memorable **art songs** from George Gershwin's opera *Porgy and Bess* (1935)—"Bess, You Is My Woman," "I Got Plenty o' Nuttin'," "It Ain't Necessarily So," "My Man's Gone Now," and "Summertime"—the accompaniment is specifically designed as an integral part of the song. Such is also the case in several songs by Jerome Kern containing **countermelodies** with which they have become indelibly associated: "I've Told Ev'ry Little Star" (1932), "The Song Is You" (1932), "Smoke Gets in Your Eyes" (1933), and "The Way You Look Tonight" (1936).

Historically, accompaniment has been an important determinant of style in popular song. "Dardanella" (1919), originally called "Turkish Tom Toms," is an early example of a song with distinctive accompaniment figures. In the 1930s, distinctive patterns of accompaniment became more important with the advent of the **rumba**, **samba**, and other dances imported from Latin America. Also at about that time, two important figured accompaniments were popularized: **boogie-woogie** and the **beguine**.

A radical change occurred in the mid-1950s, when accompaniment, which up to that time was chiefly composed of the piano and other acoustic instruments, began to feature the electric guitar and electronic instruments. Also at about that time, with the advent of **rhythm and blues**, the bass and percussion became more prominent, a situation that persisted into the age of **rock**.

See also: **Instrumentation**

ADAPTATION

Adapting music or lyrics to new use can take many forms: a new **arrangement** of a song, a translation from a foreign tongue, the reworking of a **folk song** or other song in the public domain, basing a song upon the **classics**, or **borrowing** from another writer or from oneself.

Another type of adaptation involves adding lyrics to an existing instrumental work. Hoagy Carmichael originally wrote a ragtime piece for piano in 1927; two years later, with the addition of lyrics by Mitchell Parish, it became world-famous as a ballad called "Star Dust." In 1932, the principal strain of F. D. Marchetti's "Valse Tsigane" of 1904 was given new life as the waltz "Fascination." Another waltz, originally written in 1912 as "Melody," became a standard only in 1951 when it was given words and entitled "It's All in the Game." Charles Gates Dawes, its composer, was a prominent banker who went on to become a general, a statesman, and vice president of the United States from 1925 to 1929; he died the year of his song's rebirth.

Sometimes songs go through several adaptations. A piano piece by Rudolf Friml was written in 1920 as "Chanson," put to words first as "Chansonette" in 1923, and again as "The Donkey Serenade" in 1937 for the operetta *The Firefly*, in which it was sung by Allan Jones. In its last incarnation, it remains a favorite of robust male singers.

Peter De Rose wrote an orchestral suite in 1934 from which two popular songs were extracted, again with the addition of lyrics by Mitchell Parish: "Deep Purple" and "Lilacs in the Rain" (both published in 1939). Similarly, a number of songs were extracted from suites by the Cuban composer Ernesto Lecuona, among them "The Breeze and I" (1940), from his suite *Andalucia*, and "At the Crossroads" (1942), from his suite *Malaguena*. Similarly, the song "Daybreak" (1942) was taken from Ferde Grofé's *Mississippi Suite* of 1926.

Another type of adaptation involves the addition of words to preexisting music. The march "American Patrol," written in 1885, became a hit in 1942 when it was given words as "We Must Be Vigilant." José Padilla's "La Violetera" of 1918 became famous five years later as

"Who'll Buy My Violets?" Georges Boulanger's haunting "Avant de Mourir" of 1926 achieved worldwide popularity in 1939 as "My Prayer," with lyrics by Jimmy Kennedy. A violin piece called "Violino Tsigano" became popular in 1936 as "Serenade in the Night."

The substitution of new lyrics for old is another time-honored tradition. Vincent Youmans's "Sometimes I'm Happy" (1927) started out as "Come On and Pet Me," while Irving Berlin's "Easter Parade" (1933) was originally written in 1914 as "Smile and Show Your Dimple." Rodgers and Hart's famous "Blue Moon" (1934) had previous incarnations as "Prayer" and "The Bad in Every Man" before receiving its permanent title and lyrics. Translation is another abiding means of adaptation. Countless foreign songs have been given new life in English translation.

See also: Austria; Brazil; Cuba; Foreign Influence; France; Germany; Italy; Mexico

AFRICA

The influence of Africa on American popular music has been pervasive, leading directly to such African-American musical genres as the blues, boogie-woogie, calypso, gospel, jazz, Motown, ragtime, rhythm and blues, rock 'n' roll, salsa, soul, and zydeco.

The vast continent encompasses numerous nations from Morocco to South Africa, but by far the most influential were the sub-Saharan nations of West Africa, from which many slaves embarked. From the various topographies of desert and jungle, the people pursued hundreds of tribal cultures, in all of which—as in most pre-urban cultures—life and music were inseparably intertwined. This music reached our shores along with the slaves, and many elements of it were incorporated into the music of African Americans, and eventually into the mainstream of American popular music.

Most striking was the importance of rhythm and the prominence of percussion in African tribal music. Polyrhythm—the simultaneous use of different rhythms by a series of different drums—was an essential characteristic. Another was polymeter, the use of more than one meter at the same time. Other features were the maintenance of strict time and the use of syncopation. Among other aspects of African music that found their way to the New World were the exploitation of vocal and instrumental timbre, the use of improvisation, the employment of constant repetition, call and response in singing, the use of percussion as melody, the variety of scales, and the importance of dance. All these essentially African characteristics appear in the music of the United States, Brazil, Cuba, and other countries of the Western Hemisphere.

Unlike European music, the music of nineteenth-century Africa was primarily ritualistic. No composers such as Bach or Beethoven were to be found, nor were there instrumental or vocal ensembles such as were prevalent throughout Europe. While Europeans were enjoying the symphonies of Mozart and the operas of Verdi and Wagner, Africans were participating in tribal music describing birth, death, battle, manhood, marriage, and social and political events.

To provide the music for their various ceremonies, the tribes or clans depended upon members who possessed musical ability with either voice or instrument. African instruments are very sophisticated. The *mbira*, or *kalimba*, a kind of thumb piano, is one of the most complex instruments in all of Africa. Constructed on the principle of the guitar, but utilizing springs that are plucked by the thumbnail, rather than strings, the instrument is capable of playing a melodic line of limited range. It is sometimes amplified by being played inside the shell of a very large gourd. Other percussion instruments include many types of drums in various sizes and ranges, as well as instruments of varying pitch, like the xylophone. There are also important instruments of the lyre and harp family. While these instruments were designed primarily for communication, they were also an integral part of rituals performed throughout the continent.

African musicians had no formal training to compare with their European counterparts. There was no written notation; the various tribal songs were performed from memory. When the slave trade was active, musicians were often captured and sold into slavery, thereby leaving a void in the tribe's musical history. At that point a reconstruction of the history and musical heritage of the tribe became necessary.

Melodically, Africans used a variety of scales, including the diatonic, but often based their songs upon the pentatonic, or five-tone, scale, in such configurations as C, D, E, G, A. It has been suggested that the harmonization of songs in the pentatonic scale led to the origin of the blue note.

It was usually the responsibility of the Griot, or official minstrel, to be the composer. This person was the musical storyteller and historian of the tribe. Like the European troubadours of the Middle Ages, the Griot traveled throughout tribal territory, acting as a sort of vocal news service and relating all kinds of information by song. The music of these bards was as varied as the continent's countries and tribes. Very often connected to religious ritual, it contained emotions and moods similar to European and American folk music. Just as Stephen Foster, James Bland, George Gershwin, and Irving Berlin elicited moods ranging from comedy to tragedy in their songs, so did African composers develop their songs and lyrics to elicit particular moods.

The importance of African music cannot be over-emphasized. It can indeed be stated without equivocation that popular music in the United States, as in much of the Western Hemisphere, is a synthesis of the music of two continents: Europe and Africa.

Otto Werner

Bibliography

De Lerma, Dominique-René. *Bibliography of Black Music*. 4 vols. 1981–84.

Jones, A. M. *Studies in African Music*. 2 vols. 1959.

Jones, LeRoi [Amiri Baraka]. *Blues People: Negro Music in White America*. 1980.

Kwabena Nketia, Joseph H. *The Music of Africa*. 1974.

Merriam, Alan P. *African Music in Perspective*. 1982.

Roberts, John Storm. *Black Music of Two Worlds*. 1972.

Schuller, Gunther. *Early Jazz: Its Roots and Musical Development*. 1968.

Southern, Eileen. *The Music of Black Americans: A History*. 1983.

————. *Readings in Black American Music*. 1983.

AGE

In popular song, the accent has always been on youth; there are more songs about "April Love" (1957) than about "The September of My Years" (1965). Specific ages, when mentioned, are most often confined to the adolescent years, with sixteen and seventeen the ages preferred above all others. Representative examples through the years are "When You Were Sweet Sixteen" (1898), "Sixteen Candles" (1959), "You Are Sixteen" (1959), and "At Seventeen" (1975). Also obviously very young are the protagonists of "Too Young," introduced by Nat "King" Cole in 1951.

Other well-known songs about youth are "While We're Young" (1943), "Younger Than Springtime" (1949), "Hello, Young Lovers" (1951), and "When the World Was Young" (1952). The American penchant for wanting to feel young even if one isn't is reflected in two standards: "You Make Me Feel So Young" (1946) and "Young at Heart" (1954).

Few songs are concerned with middle age, although one echoes a common complaint heard during World War II: "They're Either Too Young or Too Old" (1943); still another, "I'm Glad I'm Not Young Any More" (1958), celebrates the joys of maturity. At least four love songs are about people growing old gracefully together: "When Your Hair Has Turned to Silver (I Will Love You Just the Same)" (1930), "When I Grow Too Old to Dream" (1934), "September Song" (1938), and "Through the Years" (1980).

Then there is "Sunny Boy" (1928), about a three year old, and "It Was a Very Good Year," a 1961 song

that, in its lyrics, covers several years of a lifetime: the ages of seventeen, thirty-five, and an indeterminate age called "the autumn of the year."

Additional Songs

Forever Young (1973)
Happy Birthday, Sweet Sixteen (1961)
Last Night When We Were Young (1936)
Like Young (1958)
Love Among the Young (1955)
My Generation (1965)
Only Sixteen (1959)
Puppy Love (1959)
Sweet Little Sixteen (1958)
A Teenager in Love (1959)
When I Grow Up (To Be a Man) (1964)
When I'm Sixty-Four (1967)
Young and Foolish (1954)
Young Girl (1968)
Young Love (1956)

See also: Baby; Boy; Childhood; Girl; Pop

AIRPLANES. *SEE* TRAVEL

ALLITERATION

Alliteration, the use of two or more words with the same initial sound, is common in popular song, both in **lyrics** and titles. Cole Porter was one of its chief advocates. Hundreds of examples can be found in his lyrics, including the "sentimental centipedes" of "Let's Do It (Let's Fall in Love)" (1928), the "beat, beat, beat" and "tick, tick, tock" of "Night and Day" (1932), and the "fine finnan haddie" of "My Heart Belongs to Daddy" (1938). Porter also managed multiple alliteration in his delightful song "It's D'Lovely" (1936) with such words as "delightful," "delicious," and "delectable."

Although the **lyricist** Lorenz Hart was more partial to **rhyme** than to alliteration, he occasionally used the latter, as in the three "s" sounds in the opening line of "You Took Advantage of Me" (1928): "I'm a sentimental sap, that's all." Alliteration was a favorite device of Howard Dietz, who used it in such passages as "waltzing in the wonder" and "looking for the light," from "Dancing in the Dark" (1931), and "fill me with flaming desire," from "You and the Night and the Music" (1934).

As for other alliterative titles besides "Dancing in the Dark," three of the best known with two consonants are "Tea for Two" (1924), "Begin the Beguine" (1935), and "Where or When" (1937). Two songs with doubly alliterative titles are "The Birth of the Blues" (1926) and "Love Me or Leave Me" (1928).

Titles with three similar consonants include "Toot Toot Tootsie" (Goo'Bye) (1922), popularized by Al Jolson; "Tip Toe Through the Tulips With Me" (1929), a song much favored by tap dancers; "Bewitched (bothered and bewildered)," a bewitching ballad of 1941; "Jingle, Jangle, Jingle," a novelty song of 1942; "Chattanooga Choo Choo" (1941), a train song; and "The Poor People of Paris," a 1956 import from France.

Three extreme examples of alliterative titles, each with four similar consonants, are: "She Sells Sea-Shells (on the Seashore)" (1908); "K-K-K-Katy" (1918), promoted as "The Sensational Stammering Song Success by the Soldiers and Sailors"; and "Boogie Woogie Bugle Boy (from Company B)," introduced by the Andrews Sisters in the film *Buck Privates* (1941).

Additional Songs

Black Bottom (1926)
The Dipsy Doodle (1937)
Lovely to Look At (1935)
Magic Is the Moonlight (1930)
Rio Rita (1926)
The Sound of Silence (1964)
Teach Me Tonight (1953)
The Tender Trap (1955)
Tumbling Tumbleweeds (1934)
Willow Weep for Me (1932)

Bibliography

Davis, Sheila. *The Craft of Lyric Writing.* 1985.

Furia, Philip. *The Poets of Tin Pan Alley: A History of America's Great Lyricists.* 1990.

See also: Humor

AMERICA. *SEE* NATIONS; PATRIOTISM

ANATOMY

Parts of the body have long served as song subjects, as witness Stephen Foster's "Jeanie With the Light Brown Hair" (1854) or "My Heart at Thy Sweet Voice," from Camille Saint-Saëns's, opera *Samson and Delilah* (1876). This tradition continued into the twentieth century, when the body and its parts became a major source of inspiration to popular songwriters.

A few songs encompass literally all parts of the anatomy; "Body and Soul" (1930) is a striking example; another is "All of Me" (1931). Most songs, however, are about individual parts of the body. As might be expected, the heart is by far the most-favored body part, followed (not too closely) by the eyes, and then by the hands, face, arms, and hair.

Heart songs, of course, almost always refer to that organ only in a figurative sense. Perhaps the closest literal references occur in Lorenz Hart's lyrics for "My Heart Stood Still" (1927) and in Harold Rome's for "(All of a Sudden) My Heart Sings" (1941). There are many other kinds of heart songs, including songs about aching hearts, breaking hearts, cheating hearts, and secret hearts (see Table 2); hearts have been left in such diverse places as the Stage Door Canteen and San Francisco.

Songs about the eyes span the twentieth century, from "When Irish Eyes Are Smiling" (1912) to "Spanish Eyes" (1965) and "Can't Take My Eyes Off You" (1967). Two "eye" songs from the 1930s have shown unusual qualities of endurance: "Smoke Gets in Your Eyes" (1933) and "I Only Have Eyes for You" (1934). "Jeepers Creepers," a hit of 1938, uses the expression "Where'd ya get them peepers"—the latter a slang word for eyes.

Hands also figure prominently in popular song, but in very diverse ways. One has only to compare Ira Gershwin's jaunty lyrics for "Clap Yo' Hands" (1926) to Otto Harbach's stately words for "The Touch of Your Hand" (1933). A later generation could similarly contrast John Lennon and Paul McCartney's lyrics for "I Want to Hold Your Hand" (1963) to Stephen Sondheim's for "One Hand, One Heart" (1957).

"Face" songs include "I've Grown Accustomed to Her Face" (1956), "Put On a Happy Face" (1960), and "The First Time Ever I Saw Your Face" (1962). As for arms, they have been song subjects since as far back as 1910, when the perennial favorite "Put Your Arms Around Me Honey" was written.

The 1930s saw a flowering of anatomical songs. Two of them, Irving Berlin's "Cheek to Cheek" (1935) and Cole Porter's "I've Got You Under My Skin" (1936) are of interest for their length and unusual form. "Head" songs include "You Go to My Head" (1938), celebrated for its innovative harmony; and such more recent songs as "Goin' Out of My Head" (1964) and "Raindrops Keep Fallin' on My Head" (1969). The chorus of Kris Kristofferson's "For the Good Times" (1968) begins with the words "Lay Your Head Upon My Pillow."

There are also several striking examples of anatomical combinations in lyrics. Cole Porter, in "All of You" (1954), admires "The eyes, the arms, the mouth of you." Johnny Mercer, in his 1943 song "That Old Black Magic", manages to refer to three parts of the anatomy simultaneously in one sentence: "icy fingers," "my spine," and "your lips." "Put Your Head on My Shoulder" is the title of a 1958 song by Paul Anka.

See also: Mind; Smiling

TABLE 2

Anatomy in Song

Arms
Crazy Arms (1956)
Full Moon and Empty Arms (1946)
Here in My Arms (1925)
Put Your Arms Around Me Honey (1910)
Take Me in Your Arms (1932)

Body
Body and Soul (1930)

Brain
If I Only Had a Brain (1939)
Scatter-brain (1939)

Cheeks
Cheek to Cheek (1935)

Ears
Cheerful Little Earful (1930)

Eyes
Bette Davis Eyes (1975)
Blue Eyes Crying in the Rain (1945)
Brown Eyed Girl (1967)
Can't Take My Eyes Off You (1967)
Dark Eyes (1926)
Don't It Make My Brown Eyes Blue (1977)
Don't Let the Stars Get in Your Eyes (1953)
The Eyes of Texas (1903)
Five Foot Two, Eyes of Blue; Has Anybody Seen My Girl? (1925)
Green Eyes (1929)
I Only Have Eyes for You (1934)
Lyin' Eyes (1975)
Mal (He's Making Eyes at Me) (1921)
My Eyes Adored You (1974)
Pretty Little Angel Eyes (1961)
Smoke Gets in Your Eyes (1933)
Spanish Eyes (1965)
Star Eyes (1943)
Stars in My Eyes (1936)
Them There Eyes (1930)
Theme from *Ice Castles* (Through The Eyes of Love) 1978
There's Yes Yes in Your Eyes (1924)
When Irish Eyes Are Smiling (1912)
With My Eyes Wide Open I'm Dreaming (1934)
Your Eyes Have Told Me So (1919)

Face
Baby Face (1926)
The First Time Ever I Saw Your Face (1962)
I See Your Face Before Me (1937)
I've Grown Accustomed to Her Face (1956)
Nancy (With the Laughing Face) (1944)
Put On a Happy Face (1960)
Were Thine That Special Face (1948)
Your Smiling Face (1977)

Feet
Your Feet's Too Big (1935)

Fingers
I've Got Rings on My Fingers (1909)
Under My Thumb (1966)

Hair
I'm Gonna Wash That Man Right Outa My Hair (1949)
Scarlet Ribbons (For Her Hair) (1949)
When Your Hair Has Turned to Silver (I Will Love You Just the Same) (1930)
With the Wind and the Rain in Your Hair (1930)

Hands
Clap Yo' Hands (1926)
Hands Across the Table (1934)
Hold My Hand (1950)
I Kiss Your Hand, Madame (1929)
I Want to Hold Your Hand (1963)
One Hand, One Heart (1957)
Shake a Hand (1953)
Time on My Hands (1930)
The Touch of Your Hand (1933)

Head
Caldonia (What Makes Your Big Head So Hard?) (1945)
Goin' Out of My Head (1964)
Put Your Head on My Shoulder (1958)
Raindrops Keep Fallin' on My Head (1969)
You Go to My Head (1938)

Heart
Always in My Heart (1942)
Anema e Core (1954)
Cold, Cold Heart (1951)
Dear Heart (1964)
Deep in My Heart, Dear (1924)
The Door Is Still Open to My Heart (1955)
Good Morning Heartache (1946)
Heart and Soul (1939)
Heartaches (1931)
Heartbreak Hotel (1956)
Hearts and Flowers (1899)
I Have But One Heart (1945)
I Left My Heart at the Stage Door Canteen (1942)
I Left My Heart in San Francisco (1954)
I Let a Song Go Out of My Heart (1938)
If I Give My Heart to You (1954)
I'll Follow My Secret Heart (1934)
I'll Hold You in My Heart (Till I Can Hold You in My Arms) (1947)
Love Me With All Your Heart (1964)
Love—What Are You Doing to My Heart? (1933)
My Foolish Heart (1949)
My Heart Belongs to Daddy (1938)
My Heart Cries for You (1950)
(All of a Sudden) My Heart Sings (1945)
My Heart Stood Still (1927)
My One and Only Heart (1953)
The One Rose That's Left in My Heart (1929)
Peg 'o My Heart (1913)
The Song from *Moulin Rouge*, (Where is Your Heart?) (1953)
The Story of the Rose (Heart of My Heart) (1899)
Stouthearted Men (1928)
This Heart of Mine (1946)
Two Hearts in Three Quarter Time (1930)
With a Song in My Heart (1929)
You Belong to My Heart (1941)
Young at Heart (1954)
Your Cheatin' Heart (1952)
You're Breaking My Heart (1948)
Yours Is My Heart Alone (1931)
Zing Went the Strings of My Heart (1935)

Legs
Skinny Legs and All (1967)

Lips
Lucky Lips (1957)
The Touch of Your Lips (1936)

Skin
I've Got You Under My Skin (1936)

ANGELS

Many popular songs have been written about angels, but few refer to them as spiritual beings. One of the exceptions is the 1939 big band hit "And the Angels Sing" (1939), but even that song expresses admiration for a human being, with the words "You smile, and the angels sing."

Indeed, most songs about angels are about especially lovable persons. Songs of this kind include "Got a Date With an Angel" (1931), "I Married an Angel" (1938), "Angel Eyes" (1953), "Earth Angel (Will You Be Mine)" (1954), and at least a dozen songs simply entitled "Angel," including one co-written and performed by Madonna in 1984.

In these songs, few "angels" are less than perfect, although questions are raised in "I'll String Along With You" (1934), with the words "You may not be an angel," as well as in "Devil or Angel" (1956).

Additional Songs

The Angel in Your Arms (1976)
Angel of the Morning (1967)
Angela Mia (My Angel) (1928)
Johnny Angel (1962)
Kiss an Angel Good Morning (1971)
My Special Angel (1957)
Pretty Little Angel Eyes (1961)

> See also: Baby; Endearment; Heaven; Love; Romance

ANIMALS

Animal allusions are common in popular song. One of the best known occurs in Oscar Hammerstein's first line for "Can't Help Lovin' Dat Man," from Show Boat (1927): "Fish got to swim and birds got to fly." Although this is a love song, references to animals are more often whimsical or humorous in nature. Cole Porter, for example, lists a veritable Noah's Ark of animals in his catalogue song "Let's Do It (Let's Fall in Love)" (1928), including birds, bees, "educated fleas," electric eels "(though it shocks 'em, I know)," English soles, "sentimental centipedes," "courageous kangaroos," "heavy hippopotami," "bears in pits," and "pekineses in the Ritz," to mention only a few. Animals are also referred to en masse in the lyrics of two Academy Award winners: "Swinging on a Star," from Going My Way (1944); and "Talk to the Animals," from Dr. Dolittle (1967).

However, most songs about animals refer to singular species. One of the earliest examples refers to an insect. "The Glow-Worm," originally published in Germany as "Glühwürmchen" in 1902, became a great hit in America in 1907. More troublesome insects are alluded to in "La Cucaracha" ("The Cockroach")—first adapted from a Mexican folk song in 1916—and "Spanish Flea" (1965). The ballad "Poor Butterfly" (1916) refers of course not to the insect but to the heroine of Giacomo Puccini's opera Madama Butterfly (1904).

Domestic animals are frequent subjects of song. Dogs are represented by "Bulldog! Bulldog! Bow Wow Wow" (1911), written as a football fight song by the eighteen-year-old Porter while he was attending Yale University; by Noël Coward's humorous "Mad Dogs and Englishmen" (1931); by Bob Merrill's novelty hit of 1953, "(How Much Is That) Doggie in the Window?"; and by Jerry Leiber and Mike Stoller's "Hound Dog," made famous by Elvis Presley in 1956.

Horses are immortalized in such songs as "The Old Grey Mare (She Ain't What She Used to Be)" (1917), the two-step "My Pony Boy" (1909), the Austrian waltz "The White Horse Inn" (1931), and "The Donkey Serenade" (1937). And then there is the phonetic nonsense song of 1943, "Mairzy Doats," which is really about mares and does and little lambs that eat ivy.

Entire musicals—as diverse as The Cat and the Fiddle (1931) and Cats (1981)—have been built around felines. Cats have also been treated metaphorically, as in the songs "What's New Pussycat?" (1965) and "Alley Cat" (1962).

As for wild animals, a commonly sung parody of the circus march, "National Emblem" (1906), begins with the words "And the monkey wrapped his tail around the flagpole." "The Aba Daba Honeymoon" of 1914 is about a "chimpie" and a "monk" who are married by a "big baboon." "Who's Afraid of the Big Bad Wolf?," about a fierce animal and first presented in the film The Three Little Pigs (1933), became symbolic of the Great Depression. "Three Little Fishes" was a novelty hit of 1939. The song "Born Free" (1966), from the film of the same name, is about a pet lion.

Two jazz favorites are "Tiger Rag" (1917), about the Princeton University mascot, and "Muskrat Ramble" (1926). Christmas is a favorite time for animals, when "Rudolph the Red-Nosed Reindeer" (1949) appears, as do three smaller, electronic animals in "The Chipmunk Song" (1958). But with so many species represented in popular song, as far as can be ascertained only one song has ever been written about a rat: "Ben," from the film of the same name (1972).

The years before World War I saw a craze for ragtime dances, many of them named after animals, including the bunny hug, camel walk, grizzly bear, horse trot, kangaroo hop, lame duck, turkey trot, and walking the dog. None of them survived. But one dance that did, the fox trot, got its name not from the animal, but from a vaudeville entertainer named Harry Fox.

Additional Songs

Bird Dog (1958)
Black Dog (1972)
The Bunny Hop (1952)
The Cattle Call (1934)
Crocodile Rock (1972)
Did You Ever think as The Hearse Rolls By, or The
    Worms Crawl In, The Worms Crawl Out (1923)
Elusive Butterfly (1966)
Eye of the Tiger (1982)
Honky Cat (1972)

Hungry Like the Wolf (1983)
The Lion Sleeps Tonight (1961)
Mule Train (1949)
Ostrich Walk (1918)
Ride Your Pony (1965)
Tiger (1959)
Walking the Dog (1963)
White Rabbit (1967)
Wild Horses (1953)
Yellow Dog Blues (1928)

See also: Birds; Dance Crazes

ANTHEMS. *SEE* PATRIOTISM

ARGENTINA

Argentina's most significant contribution to European and North American music is the **tango**, a dance conceived in Buenos Aires around 1910 which quickly swept the civilized world. In the ensuing **dance craze** in the United States, several Argentine tangos became popular, including "El Choclo" (1913), which attained great popularity in 1952 as a ballad titled "Kiss of Fire"; and the famous dance "La Cumparsita" (1916), given English words only in 1932. Through the years, the tango has remained popular, and is often danced to such Argentine favorites as "Adios Muchachos" (1929), adapted with English lyrics as " I Get Ideas" in 1951; and "Caminito" (1936).

Argentina has also served as the setting of films and musicals, from *Down Argentine Way*, a 1940 film starring Betty Grable and Carmen Miranda, to *Evita*, a 1978 British musical loosely based on the life of onetime Argentine first lady Eva Perón. From the latter comes the popular tango "Don't Cry for Me Argentina."

See also: Foreign Influence; Nations

ARPEGGIO

An arpeggio is a **broken chord** performed as if it were played on the harp; that is, with its notes played upward or downward in rapid succession rather than simultaneously. The arpeggio, in various guises, is ubiquitous in popular song; it is an important component of **improvisation**, especially on piano and guitar.

Perhaps its most important function in popular song, however, is as an introduction to a ballad, especially one to be sung in a nonrhythmical style (as opposed to rhythm ballads and uptempo songs, where a **vamp** would be more appropriate). In such an instance, the arpeggio points the vocalist in the direction of the proper starting pitch. To this end, in the interest of clarity of intention, some form of the dominant seventh chord is almost always the one that is arpeggiated.

ARRANGEMENT

An arrangement is an **adaptation** of a piece of music for voices or instruments, especially for those not originally intended. Arrangement is quite distinct from orchestration; in many shows, for example, the arranger (particularly of dances) and the orchestrator are different people. In pop music, however, the arranger is very often the orchestrator as well, and produces an arrangement, also known as a chart or a score.

Throughout the history of popular music, arrangers have played a very important, if often overlooked, role. Many songwriters, even highly creative composers from the 1930s and 1940s, were unable to do more than hammer out their tunes in very simple fashion on a keyboard. Arrangers were often called upon to flesh out and improve the songwriter's initial effort; they frequently became nameless contributors to many of the songs we have come to love.

Very often the arranger takes an idea from a composer, which may be only in his head or, perhaps, on a simple **lead sheet**, and transforms it into an arrangement for voice and piano. He may, if given a free hand, change the original tempo, alter the harmonies, or even rephrase the melodic line, becoming, in fact, a collaborator.

In its usual sense, however, arrangement implies orchestration, and the arranger's compositional abilities are mostly confined to a last (in the old days called a "sock") chorus, wherein the original piece of music becomes almost another composition. Since the original material is usually written in concert **key** or for the piano, the arranger must be able to transpose each part to the key in which various instruments play. For example, if the original key is F, an alto saxophone would play in the key of D. The arranger, then, must know the **range** and limitations of each instrument in the ensemble for which he is writing.

Although arrangers for Broadway have not always been given their due in programs, successful arrangers of pop songs often have a unique style for which they become well known. In fact, some arrangers, have become almost as famous as the artists for whom they wrote their scores. When Nelson Riddle wrote arrangements for Frank Sinatra, Linda Ronstadt, and others, Riddle's name appeared on the album cover along with that of the performer. Billy May became as important as the bandleaders for whom he arranged.

Fletcher Henderson helped create the sound that made Benny Goodman's band immediately recognizable. Henderson wrote tightly knit voicings of instruments; chords moved in the style of two locked hands on a piano keyboard. He was among the first arrangers to let both the reed section and **brass** section play as individual blocks: one answering the other in a kind of call-and-response style.

Sy Oliver, well known as an arranger for Jimmie

section play as individual blocks: one answering the other in a kind of call-and-response style.

Sy Oliver, well known as an arranger for Jimmie Lunceford and later Tommy Dorsey, used spread voicings. Transferred to a keyboard, Oliver's writing would have surpassed the reach of a pianist's fingers. Oliver also broke an old rule of orchestration prohibiting parallel fifths in motion; parallel fifths were ubiquitous in his voicings. His arrangements for Tommy Dorsey of Stephen Foster's "Old Folks at Home" (1851), which he called "Swanee River," is a good example of Oliver's writing style. He was also one of the first arrangers to use five reeds in a section. After Oliver, almost all dance bands used five saxophones or reeds.

Duke Ellington's band was always recognizable on recordings or on live radio broadcasts because of the pianist-leader's distinctive style of arranging. In fact, the Ellington style of instrumental voicings was described as the "Ellington sound" even when present in other bands of the period.

Glenn Miller arranged for the Dorsey Brothers and Ray Noble before forming his own band. The "Miller sound," a phrase still used today, refers to the clarinet-lead voicing that Miller created more than fifty years ago. Miller also used arrangers Jerry Gray and Bill Finnegan; much of their writing also reflected the "Miller sound." Gray was also responsible for the hit arrangement of Cole Porter's "Begin the Beguine" (1935) for the Artie Shaw band. Finnegan left the Miller band to team up with arranger Eddie Sauter, and together they formed the legendary Sauter-Finnegan Orchestra. This concert/dance band used extra horns and percussion, thereby giving both arrangers more opportunity to experiment with orchestral colors.

Sauter had written arrangements for Red Norvo and Benny Goodman before joining forces with Finnegan in the 1950s. He had a unique writing style which appears to have been influenced by composers such as Igor Stravinsky and the French impressionists. His penchant for unorthodox combinations of instruments would be demonstrated later in several symphonic-style recordings and Broadway musical scores that he arranged. Along with Finnegan, Sauter was the first arranger to demand extra **woodwind** doubling from the reed section. Saxophonists in the Sauter-Finnegan Orchestra were required to double on flute, piccolo, oboe, bassoon, clarinet—everything but kazoo. Actually, one chart did indeed call for kazoos!

Arrangements helped make hits during the era of the **big bands**. Examples include Billy May's hard-swinging chart of Ray Noble's "Cherokee" (1938) for Charlie Barnet; Neal Hefti's laid-back arrangement of his own "Li'l Darlin'" (1958) for Count Basie; Tutti Camarata's abrupt changes of tempo in the Tommy Dorsey recording of "Green Eyes" (1929); and Wild Bill Davis's chart for Count Basie of Vernon Duke's "April

in Paris" (1932). This last arrangement is one of the best known in big band history. The song came originally from a 1934 revue called *Walk a Little Faster*. Over the years, it became a well-known standard, usually performed as a ballad. In 1944, organist-arranger Davis wrote a chart for Basie, a swinging **riff**-style arrangement that repeated the last twelve bars after the phrase "One more time," shouted by the orchestra. So popular did this arrangement become that in future years, whenever the Basie band appeared, the audience would shout "One more time" in order to hear a reprise of the last phrase.

Gil Evans attracted attention as arranger for the Claude Thornhill band, but his greatest recognition came with the recordings he made with Miles Davis and, later, with his own orchestra. The historic Columbia recordings of Davis's trumpet improvisations against Evans's modern orchestral sounds include the albums *Sketches of Spain* and *Something Blue*.

Evans is among the well-known arrangers who are also composers in their own right. Johnny Mandel, one of our finest composers, is also a talented arranger; his writing for the film *I Want to Live* is but one shining example. Composer Alec Wilder arranged Hugh Martin's score for the film *Grandma Moses*, and Martin insisted that Wilder get equal billing because he believed that Wilder's arrangements had greatly enhanced the original score. Quincy Jones, who began his career as arranger for bands such as Count Basie's, was still in the 1990s sought after as composer and arranger for film scores and major recording projects.

Many important arrangers have enriched popular music. They include William Grant Still, John Scott Trotter, Don Sebesky, Manny Albam, Marion Evans, Marty Paich, Billy Byers, Billy VerPlanck, Bill Holman, Gerry Mulligan, Bob Brookmeyer, Benny Carter, Thad Jones, Ray Ellis, Gordon Jenkins, and newcomers Mike Abene, Bill Kirchner, and Mike Crotty. Whether the sound was produced by a so-called sweet band, such as that of Hal Kemp, Kay Kyser, or Sammy Kaye, or a swing band like that of Les Brown, Woody Herman, or Benny Goodman, the arrangement was an important ingredient in determining a song's success.

The dean of popular music arrangers is probably Canadian-born Robert Farnon. Now living in the United Kingdom, Farnon is regarded by many singers and instrumentalists as the finest of all arrangers, especially for **strings**. Performers such as Tony Bennett, Lena Horne, Eileen Farrell, Singers Unlimited, Pia Zadora, and George Shearing give him a free hand to write for them as he chooses. Knowing that Farnon is also a fine composer, they can count on sensitive **accompaniment** for their solos, and introductions and interludes that are, in themselves, wonderful compositions.

Bandleaders, singers, and instrumental soloists are

always on the lookout for new material, either for a song that will bring about a hit record, or for a piece that will be perfect for an act. If they are smart and can afford it, performers also look for a talented arranger. Very often the arrangement makes the song. It is doubtful if the simple song "A String of Pearls" (1941) would have been a hit record without the Jerry Gray arrangement. And the same holds true for a multitude of other songs.

Loonis McGlohon

Bibliography

Charlton, Andrew, and John DeVries. *Jazz and Commercial Arranging.* 2 vols. 1982.

Miller, Alton Glenn. *Glenn Miller's Method for Orchestral Arranging.* 1956.

Art Song

An art song is a piece suitable for performance in a recital or concert hall. It may differ from other types of popular song in several ways: the poetic quality of its lyrics, the "semi-classical" style of its music, and its fixed—as opposed to improvised—accompaniment. Not surprisingly, many art songs stem from operetta. Among the best known of these are "Oh Promise Me," from *Robin Hood* (1890); "Gypsy Love Song" and "Romany Life," from *The Fortune Teller* (1898); "The Merry Widow Waltz" and "Vilia," from *The Merry Widow* (1907); and "Ah, Sweet Mystery of Life" and "Italian Street Song," from *Naughty Marietta* (1910). Needless to say, all the numbers from the **opera** *Porgy and Bess* (1935) qualify as art songs.

In addition, a number of art songs were written independently of the stage. They include two that were traditionally sung at weddings during the first half of the twentieth century: "Because" (1902) and "I Love You Truly" (1901)—both composed by women. Other stalwarts of the art song repertoire include "Mighty Lak' a Rose" (1901), one of Ethelbert Nevin's last songs; "From the Land of the Sky Blue Water" (1909), extracted from Charles Wakefield Cadman's *Four American Indian Songs*; "The Song of Songs" (1914), adapted from "Chanson du Coeur Brisé"; and "Without a Song" (1929), with a soaring melody by Vincent Youmans.

Oscar Hammerstein II and Jerome Kern brought the genre to new heights. Many songs from their landmark Broadway production, *Show Boat* (1927), can be considered art songs, but especially "Ol' Man River" and "You Are Love." Equally impressive examples of the genre by the same songwriting team are "The Song Is You" (1932) and "All the Things You Are" (1939). Kern's music for "Smoke Gets in Your Eyes," with its distinctive accompaniment figures and **countermelody**, is also considered by many to be an art song despite its less-than-inspired lyrics by Otto Harbach, which include the line "so I chaffed them and I gaily laughed." Among other art songs graced by Kern's music are the captivating waltzes "The Touch of Your Hand" (1933) and "I Dream Too Much" (1935).

Bibliography

Fuld, James J. *The Book of World-Famous Music: Classical, Popular and Folk.* 1985.

See also: **Golden Age**

ASCAP

ASCAP is an acronym for the American Society of Composers, Authors and Publishers, the first performance-rights licensing agency in the United States. ASCAP was founded in New York in 1914, with Victor Herbert as its first vice president. It issues licenses to radio and television stations and to other performance media, collects fees based on the number of aired performances, and distributes proceeds to its members accordingly.

In 1940, ASCAP was challenged by the broadcasting industry, and there was a temporary boycott of ASCAP music on the air. For a time, the only works that could be heard were those in the public domain; Stephen Foster's "Jeanie With the Light Brown Hair," written in 1854, suffused the airwaves. Eventually the broadcasters established their own agency, Broadcast Music Incorporated (**BMI**), which remains ASCAP's chief rival today. While ASCAP licenses most of the standard repertoire—including, of course, most popular songs written before 1940—BMI has more closely followed popular taste, concentrating on the fields of pop, rock, and country and western music. In addition, both organizations have a strong concert composer component.

Bibliography

Ewen, David. *All the Years of American Popular Music.* 1977

Rachlin, Harvey. *The Encyclopedia of the Music Business.* 1981.

Sanjek, Russell, and David Sanjek. *American Popular Music Business in the 20th Century.* 1991.

Schultz, Lucia S. "Performing-Right Societies in the United States." *Music Library Association Notes,* 35: (1978–79): 511–36.

Shemel, Sidney, and M. William Krasilovsky. *This Business of Music.* 1979.

See also: **Copyright**

Austria

Vienna, once the capital of the mighty Austro-Hungarian Empire and, since 1918, capital of the much-reduced republic of Austria, has often been called a world capital of music. This claim can certainly be justified for the period from the 1760s to the 1940s, when the city and its environs were home to such composers as Christoph Willibald Gluck, Josef Haydn, Wolfgang Amadeus Mozart, Ludwig van Beethoven, Franz Schubert, Johannes Brahms, Anton

Bruckner, Richard Strauss, Gustav Mahler, Arnold Schoenberg, Alban Berg, and Anton Webern, among others. It has seen musical revolutions as well; two examples among many were Gluck's revolutionary opera *Orfeo ed Euridice* (1762) and Schoenberg's development of his twelve-tone theory in the early 1920s.

In popular music, Austria's contribution is perhaps less striking, but hardly less revolutionary. It was here that the **waltz** developed out of the Ländler, a dance of the Austrian country-folk. It was here that it was popularized, first by Josef Lanner (1801–1843) and his rival Johann Strauss, Sr. (1804–1849), and later by Johann Strauss, Jr. (1825–1899). The latter, known as the "Waltz King," wrote marches and polkas as well as waltzes, but it was the last that brought him fame and changed the face of popular music throughout the world. In the United States, the waltz reigned supreme in the 1880s and 1890s. It reached its apogee in the first decade of the twentieth century, and its influence in popular music is felt to the present day.

Austria's effect on American popular song did not stop with the waltz. The face of **operetta** was changed forever with the New York premiere of *The Merry Widow* in 1907. First produced in Vienna in 1905, its music is by Franz Lehár (1870–1948), who was born in **Hungary** and educated in Prague but who spent most of his life in Austria. *The Merry Widow* created a new era in American musical theater, and its influence is still felt. Its beautiful melodies, especially "The Merry Widow Waltz" (also known as "I Love You So"), "Vilia," "Maxim's," and "Girls, Girls, Girls," became hits of the day and remain in the standard repertoire as does the operetta itself.

Later operettas by Lehár include *The Count of Luxembourg*, from which comes the memorable song "Say Not Love Is a Dream" (1912); *Frasquita*, with its "Frasquita Serenade," also known as "My Little Nest of Heavenly Blue" (1926); and *The Land of Smiles*, from which comes the passionate "Yours Is My Heart Alone" ("Dein ist mein ganzes Herz") (1931), popularized by Richard Tauber. Lehár's music for these works epitomizes the spirit of Vienna between the two world wars.

Another composer born in Hungary who received his initial success in Vienna was Emmerich Kálmán (1882–1953). He wrote many fabulously successful operettas in Europe, but he is best known in the United States for *Sari*, from which comes "Love's Own Sweet Song" (1914), and *Countess Maritza*, with its stirring "Play Gypsies—Dance Gypsies" (1926).

Composers born in Austria who achieved great success in the United States include Oscar Straus (1870–1954), who wrote the operettas *A Waltz Dream* (1907) and *The Chocolate Soldier* (1909), the latter most famous for the high tessitura of its aria "My Hero"; Karl Hoschna (1877–1911), composer of the hit songs "Cuddle Up a Little Closer" (1908), and "Every Little Movement (Has a Meaning All Its Own" (1910); Fritz Kreisler (1875–1962), composer of some of the most

popular violin pieces in the world and of the song "Stars in My Eyes" (1936); and Frederick Loewe (1904–1988), composer of many great songs, including those in the musical dramas *Brigadoon* (1947), *My Fair Lady* (1956), and *Camelot* (1960) and the musical film *Gigi* (1958). Songwriters from non-Austrian parts of the old Austro-Hungarian Empire are Jean Schwartz and Sigmund Romberg, both born in Hungary, and Rudolf Friml, born in what is now **Czechoslovakia**.

Very much a product of Austria was the operetta *Blossom Time* (1921), based on the music of the Viennese-born Franz Schubert as arranged by Sigmund Romberg. It was actually derived from a very successful European operetta called *Das Dreimäderlhaus (Lilac Time)*, originally produced in Vienna in 1916. A fictitious account of Schubert's supposed life and love, its most popular song is "Song of Love," borrowed from the second theme of the first movement of Schubert's *Symphony No. 8 "The Unfinished"* (*see* Classics).

Two independent Austrian songs achieved considerable success in the United States: "Just a Gigolo" (1929)—originally "Schöner Gigolo"—and "Hear My Song, Violetta" (1938). Vienna is further memorialized in the nostalgic song "Vienna, My City of Dreams" (1914) (originally "Wien du Stadt meiner Träume") and in "Intermezzo," or "Souvenir de Vienne," taken from the theme of the 1939 film *Intermezzo*, starring Ingrid Bergman and Leslie Howard. Austria also served as the venue of one of the most popular American musical dramas—*The Sound of Music* (1959), based on the book *The Trapp Family Singers*—and of numerous films, including *The Third Man* (1949), which featured a sound track entirely played on the box zither, an instrument indigenous to Austria and southern Germany.

Austria's influence on American popular song has been pervasive. Reaching a peak in the first quarter of the twentieth century, it contributed the waltz and a host of fine composers. Indirectly, it gave us even more; embedded in much of American popular music—along with powerful influences from **Britain, France, Latin America**, and other countries—may be found the Austrian traditions of soaring lyricism and melodic balance.

Bibliography

Hofmann, Paul. *The Viennese: Splendor, Twilight, and Exile.* 1988.

Spiel, Hilde. *Vienna's Golden Autumn: 1866–1938.* 1987.

Automobiles. See Travel

Awards

Many institutions concerned with popular culture honor songs on the basis of aesthetic or commercial success. Some organizations, such as *Billboard* or the National

Academy of Recording Arts and Sciences, give awards chiefly for music or musical performance. Others, primarily involved in nonmusical aspects of the entertainment industry, like the Academy of Motion Picture Arts and Sciences, grant awards to songs that enhance the quality of that industry's productions (see Table 1).

Some awards are competitive, with several songs nominated for a single award; others are won whenever a song meets some objective criteria. For example, a "gold record" award is given automatically to singles and albums that have sold 500,000 or more copies. A "platinum" award goes to records that have sold one million or more copies. Some organizations offer both types of awards. Such is the case with Billboard, which over the years has given competitive awards as well as awards for reaching the number-one position in the Billboard charts.

Other prominent awards involving popular music include the **BMI** Awards (see Table 4), the **Grammy Awards** (see Table 10), the MTV Music Video Awards, the Handy Award (given by the Blues Foundation), and the Country Music Association Awards. Many institutions also give "Hall of Fame" awards to songwriters and performers who have demonstrated exceptional talent. These include the National Academy of Popular Music, which fosters the Songwriters' Hall of Fame and gives annual songwriting awards; the Nashville Songwriters' Association; and the Rock and Roll Hall of Fame Foundation, which honors both songwriters and performers.

Ehrick V. Long

See also: **Academy Awards; Recording**

Bibliography

Siegman, Gita, ed. *Awards, Honors and Prizes.* 1991.
———. *World of Winners.* 1989.
Stambler, Irwin. *Encyclopedia of Pop, Rock & Soul.* 1989.
Walter, Claire. *Winners: The Blue Ribbon Encyclopedia of Awards.* 1978.

b

BABY

The word "baby" has been used and abused by songwriters for well over a hundred years—since as far back as 1878 when, a song called "Baby Mine" was a hit. Seldom, however, does the term actually refer to a little **boy** or **girl**. It is used instead as a colloquialism expressing familiarity or the affection of one person for another. In the few songs in which babies are referred to in a literal sense, they often serve as a basis for comparison; "Baby Face" (1926) and "You Must Have Been a Beautiful Baby" (1938) are songs about adults rather than **children**.

One early example, "Hello! Ma Baby" (1899), is in fact a **telephone** song. Celebrating the then newfangled invention, it is also a prime example of **ragtime** in popular song. Another song of the same era, "My Melancholy Baby" (1912; copyrighted in 1911 with the title "Melancholy"), may well have been the first **torch song**.

The lyricist Gus Kahn seems to have had a penchant for baby songs. He wrote at least three of them: "Pretty Baby" (1916), "Yes Sir, That's My Baby" (1925); and "My Baby Just Cares for Me" (1930). The sprightly standard "I Found a Million Dollar Baby (in a Five and Ten Cent Store)"—with lyrics by Mort Dixon and Billy Rose and music by Harry Warren—was introduced in the revue *Crazy Quilt* in 1931; the song's emphasis on **money** reflected the lack of it during the Depression years.

The 1960s saw a rash of baby, or "babe," songs, such as "Baby Love" (1964; recorded by the Supremes), "I Got You Babe" (1965; recorded by Sonny and Cher), and "Baby, You're a Rich Man" (1967; recorded by the Beatles). The word was literally spelled out in the 1966 song "B-A-B-Y."

From the Gay Nineties to the Age of Rock, the words "baby" and "babe" have of course not been confined to titles, but have also appeared in innumerable lyrics. Nor have they been confined to the English language, as witness "Ciao, Ciao, Bambina" (1959). Functioning both as a term of **endearment** and a basic component of the lyrics of popular song, "baby" has been universal in its appeal.

Additional Songs

Baby Don't Get Hooked on Me (1972)
Baby, It's Cold Outside (1948)
Baby, It's You (1961)
Baby, Won't You Please Come Home? (1923)
Be My Baby (1963)
Bye Bye Baby (1949)
Bye Bye Baby (Baby Goodbye) (1964)
Cry Baby (1963)
Don't Say Nothin' Bad (About My Baby) (1963)
Don't Worry Baby (1964)
Dream Baby, How Long Must I Dream? (1962)
(You're) Having My Baby (1974)
Hey, Baby (1961)
I Don't Want to Walk Without You (1941)
I Found a New Baby (1925)
I'm Nobody's Baby (1921)
Is You Is or Is You Ain't (Ma' Baby) (1943)
It Ain't Me Babe (1964)
Love to Love You Baby (1976)
Rock Your Baby (1974)
Rock-a-bye Your Baby With a Dixie Melody (1918)
Ruby Baby (1955)
Since I Met You Baby (1956)
Steppin' Out With My Baby (1947)
Take Good Care of My Baby (1958)
Thank You Pretty Baby (1959)
There Goes My Baby (1959)
Walkin' My Baby Back Home (1930)
When My Baby Smiles at Me (1920)

See also: **Childhood**

BALLAD

At least three types of songs can be called ballads. The first, and most traditional, is the narrative: a strophic song that tells a story. Many examples, often based on history or legend, are found in **folk song**. The narrative tradition is perpetuated in such popular songs as "Ballad for Americans" (1940), "The Ballad of Davy Crockett" (1955), "The Ballad of the Green Berets" (1966), "The Ballad of Bonnie and Clyde" (1967), and "The Ballad of Sweeney Todd" (1979).

A second type of ballad is the sentimental song in which a story is told in a series of **verses**, each followed by a more melodic **chorus**, or refrain. Such songs, very popular at the turn of the century, were usually cast in the style of a **waltz**. A typical example is "After the Ball" (1892), which has three sixty-four-bar verses, each followed by the same thirty-two-bar chorus.

Since the 1920s the term "ballad" has come to represent any popular song in slow tempo. Although the **meter** is most often 4/4 or common time, other meters are used as well. Examples abound in the literature. "All the Things You Are," "Darn That Dream," "If I Didn't Care," "Over the Rainbow," and "What's New?" are representative examples of ballads, all written within the same year: 1939.

At least two subgenres of the last category exist: the waltz ballad and the rhythm ballad. The former is, of course, a slow song in 3/4 meter time, such as "Always" (1925), "I'll See You Again" (1929), "For You" (1930), or "Fly Me to the Moon" (1954). A rhythm ballad can best be described as a slow song with a strongly pronounced beat, such as "Can't Help Lovin' Dat Man" (1927), "Ain't Misbehavin'" (1929), "All of Me" (1931), and "I Don't Know Why (I Just Do)" (1931).

In more recent years, definitions of the term have tended to coalesce, and the ballad has come to mean any slow, romantic song with a steady but unobtrusive beat. Typical of this later stage of ballad composition are such songs as "We've Only Just Begun" (1970), "The Way We Were" (1973), "What I Did for Love" (1975), and "Just the Way You Are" (1977).

BALLROOM DANCE. SEE DANCE CRAZES

BANJO. SEE STRINGS

BARBERSHOP

Barbershop is as truly American a type of music as jazz or the blues. In its heyday, from the 1890s to the 1920s, it was performed everywhere: at home, in saloons, on streetcorners, even in barbershops—in short, any place where men congregated.

Barbershop music is a form of unaccompanied part-singing by a minimum of four male singers. The distinctive four-part barbershop harmony is achieved by assigning each part a specific role; the second tenor, the

"lead," sings the melody; the first tenor usually sings above the lead; the bass supplies the foundation; and the baritone fills in the notes needed to complete the chords. Although a male quartet is most often the unit of choice, it is by no means the only ensemble size capable of producing barbershop music; choruses of one hundred more are not unknown.

The **minstrel show**, launched in 1843, gave quartets a major boost in opportunities for performance, for they featured these vocal groups as a regular part of their programs. In addition, barbershop quartets often appeared in the Chautauqua: a type of traveling tent show focusing upon lectures and dramatic readings that entertained the American public until the early 1930s. Another type of entertainment, **vaudeville**, also featured barbershop quartets, with many of the more famous groups appearing on stage, until the advent of radio and sound film put an end to vaudeville productions.

One of the high points of barbershop singing occurred in the 1890s, when a number of songs were written with this particular style in mind. A prime example is "My Sweetheart's the Man in the Moon," written in 1892 by James Thornton, who had his last success in 1898 with another barbershop song, "When You Were Sweet Sixteen." Also in this decade the nation first heard "Ta-Ra-Ra Boom-De-Ay!," a **non-sense** song written by Henry Sayers in 1891; the title phrase was supposedly created by dance hall girls in St. Louis. Another song credited to the "girls" was "A Hot Time in the Old Town" (1896), composed by Theodore Metz employing the music of an old German folk song.

Two songs interpolated into an 1892 stage show, A Trip to Chinatown, are still popular with barbershop quartets: "After the Ball," by Charles K. Harris, and "The Bowery," by Percy Gaunt. The year 1892 also saw the appearance of "Daisy Bell" by Henry Dacre, a song better known by its auxiliary title: "A Bicycle Made for Two." Several other barbershop songs written in that final decade of the nineteenth century linger on, notably "The Story of the Rose (Heart of My Heart)" and "On the Banks of the Wabash, Far Away," both written in 1899.

It was near the turn of the century that the **recording** industry got its start. In 1897, the Universal Phonograph Company was formed in New York; this firm's first recording featured a barbershop quartet and chorus. Soon, other companies were seeking out quartets for their recordings, motivated partly by the fact that there was no need to hire additional musicians to accompany the singers.

Although barbershop singing continued to be popular during the opening decade of the twentieth century, it could not sustain interest after 1925, and thereafter nearly disappeared from the musical scene. Its decline in popularity can be attributed to at least two factors: the advent of radio and film, with consequent changes in lifestyle and musical taste; and the more sophisticated harmonies of many new songs, which did not readily lend themselves to four-part harmonization.

In 1938, however, barbershop singing was revitalized thanks to two men in Tulsa, Oklahoma, who formed a local singing club. Owen C. Cash, a tax attorney, and Rupert I. Hall, an investment banker, sent letters to their friends stating:

> In this age of dictators and government control of everything, about the only privilege guaranteed by the Bill of Rights not in some way supervised or directed is the art of barbershop singing. Without a doubt, we still have the right of peaceable assembly, which we are advised by competent legal authority, includes quartet singing. . . . Therefore, we have decided to hold a songfest to encourage the enjoyment of this last remaining vestige of human liberty.

From this letter came forth the Society for the Preservation and Propagation of Barber Shop Quartet Singing in America, later changed to the Society for the Preservation and Encouragement of Barber Shop Quartet Singing in America, or SPEBSQSA.

Men in other cities learned of this new organization and formed related clubs and societies. By the 1980s the SPEBSQSA was the world's largest singing organization, with more than 40,000 members, 2,500 quartets, and 700 choruses. In 1945, a barbershop-style singing organization for women, Sweet Adelines, was formed; a second female group, Harmony Inc., started in 1958. Thus, barbershop singing is alive and well in America and growing with each passing year. With a widening repertoire of songs, barbershop quartets and choruses remain an integral part of the American scene.

Additional Songs

By the Beautiful Sea (1914)
By the Light of the Silvery Moon (1909)
Down by the Old Mill Stream (1910)
I Wonder Who's Kissing Her Now (1909)
In the Good Old Summertime (1902)
In the Shade of the Old Apple Tree (1905)
Let Me Call You Sweetheart (1910)
Mighty Lak' a Rose (1901)
(On) Moonlight Bay (1912)
Play That Barbershop Chord (Mr. Jefferson Lord) (1910)
Put Your Arms Around Me, Honey (1910)
Shine On, Harvest Moon (1908)
Take Me Out to the Ball Game (1908)
Will You Love Me in December as You Do in May? (1905)
You're the Flower of My Heart, Sweet Adeline (1903)

William D. Askin

See also: Gay Nineties

Bibliography

Heller, Ray. "From the Archives." *The Harmonizer*, 50, no. 3 (May/June 1990): 6–8.
Johnson, James Weldon. "The Origin of the 'Barber Chord.'" *The Mentor* (Feb. 1929): 53.
Martin, Deac (C. T.). *Deac Martin's Book of Musical Americana*. 1970.
———. "The Evolution of Barbershop Harmony." *Music Journal Annual*. 1965.
Spaeth, Sigmund. *Barber Shop Ballads and How to Sing Them*. 1940.

Bass Line

The bass line is the lowest-sounding part of a composition or **arrangement**. As such, it is of particular importance in popular song, where it is often the only melodic part independent of the melody itself. In practice, the bass line of popular music is usually assigned to the electric bass guitar, the left hand of the keyboard instrument, the double bass, or the tuba, or to various combinations of these instruments.

The nature of the bass line, at least as it is written in **sheet music**, has changed radically over the past one hundred years. Around the turn of the century, the bass was often written as the root note of the prevailing **harmony**. The bass line in the chorus of the 1896 song "A Hot Time in the Old Town" for example, consists of twelve bars repeating the note G (the tonic), two bars on D (the dominant), and a final two bars on G.

This simplicity continued in the bass lines of early **Tin Pan Alley**. In waltzes, a bass note almost invariably falls on the first beat of each measure, while empty spots in the melody are filled in with stepwise passages in the bass. On rare occasions, as in the sheet music arrangement of Irving Berlin's waltz "Remember" (1925), the bass line carries the melody.

In songs of the time in duple meter, movement of the bass line in fourths and fifths is common, occasionally interspersed with brief chromatic passages. Passages like this appear:

In music written for Broadway and Hollywood, bass lines, along with harmonies, tend to be more complex. For example, in the chorus of "The Girl Friend" (1926), the bass ascends chromatically with each harmonic change. In "Sophisticated Lady" (1933), it descends chromatically along with the harmonies. In "Lover" (1933), the bass line descends chromatically in fifths, parallel to the melodic line. In the release of "I Won't

Dance" (1935), the bass, like the harmony, is quite intricate: moving in fifths from A-flat to D-flat to B, and then through the **circle of fifths**, before returning to the tonic of C.

In practice, however, bass lines are seldom performed as they are written. Frequently, the written-out bass line serves only as a matrix for improvisational elaboration. A common device used both in **jazz** performance and in the **big bands,** is the so-called walking bass, usually comprised of quarter or eighth notes in predominantly stepwise motion:

Also favored in many jazz-oriented works is the distinctive *basso ostinato* known as **boogie-woogie,** consisting of insistent repetitions of a bass pattern throughout a piece.

The music of **Latin America** is noted for its provocative bass lines. In many cases, they are leading determinant factors of style, as in the **tango,** the **rumba,** the **cha cha cha,** and related genres. The **bossa nova,** in particular, is noted for its bass lines, which are sometimes as important as the melody. They frequently descend chromatically, as in "Quiet Nights of Quiet Stars" (1962). The bass line of "One Note Samba" (1961), which also descends chromatically, in fact holds much more melodic interest than the repeated one-note melody.

Beginning in the 1960s, bass lines become both louder—aided by the proliferation of amplification—and more varied. Sometimes, as in "Light My Fire" (1967), the bass consists of alternating patterns of quarter and eighth notes. At other times, as in "Hey Jude" (1968), it consists largely of repeated eighth notes. In pop-rock, bass patterns like this are common:

In striking contrast to these simple patterns, extremely complicated bass parts were also written in the 1970s

and 1980s, demonstrating that the bass line had come a long way from the two-to-the-bar bass notes of early Tin Pan Alley.

See also: Chromaticism; Improvisation; Instrumentation; Lead Sheet

BEAUTY

The words "beautiful," "lovely," "pretty," and "cute" are staples of popular song. Objects of beauty are diverse, ranging from a nation ("America, the Beautiful," 1895), to a river ("Beautiful Ohio," 1918), to a time of day ("Oh What a Beautiful Mornin'," 1943), to a friendship ("A Beautiful Friendship," 1956), and even to a balloon; the 1967 song "Up, Up and Away" begins with the words "Would you like to ride in my beautiful balloon?"

Containing three syllables, the word "beautiful" lends itself well to dotted rhythms, as shown in the perennials "Oh You Beautiful Doll" (1911) and "You Must Have Been a Beautiful Baby" (1938). It also marries well with syncopation, as in the 1973 song "The Most Beautiful Girl." Lorenz Hart and Richard Rodgers wrote two excellent songs on the subject: the ballad "You Are Too Beautiful" (1932) and the waltz "The Most Beautiful Girl in the World" (1935). Sometimes titles are taken from popular expressions; "The Night Is Young and You're So Beautiful" (1936) and "We Could Make Such Beautiful Music (Together)" (1940) are examples. In one memorable song, Gordon Jenkins's ballad "This Is All I Ask" (1958), "beautiful girls" are asked to "walk a little slower."

The word "lovely" has also appeared in many songs. Jerome Kern was particularly adept at setting it to music in songs like "Lovely to Look At" (1935), "You Were Never Lovelier" (1942), and "The Way You Look Tonight" (1936). The final stanza of the last begins with Dorothy Field's unforgettable line "Lovely, never, never change," where the word "lovely" is expressed in music by two whole notes descending an interval of a fifth. On the other hand, many songs use the word in a context far removed from personal appearance: "Isn't This a Lovely Day" (1935), "It's D'Lovely" (1936), "The Loveliest Night of the Year" (1950), and—with a Cockney accent—"Wouldn't It Be Loverly?," from *My Fair Lady* (1956).

As for "pretty," it goes at least as far back as 1900 and the song "Tell Me Pretty Maiden (Are There Many More at Home Like You?)," sung by the Floradora Girls in the revue *Floradora.* One of the most famous songs on the subject is Irving Berlin's "A Pretty Girl Is Like a Melody," from the *Ziegfeld Follies of 1919.* Roy Orbison's 1964 hit, "Oh Pretty Woman," is another case in point. The word was also used to good advantage by Stephen Sondheim in his lyrics for "I Feel Pretty" (1957), "Pretty Lady" (1976), and "Pretty Women" (1978).

"Cute" is another variation on the theme of good looks, expressed in "You Couldn't Be Cuter" (1938). But Hank Williams had a more down-to-earth approach to appearance: "Hey Good Lookin'" (1951).

Additional Songs

The Bad and the Beautiful (Love Is for the Very Young) (1953)
A Beautiful Lady in Blue (1935)
Beautiful Love (1931)
But Beautiful (1947)
Do I Love You Because You're Beautiful? (1957)
Everything Is Beautiful (1970)
If There Is Someone Lovelier Than You (1934)
It's a Lovely Day Today (1950)
It's a Lovely Day Tomorrow (1939)
Lovely Lady (1937)
A Lovely Way to Spend an Evening (1943)

See also: **Girl; Lady; Woman**

Bebop

Bebop, also known as "bop," was a style of jazz **improvisation** that developed in the 1940s, chiefly as a reaction by black musicians to the strictures and formalism of big-band **swing**. Among its characteristics were jagged melody, frequent interruptions, bold harmonies using altered chords of the eleventh and thirteenth, polyrhythm, asymmetrical accents, fast tempos, "walking" **bass lines**, and unexpected changes of direction. The appellation, originally "rebop," was derived from an onomatopoeic way of singing a characteristic motive, on the order of **scat singing**.

The bebop style of playing originated at Minton's Playhouse in **Harlem** around 1942, and shortly thereafter in the jazz clubs of West 52nd Street in New York City. Its leading exponents were alto saxophonist Charlie "Bird" Parker, trumpeters Dizzy Gillespie and Fats Navarro, pianist Thelonious Monk, drummer Kenny Clarke, and guitarist Charlie Christian.

With few exceptions—like "Round Midnight" (1944), co-authored by Monk, and Gillespie's "Be-Bop" of the same year—the repertoire consisted of standard songs. These songs were used as general outlines for fashioning entirely new pieces by avoiding the original melody and by altering the harmony and even, in some cases, the form. Many jazz instrumental pieces were written in this manner, keeping only the barest harmonic progressions of the original. Perhaps the most famous model song, and bebop's virtual anthem, was "How High the Moon" (1940); others were "What Is This Thing Called Love?" (1929) and "Embraceable You" (1930).

At the height of the bebop craze, it engendered something of a cult. Many of its adherents, like Gillespie, affected peculiar mannerisms and clothing: berets, goatees, dark glasses, impoliteness. Also at this time

(1945), several commercial songs became popular, including "Be-Baba-Luba" and "Hey! Ba-Ba-Re-Bop."

There was a brief resurgence of bebop, under the name "hard bop," in the mid-1950s. Its chief performers were Sonny Rollins (saxophone), Clifford Brown (trumpet), Earl "Bud" Powell (piano), and Art Blakey and Max Roach (drums). But in ensuing years, bebop gave way to other forms of jazz improvisation, such as "cool" and "West Coast."

Additional Songs

After You've Gone (1918)
Cherokee (1938)
Don't Blame Me (1933)
Honeysuckle Rose (1929)
I Got Rhythm (1930)
Indiana (Back Home Again in Indiana) (1917)
Lover Man (Oh Where Can You Be) (1942)
Oh, Lady Be Good (1924)
There Will Never Be Another You (1942)
You Turned the Tables on Me (1936)

Bibliography

Feather, Leonard. *Inside Be-Bop*. Reprinted as *Inside Jazz*. 1977.

Gillespie, Dizzy, with Al Fraser. *To Be or Not to Bop: Memories*. 1979.

Hodeir, André. *Jazz: Its Evolution and Essence*. 1979.

Jones, LeRoi [Amiri Baraka]. *Blues People: Negro Music in White America*. 1980.

Ulanov, Barry. *A Handbook of Jazz*. 1975.

Beginning

The subject of starting something—most often, a new romance—has resulted in a number of intriguing songs. One of them, Otto Harbach and Jerome Kern's "Let's Begin," comes from the original stage version of *Roberta* (1933). Another, "I Can't Get Started", written by Ira Gershwin and Vernon Duke in 1935, laments the singer's inability to initiate a new romance, even though he or she has—in Ira Gershwin's words—"been around the world in a plane" and "settled revolutions in Spain." Still another song, "(Where Do I Begin) Love Story," (1970), questions exactly how to get started with a new affair.

Three well-known songs are concerned with the first stages of a new relationship: "(I've Got) Beginner's Luck" (1937), "This Could Be the Start of Something Big" (1956), and "We've Only Just Begun" (1970). Several other songs contain the word "beginning" in their titles, but are really about other subjects: sudden awareness, in "I'm Beginning to See the Light" (1944); inarticulateness, in "I Can't Begin to Tell You" (1945); and the approach of the holiday season, in "It's Beginning to Look Like Christmas" (1951). But perhaps the most familiar use of the word "begin" occurs in Cole Porter's "Begin the Beguine" (1935)—a song that is more about nostalgia, and remembering "the sound of music so tender," than about beginning.

Additional Songs

Beginnings (1969)
Right Back Where We Started From (1976)
Wanna Be Startin' Somethin' (1982)

See also: Birth; Ending

BEGUINE

The beguine is a dance which probably originated on the islands of Martinique and St. Lucia; the term also refers to the distinctive music that accompanies the dance. In 4/4 meter, it resembles the **bolero** and **rumba,** but it differs from those dances in the continuity of its strongly accented first, third, and fourth beats and accented afterbeats in a configuration such as this:

A modified form of the beguine became very popular as a ballroom dance in Europe and North America in the 1930s and 1940s, largely through the efforts of Cole Porter. His "Begin the Beguine" (1935) popularized both the term and the dance. The song was so successful that Porter wrote a number of other songs compatible with the rhythm: "Easy to Love" and "I've Got You Under My Skin" in 1936, "In the Still of the Night" in 1937, "I Concentrate on You" in 1939, "You'd Be So Nice to Come Home To" in 1942, "I Love You" in 1944, and "So in Love" in 1948. Several of his earlier songs, such as "Night and Day" (1932), are also effective in the rhythm of the beguine. All these songs bear the hallmarks of Porter's melodic and harmonic sophistication, which serve to enhance the exotic rhythmic background. Many are unusual in other aspects as well: dynamics, form, length, and range. It is as if the rhythm of the beguine acts as a catalyst for innovation.

A number of melodies by other composers also lend themselves well to the rhythm of the beguine. Five enchanting songs immediately come to mind: Richard Rodgers's "I Didn't Know What Time It Was" (1939), Jerome Kern's "Dearly Beloved" and "I'm Old Fashioned" (both 1942), Kurt Weill's "Speak Low" (1943), and Leonard Bernstein's "Tonight" (1957). The rhythm

of the beguine is, in fact, adaptable to almost any nonsyncopated song in moderate tempo and duple time.

See also: **Accompaniment; Dance Crazes; Rhythm**

BELGIUM

Belgium's influence upon American popular music rests primarily with its native artists. Of special importance was the singer, composer, and author Jacques Brel. Born in Brussels, he attained early success in **France**. Among his most popular compositions in the United States were "Carousel," "If We Only Had Love," and "Marieke," all featured in the **revue** *Jacques Brel Is Alive and Well and Living in Paris*, which opened at the Village Gate **cabaret** in New York City in 1968. Belgium is also the birthplace of the singer Soeur Sourire, whose hit recording of the waltz "Dominique" (1963) led to the film *The Singing Nun* (1966).

See also: **Foreign Influence**

BIG BANDS

During their heyday—the period from the mid-1930s until the end of **World War II**—groups of ten or more musicians were known as "big bands." A typical band might consist of a leader, a rhythm section (piano, bass, guitar, drums), a woodwind section (three to five saxophones, some of them doubling on clarinet, bass clarinet, or flute), a brass section (at least two trumpets and two trombones), and a **singer** or **singing group**, but many other combinations existed. Bands, or orchestras (as they were called), appeared in ballrooms, hotels, nightclubs, and theaters, but attained their greatest renown as the result of thousands of remote **radio** broadcasts from hotels and ballrooms throughout the nation, as well as from a multitude of **recordings**.

Big bands had existed since the early 1920s; some of the best known were those headed by Paul Whiteman, Vincent Lopez, and Fred Waring. Not until 1935, however, with Benny Goodman's engagement at the Palomar Ballroom in Los Angeles, did the organizations take consistent shape and become universally popular.

In general, there were three types of big bands: swing, sweet, and novelty. However, the styles were not mutually exclusive, and most bands did not adhere to a single style. Goodman, Tommy Dorsey, Jimmy Dorsey, and Glenn Miller, for example, were equally at home in sweet and swing and were not averse to doing novelties. Sweet bands, on the other hand, rarely played swing; groups led by leaders like Guy Lombardo, Eddy Duchin, and Freddy Martin concentrated on ballads. Novelty bands, such as those of Sammy Kaye and Kay Kyser, were essentially sweet bands with innovative ideas like Kyser's "College of Musical Knowledge."

Spike Jones carved a special niche for himself and his band in the field of **humor** and mimicry.

Of primary importance to the success of the big bands (although they were seldom acknowledged) were their **arrangements** and orchestrations. Goodman owed much of his initial success to the orchestral arrangements of Fletcher Henderson; Tommy Dorsey and Jimmie Lunceford to those of Sy Oliver. A number of leaders, including Duke Ellington, Claude Thornhill, Glenn Miller, and Les Brown, used their own arrangements as well as those of others. Orchestra musicians (known as "sidemen") also occasionally doubled as arrangers; Henry Mancini, Johnny Mandel, Neal Hefti, and Nelson Riddle started their careers in this fashion.

Also of vital importance to a band's success were its singers and vocal groups, many of whom went on to long careers as soloists or in other aspects of show business. Such future stars as Frank Sinatra, Peggy Lee, and Doris Day had their first popular successes with the orchestras of Tommy Dorsey, Benny Goodman, and Les Brown, respectively. Other vocalists became indelibly identified with a band's style: Bea Wain with Larry Clinton, Bob Eberly and Helen O'Connell with Jimmy Dorsey, Jo Stafford (and Sinatra) with Tommy Dorsey, Martha Tilton with Benny Goodman, Dick Haymes and Helen Forrest with Harry James, Ray Eberle and the Modernaires with Glenn Miller, and Helen Forrest with Artie Shaw.

Thousands of popular songs were introduced by the big bands, among them such standards as "In the Mood" (1939), "I'll Never Smile Again" (1939), and "Sentimental Journey" (1944) (see Table 3). In addition, the bands popularized old standards in new arrangements—songs like "You Made Me Love You" (1913), played by Harry James; "Begin the Beguine"

(1936), by Artie Shaw; and "I Can't Get Started" (1935), by Bunny Berigan.

Every band had its own theme song, played at the beginning and end of each appearance or broadcast. Some bands had different opening and closing themes, such as Goodman's "Let's Dance" (1935) and "Good-bye" (1935). Among the best-known theme songs were Tommy Dorsey's "I'm Gettin' Sentimental Over You" (1932), Duke Ellington's "Take the 'A' Train" (1941), Harry James's "Ciribiribin" (1898), and Bunny Berigan's "I Can't Get Started" (1935) (see Table 3).

With the advent of World War II, keeping bands together became more difficult as more and more leaders and sidemen went into the service. Singers gradually began to take on more importance within the bands. Wartime shortages, particularly of gasoline, made touring difficult. All these factors contributed to the diminution in importance of the big band and the birth of a new era featuring the singer.

But the big bands never completely disappeared. Easily the most long-lasting organization was that of Lawrence Welk, which became the nucleus of the most successful dance band show ever produced on **television**. Other big bands remained popular through the 1980s, especially on college campuses and in civic centers. Usually, like a voice from the past, they retained the names of their deceased leaders—calling themselves the Tommy Dorsey Orchestra, the Guy Lombardo Orchestra, the Glenn Miller Orchestra, the Count Basie Orchestra—despite a complete change of personnel.

Bibliography

Simon, George T. *The Big Bands*. Fourth ed. 1981.
———. *The Big Bands Songbook*. 1981.

See also: Brass; Golden Age; Instrumentation; Woodwinds

TABLE 3

The Big Bands and Their Songs

Mitchell Ayres
    *You Go to My Head (1938)

Charlie Barnet
    *Cherokee (1938)

Count Basie
    *One O'Clock Jump (1938)

Bunny Berigan
    *I Can't Get Started (1935)

Will Bradley
    What Can I Say After I Say I'm Sorry? (1926)
    I Don't Stand a Ghost of a Chance With You (1932)
    It's a Wonderful World (1931)

Les Brown
    *Sentimental Journey (1944)

'Tis Autumn (1941)

Frankie Carle
    *Sunrise Serenade (1938)

Larry Clinton
    Deep Purple (1934)
    *The Dipsy Doodle (1937)
    How High the Moon (1940)
    My Reverie (1938)

Bob Crosby
    Big Noise From Winnetka (1940)
    Muskrat Ramble (1926)
    South Rampart Street Parade (1938)
    *Summertime (1935)
    What's New? (1939)

Xavier Cugat
    My Shawl (1934)

Jimmy Dorsey
Amapola (1924)
Green Eyes (1929)
I Understand (1941)
Maria Elena (1933)
*So Rare (1937)
Tangerine (1942)
Yours (1937)

Tommy Dorsey
East of the Sun (And West of the Moon) (1934)
Embraceable You (1930)
I'll Never Smile Again (1939)
*I'm Gettin' Sentimental Over You (1932)
Marie (1928)
Oh! Look at Me Now! (1941)
Once in a While (1937)
South of the Border (Down Mexico Way) (1939)
This Love of Mine (1941)

Duke Ellington
Do Nothin' Till You Hear From Me (1943)
Don't Get Around Much Anymore (1942)
I Got It Bad (And That Ain't Good) (1941)
I Let a Song Go Out of My Heart (1938)
I'm Beginning to See the Light (1944)
In a Sentimental Mood (1935)
Mood Indigo (1931)
Perdido (1942)
Prelude to a Kiss (1938)
Satin Doll (1958)
Solitude (1934)
Sophisticated Lady (1933)
*Take the 'A' Train (1941)

Benny Goodman
After You've Gone (1918)
Blue Skies (1927)
Body and Soul (1930)
Don't Be That Way (1938)
*Good-bye (1935)
*Let's Dance (1935)
Sing, Sing, Sing, Sing (1936)
Sometimes I'm Happy (1927)

Glen Gray and the Casa Loma Orchestra
Exactly Like You (1930)
For You (1930)
Happy Days Are Here Again (1929)
It's the Talk of the Town (1933)
Lazy Bones (1933)
On the Sunny Side of the Street (1930)
*Smoke Rings (1933)
Under a Blanket of Blue (1933)

Harry James
All or Nothing at All (1940)
*Ciribiribin (1898)
I Cried for You (1923)
I Don't Want to Walk Without You (1941)
I Surrender, Dear (1931)
I'll Get By (As Long as I Have You) (1928)
I've Heard That Song Before (1942)
Skylark (1942)
You Made Me Love You (1913)

Isham Jones
I'll See You in My Dreams (1924)
It Had to Be You (1924)

On the Alamo (1922)
The One I Love Belongs to Somebody Else (1924)
Star Dust (1929)
Swingin' Down the Lane (1923)

Sammy Kaye
Harbor Lights (1937)
It Isn't Fair (1933)

Hal Kemp
Got a Date With an Angel (1931)
Hands Across the Table (1934)
It's Easy to Remember (1934)
You're the Top (1934)

Stan Kenton
And Her Tears Flowed Like Wine (1943)

Wayne King
*The Waltz You Saved for Me (1930)

Kay Kyser
Praise the Lord and Pass the Ammunition (1942)
Three Little Fishes (1939)

Guy Lombardo
*Auld Lang Syne (1711)
Boo-Hoo! (1937)
Coquette (1928)
Gimme a Little Kiss, Will Ya Huh? (1926)
Heartaches (1931)
Intermezzo (A Love Story) (1940)
Little White Lies (1930)
Seems Like Old Times (1946)

Johnny Long
A Shanty in Old Shanty Town (1932)

Freddy Martin
I Look at Heaven (When I Look at You) (1942)
*Tonight We Love (1941)

Glenn Miller
At Last (1942)
Chattanooga Choo Choo (1941)
In the Mood (1938)
I've Got a Gal in Kalamazoo (1942)
*Moonlight Serenade (1939)
Pennsylvania 6-5000 (1940)
Serenade in Blue (1942)
A String of Pearls (1942)
Tuxedo Junction (1940)

Vaughn Monroe
(Ghost) Riders in the Sky (A Cowboy Legend) (1949)
*Racing With the Moon (1941)

Russ Morgan
*Does Your Heart Beat for Me? (1936)

Ray Noble
*Goodnight Sweetheart (1931)
Love Is the Sweetest Thing (1933)
The Touch of Your Lips (1936)
*The Very Thought of You (1934)

Artie Shaw
Begin the Beguine (1935)
Frenesi (1939)
Indian Love Call (1924)
Lover, Come Back to Me! (1928)

* = theme song

BILLBOARD

Billboard, a show business periodical, is best known for its charts ranking the popular songs of the day in various categories. It began in November 1894 as *Billboard Advertising*, a monthly catering to bill-posting companies and to businesses—such as fairs and exhibitions—that frequently used them. By the turn of the century, other entertainment media had also become a regular feature of the periodical. In 1900, *Billboard's* first regular column devoted to musical theater, "Footlight Flickerings," made its debut, heralding the shift from advertising to entertainment. The emphasis on show business continued to grow during the 1910s, especially regarding music performed in **minstrel shows** and **vaudeville.**

Billboard's most recognizable feature, the pop chart, has had a long, if broken, history. The first chart, published July 19, 1913, listed the top-selling **sheet music** of the day. Later that year an additional chart was published, giving an unranked listing of popular vaudeville songs. Among the songs included were George M. Cohan's "You're a Grand Old Flag" (1906) and Alfred Bryan and Fred Fisher's "Peg o' My Heart" (1913).

From 1918 to 1934, there were sporadic listings of top-selling sheet music. In 1934, a regular column was added charting the top songs played on **radio.** From 1935 to 1938, *Billboard*, along with *Variety* and other show business journals, published the "Ten Best Records," announcing the top-selling records of each major label. For example, Brunswick's best-seller for the week of this chart's debut was a performance of Cole Porter's "Me and Marie" (1935) by Johnny Green and His Orchestra. Charts were added in 1938 reflecting jukebox favorites. The first comprehensive chart of **recordings**—indicating the biggest **hit songs** nationally and by region—was published in 1940.

In the 1950s, as radio moved in the direction of all-music formats and stations sought to extend their playlists, *Billboard's* charts expanded from 20 records to 100. The first number-one hit of *Billboard's* "Top 100" chart was "Love Is a Many-Splendored Thing" (1955), sung by the Four Aces. The "Top 100" changed to the "Hot 100" in 1958, as **rock 'n' roll** became an increasingly important part of the music industry. This was demonstrated by two hits of 1958: "Rockin' Robin," recorded by Bobby Day, and "Summertime Blues," co-written and recorded by Eddie Cochran. In 1990, the "Hot 100" remained *Billboard's* principal chart, although new charts were added to indicate emerging pop markets such as **rap, dance,** and Latin American music.

Ehrick V. Long

Bibliography

Fiehl, John. *Music Trends: Characteristics of the "Billboard" Charts, 1955–1977.* 1981.

Whitburn, Joel. *Joel Whitburn's Pop Annual, 1955–1982.* 1983.

———. *Joel Whitburn's Pop Memories, 1890–1954.* 1983.

BIRDS

The species of birds represented in popular song are many and varied. Two, the robin and the blackbird, were first sighted in 1926 and have shown great endurance: "When the Red, Red Robin Comes Bob, Bob, Bobbin' Along" and "Bye Bye Blackbird." An unrelated series of **revues** called the *Blackbirds* ran sporadically in New York City from 1928 to 1939. Nightingales were spotted first in 1940 with "A Nightingale Sang in Berkeley Square," and two years later in the bolero "Nightingale," popularized by Xavier Cugat and His Orchestra.

Swallows and woodpeckers appeared in 1940, in "When the Swallows Come Back to Capistrano" and "The Woodpecker Song"—the latter an import from **Italy** originally entitled "Reginella Campagnola." Skylarks and flamingos were sighted in the 1940s, with the **big band** favorites "Flamingo" (1941) and "Skylark" (1942). Perhaps the only song to describe the love life of a bird, "Baltimore Oriole," made an appearance in 1942, while 1944 saw "The Eagle and Me"; 1950, "The Little White Duck"; and 1958, "Rockin' Robin."

Birds have sometimes been treated metaphorically, as in "A Bird in a Gilded Cage" (1899), a song noted for the banality of its lyrics, in which the heroine of the song "married for wealth, not love." Birds have also served as bearers of good fortune, as in the wartime favorite "(There'll Be Bluebirds Over) The White Cliffs of Dover" (1941).

The era of **rhythm and blues** in the late 1940s and early 1950s saw a proliferation of **singing groups** named after birds: the Ravens, the Robins, the Swallows, the Penguins, the Wrens, the Cardinals, the Orioles, and even the Feathers.

Bird songs can be generic as well: no species are specified in "When My Sugar Walks Down the Street, All the Birdies Go Tweet-Tweet-Tweet" (1924) and "Let's All Sing Like the Birdies Sing" (1932). Birds can also be deceptive: "Lullaby of Birdland" (1952) refers, of course, not to one of our feathered friends but rather to a New York ballroom named after jazz saxophonist Charlie (Bird) Parker (1920–1955).

Additional Songs

Ain't Nobody Here But Us Chickens (1946)
Albatross (1967)
Bird on the Wire (1969)
The Bluebird of Happiness (1934)
Great Speckled Bird (1937)
The Hot Canary (1948)
When Doves Cry (1984)
Yellow Bird (1957)

See also: Animals

BIRTH

Birth is, after all, a form of **beginning**. As such, it is referred to in the rollicking 1926 song "The Birth of the Blues." Very often in popular song, however, being born is viewed as a source of inequity: exploitation ("That's Why Darkies Were Born," 1931), mistreatment of animals ("Born Free," 1966), or unrequited love ("Why Was I Born?," 1929).

A much happier circumstance is found in the lyrics of the 1979 waltz "With You I'm Born Again": "Lying safe within your arms, I'm born again." Being born is also at the core of what is probably the most popular American song ever written, "Happy Birthday to You," written by two sisters, Patty Smith Hill and Mildred J. Hill, in 1893.

Additional Songs

Born in the U.S.A. (1984)
Born to Be Wild (1968)
Born to Lose (1943)
Born to the Breed (1975)
Born Too Late (1958)

BLUE. SEE COLORS

BLUE NOTE

The term "blue note," quite simply meaning a lowered note, probably derives from its frequent presence in the **blues**. Although blue notes can occur on almost any degree of the diatonic **scale**, in practice the third, sixth, or seventh scale degrees are the notes most often flattened. George Gershwin was especially fond of blue notes. They permeate his *Rhapsody in Blue* (1924): its opening motive features a flatted seventh and its closing motive a flatted third. Flatted thirds are also found in Gershwin's "Somebody Loves Me" (1924) and "My One and Only" (1927), while flatted sevenths are prominent in the **melodies** of many of his songs, including "The Man I Love" (1924), "Fascinating Rhythm" (1924), "Soon" (1929), "Bess, You Is My Woman" (1935), and "A Foggy Day" (1937).

Blue notes are prevalent in a number of other songs written from the 1920s through the 1940s. "Am I Blue?" (1929), for example, has a flatted third at each cadence. Several famous songs of the big bands are also characterized by blue notes, among them "At Last" (1942), "Serenade in Blue" (1942), and "Sentimental Journey" (1944).

With the coming of **rhythm and blues** and **rock 'n' roll**, the blue note became an essential ingredient in the melodic vocabulary of many rhythm songs. It retained this status through the 1980s, as witness the prominent flatted thirds in Stevie Wonder's "Boogie on Reggae Woman" (1974).

BLUEGRASS

Bluegrass is a type of **country and western** music that came to prominence on broadcasts of the Grand Ole Opry originating in **Nashville** during the 1940s. Its name is derived from the group that initiated those broadcasts: Bill Monroe and his Blue Grass Boys. That group, in turn, got its name from the Bluegrass State, Kentucky. Bluegrass music is by no means confined to Kentucky, however; it is found throughout the Appalachian states, from where it has spread to other parts of the United States and throughout the world.

Bluegrass music is commonly performed by groups of four to seven individuals who sing and accompany themselves on nonelectronic, or "acoustic," **instruments**—traditionally, the fiddle, mandolin, five-string banjo, lead guitar, and Dobro as melody instruments, with guitar and string bass supplying the rhythmic accompaniment. Although bluegrass musicians pride themselves on using natural sounds and avoid electronic instruments, they are not averse to microphones for amplification. The preferred vocal ideal, called "the high and lonesome sound," is achieved by using close vocal harmony in from two to four parts.

The music is usually in duple meter and played in a fast tempo. Considerable attention is paid to instrumental technique, as exemplified by the virtuosity of Monroe on the mandolin, Earl Scruggs on the banjo, and Lester Flatt on the guitar.

The bluegrass repertoire includes many traditional **folk songs**, as well as country-and-western songs that are performed in bluegrass style. Songs are for the most part conventional, with simple melodies, harmonies, and lyrics. In addition, numerous original bluegrass songs have been written, including Monroe's "Blue Moon of Kentucky" (1947) and "Uncle Pen" (1951). Scruggs's "Foggy Mountain Breakdown" (1950), sung by Flatt and Scruggs, was used as musical background for the car chase scene in the 1967 film *Bonnie and Clyde*. Bluegrass music was also used extensively in the television show *The Beverly Hillbillies*, which had as its theme the bluegrass song "Ballad of Jed Clampett" (1962), and in the 1972 film *Deliverance*, noted for its famous instrumental duet, "Dueling Banjos."

Bibliography

Artis, Bob. *Bluegrass: From the Lonesome Wail of a Mountain Love Song to the Hammering Drive of the Scruggs-Style Banjo: The Story of an American Musical Tradition.* 1975.

Hill, Fred. *Grassroots: An Illustrated History of Bluegrass and Mountain Music.* 1980.

Price, Steven D. *Old as the Hills: The Story of Bluegrass Music.* 1975.

Rosenberg, Neil V. *Bluegrass: A History.* 1985.

BLUES

The blues has manifold significance in the history of popular song: the term at once denotes an emotion, a spirit, a genre, and a form. Throughout the twentieth century, the blues also served as a source of inspiration for many related genres, including **gospel, jazz, Motown, reggae, rhythm and blues, rock, rock 'n' roll,** and **soul.** In addition, the word itself became attached to the titles of many songs, some of which are authentic blues, while others are not.

As an emotion, the blues denotes a feeling or **mood** of depression, as in the songs "Blue and Broken Hearted" (1922), "Am I Blue?" (1929), and "Bye, Bye Blues" (1930). Many songs also capitalize on the ambiguity of blue as both a **color** and an emotion.

As a spirit, the blues goes back to its origins in the nineteenth century, when it originated in the field hollers and work songs of black farmhands and shiploaders. These chants were often characterized by lowered tones, often of the flatted third and seventh, which came to be called **blue notes.** Their sentiments ranged from sorrow and despair to unabashed joy.

As a genre, the blues has many varieties. Different sections of the United States had their own types of blues at different times; for example, the "classic" blues sung by urban women in New York and Chicago in the 1920s; the country, or down-home, blues of the Mississippi delta; the southern folk blues of the early twentieth century; piano blues and **boogie-woogie;** the urban blues of Chicago; the post–World War II blues of the West Coast; **zydeco** in Louisiana; and soul blues in the 1950s and 1960s.

In many of these blues songs, the primary emotions are those of sadness and dissatisfaction: a back-breaking job, a lost love. But at the other extreme, the blues could also be "good time music," suitable for dancing and celebration. Many performers sang the blues, varying in style from country singer-guitarists like Blind Lemon Jefferson and Ledbelly, to urban singers like Muddy Waters and B. B. King, and to classic blues singers like Ma Rainey and Bessie Smith.

Blues form developed out of the form of its lyrics: two repeated lines, followed by an answering line (AAB). This poetic form readily translated itself into a musical form of twelve bars: three four-bar phrases—one for each line—distributed among tonic (I), dominant (V), and subdominant (IV) chords, as follows:

Blues form proved to be extremely flexible, both as a basis for **improvisation** and as a song form. In particular, hundreds of **boogie-woogie, rhythm-and-blues,** and **rock-'n'-roll** songs were written in blues form.

The blues reached **Tin Pan Alley** in the second decade of the century, when W. C. Handy brought his compositions to New York City. His first hit was "The Memphis Blues" (1912), followed two years later by the classic "St. Louis Blues." It is noteworthy that this, the most popular blues song (and one of the most popular songs ever written), is only partly in blues form; one of its three sections is a **tango—a dance craze** then (in 1914) at the height of its popularity. Although Handy wrote many other blues songs in subsequent years—among them "Beale Street Blues" (1916), "Joe Turner Blues" (1916), "Aunt Hagar's Blues" (1920), "The John Henry Blues" (1922), and "Yellow Dog Blues" (1928)—"St. Louis Blues" remained his crowning accomplishment.

Spencer Williams was another early songwriter who helped bring the spirit of the blues to Tin Pan Alley in songs like "Tishomingo Blues" (1917), "Royal Garden Blues" (with Clarence Williams; 1919), and the enduring "Basin Street Blues" (1928). The spirit, if not the form, of the blues was carried forth by other songwriters in such standards as "The Wang Wang Blues" (1921), "Sugar Blues" (1923), and "The Birth of the Blues" (1926). One of the most evocative blues songs ever written, Johnny Mercer and Harold Arlen's "Blues in the Night" (1941), is a tribute to Handy, not only retaining the authentic blues form, but also restoring the tripartite structure of the latter's immortal "St. Louis Blues."

It is no exaggeration to say that without the blues, the face of twentieth-century popular music would be virtually unrecognizable. In the early years of the century, it exerted some influence on Tin Pan Alley and Broadway, mainly through the efforts of such composers as George Gershwin and Harold Arlen. But after 1950, the blues spirit completely permeated almost all aspects of popular music, spurred on by such performers as Chuck Berry, Fats Domino, the Beatles, and Bob Dylan.

Additional Songs

Blowtop Blues (1947)
Bluin' the Blues (1919)
Dallas Blues (1918)
Down Hearted Blues (1923)
Every Day I Have the Blues (1952)
Evil Gal Blues (1944)
The Half of It Dearie Blues (1924)
Home Again Blues (1920)
How Long, How Long Blues (1929)
Mule Skinner Blues (1931)
Rusty Dusty Blues (1943)
Shaking the Blues Away (1927)
Singing the Blues (1954)
Subterranean Homesick Blues (1965)
The Yankee Doodle Blues (1922)

Bibliography

Bastin, Bruce. *Crying for the Carolines.* 1983.

Charters, Samuel Barclay. *The Country Blues.* 1975.

———. *The Roots of the Blues: An African Search.* 1981.

Feather, Leonard. *A History of the Blues.* 1972.

Groom, Bob. *The Blues Revival.* 1983.

Jones, LeRoi [Amiri Baraka]. *Blues People: Negro Music in White America.* 1980.

Keil, Charles. *Urban Blues.* 1966.

Murray, Albert. *Stompin' the Blues.* 1978.

Oliver, Paul. *Screening the Blues: Aspects of the Blues Tradition.* 1970.

———. *The Story of the Blues.* 1972.

———. Max Harrison, and William Balcom. *The New Grove Gospel, Blues and Jazz.* 1986.

Southern, Eileen. *The Music of Black Americans: A History.* 1983.

Titon, Jeff T. *Early Downhome Blues: A Musical and Cultural Analysis.* 1977.

BMI

Broadcast Music Incorporated (BMI) is a nonprofit organization that collects fees on behalf of popular songs listed in its catalogue. By monitoring **radio** stations and other businesses that rely on recorded songs, BMI estimates the usage of songs and computes royalty payments for its member songwriters and publishers. It then divides the fees according to contractual agreement. This benefits songwriters by eliminating the need for them to make separate performance agreements with all the venues that might play their music. Simply put, BMI, in Paul Kingsbury's words, acts as "a conduit between the owners and users of music."

BMI's function and methods are not very different from those of other performance-rights organizations, such as the American Society of Composers, Authors and Publishers (**ASCAP**). ASCAP, the first organization of its kind in the United States, was formed in February 1914 to protect and administer the proper royalties for songwriters' works. Most of the prestigious **Tin Pan Alley** publishing houses and songwriters belonged to ASCAP, and thus it developed as an influential institution throughout the 1920s and 1930s. By 1940, however, ASCAP's dominance began to cause problems within various factions of the music industry. In that year, an agreement between ASCAP and radio stations (who at that time were paying as much as five percent of their advertising income for permission to play ASCAP music) was due to expire. Many in radio became concerned about the ever-increasing fees—from $960,000 in 1931 to $4.3 million in 1939—that ASCAP wanted to play its music.

The radio industry, led by the National Association of Broadcasters, responded by establishing its own performance-rights organization, BMI, in the fall of 1939. BMI became operational on February 15, 1940, and quickly took advantage of the radio industry's concern about ASCAP's growing revenue. By offering the songs listed in its catalogue at lower prices, BMI was able to compete with the older organization, particularly in the area of broadcast music.

To meet the demand brought about by its initial success, BMI enlisted the services of songwriters who were either unpublished or had been rejected by ASCAP. It also acquired a large catalogue of newly arranged pieces in the public domain, such as Stephen Foster's "Jeanie With the Light Brown Hair" (1854), which enjoyed a measure of commercial success in the early 1940s. In 1941, E. B. Marks, one of the more prominent Tin Pan Alley publishing houses, left ASCAP and joined BMI. From that time on, BMI steadily increased its catalogue of songs, composers, and publishers, aided by the support of major radio networks that were seeking more and more non-ASCAP music.

At first, BMI was criticized for frequently using songwriters and publishers that ASCAP had already rejected. Thus, ASCAP regarded BMI as an aesthetically second-rate organization (the joke around ASCAP at the time was that BMI really stood for "Bad Music Inc."). BMI countered by saying that its "open-door policy" was designed to give an opportunity to songwriters who had been discriminated against by ASCAP on the basis of race or social status. Indeed, even so successful a songwriter as Ferdinand "Jelly Roll" Morton had considerable difficulty in joining ASCAP.

Conversely, songs by black songwriters, such as "Opus (Number) One" (1944) and "Saturday Night Fish Fry" (1949), found new access to public performance via BMI. Folk and country songs like "Goodnight Irene" (1936), "Tennessee Waltz" (1948), "Your Cheatin' Heart" (1952), and "This Land Is Your Land" (1956) were also written by BMI writers who had experienced difficulty in joining ASCAP.

In the late 1940s, BMI profited by taking in such publishing firms as Arc Music, which specialized in **rhythm-and-blues** songs. The organization's growing involvement with this type of music during the 1950s was exemplified by the number of hit songs by BMI writers like Chuck Berry—"Maybelline" (1955) and "Johnny B. Goode" (1958)—and Otis Blackwell—"Don't Be Cruel" (1956) and "All Shook Up" (1957).

During the early 1960s, BMI covered a broad spectrum of **country and western, rhythm and blues,** and **rock 'n' roll,** with such songs as Roy Orbison's "Crying" (1961), Willie Nelson's "Crazy" (1961), and Sam Cooke's "Twisting the Night Away" (1962). The organization's growing involvement with rock 'n' roll at this time seemed to confirm the suspicions of older songwriters and performers concerning BMI's supposed inferiority. One of these was Billy Rose, who had this to say (as quoted by Ian Whitcomb):

Not only are most of the BMI songs junk, but in many cases they are all obscene junk pretty much on the level with dirty comic magazines. . . . It is the current climate on radio and TV that makes Elvis Presley and his animal posturings possible. . . . When ASCAP songwriters were permitted to be heard, Al Jolson, Nora Bayes and Eddie Cantor were all big salesmen of songs. Today, it is a set of untalented twitchers and twisters whose appeal is largely to the zootsuiter and the juvenile delinquent.

Currently, BMI continues to represent many popular songs of all description, including works by such songwriters as Gloria Estefan and Steve Winwood. It also sponsors workshops for television, film, and jazz music; gives awards to its top songwriters and young composers; and publishes a periodical, *BMI Music World*. Representing some 60,000 songwriters and 35,000 publishers, BMI has a reciprocal agreement with thirty-nine other licensing agencies worldwide. In addition,

BMI gives special citations to those songs that have been performed on radio and television 1 million times or more (*see* Table 4). It is interesting to observe that only one song in the BMI catalogue, John Lennon and Paul McCartney's "Yesterday" (1965), has achieved over five million performances—needless to say, in a multitude of successful recordings.

Ehrick V. Long

Bibliography

Chappe, Steve, and Reebee Garofalo. *Rock and Roll Is Here to Pay*. 1977.

Kingsbury, Paul. *The Explosion of American Music, 1940–1990: BMI 50th Anniversary*. 1990.

Ryan, John. *The Production of Culture in the Music Industry: The ASCAP-BMI Controversy*. 1985.

Shemel, Sydney, and William Krasilovsky. *This Business of Music*. 6th ed. 1990.

Whitcomb, Ian. *After the Ball*. 1972.

See also: Awards; Recording

TABLE 4

BMI Awards

Listed here are songs that have been performed on radio and television two million times or more. Not listed here for space reasons are an additional 350 BMI songs that have been played at least one million times.

a) Five Million Performances

Song	Lyricist/Composer*	Notable Artist; Label/Rec#
Yesterday (1965)	John Lennon, Paul McCartney	Beatles Capitol (5498) Ray Charles; ABC/TRC (11009)

b) Four Million Performances

Song	Lyricist/Composer	Notable Artist; Label/Rec#
Bridge Over Troubled Water (1969)	Paul Simon	Simon & Garfunkel; Columbia 45079 Aretha Franklin; Atlantic 2650 Linda Clifford; RSO 921
By the Time I Get to Phoenix (1967)	Jim Webb	Glen Campbell Capitol 2015 Issac Hayes; Enterprise 9003 Mad Lads;; Volt 4016
Canadian Sunset (1956)	Norman Gimbel/ Eddie Heywood	Hugo Winterhalter and His Orchestra with Eddie Heywood; RCA 6537 Andy Williams; Cadence 1297 Etta Jones; Prestige 191 Sounds Orchestral; Parkway 958
Gentle on My Mind (1967)	John Hartford	Glen Campbell; Capitol 2015 Patti Page; Columbia 44556 Aretha Franklin; Atlantic 2619
Georgia on My Mind (1930)	Stuart Gorrell Hoagy Carmichael	Ray Charles; ABC-Paramount 1035 Righteous Brothers Moonglow 244 Wes Montgomery; A&M 940 Willie Nelson; Columbia 10704
I Can't Stop Loving You (1958)	Don Gibson	Don Gibson; RCA 7133 Ray Charles ; ABC-Paramount 10330

*Writers credited solely with lyrics or music are set down in that order and separated by a slash: e.g., Oscar Hammerstein II/Jerome Kern. The presence of a comma indicates that the writers are jointly credited for the music, the lyrics, or the song.

Michelle (1966)	John Lennon, Paul McCartney	Count Basie; Reprise 20170 David & Jonathan; Capitol 5563 Bud Shank; World Pacific 77814 Billy Vaughn; Dot 16809 Beatles (from *Rubber Soul*); Capitol 2442
More (Theme From *Mondo Cane*) (1963)	Norman Newell (Eng.)/ Nino Oliviero, Riz Ortolani	Kai Winding; Verve 10295 Vic Dana; Doloton 81
Mrs. Robinson (1968)	Paul Simon	Simon & Garfunkel; Columbia 44511 Booker T & the M.G.s; Stax 0037
Never My Love (1967)	Donald J. Addrisi, Dick Addrisi	Association; Warner 7074 Sandpebbles; Calla 155 Fifth Dimension; Bell 45134 Blue Suede; EMI 3627 Addrisi Brothers; Buddah 587
Something (1969)	George Harrison	Beatles; Apple 2654 Shirley Bassey; United Artists 50698 Booker T & the M.G.s; Stax 0073 Johnny Rodriguez; Mercury 73471
Strangers in the Night (1966)	Eddie Snyder, Charles Singleton/Bert Kaempfert	Frank Sinatra; Reprise 0470

c) Three Million Performances

Song	Lyricist/Composer	Notable Artist; Label/Rec#
All I Have to Do Is Dream (1958)	Boudleaux Bryant	Everly Brothers; Cadence 1348 Richard Chamberlain; MGM 13121 Glen Campbell & Bobby Gentry; Capitol 2745 Nitty Gritty Dirt Band; United Artists 655 Andy Gibb & Victoria Principal; RSO 1065 Merrilee Rush & the Turnabouts; Bell 705
Angel of the Morning (1967)	Chip Taylor	Juice Newton; Capitol 4976
Both Sides Now (1967)	Joni Mitchell	Judy Collins; Elektra 45639
Breaking Up Is Hard to Do (1962)	Neil Sedaka, Howard Greenfield	Dion; Laurie 3495 Neil Sedaka; RCA 8046, Rocket 40500
Can't Take My Eyes Off You (1967)	Bob Crewe, Bob Gaudio	Happenings; B. T. Puppy 543 Lenny Welch; Common U. 3004 Patridge Family; Bell 45235 Frankie Valli; Phillips 40446
Cherish (1966)	Terry Kirkman	Lettermen; Capitol 2054 Nancy Wilson; Capitol 2644 Association; Valiant 747 David Cassidy; Bell 45150
Everybody's Talkin' (1969)	Fred Neil	Harry Nilsson; RCA 0161
For All We Know (1970)	Robb Roger, Jimmy Griffin/Fred Karlin	Carpenters; A&M 1243
For the Good Times (1968)	Kris Kristofferson	Ray Price; Columbia 45178
The Girl From Ipanema (1963)	Norman Gimbel (Eng.)/ Antonio Carlos Jobim	Stan Getz & Astrud Gilberto; Verve 10323
Goin' Out of My Head (1964)	Teddy Randazzo, Bobby Weinstein	Little Anthony & the Imperials; DCP 119 Lettermen; Capitol 2054 Frank Sinatra; Reprise 0865
Help Me Make It Through the Night (1970)	Kris Kristofferson	Sammi Smith; Mega 0015 Joe Simon; Spring 113 O. C. Smith; Columbia 45435 Gladys Knight & the Pips; Soul 35094 Olivia Newton-John; MCA 40280
I Honestly Love You (1974)	Peter Allen, Jeff Barry	
Killing Me Softly With His Song (1973)	Charles Fox, Norman Gimbel	Roberta Flack; Atlantic 2940
The Most Beautiful Girl (1973)	Rory Bourke, Billy Sherrill, Norris Wilson	Charlie Rich; Epic 11040
My Cherie Amour (1968)	Sylvia Moy, Henry Cosby, Stevie Wonder	Stevie Wonder; Tamla 54180 Soul Train Gang; Soul Train 10995

My Way (1967)	Paul Anka/Claude François, Jacques Revaux	Frank Sinatra; Reprise 0817
		Brook Benton; Cotillion 44072
		Elvis Presley; RCA PB-11165
Never on Sunday (1960)	Manos Hadjidakis, Billy Towne/Manos Hadjidakis	Don Costa; United Artists 234
		Chordettes; Cadence 1402
		Lale Anderson; King 5478
Only You (And You Alone) (1955)	Ande Rand, Buck Ram	Platters; Mercury 70633
		Hilltoppers; Dot 15423
		Franck Poucel's French Fiddles; Capitol 4165
		Mr. Acker Bilk; Atco 6247
		Bobby Hatfield; Verve 10634
		Ringo Starr; Apple 1876
Release Me (1954)	Eddie Miller, Dub Williams, Robert Yount	Esther Phillips; Lenox 5555
		Engelbert Humperdinck; Parrot 40011
		Johnny Adams; SSS International 750
(I Never Promised You a) Rose Garden (1967)	Joe South	Lynn Anderson; Columbia 45252
Scarborough Fair/ Canticle (1966)	Paul Simon, Art Garfunkel	Simon & Garfunkel; Columbia 44465
		Sergio Mendes & Brasil '66; A&M 986
(Sittin' on the) Dock of the Bay (1968)	Steve Cropper, Otis Redding	Otis Redding; Volt 157
		King Curtis; Atco 6562
Snowbird (1970)	Gene MacLellan	Anne Murray; Capitol 2738
The Song From *Moulin Rouge* (Where Is Your Heart?) (1953)	William Engvick/ Georges Auric	Percy Faith; Columbia 39944
		Annunzio Mantovani & His Orchestra; London 1328
The Sound of Silence (1964)	Paul Simon	Simon & Garfunkel; Columbia 43396
		Peaches & Herb; Columbia 45386
Spanish Eyes (1965)	Charles Singleton, Eddie Snyder/Bert Kaempfert	Al Martino; Capitol 5542
Stand by Me (1961)	Ben E. King, Jerry Leiber, Mike Stoller	Ben E. King; Atco 6194, Atlantic 89361
		Earl Grant; Decca 25674
		Spyder Turner; MGM 13617
		David & Jimmy Ruffin; Soul 35076
		John Lennon; Apple 1881
		Mickey Gilley; Full Moon 46640
		Maurice White; Columbia 05571
Sunny (1965)	Bobby Hebb	Bobby Hebb; Phillips 40365
Tennessee Waltz (1948)	Pee Wee King, Redd Stewart	Pee Wee King; RCA 2680
		Guy Lombardo; Decca 27336
		Jo Stafford; Columbia 78-39065
		Fontane Sisters; RCA 3979
		Patti Page; Mercury 5534
		Les Paul & Mary Ford; Capitol 1316
		Spike Jones & His City Slickers; RCA 4011
		Anita O' Day; London 876
		Bobby Comstock; Blaze 349
		Jerry Fuller; Challenge 59057
		Sam Cooke; RCA 8368
Tie a Yellow Ribbon Round the Ole Oak Tree (1972)	Irwin Levine, L. Russell Brown	Dawn; Bell 45318
Traces (1969)	Buddy Buie, James B. Cobb, Emory Gordy	Classics IV; Imperial 66352
		Lettermen; Capitol 2697
Twilight Time (1944)	Morty Nevins, Al Nevins, Buck Ram, Artie Dunn	Platters; Mercury 71289
		Andy Williams; Cadence 1433
		Three Suns; Hit 7992
Up, Up and Away, or My Beautiful Balloon (1967)	Jim Webb	Fifth Dimension; Soul City 756
		Johnny Mann Singers; Liberty 55972
		Hugh Masekela; Uni 55037
We've Only Just Begun (1970)	Paul Williams	Carpenters; A&M 1217
You've Lost That Lovin' Feelin' (1964)	Barry Mann, Phil Spector, Cynthia Weil	Righteous Brothers; Philles 124
		Dionne Warwick; Scepter 12226
		Long John Baldry; EMI 8018

Darryl Hall & John
Oates; RCA 12103

d) Two Million Performances

Song	Lyricist/Composer	Notable Artist; Label/Rec#
After the Lovin' (1974)	Alan Bernstein, Ritchie Adams	Engelbert Humperdinck; Epic 50270
Alone Again (Naturally) (1972)	Gilbert O'Sullivan	Gilbert O'Sullivan; MAM 3619
Always on My Mind (1971)	Wayne Thompson Johnny Christopher, Mark James	Willie Nelson; Columbia 02741
And I Love Her (1964)	John Lennon, Paul McCartney	Beatles; Capitol 5235 Esther Phillips; Atlantic 2281
And I Love You So (1970)	Don McLean	Bobby Goldsboro; United Artists 50776 Perry Como; RCA 0906
(Hey Won't You Play) Another Somebody Done Somebody Wrong Song? (1975)	Larry Butler, Chips Moman	B. J. Thomas; ABC 12054
Baby Don't Get Hooked on Me (1972)	Mac Davis	Mac Davis; Columbia 45618
Behind Closed Doors (1973)	Kenny O'Dell	Charlie Rich; Epic 10950
Blue Bayou (1963)	Joe Melson, Roy Orbison	Roy Orbison; Monument 824 Linda Ronstadt; Asylum 45431
Blue Velvet (1951)	Lee Morris, Bernie Wayne	Statues; Liberty 55245 Bobby Vinton; Epic 9614 Tony Bennett; Columbia 39555
Born Free (1966)	Don Black/ John Barry	Roger Williams; Kapp 767 Hesitations; Kapp 878
Brazil (1939)	S. K. Russell (Eng.)/ Ary Barroso	Xavier Cugat & His Waldorf-Astoria Orchestra; Columbia 36651 Jimmy Dorsey & His Orchestra; Decca 18460 Ritchie Family; 20th Century 2218
The Breeze and I (1940)	Al Stillman (Eng.)/ Ernesto Lecuona	Jimmy Dorsey & His Orchestra; Decca 3150
Cabaret (1967)	Fred Ebb / John Kander	Herb Alpert and the Tijuana Brass; A&M 925
Call Me (1967)	Tony Hatch	Chris Montez; A&M 780
Classical Gas (1967)	Mason Williams	Mason Williams; Warner 7190
Cold, Cold Heart (1951)	Hank Williams	Dinah Washington; Mercury 72040 Tony Bennett; Columbia 39449 Fontane Sisters; RCA 4274 Eileen Wilson; Decca 27761 Tony Fontane; Mercury 5693 Hank Williams & His Drifting Cowboys; MGM 10904
El Condor Pasa (1970)	Daniel Robles, Paul Simon	Simon & Garfunkel; Columbia 45237
Crying (1961)	Joe Melson, Roy Orbison	Roy Orbison; Monument 447 Jay & the Americans; United Artists 50016 Don McLean; Millennium 11799
Cupid (1961)	Sam Cooke	Sam Cooke; RCA 7883 Johnny Rivers; Imperial 66087 Johnny Nash; JAD 220 Dawn; Elektra 45302 Spinners; Atlantic 3664
Daniel (1973)	Elton John, Bernie Taupin	Elton John; MCA 40000
Daydream Believer (1967)	John C. Stewart	Monkees; Colgems 1012, Arista 9532 Anne Murray; Capitol 4813
Don't Be Cruel (1956)	Otis Blackwell, Elvis Presley	Elvis Presley; RCA 47-6540 Bill Black's Combo; Hi 2026 Barbara Lynn; Jamie 1244
Don't Pull Your Love (1976)	Dennis Lambert, Brian Potter	Hamilton, Joe Frank & Reynolds; Dunhill 4276

Song	Writer	Performer/Recording
Dreams (1977)	Stephanie Nicks	
Dust in the Wind (1977)	Kerry Livgren	
El Paso (1959)	Marty Robbins	Glen Campbell; Capitol 4245
Eleanor Rigby (1966)	John Lennon, Paul McCartney	Fleetwood Mac; Warner 8371
		Kansas; Kirshner 4274
		Marty Robbins; Columbia 41511
		Beatles; Capitol 5715
		Ray Charles; ABC/TRC 11090
		Aretha Franklin; Atlantic 2683
Emotion (1977)	Barry Gibb, Robin Gibb	Samantha Sang; Private S. 45178
Everything Is Beautiful (1970)	Ray Stevens	Ray Stevens; Barnaby 2011
Feel Like Makin' Love (1974)	Gene McDaniels	Roberta Flack; Atlantic 3025
		Bob James; CTI 24
Feels So Good (1977)	Chuck Mangione	Chuck Mangione; A&M 2001
Fever (1956)	Eddie Cooley, John R. Davenport	Little Willie John; King 4935
		Peggy Lee; Capitol 3998
		McCoys; Bang 511
		Rita Coolidge; A&M 1398
The 59th Street Bridge Song (Feelin' Groovy) (1966)	Paul Simon	Harper's Bizarre; Warner 5890
		Simon & Garfunkel (from *Parsley, Sage Rosemary & Thyme*); Columbia 9363
Fire and Rain (1969)	James Taylor	James Taylor; Warner 7423
		R. B. Greaves; Atco 6745
		Johnny Rivers; Imperial 66453
The First Time Ever I Saw Your Face (1962)	Ewan McColl	Roberta Flack; Atlantic 2864
Games People Play (1968)	Joe South	Joe South; Capitol 2248
Go Away Little Girl (1962)	Gerry Goffin, Carole King	Steve Lawrence; Columbia 42601
		Happenings; B. T. Puppy 520
		Donny Osmond; MGM 14285
The Green, Green Grass of Home (1965)	Curly Putman	Tom Jones; Parrot 40009
Handy Man (1959)	Otis Blackwell, Jimmy Jones	Jimmy Jones; Cub 9049
		Del Shannon; Amy 905
		James Taylor; Columbia 10557
Happy Together (1966)	Garry Bonner, Alan Lee Gordon	Turtles; White Whale 244
		Dawn; Bell 45175
		Captain & Tennille; Casablanca 2264
Have You Never Been Mellow? (1974)	John Farrar	Olivia Newton-John; MCA 40349
(You're) Having My Baby (1974)	Paul Anka	Paul Anka; United Artists 454
Here Comes the Sun (1969)	George Harrison	Richie Havens; Stormy F. 656
		Beatles (from *Abbey Road*); Apple 383
Here, There and Everywhere (1966)	John Lennon, Paul McCartney	Emmylou Harris; Reprise 1346
		Beatles (from *Revolver*); Capitol 2576
Here You Come Again (1977)	Barry Mann, Cynthia Weil	Dolly Parton; RCA 11123
Hey Jude (1968)	John Lennon, Paul McCartney	Beatles; Apple 2276
(Your Love Has Lifted Me) Higher and Higher (1967)	Gary Jackson, Carl William Smith, Raynard Miner	Wilson Pickett; Atlantic 2591
		Jackie Wilson; Brunswick 55336
		Rita Coolidge; A&M 1922
Hooked on a Feeling (1968)	Mark James	B. J. Thomas; Scepter 12230
		Blue Swede; EMI 3627
How Can You Mend a Broken Heart (1971)	Barry Gibb, Robin Gibb	Bee Gees; Atco 6824
How Deep Is Your Love (1977)	Barry Gibb, Maurice Gibb, Robin Gibb	Bee Gees; RSO 882
How Sweet It Is (To Be Loved by You) (1964)	Lamont Dozier, Eddie Holland, Brian Holland	Marvin Gaye; Tamla 54107
		Jr. Walker & the All-Stars; Soul 35024
		James Taylor; Warner 8109
Hurt So Bad (1965)	Bobby Hart, Teddy Randazzo, Bobby Weinstein	Little Anthony & the Imperials; DCP 1128
		Lettermen; Capitol 2482
		Jackie DeShannon; Imperial 66452

Song	Writer	Artist
I Love a Rainy Night (1980)	David Malloy, Eddie Rabbitt, Even Stevens	Linda Ronstadt; Asylum 46624 Eddie Rabbitt; Elektra 47066
I Love How You Love Me (1961)	Larry Kolber, Barry Mann	Paris Sisters; Gregmark 6 Bobby Vinton; Epic 10397
I Will Wait for You (1964)	Norman Gimbel (Eng.)/ Michel Legrand	Vikki Carr; Pair 1082 Jack Jones; MCA 4115
I Write the Songs (1974)	Bruce Johnston	Barry Manilow; Arista 0157
I'd Really Love to See You Tonight (1975)	Parker McGee	England Dan & John Ford Coley; Big Tree 16069
If I Were a Carpenter (1966)	Tim Hardin	Bobby Darin; Atlantic 2350 Four Tops; Motown 1124 Johnny Cash & June Carter; Columbia 45064 Bob Seger; Palladium 1079 Leon Russell; Shelter 40210
If You Love Me (Let Me Know) (1974)	John Rostill	Olivia Newton-John; MCA 40209
I'm Movin' On (1950)	Hank Snow	Ray Charles; Atlantic 2043 Matt Lucas; Smash 1813 John Kay; Dunhill 4309 Hank Snow; RCA 4593
I'm So Lonesome I Could Cry (1949)	Hank Williams	B. J. Thomas; Scepter 12129 Hank Williams; M G M 13489 Hank Wilson; Shelter 7336 Terry Bradshaw; Mercury 73760 Johnny Tillotson; Cadence 1432
Imagine (1971)	John Lennon	John Lennon & the Plastic Ono Band; Apple 1840
Islands in the Stream (1983)	Barry Gibb, Robin Gibb, Maurice Gibb	Dolly Parton & Kenny Rogers; RCA 13615
It's Just a Matter of Time (1958)	Brook Benton, Clyde Otis, Belford Hendricks	Brook Benton; Mercury 71394
It's Only Make Believe (1958)	Jack Nance, Conway Twitty	Conway Twitty; MGM 12677 Glen Campbell; Capitol 2905
Jambalaya (On the Bayou) (1952)	Hank Williams	Hank Williams; MGM 10352 Fats Domino; Imperial 5779 Blue Ridge Rangers; Fantasy 689 Bobby Comstock & the Counts; Atlantic 2051 Nitty Gritty Dirt Band; United Artists 50890
King of the Road (1964)	Roger Miller	Roger Miller; Smash 1965 Jody Miller; Capitol 5402
Last Date (1960)	Floyd Cramer	Floyd Cramer; RCA 7775 Lawrence Welk; Dot 16198 Skeeter Davis; RCA 7825 Joni James; MGM 12933
Laughter in the Rain (1974)	Neil Sedaka, Phil Cody	Neil Sedaka; Rocket 40313
Let It Be (1970)	John Lennon, Paul McCartney	Beatles; Apple 2764 Joan Baez; Vanguard 35145
Let Me Be There (1973)	John Rostill	Olivia Newton-John; MCA 40101
Let Your Love Flow (1976)	Lawrence Williams	Bellamy Brothers; Warner 8169
The Long and Winding Road (1970)	John Lennon, Paul McCartney	Beatles; Apple 2832
Love Me Tender (1956)	Vera Matson, Elvis Presley	Elvis Presley; RCA 47-6643 Richard Chamberlain; MGM 13097 Percy Sledge; Atlantic 2414 Henri Rene; RCA 6728 Captain & Tennille; A&M 1672
Love Will Keep Us Together (1975)	Howard Greenfield, Neil Sedaka	Captain & Tennille; A&M 1672
Love's Theme (1973)	Barry White	Love Unlimited Orchestra; 20th Century 2069
Lucille (1976)	Roger Bowling, Hal Bynum	Kenny Rogers; United Artists 929
Lullaby of Birdland (1952)	George Shearing, George Weiss	Blue Stars; Mercury 70742
Make the World Go Away (1963)	Hank Cochran	Timi Yuro; Liberty 55587 Ray Price; Columbia 42827 Eddy Arnold; RCA 8879 Donny & Marie Osmond; MGM 14807

Mandy (1971)	Scott English, Richard Kerr	Scott English; Janus 171 Barry Manilow; Bell 45613
Margaritaville (1977)	Jimmy Buffett	Jimmy Buffett; ABC 12254
Maria Elena (1933)	Lorenzo Barcelata, Sidney K. Russell/ Lorenzo Barcelata	Los Indios Trabajaros; RCA 8216 Jimmy Dorsey & His Orchestra; Decca 3698
Memories Are Made of This (1955)	Richard Dehr, Terry Gilkyson, Frank Miller	Dean Martin; Capitol 3295 Gale Storm; Dot 15436 Mindy Carson; Columbia 40573 Drifters; Atlantic 2325
Midnight Blue (1974)	Melissa Manchester, Carole Bayer Sager	Melissa Manchester; Arista 0116
Mr. Bojangles (1968)	Jerry Jeff Walker	Jerry Jeff Walker; Atco 6594 Bobby Cole; Date 1613 Nitty Gritty Dirt Band; Liberty 56197
Misty Blue (1965)	Bob Montgomery	Eddy Arnold; RCA 91821 Joe SimoSound Stage 1508 Dorothy Moore; Malaco 1029
My Eyes Adored You (1974)	Bob Crewe, Kenny Nolan	Frankie Valli; Private S. 45003
My Special Angel (1957)	Jimmy Duncan	Bobby Helms; Decca 30423 Vogues; Reprise 0766
My Sweet Lord (1970)	George Harrison	George Harrison; Apple 2995 Billy Preston; Apple 1826
Never Can Say Goodbye (1970)	Clifton Davis	Jackson 5; Motown 1179 Issac Hayes; Enterprise 9031 Gloria Gaynor; MGM 14748
Night Train (1952)	Jimmy Forrest, Oscar Washington, Lewis C. Simpkins	Viscounts; Madison 123 Richard Hayman; Mercury 71869 James Brown; King 5614 Buddy Morrow & His Orchestra; RCA 4693
9 to 5 (1980)	Dolly Parton	Dolly Parton; RCA 12133
Nobody Does It Better (1977)	Carole Bayer Sager, Marvin Hamlisch	Carly Simon; Elektra 45413
Oh, Lonesome Me (1958)	Don Gibson;	Don Gibson; RCA 7133 Johnny Cash; Sun 355
On and On (1977)	Stephen Bishop	Stephen Bishop; ABC 12260
On Broadway (1962)	Jerry Leiber, Barry Mann, Mike Stoller, Cynthia Weil	Drifters; Atlantic 2182 George Benson; Warner 8542
Opus (Number) One (1944)	Sid Garris/Sy Oliver	Tommy Dorsey & His Orchestra; Victor 1608
Perfidia (1939)	Milton Leeds (Eng.)/ Alberto Dominguez	Ventures; Dolton 28 Xavier Cugat & His Waldorf-Astoria Orchestra; Victor 26665 Jimmy Dorsey & His Orchestra; Decca 3198 Benny Goodman & His Orchestra; Columbia 359962 Glenn Miller & His Orchestra; Bluebird 11095 Gene Krupa & His Orchestra; Okeh 5715 Four Aces; Decca 27987
Proud Mary (1968)	John C. Fogerty	Creedence Clearwater Revival; Fantasy 619 Solomon Burke; Bell 78 Ike & Tina Turner; Liberty 56216 Checkmates Ltd.; A & M 1127
Put a Little Love in Your Heart (1969)	Jackie DeShannon, Randy Myers, Jimmy Holiday	Jackie DeShannon; Imperial 66385
Reminiscing (1978)	Graham Goble	Little River Band; Harvest 4605
Rhythm of the Rain (1962)	John Gummoe	Cascades; Valiant 6026 Gary Lewis & the Playboys; Liberty 56093
The Rose (1977)	Amanda McBroom	Bette Midler; Atlantic 3656
Ruby, Don't Take Your Love to Town (1966)	Mel Tillis	Kenny Rogers & the First Edition; Reprise 0829
Save the Last Dance for Me (1960)	Doc Pomus, Mort Shuman	Drifters; Atlantic 2071 DeFranco Family; 20th Century 2088
Seasons in the Sun (1964)	Rod McKuen (Eng.)/ Jacques Brel	Terry Jacks; Bell 45432
Singing the Blues (1954)	Melvin Endsley	Aileen Stanley; Victor 18703

		Frankie Trumbauer & His Orchestra; Okeh 40772 Connee Boswell; Decca 28498 Pointer Sisters; Planet 47929
Slow Hand (1980)	John Bettis Michael Clark	
Somethin' Stupid (1967)	Carson C. Parks	Nancy & Frank Sinatra; Reprise 0561
Sometimes When We Touch (1977)	Dan Hill/ Barry Mann	Dan Hill; 20th Century 2355
Southern Nights (1974)	Allen Toussaint	Glen Campbell; Capitol 4376
Spanish Harlem (1960)	Phil Spector, Jerry Leiber	Ben E. King; Atco 6185 Aretha Franklin; Atlantic 2817
Spinning Wheel (1968)	David Clayton Thomas	Blood, Sweat & Tears; Columbia 44871 James Brown; King 6366
Stranger on the Shore (1961)	Robert Mellin/ Acker Bilk	Mr. Acker Bilk; Atco 6217 Andy Williams; Columbia 42451 Drifters; Atlantic 2143
Sukiyaki (1963)	Tom Leslie, Buzz Cason/Ei Rokusuke, Hachidai Nakamura	Kyu Sakamoto; Capitol 4945 A Taste of Honey; Capitol 4953
Summer Breeze (1971)	James Seals/Darrell Crofts	Seals & Crofts; Warner 7606 Isley Brothers; T-Neck 2253
Suspicious Minds (1968)	Fred Zambon	Elvis Presley; RCA 47-9764 Dee Dee Warwick; Atco 6810
That'll Be the Day (1957)	Jerry Allison, Norman Petty, Buddy Holly	Buddy Holly & the Crickets; Brunswick 55009 Linda Ronstadt; Asylum 35340
Theme From *Mahogany* (Do You Know Where You're Going To?) (1973)	Gerry Goffin/ Michael Masser	Diana Ross; Motown 1377
Torn Between Two Lovers (1976)	Phil Jarrell, Peter Yarrow	Mary MacGregor; Ariola American 7638
Up on the Roof (1963)	Gerry Goffin, Carole King	Drifters; Atlantic 2162 Cryan' Shames; Columbia 44457 Laura Nyro; Columbia 45230 James Taylor; Columbia 11005 Frank Sinatra; Reprise 1029
Watch What Happens (1964)	Jacques Demy, Norman Gimbel/ Michel Legrand	Michael Legrand; Verve 834827
Wedding Bell Blues (1966)	Laura Nyro	Fifth Dimension; Soul City 779
Weekend in New England (1975)	Randy Edelman	Barry Manilow; Arista 0212
What a Diff'rence a Day Makes (1934)	Stanley Adams/ Maria Grever	Dinah Washington; Mercury 71435 Esther Phillips; Kudu 925 Dorsey Brothers; Decca 283
When I Need You (1977)	Carole Bayer Sager, Albert Hammond	Leo Sayer; Warner 8332
When Will I Be Loved? (1960)	Phil Everly	Everly Brothers; Cadence 1380 Linda Ronstadt; Capitol 4050
Wildfire (1975)	Larry Cansler, Michael Murphey	Michael Murphey; Epic 50084
Windy (1967)	Ruthann Friedman	Association; Warner 7041 Wes Montgomery; A&M 883
(What a) Wonderful World (1959)	Lou Adler, Herb Alpert, Sam Cooke	Sam Cooke; Keen 2112 Herman's Hermits; MGM 13354 Art Garfunkel, Paul Simon, James Taylor; Columbia 10676
You Are My Sunshine (1940)	Jimmie Davis, Charles Mitchell	Ferko String Band; Media 1013 Johnny & the Hurricanes; Big Top 3056 Ray Charles; ABC-Paramount 10345 Mitch Ryder; New Voice 826 Bing Crosby; Decca 3952 Wayne King & His Orchestra; Victor 26767 Gene Autry; Okeh 06274
You Are So Beautiful (1973)	Billy Preston, Bruce Fisher	Joe Cocker; A&M 1641
You Belong to Me (1952)	Pee Wee King, Chilton Price, Redd Stewart	Dean Martin; Capitol 2165 Jo Stafford; Columbia 39811
You Can't Hurry Love	Lamont Dozier,	Supremes; Motown 1097

(1966)	Brian Holland, Eddie Holland	Phil Collins; Atlantic 89933
You Don't Know Me (1962)	Cindy Walker, Eddy Arnold	Jerry Vale; Columbia 40710 Lenny Welch; Cadence 1373 Ray Charles; ABC-Paramount 10345 Elvis Presley; RCA 47-9341 Micky Gilley; Epic 02172
You Send Me (1957)	L. C. Cooke	Sam Cooke; Keen 34013 Teresa Brewer; Coral 61898 Aretha Franklin; Atlantic 2518 Ponderosa Twins + One; Horoscope 102 Manhattans; Columbia 04755
You'll Never Find Another Love Like Mine (1976)	Kenneth Gamble, Leon Huff	Lou Rawls; Philadelphia International 3592

Young at Heart (1954)	Carolyn Leigh/ Johnny Richards	Frank Sinatra; Capitol 2703
		Bing Crosby with
		   Guy Lombardo & His Royal
		     Canadians; Decca 29054

Young Love (1956)	Ric Cartey, Carole Joyner	Tab Hunter; Dot 15533 Sonny James; Capitol 3602 Crew-Cuts; Mercury 71022 Donny Osmond; MGM 14583 Ray Stevens; Barnaby 618

Your Cheatin' Heart (1952)	Hank Williams	George Hamilton
		   IV; ABC-Paramount 9946
		Billy Vaughn; Dot 15936
		Ray Charles; ABC-Paramount 10375
		Joni James; MGM 11426
		Frankie Laine; Columbia 39938
		Hank Williams &
		   His Drifting Cowboys; MGM 11416

Your Song (1969)	Elton John, Bernie Taupin	Elton John; Uni 55265

Yours (Quiéreme Mucho (1937)	Augustin Rodriguez, Jack Sherr/Gonzalo Roig	Jimmy Dorsey & His
		   Orchestra; Decca 3657
		Xavier Cugat & His
		   Waldorf-Astoria
		   Orchestra; Victor 26384
		Benny Goodman; Columbia 36067
		Vera Lynn; London 1261
		Dick Contino; Mercury 70455

You've Made Me So Very Happy (1967)	Brenda Holloway, Patrice Holloway, Frank Wilson, Berry Gordy, Jr.	Brenda Holloway; Tamla 72935 Blood, Sweat & Tears; Columbia 44776 Lou Rawls; Capitol 2734

Ehrick V. Long

BOATING

A wide variety of watercraft have found their way into American popular song, ranging from rowboats ("Row, Row, Row," 1912), to submarines ("Yellow Submarine," 1966).

Mississippi River steamboats have inspired such songs as "Waiting for the Robert E. Lee" (1912), "Here Comes the Show Boat" (1927), and "Proud Mary" (1968). The landmark musical, **Show Boat** (1927), in fact, centers about such a boat: the *Cotton Blossom.* Although a song like "Cruising Down the River" (1945) could apply to almost any kind of vessel from rowboat to ocean liner, the "boat" in "There's a Boat Dat's Leavin' Soon for New York," from *Porgy and Bess* (1935), is unquestionably a coastal vessel plying between Charleston and New York. The boat required in Frank Loesser's "(I'd Like to Get You) On a Slow Boat to China" (1948), on the other hand, would most probably be a freighter—preferably the slowest one available. "Ferry-Boat Serenade" (1940), needless to say, is concerned with a ferryboat.

Sailboats are the subjects of a number of songs, including "(On) Moonlight Bay" (1912), which begins, "We were sailing along"; "Red Sails in the Sunset," the enduring British import of 1935; and Christopher Cross's award-winning "Sailing" (1979). Two songs from the West Indies are about trading vessels: "Shrimp Boats" (1951) and "The Banana Boat Song (Day-O)" (1956). Naval vessels are represented by "Anchors Aweigh" (1907), the anthem of the United States Navy; and "Don't Give Up the Ship," first heard in the 1935 film **Shipmates Forever.** Boating, along with other means of **travel,** is also mentioned in the 1964 song "Trains and Boats and Planes."

There are also metaphorical ships. In Ira Gershwin and Kurt Weill's extraordinary "My Ship" (1941), the protagonist is waiting for the ship of her dreams, carrying her "one true love," to come in. In Lorenz Hart and Richard Rodgers's "A Ship Without a Sail" (1929), the singer is "all alone, all at sea." Shirley Temple, the adorable child star, sang "On the Good Ship Lollipop" in the 1934 film **Bright Eyes;** the song was a creation of fantasy welcome in the depths of the Depression.

"Don't rock the boat" is a popular colloquialism usually unrelated to boating. It is memorialized in two songs with similar titles, "Sit Down, You're Rocking the Boat" (1913) and "Sit Down, You're Rockin' the Boat" (1950), as well as in the 1941 song "Someone's Rocking My Dreamboat." Finally, there is actually a song about a fictional ship that rolled over and sank—"The Morning After," from the film **The Poseidon Adventure** (1972).

Additional Songs

Go, Little Boat (1917)
The Love Boat (1977)
Michael (Row the Boat Ashore) 1960

Paddlin' Madelin' Home (1925)
Rock the Boat (1973)
Sail Along Silvery Moon (1937)
Sail On (1979)
Sailboat in the Moonlight (1937)
Sloop John B. (1966)

See also: **Ocean; Rivers; Trains; Waterfront**

BODY. SEE ANATOMY

BOLERO

There are two distinct types of bolero. The first, which originated in Spain in the late eighteenth century, is a dance in moderate triple **meter** best exemplified by Maurice Ravel's *Bolero* for orchestra, composed in 1928 for a ballet. Several popular songs in duple meter and slow tempo, among them "Temptation" (1933) and "What Now My Love?" (1962), feature a similar **accompaniment,** characterized by a persistent rhythm of triplets and eighth notes:

The second and predominant type of bolero originated in **Cuba** in the nineteenth century. This languid type of bolero is usually set to romantic or sentimental lyrics and is very often in *AABA* form. It is also a dance, but has duple meter and a slow-to-moderate tempo with a characteristic accompaniment featuring claves, maracas, and other percussion instruments in a configuration such as this:

Since the 1930s, many American popular songs have been set to the rhythm of the bolero, including a number originally written by Cuban or Mexican composers. Among the most popular of the latter were "Magic Is the Moonlight" (1930), "What a Diff'rence a Day Made" (1934), "Yours" (1937), "Time Was" (1941), "Always in My Heart" (1942), "Amor" (1941), "Besame Mucho" (1941), "You Belong to My Heart" (1941), and "Love Me With All Your Heart" (1964). The French song "Boléro" became a hit in 1950 as a bolero with the title "All My Love." Beginning in the 1950s, the rhythm and percussion instruments of the bolero infiltrated other types of American popular music. Elements of bolero style found a permanent place in **rhythm and blues** and **country and western** music, exemplified by such songs as "The Wayward Wind" (1956), The Lonely Bull" (1962), and "Someday Soon" (1963).

Additional Songs

Arrivederci Roma (1954)
Autumn Leaves (1947)
Ciao, Ciao, Bambina (1959)
Come Closer to Me (1940)
Misirlou (1941)
Nightingale (1942)
Perfidia (1939)
Poinciana (1936)
The Shadow of Your Smile (1965)
Summertime in Venice (1955)

Bibliography

Roberts, John Storm. *The Latin Tinge: The Impact of Latin American Music on the United States.* 1985.

See also: Rumba

BOOGALOO

The boogaloo, or *bugalú,* was a Latin American style of music of the 1960s that represented a fusion between the Cuban **mambo** and early American **rock 'n' roll.** It was an eclectic style, borrowing from jazz, rhythm and blues, gospel, and Latin American elements. Boogaloo differed from other Latin American music in its use of English lyrics. Among its most popular songs were "I Like It Like That" (1961), "Bang Bang (My Baby Shot Me Down)" (1966), and "Boogaloo Down Broadway" (1967). But the genre did not survive past 1969, although boogaloo songs remained popular during the **disco** years of the 1970s and many of its ideas were passed on to **rock** and **salsa.**

Bibliography

Roberts, John Storm. *The Latin Tinge: The Impact of Latin American Music on the United States.* 1985.

BOOGIE-WOOGIE

The term "boogie-woogie" usually refers to a style of piano playing. More specifically, it applies to a **bass line** that can be played on almost any instrument: a ground bass, or *basso ostinato,* utilizing a steady pattern of eighth notes; hence the expression "eight to the bar."

As a piano style, boogie-woogie puts the emphasis on **rhythm.** It probably originated in Chicago in the 1920s as an offshoot of the **blues;** its phrases fit nicely into the twelve-bar rhythmic-harmonic structure of the blues. The term was first used in 1929 as the title of an instrumental recording—"Boogie Woogie"—by the pianist Clarence "Pinetop" Smith (1904–1929).

As a *basso ostinato,* boogie-woogie enjoys innumerable varieties limited only by the imagination of the performer. Three of the most common types use two-bar phrases (a), one-bar phrases (b), or half-bar phrases (c).

A prototype of boogie-woogie occurs in the **accompaniment** to "Dardanella," a **novelty song** of 1919 (possibly inspired by the Turkish strait of the Dardanelles, which was then in the news). Its bass line has a family resemblance to boogie-woogie. Jerome Kern used a similar bass as accompaniment in several bars of his "Ka-lu-a" (1921); a lawsuit claiming infringement of copyright was dismissed.

In the 1930s and 1940s, boogie-woogie became very popular as a style of piano playing. It inspired a host of songs on the subject, including two popularized by the Andrews Sisters: "Beat Me Daddy, Eight to the Bar" (1940) and "Boogie-Woogie Bugle Boy" (1941).

In the 1950s and 1960s, boogie-woogie continued as an intrinsic part of **rhythm and blues** and **rock 'n' roll.** It survived into the 1970s, in **rock** and **disco,** not only as a bass pattern, but also in the titles of a number of hits. By then it had lost the "woogie," and stood alone as "boogie" in such songs as "Boogie Down" (1973) and "Boogie On Reggae Woman" (1974), "Boogie Fever" (1976), and "Boogie Oogie Oogie" (1978). The term had also acquired a peripheral meaning by the 1970s: it referred to a kind of dance using uninhibited gyrations.

Additional Songs

Blue Light Boogie (1950)
Boogie Chillun (1949)
Choo Choo Ch' Boogie (1945)
Cow-Cow Boogie (1941)
Get Up and Boogie (1976)
I'm Your Boogie Man (1977)
Jungle Boogie (1973)
Rockin' Pneumonia and the Boogie Woogie Flu (1957)

Bibliography

Kriss, Eric. *Barrelhouse and Boogie Piano.* 1974.

BOOKS. SEE WRITING

BORROWING

Borrowing is one of the oldest traditions of music. Indeed, in the fourteenth and fifteenth centuries, it was common practice to compose a piece based on a preexisting melody, or *cantus firmus*. Appropriating others' ideas manifested itself in the following centuries in the widespread use of chorale melodies and borrowed themes for variation by composers as diverse as J. S. Bach, Mozart, Beethoven, and Rachmaninoff.

In the world of twentieth-century popular song, borrowing continued apace. Sometimes it took the form of the **adaptation** of words to a previously written melody. Very often, in addition, melodies were derived from the **classics**—a practice with distinct advantages, since they are usually in the public domain and thus free of copyright protection.

Songwriters also constantly borrowed from themselves. Thus, Arthur Schwartz's music for "I Guess I'll Have to Change My Plan" (1929) began life as the official Brandt Lake Summer Camp song, "I Love to Lie Awake in Bed," while Vernon Duke's "I Can't Get Started" (1935) originated unsuccessfully as "Face the Music With Me." Before Rodgers and Hart's most famous song was called "Blue Moon" (1934), it had at various times been known as "Prayer," "Manhattan Melodrama," "The Bad in Every Man," and "Make Me a Star."

In addition, many songs, such as "The Old Grey Mare (She Ain't What She Used to Be)" (1917) and "Minnie the Moocher" (1931), were derived from **folk songs**. Others, such as "He's Got the Whole World in His Hands" (1924) and "We Shall Overcome" (1945), had a religious background.

Other countries and cultures have contributed folk music as well. From **Ireland** came "Londonderry Air," the beautiful melody of which was appropriated in "Danny Boy" (1913). The traditional Russian **gypsy** song "Otchi Tchorniya" became popular as "Dark Eyes" in 1926. From folk songs of **Mexico** and Hawaii respectively came "La Cucaracha" (1934) and "Hawaiian War Chant" (1936). New Zealand contributed "Now Is the Hour" (1948), based on a Maori folk song, "Hearere Ra." "Tzena, Tzena, Tzena" (1950) came from a traditional Yiddish song, while "Eh Cumpari" (1953) originated in **Italy**. Similarly, both "Wimoweh" (1951) and "The Lion Sleeps Tonight" (1961), are based on a traditional South-African song, while "Those Were the Days" (1968) originated as an Eastern European folk song.

In addition, a great many popular songs of the twentieth century were derived from published American songs of the previous century. For example, "The Eyes of Texas (Are Upon You)" (1903) was first known as "I've Been Working on the Railroad" (1894). The melody for "How Dry I Am," the prohibition lament, came from the 1855 hymn, "(O) Happy Day." The World War II admonition "Don't Sit Under the Apple Tree (With Anyone Else but Me)" (1942) paraphrased the 1833 song, "Long, Long Ago." The 1944 song "Dance With a Dolly" was derived from "Lubly Fan," or "Buffalo Gals (Won't You Come Out Tonight?)" written in 1844. "One Meat Ball" (1944) was based on an 1855 song called "The Lone Fish Ball," while Elvis Presley's 1956 hit "Love Me Tender" used George Poulton's music for "Aura Lea," written and published in 1861.

There were also many borrowings from abroad. Fritz Kreisler's "The Old Refrain" (1915) was indeed an "old refrain"—taken from a Viennese song published in 1887. The songs "I Get Ideas" (1951) and "Kiss of Fire" (1952) were respective adaptations of the Argentine tangos "Adios Muchachos" (1929) and "El Choclo" (1913). "Midnight in Moscow," or Moscovian Nights" (1961), was based on a song originally published in Russia. Numerous other songs over the years were based on songs originally published in foreign languages in **Brazil**, **Cuba**, **France**, **Germany**, **Italy**, **Mexico**, and elsewhere.

With the establishment of international copyright laws in 1891, borrowing became more perilous. Suits for copyright infringement became commonplace. One of the most celebrated plagiarism suits was filed in 1945. It claimed that the Andrews Sisters' hit "Rum and Coca-Cola" was based on "L'Année Passée," a song by Lionel Belasco, composed in Trinidad in 1906. Another famous case was that of "Hello Dolly," from the 1964 show of the same name, said to have been taken from "Sunflower" (1948), the state song of Kansas. Both cases were decided in favor of the plaintiffs.

In still another instance, Joe E. Howard's arranger was given credit as co-composer of the vaudeville entertainer's famous hit "I Wonder Who's Kissing Her Now" only in 1947—thirty-eight years after the song was published—after an extensive court battle.

There have been many other reputed borrowings over the years (*see* additional songs below). Indeed, suits for copyright infringement have been a conspicuous part of the landscape of twentieth-century popular song. Some of these suits have been decided in favor of the plaintiff, others not. But two mitigating, and related, factors must be borne in mind in judging the act of borrowing. First, appropriating another person's idea is very often done subconsciously. Second, the musical palette is limited to only twelve tones and resemblances are bound to occur.

In recent years, borrowing has become respectable. It is an accepted procedure in **rap** music, through the device of digital sampling, where passages from prerecorded songs are analyzed and manipulated, becoming integral parts of the newly-created work.

Additional Reputed Borrowings

Boola Boola (1898), from "La Hoola Boola" (1897)
Bye Bye Blues (1930), from "The Star" (1912)
I Can't Begin to Tell You (1945), from "When Love Is Young in Springtime" (1906)
I Didn't Raise My Boy to Be a Soldier (1915), from "How Much I Really Cared" (1914)
Little Star (1958), from "Twinkle, Twinkle Little Star" (1761)
Love Letters in the Sand (1931), from "The Spanish Cavalier" (1881)
Moonlight Cocktail (1941), from "Ripples of the Nile"
San Fernando Valley (1943), from "Sweet and Hot" (1930)
Somebody Else Is Taking My Place (1937), from "Please Go 'Way and Let Me Sleep" (1902)
There's Yes Yes in Your Eyes (1924), from "Without You the World Doesn't Seem the Same"

Bibliography

Ewen, David. *All the Years of American Popular Music.* 1977.
Fuld, James J. *The Book of World-Famous Music: Classical, Popular and Folk.* 1985.
Lax, Roger, and Frederick Smith. *The Great Song Thesaurus.* 1989.
Spaeth, Sigmund. *A History of Popular Music in America.* 1960.

See also: **Foreign Influence**

BOSSA NOVA

Bossa nova is a musical style representing a fusion between elements of West Coast progressive **jazz** and Brazilian dances like the **samba** and maxixe. Created in the 1950s by such jazz-oriented musicians as João Gilberto, Antonio Carlos Jobim, and João Donato, the bossa nova is characterized by limpid melodies; detached singing; dense harmonies, featuring major seventh and ninth chords; light rhythmic accompaniment of piano, bass, and acoustic guitar; and an oblique rhythm with many offbeats, like this:

The bossa nova became the rage in the United States in 1962 with the resounding hit "Desafinado (Slightly Out of Tune)." Performers responsible for the early success of the genre in the United States included the singer Astrud Gilberto, guitarists Bola Sete and Charlie Byrd, saxophonist Stan Getz, trumpeter Dizzy Gillespie, flutist Herbie Mann, and bandleader Sergio Mendes. The bossa nova reached a peak of popularity during the years 1962 to 1964; it even generated a protest song: "Blame It on the Bossa Nova" (1962).

Among the most striking bossa novas popular in North America were those written in whole or in part by Jobim, especially "One Note Samba" (1961), "Meditation" (1962), "Quiet Nights of Quiet Stars (Corcovado)" (1962), "The Girl From Ipanema" (1963), "How Insensitive" (1963), and "Wave" (1967). Several non-Brazilian songs have musical attributes similar to those of the bossa nova, and are often played as such. They include "Fly Me to the Moon," or "In Other Words" (1954), "The Look of Love" (1965), and "A Man and a Woman" (1966).

Bibliography

Roberts, John Storm. *The Latin Tinge: The Impact of Latin American Music on the United States.* 1985.

See also: **Brazil**

BOY

As a **subject** of popular song, a boy can be many things. He can be literally a young child—precisely three years old, in fact—as he is in "Sonny Boy." That song has the distinction of being the first song to be introduced in a film; it was sung by Al Jolson in *The Singing Fool* (1928). A boy can also be an object of affection, as in two outstanding songs: "Mad About the Boy" (1935) and "The Boy Next Door" (1943). He can be patriotic, as in George M. Cohan's "The Yankee Doodle Boy" (1904) and Ivor Novello's "Keep the Home Fires Burning"-"(Till the boys come home)"-(1915); mystical, as in "Nature Boy" (1946); a drinking companion, as in "The Boys in the Back Room" (1939); or a rustic, as in "Thank God I'm a Country Boy" (1974).

A boy can be sought after, as in "Looking for a Boy" (1925); mentioned by **name**, as in "Danny Boy" (1913), "Charley, My Boy" (1924), and "A Boy Named Sue" (1969); or be of foreign background, as in "China Boy" (1922) and "Adios Muchachos" (1929). In short, the functions of the word "boy" in popular song are, if anything, diverse.

Additional Songs

Boogie-Woogie Bugle Boy (1941)
The Boy From . . . (1966)
A Boy Like That (1957)
Dear Little Boy of Mine (1918)
He's Sure the Boy I Love (1962)

Hey There Lonely Girl/Hey There Lonely Boy (1962)
I Didn't Raise My Boy to Be a Soldier (1915)
The Little Drummer Boy (1958)
(I'm Just a) Lonely Boy (1958)
Lonely Boy (1977)
My Pony Boy (1909)
Oh Mama (The Butcher) Boy (1938)
Soldier Boy (1961)
Where the Boys Are (1960)

   See also: **Baby; Childhood; Girl; Man**

BRASS

The predominant brass instruments used in popular music are the valve trumpet and slide trombone. However, many other brass instruments have been employed, among them the cornet, valve trombone, bass trumpet, mellophone, bugle, flugelhorn, French horn, alto horn, tenor horn, baritone horn, euphonium, and tuba or sousaphone. In **Dixieland** jazz, the somewhat mellower cornet, rather than the more piercing trumpet, used to be the lead instrument of choice, while the tuba was often used as a bass instrument; it was later replaced by the stringed double bass.

In the era of the **big bands**, a number of leaders became associated with brass instruments. Foremost among these were Harry James, on trumpet, and Tommy Dorsey, on trombone—famous respectively for their solo renditions of "You Made Me Love You" (1913) and "I'm Gettin' Sentimental Over You" (1932).

The legendary cornet player Leon "Bix" Beiderbecke was also a pianist and composer. Outstanding **jazz** trumpet players have included Louis Armstrong, Muggsy Spanier, Roy Eldridge, Fats Navarro, and Clifford Brown. The trumpeter Dizzy Gillespie was one of the founders of **bebop**, while Miles Davis was a pioneer of cool jazz. Wynton Marsalis, an outstanding trumpet virtuoso, won Grammy Awards for both jazz and classical recordings in the 1980s.

Among eminent jazz trombonists were Kid Ory (reputed inventor of "tailgate trombone" in Dixieland), Miff Mole, J. C. Higgenbotham, Jack Teagarden, J. J. Johnson, Bill Harris, and Juan Tizol. The last collaborated on such songs as "Caravan" (1937) and "Perdido" (1942).

A number of song titles are associated with brass instruments, including "Bugle Call Rag" (1923), "When Yuba Plays the Rumba on His Tuba" (1931), "The Toy Trumpet" (1938), "Boogie-Woogie Bugle Boy" (1941), "Tubby the Tuba" (1948), "Fugue for Tinhorns" (1950), and "Seventy-Six Trombones" (1957).

   See also: **Improvisation; Instrumentation; Swing**

BRAZIL

Brazilian music has influenced North American popular song at least since the 1930s. However, unlike the influence of such nations as **Britain, Mexico,** and pre-Castro **Cuba,** Brazil's influence has tended to be intermittent rather than constant. Its culmination was the **bossa nova** craze of the early 1960s, after which many characteristics of Brazilian music merged with the North American mainstream.

Although the **samba** had been established as a dance and type of song in Rio de Janeiro by the 1920s, it had yet to receive worldwide recognition. Brazilian musicians were relatively unknown in the United States in the early 1930s. For instance, the 1933 film *Flying Down to Rio* introduced an Argentine-type **tango,** "Orchids in the Moonlight," and a hybrid dance-song called "Carioca," both written by North Americans.

The first truly Brazilian song to be popular in the United States was the samba "Come to the Mardi Gras" (1937), originally "Não Tenho Lagrimas." It was followed by another samba, "Aquarela do Brasil," which attained great and enduring popularity as "Brazil" (1939). The Brazilian-American singer Carmen Miranda, noted for her elaborate fruited headdresses and ultra-high heels, introduced several ersatz Brazilian songs in musical films, including "Chica Chica Boom Chic" and "I, Yi, Yi, Yi Yi, (I Like You Very Much)," from *That Night in Rio* (1941). Two real Brazilian sambas were introduced in musical films of 1944: the frenetic "Tico Tico," from the cartoon feature *Saludos Amigos* (1944), and the languid "Baia," from *The Three Caballeros* (1945).

After a long hiatus, Brazilian music returned to North American consciousness with the outstanding score for the film *Black Orpheus* (1959). Among the songs introduced in that film were the haunting "Manha de Carnaval"—given English lyrics in 1966 as "A Day in the Life of a Fool"—and "Samba de Orfeu." The film also helped familiarize the North American public with the vast variety of Brazilian percussion instruments, including the *cuica,* a type of small drum with a tube inside its head; and the *berimbau,* a form of musical bow. The persistent sound of percussion, played for the Carnival by members of competing samba schools, permeates the soundtrack of the film.

Although Luis Bonfa was the principal composer of *Black Orpheus,* parts of the score were written by Antonio Carlos Jobim, destined to become the most popular bossa nova composer in the United States. Among the latter's numerous credits are "One Note Samba" (1961), "Desafinado (Slightly Out of Tune)" (1962), "Meditation" (1962), "Quiet Nights of Quiet Stars (Corcovado)" (1962), "The Girl From Ipanema" (1963), "How Insensitive" (1963), and "Wave" (1967).

Brazilians as well as North Americans contributed to the success of the bossa nova in the United States during the early 1960s. They included, besides Bonfa and Jobim, the composer-instrumentalists João Gilberto, João Donato, Edu Lobo, Baden Powell, and Dorival

Caymmi; and the singer Astrud Gilberto. The Brazilian-born pianist and composer Sergio Mendes contributed mightily to the popularity of Brazilian music in the United States. His recordings, often featuring female voices as background, brought the sounds of Brazil to such non-Brazilian songs as "The Look of Love" (1965) and "Day Tripper" (1966).

Although the bossa nova itself lost some of its popularity, Brazilian music remained a potent influence on North American music, and on jazz in particular, during the 1970s and 1980s. Active in performance and recording, in addition to many of the composers, singers, and instrumentalists mentioned above, were the percussionist Airto Moreira, the singers Flora Purim and her sister Yana Purim, and the singer-composer Dori Caymmi, son of Dorival.

Henry Kelly

Bibliography

Appleby, David. *The Music of Brazil.* 1983.

Roberts, John Storm. *The Latin Tinge: The Impact of Latin American Music on the United States.* 1979.

Break

A break is an improvisatory passage played or sung by an instrumental or vocal soloist, usually without accompaniment. It can occur either in performance or written out in the music itself. Breaks are especially common in the improvisatory performance of bluegrass, the blues, country and western music, jazz, and swing. They may feature any instrument, although breaks are most common on the piano, bass, drums, guitar, violin, flute, clarinet, saxophone, trumpet, and trombone. In most instances, accompanying instruments temporarily cease playing.

Written-out breaks are prominent in several songs. Two consecutive ones appear, for example, just before the last line of Shelton Brooks's "Darktown Strutters' Ball" (1917). In both "After You've Gone" (1918) and "California Here I Come" (1924), a breaklike passage occurs at the close of the second section. A break also delineates the end of the release in several songs, including "Ain't She Sweet?" (1927), "Old Devil Moon" (1946), and "You Make Me Feel So Young" (1946).

See also: Improvisation; Instrumentation; Riff

Bridge. See Release

Brill Building

Located in New York City, at 1619 Broadway, near West 49th Street, the Brill Building is an eleven-story office building that has housed music publishers for over fifty years. In the 1940s, the building was considered the last outpost of Tin Pan Alley and was noted for its concentration of music publishers. Among the many offices in the building were those of Southern Music Publishing Co., Ltd., later Peer International Corporation, which specialized in importing music from Latin America; Select Music Publications, Inc., publishers of "Pennies From Heaven" (1936) and many other songs; Edwin A. Morris and Company, Inc., publishers of the music from *Guys and Dolls* (1950); and a host of very small, sometimes marginal, publishing firms.

The building was tired-looking and somewhat run-down even in the late 1940s, but was still a beehive of activity. Songwriters and would-be songwriters congregated in its lobby and in neighboring restaurants like Jack Dempsey's and Lindy's. Periodically, they made assaults on the publishers, displaying their latest creations. A fortunate few were employed as staff songwriters. The early 1950s, however, saw a gradual decline in activity, as the center of gravity of song distribution moved from sheet music to recording; more and more recording companies took direct control of song merchandising away from the publishers.

All that changed with the emergence of rock 'n' roll in the mid-1950s, when there was a renewal of activity in the Brill Building. It became the headquarters of many rock 'n' roll publishers, as well as publishers looking for a new sound. One of the largest firms, Aldon Music, was founded in 1958 by the guitarist Al Nevins and the songwriter Don Kirshner. Seeking a conciliation between Tin Pan Alley and rock 'n' roll, Aldon Music encouraged teams of budding songwriters, pairing writers like Carole King and Gerry Goffin, Barry Mann and Cynthia Weil, and Neil Sedaka and Howard Greenfield. These teams met with phenomenal success, producing over two hundred chart hits, including "Breaking Up Is Hard to Do" (1962), "Go Away, Little Girl" (1962), and "Walking in the Rain" (1964).

In 1959, the top floor of the Brill Building became the headquarters of an umbrella organization known as Eleventh Floor Music, which merged a number of firms jointly owned by publishers and entertainers like Elvis Presley. Created by Jean and Julian Aberbach, and developed largely through the efforts of their nephew, Freddie Bienstock, Eleventh Floor Music became the nucleus of a far-flung empire that eventually included London-based Carlin Music, Hill & Range Songs, and Hudson Bay Music.

Bibliography

Sanjek, Russell, and David Sanjek. *American Popular Music Business in the Twentieth Century.* 1991.

Britain

British and American popular music have had a symbiotic relationship dating back to colonial days. Aided by a common tongue, Britain has consistently been the leader among nations in foreign influence on American song. Conversely, the rich panoply of American popular song has always found a ready audience in Britain, particularly from the 1920s to the 1950s.

This mutualism changed in the 1960s with the Beatles, who opened the floodgates to a British invasion of previously unheard-of proportions. Since 1964, British songwriters and **performer-songwriters** have influenced music in the United States to such an extent that American popular music has become almost as much a British invention as an American one.

In the nineteenth century, the comic operas of W. S. Gilbert and Arthur Sullivan—especially *The Pirates of Penzance* (1879) and *The Mikado* (1885)—were a seminal influence on the American musical stage. In 1891, both "Little Annie Rooney" and "Ta-Ra-Ra Boom-De-Ay!" were music-hall favorites in London before reaching New York. Several very popular songs had British roots; Percy Gaunt, composer of "The Bowery" (1892), was of English birth, as was Harry Dacre, who wrote "Daisy Bell" in the same year.

In the early twentieth century, interaction between the London and New York stages continued. Jerome Kern, for example, interpolated his own songs in the stage musicals of both cities. British influence on American song was also manifest in Rudyard Kipling's poem "On the Road to Mandalay," put to music in 1907 by the American baritone and composer Oley Speaks. Also popular at the time were the songs of the Scottish songwriter and music-hall performer Harry Lauder, especially "Roamin' in the Gloamin'" (1911). During **World War I**, British songs popular in the United States included "Keep the Home Fires Burning" and "Pack up Your Troubles in Your Old Kit Bag and Smile, Smile, Smile" (both 1915) and "If You Were the Only Girl in the World" (1916).

The so-called **Roaring Twenties** were very much an American phenomenon. British contributions were limited to isolated songs such as "Moonlight on the Ganges" (1926), "Bless This House" (1927), and "A Garden in the Rain" (1929) until Noël Coward changed all that. This playwright, actor, and producer was an outstanding **composer-lyricist** as well, contributing such enduring favorites as "A Room With a View" (1928), "I'll See You Again" (1929), "Someday I'll Find You" (1931), and "I'll Follow My Secret Heart" (1934).

Also from Britain was the bandleader and composer-lyricist Ray Noble, whose songs include "Love Is the Sweetest Thing" (1933), "The Very Thought of You" (1934), "The Touch of Your Lips" (1936), "I Hadn't Anyone Till You" (1938), and "Cherokee" (1938). He also collaborated on the quintessential song of farewell, "Good Night Sweetheart" (1931).

The pace of British imports to the United States increased during the 1930s, with such hits as "Got a Date With an Angel" (1931), "Marching Along Together" (1933), "Isle of Capri" (1934), "Dinner for One, Please James" (1935), "These Foolish Things (Remind Me of You)," (1935), "Red Sails in the Sunset" (1935), "Harbor Lights" (1937), "Lambeth Walk" (1937), "Me and My Girl" (1937), and "At the Balalaika" (1939).

With the advent of **World War II**, contributions from abroad lessened. Among British songs finding their way to the United States at this time were "There'll Always Be an England" (1939), "A Nightingale Sang in Berkeley Square" (1940), "The Gypsy" (1945), and "Cruising Down the River (On a Sunday Afternoon)" (1945).

After the war, British contributions to American music were at first relatively sparse, and remained so throughout the 1950s. Not until 1961 did several British songs attain popularity in the United States: "Portrait of My Love" and "Stranger on the Shore." In 1962, three songs from the British musical *Stop the World—I Want to Get Off* were destined to become standards: "Gonna Build a Mountain," "Once in a Lifetime," and "What Kind of Fool Am I?," written by Anthony Newley and Leslie Bricusse. The same writers repeated their success three years later, in 1965, with *The Roar of the Greasepaint—The Smell of the Crowd*, from which came two memorable songs: "Who Can I Turn To?" and "(On) A Wonderful Day Like Today."

The aforementioned British invasion starting in the 1960s had at least two prongs: **rock** and theater music. On the one hand were the Beatles and the songs written for the most part by two of them, John Lennon and Paul McCartney, including "All My Loving" in 1963; "And I Love Her" in 1964; "Yesterday" in 1965; "Eleanor Rigby," "Here, There and Everywhere," "Michelle," and "Norwegian Wood" in 1966; "Strawberry Fields Forever" and "The Fool on the Hill" in 1967; and "Hey Jude" in 1968. On the other hand were British musicals represented by Lionel Bart's *Oliver!* of 1960, from which came such standards as "As Long As He Needs Me" and "Consider Yourself"; and by the Newley–Bricusse musicals mentioned above.

The tremendous success of the Beatles spawned a host of British performer-songwriters; the roster of **rock** stars of the past twenty-five years reads like a British *Who's Who*; Dave Clark, Paul McCartney, Barry and Robin Gibb, Mick Jagger and the Rolling Stones, Elton John, Pink Floyd, David Bowie, and many others are of British origin. Many of the songs of Tony Hatch were popular in the late 1960s; they include "Downtown" (1965), "Color My World" (1966), "Call Me" (1967), and "Don't Sleep in the Subway" (1967). Other British imports of the time were "Georgy Girl" (1966), "The Candy Man" (1970), "Sleepy Shores" (1971), and "Can't Smile Without You" (1975).

British musicals continued to storm our shores in the 1970s and 1980s. The works of the English composer Andrew Lloyd Webber met with extraordinary financial success. Several songs from his shows have become standards, in particular "I Don't Know How to Love Him," from *Jesus Christ Superstar* (1971); "Don't Cry for Me, Argentina" from *Evita* (1978); "Memory," from *Cats* (1981); "All I Ask of You," from *The Phantom of the Opera* (1986); and "Love Changes Everything," from *Aspects of Love* (1989).

British songwriters have also contributed to film. "Goldfinger" (1964), "(Theme From) You Only Live Twice" (1967), "Talk to the Animals" (1967), "Can You Read My Mind? (Love Theme From Superman)" (1978), "Against All Odds (Take a Look at Me Now)" (1984), and "Somewhere Out There" (1986) are just a few of the many songs by British writers that were introduced in films.

In sum, British influence on American popular song has existed since the two nations were one. But it became much more pervasive from the 1960s to the 1990s, enhancing all forms of popular entertainment: the stage, film, radio, recording, and television.

Bibliography

Chambers, Iain. *Urban Rhythms: Pop Music and Popular Culture*. 1985.

Gammond, Peter. *The Oxford Companion to Popular Music*. 1991.

Lee, Edward. *Music of the People: A Study of Popular Music in Great Britain*. 1970.

BROADWAY

The word "Broadway" has several meanings. It is, first of all, a thoroughfare, stretching northward within **New York City** through Manhattan Island and the Bronx, and then continuing on into Westchester. Broadway also stands for the principal theater district of New York City, located since the 1920s in and around Times Square.

Carried a step further, Broadway has come to represent the American legitimate stage and, in particular, the Broadway musical. It has become a metaphor for the entire noncinematic entertainment industry. As the cradle of **vaudeville**, the **revue, musical comedy, operetta**, and the **musical play**, Broadway has had a profound effect upon American popular song.

Tin Pan Alley, a district of New York City long associated with songwriters and publishers, has always been located on or near Broadway: beginning around 1900 on 28th Street between Broadway and Fifth Avenue; and, from the 1930s to the 1950s, in the **Brill Building**, located at 1619 Broadway, at the corner of 49th Street.

Directly, and sometimes even indirectly, Broadway has influenced popular music. Many worthy songs, such as those from the longest-running American stage show of all time, *The Fantasticks* (1960), originated in so-called off-Broadway productions presented by small, sometimes experimental theaters typically located away

from the Broadway entertainment district.

Broadway has also been the subject of a number of outstanding songs. In one of the earliest, George M. Cohan's "Give My Regards to Broadway" (1904), the words "Remember me to Herald Square" were appropriate, since most of the theaters of the time were clustered in the vicinity of 34th Street. "Forty-Five Minutes From Broadway," written by Cohan two years later, referred to the then-bucolic suburb of New Rochelle.

Many early **film musicals** used Broadway as a venue. Songs like "The Broadway Melody" (1929), "Broadway Rhythm" (1935), and "Lullaby of Broadway" (1935) all originated in Hollywood. The latter, an innovative song, was featured in a lengthy production number in the film *Gold Diggers of 1935*, with choreography by Busby Berkeley.

During **World War II**, a popular landmark just off Broadway was memorialized in Irving Berlin's poignant "I Left My Heart at the Stage Door Canteen" (1942). Other songs about the famous thoroughfare include "On Broadway" (1962) and "Boogaloo Down Broadway" (1967).

Finally, as a symbol of the entertainment industry, Broadway is the implied subject of such show-stoppers as "There's No Business Like Show Business" (1946), "Another Op'nin', Another Show" (1948), "That's Entertainment" (1953), and "Let Me Entertain You" (1959).

Bibliography

Burton, Jack. *The Blue Book of Broadway Musicals*. 1969.

Gottfried, Martin. *Broadway Musicals*. 1980.

Lewine, Richard, and Alfred Simon. *Songs of the Theater*. 1984.

Marks, Edward B., as told to J. Liebling. *They All Sang: From Tony Pastor to Rudy Vallée*. 1934.

Swain, Joseph P. *The Broadway Musical: A Critical and Musical Survey*. 1990.

See also: **Cities; Streets**

BROKEN CHORD

Melodies with pitches outlining basic triads are common throughout the history of Western music. A typical example is the U.S. national anthem, "The Star-Spangled Banner" (1814), which is a contrafactum on the melody of the English song "To Anacreon in Heaven" (c. 1778). Its opening notes outline first a descending tonic triad, then an ascending one. Another famous triadic melody is that of Johann Strauss, Jr.'s "On the Beautiful Blue Danube" (1867).

A broken chord can bring a military flavor to a melody by association with such bugle calls as "Retreat" (date uncertain), "Reveille" (c. 1836), and "Taps" (1862), each of which outlines a tonic triad. This patriotic ambiance is used to good advantage in several early twentieth-century songs, such as George M. Cohan's

"You're a Grand Old Flag" (1906) and "Over There" (1917) and Irving Berlin's "Oh How I Hate to Get Up in the Morning" (1918). In the latter, the composer-lyricist inserts an actual **quotation** of the bugle call "Reveille."

At the turn of the century, broken chords were very much in the air; they offered simplicity and directness and were easy to sing. The melody of Cohan's "Mary's a Grand Old Name" (1905) outlines an ascending triad, starting on the dominant degree of the scale an **octave** below; the melody of "Daisy Bell" (1892) does precisely the opposite. "After the Ball" (1892) starts on the mediant, ascends to the dominant, and then descends, outlining a sixth chord by picking up the submediant along the way.

Melodies outlining broken sixth chords continued to be popular as the century progressed. They are found in such diverse songs as "The Darktown Strutters' Ball" (1917), "Deep in the Heart of Texas" (1941), "How Are Things in Glocca Morra" (1947), and "Hello Dolly" (1964). The melody of "Take the 'A' Train," true to its **blues** orientation, outlines a flatted sixth.

The melody of "Who's Sorry Now" (1923) outlines an ascending tonic triad in the first inversion, as does that of the big band classic "In the Mood" (1939). On the other hand, in "All of Me" (1931), the same chord is outlined in a descending direction. In "The Varsity Drag" (1927), broken tonic and subdominant chords are emphasized by **repeated notes**. The opening notes of the 1944 song "Have Yourself a Merry Little Christmas" consist of an ascending tonic triad followed by an octave.

Few composers were immune to the charm of the broken chord as a source of melodic strength. Triadic formations are found in Jerome Kern's "The Siren's Song" (1917) and "I've Told Ev'ry Little Star" (1932), in Irving Berlin's "The Girl That I Marry" and "There's No Business Like Show Business" (both 1946), and in George Gershwin's "Oh, Lady Be Good" (1924) and "Love Walked In" (1938). In "Oh, Lady Be Good", the chord is outlined not at the song's beginning, but rather wherever the words of the title appear, outlining both tonic and dominant seventh chords. The opening motive of Ray Henderson's "Together" (1928) outlines a tonic chord in the third position (six-four). Harry Warren begins "You'll Never Know" (1943) with the same chord—ascending and then descending. Jule Styne used a broken chord in the style of a fanfare as his opening flourish in "Diamonds Are a Girl's Best Friend" (1949).

Broken chords in the minor **mode** are outlined in the melodies of "Forty-Second Street" (1932), "Sunrise, Sunset" (1964), and "Speak Softly Love"—the last derived from a theme from the film *The Godfather* (1972).

Two imports from Latin America using the device are "Mama Yo Quiero (I Want My Mama)," of 1940, and "Amor" (1941). Finally, in a burst of carefree optimism, the melody of "Happy Days Are Here Again" (1929) blithely calls attention to its broken chords, ascending and descending, by repeating each note except the first.

See also: Harmony; Interval; Modality; Repeated Notes; Sequence

C

CABARET

A cabaret is a nightclub that offers a short program of live entertainment in an intimate setting. This entertainment is usually provided by a pianist, singer, or small group. Very often, the material offers some form of social comment or satire.

Cabarets originated in Paris in the 1870s, and were established in Berlin, Munich, Vienna, and London by the early years of the twentieth century. Berlin in particular became a hotbed of cabaret activity. Berlin cabarets are the settings of both the 1930 film *The Blue Angel*—famous for Marlene Dietrich's singing of "Falling in Love Again (Can't Help It)"—and the 1966 musical play *Cabaret*, noted for its songs "Cabaret" and "Willkommen."

In the United States, cabarets proliferated in **New York City**, Chicago, New Orleans, Boston, San Francisco, Los Angeles, and other large cities during the 1930s and 1940s—many as outgrowths of speakeasies—with a varied repertoire of jazz, folk, and blues. Hundreds of small clubs existed in Manhattan alone, featuring such performers as Eartha Kitt, Barbra Streisand, Woody Allen, Mike Nichols, Elaine May, Carol Burnett, Joan Rivers, Doris Day, and Bette Midler. Among the better-known clubs in New York were the Blue Angel, the Village Vanguard, Billy Reed's Little Club, Le Ruban Bleu, and Café Society Uptown and Downtown. Perhaps the most significant performers at these and other cabarets were the pianist Cy Walters, famous for his flowing, jazz-oriented style; and the singer Mabel Mercer, renowned for her careful phrasing and lucid interpretation of the lyrics. Both artists profoundly influenced the next generation of pianists and singers.

Along with other pianists, singers, guitarists, and small groups, Walters and Mercer performed a repertoire often consisting of little-known **show tunes**, many of superior quality. Among previously obscure songs performed in little Manhattan clubs in the 1940s and 1950s were a number of tender songs by Lorenz Hart and Richard Rodgers, including "My Romance" (1935), "Glad to Be Unhappy" (1936), "My Funny Valentine" (1937), "It Never Entered My Mind" (1940), and "Wait Till You See Her" (1942).

Cole Porter's worldly lyrics and sophisticated music also appealed to discerning patrons in such favorites as "I'm in Love Again" (1925), "Miss Otis Regrets (She's Unable to Lunch Today)" (1934), "Why Shouldn't I?" (1935), and "Down in the Depths on the Ninetieth Floor" (1936).

Among other worthwhile songs to be rescued from possible oblivion by pianists and singers in cabarets were "I've Got a Crush on You" (1928), "The Folks Who Live on the Hill" (1937), "It's a Big Wide, Wonderful World" (1940), "While We're Young" (1943), "Lucky to Be Me" (1944), and "The End of a Love Affair" (1950).

Some cabarets offered **revues** on the order of *Jacques Brel Is Alive and Well and Living in Paris*, which opened at the Village Gate in New York in 1968; its songs included "Carousel," "If We Only Have Love," and "Marieke." Larger cabarets with satirical revues, as well as smaller clubs featuring such singer-pianists as Bobby Short and Michael Feinstein, continued to be popular throughout the 1980s.

Bibliography

Appignanesi, Lisa. *The Cabaret*. 1976.
———. *Cabaret: The First Hundred Years*. 1984.
Gavin, James. *Intimate Nights: The Golden Age of New York Cabaret*. 1991.

CADENCE

A cadence is a musical gesture marking the end of a phrase, period, or song. In popular music, at least through the 1950s, the strongest cadences typically occur at the end of the **verse** and at the end of the song itself. Traditionally, the **chorus** ends with a full, or authentic, cadence, which moves from dominant seventh to tonic (often with added notes) as follows:

The verse may also terminate with a full cadence, but more likely will employ a half cadence—a type that moves to the dominant seventh from any other scale degree:

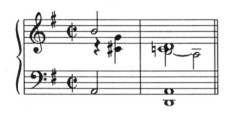

Although the vast majority of songs written in the first half of the century close with an authentic cadence, one exceptional genre comes to mind: the **tango** almost always ends with a half cadence.

Beginning in the 1960s, cadences often moved away from the traditional. For example, Paul Simon uses a plagal cadence in his song "Bridge Over Troubled Water" (1969). This type of cadence, traditionally associated with sacred music, moves from subdominant to tonic, as follows:

Other ways were found to avoid the authentic cadence. Simon's "The Sound of Silence" (1964) moves from the lowered leading tone to the tonic, giving the ending a modal sound. Hal David and Burt Bacharach's "Alfie" (1966) dresses up the final cadence with added sevenths and ninths. Bobby Hebb's "Sunny" (1965), like many other songs of its time, avoids cadences altogether by use of the **fade-out**.

The conscious use of the cadence to underline the sense of the lyrics is exemplified in Ira Gershwin and Kurt Weill's "My Ship," from *Lady in the Dark* (1941). In that song, various methods are used to avoid a feeling of finality. So-called deceptive cadences occur at the end of each eight-bar period. The first period moves to the supertonic, the second to the subdominant, the **release** to the dominant of the dominant, and the penultimate section to the dominant seventh. Only at the end of the **coda**—at the words "my own true love to me"—does an authentic cadence appear. There it is strengthened by use of the hallowed cadential formula: I-II-IV-V-I.

See also: Harmony

CAJUN. SEE ZYDECO

CAKEWALK

The cakewalk was a strutting, promenade type of dance that originated on southern plantations in the 1840s. Moving to the cities during the 1890s, it became immensely popular in the ballrooms of Europe and North America around the turn of the century.

The music accompanying the dance was at first the **march**, but with the increasing popularity of **ragtime**, melodies became more and more syncopated. Eventually, cakewalk music became indistinguishable from ragtime. By the turn of the century, the cakewalk was danced to such ragtime songs as "A Hot Time in the Old Town" (1896), "Hello! Ma Baby" (1899), and "Under the Bamboo Tree" (1902).

Bibliography

Berlin, Edward A. *Ragtime: A Musical and Cultural History*. 1980.

See also: **Coon Song; Dance Crazes; Gay Nineties; Two-Step**

CALL AND RESPONSE

Call and response—the alternation between a solo singer and vocal group or between two vocal groups—is a striking characteristic of the music of **Africa**, among other cultures. As such, it became a regular feature of African-American work songs and **gospel** music. By extension, call and response soon applied to instruments as well as voices, with contrast between instrumental soloists and ensembles in **jazz** and **swing**, where the "response" is usually improvisational in nature. A prime manifestation of call and response is the **riff**, alternating between different sections of the orchestra.

Beginning in the late 1940s, both vocal and instrumental call and response spread to such primarily African-American genres as **rhythm and blues** and **soul**, as well as to the interracial genres of **rock 'n' roll** and **rock**. Call and response also had a strong influence on Latin American music, whether as antiphonal singing in the **guaracha** and **merengue**, or as contrast between various sections of the orchestra, as in the playing of the **mambo** and **salsa**.

See also: **Improvisation; Latin America**

CALYPSO

Calypso is a type of song characterized by topical lyrics commenting wryly about personalities, social mores, and political events. It originated in Trinidad—where it was often played by steel bands—and quickly spread to other parts of the West Indies, notably the Bahamas and Jamaica.

Musically, calypso is in moderate tempo and duple meter; it uses simple harmonies of the tonic, dominant, and subdominant; and it has a lightly syncopated melody loosely outlining those harmonies by the use of broken chords alternating with repeated notes. The bass line also outlines the harmonies in a pattern such as this:

In the 1950s, calypso entered the mainstream of music in the United States, largely through the efforts of the singer Harry Belafonte. He popularized the calypso songs "Matilda, Matilda" in 1953, "Jamaica Farewell" in 1955, and "The Banana Boat Song (Day-O)" in 1956. In the following year, three calypso songs were hits: "Marianne," "Melodie d'Amour," and "Yellow Bird."

Although few calypso songs were as successful in the intervening years, the style was revived by John Denver in 1975, with his "Calypso"; and again in 1988, with the score for Walt Disney's animated film feature *The Little Mermaid*, set in the Caribbean, whose score consists almost entirely of calypso songs. The most popular of these is "Under the Sea," winner of the Academy Award for Best Song of 1988.

See also: **Reggae**

CANADA

Canada's influence on the popular music of the United States stems principally from its native songwriters and entertainment figures. Canadian-born **composer-lyricists** and **performer-songwriters** include Shelton Brooks, creator of "Some of These Days" (1910) and "The Darktown Strutters' Ball" (1917)—from Amesbury, Ontario; Paul Anka, whose many credits include "Diana" (1957) and "Put Your Head on My Shoulder" (1958) as well as the lyrics of "My Way" (1967)—from Ottawa; Leonard Cohen, who wrote "Suzanne" (1967)—from Montreal; and Joni Mitchell, writer of "Chelsea Morning" and "Both Sides Now" (both 1967)—born in McLeod, Alberta.

As for entertainers, Guy Lombardo, leader of the most popular "sweet" band of the 1930s and 1940s, was born in London, Ontario. His band, in fact, was known as the Royal Canadians. Also associated with this band was Guy's brother, Carmen, who was a singer and saxophonist with the band and co-writer of such songs as "Coquette" (1928), "Jungle Drums" (1930), "Boo-Hoo" (1937), and "Seems Like Old Times" (1946).

Other native Canadian entertainers include Giselle MacKenzie (Winnipeg), singing star of *Your Hit Parade*; Oscar Peterson (Petersborough, Ontario), famed jazz pianist; and Anne Murray (Springhill, Nova Scotia), a singer who popularized a number of hit songs including the appropriately named "Snowbird" (1970).

Other areas of influence have come from Canadian folk song and jazz. "Alouette," first published in Montreal in 1879, originated as a work song in Quebec. The after-drinking song "Show Me the Way to Go Home" (1925) was probably adapted from a Canadian folk song. The 1958 jazz classic "The Swingin' Shepherd Blues" is also of Canadian origin.

See also: **Foreign Influence; Nations**

CARDINAL POINTS

The four cardinal points of the compass, East, West, North, and South, have their place in popular song. One of the earliest and best-known modern songs to mention East and West is "The Sidewalks of New York" (1894), a simple waltz that begins with the words: "East Side, West Side, all around the town." In contrast, "East of the Sun (and West of the Moon)," written in 1934, is a sophisticated song with much more complex harmonies. East is plainly preferred over West in the opening lyrics of "Buttons and Bows" (1948): "East is east and west is west and the wrong one I have chose." Several songs refer to the South as a region of the United States, among them "When It's Sleepy Time Down South" (1931) and "That's What I Like About the South" (1944). "Just a Little Bit South of North Carolina" (1940) refers, of course, to South Carolina; "South of the Border (Down Mexico Way)" (1939), a British import, is about our neighbor to the South.

Perhaps the most memorable use of all four cardinal points in popular song is Cole Porter's employment of the words "The east, west, north and the south of you" in his song "All of You" of 1954. The same idea, with different orientation, is found in Alan and Marilyn Bergman's lyrics to Michel Legrand's "What Are You Doing the Rest of Your Life?" (1969): "North and South and East and West of your life."

See also: Cities; Nations; States

CATALOGUE SONG

The catalogue song has a long and honorable history in opera; Leporello's "Catalogue" aria from Mozart's *Don Giovanni* is perhaps the most famous example. In the same tradition are the catalogue songs of the American musical theater; they playfully list all sorts of items.

The master in this regard was Cole Porter, who tried to have at least two catalogue songs in every show. "Let's Do It (Let's Fall in Love)," from *Paris* (1928), lists countless animals (from moths to giraffes) and nationalities (from Siamese to Letts) who "do it." "You're the Top," from *Anything Goes* (1934), is a catalogue of the best things in life at the time it was written, from the Colosseum and the Louvre Museum to cellophane and Mickey Mouse. "At Long Last Love," from *You Never Know* (1938), catalogues imitations and compares them with the genuine article: "Is it Granada I see or only Asbury Park?" "Do I Love You?," from *Du Barry Was a Lady* (1939), is a list of rhetorical questions like "Doesn't one and one make two?" "Brush Up Your Shakespeare," from *Kiss Me Kate* (1948), is a pun-filled catalogue of Shakespeare's works, from *Coriolanus* to *Measure for Measure*.

But Porter was far from being the only songwriter to delight in catalogue songs. Lorenz Hart (with Richard Rodgers), in "Any Old Place With You" (1919), presents a long list of places the protagonist would like to visit with his beloved—from Timbuktu to Lake Superior; from Syria to Siberia to "I'll go to hell for ya or Philadelphia." "The Lady Is a Tramp" (1937), also by Rodgers and Hart, catalogues the reasons why "the lady is a tramp," among them getting "too hungry for dinner at eight" and never bothering "with people I hate." In "A Fine Romance," from the film *Swing Time* (1936), Dorothy Fields (with Jerome Kern) lists the many ways the budding romance is falling flat—no kisses, no clinches, no pinches—and comments wryly: "You're just as hard to land as the 'Ile de France.'"

"I Can't Get Started," written by Ira Gershwin (with Vernon Duke) in 1935, is a catalogue of the many things its protagonist has done, from going "'round the world in a plane" to settling "revolutions in Spain," but still, he "can't get started." "How About You?," written by Ralph Freed and Burton Lane in 1941, is a catalogue of things to admire: "New York in June . . . a Gershwin tune . . . potato chips . . . moonlight and motor trips."

But perhaps the ultimate catalogue is Ira Gershwin's list of fifty-one Russian composers in "Tschaikowsky," written (with music by Kurt Weill) for Danny Kaye to sing in *Lady in the Dark* (1941).

Stephen Sondheim proved that the catalogue song still survived in his song of survival, "I'm Still Here," from *Follies* (1971). The song incorporates a long list of nostalgia, going from "Windsor and Wallie's affair," to "Amos 'n Andy, Mahjongg and platinum hair."

Additional Songs

Always True to You (In My Fashion) (1948)
Anything Goes (1934)
Bewitched (1941)
How Deep Is the Ocean? (1932)
Isn't It Romantic? (1932)
Mountain Greenery (1926)
My Favorite Things (1959)
My Romance (1935)
Then I'll Be Tired of You (1934)
These Foolish Things (Remind Me of You) (1935)

Bibliography

Mast, Gerald. *Can't Help Singin': The American Musical on Stage and Screen.* 1987.

See also: Musical Comedy; Operetta

CELEBRATIONS. *SEE* OCCASIONAL SONG

CHA CHA CHA.

The cha cha cha is a type of dance music developed during the 1950s by Cuban musical ensembles called *charangas*. Both the music and the ballroom dance created a sensation in the United States in 1953 with Perez Prado's recording of "Cerazo Rosa"—originally a French song, but later given English lyrics as "Cherry Pink and Apple Blossom White" (1955). In North America, the cha cha cha was usually played by large orchestras in moderate tempo, emphasizing the persistent rhythm by the use of percussion instruments such as timbales and cowbells, in patterns such as this:

Also characteristic of the music are frequent flute solos and strong contrast between brass and woodwinds in the style of the **mambo**.

The craze for the cha cha cha was relatively short-lived; it faded away with the rise of rock 'n' roll in the 1960s. However, some standards of the genre, such as "Sweet and Gentle" (1955), are still played. The cha cha cha also contributed to the popularity of the Greek import "Never on Sunday" (1960), which is often played in that style.

Bibliography

Roberts, John Storm. *The Latin Tinge: The Impact of Latin American Music on the United States.* 1985.

See also: **Cuba; Dance Crazes; Merengue; Rumba**

Chance. *See* Luck

Charleston

The Charleston is a moderately fast dance in duple meter that flourished during the **Roaring Twenties**. It is characterized by a syncopated rhythm that anticipates the third beat in common time in this manner:

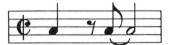

The name of the dance is derived from that of the song "Charleston"—first heard in the 1923 musical *Runnin' Wild.* The song title, in turn, is derived from the city of that name in South Carolina.

The rhythm of the Charleston became very popular throughout the 1920s and in periodic revivals thereafter. It pulsates in such songs as "Five Foot Two, Eyes of Blue; Has Anybody Seen My Girl?," (1925) "Sweet Georgia Brown" (1925), "Yes Sir, That's My Baby" (1925), "Clap Yo' Hands" (1926), "The Girl Friend" (1926), "The Varsity Drag" (1927), and "Crazy Rhythm" (1928). But the quintessential song to accompany the dance remains "Charleston."

See also: **Dance Crazes**

Childhood

Most song lyrics have to do with adult life: falling in or out of love, staying out in (or in out) of bad weather, celebrating or cursing the seasons, or listing reasons why one should visit particular cities. Less popular with songwriters are songs about childhood. Nonetheless, there are some notable ones on the subject.

In 1906, there was Gus Edwards's memorable waltz, "School Days (When We Were a Couple of Kids)." In 1928, when Al Jolson's image flashed across the silver screen in the film *The Singing Fool,* his voice was also heard singing "Sonny Boy"—a sentimental piece about a three year old that begins: "Climb upon my knee, Sonny Boy." In the 1960s jazz musicians revived it, mainly as a vehicle for instrumentalists, although Mel Tormé recorded a fine vocal version. At least twice—in 1905 and again in 1949—the phrase "Daddy's Little Girl" was used as a song title. The most recent song is frequently played at debutante balls around the country.

Oscar Hammerstein II provided a number of finely crafted lyrics about children, all set to lovely melodies by Richard Rodgers. In the Broadway production of *Carousel* (1945), the expectant father sings about his soon-to-be-born son in "Soliloquy." Then, in case the son should turn out to be a daughter, he sings a different set of Hammerstein lyrics: as pink and gentle as the son's lyrics are ruddy and muscular.

Children play important roles in another Rodgers and Hammerstein show, *The Sound of Music* (1959). For that reason, some songs from the score present a child's point of view. "Do Re Mi," based on the musical scale, correlates familiar English words with the Italian syllables for musical intervals. "My Favorite Things" conjures up pleasant images to help stave off children's fears. "Sixteen Going on Seventeen" is, obviously, a song about growing up. Other youth-oriented Rodgers and Hammerstein songs include "It Might as Well Be Spring" (1946), "Younger Than Springtime" (1949), "Hello, Young Lovers" (1951), and "I Whistle a Happy Tune" (1951). Hammerstein's lyrics about youth have a poignant and wistful quality that strikes responsive chords in all listeners.

Alec Wilder was not especially fond of children, but he wrote many pieces for and about them, most notably "While We're Young" (1943), a song whose superb William Engvick lyrics—with such rhymes as "How blue the skies, all sweet surprise"—have been called a gem of English literature.

In 1944, the comedian Phil Silvers, together with James Van Heusen, wrote an enchanting song that was dedicated to Frank Sinatra's young daughter. It was aptly called "Nancy (With the Laughing Face)," and became a late-blooming hit when Sinatra recorded it some years later.

Johnny Mercer, dean of American lyricists, wrote several song-poems about children. In 1938, he collaborated with Harry Warren on a charming song called "You Must Have Been a Beautiful Baby." Because Mercer used the conjunction "and" in the phrase "and baby, look at you now," we know that the **baby** grew up to be an even more beautiful adult. Unfortunately, some singers substitute "but" for the "and," thereby completely changing the meaning. With Hoagy Carmichael, Mercer in 1933 wrote "Lazy Bones," a languid, southern-oriented song about a young child "sleeping in the noon-day sun." In a similar vein is "Small Fry," which Carmichael wrote with Frank Loesser in 1938.

Another Mercer lyric should be mentioned, even though it has been called an accurate translation from the French original: "When the World Was Young," which begins "Ah, the apple tree" (1952). Mercer's talent for rhyme shines here. Such imagery as "On our backs we'd lie, looking at the sky" takes us back to our childhood, whether it was spent in Bordeaux or Baltimore. In this song, Mercer's poetry is perfectly married to the song's bittersweet melody.

In the score of the musical comedy *Bye Bye Birdie* (1960), there is a song by Charles Strouse and Lee Adams that presents a caustic question often posed by elders: "What's the matter with kids today?" This witty and bouncy song is appropriately called "Kids".

Several songs bridge the period between childhood and adolescence. These include Hugh Martin and Ralph Blane's lovely "The Boy Next Door" (1944); Ronny Graham's poignant "I'm in Love With Miss Logan" (1952); young Oliver's question "Where Is Love?," from the show *Oliver!* (1963); the 1951 hit song "Too Young"; and "Thank Heaven for Little Girls," from the film *Gigi* (1958). Billie Holiday and Arthur Herzog, Jr. collaborated on a song called "God Bless the Child" in 1941, and this sad ballad about the have-nots became associated with singer Holiday for the rest of her life.

Loonis McGlohon

See also: Age; Boy; Girl

CHORUS

Two words are used to define the overall musical structure of a popular song: "**verse**" and "chorus." The latter term originated in the nineteenth century to designate the main section of a popular song: often sung by a group or chorus, in contrast to the verse, usually sung by a single person. Although the term was seldom used by writers of songs for the theater — who preferred "refrain" or "burden," often with some modifier in parentheses, such as "very slowly," "at a slow even pace," "tenderly," or "leisurely" — "chorus," was the designation of choice for the majority of songwriters, including most of **Tin Pan Alley**, and remains so to this day. In jazz **improvisation**, it very often refers to the song in general—as in the expression "take another chorus"—since verses are seldom performed.

In the course of the twentieth century, the chorus has generally tended to overshadow the verse. Many songs, in fact, consist only of a chorus. Jerome Kern was a pioneer in this regard; a number of his songs are verseless, including "Smoke Gets in Your Eyes" (1933), "A Fine Romance" (1936), and "The Way You Look Tonight" (1936). After the 1950s the tendency to eliminate the verse accelerated and numerous songs were written with chorus only. However, exceptions are found in folk-oriented and country and western songs using verse-chorus (AB) **form**, as well as in throwbacks to older genres, such as the tango "Don't Cry for Me, Argentina" (1976) and the waltz "You Light Up My Life" (1976).

CHRISTMAS

More songs have been written about Christmas than about all other **holidays** combined. There are, first of all, the traditional hymns and carols of British origin: "What Child Is This?" (1861), based on "Greensleeves" (c. 1580), "The Twelve Days of Christmas" (c. 1700); "Adeste Fideles," or "O Come All Ye Faithful" (1782); "Deck the Halls" (1784); "God Rest You Merry Gentlemen" (1827); "The First Noël" (1833), and "It Came Upon a Midnight Clear," (1850). Then there are the other European contributions: the Austrian "Silent Night, Holy Night" (1818), Felix Mendelssohn's "Hark the Herald Angels Sing" (1855), the French "O Holy Night" (1858), and the Swedish "Good King Wenceslas" (c. 1860). There are, in addition, peculiarly American standbys of the season, like "Jingle Bells," or "The One Horse Open Sleigh," written in 1857 by James Pierpont, the uncle of financier J. Pierpont Morgan, and "O Little Town of Bethlehem" (1868), the words of which were written by the pastor of Trinity Church in Boston.

In addition to these religious works, which are revived each Christmas season, many songs have been written specifically for the holiday over the past one hundred years. The best known of these, and one of the most commercially successful songs ever written, is Irving Berlin's "White Christmas," initially sung by Bing Crosby in the 1942 film *Holiday Inn*. Three lively songs of the season written with children in mind are "Santa Claus Is Coming to Town" (1934), "Rudolph the Red-Nosed Reindeer" (1949), and "Frosty the Snowman" (1950). Also popular with children (and adults too) is Ross Bagdasarian's "The Chipmunk Song (Christmas Don't Be Late)" (1958), a moderate waltz that features the unforgettable electronic characters Alvin and the Chipmunks.

Several ballads are revived each Christmas season. These include the wartime affirmation "I'll Be Home for Christmas" (1943); Hugh Martin and Ralph Blane's touching song "Have Yourself a Merry Little Christmas," featured in the film *Meet Me in St. Louis* (1944); Mel Tormé and Robert Wells's "The Christmas Song" (1946), better known by either its first line, "Chestnuts roasting on an open fire," or its last, "Merry Christmas to you"; Meredith Willson's "It's Beginning to Look Like Christmas" (1951); and the 1984 song "Do They Know It's Christmas." Also periodically revived are the march "The Little Drummer Boy" (1938) and the waltz "Silver Bells" (1950). The **weather** at that time of the year, at least in the colder parts of the nation, has also inspired several songs, including "Winter Wonderland" (1934), "Let It Snow! Let It Snow! Let It Snow!" (1945), and "Sleigh Ride" (1950).

The most popular Christmas song with a rock beat is "Jingle-Bell Rock" (1957), followed in popularity by "Rockin' 'Round the Christmas Tree" (1960). Also pertaining to the holiday are such novelties as "All I Want for Christmas (Is My Two Front Teeth)" (1950) and "I Saw Mommy Kissing Santa Claus" (1952).

See also: Months; Religion; Seasons

CHROMATICISM

Chromaticism—the use of some pitches of the chromatic **scale**—can be expressed in popular music in the **melody**, in the **bass line**, or in the **harmony**. In most cases, however, the use of half steps rather than whole steps does not detract from the essential tonic-dominant **tonality** of a song.

Even so eminently chromatic a song as Cole Porter's "All Through the Night" (1934) is firmly anchored in the **key** of F major. In this example of melodic chromaticism, the melody of each A section moves inexorably downwards in half steps, while the harmony and bass line go their own way. Many other examples of melodic chromaticism exist in Porter's music, including "Let's Do It (Let's Fall in Love)" (1928), "Night and Day" (1932), and "I Concentrate on You" (1939). In another example, Duke Ellington's music for "Prelude to a Kiss" (1938), two descending chromatic passages occur in each A section—the first from b' to g', the second from g'-sharp to e'—while the harmony goes through the **circle of fifths**. Melodic chromaticism is also prominent in the melody of Jerome Kern's "I Dream Too Much" (1935).

The chromatic bass line is a staple of popular music. The bass line of Porter's "Just One of Those Things" (1935), for example, descends chromatically from d to G in each A section. Ellington uses a similar bass line in his song "In a Sentimental Mood" (1935). James Van Heusen often combines a chromatic bass line with diminished-seventh harmonies, as in "Darn That Dream" (1939), "It Could Happen to You" (1944), and "Call Me Irresponsible" (1962). Chromatic bass lines are also prominent in many **bossa novas**, like Antonio Carlos

Jobim's "One Note Samba" (1961), "Quiet Nights of Quiet Stars" (1962), and "How Insensitive" (1963), as well as in Michael Legrand's music for songs like "Watch What Happens" (1964) and "What Are You Doing the Rest of Your Life?" (1969).

Harmonic chromaticism occurs less frequently. In Francis Lai's "A Man and a Woman" (1966), the harmony and bass line descend together in three-bar segments—with the harmonies D major seventh, C-sharp seventh, C major seventh, and B seventh—while the melody consists mostly of **repeated notes**.

All three types of chromaticism are apparent in Ellington's "Sophisticated Lady": the melody, harmony, and bass line descend concurrently, twice in each A section–from G-flat to E-flat and from A-flat to F. But perhaps the most striking simultaneous chromaticism of all is that in Richard Rodgers's music for "Lover" (1932). In that enduring waltz, the chromatic nature of the melody is softened somewhat by the use of neighbor tones, but in each A section, melody, harmony (in sevenths), and bass line all descend together for five half steps, from c to G.

See also: Interval

CIRCLE OF FIFTHS

The circle of fifths may be described as an imaginary circle consisting of related **keys**, moving either clockwise, in the "sharp" direction (C, G, D, A, E, B, F-sharp), or counterclockwise, in the "flat" direction (C, F, B-flat, E-flat, A-flat, D-flat).

These simple and easily comprehended changes form the harmonic basis of many popular songs. For example, the first half of the sixteen-bar song "Ballin' the Jack" (1913) passes through the following harmonies: G seventh, C seventh, F seventh, B-flat major—with a change every two bars. Similarly, "Five Foot Two, Eyes of Blue (Has Anybody Seen My Girl?)" (1925) is built almost entirely around the circle of fifths, with these harmonic changes: C major, E seventh, A seventh, D seventh, G seventh, C major. Even in the song's **release**, the same idea is carried out: E seventh, A seventh, D seventh, G seventh. "Sweet Georgia Brown" (1925) is another case in point, descending through the harmonies of E seventh, A seventh, D seventh, and G major.

"All of Me" (1931), in ABAC **form**, passes through parts of the circle three times in succession. Its harmonies move abruptly from C major to E seventh, and then to A seventh and D minor; then through the chords of E seventh, A minor, D seventh, and G seventh; and finally back to the first chord progression. In "Prelude to a Kiss" (1938), the circle of fifths is paired with **chromaticism**; the **bass line** ascends through various segments of the circle—D, G, C, F and B, E, A, D—while the melody and harmony descend chromatically.

The opening harmonies of George and Ira Gershwin's "Nice Work If You Can Get It" (1937) also pass through the circle: B seventh, E seventh, A seventh, D seventh, before landing on the tonic of G major.

The 1965 song "The Shadow of Your Smile" is also constructed around the circle of fifths. In the key of E minor, it begins with an F-sharp seventh chord and then outlines the following harmonic progression: B seventh, E minor, A minor, D seventh, G major. Similarly, the 1981 song "Arthur's Theme (Best That You Can Do)," with a key signature of one flat, goes through the following chord changes three times in succession: D minor seventh, G seventh, C major, F major, B-flat major, before moving to E seventh and its tonic of A major.

In writing the release, which often calls for fast and remote harmonic changes, a composer will often utilize the circle of fifths. Hundreds of songs employ the device in their middle sections—from George Gershwin's "I Got Rhythm" (1930) and Harold Arlen's "I've Got the World on a String" (1932) to Stephen Sondheim's "I'm Still Here" (1971). This all goes to prove that the circle of fifths, which was almost a cliché in the 1920s, has far from outlived its usefulness to songwriters.

See also: Enharmonic Equivalence; Harmony

CIRCUS

The circus and music have long had an affinity for one another. **Marches** and **waltzes**, such as "National Emblem" (1906) and "Waves of the Danube" (1880), traditionally accompany circus acts. Songs about circus performers also have a venerable history. One example among many is "The Daring Young Man (On the Flying Trapeze)" of 1868, revived in 1933 as "The Man on the Flying Trapeze."

However, the circus entertainer dearest to the heart of the songwriter is the clown. Seldom a performer, he is usually cast in the role of a dupe or **fool**. This usage is applied in such dramatic songs as "Laugh! Clown! Laugh!" (1928), "Cathy's Clown" (1960), "Tears of a Clown" (1967), and, most notably, in "Send in the Clowns" (1973). On the other hand, the "clown" of "Be a Clown" (1948) is a person who struggles to keep up appearances in the face of adversity.

The circus and the carnival have also provided the setting for a number of outstanding stage productions. *Jumbo* (1935) is about a circus elephant. *Carousel* (1945), with its enchanting score, revolves about a carnival. The striking merry-go-round song "Love Makes the World Go Round" was introduced in the musical *Carnival* (1961). Also about revolving mechanisms are such songs as "The Merry-Go-Round Broke Down," of 1937, and Jacques Brel's "Carousel" of 1959.

In one memorable song, "It's Only a Paper Moon" (1933), the circus symbolizes tawdriness and make believe: "It's a Barnum and Bailey world, Just as phony as it can be." In another, "Circus" (1949), the circus is used as a metaphor for a failed romance: "I was the clown, you were the laughter echoing after."

See also: **Magic**.

CITIES

The city has figured prominently in the development of American popular song. Several cities come immediately to mind: **New York City**, the location of **Broadway**, **Tin Pan Alley**, **Harlem**, the **Brill Building**, and much of the publishing and **recording** industries; Los Angeles, center of the film industry and the **film musical**; New Orleans, the birthplace of **jazz**; Chicago, its incubator; **Nashville**, the hub of **country and western** music; and Memphis, an important satellite.

These cities, along with many others, foreign and domestic, have also served as **subjects** of popular song and as sources of inspiration to songwriters, with the cities of New York and Paris clearly preferred above all others (*see* Table 5).

New York City has held a fascination for songwriters since the turn of the century, as evidenced by such standards as "The Sidewalks of New York," also known as "East Side, West Side" (1894) and "The Streets of New York (In Old New York)" (1906). "Manhattan" (1925), the first hit by Lorenz Hart and Richard Rodgers, is the apotheosis of New York. Its chorus has four sets of lyrics replete with allusions to areas in or near the city: The Bronx, Staten Island, Greenwich Village, Yonkers, Coney Island, Bowling Green, Jamaica Bay, Flatbush, Central Park, and Canarsie. Both the lyrics and music have proven extremely durable, as have those of Betty Comden, Adolph Green, and Leonard Bernstein in their "New York, New York" (1944): "The Bronx is up and the Battery's down."

Another song with the same title appeared in 1977 as the theme of the film *New York, New York*. As locale, the city has also figured in countless theatrical productions and films, perhaps most notably in *West Side Story* (1957). In addition, a host of songs include references to New York in their lyrics. "How About You?" (1941) begins with the words "I like New York in June"; Park Avenue is mentioned in "Penthouse Serenade (When We're Alone)" (1931); and Fifth Avenue is the locale of Irving Berlin's "Easter Parade" (1933).

On the subject of Paris, many songs are imports from **France**. However, several American-made songs stand out as well. One of these is Vernon Duke's "April in Paris" (1932), a song revolutionary in its day for its sophisticated harmonies. Oscar Hammerstein II and Jerome Kern wrote "The Last Time I Saw Paris" in 1940, when Paris was about to fall to the Nazis. This song is notable for the romanticism of its lyrics, the poignancy of its melody, and the grace notes in its release simulating Parisian taxicabs. Cole Porter wrote his panegyric "I Love Paris" in 1953 for the musical comedy *Can-Can*. Its chief attribute is the contrast between minor and major. Paris has also figured as the locale of two outstanding film musicals: *An American in Paris* (1951), an anthology of music by George Gershwin; and *Gigi* (1958), which introduced several songs by Alan Jay Lerner and Frederick Loewe destined to become standards.

Moving on to other cities, there are at least three standards about St. Louis: "Meet Me in St. Louis, Louis" (1904), a hardy perennial, thanks to its revival in the 1944 musical film *Meet Me in St. Louis*; W. C. Handy's "St. Louis Blues" (1914), one of the most famous songs ever written; and the 1948 song "You Came a Long Way From St. Louis."

Three songs about London stand out. "Limehouse Blues" (1922) refers to a then partly Chinese district in London's East End; it was performed at Paul Whiteman's historic concert at Aeolian Hall in New York on February 12, 1924—the same concert that saw the world premiere of George Gershwin's *Rhapsody in Blue*. Another song about London, Ira and George Gershwin's "A Foggy Day" (1937), was introduced in the Fred Astaire film *A Damsel in Distress*; it opens with the lyrics "A foggy day in London town." Both songs have long been favorites of jazz musicians. Other London locales were immortalized in the 1937 song "Lambeth Walk" and in "A Nightingale Sang in Berkeley Square" (1940). London has also functioned as a locality in theatrical productions, most notably in Alan Jay Lerner and Frederick Loewe's *My Fair Lady* (1956).

One memorable song includes two different cities and a state in its lyrics: "By the Time I Get to Phoenix" (1967) contains references to Albuquerque and Oklahoma along with the title city. Nor must one forget Johnny Mercer's earthy lyrics to "Blues in the Night" (1941), with its catalogue of cities: "From Natchez to Mobile, from Memphis to St. Joe."

Cities in California are represented in at least six standard songs. Among them is one of the most popular songs of all time, "I Left My Heart in San Francisco" (1954). San Francisco is almost everybody's favorite town and has been memorialized over the years in other songs as well, including the 1936 song "San Francisco," from the film of the same name, and the 1967 song "San Francisco (Be Sure to Wear Some Flowers in Your Hair)."

Other cities of note, with two songs each, are Chicago, represented by "Chicago (That Toddling Town)" (1922) and "My Kind of Town" (1964); and San Antonio, with "On the Alamo" (1922) and "San Antonio Rose" (1940). And then there is Charleston, South Carolina, scene of the opera *Porgy and Bess* (1935) and the namesake of one of the most popular dances of the Roaring Twenties, "Charleston" (1923). Finally, two exotic cities in Myanmar (formerly Burma) and Spain are represented by art songs that stride the border between the popular and the classic: "On the Road to Mandalay" (1907) and "Granada" (1932). One can conclude from the foregoing that cities both ordinary and exotic—from Miami to Moscow, from Memphis to Managua, from Kalamazoo to Copenhagen—will continue to serve as subjects of popular song in the years to come.

See also: **Nations; States; Streets; Trains; Travel**

TABLE 5

Cities in Song

Atlantic City, New Jersey
On the Boardwalk in Atlantic City (1946)

Avalon, Santa Catalina Island, California
Avalon (1920)

Baia, Brazil
Baia (1944)

Birmingham, Alabama
Down in the Valley, or Birmingham Jail (1917)

Boston, Massachusetts
Boston Beguine (1952)

Buffalo, New York
Shuffle Off to Buffalo (1932)

Capri, Italy
Isle of Capri (1934)

Charleston, South Carolina
Charleston (1923)

Chattanooga, Tennessee
Chattanooga, Choo Choo (1941)
Chattanooga Shoe Shine Boy (1950)

Chicago, Illinois
Chicago (That Toddling Town) (1922)
My Kind of Town (1964)

City (nonspecific)
Hot Child in the City (1978)
Living for the City (1973)
Summer in the City (1966)

Copenhagen, Denmark
Wonderful Copenhagen (1952)

Dallas, Texas
Big D (1956)
Dallas Blues (1918)

Detroit, Michigan
Detroit City (1963)

Dover, England
(There'll be Bluebirds Over) The White Cliffs of Dover (1941)

El Paso, Texas
El Paso (1960)

Galveston, Texas
Galveston (1968)

Gary, Indiana
Gary, Indiana (1957)

Granada, Andalucia, Spain
Granada (1932)

Hong Kong
Hong Kong Blues (1939)

Istanbul, Turkey
Istanbul, Not Constantinople (1953)

Kalamazoo, Michigan
I've Got a Gal in Kalamazoo (1942)

Kansas City, Missouri
Kansas City (1943)
Kansas City (1959)

Lisbon, Portugal
Lisbon Antigua (In Old Lisbon) (1954)

London, England
A Foggy Day (1937)
Lambeth Walk (1937)
Limehouse Blues (1922)
London Pride (1941)
A Nightingale Sang in Berkeley Square (1940)

Los Angeles, California
Hooray for Hollywood (1937)
MacArthur Park (1968)
San Fernando Valley (1943)
Theme From *Valley of the Dolls* (1968)

Managua, Nicaragua
Managua Nicaragua (1946)

Mandalay, Burma
On the Road to Mandalay (1907)

Marrakesh, Morocco
Marrakesh Express (1969)

Memphis, Tennessee
The Memphis Blues (1912)

Mexicali, Mexico
Mexicali Rose (1923)

Miami, Florida
Miami Beach Rumba (1946)
Miami Vice Theme (1984)
Moon Over Miami (1935)

Monterey, Mexico
It Happened in Monterey (1930)

Moscow, Russia
Midnight in Moscow, or Moscow Nights (1962)

Nagasaki, Japan
Nagasaki (1928)

Naples, Italy
Neapolitan Nights (1925)

New Orleans, Louisiana
The Battle of New Orleans (1957)
The City of New Orleans (1970)
'Way Down Yonder in New Orleans (1922)

New York, New York
Autumn in New York (1932)
The Boy From New York City (1964)
Harlem Nocturne (1940)
How About You? (1941)
Manhattan (1925)
Manhattan Serenade (1928)
New York, New York (1944)
(Theme From) New York, New York (1977)
New York State of Mind (1976)
Penthouse Serenade (When We're Alone) 1931
The Sidewalks of New York, or East Side, West Side (1894)
Spanish Harlem (1960)
The Streets of New York (In Old New York) (1906)
There's a Boat Dat's Leavin' Soon for New York (1935)

Paris, France
April in Paris (1932)
Free Man in Paris (1973)
How Ya Gonna Keep 'Em Down on the Farm After They've Seen Paris? (1919)
I Love Paris (1953)
The Last Time I Saw Paris (1940)
Mademoiselle de Paree (1948)
Paris in the Spring (1935)
The Poor People of Paris (1956)
Under a Roof in Paree (1931)
Under Paris Skies (1953)

Philadelphia, Pennsylvania
Philadelphia Freedom (1974)
Philadelphia, U.S.A. (1958)

Phoenix, Arizona
By the Time I Get to Phoenix (1967)

Rio de Janeiro, Brazil
Come to the Mardi Gras (1937)
Flying Down to Rio (1933)
Rainy Night in Rio (1946)

Rome, Italy
Arrivederci Roma (1958)

St. Louis, Missouri
Meet Me in St. Louis, Louis (1904)
St. Louis Blues (1914)
You Came a Long Way From St. Louis (1948)

Salt Lake City, Utah
I Lost My Sugar in Salt Lake City (1942)

San Antonio, Texas
On the Alamo (1922)
San Antonio Rose (1940)

San Francisco, California
Hello Frisco Hello (1915)
I Left My Heart in San Francisco (1954)
San Francisco (1936)
San Francisco (Be Sure to Wear Some Flowers in Your Hair) (1967)

San Jose, California
Do You Know the Way to San Jose? (1967)

Scarborough, England
Scarborough Fair/Canticle (1966)

Sioux City, Iowa
Sioux City Sue (1945)

Sorrento, Italy
Come Back to Sorrento (1904)

Tijuana, Mexico
The Tijuana Jail (1959)
Tijuana Taxi (1965)

Town (nonspecific)
Chinatown, My Chinatown (1910)
The Darktown Strutters' Ball (1917)
Downtown (1964)
Gee, But It's Great to Meet a Friend from Your Old Home Town (1910)
Get Out of Town (1938)

A Hot Time in the Old Town (1896)
I'm the Lonesomest Gal in Town (1912)
In a Little Spanish Town (1926)
It's the Talk of the Town (1933)
Poor Side of Town (1966)
Santa Claus Is Coming to Town (1934)
(In) A Shanty in Old Shanty Town (1932)
Wake the Town and Tell the People (1954)

Venice, Italy
Summertime in Venice (1955)

Vienna, Austria
Vienna, My City of Dreams (1914)

Wichita, Kansas
Wichita Lineman (1968)

Winchester, England
Winchester Cathedral (1966)

Winnetka, Illinois
Big Noise From Winnetka (1940)

CLARINET. SEE WOODWINDS

CLASSICS

Art music from the eighteenth to the twentieth centuries has profoundly influenced American popular song. Indirectly, the classics have served as stylistic models, providing the essential building blocks of popular song. More directly, they have been major sources of **borrowing**. Songwriters have looked to them not only because of their inherent quality, but also for a more practical reason: classics are usually in the public domain and thus free of copyright protection.

This borrowing must be seen in the context of the long history of variations and paraphrases on popular themes, as exemplified by Mozart, Beethoven, and Liszt, but with a difference. In American popular song, the derivation is seldom acknowledged.

Not surprisingly, composers whose works have been borrowed most often are those whose musical styles most closely approximate the popular ideal. Thus, romantic and impressionistic composers such as Piotr Ilyich Tchaikovsky (1840–1893), Frédéric Chopin (1810–1849), Giacomo Puccini (1858–1924), Alexander Borodin (1833–1887), Edvard Grieg (1843–1907), Claude Debussy (1862–1918), and Maurice Ravel (1875–1937) have been in the forefront, while other masters such as Johann Sebastian Bach (1685–1750), Wolfgang Amadeus Mozart (1756–1791), Joseph Haydn (1732–1809), and Béla Bartók (1881–1945) have been, to a large extent, neglected.

The most popular individual composer as a source of borrowing is unquestionably Tchaikovsky. There was a rage for his music in the 1930s and 1940s, when over a hundred songs based on his music were written. In 1939, the conductor André Kostelanetz took the first theme from the second movement of Tchaikovsky's *Symphony No. 5* and adapted it into the hit song "Moon Love." In the same year, the bandleader Larry Clinton was instrumental in converting the flowing third theme of the overture-fantasy *Romeo and Juliet* into "Our Love," with the insertion—not too successfully—of non-Tchaikovskian material for the release. At least sixteen songs were based on one theme alone: the first theme of his *First Piano Concerto*, in B-flat minor. The most popular of these, "Tonight We Love," was introduced by Freddy Martin and his band in 1941. No attempt was made to hide the derivation of the music; indeed, the famous upward-moving piano chords of the concerto became an integral part of Martin's arrangement. The most obvious change from the original was one of meter: from 3/4 meter to 4/4 meter. In 1960, the same concerto was the basis of another hit song, "Alone at Last."

Chopin was recognized as a good source as far back as 1898, when Victor Herbert took the opening notes of the second theme from the first movement of the *Concerto No. 1 in E minor* for the verse of his "Gypsy Love Song." Herbert never acknowledged this, or any other, borrowing. In fact, in 1902, he won a celebrated court case for libel against an editor who had accused him of deliberately stealing from the classics. A much more substantial borrowing from Chopin occurred in 1918, when an obscure songwriter named Harry Carroll took the melody from the middle section of the *Fantaisie-Impromptu in C-sharp minor* as the principal theme of his hit song "I'm Always Chasing Rainbows." Although

Chopin's beautiful melody is essentially unchanged, except for the addition of a bridge, he was never credited as the originator of the melody of this very successful song, which became a hit again in 1946 when it was featured in the film *The Dolly Sisters*.

The craze for Chopin in the mid-1940s reached a peak with the 1945 release of his film biography, *A Song to Remember*. A recurrent theme in the film, which starred Cornel Wilde, Merle Oberon, and Paul Muni, was the *Polonaise in A-flat*, played by José Iturbi. Capitalizing on the success of the film, two songwriters took the principal theme of the *Polonaise*, added some typical Tin Pan Alley twists, and emerged with a hit song, "Till the End of Time," thus transforming a stirring martial theme into a trite, sentimental ballad.

Opera has often been favored by popular songwriters, with Puccini preferred above all other operatic composers, probably because of the sensuousness of his music. An early instance of borrowing was from the famous tenor aria "Èlucevan le stelle" from his opera *Tosca* (1900), which became the hit song "Avalon" in 1920, popularized by Al Jolson, who was also given credit as one of the writers. The aria was changed considerably by regularizing the rhythm of the melody and changing the mode from minor to major. Despite this smoke screen, the origin of the melody was recognizable, at least to Puccini's publishers in Milan, G. Ricordi & Co. They instituted a lawsuit claiming copyright infringement, as a result of which they were awarded $25,000 in damages and all future royalties from "Avalon." The recording company which put out the song was forced to go out of business.

But Puccini, in contrast to Tchaikovsky and Chopin, has seldom been borrowed from directly. Rather, his melodies have been used as possibly subconscious matrices around which new melodies have been fashioned. Thus, "Love Is a Many Splendored Thing" has been said to bear a striking resemblance to "Un bel dì," from, *Madama Butterfly* (1907), in its use of downward-moving thirds, a similarity which did not keep it from winning the Academy Award as "best original song of 1955."

Another opera composer, Giuseppe Verdi (1813–1901), was the source of a double borrowing. First, the famous "Anvil Chorus" from his opera *Il Trovatore* (1853) was deliberately parodied by Sir William Gilbert and Sir Arthur Sullivan in their operetta *The Pirates of Penzance* (1879); they appropriately called their parody "The Pirate's Chorus." Then, thirty-eight years later, in 1917, the durable melody was used by songwriter Theodore Morse for his "Hail, Hail, the Gang's All Here," without acknowledgment either to Verdi or to Sullivan.

One might also mention Jacques Offenbach (1819–1880), whose opera *Geneviève de Brabant* (1859) was the source of the melody of "The Marine's Hymn" (1919), for which the words, beginning "From the halls of Montezuma to the shores of Tripoli," were added by an anonymous hand. Ruggero Leoncavallo (1857–1919), composer of the opera *Pagliacci*, wrote a beautiful art song called "La Mattinata" in 1904. It was borrowed almost intact in 1960. With the meter changed from 3/4 meter to 4/4 meter, it became a sentimental ballad entitled "You're Breaking My Heart."

Although impressionist composers have continually served as models for popular songwriters, few have been borrowed from directly. Most notable are Debussy and Ravel, both of whom were rediscovered in the late 1930s. Debussy had written a haunting piece for piano entitled *Reverie* in 1895. Forty-three years later, in 1938, its principal theme was converted into a hit song by the bandleader Larry Clinton. Scarcely bothering to change the title, he called it "My Reverie." Only the bridge, with its stepwise melodic sequence, is newly composed. A year later, riding the impressionist wave, three songwriters converted the secondary theme of Ravel's *Pavane pour une enfante défunte* of 1899 into the big band hit "The Lamp Is Low."

In the age of rock, borrowing from the classics went on apace, but often without acknowledgment. Thus the hit "Can't Help Falling in Love," introduced by Elvis Presley in the film *Blue Hawaii* in 1961, bears a resemblance to the French air *Plaisir d'Amour*, composed in the 1790s by the German-French organist/composer Jean Paul Egide Martini (1741–1816). The Original song, widely available in English translation as *The Joy of Love*, is clearly recognizable, although the initial three notes after the pickup have been changed from their original stepwise pattern to one of jumps of a fifth. A brief bridge brings in new material.

In 1971, homage was paid to Felix Mendelssohn (1809–1847) when a melody reminiscent of the principal theme of the second movement of his *Violin Concerto in E minor* (1844) was composed by Andrew Lloyd Webber for his song "I Don't Know How to Love Him," introduced in *Jesus Christ Superstar*. Although changes were made, including one of meter (from 6/8 to 4/4), the similarity of the melody is clear.

A more obscure composer was the Romanian bandleader Ion Ivanovici (1845–1902). In 1880, he wrote a waltz called *The Waves of the Danube*, which became very popular, especially in circus productions, throughout the world. In 1947, Al Jolson — no stranger to borrowing—took the famous first and second strains of this waltz and, with no changes other than the addition of lyrics, emerged with a hit song entitled "Anniversary Song," included in the biographical film *The Jolson Story* (1946). With its opening lyrics— "Oh how we danced on the night we were wed" — it has become a signature song, played and danced whenever people celebrate their anniversaries, without mention of its original composer, Ivanovici. In the same year

(1947), Jolson had a hand in another popular song called "All My Love," based on the principal theme of Emil Waldteufel's famous waltz *Dolores* (1880).

Although, as we have seen, borrowing from the classics has been frequently done without acknowledgment, there have been instances where songwriters have admitted openly to the origins of their ideas. Such a case was the operetta *Blossom Time*, in which Franz Schubert (1797–1828) was at once the protagonist of the show and the source of its music. Originally written as *Das Dreimäderlhaus* by the Hungarian composer Heinrich Berté in 1916, it was presented in English with musical arrangements by Sigmund Romberg in New York in 1921. The hit of that show was "Song of Love," based on the second theme of the first movement of Schubert's *Symphony No. 8 in B minor (the Unfinished)*.

Within the tradition of respect for the classics, two songwriters named George Forrest and Robert Wright wrote an operetta in 1944 called *Song of Norway*, based on the life and music of Edvard Grieg. The hit of that show was "Strange Music," artistically fashioned out of two piano pieces by Grieg: "*Wedding Day in Troldhhaugen*" and "*Nocturne*." The songwriters created a new melody built around the melodic outlines of "Wedding Day," while preserving its distinctive harmonies.

Nine years later, in 1953, Wright and Forrest re-peated their success by taking the music of the Russian scientist and composer Alexander Borodin and converting it into the operetta *Kismet*. Three outstanding songs came out of that show: "Stranger in Paradise," "Baubles, Bangles, and Beads," and "And This is My Beloved." In some respects, these fare better as songs than as their originals, which were, respectively, the "Polovtsian Dances" from *Prince Igor* and the second and third movements of the *String Quarter No. 2 in D major*. Unquestionably, they brought Borodin more popularity than he had ever achieved in his lifetime.

To summarize, the classics have been an unwavering source of inspiration to American songwriters. Sometimes the results have been good; at other times they have been dreadful. Occasionally classical sources have been acknowledged, but more often they have not. This is to be lamented, because borrowing is one of the oldest traditions in music, and not to be hidden or denied.

Bibliography

Ewen, David. *All the Years of American Popular Music*. 1977.

Lax, Roger, and Frederick Smith. *The Great Song Thesaurus*. 1984.

Spaeth, Sigmund. *A History of Popular Song in America*. 1948.

See also: Austria; Folk Song; Foreign Influence; France; Germany; Italy; Quotation

TABLE 6

The Classics and Popular Song

Isaac Albéniz
Tango in D	Moonlight Masquerade (1941)	

Johann Sebastian Bach (attrib.)
Minuet in G	A Lover's Concerto (1965)

Ludwig van Beethoven
Minuet in G	When the Lights Go On Again (All Over the World) (1942)
Symphony No. 5, i	A Fifth of Beethoven (1976)
Symphony No. 9, iv	Joy (1972)

Alexander Borodin
Prince Igor, "Polovtsian Dances"	Stranger in Paradise (1953)
String Quartet No. 2, ii (Scherzo)	Baubles, Bangles, and Beads (1953)
String Quartet No. 2, iii (Notturno)	And This Is My Beloved (1953)

Georges Boulanger
Avant de Mourir	My Prayer (1939)

Johannes Brahms
Hungarian Dance No. 4	As Years Go By (1947)

Emmanuel Chabrier
España	Hot Diggity (1956)

Frédéric Chopin
Fantaisie-Impromptu in C-sharp minor	I'm Always Chasing Rainbows (1918)
Nocturne in E-flat	My Twilight Dream (1939)
Piano Concerto No. 1, i	Gypsy Love Song (1898)
Polonaise in A-flat	Till the End of Time (1945)

Alphonse Czibulka
Wintermärchen	Hearts and Flowers (1899)

Claude Debussy
Reverie	My Reverie (1938)

Antonin Dvorák
Humoresque	I'd Climb the Highest Mountain (1926)
Symphony from the New World Largo	Goin' Home (1922)

Zdenko, Fibich
Poème — My Moonlight Madonna (1933)

Enrique Granados
Goyescas — Besame Mucho (1941)

Edvard Grieg
Piano Concerto, i — I Look at Heaven (1942)
Wedding Day in Troldhaugen — Strange Music (1944)

Ion Ivanovici
The Waves of the Danube — Anniversary Song (1946)

Ernesto Lecuona
Andalucia — The Breeze and I (1940)
Malagueña — At the Crossroads (1942)

Edwin H. Lemare
Andantino in D-flat — Moonlight and Roses (Bring Mem'ries of You) (1925)

Ruggero Leoncavallo
La Mattinata — You're Breaking My Heart (1948)

Franz Liszt
Hungarian Rhapsody No. 2 — Music! Music! Music! (1950)
Les Préludes — Good Night Sweetheart (1931)

Jean Paul Egide Martini
Plaisir d'Amour — Can't Help Falling in Love (1961)

Felix Mendelssohn
Spring Song — That Mesmerizing Mendelssohn Tune (1909)
Violin Concerto, ii — I Don't Know How to Love Him (1970)

Wolfgang Amadeus Mozart
Piano Sonata No. 3, C major — In an Eighteenth-Century Drawing Room (1939)

Modest Mussorgsky
A Night on Bald Mountain — Night on Disco Mountain (1977)

(Carl) Otto Nicolai
Overture, *The Merry Wives of Windsor* — Marcheta (1913)

Jacques Offenbach
Geneviève de Brabant, "Couplets des Deux Hommes d'Armes" — The Marine's Hymn (1919)

F. Poliakin
Le Canari — The Hot Canary (1948)

Amilcare Ponchielli
La Gioconda, Act III, "Dance of the Hours" — "Hello Muddah, Hello Fadduh (1963)

Giacomo Puccini
La Bohème, "Musetta's Waltz" — Don't You Know (1959)
Madama Butterfly, "Un bel dì" — Love Is a Many-Splendored Thing (1955)
Tosca, "Èlucevan le stelle" — Avalon (1920)

Sergei Rachmaninoff
Piano Concerto No. 2, i — Full Moon and Empty Arms (1946)

Maurice Ravel
Pavane pour une enfante défunte — The Lamp Is Low (1939)

Juventino P. Rosa
Over the Waves — The Loveliest Night of the Year (1950)

Anton Rubinstein
Romance in E-flat — If You Are But a Dream (1941)

Pablo de Sarasate
Zigeunerweisen — You'd Be So Nice to Come Home To (1942)

Franz Schubert
Symphony No. 8, i — Song of Love (1921)

Robert Schumann
Wilder Reiter — Wild Horses (1953)

Sir Arthur Sullivan
The Mikado, "If you want to know who we are" — The Music Goes 'Round and 'Round (1935)
The Pirates of Penzance, "Come friends who plow the sea" — Hail, Hail, the Gang's All Here (1917)

Piotr Ilyich Tchaikovsky
First Piano Concerto, i — Alone at Last (1960) / Tonight We Love (1941)
June Barcarolle — Lover Come Back to Me! (1928)
Melodie, op. 24, no. 3 — The Things I Love (1941)
Romeo and Juliet, fantasy-overture — Our Love (1939)
String Quartet in D, ii — On the Isle of May (1940)
Symphony No. 5, ii — Moon Love (1939)
Symphony No. 6, i — The Story of a Starry Night (1941)

Emil Waldteufel
Dolores — All My Love (1947)

CLOSENESS

It has long been recognized that proximity is a necessary adjunct to the pursuit of **romance**. Being near someone is an obvious advantage when **love** is the objective. Songwriters have elaborated on the importance of nearness or closeness in such diverse songs as "Cuddle Up a Little Closer, Lovey Mine" (1908), "Come Closer to Me" (1940), "The Nearness of You" (1937), "Close as Pages in a Book" (1944), "Beside You" (1947), "Near You" (1947), "Too Close for Comfort" (1956), "The Closer You Are" (1956), "(They Long to Be) Close to You" (1963), and "Don't Stand So Close to Me" (1980).

Conversely, the fact that being apart can be devastating to the maintenance of a relationship is emphasized in the lyrics of a 1946 song from *Finian's Rainbow*, "When I'm Not Near the Girl I Love," which state: "When I'm not near the girl I love, I love the girl I'm near."

CLOTHING

Popular song often reflects changes in fashion through the years. For example, songs about hats, very popular around the turn of the century, more or less disappeared after the 1940s (a notable exception being "The Ballad of the Green Berets" of 1966, which is really not about hats). Bonnets, which are hats held in place by ribbons, are referred to in two famous songs: "Put On Your Old Grey Bonnet" (1909) and Irving Berlin's "Easter Parade" (1933), which begins: "In your Easter bonnet." In 1935, another antiquated headpiece, along with other articles of formal attire, appeared in another Berlin song, "Top Hat, White Tie and Tails." By 1949, however, hats were out of fashion; only the ribbons remained, as in "Scarlet Ribbons (For Her Hair)."

At the other extreme of dress are shoes. During the **Depression years**, there seems to have been a preoccupation with keeping them shined, as demonstrated in the songs "A Shine on Your Shoes" (1932) and "Shoe Shine Boy" (1936). Later on, however, shoes took on a more personal meaning, as in "Sand in My Shoes" (1941), "The Old Soft Shoe" (1951), and "Blue Suede Shoes" (1955).

Very often, articles of clothing are peripheral to the real thrust of a song. Thus, "Who Threw the Overalls in Mrs. Murphy's Chowder?" (1899) is a humorous song, while "Alice Blue Gown" (1919) is more about Alice Roosevelt Longworth's favorite color than about a gown. "Button Up Your Overcoat" (1928) pleads with a loved one: "Take good care of yourself." "You Forgot Your Gloves" (1931) is a ploy to meet someone. "Satin Doll" (1958) is concerned not with a type of fabric, but rather with the person who wears the clothing, the "doll." Similarly, "Black Denim Trousers and Motorcycle Boots" (1955) is a song about cult dressing, "Bobby Sox to Stockings" (1959) is really about grow-

ing up, and "Lipstick on Your Collar" (1959) refers to the traces of another woman.

Clothing has its place, too, in lyrics. One famous example occurs in "I Guess I'll Have to Change My Plan" (1929)—known as the "blue pajama" song because of this lyric by Howard Dietz: "Why did I wear those blue pajamas before our love affair began." Still another Berlin song does away with the need for an overcoat or gloves in cold weather: "I've Got My Love to Keep Me Warm" (1937).

Additional Songs

Coat of Many Colors (1969)
Raspberry Beret (1985)
A White Sport Coat and a Pink Carnation (1957)
See also: Colors; Jewelry; Subjects

CLOUDS. SEE SKY

CLOWNS. SEE CIRCUS

CODA

A coda is a closing gesture that occurs after the structural conclusion of a piece. Codas were unusual in popular song during the early years of the century, when sixteen- and thirty-two-bar lengths were *de rigueur*, but after the 1950s they became increasingly more common.

Some of the earliest codas involve mere repetition of the last phrase of a piece. Such is the case in "The Way You Look Tonight" (1936), which repeats both words and music along with a hummed interlude. More adventurous is the 1938 song "You Go to My Head," which grafts an additional eight bars, consisting mostly of quarter-note **triplets**, onto the basic thirty-two-bar **AABA** form. In "That Old Black Magic" (1942), the coda consists of **repeated notes**, at the words "In a spin, loving the spin I'm in, under that old black magic called love." Short but distinctive codas are also found in "Begin the Beguine" (1935) and "Moonlight in Vermont" (1944). Codas of some songs, like "Over the Rainbow" (1939) and "Some Enchanted Evening" (1949), consist of material previously presented in the **release**.

Several big-band **arrangements** of the 1930s and 1940s employ codas for special effects. Two of the most famous—the codas of "In the Mood" (1938) and "Tuxedo Junction" (1940) as played by Glenn Miller and His Orchestra—consist of three or four repetitions of the principal theme at a steadily decreasing dynamic level followed by one very loud and conclusive repetition. Equally well known is the clangorous coda at the end of the arrangement of "April in Paris" (1932) used by Count Basie and His Orchestra.

Codas became more commonplace in the 1960s

with the loosening of popular song from the confines of rigid structure. "Cabaret" (1966), for example, has an added six bars of repeated and elongated notes which help bring the song to a stirring conclusion. The French import "A Man and a Woman" (1966) has an especially interesting coda of nineteen bars, contrasting both in meter (3/4 meter, as against 4/4 meter) and key (E major, as against D major) with the body of the song.

Codas were appended to songs with greater frequency as the years progressed. Some of them, like the codas of "Raindrops Keep Fallin' on My Head" (1969) and "(They Long to Be) Close to You" (1963), are relatively short. The coda of "The Way We Were" (1973), on the other hand, is longer and brings the song to a resounding climax. Some codas reach unprecedented lengths; that of "The Wind Beneath My Wings" (1982), at twenty-seven bars, is longer than many entire songs.

See also: Form

COLLABORATION

From the time of W. S. Gilbert and Arthur Sullivan to the present, the craft of songwriting has most often been the joint intellectual endeavor of a **composer** and a **lyricist**, who, until the 1950s, usually maintained their separate identities in the creative process. After that decade, however, it became the custom to make no distinction as to credits for the creation of words and music. Increasingly, the designations "music by" and "lyrics by" were replaced by the collective term "music and lyrics by" in collaborations like those of John Lennon and Paul McCartney, Jerry Leiber and Mike Stoller, Mick Jagger and Keith Richards, and Cynthia Weil and Barry Mann. This custom coincided with the rise of the **performer-songwriter**. Indeed, Lennon and McCartney, as members of the Beatles, introduced all of their own collaborative efforts themselves, including the standards "And I Love Her" (1964); "Can't Buy Me Love" (1964); "Yesterday" (1965); "Here, There and Everywhere," "Michelle" and "Norwegian Wood" (1966); and "Hey Jude" (1968).

Nonetheless, a number of songwriting teams in the older tradition of separate credits for music and lyrics stand out for the quality and consistency of their output. As with Gilbert and Sullivan, their combined work sometimes seems to be better than the sum of its individual parts. Foremost in this regard were the collaborations of Ira and George Gershwin, Lorenz Hart and Richard Rodgers, Oscar Hammerstein II and Richard Rodgers, and Alan Jay Lerner and Frederick Loewe. Among other productive collaborations were those of Howard Dietz and Arthur Schwartz, Dorothy Fields and Jimmy McHugh, Johnny Burke and James Van Heusen, Al Dubin and Harry Warren, Mack Gordon and Harry Warren, and Hal David and Burt Bacharach.

There have also been several long-lasting collaborations between lyricists alone, including those of Buddy DeSylva and Lew Brown, Betty Comden and Adolph Green, and Alan and Marilyn Bergman.

A rather unusual collaboration of brothers was that of Ira and George Gershwin, who wrote hundreds of songs together from 1924 until George's untimely death in 1937. Writing for both Broadway and Hollywood, the team produced such classics as "Someone to Watch Over Me" (1926), "He Loves and She Loves" (1927), "How Long Has This Been Going On?" (1927), "I've Got a Crush on You" (1928), "But Not for Me" (1930), "Embraceable You" (1930), and "Who Cares?" (1931).

Richard Rodgers had the distinction of working with two longtime collaborators, resulting in two quite different bodies of work. Together with Lorenz Hart, he enjoyed over twenty years of success as a member of Broadway's foremost songwriting team. The songs of Rodgers and Hart are in a league by themselves, possessing a lightheartedness and seamlessness of words and music seldom found elsewhere. Among their hundreds of magical songs were "Little Girl Blue" (1935), "My Romance" (1935), "There's a Small Hotel" (1936), "My Funny Valentine" (1937), "Where or When?" (1937), and "This Can't Be Love" (1938).

Rodgers's second collaboration, with Oscar Hammerstein II, began in 1943 with the landmark show *Oklahoma!* It continued with a string of Broadway successes, including *Carousel* (1945), *South Pacific* (1949), and *The King and I* (1951), and ended a year before Hammerstein's death with *The Sound of Music* (1959). Rodgers and Hammerstein's songs were perhaps more sentimental and less sophisticated than those of Rodgers and Hart. Nevertheless, they have proved equally enduring, and include such standards as "If I Loved You" (1945), "You'll Never Walk Alone" (1945), "It Might as Well Be Spring" (1946), "Getting To Know You" (1951), "I Have Dreamed" (1951), and "Something Wonderful" (1951).

The team of Alan Jay Lerner, lyricist, and Frederick Loewe, composer, was formed in 1942. Their career on Broadway took wing with *Brigadoon* in 1947, blossomed forth with *Paint Your Wagon* in 1951, exploded with *My Fair Lady* in 1956, and ended with *Camelot* in 1960—with a short excursion to Hollywood for the film *Gigi* in 1958. Loewe's Viennese background blended well with Lerner's witty and sometimes acerbic lyrics in such exquisite songs as "Come to Me, Bend to Me" (1947), "I've Grown Accustomed to Her Face" (1956), "Show Me" (1956), "I'm Glad I'm Not Young Anymore" (1958), "How to Handle a Woman" (1960), and "If Ever I Would Leave You" (1960).

Lyricist Howard Dietz and composer Arthur Schwartz wrote songs as a team for a succession of **revues**, beginning with *The Little Show* (1929). They continued to collaborate off and on into the 1960s, producing such lasting songs as "I Guess I'll Have to Change My Plan" (1929), "Something to Remember You By" (1930), "Dancing in the Dark" (1931), "Alone Together" (1932), "You and the Night and the Music" (1934), "By Myself" (1937), "I See Your Face Before Me" (1937), and "That's Entertainment" (1953).

Dorothy Fields began her long career in 1928, as lyricist for the Cotton Club Revues in collaboration with composer Jimmy McHugh. Although she later went on to write with many other composers—among them Jerome Kern, Fritz Kreisler, and Sigmund Romberg—her collaboration with McHugh brought forth many standards, including "I Can't Give You Anything But Love" (1928), "Exactly Like You" (1930), "On the Sunny Side of the Street" (1930), and "Don't Blame Me" (1933).

The team of Johnny Burke (lyrics) and James Van Heusen (music) is remembered chiefly for its contribution to the **film musical**, producing a superior body of work including "Imagination" (1940), "It's Always You" (1941), "It Could Happen to You" (1944), and "But Beautiful" (1947).

Another prolific composer for the movies, Harry Warren, enjoyed two fruitful collaborations. His first, with Al Dubin, began in 1932 with the film *Forty-Second Street*; it resulted in songs like "You're Getting to Be a Habit With Me" (1932), "I Only Have Eyes for You" (1934), "Lullaby of Broadway" (1935), and "September in the Rain" (1937). Warren's second collaboration, with Mack Gordon, produced show-stoppers like "Chattanooga Choo Choo" (1941) and "I've Got a Gal in Kalamazoo" (1942), as well as such lovely ballads as "I Had the Craziest Dream," "Serenade in Blue," "There Will Never Be Another You," (all 1942), and "You'll Never Know" (1943).

The songwriting team of Hal David (lyrics) and Burt Bacharach (music) carried the tradition of separately credited music and lyrics into the 1960s and 1970s. Among their innovative songs were "(They Long to Be) Close to You" (1963), "A House Is Not a Home" (1964), "Alfie" (1966), "I Say a Little Prayer" (1967), "Do You Know the Way to San Jose?" (1967), "I'll Never Fall in Love Again" (1968), "This Guy's in Love With You" (1968), and "Raindrops Keep Fallin' on My Head" (1970).

Perhaps the longest collaboration of any two persons on record is that of the lyricists, librettists, and performers Betty Comden and Adolph Green; they have written solely with each other since the 1930s. This long-lasting team has, in turn, collaborated with many different composers, most notably with Leonard Bernstein on *On the Town* (1944) and *Wonderful Town* (1953); and with Jule Styne on *Bells Are Ringing* (1956) and *Do Re Mi* (1960). Among their co-authored lyrics are "Lucky to Be Me" (1944), "Never Never Land"

(1954), "Just in Time" (1956), "The Party's Over" (1956), and "Make Someone Happy" (1960).

Another successful collaboration of lyricists was that of Buddy DeSylva and Lew Brown, who most often wrote with composer Ray Henderson. This unusual three-man team began working together on *George White's Scandals of 1926* and continued into the 1930s, producing such standards as "The Birth of the Blues" (1926), "Button Up Your Overcoat!" (1928), "You're the Cream in My Coffee" (1928), and "Sunny Side Up" (1929).

Still another successful team of lyricists is that of Alan and Marilyn Keith Bergman, husband and wife. They have themselves written in collaboration with many composers, among them Norman Luboff, Michel Legrand, and Marvin Hamlisch. Their lyrics include "Yellow Bird" (1957), "What Are You Doing the Rest of Your Life?" (1969), "The Summer Knows" (1971), "Brian's Song" (1972), and "The Way We Were" (1973).

A host of other collaborations have borne fruit over the years: Sheldon Harnick and Jerry Bock; Arthur Freed and Nacio Herb Brown; Fred Ebb and John Kander; Hugh Martin and Ralph Blane; Sammy Cahn and Jule Styne; Gerry Goffin and Carole King; Brian Holland, Eddie Holland, and Lamont Dozier; and Barry Gibb, Maurice Gibb, and Robin Gibb; among others. In contrast, many individual writers have chosen to play the field, working with a wide variety of partners. But except for the relatively few **composer-lyricists**, like George M. Cohan, Irving Berlin, Cole Porter, and Stephen Sondheim, who have been able to write their songs single-handedly, songwriting has remained a collaborative effort of partners working in close association on both the music and lyrics.

Bibliography

Gibb, Barry, Robin Gibb, and Maurice Gibb. *Bee Gees: The Authorized Biography*. 1979.

Green, Stanley. *The Rodgers and Hammerstein Story*. 1980.

Kimball, Robert, and Alfred Simon. *The Gershwins*. 1980.

Marx, Samuel, and Jan Clayton. *Rodgers and Hart: Bewitched, Bothered, and Bedevilled*. 1977.

Nolan, Frederick. *The Sound of Their Music: The Story of Rodgers and Hammerstein*. 1979.

Palmer, Robert, and John Lahr. *Baby, That Was Rock and Roll: The Legendary Leiber and Stoller*. 1978.

Rosenberg, Deena. *Fascinating Rhythm: The Collaboration of George and Ira Gershwin*. 1991.

Taylor, Deems. *Some Enchanted Evenings: The Story of Rodgers and Hammerstein*. 1972.

COLORS

Although virtually every color of the rainbow may be found in popular song (*see* Table 7), blue is preferred above all others. Perhaps this is because it can be taken in two ways, either as a color or a mood. One of the first songs to use blue as a color, "Alice Blue Gown" (1919), is a simple waltz describing the favorite shade of Alice Roosevelt Longworth, the daughter of President Theodore Roosevelt. Other popular "blue" songs of that period are "Five Foot Two, Eyes of Blue; Has Anybody Seen My Girl?" (1925), "Blue Room" (1926), "Blue Skies" (1927), and "My Blue Heaven" (1927).

"Am I Blue?" (1929) is one of the songs that uses blue in its second sense, as a mood of sadness or depression. Its melody reflects the "blueness" of its lyrics in its recurrent use of **blue notes**. From the 1930s on, mood songs became predominant, often with a nod to the **blues**. "Mood Indigo" (1931) is quite literally a mood song, albeit about a darker shade of blue. "Serenade in Blue" (1942) became a favorite of the big bands, while "When Sunny Gets Blue" (1956) became a jazz classic.

Sometimes the two meanings of blue are intertwined, as in the lyrics of "Blue Moon" (1934). In this case, one cannot be sure whether the lyricist (Lorenz Hart) is referring to a moon that is actually colored blue or to one that reflects the mood of the protagonist; although the "moon turns to gold" when a lover suddenly appears before him or her, the meaning remains ambiguous. In Irving Berlin's "Blue Skies" (1927), on the other hand, blue is used as a symbol of happiness; at various places in the song, it refers to a color, a mood, and a bird. Probably the very ambiguity of the word "blue" accounts for its continued attraction for songwriters.

Green has a number of vivid entries, starting with the Lorenz Hart and Richard Rodgers classic "Mountain Greenery" (1926). Another durable song is "Green Eyes" (1941); originally written in Cuba as "Aquellos Ojos Verdes" in 1929, it achieved great popularity in an arrangement played by the Jimmy Dorsey Band and sung by Helen O'Connell. "On Green Dolphin Street," taken from the score of the 1947 film *Green Dolphin Street*, is another jazz standard. "Evergreen," a distinctive song, was first heard as the love theme in the film *A Star Is Born* (1975).

Red songs are generally less distinguished, with references to **flowers**—"When You Wore a Tulip and I Wore a Big Red Rose" (1914), "Red Roses for a Blue Lady," (1948); **birds**—"When the Red, Red Robin Comes Bob, Bob, Bobbin' Along" (1926); **clothing**—"Scarlet Ribbons (For Her Hair)" (1949); and **animals**—"Rudolph the Red-Nosed Reindeer" (1949), among others.

Three of the most famous color songs of all are achromatic: "Put On Your Old Grey Bonnet" (1909), "White Christmas" (1942), and "That Old Black Magic" (1943). As for other color songs, one of the most evocative is "Deep Purple" (1939), an adaptation by Peter De Rose from a suite of his own written in 1934. It is a striking example of the significance of color in American popular song.

TABLE 7
Colors In Song

Black

Black Bottom (1926)
Black Denim Trousers and Motorcycle Boots (1955)
Bye Bye Blackbird (1926)
Paint It Black (1966)
That Old Black Magic (1943)

Blue

Alice Blue Gown (1919)
Am I Blue? (1929)
Between the Devil and the Deep Blue Sea (1931)
Beyond the Blue Horizon (1930)
Blue (And Broken Hearted) (1922)
Blue Bayou (1963)
Blue Champagne (1941)
Blue Hawaii (1937)
Blue Monday (1957)
Blue Moon (1934)
Blue Orchids (1939)
Blue Room (1926)
Blue Skies (1927)
Blue Suede Shoes (1955)
Blue Velvet (1951)
Blueberry Hill (1940)
Dream (When You're Feeling Blue) (1945)
Five Foot Two, Eyes of Blue, Has Anybody Seen My Girl?
   (1925)
Have You Ever Been Lonely (Have You Ever Been Blue?)
   (1933)
It's a Blue World (1939)
Little Girl Blue (1935)
Love Is Blue (1968)
Midnight Blue (1974)
Mister Blue (1959)
Misty Blue (1965)
Mood Indigo (1931)
My Blue Heaven (1927)
Serenade in Blue (1942)
Song Sung Blue (1972)
True Blue (1986)
Under a Blanket of Blue (1933)
When Sunny Gets Blue (1956)

Brown

Fine Brown Frame (1944)

Color (nonspecific)

Color My World (1966)
Colour My World (1970)
My Coloring Book (1962)

Color Combinations

Black & White (1956)
Cherry Pink and Apple Blossom White (1955)
Coat of Many Colors (1969)
Don't It Make My Brown Eyes Blue? (1977)
Ebony and Ivory (1982)
Red Roses for a Blue Lady (1948)
When My Blue Moon Turns to Gold Again (1941)
Where the Blue of the Night Meets the Gold of the Day
   (1931)
(There'll Be Bluebirds Over) The White Cliffs of Dover
   (1941)
A White Sport Coat and a Pink Carnation (1957)

Green

The Ballad of the Green Berets (1966)
Evergreen (Love Theme From *A Star Is Born*) (1975)
Green Eyes (1929)
The Green, Green Grass of Home (1965)
The Green Leaves of Summer (1960)
Green-Up Time (1948)
Little Green Apples (1968)
Mountain Greenery (1926)
On Green Dolphin Street (1947)

Grey

The Old Grey Mare (She Ain't What She Used to Be)
   (1917)
Put On Your Old Grey Bonnet (1909)
Touch of Grey (1987)

Orange

Orange Colored Sky (1950)

Purple

Deep Purple (1939)
Purple Haze (1967)

Red

The Lady in Red (1935)
Raspberry Beret (1985)
Red Sails in the Sunset (1935)
Rudolph the Red-Nosed Reindeer (1949)
Scarlet Ribbons (For Her Hair) (1949)
When the Red, Red Robin Comes Bob, Bob Bobbin' Along
   (1926)
When You Wore a Tulip and I Wore a Big Red Rose
   (1914)

Rose

La Vie en Rose (1946)

Silver

By the Light of the Silvery Moon (1909)
Look for the Silver Lining (1920)
Silver Bells (1950)
That Silver-Haired Daddy of Mine (1932)
When Your Hair Has Turned to Silver (I Will Love You
   Just the Same) (1930)

White

The Little White Cloud That Cried (1951)
Little White Lies (1930)
Top Hat, White Tie and Tails (1935)
White Christmas (1942)
The White Horse Inn (1931)
White Room (1968)
A Whiter Shade of Pale (1967)

Yellow

Big Yellow Taxi (1975)
Mellow Yellow (1966)
The Moon Was Yellow (1934)
Tie a Yellow Ribbon Round the Old Oak Tree (1972)
Yellow Bird (1957)
The Yellow Rose of Texas (1955)
Yellow Submarine (1966)

COMPARATIVES

"More" is the comparative of choice in popular song. A number of enduring songs have the word in their titles, most notably the ballads "More Than You Know" (1929) and "The More I See You" (1945), and the striking theme from the Italian film *Mondo Cane* (1963), known in English as "More." Among other "more" songs are "More and More" (1944), "More I Cannot Wish You" (1950), and "More Than a Woman" (1977).

Other comparatives in popular song include "closer," as in the rumba "Come Closer to Me" (1940); "younger," as in "Younger Than Springtime," from *South Pacific* (1949); "sweeter," as in "Kisses Sweeter Than Wine" (1951); and "better," as in "Nobody Does It Better" (1977). Another, very competitive song about doing better is Irving Berlin's "Anything You Can Do," from *Annie Get Your Gun* (1946).

See also: **Superlatives**

COMPOSER-LYRICISTS

Songwriting is most often a collaborative effort, involving two or more persons. However, a few single individuals have been able to combine the functions of both **lyricist** and **composer** in the production of an enduring, and in some cases superior, body of work. The most esteemed members of this elite group were Irving Berlin and Cole Porter. Other prominent composer-lyricists include George M. Cohan, Noël Coward, Meredith Willson, Harold Rome, Frank Loesser, Stephen Sondheim, and Jim Webb. In addition, increasingly since the 1960s, many composer-lyricists have also functioned as **performer-songwriters,** among them such multitalented entertainer-songwriters as Elton John, Billy Joel, Stevie Wonder, Paul Simon, Carole King, and Bob Dylan.

Irving Berlin's songwriting career lasted over four decades. Born in Russia in 1888—he died in 1989—he came to the United States at age five. He began as a singing waiter in New York's Chinatown, eventually becoming a **song plugger** for publisher Harry Von Tilzer. At first he collaborated with various composers, writing only the lyrics for his first published song, "Marie From Sunny Italy" (1907), and for several succeeding songs. However, by 1909 he had become a composer-lyricist in his own right.

In his early years, Berlin occasionally borrowed, as in "That Mesmerizing Mendelssohn Tune" (1909)—a ragtime version of Felix Mendelssohn's "Spring Song"— or employed **quotation,** as in "Alexander's Ragtime Band" (1911), his first great hit, which incorporates a bugle call. Berlin soon branched out on his own, however, writing a host of memorable songs. His output is remarkable for both quantity and stylistic range, encompassing almost all varieties of popular song.

Equally adept at writing for **Tin Pan Alley, Broad-way,** or film, Berlin wrote songs for **holidays:** "Easter Parade" (1933), "White Christmas" (1942); for soldier shows in two world wars: *Yip Yip Yaphank* (1917), *This Is the Army* (1942); and a song that has become a second national anthem: "God Bless America" (written in 1918, but published only in 1939).

Berlin was neither a trained musician nor an inspired lyricist. Yet many of his songs, especially those written for films, show surprising melodic and harmonic sophistication. Examples of these are "Cheek to Cheek" (1935), "Top Hat, White Tie and Tails" (1935), "Let's Face the Music and Dance" (1936), and "Change Partners" (1938). At the other extreme, he was able to write such simple and heartfelt songs as "What'll I Do?" (1924) and "Always" (1925). More than any other composer-lyricist, he was able to suit a song to its occasion.

Cole Porter (1891–1964) was the epitome of the composer-lyricist. He always wrote alone, excelling in both **lyrics** and music. Much of his output shows a cohesiveness and seamlessness often lacking in the products of collaborators. Although he is best known for the wittiness and worldliness of his lyrics, Porter's music is also of the highest quality, giving evidence of the extent of his considerable musical training.

His career lasted over thirty years, almost always in **musical comedy,** although he wrote for **film** as well. From 1919 to 1955, he wrote songs for a succession of theater pieces and films. Among them were many destined to become standards: "Let's Do It (Let's Fall in Love" (1928), "What Is This Thing Called Love?" (1929), "Night and Day" (1932), "Anything Goes" (1934), "I Get a Kick Out of You" (1934), "Begin the Beguine" (1935), "I've Got You Under My Skin" (1936), and "Don't Fence Me In" (1944).

Innovation in both words and music is shown in such superior songs as "You're the Top" (1934), "Just One of Those Things" (1935), "Easy to Love" (1936), "In the Still of the Night" (1937), "Get Out of Town" (1938), "I Concentrate on You" (1940), "You'd Be So Nice to Come Home To" (1943), "I Love You" (1943), and "So in Love" (1949). Porter helped bring sophistication to American popular song by freeing it from its thirty-two-bar cocoon and by his frequent use of dissonance and the minor mode. He was an original, uniquely able to combine words and music to maximum effect.

Of the other composer-lyricists, George M. Cohan (1878–1942) was a vaudeville performer with a knack for writing songs which achieved great popularity. He received the Congressional Medal of Honor for his stirring song "Over There" (1917). Cohan wrote straightforward lyrics and simple melodies, sometimes, like Berlin, employing quotation. Although many of his songs—such as "The Yankee Doodle Boy" (1904), "You're a Grand Old Flag" (1906), and the aforementioned "Over There"—are on patriotic themes, he was equally adept with ballads and novelties like "Give My Regards to Broadway" (1904), "Mary's a Grand Old Name" (1905), and "Harrigan" (1908).

Noël Coward (1899–1973), born in **Britain**, was associated with the theater as playwright, actor, and producer, as well as songwriter. Although he had no formal musical education, he wrote both words and music for a number of lasting songs designed for a succession of his own musical plays. Among his songs most popular in the United States were: "A Room With a View" (1928), "I'll See You Again" and "Zigeuner" (both 1929), "Mad Dogs and Englishmen" and "Someday I'll Find You" (both 1931), "I'll Follow My Secret Heart" (1934), "Mad About the Boy" (1935), "You Were There" (1936), and "London Pride" (1941). His songs are characterized by witty lyrics and romantic melodies.

Meredith Willson (1902–1984) had a varied career as flutist, arranger, orchestrator, conductor, and composer. His best-known work is *The Music Man* (1957), a musical comedy for which he wrote the book, as well as the music and lyrics. The most popular songs from that production are the march "Seventy-Six Trombones" and the ballad "Till There Was You."

Harold Rome (b. 1908) has worked both as lyricist and composer-lyricist. In the first capacity, he collaborated on many songs, including the French import "(All of a Sudden) My Heart Sings" of 1941. As composer-lyricist he wrote several successful Broadway shows, including *Wish You Were Here* (1952) and the enchanting *Fanny* (1954).

Frank Loesser (1910–1969) also began his career as a lyric writer, chiefly for film—collaborating in the 1930s with such composers as Hoagy Carmichael, Alfred Newman, and Louis Alter. During World War II, he started writing both words and music while he was in the United States Army, producing such hits as "Praise the Lord and Pass the Ammunition" (1942). He achieved great popularity as composer-lyricist after the war with a succession of diverse songs, including the ballad "Spring Will Be a Little Late This Year" (1944) and the novelties "Baby, It's Cold Outside" and "On a Slow Boat to China" (both 1948). In addition, many standards emanated from his Broadway productions *Where's Charley?* (1948), *Guys and Dolls* (1950), and *The Most Happy Fella* (1956).

Stephen Sondheim (b. 1930) started his career as a lyricist as well. Nevertheless, he was thoroughly trained in composition, having studied at Princeton University with the modernist composer Milton Babbitt. Sondheim successfully wrote lyrics with the composers Leonard Bernstein, Jule Styne, and Richard Rodgers, collaborating on their respective shows *West Side Story* (1957), *Gypsy* (1959), and *Do I Hear a Waltz?* (1965). He also made his mark in the musical theater as composer-lyricist, first with *A Funny Thing Happened on the Way to the Forum* (1962), and then with a succession of other musicals, including *A Little Night Music* of 1973, which introduced the striking "Send in the Clowns." Especially known for the wittiness of his lyrics, Sondheim demonstrates eclecticism in his scores, often dictated by the demands of the libretto, in a style that can verge on the operatic.

Jim Webb (b. 1946) has produced a number of unusual and often innovative songs without collaboration, among them "By the Time I Get to Phoenix" and "Up, Up and Away," both 1967; and several songs about cities, including "MacArthur Park" and "Wichita Lineman," both 1968, and "Galveston" (1969).

Other composer-lyricists of note include Herman Hupfeld ("As Time Goes By," 1931), Ray Noble ("The Very Thought of You," 1934), and Jerry Herman ("Hello, Dolly," 1964)—as well as a host of performer-songwriters like Sam Cooke, Bobby Darin, Billy Joel, Stevie Wonder, Paul Simon, Rod McKuen, Don McLean, Lionel Richie, and William "Smokey" Robinson, who frequently used their own material. There have also been a number of songwriters known primarily as composers or lyricists who on occasion combined both functions. Thus, the composer Richard Rodgers wrote both music and lyrics for the show *No Strings* in 1962, which included the songs "No Strings" and "The Sweetest Sounds"; while the lyricist Johnny Mercer wrote both words and music for "I'm an Old Cow Hand (From the Rio Grande)" (1936), "Dream" (1944), "Something's Gotta Give" (1955), and other songs.

Bibliography

Bergreen, Laurence. *As Thousands Cheer: The Life of Irving Berlin*. 1990.

Eels, George. *The Life That Late He Led: A Biography of Cole Porter*. 1972.

Freedland, Michael. *Irving Berlin*. 1978.

McCabe, John H. *George M. Cohan: The Man Who Owned Broadway*. 1977.

McKuen, Rod. *Finding My Father: One Man's Search for Identity*. 1977.

Marchant, William. *The Privilege of His Company: Noël Coward Revisited*. 1975.

Mast, Gerald. *Can't Help Singin': The American Musical on Stage and Screen*. 1987.

Rimler, Walter. *Not Fade Away: A Comparison of Jazz Age With Rock Era Composers*. 1984.

Schwartz, Charles. *Cole Porter: A Biography*. 1979.

Wilder, Alec. *American Popular Song: The Great Innovators 1900–1950*. 1972.

Willson, Meredith. *And There I Stood With My Piccolo*. 1976.

Zadan, Craig. *Sondheim and Company*. 1976.

COMPOSERS

There are two sides to the songwriting equation, the

literary and the musical, and they are considered by many to be of equal importance in the creation of popular song. Yet very often it is the music, rather than the lyrics, that comes to mind when one recalls a song. Just as in opera, where the composer is generally given more attention than the librettist, the public is more aware of the composer of popular song than of the **lyricist**.

The concept of the composer as solely responsible for the music is central to the Western musical tradition. As such, it was carried over into American popular song, but with an important difference from the classics. With few exceptions, the composer of popular, as opposed to classical, music supplies only the melodic line and a suggestion of the harmonies. The rest of the scoring is left to an arranger, who becomes in fact an anonymous collaborator on the song (*see* Arrangement).

Six outstanding composers have dominated the composition of American popular music: Jerome Kern, Irving Berlin, Cole Porter, George Gershwin, Richard Rodgers, and Harold Arlen. Two of these, Irving Berlin and Cole Porter, wrote their own lyrics as well (*see* Composer-Lyricists). Other influential composers who wrote a significant number of standards include Victor Herbert, Rudolf Friml, Sigmund Romberg, Harry Warren, Jimmy McHugh, Nacio Herb Brown, Ray Henderson, Vincent Youmans, Duke Ellington, Hoagy Carmichael, Kurt Weill, Arthur Schwartz, Frederick Loewe, Vernon Duke, Jule Styne, John Green, Burton Lane, James Van Heusen, Leonard Bernstein, Henry Mancini, Burt Bacharach, and Marvin Hamlisch.

Jerome Kern (1885–1945) is widely considered the most influential of non-lyric-writing American popular composers. Born in New York City, he studied at the New York College of Music and made frequent trips to England as a young man. His music is extraordinary, characterized by lyrical melodies and graceful harmonies. In particular, his adventuresome **modulations** brought a new dimension to American popular song, moving it closer to the European **art song** tradition with such works as "The Song Is You" (1932) and "Smoke Gets in Your Eyes" (1933).

Kern worked with many lyricists, including P. G. Wodehouse, Otto Harbach, Oscar Hammerstein II, Dorothy Fields, Clifford Grey, Johnny Mercer, E. Y. Harburg, and Ira Gershwin. On occasion, as in "Till the Clouds Roll By" (1917), he even collaborated on the lyrics himself. He wrote almost exclusively for the musical theater in London and New York from 1902 to 1935. During World War I, his shows at the Princess Theater in New York were instrumental in drawing public taste away from the prevailing style of **operetta** and in moving it in the direction of **musical comedy**. His ballad in 4/4 meter, "They Didn't Believe Me," interpolated in the show *The Girl From Utah* in 1914, was

a complete departure from the waltzes which dominated operetta. It has long been considered a landmark of American popular song, differing from its predecessors in aspects of melody, harmony, and form.

Another landmark was the pathbreaking **musical play** *Show Boat*. It opened in New York in 1927 with book and lyrics by Oscar Hammerstein II and contained some of Kern's best-known melodies: "Can't Help Lovin' Dat Man," "Make Believe," "Ol' Man River," and "Why Do I Love You?" But Kern's most unusual song, melodically and harmonically, was "All the Things You Are," written for a show that was a failure, *Very Warm for May* (1939). Even with its complexity, and in spite of reservations by both Kern and Hammerstein about its acceptance by the public, the song became a hit.

In the early 1930s, Kern started writing for Hollywood. Some of his finest songs were written for film **musicals**, including "I Won't Dance" (1935), "A Fine Romance" (1936), "The Way You Look Tonight" (1936), and "Long Ago (And Far Away)" (1944).

Irving Berlin (1888–1989) is usually thought of as the consummate songwriter rather than as a composer. Nevertheless, his music stands on its own, varying in nature from simplicity and directness—as in "God Bless America" (1939)—to rhythmic and harmonic compexity—as in "Puttin' On the Ritz" (1929).

The music of Cole Porter (1891–1964), like that of the other great composer-lyricist, Berlin, has seldom been considered on its own merits; it has often been overshadowed by his lyrics. Yet Porter was one of America's most innovative and influential composers of popular music, as demonstrated in such remarkable compositions as "I Concentrate on You" (1940) and "From This Moment On" (1950).

George Gershwin (1898–1937) brought the legacy of the **blues** and **jazz** into American show music. He also sought to reconcile the worlds of popular and "serious" music in such concert works as *Rhapsody in Blue* (1924), *Concerto in F* (1925), and *An American in Paris* (1929). His many songs bear the mark of melodic and harmonic sophistication as well as rhythmic vitality.

Born in New York City, Gershwin had little musical education. At age fifteen, he worked as a pianist and **song plugger** for Remick Music Corporation. Shortly thereafter, he became a staff composer for T. B. Harms. He collaborated most often with his brother Ira, a talented lyricist, but also worked at various times with Irving Caesar, B. G. DeSylva, Oscar Hammerstein II, Otto Harbach, and Gus Kahn.

Like Kern, Gershwin started on Broadway and ended in Hollywood. His first resounding success was "Swanee," written in 1919. This was followed by a string of hits written for musical comedy, including "The Man I Love" (1924), "Oh, Lady Be Good" (1924), "Someone to Watch Over Me" (1926), "'S Wonderful"

(1927), "Embraceable You" (1930), and "I Got Rhythm" (1930).

His landmark **opera**, *Porgy and Bess*, written with Ira and DuBose Heyward in 1935, was a highlight of Gershwin's career. Its music—including that of the enchanting lullaby, "Summertime" and the rousing spiritual "I Got Plenty o' Nuttin'"—is in a class by itself.

Gershwin spent the three remaining years of his short lifetime writing for film. Like Kern, some of his best songs came out of Hollywood, among them "A Foggy Day" (1937), "They Can't Take That Away From Me" (1937), "Love Is Here to Stay" (1938), and "Love Walked In" (1938).

Richard Rodgers (1902–1979) had one of the longest careers of any popular composer; his songs were published continually over a period of sixty years, from 1919 to 1979. Although most of them were written for the musical theater, often with specific dramatic situations in mind, many of his songs seem to have a life of their own. They are consistently excellent, showing musical sensitivity and their composer's fine sense of craftsmanship.

Rodgers was born in New York City and educated at Columbia University. His career can be divided into three phases, defined by his lyricists: the first, from 1920 to 1943, with Lorenz Hart; the second, from 1943 to 1960, with Oscar Hammerstein II; and the third, from 1960 to 1979, with a variety of lyricists, including himself, Stephen Sondheim, Sheldon Harnick, and Martin Charnin. The periods with Hart and Hammerstein were by far the most fruitful both for him and for American popular song (*see* Collaboration).

Harold Arlen (1905–1986) was perhaps the most blues-oriented of popular composers. His music is noted for its experimentation, particularly in **length** and **form**—evidenced in such songs as "Blues in the Night" (1941) and "The Man That Got Away" (1954). He collaborated with many lyricists, among them Ted Koehler, E. Y. Harburg, Johnny Mercer, and Ira Gershwin.

Born in Buffalo, New York, Arlen was by age fifteen a professional pianist on the steamers that plied Lake Erie. Soon thereafter, he started playing for **revues** in New York City; before long, he was writing songs for them. Among his early hits were two songs written in 1933: "It's Only a Paper Moon" and "Stormy Weather." Later Arlen achieved great success with songs written specifically for films, such as "Over the Rainbow," for *The Wizard of Oz* (1939), and "That Old Black Magic," for *Star-Spangled Rhythm* (1942).

Turning now to the second tier of composers, a triumvirate of European-born composers dominated the field of **operetta** in the early twentieth century: Victor Herbert (1859–1924), Rudolf Friml (1879–1972), and Sigmund Romberg (1887–1951). They carried on in the Viennese tradition of soaring melodies and graceful harmonies, as it was brought to the United States by Franz Lehár, Emmerich Kálmán, and Oscar Straus.

Harry Warren (1893–1981), although not as well known as the operetta composers, was probably the most successful composer for the early film musical. He wrote with many lyricists, including Al Dubin, Johnny Mercer, Mack Gordon, and Sammy Cahn. A remarkable number of his songs have endured, including "I Only Have Eyes for You" (1934), "Lullaby of Broadway" (1935), "September in the Rain" (1937), and "You'll Never Know" (1943).

Jimmy McHugh (1894–1969), another composer who wrote primarily for Hollywood, collaborated with lyricists like Dorothy Fields, Harold Adamson, Ned Washington, and Johnny Mercer. Among his credits are "I Can't Give You Anything But Love" (1928), "Exactly Like You" (1930), "On the Sunny Side of the Street" (1930), and "I'm in the Mood for Love" (1935).

Nacio Herb Brown (1896–1964) wrote innovative music, primarily for early film musicals. Among his lyricists were Arthur Freed, B.G. DeSylva, Gus Kahn, and Leo Robin. His songs include the standards "Singin' in the Rain" (1929), "Temptation" (1933), "Alone" (1935), and "You Stepped Out of a Dream" (1940).

Ray Henderson (1896–1970) is best known for the music he wrote in collaboration with the lyric-writing team of B. G. DeSylva and Lew Brown, including "The Birth of the Blues" (1926), "It All Depends on You" (1926), "The Best Things in Life Are Free" (1927), and "You're the Cream in My Coffee" (1928). He also wrote the music for such standards as "Five Foot Two, Eyes of Blue; Has Anybody Seen My Girl?" (1925) and "Bye Bye Blackbird" (1926).

Vincent Youmans (1898–1946), a talented composer, was equally adept at ballads and novelty songs. He wrote chiefly for the New York musical theater, with such collaborators as Ira Gershwin, Otto Harbach, Herbert Stothart, and Irving Caesar. Among his hits were "Tea for Two" (1924), "Sometimes I'm Happy" (1927), "More Than You Know" (1929), and "Time on My Hands" (1930).

Edward Kennedy (Duke) Ellington, (1899–1974) was a bandleader and pianist as well as a composer. His music is noted for its wistful melodies and pungent harmonies. He collaborated with many writers of both music and lyrics, including Billy Strayhorn, Irving Mills, Mitchell Parish, Eddie DeLange, Bob Russell, Irving Gordon, and Carl Sigman. Best known of his own compositions are "Sophisticated Lady" (1933), "Solitude" (1934), and "Don't Get Around Much Anymore" (1934).

Howard Hoagland (Hoagy) Carmichael (1899–1981) was an entertainer and lyricist as well as a composer. He collaborated with a number of lyricists, including Johnny Mercer, Mitchell Parish, Frank

Loesser, and Stanley Adams. Although best known for his landmark song "Star Dust" (1929), Carmichael also wrote the music for such standards as "Georgia on My Mind" (1930) and "The Nearness of You" (1937).

Kurt Weill (1900–1950) achieved his first success in Germany, with *Die Dreigroschenoper* written with Bertolt Brecht in 1928. It was produced in 1953 in New York as *The Threepenny Opera*, with English words by Marc Blitzstein (in probably the best-known translation), and included the memorable song "Mack the Knife." Weill's later lyricists included Ira Gershwin, Ogden Nash, Maxwell Anderson, and Alan Jay Lerner. He wrote almost exclusively for the musical theater, composing such lasting songs as "September Song" (1938), "Speak Low" (1943), and "Lost in the Stars" (1949).

Arthur Schwartz (1900–1984) was a producer for stage and screen as well as a composer. His chief lyricists were Howard Dietz, Dorothy Fields, Johnny Mercer, and Ira Gershwin. Among his best-known songs are "Something to Remember You By" (1930), "Dancing in the Dark" (1931), and "Alone Together" (1932).

Frederick Loewe (1901–1988) was born in Vienna. He wrote with only one lyricist, Alan Jay Lerner, with whom he received worldwide acclaim as composer of the Broadway shows *My Fair Lady* (1956) and *Camelot* (1960), and the film classic *Gigi* (1958).

Vernon Duke (1903–1969), born in Russia, was a composer not only of popular song but also, under his original name of Vladimir Dukelsky, of "serious" works. Among his lyricists were E. Y. Harburg, Ira Gershwin, Ogden Nash, Howard Dietz, John Latouche, and himself. Perhaps his best-known songs are "April in Paris" (1932), "Autumn in New York" (1934), "I Can't Get Started" (1935), and "Taking a Chance on Love" (1940).

Jule Styne (b. 1905) has had a long career as composer, publisher, and producer. His chief lyricists were Sammy Cahn, Leo Robin, Betty Comden and Adolph Green, Bob Merrill, and Stephen Sondheim. His songs run the gamut from Tin Pan Alley to Broadway and Hollywood, from ballads to novelties, and include "I Don't Want to Walk Without You" (1941), "It's Been a Long, Long Time" (1945), "Diamonds Are a Girl's Best Friend" (1949), "Just in Time" (1956), and "People" (1964).

John Green (1908–1989) was known as a conductor and pianist as well as a composer. He was executive-in-charge of music at MGM Studios from 1949 to 1958. Among his lyricists were Edward Heyman, E. Y. Harburg, Johnny Mercer, Ira Gershwin, and Robert Sour. His most innovative and enduring works were written in the early 1930s, and include "Body and Soul" (1930), "I'm Yours" (1930), "(You Came Along From) Out of Nowhere" (1931), and "I Cover the Waterfront" (1933).

Burton Lane (b. 1912) has collaborated with lyricists Harold Adamson, E. Y. Harburg, Ralph Freed, Al Dubin, Alan Jay Lerner, Ira Gershwin, and Dorothy Fields on such songs as "How About You?" (1941), "How Are Things in Glocca Morra?" (1947), and "On a Clear Day You Can See Forever" (1966).

James Van Heusen (1913–1979) is the pen name of Edward Chester Babcock. He wrote mainly for film; a number of his songs won Academy Awards. His chief lyricists were Johnny Burke, Sammy Cahn, Johnny Mercer, and Eddie DeLange. Among his best-known songs, many popularized by his friend Frank Sinatra, were "It Could Happen to You" (1944), "Here's That Rainy Day" (1953), "The Second Time Around" (1960), and "Call Me Irresponsible" (1962).

Leonard Bernstein (1918–1990) was a conductor and pianist, as well as a composer of both serious and popular works. His most important contribution to American popular song was the score for the landmark musical *West Side Story* (1957), with lyrics by Stephen Sondheim. Among his other collaborators were Richard Wilbur and Betty Comden and Adolph Green.

Henry Mancini (b. 1924) is best known as a conductor and composer of film scores. He worked with the lyricist Johnny Mercer on such well-known songs as "Moon River" (1961), "The Days of Wine and Roses" (1962), and "Charade" (1963), all of which achieved success independent of the films in which they first appeared. He has also worked with other lyricists, including Leslie Bricusse and Alan and Marilyn Bergman.

Burt Bacharach (b. 1928) was the musical half of a successful songwriting team with Hal David; they produced such hits as "(They Long to Be) Close to You" (1963), "The Look of Love" (1965), "Alfie" (1966), "I'll Never Fall in Love Again" (1968), and "Raindrops Keep Fallin' on My Head" (1969). Bacharach also has collaborated with other lyricists, among them Mack David, Paul Anka, and Bob Hilliard.

Marvin Hamlisch (b. 1944) has written music for both plays and films. His lyricists include Alan and Marilyn Bergman, Edward Kleban, and Carol Bayer Sager. Among his best-known songs are "The Way We Were" (1973), "One" (1975), and "What I Did for Love" (1975).

In addition to the above composers, three from abroad have contributed more than their share to American popular song: Michel Legrand, from **France**; Antonio Carlos Jobim, from **Brazil**; and Andrew Lloyd Webber, from **Britain**. For information about other American and foreign composers, see Part II: Catalogue of Songs.

Bibliography

ASCAP Biographical Dictionary. 4th ed. 1980.

Bordman, Gerald. *Jerome Kern: His Life and Music*. 1980.

Carmichael, Hoagy. *The Stardust Road*. 1969.

Craig, Warren. *The Great Songwriters of Hollywood.* 1980.

Ellington, Duke. *Music Is My Mistress.* 1976.

Freedland, Michael. *Jerome Kern: A Biography.* 1978.

Jablonski, Edward. *Gershwin.* 1987.

————. *Harold Arlen: Happy With the Blues.* 1961.

Marx, Samuel, and Jan Clayton. *Rodgers and Hart: Bewitched, Bothered, and Bedevilled.* 1977.

Nolan, Frederick. *The Sound of Their Music: The Story of Rodgers and Hammerstein.* 1979.

Sanders, Ronald. *The Days Grow Short: The Life and Times of Kurt Weill.* 1980.

Schwartz, Charles M. *George Gershwin: A Selective Bibliography and Discography.* 1974.

———— *Gershwin: His Life and Music.* 1979.

Taylor, Theodore. *Jule: The Story of Composer Jule Styne, A Revue in Many Acts and Scenes.* 1978.

Thomas, Tony. *Harry Warren and the Hollywood Musical.* 1975.

Waters, Edward Neighbor. *Victor Herbert: A Life in Music.* 1978.

Wilder, Alec. *American Popular Song: The Great Innovators, 1900–1950.* 1972.

See also: Performer-Songwriters

CONGA

The conga is a communal dance in moderate **tempo**, in which the participants form an ever-growing line as they execute a pronounced kick on the fourth beat of each measure. This beat is strongly accentuated in the orchestra by percussion, as follows:

Having originated in **Cuba** around 1935 as a carnival dance, the conga initiated a **dance craze** in the United States in 1939, largely through the efforts of singer Desi Arnaz and orchestra leader Xavier Cugat. It remained popular at festivals and celebrations through the 1980s, danced to such songs as Eliseo Grenet's "La Conga" (1938) and Enrique Garcia's "Conga" (1985).

See also: **Mambo; Rumba; Salsa**

CONTRACTIONS

The shortening of a word can serve two functions in popular song, either bringing forth the vernacular or accommodating the music. Contraction may entail the elision of a consonant, as in "Makin' Whoopee" (1928); of a vowel, as in "Ev'ry Time We Say Goodbye" (1944); or both, as in "Ev'rything I've Got" (1942). Hundreds of songs begin with the contractions "Can't," "Don't," "Isn't," "I'll," "I'm," "It's," "Let's," "That's," "There's," and "You're." The most popular contraction of all, "ain't," is almost always associated with **dialect**, as in "It Ain't Necessarily So" (1935), or **slang**, as in "Is You Is or Is You Ain't Ma' Baby" (1943).

Irving Berlin, always responsive to the speech patterns of the American public, was a consummate user of contraction. It is an essential component of his **lyrics**, as, for example, in the famous opening words of the chorus of "Alexander's Ragtime Band" (1911): "Come on 'n' hear." Many of his titles are built on contractions: "Doin' What Comes Natur'lly" (1946), "Everybody's Doin' It Now" (1911), "The Hostess With the Mostes' on the Ball" (1950), "Isn't This a Lovely Day" (1935), "Let's Face the Music and Dance" (1936), "Puttin' on the Ritz" (1929), "Steppin' Out With My Baby" (1947), "There's No Business Like Show Business" (1946), "You'd Be Surprised" (1919).

Cole Porter was another songwriter who was fond of contraction. He shortened words in his lyrics in such phrases as "You have the pow'r to hypnotize me," from "You Do Something to Me" (1929), and "'Cause you'd be oh, so easy to love," from "Easy to Love" (1936). Among his song titles using contractions are "Ev'rything I Love" (1941), "It's All Right With Me" (1953), "I've Got You Under My Skin" (1936), "Let's Do It (Let's Fall in Love)" (1928), "Why Can't You Behave?" (1949), "Why Shouldn't I?" (1943), "You'd Be So Nice to Come Home To" (1934), and "You're the Top" (1934).

Ira Gershwin also often contracted his words. The verse of "Someone to Watch Over Me," for example, begins: "Lookin' ev'rywhere, haven't found him yet." His titles include "Bidin' My Time" (1930), "Clap Yo' Hands" (1926), "I've Got a Crush on You" (1928), "Liza (All the Clouds'll Roll Away)" (1929), and what is perhaps the quintessential contraction song—"'S Wonderful" (1927). The latter, built entirely around contractions, includes such memorable passages as: "'S awful nice! 'S paradise—'S what I love to see!"

Bibliography

Furia, Philip. *The Poets of Tin Pan Alley: A History of America's Great Lyricists.* 1990.

Mast, Gerald. *Can't Help Singin': The American Musical on Stage and Screen.* 1987.

COON SONG

"Coon song" was a derogatory term used in the nineteenth and early twentieth centuries to denote a song in black **dialect**. In performance, more often than not, it involved shouting rather than singing. Long a staple of the **minstrel show**, the coon song was often done by white performers in blackface. This tradition continued in **vaudeville** until about 1912. The genre flourished until about that time on **Tin Pan Alley** as well.

From the **Gay Nineties** on, coon songs were often equated with **ragtime**, even though many of them lacked the syncopation inherent to that genre. Lyrics were very often offensive, resorting to racial stereotypes. A prime example is "All Coons Look Alike to Me" (1896), which was in fact written by a black composer, Ernest Hogan.

After the turn of the century, the lyrics of the coon song tended to be toned down somewhat. Many erstwhile coon songs, such as "A Hot Time in the Old Town" (1896), "Hello! Ma Baby" (1899), "Under the Bamboo Tree" (1902), "Bill Bailey, Won't You Please Come Home?" (1902), and "Waiting for the Robert E. Lee" (1912), joined the musical mainstream. Some songs lost their dialects in the process. Others, like "My Gal Is a High Born Lady" (1896), "Mister Johnson, Turn Me Loose" (1896), and "At a Georgia Camp Meeting" (1897), became successes in vaudeville or as dances. It became customary to publish many of the best-known coon songs in piano arrangements.

From around 1910 on, the coon song merged with the sentimental **ballad**, resulting in such hybrid songs as "Some of These Days" (1910) and "You Made Me Love You" (1913).

Bibliography

Berlin, Edward A. *Ragtime: A Musical and Cultural History.* 1980.

See also: **Cakewalk**

COPYRIGHT

Copyright laws have offered protection to songwriters within the United States since 1790. At first they applied only to **sheet music**, providing for a royalty for each copy of a registered song that was sold. Not until 1891, however, was there an international copyright agreement; songs written prior to that date had been pirated freely in both directions between the United States and Europe. British songs, such as those of Gilbert and Sullivan, were particular favorites for pirating, and were widely performed in America with no recompense to their authors. The International Copyright Act of 1891 was designed to alleviate these conditions and to protect writers on both sides of the Atlantic.

The United States Copyright Act of 1909 protected songwriters for a period of twenty-eight years after the date of copyright—a term that was renewable. It also was the first law to apply specifically to the mechanical reproduction of music, giving publishers, composers, and authors a royalty of two cents for each phonograph record or piano roll that was produced.

The next major act was the Copyright Law of 1976, which took effect on January 1, 1978. This far-reaching law offers automatic copyright for a work from the time that it is created. It further calls for an annual fee of eight dollars for each existing **jukebox**, and extends the duration of copyright to fifty years after the death of the last surviving author. Works copyrighted before 1976 are given protection at least until the year 2027.

The two chief performance-rights organizations in the United States are **ASCAP** and **BMI**. These licensing agencies collect fees on some types of public performance of copyrighted works—mainly on **radio** and **television**—and pass them on to the authors.

Bibliography

Erickson, J. Gunna, Edward R. Hearn, and Mark. E Halloran. *Musician's Guide to Copyright.* 1983.
Sanjek, Russell, and David Sanjek. *American Popular Music Business in the Twentieth Century.* 1991.
Shemel, Sidney, and M. William Krasilovsky. *This Business of Music.* 1990

See also: **Recording; Tin Pan Alley**

COUNTERMELODY

A countermelody is a melodic line that is subordinate to the principal melody and functions as part of the **accompaniment**. It is sometimes ornamental in nature, using neighboring tones like the F-sharp and G-sharp surrounding the A minor tonality of George Gershwin's "Summertime" (1935).

Countermelodies gain special importance in the music of Jerome Kern; in some cases they form integral parts of his songs. For example, in "I've Told Ev'ry Little Star" (1932), each of the three A-sections ends with a similar countermelody. In "The Song Is You" (1932), a countermelody in triplets appears both at the halfway point and at the end of the song. In "Smoke Gets in Your Eyes" (1933), there are two different countermelodies, positioned at the ends of each of the four main sections (AABA) of the song; they exhibit the contrasting form abab. "The Way You Look Tonight" (1936) has a chordal accompaniment with a distinctive, wispy countermelody at the end of each A-section.

Countermelodies are found in the music of other composers as well: Jule Styne's "Make Someone Happy" (1960) has a chromatic **vamp** which functions both as accompaniment and countermelody. But seldom have they been used to such enchanting effect as in Kern's songs.

See also: **Counterpoint**

COUNTERPOINT

Counterpoint, the simultaneous use of two or more melodic lines, is a rare component of popular song. One of its first advocates was Irving Berlin, whose "Play a Simple Melody," from the 1914 revue *Watch Your Step*, puts together two seemingly incompatible **melodies**: one syncopated in the manner of ragtime; the other legato in the style of a ballad. Thirty-six years later, Berlin produced another contrapuntal hit, "You're Just in Love," written specifically for the 1950 show *Call Me Madam*. In similar fashion, it places two equally important melodic lines—one flowing, the other syncopated—against one another.

Other instances of counterpoint occur primarily in duets and trios of the musical theater. For example, in "Mine," from George and Ira Gershwin's *Let 'Em Eat Cake* (1933), two different melodies are sung variously in three refrains. First the primary melody is sung by a soloist; then the second melody is sung by the chorus; and finally both melodies are sung together in counterpoint. The famous "Fugue for Tinhorns," from Frank Loesser's *Guys and Dolls* (1950), is a trio in counterpoint about playing the ponies and reading the racing form, beginning with the words "I've got the horse right here." The song "One," from Edward Kleban and Marvin Hamlisch's *A Chorus Line* (1975), consists of two disparate melodies and sets of lyrics which are sung first individually and then together.

See also: Countermelody; Texture

COUNTRIES. SEE NATIONS

COUNTRY AND WESTERN

Country and western, or country music, is a flourishing genre of popular music that developed in the United States and spread throughout the world. It began as folk music in its literal sense: music made not by urban outsiders, but rather by the people indigenous to the culture from which it emanates.

Country music had been part of southern folk culture from the time European settlers first moved into the southeastern region of the United States. Derived from **folk song**, it gradually moved westward through the states of Oklahoma and Texas, where it acquired the rubric "country and western." Until the advent of phonograph records and **radio**, the music was mostly rural and largely untouched by outside influences, although its early makers, in their wanderings, were always receptive to new styles.

Many aspects of country music could be traced back to the ballads and dances of the "common man" living in seventeenth- and eighteenth-century Europe, and particularly the British Isles. The structure of the music, similar to that of mainstream American popular song, is also European in origin, often consisting of a verse and a thirty-two-bar chorus in **AABA** form. Dances, each with a distinctive rhythmic flavor, were based on preexisting types: the reel, scottische,

and polka, in duple meter; and the jig, ländler, and waltz, in triple meter. The quality of vocal performance was also distinctive: usually rough and strong and sung in a high-pitched wail.

The main instruments used by early immigrants were the fiddle and dulcimer, later augmented by the dobro, harmonica, and steel guitar. The method of playing stringed instruments differed from the strumming sound found in other styles; instruments were often picked, twanged, and scraped. In addition, early settlers absorbed cultural influences from other new arrivals, most notably from the black slave population, which contributed the spiritual and the **blues**, as well as a new instrument: the banjo. As settlers moved westward, they were also introduced to the **guitar** by the Spanish-speaking people of that region.

The music that evolved was not of the upper classes. It was simple and narrative in nature, developing out of loneliness and hard times. A good deal of its content was religious, derived from church services and revival meetings.

Prior to World War I, country music was mostly confined to the regions where it was created and performed. With the coming of war, however, the situation changed dramatically, resulting in a cross-cultural exchange between rural and urban populations. Young men from urban areas were sent to military camps in the nation's rural areas, while country families moved to the cities to find work in defense plants.

When the war ended, phonograph records became popular and radio broadcasts reached an ever-widening audience. This opened the door for country and western music to be heard nationally. On July 1, 1922, a fiddler named A. C. "Eck" Robertson earned the distinction of being the first southern white performer to make a commercial **recording**—for the Victor Talking Machine Company.

Soon record companies affixed the term "hillbilly" to this type of music. Hit songs began to emerge, including "The Prisoner's Song," or "If I Had the Wings of an Angel"—which sold about one million records and one million copies of sheet music—and "The Wreck of the Southern Old 97," the first country song about railroads; both songs were recorded in 1924 by Vernon Dahlhart. In 1925, radio station WSM was inaugurated in **Nashville** and it began broadcasting the popular *WSM Barn Dance*, retitled two years later as *Grand Ole Opry*. No other single show has so dominated the field; it became the preeminent platform enabling a country song to become a standard. This was also the year (1927) that Darby and Tarlton made the first recording of the traditional folk song "Down in the Valley," or "Birmingham Jail."

Two stage acts, the Carter Family and Jimmie Rodgers, came out of this period. They left an indelible mark, not only on country and western music, but on other genres of popular music as well. The Carter

Family represented the epitome of the traditional, religious Appalachian singing family. The values of home, family, decency, and modesty were always at the forefront of their songs. Their simple and easy singing style enabled their songs to be perpetuated, and they influenced many folk musicians to come. They were inventive in their use of the guitar and autoharp as accompaniment. They recorded over three hundred songs, including "Wildwood Flower," the unofficial anthem of country music, in 1928.

Jimmie Rodgers was the first country superstar and was considered by many to be the "father of country music," His recordings were loved by people in all walks of American society. In contrast to the Carters, Rodgers sang about life's temptations and about men who favored the open road; his songs are populated with gamblers, hoboes, convicts, and carousers. His vocal stylings and **instrumentation** tapped into melodies found in folk, dixieland, blues, and jazz. Rodgers recorded 113 songs for RCA Victor, among them "T for Texas" (originally known as "Blue Yodel No. 1") in 1927 and "Mule Skinner Blues," or "Blue Yodel No. 8," in 1931. As a testament to their talents, both the Carters and Rodgers sold records during the Great Depression when other artists could not. Rodgers died in 1933 and the Carter Family disbanded in 1943, but their songs live on to this day.

Although the Depression curtailed the sale of records, country music could be heard without cost over the radio. Singing cowboys in motion pictures contributed to the spread of country and western music as well, with songs like Gene Autry and Jimmy Long's "That Silver-Haired Daddy of Mine" (1932) and Jimmy Davis and Charles Mitchell's "You Are My Sunshine" (1940).

About this time, Bob Wills and his Texas Playboys blended a mixture of country, jazz, and blues into a song called "Steel Guitar Rag" (1941), in a style that came to be known after World War II as "western swing." "San Antonio Rose," a 1940 hit for Bob Wills, was recorded the following year by Bing Crosby; it was one of the first examples of a country-to-pop **crossover**. Among other hits of this period were "Tumbling Tumbleweeds" (1934); "I Want to Be a Cowboy's Sweetheart," recorded by Patsy Montana in 1936; and "The Great Speckled Bird," recorded by Roy Acuff in 1937. The last is one of the most famous songs in country music and was adopted as an anthem by many Pentecostal groups.

During **World War II**, country and western music expanded its influence as more radio stations broadcast it than ever before. The music's rural identity dissipated as the war years saw the growth and dispersal of the southern urban working class and its changing socioeconomic status. Adjustment was difficult for many of these people, who sought solace over a bottle of beer in

a "honky-tonk." Thus, the seeds were planted for a new style of country music. For the most part the subjects were still love, work, and home, but in addition there were new themes: adultery, divorce, and drinking. While the fully realized honky-tonk sound was yet to come—the actual term would not be used until the 1960s—early examples of honky-tonk song appeared in the 1940s, among them Ernest Tubb's "Walking the Floor Over You" (1941), "When My Blue Moon Turns to Gold Again" (1941), "Born to Lose" (1943), and the biggest honky-tonk song of this period, Al Dexter's "Pistol Packin' Mama" (1943). This song, along with "There's a Star-Spangled Banner Waving Somewhere" (1942)—the major patriotic song of the war—quickly crossed over into the musical mainstream.

At war's end, Eddy Arnold was the leading country and western singer in America and a prime factor in the music's postwar move toward national commercial acceptance. After his recording of "The Cattle Call" in 1944, almost all of his hits crossed over to the pop charts, including "I'll Hold You in My Heart (Till I Can Hold You in My Arms)" in 1947 and "Just a Little Lovin' (Will Go a Long Way)" in 1948. Also in 1948, Redd Stewart and Pee Wee King's "Tennessee Waltz" proved once and for all the enormous crossover potential of country song when Patti Page and six other major pop artists made the charts with their own hit versions.

In 1949, Hank Williams made his initial appearance at the Grand Ole Opry. By the time of his untimely death at age twenty-nine on January 1, 1953, he had inherited the mantle left by Jimmie Rodgers as the preeminent star of country and western music. As writer and performer, Williams had an innate ability to create an oeuvre to which listeners could relate. His songs, many written in collaboration with music publisher Fred Rose, broadened the base of country music's acceptance. Among his many crossover hits were "Cold, Cold Heart" (recorded by Tony Bennett in 1951), "Jambalaya (On the Bayou)" (recorded by Jo Stafford in 1952), and one of his best-known songs, "Your Cheatin' Heart" (a major pop hit for Joni James in 1953). Among Williams's other lasting songs were "I'm So Lonely I Could Cry" (1949), "Hey Good Lookin'" (1951), and "Kaw-Liga" (1952)

Because of the crossover success of Williams and others, it was not long before country music began to mutate into pop form. Country writers and artists began to adapt their styles to fit the musical mainstream. In 1955, such country performers as Bill Haley and the Comets and Elvis Presley turned the music world upside down with their recordings of "(We're Gonna) Rock Around the Clock" (1953) and "That's All Right" (1947).

Record companies, feeling the pressure of teenaged youth, now encouraged their country artists to perform **rock 'n' roll**. The result was a melding together of western swing, **rhythm and blues,** and honky-tonk known as **rockabilly.** Not every one was happy. Youth loved the new sound, but admirers of traditional country music feared that their music would soon fade away.

In 1955, Tennessee Ernie Ford made one of the fastest-selling records in music history: Merle Travis's "Sixteen Tons," written in 1947. Although it was not rockabilly, part of its success could be attributed to its mild rocking beat. "Young Love" (1956), as sung by Sonny James, also helped usher in the growing blend of pop and country. With its similarity to a rock ballad, it appealed to young listeners; with instrumentation veering far away from traditional country music, it was one of the first country songs to feature a choral background.

Most country-pop songs of this type bear little resemblance to true country and western music. Steel guitars and fiddles are absent, choral backgrounds are very evident, and the instrumentation is a vague mixture of rock 'n' roll, pop, and country. In many cases, the only connection these songs have with country and western is that the performer is a "country" singer; Marty Robbins's "A White Sport Coat and a Pink Carnation" (1957) is a perfect example.

Among other standards dating from this period were Johnny Cash's rockabilly-influenced "I Walk the Line" and Ray Price's recording of "Crazy Arms," a song derived from traditional honky-tonk. Both were released in 1956. A year later, Bobby Helms recorded "My Special Angel" as well as the enduring Christmas favorite "Jingle-Bell Rock." In 1958, Conway Twitty, who went on to become a driving force in country music in the 1970s, had a major hit with "It's Only Make Believe."

An offshoot of country-pop called the "saga" song appeared in the late 1950s. This is a song telling a tale of a true or fictional event. Examples of this genre are "The Battle of New Orleans" (1957), based on a fiddle tune written to celebrate the last battle of the War of 1812; "El Paso," recorded by Marty Robbins in 1959; the legendary Lefty Frizzell's recording of "Long Black Veil" (1959); Jimmy Dean's "Big Bad John" (1961); Bobbie Gentry's "Ode to Billie Joe" (1967), and Tom T. Hall's "The Harper Valley P.T.A." (1967).

In the 1960s, Chet Atkins (renowned guitarist and chief of RCA's country and western arm) and Owen Bradley (famous Nashville producer, musician, and executive) were separately but concurrently trying to preserve traditional country sounds while at the same time providing new fans with music they could enjoy. The resulting middle-of-the-road pop has been variously called "country-politan" and the "Nashville sound." While this type of music was basically country in content and vocal approach, its instrumentation, which now included drums, vibraphone, strings, piano, and bass, was relaxed and sophisticated pop.

Many artists rushed to record in this new style of country-pop, but few were consistently successful. Jim Reeves was the leading male singer of the genre. His most famous recording was "He'll Have to Go" in 1960. Although he died in a plane crash in 1964, Reeves had hits on the country charts into the 1980s. Patsy Cline, the leading female exponent of the Nashville sound, had many hits, including her recordings of Hank Cochran and Harlan Howard's "I Fall to Pieces" and Willie Nelson's "Crazy" in 1961. Cline also died in a plane crash, in 1963.

Ray Charles helped solidify country and western music's acceptance all over the world with his 1962 album *Modern Sounds of Country and Western Music.* The biggest single hit from that album was Don Gibson's "I Can't Stop Loving You." When Charles—the advocate of soul, rhythm and blues, jazz, blues, and rock—was asked by reporters how he had come to record country music, he gave credit to the Grand Ole Opry, which he said he had listened to since he was a child.

By the 1960s, most standards were recorded in Nashville, which by then had become the mecca of country and western music. One song covered by countless artists was George Jones's "She Thinks I Still Care" (1962). Roger Miller moved way beyond country acceptance with his universally popular "King of the Road" in 1964. Eddy Arnold's career was revitalized with numerous hits, notably Hank Cochran's "Make the World Go Away" of 1963. Glen Campbell, a prolific studio musician, became a star with John Hartford's "Gentle on My Mind" and Jim Webb's "By the Time I Get to Phoenix" in 1967. Merle Haggard, a living legend of country music, recorded "Mama Tried" in 1968 and "Hungry Eyes" in 1969; both refer in a semi-autobiographical way to his wild childhood and prison record. Tammy Wynette had a best-selling record in 1968, with "Stand By Your Man."

While country music was reaching acceptance with its new sound in the 1960s, many fans also expressed interest in a revival of older styles. Honky-tonk attracted new interest because it addressed itself effectively to the suffering found in the human condition. **Bluegrass,** invented in the mid-1940s by Bill Monroe and his Blue Grass Boys, also was revived in the 1960s, carried along by the folk music boom and the development of bluegrass festivals across the nation.

In the late 1960s and early 1970s, America was torn apart by conflicting ideologies concerning the Vietnam War and racial issues. A few country stars spoke out on the side of the conservative political right. For the first time, country and western music became equated with establishment values. But once the Vietnam War ended, the music placed renewed emphasis on the shared traits of all people.

With the new decade, rock 'n' roll performers showed more interest in country sounds, resulting in a fusion of musical genres sometimes called "country rock." The Byrds, with new band member Gram Parson, released the first country rock album, *Sweetheart of the Rodeo*, in 1968. A year later, Bob Dylan—who never hid the fact that Hank Williams was one of his favorite singers—released his album *Nashville Skyline*, which featured a duet with Johnny Cash. Dylan repaid the favor by appearing on Cash's network television show, which was broadcast from the Ryman Auditorium, the home of the Grand Ole Opry.

Among other country rock artists of this period were Linda Ronstadt, Poco, the Eagles, the Ozark Mountain Daredevils, Pure Prairie League, and the Flying Burrito Brothers. In 1972, the Nitty Gritty Dirt Band released its best-selling album, *Will the Circle Be Unbroken?*, which featured such legends of country music as Doc Watson, Merle Travis, Earl Scruggs, Roy Acuff, and Maybelle Carter.

The 1970s saw Nashville and the country music industry grow by leaps and bounds. Most major record companies established country and western branches. At this time, the industry was more interested in the crossover hit and the artist than in the song itself. As a result, there were a number of hits but not many songs that became standards. Many songs became so fully identified with the original singer that other artists dared not to **cover** them: for example, the autobiographical "Coal Miner's Daughter" (1969) by Loretta Lynn and "Coat of Many Colors (1969) by Dolly Parton. Although there have been few black country stars, Charley Pride had a major success with his recording of Ben Peters's "Kiss an Angel Good Morning" in 1971. John Denver, never strictly a country artist, performed two enduring country standards: "Take Me Home, Country Roads" in 1971 and "Thank God I'm a Country Boy" in 1975. Kris Kristofferson, an artist who was all country, seemed to write and perform nothing but standards, including "For the Good Times" (1968), "Me and Bobby McGee" (1969, with Fred L. Foster), "Help Me Make It Through the Night" (1970), and "Loving Her Was Easier (Than Anything I'll Ever Do Again)" (1970).

Tanya Tucker recorded the much-covered "Delta Dawn" in 1972 at the age of fourteen. Prior to that, the youngest female country artist to have had a hit was Brenda Lee, with Ronnie Self's "Sweet Nothin's" in 1959. Charlie Rich, originally a rockabilly artist, had such hits as "Behind Closed Doors" and "The Most Beautiful Girl" (both in 1973). Waylon Jennings was a self-styled "outlaw"; the songs he sang were about self-doubt and alienation, mostly couched in the imagery of the Old West, as in his own "Are You Sure Hank Done It This Way?" (1975).

Also in 1975, Freddy Fender became a star with a new approach to country sound, featuring a lispy and hurt-sounding voice that seemed surrounded by a claustrophobic presence, in such songs as "Before the Next Teardrop Falls" (1967) and "Wasted Days Wasted Nights" (1975). Loretta Lynn's younger sister, Crystal Gayle, made it big in 1977 with Richard Leigh's catchy "Don't It Make My Brown Eyes Blue."

Three performers reached superstardom in the 1970s: Conway Twitty, Willie Nelson, and Kenny Rogers. Twitty started out as Harold Jenkins, a rockabilly artist for Sun Records in the 1950s. Between 1970, with "Hello Darlin'," and 1977, with "I've Already Loved You in My Mind," he recorded ten of his own compositions that reached Number One on the charts. Nelson, a prolific songwriter, began supplying songs to other performers in the 1960s. In 1975, he recorded a remarkable concept album, *The Red Headed Stranger*, which included the national crossover hit "Blue Eyes Crying in the Rain" (1945) a song he did *not* write, but which established him as a nationally known figure. Rogers had not always been a country performer. He started in the 1960s as a member of various folk-country-pop groups until he decided to go full-blown country in the mid-1970s. In 1977, his recording of "Lucille" was Number One on the country chart and Number Five on the pop chart. His dominance of both charts continued well into the 1980s.

A new breed of young country performers entered the fold in the 1980s, including Randy Travis, Reba McEntire, K. T. Oslin, Clint Black, Alabama, and Garth Brooks. Brooks's 1990 album, *No Fences*, sold over five million copies; his 1991 album *Ropin' the Wind*, sold more than four million. Many artists, like Dwight Yoakam, k. d. lang, and Lyle Lovett, returned to updated versions of traditional songs and styles, sometimes ruffling the feathers of the then-current country and western establishment.

By 1990, country music had been embraced by fans throughout the world. **Britain** became a major supporter of the music, with a legion of its own country performers and recording artists. Country music also moved to other media. Many motion pictures dealt with the subject, for example, *Nashville* (1975), *Urban Cowboy* (1980), and *Sweet Dreams* (1985). *Hee Haw*, a country music and comedy show, had run on television uninterruptedly since 1969. In 1985, *Big River*—with music and lyrics by Roger Miller—won the Tony Award for best Broadway musical of the year.

In the June 1952 issue of the magazine *Country Song Roundup*, Frank "Pee Wee" King closed his column with these words:

> Yes sir, it does a folk (country) artist a world of good to know that our music is here to stay— I say "Our" music because it's yours and mine and everyone's music. It was given to us by our grandpappys and given to them by their grandpappys and it's been happenin' that way for generation after generation, which proves one thing—"Country Music is Real Music!"

Additional Songs

Act Naturally (1963)
Always on My Mind (1971)
Any Time (1921)
Bouquet of Roses (1948)
Cool Water (1936)
Detroit City (1963)
Funny How Time Slips Away (1961)
The Grand Tour (1974)
Green, Green Grass of Home (1965)
Half as Much (1951)
I Can't Help It (If I'm Still in Love With You) (1951)
I Love You a Thousand Ways (1951)
I Love You Because (1949)
If You've Got the Money, I've Got the Time (1950)
I'm Movin' On (1950)
It Wasn't God Who Made Honky Tonk Angels (1952)
Orange Blossom Special (1938)
Singing the Blues (1954)
Six Days on the Road (1963)
Slippin' Around (1949)
Take These Chains From My Heart (1952)
Take This Job and Shove It (1977)
There Stands the Glass (1951)
Welcome to My World (1961)
The Wild Side of Life (1952)

Jeffrey Cahn

Bibliography

Dellar, Fred, and Roy Thompson, with Douglas B. Green. *The Illustrated Encyclopedia of Country Music*. 1977.

Dew, Joan. *Singers and Sweethearts: The Women of Country Music*. 1977.

Gentry, Linnell, ed. *A History and Encyclopedia of Country, Western, and Gospel Music*. 1969.

Green, Douglas B. *Country Roots: The Origins of Country Music*. 1976.

Guralnick, Peter. "Ray Charles." *The Rolling Stone Illustrated History of Rock and Roll*. 1980.

Hemphill, Paul. *The Nashville Sound: Bright Lights and Country Music*. 1970.

King, Frank "Pee Wee." "King's Corn Fab." *Country Song Roundup* (June 1952).

Malone, Bill C. *Country Music, U.S.A.: A Fifty-Year History*. 1968.

———. *The Smithsonian Collection of Classic Country Music*. Liner notes to record album (n.d.).

Morris, James R. *The Smithsonian Collection of Classic Country Music*. Liner notes to record album (n.d.).

Shestack, Melvin. *The Country Music Encyclopedia*. 1974.

Stambler, Irwin, and Grelun Landon. *Encyclopedia of Folk, Country, and Western Music*. 1975.

———. *Golden Guitars: The Story of Country Music*. 1971.

COVER

Generally, the term "cover" means simply a recorded version of a song other than the original. But in the 1950s, during the early years of **rock 'n' roll**, the term specifically referred to a second version by a white artist(s), on a major label, of a song first recorded by a black artist(s) for a smaller, independent label.

During this period, the big 50,000-watt stations would not play **rhythm and blues** (R&B) because of its "black sound," and so a significant number of white listeners were unaware that these originals existed. The charts were similarly segregated, with separate lists for both R&B and pop. Thus, when an Artist and Repertory (A&R) man at one of the major record companies learned of a black disc on an independent label that showed hit potential, he would quickly cover the song with a recording by one of his white artists, making a record that extracted the catchy elements from the black version but polished and sweetened them for white ears. So Bill Haley and the Comets' version of "Shake, Rattle and Roll" for Decca (1954) eliminated the sexual innuendo of Joe Turner's recording for Atlantic, while the Crew Cuts' version of "Sh-Boom" (1954) for Mercury altered the vocal harmony of the original Chords' recording on the Cat label to **barbershop** style and added a lush orchestral background.

Cover versions received wider airplay on the more powerful stations that featured white music and, therefore, usually achieved greater commercial success than the original versions. In 1957, for example, the Diamonds' version of "Little Darlin'" managed to reach Number Three on the R&B chart and Number Two on the pop chart, while the Gladiolas' original on the Excello label scored on the R&B chart only. An example of a black covering a black was Chubby Checker's version of Hank Ballard's "The Twist" (1959), which buried the Hank Ballard original and became a Number One hit not once but twice! The Crew Cuts' version of "Sh-Boom" even beat the original on the R&B chart, peaking at Number Five, while the Chords could do no better than Number Nine.

While the majors were attentive to the independents for songs they could cover, they were frequently apprised of potential cover tunes by the smaller labels themselves, who could not compete with the majors in terms of distribution. What the smaller companies lost in record sales, they might possibly recoup in royalties, for they usually owned the copyright to the material recorded by black artists. Inevitably, it was the black artists who were the losers, although they might benefit indirectly from their association with a hit established by white performers.

The covering of non-pop material by pop artists was first practiced consistently in the early 1950s by Mitch Miller, then A&R chief for Columbia and later a staunch opponent of the new rock music. Miller had several of Columbia's top pop vocalists cover **country and western** hits: Tony Bennett recorded Hank Williams's "Cold, Cold Heart" in 1951, while Jo Stafford recorded his "Jambalaya" the following year.

Many of the larger record companies indulged in the practice of covering black rhythm and blues; Dot and Mercury were probably the two most significant. For Mercury, the Crew Cuts recorded, in addition to "Sh-Boom," "Earth Angel, (Will You Be Mine)" (1954; original by the Penguins), "Don't Be Angry" (1955; original by Nappy Brown), and "A Story Untold" (1955; original by the Nutmegs); while the Diamonds, in addition to "Little Darlin'," covered "Why Do Fools Fall in Love?" (1956; original by Frankie Lymon and the Teenagers), "Church Bells May Ring" (1956; original by the Willows), and "Silhouettes" (1957; original by the Rays). Mercury also recorded Georgia Gibbs and Patti Page, both of whom released cover material. Dot released cover versions by Pat Boone of, for example, Fats Domino's "Ain't That a Shame" (1955), Little Richard's "Tutti-Frutti" (1955), and the Flamingos' "I'll Be Home" (1956), as well as covers by other pop artists such as Gale Storm, who recorded "I Hear Your Knocking" (1955; original by Smiley Lewis), "Why Do Fools Fall in Love?" (1956), and "Ivory Tower" (1956; original by Otis Williams and the Charms).

As disc jockeys, following the lead of such pioneers as Alan Freed, Dewey Phillips, and Wolfman Jack, began playing more of the original recordings, and exposure of black artists increased through rock 'n' roll concerts, white listeners grew more aware of black rhythm and blues, and so the practice eventually disappeared.

Barry Keith Grant

Bibliography

Gillett, Charlie. *The Sound of the City: The Rise of Rock and Roll*. 1970.

See also: Crossover

CRAZINESS. *SEE* MADNESS

CROSSOVER

"Crossover" is a term used to describe a song or performer equally at home in two or more genres. Although the word itself was added to our vocabulary only in the 1970s, the practice of crossing over goes back to music's beginnings. Among the many masters of crossover were J. S. Bach, Mozart, Liszt, and Rachmaninoff—all of whom used popular themes as subjects.

The varieties of crossover in twentieth-century popular song are bewildering. Included are songs like "Have I Told You Lately That I Love You" (1945) and "Take Me Home, Country Roads" (1971) that have moved into the city from their rural beginnings. In the other direction are such songs as "Star Dust" (1929) and "Blue Moon" (1934), which have made the transition from Tin Pan Alley to country and western. Songs in

the early British rock style of the Beatles have won acceptance in the fields of jazz and easy listening; virtually every type of performer in every field has done "Yesterday" (1965) in one style or another. On the other hand, mainstream songs like "I Only Have Eyes for You" (1934) have made the transition from love ballad to pop-rock.

Many jazz-oriented songs have crossed over from their original presentation to middle-of-the-road acceptance. An example is "Misty" (1954), originally conceived by pianist Erroll Garner as a jazz ballad. The uptempo country arrangement recorded by Willie Nelson is completely at variance with the composer's intentions, but nevertheless won new fans for the song. "Lullaby of Birdland" (1952) was first recorded by its composer, George Shearing, but has since been embraced by a number of artists in diverse fields. Such songs as "Lover Man (Oh Where Can You Be?)" (1942) and "'Round Midnight" (1944) also eventually gained an audience much broader than simply the jazz aficionados who first knew them.

An early modern crossover performer was the soprano Eileen Farrell, who made the transition from opera to popular music in the late 1950s. Farrell was in Italy performing operatic arias when Louis Armstrong was booked to appear with her on a television program. Armstrong became ill and the operatic soprano offered to fill in for him with some songs by Rodgers and Hart. Since then, she has moved comfortably between Giacomo Puccini and Harold Arlen.

Linda Ronstadt is another crossover performer, equally at home in the fields of Tin Pan Alley and the Top Forty; she also has appeared in opera. Toni Tennille, another singer, has surprised audiences by handling both contemporary pop material and standard show tunes. Willie Nelson, without changing the timbre of his voice, often strays from his home ground, country music, to sing a standard song. Versatility indeed became a hallmark of performance from the 1970s onward, when crossing over became the rule rather than the exception.

Loonis McGlohon

See also: Cover

CRYING

The subject of crying has a long history in popular song, encompassing more than half a century: from "I Cried for You" (1923) to "Don't Cry Out Loud" (1976).

Perhaps the best-known song about crying is "Misty," a song so popular that the expression "Play 'Misty' for me," usually addressed to piano players, has become part of the vernacular. The expression has even been used as the title of a film about a radio disc jockey. The song was composed by the jazz pianist Erroll Garner in 1954, and its blue notes, major sevenths, and major ninths have made it a favorite of jazz musicians, along with the similarly constructed "Cry Me a River" (1953). Crying is also the theme of a very popular tango "Don't Cry for Me, Argentina," from *Evita* (1978).

Tears are, of course, a primary manifestation of crying and, as such, have led to a number of songs, including "Dancing With Tears in My Eyes" (1930), "And Her Tears Flowed Like Wine" (1944), "Tears of a Clown" (1967), and "Before the Next Teardrop Falls" (1967).

Since crying is merely an outward expression of inner sorrow, it is perhaps appropriate that so many songs on the subject use the characteristically expressive devices of blue notes, dissonant intervals, and minor keys.

Additional Songs

Big Girls Don't Cry (1962)
Blue Eyes Crying in the Rain (1945)
Boo-Hoo! (1937)
Cry (1951)
Cry Baby (1963)
Cry Like a Baby (1968)
Crying (1961)
Crying in the Chapel (1953)
Crying Time (1964)
Don't Let the Sun Catch You Crying (1964)
I Cried a Tear (1958)
I'm So Lonesome I Could Cry (1949)
Judy's Turn to Cry (1963)
The Little White Cloud That Cried (1951)
Lonely Teardrops (1958)
Moanin' Low (1929)
My Heart Cries for You (1950)
96 Tears (1966)
She Cried (1962)
Teardrops From My Eyes (1950)
Tears on My Pillow (1958)
When a Gypsy Makes His Violin Cry (1935)
When Doves Cry (1984)
Willow Weep for Me (1932)
You've Got Me Crying Again (1933)

See also: Loneliness

CUBA

The music of Cuba, with its mixture of Spanish and African elements, exerted a major influence on mainstream popular music in the United States as early as the mid-1920s. Besides being the source of such **dance crazes** as the habañera, the son, the **rumba**, the mambo, the **conga**, and the **cha cha cha**, the island nation was the place of origin of numerous attractive songs and also the birthplace of the celebrated composer Ernesto Lecuona (1896–1963).

Lecuona, who graduated from the National Conservatory of Havana in 1911, wrote numerous songs that achieved worldwide popularity. Among them were "Siboney" (1929), "Jungle Drums" (1933), "Say 'Si Si'"

(1936), "Two Hearts That Pass in the Night," (1941), and "Always in My Heart," (1942). He also collaborated on several **adaptations** from his own suites, including "The Breeze and I" (1940, from his suite *Andalucía*) and "At the Crossroads" (1942, from his suite *Malagueña*).

One of the first rumbas to sweep the United States (and the world) was "The Peanut Vendor (El Manicero)," introduced in 1930 by Don Azpiazú's Havana Casino Orchestra at the Palace Theater in New York. It was the forerunner of a flood of Cuban imports, among them "Mama Inez" (1931), "Green Eyes" ("Aquellos Ojos Verdes," 1931), and "Perhaps, Perhaps, Perhaps" ("Quizas, Quizas, Quizas," 1947).

A series of new dances emanated from Cuba in the 1950s. First came the mambo, popularized with the songs "Cuban Mambo" (1950), "Mambo Jambo" (1950), and "Sway" ("Quien Sera," 1953). Next came the cha cha cha, which became enormously popular in the United States in 1955 when the French import "Cherry Pink and Apple Blossom White" was recorded as "Cerazo Rosa" by Perez Prado and His Orchestra. Many other songs were recorded as cha cha chas, including the Cuban "Sweet and Gentle" (originally "Me Lo Dijo Adela," 1955) and the Greek "Never on Sunday" (1960).

When Fidel Castro assumed power on February 16, 1959, direct Cuban influence on American popular song virtually ceased, with some isolated exceptions such as "Guantanamera," popularized by folksinger Pete Seeger in 1966. But indirectly, Afro-Cuban influence continued to be felt in the waning years of the century in such manifestations as the **boogaloo** and **salsa.**

Bibliography

Roberts, John Storm. *The Latin Tinge: The Impact of Latin American Music on the United States.* 1979.

See also: Latin America; Mexico; Nations

CZECHOSLOVAKIA

Czechoslovakia's contribution to American popular music is twofold. First, its capital city, Prague, was the birthplace of Rudolf Friml (1879–1972), an outstanding composer of **operettas,** who wrote such classic songs as "Gianina Mia" (1912), "Sympathy" (1912), "L'Amour Toujours l'Amour" (1922), "Indian Love Call" (1924), "Rose Marie" (1924), "Only a Rose" (1925), and "The Donkey Serenade" (1937).

Czechoslovakia's second contribution to American music was a song called "The Beer Barrel Polka (Roll Out the Barrel)," originally written in 1934 as "Skoda Lasky," or "Lost Love." The song attained worldwide popularity after its recording by the Andrews Sisters in 1939, and remains a standard **polka** to this day.

See also: Foreign Influence

d

DANCE CRAZES

Dozens of dance crazes have come and gone in the United States over the last hundred years. There were, however, a few periods when veritable explosions of dance fever erupted: before **World War I**, before **World War II**, and in the late 1970s. Inevitably, songs were written to accompany these dances. In some instances, as in "Ballin' the Jack" (1919) and "Charleston" (1923), the song and the dance were one. Most songs, however, were merely written in the meter and tempo appropriate to the dance.

Around the turn of the century, the **waltz** was triumphant, overshadowing other dances imported from Europe, such as the scottische and **polka**. It was danced to several tempos. As the traditional Viennese waltz in fast tempo, it was danced to such operetta favorites as "The Merry Widow Waltz" and "A Waltz Dream" (both 1907). In moderate tempo, it was danced to Tin Pan Alley songs like "After the Ball" (1892) and "Take Me Out to the Ball Game" (1908). Around 1910, a still slower variety of waltz, called the Boston, or American, waltz, became the rage, danced to such sentimental songs as "Let Me Call You Sweetheart" (1910) and "Alice Blue Gown" (1919).

But the waltz was far from being the only dance of the time. Walking to **march** music was also in vogue, as were the **two-step** and a strutting sort of dance called the **cakewalk**. As melodies became more syncopated, **ragtime** took hold, with songs like "A Hot Time in the Old Town" (1896) and "Hello! Ma Baby" (1899).

The first explosion of dance fever started around 1910, with a craze for ragtime dances. These included a veritable menagerie of "**animal**" dances: the grizzly bear, turkey trot, bunny hug, camel walk, kangaroo hop, horse trot, lame duck, and walking the dog. Many of these dances involved grotesque movements of the arms and legs. When Irving Berlin wrote "Everybody's Doin' It Now" in 1911, he was referring to the turkey trot, but "it" could have applied just as well to any of a dozen other dance fads of the day.

The most popular dance team of the day was Vernon and Irene Castle. They popularized many new dances, instituted tea dances in **New York City** cafés and restaurants, established dance schools, and conducted dance contests. They introduced the Argentine **tango** in 1913. Danced to still-popular songs, such as "El Choclo" (1913) and "La Cumparsita" (1916), the tango became the rage in New York. The Castles also invented new figures for that old standby, the waltz, with the Castle Hesitation Waltz, the Castle Classic Waltz, and the Castle Innovation Waltz, and devised new dances with names like the Castle Walk, the Castle Maxixe, the Castle Lame Duck, the Castle Tango, and the Castle House Rag.

The vogue for new dances led to one of the first dance-instructional songs, "Ballin' the Jack"—the lyrics of which tell the neophyte where to put his or her feet—in 1913. But a far more important development that year was the introduction of a dance destined to become universally popular, the **fox trot**. Introduced by a vaudevillian named Harry Fox, it involved promenading up and down stage with several pulchritudinous partners and came to be called "Mr. Fox's Trot." It remains the most indestructible of dances, suitable for thousands of songs in slow or moderate tempo and duple meter. Other shorter-lived dance crazes of the time were the toddle and the shimmy shawobble, the latter inspired by the song "I Wish I Could Shimmy Like My Sister Kate" in 1919. There also were faster dances like the **one-step**, which led in the 1920s to the **peabody**.

The **Roaring Twenties** saw a proliferation of new dances. Many were uptempo and in duple meter, reflecting the carefree spirit of the age. The song "Charleston" (1923) became the namesake of a dance craze of its own, which lasted through the 1920s. Flappers and their beaus danced in speakeasies to dance-inspired songs like "Black Bottom" (1926) and "The Varsity Drag" (1927). Other dances of the 1920s included the Java, the flea hop, the sloppy sailor walk, the sugar foot stomp, and a dance called the Lindy hop, commemorating Charles Lindbergh's solo flight across the Atlantic in 1927.

Ballroom dancing became the vogue in the 1930s, aided and abetted by the rise of the **big bands**. Spacious ballrooms like the Palladium, Meadowbrook, Avalon, Glen Island Casino, and Roseland sprang up throughout the country, and there was dancing in hotel nightclubs as well. The fox trot and the waltz were still popular, but a new type of dance developed out of **swing**. The intoxicating rhythm of this new music caused a revival of the Lindy hop and the emergence of other hopping dances, such as the Hoosier hop, Dixie stomp, Roosevelt hop, Westchester, shag, trucking, Susy-q, big apple, and pecking. There was also a dance, characterized by elaborate footwork, jumps, and lifts, that came out of Harlem. It was called the "jitterbug," because of its resemblance to "jittery bugs"; the name became a general term for dancing to swing music.

A love affair of the North American public with the music of **Latin America** began in 1930 with Don Azpiazú's recording of the Cuban song "The Peanut Vendor." It spawned a series of Latin dance crazes that lasted for decades, including the **rumba** (1930), siboney (1931), **samba** and **conga** (1939), Balboa (1942), **mambo** (1949), **cha cha cha** (1950), **merengue** (1951), la plena (1955), pachanga (1959), cumbia (1959), and **bossa nova** (1960). Among other Latin American dances to take hold in subsequent years were the **salsa** and lambada.

Another dance from abroad was the Lambeth walk, introduced by a song of that name in the British musical *Me and My Girl* (1937). Dances were also manufactured by American filmmakers. The most prominent dance team of the 1930s, Fred Astaire and Ginger Rogers, introduced several made-to-order songs as dance numbers for their films: "Carioca," in *Flying Down to Rio* (1933); "The Continental," in *The Gay Divorcee* (1934); and "The Piccolino," in *Top Hat* (1935). Although none of these numbers became popular as dances, they remain as songs in the standard repertoire.

Another development in dance was the polka revival of 1939, inspired by the success of the Czech import "Beer Barrel Polka (Roll Out the Barrel)." Other songs that inspired similarly titled dances were "Truckin'" (1935), "Peckin'" (1937), "Boomps-a-Daisy" (1940), and "The Bunny Hop" (1952).

With the emergence of **rock 'n' roll**, an entirely new style of dancing arose. Couples no longer remained in close contact, but were separated and faced one another—each person interpreting the music in his or her own way. The first dance of this sort was the twist. Beginning in 1959 with Hank Ballard's "The Twist," popularized by Chubby Checker in 1962, the craze continued with "Twistin' U.S.A." (1960), "Twist and Shout" (1960), "Let's Twist Again" (1961), and "Twisting the Night Away" (1962). Other rock 'n' roll dances came and went: the hully gully, mashed potato, fly, duck, swim, **boogaloo**, fish, Watusi, frug, jerk, monkey shake, funky chicken, and more.

A new dance craze erupted in 1975, marked by the appearance of a song called "The Hustle." **Disco** involved frantic and uninhibited dancing to very loud recorded music supplied by **disc jockeys**. Unlike some of its predecessors, disco dancing lasted a relatively short time: only five years, In sharp contrast, ballroom dances like the fox trot, waltz, rumba, and tango—all of which began as dance crazes long ago—live on.

Bibliography

Ellfeldt, Lois, and Virgil L. Morton. *This Is Ballroom Dance.* 1974.

Erenberg, Lewis A. *Steppin' Out: New York Nightlife and the Transformation of American Culture, 1890–1930.* 1984.

See also: Charleston; Dancing

DANCING

Many songs have been written on the subject of dancing. Irving Berlin, always sensitive to popular trends, wrote at least a dozen. They include the 1921 hit "Everybody Step"; "It Only Happens When I Dance With You," written for the 1948 film *Easter Parade*; and three memorable songs first sung and danced in cinema by the magical team of Fred Astaire and Ginger Rogers: "Cheek to Cheek" (1935), "Let's Face the Music and Dance" (1936), and "Change Partners" (1938).

Songs about dancing tend to focus upon four different aspects of the dance: invitations, descriptions, marathons, and ballrooms. In the category of invitations are two songs called "Shall We Dance?" The first was written by Ira and George Gershwin for the 1937 film of the same name; the second, by Oscar Hammerstein II and Richard Rodgers, for the 1951 musical *The King and I*. Other invitational songs are Benny Goodman's theme "Let's Dance" (1935), "Papa, Won't You Dance With Me?" (1947), "Dance With Me Henry" (1955), and "Save the Last Dance for Me" (1960).

Descriptive songs include the tearful "Dancing With Tears in My Eyes" of 1930, the joyful and imaginative "Dancing on the Ceiling" of 1930, the romantic "Dancing in the Dark" of 1931, the early rock 'n' roll standard "Shake, Rattle and Roll" of 1954, and the frenzied disco number "Flashdance . . . What a Feeling" of 1983.

Dance marathons were contests of endurance popular in the 1930s. They live on in the titles of several songs, such as "I Could Have Danced All Night," from *My Fair Lady* (1956); and the disco favorites "Keep on Truckin'" (1973) and "Dancing Machine" (1974).

Ballrooms are represented in popular song by the early sheet-music favorite "After the Ball" (1892), the two-step "The Darktown Strutters' Ball" (1917), and the disc jockey theme "It's Make Believe Ballroom Time" (1940). "Ten Cents a Dance" (1930) is the lament of a dance hall hostess who complains: "Trumpets are tearing my eardrums, Customers crush my toes."

Finally, a tongue-in-cheek refusal to dance is featured in the 1935 musical film *Roberta*, when Astaire sings to Rogers the lovely Dorothy Fields–Jerome Kern song "I Won't Dance."

Additional Songs

Arthur Murray Taught Me Dancing in a Hurry (1942)
Come Dance With Me (1959)
Could I Have This Dance (1980)
Dance With a Dolly (1944)
Dance With Me (1959)
Dancing in the Dark (1984)
Dancing in the Street (1964)
Dancing Queen (1977)
I'll Dance at Your Wedding (1947)
I'm in a Dancing Mood (1936)
Last Dance (1977)
Let's Dance (1983)
Play Gypsies—Dance Gypsies (1926)
Shadow Dancing (1978)
Stompin' at the Savoy (1934)
Twisting the Night Away (1962)
When Francis Dances With Me (1921)
When You Dance (1955)
You Make Me Feel Like Dancing (1977)
You Should Be Dancing (1976)

See also: Dance Crazes

DAY

The day, like the **night**, has long been a favorite subject of songwriters. As far back as 1907, Gus Edwards introduced his unpretentious waltz "School Days (When We Were a Couple of Kids)" into his vaudeville act. Three years later, in 1910, Sophie Tucker introduced another famous "day" song into her act: "Some of These Days" by Shelton Brooks; Tucker used it thereafter as her theme song.

Two "day" songs deserve special mention for their quality and endurance. Cole Porter's "Night and Day" (1932) is a remarkable marriage of words and music: a romantic song replete with interesting harmonies, exciting lyrics, repeated notes, and chromaticism. Maria Grever's "What a Diff'rence a Day Made?" (1934) originated in Mexico as a tango, but has been performed as rumba, foxtrot, ballad, and disco song.

Several interesting "day" songs have to do with the **weather**. They include "A Foggy Day" (1937), "Here's That Rainy Day" (1953), "Those Lazy Hazy Crazy Days of Summer" (1964), "On a Clear Day" (1966), and

"Rainy Days and Mondays" (1970). Two very sophisticated songs on the subject are Johnny Mercer and Rube Bloom's "Day In—Day Out" (1939) and Oscar Hammerstein II and Jerome Kern's "All Through the Day" (1946). The song "Daybreak" (1942) was extracted from Ferde Grofé's *Mississippi Suite* of 1926.

The subject seems to have attracted its share of "twins": two songs with similar titles. There have been two songs called "Day by Day," one in 1946, the other in 1971. There are two "days in the life": "A Day in the Life of a Fool," a Brazilian import of 1966, and the Beatles' "A Day in the Life," imported from Britain a year later. Three "lovely day" songs were written by Irving Berlin: "Isn't This a Lovely Day" in 1935, "It's a Lovely Day Tomorrow" in 1939, and "It's a Lovely Day Today" in 1950. Two of a number of "daydream" songs are "Daydream" (1966) and "Daydream Believer" (1967). But only one song bears the enigmatic title "A Hard Day's Night": the famous song introduced by the Beatles in 1964.

There have been joyful songs on the subject, such as "A Perfect Day" (1910), "Lucky Day" (1926), "Great Day!" (1929), "Happy Days Are Here Again" (1929), "It's a Most Unusual Day" (1948), and "(On) A Wonderful Day Like Today" (1964); nostalgic songs like "Golden Days" (1924), "Days of Wine and Roses" (1962), and "Those Were the Days" (1968); and songs of hope and expectation like "Some Day I'll Find You" (1931), "Some Day My Prince Will Come" (1937), and "Some Day We'll Be Together" (1970).

Then there are songs about days past and days to come. Three famous examples are Otto Harbach and Jerome Kern's "Yesterdays" (1933), John Lennon and Paul McCartney's "Yesterday" (1965), and Charles Aznavour and Herbert Kretzmer's "Yesterday, When I Was Young" (1965). Songs about the future include "Domani" (1955), "Mañana (Is Soon Enough for Me)" (1948), "There's No Tomorrow" (1949), "Till Tomorrow" (1959), and "Tomorrow" (1977).

Additional Songs

All Day and All of the Night (1964)
Every Day Is Ladies' Day With Me (1906)
I Won't Last a Day Without You (1972)
It's a Good Day (1946)
It's a Great Day for the Irish (1940)
Let a Smile Be Your Umbrella (On a Rainy Day) (1927)
Many a New Day (1943)
One Fine Day (1963)
Some Day I'll Find You (1931)
Some Day You'll Want Me to Want You (1946)
That Great Come-and-Get-It Day (1946)
Wasted Days Wasted Nights (1975)
When Day Is Done (1926)
Where the Blue of the Night Meets the Gold of the Day (1931)

See also: Days of the Week; Memory; Time of Day

DAYS OF THE WEEK

As subjects of popular song, weekends are preferred over all other **days** of the week. Far more songs have been written about Saturday and Sunday than about any other day. "Don't Get Around Much Anymore" (1943) qualifies for inclusion in this category because of its famous opening line: "Miss the Saturday dance." Other songs about Saturday include the big band favorite of 1944, "Saturday Night (Is the Loneliest Night of the Week" (its message applied to millions of lonely women when the song was written, at the height of World War II) and "Come Saturday Morning," a gentle waltz introduced in the 1969 film *The Sterile Cuckoo.*

Another waltz, this time about Sunday, was the lasting "On a Sunday Afternoon" (1902). More than a half-century later, a very different type of Sunday song appeared: "Never on Sunday," from the film of the same name. Written by the eminent Greek composer Manos Hadjidakis, it won the Academy Award for best song in 1960. It is actually a *rebetiko*, a type of Greek urban folk song, but is very often performed as a cha cha cha. Another enduring song about the day is "Sunday Mornin'," introduced in 1968 by Spanky and Our Gang.

Other days of the week are poorly represented in the literature; there are no songs at all about Thursday or Friday. However, Monday is mentioned in several songs, including "Monday, Monday," popularized by the Mamas and the Papas in 1966, and "Rainy Days and Mondays," popularized by the Carpenters in 1970. Tuesday makes a brief but unforgettable appearance in Ira Gershwin's lyrics for "The Man I Love" (1924): "Maybe Tuesday will be my good news day."

Additional Songs

Another Saturday Night (1963)
Blue Monday (1957)
Eight Days a Week (1964)
Saturday in the Park (1972)
Saturday Night (1976)
Saturday Night at the Movies (1964)
Saturday Night Fish Fry (1949)
A Sunday Kind of Love (1946)
Sunday, Monday or Always (1943)
Wednesday's Child (1967)

See also: Night; Time of Day

DENMARK

Denmark's contribution to American popular music is minor but nevertheless striking. The country is the birthplace of Jacob Gade (1879–1963), composer of one of the most popular **tangos** of all time, "Jalousie" in 1925—given English words as "Jealousy." Denmark is also the place of origin of the **novelty song** "Alley Cat" (1961)—first called "Omkring et Flygel," or "Around the Piano."

See also: Foreign Influence

DEPRESSION YEARS

On October 28, 1929, one day before the infamous stock market crash, Paul Whiteman and His Orchestra made a recording of "Great Day," from the musical of the same name (1929). It was to be the last "great day" America would see for more than a decade.

The 1920s can be characterized as a period when enjoyment of prosperity reigned supreme (*see* Roaring Twenties). The nightmare of World War I was over, life was carefree, and the music of the nation reflected this. "Runnin' Wild," a hit song of 1922, served as the unofficial anthem of the times. It was the age of **jazz**, the automobile, motion pictures, and stock market deals. F. Scott Fitzgerald painted a picture of American youth wearing raccoon coats, drinking out of hip flasks, necking in Ford roadsters, and attending wild parties held in speakeasies.

But all that came to an end on October 29, Black Tuesday. The decade that came in "roaring" would go out with a moan. After that fateful day in 1929, the economy began a long spiral downward. By the winter of 1932, nine thousand banks had closed. Unemployment was at an all-time high; millions of Americans were out of work. One of the country's best **blues** singers, Bessie Smith, summed up the tragic situation with her last recording hit in 1929: "Nobody Knows You When You're Down and Out" (written in 1923). People went from being homeowners to vagabonds. "A Cottage for Sale" became a popular song on the **radio** in 1930.

Displaced people queued up on bread lines for any morsel to eat. This was a time when street vendors sold apples for pennies and people could not afford to buy them. The lucky ones who worked earned only a few cents an hour, but their employers still had difficulty showing a profit.

During the Depression years, radio became a lifeline to those who were able to afford one. The price of live entertainment and phonograph records was prohibitive for most people, but radio entertainment, musical and otherwise, provided a free alternative. In 1929, Thomas Alva Edison's record business closed due to declining sales; he turned to radio production.

While political and economic events have always shaped the course of music, seldom have writers based so many songs on one central theme. It was almost as if **Tin Pan Alley** exalted in its new-found inspiration.

Songs written about and inspired by the Great Depression took three different directions. At one end of the spectrum, they were melancholy in nature, often contained a high degree of self-pity, and were frequently performed by female entertainers known as "torch singers." These singers had started appearing in nightclubs, cabarets, and Broadway shows at the end of World War I. They would sing about how their man had "done them wrong" by loving them and leaving them and how, as a result, their lives were hopeless and bankrupt. As radio grew in popularity, these singers gained a new forum in which to be heard. Within the context of the Depression, their songs became metaphors for the despondency in so many lives. They were carrying the torch not only for the man that got away, but also for the good life that was now gone. Songs of this type include "Moanin' Low" and "Why Was I Born?" from 1929; "Ten Cents a Dance," "Love for Sale," and "Body and Soul," from 1930; and "Remember My Forgotten Man," from 1933.

At the opposite end of the spectrum were the songs written to keep people's spirits up and give them the courage to go on. Some examples are "Life Is Just a Bowl of Cherries" and "(Potatoes Are Cheaper—Tomatoes Are Cheaper) Now's the Time to Fall in Love" (both from 1931). "When My Ship Comes In" was a lighthearted and uplifting song from 1934. But perhaps the ultimate song of inspiration was "Happy Days Are Here Again," first released on record in 1930, and adopted by Franklin D. Roosevelt as his presidential campaign song in 1932.

Positioned between these two points on the spectrum were songs that shared characteristics both melancholy and inspirational. These songs were dark and foreboding in tone, as if their characters were frightened by the circumstances in which they found themselves, unsure of what was on the horizon, but nevertheless determined to carry on. Four examples are "Dancing in the Dark" and "Just a Gigolo," from 1931; "Got the Jitters" (1934); and "Let's Face the Music and Dance" (1936).

There were, in addition, songs that used geography, space, and the forces of nature as allusions for good and bad times. Examples are "River, Stay 'Way From My Door" (1931), "Stormy Weather" and "It's Only a Paper Moon" (both from 1933), and "Where the Blue of the Night Meets the Gold of the Day" and "When the Moon Comes Over the Mountain" (both from 1931).

When the Depression began, the three most famous romantic singers in the United States were Russ Columbo, Rudy Vallée, and Harry Lillis (Bing) Crosby. Columbo, who co-wrote many of his own songs, among them "Prisoner of Love" in 1931, died from an accidental shooting in 1934. Vallée, whose many hits included "Let's Put Out the Lights (And Go to Sleep)" in 1932, was a tremendously popular singer who failed to sustain his career after the mid-1940s. And then there was Bing. His voice was the panacea that America so desperately needed. With his resonant baritone, his breezy persona, and his intimate "crooning" style, he wrote a new chapter in popular song. He remained one of America's greatest stars until his death in 1977. Bing made standards of many Depression-era songs, including "Wrap Your Troubles in Dreams" (1931), "Just One More Chance" (1931), "June in January" (1934), "It's Easy to Remember" (1934), "Pennies from Heaven" (1936), and—the definitive song of the Depression—"Brother, Can You Spare a Dime?" (1932).

After President Franklin Delano Roosevelt launched the first federal relief programs in 1933, the economy started to turn around slightly. The repeal of Prohibition stimulated the opening of thousands of bars and cocktail lounges, many equipped with jukeboxes. Records were now reaching a new market and becoming affordable, dropping in price from seventy-five cents to thirty-five cents. Reflecting the upswing in the economy, "Are You Makin' Any Money?" became a hit song of 1933.

In that same year Warner Brothers produced two great film musicals, Gold Diggers of 1933 and Forty-Second Street, which proved to be fabulous escapes for many desolate Americans. From his starring roles in these movies, Dick Powell emerged as a popular musical performer. Among the uplifting songs he introduced were "We're in the Money," also known as "The Gold Diggers' Song" (1933); "I Only Have Eyes for You" (1934); and "With Plenty of Money and You" (1936). These songs and several others mentioned above were written by the songwriting team of Al Dubin and Harry Warren, among the most prolific writers working in film musicals.

Film operettas were also very successful in the 1930s. Two of the biggest stars of this genre were Jeanette MacDonald and Nelson Eddy who, in 1936, had a hit recording of Rudolf Friml's "Indian Love Call," from the film Rose Marie.

Not all songwriters fared as well in Hollywood. In 1932, Cole Porter's entire score for the film The Gay Divorcée was rejected, except for "Night and Day"; Richard Rodgers and Lorenz Hart failed miserably with their musical film Hallelujah, I'm a Bum.

By 1939, the worst was over. The Depression had made a hero of everyone who survived. Americans began looking forward to the 1940s in the hope of better times. "Over the Rainbow," sung by Judy Garland in the 1939 film The Wizard of Oz, was an appropriate song to end the decade.

Jeffrey Cahn

Bibliography

Goldston, Robert. The Great Depression: The United States in the Thirties. 1968.

Hughes, Jonathan. American Economic History. 1983.

Whitcomb, Ian. After the Ball: Pop Music From Rag to Rock. 1972.

See also: Golden Age; Money; Musical Comedy; Revues

DEPTH

As a subject, depth has long been of interest to songwriters. Perhaps this is because of the ambiguity and versatility of the word "deep." Songs have been written about the depths of bodies of water—"Deep River" (1917), "Between the Devil and the Deep Blue

Sea"; the depth of one person's **love** for another—"How Deep Is the Ocean?" (1932), "How Deep is Your Love" (1977); a shade of **color**—"Deep Purple" (1939); a **state**—"Deep in the Heart of Texas" (1941); and even, in a humorous vein, about a skyscraper—"Down in the Depths, on the Ninetieth Floor" (1936).

Written in the waning years of the nineteenth century, "Asleep in the Deep" (1897) remains a favorite of bass singers, who use it to demonstrate the depth of their **range**, which reaches its lowest point on the word "beware." A high point of Sigmund Romberg's 1924 operetta *The Student Prince* is the waltz "Deep in My Heart, Dear." Other songs on the subject include "Deep Night" (1921) and "Deep in a Dream" (1938). Many of the above songs convey a sense of deepness by the jagged contours of their melodies, the abundance of their long-held notes, and the wideness of their ranges.

See also: Height

DESPAIR. *SEE* CRYING

DIALECT

Regional dialects have had a place in American popular song since colonial days. The nineteenth-century **coon song**, for example, a regular feature of the **minstrel show**, was always in southern dialect. It led directly to such turn-of-the-century **ragtime** songs as "A Hot Time in the Old Town" (1896) and "Under the Bamboo Tree" (1902). Most of the dialect in these songs is deliberately ungrammatical and contains frequent misspellings. The verse of "A Hot Time," for example, contains such passages as "Dere's gwine to be a meeting" and "Where you knowded ev'rybody and dey all knowded you," while the chorus of "Under the Bamboo Tree" begins with the famous line: "If you lak-a-me-lak I lak-a you." Among other dialect songs of this period were "Just A-Wearying for You" (1901), "Mighty Lak' a Rose" (1901), and "Bill Bailey, Won't You Please Come Home?" (1902).

Around 1911 there was a vogue for songs in Scottish dialect, sparked by the popularity of Sir Harry Lauder's songs "Roamin' in the Gloamin'" and "A Wee Deoch-an-Doris." Tin Pan Alley also often resorted to Yiddish and Italian dialect (among others) in such songs as "My Yiddishe Momme" (1925) and "Where Do You Work-a John?" (1926).

But most of the lasting songs in dialect originated in the musical theater. In Oscar Hammerstein II and Jerome Kern's *Show Boat* (1927), there is a dichotomy between literal numbers sung by white characters and songs in dialect performed by blacks. For example, the **lyrics** of "Make Believe" and "Why Do I Love You?" are written in normal speech patterns, and are even florid in the operatic style of the day. In contrast, "Ol' Man River" contains passages like "Bend yo' knees an' bow yo' head, an ' pull dat rope until yo're dead," as well as

a liberal sprinkling of such words as "sumpin'," " 'taters," and "rollin.'" "Can't Help Lovin' Dat Man," sung by a mulatto character, includes such words as "dere," "sumpin'," "chimbley," and "wid"—for "there," "something," "chimney," and "with." In sharp contrast are the lyrics of "You Are Love," containing such literate passages as "Once a wand'ring ne'er-do-well" and "like a lonely Punchinello."

The opera *Porgy and Bess* (1935) is written entirely in the dialect of Charleston, South Carolina, the location of the fictional Catfish Row. The song titles alone are a giveaway: "Bess, You Is My Woman," "I Got Plenty o' Nuttin'," "I Loves You Porgy," "It Ain't Necessarily So," "My Man's Gone Now," "There's a Boat Dat's Leavin' Soon for New York," and "A Woman Is a Sometime Thing."

As the **musical play** evolved, its creators often resorted to regionalism and many songs were written in real or imaginary dialect. Rodgers and Hammerstein's first successes, *Oklahoma!* (1943) and *Carousel* (1945), include a number of songs in the country dialects of the Southwest and New England, respectively. Examples are "I Cain't Say No" and "Oh What a Beautiful Mornin'" from *Oklahoma!*, and "June Is Bustin' Out All Over" and "What's the Use of Wond'rin'?" from *Carousel*. Other examples of dialect are the title song (in Italian dialect) of *The Most Happy Fella* and "Wouldn't It Be Loverly?" (in English cockney) from *My Fair Lady* (both 1956).

Additional Songs

Ain't It a Shame? (1922)
Ain't Misbehavin' (1929)
Ain't No Mountain High Enough (1967)
Ain't No Stoppin' Us Now (1979)
Ain't No Way to Treat a Lady (1974)
Can't Yo' Heah Me Callin', Caroline? (1914)
I Ain't Got Nobody (1916)
I Gotta Right to Sing the Blues (1932)
Is You Is or Is You Ain't Ma' Baby (1943)
It Ain't Gonna Rain No' Mo' (1923)
You Ain't Seen Nothin' Yet (1974)
Your Feet's Too Big (1935)

Bibliography

Furia, Philip. *The Poets of Tin Pan Alley: A History of America's Great Lyricists*. 1990.

See also: Contractions, Foreign Influence; Slang

DIATONIC SCALE. *SEE* SCALE

DIRECTION. *SEE* CARDINAL POINTS

DISC JOCKEY

The disc jockey came to the forefront on **radio** shortly after 1932, when Al Jarvis played records and commented about them on a program called *The World's*

Largest Make Believe Ballroom, heard over radio station KJWB in Los Angeles. In 1935 Martin Block presented the same format in his *Make Believe Ballroom* on WNEW in New York. The program became extremely popular and was introduced by its own theme song,"It's Make Believe Ballroom Time" (1936).

Many other disc jockeys followed suit in cities throughout the United States and Canada; some of the most prominent were Dick Clark, Alan Freed, Bill Randle, Sidney Torin (Symphony Sid), and William B. Williams. All had in common what has been described as "the gift of gab." Several disc jockeys, such as Arthur Godfrey and Soupy Sales, went on to careers in other aspects of show business.

Initially, disc jockeys—or deejays, as they came to be called—promoted the **big bands.** In the 1950s, however, they were instrumental in changing public taste in the direction of the **singer.** Deejays became kings of the airwaves by relentlessly promoting and playing **recordings** by such performers as Nat "King" Cole, Perry Como, Dick Haymes, Peggy Lee, Johnny Mathis, Patti Page, and Frank Sinatra. Inevitably, "payola"—a practice as old as music itself—took over. Scandals involving the bribing of disc jockies to promote records erupted in 1959 and again in 1972.

In the 1950s, the disc jockey remained an abiding force in radio. By that time deejays had also infiltrated **television,** notably with Dick Clark's *American Bandstand* (originally called *Philadelphia Bandstand*), a major promoter of **rock 'n' roll.** With the coming of cable television in the 1980s, video jockeys, called veejays became influential in the placing of music videos on cable channels such as MTV and VH-1.

A multitude of songs have been popularized by disc jockeys, including such standards as "Harbor Lights" (1937), "I'll Be Seeing You" (1938), "And the Angels Sing" (1939), "You'll Never Know" (1943), "Nature Boy" (1946), "Near You" (1947), "Good Night Irene" (1950), and "Cry" (1952). Beginning in the 1950s, a radical change in radio programming occurred with the advent of the **Top Forty** format. With the arrival of **disco** in the 1970s, the disc jockey—both on radio and in the ballroom—became more ubiquitous than ever. The concept even spread to ballrooms, catering halls, nightclubs, and restaurants, which often employed deejays in lieu of live musicians.

Bibliography

Ewen, David. *All the Years of American Popular Music.* 1977.
Sanjek, Russell. *American Popular Music and Its Business: The First Four Hundred Years.* Vol. 3: *From 1900 to 1984.* 1988.

See also: **Song Plugger**

DISCO

The word "disco" can be used in two ways: as an abbreviation and as a description of a musical style. As an abbreviation, it is short for "discothèque," a type of dance hall that originated in France in the early 1960s that used recorded rather than live music. As a musical style, disco developed in the United States during the 1970s. It is characterized by excessive loudness and by a steady 4/4 meter pulse emphasizing percussion and bass, aided by electronic amplification.

Discos started in the United States as nightclubs. One of the preeminent disco clubs in New York City was the Peppermint Lounge, featuring Joey Dee and the Starlighters. In these clubs, house bands provided live versions of the latest Top Forty **dance crazes:** the twist, mashed potato, slop, fly, frug, or hustle. The last-named dance originated in a song, "The Hustle," written and recorded in 1975 by Van McCoy. It was so successful that it swept the nation off its feet.

In the course of the 1960s, **rock 'n' roll** evolved into **rock** and gained respectability. Groups were now considered "artists" and albums became an art form. Dancing fell out of fashion and attending rock shows became the "in" thing to do.

In the early 1970s, rock fans grew disenchanted; they felt that big business was dictating their tastes and that the music was becoming complacent and dull. In the burgeoning underground clubs in New York and Europe, those who felt ostracized by mainstream rock—especially gay men, blacks, and women—took solace in the frenzy of this sensuous, driving, and liberating new music. Whereas in the past a band had provided the beat, now a club **disc jockey,** relying on skill and timing, mixed different records together to provide the musical flow.

Disco music was a **pop** genre virtually without roots. Although related to the black urban **soul** emanating from Philadelphia, it essentially owed nothing to rock 'n' roll and its progenitors, country and blues. Rather than focusing on artists and albums, disco's main function was to provide a steady, unsyncopated, danceable 4/4 meter beat.

Because the beat *was* the music, disco offered no basis for establishing artists and their careers. It was a music made up predominantly of "one-hit wonders." By 1974, **Top Forty** radio could no longer ignore disco music; the first major hits to make their mark were "Rock the Boat," performed by Hues Corporation and "Rock Your Baby," performed by George McRae.

Disco was "happening," and producers now searched for anything that could be cranked out in disco style. There were new arrangements of **Tin Pan Alley** songs such as "Baby Face" (1975); big band chestnuts like "What a Diff'rence a Day Made" (1936), "Brazil" (1939), and "Tangerine" (1942); soul standards like "Knock on Wood" (1966); and a recent **Motown** remake, "Never Can Say Goodbye" (1971).

Europeans, growing tired of borrowing from pop's past, tried to extend the boundaries of disco music with music that came to be known as "Eurodisco." It was built around long, almost symphonic-like compositions (usually enough to fill one side of an lp) and was propelled by one rhythmic pulse and a variety of melodies. Americans, ever enamoured of new products from abroad, started importing these records. A big hit from Germany in 1975 was "Fly, Robin, Fly," performed by Silver Convention. Since the songs coming out Europe were much longer than the American ones, record companies were forced to develop the twelve-inch single. Not only could this format contain an entire song without splitting it in half (as was the custom with standard 45s), it also gave companies the potential for greater profit because a greater amount of music could subsequently be remixed for club play.

Donna Summer, an American singer working in Munich under the supervision of Italian producer Giorgio Moroder, recorded "Love to Love You Baby" in 1976. This recording, more than sixteen minutes in duration, was nothing more than Summer repeating the title and moaning in orgasmic ecstasy. Nevertheless, it raised her to the throne of the disco craze. Summer became the first Queen of Disco. Some of her other hits were "I Feel Love" (1977), "Last Dance" (1978), and "Hot Stuff" (1979).

There was never a Disco King, but the most prolific male artist was a Florida record producer named Harry Wayne Casey. With his group, KC and the Sunshine Band, he went on to produce five Number One records: "Get Down Tonight" (1975), "That's the Way (I Like It)" (1975), "(Shake, Shake, Shake) Shake Your Booty" (1976), "I'm Your Boogie Man" (1977), and "Please Don't Go" (1979).

In 1977, disco entered the mainstream with the box office movie hit *Saturday Night Fever*. The film's soundtrack quickly became the best-selling album in the history of popular music up to that time. Its theme song, "Night Fever," was written and recorded by the Bee Gees, a group of consistent hit-makers from the late 1960s on. Established pop stars now jumped on the disco bandwagon. Rod Stewart rose to stardom with "Do You Think I'm Sexy?" in 1979. With the exceptions of Summer and KC, however, few performers fully exploited the music. There were, in fact, no other stars to spearhead the disco movement.

Outside the big cities, disco never caught on. People were reluctant to embrace it, partly because it was seen as an entertainment for the idle rich, partly because the music was always associated with its creators, who were predominantly gay and black, and with other homosexual groups. One such group was the Village People. They not only gave disco some of its last hits, but also drove the final nail into disco's coffin. The members of the group were all alleged homosexuals who would appear on television strutting like male strippers and lip-syncing their hits: "Macho Man" (1978), "Y.M.C.A." (1978), and "In the Navy" (1979).

After that, disco as a genre died a fast death. By 1980, it was all over.

Disco did make some contributions. Whether one likes them or loathes them, the synthesizer and drum machine grew out of the disco movement. The beat of disco—pervasive and unrelenting—continued to be heard in the dance grooves of the 1980s. Perhaps disco's greatest contribution was to remind audiences that pop music could make people want to dance as well as listen.

Additional Songs

Boogie Oogie Oogie (1978)
Dancing Queen (1977)
Disco Inferno (1977)
Disco Lady (1976)
Doctor's Orders (1974)
Everlasting Love (1967)
I Just Want to Be Your Everything (1977)
I Love the Nightlife (1977)
If I Can't Have You (1977)
Right Back Where We Started From (1976)
Shame, Shame, Shame (1974)
You Make Me Feel Like Dancing (1977)
You're the First, the Last, My Everything (1974)

Jeffrey Cahn

Bibliography

Smucker, Tom. "Disco." *The Rolling Stone Illustrated History of Rock and Roll*. 1980.

Tucker, Ken. "Outsider Art: Disco and Funk." *Rock of Ages—The Rolling Stone History of Rock and Roll*. 1986.

DIXIELAND

Dixieland is a form of **jazz** involving collective **improvisation**. Developed in the Storyville district of New Orleans in the second decade of the twentieth century, it was typically played by small groups consisting of cornet, clarinet, trombone, drums, and sometimes piano and tuba. A military sort of music, Dixieland was customarily played for marches and parades.

The chief characteristics of the music are two beats to the bar, simple harmonies, little **syncopation**, slow **harmonic rhythm**, and few changes in **dynamics**. A common feature is the use of a "tailgate trombone," so called because the trombonist was usually placed at the rear of the bandwagon so that he could freely activate his slides. Edward "Kid" Ory was said to have originated this style, which featured many glissandos between bass notes.

As a style, Dixieland came to world attention in 1917, when the Original Dixieland Jazz Band (ODJB), led by Nick La Rocca on cornet, opened at Reisenweber's Café in New York City. The band soon created a stir with its first recording for Victor: "Livery Stable Blues" (1916) and "Original Dixieland One-Step" (1918). Other recordings followed, most notably "Tiger Rag"

(1917), "At the Jazz Band Ball" (1918), "Ostrich Walk" (1918), and "The Jazz Me Blues" (1921).

A similar performing style was developed in the early 1920s by the New Orleans Rhythm Kings, led by Paul Mares and featuring clarinetist Leon Rappolo. Among the songs they co-wrote are "Farewell Blues" (1923), "Tin Roof Blues" (1923), and "Milenberg Joys" (1925).

Dixieland style survived through the years, played by numerous bands, many of whom considered it to be the "purest" kind of jazz. Their repertoire included such songs as "When the Saints Go Marching In" (1896), "12th Street Rag" (1914)'," Way Down Yonder in New Orleans" (1922), "Bugle Call Rag" (1923), "Muskrat Ramble" (1926), and "South Rampart Street Parade" (1938).

Additional Songs

Dixieland Band (1935)
I Ain't Gonna Give Nobody None o' This Jelly Roll (1919)
King Porter Stomp (1924)
Sugar Foot Stomp (1926)
That's a Plenty (1909)

Bibliography

Brunn, Harry O. *The Story of the Original Dixieland Jazz Band.* 1977.

Rose, Al. *Storyville, New Orleans: Being an Authentic Illustrated Account of the Notorious Red-Light District.* 1974.

————, and Edmond Souchon. *New Orleans Jazz: A Family Album.* 1984.

Schuller, Gunther. *Early Jazz: Its Roots and Musical Development.* 1968.

See also: Instrumentation; Ragtime; Roaring Twenties

DOLL

As a minor subject of popular song, "doll" is usually taken in its **slang** context: that of an attractive female. One of the first and most lasting songs of this nature is "Oh, You Beautiful Doll," written in 1911. Its light-hearted melody is the product of Nat D. Ayer, an English composer. The wistful "Paper Doll"—"I'm gonna buy a paper doll that I can call my own"—written in 1915, has enjoyed a number of revivals, most notably that of 1942. It is best known as the theme song of the Mills Brothers.

In 1950, Damon Runyon's short story "The Idyll of Miss Sarah Brown" was used as the basis of the musical comedy *Guys and Dolls,* which has a memorable score by Frank Loesser and a title song that has shown some longevity.

But perhaps the best-known song on the subject is "Satin Doll" (1958), a favorite subject of improvisation for jazz musicians worldwide. "Rag Doll" was a Number One record for the Four Seasons in 1964. Other "doll"

songs include "Dance With a Dolly," written in 1944 but based on "Buffalo Gals (Won't You Come Out Tonight?)" or "Lubly Fan" (1844); the memorable theme from the film *Valley of the Dolls,* which is, of course, the San Fernando Valley of Los Angeles; and "The Wedding of the Painted Doll," written for the film *Broadway Melody* in 1929. The last, historically important as one of the first extended dance sequences in motion pictures, is also one of the few songs that treat a doll as a toy rather than as a human being.

See also: Baby; Childhood; Girl; Woman

DOO-WOP

Derived from two of the many **nonsense** syllables sung by backup vocalists, "doo-wop" is a revisionist name for the style of vocal **rhythm and blues** (R&B) popular from the late 1940s through the early 1960s, particularly with urban ethnic groups. These groups, usually black, would often rehearse on street corners and in subway stations; they sometimes made *a cappella* recordings as well.

Evolving out of the **gospel** tradition, the doo-wop style features background harmonies that become an essential part of the melody—indeed, they function virtually as **countermelodies**. These background vocals are used to fill out lines or to provide color behind held notes. Most doo-wop tunes are concerned with **romance**, treating it in an excessively sentimental manner that recalls the self-effacement of the suitor in the medieval tradition of courtly **love**. So while doo-wop songs tend to be relatively simple and extremely formulaic in terms of both subject and structure, their appeal depends in large measure on their individual vocal embellishments.

Doo-wop developed from pre-rock black vocal groups such as the Mills Brothers and, most importantly, the Ink Spots, whose **ballad** style, featuring the interplay of lead singer Bill Kenny and bassman "Hoppy" Jones, was extremely popular from the late 1930s through the early 1940s. The Ink Spots were followed by such groups as the Ravens and the Orioles, the former featuring bass singer Jimmy Ricks and the latter tenor Sonny Til, who were influenced by Jones and Kenny, respectively. These groups, and the many that soon followed them, added rougher harmonies and falsetto accompaniment behind the lead vocal. The Orioles' "Crying in the Chapel" (1953) was the first doo-wop recording to gain acceptance with a white audience.

The mid-1950s, clearly, was the golden age of doo-wop. For example, "Earth Angel (Will You Be Mine)" (the Penguins, 1954), "In the Still of the Night" (the Five Satins, 1956), and "Tonight" (the Mellowkings, 1957), generally considered among the greatest of doo-wop records, were released during this period. Such groups as the Drifters and the Coasters added a stronger beat and more pronounced gospel elements—eventually leading to what would become known as "**soul** music."

By the end of the 1950s, doo-wop was fading in competition with the manufactured teen idols of the period who were coming to dominate the charts. Although doo-wop groups tried to offset this competition by introducing novelty appeal (the Monotones' "Book of Love" in 1958) and baroque excess (the Marcels' "Blue Moon" in 1961), they were soon overshadowed by white groups. As examples, the Fleetwoods and the Skyliners began recording doo-wop in a pop style (the latter group's "Since I Don't Have You" in 1959 featured an elaborate orchestral arrangement) that further removed doo-wop from its black R&B and gospel roots. Additional competition came from overseas. In 1964, the British Invasion, with its instrumental emphasis on the electric guitar, effectively finished off doo-wop's broad commercial appeal, even as some British groups covered R&B material (e.g., Manfred Mann's version of the Shirelles' "Sha-La-La").

Doo-wop enjoyed a brief resurgence of nostalgic appeal in the 1970s due in large measure to the popularity of groups such as Manhattan Transfer and Sha-Na-Na (their name taken from part of the background harmony of the Silhouettes' 1958 doo-wop classic, "Get a Job").

Barry Keith Grant

See also: Rock 'n' Roll; Singing Groups

DOUBLE BASS. *SEE* STRINGS

DREAMS

A dream can be many things: an image occurring in sleep; an abstraction; a daydream; an aspiration; a wild hope; or merely something wonderful. In popular song, it has been all these and more. It has remained one of the most frequently used subjects for over a hundred years.

At the turn of the century, when the **waltz** was king, "dream" songs lent themselves well to three-quarter time. Two imports from **Austria** became popular in English translation: Oscar Straus's "A Waltz Dream" (1907), from his operetta of the same name, and Franz Lehár's "Say Not Love Is a Dream" (1912), from his operetta *The Count of Luxembourg*. Both are characterized by enchanting melodies in the Viennese tradition.

Another waltz, "You Tell Me Your Dream, I'll Tell You Mine" (1908), better known by its opening line: "I had a dream dear," remains to this day a favorite of **barbershop** harmonizers, although it is usually sung in duple time. Two outstanding "dream" waltzes of 1935 are Sigmund Romberg's "When I Grow Too Old to Dream" (1934) and Jerome Kern's "I Dream Too Much"

(1935). They contrast vividly: an old-fashioned waltz and an **art song** of great beauty. The famous Austrian import "Vienna, My City of Dreams" (1914), originally entitled "Wien du Stadt meiner Traümer," has a nostalgic quality of longing for the city of one's dreams.

A surprising number of "dream" songs came out of Hollywood in the 1930s and 1940s. Such standards as "I'm a Dreamer, Aren't We All" (1929), "Boulevard of Broken Dreams" (1933), "Did You Ever See a Dream Walking?" (1933), "With My Eyes Wide Open I'm Dreaming" (1934), "You Stepped Out of a Dream" (1940), and "I Had the Craziest Dream" (1943) were specially written for film musicals. Of these, "You Stepped Out of a Dream" is one of the most innovative, while "Boulevard of Broken Dreams" epitomizes the **Depression years** in which most of these songs were written.

Three "dream" songs, written in three different generations, stand above the rest for their endurance. "I'll See You in My Dreams" (1924) is the quintessential song of **farewell**. "Dream" (1944) is a product of the lonely years just before the end of World War II. "The Impossible Dream," also known as "The Quest," is a strikingly original song written for the musical play *Man of La Mancha* (1965).

Over the years, dreams have often led to memorable songs. But in popular song as in real life, dreams are not always what they seem. For example, "Meet Me Tonight in Dreamland" (1909) is not about some never-never land. It was written for the opening of an amusement park called Dreamland in New York's Coney Island.

Additional Songs

All I Do Is Dream of You (1934)
California Dreaming (1965)
Darn That Dream (1939)
Deep in a Dream (1938)
Dream a Little Dream of Me (1931)
Dream Baby, How Long Must I Dream? (1962)
Dream Lover (1959)
The Dream of Olwen (1947)
Dreams (1977)
Drifting and Dreaming (1925)
Girl of my Dreams (1927)
Hit the Road to Dreamland (1942)
I Can Dream, Can't I? (1937)
I Have Dreamed (1951)
If You Are But a Dream (1941)
In Dreams (1963)
In My Dreams (1984)
I've Got a Pocketful of Dreams (1938)
Jeannine, I Dream of Lilac Time (1928)
A Kiss to Build a Dream On (1935)
Making Our Dreams Come True (1976)
My Reverie (1938)
Out of My Dreams (1943)
Smoke Dreams (1936)

Someone's Rocking My Dreamboat (1941)
(On the) Street of Dreams (1932)
Wrap Your Troubles in Dreams (And Dream Your Troubles
Away) (1931)

  See also: Sleep; Wishing

DRINK. *SEE* FOOD AND DRINK

DUMMY LYRICS

It was customary in the early days of **Tin Pan Alley** to write the music before the **lyrics**. In such instances, the composer would produce a melody to which the lyricist would set temporary words, called "dummy lyrics." Very often these words were nonsense, merely indicating the number and stresses of the syllables needed to accommodate the music.

In at least two celebrated instances, however, the dummy lyrics remained the permanent ones. Irving Caesar's silly words, temporarily dashed off to illustrate Vincent Youmans's striking melody, were too good to discard. They became the basis of "Tea for Two" (1924): "Picture you upon my knee; just tea for two and two for tea." Similarly, the distinctive musical rhythm of Ira Gershwin's dummy title, "It Ain't Necessarily So" (1935), set to his brother George's melody, begat an entire song. As Ira himself pointed out, the opening eight-syllable line (and title) of the song could just as easily have been "Tomorrow's the *Fourth* of *July*" or "An *order* of *bacon* and *eggs*."

Bibliography

Furia, Philip. *The Poets of Tin Pan Alley: A History of America's Great Lyricists.* 1990.

Gershwin, Ira. *Lyrics on Several Occasions: A Selection of Stage and Screen Lyrics.* 1978.

DYNAMICS

Dynamics, the degree of loudness or softness within a song, is seldom of concern to the popular music composer. Generally speaking, the dynamic level set at the beginning of a piece holds throughout. The majority of songs are marked either *p* (soft), *mp* (moderately soft), or *mf* (moderately loud). *Crescendos* (increasing loudness), *decrescendos* (decreasing loudness), and *sforzandos* (sudden accents) are used to small effect, if at all.

But there are exceptions. Many of them stem from the pen of that most experimental of composers, Cole Porter, who often used dynamics as an integral part of his musical and literary ideas. The dynamic level of "Begin the Beguine" (1935), for example, builds up inexorably from *p*, at the beginning, to *mf*, at the first occurrence of the words "Let them begin," to *f*, at the words' second appearance. There is a sudden quiescence to *p* at the words "And we suddenly know," and the song ends with a decrease in volume (*diminuendo*) to *pp* (*pianissimo*).

The striking **release** of another Porter song, "I've Got You Under My Skin" (1936), is marked *poco a poco cresc(endo) ed appassionato*. The dynamic level steadily increases in volume over a period of five bars, before suddenly changing to *p* at "A warning voice that comes in the night." This, in turn, leads to a *molto cresc(endo)*, followed by an *f* at "Don't you know, little fool."

Porter's "In the Still of the Night" (1937) begins quietly at *p*, moves to *f* at the words "Do you love me?," and ends *morendo*, fading away to *piano pianissimo* (*ppp*). In his "Get Out of Town" (1938), a *crescendo* is followed by a *sforzando* at "So on your mark, get set." This, in turn, is followed by a **break** and a sudden change to *mp*.

Of course, other composers have also been concerned with dynamics. In Ira and George Gershwin's "Sweet and Low-Down" (1925), for example, the main motive rises in pitch as well as dynamics (from *p* to *mf*) whenever it appears. Dynamics have also been used to especially telling effect in many Broadway scores, like *Porgy and Bess* (1935) and *West Side Story* (1957).

An entirely new dynamic aesthetic arose with the emergence of electronic instruments and the triumph of amplification in the 1960s. Very often, the ideal sound became one of earsplitting loudness, especially in the **disco** years of the 1970s. Nevertheless, soft sounds still found a place, particularly in theater music. Stephen Sondheim's "Send in the Clowns," from *A Little Night Music* (1973), stays at one dynamic level throughout, *piano*. The dynamics of Andrew Lloyd Webber's "Memory," from *Cats* (1981), move at terraced levels from moderately soft (*mp*) to very loud (*ff*) to soft (*p*).

  See also: **Fade-Out**

e

ENDEARMENT

Terms of endearment, as used in popular song, fall into three categories. There are, first of all, terms expressing a sense of rarity or value by using words like "dear," "darling," or "precious." Then there are terms that convey a feeling of smallness, either by using such words as **baby**, babe, or **doll** or by adding the diminutive suffix "ie"—as in "dearie." Finally, there are those that convey some variation on the theme of **sweetness**: sweetheart, honey, sugar, or the like.

"Dear," the oldest and most commonly used of these terms, is found in a number of songs, including "Dear Old Girl" (1903), "Deep in My Heart, Dear" (1924), "Dearly Beloved" (1942), "Dear Hearts and Gentle People" (1950), and "Dear Heart" (1964). One song, "Dearie" (1950), even combines it with the diminutive. "Dear" also occurs in French and Italian in such songs as "Cherie" (1921), "Cara Mia" (1954), and "My Cherie Amour" (1968).

The word "darling" gained a reputation for affectation, in part because of its overuse in films, and fell out of favor after the 1950s. However, several older songs use it, including the show tune "My Darling" (1932); Hildegarde's theme song, "Darling, Je Vous Aime Beaucoup" (1935); Frank Loesser's "My Darling, My Darling," from *Where's Charley?* (1948); and "Little Darlin'" (1957). In contrast, the 1946 song "You Call Everybody Darling" is more an expression of reproach than of endearment.

See also: Falling in Love; Love

ENDING

The word "end" seems to have gone out of fashion in popular song around the middle of the twentieth century; its place was taken by "stop." For example, Carrie Jacobs-Bond began her song "A Perfect Day" (1910) with the words: "When you come to the end of a perfect day," while Don Gibson, in a popular song of 1958, intoned "I Can't Stop Lovin' You."

Other "end" songs are "The Song Is Ended But the Melody Lingers On" (1927), "Till the End of Time" (1945), and "The End of a Love Affair" (1950). "Stop" songs include "Stop and Think It Over" (1964), "Stop! In the Name of Love" (1965), "Who'll Stop the Rain" (1970), "They Just Can't Stop It (The Games People Play)" (1975), and "Don't Stop 'Til You Get Enough" (1978).

Other kinds of "endings" expressed in popular song include "When Day Is Done" (1926), "Breaking Up Is Hard to Do," (1959), "Wipe Out" (1963), and "It's Over" (1964). At the opposite extreme are songs about never-ending **love**, like "Endlessly" (1959) and "Endless Love" (1981).

See also: Beginning; Enduring Love

ENDURING LOVE

The subject of enduring love, long a favorite of poets, has understandably been of interest to songwriters as well. Irving Berlin promised that his **love** would endure forever in the autobiographical "Always," written in 1925; Cole Porter hedged a bit in his sardonic "Always True to You (In My Fashion)" (1948).

George and Ira Gershwin wrote two exceptional songs about enduring love: "Love Is Here to Stay" (1938) and "For You, For Me, For Evermore" (1946). Ironically, they were both published posthumously, after George Gershwin's untimely death in 1937. Charles Chaplin's theme from his film *Limelight*, of 1953, was given lyrics and popularized as "Eternally." In the same year, another song about eternity appeared: the title song of the film *From Here to Eternity*. More recently, similar sentiments have been expressed in such songs as "Everlasting Love" (1967), "Through the Years" (1980), and "Endless Love" (1981).

Enduring love is the subject of several imported songs as well, including "Always in My Heart" (1942), from **Cuba**; "As Long as He Needs Me" (1963), from **Britain**; and "I Will Wait for You" (1964), from **France**. **Waiting** for one's love to return was given its reward in the song "It's Been a Long, Long Time," written in 1945, near the end of **World War II**. With its carefree lyrics—"Kiss me once and kiss me twice and kiss me once again "—it was a fitting antidote to a war that had seemed to last forever.

Additional Songs

As Long as I Live (1934)
Endlessly (1959)
Here I'll Stay (1948)
I'll Always Love You (1987)
I'm Still in Love With You (1972)
Only Forever (1940)
Till the End of Time (1959)
You Belong to My Heart (1941)

ENGLAND. SEE BRITAIN

ENHARMONIC EQUIVALENCE

Enharmonic equivalence refers to two pitches that sound the same, even though they are "spelled" differently: for example F-sharp and G-flat. It became possible only with the universal adoption of equal temperament in the eighteenth century.

Enharmonic equivalence was an essential tool of nineteenth-century Romantic music, which often required **modulation** to remote **keys**. However, it has been far less common in twentieth-century popular music. One of its chief advocates was Jerome Kern. His "Smoke Gets in Your Eyes" (1932), in the key of E-flat major, changes both key and key signature to B major (rather than C-flat major) in its **release**. Kern also used enharmonic equivalence in the service of modulation in a number of his songs, particularly at transitions between sections. In "All the Things You Are" (1939), for example, the transition from the release (ending on E major) to the recapitulation (beginning on F minor) is accomplished by means of an A-flat augmented, rather than a G-sharp augmented, chord. The release of his "I Won't Dance" (1935) passes through the keys of A-flat major and D-flat major, and then moves to B major—the enharmonic equivalent of C-flat major.

Later composers did not always resort to enharmonic equivalence. Leonard Bernstein's "Somewhere," from *West Side Story* (1957)—which is in the key of E-flat major—digresses to C-flat and G-flat major rather than to B and F-sharp. Stephen Sondheim's "I'm Still Here" (1971), in G major, has modulatory passages in C-sharp and F-sharp major rather than in D-flat and G-flat. But Andrew Lloyd Webber carries on the old tradition in a piece such as "The Music of the Night," from *The Phantom of the Opera* (1986). In the key of D-flat major, it twice changes both key and key signature to E major over a period of only three bars.

See also: Harmony

EVENING. SEE NIGHT

EYES. SEE ANATOMY

FADE-OUT

A fade-out is a gradual softening of sound, or *diminuendo*, occurring at the close of a piece. It flourished as a device of songwriters from the 1960s on, often replacing a final **cadence**. Widespread use of the fade-out was aided by development of electronic instruments and the technical accomplishments of recording engineers. An early example occurs at the end of the 1963 ballad "(They Long to Be) Close to You," in which the words "Just like me, they long to be close to you" are repeated with a fade-out.

Countless other songs used the fade-out, especially those written in the early years of **rock**. Among songs using the device were "Downtown" (1964), "Goin' Out of My Head" (1964), "Sunny" (1965), "Georgy Girl" (1966), and "Spinning Wheel" (1968). Several songs, including "Hey Jude" and "My Cherie Amour" (both 1968), fade out to **vamp**-like passages.

The fade-out continued to be used in the following decades, but it sometimes took on the appearance of a mannerism or affectation seeking ambiguity by avoidance of a final **cadence** at any cost.

Additional Songs

Both Sides Now (1967)
The Candy Man (1970)
Come Saturday Morning (1969)
(Sittin' on) The Dock of the Bay (1968)
Everybody's Talkin' (1967)
Everything Is Beautiful (1970)
Feelings (¿Dime?) (1974)
Honky Tonk Women (1969)
Leaving on a Jet Plane (1967)
Monday, Monday (1966)
The Most Beautiful Girl (1973)
One (1975)
Proud Mary (1968)
Up, Up and Away (1967)

    See also: Dynamics

FAITHFULNESS. *SEE* ENDURING LOVE

FALLING IN LOVE

Since **love** is the most favored subject of popular song, it is understandable that the act of falling in love has received considerable attention from songwriters. Two contrasting songs written almost sixty years apart illustrate changes in style over the years. Rida Johnson Young and Victor Herbert's "I'm Falling in Love With Some One" (1910) is a Boston waltz, a slow variety of the dance much favored in the early years of the century; Hal David and Burt Bacharach's "I'll Never Fall in Love Again" (1968) is a rhythm ballad with an infectious beat.

The subject has inspired other waltzes as well. "Falling in Love Again (Can't Help It)," imported from Germany, was introduced by Marlene Dietrich in the film *The Blue Angel* in 1930. "Falling in Love With Love," with its cynical lyrics about falling for make-believe, was introduced in the musical comedy *The Boys From Syracuse* in 1938. It was one of several songs in which composer Richard Rodgers helped to revivify the waltz in a faster tempo.

A number of memorable ballads on the subject were introduced in films. These include "Let's Fall in Love," composed by Harold Arlen for the musical film of the same name (1933); "I Fall in Love Too Easily," introduced by Frank Sinatra in *Anchors Aweigh* (1944); "When I Fall in Love," with a beautiful melody by Victor Young, from *One Minute to Zero* (1951); and "Can't Help Falling in Love," introduced by Elvis Presley in *Blue Hawaii* (1961).

In addition, several uptempo songs stand out. In Cole Porter's "Let's Do It (Let's Fall in Love)" (1928) the intoxicating lyrics tell about animals and peoples (including Letts) who "do it"—that is, fall in love. In 1929, "I've Got a Feeling I'm Falling" was introduced by one of its writers, Thomas "Fats" Waller. During the Depression years, Eddie Cantor was instrumental in popularizing a song of the times: "(Potatoes Are Cheaper, Tomatoes Are Cheaper) Now's the Time to Fall in Love" (1931).

As the century progressed, questions about falling in love sometimes arose, as in the 1956 song "Why Do Fools Fall in Love?" Other songs on the subject include "Since I Fell for You "(1948) and "A Rockin' Good Way (To Mess Around and Fall in Love)" (1960). By the 1970s, falling in love commonly happened more than once in a lifetime, as illustrated by such titles as "Fallin' in Love (Again)" (1974) and "I Just Fall in Love Again" (1977).

FANTASY. *SEE* IMAGINATION; MAGIC

FAREWELLS

Songs of farewell have long been associated with traditional forms of saying "goodbye"; they occur in every historical period and in every language. Most often this type of song is directed to a particular person, place, or event. It can also reflect the historical period in which it was written: "Goodbye Broadway, Hello France" exemplified well the 1917 date of composition. "Toot Toot Tootsie (Goo' Bye)" of 1922 and "Bye, Bye Blackbird" of 1926 were typically lively songs of the Roaring Twenties; "Goodnight Irene" (1936) signalled the folk song revival; "I'll Be Seeing You" (1938) was a perfect expression for the upcoming world war. Titles can be of one word, as in Benny Goodman's 1935 theme song "Goodbye," or of many, as in Woody Guthrie's 1939 song "So Long (It's Been Good to Know Yuh)."

In addition, many **foreign-language** ways of saying goodbye have taken root in America. There are at least three farewell songs employing German: "Auf Wiederseh'n" (1915), "Auf Wiederseh'n, My Dear" (1932), and "Auf Wiederseh'n, Sweetheart" (1952); three employing Italian: "Arrivederci Roma" (1958), "Ciao, Ciao Bambina" (1959), and "Addio, Addio" (1962); two employing Spanish: "Adios" (1931) and "Adios Muchachos" (1932); two using Hawaiian: "Aloha Oe" (1878) and "To You Sweetheart, Aloha" (1936); and two using French: "Say 'Au Revoir' But Not "Goodbye'" (1893) and "Au Revoir, Pleasant Dreams" (1930).

The good-night song is a special category of farewell. Played or sung at the end of an evening's festivities, it affirms that the party is indeed over. Songs of this type go back to the nineteenth century and the Christie Minstrels' "Good Night Ladies," or "Merrily We Roll Along," of 1847. In the present century, they include "I'll See You in My Dreams" (1924), "Good Night Sweetheart" (1931), "Dream" (1944), and (inevitably) "The Party's Over" (1956). A more subtle song about saying goodbye is "You Better Go Now," from *New Faces*

of 1936; it is sometimes used by musicians as a gentle hint that it's time to go home.

Additional Songs

Bye Bye Baby (1949)
Bye Bye Baby (Baby Goodbye) (1964)
Bye Bye Blues (1930)
Bye Bye Love (1957)
Ev'ry Time We Say Goodbye (1944)
Farewell Blues (1923)
Good Night (1968)
Goodbye, My Lady Love (1904)
Goodbye Yellow Brick Road (1973)
Goodnight, My Love (1936)
Goodnight My Someone (1957)
Goodnight Sweetheart, Well It's Time to Go (1954)
Goodnight Tonight (1979)
Hello Goodbye (1968)
Hello My Lover, Goodbye (1931)
I'll See You Again (1929)
It's a Pity to Say Goodnight (1946)
Jamaica Farewell (1957)
Kiss and Say Goodbye (1976)
Never Can Say Goodbye (1970)

   See also: Greetings; Sleep

FATHERS

Songs about fathers, like songs about **mothers,** range from sentimentality to lightheartedness, with a decided emphasis on the latter. In fact, most songs using such synonyms as "daddy" or "papa"—like "Beat Me Daddy, Eight to the Bar" (1940) and "Papa, Won't You Dance With Me?" (1947)—have little or nothing to do with fatherhood. The idea of the "sugar daddy," in particular goes back a long way, at least to 1892 and the British music-hall song "Daddy Wouldn't Buy Me a Bow-Wow." One of the best-known examples of the sugar daddy song is Cole Porter's "My Heart Belongs to Daddy," which uses the melismatic incantation: "da-da-, da-da-da, da-da-da-ad." It was unforgettably sung by Mary Martin in the 1938 musical *Leave It to Me.*

There are, however, a few songs about actual devotion to one's father. "That Silver-Haired Daddy of Mine," written in 1932 by cowboy star Gene Autry in collaboration with his father-in-law, Jimmy Long, was a great success. An import from Switzerland, originally known as "O Mein Papa," became a Number One hit for Eddie Fisher, as "Oh! My Pa-Pa," in 1953.

Additional Songs

Color Him Father (1969)
Daddy (1941)
Daddy's Home (1961)
Daddy's Little Girl (1905)
Daddy's Little Girl (1949)
Hello Muddah, Hello Fadduh (1963)
I Want a Girl Just Like the Girl That Married

Dear Old Dad (1911)
My Dad (1962)
Papa Don't Preach (1986)
Papa Loves Mambo (1954)
Papa Was a Rollin' Stone (1972)
Papa's Got a Brand New Bag (1965)
Soliloquy (1945)
What's the Matter With Father? (1910)

See also: **Boy; Childhood; Girl; Man**

FEELING

As a subject of popular song, the word "feeling" has little to do with the sense of touch. Rather, it conveys a degree of emotionalism—expressed somewhat vaguely in the early years, but growing increasingly more specific as the century unfolded. In line with broad changes in society, the generalities of "That Certain Feeling" (1925), "I've Got a Feeling I'm Falling" (1929), "That Old Feeling" (1937), and "Dream" (When you're feeling blue)," (1944) eventually gave way to the specifics of "I Feel Fine" (1964), "The 59th Street Bridge Song (Feelin' Groovy)" (1966), and "Feels So Good" (1977).

The sense of vagueness inherent in the concept of feeling never disappeared completely, however, as exemplified in the amorphous lyrics of the 1975 hit "Feelings (¿Dime?)": "Feelings, wo wo wo feelings." To a more particular end are the feelings of "I Feel a Song Comin' On" (1935), "Feel Like Makin' Love" (1973), and "You Make Me Feel Like Dancing" (1977). Finally, feelings of youthfulness and attractiveness are celebrated in songs like "You Make Me Feel So Young" (1946) and "I Feel Pretty" (1957).

Additional Songs

Hooked on a Feeling (1968)
I Feel for You (1979)
I Feel Love (1977)
I Feel the Earth Move (1971)
I Got You (I Feel Good) (1966)
More Than a Feeling (1976)
(You Make Me Feel Like) A Natural Woman (1967)
Only the Lonely (Know the Way I Feel) (1966)
Sometimes I Feel Like a Motherless Child (1899)
The Way You Make Me Feel (1987)
You Make Me Feel Brand New (1974)
You've Lost That Lovin' Feelin' (1964)

See also: **Love; Moods; Romance; Sentiment**

FILM MUSIC

Music has been an essential part of the cinema almost from its inception. In the first film to feature talking and singing, *The Jazz Singer* (1927), Al Jolson's rendition of "My Mammy" (1918) caused a sensation and helped to hasten the end of the silent era in film. When Jolson declared in the movie, "You ain't seen nothin' yet," it was a prophetic remark and, if anything, an understatement.

Music has also been of crucial importance in the development of the **film musical**, a distinct genre in which many standards were introduced. Although few can remember in which movies songs like "Singin' in the Rain" (1929), "The Way You Look Tonight" (1936), "White Christmas" (1942), and "I'm in the Mood for Love" (1944) first appeared, the songs themselves are instantly recognizable (*See* Table 9).

Even silent films produced their share of hit songs. One, called "The Perfect Song" was used to accompany the 1915 film *The Birth of a Nation* (the song was revived in 1928 as the opening theme of the *Amos 'n' Andy* radio show). The perennial waltz "Charmaine" was expressly written to accompany the film *What Price Glory?* (1926). Another waltz, "Diane," was first heard in the 1927 film *Seventh Heaven*. Still another waltz, "Ramona" (1927), was the title song of a film starring Dolores Del Rio. Two other waltzes, "Jeannine, I Dream of Lilac Time" and "Pagan Love Song," were introduced respectively in the films *Lilac Time* (1928) and *The Pagan* (1929).

In addition, many songs were derived from themes for nonmusical films; some have transcended their original functional contexts to become popular favorites (*see* Table 9). For instance, the haunting theme of the dramatic film *Laura*, composed by David Raksin in 1945, was later given lyrics by Johnny Mercer; it has since become a standard as "Laura." Other examples are Victor Young's themes for both *The Uninvited* (1946) and *Around the World in Eighty Days* (1956), which became, respectively, "Stella by Starlight" and "Around the World"; Henry Mancini's "Moon River," from *Breakfast at Tiffany's* (1961), and "Days of Wine and Roses" (1962), from the film of the same name; Maurice Jarre's "Somewhere My Love," from *Doctor Zhivago* (1965); "Speak Softly Love," taken from Nino Rota's theme for *The Godfather* (1972); and Marvin Hamlisch's title song from *The Way We Were* (1973).

Songs originally from **Tin Pan Alley** and the musical stage were often interpolated into films. A striking example is "As Time Goes By," originally written in 1931, but attaining its greatest popularity only after its appearance in the 1942 film *Casablanca*. Other early interpolations include the German waltz "Falling in Love Again (Can't Help It)," added as a vehicle for Marlene Dietrich in the 1930 film *The Blue Angel;* "I Cover The Waterfront," written as a promotional song for the film of the same name; and "Two Sleepy People," interpolated in the 1938 film *Thanks for the Memory*, starring Bob Hope. Countless songs have since been heard over and over in film productions.

The popularity such songs could achieve encouraged filmmakers to incorporate a potential hit song into the majority of their films, no matter how inappropriate the context. Thus, Paul Newman, Robert Redford, and Katharine Ross take time out from the plot of *Butch Cassidy and the Sundance Kid* (1969) to cavort on a bicycle to the musical accompaniment of B. J. Thomas singing "Raindrops Keep Fallin' on My Head."

Such commercial appeal was sometimes strong enough to allow character and plot to be subordinated to the hit music. Thus, Anne Bancroft's character in *The Graduate* (1968) was derived from the protagonist of the hit song, "Mrs. Robinson," which had been previously recorded by the folk-rock duo of Simon and Garfunkel. George Lucas's *American Graffiti* (1973), although not actually a musical, employed a nonstop soundtrack of rock oldies, showing Hollywood that movies could be sold primarily on the strength of the pop music they incorporated. Extreme examples of this tendency are those films named after and built around specific songs: for instance, *Play Misty for Me* (1971), *Someone to Watch Over Me* (1988), and *Sea of Love* (1989).

It is a misconception to think of films before the coming of sound as "silent movies," for even though they lacked a synchronized soundtrack, they were almost always *experienced* with musical accompaniment. In the days of the nickelodeon, piano players sitting in the pit beneath the screen riffed their way through standard tunes and familiar classical pieces, underscoring the action on the screen—making the chase seem more exciting, the love scene more romantic, the villain more dastardly.

In addition, many silent films were shot to the accompaniment of atmospheric music, played on the set by piano or phonograph in order to smother the sound of the grinding cameras and put the actors in the right mood. The actor John Gilbert, for instance, is said to have liked listening to "Moonlight and Roses (Bring Mem'ries of You)" (1925) in the course of filming *The Big Parade* in the same year. The director King Vidor, on the other hand, had Tchaikovsky's *"Pathétique" Symphony* played on the set while he was filming his classic *The Crowd* (1928).

The instrument initially engaged for the musical accompaniment of silent film was the piano, but within a very short time, pianos were replaced by theater organs, which were equipped with devices to imitate sounds as diverse as a snare drum and a harp. After World War I, it was not uncommon to find a full orchestra replacing the theater organist. This was the era in which the performance of a musical overture often preceded the film screening, which in turn was accompanied with preselected passages from the popular classics, provided on cue sheets by the studio. As early as 1910, the Edison kinescope of *Frankenstein* was released with a cue sheet calling for music from widely different sources: from "Annie Laurie" (1838) and from *Der Freischütz* (1821), an opera by Carl Maria von Weber. This last-named source provided musical accompani-

ment whenever the creature Frankenstein appeared on the screen.

D. W. Griffith's masterpiece, *The Birth of a Nation* (1915), was one of the first movies to feature music composed expressly for it. By the 1920s, many major films were distributed with accompanying scores composed specifically for them. Even as late as 1939, Erich Wolfgang Korngold's score for *The Private Lives of Elizabeth and Essex* was performed live, in concert, by a full orchestra at the time of the film's opening in Los Angeles.

By the 1930s, it was standard practice for a movie to have original music mixed into its soundtrack. Hollywood studios developed their own music departments with house orchestras; composers, like actors, screenwriters, and cinematographers, were signed to exclusive contracts. Studios unable to afford such expenses often resorted to the old practice of recycling the classics. Even Universal had its orchestra repeat Tchaikovsky's *Swan Lake* for more than one of the many horror pictures it produced in this period.

Regardless of a particular studio's financial resources or the quality of its musical staff, the use of music in film became, for the most part, decidedly conventional. Although the soundtrack allowed for the inclusion of music, ambient noise, sound effects, and dialogue, it was the latter that naturally assumed a privileged position in picture-making. Actors were no longer required to express themselves in unrealistic gestures; they could employ a more subtle use of their bodies because their voices could give words a wide range of inflections. Accordingly, film acting became distinctly different from that for the stage. Movies were therefore increasingly focused upon conversation—what Alfred Hitchcock disparagingly called "talking heads."

As a result, the primary function of film music, now original rather than borrowed, remained the same as it had been in the silent film era: to provide emotional support to the story and to enhance the "reality effect" by evoking a particular time or place. Such use of music is aptly called "mickey-mousing." The method is perhaps nowhere more obvious than in the rhythmic, electronically produced music invariably used in the frightening sequences in contemporary horror films or in the swelling strings used during the love scenes in domestic melodramas. How effective, one might ask, would Steven Spielberg's partially submerged camera be without John Williams's ominous musical accompaniment in *Jaws* (1975)?

The use of musical motives to signify persons, places, things, events, and emotions—an idea borrowed from the leitmotif principle of Wagnerian opera—became a standard procedure for Hollywood film scores. In fact, actual Wagnerian leitmotifs made their appearance in film scores. For example, Griffith inserted motifs from Wagner's *The Flying Dutchman* and *The Ride of the Valkyries* (used again decades later to superb effect by Francis Ford Coppola in *Apocalypse Now*, 1979) into his score for *The Birth of a Nation*. Griffith as well as Korngold helped to establish the leitmotif style of film music, while others—Miklos Rosza, Max Steiner, and Alfred Newman—raised it to an art form. Bernard Herrmann, whose forty-eight film credits include several outstanding scores for Alfred Hitchcock, brought the leitmotif style to perfection, perhaps most clearly in Orson Welles's monumental *Citizen Kane* (1941), wherein some characters are associated with multiple themes.

One of the most crucial questions facing composers as well as filmmakers concerns the role of music in the filmmaking process: should film music play a secondary role, one among many elements used to highlight the drama unfolding on the screen, or should it play a partnership role, having a life of its own without causing undue distraction from the drama? Some composers who have written about the art of film music—Bernard Herrmann, Kurt Weill, Dmitri Tiomkin, Maurice Jaubert, George Antheil, Constant Lambert, and Virgil Thomson, among others—argue for the integrity of the music itself even while they acknowledge that music must serve a unified function within the entire movie. According to Herrmann, "no one person has complete expression because film is a mosaic art, and if you work in films, you have to partake of a community expression." Yet, as Kurt London wrote in 1936 in one of the first books on the subject of film music, if music "is employed to strain after effects which the film itself cannot induce, then it degrades the film and itself."

There are, of course, notable examples of film scores rising above the conventional format. In 1939, the famous Soviet filmmaker Sergei Eisenstein made *Alexander Nevsky*, wherein dialogue is considerably less important than the original music by Sergei Prokofiev. Both artists sought to create a work that would present a harmonious and equal combination of image and music. For some sequences, the music was composed first, and then the director composed his images and edited them according to the musical material; in others, the process was reversed. The legacy of these two artists is discernible in the work of certain directors whose films gain much of their aesthetic effect from the music. This is most apparent whenever a director has worked consistently with the same composer, for he develops a trademark as a result of the partnership. For example, imagine Alfred Hitchcock's blend of comedy and suspense without the music of Bernard Herrmann, Federico Fellini's movies without the whimsical music of Nino Rota, the intellectual art films of Peter Greenaway without the relentless, serial-like compositions of Michael Neyman, or the spaghetti westerns of Sergio Leone without Ennio Morricone's distinctive accompaniment.

Music not only can contribute to the overall aesthetic quality of a film; it also can be aesthetically pleasing on its own terms, as the history of film music clearly demonstrates. Arthur Penn's *Bonnie and Clyde* (1967), for example, was a popular mainstream movie that seemed to fulfill Eisenstein's call, in his famous "Sound Manifesto" of 1930, for the contrapuntal use of music. The film is structured like a folk ballad in which Flatt and Scruggs's banjo picking functions like a refrain after the verses in a narrative ballad. The banjo picking also provides frequent ironic commentary upon the violent actions taking place. Coincidentally, a folk ballad, "The Ballad of Bonnie and Clyde," was this film's legacy to popular song.

Another example is Herrmann's striking music for Hitchcock's *Psycho* (1959), which is scored entirely for strings. The plucking of the violins functions on two levels: during the shower scene it effectively unnerves the viewer; during the entire film, it is equated with a bird motif.

Some filmmakers have consciously sought experimental or contemporary sounds for their scores. Anton Karas's music for *The Third Man* (1949) is unique in that it is scored solely for a zither; yet the composer manages to elicit a surprising range of expression from that singular instrument. Panpipes in the Australian film *Picnic at Hanging Rock* (1975) provide an appropriate accompaniment for a story dealing with the ineffable mysteries of nature. The "weird" genres of science fiction provide convenient futurist trappings for Louis and Beebe Barron's electronic music in *Forbidden Planet* (1956), while horror provides the same excuse for Remi Gassmann and Oskar Sala in Hitchcock's *The Birds* (1963). Philip Glass's minimalist-styled scores for Godfrey Reggio's two films, *Koyaanisqatsi* (1983) and *Powaqqatsi* (1988), work effectively to build and sustain the emotional power of the director's relentlessly moving style.

The contemporary idiom of jazz—initially restricted by a kind of guilt by association to film subjects dealing with decadence, sleaziness, and urban nightlife—has emerged as an important style of film music. In *I Want to Live* (1958), the immoral "goodtime girl" played by Susan Hayward makes a point of boasting that she knows all the recordings of Gerry Mulligan, who has provided the movie's effective musical score and who can be seen performing in the initial scene of the film, set in a smokey nightclub inhabited by pot smokers and sundry hustlers. Hayward's comment sums up the connotations of immorality that tainted so many early uses of jazz in the movies. Relevant examples of films using jazz include *A Streetcar Named Desire* (1951), with music by Alex North, and Otto Preminger's film about drug addiction, *The Man With the Golden Arm* (1955), with its brassy score by Elmer Bernstein.

It was Henry Mancini's successful use of jazz for the television series *Peter Gunn* (1957) that launched jazz musicians into composing film scores. Among the more memorable of these scores are the following: Duke

Ellington's for Preminger's *Anatomy of a Murder* (1959), Stan Getz's for *Mickey One* (1965), Sonny Rollins's for *Alfie* (1966), and Gato Barbieri's for *Last Tango in Paris* (1973). The title songs of the last two films have become standards.

The animated cartoon boasts some of the most experimental and creative uses of popular music to be found in the movies. On the one hand, cartoon music tends to be quite simple. In the words of cartoonist Chuck Jones, cartoon music is comprised of "the hackneyed, the time-worn, the proverbial." Indeed, to a large extent, cartoon scores are often little more than pastiches of easily recognizable popular and folk tunes. As the important and innovative cartoon composer Scott Bradley has remarked, "it seemed . . . that almost anybody could collect a lot of nursery jingles and fast moving tunes, throw them together along with slide whistles and various noise makers, and call that a cartoon score." Further, since cartoons are often relatively short, and events in them usually take place at a breakneck pace, the musical technique involved tends toward "aphoristic brevity" and seemingly offers little opportunity for elaboration of musical ideas.

On the other hand, many cartoons—Walt Disney's *The Band Concert* (1935) and the feature-length *Fantasia* (1940), Chuck Jones's *The Rabbit of Seville* (1950) and *What's Opera, Doc?* (1957), Ralph Bakshi's feature-length *American Pop* (1980), to name but a few—have come into being entirely for the purpose of providing imagery to accompany familiar music. Certainly it is no accident that the important Hollywood cartoon series have names like "Silly Symphonies" (Disney), "Swing Symphonies" (Walter Lantz), "Screen Songs" and "Car-Tunes" (the Fleischer Brothers), and, of course, "Loonie Tunes" and "Merrie Melodies" (Warner Brothers).

There evolved distinctly discernible types, perhaps even subgenres, of cartoons, some of which could be defined largely by their use of music. In the early 1920s, the Fleischer Studio released a series of Betty Boop cartoons, combining Betty, her friends Bimbo and Ko-Ko, and jazz artists such as Cab Calloway and Louis Armstrong through the technique of rotoscoping (the tracing of movement photographed by the camera onto animation cels, which resulted in extremely realistic animated movement). In the early 1940s, short animated loops for jukeboxes known as "soundies" appeared; they were rear-projected and featured the top jazz and pop performers of the period. Eventually, "soundies" were withdrawn because of pressure from theatrical distributors who viewed them as competition.

The documentary is another type of film that has generated a great deal of fine film music. The British documentary *Night Mail* (1936), for example, joins Benjamin Britten's music with W. H. Auden's poetry to dramatically contrast the changing rhythms of the mail

train in its slow ascent into the highlands and its rapid descent toward Glasgow, its final destination. A rather novel use of music occurs in Luis Buñuel's self-reflective documentary, *Land Without Bread* (1932), in which music by Brahms flows contrapuntally with images of poverty and disease among the Hurdanos in the Spanish mountains.

The cinema verité documentary (using portable 16mm cameras and lightweight, synchronized sound equipment) focuses on individual stars and personalities such as Marlon Brando, Jane Fonda, and racecar driver Eddie Sachs. The accompanying music tends, therefore, to concentrate on rock performers. The first such documentary was the Canadian *Lonely Boy* (1961), which is about the pop singer Paul Anka.

The decade of the 1960s saw the development of another form of documentary, the "rockumentary," with notable examples such as *The Beatles in the U.S.A.* (1964); *Don't Look Back* (1966), which documents Bob Dylan's first British tour; and *Monterey Pop* (1968). These films ranged in perspective from the celebratory (*Woodstock*, 1970) to the demystifying (*Gimme Shelter*, 1970). The form may have reached its apogee with *This Is Spinal Tap* (1984), a clever parody about an imaginary heavy metal band that was almost convincing enough to launch the actors on their own musical careers.

Another relatively new film genre, one which harkens back to Jack Webb's *Pete Kelly's Blues* (1955), is the film biography of a famous jazz musician that places the subject's music in the foreground. Examples of this type are *Artie Shaw: Time Is All You've Got* (1985); *Straight, No Chaser* (1989), about Thelonious Monk; and *'Round Midnight* (1986), a thinly disguised treatment of the life of pianist Bud Powell, featuring the sinuous saxophone of Dexter Gordon. In Clint Eastwood's *Bird* (1987), which is about the life of legendary alto saxophonist Charlie Parker, Bird's solos were electronically lifted out of their original ensemble context and remixed with new accompaniment by contemporary jazz musicians.

Barry Keith Grant

Bibliography

Eisler, Hans. *Composing for the Films*. 1947.

Evans, Mark. *Soundtrack: The Music of the Movies*. 1975.

Flinn, Caryl. *Strains of Utopia: Gender, Nostalgia, and Hollywood Film Music*. 1992.

Gorbman, Claudia. *Unheard Melodies: Narrative Film Music*. 1987.

Hofmann, Charles. *Sounds for Silents*. 1970.

Huntley, John. *British Film Music*. 1972.

Limbacher, James, ed. *Film Music: From Violins to Video*. 1974.

Manvell, Roger, and John Huntley. *The Technique of Film Music*. 1975.

Prendergrast, Roy M. *A Neglected Art: A Critical Study of Music in Films*. 1977.

Smith, Steven L. *A Heart at Fire's Center: The Life and Music of Bernard Herrmann*. 1991.

Thomas, Tony. *Music for the Movies.* 1973.

TABLE 8

Songs Associated With Non-Musical Films

An Affair to Remember (1957)
An Affair to Remember

Against All Odds (1984)
Against All Odds (Take a Look at Me Now)

The Alamo (1960)
The Green Leaves of Summer

Alfie (1966)
Alfie

Anastasia (1956)
Anastasia

Anna (1951)
Anna

Around the World in Eighty Days (1958)
Around the World

Arthur (1981)
Arthur's Theme (Best That You Can Do)

The Bad and the Beautiful (1953)
The Bad and the Beautiful (Love Is For the Very Young)

Beaches (1988)
The Wind Beneath My Wings

Ben (1972)
Ben

The Birth of a Nation (1915)
The Perfect Song

Blackboard Jungle (1955)
(We're Gonna) Rock Around the Clock

The Blue Angel (1930)
Falling in Love Again (Can't Help It)

Bonnie and Clyde (1967)
The Ballad of Bonnie and Clyde

Born Free (1966)
Born Free

Breakfast at Tiffany's (1961)
Moon River

The Bridge on the River Kwai (1957)
The River Kwai March

Butch Cassidy and the Sundance Kid (1969)
Raindrops Keep Fallin' on My Head

The Caddy (1953)
That's Amore

Canyon Passage (1946)
Ole Buttermilk Sky

Captain Carey, U.S.A. (1950)
Mona Lisa

Casino Royale (1967)
The Look of Love

A Certain Smile (1958)
A Certain Smile

Charade (1963)
Charade

Davy Crockett (1955)
The Ballad of Davy Crockett

Days of Wine and Roses (1962)
Days of Wine and Roses

Dear Heart (1965)
Dear Heart

Deliverance (1973)
Dueling Banjos

Destry Rides Again (1939)
(See What the) Boys in the Back Room (Will Have)

Doctor Zhivago (1965)
Somewhere My Love (Lara's Theme)

Down Mexico Way (1941)
Maria Elena

Dude Ranch (1931)
Out of Nowhere

Endless Love (1981)
Endless Love

Exodus (1960)
Theme From *Exodus*

Father Goose (1965)
Pass Me By

Fireworks (1953)
Oh! My Pa-pa

Forest Rangers (1942)
Jingle, Jangle, Jingle

Friendly Persuasion (1956)
Friendly Persuasion

From Here to Eternity (1953)
From Here to Eternity

From Russia With Love (1963)
From Russia With Love

Georgy Girl (1966)
Georgy Girl

The Godfather (1972)
Speak Softly Love

Golden Earrings (1947)
Golden Earrings

Goldfinger (1964)
(Theme From) Goldfinger

Gone With the Wind (1939)
Tara Theme

The Good, the Bad and the Ugly (1968)
The Good, the Bad and the Ugly

The Graduate (1967)
Mrs. Robinson

Green Dolphin Street (1947)
On Green Dolphin Street

The Happy Ending (1969)
What Are You Doing the Rest of Your Life?

The High and the Mighty (1954)
The High and the Mighty

High Noon (1952)
High Noon (Do Not Forsake Me)

High Time (1960)
The Second Time Around

The Hurricane (1937)
The Moon of Manakoora

I Cover the Waterfront (1933)
I Cover the Waterfront

Ice Castles (1979)
Theme From *Ice Castles* (Through the Eyes of Love)

The Inn of the Sixth Happiness (1958)
The Children's Marching Song (This Old Man)

Intermezzo (1939)
Intermezzo

Invitation (1952)
Invitation

The Joker Is Wild (1957)
All the Way

Kill That Story (1934)
Two Cigarettes in the Dark

Laura (1944)
Laura

The Lemon Drop Kid (1951)
Silver Bells

Lilac Time (1928)
Jeannine, I Dream of Lilac Time

Limelight (1953)
Eternally

Love Affair (1939)
Wishing (Will Make It So)

Love Is a Many-Splendored Thing (1955)
Love Is a Many-Splendored Thing

Love Letters (1945)
Love Letters

Love Me Tender (1956)
Love Me Tender

Love Story (1970)
(Where Do I Begin) Love Story

Lovers and Other Strangers (1970)
For All We Know

Mahogany (1975)
Theme From *Mahogany* (Do You Know Where You're Going To?)

A Man and a Woman (1966)
A Man and a Woman

A Man Could Get Killed (1966)
Strangers in the Night

The Man Who Knew Too Much (1956)
Whatever Will Be, Will Be (Que Sera, Sera)

Marjorie Morningstar (1958)
A Very Precious Love

M*A*S*H (1970)
Song From M*A*S*H (Suicide Is Painless)

Midnight Cowboy (1969)
Everybody's Talkin'
Midnight Cowboy

Modern Times (1954)
Smile

Mondo Cane (1963)
More

Moulin Rouge (1953)
The Song From *Moulin Rouge* (Where Is Your Heart?)

My Foolish Heart (1949)
My Foolish Heart

Never on Sunday (1960)
Never on Sunday

New York, New York (1977)
(Theme From) New York, New York

The Odd Couple (1968)
The Odd Couple

The Old Barn Dance (1938)
You're the Only Star in My Blue Heaven

One Minute to Zero (1951)
When I Fall in Love

The Pagan (1929)
Pagan Love Song

Paleface (1948)
Buttons and Bows

Papa's Delicate Condition (1963)
Call Me Irresponsible

Picnic (1956)
(Theme From) Picnic

Pieces of Dreams (1970)
Pieces of Dreams

The Poseidon Adventure (1972)
The Morning After

The Prime of Miss Jean Brodie (1969)
Jean

Ramona (1927)
Ramona

The Razor's Edge (1947)
Mam'selle

Riders in the Sky (1949)
(Ghost) Riders in the Sky (A Cowboy Legend)

Rocky (1977)
Gonna Fly Now

Romeo and Juliet (1969)
A Time for Us

The Rose (1979)
The Rose

Ruby Gentry (1953)
Ruby

Sadie McKee (1934)
All I Do Is Dream of You

St. Elmo's Fire (1985)
Love Theme From *St. Elmo's Fire* (For Just a Moment)

The Sandpiper (1965)
The Shadow of Your Smile

Santa Fe Trail (1940)
Along the Santa Fe Trail

Sentimental Journey (1946)
Sentimental Journey

Seventh Heaven (1927)
Diane

Shane (1953)
The Call of the Far-Away Hills

The Singing Nun (1966)
Dominique

A Star Is Born (1954)
The Man That Got Away

A Star Is Born (1976)
Evergreen (Love Theme From *A Star Is Born*)

The Sterile Cuckoo (1969)
Come Saturday Morning

The Stripper (1963)
The Stripper

Summer of '42 (1971)
The Summer Knows

A Summer Place (1959)
Theme From *A Summer Place*

Superman (1979)
Can You Read My Mind?

Suzy (1936)
Did I Remember?

Sweet Bird of Youth (1962)
Ebb Tide

The Tender Trap (1955)
The Tender Trap

The Thomas Crown Affair (1968)
The Windmills of Your Mind

Three Coins in the Fountain (1954)
Three Coins in the Fountain

Till the End of Time (1946)
Till the End of Time

To Each His Own (1946)
To Each His Own

To Have and Have Not (1945)
How Little We Know

The Trail of the Lonesome Pine (1936)
A Melody From the Sky
Twilight on the Trail

The Trespasser (1929)
Love, Your Magic Spell Is Everywhere

The Umbrellas of Cherbourg (1964)
I Will Wait for You
Watch What Happens

Unchained (1955)
Unchained Melody

Underwater (1955)
Cherry Pink and Apple Blossom White

The Uninvited (1944)
Stella by Starlight

Valley of the Dolls (1968)
(Theme From) Valley of the Dolls

The Way We Were (1973)
The Way We Were

What Price Glory? (1926)
Charmaine

What's New Pussycat? (1965)
What's New Pussycat

When the Lights Go On Again (1942)
When the Lights Go On Again

Willy Wonka and the Chocolate Factory (1971)
The Candy Man

Wives and Lovers (1963)
(Hey, Little Girl) Wives and Lovers

A Woman Commands (1932)
Paradise

Yentl (1983)
The Way He Makes Me Feel

You Light Up My Life (1977)
You Light Up My Life

You Only Live Twice (1967)
(Theme From) You Only Live Twice

Youth on Parade (1943)
I've Heard That Song Before

See also: Table 9: Songs Introduced in Film Musicals

FILM MUSICALS

The film musical, although inspired by **vaudeville** and the musical theater, quickly developed into a genre that was unique to the cinematic medium. Whereas westerns evolved from the dime novel, gangster films from pulp magazines and contemporary headlines, and horror movies from gothic novels, the musical movie—with its combination of song-and-dance numbers set in an imaginary space, yet contained within a narrative framework—was a new form that developed along with Hollywood.

Warner Brothers' *The Jazz Singer*, released in 1927, was at once the first feature-length sound film (although parts of it were silent, relying on titles) and the first musical, with Al Jolson singing several already established songs, including "My Mammy" (1920), "Toot, Toot, Tootsie (Goo' Bye)" (1922), and "Blue Skies" (1927). *The Singing Fool*, also starring Jolson, was released the following year. Jolson's rendition of "Sonny Boy" in that film started the tradition of introducing new songs in film musicals. By the end of the 1920s, singing on film had caught the public's imagination, and musicals were destined to become a Hollywood staple. According to one historian, by 1930, "studios turned out musicals like sausages."

In the 1930s, Broadway composers started moving to the West Coast in search of steady employment. Soon virtually all the successful Broadway songwriters were working for the movies: Irving Berlin, Cole Porter, Vincent Youmans, Rodgers and Hart, Jerome Kern, Sigmund Romberg, Harold Arlen, and the Gershwins. It should come as no surprise, then, that in subsequent years, many remarkable songs were first heard in films: "Cheek to Cheek" from *Top Hat* (1935); "I've Got You Under My Skin" from *Born to Dance* (1936); "A Foggy Day" from *A Damsel in Distress* (1937); "Over the Rainbow" from *The Wizard of Oz* (1939); "White Christmas" from *Holiday Inn* (1942); and "The More I See You" from *Diamond Horseshoe* (1945) (see Table 9).

In 1929, just two years after *The Jazz Singer*, at least six movies significant to the genre's development appeared: *The Desert Song*, based on the operetta of the same name, was Warner's first "100% all talking, 100% all singing" film; *Hollywood Revue of 1929* introduced the variety format of loosely related numbers, not unlike its obvious predecessor, vaudeville; *The Love Parade* established the fantastic middle-European setting that was to prove a durable convention for at least another decade; *Hallelujah* combined location photography with regional music; *The Broadway Melody* was the first movie to employ the "backstage" narrative formula; and *Applause*, with its backstage locale, added a degree of social realism uncharacteristic of the genre but also present in such later, anomalous films as *West Side Story* (1961) and *Pennies From Heaven* (1981).

The backstage, or show-within-a-show, narrative provided a convenient pretext for the inclusion of the production numbers which, after all, constitute the genre's primary appeal. But the musical numbers soon chafed against their slim and confining narrative frames. By 1933, musical choreography was clearly stretching beyond the boundaries of narrative realism. *Flying Down to Rio*, for instance, features a musical climax wherein the "dancers," their waists tied to the wings of airplanes, move their arms to music played by the band on the ground below as the planes swoop by in formation. This feat is not only aerodynamically unlikely, it is also spatially impractical. The women on the planes would not be able to hear the music below; the observers on the ground would not be able to see much of the performance above.

Similarly, Busby Berkeley's choreography and camerawork for his series of Warner musicals consistently create spectacles that deny the theatrical spaces in which they are supposedly occurring. His dance routines are often organized not for the theatrical spectators present within the movie's story, but for the bird's-eye view of the camera and film viewer. The musical, then, became the only genre that continually worked against the otherwise inviolable tenets of classic Hollywood realism. Certainly it is the only genre wherein characters address the camera directly (in performance) without breaking the suspension of disbelief so essential to conventional narrative construction.

These musical sequences and their narrative contexts are not merely escapist entertainment; they function thematically. For example, in *Gold Diggers of 1933*, the contemporary reality of the Depression significantly informs both the backstage narrative and the production numbers. The film begins with Ginger Rogers singing "We're in the Money," but the escapist fantasy of being wealthy and the spectacle of seminude women clad only in the largess of giant coins is undercut by Depression reality when the sheriff abruptly appears, halts the number, and closes the show because the producers have run out of money. The last number of the film, the justly famous "Remember My Forgotten Man," is about neglected World War I veterans and uses wounded and maimed soldiers in its choreography.

In the film musicals of the 1930s, given the context of the Depression, social harmony and group cooperation were important themes, both in the stories and in the production numbers. Thus, just as in the narrative of *Gold Diggers* Dick Powell finds it necessary to forego personal considerations (he must abandon his elite Boston "blueblood" heritage for the guise of a common man) for the good of the group, so in the dance numbers Berkeley's rigid, geometrical deployment of the dancers expresses the need for communal cooperation in which individual action is subordinated to the symmetry of the entire design.

In *Forty-Second Street* of 1933 (which introduced such memorable songs as the title song, "Shuffle Off to Buffalo," and "You're Getting to Be a Habit With Me"), mounting the show demands everyone's participation and cooperation; it becomes a metaphor for a national effort to salvage the ship of state foundering in the stormy weather of a troubled economy. As the show's opening approaches, everyone sacrifices for the collective good: Ginger Rogers declines her golden opportunity to play the lead part because she knows Ruby Keeler is better suited for the job, and Bebe Daniels, the intended star now sidelined with a broken ankle, overcomes her jealousy and resentment toward Keeler and sends her out with a stirring speech. Perhaps most explicit in this context is the climactic "Shanghai Lil" number of *Footlight Parade* (1933), in which the chorines, like a college football cheering section, turn over cards to reveal first the Blue Eagle of the National Recovery Administration and then the face of Franklin Delano Roosevelt.

As the urgency of the Depression began to fade, the genre's notion of community shifted from the social sphere to the personal, from economics and politics to romance. In *Swing Time* (1936), the image of Astaire riding a freight train in top hat and tails graphically suggests the extent to which social reality has been pushed aside. It is here, in romantic fantasy rather than in social consciousness, that the film musical discovered its essential charm.

In the film musical, emotion is articulated by movement and sound, and thus the genre consistently exploits these two basic elements, as well as the basic appeal of the film medium itself. Precisely for this reason, musicals are, in the phrase of French director Jean-Luc Godard, "the idealization of cinema." Indeed, classic musicals depict a Utopian integration of mental and physical life, of mind and body, where intangible feeling is given form as concrete yet gracious physical action. Characters in musicals always give physical expression to their feelings, never permitting unwholesome repression to dominate. As Gene Kelly shouts in *Singin' in the Rain* (1952), "Gotta dance!"

Not surprisingly, romance in the musical is usually depicted in terms of the great clichés of pop music. Typically, it is of the wonderful "some-enchanted-evening" variety, where lovers are destined for each other; after the inevitable series of delays and obstacles, they get together. In *An American in Paris* (1951), Gene Kelly is blind to the obvious charms of Nina Foch but irredeemably smitten with Leslie Caron upon his first view of her. Film critic Pauline Kael is therefore quite correct in her description of the musical as "the apotheosis of romance."

Beginning with the Fred Astaire–Ginger Rogers cycle, musicals offered model romantic relationships by inventing a dramatic conflict between the opposing values of desire and restraint, represented by the two lead players. Their initial opposition results in their inability to commit themselves to a relationship, but the narrative conflict is resolved when the couple's differences are reconciled, generally through the mediating power of musical performance, resulting in, of course, marriage or its promise. And the couple's reconciliation is itself inevitably expressed in musical performance, usually a finale. As one critic has succinctly put it, in the Astaire-Rogers films, "the question of will-they-or-won't-they get together inevitably translates into will-they-or-won't-they dance."

The "never never change" sentiment of "The Way You Look Tonight," from *Swing Time* becomes the musical's equivalent to living happily ever after. The attitude of these films regarding sex and romance is perhaps best summed up in this comic exchange between Eric Blore's hotel manager and Rogers in *Shall We Dance* (1937): being assured that she and Astaire are indeed married, he sighs, "Now I can go to bed with a clear conscience," to which she replies, "So can I." As in *Swing Time*, heterosexual coupling is more often than not "A Fine Romance," "with no kisses" until the lovers demonstrate their betrothal in song and/or dance.

The appropriately named musical *Let's Make Love* (1960) expresses both Yves Montand's desire for Marilyn Monroe as well as the romantic preoccupation of the whole genre. Ginger Rogers makes this clear enough to Astaire in the first film of their series, *The Gay Divorcée* (1934), when she sings to him about "The Continental," in which "You tell of your love while you dance." So when Gene Kelly, telling Judy Garland that he is upset about his falling out with his girlfriend and leading lady, Gloria de Haven, in *Summer Stock* (1950), comments that "This has nothing to do with getting married; it's all part of putting on the show," it becomes obvious that he is with the wrong partner, that ultimately he must end up with Garland, for performance and romance are inseparable in these movies.

Thus the characters who initially embody unbridled sexual desire inevitably become monogamous and romantic in the end. In *Top Hat* (1935), for instance, Astaire is a ladies' man who proclaims, in response to comic foil Edward Everett Horton's suggestion that he get married, that he has "No Strings": "I'm fancy free and free for anything fancy." Later, his aggressive dancing in his hotel room disturbs Rogers in the room below, and when she comes up to protest, her effect on Astaire is immediate: after she leaves, he sprinkles some sand on the floor and does a soft-shoe which soothes her to sleep. Similarly, when Astaire sings "They Can't Take That Away From Me," in the climax of *Shall We Dance* amid a sea of women all wearing identical Ginger Rogers masks ("If he couldn't dance with you, he'd dance with images of you," she is told), Rogers joins the crowd, momentarily reveals her true self, and then makes Astaire search her out, rejecting the others, before they can dance alone.

In *The Pirate* (1948), one of the musicals most obviously concerned with sexuality, Gene Kelly, in the role of the pirate Serafin, is initially depicted as sexually active and indiscriminate. A social rebel, Serafin in his first number, "Nina," expresses his desire for all beautiful women. His athletic dance in this number gives a choreographed shape to his lust; near its conclusion, a cigarette disappears within his mouth as he kisses one of these lovely women, after which it emerges again, smoking away! By the end of the film, Manuela (played by Judy Garland) tames Serafin in love, so that they can come together and joyously perform the finale, claiming "the best is yet to come."

If we understand "getting together" as love making, then dance is, to be sure, an appropriate metaphor: ideally, two bodies move as one, like John Donne's twin compasses, in utter harmony. Also, dance as a sexual metaphor offers an appealing fantasy indeed: to imagine that making love is always as smooth as Astaire and Rogers's dancing makes sex seem significantly less threatening, definitely more comforting. Moreover, the dance metaphor neatly solves the problem of censorship for the genre better than the discreet but obvious and cumbersome fade-out.

The idea of music signifying community, a spirit of selfless cooperation, is the very *raison d'être* of the musical. The genre's vision of community is nothing less than, to quote the title of one film musical, *Seven Brides for Seven Brothers* (1954). Indeed, the musical's expression of and concern for community ranges from endorsement of the nuclear family as in *Meet Me in St. Louis* (1944) even to a narcissistic concern for the Self, as in *All That Jazz* (1979), wherein Scheider has to get together not only the show, but his own psyche as well. *Silk Stockings* (1957), a musical remake of *Ninotchka* (1939), manages to reduce the contemporary political tensions of the Cold War to the play of heterosexual seduction and conquest: "Music will dissolve the iron curtain," asserts the red-blooded all-American Astaire.

So it is that characters in musicals almost never remain loners, like the western hero riding off into the sunset, or the detective walking alone down mean streets. In *The Bandwagon* (1953), Fred Astaire's solitary singing of "By Myself" (1937) is effectively countered by the surprise party mounted by his supportive cast. Similarly, Astaire's performance of "A Shine on Your Shoes" (1932), from the same film, enables him to express directly the loneliness he feels on modern Broadway, and thereby to cope with it, just as Gene Kelly could tell Debbie Reynolds of his love for her in *Singin' in the Rain* only after setting up a production number on a sound stage.

But despite the attractive utopian optimism of the genre, the musical began to founder in the 1950s, even in the midst of its so-called Golden Age (the period of Arthur Freed's unit at Metro-Goldwyn-Mayer, which included, among others, Gene Kelly, Judy Garland, Stanley Donen, Vincente Minnelli, Michael Kidd, and Betty Comden and Adolph Green). Some of the best works of the genre appeared in the early 1950s: *An American in Paris, Singin' in the Rain, The Bandwagon, Gentlemen Prefer Blondes, It's Always Fair Weather,* and *Oklahoma!* But then, quite suddenly it seemed, beginning in the second half of the decade, the genre suffered a surprising decline in production, quality, and popularity. In 1943, during World War II, Hollywood studios released sixty-five musicals; a decade later the number was down to thirty-eight, and in 1963 there were only four. Musical production was declining even as the use of color and widescreen, technical advances that should have worked to the genre's advantage, were becoming increasingly common.

It is true that by the late 1930s, rising costs were making the production of lavish musicals prohibitive; yet it was not this economic constraint that threatened the musical's existence. After he left Warners, Busby Berkeley's later musicals at MGM, beginning in 1939 with *Babes in Arms*, showed that even with greatly reduced budgets, musicals could still be both innovative and commercially successful. Even in the late 1960s, studios were still spending huge sums on musicals they hoped would be blockbusters; 20th Century–Fox, for example, spent $15 million on *Star!* and $23 million on *Hello, Dolly!*

The rapid decline of musicals in the late 1950s seems better explained by the existence of an ever-widening gap between the music used in the movies the studios were making and the music an increasing percentage of the nation was actually listening to, namely the new rock 'n' roll. In the late 1960s, after the British invasion had made rock music even more popular, such musicals as *Doctor Dolittle* (1967), *Hello, Dolly!* (1968), *Paint Your Wagon*, and *Goodbye, Mr. Chips* (both 1969) were commercially unsuccessful, while, by contrast, the two Beatles films directed by Richard Lester, *A Hard Day's Night* (1964) and *Help!* (1965), were extremely popular. In the early 1970s, with the exception of *Fiddler on the Roof* (1971), most other musicals in the classical mold, such as *The Boy Friend* (1971), *1776* (1972), and *The Little Prince* (1974), were unsuccessful, while *Woodstock* (1970) proved to be a box-office bonanza. In 1973, George Lucas's *American Graffiti*, which, although it was not a musical, featured a continuous soundtrack of rock oldies, was one of the most popular movies of the year. Since then, musicals have concentrated primarily on more contemporary rock sounds.

By the close of that affluent decade of the 1950s, the youth audience (the same group that constituted rock's primary audience) accounted for the vast majority of the commercial film audience. Obviously Hollywood needed to incorporate rock music into its films to attract the majority of its potential audience. Within less than twenty years, rock came to dominate the genre's big-budget glossy releases, either in terms of the music or of the stars.

As a result, the genre has changed drastically from the classic musicals of the 1930s and 1950s. Clearly no sane person today would suddenly begin dancing amid the frightening bustle of New York City, as Kelly, Frank Sinatra, and Jules Munshin do in *On the Town* (1949), the first musical shot on location. Nor, after Love Canal, would anyone wish to "Shuffle Off to Buffalo" (1932). True, one might have been more disposed to singing in the rain shortly after World War II than now—unless that rain happened to be glistening on the mean streets of the then-popular *film noir*. However, these days the better part of valor inclines us not to draw too much attention to ourselves in a crowd. Even back in 1961, when the Jets began to dance in the street at the beginning of the on-location *West Side Story*, more than one viewer paused to wonder whether they might be gay or under the influence of drugs.

Such observations suggest the extent to which the romance of the classic musical has been undermined by the more straightforward eroticism of both rock music and contemporary dance. The physical, the earthy, is now preferred over the elegant flights of romantic fancy that characterized the older examples of the genre.

At first, rock 'n' roll stars were forced into the pattern of the traditional musical. So Elvis Presley, to take the most notorious example, began as a fiery, rebellious character not dissimilar from himself in *Loving You* (1956), *Jailhouse Rock* (1957), and *King Creole* (1958); but in short order he became a nice all-American boy in movies like *G.I. Blues* (1960). In his next-to-last film, *Change of Habit* (1969), Presley is cast as a crusading ghetto doctor, socially acceptable enough that Mary Tyler Moore can contemplate leaving the convent for a secular marriage with him without alienating the movie audience. Similarly, recent movies like *Grease* (1978) seek to employ nostalgia by consciously fitting rock music into the old generic structures.

Today, to dance "cheek to cheek" means to grind buttocks, as in *Dirty Dancing* (1987). Even the style of the musical numbers in newer musicals seeks to be "more muscular" than before, and this is true even of Gene Kelly's acrobatic choreography. Whereas the best cinematography for Astaire or Kelly was to let the camera keep them fully in frame, dance numbers in contemporary musicals tend to be composed of numerous short shots combined with dizzy montage effects and peripatetic camera movement. Such a style seems a suitable visual accompaniment for the more frenetic kind of music and dance—as in *Fame* (1980), *Flashdance* (1983), and *Footloose* (1984). But it suggests a frantic self-determination and even narcissism—see, for example, Prince's choreography in *Purple Rain* (1984)—that leaves little room for traditional romance.

Every now and then, new film musicals, like the Howard Ashman-Alan Menken animated features *The Little Mermaid* (1989) and *Beauty and The Beast* (1991), come along to capture the audience's imagination. However, because of the antithetical relation between contemporary popular music and the established generic formulas, the musical today lacks much of the appeal it possessed in the past. Whether it can regain this appeal in the era of short, punchy music videos is, alas, doubtful.

Barry Keith Grant

Bibliography

Altman, Rick. *The American Film Musical*. 1987.
———. *Genre: The Musical*. 1981
Aylesworth, Thomas G. *History of Movie Musicals*. 1984.
Delamater, Jerome. *Dance in the Hollywood Musical*. 1981.
Fever, Jane. *The Hollywood Musical*. 1982.
Green, Stanley. *Encyclopedia of the Musical Film*. 1981.
Hirschhorn, Clive. *The Hollywood Musical*. 1981.
Mast, Gerald. *Can't Help Singin': The American Musical on Stage and Screen*. 1987.
Mordden, Ethan. *The Hollywood Musical*. 1981.
Sennett, Ted. *Hollywood Musicals*. 1981.
Stern, Lee Edward. *The Movie Musical*. 1974.

See also: Depression Years; Film; Film Music; Music; Musical Comedy; Revues

TABLE 9

Songs Introduced in Film Musicals

Always in My Heart (1942)
Always in My Heart

An American Tail (1986)
Somewhere Out There

Anchors Aweigh (1945)
I Fall in Love Too Easily
(All of a Sudden) My Heart Sings

And the Angels Sing (1944)
It Could Happen to You

April Love (1957)
April Love

Babes on Broadway (1941)
How About You?

Beauty and the Beast (1991)
Beauty and the Beast

Belle of the Nineties (1934)
My Old Flame

Bells of Capistrano (1927)
At Sundown

The Big Broadcast (1932)
Where the Blue of the Night Meets the Gold of the Day

The Big Broadcast of 1936
Thanks for the Memory

The Big Pond (1930)
You Brought a New Kind of Love to Me

Blonde Crazy (1931)
When Your Lover Has Gone

Blue Hawaii (1961)
Can't Help Falling in Love

Blues in the Night (1941)
Blues in the Night

Born to Dance (1936)
Easy to Love
I've Got You Under My Skin

Broadway Melody (1929)
The Broadway Melody
The Wedding of the Painted Doll
You Were Meant for Me

Broadway Melody of 1936
Broadway Rhythm
I've Got a Feelin' You're Foolin'

Calamity Jane (1953)
Secret Love

Can't Help Singing (1944)
Can't Help Singing

Carefree (1938)
Change Partners

Casino de Paree (1935)
About a Quarter to Nine

Centennial Summer (1946)
All Through the Day
In Love in Vain

Cinderella (1949)
A Dream Is a Wish Your Heart Makes

College Rhythm (1934)
Stay as Sweet as You Are

Cover Girl (1944)
Long Ago (And Far Away)

The Cuban Love Song (1931)
Cuban Love Song

Daddy Long Legs (1955)
Something's Gotta Give

Dames (1934)
I Only Have Eyes for You

A Damsel in Distress (1937)
A Foggy Day
Nice Work If You Can Get It

Dancing Lady (1933)
Everything I Have Is Yours

A Date With Judy (1948)
It's a Most Unusual Day

Diamond Horseshoe (1945)
The More I See You

Dixie (1943)
Sunday, Monday or Always

Doctor Dolittle (1967)
Talk to the Animals

Easter Parade (1948)
A Couple of Swells
It Only Happens When I Dance With You
Steppin' Out With My Baby

Every Night at Eight (1935)
I Feel a Song Comin' On
I'm in the Mood for Love

Flashdance (1983)
Flashdance (What a Feeling)

The Fleet's In (1942)
Arthur Murray Taught Me Dancing In a Hurry
I Remember You
Tangerine

Flying Down to Rio (1933)
The Carioca
Flying Down to Rio
Orchids in the Moonlight

Follow the Boys (1944)
Is You Is or Is You Ain't (Ma' Baby)

Follow the Fleet (1936)
I'm Putting All My Eggs in One Basket
Let Yourself Go
Let's Face the Music and Dance

Footlight Parade (1933)
By a Waterfall
Shanghai Lil

Forty-Second Street (1933)
Forty-Second Street
Shuffle Off to Buffalo
You're Getting to Be a Habit With Me

The Gay Divorcée (1934)
The Continental

Gigi (1958)
Gigi
I Remember It Well
I'm Glad I'm Not Young Anymore
The Night They Invented Champagne
Thank Heaven for Little Girls

Gilda (1946)
Put the Blame on Mame

Give Out, Sisters (1942)
Pennsylvania Polka

Going Hollywood (1933)
Temptation

Going My Way (1944)
Swinging on a Star

Going Places (1938)
Jeepers Creepers

Gold Diggers of 1933
Remember My Forgotten Man
Shadow Waltz
We're in the Money

Gold Diggers of 1935
Lullaby of Broadway

Gold Diggers of 1937
With Plenty of Money and You

The Great Caruso (1951)
The Loveliest Night of the Year

The Great Ziegfeld (1936)
It's Been So Long
You (Gee But You're Wonderful)

Hallelujah, I'm a Bum (1933)
You Are Too Beautiful

Hans Christian Andersen (1952)
Anywhere I Wander
No Two People
Wonderful Copenhagen

A Hard Day's Night (1964)
A Hard Day's Night

The Harvey Girls (1946)
On the Atchison, Topeka and the Santa Fe

Hello, Frisco, Hello (1943)
You'll Never Know

Here Come the Waves (1944)
Ac-cent-tchu-ate the Positive

Here Is My Heart (1935)
June in January
Love Is Just Around the Corner

Hi Neighbor (1941)
Deep in the Heart of Texas

High Society (1956)
True Love

High, Wide and Handsome (1937)
Can I Forget You?
The Folks Who Live on the Hill

Holiday Inn (1942)
Be Careful, It's My Heart
Happy Holiday
White Christmas

Hollywood Canteen (1944)
Don't Fence Me In

Hollywood Hotel (1938)
Hooray for Hollywood

Hollywood Revue (1929)
Singin' in the Rain

I Dream Too Much (1935)
I Dream Too Much

Iceland (1942)
There Will Never Be Another You

I'll Take Romance (1937)
I'll Take Romance

The King of Burlesque (1936)
I'm Shooting High
Lovely Lady

King of Jazz (1930)
It Happened in Monterey

The King Steps Out (1936)
Stars in My Eyes

Kiss the Boys Goodbye (1941)
Sand in My Shoes

The Kissing Bandit (1948)
Love Is Where You Find It

Lady Sings the Blues (1972)
Happy

Let's Fall in Love (1934)
Let's Fall in Love

Lili (1953)
Hi-Lili, Hi-Lo

The Little Mermaid (1989)
Under the Sea

Love Me Tonight (1932)
Isn't It Romantic?
Lover
Mimi

Manhattan Parade (1932)
I Love a Parade

Mary Poppins (1964)
Chim Chim Cher-ee
A Spoonful of Sugar
Supercalifragilisticexpialidocious

Meet Me in St. Louis (1944)
The Boy Next Door
Have Yourself a Merry Little Christmas
The Trolley Song

Mississippi (1935)
It's Easy to Remember
Soon

Monte Carlo (1930)
Beyond the Blue Horizon

Murder at the Vanities (1934)
Cocktails for Two

A Night at the Opera (1935)
Alone

A Night in Casablanca (1946)
Moonlight Cocktail

The Night Is Young (1935)
When I Grow Too Old to Dream

On the Avenue (1937)
I've Got My Love to Keep Me Warm

On With the Show (1929)
Am I Blue?

One Hour With You (1932)
(I'd Love to Spend) One Hour With You

One Night of Love (1934)
One Night of Love

Orchestra Wives (1942)
I've Got a Gal in Kalamazoo
Serenade in Blue

Pennies From Heaven (1936)
Pennies From Heaven

Pinocchio (1940)
When You Wish Upon a Star

The Pirate (1948)
Be a Clown

Playboy of Paris (1930)
My Ideal

Private Buckaroo (1942)
Don't Sit Under the Apple Tree (With Anyone Else But Me)

Ready, Willing and Able (1937)
Too Marvelous for Words

Rhythm on the Range (1936)
I'm an Old Cow Hand (From the Rio Grande)

Rhythm on the River (1940)
Only Forever

Ride 'em Cowboy (1942)
I'll Remember April

Ride, Tenderfoot Ride (1940)
The Woodpecker Song

The Road to Morocco (1942)
Moonlight Becomes You
The Road to Morocco

The Road to Rio (1947)
But Beautiful

The Road to Utopia (1945)
Personality

The Road to Zanzibar (1941)
It's Always You

Roberta (1935)
I Won't Dance

Romance on the High Seas (1948)
It's Magic

Royal Wedding (1951)
How Could You Believe Me When I Said I Love You When
    You Know I've Been a Liar All My Life?
Too Late Now

Saludos Amigos (1944)
Brazil
Tico Tico

San Antonio Rose (1941)
Hut Sut Song
San Antonio Rose

Saturday Night Fever (1977)
How Deep Is Your Love
More Than a Woman
Stayin' Alive

Say It With Music (1933)
Love Is the Sweetest Thing

The Seven Hills of Rome (1957)
Arrivederci Roma
Memories Are Made of This

Shall We Dance (1937)
(I've Got) Beginner's Luck
Let's Call the Whole Thing Off
Shall We Dance
Slap That Bass
They All Laughed
They Can't Take That Away From Me

She Loves Me Not (1934)
Love in Bloom

Shipmates Forever (1935)
Don't Give Up the Ship

The Shocking Miss Pilgrim (1947)
For You, for Me, for Evermore

Shoot the Works (1934)
With My Eyes Wide Open I'm Dreaming

Sing, Baby, Sing (1936)
You Turned the Tables on Me

The Singing Fool (1928)
Sonny Boy

The Singing Hill (1941)
Blueberry Hill

Sitting Pretty (1934)
Did You Ever See a Dream Walking?

The Sky's the Limit (1943)
My Shining Hour
One for My Baby (And One More for the Road)

Snow White and the Seven Dwarfs (1937)
Heigh-Ho
Some Day My Prince Will Come
Whistle While You Work

Something to Shout About (1943)
You'd Be So Nice to Come Home To

Song of the South (1946)
Zip-A-Dee-Doo-Dah

Springtime in the Rockies (1942)
I Had the Craziest Dream

State Fair (1945)
It Might as Well Be Spring
It's a Grand Night for Singing
That's for Me

Stepping High (1928)
I'll Always Be in Love With You

Sunny Side Up (1929)
If I Had a Talking Picture of You

Sweater Girl (1942)
I Don't Want to Walk Without You

The Swing Parade of 1946
Caldonia (What Makes Your Big Head So Hard?)

Swing Time (1936)
A Fine Romance
The Way You Look Tonight

That Night in Rio (1941)
Chica Chica Boom Chic
I Yi Yi Yi Yi (I Like You Very Much)

Thoroughly Modern Millie (1967)
Thoroughly Modern Millie

The Three Caballeros (1944)
Baia
You Belong to My Heart

Three Little Girls in Blue (1946)
On the Boardwalk in Atlantic City
You Make Me Feel So Young

The Three Little Pigs (1933)
Who's Afraid of the Big Bad Wolf?

Thrill of a Romance (1945)
I Should Care

The Time, the Place and the Girl (1946)
A Gal In Calico
Rainy Night in Rio

The Toast of New Orleans (1950)
Be My Love

Top Hat (1935)
Cheek to Cheek
Isn't This a Lovely Day
The Piccolino
Top Hat, White Tie and Tails

Twenty Million Sweethearts (1934)
I'll String Along With You

Under the Clock (1948)
If I Had You

Waikiki Wedding (1937)
Blue Hawaii
Sweet Leilani

The Wizard of Oz (1939)
Ding, Dong! The Witch Is Dead
If I Only Had a Brain
Over the Rainbow
We're Off to See the Wizard

You Were Never Lovelier (1942)
Dearly Beloved
I'm Old Fashioned
You Were Never Lovelier

Ziegfeld Girl (1941)
You Stepped Out of a Dream

See also: Table 9: Songs Associated With Non-Musical Films

FIRE

The subject of fire has been treated in various ways in popular song. As a symbol of domestic bliss, the fireplace has found its way into several memorable songs. During World War I, "Keep the Home Fires Burning," imported from Britain in 1915, was an admonition to American civilians that spoke for itself. Similarly, in the depths of the Great Depression, "Throw Another Log on the Fire" (1933) was a heartwarming song. Shortly after the end of World War II, "The Christmas Song" (1946) celebrated the return to normalcy with its opening line: "Chestnuts roasting on an open fire."

A very different kind of fire, that of desire, is the subject of a number of worthy songs (the convenient rhyme of "fire" and "desire" has not been overlooked by lyric writers). The aptly named torch song "My Old Flame" was introduced in the 1934 musical film *Belle of the Nineties*, which starred Mae West and Duke Ellington. Similar conflagrations occur in "Kiss of Fire," a 1952 song borrowed almost note for note from A. G. Villoldo's famous Argentine tango "El Choclo" of 1913, and in the rock standard "Light My Fire" (1967).

To round out its versatility, the subject of fire has served other functions in popular song: as a symbol of a free Russia, in the rousing title song of the 1925 operetta *Song of the Flame*; as a metaphor for losing one's "ambition for worldly acclaim," in the 1941 hit "I Don't Want to Set the World on Fire"; and as an allusion to rock 'n' roll, in "Great Balls of Fire," recorded by Jerry Lee Lewis in 1957.

Additional Songs

Burning Love (1972)
Fire (1974)
Fire and Rain (1975)
I'm on Fire (1984)
Wildfire (1975)

FLOWERS

Flowers have a long history in popular song, as exemplified by two sentimental ballads written almost eighty years apart: "Hearts and Flowers" (1899) and "You Don't Bring Me Flowers" (1977). The melody of "Hearts and Flowers" was borrowed intact from the piano piece *Wintermärchen*, which had been written by the Hungarian composer Alphonse Czibulka; the music of "You Don't Bring Me Flowers" was written by one singer, Neil Diamond, and popularized by another singer, Barbra Streisand. Flowers are also used as a metaphor for young people in Pete Seeger's protest song of 1961, "Where Have All the Flowers Gone?"

Most other significant flower songs are about individual species rather than the floral kingdom as a whole. Of all species, the rose is by far the flower of preference. Very often, as in songs such as "Honeysuckle Rose" (1929) and "La Vie en Rose" (1950), its meaning as a flower is obscured; it may refer as much to a **name** as to a **color**. Purely as a flower, however, the rose reigns supreme in such early perennials as "Mighty Lak' a Rose" (1901), "Roses of Picardy" (1916), "Moonlight and Roses" (Bring Mem'ries of You)" (1925), "Only a Rose" (1925), and "The One Rose That's Left in My Heart" (1929). More recently, the rose has appeared as a symbol of the good life in such songs as "Everything's Coming Up Roses" (1959), "Lollipops and Roses" (1960), "Days of Wine and Roses" (1962), and "I Never Promised You a Rose Garden" (1967).

The tulip blossoms in two lively songs: "When You Wore a Tulip and I Wore a Big Red Rose" (1914) and "Tip Toe Through the Tulips With Me" (1929). Violets take their turn in the barbershop favorite "Sweet Violets" (1882)—a song that has been unmercifully parodied—and in "Who'll Buy My Violets?"—a 1923 adaptation of the Spanish "La Violetera."

Lilacs bloom in "Jeannine I Dream of Lilac Time," taken from the soundtrack of the film *Lilac Time* (1928), and in "Lilacs in the Rain" (1939), adapted by Peter DeRose from his own *Deep Purple Suite*.

One of the most beautiful flowers is represented by one of the most beautiful songs. "Orchids in the Moonlight" has the distinction of being introduced in the first film musical starring Fred Astaire and Ginger Rogers, *Flying Down to Rio* (1933). A rare example of an American tango, the striking melody was written by Vincent Youmans.

Additional Songs

Blue Orchids (1939)
Bouquet of Roses (1948)
Flowers on the Wall (1965)
I'll Be With You in Apple Blossom Time (1920)
It Looks Like Rain in Cherry Blossom Lane (1937)
Love in Bloom (1934)
Orange Blossom Special (1938)
San Francisco (Be Sure to Wear Some Flowers in Your Hair) (1967)
When It's Apple Blossom Time in Normandy (1912)
A White Sport Coat and a Pink Carnation (1957)
Wildwood Flower (1928)
The Yellow Rose of Texas (1955)
You're the Flower of My Heart, Sweet Adeline (1903)
  See also: Trees

FOLK ROCK

Folk rock is a hybrid genre combining the elements of **folk song** with the electronic amplification of **rock**. However, it differs from traditional folk music in several other important respects: its provenance is more often urban than rural, it is transmitted in writing rather than by oral tradition, its writers are known rather than unknown, it is intended for mass consumption rather than for small gatherings, its form is fixed rather than changeable, and its content is more often sophisticated than simple.

One of the earliest proponents of folk rock was the Kingston Trio. Their first hit was "Tom Dooley" (1958), which one of their founders, Dave Guard, adapted from a folk song of 1868. They followed this with another hit, "The Tijuana Jail," in 1959. But folk rock did not really capture the public's imagination until Bob Dylan went "electric" with his group at the Newport Jazz and Folk Festival in 1965. Its hold on the public was confirmed in the same year with the Byrds' cover version of Dylan's "Mr. Tambourine Man" (1964) in folk-rock style.

The merging of the two styles continued apace with the duo of Simon and Garfunkel. One of their first hits was an adaptation of the Old English air "Scarborough Fair," as "Scarborough Fair/Canticle" (1966). Simon himself wrote many other songs which the duo performed in folk-rock style: "The Sound of Silence" (1964), "I Am a Rock" (1964), "The Dangling Conversation" (1966), "Mrs. Robinson" (1968), "The 59th Street Bridge Song (Feelin' Groovy)" (1966), "Cecilia" (1970), and, most notably, "Bridge Over Troubled Water" (1969).

Folk-rock style was adapted by a host of other **performer-songwriters**, among them Carole King ("You've Got a Friend," 1971), Carly Simon ("Anticipation," 1971), and James Taylor ("Country Road," 1970). It became part and parcel of pop style, with which it merged imperceptibly during the 1970s, and was closely allied to the electrification of **country and western** music by such performers as John Denver, Seals and Crofts, and Kris Kristofferson.

FOLK SONG

By definition, folk song is music of the people: passed on by oral transmission and usually of rural provenance. It is traditionally simple in style, consisting of a short, catchy **melody** which is repeated over simple harmonies uncluttered by **chromaticism**. In **form** it is most often strophic (either AAA or verse-chorus) and in **texture** homophonic (most commonly, voice accompanied by acoustic guitar). Its **subjects** encompass the totality of human experience: birth, love, anger, death, and problems of life.

The origins of American folk song are diverse. Some enduring songs, like "Billy Boy" (1824), originated in **Britain**. Others, such as "I Gave My Love a Cherry," or "The Riddle Song" (c. 1850), originated in the southern Appalachian Mountains. Still others were derived from black spirituals–"Go Down Moses (Let My People Go)" (1861) and "Nobody Knows de Trouble I've Seen" (1867); black work songs–"Michael (Row the Boat Ashore)" (pub. 1960); or black recreational music "Short'nin' Bread" (pub. 1925). Another important part of the folk tradition was the **blues**, a seminal influence

on American popular song.

Various occupations inspired other forms of folk music. The sea chantey is memorialized in such classics as "Shenandoah," or "Across the Wide Missouri" (c. 1826), and "Blow the Man Down" (1880). The American cowboy song is exemplified by "(Whoopee Ti Yi Yo) Git Along Little Dogies" (pub. 1893). The coming of the railroad left a legacy of songs: "John Henry" (1873), "I've Been Working on the Railroad" (c. 1880), "She'll Be Comin' Round the Mountain" (published in 1899 with the title "When the Chariot Comes)," "Casey Jones" (1909), "Where Do You Work-a John?" (1926), and "Wabash Cannonball" (1940), among others.

Folk songs, or songs written in folk style, were staples of the **minstrel show**. Among the best known of the latter were "Buffalo Gals Won't You Come Out Tonight?," or "Lubly Fan" (1844); Stephen Foster's "De Camptown Races (Gwine to Run All Night)" (1850), "Old Folks at Home (Way Down Upon the Swanee River)" (1851), and "Old Black Joe" (1860); and James A. Bland's "Carry Me Back to Old Virginny" (1878) and "(Oh Dem) Golden Slippers" (1879).

The 1930s and 1940s saw a new surge of interest in the rich heritage of American folk song, inspired largely by the efforts of song collectors and scholars like John A. Lomax and his son, Alan, Carl Sandburg, Cecil J. Sharp, and Charles Seeger. One of the chief balladeers of the period was the singer-guitarist Leadbelly (Huddy Leadbetter) who, with John Lomax, revived the traditional folk ballad "Goodnight Irene" in 1936. Other singers included John Jacob Niles, who sang the traditional mountain song "Black Is the Color of My True Love's Hair" (c. 1875); Burl Ives, famous for his revival of the 1846 song "Jimmy Crack Corn (The Blue Tail Fly)" and many others; and Oscar Brand, whose adaptation of the traditional folk ballad "A Guy Is a Guy," became a hit in 1951 when it was recorded by Doris Day. Also active during this period was the Carter Family, who sang in both the folk and **country and western** traditions.

Two of the most important figures in twentieth-century American folk song were Woody Guthrie and Pete Seeger. Guthrie, who sang and accompanied himself on guitar and harmonica, epitomized the hobo lifestyle and was considered by many to be a spokesman for the people. The most famous of his songs in folk style—which he wrote himself—were "So Long (It's Been Good to Know Yuh)" (1939) and "This Land Is Your Land" (1956). Together with Seeger, he formed the Almanac Singers. Seeger (the son of Charles) was the dominant figure in the folk revival of the 1950s and 1960s. He wrote most of his own material, including "If I Had a Hammer" (1958, with Lee Hays), "Where Have All the Flowers Gone?" (1961), "Turn! Turn! Turn!"(1962), and "Guantanamera" (1963, with Hector Angulo). Seeger was also a co-founder in 1949 of the influential singing group the Weavers. Among the Weavers' many hits were their recordings of "Goodnight Irene," "Kisses Sweeter Than Wine" (1951), and the traditional folk song "On Top of Old Smokey" (adapted by Seeger in 1951).

A folk-song renaissance began in the 1950s, with renewed attention to early songs and hootenannies common occurrences on college campuses. Many songs reflected the demands of youth for social and political change. Increasingly, lyrics carried messages of deeper meaning. The era of the **protest song** had arrived with songs like "If I Had a Hammer," a call against apathy; and "Where Have All the Flowers Gone?," the quintessential antiwar song.

The leading figure in this protest movement was Bob Dylan. His songs, like "Hard Rain's A-Gonna Fall" (1963) and "Masters of War" (1963), carried trenchant messages. His most famous hymn of protest, "Blowin' in the Wind" (1962), was followed two years later by "Mr. Tambourine Man." A year later, Dylan went "electric" with his group at the Newport Jazz and Folk Festival. After that, he moved on to other styles—**folk rock**, country and western, and **rock**—as well as continuing in the folk tradition.

One of the most prominent **performer-songwriters** in the folk tradition was Canadian-born Joni Mitchell. Her songs—such as "Urge for Going" (1966), "Both Sides Now (Clouds)" (1967), "Chelsea Morning" (1967), "Cactus Tree" (1968), "Woodstock" (1969), and "Help Me" (1972)—were often emotional expressions of particular appeal to women. Joan Baez, sometimes called "queen of folksingers," was primarily a performer rather than a songwriter. She sang traditional folk songs, like "Look Down, Look Down That Lonesome Road" (1865), as well as songs of protest, such as Dylan's "I Shall Be Released" (1967). She was at first very active in political causes, but her later songs, like "Diamonds and Rust" (1975), were of a more personal nature.

Judy Collins, like Baez, started her career singing songs of protest, such as Dylan's "Masters of War," and then moved on to personal songs such as Mitchell's "Both Sides Now." Her biggest hits were her versions of the eighteenth-century hymn "Amazing Grace" and Pete Seeger's "Turn! Turn! Turn!" She popularized several of her own songs as well, including "Albatross" (1967) and "Born to the Breed" (1975). Similarly eclectic was the repertoire of Buffy Sainte-Marie, a Cree Indian who wrote songs against war ("The Universal Soldier," 1964) and drugs ("Cod'ine," 1964), as well as about ordinary problems of life ("Until It's Time for You to Go," 1965).

Among other performer-songwriters in the folk tradition were Phil Ochs ("The Bells," "Bound for Glory," both 1963), Tom Paxton ("What Did You Learn in School Today?," 1962; "Bottle of Wine," 1963), and Arlo Guthrie, son of Woody ("Alice's Restaurant," 1966). By the mid-1960s, folk music had largely become commercialized, performed by such groups as the New Christy Minstrels "The Big Rock Candy Mountain," (1885) and Peter, Paul and Mary "Puff (The Magic Dragon)," (1963), and often tended to merge, almost imperceptibly, with mainstream pop.

Folk song lived on into the 1990s, sometimes expressing environmental concerns (as in Pete Seeger's collection of songs marking the environmental mission of the Hudson River boat *The Clearwater*) or current events (such as the songs created at the beginning of the Gulf War of 1991 and sung as the troops embarked from bases on the Atlantic and Pacific).

Bibliography

Baggelaar, Kristin, and David Milton. *The Folk Music Encyclopaedia*. 1977.

Bookbinder, David. *What Folk Music Is All About*. 1979.

Brand, Oscar. *The Ballad Mongers: The Rise of Modern Folk Song*. 1979.

Forcucci, Samuel L. *A Folk Song History of America*. 1984.

Grafman, Howard, and B. T. Manning. *Folk Music, U.S.A.* 1962.

Lawless, Ray McKinley. *Folksingers and Folksongs in America: A Handbook of Biography, Bibliography, and Discography*. 1981.

Lomax, Alan. *Folk Song Style and Culture*. 1968.

Nettl, Bruno. *Folk Music in the United States: An Introduction*. 1976.

Sandberg, Larry, and Dick Weissman. *The Folk Music Sourcebook*. 1976.

Stambler, Irwin, and Grelun Landon. *Encyclopedia of Folk, Country, and Western Music*. 1975.

See also: Women as Songwriters

FOLLIES. SEE REVUES.

FOOD AND DRINK

Beverages outshine solid food as subjects of popular song, with coffee holding its own as America's favorite drink. Of the many songs about coffee, four stand out: "I Love Coffee, I Love Tea" (1915), "You're the Cream in My Coffee" (1928), "Let's Have Another Cup of Coffee" (1932), and "The Coffee Song (They've Got an Awful Lot of Coffee in Brazil)" (1946).

By far the most important song about tea is "Tea for Two" (1924). Its words were written by Irving Caesar as **dummy lyrics**: a model for a later, more polished version. However, they fit Vincent Youmans's music so well that the writers decided to keep them as they were, with such obvious and silly rhymes as "And start to bake/A sugar cake."

Turning to alcoholic drinks, champagne is the beverage of choice, figuring in at least three titles: "The Champagne Waltz" (1934), "Blue Champagne" (1941), and "The Night They Invented Champagne" (1958).

Champagne also figures prominently, if in a negative way, in the opening line of Cole Porter's "I Get a Kick Out of You" (1934): "I get no kick from champagne" (the last word was originally "cocaine").

Beer, a more plebeian drink, is featured in several early songs, including "Down Where the Wurzburger Flows" (1902)—often mistakenly thought to refer to a river—and the "Drinking Song," from Sigmund Romberg's operetta *The Student Prince* (1924). A great hit of 1939 was "Beer Barrel Polka (Roll Out the Barrel)," an import from Czechoslovakia given English words: "Roll out the barrel/We'll have a barrel of fun."

Perhaps the epitome of art-deco sophistication in the early 1930s was "Cocktails for Two" (1934). Another popular mixed drink of its time (1945) forms the title of "Rum and Coca Cola." There are also a number of **rhythm-and-blues** songs about hard liquor, such as "Who Threw the Whiskey in the Well?" (1945), "Bad, Bad Whiskey" (1950), and "One Mint Julep" (1952). At the other (nonalcoholic) extreme is the Prohibition lament "How Dry I Am" (1921).

As for songs about food itself, most of them are humorous in nature. One of the funniest is the **novelty song** "Yes! We Have No Bananas" (1923). Its absurd title is reputed to have been suggested by the words of a Greek fruitdealer. Many fruits and vegetables are referred to in the lyrics: from "peaches and scallions" to "Long Island potatoes." One humorous song, "Who Threw the Overalls in Mrs. Murphy's Chowder?" (1899), manages to combine soup with **clothing**.

Several food songs came out during the **Depression years**, when food was sometimes scarce. They include "Life Is Just a Bowl of Cherries" (1931), with its uplifting words about life: "don't take it serious." "(Potatoes Are Cheaper—Tomatoes Are Cheaper) Now's the Time to Fall in Love" was popularized by Eddie Cantor in the same year. The same two vegetables, which rhyme so conveniently, were used to illustrate the differences between two lovers in Ira and George Gershwin's "Let's Call the Whole Thing Off" (1937): "You say potatoes and I say potah-toes/You say tomatoes and I say tomah-toes."

In 1950, "If I Knew You Were Comin' I'd've Baked a Cake" sold over a million records. In the following years, several songs about the transportation of food appeared, among them "Shrimp Boats" (1951) and "The Banana Boat Song" (1957). Dessert came later, in such songs as "Lollipops and Roses" (1960), "Little Green Apples" (1968), and "The Candy Man" (1970). In Don McLean's "American Pie" (1971), a song full of symbolism, only the title refers to an item of food.

Finally, in a cry for sustenance, a chorus of hungry boys raise their voices in song for any kind of "Food, Glorious Food" in Lionel Bart's musical play *Oliver!* (1960).

Additional Songs

Alice's Restaurant (1969)
And Her Tears Flowed Like Wine (1944)
Cherry Pie (1954)
Cherry Pies Ought to Be You (1950)
Days of Wine and Roses (1962)
Dinner for One, Please James (1935)
Java Jive (1940)
Kisses Sweeter Than Wine (1951)
Make It Another Old-Fashioned, Please (1940)
One for My Baby (And One More for the Road) (1943)
Scotch and Soda (1959)
Sing for Your Supper (1938)
Struttin' with Some Barbecue (1927)
Supper Time (1933)
Tequila (1958)
There Stands the Glass (1951)
When I Take My Sugar to Tea (1931)

See also: Sweetness

FOOLS

In popular song, fools are rarely buffoons; they are merely persons who expect to be deceived in the near future. Such an individual is the protagonist of the 1940 song "Fools Rush In," who at song's end declares: "So open up your heart and let this fool rush in." The title and following lyrics, of course, are taken directly from Alexander Pope's *An Essay in Criticism*: "For fools rush in where angels fear to tread."

Equally wary is the character in "My Foolish Heart," a sentimental ballad taken from the soundtrack of the 1949 film of the same name; he continually warns his "foolish heart" to "beware." Similar sentiments are expressed in "A Day in the Life of a Fool" (1966)—set to a haunting melody from Brazil—and in the 1956 song "Why Do Fools Fall in Love?"

A quite different sort of fool is found in "What Kind of Fool Am I?," a show-stopping ballad introduced by Anthony Newley in the British musical *Stop the World— I Want to Get Off* (1962); this fool is an "empty shell" who has never fallen in love. Also from Britain came the rhythmic "The Fool on the Hill," introduced by the Beatles in 1967.

Finally, another British import takes the word in an entirely different context. "These Foolish Things (Remind Me of You)" (1935), with its nostalgic lyrics— "A tinkling piano in the next apartment"—has nothing to do with a fool. It is really a song about remembrance of a lost love.

Additional Songs

The April Fools (1969)
Chain of Fools (1967)
Everybody Plays the Fool (1971)
Fool, Fool, Fool (1951)
A Fool in Love (Tell Me What's Wrong) (1960)

I've Got a Feelin' You're Foolin' (1935)
Poor Little Fool (1958)
She's a Fool (1963)
What a Fool Believes (1978)

FOREIGN INFLUENCE

The influence of American popular music abroad is well documented. Ragtime and jazz, for example, have inspired a host of European composers both "serious" and popular. Less obvious, at least until recent years, have been the steady contributions foreign **nations** have made to our music either directly, by giving us their songs, or indirectly, as birthplaces of songwriters and performers.

By far the greatest contributor, in both respects, has been **Britain**, with a veritable invasion of songwriters and performers since the Beatles' first appearance on Ed Sullivan's television show in 1964. In second place is **France**, whose contribution to American music has been steadier throughout the century. Not as direct an influence, but surely as significant a one, has been that of the continent of **Africa**.

Among other countries greatly affecting American popular music have been **Austria, Brazil, Cuba, Germany, Italy,** and **Mexico.** Lesser influences have come from **Argentina, Belgium, Canada, Czechoslovakia, Denmark, Greece, Hungary, Ireland,** and **Russia.**

Of course, foreign influence does not stop there. American popular music has absorbed numerous aspects of music from other parts of the world and continues to do so. In recent years, songs, styles, and performers have increasingly come from more diverse areas: places as differing as Australia, Iceland, Indonesia, Israel, New Zealand, Portugal, South Africa, Spain, Sweden, and Switzerland.

See also: Foreign Language

FOREIGN LANGUAGE

An interesting category of song intersperses foreign-language words or expressions within predominantly English lyrics. While most of these songs originated in the United States, some were imported from other **nations.** Many of these are songs of **love** or **farewell.**

One of the earliest songs to use a French expression was "Say 'Au Revoir' But Not Goodbye," written in 1893. Love everlasting is celebrated in the waltz "L'Amour Toujours l'Amour" (1922), with music by Rudolf Friml. The song "Au Revoir, Pleasant Dreams" (1930) became the theme song of the bandleader Ben Bernie, while "Darling Je Vous Aime Beaucoup" was written for the singer Hildegarde in 1935.

After World War II, the number of songs using French words and expressions increased. "La Vie en Rose" became popular in the United States in 1950. Introduced in France by Edith Piaf, it was given English lyrics first as "You're Too Dangerous, Cherie" and later as "Take Me to Your Heart Again," before attaining its greatest popularity as "La Vie en Rose," with English-French lyrics by Mack David. In 1947, the American song "Mam'selle" became a hit, followed by two songs from **France**: "Comme Ci, Comme ça" (1949) and "C'est Si Bon" (1950). The Beatles' "Michelle" (1966) also incorporates French words, with the expression "Ma belle."

Cole Porter, whose fondness for things French is well known, used French expressions in at least three songs: "Allez-Vous En, Go Away" and "C'est Magnifique," both from the 1953 musical comedy *Can-Can,* and "Ca, C'est l'Amour" (1957), from *Les Girls* (itself a French-English hybrid). Other songs using French words are "Dites-Moi," from *South Pacific* (1949); "Melodie d'Amour" (1949); "Chantez-Chantez" (1957); "Chanson d'Amour" (1958); and "Deja Vu" (1979). "My Cherie Amour," popularized by Stevie Wonder in 1969, manages to consolidate two different languages in its title.

One of the first songs to combine English with Italian was "Ciribiribin," which originated in **Italy** and was given English words in 1898. But the invasion of English-Italian songs didn't really begin until the 1950s, with "Botch-A-Me" written in 1952 as a phonetic way of asking for a kiss. The following year saw "Non Dimenticar" (Italian for "don't forget") and "Eh Cumpari," an **adaptation** of a traditional Italian song. "Anema e Core" and "Cara Mia" were popularized in 1954, while "Arrivederci Roma" and "Volare (Nel Blu, Dipinto di Blu)" were great hits in 1958. Two Italian ways of saying goodbye were expressed in "Ciao, Ciao, Bambina" (1959) and "Addio, Addio" (1961); the following year also saw a song of love: "Canto d'Amore."

Songs combining Spanish and English include "Adios" (1931), "Frenesi" (1940), "Amor" (1941), "Besame Mucho" (1941), "Vaya con Dios" (1953), and "Whatever Will Be, Will Be (Que Sera, Sera)" (1955). The German language is represented by three songs of farewell written over three generations—"Auf Wiederseh'n" (1915), "Auf Wiederseh'n, My Dear" (1932), and "Auf Wiederseh'n Sweetheart)" (1952) (only the last of which originated abroad)—and by the 1963 song "Danke Schoen."

Other foreign languages used in American song include Yiddish, with "Bei Mir Bist Du Schön, (Means That You're Grand)" (written in 1933, but popularized by the Andrews Sisters in 1938); Gaelic with "Too-ra-loo-ra-loo-ral, That's an Irish Lullaby," (written in 1914, but attaining its greatest popularity only in 1944 when sung by Bing Crosby in the film *Going My Way*); and Flemish, freely interspersed with English in Jacques Brel's "Marieke" (1961).

See also **Foreign Influence; Greetings**

FORGETTING

Forgetting is, of course, at the opposite pole of remembering. Therefore, it is often placed in a negative context: in Oscar Hammerstein II and Jerome Kern's hymn-like "Can I Forget You?" (1937) it poses a rhetorical question to which the answer is "no." Similarly negative in context are the songs "Unforgettable" (1951), popularized by Nat "King" Cole; and "Non Dimenticar (Don't Forget)," introduced in the Italian film *Anna* (1953). Also from Italy is the 1965 song "Forget Domani," a plea to live for today.

Forgetfulness used as a ploy to meet someone is the thrust of "You Forgot Your Gloves" (1931). Several songs juxtapose remembering and forgetting. This is the case in Rodgers and Hart's "It's Easy to Remember" ("and so hard to forget")—sung by Bing Crosby in the 1935 film *Mississippi*; and in Irving Berlin's "Remember" (1925), which ends with the wistful lyrics "But you forgot to remember." More direct is the message of a song of 1963: "Forget Him."

See also: Memory

FORGIVENESS

Asking forgiveness is the subject of a number of songs. One of the best known is the 1933 ballad "Don't Blame Me," which asks forgiveness for **falling in love**, with the words: "I'm under your spell, so how can I help it?" The mirror image of that plea occurs in the 1941 song "I Understand," which grants forgiveness, stating "And darling, you are not to blame."

Other songs on the subject include many in the form of apologies: "What Can I Say After I Say I'm Sorry?" (1926), "Forgive Me" (1927), "I Apologize" (1931), and at least two songs entitled "I'm Sorry" (1960 and 1975). In only one song, "Guilty" (1931), does the protagonist accept responsibility for his or her actions, but even there the person hedges: "If it's a crime then I'm guilty, guilty of loving you."

FORM

The form of a song is its musical structure, and usually involves some degree of either repetition after contrast or simple repetition. Countless formal plans have been used in popular songs over the past hundred years, but several stand out as favorites: verse/chorus, **blues** form, and plans that can be schematized as ABAB, ABAC, AABA, and AAA. However, these plans should not be thought of as procrustean beds; they are subject to an almost infinite number of modifications and variations.

Verse/chorus form was popular around the turn of the century and again from the 1970s onward. In this form, the narrative is told in a number of **verses** with changing **lyrics**, each followed by a **chorus**. Early examples were "After the Ball" (1892, with three verses) and "Meet Me in St. Louis, Louis" (1904, with two verses). More recent examples of verse/chorus form are "I Write the Songs" (1974) and "Nobody Does It Better" (1977).

The blues form is a simple twelve-bar pattern that can be summarized lyrically as AAB, wherein the first line is repeated and followed by new lyrics. As a musical form, it is harmonically oriented, starting each four-bar phrase respectively on the tonic (I), subdominant (IV), and dominant (V), and ending each time on the tonic. The most famous blues song, "St. Louis Blues" (1914) consists of three sections in blues form and a fourth section of sixteen bars, a tango in ABAB form.

The formal plans schematized as ABAB and ABAC were very popular in the first quarter of the twentieth century. In ABAB form, the initial idea (A) is followed by a second idea (B), after which both themes are repeated. Very often, as in the choruses of such songs as "Swanee" (1919) and "April Showers" (1921), the repetition of the second idea is modified to make an ending (B'). In ABAC form, a third idea (C) appears toward the end of the chorus, examples are George M. Cohan's "Give My Regards to Broadway" (1904) and "Mary's a Grand Old Name" (1905), and George Gershwin's "Embraceable You" (1930).

It should be emphasized that the overall form of a popular song includes the verse and chorus and their repetitions, as well as any introductions, **vamps, patters,** or **codas** that may occur. Nevertheless, many songs from the 1930s onward consist of choruses alone, including Jerome Kern's "Yesterdays" (1933) and Stevie Wonder's "You Are the Sunshine of My Life" (1972).

AABA form—usually in a **length** of thirty-two bars—was the most popular song form from about 1925 through the 1950s. But this versatile plan has been used in many songs since that time. In it, an initial idea (A) is repeated and then followed by a contrasting idea (B), called the **release** or bridge; after this, the first idea is recapitulated. Innumerable songs, including some of the most innovative standards, fall into this pattern: "Ol' Man River" (1927) and "The Way We Were" (1973) are examples from two different periods.

Although the majority of songs written in the first half of the twentieth century were written in ABAB', ABAC, or AABA form, it would be a mistake to think that they were the only forms employed; many other plans were used. For example, in the 1910 song "Some of These Days," repetition never occurs—a plan that can be represented as ABCD. Some songs are written in true ternary, or song, form (ABA): their initial idea is brought back only at the recapitulation. Examples are "Bidin' My Time" (1930) and "I'll Remember April" (1941). In other songs, interesting variations occur. "Night and Day" brings back only the second half of its principal theme at the recapitulation, in a plan that can be designated as ABABCB'. The plan of "I'm Old Fashioned" is ABCA', followed by a coda.

With the **folk song** revival and **rock** revolution of the 1960s, there was a powerful reaction against traditional formal plans. This reaction manifested itself in a return to many much older forms. One of the oldest and simplest consists of one musical idea that is repeated a number of times (AAA), as in "Gentle on My Mind" and "By the Time I Get to Phoenix" (both 1967). Many **protest songs** and songs of social conscience used this format, including "We Shall Overcome" (1945) and "Where Have All the Flowers Gone?" (1961). Also returned to favor were the verse/chorus "(Don't Cry Out Loud," 1976) and ABAB ("Hello," 1984) forms.

In fact, it can truly be said that no form has ever fallen completely out of favor. All have been used time and again—sometimes with such modifications as instrumental interludes or modulations to other keys—in the service of popular song.

Bibliography

Davis, Sheila. *The Craft of Lyric Writing*. 1985.
Hamm, Charles. *Yesterdays: Popular Song in America*. 1979.
Wilder, Alec. *American Popular Song: The Great Innovators 1900–1950*. 1972.

Fox Trot

The fox trot originated as a dance, but the term has also become generic for most American dance music in 4/4 or 2/4 **meter**, exclusive of rock. As such, it is set apart from the **waltz**, the **tango**, the **rumba**, the **bossa nova**, and other Latin American dances.

The fox trot originated in 1913 as one of a myriad of **dance crazes**. It was introduced by a vaudeville entertainer named Harry Fox, who liked to "trot" around the stage with various female partners in what came to be called "Mr. Fox's Trot." When Vernon and Irene Castle made social dancing the rage a few years later, the fox trot became the dance of choice. It has remained so through the years.

Tens of thousands of popular songs are known as fox trots. Some, like "A Pretty Girl Is Like a Melody" (1919), are in slow **tempo**. Others, such as "The Lady Is a Tramp" (1937), are often played uptempo—in so-called **society tempo**. Most commonly, however, the fox trot is danced in moderate tempo, to songs like "I Don't Know Why (I Just Do)" (1931) and "Call Me Irresponsible" (1962).

See also: Peabody; Swing; Two-Step

France

French influence on popular music in the United States is second among foreign **nations** only to that of **Britain**. It has grown steadily, especially since the end of World War II, culminating in the film music of Michel Legrand (*The Umbrellas of Cherbourg*, 1965) and the theater music of Claude-Michel Schönberg (*Les Misérables*, 1980).

Less well known is the fact that many postwar popular hits in America originated in France. These include "La Vie en Rose" (1950), the theme song of Edith Piaf; "Autumn Leaves" (1947), originally "Les Feuilles Mortes"; "Beyond the Sea" (1947), which began life as Charles Trenet's "La Mer"; "I Wish You Love" (1955), formerly Trenet's 1946 French hit "Que Reste-t-il de Nos Amours?"; "Cherry Pink and Apple Blossom White" (1955); "Let It Be Me" (1955), originally "Je T'Appartiens," "What Now My Love?," originally "Et Maintenant"; "The Good Life," popularized by Tony Bennett in 1963; "Love is Blue" (1968), originally "L'Amour Est Bleu"; the quintessential "American" song, "My Way" (1967), first called "Mon Habitude," which achieved great popularity with English lyrics by Paul Anka; and "The Old Fashioned Way" (1972), originally "Les Plaisirs Démodés."

Early in the twentieth century, French influence was relatively minor, confined to such imports as "Because" (1902), an art song often sung at weddings; the World War I favorite "Madelon" (1918); Fanny Brice's theme song, "My Man" (1921), originally "Mon Homme"; the ballad "When Day Is Done" (1926); and the lively two-step "Valentine" (1926), popularized by Maurice Chevalier.

The pace quickened in the early 1930s when several popular French songs of the time were translated almost literally into English: "Sous les Toits de Paris" turned into "Under a Roof in Paree," both in 1931; the European favorite "Parlez-Moi d'Amour" was reborn as "Speak to Me of Love" in 1932. With the advent of World War II, translations were prone to delays of as much as ten or more years. For example, Charles Trenet's French hits "J'ai Ta Main" and "Vous Qui Passez sans Me Voir," both originally written in 1937, achieved popularity in the United States only after war's end, as "Holding Hands" (1945) and "Passing By" (1947), respectively. "J'Attendrai"(1938), the theme song of Jean Sablon, became "I'll Be Yours" in 1945. "Sous les Ponts de Paris" became "Under the Bridges of Paris" only in 1953. One of the few songs to be imported during the war years was the French-American hybrid "(All of a Sudden) My Heart Sings" (1941), noted for its persistent use of the diatonic scale.

Several songs of French origin are **adaptations**, or are derived from the **classics**. These include "Fascination" (1932), based on F. D. Marchetti's Valse Tsigane of 1904; "My Prayer" (1939), taken from Georges Boulanger's Avant de Mourir; "My Reverie" (1938), from Claude Debussy's Reverie of 1895; and "The Lamp Is Low" (1939), from Maurice Ravel's Pavane pour une enfante défunte, written in 1899.

In the immediate postwar years, French songs became the rage in America, spurred on by the universal popularity of such singers as Edith Piaf, Charles Trenet,

Jacqueline François, Lucienne Boyer, and Jean Sablon. The first few years after the war saw such hits as "Symphony" (1945); "Comme Ci, Comme Ça" (1947), originally "Clopin-Clopant; "C'est Si Bon" (1947); "Mademoiselle de Paree" (1948); "Pigalle" (1948); "The River Seine" (1953); and "If You Love Me, Really Love Me" (1953), originally "Hymne à l'Amour."

In the 1950s, French contributions to American song continued unabated, with "Domino" (1950); "Under Paris Skies" (1951), originally "Sous le Ciel de Paris"; two English versions of "L'Âme des Poètes": "At Last! At Last!" (1951) and "The Poet's Dream" (1959); "The Song From Moulin Rouge (Where Is Your Heart?)" (1953), with music by the eminent French composer Georges Auric; "Back Track!" (1954), from "Passe Ton Chemin"; and "The Poor People of Paris" (1956), originally "La Goulant du Pauvre Jean."

In Michel Legrand, France produced a popular composer whose music is imbued with the classical tradition, yet remains highly contemporary. Born in Paris in 1932, he has written scores for over one hundred films. Many songs from these films have attained great popularity in the United States, starting with "I Will Wait for You" and "Watch What Happens" both from *The Umbrellas of Cherbourg* (1964). In subsequent years, a number of his songs were given English lyrics by the husband-and-wife team of Alan and Marilyn Bergman, including "The Windmills of Your Mind," the theme from *The Thomas Crown Affair*, (1968); "What Are You Doing the Rest of Your Life?" (1969); "Pieces of Dreams" (1970); "The Summer Knows" (1971); "Brian's Song" (1972); and "The Way He Makes Me Feel" (1983).

Victor Hugo's classic novel *Les Misérables* was converted into an extremely successful musical by the lyricist Alain Boublil and the composer Claude-Michel Schönberg. It opened at the Palais des Sports in Paris in 1980, was given English lyrics by Herbert Kretzmer, and became a sensation in London in 1985, attaining equal success in New York in 1986. Its remarkable score includes the songs "I Dreamed a Dream," "Castle on a Cloud," "Master of the House," and "On My Own."

Just as French food and wine have upheld their reputation through the years, French music has maintained its hold on the American public through good and bad times, war and peace.

See also: Foreign Influence; Foreign Language

Freedom Song

Many songs sung in the 1960s during the initial events of the nonviolent civil rights movement in the South began as protests against racial segregation at public facilities. Later, as the movement gained momentum, especially among adherents from both black and white college communities, the focus of the repertoire shifted from the "protest" to the "freedom" song.

The musical backbone for these freedom songs came from the slow-paced spiritual and the fast-paced jubilee gospel song, among others. Adapting music that had all but disappeared from the black communities instilled a feeling of pride in those fighting for their rights as Americans. This adaptation of well-known tunes to new lyrics was the brainchild of Guy Carawan, a young white folksinger who had been researching black folk music at the time that the lunch counter sit-ins began. Carawan understood that the success of the civil rights movement depended upon unity of spirit and purpose, and he saw the revitalization of black song as a means to accomplish this task.

The theme song of the civil rights movement was "We Shall Overcome." Its origins are somewhat blurred, with one version attributed to C. A. Tindle. At the very least, it is known that the song appeared in an early twentieth-century Baptist hymnal under the title "I'll Overcome Someday"; the words read in part: "I'll be all right, I'll be like Him, . . . I'll overcome." In the 1940s, the Negro Textile Union Workers adapted the hymn for their own use and soon thereafter brought their version of it to the attention of the Highlander Folk School in Monteagle, Tennessee. There it became not only that school's theme song but also a signature song for Zilphia Horton's performances at union rallies in southern states. Zilphia in turn introduced the song to Pete Seeger, who popularized it (albeit with new lyrics) in the northern states.

Guy Carawan, who was associated with the Highlander School, brought "We Shall Overcome" in its present form to the attention of student activists in the Southern Freedom Movement. Along with other freedom songs, "We Shall Overcome" was sung at mass meetings, before Freedom Rides, during prayer vigils, and in jails holding many who had taken part in nonviolent demonstrations.

"We Shall Overcome" is copyrighted in the arrangement of words and music by Zilphia Horton, Frank Hamilton, Guy Carawan, and Pete Seeger. Although this song is not "folk" in origin, it functions like a folk song, for it is known and used throughout the world wherever a rallying cry for freedom is raised.

Hermine W. Williams

Bibliography

Carawan, Guy, and Candie Carawan, compilers. *We Shall Overcome!: Songs of the Southern Freedom Movement.* 1963.

See also: Borrowing; Form; Gospel; Protest Song

Friendship

The subject of friendship has a long history in popular song. As far back as 1898, it was celebrated in the convivial favorite "A Stein Song," which begins: "For it's always fair weather, when good fellows get together." Another unofficial anthem of friends whenever they meet is "Hail, Hail, the Gang's All Here," with a melody borrowed from Giuseppe Verdi by way of Sir Arthur Sullivan (*see* Classics).

The subject of friendship has been of special interest to **barbershop** singers. They embrace it in such old favorites as "Gee, But It's Great to Meet a Friend From Your Home Town" (1910), "Oh! What a Pal Was Mary" (1919), and "(The Gang That Sang) Heart of My Heart" (1926).

The waltz "My Buddy" was a great hit of 1922, notwithstanding its similarity to Jerome Kern's "The Siren's Song," written five years earlier. Kay Swift wrote a memorable melody called "Can't We Be Friends?" for the first edition of *The Little Show* in 1929.

Cole Porter treated the subject sardonically in two songs: "Friendship" (1939) and "Let's Be Buddies" (1940). The song "A Beautiful Friendship" (1956) is about a friendship that blossomed into love. The 1961 waltz "Moon River" is noted for Johnny Mercer's enigmatic allusion to "My huckleberry friend." More recently, Carole King won a Grammy Award for her recording of "You've Got a Friend" (1971), and friendship through "good times and bad times" and "forever more" is pledged in "That's What Friends Are For" (1982).

True, self-effacing friendship is expressed in such songs as "Bridge Over Troubled Water" (1969) and "The Wind Beneath My Wings" (1982). But a more cynical view of friendship is shown in a song introduced in 1949 by Carol Channing in *Gentlemen Prefer Blondes*: "Diamonds Are a Girl's Best Friend."

Additional Songs

Friendly Persuasion (1956)
The Girl Friend (1926)

Just a Friend (1989)
Just Friends (1931)
Leader of the Pack (1964)
Playmates (1940)
With a Little Help From My Friends (1967)
   See also: **People; Togetherness**

FUNK

The term "funky" can apply to any uninhibited music performed in a campy or outlandish manner. But more specifically, "funk" refers to a type of black popular music that flourished in the late 1960s and 1970s as a reaction to what was seen as the commercialization of **soul** and the intellectualism of West Coast **jazz**.

The music of funk was conceived as honest, down-to-earth, uncompromising, and raw, and contained many elements of the **gospel** sound. Very often, it was highly syncopated and used hymn-like subdominant progressions and the minor mode. It was also eclectic, incorporating elements of **bebop, rhythm and blues, rock 'n' roll, calypso**, Latin music, and **rock**. James Brown was an early influence.

A banner year for funk was 1974, when Kool and the Gang presented such hits as "Hollywood Swinging" and "Jungle Boogie." Other important funk groups included Charlie Wright and the Watts 103rd Street Rhythm Band; Earth, Wind and Fire; Parliament; and Funkedelic—the last two presided over by the irrepressible George Clinton. One of the first successful songs to use the word in its title was "Funky Broadway," introduced by Dyke and the Blazers in 1967. Among other songs to follow were "Play That Funky Music" (1976) and "Funkytown" (1980).

g

GAY NINETIES

The last decade of the nineteenth century has been variously called the Gay Nineties, the Mauve Decade, and the Naughty Nineties. But the 1890s cannot be so simplistically categorized; the period was by no means as happy and carefree as these sobriquets would suggest, and saw more than its share of war, poverty, and discrimination.

Nevertheless, the 1890s were seminal years in the development of American popular song, a period when the seeds of jazz were sown with **ragtime**, when new life was given to the American musical theater by composers like Victor Herbert, when **vaudeville** became an important venue for introducing new music, when technological advances such as the phonograph, kinescope, and **player piano** offered new modes of transmission, and when songwriting became a profession and music publishing became big business. They were the years when **Tin Pan Alley** began and when sales of **sheet music** first rose into the millions with such songs as "Daisy Bell" (1892), "The Sidewalks of New York" (1894), and "You Tell Me Your Dream, I'll Tell You Mine" (1899).

The first million-dollar seller was "After the Ball," written and published by Charles K. Harris in 1892 at the age of twenty-five. Harris had been interested in **minstrel shows** as a boy, fashioning himself a banjo from an oyster can and wire strands. He first wrote songs at the age of sixteen, opening his own publishing firm in Milwaukee with a sign out front which said: "Songs Written To Order." His first hit, "After the Ball," was a flop when introduced. But Harris, not to be denied, paid a popular performer of the day $500 and gave him a percentage of the sheet music sales to include it in his performance. "After the Ball" was an "instant" hit and within days Harris had an order for 75,000 copies. Within a year he was drawing a profit of $25,000 a week from sheet music sales; the waltz-ballad eventually sold over five million copies.

Harris soon moved his firm to New York City to join other music publishers in the area around 14th Street known as Union Square. Some other firms that got their start there included M. Witmark and Sons, Jerome H. Remick Company, Joseph W. Stern, and Leo Feist and Company. The song that made Witmark a major publisher was "The Picture That's Turned Toward the Wall" (1891). Prior to "Picture," Witmark had sold song sheets in the hundreds, but with this song, sales zoomed into the thousands, making Witmark a major force in the music publishing industry.

The public in the Gay Nineties sought more and more sentimental ballads, and composers were more than happy to oblige. A fine example of the sentimental song of the time was "When You Were Sweet Sixteen" (1898). The song was anything but an instant hit; it was sold originally for $20 and then lingered on a publisher's shelf before being sold again for $15. It finally found its spot in vaudeville, and its sheet music sales went well over the million mark. "You're the Flower of My Heart, Sweet Adeline," although published in 1903, was written in 1896 and went through a number of name-changes before becoming part of the repertoire of every **barbershop** group in the nation. Originally called "Down Home In New England," it then became "You're the Flower of My Heart, Sweet Rosalie," before acquiring its final name.

The Gay Nineties had something for everyone when it came to popular music. In addition to the ballad, there was the "**nonsense song**"; the best known of these was "Ta-Ra-Ra Boom-De-Ay!" (1891). The original lyrics of this song were so ribald that it was performed secretly for years before it was cleaned up and became a classic. The first sheet music of this nonsense song sold at the astronomical price of one dollar a copy. Competitive publications brought the price down to two cents a copy, and later it was even given away free with a purchase of a popular tea.

Patriotism had its day in the period with the publishing of "America the Beautiful" (1898), a song which started life as a poem. The words were set to the music of a hymn, "O, Mother Dear, Jerusalem" (1888), but the song found its true niche in American music as a substitute national anthem. Another patriotic song of the decade was John Philip Sousa's "The Stars and Stripes Forever" (1897), conceived as the composer returned from a European journey. The bandmaster was said to have received a million dollars from sales and royalties of the **march**, to which he added his own words. Sousa also composed numerous other marches during this period. **Operetta** also had its influence on popular music with the success of "Oh Promise Me," from Reginald De Koven's *Robin Hood* (1890).

The Gay Nineties was a period of change, and one such change has remained to this day: the emphasis on the **chorus** rather than the **verse**. Prior to the turn of the century, verses tended to be far longer than choruses. In this decade, the chief melodic material now moved to the chorus, as in "The Bowery" (1892). This popular song had six verses, but as the decade continued, the trend was to fewer verses (two or three).

One composer who might be called typical of the Gay Nineties was Harry Von Tilzer, who claimed to have written 8,000 songs, of which "3,000 came before [his] first hit," "My Old New Hampshire Home" (1898), which sold two million copies. Two years later, Von Tilzer composed "A Bird in a Gilded Cage" (1899) in a brothel. In keeping with the innocence of the time, the lyricist (Arthur J. Lamb) made it very clear that the "lady" in the song was a millionaire's wife, not his mistress.

One successful song of the mid-1890s, "The Little Lost Child" (1894), gained fame through an innovative method of song plugging, the song slide. This consisted of a series of pictures projected on a screen as a singer performed a song. "Lost Child" sold over two million copies of sheet music through this gimmick. Two years later, the song "Mother Was a Lady," or "If Jack Were Only Here" (1896) sold even more copies of sheet music employing projected slides.

In 1899, Paul Dresser composed "On the Banks of the Wabash Far Away," a song that later became the state song of Indiana. "Wabash" was followed by another major success, "The Curse of the Dreamer" (1899). The latter song made Dresser even more famous than his brother, the novelist Theodore Dreiser, who spelled the family name differently.

However, the most popular song to make its debut during the so-called Gay Nineties was not written by a famed composer on Tin Pan Alley, but rather by two sisters who were kindergarten teachers. The song, "Happy Birthday to You" (1893), was originally written as a children's song called "Good Morning to All." According to the *Guinness Book of World Records*, "Happy Birthday to You" is the most frequently sung song in the

English language. (The two runners-up are "For He's a Jolly Good Fellow" and "Auld Lang Syne.") It is a fitting reminder of a most important decade for American popular song.

Additional Songs

Asleep in the Deep (1897)
The Band Played On (1895)
Break the News to Mother (1897)
Comrades (1894)
Doan Ye Cry Mah Honey (1899)
Elsie From Chelsea (1896)
Forgotten (1894)
Georgia Camp Meeting (1897)
Gypsy Love Song (1898)
Hearts and Flowers (1899)
Hello! Ma Baby (1899)
I Don't Want to Play in Your Yard (1894)
I've Been Working on the Railroad (1894)
Kentucky Babe (1896)
Little Annie Rooney (1890)
Mandy Lee (1899)
My Gal Is a High Born Lady (1896)
My Sweetheart's the Man in the Moon (1892)
My Wild Irish Rose (1899)
Put Me Off at Buffalo (1895)
Say "Au Revoir" But Not "Goodbye" (1893)
The Story of the Rose (Heart of My Heart) (1899)
There'll Be a Hot Time in the Old Town (Tonight) (1896)

William D. Askin

Bibliography

Ewan, David, *All the Years of American Popular Music: A Comprehensive History.* 1977.
———. *Panorama of American Popular Music.* 1957.
———. *The World of Twentieth Century Music.* 1968.
Fremont, Robert A., ed. *Favorite Songs of the Nineties: Complete Original Sheet Music for 89 Songs.* 1973.
Hamm, Charles, *Yesterdays: Popular Song in America.* 1979.
Marks, Edward B. *They All Sang: From Tony Pastor to Rudy Vallee.* 1934.
Spaeth, Sigmund, *A History of Popular Music in America.* 1960.
Taws, Nicholas, *A Music for the Millions: Antebellum Democratic Attitudes and the Birth of American Popular Music.* 1984.

GENTLENESS. *SEE* TENDERNESS

GERMANY

Despite the interruption of two world wars, the German contribution to popular music in America has been fairly consistent since the 1920s. One of the earliest German songs to reach these shores was "Parade of the Wooden Soldiers," a novelty originally written in 1905 as "Die Parade der Holzsoldaten." The song attained great popularity in the United States after its presentation in the revue *Chauve-Souris* (1922).

In 1928, Bertolt Brecht and Kurt Weill's *Die Dreigroschenoper* opened in Berlin to great acclaim. First produced in America five years later as *The Threepenny Opera*, it is perhaps best known in English in a later (1954) translation with lyrics by Marc Blitzstein; its most enduring songs are "Mack the Knife" (also known as "Moritat") and "Pirate Jenny." Brecht and Weill also wrote "The Bilbao Song" in 1929, which was given English lyrics by Johnny Mercer in 1961. Weill later composed many other fine songs in America, using a succession of different lyricists, and is perhaps our most significant German-born popular composer.

Between the wars, several German **tangos** became popular in the United States, among them "I Kiss Your Hand, Madame" (1929) and "Take Me in Your Arms" (1932). The **waltz**, always dear to the German soul, is represented by "Falling in Love Again (Can't Help It)," sultrily introduced by Marlene Dietrich in the film *The Blue Angel* (1930); and by "Answer Me, My Love," recorded successfully by Nat King Cole in 1954.

A special case can be made of the little **march** "Lili Marleen" (1940). The words were originally written by a German soldier, Hans Leip, in 1915 and were set to music in 1938 by Norbert Schultze. During **World War II**, the song was revived, and became extremely popular on both German and Allied sides.

After the war, several West German songs became popular in the United States: "Auf Wiederseh'n, Sweetheart," sung by Vera Lynn in 1952; "The Happy Wanderer (Val-de Ri—Val-de Ra)," a novelty of 1954; "Danke Schoen," recorded by Wayne Newton in 1963; "A Walk in the Black Forest (1965); and, especially, "Strangers in the Night" (1966), most successfully recorded by Frank Sinatra.

> *See also:* **Austria; Foreign Influence; Foreign Language; Nations**

GIRL

Songs on the subject of **woman** abound; so, too, do the words used to address them: **angel**, babe, **baby**, belle, dame, **doll**, honey, **lady**, madam, mademoiselle, maiden, **mother**, siren, and sweetheart, among others. But the most popular designation of all is "girl."

As in the case of "**boy**," few songs about girls have to do with **childhood**; most refer to adult women. Exceptions are "Daddy's Little Girl" (1905) and "Thank Heaven for Little Girls" (1958), both of which could apply as well to children as to adults, and the section of "Soliloquy," from *Carousel* (1945), that starts with the words "My little girl," which is indeed about a child.

In songs about women, girls are portrayed in a variety of ways. They are: pretty, in "A Pretty Girl Is Like a Melody" (1919); beautiful, in "The Most Beautiful Girl in the World" (1935) and "The Most Beautiful Girl" (1973); objects of desire, in "If You Were the Only Girl in the World" (1916) and "Girl of My Dreams" (1927); prospective spouses, in "I Want a Girl Just Like the Girl That Married Dear Old Dad" (1911) and "The Girl That I Marry" (1946); from exotic places, in "The Girl From Ipanema" (1963); somewhat cynical, in "Diamonds Are a Girl's Best Friend" (1949); dejected, in "Little Girl Blue" (1935); or just plain bad, in "Bad Girls" (1978).

Entire musical comedies have been written about girls, among them *The Girl Friend* (1926), *Girl Crazy* (1931), *Me and My Girl* (1938), and *Funny Girl* (1964). Girls perform the can-can in *The Merry Widow* (1907) to the strains of "Girls, Girls, Girls." There are also a number of songs from the first half of the twentieth century that use the informal equivalent of girl, "gal," a designation now out of favor. These include "My Gal Sal" (1905), "For Me and My Gal" (1917), "Somebody Stole My Gal" (1918), "Sleepy Time Gal" (1924), and "I've Got a Gal in Kalamazoo" (1942). But perhaps the proudest girl of all is the one in *Flower Drum Song* (1958), who sings "I Enjoy Being a Girl."

Additional Songs

All I Need Is the Girl (1959)
Big Girls Don't Cry (1962)
Candy Girl (1963)
Cowboys to Girls (1968)
Daddy's Little Girl (1949)
Dear Old Girl (1903)
A Fellow Needs a Girl (1947)
Five Foot Two, Eyes of Blue, Has Anybody Seen My Girl? (1925)
Georgy Girl (1966)
The Girl Friend (1926)
The Girl Is Mine (1982)
Girl Watcher (1968)
Go Away, Little Girl (1962)
Happiest Girl in the Whole U.S.A. (1971)
Heaven Will Protect the Working Girl (1909)
Hey, Girl (1963)
Hey There Lonely Girl/Hey There Lonely Boy (1970)
Island Girl (1975)
Just a Girl That Men Forget (1923)
Material Girl (1984)
Me and My Girl (1938)
Music to Watch Girls By (1966)
When I'm Not Near the Girl I Love (1946)
Who's That Girl? (1987)
You're My Girl (1947)

GOLDEN AGE

Writers have noted a period of exceptional achievement in the history of American popular song, one sparked by the music and lyrics of Irving Berlin, Jerome Kern, George and Ira Gershwin, Cole Porter, Richard Rodgers, Harold Arlen, Lorenz Hart, Oscar Hammerstein II, Johnny Mercer, and many others. Often referred to as a "golden age," the period is difficult to define precisely, although the years 1925 and 1945 approximate its beginning and ending.

Those twenty golden years saw the rise of Rodgers and Hart, the Gershwins, and Porter in **musical comedy**; the appearance of the landmark **musical plays** *Show Boat* (1927) and *Oklahoma!* (1943), and of the **opera** *Porgy and Bess* (1935); the rise of **radio**, the **big bands** and the **film musical**; and the final glow of **Tin Pan Alley**.

Ironically, by far the most productive years of this golden age coincided with the **Depression years** from 1929 to 1939. Many innovative **standards** were written at this time. They include "Star Dust" in 1929; "Body and Soul" and "Embraceable You" in 1930; "Dancing in the Dark" and "Mood Indigo" in 1931; "April in Paris," "Night and Day," and "The Song Is You" in 1932; "Lover," "Smoke Gets in Your Eyes," "Sophisticated Lady," and "Yesterdays" in 1933; "Autumn in New York," "I Get a Kick Out of You," and "You're the Top" in 1934; "Begin the Beguine" in 1935; "I've Got You Under My Skin" and "The Way You Look Tonight" in 1936; "A Foggy Day" and "My Funny Valentine" in 1937; "September Song" in 1938; and "All the Things You Are" in 1939.

The same ten years also saw hundreds of other less innovative but equally enduring standards. Among these are "Ain't Misbehavin'" and "More Than You Know" (1929); "As Time Goes By," "Georgia on My Mind," and "On the Sunny Side of the Street" (1930); "All of Me" and "Penthouse Serenade" (1931); "I Don't Stand a Ghost of a Chance With You" (1932); "Easter Parade" and "It's Only a Paper Moon" (1933); "Blue Moon" and "Deep Purple" (1934); "Cheek to Cheek" and "I Can't Get Started" (1935); "Pennies From Heaven" (1936); and "Over the Rainbow" (1939).

If one adds the years of the late 1920s and early 1940s to this golden age, one can include such evergreens as "Always" and "Manhattan" (1925), "Blue Room" and "Someone to Watch Over Me" (1926), "Blue Skies" and "My Blue Heaven" (1927), "I Can't Give You Anything But Love" and "If I Had You" (1928), "How High the Moon" and "The Nearness of You" (1940), "Bewitched" and "Blues in the Night" (1941), "That Old Black Magic" (1942), "Oh, What a Beautiful Mornin'" and "You'll Never Know" (1943), "It Could Happen to You" (1944), and "If I Loved You" and "Laura" (both 1945).

Whether it lasted ten years or twenty, there is no denying that this remarkable outpouring of songs produced a golden age of American popular song. It has left us a rich legacy of standards—enduring songs that have been adapted in diverse ways and that have become part of the American consciousness.

See also: **Collaboration; Composers; Composer-Lyricists; Landmarks of Stage and Screen; Lyricists; Roaring Twenties; World War II**

GOODBYES. *SEE* FAREWELLS

GOSPEL

"Real gospel music," according to Harold Bailey (leader of a Chicago-based group of gospel singers), "is an intelligible sermon in song." It is also a medium through which personal religious experiences are expressed. The success of gospel musicians—be they ecstatic soloists, quartets, or choirs—is measured by their commitment to a Christian way of life and by their dedication to bringing the "good news" to believers and nonbelievers alike. The message and the musician are of equal importance in "traditional" gospel music.

It is difficult to define this uniquely American art form, for gospel music assumes many and varied guises: white gospel or black gospel, religious folksong or strophic hymn, sentimental ballad or country-western song, "traditional" gospel (which remains closely aligned with the church) or "conventional" gospel (which popularizes the form by allowing the "message" to be swallowed up by the performance).

White Gospel Music

White gospel music represents a simple, straightforward means to communicate an evangelical Protestant message. The need for this type of musical expression arose during successive eras of revivalism that swept across American soil, most notably those of 1800–30, 1870–1900, and the 1950s. Influences upon white gospel have come from such disparate sources as the eighteenth-century hymnody of Isaac Watts and John Newton, camp-meeting spirituals, Appalachian folk hymnody, Civil War marching songs, Sunday school songs, and popular secular songs.

Typical of pre-1860 collections containing folk and urban revival hymnody is Joshua Leavitt's *The Christian Lyre* (1831). It has New England psalm tunes, a German chorale, American folk hymns, newly created "social" songs, and popular secular songs (such as "Home Sweet Home," set to a sacred parody of its original lyrics). Music associated with the secular world was intentionally introduced to entice the general public to attend revival meetings.

White gospel music was usually cast in the mold of a four-part strophic hymn, with a verse-refrain format, simple harmonic vocabulary, dotted rhythms, and a homophonic texture relieved by the interjection of "echo parts" (the **call-and-response** effect of soprano-alto parts rhythmically echoed by tenor-bass parts). Texts had an immediacy about them. They focused on specific questions ("Brother, art thou worn and weary?") and issued direct commands ("Brighten the corner where you are!").

Gospel hymnody spread rapidly, first as a corpus of relevant songs for Sunday schools and "services of sacred song" featuring renowned singers such as Philip

Phillips, and later as a medium for bringing the "message" to the general public by way of revival preacher–singer teams. One of the most famous teams was that of Dwight Moody, an evangelist, and Ira Sankey, a singer, composer, and compiler of gospel songs; they worked together in Great Britain and the United States from 1879 to 1910. Among the next generation's teams was the well-known 1910–30 duo of William "Billy" Sunday, evangelist, and Homer Rodeheaver, singer, trombonist, publisher, and owner of Rainbow Records.

Most white evangelists, including Billy Graham, engaged musicians—singers, composers, choral groups—to increase the entertainment value of their mass revival meetings. In fact, meetings like those organized by Moody were even advertised in the entrainment section of newspapers. Publishers and recording companies were also added to the support roster.

The ecstatic emotionalism of revival singing in the early decades of the nineteenth century was tempered in the Moody-Sankey era into a very controlled but sentimental performance style. With the advent of the twentieth century came a change in the mood of white gospel music. Whereas the hymnody of Moody and Sankey was intended for use in services of worship and devotional meetings, that of subsequent generations was designed, according to Rodeheaver, "to bridge the gap between the popular song of the day and the great hymns and gospel songs." The idea was to provide religious songs that could be learned quickly and easily. Singing conventions, commercial publications, and recordings promoted the new gospel music, much of which could be labeled "pop gospel," with its country-western flavoring of **bluegrass** and hillbilly styles.

One of the best-known white gospel groups in the 1960s and 1970s was the Gaither Trio, with the Gaither brothers, Bill and Danny, and their sister Mary Ann as founding members. Bill Gaither seems to have been the driving force of this trio, for he was not only a performer and composer of gospel music, but also a publisher. His Gaither Music Company was formed for the sole purpose of publishing his original compositions and his song collections. In 1971, Gaither's "Because He Lives" was named "song of the year" by the Gospel Music Association. Gaither himself was named "songwriter of the year," winning the Dove Award in eight consecutive years. He also was awarded seven **Grammy Awards** and was honored for having the first gold album by a gospel artist on a gospel label.

Although gospel music was popular, it was quite evident that the momentum behind the million-selling gospel records was due in large measure to recording artists who were superstars. Not all white gospel artists considered themselves "religious" artists, nor did they make their living solely from proclaiming the Christian message in song. Elvis Presley, to name but one, falls into this category, for he pursued a dual career in gospel and **rock 'n' roll**. From the 1950s until his death in 1977, Presley never divorced himself from the Pentecostal environment in which he was born and raised.

Pentecostalism took root in the southern regions of the United States at the beginning of this century. It was noted for its unwavering allegiance to traditional and conservative religious values and was distinguished by its adherents' speaking in tongues (glossolalia), a sign of their empowerment by the Holy Spirit.

Presley's earliest recordings were made with a backup gospel quartet, the Jordanaires. His first gospel album was *His Hand in Mine*; it featured many gospel standards, to which Presley added a stirring rhythmical beat. In the late 1950s, he recorded Thomas A. Dorsey's "Precious Lord, Take My Hand" (1932) and "Peace in the Valley" (1939), selling over a million copies of each, and in 1968 his album *How Great Thou Art* (made with the Jordanaires and the Imperials) became a gold record.

Black Gospel Music

At the time of the first and second Great Awakenings, white pioneers expressed the fervor of Christian revivalism in songs that reflected their ecstatic emotions. Black slaves witnessed these revivals; they heard the songs and used them, along with their own newly created camp-meeting spirituals, as a wellspring for developing black gospel music. They adapted the pioneers' favorite hymn texts by Isaac Watts and John Newton, among others, to African-American styles of performance, with call-and-response delivery, syncopated and repeated rhythmic patterns, and flexible pitches including **blue notes**.

Blacks were, and continue to be, attracted to the Watts and Newton hymns because many of the texts speak directly to life's daily experiences. For example, "Father I Stretch My Hand" by Watts portrays the despair and loneliness of living if one is deprived of divine help and guidance: "If thou withdraw Thyself from me, whither shall I go?" "The Day Is Past and Gone," also by Watts, addresses the finality of life: "O may we all remember well, the night of death draws near." "Amazing Grace" by Newton, the number one standard for both black and white gospel singers (albeit with significant variation in stanzas), describes the hardships of people living "through many dangers, toils, and snares."

One of the first hymnals designed specifically for use by black congregations was Richard Allen's *A Collection of Spiritual Songs and Hymns Selected From Various Authors*, which went through at least eight editions from 1801 to 1954. In addition to spirituals, camp-meeting songs, and eighteenth-century hymn texts (many of which were adapted to popular tunes), this collection presented some new hymns such as "When I Can Read My Title Clear" and "There Is a Land of Pure Delight."

Among other collections that have played an important role in the history of black gospel is Charles A. Tindley's *New Songs of Paradise* (1916). Tindley was not only a well-known minister of the East Calvary Methodist Episcopal Church, which he founded in Philadelphia in 1870, but also an influential black gospel songwriter. His music is "a cross between the music of spirituals and the texts of hymns," which, for lack of a better word, might be described as gospel **folk song**. He uses a **blues** format for the melody and creates opportunities for improvisation in the form of vocal interpolations and jazz syncopations. Among Tindley's songs that have become standards are "I'll Overcome Some Day" (1901), "Stand By Me" (1905) and "Leave It There" (1910).

Tindley was an inspiration for the next generation of gospel songwriters, especially for Thomas A. Dorsey, the son of a southern Baptist minister. Dorsey, known professionally as "Georgia Tom," made his living initially as a blues and ragtime pianist, singer, and composer. The first glimpse of his gospel songwriting talents appears in a publication of the best-loved songs sung by black congregations, *Gospel Pearls* (1921), in which Dorsey is the featured composer. It is immediately apparent that many of Dorsey's songs come straight out of Tindley's style of gospel music, with their blues-colored melodies and texts that speak directly to the poor and oppressed.

Dorsey is usually singled out as the person who had the greatest impact upon black gospel music in the 1920s and 1930s. In fact, Dorsey claims he "coined the words 'gospel songs' after he first heard a gospel choir" sing what he would previously have termed evangelistic songs. Dorsey's gospel blues accompanied by jazz riffs became both acceptable for use in mainline black churches and popular with white southerners. Among Dorsey's songs, several continue to be standards: "If You See My Savior, Tell Him That You Saw Me" (1926), recorded in 1931 by the Blue Jay Quartet, the first group to record a Dorsey gospel song; "It's My Desire," popularized in the late 1940s by Guy Lombardo; "Precious Lord, Take My Hand" (1932), recorded by almost all the major gospel singers and translated into many different languages; "Peace in the Valley" (1939), a song often heard at the funeral services of gospel artists; and "I'm Gonna Live the Life I Sing About in My Song (c. 1940)" prompted by Dorsey's disgust for musicians who were making a living singing gospel but had no respect for the message of the songs or the tradition.

The decade of the 1930s was a crucial one for Dorsey as he began his mission of disseminating gospel music throughout the United States, both in and out of services of worship. Prior to 1930, Dorsey's songwriting had produced many fans, but few of the "established" black churches (Baptist and Methodist) sanctioned his music for regular use. All that changed in 1930 when two of Dorsey's songs—"Did You See My Savior?" and "How About You?"—were enthusiastically received at the National Baptist Convention for blacks in Chicago. It should be noted, however, that not until 1977, with the publication of *The New National Baptist Hymnal*, did the National Baptist Convention officially declare gospel to be the hymnody of choice for Baptist congregations.

Dorsey was also responsible for seeing that choirs, especially all-female choirs, could play a major role in promoting gospel music. In 1931, he and Theodore Frye formed a gospel choir at the Ebenezer Baptist Church in Chicago. A year later, Dorsey, together with one of his many associates, Sallie Martin, convened the National Convention of Gospel Choirs and Choruses. The convention was held at the Pilgrim Baptist Church where Dorsey had recently been appointed choir director and minister of music. From this very influential church position, which Dorsey held continuously for forty years, he was able to steer the course of gospel music from within the church's organization.

Other important activities of Dorsey in the 1930s include founding the Thomas A. Dorsey Gospel Songs Music Publishing Company, the first publishing firm dedicated to black gospel music, and the formation of the Dorsey Trio in 1933 for the purpose of promoting Dorsey's songs. Last, but not least, Dorsey was involved for more than ten years (1932–44) in "Evenings With Dorsey" which were gospel music concerts performed throughout the United States by Dorsey, Sallie Martin, Roberta Martin, and Mahalia Jackson, among others. This touring gospel "act" paved the way for what was to become the golden age of gospel: 1945–60.

There have been many outstanding black female gospel singers, but none is better known than Mahalia Jackson. Her choice of repertoire and her distinctive style of performing bear the stamp of her childhood years in New Orleans. She was raised in a devout Baptist family, attended Sunday services in a southern Baptist church, was exposed to the "Holiness" workship experience in the Sanctified church next to her home, had knowledge of professional entertainers through her relatives, and heard jazz and blue played by street musicians.

In 1927, Jackson set out for Chicago, where many of the great gospel soloists were in residence or appeared on tour. Jackson's performance style was typically southern, for she vocally stretched the phrasing of her songs, interpolated moans and growls, improvised upon melody and meter, and moved her body in much the same way that black preachers did when delivering their sermons. When she toured with Dorsey in the 1940s, her distinctive manner of singing his "Precious Lord" and "If You See My Savior" disturbed Dorsey, for her performances rendered his songs unrecognizable from his conception of them.

In the late 1930s, Jackson cut several records, singing old favorites ("God's Gonna Separate the Wheat From the Tares") as well as new creations ("God Shall Wipe All Tears Away"). A decade later she recorded W. Herbert Brewster's "Move On Up a Little Higher (1946)," which sold over a million copies. As the title suggests, the success of this recording helped Jackson move up a little higher in the popularity ratings, soon becoming known as the Gospel Queen. This recording is important for another reason; in it, Jackson introduced the "vamp." A **vamp** involves multiple repetitions of a simple chord progression in the accompaniment, over which the soloist improvises melody and/or text. So effective was this special feature that the vamp was incorporated by many soloists into their gospel performances.

Other Brewster songs from the late 1940s, such as "Just Over the Hill," "How I Got Over," and "These Are They," gave Jackson suitable material to build her emotion-packed performances, not only in churches but also in stadiums and concert halls. She was featured on radio and TV programs, sang at the 1958 Newport Jazz Festival, and even gave several concerts in Carnegie Hall during the 1950s and 1960s.

Jackson's popularity with both black and white audiences allowed her to be active in political events. For example, through her inclusion of "We Shall Overcome" in many of her major concerts, she drew attention to the civil rights movement and Dr. Martin Luther King, Jr. She also shared a moment in the political spotlight when she sang at the inauguration of President John F. Kennedy in 1961.

Many other female singers have played significant roles in the history of black gospel. Clara Ward popularized gospel at the 1957 Newport Jazz Festival. Aretha Franklin, protégé of Thomas Dorsey, had a gold record with her 1972 recording of "Amazing Grace." Shirley Caesar made a name for herself as a singer-preacher. Others who should be mentioned include Sallie Martin, Roberta Martin, Rosetta Tharpe, Willie Mae Ford, Bessie Griffin, Dorothy Love, Marion Williams, and Tramaine Hawkins.

Several of the singers mentioned above were members of Holiness or Sanctified churches, a factor that greatly influenced their gospel performances. Not only did Holiness services of worship emphasize singing, dancing, hand-clapping, and the use of many different kinds of musical instruments, they also focused upon that most unique of all worship ingredients, "shouting." A "shout" is a bodily movement peculiar to each worshiper's response to the spiritual impact of the worship experience. The individual "shout" can be as controlled as a gentle swaying of the body or as violent as a frenetic dance that ends in spirit possession. An example of a "shout" number is W. Herbert Brewster's "Surely God Is Able" (1949), made famous by performances and a recording cut by the Ward Singers and Marion Williams.

Among the most popular male gospel soloists of the 1960s was James Cleveland. Born in Chicago in 1932 and musically nurtured in the Pilgrim Baptist Church, where, as a boy soprano, he sang under the direction of Thomas A. Dorsey, Cleveland quickly rose to prominence as a singer, a director of choirs, and a composer of more than three hundred gospel songs. His voice was rough and raspy, and it was often described as "the worst voice I have ever heard." Nevertheless, his performances earned for him the nickname "King James" and "Crown Prince of Gospel." Cleveland made arrangements of old spirituals ("It's Me O Lord" and "Old Time Religion"), composed new tunes for old standards ("Stand By Me"), and wrote his own gospel songs ("Sit Down Servant") both c.1955. He cut a number of records in the 1950s, several with well-disciplined choirs. Not until the next decade, however, did he enjoy his first taste of national acclaim: together with the Angelic Choir, he produced an album that sold 800,000 copies. The title song was "Peace Be Still," an eighteenth-century madrigal which Cleveland recast as a Holiness shout.

Cleveland founded the Gospel Singers Workshop Convention, an annual meeting of some of the best young gospel musicians in the nation. At these conventions, Cleveland encouraged musicians (many still in their teens) to expand the horizons of gospel sound and to create new means to combine gospel and pop without sacrificing the spirit of the art form. Evidence of Cleveland's ideas are forever captured on Savoy Records, his albums consistently selling more than 50,000 copies each.

By the end of the 1960s, black gospel music showed signs of developing in two different directions. One path was committed to maintaining traditional gospel, conceived for and performed in churches or halls where congregations of believers had assembled. The other path was designed for consumption by the secular world. Instead of singing about the love of God, the musicians were singing about love of one's neighbor and about societal issues. Cleveland had straddled the two paths without giving in to either one. Those who followed him were more prone to adopting one of the two paths.

Cleveland laid the groundwork for the transformation wrought by Edwin Hawkins, whose 1969 arrangement of the traditional Baptist hymn "Oh, Happy Day" catapulted gospel into a new era. Hawkins's arrangement, influenced by **rhythm and blues**, was recorded with the North California State Youth Choir (later known as the Edwin Hawkins Singers) and sold two million copies.

Another influential gospel group that rose to prominence in the 1970s was the **folk-rock** Staple Singers, led by Roebuck Staples. Representative songs are "I'll Take Your There" and "Respect Yourself," both from a 1971 album. These and other Staple Singers songs from the 1970s make use of pop and soul as their musical palette and rarely make any explicit reference to the divine presence of God; hence their recordings are deemed acceptable for broadcast on regular radio programs.

Other contemporary gospel groups, like BeBe and CeCe Winans, are achieving gold records status, receiving number one ratings on the *Billboard* rhythm-and-blues charts, and winning the coveted Grammy Award. Examples of the Winans's songs are "Addictive Love" and "Depend on You."

Tramaine Hawkins released "Fall Down," a single that was played frequently in discos. In response to the criticism she received from traditional gospel artists, Hawkins indicated that she was not selling out to the secular world. Instead, her music was reaching out to a wider audience, one that she hoped could be brought into the realm of traditional gospel. Her motives are echoed in the production philosophy of other groups such as Take Six and Sounds of Blackness.

One of the biggest traditional gospel hits of the 1980s was "(I'm Comin Up) The Rough Side of the Mountain," a duet by Janice Brown and F. C. Barnes, co-pastors of a North Carolina church. The lyrics mirror the bad economic climate of the early 1980s, but they also proclaim the "good news" in a traditional gospel style, allowing the message to shine as a beacon in hard times. Sales of this single surpassed all expectations, and proved that traditional gospel can and will continue to hold its own against contemporary gospel.

No discussion of black gospel music would be complete without mention of the important role played by quartets and choirs. The male quartet and the male evangelical preacher—the song and the sermon—formed the cornerstone of traditional black services of worship beginning in the 1920s. Most of the early quartets, of which the Heavenly Gospel Singers are representative, performed *a cappella* in close four-part harmony. In the 1930s and 1940s, groups such as the Golden Gate Jubilee Quartet incorporated novelty techniques to expand their *a cappella* performances: they used "vocal percussion" to imitate instrumental sounds and emphasized the extremes of their vocal registers by contrasting falsetto with bass parts. With the increased influence of Sanctified services of worship, the quartets introduced instrumental accompaniments (piano, guitar, harmonica, and especially tambourine) and moved away from the four-part hymn structure to one using a strong vocal line backed by a group. Such an arrangement allowed for extensive vocal improvisation over a vamp and textual interpolations by the lead, as well as for the use of the call and response between lead and quartet.

Ira Tucker (tenor) and the Dixie Hummingbirds exemplify well the various facets of the 1950s quartet style, especially in the title song of the album *In the Morning*. Another Hummingbirds' recording includes one of their best-known songs, "Trouble in My Way," with its opening twelve bar blues-type format. Although Tucker and the Hummingbirds appeared at the 1966 Newport Jazz Festival, they never succumbed to the contemporary style of gospel.

For a brief period in the 1960s, quartets tried the so-called hard gospel approach, but softer, more mellow performance styles soon came back into vogue. Several groups in particular who helped restore the popularity of the male gospel quartet were the Mighty Cloud of Joy, the Jackson Southernaires, and the Williams Brothers.

Since the 1930s, gospel choirs (many made up exclusively of women) have augmented or even supplanted the "senior" choirs in black Baptist churches. Beginning with the Thomas A. Dorsey and Theodore Frye choir, the number of gospel choirs organized for churches and college campuses is legion. Some choirs excel in a disciplined style of singing; others are known for their encouragement of spontaneous singing, shouting, and dancing.

The St. Paul's Baptist Church choir was one of the first to achieve a hit recording. The choir did so in 1947 singing Dorsey's "We Sure Do Need Him Now" and "God Be With You."

With the organization in 1968 of the Gospel Music Workshop of America (GMWA) by James Cleveland, Mattie Clark, and others, the standards of gospel choir performance were set forth and have influenced gospel choir singing ever since. With membership at well over half a million, the GMWA can perhaps take credit for the establishment not only of college-based choirs but also of gospel festivals all over the nation.

Although there has been considerable **crossover** between black and white gospel and between traditional and contemporary gospel, the traditional black artists are fighting to preserve an art form that brings unambiguously a distinctive message in religious words to the downtrodden and poor, a message supported, not overpowered, by a rich and ever-changing musical language.

Hermine W. Williams

Bibliography

Cusic, Don. *The Sound of Light: A History of Gospel Music.* 1990.

Eskew, Harry, James Downey, and Horace Boyer. "Gospel Music." In *The New Grove Dictionary of American Music.* 1986.

Harris, Michael W. *The Rise of Gospel Blues: The Music of Thomas Andrew Dorsey in the Urban Church.* 1992.

Heilbut, Anthony. *The Gospel Sound: Good News and Bad Times.* 1985.

Oliver, Paul. "Gospel." In *The New Grove Gospel, Blues, and Jazz.* 1980–86.

GRAMMY AWARDS

One of the best known of popular song **awards** is the "Grammy," which has been bestowed upon songwriters and performers by the National Academy of Recording Arts and Sciences since 1958, when "Volare," or "Nel Blu Dipinto di Blu," won the award for both Record of the Year and Song of the Year (*see* TABLE 10). Over the course of its existence, the Grammy Award has attempted to reflect many aspects of the music industry. For example, Grammys have been given in the area of jazz, as well as for religious, classical, folk, and Latino music. They have also honored technical expertise with such awards as Best Engineer and Best Producer.

It must be pointed out that various categories have come and gone over the years. Awards in some, like Best Rock Vocal Performance (both male and female), were first presented considerably after the Grammy came into existence. Other categories, like Best Rhythm and Blues Recording, have long since been abandoned. Still others—Best Country Single, for instance—lasted for only one or two years.

Ehrick V. Long

Bibliography

The National Academy of Recording Arts and Sciences (NARAS). *The Grammy Winners Book.* 1986.

Siegman, Gita, ed. *Awards, Honors and Prizes.* 1991.

———. *World of Winners.* 1989.

Stambler, Irwin. *Encyclopedia of Pop, Rock, and Soul.* 1989.

Walter, Claire. *Winners: The Blue Ribbon Encyclopedia of Awards.* 1978

See also: Academy Awards; BMI; Recording

TABLE 10

Grammy Awards

a) Record of the Year

Year	Record Title	Artist(s)	Lyricist/Composer*	Label/Rec.#
1958	Volare, or Nel Blu Dipinto di Blu	Domenico Modugno	Mitchell Parrish/Domenico Modugno	Decca 30677
1959	Mack the Knife	Bobby Darin	Marc Blitzstein/Kurt Weill	Atco 6147
1960	Theme from *A Summer Place*	Percy Faith	Max Steiner	Columbia 41490
1961	Moon River	Henry Mancini	Johnny Mercer / Henry Mancini	RCA 7916
1962	I Left My Heart in San Francisco	Tony Bennett	Douglass Cross/George Cory	Columbia 42332
1963	Days of Wine and Roses	Henry Mancini	Johnny Mercer/Henry Mancini	RCA 8120
1964	The Girl From Ipanema	Stan Getz and Astrud Gilberto	Norman Gimbel/ Antonio Carlos Jobim	Verve 10323
1965	A Taste of Honey	Herb Alpert & the Tijuana Brass	Ric Marlow/ Bobby Scott	A&M 775
1966	Strangers in the Night	Frank Sinatra	Charles Singleton, Eddie Snyder/Bert Kaempfert	Reprise 0470
1967	Up, Up and Away	The Fifth Dimension	Jim Webb	Soul City 756
1968	Mrs. Robinson	Simon & Garfunkel	Paul Simon	Columbia 44511
1969	Aquarius/Let the Sunshine In	The Fifth Dimension	Gerome Ragni, James Rado/Galt MacDermot	Soul City 772
1970	Bridge Over Troubled Water	Simon & Garfunkel	Paul Simon	Columbia 45079
1971	It's Too Late	Carole King	Toni Stern/ Carole King	Ode 66015
1972	The First Time Ever I Saw Your Face	Roberta Flack	Ewan MacColl	Atlantic 2864

1973	Killing Me Softly With His Song	Roberta Flack	Norman Gimbel, Charles Fox	Atlantic 2940
1974	I Honestly Love You	Olivia Newton-John	Peter Allen, Jeff Barry	MCA 40280
1975	Love Will Keep Us Together	The Captain & Tennille	Howard Greenfield/ Neil Sedaka	A&M 1672
1976	This Masquerade	George Benson	Leon Russell	Warner 8209
1977	Hotel California	The Eagles	Don Felder, Don Henley, Glenn Frey	Asylum 45386
1978	Just the Way You Are	Billy Joel	Billy Joel	Columbia 10646
1979	What a Fool Believes	The Doobie Brothers	Kenny Loggins, Michael McDonald	Warner 8725
1980	Sailing	Christopher Cross	Christopher Cross	Warner 49507
1981	Bette Davis Eyes	Kim Carnes	Donna Weiss/ Jackie DeShannon	EMI America 8077
1982	Rosanna	Toto	David Paich	Columbia 02811
1983	Beat It	Michael Jackson	Michael Jackson	Epic 03759
1984	What's Love Got to Do With It?	Tina Turner	Terry Britten, Graham Lyle	Capitol 5354
1985	We Are the World	USA for Africa	Michael Jackson, Lionel Richie, Jr.	Columbia 40043
1986	Higher Love	Steve Winwood	Will Jennings/ Steve Winwood	Island 28710
1987	Graceland	Paul Simon	Paul Simon	Warner 8349
1988	Don't Worry, Be Happy	Bobby McFerrin	Bobby McFerrin	EMI 50146
1989	The Wind Beneath My Wings	Bette Midler	Larry Henley, Jeff Silbar	Atlantic 88972
1990	Another Day in Paradise	Phil Collins	Phil Collins	Virgin 1234
1991	Unforgettable	Natalie Cole, Nat "King" Cole	Irving Gordon	Elektra 961049-2

*Writers credited solely with lyrics or music are set down in that order and separated by a slash: e.g., Oscar Hammerstein II/Jerome Kern. The presence of a comma indicates that the writers are jointly credited for the music, the lyrics, or the song.

b) Song of the Year

Year	Song Title	Lyricist/Composer	Artist(s); Label/Rec.#
1958	Volare, or Nel Blu Dipinto di Blu	Mitchell Parrish Domenico Modugno	Domenico Modugno; Decca 30677
1959	The Battle of New Orleans	Jimmy Driftwood	Johnny Horton; Columbia 41399 Vaughn Monroe; RCA 7495
1960	Theme From *Exodus*	M. Ernest Gold	Ferrante & Teicher; United Artists 274
1961	Moon River	Johnny Mercer/ Henry Mancini	Henry Mancini; RCA 7916 Jerry Butler; Vee Jay 405
1962	What Kind of Fool Am I?	Leslie Bricusse, Anthony Newley	Sammy Davis, Jr.; Reprise 20048 Anthony Newley; London 9546 Robert Goulet; Columbia 42519
1963	Days of Wine and Roses	Johnny Mercer Henry Mancini	Henry Mancini; RCA 8120 Andy Williams; Columbia 42674
1964	Hello Dolly	Jerry Herman	Louis Armstrong; Kapp 573
1965	The Shadow of Your Smile (Love Theme from *The Sandpiper*)	Paul Francis Webster/Johnny Mandel	Tony Bennett; Columbia 43431
1966	Michelle	John Lennon, Paul McCartney	David & Jonathan; Capitol 5563 Bud Shank; World 77814 Billy Vaughn; Pacific Dot 16809 Beatles (from *Rubber Soul*); Capitol 2442
1967	Up, Up and Away	Jim Webb	The Fifth Dimension; Soul City 756
1968	Little Green Apples	Bobby Russell	O. C. Smith; Columbia 44616 Roger Miller; Smash 2148 Patti Page; Columbia 44556
1969	Games People Play	Joe South	Joe South; Capitol 2248
1970	Bridge Over Troubled Water	Paul Simon	Simon & Garfunkel; Columbia 45079
1971	You've Got a Friend	Carole King	James Taylor; Warner 7498 Roberta Flack & Donny Hathaway; Atlantic 2837

1972	The First Time Ever I Saw Your Face	Ewan MacColl	Roberta Flack; Atlantic 2864
1973	Killing Me Softly With His Song	Norman Gimbel, Charles Fox	Roberta Flack, Atlantic 2940
1974	The Way We Were	Marilyn Bergman, Alan Bergman/ Marvin Hamlisch	Barbra Streisand; Columbia 45944
1975	Send in the Clowns	Stephen Sondheim	Judy Collins Elektra 45253
1976	I Write the Songs	Bruce Johnston	Barry Manilow; Arista 0157
1977	Evergreen (Love Theme From A Star Is Born)	Paul Williams/ Barbra Streisand	Barbra Streisand; Columbia 10450
1978	Just the Way You Are	Billy Joel	Billy Joel; Columbia 10646
1979	What a Fool Believes	Kenny Loggins, Michael McDonald	The Doobie Brothers; Warner 8725
1980	Sailing	Christopher Cross	Christopher Cross; Warner 49507
1981	Bette Davis Eyes	Donna Weiss/ Jackie DeShannon	Kim Carnes; EMI America 8077
1982	Always on My Mind	Wayne Thompson, Mark James, Johnny Christopher	Willie Nelson; Columbia 02741
1983	Every Breath You Take	Gordon Sumner /(Sting)	Police; A&M 2542
1984	What's Love Got to Do With It?	Terry Britten, Graham Lyle	Tina Turner; Capitol 5354
1985	We Are the World	Michael Jackson, Lionel Richie, Jr.	USA for Africa; Columbia 40043
1986	That's What Friends Are For	Burt Bacharach, Carole Bayer Sager	Dionne (Warwick) & Friends (Elton John, Gladys Knight, & Stevie Wonder); Arista 9422
1987	Somewhere Out There	James Horner, Barry Mann, Cynthia Weil	James Ingram & Linda Ronstadt; MCA 1132
1988	Don't Worry, Be Happy	Bobby McFerrin	Bobby McFerrin; EMI 50146
1989	The Wind Beneath My Wings	Larry Henley, Jeff Silbar	Bette Midler; Atlantic 88972
1990	From a Distance	Julie Gold	Bette Midler; Atlantic 7820
1991	Unforgettable	Irving Gordon	Nat "King" Cole; Capitol 1808 Natalie Cole, Nat "King" Cole; Elektra 9 61049-2

c) Best Vocal Performance, Female

Year	Artist	Performance	Album*	Lyricist/Composer	Label/Rec. #
1958	Ella Fitzgerald	*Ella Fitzgerald Sings the Irving Berlin Songbook*			Verve 4019-2
1959	Ella Fitzgerald	But Not for Me	*Ella Fitzgerald Sings the George and Ira Gershwin Songbook*	Ira Gershwin/George Gershwin	Verve V-29-5
1960	Ella Fitzgerald	Mack the Knife	*Ella in Berlin*	Marc Blitzstein/ Kurt Weill	Verve 4041
1961	Judy Garland	*Judy at Carnegie Hall*			Capitol 1569
1962	Ella Fitzgerald	*Ella Swings Brightly With Nelson Riddle*			Verve 4055
1963	Barbra Streisand	*The Barbra Streisand Album*			Columbia 8807
1964	Barbra Streisand	People		Bob Merrill/ Jule Styne	Columbia 42965
1965	Barbra Streisand	*My Name is Barbra*			Columbia 9136
1966	Eydie Gorme	If He Walked Into My Life		Jerry Herman	Columbia 43660
1967	Bobbie Gentry	Ode to Billie Joe		Bobbie Gentry	Capitol 5950

*Album listed only if the performance was a track from that album, but not released as a single. Also songwriters are listed only for singles and album tracks.

d) Best Vocal Performance, Male

Year	Artist	Performance	Album*	Lyricist/Composer	Label/Rec. #
1958	Perry Como	Catch a Falling Star		Paul Vance, Lee Pockriss	RCA 7128
1959	Frank Sinatra	*Come Dance With Me*			Capitol 789
1960	Ray Charles	Georgia on My Mind	*The Genius of Ray Charles*	Stuart Gorrell/ Hoagy Carmichael	ABC-1035 Paramount
1961	Jack Jones	Lollipops and Roses		Tony Velona	Kapp 435
1962	Tony Bennett	I Left My Heart in San Francisco		Douglas Cross/ George Cory	Columbia 42332
1963	Jack Jones	(Hey Little Girl) Wives & Lovers		Hal David/ Burt Bacharach	Kapp 551
1964	Louis Armstrong	Hello Dolly		Jerry Herman	Kapp 573
1965	Frank Sinatra	It Was a Very Good Year		Ervin Drake	Reprise 0429
1966	Frank Sinatra	Strangers in the Night		Charles Singleton Eddie Snyder/Bert Kaempfert	Reprise 0470
1967	Glen Campbell	By the Time I Get to Phoenix		Jim Webb	Capitol 2015

*Album listed only if the performance was a track from that album, but not released as a single. Also, songwriters are listed only for singles and album tracks.

e) Best Contemporary Recording

Year	Title	Artist(s)	Lyricist/Composer*	Label/Rec.#
1959	Midnight Flyer	Nat "King" Cole	Mayme Watts, Robert Mosley	Capitol 4248
1960	Georgia on My Mind	Ray Charles	Stuart Gorrell/ Hoagy Carmichael	ABC-Paramount 10135
1961	Let's Twist Again	Chubby Checker	Kal Mann, Dave Appel	Parkway 824
1962	Alley Cat	Bent Fabric	Frank Bjorn	Atco 6226
1963	Deep Purple	Nino Tempo & April Stevens	Mitchell Parrish/ Peter DeRose	Atco 6273
1964	Downtown	Petula Clark	Tony Hatch	Warner 5494
1965	King of the Road	Roger Miller	Roger Miller	Smash 1965
1966	Winchester Cathedral	The New Vaudeville Band	Geoff Stevens	Fontana 1562
1967	*Sgt. Pepper's Lonely Hearts Club Band*	The Beatles		Capitol 2653
1968	Up, Up and Away	The Fifth Dimension	Jim Webb	Soul City 756

*Songwriters are listed only for singles.

f) Best Contemporary Pop Vocal Performance, Female

Year	Artist	Performance	Lyricist/Composer*	Label/Rec.#
1965	Petula Clark	I Know a Place	Tony Hatch	Warner 5612
1966	No award			
1967	Bobbie Gentry	Ode to Billie Joe	Bobbie Gentry	Capitol 5950
1968	Dionne Warwick	Do You Know the Way to San Jose?	Hal David/ Burt Bacharach	Scepter 12216
1969	Peggy Lee	Is That All There Is?	Jerry Leiber, Mike Stoller	Capitol 2602
1970	Dionne Warwick	*I'll Never Fall in Love Again*	Hal David/ Burt Bacharach	Scepter 12273
1971	Carole King	*Tapestry*		Ode 77009
1972	Helen Reddy	I Am Woman	Helen Reddy/ Ray Burton	Capitol 3350
1973	Roberta Flack	Killing Me Softly With His Song	Norman Gimbel, Charles Fox	Atlantic 2940
1974	Olivia Newton-John	I Honestly Love You	Peter Allen, Jeff Barry	MCA 40280
1975	Janis Ian	At Seventeen	Janis Ian	Columbia 10154
1976	Linda Ronstadt	*Hasten Down the Wind*		Asylum 1072
1977	Barbra Streisand	Evergreen (Love Theme From *A Star Is Born*)	Paul Williams/ Barbra Streisand	Columbia 10450
1978	Anne Murray	You Needed Me	Randy Goodrum	Capitol 4574
1979	Dionne Warwick	I'll Never Love This Way Again	Richard Kerr, Will Jennings	Arista 0419

1980	Bette Midler	The Rose	Amanda McBroom	Atlantic 3656
1981	Lena Horne	*Lena Horne: The Lady and Her Music Live on Broadway*		Qwest 66108
1982	Melissa Manchester	You Should Hear How She Talks About You	Tom Snow, Dean Pitchford	Arista 0676
1983	Irene Cara	Flashdance . . . What a Feeling	Keith Forsey, Irene Cara/Giorgio Moroder	Casablanca 811440
1984	Tina Turner	What's Love Got to Do With It?	Terry Britten, Graham Lyle	Capitol 5354
1985	Whitney Houston	Saving All My Love for You	Gerry Goffin/ Michael Masser	Arista 9381
1986	Barbra Streisand	*The Broadway Album*		Columbia 40092
1987	Whitney Houston	I Wanna Dance With Somebody (Who Loves Me)	George Merrill, Shannon Rubicam	Arista 9598
1988	Tracy Chapman	Fast Car	Tracy Chapman	Elektra 73
1989	Bonnie Raitt	*Nick of Time*		Capitol 91268
1990	Mariah Carey	Vision of Love	Mariah Carey, Ben Margulies	CBS 4668151
1991	Bonnie Raitt	Something to Talk About	Shirley Elkhard	Capitol CL619

*Songwriters are listed only for singles.

g) Best Contemporary Pop Vocal Performance, Male

Year	Artist	Performance	Lyricist/Composer*	Label/Rec.#
1965	Roger Miller	King of the Road	Roger Miller	Smash 1965
1966	Paul McCartney (The Beatles)	Eleanor Rigby	John Lennon, Paul McCartney	Capitol 5715
1967	Glen Campbell	By the Time I Get to Phoenix	Jim Webb	Capitol 2015
1968	Jose Feliciano	Light My Fire	The Doors (John Densmore, Robert Krieger, Raymond Manzarek, Jim Morrison)	RCA 9550
1969	Harry Nilsson	Everybody's Talkin'	Fred Neil	RCA 0161
1970	Ray Stevens	Everything Is Beautiful	Ray Stevens	Barnaby 2011
1971	James Taylor	You've Got a Friend	Carole King	Warner 7498
1972	Harry Nilsson	Without You	Thomas Evans, William Peter Ham	RCA 0604
1973	Stevie Wonder	Your Are the Sunshine of My Life	Stevie Wonder	Tamla 54232
1974	Stevie Wonder	*Fulfillingness First Finale*		Tamla 332
1975	Paul Simon	*Still Crazy After All These Years*		Columbia 33540
1976	Stevie Wonder	*Songs in the Key of Life*		Tamla 340
1977	James Taylor	Handy Man	Otis Blackwell, Jimmy Jones	Columbia 10557
1978	Barry Manilow	Copacabana (At the Copa)	Barry Manilow, Bruce Sussman, Jack Felder	Arista 0339
1979	Billy Joel	*52nd Street*		Columbia 35609
1980	Kenny Loggins	This Is It	Kenny Loggins, Michael McDonald	Columbia 11109
1981	Al Jarreau	*Breakin' Away*		Warner 3576
1982	Lionel Richie, Jr.	Truly	Lionel Richie, Jr.	Motown 1644
1983	Michael Jackson	*Thriller*		Epic 38112
1984	Phil Collins	Against All Odds (Take a Look at Me Now)	Phil Collins	Atlantic 89700
1985	Phil Collins	*No Jacket Required*		Atlantic 81240

1986	Steve Winwood	Higher Love	Will Jennings/ Steve Winwood	Island 28710
1987	Sting	*Bring on the Night*		A&M Bring 1
1988	Bobby McFerrin	Don't Worry, Be Happy	Bobby McFerrin	EMI 50146
1989	Michael Bolton	How Am I Supposed to Live Without You	Michael Bolton, Doug James	Columbia 55397
1990	Roy Orbison	Oh, Pretty Woman	Roy Orbison, Bill Dees	Virgin 2601
1991	Michael Bolton	When a Man Loves a Woman	Calvin H. Lewis, Andrew Wright	Columbia 4678121

*Songwriters are listed only for singles.

h) Best Pop Duo or Group with Vocal Performance

Year	Artist(s)	Performance	Lyricist/Composer*	Label/Rec.#
1965	The Statler Brothers	Flowers on the Wall	Lewis DeWitt	Columbia 43315
1966	The Mamas & the Papas	Monday, Monday	John Phillips	Dunhill 4026
1967	The Fifth Dimension	Up, Up and Away	Jim Webb	Soul City 756
1968	Simon & Garfunkel	Mrs. Robinson	Paul Simon	Columbia 44511
1969	The Fifth Dimension	Aquarius/Let the Sunshine In	Gerome Ragni, James Rado/Galt MacDermot	Soul City 772
1970	The Carpenters	(They Long to Be) Close to You	Hal David/Burt Bacharach	A&M 1183
1971	The Carpenters	Carpenters		A&M 3502
1972	Roberta Flack & Donny Hathaway	Where Is the Love?	Ralph McDonald, William Salter	Atlantic 2879
1973	Gladys Knight & the Pips	Neither One of Us	Jim Weatherly	Soul 35098
1974	Paul McCartney & Wings	Band on the Run	Paul McCartney, Linda McCartney	Apple 1873
1975	The Eagles	Lyin' Eyes	Don Henley, Glenn Frey	Asylum 45279
1976	Chicago	If You Leave Me Now	Peter Cetera	Columbia 10390
1977	The Bee Gees	How Deep Is Your Love	Barry, Robin, and Maurice Gibb	RSO 882
1978	The Bee Gees	*Saturday Night Fever*		RSO 4001
1979	The Doobie Brothers	Minute by Minute	Lester Abrams, Michael McDonald	Warner 3193
1980	Barbra Streisand & Barry Gibb	Guilty	Barry, Robin, and Maurice Gibb	Columbia 11390
1981	Manhattan Transfer	The Boy From New York City	John Taylor	Atlantic 3816
1982	Jennifer Warnes & Joe Cocker	Up Where We Belong	Jack Nitzsche, Will Jennings, Buffy Sainte-Marie	Island 99996
1983	Police	Every Breath You Take	Gordon Sumner (Sting)	A&M 2542
1984	Pointer Sisters	Jump (For My Love)	Marti Sharron, Steve Mitchell, Gary Skardina	Planet 13780
1985	USA for Africa	We Are the World	Michael Jackson, Lionel Richie, Jr.	Columbia 40043
1986	Dionne (Warwick) & Friends (Elton John, Gladys Knight, & Stevie Wonder)	That's What Friends Are For	Burt Bacharach, Carole Bayer Sager	Arista 9422
1987	Bill Medley & Jennifer Warnes	(I've Had) The Time of My Life [from *Dirty Dancing* soundtrack]	Frankie Previte/John DeNicola, Donald Markowitz	RCA 86408
1988	Manhattan Transfer	*Brasil*		Atlantic 81803
1989	Linda Ronstadt & Aaron Neville	All I Need to Know (Dont' Know Much) [from *Cry Like a Rainstorm, Howl Like the Wind*]	Cynthia Weil, Tom Snow, Barry Mann	Elektra 60872-2

| 1990 | Linda Ronstadt & Aaron Neville | All My Life [from *Cry Like a Rainstorm, Howl Like The Wind*] | Karla Bonoff | Elektra 60872-2 |
| 1991 | R.E.M. | Losing My Religion | Bill Berry, Peter Buck, Mike Mills, Michael Stipe | Warner Brothers W 0015 |

*Songwriters are listed only for singles.

i) Best Rock Vocal Performance, Female

Year	Artist	Performance	Lyricist/Composer*	Label/Rec. #
1979	Donna Summer	Hot Stuff	Pete Bellotte, Harold Faltermeier, Keith Forsey	Casablanca 978
1980	Pat Benatar	*Crimes of Passion*		Chrysalis 1275
1981	Pat Benatar	Fire & Ice	Pat Benatar, Scott Sheets, Tom Kelly	Chrysalis 2529
1982	Pat Benatar	Shadows of the Night	David Leigh Byron	Chrysalis 2647
1983	Pat Benatar	Love Is a Battlefield	Mike Chapman, Holly Knight	Chrysalis 42732
1984	Tina Turner	Better Be Good to Me	Holly Knight, Mike Chapman, Nicky Chinn	Capitol 5387
1985	Tina Turner	One of the Living	Holly Knight	Capitol 5518
1986	Tina Turner	Back Where You Started	Bryan Adams, Jim Vallance	Capitol 2081
1987	No award			
1988	Tina Turner	*Tina Live in Europe*		Capitol ESTD1
1989	Bonnie Raitt	*Nick of Time*		Capitol 91268
1990	Alannah Myles	Black Velvet	David Tyson, Christopher Ward	Atlantic 8742
1991	No award			

*Songwriters are listed only for singles.

j) Best Rock Vocal Performance, Male

Year	Artist	Performance	Album*	Lyricist/Composer	Label/Rec. #
1979	Bob Dylan	Gotta Serve Somebody		Bob Dylan	Columbia 11072
1980	Billy Joel	*Glass Houses*			Columbia 36384
1981	Rick Springfield	Jessie's Girl		Rick Springfield	RCA 12201
1982	John Cougar Mellencamp	Hurts So Good		John Cougar Mellencamp, George Michael Green	Riva 209
1983	Michael Jackson	Beat It		Michael Jackson	Epic 03759
1984	Bruce Springsteen	Dancing in the Dark		Bruce Springsteen	Columbia 04463
1985	Don Henley	The Boys of Summer		Don Henley, Mike Campbell	Geffen 29141
1986	Robert Palmer	Addicted to Love		Robert Palmer	Island 99570
1987	No award				
1988	Robert Palmer	Simply Irresistible	*Simply Irresistible*	Robert Palmer	EMI 65
1989	Don Henley	*The End of Innocence*			Geffen 253
1990	Eric Clapton	Bad Love		Eric Clapton, Mick Jones	Reprise/Duck w 2644
1991	No award				

*Album listed only if the performance was a track from that album, but not released as a single. Also, songwriters are listed only for singles and album tracks.

k) Best Rock Vocal Performance, Solo

Year	Artist	Performance	Label/Rec#
1987	Bruce Springsteen	*Tunnel of Love*	Columbia 40999

l) Best Rock Performance by a Duo or Group With Vocal

Year	Artist(s)	Performance	Lyricist/Composer*	Label/Rec.#
1979	Eagles	Heartache Tonight	Bob Seger, Don Henley, J. D. Souther, Glen Frey	Asylum 46545
1980	Bob Seger & The Silver Bullet Band	Against the Wind	Bob Seger	Capitol 4863
1981	Police	Don't Stand So Close to Me	Gordon Sumner (Sting)	A&M 2301
1982	Survivor	Eye of the Tiger	Jim Peterik, Frank Sullivan	Scotti Brothers 02912
1983	Police	*Synchronicity*		A&M 3735
1984	Prince & The Revolution	*Purple Rain —Music from the Motion Picture*		Warner 25110
1985	Dire Straits	Money for Nothing	Gordon Sumner (Sting), Mark Knopfler	Warner 28950
1986	Eurythmics	Missionary Man	Annie Lennox, Dave Stewart	RCA 14414
1987	U2	*The Joshua Tree*		Island 90581
1988	U2	Desire	Bono	Island 400
1989	Traveling Wilburys	*Traveling Wilburys Vol. I*		Wilbury/ Warner 224
1990	Aerosmith	Janie's Got a Gun [from *Pump*]	Steven Tyler Tom Hamilton	Geffen 24254
1991	Bonnie Raitt & Delbert McClinton	Good Man, Good Woman [from *Luck of the Draw*]	C. Womack, L. Womack	Capitol 2145

*Songwriters are listed only for singles.

m) Best Rhythm & Blues Recording

Year	Title	Artist(s)	Lyricist/Composer	Label/Rec. #
1958	Tequila	The Champs	Chuck Rio	Challenge 1016
1959	What a Diff'rence a Day Made	Dinah Washington	Stanley Adams/Maria Grever	Mercury 71435
1960	Let the Good Times Roll	Ray Charles	Sam Theard, Fleecie Moore	Atlantic 2047
1961	Hit the Road, Jack	Ray Charles	Percy Mayfield	ABC-Paramount 10244
1962	I Can't Stop Loving You	Ray Charles	Don Gibson	ABC-Paramount 10330
1963	Busted	Ray Charles	Harlan Howard	ABC-Paramount 10481
1964	(You Don't Know) How Glad I Am	Nancy Wilson	Jimmy Williams, Larry Harrison	Capitol 5198
1965	Papa's Got a Brand New Bag	James Brown	James Brown	King 5999
1966	Crying Time	Ray Charles	Buck Owens	ABC-Paramount 10739
1967	Respect	Aretha Franklin	Otis Redding	Atlantic 2403

n) Best Rhythm & Blues Vocal Performance, Female

Year	Artist	Performance	Album*	Lyricist/Composer	Label/Rec. #
1967	Aretha Franklin	Respect		Otis Redding	Atlantic 2403
1968	Aretha Franklin	Chain of Fools		Don Covay	Atlantic 2464
1969	Aretha Franklin	Share Your Love With Me		Deadric Malone, Al Braggs	Atlantic 2650
1970	Aretha Franklin	Don't Pay That Song (You Lied)		Ahmet Ertegun, Betty Nelson	Atlantic 2751
1971	Aretha Franklin	Bridge Over Troubled Water		Paul Simon	Atlantic 2796
1972	Aretha Franklin	*Young Gifted and Black*			Atlantic 7213
1973	Aretha Franklin	Master of Eyes		Bernie Hart, Aretha Franklin	Atlantic 2941
1974	Aretha Franklin	Ain't Nothing Like the Real Thing		Nickolas Ashford, Valerie Simpson	Atlantic 3200

Year	Artist	Performance	Album	Lyricist/Composer	Label/Rec. #
1975	Natalie Cole	This Will Be (An Everlasting Love)		Marvin Yancy, Chuck Jackson	Capitol 4109
1976	Natalie Cole	Sophisticated Lady (She's a Different Lady)		Marvin Yancy, Chuck Jackson Natalie Cole	Capitol 4259
1977	Thelma Houston	Don't Leave Me This Way		Kenny Gamble, Leon Huff, Cary Gilbert	Tamla 54278
1978	Donna Summer	Last Dance		Paul Jabara	Casablanca 926
1979	Dionne Warwick	Deja Vu		Adrienne Anderson/ Isaac Hayes	Arista 0459
1980	Stephanie Mills	Never Knew Lovee Like This Before		James Mtume, Reginald Lucas	20th Century 2460
1981	Aretha Franklin	Hold On (I'm Coming)	*Love All the Hurt Away*	David Porter, Isaac Hayes	Arista 1170
1982	Jennifer Holliday	And I Am Telling You I'm Not Going		Tom Eyen/ Henry Krieger	Geffen 29983
1983	Chaka Khan	*Chaka Khan*			Warner 23792
1984	Chaka Khan	I Feel for You		Prince Rogers Nelson	Warner 29195
1985	Aretha Franklin	Freeway of Love		Jeffrey Cohen, Narada Michael Walden	Arista 9354
1986	Anita Baker	*Rapture*			Elektra 60444
1987	Aretha Franklin	*Aretha*			Arista 8442
1988	Anita Baker	Giving You the Best That I Got	*Giving You the Best That I Got*	Anita Baker, Skip Scarborough, Randy Holland	Elektra 60827
1989	Anita Baker		*Giving You the Best That I Got*		Elektra 60287
1990	Anita Baker		*Compositions*		Elektra 9 60827-2
1991	Lisa Fischer	How Can I Ease the Pain	*So Intense*	Lisa Fischer, Narada Michael Walden	Elektra Asylum 60889
	Patti Labelle		*Burnin'*		MCA MCAD-10439

*Songwriters are listed only for singles or album tracks.

o) Best Rhythm & Blues Vocal Performance, Male

Year	Artist	Performance	Album	Lyricist/Composer*	Label/Rec. #
1966	Ray Charles	Crying Time		Buck Owens	ABC-Paramount 10739
1967	Lou Rawls	Dead End Street		Ben Raleigh/ David Axelrod	Capitol 5869
1968	Otis Redding	Sittin' On the Dock of the Bay		Otis Redding, Steve Cropper	Volt 157
1969	Joe Simon	The Chokin' Kind		Harlan Howard	Sound 2628 Stage
1970	B. B. King	The Thrill Is Gone		B.G. DeSylva, Lew Brown/ Ray Henderson	Bluesway 61032
1971	Lou Rawls	A Natural Man		Bobby Hebb, Sandy Baron	MGM 14262
1972	Billy Paul	Me & Mrs. Jones		Kenny Gamble, Leon Huff, Cary Gilbert	Philadelphia International 3521
1973	Stevie Wonder	Superstitions		Stevie Wonder	Tamla 54226
1974	Stevie Wonder	Boogie On Reggae Woman		Stevie Wonder	Tamla 54254
1975	Ray Charles	Living for the City		Stevie Wonder	Crossover 981
1976	Stevie Wonder	I Wish		Stevie Wonder	Tamla 54274
1977	Lou Rawls	*Unmistakably Lou*			Philadelphia International 34488
1978	George Benson	On Broadway		Jerry Leiber, Mike Stoller, Barry Mann, Cynthia Weil	Warner 8542
1979	Michael Jackson	Don't Stop 'Til You Get Enough		Michael Jackson	Epic 50742

1980	George Benson	Give Me the Night			Warner 3453
1981	James Ingram	One Hundred Ways	The Dude (by Quincy Jones)	Tony Coleman, Benjamin Wright, Kathy Wakefield	A&M 3721
1982	Marvin Gaye	Sexual Healing		Marvin Gaye	Columbia 03302
1983	Michael Jackson	Billie Jean		Michael Jackson	Epic 03509
1984	Billy Ocean	Caribbean Queen (No More Love on the Run)		Billy Ocean, Keith Diamond	Jive 9199
1985	Stevie Wonder	In Square Circle			Tamla 6134
1986	James Brown	Living in America	Gravity	Dan Hartman, Charlie Midnight	Scotti Brothers 57108
1987	Smokey Robinson	Just to See Her		Lou Pardini, Jimmy George	Motown 41147
1988	Terrence Trent D'Arby	Introducing the Hardline line According to Terrence Trent D'Arby			Columbia 40964
1989	Bobby Brown	Every Little Step		L.A.Reid (Antonio Reid), Babyface (Kenny Edmunds)	MCA 53618
1990	Luther Vandross	Here and Now	The Best of Luther Vandross: The Best of Love	Terry Steele, David L. Elliott	Epic 45320
1991	Luther Vandross		Power of Love		Epic 46789

*Songwriters are listed only for singles or album tracks.

p) Best Rhythm & Blues Performance by a Duo or Group With Vocal

Year	Artist(s)	Performance	Album	Lyricist/Composer*	Label/Rec. #
1966	Ramsey Lewis	Hold It Right There	Wade in the Water	Eddie "Mr. Cleanhead" Vinson	Cadet 775
1967	Sam & Dave	Soul Man		Isaac Hayes, David Porter	Stax 231
1968	Temptations	Cloud Nine		Barrett Strong, Norman Whitfield	Gordy 7081
1969	Isley Brothers	It's Your Thing		Rudolph Isley, Ronald Isley, O'Kelly Isley	T-Neck 901
1970	Delfonics	Didn't I (Blow Your Mind This Time)		Thom Bell, William Hart	Philly Grove 161
1971	Ike & Tina Turner	Proud Mary		John C. Fogerty	Liberty 56216
1972	Temptations	Papa Was a Rollin' Stone		Barrett Strong, Norman Whitfield	Gordy 7121
1973	Gladys Knight & the Pips	Midnight Train to Georgia		Jim Weatherly	Buddah 383
1974	Rufus	Tell Me Something Good		Stevie Wonder	ABC 11427
1975	Earth, Wind & Fire	Shining Star		Maurice White, Philip Bailey, Larry Dunn	Columbia 10090
1976	Marilyn McCoo & Billy Davis, Jr.	You Don't Have to Be a Star (To Be in My Show)		James Dean, John Henry Glover, Jr.	ABC 12208
1977	Emotions	Best of My Love		Maurice White, Albert McKay	Columbia 10544
1978	Earth, Wind & Fire	All 'n' All			Columbia 34905
1979	Earth, Wind & Fire	After the Love Has Gone		David Foster, Jay Graydon, Bill Champlin	ARC 11033
1980	Manhattans	Shining Star		Leo Graham, Jr., Paul Richmond	Columbia 10310
1981	Quincy Jones	The Dude			A&M 3721
1982	Dazz Band	Let It Whip		Leon Chancler, Reginald	Motown 1609

			Andrews Maurice White, Wayne Vaughn	ARC 02688
1983	Rufus & Chaka Khan	Ain't Nobody	David Wolinski	Warner 29555
1984	James Ingram & Michael McDonald	Yah Mo B There	James Ingram, Michael McDonald, Rod Temperton, Quincy Jones	Qwest 29394
1985	Commodores	Nightshift	Walter Orange, Dennis Lambert, Frannie Golde	Motown 1773
1986	Prince & the Revolution	Kiss	Prince Rogers Nelson	Paisley Park 28751
1987	Aretha Franklin & George Michael	I Knew You Were Waiting (For Me)	Simon Climie, Dennis Morgan	Arista 9559
1988	Gladys Knight & the Pips	Love Overboard	Reggie Calloway	MCA 1223
1989	Soul II Soul	Back to Life	Simon Laws, Caron Wheeler, Nelle Hooper, Bereford Romeo	Virgin 65370
1990	Ray Charles & Chaka Khan	I'll Be Good to You	Louis Johnson, George Johnson, Senora Sam	Qwest/ Warner Brothers W 2697 Motown 37463-6320-2
1991	Boyz II Men	*Cooley high harmony*		

*Songwriters are listed only for singles or album tracks.

q) Best Rhythm & Blues Song (Songwriter's Award)

Year	Song Title	Lyricist/Composer	Artist(s);Label/Rec. #
1968	(Sittin' on) The Dock of the Bay	Otis Redding, Steve Cropper	Otis Redding; Volt 157 King Curtis; Atco 6562
1969	Color Him Father	Richard Spencer	Winstons; Metromedia 117
1970	Patches	Ronald Dunbar, General Johnson	Clarence Carter; Atlantic 2726
1971	Ain't No Sunshine	Bill Withers	Bill Withers; Sussex 219
1972	Papa Was a Rollin' Stone	Barrett Strong, Norman Whitfield	Temptations; Gordy 7121 Undisputed Truth; Gordy 7117
1973	Superstition	Stevie Wonder	Stevie Wonder; Tamla 54226
1974	Living for the City	Stevie Wonder	Stevie Wonder; Tamla 54242
1975	Where Is the Love?	Harry Wayne Casey, Richard Finch, Willie Clarke, Betty Wright	Betty Wright; Alston 3713
1976	Lowdown	Boz Scaggs, David Paich	Boz Scaggs; Columbia 10367
1977	You Make Me Feel Like Dancing	Leo Sayer, Vini Poncia	Leo Sayer; Warner 8283
1978	Last Dance	Paul Jabara	Donna Summer; Casablanca 926
1979	After the Love Has Gone	David Foster, Jay Graydon, William Champlin	Earth, Wind & Fire; Arc 11033
1980	Never Knew Love Like This Before	Reginald Lucas, James Mtume	Stephanie Mills; 20th Century 2460
1981	Just the Two of Us	Bill Withers, William Salter, Ralph McDonald	Grover Washington; Elektra 47103 Jr. (with Bill Withers);
1982	Turn Your Love Around	Jay Graydon, Steve Lukather, Bill Champlin	George Benson; Warner 49846
1983	Billie Jean	Michael Jackson	Michael Jackson; Epic 03509 Club House (medley with "Do It Again"); Atlantic 89795
1984	I Feel for You	Prince Rogers Nelson	Chaka Khan; Warner 29195
1985	Freeway of Love	Narada Michael Walden, Jeffrey Cohen	Aretha Franklin; Arista 9354
1986	Sweet Love	Anita Baker, Louis A. Johnson, Gary	Anita Baker; Elektra 69557

1987	Lean on Me	Bias Bill Withers	Club Noveau; Warner 28430 (originally on Tommy Boy)
1988	Giving You the Best That I Got	Anita Baker, Skip Scarborough, Randy Holland	Anita Baker; Elektra 60827
1989	If You Don't Know Me by Now	Kenny Gamble, Leon Huff	Simply Red; Elektra 960828-2
1990	U Can't Touch This	M.C. Hammer, Rick James, Alonzo Miller	M.C. Hammer; Capitol 961049-2
1991	Power of Love/Love Power	Luther Vandross, Marcus Miller, Teddy Vann	Luther Vandross; Epic 6568227

r) **Best Country Single**

Year	Record Title	Artist	Lyricist/Composer	Label/Rec. #
1964	Dang Me	Roger Miller	Roger Miller	Smash 1881
1965	King of the Road	Roger Miller	Roger Miller	Smash 1965

s) **Best Country & Western Performance**

Year	Artist(s)	Performance	Album	Lyricist/Composer*	Label/Rec. #
1958	Kingston Trio	Tom Dooley		Dave Guard	Capitol 4049
1959	Johnny Horton	The Battle of New Orleans		Jimmy Driftwood	Columbia 41339
1960	Marty Robbins	El Paso		Marty Robbins	Columbia 41511
1961	Jimmy Dean	Big Bad John		Jimmy Dean	Columbia 42175
1962	Burl Ives	Funny Way of Laughin		Hank Cochran	Decca 31371
1963	Bobby Bare	*Detroit City*			RCA 8183
1964	No award				
1965	No award				
1966	Davis Houston	Almost Persuaded		Billy Sherrill, Glenn Sutton	Epic 10025
1967	Glen Campbell	*Gentle on My Mind*			Capitol 2809

*Songwriters are listed only for singles.

t) **Best Country & Western Performance, Female**

Year	Artist	Performance	Album	Lyricist/Composer*	Label/Rec. #
1964	Dottie West	Here Comes My Baby Back Again		Dottie West, Bill West	RCA 8374
1965	Jody Miller	Queen of the House		Mary Taylor/ Roger Miller	Capitol 5402
1966	Jeanie Seely	Don't Touch Me		Hank Cochran	Monument 933
1967	Tammy Wynette	I Don't Wanna Play House		Glenn Sutton, Billy Sherrill	Epic 2275
1968	Jeannie C. Riley	The Harper Valley PTA.		Tom T. Hall	Plantation 3
1969	Tammy Wynette	*Stand by Your Man*			Epic 26451
1970	Lynn Anderson	Rose Garden		Joe South	Columbia 45252
1971	Sammie Smith	Help Me Make It Through the Night		Kris Kristofferson	Mega 0015
1972	Donna Fargo	Happiest Girl in the Whole USA		Donna Fargo	Dot 17409
1973	Olivia Newton-John	Let Me Be There		John Rostill	MCA 40101
1974	Anne Murray	*Love Song*			Capitol 11266
1975	Linda Ronstadt	I Can't Help It (If I'm Still in Love With You)		Hank Williams	Capitol 3990
1976	Emmylou Harris	*Elite Hotel*			Reprise 2236
1977	Crystal Gayle	Don't It Make My Brown Eyes Blue		Richard Leigh	United Artists 1016
1978	Dolly Parton	*Here You Come Again*			RCA 2544
1979	Emmylou Harris	*Blue Kentucky Girl*			Warner 3318
1980	Anne Murray	Could I Have This Dance		Wayland Holyfield, Bob House	Capitol 4920
1981	Dolly Parton	9 to 5		Dolly Parton	RCA 12133
1982	Juice Newton	Break It to Me Gently		Diane Lampert, Joe Seneca	Capitol 5148

1983	Anne Murray	A Little Good News		Charlie Black, Rory Bourke, Thomas Rocco	Capitol 5264
1984	Emmylou Harris	In My Dreams	*White Shoes*	Paul Kennerley	Warner 923961
1985	Rosanne Cash	I Don't Know Why You Don't Want Me		Rosanne Cash, Rodney Crowell	Columbia 08401
1986	Reba McEntire	Whoever's in New England	*Whoever's in New England*	Quentin Powers, Kendall Franceschi	MCA 5691
1987	K. T. Oslin	80's Ladies	*This Woman*	K. T. Oslin	RCA 8369
1988	Emmylou Harris	Hold Me			MCA
1989	k. d. lang	*Absolute Torch and Twang*			Sire 259
1990	Kathy Mattea	Where've You Been		Don Henry, Jon Vezner	Mercury MER 338
1991	Mary-Chapin Carpenter	Down at the Twist and Shout	*Shootin' Straight in the Dark*	Mary-Chapin Carpenter Columbia CK-46077	

*Songwriters are listed only for singles or album tracks

u) Best Country Vocal Performance, Male

Year	Artist	Performance	Album	Lyricist/Composer*	Label/Rec. #
1964	Roger Miller	Dang Me		Roger Miller	Smash 1881
1965	Roger Miller	King of the Road		Roger Miller	Smash 1965
1966	David Houston	Almost Persuaded		Billy Sherrill, Glen Sutton	Epic 10025
1967	Glen Campbell	Gentle on My Mind		John Hartford	Capitol 5939
1968	Johnny Cash	Folsom Prison Blues		Johnny Cash	Columbia 44513
1969	Johnny Cash	A Boy Named Sue		Shel Silverstein	Columbia 44944
1970	Ray Price	For the Good Times		Kris Kristofferson	Columbia 45178
1971	Jerry Reed	When You're Hot, You're Hot		Jerry Reed	RCA 9976
1972	Charley Pride	*Charley Pride Sings Heart Songs*			RCA 4617
1973	Charlie Rich	Behind Closed Doors		Kenny O'Dell	Epic 10950
1974	Ronnie Milsap	Please Don't Tell Me How the Story Ends		Kris Kristofferson	RCA 0313
1975	Willie Nelson	Blue Eyes Crying in the Rain		Fred Rose	Columbia 10176
1976	Ronnie Milsap	I'm a Stand by Your Woman Man	*20-20 Vision*	Kent Robbins, Billy Sherrill, Tammy Wynette	RCA 3278
1977	Kenny Rogers	Lucille		Roger Bowling, Hal Bynum	United Artists 929
1978	Willie Nelson	Georgia on My Mind		Stuart Gorrell/ Hoagy Carmichael	Columbia 10704
1979	Kenny Rogers	The Gambler		Don Schlitz	United Artists 1250
1980	George Jones	He Stopped Loving Her Today	*I Am What I Am*	Bobby Bradock, Curly Putman	RCA 1105
1981	Ronnie Milsap	(There's) No Gettin' Over Me		Tom Brasfield, Walt Aldredge	RCA 12264
1982	Willie Nelson	Always on My Mind Mind		Wayne Thompson, Mark James, Johnny Christopher	Columbia 02741
1983	Lee Greenwood	I.O.U		Kerry Chater, Austin Roberts	MCA 52199
1984	Merle Haggard	That's the Way Love Goes	*That's the Way Love Goes*	Whitey Shafer, Lefty Frizzell	Epic 25537
1985	Ronnie Milsap	Lost in the Fifties Tonight (In the Still of the Night)	*Lost in the Fifties Tonight*	Troy Seals, Mike Reid, Frederick Parris	RCA 81794
1986	Ronnie Milsap	*Lost in the Fifties Tonight*			RCA 81794
1987	Randy Travis	*Always and Forever*			Warner 25568
1988	Randy Travis	*Old 8x10*			Warner 25738
1989	Lyle Lovett	*Lyle Lovett and His Large Band*			MCA 6037
1990	Vince Gill	When I Call Your Name	*When I Call Your Name*	Vince Gill, Tim Dubois	MCA 4232

1991	Garth Brooks	Ropin' the Wind			Capitol C2-96330

*Songwriters are listed only for singles or album tracks.

v) Best Country Performance by a Duo or Group With Vocal

Year	Artist(s)	Performance	Album	Lyricist/Composer*	Label/Rec. #
1967	Johnny Cash & June Carter	*Jackson*			Columbia 33120
1968	No award				
1969	Waylon Jennings & the Kimberlys	MacArthur Park		Jim Webb	RCA 021
1970	Johnny Cash & June Carter	If I Were a Carpenter		Tim Hardin	Columbia 45064
1971	Conway Twitty & Loretta Lynn	After the Fire Is Gone		L. E. White	Decca 32776
1972	Statler Brothers	Class of '57		Harold Reid, Don Reid	Mercury 870442
1973	Kris Kristofferson & Rita Coolidge	From the Bottle to the Bottom	*Full Moon*	Kris Kristofferson	A&M 64403
1974	Pointer Sisters	Fairytale		Bonnie & Anita Pointer	Blue Thumb 254
1975	Kris Kristofferson & Rita Coolidge	Lover, Please	*Breakaway*	Billy Swan	CBS 32775
1976	Amazing Aces	The End Is Not in Sight (The Cowboy Tune)		H. Russell Smith	ABC 12202
1977	Kendalls	Heaven's Just a Sin Away		Jerry Gillespie	Ovation 1103
1978	Waylon Jennings & Willie Nelson	Mammas Don't Let Your Babies Grow Up to Be Cowboys		Ed Bruce, Patsy Bruce	RCA 11198
1979	Charlie Daniels Band	The Devil Went Down To Georgia		Tom Crain, Taz DiGregorio, Fred Edwards, Jim Marshall, Charles Hayward, Charlie Daniels	Epic 50700
1980	Roy Orbison & Emmylou Harris	That Lovin' You Feelin' Again		Roy Orbison, Chris Price	Warner 49262
1981	Oak Ridge Boys	Elvira		Dallas Frazier	MCA 51084
1982	Alabama	*Mountain Music*			RCA 4229
1983	Alabama	*The Closer You Get*			RCA 4663
1984	Judds	Mama He's Crazy		Kenny O'Dell	RCA 49917
1985	Judds	*Why Not Me*			RCA/Curb 5319
1986	Judds	Grandpa (Tell Me 'Bout the Good Old Days)	*Rockin' With the Rhythm*	Jamie O'Hara	RCA 87042
1987	Dolly Parton, Emmylou Harris & Linda Ronstadt	*Trio*			Warner 25491
1988	Judds	*Give a Little Love*			RCA 90011
1989	Nitty Gritty Dirt Band	*Will the Circle Be Unbroken, Vol. II*			Universal/MCA 9001
1990	Kentucky Headhunters		*Pickin' on Nashville*		Phonogram 8387441
1991	Judds	Love Can Build a Bridge	*Love Can Build a Bridge*	Naomi Judd, John Jarvis, Paul Overstreet	RCA 90531

*Songwriters are listed only for singles or album tracks.

w) Best Country Song (Songwriter's Award)

Year	Song Title	Lyricist/Composer	Artist(s)Label/Rec. #
1964	Dang Me	Roger Miller	Roger Miller; Smash 1881
1965	King of the Road	Roger Miller	Roger Miller; Smash 1965 Jody Miller (as "Queen of the House"); Capitol 5402
1966	Almost Persuaded	Billy Sherrill, Glen Sutton	Davis Houston; Epic 10025 Ben Colder (pseudonym of Sheb Wooley, who recorded tune as "Almost Persuaded No. 2"); MGM 13590

1967	Gentle on My Mind	John Hartford	Glen Campbell; Capitol 5939
1968	Little Green Apples	Bobby Russell	O. C. Smith; Columbia 44616 Roger Miller; Smash 2148 Patti Page; Columbia 44556
1969	A Boy Named Sue	Shel Silverstein	Johnny Cash; Columbia 44944
1970	My Woman, My Woman My Wife	Marty Robbins	Marty Robbins; Columbia 45091
1971	Help Me Make It Through the Night	Kris Kristofferson	Sammi Smith; Mega 0015
1972	Kiss An Angel Good Mornin'	Ben Peters	Charley Pride; RCA 0550
1973	Behind Closed Doors	Kenny O'Dell	Charlie Rich; Epic 1095
1974	A Very Special Love Song	Norro Wilson, Billy Sherrill	Charlie Rich; Epic 11091
1975	(Hey Won't You Play) Another Somebody Done Somebody Wrong Song	Chips Moman, Larry Butler	B. J. Thomas; ABC 12054
1976	Broken Lady	Larry Gatlin	Larry Gatlin; Columbia 38337 (With Family and Friends)
1977	Don't It Make My Brown Eyes Blue	Richard Leigh	Crystal Gayle; United Artists 101
1978	The Gambler	Don Schlitz	Kenny Rogers; United Artists 1250
1979	You Decorated My Life	Debbie Hupp, Bob Morrison	Kenny Rogers; United Artists 1315
1980	On the Road Again	Willie Nelson	Willie Nelson; Columbia 11351
1981	9 to 5	Dolly Parton	Dolly Parton; RCA 12133
1982	Always on My Mind	Johnny Christopher, Mark James, Wayne Thompson	Willie Nelson; Columbia 02741
1983	Stranger in My House	Mike Reid	Ronnie Milsap; RCA 13470
1984	The City of New Orleans	Steve Goodman	Arlo Guthrie; Reprise 1103
1985	Highwayman	Jim. Webb	Waylon Jennings, Willie Nelson, Kris Kristofferson & Johnny Cash (*Highwayman*); Columbia 26466
1986	Grandpa (Tell Me 'Bout the Good Old Days)	Jamie O'Hara	Judds (*Rockin in Rhythm*); RCA 87042
1987	Forever and Ever, Amen	Paul Overstreet, Don Schlitz	Randy Travis; Warner 25568 (*Always & Forever*)
1988	Hold Me	K. T. Oslin	K. T. Oslin (*This Woman*); RCA 8369
1989	After All This Time	Rodney Crowell	Rodney Crowell; Columbia 460873 (*Diamonds and Dirt*)
1990	Where've You Been	Don Henry, John Vezner	Kathy Mattea; Mercury MER 338
1991	Love Can Build a Bridge	Naomi Judd, John Jarvis, Paul Overstreet	The Judds; (*Love Can Build a Bridge*); RCA 90531

Ehrick V. Long

GREAT DEPRESSION. SEE DEPRESSION YEARS

GREECE

Greek composers have contributed several striking songs to the repertoire of popular song in America. One of them, "Misirlou" (1941), has a melody reminiscent of the ancient Greek **modes**; it is often performed as a **rumba**. Another, "Never on Sunday" (1960), with music by the renowned composer and conductor Manos Hadjidakis, was introduced by the actress and singer Melina Mercouri in the film of the same name. It won the **Academy Award** for best song of its year, and is to this day very often performed as a **cha cha cha**. Mike Theodorakis's theme from the 1965 film *Zorba the Greek* is in fact a popular Greek dance, the *syrtaki*; its infectious, accelerating rhythm assured it continuing popularity. Both of these works, characterized by metrical intensity, are based on a duple pattern. But Greek folk dances are more often based on asymmetrical metrical patterns such as 5/8 (2 3), 7/8 (3 2 2), and 9/8 (2 2 2 3).

See also: **Foreign Influence**

GREEN. SEE COLORS

GREETINGS

Popular songs of greeting and salutation have been abundant in the literature for well over a century. They are almost equally divided in number between those beginning with "hello" and those beginning with "hey." There are also a few songs beginning with "hi," or containing a foreign word of greeting.

"Hello" songs span the century, from the ragtime song "Hello! Ma Baby," of 1899, to Lionel Richie's Number One hit "Hello," of 1984. Perhaps the most famous is "Hello, Dolly!" from the 1964 show of the same name. Its hold on the public was strengthened with a famous Decca recording by Louis Armstrong. Another memorable song that emanated from a show is the graceful waltz "Hello Young Lovers," from *The King and I* (1951).

A group of "hello" songs have been written about the **telephone**; one of the best known is the narrative song "Hello Central, Give Me Heaven," of 1901. Other songs are about events, like the **World War I** song "Good-bye Broadway, Hello France" (1917). The Beatles also contributed several songs of greeting, including "Hello Little Girl" (1963) and "Hello, Goodbye" (1967).

Although few songs beginning with the word "hey" were written in the first third of the century, such songs became increasingly abundant as the years progressed. Lionel Hampton's "Hey! Ba-Ba-Re-Bop" of 1945 was a mixture of greeting and **nonsense** syllables. Hank William's "Hey Good Lookin'" of 1951, originally a country and western song, became an early **crossover** hit. Two different Broadway shows introduced, respectively, the poignant ballad "Hey There," from *The Pajama Game* (1954), and the sprightly **march** "Hey, Look Me Over," from *Wildcat* (1960). The Beatles introduced the innovative "Hey Jude" in 1968.

Songs beginning with "hi" are much less common. Best Known is "Hi-Lili, Hi-Lo," from the 1953 film *Lili*—another song that features nonsense syllables. As for **foreign-language** greetings in song, they include the Hawaiian "Aloha Oe" (1878) and "To You Sweetheart, Aloha" (1936), the Hebrew "Shalom" (1961), and the German "Willkommen" (1966).

Additional Songs

Hello Frisco Hello (1915)
Hello, I Love You (1968)
Hello, It's Me (1968)
Hello Muddah, Hello Fadduh (1963)
Hello, My Lover, Goodbye (1931)
Hey, Baby (1961)
Hey, Girl (1963)
Hey! Jealous Lover (1956)
Hey, Mr. Banjo (1955)
Hey, Paula (1963)
Hey There, Good Times (1977)
Hey There, Lonely Girl/Hey There, Lonely Boy (1962)
Hi, Neighbor (1941)
Welcome Back (1976)

See also: **Farewells**

GUARACHA

The guaracha is a song-and-dance genre characterized by satirical lyrics, **call-and-response** vocal exchanges, and improvisational instrumental passages. It originated in **Cuba**, where it was often performed by urban dance ensembles.

One of the many Latin American **dance crazes** that reached the United States in the 1940s, the guaracha is performed in fast tempo and duple meter and is similar to the **mambo** in its use of polyrhythm and exchange between soloists and sections of the orchestra. Among the most popular guarachas in the United States were "Cachita" (1936), "Cuanto le Gusta" (1940), and "El Cumbanchero" (1943). Guarachas were later taken up by **salsa** groups, and became part of their repertoire during the 1970s.

See also: **Conga**; **Rumba**

GUILT. SEE FORGIVENESS

GUITAR

The guitar has been played in America since pre-Colonial times. Because of its portability, versatility, and relative inexpensiveness, it had long been the quintessential accompanying instrument of **folk song,** the **blues,** and **country and western** music. But its popularity began in earnest only when it was amplified in the 1940s and used for **rhythm and blues,** and when it was adapted to **rock 'n' roll** in the 1950s.

Early guitarist-composers included Huddie Leadbetter (Leadbelly), co-writer of "Goodnight Irene" (1936), and Clarence "Blind Lemon" Jefferson, both were famous for their folk blues. Jimmie Rodgers, a pioneer of country and western music, played both banjo and guitar, one of his most popular songs was "Mule Skinner Blues" (1931). Woody Guthrie, who played both harmonica and guitar, was largely responsible for the folk song revival with such songs as "So Long (It's Been Good to Know Yuh)" (1939).

The guitar was used less extensively in **jazz,** where it was primarily part of the rhythm section. There were, however, a number of eminent solo improvisers, such as Charlie Christian, Django Reinhardt, Barney Kessel, and Les Paul, who helped bring the guitar out of the cellar, so to speak.

The 1960s—the age of **rock** and the **performer-songwriter**—saw an explosion of guitar-playing composers, among them members of the Beatles and Bob Dylan. Three types of guitar playing became the rule, respectively emphasizing melody, rhythm, and bass with widespread electronic manipulation of guitar tone and texture. The guitar was also used extensively in the performance of **bossa nova.** Outstanding in this regard were the American guitarist Charlie Byrd and the Brazilian Bola Sete. The outstanding Brazilian composer, Antonio Carlos Jobim, who wrote "The Girl From Ipanema" (1963) and many other standards, was a guitarist as well as a pianist. Among other renowned performers on the instrument were B. B. King, Muddy Waters, Carlos Santana, and Jimi Hendrix.

See also: **Improvisation; Instrumentation; Strings**

GYPSY MUSIC

Gypsy music knows few national boundaries. There are, among others, the flamenco music of Spain; the music of the Russian Gypsies, like "Otchi Tchorniya," adapted by Harry Horlick in 1926 as "Dark Eyes"; the

French *valse-tsigane,* "Fascination," given English words in 1932; and the Danish *tango-tsigane,* "Jalousie," which became "Jealousy" in 1925.

The best-known music of the Gypsies is that of **Hungary** and **Romania,** typically played by ensembles of two violins, double bass, and cimbalom. The music often uses a modified harmonic minor **scale**—c, d, e-flat, f-sharp, g, a-flat, b, c'—and is further characterized by sudden and unexpected changes of **tempo** and **dynamics.**

Gypsy music has had relatively little influence in the development of American popular song. Several European works on Gypsy themes were popular here, including Franz Lehár's *Gypsy Love* (1912), which included the popular song "Gypsy Maiden." Emmerich Kálmán's *Countess Maritza* was very successful in New York City in 1926; its most striking song was "Play Gypsies—Dance Gypsies," which was more cosmopolitan Hungarian than Gypsy in spirit. Similarly Hungarian in spirit is Noël Coward's "Zigeuner," from his play *Bitter Sweet* (1929). Hardly more in the Gypsy tradition were two songs written in part by the "Gypsy" violinist Emery Deutsch: "Play Fiddle Play" (1932) and "When a Gypsy Makes His Violin Cry" (1935).

Other songs bearing the appellation "Gypsy" exhibit few traditional characteristics of the music. Victor Herbert's "Gypsy Love Song," of 1898, is a fairly ordinary song of its time, although its verse—of which the chorus of "Play Fiddle Play" is reminiscent—is in a minor key.

The word "Gypsy," as it is used in a number of songs, has no relationship to Gypsy music, however; it has more to do with restlessness. Songs in this category are "The Gypsy in Me" (1934) and "The Gypsy in My Soul" (1937). A similar idea appears in Ira Gershwin's famous line from "Embraceable You" (1930): "You and you alone bring out the Gypsy in me." Also unrelated to Gypsy music are the songs "The Gypsy" (1945), "Gypsies, Tramps and Thieves" (1971), "Gypsy Man" (1973), and "Say Has Anybody Seen My Sweet Gypsy Rose" (1973). The latter may have been inspired by the enormous success of the 1959 musical comedy *Gypsy,* which was in turn inspired by the career of entertainer Gypsy Rose Lee.

See also: **Austria; Foreign Influence; Russia**

h

HAPPINESS

Happiness, in popular song, is most often expressed in the form of an adjective. Examples through the years include "Happy Birthday to You" (1893), "Get Happy" (1930), "Happy Holiday" (1942), "The Happy Wanderer" (1954), "Put On a Happy Face" (1960), "Love Can Make You Happy" (1969), and "Happy Days" (1974).

Vincent Youmans wrote the music for two of the best "happy" songs: "I Want to Be Happy," from *No, No, Nanette* (1924), and "Sometimes I'm Happy," from *Hit the Deck* (1927). One of the most familiar songs on the subject is the rousing "Happy Days Are Here Again" (1928), often revived at political conventions. "Happy" is also the title of the love theme from the film *Lady Sings the Blues* (1972), based on the life of singer Billie Holiday.

As for "happiness" in the form of a noun, two songs are worthy of mention. The haunting "Happiness is (Just) a Thing Called Joe" was written by E. Y. Harburg and Harold Arlen for the film version of the musical play *Cabin in the Sky* (1942). The folk-like "My Happiness," written in 1933, was successfully revived in 1948, and again in 1958.

At the opposite extreme, "unhappiness" is the tongue-in-cheek subject to the poignant ballad "Glad to Be Unhappy," written in 1936 by Lorenz Hart and Richard Rodgers.

Additional Songs

Aren't You Glad You're You? (1946)
Bluebird of Happiness (1934)
Happiest Girl in the Whole U.S.A. (1971)
Happy Talk (1949)
Happy Together (1967)
(You Don't Know) How Glad I Am (1975)
I Whistle a Happy Tune (1951)
If You Wanna Be Happy (1962)
I'm Glad There Is You (1941)
It's a Hap-Hap-Happy Day (1939)
The Most Happy Fella (1956)
You've Made Me So Very Happy (1967)
   See also: Heaven; Luck; Sun

HARLEM

Harlem, a district of **New York City** located in Manhattan north of 110th Street, has been a center of black culture since the 1930s. It has greatly influenced American popular song, especially through its theaters, nightclubs, and ballrooms. The Apollo Theatre, located at 253 West 125th Street, between Seventh and Eighth Avenues, has offered **vaudeville** by black entertainers, as well as music of the **big bands** since 1934. Stars featured there included Duke Ellington, Billie Holiday, Ella Fitzgerald, Dionne Warwick, and Smokey Robinson. The Apollo has also long been a center of **rhythm and blues, gospel, and soul.**

The Cotton Club, located at 644 Lenox Avenue, at 142nd Street, was founded in 1922. It was famous for providing late-night black entertainment for white patrons. Such bands as those of Ellington, Cab Calloway, and Jimmie Lunceford, and singers like Ethel Waters and Lena Horne, were regulars. The Cotton Club also offered a series of **revues.** Such songs as "I've Got the World on a String" (1932), "Stormy Weather" (1933), and "As Long as I Live" (1934) were written for Cotton Club Revues.

The most famous ballroom in Harlem was the Savoy, located at 596 Lenox Avenue, which opened in 1926. Ella Fitzgerald got her start there, singing with Chick Webb and His Orchestra. The Savoy Ballroom was famous for its introduction of many **dance crazes** and for its battles of the bands. It is best remembered as part of the title of the jazz standard "Stompin' at the Savoy" (1934).

A number of songs have been written about Harlem, among them "Bojangles of Harlem" (1936) and "Harlem

Nocturne" (1940). Jerry Leiber and Phil Spector's 1960 song "Spanish Harlem" refers to the Latin American enclave in New York City just east of Harlem.

Bibliography

Cooper, Ralph, with Steve Dougherty. *Amateur Night at the Apollo: Ralph Cooper Presents Five Decades of Great Entertainment.* 1990.

HARMONIC RHYTHM

The relative speed of harmonic changes within a piece of music is known as its harmonic rhythm. Historically, the harmonic rhythm of popular song has varied from very slow to very fast, with the majority of songs falling somewhere in between.

In the 1890s, slow harmonic rhythm was the rule; harmonies tended to be maintained for four or more bars. Thus, in the chorus of "A Hot Time in the Old Town" (1896), the tonic triad is held for twelve bars in common time. Similarly, the dominant seventh **harmony** in the chorus of "The Band Played On" (1895) is maintained for eight consecutive bars, while the tonic harmony in "After the Ball" (1892) is unchanged for six bars (both in 3/4 **meter**). This tendency toward slow harmonic rhythm continued after the turn of the century in such songs as "Bill Bailey, Won't You Please Come Home?" (1902) and in the performance of **Dixieland** (the slow-moving harmonies of "When the Saints Go Marching In" (1896) are a classic example).

Faster harmonic rhythm began to manifest itself with the development of **jazz**. Songs with interesting and more frequent "changes," like "Rose Room" (1917), "After You've Gone" (1918), and "I Can't Get Started" (1935), became of interest to jazz musicians as bases for **improvisation**. The harmonies of Duke Ellington's "Sophisticated Lady" (1937) and "Prelude to a Kiss" (1938) change as often as every beat. During the same era, the **art song** showed similar characteristics, with three changes to a bar a common occurrence, as in Jerome Kern's waltzes "The Touch of Your Hand (1933) and "I Dream Too Much" (1935).

The dichotomy between slow and fast harmonic rhythm continued into the following decades, simultaneously pairing songs in slow harmonic rhythm— "In the Mood" (1939), "Deep in the Heart of Texas" (1941), "Sentimental Journey" (1944), "Eleanor Rigby" (1966), "Strangers in the Night" (1966), "Gentle on My Mind" (1967)—with songs in fast harmonic rhythm— "Yesterday" (1965), "Georgy Girl" (1966), "Up, Up and Away" (1967), "Theme From *Mahogany*," (Do You Know Where You're Going To?)" (1973).

However, in the vast majority of popular songs, like "A Taste of Honey" (1960), "Moon River" (1961), and "My Way" (1967), harmonic change occurs approximately once in every bar. Occasionally there may be episodes of either fast harmonic rhythm—as in the **release** of "Have You Met Miss Jones?" (1937)—or of slow harmonic rhythm—as in the notes held for four bars in "Aquarius" (1967).

HARMONY

Harmony is the vertical relationship of tones to one another: the way they sound together. In its broadest sense, the term embraces the **tonality** of a piece: the **key** in which it is written, as well as any **modulations** that may occur within it. But most often in popular song, the term "harmony," in a narrower sense, refers to the chords that are used.

The harmonic vocabulary of popular song is extremely variable, ranging from the simplest to the most complex. The simplest chords—tonic and subdominant triads and dominant sevenths—are characteristic of many waltzes dating from around the turn of the century. Many songs of the time, like "The Band Played On" (1895), are in slow **harmonic rhythm**; the opening harmonies of its chorus are as follows: A (4 bars), E7 (8 bars), A (4 bars). Very often, as in "Daisy Bell" (1892), the **melody** is simple too, outlining **broken chords**.

Simple harmony is also a prominent feature of much **folk song, country and western,** and **rock 'n' roll** music. It has even found its way to Broadway in Songs with a folk flavor, like "Oh What a Beautiful Mornin'," from *Oklahoma!* (1943). Another folk-like song, "Gentle on My Mind" (1967), vacillates between only two chords: C major and D minor. Many of the most popular songs of the 1960s, such as "Blowin' in the Wind" (1962) and "Both Sides Now" (1967), alternate almost entirely between chords of the tonic, subdominant, and dominant.

At the other extreme are the sophisticated harmonies of many of the songs written in the first half of the twentieth century. In this regard, the coloristic harmony of sevenths and ninths used by Claude Debussy at the turn of the century greatly influenced popular composers of the 1930s. Duke Ellington's "Sophisticated Lady" (1933), for example, has two chromatic chord progressions: G-flat7, F7, E7, E-flat 7, and A-flat7, G7, G-flat7, F7; his "Prelude to a Kiss" (1938) begins with the harmonies: D9, G7+5, C9, Fmaj7, B9, E9, A7, Dm.

Chords of the major and minor seventh are especially characteristic of popular song. Songs like "The Girl From Ipanema" (1963) and "A Man and a Woman" (1966) consist of successions of seventh chords. "Goin' Out of My Head" (1964) constantly reiterates the tonic minor seventh chord. The most prominent feature of "On a Clear Day You Can See Forever" (1966) is its use of major sevenths, ninths, elevenths, and thirteenths. "Killing Me Softly With His Song" (1972) emphasizes the minor seventh.

Songs with particularly interesting harmony frequently become favorite subjects of jazz **improvisa-**

tion. The chorus of "Body and Soul" (1930), for one, begins with a minor chord on the second scale degree and has highly unusual changes throughout. "Night and Day" (1932) begins with a very provocative C-flat major seventh chord, producing a striking dissonance against the repeated B-flats of the melody. "Out of Nowhere" (1931) is noteworthy for its major ninth chords: first on the lowered sixth and then on the sixth degree of the scale. The juxtaposition of the major and minor **mode** is another much-used harmonic device in jazz standards; examples are "How High the Moon" (1940) and "Here's That Rainy Day" (1953). The chorus of the 1943 waltz "The Boy Next Door" is of special interest because of its suspended dominant ninth chords descending sequentially. Interesting chord changes also occur in such jazz standards as "Autumn in New York" (1934) and "Moonlight in Vermont" (1944). In these and many other songs, the element of harmony has contributed to the distinctiveness of much American popular music.

Bibliography

Wilder, Alec. *American Popular Song: The Great Innovators 1990–1950.* 1972.

See also: Cadence; Chromaticism; Circle of Fifths; Counterpoint; Enharmonic Equivalence; Interval; Pedal Point

HEART. SEE ANATOMY

HEAVEN

Popular songs using heaven in its celestial sense, as a place in the **sky**, are relatively few in number. Nevertheless, they include three well-known songs "Heaven Will Protect the Working Girl" (1909), "Pennies From Heaven" (1936), and "Thank Heaven for Little Girls" (1958).

Most often, the word "heaven" refers to a place of supreme **happiness** aided by the presence of a loved one. Examples include Charles K. Harris's early telephone song, "Hello Central, Give Me Heaven" (1901): "My Little Nest of Heavenly Blue" (1923), the English-language version of Franz Lehár's "Frasquita Serenade"; and George Whiting and Walter Donaldson's enduring song "My Blue Heaven" (1927). In the film *Top Hat* (1935), Fred Astaire sings "Heaven, I'm in heaven," while he is dancing "Cheek to Cheek" with Ginger Rogers. Paradise is also referred to in several songs, notably George and Ira Gershwin's "I'll Build a Stairway to Paradise" (1922) and the 1931 waltz "Paradise." A popular song of 1939, "Heaven Can Wait," refers to paradise as well: "This is paradise/Just being here with you."

But heaven can also apply to one person in particular, as in Gene Autry's 1938 country hit "You're the Only Star in My Blue Heaven" or the 1942 song derived from Edvard Grieg's *Piano Concerto in A Minor:* "I Look at Heaven" ("When I look at you"). Similarly, one place alone can be heavenly; examples are Ernest R. Ball's paean to the land of his ancestors, "A Little Bit of Heaven, Shure They Call It Ireland" (1914); and the often-revived 1946 song about heaven on earth called "Shangri-La."

The 1960s and 1970s saw a revival of interest in songs about heaven, from "Heaven Must Have Sent You" (1966) to "Heaven Help Us All" (1970).

Additional Songs

Heaven Is a Place on Earth (1987)
Heaven Knows (1978)
Heaven Must Be Missing an Angel (1976)
Heaven on the Seventh Floor (1977)
Home Sweet Heaven (1964)
Stairway to Heaven (1960)
The Sweetest Music This Side of Heaven (1934)
When Did You Leave Heaven? (1936)
You'll Never Get to Heaven (1964)

See also: Angels; Religion

HEAVY METAL

The term "heavy metal" denotes a high-decibel type of **rock** music characterized by all-encompassing amplification of **guitar** and bass guitar with emphasis on the lower spectrum of sound. Among its other stylistic features are heavy and repetitive **riffs**, extended drum solos, and frequent resort to sound distortion and feedback. With sheer loudness as its ideal, heavy metal served as a symbol of teenage frustration and rebellion. The expression is said to have been first applied to rock music by the British group Steppenwolf, who used it in their 1968 recording of "Born to Be Wild."

Heavy metal began in the late 1960s in **Britain**, Europe, and the United States; often associated with drug use and the lower classes, it flourished into the 1980s. One of its early exponents was the American guitarist Jimi Hendrix, who with his group The Jimi Hendrix Experience, formed in London in 1966, had a hit with "Purple Haze" (1967). Another heavy-metal forerunner was "In-a-gadda-da-vida," performed by the group Iron Butterfly, and released by Atlantic Records in 1968. The British group Cream, with guitarist Eric Clapton, also had several successful records of the genre, including "Sunshine of Your Love" (1968), "White Room" (1968), and "Badge" (1969).

By far the most successful and lasting heavy-metal band was the British group Led Zeppelin, founded by Jimmy Page on guitar, with Robert Plant on vocals, John Paul Jones on keyboards, and John Bonham on drums. The group's many hits from albums included "Whole Lotta Love" (1969), "Immigrant Song" (1970), "Black Dog" (1972), "D'Yer Mak'er" (1973), and their most popular, "Stairway to Heaven" (1972), a song that was never released as a single. An American group, Grand Funk Railroad, also produced a number of heavy-metal hits, including "We're an American Band" (1973) and a 1974 **cover** of "The Loco-Motion," first sung by Little Eva twelve years before.

Bibliography

Gammond, Peter. *The Oxford Companion to Popular Music.* 1991.

Halfin, Ross, and Pete Makowski. *Heavy Metal.* 1982.

Harrigan, Brian, and Malcolm Dome. *Encyclopaedia Metallica: The Bible of Heavy Metal.* 1981.

———. *Heavy Metal A–Z: The Definitive Encyclopedia of Heavy Metal, From AC/DC Through Led Zeppelin to ZZ Top.* 1981.

Jasper, Tony, Derek Oliver, Steve Hammond, and David Reynolds. *The International Encyclopedia of Hard Rock and Heavy Metal.* 1983.

Martyn, Lee. *Masters of Metal.* 1984.

Miller, Jim, ed. *The Illustrated History of Rock & Roll.* 1980.

Obrecht, James, ed. *Masters of Heavy Metal.* 1984.

See also: Punk Rock

HEIGHT

Not surprisingly, many songs having to do with height are concerned with hills or **mountains**; some examples are "I'd Climb the Highest Mountain" (1926), "High on a Windy Hill" (1940), "The Mountains High" (1961), "Ain't No Mountain High Enough" (1967), and "Rocky Mountain High" (1972). Other songs go to even greater heights, for instance, "Up, Up and Away," (1967), and "Sky High" (1975).

But probably the best-known song on the subject of height is the perennial jazz and bebop standard "How High the Moon" (1950). The word "high" is also frequently used in popular song as a synonym for feeling good; examples are "Ridin' High" (1936) and "(Your Love Has Lifted Me) Higher and Higher" (1967). Among other songs alluding to height in one way or another are "You're a Builder Upper" (1934), "I'm Shooting High" (1935), "The High and the Mighty" (1954), "Long Tall Sally" (1956), "High Hopes" (1959), "Eight Miles High" (1966), and "I Want to Take You Higher" (1968).

See also: Depth; Sky

HELLO. SEE GREETINGS

HIT PARADE. SEE YOUR HIT PARADE

HIT SONG

A hit song can be described as one that is commercially successful, but such a definition is far too simplistic in today's pop music market. In practice, it is best to qualify the term by using modifying adjectives like "major," "minor," "only," "blockbuster," or "regional." For example, the song "The Impossible Dream" was the hit song from the musical *Man of La Mancha* (1965), but was only a minor hit for Jack Jones in the *Billboard* chart (Number 35 in 1966). Nevertheless, it was "the" hit song from the show.

Historically, the first gauge of a hit was the number of copies of **sheet music** it sold. As early as 1892, major hit songs were selling millions of copies ("After the Ball" reportedly sold five million). Sheet music sales remained the primary indicator of hit status until the Great Depression began in late 1929, and sales fell off drastically. During the 1920s, many hit songs routinely sold between 750,000 and one million copies of sheet music annually. In contrast, in the early 1930s annual sales averaged only half a million.

In the impoverished economy of the Depression, **radio** became the most important hit-making medium, because once a receiver was purchased the entertainment was free. Therefore, radio airplay became increasingly important as a hit-making avenue and a major indicator of hit songs.

In 1935, when *Your Hit Parade* premiered on radio, information was gathered from music shops regarding sales of records and sheet music, from radio stations on the amount of airplay each song received, from **jukebox** operators on songs that were most played, and from important bandleaders as to the songs most frequently requested. For the next several years, the accepted barometer of a hit song was its appearance on *Your Hit Parade*. Still, many songs now considered **standards** never appeared on the radio show. "Star Dust" (1929), "Begin the Beguine" (1935), and "September Song" (1938) were selected by **ASCAP** for its "All Time Hit Parade," but did not make *Your Hit Parade*. Neither did "Summertime" (1935), "My Funny Valentine" (1937), "God Bless America" (1939), or these famous recordings: Tommy Dorsey's version of "Boogie Woogie" (1928; recorded in 1938), the Andrews Sisters' "Boogie Woogie Bugle Boy" (1931), or Glenn Miller's "Tuxedo Junction" (1940).

Variety and *Billboard* began running weekly pop charts in the early 1940s; the measure of a hit song was its appearance in the Top Ten of at least one of these charts. Each of the charting organizations obtained their information from different sources, and of course each claimed to be the most accurate.

The postwar boom in the **recording** industry began in 1946, when sales of records went up 100 percent over 1945 figures. From that time on, record sales (specifically of singles) became a more accurate indicator of hit status.

Cash Box joined the charters in 1950, but over the years **Billboard** became the best known of the charts;

its Hot 100 and **Top Forty** are posted in most record stores. In addition, its **Rhythm and Blues** (now called Black) and **Country and Western** charts are usually posted. Songs that make the Top Forty on any of these charts receive a "rack" order and are stacked by most stores.

Before 1958, gold records (signifying one million or more units sold or $1 million in album sales) were given to artists on a rather informal basis. Since then, however, gold discs have been certified by RIAA (Record Industry Association of America). In the early years, a gold record was considered quite an achievement, but by the 1980s, many songs reached platinum status, signifying two million units sold for singles or $2 million in revenue for albums.

Technically, a song is a hit in its category if it makes the weekly Top Forty on any particular chart (Black, Country, Adult Contemporary, Pop Singles, Dance, or Jazz). A song that makes the Top Ten on any chart may be considered a major hit in that category. The most prestigious categories, because they are the most lucrative, are the Top Pop Albums and Top Pop Singles. A Top Forty Country hit is minor in comparison to a Top Forty Pop hit.

Therefore, by any measure, the word "hit" must be taken with caution, and liberally qualified by modifiers describing the type or degree.

Don Tyler

Bibliography

Tyler, Don. *Hit Parade, 1920–1955*. 1985.

Whitburn, Joel. *The Billboard Book of Top 40 Hits*. Revised and enlarged. 1992

Williams, John R. *This Was Your Hit Parade*. 1973.

See also: BMI

HOLIDAYS

A number of songs are traditionally associated with holidays. No New Year's Eve would be complete without "Auld Lang Syne" (1711). "My Funny Valentine" is certainly appropriate for St. Valentine's Day (February 14), while any song about **Ireland** or the Irish will do for St. Patrick's Day (March 17). Easter is well represented by Irving Berlin's "Easter Parade" (1933) and by the 1950 song "Peter Cottontail." As for the Fourth of July, almost any song emphasizing **patriotism** will do.

But all these pale in significance before the sheer number of songs associated with **Christmas** and the holiday season. The best known of these, and one of the most popular songs ever written, is Berlin's "White Christmas," introduced by Bing Crosby in *Holiday Inn* (1942), a film built around songs associated with favorite holidays of the year. For the film, Berlin wrote a song for every major holiday of the year, including "Let's Start the New Year Right" for New Year's Day and

"Plenty to Be Thankful For," for Thanksgiving. Of these, aside from "White Christmas" and "Easter Parade" (which was also featured in the film), only the ballad "Be Careful, It's My Heart" and the picture's theme song, "Happy Holiday," survive.

Additional Songs

Holiday (1967)
(There's No Place Like) Home for the Holidays (1955)

See also: Months; Religion; Seasons

HOME

Home, along with motherhood, was one of the most popular **subjects** of song during the nineteenth century. Typically, songs about home were sentimental and emotional, bearing such titles as "Home! Sweet Home!" (1823), "Old Folks at Home" (1851), "My Old Kentucky Home" (1853), "Home on the Range" (1873), and "I'll Take You Home Again Kathleen" (1876).

In the early twentieth century, the sentimental aspect sometimes disappeared, and home became a place more of refuge than of emotional attachment. The subject was often used frivolously or humorously, as in "Tell Me Pretty Maiden (Are There Many More at Home Like You?)," from *Floradora* (1900); "Bill Bailey, Won't You Please Come Home?" (1902); "Baby, Won't You Please Come Home?" (1923); "Paddlin' Madelin' Home" (1925); and "Walkin' My Baby Back Home" (1930). Occasionally, as in the prohibition lament "Show Me the Way to Go Home" (1925), there were even alcoholic overtones.

But at the same time, songs continued to be written in the earlier sentimental mode, as exemplified by the location songs "My Old New Hampshire Home" (1898), "Little Grey Home in the West" (1911), and "Indiana (Back Home Again in Indiana)" (1917). The song "Goin' Home" was adapted in 1922 from Anton Dvořak's symphony *From the New World* of 1893. One of the most enduring songs about home, beginning with the words "When shadows fall . . .," is entitled simply "Home" (1931).

During times of war, thoughts of home naturally come to mind. In the Civil War, it was "When Johnny Comes Marching Home" (1863); in **World War I**, "Keep the Home Fires Burning" (1915); and in **World War II**, "I'll Be Home for Christmas" (1943). Home can also be where the heart is, as in Cole Porter's wistful "You'd Be So Nice to Come Home To" (1942), or a refuge from the perils of the big city, as in the John Denver hit "Take Me Home, Country Roads" (1971). Then, too, there are songs about specific homes; Paul Simon's "Graceland" (1986) is about Elvis Presley's famous home in Tennessee.

A house can be a home as well, whether it is expensive, as in "Penthouse Serenade (When We're

Alone)" (1931), or humble, as in "A Shanty in Old Shanty Town" (1932). As a matter of fact, during the **Depression years**, a house was very often "A Cottage for Sale" (1930). But a clear distinction between a house and a home is made in Hal David's lyrics for "A House Is Not a Home" (1964): a house is "not a home when there's no one there. . . ."

Additional Songs

Bring It On Home to Me (1962)
Come On-a My House (1950)
Flying Home (1941)
The Green, Green Grass of Home (1967)
(There's No Place Like) Home for the Holidays (1955)
Homeward Bound (1966)
It's So Nice to Have a Man Around the House (1950)
She's Leaving Home (1967)
Take Me Home (1979)
This Ole House (1954)

HOPE. SEE INSPIRATION

HUMOR

The underlying basis of humor in popular song, as in all other aspects of life, is incongruity. It can be manifested in various ways: humorous **rhyme**, puns, double entendre, parody, satire, comic word juxtaposition, exaggerated **alliteration**, absurd performance, utter **nonsense** or hyperbole. Many humorous songs were first heard in vaudeville, revue, or musical comedy, although Tin Pan Alley and Hollywood have provided their share as well.

Examples of humorous rhyme abound in the works of Lorenz Hart, Cole Porter, Ira Gershwin, and numerous other **lyricists**. For instance, in "Johnny One Note" (1937), Hart rhymed "willy-nilly" with "until he." Similarly, Porter could effortlessly rhyme "a custom tailored vet" with "something wet" and "begins to pet," in his slightly risqué "Always True to You (In My Fashion)" (1948). Another humorous rhyme, in Gershwin's "Who Cares?" (1931), pairs "Yonkers" with "a kiss that conquers."

Porter was also a master of the pun, particularly in his **catalogue songs**. A celebrated example occurs in "Let's Do It (Let's Fall in Love)" (1928), wherein he lists nationalities that "do it," that is fall in love: French, Dutch, Finns, Lapps, Lithuanians, and—inevitably—Letts. Another pun on a title occurs at the very end of Gershwin's "But Not for Me" (1930), a song about tying the marriage knot. The lyrics of the last line read: "And there's no knot for me."

A sterling example of double entendre in song occurs in Johnny Burke's **lyrics** for the 1945 song "Personality." The words "She has the cutest personality" clearly refer by innuendo to a physical attribute rather than to behavior or character. Similarly, Stephen

Sondheim makes it clear in his lyrics for "Can That Boy Fox-Trot!" (1971) that he is not referring to terpsichorean proficiency; in fact, the lyrics explicitly state that the boy has one flaw: "He can't dance."

Putting new lyrics to existing melodies is one of the oldest forms of parody in music. There are numerous examples in popular song. In 1940, Milton Berle parodied the serious 1932 song "Lawd, You Made the Night Too Long" as "Sam, You Made the Pants Too Long." In the 1963 hit song "Hello Muddah, Hello Fadduh," Allan Sherman put a child's letter from summer camp to the well-known melody of Ponchielli's "Dance of the Hours," from the opera *La Gioconda* (1876). In the 1960s, Noël Coward wrote a somewhat scandalous parody of Cole Porter's "Let,s Do It," referring to the habits of real people, like Louella Parsons and Liberace, instead of those of animals and nationalities. Even titles can sometimes be parodied to humorous effect, when service is slow at a restaurant, an appropriate version of the waltz "Some Day My Prince Will Come," from *Snow White and the Seven Dwarfs* (1937), might be "Some Day My Blintz Will Come."

Satirical songs may be divided into the political and the nonpolitical. Political satire is the essence of several comic songs from musicals, such as "Wintergreen for President," from *Of Thee I Sing* (1931), and the title song of *Let 'Em Eat Cake* (1933). Graft and corruption figure prominently in two songs from *Fiorello* (1959): "(In My) Little Tin Box" and "Politics and Poker." Far removed from politics, but still satirical, are two songs from *Finian's Rainbow* (1947), the titles of which speak for themselves: "When I'm Not Near the Girl I Love"—"(I love the girl I'm near)"—and "When the Idle Poor Become the Idle Rich."

Sir William S. Gilbert, in his operettas with Sir Arthur Sullivan, was a master of word juxtaposition. The tradition was carried over to popular music in such songs as "Who Threw the Overalls in Mrs. Murphy's Chowder?" (1899) and "Yes! We Have No Bananas" (1923). In Noël Coward's "Mad Dogs and Englishmen" (1931), only two creatures "go out in the noonday sun." The "Boston Beguine," from the revue *New Faces* (1952), incongruously pairs an exotic and romantic dance with a rather mundane locale. Incongruous pairings in Alan Jay Lerner's lyrics for "Come Back to Me" (1965) include "On a mule, In a jet"; "Hop a freight, Grab a plane"; "To the moon or the corner saloon."

Perhaps the supreme example of exaggerated alliteration put to comic effect is the tongue-twisting "She Sells Sea-Shells (on the Seashore)" (1908). Among other examples are "K-K-K-Katy" (1918) and "Boogie-Woogie Bugle Boy" ("from Company B") (1941).

Absurd performance was the province of the bandleader Spike Jones during the 1940s and 1950s. Known as the King of Corn, he and his City Slickers mocked songs in ridiculous arrangements using such sound effects as cowbells, horns, whistles, guns, and saws. His first hit was "Der Fuehrer's Face" in 1942, followed by his preposterous arrangements of "Chloe" (1927), "Cocktails for Two" (1934), "Hawaiian War Chant" (1936), and "You Always Hurt the One You Love" (1944).

Even a "straight" song can be made humorous in performance. A case in point is the ballad, "I Believe in You" sung by the hero of *How to Succeed in Business Without Really Trying* (1961) to himself in a mirror, while shaving.

Although nonsense songs form a category of their own, one of them derives humor from the sheer length of its title. "Supercalifragilisticexpialidocious," from the film *Mary Poppins* (1964).

As for overstatement, two lengthy titles tell it all: "I'm Looking for a Guy Who Plays Alto and Baritone and Doubles on the Clarinet and Wears a Size Thirty-seven Suit" (1940) and "How Could You Believe Me When I Said I'm Sorry When You Know I've Been a Liar All My Life?" (1950).

Additional Songs

Adelaide's Lament (1950)
I Cain't Say No (1943)
Just You Wait (1956)
A Puzzlement (1951)
Why Can't the English? (1956)

Bibliography

Davis, Sheila. *The Craft of Lyric Writing*. 1985.

Furia, Philip. *The Poets of Tin Pan Alley: A History of America's Great Lyricists*. 1990.

HUNGARY

Hungary has the distinction of being the birthplace of two outstanding composers of **operetta**, Franz Lehár (1870–1948) and Emmerich Kálmán (1882–1953), both of whom had active careers in **Austria**. Among Lehár's most popular songs in the United States were "The Merry Widow Waltz" and "Vilia" from *The Merry Widow* (1907); and "Yours Is My Heart Alone" from *The Land of Smiles* (1931). Kálmán's greatest popularity came with the rousing "Play Gypsies—Dance Gypsies" from *Countess Maritza* (1926).

Also born in Hungary were two songwriters who pursued their careers in the United States: Jean Schwartz (1878–1956) and Sigmund Romberg (1887–1951). Schwartz was a lyricist who had a string of hits, including "Chinatown, My Chinatown" (1910), "Rock-a-Bye Your Baby With a Dixie Melody" (1918), "Au Revoir, Pleasant Dreams" (1930), and "Trust in Me" (1934). Romberg was one of the most famous composers of his day, writing many operettas in the Viennese tradition. Among the many songs from these productions are "Will You Remember, from *Maytime* (1917); "Song of Love", from *Blossom Time* (1921); "Deep in My Heart, Dear" and "Serenade," from *The Student Prince* (1924); "The Desert Song" and "One Alone," from *The Desert Song* (1926); "Lover, Come Back to Me!" "One Kiss," "Softly, as in a Morning Sunrise," "Stouthearted Men," and "Wanting You" (1928), from *The New Moon* (1935); and "Close as Pages in a Book," from *Up in Central Park* (1945).

See also: **Foreign Influence; Gypsy Music**

IMAGINATION

Popular songs often conjure up imaginary mental images. Irving Caesar's "Picture you upon my knee," from "Tea for Two" (1924), is an image of happy domesticity. Similarly, Oscar Hammerstein II begins the verse of his and Jerome Kern's "Make Believe," from *Show Boat* (1927), with the words: "The game of 'just supposing' is the sweetest game I know." Among other songs relying on the imagination are "I'll Build a Stairway to Paradise" (1922), "'Sposin'" (1929), and "Stairway to the Stars" (1939). One of the most popular songs of the big band era, Johnny Burke and James Van Heusen's "Imagination" (1940), begins with the words: "Imagination is funny, it makes a cloudy day sunny."

Sometimes songs about the imaginary approach pure fantasy, as in "Over the Rainbow," from the film musical *The Wizard of Oz* (1939), or "Somewhere Out There," from the animated feature *An American Tail* (1986). At other times, the imagination is conjured up in pursuit of peace and brotherhood, as in John Lennon's "Imagine" (1971).

Additional Songs

I'm Making Believe (1944)
Imaginary Lover (1978)
It's Make Believe Ballroom Time (1940)
It's Only Make Believe (1958)
I've Got to Use My Imagination (1973)
Just Imagine (1927)
Pretend (1952)
Use Your Imagination (1950)

   See also: Magic

IMPROVISATION

Improvisation has long been recognized as the very heart and soul of jazz. But in a wider sense, it is at the core of all popular music, whether it be **bebop, bluegrass,** the **blues, country and western, folk song,** music from **Latin America, Motown, rhythm and blues, rock, rock 'n roll, show tunes, soul,** or **swing.**

Far from breaking new ground, the twentieth-century art of improvisation marked a return to the pre-Classic ideals of improvised accompaniment and ornamentation: ideals that had been largely forgotten—except for cadenzas—in the nineteenth century.

The melodic lines and chords of sheet music **arrangements** or **lead sheets** are seldom meant to be played as written. Rather, they are usually intended as guideposts to the basic melodic and harmonic structure of a piece. Thus, unlike the **art song,** the average popular song is incomplete: it is a theme waiting for the spontaneous variation of the performer.

The scope of improvisation varies widely: from mere embellishment of the melodic line to the invention of entirely new themes, from the addition of passing tones to the substitution of entirely new harmonies, from occasional chromatic bass notes to walking **bass lines.** Some of the most striking departures from the written notes were associated with the bebop era around 1950, when improvised interpretations veered far from the originals—indeed, creating entirely new pieces based on such standards as "Song of the Islands" (1915), "Body and Soul" (1930), "How High the Moon" (1940), "Early Autumn" (1949), "All of You" (1954), and "My Favorite Things" (1959).

Improvisation changed in the course of the twentieth century. In the first half, the **piano** was the king of solo improvisatory instruments; in the second half, it was the **guitar.** In **Dixieland** bands and other small jazz ensembles, a form of collective improvisation existed, with each member having an equal hand. In contrast, the improvised banjo and guitar solos of bluegrass are legendary. In the swing arrangements of the **big band** era, improvisation was usually confined to isolated solos by singers and instrumentalists. Rock 'n roll and its offshoots, on the other hand, offered numerous opportunities for improvisation, especially by voice, electronic instruments (keyboard and guitar), and tenor saxophone. But however it was executed, improvisation had—and still maintains—a leading role in the performance of popular song. Its importance cannot be overemphasized.

Bibliography

Berendt, Joachim. *The Jazz Book: From New Orleans to Rock and Free Jazz.* 1975.

Coker, Jerry. *Improvising Jazz.* 1964.

Hodeir, André. *Jazz: Its Evolution and Essence.* 1979.

See also: Brass; Instrumentation; Percussion; Scat Singing; Vocalese; Woodwinds

INSPIRATION

Songs of inspiration carry messages of hope and encouragement. Two songs in particular have served as sources of inspiration to many: "You'll Never Walk Alone," from *Carousel* (1945), and "The Impossible Dream (The Quest)," from *Man of La Mancha* (1965). The first urges one to "walk on, walk on, with hope in your heart"; the second is a call to "reach the unreachable stars."

Other songs that focus upon a positive attitude in **life** include "Look for the Silver Lining" (1920), "Sunny Side Up" (1929), and "Ac-cent-tchu-ate the Positive" (1945). In the last song, one is advised by Johnny Mercer to "eliminate the negative, latch on to the affirmative," and "don't mess with Mister In-between." Inspiration of a more personal kind is delineated in the 1984 song "You're the Inspiration," popularized by the group Chicago.

Mountains are sometimes used symbolically in songs of inspiration; examples are "Climb Ev'ry Mountain" (1959), "Gonna Build a Mountain" (1961), and "Anyone Can Move a Mountain" (1966). Another call for perseverance in the face of adversity is "High Hopes" (1959), a song that uses as an inspirational example an ant trying to move a "rubber tree plant."

See also: Happiness; Religion; Smiling

INSTRUMENTATION

Virtually every Western instrument known to man—as well as many from the Third World—has been used in the performance of popular music in America over the past one hundred years. But two have figured most prominently: the **piano** and the **guitar.**

The dominance of these two instruments has been far from consistent, however. Indeed, the years of the late 1950s can be regarded as a watershed clearly delineating two different types of instrumentation. In the first type, which held forth from the 1890s to the early 1950s, the piano was the chief instrument of **accompaniment,** and nonelectronic (later called "acous-

tic") instruments belonging to the traditional instrumental families of **strings, brass, woodwinds,** and **percussion** were the rule. In the second period, dating from the beginning of **rock 'n' roll,** the guitar (often amplified) was king, and electronic instruments and synthesizers prevailed.

A vast array of electronic instruments were introduced to popular music in the 1960s; with them came an invasion of new sounds, coinciding with the **rock** revolution. The synthesizer, invented by R. A. Moog in the late 1950s, spawned a myriad of keyboard instruments. With its infinite capability of producing abstract sounds, the synthesizer can imitate almost any instrument and, in addition, produce a remarkable variety of new timbres. Almost every conventional instrument has been electrified as well, producing still other variations of tone color.

Another instrument used in popular music is the organ, promoted as a jazz instrument by Fats Waller. It has also been used extensively in **rhythm and blues,** in combination with guitar or saxophone. Among the many other instruments employed in the performance of popular music are the piano accordion (particularly in **zydeco** and **polka** music) and the harmonica, the recorder, and the dulcimer (in **folk song**).

Bibliography

Berendt, Joachim. *The Jazz Book: From New Orleans to Rock and Free Jazz.* 1975.

Donington, Robert. *The Instruments of Music.* 1962.

Feather, Leonard. *The Book of Jazz: From Then Till Now: A Guide to the Entire Field.* 1965.

Marcuse, Sibyl. *Musical Instruments: A Comprehensive Dictionary.* 1975.

Sadie, Stanley, ed. *The New Grove Dictionary of Musical Instruments.* 1984.

Schuller, Gunther. *Early Jazz: Its Roots and Musical Development.* 1968.

———. *The Swing Era: The Development of Jazz, 1930–1945.* 1989.

Ulanov, Barry, *A Handbook of Jazz.* 1975.

See also: Improvisation

INTERVAL

An interval can be defined as the distance between any two pitches. Certain intervals dominate the **melodies** of American popular song. It has been pointed out, by Alec Wilder and others, that the sixth degree of the **scale,** the submediant, often gives music a peculiarly "American" flavor. This supposition may stem partly from the fact that Jerome Kern was fond of major sixths: they are prominent in the melodies of his "Who?" (1925), "She Didn't Say 'Yes'" (1931), and "Nobody Else But Me" (1946), among other songs.

But sixths, of course, are far from being an American

preference. The German-born Kurt Weill employed them in "Moritat" (1928), later "Mack the Knife" long before he came to the United States. They are also a staple of French songs: they are prominent in the melody of "My Way" (1967), while in "(Where Do I Begin) Love Story" (1970), the melody is built on major and minor sixths descending in **sequence**. Among the many American songs that feature the major sixth are "Mine" (1933), "Day In—Day Out" (1939), "Fools Rush In" (1940), "Skylark" (1942), and "I'm Still Here" (1971). The minor sixth is prominent in "So in Love" (1948).

The seventh, major or minor, is another interval important to American song. Indeed, inspired by the examples of Claude Debussy and other turn-of-the-century classical composers, the major seventh has become a staple of jazz improvisation. The song "A Man and a Woman," taken from the soundtrack of the French film of the same name (1966), consists of a chain of major sevenths descending chromatically. Major sevenths also figure prominently in the melodies of such American songs as "I've Got a Crush on You" (1928), "Dancing in the Dark" and "Who Cares?" (both 1931), "I Cover the Waterfront" (1933), "Laura" (1945), "Stella by Starlight" (1946), "Day by Day" (1971), and "One" (1975). The melody of Cole Porter's "I Love You" (1943) features descending intervals of the major seventh, while that of his "What Is This Thing Called Love?" (1929) somewhat audaciously begins on a minor seventh, which is then repeated. Minor sevenths are also found in George Gershwin's "I'll Build a Stairway to Paradise" (1922) and "The Man I Love" (1924).

Major ninths—another staple of jazz improvisation inherited from the French impressionists—are prominent in the melodies of "Mr. Lucky" (1959) and "On a Clear Day (You Can See Forever)" (1966); the latter begins with a **broken chord** outlining a major seventh with an added major ninth.

As for the use of other intervals, the melody of Jerome Kern's "All the Things You Are" (1939) is built on perfect fourths moving downward in sequence, while that of Richard Rodgers's "Blue Room" (1926) starts with successive intervals of the fourth, fifth, major sixth, minor seventh, and **octave**. Major thirds are prominent in many songs, including "My Buddy" and "Carolina in the Morning" (both 1922), "What Can I Say After I Say I'm Sorry?" (1926) "The Trolley Song" (1943), and "Don't Fence Me In" (1944). One of the widest intervals to occur in the melody of a popular song is the ascending leap of a major tenth found between the second and third notes of the aria-like song "Alone," appropriately introduced in the film *A Night at the Opera* (1935).

Bibliography

Wilder, Alec. *American Popular Song: The Great Innovators, 1900–1950.* 1972.

See also: **Harmony; Scale**

IRELAND

Ireland is at the heart of a number of American songs dating chiefly from the first two decades of the twentieth century. Second- and third-generation Irish-Americans, proud of their heritage, wrote many of these songs. Two of these songwriters, Chauncey Olcott (1858–1932) and Ernest R. Ball (1878–1927), were responsible in whole or in part for many standards relating to Ireland, including "My Wild Irish Rose" (1899), "Mother Machree" (1910), "When Irish Eyes Are Smiling" (1912), and "A Little Bit of Heaven, Shure They Call It Ireland" (1914). Another Irish-American who often wrote on Irish themes was George M. Cohan (1878–1942). The protagonist of Cohan's song "Harrigan" (1908) is "proud of all the Irish blood that's in me."

Some songs stem from the rich Irish folk heritage. One of the most famous, "Danny Boy" (1913), uses the melody of the traditional Irish ballad "Londonderry Air," written in 1855. The dotted rhythms found in such an Irish folk dance as "Irish Washerwoman" (c. 1790) are also a distinguishing feature of the American song "MacNamara's Band" (1914).

Successful songs often had sequels. Two examples are "Sweet Rosie O'Grady" (1896), followed by "The Daughter of Rosie O'Grady" (1918), and "Mother Machree," followed by "She's the Daughter of Mother Machree" (1915). Although "Where the River Shannon Flows" was a great success in 1905, it had no sequel. Nor did "The Rose of Tralee," sung by the celebrated Irish tenor John McCormack in 1912. Another song of this period, "Too-ra-loo-ra-loo-ral, That's an Irish Lullaby" (1914), attained its greatest popularity thirty years after it was written, when it was sung by Bing Crosby in the 1944 film *Going My Way*.

As the century progressed and Irish-Americans became more assimilated, Irish themes continued to hold favor, but to a much lesser extent. "Did Your Mother Come From Ireland?" was popular in 1936, and "It's a Great Day for the Irish," in 1940. In 1947 an entire musical play, *Finian's Rainbow*, had Ireland as its fictional locale; the quintessentially Irish song from that musical—although not written by an Irish-American—is "How Are Things in Glocca Morra?"

One composer of exceptional merit, born in Ireland but raised and educated in Germany, was Victor Herbert (1859–1924). He settled in the United States in 1886 and became best known for his many **operettas** and as one of the founders of **ASCAP**. Few of Herbert's works were on Irish themes, an exception being his operetta *Eileen* (1917), originally entitled *Hearts of Erin*. Among its songs are "Eileen," "Thine Alone," and "When Shall I Again See Ireland?," all with lyrics by the American-born Henry Blossom.

See also: **Britain, Foreign Influence; Nations**

ITALY

The music of Italy has influenced American popular music for well over a hundred years. In particular, the lyrical melodies of the **opera** composers Ruggiero Leoncavallo (1857–1919), Giacomo Puccini (1858–1924), and Pietro Mascagni (1863–1945) have had a profound effect. Indeed, a number of American popular songs, including "Avalon" (1920) and "You're Breaking My Heart" (1948) were based on arias and songs by these and other Italian composers (*see* Classics).

An early Italian song popular in the United States was "Ciribiribin." Composed by Alberto Pestalozzi in 1898, it was given English lyrics by Rudolf Thaler, and was popularly revived in 1945 to become the theme song of Harry James and His Orchestra. Sometimes, too, Italian songs have been borrowed without acknowledgment; for example, the famous song "The Bowery" (1892) is markedly similar to the Neapolitan song "La Spagnola." A striking case is that of the Neapolitan composer Eduardo di Capua, who wrote a song called "O Sole Mio" in 1898, but sold it outright to his publisher for a few lire and died penniless in 1917. Di Capua's famous melody has been used in at least two songs, "There's No Tomorrow" (1949) and "It's Now or Never" (1960), neither of which give him credit as composer. Another Neapolitan song, "Torna a Sorrento," became "Surrender" in 1960, the title resembling its source phonetically if not in meaning.

Italian songs translated into English often preserve remnants of their language of origin (*see* Foreign Language). Examples are "Botch-A-Me" (1952), a phoneticized version of "Ba-Ba-Baciami Piccina"; three hits of 1953: "Eh Cumpari!," "Non Dimenticar," and "That's Amore"; "Anema e Core" (1954); "Arrivederci Roma" and "Domani" (1955); the international hit "Volare (Nel Blu Dipinto di Blu)," of 1958; "Ciao Ciao Bambina" (1959); and "Addio, Addio" (1961), "Canto d'Amore" (1962), and "Quando, Quando, Quando" (1962).

Other songs from Italy have become popular in English without reference to the Italian language. A prime example is "More," a beautiful song derived from the soundtrack of a sensationalist Italian film called *Mondo Cane* (1963). Another song, "Speak Softly, Love" (1972), was taken from the score of the film *The Godfather* (1972). Its composer, Nino Rota, also wrote the music for several other outstanding songs derived from films, including "Stars Shine in Your Eyes," from *La Strada* (1956); "A Time for Us," from *Romeo and Juliet* (1969); and "Waltz Theme From The Godfather" (1972).

Among the many other songs of direct Italian origin are "Oh Mama (The Butcher Boy)" (1938), "Summertime in Venice" (1955), "Autumn Concerto" (1956), "Softly as I Leave You" (1960), "My Love, Forgive Me" (1964), and "A Man Without Love" (1968).

See also: **Foreign Influence; Nations**

Jazz

The word "jazz" is often used as an umbrella term embracing much of twentieth-century popular music. But it also describes a specific succession of performance styles extending from the 1920s on. Two elements almost always associated with jazz are **improvisation** and a rhythmic substructure, but the term itself—like so many others in popular music—is subject to a number of interpretations.

Its origins too are eclectic: a mélange of American and European, black and white, North and South, schooled and unschooled. Jazz democratically makes use of **blue notes**; of elements of **ragtime** and the **blues**; of the harmonies of Debussy, Ravel, Tchaikovsky, and Puccini; and of the rhythms of **Africa** and Latin America—creating a uniquely American music that is vastly popular throughout the world.

Above all, jazz is a showcase for extemporization—for countless variations on the themes of hundreds of songs favored by jazz instrumentalists and singers. Although almost any song can be grist for the jazz mill, certain songs have proved to be fertile grounds for improvisation. Some of them, like "Here's That Rainy Day" (1953) and "Misty" (1954), are characterized by interesting harmonic changes. In others, such as "A String of Pearls" (1941) and "Sentimental Journey" (1944), the deciding factor seems to be their absence of changes, or slow **harmonic rhythm.**

The history of jazz is extremely well documented in hundreds of books and articles. Most of them concentrate on the performers, their instruments, or on specific schools of jazz, such as **Dixieland, swing, bebop,** cool jazz, free jazz, or jazz-rock fusion.

Oddly, for so widely discussed a genre, the origins of jazz are obscure. It appears to have emerged around the turn of the century in and about New Orleans, chiefly as contrapuntal ensemble playing. The first jazz **recordings** were those of "Indiana (Back Home Again in

Indiana)" and "The Darktown Strutters' Ball" (both 1917) by the Original Dixieland Jass (sic) Band. In the early years of jazz, **syncopation** was rampant, but it was later largely supplanted by dotted notes.

By the mid-1920s, the center of jazz's development moved to Chicago, where groups such as those headed by Louis Armstrong, Jelly Roll Morton, and Johnny Dodds held sway. This was also the time of "two-beat jazz," of classic blues singers like Bessie Smith, and of instrumentalists like Bix Beiderbecke.

The 1930s saw the development of swing, the predominance of "four-beat jazz," and the emergence of the **big bands** and such virtuoso instrumental soloists as Benny Goodman, Gene Krupa, Coleman Hawkins, Johnny Hodges, and Bunny Berigan.

A more emotional and fragmented type of jazz, called "bebop," developed in Kansas City and New York's **Harlem** in the 1940s, under the aegis of such musicians as Dizzy Gillespie, Charlie Parker, Thelonious Monk, and Charlie Christian. The 1950s saw a trend toward a more relaxed, or "cool," style of jazz, inspired by trumpeter Miles Davis and the Modern Jazz Quartet, under pianist and arranger John Lewis. The cool style of playing was carried on by pianist Lenny Tristano and by many musicians on the West Coast.

Free jazz—breaking down many of the strictures of traditional jazz—was a development of the 1960s. It involved less emphasis on a steady beat, a movement away from **tonality**, and the introduction of non-European musical elements into jazz. More attention was paid to **dynamics** and to the introduction of new sounds, such as those of electronic instruments.

In the 1970s and 1980s, elements of free jazz were combined with those of Indian music and **rock**, forming a jazz-rock fusion. There was much greater use of electronic keyboards, synthesizers, amplified guitars, and other electronic instruments and devices. This period also saw the development of the collective solo, by groups such as that of bassist Charlie Mingus, and—at the opposite extreme—the unaccompanied solo, as played by such pianists as Chick Corea, Keith Jarrett, and Cecil Taylor.

Bibliography

Berendt, Joachim Ernst. *The Jazz Book: From New Orleans to Rock and Free Jazz.* 1976.

———. *The New Jazz Book: A History and Guide.* 1970.

Blesh, Rudi. *Shining Trumpets: A History of Jazz.* 1975.

Claghorn, Charles Eugene. *Biographical Dictionary of Jazz.* 1983.

Coker, Jerry. *Improvising Jazz.* 1964.

Collier, James Lincoln. *The Making of Jazz: A Comprehensive History.* 1981.

Coryell, Julie, and Laura Friedman. *Jazz-Rock Fusion: The People—the Music.* 1978.

Feather, Leonard Geoffroy. *The Book of Jazz: From Then Till Now: A Guide to the Entire Field.* 1965.

———. *The Encyclopedia of Jazz in the Sixties.* 1978.

———. *The New Edition of the Encyclopedia of Jazz.* 2nd ed., 1968.

———, and Ira Gitler. *The Encyclopedia of Jazz in the Seventies.* 1978.

Gitler, Ira. *Jazz Masters of the Forties.* 1982.

Goldberg, Joe. *Jazz Masters of the Fifties.* 1980.

Hodeir, André. *Jazz: Its Evolution and Essence.* 1979.

———. *The Worlds of Jazz.* 1972.

Jost, Ekkehard. *Free Jazz.* 1981.

Litweiler, John. *The Freedom Principle: Jazz After 1958.* 1984.

Meadows, Eddie S. *Jazz Reference and Research Materials: A Bibliography.* 1980.

Schuller, Gunther. *Early Jazz: Its Roots and Musical Development.* 1968.

———. *The Swing Era: The Development of Jazz, 1930–1945.* 1989.

Shapiro, Nat, and Nat Hentoff, eds. *Hear Me Talkin' to Ya: The Story of Jazz by the Men Who Made It.* 1982.

Stearns, Marshall W. *The Story of Jazz: New Edition.* 1970.

Tanner, Paul, and Maurice Gerow. *A Study of Jazz.* 1984.

Tirro, Frank. *Jazz: A History.* 1977.

Ulanov, Barry. *A History of Jazz in America.* 1975.

See also: **Instrumentation**

JAZZ AGE. SEE ROARING TWENTIES

JEWELRY

Rings are the most common variety of jewelry in popular song, found in "I've Got Rings on My Fingers" (1909), "Too Many Rings Around Rosie" (1924), "When Your Old Wedding Ring Was New" (1935), and "This Diamond Ring" (1964). Diamonds, specified in the last song, are also at the heart of "Diamonds Are a Girl's Best Friend," a somewhat cynical song introduced by Carol

Channing in the musical *Gentlemen Prefer Blondes* (1949). On the other hand, the word "diamonds" in the Beatles' "Lucy in the Sky With Diamonds" (1967) has nothing to do with jewelry, but is reputed to be part of a slang term for LSD, a hallucinogenic substance popular during the drug culture of the 1960s.

More down to earth is the Glenn Miller favorite of 1941, "A String of Pearls." From the Russian composer Alexander Borodin, by way of the Broadway musical *Kismet* (1953), comes the haunting waltz "Baubles, Bangles and Beads." Even artificial jewelry has its day in song, in "Rhinestone Cowboy," recorded by Glen Campbell in 1975.

See also: **Clothing**

JOY. SEE HAPPINESS

JUKEBOX

The jukebox is a coin-operated machine equipped with push buttons for the selection of records; it is often encased in a gaudy cabinet with elaborate lighting. Originating in the South in the 1920s, jukeboxes spread from there throughout North America. During the **Depression years**, they were widely used for music to dance as well as listen to. Hundreds of thousands of them could be found in bars, roadhouses, diners, restaurants, soda shops, and other gathering places throughout the land. Jukeboxes contributed mightily to the success of many songs during and after **World War II.** Among these were the **novelty songs** "The Music Goes 'Round and 'Round" (1935), "Bei Mir Bist Du Schön (Means That You're Grand)," (1937) "A-Tisket, A-Tasket" (1938), "Beer Barrel Polka (Roll Out the Barrel)" (1939), and "Three Little Fishes" (1939); as well as the **ballads** "You Are My Sunshine" (1940) and "White Christmas" (1942).

The principal manufacturers of jukeboxes were the J. P. Seeburg Company and the Wurlitzer Company; the latter stopped production in 1974. Although the jukebox's importance to the dissemination of popular songs diminished somewhat in later years—the 700,000 jukeboxes of the 1950s dwindled to only 300,000 by 1980—jukeboxes were still being manufactured and installed in the 1990s. They remain to this day a large source of income for both operators and location owners.

Bibliography

Krivine, John. *Juke Box Saturday Night.* 1977.

Lynch, Vincent, and Bill Henkin. *Jukeboxes: The Golden Age.* 1981.

Sanjek, Russell, and David Sanjek. *American Popular Music Business in the Twentieth Century.* 1991.

See also: **Recording**

K

KEY

Several aspects of key apply to popular song: **tonality** internal key change, and key preference. The concept of tonality refers to the prevalence of a tonal center. As for change of key within a song, it can occur either between the **chorus** and **verse** or between other sections of a song. In the first instance, "Alexander's Ragtime Band" (1911) moves from a verse in C major to a chorus in F major; "All the Things You Are" (1939) has a verse in G major and a chorus in A-flat major. The **release** can differ in key as well; that of "Smoke Gets in Your Eyes" (1933)—a song in E-flat major—is in B major. As for key change within other sections of a song, the "Theme From *Mahogany* (Do You Known Where You're Going To?)" (1973) moves through the following major keys (with appropriate key signatures): G-flat, E-flat, C, E-flat, C, E-flat, C, A, G-flat, and E-flat.

Choice of key has gone through some interesting changes over the past hundred years. Each song has an "original" key, in which it is usually played or sung (with allowances for differing vocal compasses). Theoretically, any of the twelve major keys or twelve minor keys could be used, but through the years certain keys have been preferred over others during certain periods. The choice of key has most often been a function of the accompanying medium, usually instrumental.

Around the turn of the twentieth century, when **sheet music** was primarily meant for amateur players and singers and when almost every home had a piano, "simple" keys were *de rigueur*. Virtually every song was set in a key with few or no accidentals, such as G major ("Down by the Old Mill Stream," 1910), F major ("After the Ball," 1892), or C major ("In the Good Old Summertime," 1902). Less commonly, songs were set in B-flat major ("Girl of My Dreams") or E-flat major ("The Bowery", 1892), and very rarely in A-flat major ("In My Merry Oldsmobile," 1905) or D major ("Take Me Out

to the Ball Game," 1908). Relatively few American songs of the time were in the minor **mode**.

By the second quarter of the century a different performing medium had come to the forefront, involving **brass** and **woodwind** instruments. Since the cornets, trumpets, saxophones, and clarinets used in **jazz** and by the **big bands** were almost all transposing instruments in B-flat or E-flat, keys favorable to those instruments were often chosen. E-flat major, which transposed as C major for E-flat instruments, became the original key of thousands of songs such as "My Silent Love" (1932), "I've Got You Under My Skin" (1936), and "Secret Love" (1954). Next in popularity was B-flat major, which transposed as C for B-flat instruments and is the key of such songs as "Poor Butterfly" (1916), "After You've Gone" (1918), and "Let's Do It (Let's Fall in Love)" (1928).

The keys of F and A-flat major, still favorable to brass and woodwinds, also were used: "Where or When?" (1937) is in F, "Why Do I Love You?" (1927) is in A-flat. At the same time, many songs were still written in C ("Mountain Greenery," 1926) and G major ("Makin' Whoopee," 1928). The key of D-flat major was used as well, in such songs as "Star Dust" (1929), "Body and Soul" (1930), and "My Romance" (1935). In addition, songs in the minor mode were on the increase, especially those in C minor ("You and the Night and the Music," 1934) and D minor ("Alone Together," 1932). Very rarely used, on the other hand, were the "sharp" keys of D, A, E, and B major.

The mid-1950s and ensuing years saw a different tonal orientation centering around the **guitar**, the pivotal instrument of **folk music**, **country and western**, and **rock**. Keys more congenial to that instrument were often chosen, with a shift in the direction of the sharp keys: G, D, A, and E major. Thus, "Love Me Tender" (1956) is in G major, "I Don't Know How to Love Him" (1970) in D major, "Evergreen (Love Theme From *A*

Star Is Born)" (1975) in A major, and "The Long and Winding Road" (1970) in E major. Keys with few or no accidentals, such as F, C, and B-flat major, also remained popular, as, to a lesser extent, did the keys of E-flat, A-flat, and D-flat major.

By the late 1970s and 1980s, there was no discernible preference for particular keys. Almost every key was found in popular song, running the gamut from B major ("Sir Duke," 1976) to G-flat major ("Those Good Old Dreams," 1981) and from C-sharp minor ("That Girl," 1981) to E-flat minor ("Woman in Love," 1980). The fashion in choice of key signature had changed from few accidentals at the beginning of the century to many accidentals at the end. It had also become commonplace for a song to undergo numerous changes of key signature. As an example, "The Phantom of the Opera" (1986) moves through the following keys: D minor, G minor, E minor, F minor, G minor, A minor.

See also: Enharmonic Equivalence; Harmony; Modulation; Scale

KISSING

The act of kissing, so closely related to **love** and **romance**, has understandably proven of interest to songwriters. To some extent, song titles mirror the cultural backgrounds of their time. The formality of the early years of the century finds an echo in four stately waltzes: "Kiss Me Again" (1905), "I Wonder Who's Kissing Her Now" (1909), "A Kiss in the Dark" (1922),

and "One Kiss" (1928). More down to earth and saucy, in the style of the Roaring Twenties, are the fox trots "Gimme a Little Kiss, Will Ya, Huh?" (1926) and "Ooh That Kiss" (1931).

Songs of the 1950s tend to be analytical, as in "Kiss of Fire" (1952) and "Kisses Sweeter Than Wine" (1957). The former song, an adaptation of the Argentine tango "El Choclo" (1913), is one of a number of "kiss" songs from abroad: "(Just) A Little Love, a Little Kiss" (1912), from France; "I Kiss Your Hand, Madame," from Germany; "Besame Mucho" (1941), from Mexico; and "Botch-A-Me" (1952) (originally "Ba-Ba Baciami Piccina"), from Italy. Other noteworthy songs on the subject are the ballads "Prelude to a Kiss," popularized by Duke Ellington in 1938; and "We Kiss in a Shadow," from *The King and I* (1951). The World War II hit song "It's Been a Long, Long Time" (1945) begins with the evocative words: "Just kiss me once, then kiss me twice, Then kiss me once again."

Additional Songs

I Saw Mommy Kissing Santa Claus (1952)
Kiss (1986)
Kiss and Say Goodbye (1976)
A Kiss to Build a Dream On (1935)
Kiss You All Over (1978)
Kissin' Time (1959)
Sealed With a Kiss (1960)
This Year's Kisses (1937)
Til I Kissed You (1959)

See also: Falling in Love

LADY

Along with the **doll**, the **girl**, and the **woman**, the lady has been the **subject** of more than her share of popular songs. As far back as 1896, "Mother Was a Lady," or "If Jack Were Only Here," was the rage, while ten years later, "Every Day Is Ladies' Day With Me" created a sensation when it was introduced in *The Red Mill*. In 1924, Ira and George Gershwin's standard "Oh, Lady Be Good" was introduced in the musical comedy of the same name. Other memorable ladies in popular song over the years have been worldly ("Sophisticated Lady," 1933), spry ("Little Old Lady," 1936), insouciant ("The Lady Is a Tramp," 1937), forlorn ("Red Roses for a Blue Lady," 1948), and enticing ("Lady," 1982). The "lady" in a 1954 song, "The Naughty Lady of Shady Lane," turns out to be, quite surprisingly, a baby.

Additional Songs

Foxy Lady (1967)
Good Bye My Lady Love (1904)
Lady Madonna (1968)
Lady Marmalade (1974)
Lady of Spain (1931)
Lady of the Evening (1922)
Lady, Play Your Mandolin (1930)
The Lady's In Love With You (1939)
Lovely Lady (1935)
Luck Be a Lady (1950)
Pretty Lady (1976)
She's a Lady (1968)

LANDMARKS OF STAGE AND SCREEN

Between 1890 and 1990 popular music went through many changes, mirroring the myriad changes in American society that occurred during those years. Most of these changes happened gradually, but several landmarks of stage and screen stand out like beacons on a darkened shore for their contributions to American popular song.

1. *The Merry Widow* (1907)

Franz Lehár's **operetta** *The Merry Widow* was originally presented in Vienna in 1905. It had a gala opening in New York at the New Amsterdam Theater on October 21, 1907. The memorable score included a striking title song in waltz time and a number of eminently singable melodies, ending with a lively can-can in the spirit of Jacques Offenbach. This important operetta launched a new era in the American musical theater. Its influence extends to the present day.

2. *The Girl From Utah* (1914)

The year 1914 marked not only the beginning of **World War I**; it was also a banner year for popular song. It was the year a **musical comedy** called *The Girl From Utah* opened in New York with a song by a young composer named Jerome Kern that was destined to become a model for all future writing for the musical stage. Doing away with the waltz, the show established the love **ballad** in 4/4 meter as its mainstay. The song, "They Didn't Believe Me," brought a new dimension to the musical theater, owing to the sophistication of its melody and harmonies—which sound to modern ears as if the song could well have been written in the 1980s rather than in 1914.

3. *Show Boat* (1927)

Show Boat has been called the first truly American **musical play** because of its American setting and the "American" quality of some of its songs. With lyrics by Oscar Hammerstein II and music by Jerome Kern, it opened on Broadway on December 27, 1927. Adapted from Edna Ferber's novel, it had a magnificent score including such standards as "Can't Help Lovin' Dat Man," "Why Do I Love You?," "Make Believe," and "Ol' Man River." It served as a model for many musical plays to follow.

4. *Jubilee* (1935)

The musical comedy *Jubilee* opened in 1935 and closed shortly thereafter. Despite the show's refreshing music and lyrics—written by an immensely talented **composer-lyricist** from Indiana named Cole Porter—the show did not catch on. Nevertheless, two of its songs did: "Just One of Those Things" and "Begin the Beguine." The latter certainly qualifies as a landmark if only because of its **length**: at 108 measures, it is one of the longest songs ever written. Like much of Porter's output, the song is experimental in other ways as well: its exotic lyrics, its unusual form, its unique rhythmic accompaniment, and its use of the **beguine**, which Porter is said to have picked up after a trip to the Carribean.

5. *Porgy and Bess* (1935)

Porgy and Bess, widely recognized as the first popular American folk **opera**, was first produced in New York on October 10, 1935. Set in Charleston, South Carolina, in the 1920s, its music was by George Gershwin, with lyrics by DuBose Heyward and Ira Gershwin. *Porgy and Bess* brought elegant and complex music to Broadway, music far removed from the simple tunes that emanated from Tin Pan Alley. Yet many of its songs stand alone, including the standards "Summertime," "It Ain't Necessarily So," "I Got Plenty o' Nuttin'," and "Bess, You Is My Woman."

6. *The Wizard of Oz* (1939)

The magical **film musical** *The Wizard of Oz* had an unforgettable score, with music by Harold Arlen and lyrics by E. Y. "Yip" Harburg. Its most famous song, "Over the Rainbow," was sung in the movie by Judy Garland, who was then seventeen years old. Notable for its opening motive with an **octave** leap, it was awarded an Oscar for best song by the Academy of Motion Picture Arts and Sciences. More than fifty years after it was written, it remains one of the most beloved of standards.

7. *Very Warm for May* (1939)

The show *Very Warm for May*, which opened in New York in 1939, could hardly be called successful, since it lasted for only fifty-nine performances. Nevertheless, it contained one song that seems destined to remain immortal: "All the Things You Are." With lyrics by Oscar Hammerstein II, it is a curious song combining inventiveness and harmonic complexity. Its composer, Jerome Kern, did not expect it to become a hit because it is difficult to sing and harmonically surprising. Yet it remains a standard as well as a masterpiece.

8. *Holiday Inn* (1942)

The musical film *Holiday Inn*, starring Bing Crosby and Fred Astaire, had a song for virtually every **holiday** of the year, written by Irving Berlin—by then the Dean of American songwriters. One of them, "White Christmas," is probably the most valuable song ever written. Its Decca recording by Bing Crosby alone sold over 25 million copies. It held first place on the radio show *Your Hit Parade* for thirty-eight weeks, longer than any other song, and won the **Academy Award** for best song of 1942.

8. *Casablanca* (1943)

Casablanca, the Michael Curtiz **film** starring Humphrey Bogart and Ingrid Bergman, was an outstanding success in 1943. Its haunting theme song, "As Time Goes By," was an integral part of the plot. Played and sung by Dooley Wilson, the song had been written twelve years earlier by the composer-lyricist Herman Hupfeld. Because of its prominent role in the film "As Time Goes By," with its striking verbal images and sequential melody, has become part of American legend.

9. *Oklahoma!* (1943)

If *Porgy and Bess* was the first American folk opera, then *Oklahoma!* can be called the first American folk operetta. It opened to rave reviews on March 31, 1943. With lyrics by Oscar Hammerstein II and music by Richard Rodgers, it included such memorable songs as "Oh, What a Beautiful Mornin'" (which brought back the waltz), "The Surrey With the Fringe on Top," and the ballad "People Will Say We're in Love" (which holds the record for number of appearances on the radio show *Your Hit Parade*).

10. *West Side Story* (1957)

Another landmark of the musical theater, *West Side Story*, opened in New York on September 26, 1957. A twentieth-century version of Shakespeare's *Romeo and Juliet*, it had a haunting and unforgettable score, with lyrics by Stephen Sondheim and music by Leonard Bernstein. Its integration of book, lyrics, music, and dance set a standard for all musicals to follow. Among its enduring songs are "Tonight," "Maria," and "Somewhere."

11. *A Little Night Music* (1973)

Stephen Sondheim's score for *A Little Night Music*, a musical play based on Ingmar Bergman's film *Smiles of a Summer Night*, is written almost entirely in waltz time. However, the most popular song from the show is not in three-quarter time, but rather in 6/8 meter. Innovative and touching, "Send in the Clowns" showed that—in spite of the incursions from abroad—there was still life and originality in the American musical theater.

LATIN AMERICA

From Tijuana to Tierra del Fuego, the music of Latin America has profoundly influenced popular music in the United States. This effect has been felt at least since the last half of the nineteenth century, when New Orleans was a cultural melting-pot with Latin music as one of its ingredients. Many Latin elements went into ragtime and jazz around the turn of the century.

The most substantial contributions to twentieth-century popular song in the United States have come from our two closest neighbors, **Cuba** and **Mexico**. But significant and innovative ideas have emanated from more-distant nations like **Brazil** and **Argentina**, contributors respectively of the **bossa nova** and the **tango**.

It is important to note that many other areas of the West Indies and Central and South America have influenced our music as well. Immigrants from Puerto Rico and Santo Domingo, in particular, have been active in the development of the **salsa** and the importation of other native genres, like the aguinaldo, bomba, jíbaro, and plena. Many of these developments have taken place in El Barrio, a district of **New York City's** East Harlem, and in similar barrios in other large cities throughout the United States.

Numerous song and dance genres originated in Latin America, most notably the baiao, **beguine, bolero, cha cha cha, conga, guaracha, mambo,** maxixe, **merengue,** pachanga, **rumba,** salsa, **samba,** and son.

Bibliography

Roberts, John Storm. *The Latin Tinge: The Impact of Latin American Music on the United States.* 1979.

See also: **Foreign Influence**

LEAD SHEET

A lead sheet is a type of musical shorthand enabling a musician to improvise around the **melody** and **harmony** of a piece. Generally consisting of a single stave in treble clef, it includes the melodic line as well as the harmony, indicated in the abbreviated form as follows: Dm7, E maj7, C#m7-5, F7 (add 6), G+, or D# dim—which respectively represent the following chords: D minor seventh; E major seventh; C-sharp minor seventh, with flatted fifth; F seventh, with added sixth; G augmented, and D-sharp diminished.

Although the **bass line** is usually not given, bass notes that are not in root position, or are foreign to the chord under which they are written, may be indicated by a preceding slash, as follows: Abmaj 7 / C, or D / E—respectively representing an A-flat major seventh chord with C bass and a D major chord with E bass. A **pickup,** or other passage where no chord is to be played, may be indicated by the notations "N.C." or "tacet."

Despite its apparently cryptic nature, the lead sheet is a valuable tool for the performing musician, giving him or her a structural background for the **improvisation** that is vital to the performance of popular music.

See also: **Sheet Music**

LENGTH

Over the past hundred years the average length of American popular song has grown gradually but perceptibly. Around the turn of the century sixteen- or thirty-two-bar choruses were the norm, as in the sixteen-bar **waltz** "The Bowery" (1892) or the thirty-two bar waltz "The Sidewalks of New York" (1894). From the 1900s through the 1950s, the thirty-two-bar song prevailed. From the 1960s onward, however, lengths tended to be more variable and less likely to be in multiples of eight.

One of the shortest songs is also one of the most popular: "Happy Birthday to You" (1893) consists of a mere eight bars in triple **meter.** A number of songs have choruses of only sixteen bars, among them "Put on Your Old Grey Bonnet" (1909), "Every Little Movement" (1910), "Lovely to Look At" (1935), and "Oh, What a Beautiful Morning" (1943). "Ja-Da" (1918), although also sixteen bars in length, is almost always performed with a two-bar tag, or **coda.** Also eighteen bars in length is Irving Berlin's "Mandy" (1919). Among songs twenty bars long are "After You've Gone" (1918), "I Guess I'll Have to Change My Plan" (1929), and "She Didn't Say 'Yes'" (1931).

Several very lengthy songs came out of **film musicals,** where they were used as production numbers. They include Arthur Freed and Nacio Herb Brown's "The Wedding of the Painted Doll," from *Broadway Melody* (1929); Herb Magidson and Con Conrad's "The Continental," from *The Gay Divorcée* (1934); and Al Dubin and Harry Warren's "Lullaby of Broadway," from *The Gold Diggers of 1935.* Cole Porter, one of the most experimental of composers, wrote many songs of unusual length, including "Night and Day" (1933), with forty-eight bars; "I've Got You Under My Skin" (1936), fifty-six bars; "Blow, Gabriel, Blow" (1934), seventy bars; and—one of the longest songs ever written—the evocative "Begin the Beguine" (1935), 108 bars.

Harold Arlen, another innovative composer, often departed from the standard thirty-two-bar song, as shown in his music for "Blues in the Night" (1941), fifty-eight bars; "Stormy Weather" (1933), seventy bars; and "That Old Black Magic" (1943), seventy-two bars. Irving Berlin, usually very conservative, departed from the thirty-two-bar mold in "Cheek to Cheek" (also a production number, from the film *Top Hat,* 1935), which is seventy-two bars long. Hugh Martin's "The Trolley Song," sung by Judy Garland in the musical film *Meet Me in St. Louis* (1944), is eighty bars in length.

In recent years, unusual and extended lengths have become the rule rather than the exception. "You Don't Bring Me Flowers" (1977) is seventy-four bars long; "Evergreen (Love Theme From *A Star Is Born*)" (1975) is seventy-eight. The vocal part alone of Jim Webb's "MacArthur Park" (1968) is 119 bars, and that does not include an instrumental section of sixty-eight bars in double time. The performer-songwriter Billy Joel is partial to extremely drawn-out songs, as exemplified by his 1977 hit "Just the Way You Are," which is 139 bars in length.

See also: Chorus; Form; Verse

LETTERS. *SEE* WRITING

LIFE

Life has been depicted in curious ways in popular song: as a bowl of fruit, in "Life Is Just a Bowl of Cherries" (1931); with cynicism, in "The Good Life" (1963); as discouraging, in "That's Life" (1964); and even as a metaphor for a supper club, in "Cabaret" (1966). The joys of living are emphasized in such songs as "I'm Gonna Live Till I Die" (1950) and "A Lot of Livin' to Do" (1960). In one of the happiest songs of all—"To Life (L'Chaim)," from *Fiddler on the Roof* (1964)—life is used as the object of a toast.

Additional Songs

Back to Life (1989)
A Day in the Life (1967)
If He Walked Into My Life (1966)
Into Each Life Some Rain Must Fall (1944)
Life, Love and Laughter (1945)
Live and Let Die (1973)
Live for Life (1967)
Living for the City (1973)
Living in America (1985)
She's Out of My Life (1979)
Someone Saved My Life Tonight (1974)
The Wild Side of Life (1952)
You Decorated My Life (1978)
You Light Up My Life (1976)

    See also: Happiness; Inspiration

LONELINESS

Catchwords have often characterized songs about being alone. An early one was "lonesome," as in "I'm the Lonesomest Gal in Town" (1912) and "Are You Lonesome Tonight?" (1926). Another early synonym was "blue," as in "Have You Ever Been Lonely, Have You Ever Been Blue?" (1933), or in the lyrics of Irving Berlin's "All Alone" (1924): "All alone feeling blue."

A number of memorable songs deal with loneliness. Duke Ellington's melody for "Solitude" (1934), with its sustained notes and descending sixths, expresses the feeling perfectly. So does the inner rhyme of Howard Dietz's lyrics for "By Myself" (1937): "No one knows better than I myself, I'm by myself alone." But for sheer melodic expansiveness—if not in keeping with its subject—these songs are overshadowed by the semi-oper-

atic "Alone," sung by Allan Jones in the 1935 Marx Brothers film *A Night at the Opera.*

Loneliness was very much a symptom of the times during **World War II**, reflected in such songs as "I'll Walk Alone" (1944), "A Little on the Lonely Side" (1944), and "Saturday Night (Is the Loneliest Night of the Week" (1944). "You'll Never Walk Alone," from *Carousel* (1945), was more a song of **inspiration** than of loneliness, urging one to "Walk on, walk on, with hope in your heart, and you'll never walk alone." Two expressive melodies particularly evocative of loneliness are Leonard Bernstein's for "Lonely Town," from *On the Town* (1944), and Kurt Weill's for "Lonely House," from *Street Scene* (1947).

There are several British songs on the subject. Two by John Lennon and Paul McCartney are "Eleanor Rigby" (1966), with its repeated refrain "All the lonely people," and "Sergeant Pepper's Lonely Hearts Club Band" (1967). Gilbert O'Sullivan's "Alone Again (Naturally)" was a hit of 1972.

Two enduring standards are about a happier situation, that of two people who are isolated from the outside world but yet are together: "When We're Alone," better known as "Penthouse Serenade" (1931), and "Alone Together" (1935).

Additional Songs

Alone at Last (1960)
Anything But Lonely (1989)
Don't Let Me Be Lonely Tonight (1972)
I'm So Lonesome I Could Cry (1949)
(I'm Just a) Lonely Boy (1958)
Lonely Days (1970)
Lonely Teardrops (1958)
Lonesome Town (1958)
Long Lonely Nights (1957)
Oh, Lonesome Me (1958)
Only the Lonely (Know the Way I Feel) (1960)
Tired of Being Alone (1971)

    See also: Crying

LOVE

Of all **subjects** of popular song, love stands supreme. In fact, in one way or another, love is the essence of the vast majority of songs.

Many aspects of love are considered. There are, for example, the attempts to define it, or, as Cole Porter put it, "What Is This Thing Called Love?" (1929). These attempts to describe love sometimes have a humorous quality: "Love Is Like a Firefly" (1912), "Love Is the Sweetest Thing" (1933), "Love Is Like a Violin" (1945), "Love Is Where You Find It" (1948), "Love Is a Simple Thing" (1952), "Love Is a Many-Splendored Thing" (1955), "Love Makes the World Go 'Round" (1961), "Love Is a Hurtin' Thing" (1966), "Love Is Blue" (1968).

Then there are the various ways of saying the three

little words "I love you" which are the focus of the 1930 song "Three Little Words." A number of songs are entitled simply "I Love You"; two of the best known of these are by Harlan Thompson and Harry Archer, from *Little Jesse James* (1923), and by Cole Porter, from *Mexican Hayride* (1944). There is also Carrie Jacobs-Bond's "I Love You Truly" (1901), which for many years was traditionally sung at wedding ceremonies. Another song, "I Love You, Sweetheart of All My Dreams" (1928), gets its message across rather insistently, by beginning: "I love you, I love you, I love you." Variations on the theme are expressed in four famous songs: "Why Do I Love You?" (1927), "Do I Love You?" (1939), "If I Love You" (1945), and "I Just Called to Say I Love You" (1984).

All phases of a romance are depicted in popular song, from its inception—"Love Your Magic Spell Is Everywhere," (1929), "Love in Bloom" (1934), "Love Walked In" (1938), "The Look of Love" (1965)—to its development and growth—"Love Is Here to Stay" (1938), "Dearly Beloved" (1942), "Love and Marriage" (1955), "Love Me With All Your Heart" (1961), "Love Will Keep Us Together" (1975)—to its demise—I'm Thru With Love" (1931), "In Love in Vain" (1946), "The End of a Love Affair" (1950), "What Now My Love?" (1962), "What I Did for Love" (1975). There is even a song of instruction, "The Glory of Love" (1936), which tells one how to conduct an affair: "You've gotta give a little, take a little."

There are, in addition, innumerable songs about the state of being in love, among them "The Man I Love" (1924), "Can't Help Lovin' Dat Man" (1927), "People Will Say We're in Love" (1943), and "A Woman In Love" (1955). Finally, love in a much broader sense, for one's fellow man, is the subject of the 1965 waltz "What the World Needs Now Is Love"—a call for love "not for some, but for everyone."

Additional Songs

After the Love Has Gone (1979)
After the Lovin' (1974)
Amor (1941)
L'Amour, Toujours l'Amour (1922)
April Love (1957)
At Long Last Love (1938)
Best of My Love (1977)
Bye Bye Love (1957)
Feel Like Makin' Love (1973)
Freeway of Love (1985)
The Greatest Love of All (1977)
I Can't Stop Loving You (1958)
I'm in the Mood for Love (1935)
The Language of Love (1984)
Like Someone in Love (1944)
Love (1945)
Love Changes Everything (1989)
Love for Sale (1930)
Love Is Just Around the Corner (1934)

Love Is Sweeping the Country (1931)
Love Letters (1945)
Love Letters in the Sand (1931)
Love, Look Away (1958)
Love Me Do (1962)
Love Me or Leave Me (1928)
Love Me Tender (1956)
The Love Nest (1920)
Love on the Rocks (1980)
Love Thy Neighbor (1934)
Love to Love You Baby (1976)
Love Train (1972)
Love—What Are You Doing to My Heart? (1933)
Love Will Find a Way (1978)
Moon Love (1939)
My Love (1973)
My Silent Love (1932)
Never My Love (1967)
Only Love Can Break a Heart (1962)
Our Love (1939)
Prisoner of Love (1931)
P.S. I Love You (1934)
Puppy Love (1959)
Secret Love (1954)
She Loves You (1964)
So in Love (1948)
Somebody Loves Me (1924)
Speak to Me of Love (1932)
Stop in the Name of Love (1965)
Sweet Love (1986)
That's Amore (1953)
This Can't Be Love (1938)
This Guy's in Love With You (1968)
True Love (1956)
Why Do Fools Fall in Love? (1956)
Woman in Love (1980)
A World Without Love (1964)
You Are Love (1927)
Young Love (1957)
You've Lost That Lovin' Feelin' (1964)

See also: Enduring Love; Falling in Love; Feeling; Lovers

LOVELINESS. SEE BEAUTY

LOVERS

Many songs have been written about lovers. One of the most enduring, entitled simply "Lover," was written by Lorenz Hart and Richard Rodgers for the 1932 film *Love Me Tonight*, which starred the unlikely team of Jeanette MacDonald and Maurice Chevalier. "Lover" is a most unusual song, giving a new dimension to the **waltz** in its use of **chromaticism**. Rodgers again used the waltz to accommodate lovers in "Hello, Young Lovers," from *The King and I* (1951). His collaborator on that musical play, Oscar Hammerstein II, had long before written another famous "lover" song with Sigmund Romberg, the ballad "Lover, Come Back to Me!," from

The New Moon (1928).

Among other notable songs on the subject are "I'm Just a Vagabond Lover," Introduced by Rudy Vallée in the film *The Vagabond Lover* (1929); the torch songs "When Your Lover Has Gone" (1931) and "Lover Man (Oh Where Can You Be)" (1942)—the latter remembered for its haunting recording by Billie Holiday; and Hal David and Burt Bacharach's "(Hey, Little Girl) Wives and Lovers," popularized by Jack Jones in 1963.

Additional Songs

Dream Lover (1959)
Everybody Loves a Lover (1958)
Fifty Ways to Leave Your Lover (1975)
Hey! Jealous Lover (1956)
I'm Just a Vagabond Lover (1929)
Imaginary Lover (1978)
Lover, Please (1961)
A Lover's Concerto (1965)
Torn Between Two Lovers (1976)

See also: Enduring Love; Falling in Love; Love; Romance

LUCK

Songs about luck come in several varieties. There are, first of all, those about good fortune: songs like "Lucky Day" (1926), "You Are My Lucky Star" (1935), "(I've Got) Beginner's Luck" (1937), "Lucky to Be Me" (1944), "I'm Just a Lucky So and So" (1945), and "Mr. Lucky" (1959). On a more somber note are such Depression ballads as "Just One More Chance" (1931) and "I Don't Stand a Ghost of a Chance With You" (1931). Then there are songs about the uncertainty of love, like "Taking a Chance on Love" (1940) and "Chances Are" (1957). Superstition in pursuit of good luck plays a role in "Three Coins in the Fountain" (1954) and "Good Luck Charm" (1962). Finally, there is gambling, the subject of two memorable show tunes: "Luck Be a Lady," from *Guys and Dolls* (1950), and "With a Little Bit of Luck," from *My Fair Lady* (1956).

Additional Songs

How Lucky Can You Get (1975)
Lucky Lips (1957)
Lucky Star (1983)
The Wheel of Fortune (1952)

See also: Happiness

LULLABY. *SEE* SLEEP

LYRICIST-COMPOSERS. *SEE* COMPOSER-LYRICISTS

LYRICISTS

In the creative process of songwriting, the person who writes the **lyrics** generally receives less attention than the **composer**. Yet a number of outstanding lyricists have contributed to popular song, especially in its **golden age**. Indeed, in some instances, their words transcend the music. Until the 1950s, lyricists—like composers—usually maintained their separate identities. But after that decade, songs more often became collaborative efforts, written by songwriting teams and **performer-songwriters** rather than by individually credited lyricists and composers.

Six lyricists dominate the literature of American popular song: Irving Berlin, Cole Porter, Oscar Hammerstein II, Lorenz Hart, Ira Gershwin, and Johnny Mercer; of these, Berlin and Porter habitually wrote their own music as well. Other important lyricists include Gus Kahn, Al Dubin, Lew Brown, Buddy DeSylva, Howard Dietz, E. Y. "Yip" Harburg, Leo Robin, Dorothy Fields, Mack Gordon, Johnny Burke, Sammy Cahn, Alan Jay Lerner, Betty Comden, Adolph Green, and Hal David.

Irving Berlin (1888–1989), along with Cole Porter, is a member of a select group of **composer-lyricists**, equally adept in words and music. Although Berlin's melodies are well known, his lyrics have received less attention. Yet he was among the most versatile of lyricists, writing lyrics about ordinary days and **holidays**, **love** and **patriotism**, peace and war, ordinary people and sophisticates—all slated for the varying markets of **Tin Pan Alley**, Broadway, and Hollywood. He often "ragged" his lyrics, using a vernacular phrase, as in "Come on along, come on along," from "Alexander's Ragtime Band" (1911). The language of everyday life was his specialty, and he frequently employed catchwords and **contractions**, as in "Everybody's Doin' It Now" (1911) and "What'll I Do?" (1924).

In contrast to those of Berlin, the lyrics of Cole Porter (1891–1964) have attracted more attention than his music. The glittery wit of his words often overshadows his numerous musical innovations. Yet Porter's lyrics are not consistently clever. They range from sophistication to banality, from sensational **catalogue songs** like "You're the Top" (1934) to sentimental trivialities like "True Love" (1956). In the lyrics of his songs, Porter accurately reflected the mid-century society in which he moved.

Oscar Hammerstein II (1895–1960) was a seminal influence in the art of writing for the musical theater. He was born into a New York City theatrical family and was educated at Columbia University and its law school. Along with two other undergraduates, Lorenz Hart and Richard Rodgers, he wrote and acted in the Varsity Shows at Columbia. Hammerstein's lyrics were rooted in **operetta**. His **rhymes** are never too assertive, but concentrate instead on "phonetics": the manipulation of open vowels. He was instrumental in the development of the **musical play**, integrating his lyrics and librettos into the dramatic contexts of such landmark shows as *Show Boat* (1927) and *Oklahoma!* (1943). Hammerstein's chief collaborators were Richard Rodgers, Jerome Kern, and Sigmund Romberg, but he also wrote at various times with Rudolf Friml, Herbert Stothart, Vincent Youmans, Arthur Schwartz, and Otto Harbach.

Except for a brief and unhappy foray in Hollywood in the late 1930s, Hammerstein wrote almost exclusively for Broadway, collaborating with Harbach, Friml, and Stothart on the operetta *Rose-Marie* (1924) and with Harbach and Romberg on *The Desert Song* (1926)—shows known respectively for their songs "Indian Love Call" and "One Alone." His first resounding success as lyricist and librettist on his own was in *Show Boat*, with music by Jerome Kern. He wrote two types of lyrics for that show: poetic ones, like "Why Do I Love You?," for the white characters, and songs in **dialect,** such as "Ol' Man River," for the blacks. Hammerstein went on to write other memorable songs with Kern, including "The Song Is You" (1932), "All the Things You Are" (1939), and "The Last Time I Saw Paris" (1940).

In 1943, Hammerstein's seventeen-year association with Richard Rodgers began with *Oklahoma!,* introducing such standards as "Oh, What a Beautiful Mornin'" and "People Will Say We're in Love." Rodgers and Hammerstein's succeeding musical plays—notably *Carousel* (1945), *South Pacific* (1949), *the King and I* (1951), and *The Sound of Music* (1959)—went on to make Broadway history, and brought forth such enduring songs as "You'll Never Walk Alone," "Some Enchanted Evening," "Hello, Young Lovers," and "The Sound of Music."

Lorenz Hart (1895–1943), like Hammerstein, was a native New Yorker who wrote for the Varsity Shows at Columbia University. But the resemblance stops there. Hart's lyrics are in a class by themselves. His forte was rhyme, in the context of the vernacular. Along with his only collaborator, Richard Rodgers, he wrote such quotable lines as: "And tell me what street compares with Mott Street in July, Sweet pushcarts gently gliding by" (from "Manhattan," 1925). Hart's sparkling lyrics enliven dozens of remarkable songs, mostly written for Broadway; the songwriting team of Rodgers and Hart became legendary. Among their songs were the standards "Dancing on the Ceiling" (1930), "Blue Moon" (1934), "My Funny Valentine" (1937), "Where or When" "(1937), and "Bewitched," (1941).

Ira Gershwin (1896–1983), also born in New York, is perhaps best known for the songs he wrote in collaboration with his famous brother, George. But he wrote with many other composers as well: Harold Arlen, Vernon Duke, Jerome Kern, Burton Lane, Arthur Schwartz, Vincent Youmans, Harry Warren, and Kurt Weill. According to Ira himself, his intention in writing lyrics was to fit the words "mosaically" to the music. To this end, he used catch-phrases, slang, and contractions whenever possible; the Gershwins' 1927 song "'S Wonderful" is a sterling example. He wrote for stage and screen, and was the first lyricist to receive the Pulitzer Prize (in 1932, for *Of Thee I Sing*). Among the best-known songs by the team of Gershwin and Gershwin are "The Man I Love" (1924), "Someone to Watch Over Me" (1926), "I've Got a Crush on You" (1928), "Embraceable You" (1930), "They Can't Take That Away From Me" (1937), and "Love Is Here to Stay" (1938). Songs written in collaboration with other composers include "I Can't Get Started" (1935), with Duke; "My Ship" (1941), with Weill; "Long Ago (And Far Away)" (1944), with Kern; and "The Man That Got Away" (1954), with Arlen.

Johnny Mercer (1909–1976), born in Savannah, Georgia, was an actor and singer as well as one of the most versatile of lyricists. He wrote hundreds of lyrics for many different composers (including himself) and in many different styles. His chief collaborators were Harold Arlen, Richard Whiting, Hoagy Carmichael, Harry Warren, Gene DePaul, Victor Schertzinger, Henry Mancini, Jerome Kern, Duke Ellington, Billy Strayhorn, Gordon Jenkins, Rube Bloom, Arthur Schwartz, and James Van Heusen.

Mercer was a master of slang and the vernacular. In his "Blues in the Night" (1941, with Arlen), the opening line, "My momma done tol' me," perfectly sets the mood for the piece. He could also be sophisticated, as in his lyrics for "Satin Doll" (1958, with Strayhorn and Ellington): "Telephone numbers well you know, doing my rhumbas with uno." He also set words to jazz instrumentals ("Midnight Sun," 1947), movie themes ("Moon River," 1961), and foreign songs ("Autumn Leaves," 1950). Among his many other lyrics are "Too Marvelous for Words" (1937), "You Must Have Been a Beautiful Baby" (1938), "That Old Black Magic" (1942), "Ac-cent-tchu-ate the Positive" (1945), and "Laura" (1945).

Of the second tier of lyricists, Gus Kahn (1886–1941) wrote with a string of composers in a wide range of styles. Born in Coblenz, Germany, he came to New York at age five. Kahn wrote for Tin Pan Alley, vaudeville, the musical theater, and film. He is the subject of a biographical film: *I'll See You in My Dreams,* (1951). Kahn's chief collaborators were Egbert Van Alstyne, Richard Whiting, B. G. DeSylva, Walter Donaldson, Isham Jones, Vincent Youmans, George Gershwin, Harry Akst, Sigmund Romberg, and Harry Warren. Among his many standards are "Memories" (1915), "Ain't We Got Fun?" (1921), "Carolina in the Morning" (1922), "Toot Toot Tootsie (Goo'Bye)" (1922), "I'll See You in My Dreams" (1924), "It Had to Be You" (1924), "Yes Sir, That's My Baby" (1925), and "Makin' Whoopee" (1928).

Al Dubin (1891–1945) was born in Zurich, Switzerland, and came to New York when he was two. He wrote principally for film and is best known for the songs he wrote with Harry Warren, including "Forty-Second Street" (1932), "The Boulevard of Broken Dreams" (1933), "We're in the Money" (1933), "I Only Have Eyes for You" (1934), "Lullaby of Broadway" (1935), and "September in the Rain" (1937). Among his other collaborators were Joe Burke, J. Fred Coots, Jimmy McHugh, Sammy Fain, Victor Herbert, and Burton Lane.

Lew Brown (1893–1958) was born in Odessa, Russia, and came to New York when he was five years old. He worked primarily in New York and Hollywood, usually in collaboration with the lyricist B. G. DeSylva and the composer Ray Henderson. He wrote at other times with Albert Von Tilzer, Con Conrad, Harry Warren, Harry Akst, Jay Gorney, Harold Arlen, Sammy Fain, and Charles Tobias. Among his most popular songs are "The Birth of the Blues" (1926), "The Best Things in Life Are Free" (1927), "You're the Cream in My Coffee" (1928), and "Beer Barrel Polka" (Roll out the Barrel)" (1939).

B. G. "Buddy" DeSylva (1895–1950), born in New York, was Brown's co-lyricist in the songwriting and music-publishing team of DeSylva, Brown, and Henderson. Before joining them, he wrote for the Broadway stage, and collaborated at various times with such lyricists and composers as George Gershwin, Gus Kahn, Jerome Kern, Al Jolson, Joseph Meyer, Victor Herbert, Emmerich Kálmán, Nacio Herb Brown, Richard Whiting, and Vincent Youmans. His songs include "Look for the Silver Lining" (1920), "Avalon" (1920), "April Showers" (1921), "California, Here I Come" (1924), "A Kiss in the Dark" (1922), and "I'll Build a Stairway to Paradise" (1922).

Howard Dietz (1896–1983), also born in New York, attended the Columbia University School of Journalism. He began his career in advertising and later became publicity director for Metro-Goldwyn-Mayer in Hollywood. His chief collaborator was Arthur Schwartz, with whom he wrote the songs for a string of intimate **revues**, from *The Little Show* (1929) to *Between the Devil* (1937). Among his other collaborators were Vernon Duke, Jerome Kern, Jimmy McHugh, Ralph Rainger, Sammy Fain, and George Gershwin. His distinctive songs include "I Guess I'll Have to Change My Plan" (1929), "Something to Remember You By" (1930), "Dancing in the Dark" (1931), "Alone Together" (1932), "You and the Night and the Music" (1934), and "By Myself" (1937).

E. Y. "Yip" Harburg (1898–1981) was another New Yorker. He graduated from City College of New York and began his career as a playwright. Harburg wrote carefully wrought lyrics for Tin Pan Alley, Broadway, and Hollywood to the music of such composers as Harold Arlen, Vernon Duke, Jay Gorney, Burton Lane, John Green, and Arthur Schwartz. His songs include "April in Paris" (1932), "Brother, Can You Spare a Dime?" (1932), "It's Only a Paper Moon" (1933), "Over the Rainbow" (1939), and "How Are Things in Glocca Morra?" (1946).

Leo Robin (1900–1984) was born in Pittsburgh and educated at the University of Pittsburgh Law School. His early career was as a newspaper reporter, after which he became a playwright and finally found his true métier in writing lyrics for film and, later, for the musical stage. His chief collaborators were Ralph Rainger, Vincent Youmans, Clifford Grey, Richard Whiting, Sam Coslow, Harry Warren, Jerome Kern, Arthur Schwartz, John Green, Harold Arlen, Jule Styne, and Nacio Herb Brown. Among his many songs are "Hallelujah!" (1927), "Louise" (1929), "Beyond the Blue Horizon" (1930), "Prisoner of Love" (1931), and "Love in Bloom" (1934).

Dorothy Fields (1905–1974) was the daughter of comedian Lew Fields. She was born in Allenhurst, New Jersey, and began writing lyrics in New York for the Cotton Club revues of the late 1920s, after which she went to Hollywood. One of the few successful woman lyricists of her time, she was as adept at colloquialisms, catch-phrases, and slang as any of her male colleagues. Among her collaborators were Jimmy McHugh, Jerome Kern, Arthur Schwartz, Fritz Kreisler, Sigmund Romberg, Harold Arlen, Harry Warren, Burton Lane, Albert Hague, and Cy Coleman. Her songs include "I Can't Give You Anything But Love" (1928), "Exactly Like You" (1930), "On the Sunny Side of the Street" (1930), "Don't Blame Me" (1933), "I'm in the Mood for Love" (1935), and "The Way You Look Tonight" (1936).

Mack Gordon (1915–1959) was born in Warsaw, Poland, but came to New York at an early age. He began his career as a boy soprano in a minstrel show, but graduated to vaudeville, where he performed as a comedian and singer. He worked as a lyricist on Broadway and in Hollywood with such composers as Harry Revel, Harry Warren, Josef Myrow, Ray Henderson, James Van Heusen, Vincent Youmans, and James Monaco. His songs include "Time on My Hands" (1930), "Did You Ever See a Dream Walking?" (1933), "Chattanooga Choo-Choo" (1941), "I Had the Craziest Dream" (1942), "There Will Never Be Another You" (1942), "You'll Never Know" (1943), and "The More I See You" (1945).

Johnny Burke (1908–1984) was born in Antioch, California, and studied at the University of Wisconsin. He wrote primarily for film, with James Van Heusen as his main composer. Among his other collaborators were James Monaco, Arthur Johnston, Victor Schertzinger, Harold Spina, Bob Haggart, and Erroll Garner. His songs include "Pennies from Heaven" (1936), "Imagination" (1940), "Swinging on a Star" (1944), "It Could Happen to You" (1944), "Here's That Rainy Day" (1953), and "Misty" (1954).

Sammy Cahn was born in New York in 1913 and began his career as a violinist in a vaudeville orchestra.

He wrote for Tin Pan Alley as well as for Hollywood. Many of his songs, written with such composers as Jule Styne, James Van Heusen, Saul Chaplin, Gene De Paul, and George Barrie, were popularized by Frank Sinatra. His lyrics include "I'll Walk Alone" (1944), "It's Been a Long, Long Time" (1945), "Time After Time" (1947), "Teach Me Tonight" (1953), "Three Coins in the Fountain" (1954), "All the Way" (1957), "The Second Time Around" (1960), and "Call Me Irresponsible" (1962).

Alan Jay Lerner (1918–1986) is best known for his collaboration with the composer Frederick Loewe on the songs for the musical plays *Brigadoon* (1947), *My Fair Lady* (1956), and *Camelot* (1960), and for the musical film *Gigi* (1958). But he also wrote with other composers, notably Burton Lane, Ira Gershwin, and Kurt Weill. Among his songs are "Almost Like Being in Love" (1947), "On the Street Where You Live" (1956), "Thank Heaven for Little Girls" (1958), "If Ever I Would Leave You" (1960), and "On a Clear Day You Can See Forever" (1966).

Betty Comden (b. 1919) and Adolph Green (b. 1915) have worked together as co-lyricists and co-librettists for a number of shows and screenplays, including *On the Town* (1944), *Singin' in the Rain* (1952), and *Bells Are Ringing* (1956). Their musical collaborators include Leonard Bernstein, Jule Styne, André Previn, and Cy Coleman. Among their songs are "Lucky to Be Me" (1944), "Just in Time" (1956), "The Party's Over" (1956), and "Make Someone Happy" (1960).

Hal David, born in New York in 1921, is best known for his collaboration with Burt Bacharach, but he has also worked with Sherman Edwards, Henry Mancini, Joe Raposo, and John Barry. He wrote for film, stage, and recordings. Among his songs, co-authored with Bacharach, are "(They Long to Be) Close to You" (1963), "What the World Needs Now Is Love" (1965), "The Look of Love" (1965), "Alfie" (1966), "I'll Never Fall in Love Again" (1968), and "Raindrops Keep Fallin' on My Head" (1969).

Stephen Sondheim, a protégé of Hammerstein, was born in New York in 1930. He is perhaps best known as composer-lyricist of a string of Broadway shows, including *A Funny Thing Happened on the Way to the Forum* (1962), *Company* (1970), *Follies* (1971), *A Little Night Music* (1973), and *Sweeney Todd* (1979). Before these successes, however, he acted as lyricist to Leonard Bernstein on the landmark show *West Side Story* (1957); to Jule Styne, on *Gypsy* (1959); and to Richard Rodgers, on *Do I Hear a Waltz?* (1965). Songs from these shows include "Maria" and "Tonight" (1957); "Everything's Coming Up Roses" and "Let Me Entertain You" (1959); and "Do I Hear a Waltz?" (1965).

For additional lyricists, see "Part II: Catalogue of Songs."

Bibliography

ASCAP Biographical Dictionary. 4th ed. 1980.

Cahn, Sammy. *I Should Care: The Sammy Cahn Story.* 1975.

Dietz, Howard. *Dancing in the Dark.* 1974.

Engel, Lehman. *Their Words Are Music: The Great Theater Lyricists and Their Lyrics.* 1975.

Furia, Philip. *The Poets of Tin Pan Alley: A History of America's Great Lyricists.* 1990.

Gershwin, Ira. *Lyrics on Special Occasions: A Selection of Stage and Screen Lyrics.* 1978.

Gottfried, Martin. *Broadway Musicals.* 1980.

Hammerstein, Oscar, II. *Lyrics.* 1949.

Hart, Dorothy, ed. *Thou Swell, Thou Witty.* 1976.

Hischak, Thomas S. *Word Crazy: Broadway Lyricists From Cohan to Sondheim.* 1991.

Lerner, Alan Jay. *The Street Where I Live: The Story of "My Fair Lady," "Gigi," and "Camelot."* 1980.

Mast, Gerald. *Can't Help Singin': The American Musical on Stage and Screen.* 1987.

Mercer, Bob and Ginger. *Our Huckleberry Friend: The Life, Times, and Lyrics of Johnny Mercer.* 1982.

See also: Collaboration; Film Musicals; Musical Comedy; Vaudeville

LYRICS

In popular song, the words—collectively known as the lyrics—have often been considered subservient to the music. Yet they are of primary importance to a song, largely determining whether it will be happy or sad, serious or comic, simple or convoluted, intelligible or inane. In fact, a perfect song has been called a "marriage of equal partners."

At the turn of the century, lyrics typically told a story in a number of **verses**, which alternated with a more melodious **chorus**. One of the most celebrated examples is Charles K. Harris's sentimental ballad "After the Ball" (1892), wherein an uncle tells his niece that he never married because long ago at a ball he saw another man kiss his sweetheart; only years later did he find out that the other man was her brother. Even so vibrant a chorus as that of "In the Shade of the Old Apple Tree" (1905) is contrasted with a lugubrious verse explaining that a man's sweetheart is buried beneath the apple tree.

With the emergence of **ragtime** and the **coon song**, a new tendency in lyric-writing began. **Lyricists** made use of **dialect**, **slang**, and **contraction**, as in the 1902 song "Bill Bailey, Won't You Please Come Home?": "I knows I'se to blame; well, ain't dat a shame?" The standardization of thirty-two-bar song **form** in the 1920s required a new style of lyrics, combining colloquialism and elegance. Lyrics were often tailored to fit the music, as in "Who?" (1925), which matches long notes on "who" and "to" in the phrase "*Who* would I answer 'yes' *to?*"

Since the words were customarily written to fit the music, lyricists often wrote **dummy lyrics**; on occasion, as in "Tea for Two" (1924), these ended up as real lyrics. Lyricists also employed a whole arsenal of effects derived from poetry. The most prominent of these were **rhyme** and **alliteration**. Among other time-honored devices found in the lyrics of popular song are allusion: "rich as Rockefeller," in "On the Sunny Side of the Street" (1930); anaphora (repetition at the start of each line): "I got music . . . I got my man," in "I Got Rhythm" (1930); simile: "restless as a willow in a windstorm," in "It Might as Well Be Spring" (1946); pure repetition: Let It Snow! Let It Snow! "Let It Snow!" (1945); metaphor: "If I were a gate I'd be swinging," in "If I Were a Bell" (1950); and apostrophe (addressing an absent person or thing): "Hello darkness, my old friend," in "The Sound of Silence" (1964).

The second half of the twentieth century saw many changes in **subject** matter as well as in musical style. But lyrics did not change as much as one might expect. Anachronisms remained, such as "the warmth of thee," in "A Taste of Honey" (1960). Narratives continued to be told in the style of the 1890s in such songs as "Alice's Restaurant" (1966). Banalities abounded, as in "Forever you'll stay in my heart," in "You Are the Sunshine of My Life" (1972). The tried and true formulas of over one hundred years still applied, as exemplified in the 1986 song "Somewhere Out There," which rhymes "see us through" with "dreams come true."

Bibliography

Cooper, B. Lee. *Popular Music Perspectives: Ideas, Themes, and Patterns in Contemporary Lyrics.* 1991.

Davis, Sheila. *The Craft of Lyric Writing.* 1985.

Engel, Lehman. *Their Words and Music: The Great Theater Lyricists and Their Lyrics.* 1975.

Furia, Philip. *The Poets of Tin Pan Alley: A History of America's Great Lyricists.* 1990.

Gershwin, Ira. *Lyrics on Special Occasions: A Selection of Stage and Screen Lyrics.* 1978.

Hammerstein, Oscar, II. *Lyrics.* 1949.

Mast, Gerald. *Can't Help Singin': The American Musical on Stage and Screen.* 1987.

Mercer, Bob and Ginger. *Our Huckleberry Friend: The Life, Times, and Lyrics of Johnny Mercer.* 1982.

See also: **Catalogue Song; Humor; Novelty Song; Protest Song**

m

MADNESS

Madness, in popular song, most often refers to **love**, or more precisely to the immoderate infatuation of one person for another. Such is the case in "(I Got a Woman Crazy for Me) She's Funny That Way" (1928). Other departures from normalcy are found in "You're Driving Me Crazy" (1930), "You Call It Madness (Ah, But I Call It Love)" (1931), "Sweet Madness" (1933), "Losing My Mind" (1971), and "Crazy Love" (1978). Love is also the subject of the protagonist's dream in "I Had the Craziest Dream" (1943).

There are also other forms of madness in popular song. "Crazy Rhythm" (1928) is a study in syncopation, relying on persistent rhythmic repetition for its effect. The "crazy" in the title of the 1964 song "Those Lazy Hazy Crazy Days of Summer" appears to be there only for the convenience of its rhyme.

Noël Coward used madness to great effect in several interesting songs. "Mad Dogs and Englishmen" (1931) is a humorous narrative about the only beings in the tropics who "go out in the midday sun." His "Mad About the Boy" (1935), a striking song in the minor mode about love, returns us to the primary meaning of "madness" in popular song.

Additional Songs

Crazy (1961)
Crazy Arms (1956)
Crazy for You (1983)
The Crazy Otto Rag (1955)
It's a Mad, Mad, Mad, Mad World (1963)
K-ra-zy for You (1928)
You Could Drive a Person Crazy (1970)

> *See also:* **Fools; Mind**

MAGIC

Very often, in popular song, the supernatural is called upon in the pursuit of **love**. One of the earliest songs to employ this device was "Love Your Magic Spell Is Everywhere," from the 1929 film *The Trespasser*, starring Gloria Swanson. In the same year, Cole Porter brought magic to his "You Do Something to Me," with the words: "Do do that voodoo that you do so well." A year later, Maria Grever's Mexican song "Te Quiero Dijiste" was given English words as "Magic Is the Moonlight." In 1941, Rodgers and Hart created their own spell with their ballad "Bewitched."

Johnny Mercer and Harold Arlen brought a new dimension to the "magic" ballad with "That Old Black Magic" (1943); a song with sleek harmonies, unusual length, and evocative lyrics. Another song about magic, "Old Devil Moon," was introduced in the 1946 musical *Finian's Rainbow*, itself about in enchanted village in Ireland. In much the same spirit is "Witchcraft," published in 1957. More conventional are two ballads on the subject, published ten years apart: "It's Magic" (1948) and "Magic Moments" (1958).

A different sort of magic, the world of fantasy, reigns supreme in the 1939 film *The Wizard of Oz*. Its most famous song, "Over the Rainbow," captures the magic world of a child's **imagination**, taking its heroine, Dorothy, to an enchanted land "where troubles melt like lemon drops." Witches and wizards also have their day in two other songs from that film: "We're Off to See the Wizard" and "Ding Dong! The Witch Is Dead."

On the other hand, "Puff (The Magic Dragon)," introduced by Peter, Paul and Mary in 1963, has nothing to do with magic; it is instead an allusion to the drug culture of its day.

Additional Songs

Aquarius (1967)
Between the Devil and the Deep Blue Sea (1931)
Black Magic Woman (1968)
Could This Be Magic (1957)
The Devil Went Down to Georgia (1979)
Do You Believe in Magic? (1965)

Magic (1980)
This Magic Moment (1960)
Witch Doctor (1958)
    See also: Luck

MAJOR, MINOR. *SEE* MODE

MAMBO

Derived from the music of Afro-Cuban carnival groups called *conjuntos*, the mambo developed as a moderate-to-fast dance music genre in **New York City** during the late 1940s and early 1950s. Strongly influenced by **swing** and typically performed by big bands, it featured strong contrast between saxes, trumpets, and trombones, as well as an extensive **percussion** section including timbale, cowbell, and conga-drum. **Riffs**, phrases alternating between **woodwind** and **brass** sections, were characteristic of the **arrangements**.

Leaders in the development of the mambo were the singer Tito Rodriguez, the *timbalero* Tito Puente, and the pianists Noro Morales and Perez Prado. The activities of their orchestras, as well as others, often centered around the Palladium Ballroom in New York. Among the hundreds of mambos written during the period of its popularity were "Cuban Mambo" and "Mambo Jambo" in 1950, "Sway (Quien Sera)" in 1953, and "Mambo Italiano," "Papa Loves Mambo," and "They Were Doing the Mambo" in 1954.

Bibliography

Roberts, John Storm. *The Latin Tinge: The Impact of Latin American Music on the United States.* 1985.

    See also: **Cha Cha Cha; Conga; Cuba; Dance Crazes; Rumba**

MAN

The word "man" appears in the titles of a great many songs, though hardly as many as does the word **"woman."** Often a man is depicted as an object of desire. An example is "My Man," an import from France originally called "Mon Homme"; it was introduced in the United States by Fanny Brice in 1921. An especially important standard about a woman's **love** for a man is Ira and George Gershwin's "The Man I Love," written in 1924. In the same loving spirit is Oscar Hammerstein II and Jerome Kern's "Can't Help Lovin' Dat Man," from their musical play *Show Boat* (1927).

The search for a man is more properly at the core of such songs as "A Good Man Is Hard to Find" (1918), "Lover Man (Oh Where Can You Be?)" (1942), and "You Can't Get a Man With a Gun" (1946). Appreciation of a man is the essence of "It's So Nice to Have a Man Around the House" (1950). **Forgetting** a man is the subject of "I'm Gonna Wash That Man Right Outa

My Hair," from *South Pacific* (1949). Losing a man is the lament of both "My Man's Gone Now," from *Porgy and Bess* (1935), and "The Man That Got Away," sung by Judy Garland in the 1954 film *A Star Is Born*. **Loneliness** is the subject of "A Man Without Love," imported from Italy in 1968.

There are also a number of occupational songs about men. In this category one finds such diverse characters as **circus** performers ("The Daring Young Man on the Flying Trapeze," 1868), gamblers ("The Man Who Broke the Bank at Monte Carlo," 1892), troopers ("Stouthearted Men," 1928), sailors ("Popeye the Sailor Man," 1931), salesman ("Travelin' Man," 1960), railroad men ("Wichita Lineman," 1968), peddlers ("The Candy Man," 1970), and musicians ("Piano Man," 1974).

A man can also be a "guy," as in "Wonderful Guy" (1949), "Guys and Dolls" (1950), and "This Guy's in Love With You" (1968). He can be a "fellow" too, as in "A Fellow Needs a Girl" (1947) and "The Most Happy Fella" (1956). As a symbol, man is also the subject of such songs as "My Sweetheart's the Man in the Moon" (1892), "The Japanese Sandman" (1920), and "Ol' Man River."

In 1958, the teen idol Fabian sang "I'm a Man," one of at least three songs with that title. An ironic song of humorous bent is "I'm an Ordinary Man," memorably spoken by Rex Harrison in *My Fair Lady* (1956). Woman enters the picture in several songs, among them "When a Man Loves a Woman" (1961), "You Are Women (I Am Man)" (1964), and "A Man and a Woman" (1966). To complete the roster are two decidedly uncomplimentary songs about men: "The Gentleman Is a Dope" (1947) and "I Hate Men" (1949).

Additional Songs

Big Man (1958)
The Children's Marching Song (This Old Man) (1958)
The Fat Man (1950)
Handy Man (1959)
I Never Loved a Man (The Way I Love You) (1966)
I'm Your Boogie Man (1977)
It's a Man's, Man's World (But It Wouldn't Be Nothing Without a Woman . . .) (1966)
Macho Man (1978)
Man With the Banjo (1953)
A Natural Man (1971)
Nowhere Man (1965)
Old Man (1972)
Ramblin' Man (1973)
Sixty Minute Man (1951)
Sooner or Later (I Always Get My Man) (1990)
Stand by Your Man (1968)
Walk Like a Man (1963)
A Well Respected Man (1965)

    See also: **Boy; Names**

MARCH

A march is a composition, usually in duple or 6/8 **meter**, that is suitable for measured walking. Around the turn of the century, marches were often used to accompany dances like the **cakewalk** and **two-step**. They were also important in the development of **ragtime**.

Two types of marches may be distinguished in popular song, the military and the nonmilitary. In the first category are the United States service songs "Anchors Aweigh" (1907); "The U.S. Field Artillery March," or "The Caissons Go Rolling Along" (1918); "The Marine's Hymn," or "From the Halls of Montezuma to the Shores of Tripoli" (1919); and "The Army Air Corps" (1939). Also of patriotic bent are George M. Cohan's "The Yankee Doodle Boy" (1904), "You're a Grand Old Flag" (1906), and "Over There" (1917)—the last a favorite marching song of **World War I**.

In the second category of marches are songs customarily used to accompany processions of various sorts: "Pomp and Circumstance" (1902), "Tramp! Tramp! Tramp! Along the Highway" (1910), "Stouthearted Men" (1928), "Marching Along Together" (1933), and "Hey, Look Me Over" (1960). In addition, a number of college songs are often used as marches, among them "On Wisconsin" (1909), the song of the University of Wisconsin, and "Stein Song," the song of the University of Maine (1910).

Another march, "Buckle Down, Winsockie," refers to a fictional college first presented in the musical comedy *Best Foot Forward* (1941). Other marches from the musical theater include. "Song of the Flame" (1925), from the show of that name; "Strike Up the Band" (1927), from the show of that name; "Wintergreen for President," from *Of Thee I Sing* (1931); and "Seventy-Six Trombones, from *The Music Man* (1957).

Additional Songs

I Love a Parade (1931)
It's a Long Way to Tipperary (1912)
March of the Musketeers (1928)
March of the Toys (1903)
Parade of the Wooden Soldiers (1905)
The Rangers' Song (1926)
We're Off to See the Wizard (1939)

> *See also:* **Patriotism; World War II**

MARRIAGE

To paraphrase the lyrics of the song "Love and Marriage" (1955), popular songs and marriage go together "like a horse and carriage." Two types of songs can be distinguished: those about marriage as an institution and those on the subject of weddings.

Songs about marriage include such long-time standards as "It's Delightful to Be Married" (1906) and "I

Want a Girl Just Like the Girl That Married Dear Old Dad" (1911). At least six show tunes also fall into this category: "I Married an Angel" (1938), from the musical comedy of the same name; "I Wanna Get Married," from *Follow the Girls* (1944); "When I Marry Mister Snow," from *Carousel* (1945); "The Girl That I Marry," from *Annie Get Your Gun* (1946); "Marrying for Love," from *Call Me Madam* (1950); and "If Momma Was Married," from *Gypsy* (1959).

Songs on the subject of weddings include "The Hawaiian Wedding Song (Ke Kali Nei Au)" "Wedding Bells Are Breaking Up That Old Gang of Mine" and "The Wedding of the Painted Doll" (both 1929), "When Your Old Wedding Ring Was New" (1935), "I'll Dance at Your Wedding" (1947), and "Wedding Bell Blues" (1966).

There also are a number of songs traditionally associated with marriage, such as "Anniversary Song" (1946), based on Ion Ivanovici's *Waves of the Danube* (1880); "Get Me to the Church on Time" from *My Fair Lady* (1956); and "Matchmaker, Matchmaker" from *Fiddler on the Roof* (1964). The German children's song "Der Kirmessbauer," known in English as "The Farmer in the Dell" (1883), is traditionally sung at wedding receptions to the words "the bride cuts the cake."

Last, but not least, some songs performed in connection with the actual wedding ceremony have been used so frequently that they have become part of the traditional corpus of music heard on these occasions. In the first half of this century, "Oh Promise Me" (1887), "I Love You Truly" (1901), and "Because" (1902) were among the standards performed. From the 1960s to the present—a period during which guitar-accompanied songs have been sanctioned for liturgical use, many different types of songs have been incorporated into the ceremony. Among those which have found repeated use are "Now May There Be a Blessing" (from Douglas Moore's opera *The Devil and Daniel Webster*, 1939), "Evergreen (Love Theme From *A Star Is Born*)" (1976), "Wedding Song (There Is Love)" (1971), and "Sunrise, Sunset" (from *Fiddler on the Roof*, 1964).

Additional Songs

The Anniversary Waltz (1941)
I Never Will Marry (1958)
I Went to Your Wedding (1952)
I'm Gonna Get Married (1959)
Married I Can Always Get (1956)
My Woman, My Woman, My Wife (1969)
This Diamond Ring (1964)
(Hey, Little Girl) Wives and Lovers (1963)

> *See also:* **Enduring Love; Love; Man; Occasional Song; Opera; Woman; Women As Songwriters**

MARY. SEE NAMES

MEETING

Judging from the dates of the songs on the subject, the concept of meeting is somewhat old-fashioned. Typical examples are "At a Georgia Camp Meeting," the popular cakewalk number of 1897, and "Meet Me in St. Louis, Louis," the waltz written to celebrate the Louisiana Purchase Exposition, held in St. Louis in 1904. Several older songs, like "Gee But It's Great to Meet a Friend From Your Old Home Town" (1910) and "(Just a) Little Street Where Old Friends Meet" (1932), pertain to meeting friends. But most meetings are in pursuit of **love,** as in the romantic waltz "Meet Me Tonight in Dreamland" (1909) or the song of chastisement "She Was Happy Till She Met You" (1899).

Two of the best-known songs about meeting in pursuit of love underline the pangs of separation during wartime: "Till We Meet Again" (1918) and "We'll Meet Again" (1939). But perhaps the most prolonged meeting of all occurs in Lorenz Hart's lyrics for "Have You Met Miss Jones?" (1937), in which the singer declares that now that he's met Miss Jones, "we'll keep meeting till we die, Miss Jones and I."

See also: **Farewells; Friendship; Greetings**

MELODY

The melody of a popular song is perhaps its most immediately recognizable musical feature. At its simplest, a melody may be conceived of as a succession of pitches of varying duration. Melodic material may be new, as in the great majority of songs, or derived: borrowed from the **classics** or from other sources.

Popular song melodies almost always function as primary thematic material, with one or more themes. In certain songs, on the other hand, a melody can have a secondary function: as **countermelody, riff,** or part of a specialized **bass line** such as **boogie-woogie.**

Most popular melodies are rooted either in the **folk song** tradition or in the musical styles of the Classic and Romantic periods of the eighteenth and nineteenth centuries. As such, they are largely diatonic and most often in the major **mode.** However, both the minor mode and **chromaticism** are also well represented in popular song. A special characteristic of many American melodies is use of the **blue note,** as exemplified in "The Man I Love" (1924).

Of necessity, popular melodies must be singable. For this reason, they are usually idiomatic for the voice, of relatively narrow **range,** and without too many difficult leaps. Three types of melodies are common: those based on **broken chords** ("Daisy Bell," 1892), **scales** ("Where or When" 1937), and **repeated notes** ("They Can't Take That Away From Me" 1937). Another type of melody outlines various **intervals;** those of the sixth, seventh, and **octave** are especially common. Although melodies can be typed to a degree, most, when viewed in their entirety, present a varying mixture of these elements. The melody of "When I Fall in Love" (1951), for example, moves stepwise as well as in intervals of the third, fourth, fifth, and sixth.

Melodic procedure often involves the use of ascending **sequence** ("As Time Goes By," 1931), descending sequence ("All the Things You Are," 1939), or repetition ("Feelings (¿Dime?)" 1974). Melodic movement can be by step ("My Heart Stood Still," 1927), skip ("I Cried for You," 1923), or, most commonly, a combination of both ("What I Did for Love," 1975).

The diversity of melodic shapes in popular song is extraordinary. Some of the most beautiful melodies develop continuously, describing a series of ever-climbing curves, as in Leonard Bernstein's soaring "Somewhere" (1957). Other themes, like that of Jule Styne's "People" (1964), alternate between the lower and upper register. Still other melodic lines are extended by the use of arpeggiation ("I Could Have Danced All Night," 1956) or ornamentation ("Smoke Gets in Your Eyes," 1933).

But no melody can stand alone in a song. It is shaped and controlled by all the other elements of music, in particular **harmony** and **rhythm.** In addition, the relation of the melody to the **lyrics** is of overriding importance. For example, the melody and lyrics of Cole Porter's "Night and Day" (1932) form a perfect union: one would be inconceivable without the other.

The very words "melody" and "tune" have proved attractive to songwriters, who have used them in a host of song titles over the years: from "That Mesmerizing Mendelssohn Tune" (1909) to "My Melody of Love" (1973).

Additional Songs

Bernie's Tune (1953)
The Broadway Melody (1929)
Elmer's Tune (1941)
I Like to Recognize the Tune (1939)
I Whistle a Happy Tune (1951)
Melodie d'Amour (1949)
A Melody From the Sky (1935)
Play a Simple Melody (1914)
A Pretty Girl Is Like a Melody (1919)
Rock-a-Bye Your Baby With a Dixie Melody (1918)
The Song Is Ended But the Melody Lingers On (1927)

Bibliography

Szabolcsi, Bence. *A History of Melody.* 1965.

Wilder, Alec. *American Popular Song: The Great Innovators 1900–1950.* 1972.

See also: **Music**

MEMORY

Remembrance lends itself well to music; numerous songs have been written on the subject over the years.

An inordinate number of them are **waltzes**, not surprising considering that dance's nineteenth-century origin. Included in this category are Gus Kahn and Egbert Van Alstyne's "Memories," of 1915; two waltzes by Sigmund Romberg: "Will You Remember (Sweetheart)," from *Maytime* (1917), and "Golden Days," from *The Student Prince* (1924); Irving Berlin's "Remember" (1925); and the deliberately nostalgic "Try to Remember" from *The Fantasticks* (1960).

The predominance of the **fox trot** over the waltz beginning in the 1920s resulted in a rash of slow ballads on the subject, including "Among My Souvenirs" and "Just a Memory" in 1927, "Memories of You" and "Something to Remember You By" in 1930, "It's Easy to Remember" in 1934, "Did I Remember?" and "These Foolish Things (Remind Me of You)" in 1935, and "Remember Me" and "Thanks For the Memory" in 1937.

Two sophisticated songs of remembrance appeared in 1942 Films: "I Remember You" and "I'll Remember April." More to the popular taste were the songs "Moments to Remember" and "Memories Are Made of This" (both 1955). The broadly realized theme from the film *An Affair to Remember* became a hit song in 1957.

Finally, capping a long tradition of remembering in music, came "Memory," from *Cats*, in 1981: a song appropriately reminiscent of years gone by.

Additional Songs

I Remember It Well (1958)
I'm Stepping Out With a Memory Tonight (1940)
Remember Pearl Harbor (1941)
There's Always Something There to Remind Me (1964)
Those Were the Days (1968)
Yesterday (1965)
Yesterday Once More (1973)
Yesterday, When I Was Young (1965)
Yesterdays (1933)

See also: Forgetting

MERENGUE

The merengue is a type of song and dance in fast tempo and duple meter, with a characteristic **rhythm**:

It originated as a folk dance in the Dominican Republic where, in its rural form, it was characterized by call-and-response singing and accompanied by accordion, two-headed drums, and metal scrapers. The merengue spread rapidly to the cities and to other countries of **Latin America** and, by the early 1950s, reached **New York City**. There, in its urban form, it was typically performed by big bands at ballrooms and in concerts. Among the best-known merengues are two Spanish-language songs: "Compadre Pedro Juan" and "El Negrito del Batey" (both 1955).

Bibliography

Roberts, John Storm. *The Latin Tinge: The Impact of Latin American Music on the United States*. 1985.

See also: **Dance Crazes; Guaracha; Mambo; Samba**

METER

Duple meter, consisting of two dominant beats, is by far the most common metrical organization in American popular song. As 2/4 meter, indicating two quarter notes to the bar, it was popular in the Gay Nineties and during the first two decades of the twentieth century, especially in dances such as the **cakewalk, one-step,** and **tango.** As 4/4, indicating that each measure consists of four quarter notes or their equivalent, duple meter was favored from the 1920s on. This time signature is often written as "C" (common time) or "₵" (cut time): the latter indicates that the first and third beats of each measure are to be stressed.

Triple meter, with a time signature of 3/4 meter, consists of three quarter notes or their equivalent to a bar. This meter was very popular around the turn of the century, especially in songs based upon the **waltz.** To a lesser extent, it remained in use throughout the century.

Usually, only one meter prevails throughout a piece, but there are exceptions. The **verse** of "I Left My Heart in San Francisco" (1954), for example, is in 3/4 meter, while its **chorus** is in common time. Similarly, Rodgers and Hart's "Little Girl Blue" (1935), in cut time, has a contrasting section in 3/4 meter.

Beginning in the late 1950s, mixing meters within a song became a part of a wider attempt to get away from the thirty-two-bar, common-time mold established by Tin Pan Alley . "Something's Coming," from *West Side Story* (1957), persistently alternates 3/4 meter with 2/4 meter. "A Taste of Honey" (1960) has an A section in 3/4 meter and a B section in 4/4 meter. In "A Man and a Woman" (1966), the song's basic metrical structure in cut time is repeatedly disrupted by the insertion of bars written in 2/4; the effect is that of 6/4 alternating with 4/4. To further complicate matters, the song's **coda** is in 3/4. The narrative song "Is That All There Is?" (1966) alternates sections in 3/4, 4/4, and 6/8 meters. Lennon and McCartney's "The Fool on the Hill" (1967) has an A section in 3/4 meter and a B section in 4/4. An extreme example of the tendency of mixing meters is "Theme From *Valley of the Dolls*" (1967), which consists of a series of diminishing meters—4/4, 3/4, 2/4—in its A section. Its **release**, on the other hand, consists of four bars in 4/4 meter and four bars in 3/4 meter. The song "Day by Day," from *Godspell* (1971), begins in 3/4 meter and subsequently repeats its principal theme in 4/4.

Compound meter, in which the basic pulse is subdivided into groups of three, is less common in popular song. It is used as 6/4, a compound duple meter, in Jacques Brel's "Marieke" (1961). As 6/8, another compound duple meter, it has traditionally been employed in **marches**, such as "The Army Air Corps" (1939). It later was used in several show tunes, including "More I Cannot Wish You," from *Guys and Dolls* (1950), and "America," from *West Side Story.* More recently, 6/8 meter also appeared in independent songs like "Hopelessly Devoted to You" (1978).

Perhaps the most popular song in compound triple, or 9/8 meter is "The Impossible Dream," from *Man of La Mancha* (1965). The 1970s and 1980s saw increasing use of 12/8 meter, a compound duple meter, which is actually a subdivided 4/4. Songs in that meter include "Colour My World" (1970), "Send in the Clowns" (1973), "Saving All My Love for You" (1978), and "Memory" (1981). Yet in the vast majority of popular songs, from blues to country to rock, simple 4/4 meter prevails.

See also: Rhythm; Tempo

MEXICO

Not surprisingly, our closest neighbor to the south has had a strong influence on, and has in turn been strongly influenced by, popular music in the United States. Far removed from the typical sound of the mariachi bands—trumpets, violins, guitar, and bass guitar—heard in some of the border states are the many Mexican songs that have become standards in the United States. Four types can be distinguished: **waltzes, boleros, ballads,** and uptempo songs.

The waltz has long been popular in Mexico. In fact, one of the most popular Viennese-style waltzes, "Over the Waves," is Mexican: it was written as "Sobre los Olas" by the composer Juventino Rosas in 1888. In 1950, its first two strains were used as the basis of a popular song called "The Loveliest Night of the Year." The international waltz favorite "Cielito Lindo (Ay, Ay, Ay)" was written in 1919 by the Mexican composer Querino Mendoza y Cortez. Another international favorite "Granada" (1932), was written by the self-taught Mexican popular composer Agustín Lara. A more sedate waltz, entitled "Maria Elena," was composed in 1932 by Lorenzo Barcelata and dedicated to the wife of then-president Emilio Portes Gil, who bore the name Maria Elena. A lighter waltz, the novelty song "Ti-Pi-Tin," was popular in 1938.

Maria Grever, composer of "Ti-Pi-Tin," also wrote two outstanding boleros: "Magic Is the Moonlight" (originally "Te Quiero Dijiste") in 1930, and "What a Diff'rence a Day Made" (originally "Cuando Vuelva a Tu Lado") in 1934. Although both originated as **tangos,** these enduring songs have been performed over the years in a variety of ways: as boleros, ballads, jazz, swing, and disco. Another Mexican composer, Alberto Dominguez, wrote two boleros that were destined to become stateside favorites of the big bands: "Frenesi" and "Perfidia" (both 1939). Still another international bolero, Lara's "Solamente Una Vez," became very popular in 1941 as "You Belong to My Heart." Other lasting Mexican boleros show Cuban influence—among them are "Come Closer to Me" (originally "Acercate Mas," 1940), "Besame Mucho" (1941), and "Amor" (1941).

Ballads in common time have a long tradition in Mexico. An early ballad-like song, Manuel M. Ponce's "Estrellita," was first published in 1914, and has since been revived many times and in many ways. The romantic Mexican song "Cuando Caliente el Sol," became "Love Me With All Your Heart" in 1966; while "Somos Novos" was converted into "It's Impossible" in 1971.

Among Mexican uptempo numbers to attain popularity north of the border is the national dance, "Popular Jarabe Tapatio," known here as the "Mexican Hat Dance" (1919). The eighteenth-century folk dance "La Bamba," noted for its cross-rhythms and first popularized in the United States by Ritchie Valens in 1958, became the title song of the 1987 film *La Bamba.* Another authentic Mexican folk song of unknown vintage "La Cucaracha" was first popularized here in 1916. Among other enduring Mexican uptempo numbers are "(Alla en) El Rancho Grande" (1934), "A Gay Ranchero" (1936), "El Cumbanchero" (1940), and "Cuanto le Gusta" (1940).

All of the above represent only part of the rich cross-fertilization between the music of Mexico and the United States that has gone on for well over a century.

Bibliography

Roberts, John Storm. *The Latin Tinge: The Impact of Latin American Music on the United States.* 1979.

See also: Cuba; Foreign Influence; Latin America; Nations

MIND

Although it takes a distant second place to the body as a **subject** of popular song, the mind has been featured in some attractive standards. John Hartford's **country and western** crossover hit "Gentle on My Mind" won a

Grammy Award in 1967, while the intricate melody of Michel Legrand's "The Windmills of Your Mind" taken from the soundtrack of the film *The Thomas Crown Affair*, brought him and his lyricists, Alan and Marilyn Bergman, the Academy Award for best song in 1968. Similarly, John Williams's stirring melody for "Can You Read My Mind?" enhanced the 1978 film *Superman*.

One of the oldest standards with the word "mind" in its title is Hoagy Carmichael's "Georgia on My Mind" (1930), but that is more properly a **state** song. Other songs on the subject include "My Heart Has a Mind of Its Own" (1960), "You Were on My Mind" (1965), "If You Could Read My Mind" (1969), and "Always on My Mind" (1971).

Two lovely songs about unrequited **love**, written more than thirty years apart, are particularly inspired. Richard Rodgers and Lorenz Hart's "It Never Entered My Mind" (1940) is notable for its internal rhymes, such as "what I lack myself" and "scratch my back myself." Stephen Sondheim's "Losing My Mind" (1971) has a melody of great power characterized by persistent syncopation, along with lyrics to match.

Additional Songs

Did You Ever Have to Make Up Your Mind? (1965)
I Almost Lost My Mind (1950)
Playground in My Mind (1971)
Suspicious Minds (1968)

> *See also:* Anatomy, Feeling; Madness; Moods; Thinking

MINSTREL SHOW

As provider of the first secular music with uniquely American characteristics, the minstrel show became widely popular in the 1840s, reached its zenith shortly before the Civil War, and survived until around the turn of the century. The subsequent emergence of the variety show and **vaudeville**, as well as a consciousness of the racist nature of minstrelsy, inevitably brought about its decline.

The minstrel show originated as a form of black entertainment, informal and spontaneous in nature, with black fiddlers providing music for both white and black social gatherings. White entertainers began to imitate and parody these performers, singing "plantation" or "coon songs." These imitations eventually evolved into two clear black stereotypes: Jim Crow and Zip Coon (also known as Dandy Jim). The former was an uncouth but joyous plantation or riverboat hand; the latter, an urban dandy with elegant clothes and exaggerated manners. The most famous pre-minstrel black impersonator was Thomas Dartmouth Rice, famous for his Jim Crow song-and-dance routine inspired by a comic jig he once saw performed by a black stablehand.

By the 1830s, blackface singing and dancing with banjo accompaniment was a common feature of the **circus**. Dan Emmett, a blackface performer during this period, got together with three other performers in 1843 and formed the Virginia Minstrels, the first such troupe to use the classic **instrumentation** of fiddle, banjo, bones, and tambourine. The troupe was an immediate success and quickly spawned several imitators, most notably Bryant's Minstrels and Edwin P. Christy's Minstrels.

As the minstrel show grew in popularity, it assumed other distinctive formal qualities. A minstrel troupe's arrival in a town would be signalled by a parade that concluded at the theater where the evening's performance was to be given. On stage, the performers sat in a semicircular arrangement; in the middle were the banjo and fiddle player, on the ends were "Tambo" and "Bones," a kind of primitive rhythm section. The show itself was comprised of three parts: the show proper, featuring jokes by the end-man and the interlocutor (who sat in the middle of the semicircle and functioned as the host); the *olio*, or series of solo acts (songs, dances, satirical skits); and a playlet or stage parody. The show would conclude with a walk-around finale that became popularly known as the **cakewalk**.

Although it disappeared around the turn of the century, the minstrel show greatly influenced the development of American popular music in the twentieth century. Many important singers (Bessie Smith, Ma Rainey) sang with minstrel troupes, and important American songwriters (Emmett, Stephen Foster, James Bland) wrote many "Ethiopian songs" that became standards of the minstrel repertoire. No less important a figure in American music than W. C. Handy (1873–1958) began his career with a minstrel troupe. Such lasting songs as "In the Good Old Summertime" (1902) and "Ida, Sweet as Apple Cider" (1903) were introduced in minstrel shows. Entertainers such as Eddie Cantor and Al Jolson brought the blackface tradition to the medium of **film**. Finally, the series of acts that comprised the *olio* was a major contributor to the development of vaudeville.

Barry Keith Grant

Bibliography

Nathan, Hans. *Dan Emmett and the Rise of Early Negro Minstrelsy*. 1962.

Paskman, Daily, and Sigmund Spaeth. *"Gentlemen, Be Seated!": A Parade of the Old-Time Minstrels*. 1953.

Toll, Robert C. *Blacking Up: The Minstrel Show in Nineteenth-Century America*. 1974.

Wittke, Carl. *Tambo and Bones: A History of the American Minstrel Stage*. 1930.

> *See also:* Gay Nineties; Tin Pan Alley

MODALITY

Modality, the use of **modes** other than major and minor, is rare in American popular song. The traditional church modes of Dorian, Phrygian, Lydian, and Mixolydian are mainly confined to jazz **improvisation**, where they were used to some extent by performers like Miles Davis.

On the other hand, some music of East European or Asian derivation shows evidence of modality. For example, both the Greek "Misirlou" (1941) and the Israeli "Hava Nagila" (1963) possess the lowered seconds characteristic of the Phrygian mode.

One of the earliest examples of modality in an American song is "Old Devil Moon," from *Finian's Rainbow* (1947), which emphasizes the lowered seventh of the Mixolydian mode. The Mixolydian also appears in Lennon and McCartney's "Norwegian Wood" (1965) and in Johnny Nash's "I Can See Clearly Now" (1972). The lowered seventh, in fact, became a signature of the early **rock** era, in songs like "Goin' Out of My Head" (1964) and "Georgy Girl" (1966).

Exceedingly rare, however, are songs entirely in one of the church modes. One of the few to hold this distinction is Paul Simon's "The Sound of Silence" (1964), which is from beginning to end in the Dorian mode.

See also: Interval; Scale

MODE

Major and minor have been the modes of choice in popular music, with only occasional digressions into **modality**. Although the vast majority of popular songs are written in major **keys**, a significant number of songs are partly or wholly in minor.

At the turn of the century, passages in minor were rare, confined for the most part to **tangos** or to songs imported from **Italy**. "St. Louis Blues" (1914) was an early American exception, starting with a tango in G minor and continuing with two **blues** sections in the parallel major key of G. Minor keys were more commonly used in the **verse** of a song, with the **chorus** in the parallel major, as in "Gypsy Love Song" (1898), "Swanee" (1919), "The Desert Song" (1926), and "Sonny Boy" (1928).

One of the earliest songs with a chorus completely in minor is Irving Berlin's "Russian Lullaby" (1927), which begins in F minor, moves to the relative major of A-flat, and ends again with F minor. Among the many other songs in minor keys through the years are "Softly, as in a Morning Sunrise" (1928) and "Sealed With a Kiss" and "A Taste of Honey" (both 1960). In Berlin's song "Blue Skies," each principal strain modulates from the minor (D minor) to the relative major (F major). In his "Let's Face the Music and Dance" (1936), a similar device is used, modulating this time to the parallel major.

Cole Porter can arguably be called the Franz Schubert of American popular song, if only because, like Schubert, he often made use of the device of major-minor contrast. Many of his songs, including "Love for Sale" (1930), "My Heart Belongs to Daddy" (1938), and "I Love Paris" (1953), exploit this contrast by repeating similar motives in both major and minor. Among other Porter songs playing on the difference between the major and minor third are "Just One of Those Things" (1935), "Get Out of Town" (1938), "You'd Be So Nice to Come Home To" (1942), "So in Love" (1948), "From This Moment On" (1950), and "It's All Right With Me" (1953). Even his lyrics for "Ev'ry Time We Say Goodbye" (1944) exploit the difference: "how strange the change from major to minor."

Although few other composers made as much use of the minor mode as Porter, there are several outstanding examples: Jerome Kern's "Yesterdays" (1933), George Gershwin's "Summertime" and "It Ain't Necessarily So" (both from *Porgy and Bess*, 1935), Richard Rodgers's "My Funny Valentine" (1937) and "The Gentleman Is a Dope" (1947), and Arthur Schwartz's "Alone Together" (1932) and "You and the Night and the Music" (1934).

During the early **Depression years**, songs using the minor mode became more prevalent, perhaps reflecting the general mood of despair. Among them are "The Thrill Is Gone" (1931); "I Surrender Dear," "Lullaby of the Leaves," "Play, Fiddle, Play," and "Forty-Second Street" (all 1932); "The Boulevard of Broken Dreams" (1933); and "Mad About the Boy" (1935).

Many songs from **France** employ the minor mode; "Autumn Leaves" (1947), "Pigalle" (1948), and "Domino" (1951) are examples. In the French songs "Under Paris Skies" and "April in Portugal" (both 1953), there are alternating strains of major and minor. Michel Legrand uses major-minor contrast to good effect in many of his songs, including "I Will Wait for You" (1964), "The Windmills of Your Mind" (1968), "What Are You Doing the Rest of Your Life" (1969), and "The Way He Makes Me Feel" (1983). Songs from Britain occasionally exploit major-minor contrast as well; the Beatles' "And I Love Her" (1964) and "Eleanor Rigby" (1966) are examples.

The minor mode has also been used to enhance ethnic background in stage and film, as in "Charade," from the film of the same name (1963); "Sunrise, Sunset," from *Fiddler on the Roof* (1964); and "Speak Softly, Love," from *The Godfather* (1972). Despite this seeming diversity, it must be remembered that minor is not the mode of choice in popular song; in at least 95 percent of the songs, the "happier" mood of the major mode prevails.

Additional Songs in Minor

Anniversary Song (1946)
Bei Mir Bist Du Schön (Means That You're Grand) (1937)
Besame Mucho (1941)

Cry Me a River (1953)
Is You Is or Is You Ain't (Ma' Baby) (1943)
Nature Boy (1946)
The Shadow of Your Smile (1965)
This Masquerade (1972)
A Time for Us (1968)
Time in a Bottle (1971)

See also: Harmony; Interval; Scale

MODULATION

Modulation refers both to the process of moving from one tonal center to another and to the results of that movement, more properly known as tonality. In popular song, the procedures of modulation are well grounded in Western harmony: employing pivot chords, using passing modulations, or moving through the circle of fifths.

Jerome Kern was an acknowledged master of modulation; it permeates his output. "All the Things You Are" (1939), for example, has a verse in G major and a chorus in A-flat major, which begins with an F minor chord; the modulation between the two uses a C dominant-seventh chord as a pivot. The release of Kern's "I Won't Dance" (1935) also offers some interesting modulations, moving through such remote tonal areas as A-flat, D-flat, and B before returning to the C tonic by means of a descending circle of fifths. One of his last songs, "All Through the Day" (1946), in F major, is celebrated for its sudden movement to the tonality of A-flat just before its ending and its quick modulation back to the tonic using a C dominant-seventh as pivot chord.

Another interesting series of modulations occurs in the release of Richard Rodgers's "Have You Met Miss Jones?" (1937), which passes through the following chord changes before returning to its F major tonic: B-flat, D-flat seventh, G-flat, A seventh, D, D-flat seventh, G-flat, C seventh. Rodgers's "I Have Dreamed," from The King and I (1951), in E-flat major, repeats the principal theme in several different keys, F major and G major, before returning to its primary tonality. In similar fashion, the principal theme of "Climb Ev'ry Mountain," from The Sound of Music (1959), is stated in the dominant key of G major at its recapitulation, but nevertheless ends on the C tonic.

Notable examples of modulation exist throughout the literature of popular song. One might cite as an example Leonard Bernstein's "Somewhere," from West Side Story (1957). Written with a key signature of three flats, it starts with a B-flat major chord and modulates through such remote tonal centers as G-flat and C-flat before ending on A-flat major. So constant is the song's modulation that it does not contain a single E-flat major chord despite its key signature. Striking and continuous modulations also occur in such songs as "Up, Up

and Away" (1967), and the theme from the film Mahogany, "Do You Know Where You're Going To?" (1973).

See also: Chromaticism; Enharmonic Equivalence; Interval; Scale

MONEY

Songs about money have an ancient heritage; a favorite topic of the sixteenth century had to do with the advantages of being a beggar rather than a king. (A modern counterpart of that idea occurs in the 1927 song "The Best Things in Life Are Free.") The temper of the times was very different during the Depression years of the 1930s, when not having money was not considered particularly advantageous. Not surprisingly, money, or its absence, became almost everyone's preoccupation at that time. This is reflected in a number of songs on the subject. One of them, "Ten Cents a Dance" (1930), is about a dance hostess who works "at the Palace Ballroom . . . at exactly a dime a throw." A year later, in 1931, three money songs appeared: the sprightly "I Found a Million Dollar Baby (In a Five and Ten Cent Store)"; the doleful "Minnie the Moocher"; and the joyful "I've Got Five Dollars"—the latter famous for its closing line: "Everything I've got belongs to you."

By 1932, in the depths of the Depression, "Brother, Can You Spare a Dime?" had become the hymn of the homeless and of the down and out. Two songs about money appeared in 1933, one a question, the other an affirmation: "Are You Makin' Any Money?" and "We're in the Money" (also known as "The Gold Diggers' Song"). Things were looking decidedly brighter by 1936, when "With Plenty of Money and You" appeared.

With the return of generally good times, nickels and dimes lost their interest as inherent objects of desire, although possessing them still might lead to better things if one tossed them into a fountain, as in "Three Coins in the Fountain" (1954). Wishful thinking is also the substance of "If I Were a Rich Man," from Fiddler on the Roof (1964).

Through the years, a number of songs have been concerned with the idea of being penniless but in love. They are in a wide range of styles, from "I Can't Give You Anything But Love" (1928) to "I Got Plenty o' Nuttin'" (1935); from "I Got the Sun in the Morning" (1946) to "Can't Buy Me Love" (1964).

No discussion of money would be complete without mentioning three "penny" songs, all using the coin symbolically. The theme from The Threepenny Opera, better known as "Mack the Knife," (1952) is a famous song taken from Kurt Weill's outstanding Berlin success Die Dreigroschenoper (1928), with a libretto adapted by Bertolt Brecht from The Beggar's Opera, written in 1728 by John Gay. "Pennies From Heaven," with its opening line, "Every time it rains, it rains pennies from heaven," is of course about counting one's blessings. "Penny Lane" (1967), by John Lennon and Paul McCartney, refers to a thoroughfare in their home town of Liverpool. In the same year, the Beatles wrote another "count your blessings" song, "Baby, You're a Rich Man."

Additional Songs

Big Spender (1965)
I've Got Sixpence (As We Go Rolling Home) (1941)
Money (That's What I Want) (1959)
Money for Nothing (1985)
Money Honey (1953)
The Money Song (1967)
The Money Tree (1956)
Rags to Riches (1953)
Rich Girl (1976)
When the Idle Poor Become the Idle Rich (1946)

MONTHS

More songs have been written about the months of April and September than about all other months combined. This is probably due to a combination of factors: the euphony of the very names of those months, their often commendable **weather**, and the changing **seasons** they represent.

Songs about April include the hardy perennial "April Showers," written in 1921, assuring us that though April showers may come our way, "they bring the flowers that bloom in May"; Vernon Duke's striking "April in Paris" of 1932; the haunting "I'll Remember April," written in 1941; the Portuguese import "April in Portugal" of 1953; "April Love," sung by Pat Boone in the 1957 film of the same name; and "The April Fools," written by Hal David and Burt Bacharach in 1969.

September is represented by the enduring ballad "September in the Rain," written in 1937, and by one of the most outstanding songs of all: "September Song," a perfect blend of music and lyrics concocted by Maxwell Anderson and Kurt Weill in 1938. In its poignant lyrics, the months of May, September, November, and December are used to symbolize different stages of life. September is also represented in a series of songs of more recent vintage: "See You in September" (1959), "Try to Remember" ("The kind of September") (1960), "It Might as Well Rain Until September" (1962), "Sweet September" (1962), and "The September of My Years" (1965).

Songs comparing one month with another form an interesting subgenre. They include "Will You Love Me in December as You Do in May?" (1905) and "June in January" (1934).

June makes appearances in the 1902 waltz "On a Sunday Afternoon," the lyrics of which continue: "In the merry month of June"; in the 1924 song "June Night," which begins: "Just give me a June night, the moonlight and you"; in "How About You?" of 1941,

which opens with the words: "I Like New York in June, how about you?"; and in "June Is Bustin' Out All Over," a hit song from the Broadway show *Carousel* of 1945.

May has at least one lovely song to its credit: Hoagy Carmichael's "One Morning in May," written in 1933. December is represented by "December 1963 (Oh What a Night)" of 1975. As for the months of February, March, July, August, October, and November, they are conspicuous by their absence. Apparently, very cold, very hot, or very dreary months are nothing to sing about.

See also: **Age**

MOODS

Moods are usually transitory and adapt well to popular song, itself a transitory art. Especially popular as subjects in the 1930s and 1940s, moods are often self-explanatory, as in two songs of 1935: "In a Sentimental Mood" and "I'm in the Mood for Love." Less specific is the mood of "In the Mood" (1939), but it would appear to be one of **happiness**. It remains a perennial favorite, usually in its original Glenn Miller arrangement. Somewhat darker moods are expressed in "Mood Indigo" (1931) and "Can't Get Out of This Mood" (1942).

See also: **Feeling; Love; Sentiment**

MOON

The moon and **love** seem to have a symbiotic relationship with one another in popular song: each benefits by the presence of the other. The relationship is of long standing, going back to "My Sweetheart's the Man in the Moon" (1892) and "Shine On, Harvest Moon" (1908).

The legendary attraction of the moon to lovers is exemplified in such songs as "Moonglow" (1934), "I Wished on the Moon" (1935), and "Moon Love" (1939). Conversely, when things go awry with love, the moon is treated ironically, as in "Racing With the Moon" (1941), "Old Devil Moon" (1946), and "Full Moon and Empty Arms" (1946).

Over the years the moon has been known to vary in **color**: "By the Light of the Silvery Moon" (1909), "Blue Moon" (1934), "The Moon Was Yellow" (1934), "Polka Dots and Moonbeams" (1940); location: "Carolina Moon" (1928), "Moon Over Miami" (1935), "The Moon of Manakoora" (1937); distance: "How High the Moon" (1940), "Fly Me to the Moon" (1954); and orientation: "When the Moon Comes Over the Mountain" (1931), "East of the Sun (And West of the Moon)" (1934). In 1961 it was combined metaphorically with another favorite subject of song, the **river**, to fashion "Moon River"; a song, introduced in the film *Breakfast at Tiffany's*, which has shown great staying power.

Then there is the moonlight a subject always dear

to a poet's heart. The reflection of moonlight, on the water has inspired such songs as "(On) Moonlight Bay" (1912) and "Moonlight on the Ganges" (1926). In tandem with **flowers**, it has led to "Moonlight and Roses (Bring Mem'ries of You)" (1925) and "Orchids in the Moonlight" (1933). Shining on a loved one, the moonlight has brightened up a host of love songs: "(Just Give Me a) June Night, (The Moonlight and You)" (1924), "My Moonlight Madonna" (1933), "In the Chapel in the Moonlight" (1936), "Moonlight Serenade" (1939), "Moonlight Cocktail" (1941) and "Moonlight Becomes You" (1942). Shining on a state famous for its skiing, it has also inspired a jazz classic: "Moonlight in Vermont" (1944).

Judging from these songs, love would be difficult without a moon. This is confirmed in "It's Only a Paper Moon" (1933), where the moon is "shining over a cardboard sky," when the lyrics go on to say: "But it wouldn't be make believe if you belonged to me." Finally, with "No Moon at All" (1949), love hasn't a chance.

Additional Songs

The Alabama Song (Moon of Alabama) (1928)
Allegheny Moon (1956)
Bad Moon Rising (1969)
Blue Moon of Kentucky (1947)
Everyone's Gone to the Moon (1965)
Magic Is the Moonlight (1930)
Moon Shadow (1970)
Moonlight Masquerade (1941)
Sail Along Silvery Moon (1937)
Silver Moon (1927)
Wabash Moon (1931)

See also: **Heaven; Sky; Stars**

MOTHERS

Some of the most sentimental songs of the nineteenth century were on the themes of **home** and motherhood, and this tradition continued well into the twentieth century. Sometimes the word "mother" was literally spelled out, as in the ballad "M-O-T-H-E-R (A Word That Means the World to Me)" (1915). At other times, the maternal image was cleverly disguised, as in "I Want a Girl Just Like the Girl That Married Dear Old Dad" (1911). The arrival of immigrants around the turn of the century also led to a flurry of ethnic "mother" songs, like "Mother Machree" (1910), "Ireland Must Be Heaven for My Mother Came From There" (1916), and "My Yiddishe Momme" (1925).

With the coming of the **Roaring Twenties**, the subject of motherhood took a decided turn away from devotion and toward frivolity in such songs as "Ma! (He's Making Eyes at Me)" (1921) and "(Does Your Mother Know You're Out) Cecilia?" (1925). This humorous approach to motherhood continued with nov-

elty songs like "Oh Mama (The Butcher Boy)" (1938), "Pistol Packin' Mama" (1943), "I Saw Mommy Kissing Santa Claus" (1952), "Hello Muddah, Hello Fadduh" (1963), and "Look What They've Done to My Song, Ma" (1970). Mothers also appeared in several rumbas, including "Mama Inez" (1931) and "Mama Yo Quiero (I Want My Mama)" (1940).

Yet the old sentimental tradition of motherhood died hard; it survived in such sentimental ballads as "My Mammy," sung by Al Jolson in 1918; "My Mother's Eyes," sung by George Jessel in 1928; and "Did Your Mother Come From Ireland?," sung by Bing Crosby in 1936.

Additional Songs

Break the News to Mother (1897)
If Momma Was Married (1959)
Mama (1946)
Mama Can't Buy You Love (1977)
Mama Told Me (Not to Come) (1966)
Mama Tried (1968)
Mother Was a Lady, or If Jack Were Only Here (1896)
Mother-in-Law (1961)
Mother's Little Helper (1966)
Sometimes I Feel Like a Motherless Child (1918)
Tell Mama (1968)
You Remind Me of My Mother (1922)

See also: **Childhood; Fathers; Woman**

MOTOWN

The most successful black record company in the history of popular music, Motown (the name is a contraction for "Motor Town") was founded and developed in Detroit by Berry Gordy, Jr. Under his autocratic control, Motown dominated the charts in the 1960s by successfully combining elements of black **gospel** and **blues** roots with mainstream **pop**.

Gordy's musical career moved from his owning a jazz record shop to his being a **rhythm and blues** songwriter in the early 1950s. His first hit was "Reet Petite" (1957), an uptempo number recorded by Jackie Wilson for the Brunswick label. He quickly followed this with several other songs for Wilson, including one of the singer's biggest hits, "Lonely Teardrops" (1958). Berry then moved into independent production; with local Detroit singer Mary Johnson, he wrote and produced several records through United Artists—two of which became Top Ten hits—and with Barrett Strong (later to become a Motown writer) he did "Money (That's What I Want)" (1959), probably the funkiest tune he has written, released on the Anna label, owned by Gordy's sister.

His success prompted him to start his own label, Tamla. The label's first major hit was "Shop Around" (1960), by Smokey Robinson and the Miracles, another local act, which climbed to the Number Two position on the pop charts. Gordy and Robinson both wrote hit material for the growing list of artists signed by the company. By 1962, Gordy had inaugurated two more labels, Motown and Gordy (later, Soul, V.I.P., and Rare Earth were added), and had signed such important pop stars as Mary Wells, the Marvelettes, and Marvin Gaye. Soon Stevie Wonder, the Four Tops, Jr. Walker and the All-Stars, the Supremes, the Jackson 5, and others would also record for Motown.

Early on, Motown's records possessed a plurality of sounds almost as numerous as its artists. The Contours' R&B hit "Do You Love Me?," for example, was considerably raunchier than the Marvelettes' "Beechwood 4-5789" (both 1962), with its adolescent girl group sound. However, largely through the efforts of the songwriting team of Lamont Dozier, Brian Holland, and Eddie Holland, Motown began producing hits in a manner akin to the assembly-line production method of the city's big auto manufacturers (Berry himself had at one point worked on the Ford line). In 1963, their song "Heat Wave," recorded by Martha and the Vandellas, initiated an astounding string of twenty-eight Top Twenty hits for Holland-Dozier-Holland in the short span of three years.

Emblematic of Motown's production method is the team's "I Can't Help Myself," a big hit for the Four Tops in 1965. They quickly followed it with the appropriately titled "It's the Same Old Song," based on the same chord progressions as the earlier song; it, too, was a Top Ten hit. Through the consistent work of Holland, Dozier, and Holland, as well as other producer-writers like Smokey Robinson, Norman Whitfield, and Nickolas Ashford and Valerie Simpson, Motown's hit ratio by 1966 was approximately 75 percent.

All the while, Berry himself exerted what he called "quality control" over the company, its artists, and its product. For example, even though the recording artists were producing millions of dollars in record sales for the company, many of them were given relatively small allowances so they would not spend their money unwisely. Motown's studio band, Earl Van Dyke and the Soul Brothers, was paid a flat salary and forced to toil anonymously behind the star vocalists. (Even Jr. Walker, the company's one instrumental star, was eventually coaxed into singing.) Berry established his "International Talent Management Incorporated" (I.T.M.I.), described by one writer as "a kind of finishing school for Motown stars," and pushed his artists into upscale venues like supper clubs and Las Vegas. The Supremes epitomized Berry's approach; discovered and groomed by him, they climbed from Detroit's ghetto to become the decade's most potent icon of upscale black glamour, garnering twelve Number One hits along the way. Among other prolific Motown groups were the Temptations, the Jackson 5, and Martha and the Vandellas.

Eventually some of the artists rebelled. In 1967,

Holland, Dozier, and Holland, discontent with Berry's tight financial management over royalties, left the company. In 1971, both Stevie Wonder and Marvin Gaye, with growing musical ambitions that exceeded the formula limitations imposed by Motown, negotiated new contracts giving them greater artistic control. Gordy himself was spending more time with Diana Ross, preparing her for a Hollywood acting career. Other major artists eventually left Motown, and finally, Philadelphia International's Gamble and Huff, pioneering a smoother **disco** sound, surpassed Motown in record sales.

Motown's sound was characterized by a winning combination of the **call-and-response** vocal and the use of tambourines (both gospel elements), rhythm and blues horns, a firm **rock** back-beat, string arrangements played by the Detroit Symphony Orchestra, and a vocal style that mixed blues shouting with smooth pop delivery. Motown's lasting legacy is that the success of this stylistic mixture brought black music out of the "race" category and made R&B acceptable to the mainstream white audience.

Additional Songs

ABC (1970)
Baby Love (1964)
Back in My Arms Again (1965)
Come See About Me (1964)
Dancing in the Street (1964)
I Can't Get Next to You (1969)
I Can't Help Myself (1965)
I Hear a Symphony (1965)
I Heard It Through the Grapevine (1966)
I Want You Back (1969)
I'll Be There (1970)
Just My Imagination (Running Away With Me) (1971)
Love Child (1968)
The Love You Save (1970)
My Girl (1964)
My Guy (1964)
Papa Was a Rollin' Stone (1972)
Reach Out I'll Be There (1966)
Some Day We'll Be Together (1969)
Stop! In the Name of Love (1965)
You Can't Hurry Love (1966)
You Keep Me Hangin' On (1966)

Barry Keith Grant

Bibliography

Garland, Phyl. *The Sound of Soul: The Story of Black Music.* 1971.

Hirshey, Gerri. *Nowhere to Run: The Story of Soul Music.* 1984.

See also: **Performer-Songwriters; Singing Groups; Soul**

MOUNTAINS

Mountains have a place in popular song, as do their smaller cousins, hills. Often a folk element is involved. "She'll Be Comin' Round the Mountain" (1899) and "On Top of Old Smokey" (1951) were adapted from folk songs. Other songs, like "The Trail of the Lonesome Pine" (1913)—which begins "In the Blue Ridge Mountains of Virginia"—and "When It's Springtime in the Rockies" (1929), have a folk-like flavor.

Somewhat more sophisticated are two songs written in 1926: "Mountain Greenery" and "I'd Climb the Highest Mountain." The former was one of the first efforts of the songwriting team of Lorenz Hart and Richard Rodgers; the latter is based on Anton Dvořák's "Humoresque." In 1931, a waltz called "When the Moon Comes Over the Mountain" was introduced; it became famous as Kate Smith's theme song. This was followed two years later by "I Like Mountain Music."

Starting in the late 1930s, mountains were frequently reduced to hills. A lovely song called "The Folks Who Live on the Hill" emanated from the film *High, Wide and Handsome* (1937). From another film, *The Singing Hill*, came "Blueberry Hill" (1940), a song that has been often revived. "High on a Windy Hill" was a favorite of the big bands in 1940. Subsequent "hill" songs include "The Heather on the Hill" (1947), "Mocking Bird Hill" (1949), "The Call of the Far-Away Hills" (1952), and the Beatles' "The Fool on the Hill" (1967).

At the same time, mountains continued to exert their influence. Ira Gershwin used them as a contrast to **enduring love** in "Love Is Here to Stay" (1938): "In time, the Rockies may tumble, Gibraltar may crumble." "Bali Ha'i," from *South Pacific* (1949), is a song about a sacred mountain on the island of Moorea. Other mountains serve as sources of **inspiration**: "Climb Ev'ry Mountain" (1959), "Gonna Build a Mountain" (1961), "Anyone Can Move a Mountain" (1966).

Additional Songs

Ain't No Mountain High Enough (1967)
Foggy Mountain Breakdown (1950)
The Mountains High (1961)
Night on Disco Mountain (1977)
Over the Mountain Across the Sea (1957)
Rocky Mountain High (1972)
(There'll Be Blue Birds Over) The White Cliffs of Dover (1941)

   See also: Ocean; Rivers

MOVIES. SEE FILM MUSIC; FILM MUSICALS

MUSIC

Hundreds of popular songs have been written on the **subject** of music or on its various aspects. Irving Berlin used music as a background for **romance** in several songs, including "Say It With Music" (1921), "The Song Is Ended But the Melody Lingers On" (1927), "Soft Lights and Sweet Music" (1932), and "Let's Face the Music and Dance" (1936). In "A Pretty Girl Is Like a Melody," Berlin compares a woman to a "strain of a haunting refrain." In "Play a Simple Melody" (1914), he contrapuntally juxtaposes an old-fashioned melody with an "up-to-date" one in syncopated ragtime.

Many other songwriters have also been attracted to the subject of music, as exemplified in such lasting ballads as "You and the Night and the Music" (1934), "Music, Maestro, Please" (1938), "We Could Make Such Beautiful Music (Together)" (1940), "Strange Music" (1944), and "The Sound of Music" (1959). There have also been several notable **novelty songs** on the subject, including "The Music Goes 'Round and 'Round" (1935), "Music! Music! Music!" (1950), and "Music to Watch Girls By" (1966).

In addition, songs have been written about such elements of music as **melody** ("I Whistle a Happy Tune," 1951), **harmony** ("Play That Barbershop Chord," (1910), **rhythm** ("Fascinating Rhythm," 1924), and **meter** ("Two Hearts in Three Quarter Time," 1930). In the musical play *The Sound of Music* (1959), there is even a memorable song about solfeggio called "Do-Re-Mi."

Certain genres of music have been used as subjects of popular song as well, among them the *waltz*: ("Casey would waltz with a strawberry blonde, and") "The Band Played On" (1895); the rhapsody: "I Hear a Rhapsody" (1941); the symphony: "Symphony" (1945); and the serenade: "Serenade in Blue" (1942).

But the most favored musical genre of all is song itself. Among the many songs about song are: "The Song of Songs" (1914), "Song of Love" (1921), "With a Song in My Heart" (1929), "Without a Song" (1929), "The Song Is You" (1932), "I Let a Song Go Out of My Heart" (1938), "I've Heard That Song Before" (a double entendre; 1942), "Song Sung Blue" (1972), "I Write the Songs" (1974), (Hey Won't You Play) Another Somebody Done Somebody Wrong Song" (1975), and "They're Playing Our Song" (1978).

Additional Songs

Autumn Serenade (1945)
Beat Me Daddy, Eight to the Bar (1940)
Brian's Song (1972)
The Donkey Serenade (1937)
Don't Play That Song (You Lied) (1962)
I Hear a Symphony (1975)
I Hear Music (1940)
I'd Like to Teach the World to Sing (1971)
It Don't Mean a Thing (If It Ain't Got That Swing) (1932)
It's the Same Old Song (1965)
Johnny One Note (1937)
Killing Me Softly With His Song (1973)
A Lover's Concerto (1965)
Manhattan Serenade (1928)

The Music of the Night (1986)
My Melody of Love (1973)
The Old Refrain (1915)
Our Song (1937)
Penthouse Serenade (When We're Alone) (1931)
Rock and Roll Music (1957)
Serenade (1924)
Serenade in the Night (1936)
Sunrise Serenade (1938)
The Sweetest Sounds (1962)
A Very Special Love Song (1974)

See also: Instrumentation

MUSIC PUBLISHING. *SEE* TIN PAN ALLEY

MUSIC VIDEOS. *SEE* TELEVISION

MUSICAL COMEDY

Musical comedy grew out of the **minstrel show** and **vaudeville** toward the end of the nineteenth century. Developing principally in New York City, it became a peculiarly American phenomenon, reaching its apogee during the 1920s and 1930s. In style, musical comedy is similar to **operetta**, consisting of lighthearted songs and a flimsy libretto. Unlike operetta, however, the plot often has contemporary overtones and the songs are usually more akin to **Tin Pan Alley** than to opera. As with other genres of the musical theater, it is sometimes difficult to draw a line of distinction between an operetta, a musical comedy, or a **musical play** (a genre combining features of both). Aside from the hundreds of lasting **show tunes** introduced in the medium (*see* Table 11), musical comedy's importance lies in the fact that is served as an incubator and training ground for **lyricists** and **composers**, many of whom went on to write songs for more serious theatrical works and for **film musicals**. Outstanding among these songwriters were George M. Cohan, Jerome Kern, George Gershwin, Ira Gershwin, Vincent Youmans, Richard Rodgers, Lorenz Hart, Cole Porter, Frank Loesser, Kurt Weill, Stephen Sondheim, Jule Styne, and Leonard Bernstein.

An early precursor of musical comedy was the play *A Trip to Chinatown* (1892), in which the songs "After the Ball" and "The Bowery" were interpolated. During the first decade of the new century, the **composer-lyricist** and performer George M. Cohan produced a series of musical comedies, including three hits: *Little Johnny Jones* (1904), *Forty-Five Minutes From Broadway* (1906), and *George Washington, Jr.* (1906), which introduced the standards "Give My Regards to Broadway," "The Yankee Doodle Boy," "Mary's a Grand Old Name," and "You're a Grand Old Flag," among others.

Jerome Kern was the next important composer of musical comedies. In fact, he revolutionized the course of the musical theater with his landmark song "They Didn't Believe Me," from *The Girl From Utah* (1914; *see* Landmarks of Stage and Screen). Over the next twenty years, Kern wrote the music for a string of musical comedies, including *Oh, Boy!* (1917), *Sally* (1920), and *Sunny* (1925), in which the songs "Till the Clouds Roll By" (1917), "Look for the Silver Lining" (1920), and "Who?" (1925) were first heard. After the historical success of *Show Boat* (1927)—widely considered to be the first musical play—Kern reverted to musical comedy in 1933 with *Roberta*, from which come the beautiful songs "Smoke Gets in Your Eyes," "The Touch of Your Hand," "Yesterdays," and "You're Devastating," all with lyrics by Otto Harbach.

George and Ira Gershwin wrote some of their most evocative songs for musical comedy. From their shows *Lady, Be Good!* (1924), *Oh, Kay!* (1926), and *Funny Face* (1927) come the standards "Oh, Lady Be Good" and "Fascinating Rhythm" (both 1924), "Someone to Watch Over Me" and "Clap Yo' Hands" (both 1926), and "He Loves and She Loves" and "'S Wonderful" (both 1927). In 1931, the Gershwins collaborated on *Girl Crazy*, which introduced four abiding standards: "Bidin' My Time," "But Not for Me," "Embraceable You," and "I Got Rhythm."

Vincent Youmans is best remembered as the composer of two pre-Depression musical comedies, *No, No, Nanette* (1925) and *Hit the Deck!* (1927), from which come the memorable songs "Tea for Two" and "I Want to Be Happy" (from the former), and "Hallelujah!" and "Sometimes I'm Happy" (from the latter).

Richard Rodgers and Lorenz Hart followed up their previous success in **revue** with several important musical comedies: *Dearest Enemy* (1925), *A Connecticut Yankee* (1927), *On Your Toes* (1936), *The Boys From Syracuse* (1938), and *Pal Joey* (1940). Songs from these shows include "Here in My Arms" (1925), "My Heart Stood Still" and "Thou Swell" (both 1927), "There's a Small Hotel" (1936), "Falling in Love With Love" and "This Can't Be Love" (both 1938), "I Could Write a Book" (1940), and "Bewitched" (1941).

The essence of musical comedy is perhaps best epitomized in Cole Porter's racy lyrics and sassy melodies. His career in musical comedy lasted over twenty years with such gems as *Paris* (1928), *Fifty Million Frenchmen* (1929), *The New Yorkers* (1930), *The Gay Divorce* (1932), *Jubilee* (1935), *Red, Hot and Blue!* (1936), *Leave It to Me!* (1938), *Du Barry Was a Lady* (1939), and *Mexican Hayride* (1944). Some of his most enduring songs come from these productions, including, to mention only a few, "Let's Do It (Let's Fall in Love)," "You Do Something to Me" (1929), "Night and Day" (1932), and "Begin the Beguine" (1935). But two Porter musicals were most productive: *Anything Goes* (1934) and *Kiss Me, Kate* (1948), which together brought forth at least nine standards, including "I Get a Kick Out of You" and

"You're the Top," from the former; and "So in Love" and "Wunderbar," from the latter.

Frank Loesser, another composer-lyricist, was responsible for three song-filled musical comedies: *Where's Charley?* (1948), *Guys and Dolls* (1950), and *How to Succeed in Business Without Really Trying* (1961). Stephen Sondheim served musical comedy in a dual capacity: as lyricist and as composer-lyricist. In the first capacity, he worked with Jule Styne on the score for *Gypsy* (1959); and in the second, he wrote the songs for *A Funny Thing Happened on the Way to the Forum* (1962), *Company* (1970), and *Follies* (1971).

Among other notable lyricists and composers of musical comedy were Ira Gershwin and Kurt Weill (*Lady in the Dark*, 1941), Ogden Nash and Kurt Weill (*One Touch of Venus*, 1943), Betty Comden, Adolph Green, and Leonard Bernstein (*On the Town*, 1944), Irving Berlin (*Annie Get Your Gun*, 1946), E. Y. Harburg and Burton Lane (*Finian's Rainbow*, 1947), Richard Adler and Jerry Ross (*The Pajama Game*, 1954, *Damn Yankees*, 1955), Meredith Willson (*The Music Man*, 1957), Lee Adams and Charles Strouse (*Bye Bye Birdie*, 1960), Jerry Herman (*Hello, Dolly!*, 1964; *Mame*, 1966), and Edward Kleban and Marvin Hamlisch (*A Chorus Line*, 1975).

Bibliography

Bordman, Gerald. *American Musical Comedy: From Adonis to Dreamgirls*. 1982.

Ewen, David, *New Complete Book of the American Musical Theater*. 1970.

Gottfried, Martin. *Broadway Musicals*. 1980.

Green, Stanley. *Encyclopedia of the Musical*. 1977.

TABLE 11

Songs Introduced in Musical Comedies

Annie (1977)
lyrics: Martin Charnin, music: Charles Strouse
Tomorrow

Annie Get Your Gun (1946)
lyrics and music: Irving Berlin
Doin' What Comes Natur'lly
The Girl That I Marry
I Got the Sun in the Morning
There's No Business Like Show Business
They Say It's Wonderful

Anything Goes (1934)
lyrics and music: Cole Porter
All Through the Night
Anything Goes
Blow, Gabriel, Blow
I Get a Kick Out of You
You're the Top

Babes in Arms (1937)
lyrics: Lorenz Hart, music: Richard Rodgers
I Wish I Were in Love Again
Johnny One Note
The Lady Is a Tramp
My Funny Valentine
Where or When?

Between the Devil (1937)
lyrics: Howard Dietz, music: Arthur Schwartz
By Myself
I See Your Face Before Me

Big Boy (1925)
lyrics and music: B. G. DeSylva, Joseph Meyer, Al Jolson
California, Here I Come
lyrics and music: B. G. De Sylva, Joseph Meyer
If You Knew Susie Like I Know Susie
lyrics and music: B. G. DeSylva, Lew Brown, Ray Henderson
It All Depends on You

The Boys From Syracuse (1938)
lyrics: Lorenz Hart, music: Richard Rodgers
Falling in Love With Love
This Can't Be Love

By Jupiter (1942)
lyrics: Lorenz Hart, music: Richard Rodgers
Ev'rything I've Got
Wait Till You See Her

Bye Bye Birdie (1960)
lyrics: Lee Adams, music Charles Strouse
A Lot of Livin' to Do
Put On a Happy Face

Cabin in the Sky (1940)
lyrics: John Latouche, music: Vernon Duke
Cabin in the Sky
Taking a Chance on Love

La Cage aux Folles (1983)
lyrics and music: Jerry Herman
The Best of Times
I Am What I Am

Call Me Madam (1950)
lyrics and music: Irving Berlin
It's a Lovely Day Today
You're Just in Love

Can-Can (1953)
lyrics and music: Cole Porter
Allez-Vous En, Go Away
C'est Magnifique
I Love Paris
It's All Right With Me

Carnival (1961)
lyrics and music: Bob Merrill
Love Makes the World Go Round

A Chorus Line (1975)
lyrics: Edward Kleban, music: Marvin Hamlisch
One
What I Did for Love

Company (1970)
lyrics and music: Stephen Sondheim
Another Hundred People
Side by Side by Side

A Connecticut Yankee (1927)
lyrics: Lorenz Hart, music: Richard Rodgers
My Heart Stood Still
Thou Swell

Damn Yankees (1955)
lyrics and music: Richard Adler, Jerry Ross
(You've Got to Have) Heart
Whatever Lola Wants

Dearest Enemy (1925)
lyrics: Lorenz Hart, music: Richard Rodgers
Here in My Arms

Do Re Mi (1960)
lyrics: Betty Comden, Adolph Green; music: Jule Styne
Make Someone Happy

Du Barry Was a Lady (1939)
lyrics and music: Cole Porter
Do I Love You?
Friendship

Face the Music (1932)
lyrics and music: Irving Berlin
Let's Have Another Cup of Coffee
Soft Lights and Sweet Music

The Fantasticks (1960)
lyrics: Tom Jones, music: Harvey Schmidt
Soon It's Gonna Rain
They Were You
Try to Remember

Fifty Million Frenchmen (1929)
lyrics and music: Cole Porter
You Do Something to Me
You've Got That Thing

Finian's Rainbow (1947)
lyrics: E. Y. Harburg, music: Burton Lane
How Are Things in Glocca Morra?
If This Isn't Love
Look to the Rainbow
Old Devil Moon
That Great Come-and-Get-It Day
When I'm Not Near the Girl I Love

Follies (1971)
lyrics and music: Stephen Sondheim
I'm Still Here
Losing My Mind

Follow the Girls (1944)
lyrics: Dan Shapiro, Milton Pascal; music: Philip Charig
I Wanna Get Married

Forty-Five Minutes From Broadway (1906)
lyrics and music: George M. Cohan
Forty-Five Minutes From Broadway
Mary's a Grand Old Name

Funny Face (1927)
lyrics: Ira Gershwin, music: George Gershwin
Funny Face
He Loves and She Loves
My One and Only
'S Wonderful

Funny Girl (1964)
lyrics: Bob Merrill, music: Jule Styne
Don't Rain on My Parade
People
You Are Woman

A Funny Thing Happened on the Way to the Forum (1962)
lyrics and music: Stephen Sondheim
Comedy Tonight

The Gay Divorce (1932)
lyrics and music: Cole Porter
Night and Day

Gentlemen Prefer Blondes (1949)
lyrics: Leo Robin, music: Jule Styne
Diamonds Are a Girl's Best Friend

George Washington, Jr. (1906)
lyrics and music: George M. Cohan
You're a Grand Old Flag

Girl Crazy (1931)
lyrics: Ira Gershwin, music: George Gershwin
Bidin' My Time
But Not for Me
Embraceable You
I Got Rhythm

The Girl Friend (1926)
lyrics: Lorenz Hart, music: George Gershwin
Blue Room
The Girl Friend
Mountain Greenery

The Girl From Utah (1914)
lyrics: Herbert Reynolds, music: Jerome Kern
They Didn't Believe Me

Good News (1927)
lyrics: B. G. DeSylva, Lew Brown; music: Ray Henderson
The Best Things in Life Are Free
The Varsity Drag

Guys and Dolls (1950)
lyrics and music: Frank Loesser
A Bushel and a Peck
Fugue for Tinhorns
Guys and Dolls
If I Were a Bell
I'll Know
I've Never Been in Love Before
Luck Be a Lady
Sit Down, You're Rockin' the Boat

Gypsy (1959)
lyrics: Stephen Sondheim, music: Jule Styne
All I Need Is the Girl
Everything's Coming Up Roses
Let Me Entertain You
Small World

Hair (1967)
lyrics: Gerome Ragni, James Rado; music: Galt MacDermot
Aquarius
Good Morning Starshine

Hello, Dolly! (1964)
lyrics and music: Jerry Herman
Hello Dolly

Hit the Deck (1927)
lyrics: Clifford Grey, Leo Robin; music: Vincent Youmans
Hallelujah!
Sometime's I'm Happy

How to Succeed in Business Without Really Trying (1961)
lyrics and music: Frank Loesser
I Believe in You

I Married an Angel (1938)
lyrics: Lorenz Hart, music: Richard Rodgers
I Married an Angel
Spring Is Here

I'd Rather Be Right (1937)
lyrics: Lorenz Hart, music: Richard Rodgers
Have You Met Miss Jones?

Irene (1919)
lyrics: Joseph McCarthy, music: Harry Tierney
Alice Blue Gown
Irene

Jubilee (1935)
lyrics and music: Cole Porter
Begin the Beguine
Just One of Those Things

Jumbo (1935)
lyrics: Lorenz Hart, music: Richard Rodgers
Little Girl Blue
The Most Beautiful Girl in the World
My Romance

Kiss Me, Kate (1948)
lyrics and music: Cole Porter
Always True to You (In My Fashion)
Another Op'nin', Another Show
Brush Up Your Shakespeare
I Hate Men
So in Love
Why Can't You Behave?
Wunderbar

Lady, Be Good! (1924)
lyrics: Ira Gershwin, music: George Gershwin
Fascinating Rhythm
Oh, Lady Be Good

Lady in the Dark (1941)
lyrics: Ira Gershwin, music: Kurt Weill
My Ship
Jenny
This Is New

Leave It to Jane (1917)
lyrics: P. G. Wodehouse, music: Jerome Kern
The Siren's Song

Leave It to Me! (1938)
lyrics and music: Cole Porter
From Now On
My Heart Belongs to Daddy

Little Jessie James (1925)
lyrics: Harlan Thompson, music: Harry Archer
I Love You

Little Johnny Jones (1904)
lyrics and music: George M. Cohan
Give My Regards to Broadway
The Yankee Doodle Boy

Love Life (1948)
lyrics: Alan Jay Lerner, music: Kurt Weill
Green-Up Time
Here I'll Stay

Madame Sherry (1910)
lyrics: Otto Harbach, music: Karl Hoschna
Every Little Movement
Put Yours Arms Around Me, Honey

Mame (1966)
lyrics and music: Jerry Herman
If He Walked Into My Life
Mame

Mary (1920)
lyrics: Otto Harbach, music: Louis A. Hirsch
The Love Nest

Me and Juliet (1953)
lyrics: Oscar Hammerstein II, music: Richard Rodgers
No Other Love

Me and My Girl (1937)
lyrics and music: Douglas Furber, Noel Gay, Arthur Rose
Lambeth Walk
Me and My Girl

Mexican Hayride (1944)
lyrics and music: Cole Porter
I Love You

Mr. Wonderful (1956)
lyrics and music: Jerry Bock, Larry Holofcener, George Weiss
Mr. Wonderful
Too Close for Comfort

Music in the Air (1932)
lyrics: Oscar Hammerstein II, music: Jerome Kern
I've Told Ev'ry Little Star
The Song Is You

The Music Man (1957)
lyrics and music: Meredith Willson
Goodnight My Someone
Lida Rose
Seventy-Six Trombones
Till There Was You

The New Yorkers (1930)
lyrics and music: Cole Porter
Love for Sale

No, No, Nanette (1924)
lyrics: Irving Caesar, music: Vincent Youmans
I Want to Be Happy
Tea for Two

No Strings (1962)
lyrics and music: Richard Rodgers
No Strings
The Sweetest Sounds

Oh, Boy! (1917)
lyrics: P. G. Wodehouse, Jerome Kern; music: Jerome Kern
Till the Clouds Roll By

Oh, Kay! (1926)
lyrics: Ira Gershwin, music: George Gershwin
Clap Yo' Hands
Do, Do, Do
Maybe
Someone to Watch Over Me

On the Town (1944)
lyrics: Betty Comden, Adolph Green; music: Leonard
Bernstein
Lonely Town
Lucky to Be Me
New York, New York

On Your Toes (1936)
lyrics: Lorenz Hart, music: Richard Rodgers
Glad to Be Unhappy
There's a Small Hotel

One Touch of Venus (1943)
lyrics: Ogden Nash, music: Kurt Weill
Speak Low

Out of This World (1950)
lyrics and music: Cole Porter
From This Moment On

The Pajama Game (1954)
lyrics and music: Richard Adler, Jerry Ross
Hernando's Hideaway
Hey There
Steam Heat

Pal Joey (1940)
lyrics: Lorenz Hart, music: Richard Rodgers
Bewitched
I Could Write a Book

Panama Hattie (1940)
lyrics and music: Cole Porter
Let's Be Buddies

Paris (1928)
lyrics and music: Cole Porter
Let's Do It (Let's Fall in Love)

Red, Hot and Blue (1936)
lyrics and music: Cole Porter
Down in the Depths on the Ninetieth Floor
It's D'Lovely

The Red Mill (1906)
lyrics: Henry Blossom, music: Victor Herbert
Because You're You
Every Day Is Ladies' Day With Me
The Streets of New York (In Old New York)

Revenge With Music (1934)
lyrics: Howard Dietz, music: Arthur Schwartz
If There Is Someone Lovelier Than You
You and the Night and the Music

Roberta (1933)
lyrics: Otto Harbach, music: Jerome Kern
Let's Begin
Lovely to Look At
Smoke Gets in Your Eyes
The Touch of Your Hand

Yesterdays
You're Devastating

Sally (1920)
lyrics: B. G. DeSylva, music: Jerome Kern
Look for the Silver Lining

Silk Stockings (1955)
lyrics and music: Cole Porter
All of You

Simple Simon (1930)
lyrics: Lorenz Hart, music: Richard Rodgers
Dancing on the Ceiling
Ten Cents a Dance

Sinbad (1918)
lyrics: Sam M. Lewis, Joe Young; music: Jean Schwartz
Rock-A-Bye Your Baby With a Dixie Melody
lyrics: Irving Caesar, music: George Gershwin
Swanee

Sunny (1925)
lyrics: Otto Harbach, Oscar Hammerstein II; music: Jerome
Kern
Sunny
Who?

Too Many Girls (1939)
lyrics: Lorenz Hart, music: Richard Rodgers
I Didn't Know What Time It Was

A Trip to Chinatown (1892)
lyrics and music: Charles K. Harris
After the Ball
lyrics: Charles H. Hoyt, music: Percy Gaunt
The Bowery

Very Warm for May (1939)
lyrics: Oscar Hammerstein II, music: Jerome Kern
All the Things You Are

Wake Up and Dream (1929)
lyrics and music: Cole Porter
What Is This Thing Called Love?

Where's Charley? (1948)
lyrics and music: Frank Loesser
My Darling, My Darling
Once in Love With Amy

Whoopee (1928)
lyrics: Gus Kahn, music: Walter Donaldson
Love Me or Leave Me
Makin' Whoopee

Wildcat (1960)
lyrics: Carolyn Leigh, music: Cy Coleman
Hey, Look Me Over

Wish You Were Here (1952)
lyrics and music: Harold Rome
Wish You Were Here

Wonderful Town (1953)
lyrics: Betty Comden, Adolph Green; music: Leonard
Bernstein
Ohio

You Never Know (1938)
lyrics and music: Cole Porter
At Long Last Love

MUSICAL PLAYS

A musical play can perhaps best be described as a stage work more serious in tone than a **musical comedy** and more dramatic in substance than an **operetta**. Some musical plays of the late twentieth century are, in fact, practically indistinguishable from **opera**. One of the hallmarks of the musical play is its successful integration of songs within the plot. Yet many songs that originated in musical plays stand on their own as standards (*see* Table 12). As is the case with other musical works for the stage, the lines of distinction between genres frequently tend to blur; this is particularly so between the genres of musical play, opera, and operetta.

The show *Oklahoma!*, which opened in New York in 1943, has sometimes been called the first musical play. However, it was not without precedent as an integrated musical. Oscar Hammerstein II, creator of both its book and lyrics, had also written the book and lyrics of an integrated show sixteen years previously. *Show Boat*, a landmark musical show based on Edna Ferber's novel of the same name, had an unforgettable score by Jerome Kern which included such future standards as "Bill," "Can't Help Lovin' Dat Man," "Make Believe," "Ol' Man River," and "Why Do I Love You?" On the basis of these two works alone, Hammerstein can indeed be called the founding father and chief architect of the musical play.

The Gershwin brothers, Ira and George, also participated in several musical plays. Two of them, both political satires, reached Broadway in 1930 and 1931 respectively. The first, *Strike Up the Band*, presented the lasting songs "I've Got a Crush on You," "Soon," and the title song, among others. From the second, *Of Thee I Sing*, came such songs as "Love Is Sweeping the Country," "Who Cares?," and the title song.

Oklahoma! can be considered a landmark musical in more ways than one. It has been called a "folk operetta" as well as a musical play, partly because it deals with the real world rather than with the imaginary world of musical comedy or operetta. Its music, by Richard Rodgers, is frequently folklike in quality, particularly in such lasting numbers as "Oh, What a Beautiful Mornin'," "People Will Say We're in Love," "The Surrey With the Fringe on Top," and the title song.

The partnership of Rodgers and Hammerstein revolutionized the musical theater through their subsequent shows, especially *Carousel* (1945), *South Pacific* (1949), *The King and I* (1951), and *The Sound of Music* (1959). The first, a mixture of tragedy and fantasy based on Ferenc Molnar's *Liliom*, introduced the lyrical ballad "If I Loved You" and the hymn-like "You'll Never Walk Alone." *South Pacific*, derived from a story in James Michener's *Tales of the South Pacific*, had one of the most song-rich scores ever written, including the standards "Bali Ha'i," "I'm Gonna Wash That Man Right Outa My Hair," "A Wonderful Guy," "Some Enchanted Evening,"

and "Younger Than Springtime."

The King and I, based on the book *Anna and the King of Siam*, brought a note of exoticism to the musical theater in a tale about a governess to the children of the Siamese King. Its memorable score included the songs "Getting to Know You," "Hello, Young Lovers," "I Whistle a Happy Tune," "Shall We Dance?," "Something Wonderful," and "We Kiss in a Shadow." Rodgers and Hammerstein's final **collaboration**, *The Sound of Music*, was based on the book *The Trapp Family Singers* and was set in Austria shortly before the German invasion of 1938. Its sentimental score included the favorites "Climb Ev'ry Mountain," "Edelweiss," "My Favorite Things," and the title song.

Another songwriting team important in the development of the musical play was that of Alan Jay Lerner and Frederick Loewe. Among their most popular shows were *My Fair Lady* (1956) and *Camelot* (1960). Based on George Bernard Shaw's *Pygmalion*, *My Fair Lady* combined an extraordinarily strong story with a moving score, including the songs "Get Me to the Church on Time," "I Could Have Danced All Night," "I've Grown Accustomed to Her Face," and "On the Street Where You Live." *Camelot*, derived from the legends of King Arthur and T. H. White's *The Once and Future King*, had a less successful but nonetheless compelling score including the title song and the ballad "If Ever I Would Leave You."

West Side Story, which opened in New York in 1957, is unquestionably one of the most important works ever produced for the musical theater. Based on Shakespeare's *Romeo and Juliet*—updated to involve a feud between Puerto Ricans and native-born white New Yorkers—it offered a strong plot, distinctive dancing, and a superior score with music by Leonard Bernstein and lyrics by Stephen Sondheim. Among its evocative songs were "I Feel Pretty," "Maria," "Somewhere," and "Tonight."

Several quasi-operettas with music and lyrics credited to Robert Wright and George Forrest were derived from the music of the **classics**. Edvard Grieg was the real star of *Song of Norway* (1944), a fictionalized account of the Norwegian composer's life. Its most famous song was "Strange Music." The music of the Russian composer Alexander Borodin was adapted for the extravaganza *Kismet* in 1953. Set in ancient Bagdad, its memorable score include "And This Is My Beloved," "Baubles, Bangles and Beads," and "Stranger in Paradise."

Among other important musical plays were *The Most Happy Fella* (1956), *Fiddler on the Roof* (1964), *Man of La Mancha* (1965), and *A Little Night Music* (1973). The late 1970s and 1980s saw an invasion of musical plays from abroad, including *Evita* (1978), *Cats* (1981), *Les Misérables* (1985), *The Phantom of the Opera* (1986), and *Aspects of Love* (1989); many of them were closely akin to opera.

See also: **Landmarks of Stage and Screen**

Bibliography

Bordman, Gerald. *American Operetta: From H.M.S. Pinafore to Sweeney Todd.* 1981.

Ewen, David. *New Complete Book of the American Musical Theater.* 1970.

Gottfried, Martin. *Broadway Musicals.* 1980.

Green, Stanley. *Encyclopedia of the Musical.* 1977.

Jackson, Arthur. *The Book of Musicals: From Showboat to Evita.* 1979.

Laufe, Abe. *Broadway's Greatest Musicals.* 1978.

Mast, Gerald. *Can't Help Singin': The American Musical on Stage and Screen.* 1987.

TABLE 12

Songs Introduced in Musical Plays[*]

Allegro (1947)
lyrics: Oscar Hammerstein II, music: Richard Rodgers
A Fellow Needs a Girl
The Gentleman Is a Dope
So Far
You Are Never Away

Aspects of Love (1989)
lyrics: Don Black and Charles Hart, music: Andrew Lloyd Webber
Anything But Lonely
Love Changes Everything

Brigadoon (1947)
lyrics: Alan Jay Lerner, music: Frederick Loewe
Almost Like Being in Love
Come to Me, Bend to Me
The Heather on the Hill
There But for You Go I

Camelot (1960)
lyrics: Alan Jay Lerner, music: Frederick Loewe
Camelot
Follow Me
How to Handle a Woman
I Loved You Once in Silence
If Ever I Would Leave You

Carousel (1945)
lyrics: Oscar Hammerstein II, music: Richard Rodgers
If I Loved You
June Is Bustin' Out All Over
Soliloquy
What's the Use of Wond'rin'?
When I Marry Mister Snow
You'll Never Walk Alone

Cats (1981)
lyrics: T. S. Eliot and Trevor Nunn, music: Andrew Lloyd Webber
Memory

Evita (1978)
lyrics: Tim Rice, music: Andrew Lloyd Webber
Don't Cry for Me, Argentina

Fanny (1954)
lyrics and music: Harold Rome
Fanny
I Have to Tell You
Restless Heart

Fiddler on the Roof (1964)
lyrics: Sheldon Harnick, music: Jerry Bock
If I Were a Rich Man
Matchmaker, Matchmaker
Sunrise, Sunset
To Life (L'Chaim)

The King and I (1951)
lyrics: Oscar Hammerstein II, music: Richard Rodgers
Getting to Know You
Hello, Young Lovers
I Have Dreamed
I Whistle a Happy Tune
Shall We Dance?
Something Wonderful
We Kiss in a Shadow

Kismet (1953)
lyrics and music: Robert Wright and George Forrest, based on the music of Alexander Borodin
And This Is My Beloved
Baubles, Bangles and Beads
Stranger in Paradise

A Little Night Music (1973)
lyrics and music: Stephen Sondheim
Send in the Clowns

Man of La Mancha (1965)
lyrics: Joe Darion, music: Mitch Leigh
Dulcinea
The Impossible Dream
Man of La Mancha

Les Misérables (1985)
English lyrics: Herbert Kretzmer, music: Claude-Michel Schönberg
Bring Him Home
I Dreamed a Dream
On My Own

The Most Happy Fella (1956)
lyrics and music: Frank Loesser
Big D
The Most Happy Fella
Standing on the Corner

My Fair Lady (1956)
lyrics: Alan Jay Lerner, music: Frederick Loewe
Get Me to the Church on Time
I Could Have Danced All Night
I'm an Ordinary Man
I've Grown Accustomed to Her Face
A Little Bit of Luck
On the Street Where You Live
The Rain in Spain

Show Me
Wouldn't It Be Loverly

Of Thee I Sing (1931)
lyrics: Ira Gershwin, music: George Gershwin
Love Is Sweeping the Country
Of Thee I Sing
Who Cares?

Oklahoma! (1943)
lyrics: Oscar Hammerstein II, music: Richard Rodgers
I Cain't Say No
Oh, What a Beautiful Mornin'
Oklahoma!
Out of My Dreams
People Will Say We're in Love
The Surrey With the Fringe on Top

Paint Your Wagon (1951)
lyrics: Alan Jay Lerner, music: Frederick Loewe
I Talk to the Trees
They Call the Wind Maria

The Phantom of the Opera (1986)
lyrics: Charles Hart, music: Andrew Lloyd Webber
All I Ask of You
The Music of the Night
The Phantom of the Opera
The Point of No Return
Prima Donna

Show Boat (1927)
lyrics: Oscar Hammerstein II, music: Jerome Kern
Bill
Can't Help Lovin' Dat Man
Here Comes the Show Boat
Make Believe
Ol' Man River
Why Do I Love You?
You Are Love

Song of Norway (1944)
lyrics and music: Robert Wright and George Forrest, based on
the music of Edvard Grieg

I Love You
Strange Music

The Sound of Music (1959)
lyrics: Oscar Hammerstein II, music: Richard Rodgers
Climb Ev'ry Mountain
Do-Re-Mi
Edelweiss
My Favorite Things
The Sound of Music

South Pacific (1949)
lyrics: Oscar Hammerstein II, music: Richard Rodgers
Bali Ha'i
A Cock-Eyed Optimist
Dites-moi
Happy Talk
Honey Bun
I'm Gonna Wash That Man Right Outa My Hair
A Wonderful Guy
Some Enchanted Evening
There Is Nothin' Like a Dame
This Nearly Was Mine
Younger Than Springtime

Strike Up the Band (1930)
lyrics: Ira Gershwin, music: George Gershwin
I've Got a Crush on You
Soon
Strike Up the Band

West Side Story (1957)
lyrics: Stephen Sondheim, music: Leonard Bernstein
America
I Feel Pretty
Jet Song
Maria
One Hand, One Heart
Something's Coming
Somewhere
Tonight

*Dates are of the first stage presentation in English, whether in London or New York.

MUZAK

Muzak, a registered trademark of Muzak Limited Partnership, has been a subliminal force in the United States for over half a century. It is the most prominent of several companies that supply background music for countless places of public gathering, ranging from hotels, restaurants, lobbies, elevators, and department stores to medical and dental offices, airport terminals, and factories.

Muzak originated in New York City in 1934 and at first used telephone lines. Since then, it has undergone many technological advances and in recent years has made use of recordings and tapes as well as piped music.

Musical selections tend to be unobtrusive, derived for the most part from **standards** which avoid vocals and harsh music and emphasize strings. Programs usually vary according to the time of day and the venue of their airing. For example, fast music has been found to encourage production in factories, while slower music is more suitable for the lobbies of office buildings. Similarly, tempos and liveliness of the music tend to increase as the day progresses from daytime to nighttime.

In recent years, Muzak has also supplied its customers with "Tones" (which it describes as "foreground music"). These are selections of tapes to be played on Muzak's equipment; included are such programs as Light Symphony Favorites, Classical Chamber, Solo Piano, and Contemporary Jazz.

Bibliography

Sanjek, Russell, and David Sanjek. *American Popular Music Business in the 20th Century.* 1991.

n

NAMES

People's names have long been a source of inspiration to American songwriters. As far back as 1848, Stephen Collins Foster wrote "Oh! Susanna"; he followed it up in 1854 with "Jeanie With the Light Brown Hair." Songs about females have always far outnumbered those about males and, quite fittingly, songs about **romance** and **love** have always been predominant. The **lyrics** of "Margie" (1920), for example, state: "After all is said and done, there is really only one, Oh, Margie, Margie, it's you!," while John Lennon and Paul McCartney, in "Michelle" (1966), go a step further and declare quite unabatedly: "I love you, I love you, I love you."

An aspect of many songs is the celebration of a woman's charms. For example, "Linda" (1947) begins with the words: "When I fall asleep, I never count sheep, I count all the charms about Linda." "If You Knew Susie Like I Know Susie" (1925) proclaims: "There's no one classy as this fair lassy." "Dinah" (1925) begins: "Dinah, is there anyone finer, in the state of Carolina?" Then there is "Diane" (1927), with its opening line: "I'm in heaven when I see you smile."

Another favorite attribute of ladies named in song is their **sweetness**. Some examples are "Sweet Rosie O'Grady" (1896), "You're the Flower of My Heart, Sweet Adeline" (1903), "Ida, Sweet as Apple Cider" (1903), "Sweet Georgia Brown" (1925), "Sweet Lorraine" (1928), "Sweet Sue" (1928), and "Sweet Leilani" (1937). In "Candy" (1944), the singer calls his "sugar" Candy because he's "sweet on candy, and Candy's sweet on me."

If love is the most popular theme, love "gone bad" is a runner-up. Among many "name" songs about unrequited love are "Cathy's Clown" (1960), "Ramblin' Rose" (1962), "Hooray for Hazel" (1966), and the melodramatic "Delilah" (1968).

The name most frequently found in song titles is Mary, and its many variations—as in George M. Cohan's "Mary's a Grand Old Name" (1905), Irving Berlin's "Marie" (1928), and Oscar Hammerstein II and Sigmund Romberg's "Marianne" (1928). Other "Mary" songs worthy of mention are "Hello, Mary Lou" (1961), "Proud Mary" (1968), and several "Maria" songs, especially the "Maria" of Stephen Sondheim and Leonard Bernstein's *West Side Story* (1957).

Annie is another frequently used name, spanning two centuries from "Annie Laurie" (1838) and "Little Annie Rooney" (1890) to two country crossover hits: "Polk Salad Annie" (1969) and "Annie's Song" (1974), to name but a few.

Two women's names have been of special interest to songwriters, perhaps owing to their imagery: both are associated with the **color** red. One, Rose, is also a **flower**, while the other, Ruby, is also a gemstone. Examples are "Rose of Washington Square" (1920), "Second Hand Rose" (1921), "Rose-Marie" (1924), "Cracklin' Rosie" (1970), "Ruby" (1953), "Ruby Baby" (1955), and "Ruby Tuesday" (1967).

Although most songs cast the **lady** as an object of affection, there are several that make her an actual character with a story of her own. These include "Hard Hearted Hannah (The Vamp of Savannah)" (1924), "Minnie the Moocher" (1931), "Lulu's Back in Town" (1935), and "Lili Marleen" (1940). In addition, several songs use surnames rather than given names, including "Miss Otis Regrets (She's Unable to Lunch Today)" (1934), "Have You Met Miss Jones?" (1937), "Tom Dooley" (1958), "Mrs. Robinson" (1968), and "Me and Mrs. Jones" (1972).

Songs discussed above were usually designed for a **man** to sing about a **woman**. However, several songs about women were popularized by women; they include "Whatever Lola Wants" (1955), "Tammy" (1957), and "Delta Dawn" (1972). On the other hand, songs in which women sing about men include "Oh Johnny, Oh Johnny, Oh!" (1917), "I'm Just Wild About Harry" (1921), "Bill" (1927), "Happiness Is a Thing Called Joe"

(1942), and "Alfie" (1966). A number of songs about men were popularized by male singers, including "Danny Boy" (1913), "Elmer's Tune" (1941), "Open the Door, Richard!" (1947), "Sam's Song" (1950), "Stagger Lee" (1958), "Daniel" (1973), and Chuck Berry's "Johnny B. Goode" (1958)—the only **rock 'n' roll** song included on the *Sounds of the Earth* record enclosed in NASA's "Voyager" interplanetary space probe.

There are also songs about both genders, such as "The Ballad of Bonnie and Clyde" (1967) and "Frankie and Johnny," The latter, a traditional folk song dating from the early 1870s, has been recorded in numerous versions by pop artists. Two songs that confuse genders in a humorous vein are "A Boy Named Sue" (1969) and "My Girl Bill" (1974).

Many song titles with names emanate from the musical theater and film. When a songwriter has the task of writing a dozen or more songs for a production, he can come closer to his goal by entitling one of them after a leading character or by the name of the show. Sometimes these are one and the same, as in "Ramona" (actually written to promote the silent film of the same name in 1927), "Gigi" (1958), "Hello, Dolly!" (1964), and "Mame" (1966).

Rock 'n' roll, and later **rock**, produced several "name" songs that have become staples in any amateur rock band's repertoire: "Peggy Sue" (1958); "Louie Louie" (1963), famous despite its almost indecipherable lyrics; "Help Me Rhonda" (1965); and "Gloria" (1965), written by Van Morrison with the famous G-L-O-R-I-A shout.

In the last half of the 1960s, several allegorical rock songs using names were produced, such as "Along Comes Mary" (1965), Bob Dylan's "Maggie's Farm" (1965), Leonard Cohen's "Suzanne" (1966), and two songs by John Lennon and Paul McCartney: "Eleanor Rigby" (1966) and "Lucy in the Sky With Diamonds" (1968).

There have also been songs inspired by real people, such as "Joltin' Joe Di Maggio" (1941); "The Ballad of Davy Crockett" (1955); "Vincent (Starry, Starry Night)," Don McLean's homage to Vincent Van Gogh, written in 1971; and a song written about three people, Abraham Lincoln, Martin Luther King, Jr., and John F. Kennedy: "Abraham, Martin and John" (1968).

Some songs using people's names are not about people at all: "Rockin' Robin" (1958) is concerned with a bird and "Ben" (1972) is about a rat.

Finally, there are songs about names in general. "What's Your Name?" (1961) is about a fellow's persistence in trying to find out the name of a certain lady. "The Name Game" (1964) was a phenomenally popular **novelty song** using a "pig Latin" type of language for any and all names.

Additional Songs

Alexander's Ragtime Band (1911)

Alice Blue Gown (1919)
Anastasia (1956)
Anna (1953)
Bad Bad Leroy Brown (1972)
Barney Google (1923)
Bess, You Is My Woman (1935)
Betty Co-Ed (1930)
Big Bad John (1961)
Bill Bailey, Won't You Please Come Home? (1902)
Billie Jean (1982)
Blow, Gabriel, Blow (1934)
Bo Diddley (1955)
Cecilia (1925)
Cecilia (1970)
Charley, My Boy (1924)
Charlie Brown (1959)
Charmaine (1926)
Christopher Columbus (1936)
Daisy Bell (1892)
Dance With Me Henry (1955)
Diana (1957)
Eadie Was a Lady (1932)
Elenore (1968)
Eli's Coming (1967)
Elvira (1965)
Fanny (1954)
Five Guys Named Moe (1941)
Georgy Girl (1966)
Good Golly Miss Molly (1958)
Goodnight Irene (1936)
Hey Joe (1965)
I Wonder What's Become of Sally (1924)
Irene (1919)
Jean (1969)
Jeannine, I Dream of Lilac Time (1928)
K-K-K-Katy (1918)
Laura (1945)
Lawdy Miss Clawdy (1952)
Liza (All the Clouds'll Roll Away) (1929)
Lola (1970)
Long Tall Sally (1956)
Louise (1929)
Lucille (1976)
Mandy (1919)
Mandy (1971)
Maria Elena (1941)
Marianne (1955)
Matilda, Matilda (1953)
Maybelline (1955)
Me and Bobby McGee (1969)
Message to Michael (1963)
Mr. Bojangles (1968)
Mona Lisa (1949)
My Gal Sal (1905)
Nancy (With the Laughing Face) (1944)
Ode to Billie Joe (1967)
Oh! Carol (1959)
Once in Love With Amy (1948)
Rosalie (1937)
Rosanna (1982)
Short Fat Fannie (1957)

Sioux City Sue (1945)
Stella by Starlight (1946)
Tangerine (1942)
They Call the Wind Maria (1951)
Think of Laura (1984)
Thoroughly Modern Millie (1967)
Wait Till the Sun Shines, Nellie (1905)
Wake Up Little Susie (1957)
Who Threw the Overalls in Mrs. Murphy's Chowder? (1899)
The Wind Cries Mary (1967)

Jeffrey Cahn

See also: Subjects

NASHVILLE

Nashville, the capital of the **state** of Tennessee, is also the capital of **country and western** music. The city's prominence began in 1925 with a **radio** program on station WSM in Nashville called *National Barn Dance,* which had originated on station WLS in Chicago the year before. In 1927—with its name changed to *Grand Ole Opry*—the show began its longtime, seemingly endless run as the international showcase of country and western music.

Following the lead of Capitol Records in 1950, most major **recording** companies maintained studios in Nashville. The city became not only a recording and publishing center for all kinds of music, but also a forum for booking acts and a venue for producing advertising commercials. Nashville's Music Row has challenged New York City's **Tin Pan Alley** in both record production and music publishing since the 1950s.

The city is also noted for what has been called the "Nashville Sound," an appellation which has changed in meaning through the years, sometimes designating nasal voices accompanied by acoustic guitars, at other times more artful voices accompanied by electronic instruments and drums. In addition, Nashville is the home of the Country Music Hall of Fame and the Opryland, U.S.A. complex. Although sometimes challenged through the years by such cities as Austin and Memphis, Nashville has retained into the 1990s its status as a world-class music center.

Bibliography

Corbin, Everett J. *Storm Over Nashville: A Case Against "Modern" Country Music.* 1980.
Hurst, Jack. *Nashville's Grand Ole Opry.* 1975.
Tassin, Myron. *Fifty Years at the Grand Ole Opry.* 1975.

See also: Bluegrass; Cities; New York City

NATIONS

Many nations of the **world** and their inhabitants have been **subjects** of popular song. Of these, **Ireland** has been by far the most popular, followed by the United States, Spain, England, and China, with lesser contributions from elsewhere abroad.

Songs with an Irish background were very much in vogue around the turn of the century, when Chauncey Olcott, a prominent singer and actor of the day, wrote such hits as "My Wild Irish Rose" (1899) and "When Irish Eyes Are Smiling" (1912)—the latter with music by Ernest R. Ball. Two other popular Irish-centered songs were published in 1914: "A Little Bit of Heaven, Shure They Call It Ireland" and "Too-ra-loo-ra-loo-ral, That's an Irish Lullaby."

A resurgence of Irish Patriotism occurred in the late 1930s with "Did Your Mother Come From Ireland?" (1936), followed in 1940 by "It's a Great Day for the Irish" and "It's the Same Old Shillelagh." In 1947, the quintessentially Irish ballad "How Are Things in Glocca Morra?" was the hit of the Broadway show *Finian's Rainbow.*

Songs about the United States run the gamut from patriotism in the early years to disillusionment in the later ones: from "America, the Beautiful" (1895) and "America, I Love You" (1915) to "American Pie" (1972) and "Born in the USA" (1984). A lighter touch is found in such songs as "America," from *West Side Story* (1957); "Only in America" (1963); and "Living in America" (1986).

Songs about **Britain** and the English include Noël Coward's "Mad Dogs and Englishmen" (1931), the patriotic "There'll Always Be an England" (1939), and Professor Higgins's plea from *My Fair Lady*: "Why Can't the English?" (1956).

Spain is represented in song by the tinkly "In a Little Spanish Town" of 1926; the paso doble "Lady of Spain" of 1931; the tango "The Rain in Spain" (Eliza's memorable elocution lesson in *My Fair Lady*, 1956); the German import "Spanish Eyes" (1965); and the sprightly **novelty song** "Spanish Flea" of 1965.

The Chinese are represented in two early songs, "Chinatown, My Chinatown" (1910) and "China Boy" (1922), while China is used as a conveniently distant destination in Frank Loesser's "On a Slow Boat to China" (1948).

Other Asian countries referred to in song are India, with "Hindustan" (1918); Japan, with "The Japanese Sandman" (1920); Iran, with "In a Persian Market" (1920); and Arabia, with "The Sheik of Araby" (1921). Pure exoticism—a form of escape during World War II—is celebrated in a song about Africa, "The Road to Morocco" (1942).

Other parts of Europe memorialized in song include **Russia**, with "Russian Lullaby" (1927) and "From Russia With Love" (1964); **France**, with "Roses of Picardy" (1916); and Norway, with "Norwegian Wood" (1966).

North American countries other than the United States represented in song include **Canada**, with "Canadian Capers" (1915) and "Canadian Sunset" (1956); Jamaica, with "Jamaica Farewell" (1955); **Mexico**, with "South of the Border (Down Mexico Way)" (1939), "Mexican Joe" (1953), and "(My Heart's in) Mexico" (1961); and **Cuba**, with "Cuban Love Song" (1931) and "Cuban Pete" (1936).

As for South America, there are several songs about **Brazil**, including the samba "Brazil" (1939) and the 1947 novelty "The Coffee Song (They've Got an Awful Lot of Coffee in Brazil)." **Argentina** is mentioned in such songs as "Down Argentina Way" (1940) and "Don't Cry for Me, Argentina" (1976). South America also has the distinction of being the only entire continent memorialized in song in two contrasting songs, one in favor and one against: "South American Way" (1939) and "South America, Take It Away" (1946).

> *See also*: Foreign Influence; Foreign Language; Patriotism

New York City

New York City towers over all other cities as the heartbeat of American popular song. Its significance is manifold: it is the location of **Broadway, Harlem, Tin Pan Alley,** and the **Brill Building**; the center of music publishing; the venue of **vaudeville, opera, operetta, revue,** and numerous **dance crazes**; the birthplace of **musical comedy** and the **musical play**; a center of **jazz** activity; and an important location of ballrooms, **cabarets,** nightclubs, and theaters.

Several New York theaters have been of seminal importance in the introduction of popular song. The New Amsterdam Theatre, on West 42nd Street, was the home of such important productions as *The Merry Widow* (1907), *The Ziegfeld Follies* (1908–36), and *The Band Wagon* (1931), which brought forth such hits as "Vilia" (1907), "Shine On Harvest Moon" (1908), and "Dancing in the Dark" (1931). The Princess Theatre, on West 39th Street, was the scene of Jerome Kern's first success as composer of the musical comedies *Very Good, Eddie!* (1915), *Oh, Boy!* (1917), and *Oh, Lady! Lady!* (1918). The Music Box Theatre, built on West 45th Street in 1920 by Sam H. Harris and Irving Berlin, became a showcase of Berlin songs in the *Music Box Revues* (1920–24), which introduced the songs "Say It With Music" (1921) "What'll I Do?" (1924), and "All Alone" (1924), among others.

With the advent of the **big bands**, nightclubs like the Paradise Restaurant and Birdland became important. The former introduced the nation to the sounds of Glenn Miller and His Orchestra. The latter, named for alto-saxophonist Charlie Parker, opened in 1948 and is immortalized in the jazz standard "Lullaby of Birdland" (1952). Many hotels—such as the Pennsylvania, New Yorker, McAlpin, Roosevelt, and Waldorf-Astoria—and ballrooms like Roseland were also favored by the

sounds of the big bands. Still other ballrooms brought the sounds of **Latin America** to New York, introducing to the United States such dances as the rumba, guaracha, conga, mambo, cha cha cha, and salsa.

Since the 1960s, New York City has given up its monopoly as the sole headquarters of American popular music. Many of its former activities have moved to such distant places as Los Angeles, **Nashville,** Memphis, and Detroit. But into the 1990s, enough musical life remained in the "Big Apple" for New York City to retain its position as the capital of American popular song.

> *See also*: Cities

Night

Far more songs have been written about the night than the **day**, possibly because the hours of darkness are the traditional time for the pursuit of **love** and **romance**. Of the hundreds of songs on the subject, several stand out. Cole Porter wrote three haunting ballads on the theme—"Night and Day" (1932), "All Through the Night" (1934), and "In the Still of the Night" (1937). Romantic songs by others include "Tonight We Love" (1934), "You and the Night and the Music" (1934), "The Night Is Young and You're So Beautiful" (1936), "I Could Have Danced All Night" (1956), "Tonight" (1957), and "Strangers in the Night" (1966).

There are also songs wherein the night serves as a backdrop for such activities as **kissing** ("A Kiss in the Dark," 1922), **dancing** ("Dancing in the Dark," 1931 and 1984), singing ("It's a Grand Night for Singing," 1945), or celebrating ("The Night They Invented Champagne," 1958).

But songs about the night are not always songs of joy. Nights can be restless, as in "I Couldn't Sleep a Wink Last Night" (1943); bleak, as in "Blues in the Night" (1941); or lonely, as in "Help Me Make It Through the Night" (1970). There are, in addition, a great many **farewell** songs about saying good night—on the order of "Good Night Sweetheart" (1931)—as well as songs that deal with specific nights of the week, such as "Saturday Night (Is the Loneliest Night of the Week)" (1944) and "Saturday Night" (1976).

Additional Songs

Deep Night (1929)
Give Me the Night (1980)
Here Comes the Night (1965)
I Love a Rainy Night (1980)
In the Blue of Evening (1942)
In the Cool, Cool, Cool of the Evening (1951)
June Night (1924)
Last Night (1961)
Last Night on the Back Porch, I Loved Her Best of All (1923)
Last Night When We Were Young (1936)
The Loveliest Night of the Year (1950)

The Night Chicago Died (1974)
Night Fever (1977)
The Night Has a Thousand Eyes (1948)
The Night the Lights Went Out in Georgia (1972)
Night Train (1952)
The Night Was Made for Love (1931)
Nights in White Satin (1967)
Oh, What a Night (1956)
One Night of Love (1934)
One of These Nights (1975)
One Summer Night (1958)
Serenade in the Night (1936)
Southern Nights (1977)
(This Is) The Story of a Starry Night (1941)
Summer Night (1936)
Tonight's the Night (It's Gonna Be Alright) (1976)
Twilight on the Trail (1936)
Twilight Time (1944)
Twistin' the Night Away (1962)
Whatever Gets You Through the Night (1974)
Where the Blue of the Night Meets the Gold of the Day
(1931)
Wild Night (1971)

    See also: **Days of the Week; Sleep; Time of Day**

NIGHTCLUB. *SEE* CABARET

NONSENSE

Unintelligible syllables have always fascinated the American public—especially when they are put to music. A case in point is the rousing "Ta-Ra-Ra-Boom-De-Ay!," a British song which created a sensation when it was introduced in New York in 1891. Blanche Ring's hit of 1909, "I've Got Rings on My Fingers," bore the interesting subtitle "Mumbo Jumbo Jijiboo O'Shea." Another nonsense song, "The Aba Daba Honeymoon" (1914), tells the absurd story of a "chimpie" and a "monk" who are married by a "big baboon." World War I saw several nonsense songs, including "Ja Da" and "Hinky Dinky Parlay Voo" (both 1918); the latter—also known as "Mad'moiselle From Armentières"—is at least partially based on the French language.

Some songs which seem to be utter nonsense actually are functional. "Inka Dinka Doo" (1933), for example, long served comedian Jimmy Durante as his theme song. Larry Clinton's "The Dipsy Doodle," of 1937, describes a game wherein one says things in reverse, like "You love I and me love You." "Boomps-a-Daisy," from *Hellzapoppin'* (1939), describes a somewhat clumsy dance that entails bumping one's partner in the rear.

Aided and abetted by the Walt Disney Studios, a series of nonsense songs emanated from Hollywood, beginning with the dwarfs' marching song "Heigh-Ho," from *Snow White and the Seven Dwarfs* (1937). This was followed by "Hi-Diddle-Dee-Dee (An Actor's Life for Me)," from *Pinocchio* (1940); "Zip-a-Dee-Doo-Dah," from *Song of the South* (1947); and "Bibbidi-Bobbidi-Boo," from *Cinderella* (1949). Louis Armstrong contributed to the genre by singing the song "Jeepers Creepers" to a racehorse of that name in the film *Going Places* (1938), while Carmen Miranda introduced the nonsensical "Chica Chica Boom Chic" in the movie *That Night in Rio* (1941).

The grim years of World War II were somewhat counteracted by several songs in double talk, including "Hut Sut Song" (1939) and "Mairzy Doats" (1943); the latter is a play on the words "Mares eat oats and does eat oats and little lambs eat ivy." Some songs, like "Hey Ba-Ba-Re-Bop" (1945), were an outgrowth of **scat singing**.

The 1960s began with gibberish, in the classic "Who Put the Bomp (In the Bomp Ba Bomp Ba Bomp)" (1961). The film *Mary Poppins* (1964) actually boasted two nonsense songs: "Chim Chim Cher-ee" and—with what is certainly the longest one-word title, nonsensical or otherwise—"Supercalifragilisticexpialidocious." The Beatles had their hands in several nonsense songs as well, among them "Helter Skelter" (1968) and "Ob-La-Di Ob-La-Da" (1968).

Additional Songs

Alley Oop (1960)
Be-Bop-A-Lula (1956)
Bim Bam Boom (1941)
Boola Boola (1898)
Chitty Chitty Bang Bang (1968)
Da Doo Ron Ron (When He Walked Me Home) (1963)
Diga Diga Doo (1928)
Do Wah Diddy Diddy (1963)
Flat Foot Floogie (1938)
(Whoopee Ti Yi Yo) Git Along Little Dogies (1893)
Hi-Lili, Hi-Lo (1952)
Hot Diggity (1956)
In-a-gadda-da-vida (1968)
Nana, Hey, Hey, Kiss Him Goodbye (1969)
Ooby Dooby (1956)
Sh-Boom (1954)
Shimmy, Shimmy, Ko-Ko-Bop (1959)
Ti-Pi-Tin (1938)
Yakety Yak (1958)
Yip-I-Addy-I-Ay (1908)

    See also: **Dance Crazes; Humor; Novelty Songs**

NOVELTY SONG

Music publishers and songwriters have long used the term "novelty song" to describe any song that is not on the **subject** of love. This definition subsumes a wide range of genres, including dance songs ("Charleston," 1923), comic songs ("Does the Spearmint Lose Its Flavor on the Bedpost Overnight?," 1924), **dialect** songs ("Where Do You Work-a John?," 1926), place songs ("My Little Grass Shack in Kealakekua, Hawaii,"

1933), **foreign-language** songs ("Bei Mir Bist Du Schön [Means That You're Grand]," 1937), and **nonsense** songs ("Mairzy Doats," 1943).

Novelty songs grew out of **coon songs** like "Hello! Ma Baby" (1899) and "Bill Bailey, Won't You Please Come Home?" (1902). The phenomenal success of Irving Berlin's "Alexander's Ragtime Band" in 1911 gave novelties a permanent position in the songwriter's repertoire. A proliferation of novelties occurred in the 1920s, with such songs as "Barney Google" (1923) and "When the Red Red Robin Comes Bob Bob Bobbin' Along," (1926). But the most sensational novelty song of that decade was "Yes! We Have No Bananas" (1923), a title reputed to have been suggested to the songwriters by the confusing statement of a Greek fruit peddler to a customer.

In the **Depression years**, publishers clamored for novelty songs both as an antidote to the nation's ills and as a source of income. Songwriters obliged, with such hits as "The Music Goes 'Round and 'Round" (1935), "A-Tisket, A-Tasket" (1938), and "Beer Barrel Polka (Roll Out the Barrel)" (1939). During **World War II**, a number of songs about **trains**, like "Chattanooga Choo Choo" and "On the Atchison, Topeka, and the Santa Fe" (1945), offered another form of escape.

The **jukebox** brought many novelty songs to fame. "Music! Music! Music!," also known by its first line, "Put another nickel in," was a sensation in 1950. Rosemary Clooney popularized several novelty songs in dialect, including "Come On-a-My House" (1950) and "Botch-A-Me" (1952). The following years saw **animal** songs like "(How Much Is That) Doggie in the Window?" (1953) and **rock 'n' roll** songs such as "Shake, Rattle and Roll" (1954)—foreshadowing the deluge of novelty songs to follow in the age of **rock**, when songs about love distinctly became members of the minority.

Additional Songs

Are You From Dixie, 'Cause I'm From Dixie Too (1915)
Boogie-Woogie Bugle Boy (1941)
Crazy Rhythm (1928)
The Darktown Strutters' Ball (1917)
Itsy Bitsy Teenie Weenie Yellow Polkadot Bikini (1960)
Johnny One Note (1937)
Mr. Bojangles (1971)
Winchester Cathedral (1966)

> *See also*: **Birds; Christmas; Clothing; Dance Crazes; Food and Drink; Humor; Ragtime; Travel**

O

OCCASIONAL SONG

Among happy occasions celebrated in song are birthdays, anniversaries, and weddings. The simple strains of "Happy Birthday to You" (1893) have been set to accommodate the names of countless birthday celebrants over the years. This song—originally written for schoolchildren as "Good Morning to All" by two sisters, Patty Smith Hall and Mildred J. Hall—is one of the most popular songs of all time, not only in the United States but all over the world. Almost a century after it was written, the owners of its copyright were still collecting substantial royalties. Several other birthday songs have appeared in more recent years, among them "Happy, Happy Birthday Baby" (1957) and "Happy Birthday, Sweet Sixteen" (1961).

"Happy Birthday to You" is also used to celebrate other happy occasions, especially anniversaries, in which case the melody is given two added eighth notes in order to accommodate the extra syllables in "anniversary." But the supreme anniversary song is called just that: "The Anniversary Song." Derived from the first two strains of Ion Ivanovici's famous waltz of 1880, *Danube Waves (Über den Wellen)*, it was introduced by Al Jolson—who also is credited as one of its writers—in the 1946 film *The Jolson Story*. It remains by far the most popular anniversary song; it is customary for the honored couple to dance to its strains at anniversary celebrations. This song is not to be confused with another, less popular anniversary song, "The Anniversary Waltz," which preceded it in 1941.

Marriage is another occasion celebrated in songs, such as "Love and Marriage" (1955) and "Sunrise, Sunset" (1964). Increasingly since the 1960s, another occasion has been cause for celebration as well: the second marriage. The proper song for *that* occasion is "The Second Time Around" (1960).

See also: **Christmas; Happiness; Holidays**

OCEAN

The ocean has a long and honorable tradition in music. Such works as "My Bonnie Lies Over the Ocean" (1881) and "Over the Waves" (1888) attest to its popularity as a subject during the nineteenth century. The United States Navy anthem, "Anchors Aweigh" (1907), is a stirring reminder of the sea.

Appropriately enough, some of the most popular songs about the ocean have come from across it. In 1939, "La Mer"—a song written and introduced in **France** by Charles Trenet—became a great success throughout Europe. Eight years later, in 1947, it became a hit in the United States as "Beyond the Sea." **Britain**, ever conscious of the seas surrounding it, has given us such nautical hits as "Red Sails in the Sunset" (1935) and "Harbor Lights" (1937), as well as songs about the **waterfront**, like "Stranger on the Shore" (1961) and "Sleepy Shores" (1971).

Very often, songs emphasize the recreational aspects of the ocean. The joys of ocean bathing are celebrated in such early songs as the tongue-twister "She Sells Sea-Shells (On the Seashore)" (1908) and the perennial "By the Beautiful Sea" (1914). "On the Boardwalk in Atlantic City" appeared in 1946, followed quite logically by "Under the Boardwalk" in 1964. The surfing explosion of the 1960s led to such hits as "Surfin' Safari" (1962) and "Surf City" (1963), sung by the Beach Boys, and "Surfin' U.S.A." (1963), sung by Chuck Berry.

The ocean is used metaphorically in such songs as "Between The Devil and the Deep Blue Sea" (1931), "How Deep Is the Ocean?" (1932), and "Sea of Love" (1959). Its beauty is sung about in the haunting "Ebb Tide" (1953). Life in its depths is fantasized about in the calypso song "Under the Sea," from the animated film *The Little Mermaid* (1989). The sea can also be a place of romance, as in Irving Berlin's "I Threw a Kiss in the Ocean" (1942). But Berlin's treatment of the subject is less complimentary in "We Saw the Sea," from the 1936 film *Follow the Fleet*. It is sung by sailors who "joined the Navy to see the world," and "What'd we see? We saw the sea."

> *See also*: Boating; Depth; Rivers

OCTAVE

A special characteristic of several songs is their prominent use of the octave, or **interval** of the eighth, as part of the **melody**. One of the best known of these songs is "Over the Rainbow" (1939), the melody of which is given a poignant quality by rising an octave on the tonic at the opening word "Somewhere." A similar quality is given to the melody of the 1940 song "When You Wish Upon a Star," which rises an octave on the first two syllables, but this time the rise occurs on the dominant. The dominant octave is also prominent in the melody of "Deep Purple" (1934), but here an interval of a second is interspersed between the lower and higher dominant tones.

Upward leaps of an octave give an air of buoyancy to several waltzes, among them "Take Me Out to the Ball Game" (1908) and "It's a Grand Night for Singing" (1945). A number of other songs using octaves move from the **pickup** to the first note on the beat. These include "Two Loves Have I" (1931), "It's Only a Paper Moon" (1933), "It Ain't Necessarily So" (1935), "Just One of Those Things" (1935), and "Camelot" (1960).

Downward leaps are far less common. They are found in Cole Porter's "It's D' Lovely" (1936), Irving Berlin's "There's No Business Like Show Business" (1946), and—in an extreme case—Nacio Herb Brown's "You Are My Lucky Star" (1935), the melody of which is literally built around downward leaps of the octave on the dominant, a procedure that is repeated ten times in the chorus.

The octave is used to great advantage in the chorus of "My Hero," from Rudolf Friml's operetta *The Chocolate Soldier* (1909). Here the entire opening phrase of eight tones is repeated an octave higher at the end of the song, bringing it to a most effective climax.

ONE-STEP

The one-step was a social dance that was popular in the first and second decades of the twentieth century. It was danced to songs in very fast **tempo** (approximately ♩ = 132) and in duple **meter**, such as "My Pony Boy" (1909), "Chinatown, My Chinatown" (1910), and "The World Is Waiting for the Sunrise" (1919). Around 1920, the one-step gave way to a gliding dance in similar tempo called the **Peabody**.

> *See also*: Dance Crazes; Charleston; Two-Step

OPERA

It is a well-known fact that the **classics** have supplied composers of American popular song with a wealth of musical material. Included among these classics are nineteenth- and twentieth-century operas from which the music is either quoted verbatim, paraphrased, or parodied. For example, Irving Berlin parodied the famous sextet from Gaetano Donizetti's *Lucia di Lammermoor* (1935) in his "Ragtime Sextet" (1912). Joseph Sullivan used a recognizable leitmotif from Richard Wagner's *Lohengrin* (1846) for "Where Did You Get That Hat?" (1888). Other examples show that Sammy Kaye drew upon "Vesti la giubba," an aria in Ruggiero Leoncavallo's *I Pagliacci* (1892), for "Tell Me You Love Me," which was popular in 1951; Dorcas Cochran and Harold Grant created "Here" (1954) from "Caro nome," an aria in Giuseppe Verdi's *Rigoletto* (1851); and Robert Wright and George Forrest dipped into the Polovtsian Dances in Alexander Borodin's *Prince Igor* (1890) for "Stranger in Paradise," one of the hit songs in their Broadway musical *Kismet* (1953).

The tune for "Hail, Hail, the Gang's All Here," in its 1917 version by D. A. Esrom and Theodore Morse, was borrowed from the Anvil Chorus in Verdi's *Il Trovatore* (1853). This borrowing, however, did not come directly from the opera; rather, it came by way of a parody of the Verdi melody that appears in Act II of Gilbert and Sullivan's *The Pirates of Penzance* (1879).

Jacques Offenbach's *Geneviève di Brabant* (1868), an *opéra bouffe*, may not be known to many opera fans, but the melody from one of its arias, "Complets des deux hommes d'armes," can surely be hummed by every American acquainted with "The Marine's Hymn" (1919) with the opening line, "From the Halls of Montezuma." What is interesting about the Offenbach opera is that it parodied preexisting materials from eighteenth-century vaudeville and Italian comic opera. Thus, "The Marine's Hymn" melody may be based upon a source even older than the Offenbach opera.

An example of an entire opera being usurped for the creation of a Broadway musical is offered by Georges Bizet's *Carmen* (1875), from which Oscar Hammerstein II fashioned *Carmen Jones* (1943). New lyrics were set to the original music, transforming the eighteenth-century European setting into a twentieth-century American locale in the South, complete with an all-black cast. What was once the "Toreador Song" became "Stan' Up an' Fight" and the "Habanera" became "Dat's Love."

Sometimes songwriters drew upon contemporary operas, thereby exposing their borrowings to questions of copyright violation. One such example concerns the melody for "Avalon" (1920), which Vincent Rose and Al Jolson borrowed from "É lucevan le stelle," an aria in Giacomo Puccini's *Tosca* (1900). The borrowing was somewhat disguised, for the minor key of the aria was transposed to a major key for "Avalon." Nonetheless, the unauthorized use of material did not escape notice by Puccini's publishers and quite possibly by Puccini himself, since he was still alive when this incident took place. Ricordi sued and won a sizable financial settlement.

The plot rather than the music of Puccini's *Madama Butterfly* (1904) was the inspiration for "Poor Butterfly" (1916), a song created by John Golden and Raymond Hubbell for *The Big Show*, an "extravaganza" staged in New York City's Hippodrome. "Poor Butterfly" was intended for a particular opera singer, Tamaha Miura, who had been performing the leading role in the Metropolitan Opera production of *Madama Butterfly*. Miura, however, was not asked to sing in the show and therefore "Poor Butterfly" was introduced by a singer of more modest talent. The song became a standard, selling more than two million copies.

"Poor Butterfly" spawned a spoof of itself: "Poor Little Butterfly Is a Fly Girl Now" (1919), with lyrics by Sam Lewis and Joe Young and music by M. K. Jerome. To appreciate the humor of this musical parody, one need look no further than the song's lyrics: "[Butterfly] knows that 'Ballin' the Jack' will bring Pinkerton back."

In the 1950s, Bobby Worth used "Musetta's Waltz" from Puccini's *La Bohème* (1896) for his ballad "Don't You Know" (1959), the recording of which achieved gold status. Other instrumental numbers from operas that made their way into popular song include the "Dance of the Hours" from Amilcare Ponchielli's *La Gioconda* (1876) and the Overture to Otto Nicolai's *Die lustigen Weiber von Windsor* (*The Merry Wives of Windsor*, 1849)—the main theme of the overture serving as the melody for Victor Schertzinger's 1913 hit "Marcheta."

Rare are examples of American popular song invading the realm of opera. One unusual example comes to mind: *Joe Hill, the Man Who Never Died* by Barnie Starvis (libretto) and Alan Bush (music), an opera staged at the Staatsoper in Berlin in 1970. This work included four popular songs by Joe Hill, whose lyrics (wed to popular melodies) promoted labor unions in America during the early decades of this century when the Industrial Workers of the World were being organized. Hill was killed in the course of his union crusade, but his life was immortalized not only by the 1970 opera but also by two different ballads entitled simply "Joe Hill." One was written by Earl Robinson in 1938, his music setting a poem about the martyred organizer by Alfred Hayes. A second "Joe Hill" was composed by Phil Ochs in 1966. It was the Robinson ballad, however, that Joan Baez sang at Woodstock in 1969; she repeated it two years later on the soundtrack for the film *Joe Hill*. Another example is provided by "'Tis the Last Rose of Summer" (1813). This popular song was interpolated into Friedrich von Flotow's opera *Martha* (1847).

A number of airs or arias from twentieth-century operas (and *musical plays*, which are sometimes so closely akin to operas as to be indistinguishable from them) have moved directly from the stage into the commercial market, thereby contributing substantially to the corpus of American popular song. How one defines what is an "opera" or a "musical" is often simply a matter of arbitrary classification. Works launched on Broadway or in Off-Broadway theaters tend to be labeled "musicals" whereas those staged by opera companies are deemed to be "operas." **Crossovers** between the two theatrical arenas abound, further complicating classification. For example, George and Ira Gershwin and DuBose Heyward's *Porgy and Bess* (1935) played on Broadway for many years before being incorporated into the Metropolitan Opera repertoire. Frank Loesser's *The Most Happy Fella* (1956), in 1991 and 1992 revivals, played on Broadway and on the stage of the New York City Opera during the same season. *Les Misérables* (1985), on Broadway at this writing, is every inch an opera, yet it remains in the realm of the musical play. What follows is a sampling of popular songs contained in works which, in the broadest sense of the term, can be called operas.

In 1935, Kurt Weill came to the United States from Germany and brought with him his palette of operatic successes; not the least of these was his *Die Dreigroschenoper* (*The Threepenny Opera*, 1928). Weill's pre-1935 operas, especially *The Czar Has Himself Photographed* (1928) and *The Rise and Fall of the City of Mahagonny* (1929), show his thorough acquaintance with American popular music, for his scores are flavored with the blues, ragtime, and jazz. Thus, upon immigration, it was easy for Weill to quickly assimilate his music into the American scene.

In the 1950s, Marc Blitzstein (an opera composer in his own right) prepared *The Threepenny Opera* for an Off-Broadway production, having fitted Weill's score with English lyrics. Out of this English version came the hit song "Mack the Knife" (originally "Moritat" in the Brecht-Weill opera), introduced first in concert performance in 1952 and then in the theatrical production of 1954. "Mack the Knife" was represented on *Your Hit Parade* and had numerous recordings, with three of the best-selling ones being by Louis Armstrong (1957), Bobby Darin (1959), and Ella Fitzgerald (1962). The Darin recording sold over two million copies and won a Grammy.

From another Weill opera, *Happy End* (1929), comes "The Bilbao Song"; it became popular in 1961 with Johnny Mercer's English lyrics.

Douglas Moore's one-act opera *The Devil and Daniel Webster* (1939) contains "Now May There Be a Blessing." The aria's text, adapted by Stephen Vincent Benét from Hebrew scripture, concerns the pledge made between Ruth and Naomi. In 1941, this aria was published under the title "A Nuptial Blessing." It became, and remains today, a standard among wedding songs.

Reginald de Koven's comic opera *Robin Hood* (1890)

contains another wedding classic, "Oh Promise Me" (1887), a song not originally intended for the opera. When it was decided that the wedding scene in Act II of *Robin Hood* needed additional music, De Koven drew upon his and Clement Scott's previously written and published "Oh Promise Me" and incorporated it into the score. The song quickly became associated with weddings, for which it remained a popular standard for more than fifty years.

Porgy and Bess has sometimes been labeled a "folk opera," for it combines the compositional mold of classical opera with aspects of popular music. The opera opened on Broadway in 1935, had an extremely long run on Broadway in its 1942 revival, and was made into a film, whose soundtrack won a Grammy in 1959. All this happened before the original score, with its recitatives (instead of spoken dialogue) was fully revealed to the public in a 1975 concert version and a subsequent Metropolitan Opera production in the mid-1980s. Out of this truly remarkable American opera have come several standards: "Summertime," "I Got Plenty o' Nuttin'," "Bess You Is My Woman," and "It Ain't Necessarily So," among others.

Show Boat (1927) by Oscar Hammerstein II and Jerome Kern is one of the Broadway musicals that crossed over into the opera repertoire, having been incorporated into the regular repertory at the New York City Opera in 1954. Among its most memorable songs are "Ol' Man River," "Make Believe," and "Why Do I Love You?"

Other crossovers include Loesser's *The Most Happy Fella* (1956), with "Somebody, Somewhere" and "Standing on the Corner" among its hit songs. Leonard Bernstein's *West Side Story* (1957), with lyrics by Stephen Sondheim, found its way not only into American opera houses but also into European ones as well, such as the Volksoper in Vienna. "Maria," "Tonight," and "I Feel Pretty" are some of its most popular songs. Sondheim produced his own crossovers as well: the best known are *A Little Night Music* (1973) with "Send in the Clowns" (which earned a Grammy in 1976) and *Sweeney Todd* (1978) with "Pretty Women" and "Not While I'm Around."

In the 1960s, the rock opera *Hair* (lyrics by Gerome Ragni and James Rado, music by Galt MacDermot) captured the attention of the public with "Aquarius" in its 1967 Off-Broadway production and "Let the Sunshine In" in the 1968 Broadway run. Both songs were on the recording that won the Grammy Award for Record of the Year in 1969.

Hermine W. Williams

Bibliography

Grout, Donald Jay, with Hermine Weigel Williams. *A Short History of Opera*. 3rd ed. 1988.

See also: Marriage; Operetta

OPERETTA

An operetta may be described as a musical stage work with spoken dialogue that is lighter in tone than an **opera** but more substantial in plot and music than a **musical comedy**. The genre reached its zenith in the United States in the 1920s, after which many of its characteristics were absorbed into the conception of the **musical play**. Although the lines of distinction between these various genres of musical theater are frequently blurred, certain characteristics of twentieth-century operettas can be noted. They are lighthearted and very often set in exotic or far-away places. As for their songs, they are often more akin to the arias and ariettas of opera than to other types of popular song, exhibiting wider ranges, more melismatic melodies, and more elaborate verses.

Operetta originated in Europe in the mid-nineteenth century with Jacques Offenbach, who composed over ninety of them, chiefly in Paris. He, in turn, passed on the tradition to such Viennese composers as Franz von Suppé and Johann Strauss, Jr. In the early twentieth century, Franz Lehár, Emmerich Kálmán, and Oscar Straus brought Viennese operetta to the United States. Operetta in this country was also strongly influenced by the works of W. S. Gilbert and Sir Arthur Sullivan, especially *H. M. S. Pinafore* (1879), *The Pirates of Penzance* (1879), and *The Mikado* (1885).

Unquestionably the most popular and influential operetta of the early twentieth century was Lehár's *The Merry Widow*, which opened in New York, in English translation, in 1907. Its songs, still popular, include "The Merry Widow Waltz (I Love You So)," the striking "Maxim's," the two-step "Girls, Girls, Girls," and the ballad "Vilia." Although Lehár was never later able to equal the tremendous success of *The Merry Widow* in America, Kálmán received considerable acclaim here for his operettas *Sari* (1914) and *Countess Maritza* (1926)—the latter featuring the impressive "Play Gypsies—Dance Gypsies."

After *The Merry Widow*, several European-born composers took up the torch of operetta in America. The most successful of these were Sigmund Romberg, Victor Herbert, Rudolf Friml, and Oscar Straus.

Romberg, born in **Hungary** in 1887, wrote over seventy operettas, most of them in the United States. Among his most successful were *Maytime* (1917), *The Student Prince* (1924), *The Desert Song* (1926), *My Maryland* (1927), and *The New Moon* (1929). He also adapted the music of Franz Schubert for his operetta *Blossom Time* (1921), loosely based on Schubert's life. Among the most enduring songs from these works are "Will You Remember?" "Serenade," "The Desert Song," and "Lover Come Back to Me!"

Herbert, born in **Ireland** in 1859, is chiefly remembered for his operettas *The Fortune Teller* (1898), *Naughty Marietta* (1910), and **Sweethearts** (1913). His most lasting songs from these works are "Gypsy Love Song," "Ah, Sweet Mystery of Life," "I'm Falling in Love With Some One," and "Sweethearts."

Friml, born in **Czechoslovakia** in 1879, is best known for his operettas *The Firefly* (1912), *Rose-Marie* (1924), and *The Vagabond King* (1925) and his songs "Indian Love Call" and "Rose-Marie."

Oscar Straus, born in **Austria** in 1870, was most successful in the United States with his operettas *A Waltz Dream* (1908) and *The Chocolate Soldier* (1909), the latter best known for the aria-styled "My Hero."

It can be said that with *The New Moon*, operetta in the Viennese tradition reached its apogee in the United States. Two years earlier, when *Show Boat* opened on *Broadway*, a new breed of musical theater—the musical play—had been born. It contained many of the elements of operetta, but was quite distinct from it in the seriousness of its story and the more "American" character of its songs.

Bibliography

Bordman, Gerald. *American Operetta: From H.M.S. Pinafore to Sweeney Todd.* 1981.

Ewen, David. *New Complete Book of the American Musical Theater.* 1970.

Lubbock, Mark. *The Complete Book of Light Opera. With an American Section by David Ewen.* 1962.

TABLE 13

Songs Introduced in Operettas

Apple Blossoms (1919)
lyrics: William Le Baron, music: Victor Jacobi
You Are Free

Bitter Sweet (1929)
lyrics and music: Noël Coward
I'll See You Again
Zigeuner

Blossom Time (1921)
lyrics: Dorothy Donnelly, music: adapted from Franz
Schubert by Sigmund Romberg
Serenade
Song of Love

The Chocolate Soldier (1909)
lyrics: Stanislaus Stange, music: Oscar Straus
My Hero

Countess Maritza (1926)
lyrics: Harry B. Smith, music: Emmerich Kálmán
Play Gypsies—Dance Gypsies

The Desert Song (1926)
lyrics: Otto Harbach and Oscar Hammerstein II, music:
Sigmund Romberg
The Desert Song
One Alone
The Riff Song
Romance

The Firefly (1912)
lyrics: Otto Harbach, music: Rudolf Friml
Gianina Mia
Love Is Like a Firefly
Sympathy

The Fortune Teller (1898)
lyrics: Harry B. Smith, music: Victor Herbert
Gypsy Love Song
Romany Life

Maytime (1917)
lyrics: Rida Johnson Young, music: Sigmund Romberg
Will You Remember?

The Merry Widow (1907)
lyrics: Adrian Ross, music: Franz Lehár
Girls, Girls, Girls
Maxim's
The Merry Widow Waltz (I Love You So)
Vilia

My Maryland (1927)
lyrics: Dorothy Donnelly, music: Sigmund Romberg
Silver Moon

Naughty Marietta (1910)
lyrics: Rida Johnson Young, music: Victor Herbert
Ah, Sweet Mystery of Life
I'm Falling in Love With Some One
Italian Street Song
Tramp! Tramp! Tramp! Along the Highway

The New Moon (1929)
lyrics: Oscar Hammerstein II, music: Sigmund Romberg
Lover Come Back to Me!
Marianne
One Kiss
Softly, as in a Morning Sunrise
Stouthearted Men
Wanting You

Rio Rita (1927)
lyrics: Joseph McCarthy, music: Harry Tierney
The Rangers' Song
Rio Rita

Robin Hood (1890)
lyrics: Clement Scott, music: Reginald De Koven
Oh Promise Me

Rose-Marie (1924)
lyrics: Otto Harbach and Oscar Hammerstein II, music:
Rudolf Friml
Indian Love Call
Rose Marie

Sari (1914)
lyrics: C. C. S. Cushing and E. P. Heath, music: Emmerich
Kálmán
Love's Own Sweet Song (Sari Waltz)

The Student Prince (1924)
lyrics: Dorothy Donnelly, music: Sigmund Romberg
Deep in My Heart, Dear
Drinking Song
Golden Days
Serenade

Sweethearts (1913)
lyrics: Robert B. Smith, music: Victor Herbert
Sweethearts

The Three Musketeers (1928)
lyrics: P. G. Wodehouse and Clifford Grey, music: Rudolf Friml
March of the Musketeers

The Vagabond King (1925)
lyrics: Brian Hooker, music: Rudolf Friml
Only a Rose
Song of the Vagabonds

A Waltz Dream (1908)
lyrics: Joseph W. Herbert, music: Oscar Straus
Love's Roundelay

OSCARS. SEE ACADEMY AWARDS

P

PARTING. *SEE* FAREWELLS

PATRIOTISM

The United States of America has inspired numerous songs of support and devotion. The earliest in common use is also our official national anthem. The words of the "The Star-Spangled Banner" (1814) were written by Francis Scott Key to the music of the English song "To Anacreon in Heaven" (c. 1780). It is a stirring song, but its skipping melody and wide range (an octave and a half) make it difficult to sing. A second, unofficial anthem, "America (My Country 'Tis of Thee)" (1832), obviates these deficiencies by its stepwise melody and narrow range of only a seventh. Its words were set by Samuel Francis Smith to the music of the British national anthem, "God Save the King" (1744), a durable melody that has also been used for the Prussian and Russian state anthems.

Two patriotic songs of the past one hundred years have joined—and, in some ways, surpassed—these traditional anthems. The words of the first, "America, the Beautiful" (1895), were written by the poet Katharine Lee Bates to the music of Samuel Augustus Ward's "Materna." The second, "God Bless America" (1939), had been written by Irving Berlin for his soldier show, *Yip! Yip! Yaphank*, 1918. At that time, however, Berlin thought the song inappropriate for men in uniform to sing in a show, and he accordingly filed it away. Twenty years later, with war clouds gathering, he resurrected it as a vehicle for Kate Smith in her radio show. It met with immediate success and remains perhaps the most popular of our unofficial anthems. "America the Beautiful" and "God Bless America" have several characteristics in common. Their melodies are easy to sing, moving in stepwise motion within a range of a ninth. Their harmonies are simple. Their words express heartfelt devotion to one's country and call on the divinity.

Besides Berlin, another **composer-lyricist** famous for his patriotic songs was George M. Cohan. Early in the century, he displayed his own brand of hard, unsentimental patriotism in his songs "The Yankee Doodle Boy" (1904) and "You're a Grand Old Flag" (1906). Both songs rely on **quotation**: "Yankee Doodle" (1767) in the former, "Auld Lang Syne" (c. 1711) in the latter. So unsentimental was Cohan, in fact, that "You're a Grand Old Flag" began life with the opening line, "You're a grand old rag." Only the intervention of several patriotic societies forced Cohan to change the line to coincide with the title.

It is well established that wars bring out patriotism, and **World War I** and **World War II** were no exceptions. Cohan's famous "Over There" (1917), popularized by such notables as Nora Bayes and Enrico Caruso, became a battle cry of the war. Based on a simple bugle call, its verse literally quoted the 1886 call to arms "Johnny Get Your Gun." Berlin expressed his patriotism in two soldier shows, one for each war: *Yip! Yip! Yaphank* and *This Is the Army* (1942). However, the songs he wrote for these shows—like "Oh, How I Hate to Get Up in the Morning" (1918) and "I Left My Heart at the Stage Door Canteen" (1942)—were more about the everyday life of the ordinary soldier than about love for one's country. Perhaps the most patriotic songs of World War II were "Praise the Lord and Pass the Ammunition" and "There's a Star Spangled Banner Waving Somewhere" (both 1942), and "Comin' In on a Wing and a Prayer" (1943).

Each of the major armed services has a march-anthem of its own. These **marches** have become universally popular and are played and sung at parades and patriotic gatherings everywhere. The earliest, "Anchors Aweigh," was written as a rallying song for the Class of 1907 at the Naval Academy in Annapolis. Originally entitled "Sail Navy Down the Field," it has stirring music by Charles A. Zimmerman. "The Caissons Go Rolling Along" is set to "The U.S. Field Artillery March," written in 1918 by Brigadier General

Edmund L. Gruber. The author of "The Marine's Hymn" (1919)—also known by its first line, "From the halls of Montezuma to the shores of Tripoli"—is unknown, but the music is derived from an aria in Jacques Offenbach's opera *Geneviève de Brabant* (1868). The most recent service song, "The U.S. Air Force Song," was written as "The Army Air Corps Song" by Robert Crawford in 1939. The song, with its stirring opening line, "Off we go into the wild, blue yonder," became very popular during World War II. These four service songs share several characteristics: triadic melodies, simple harmonies, and dotted rhythms.

Among other patriotic marches that have been supplied with words are "American Patrol" (1885)—also known as "We Must Be Vigilant" and given words only in 1942—and John Philip Sousa's famous "The Stars and Stripes Forever" (1897), given words by Sousa himself.

As for songs about America as a **nation**, there are many, of varying sentiments, including Edgar Leslie and Archie Gottler's "America, I Love You" (1915); Woody Guthrie's "This Land Is Your Land" (1956); Stephen Sondheim and Leonard Bernstein's "America," from *West Side Story* (1957); Don McLean's "American Pie" (1971); Neil Diamond's "America" (1980); and Bruce Springsteen's "Born in the U.S.A." (1985).

Bibliography

Ewen, David. *All the Years of American Popular Music.* 1977.

Fuld, James J. *The Book of World-Famous Music: Classical, Popular and Folk.* 1985.

Scheurer, Timothy E. *Born in the U.S.A.: The Myth of America in Popular Music From Colonial Times to the Present.* 1991.

See also: **Cities, States**

PATTER

A patter is a lyric that is sung glibly and at a fairly rapid pace. Patters, often humorous in nature, abound in the works of Gilbert and Sullivan. They later became staples of the British music hall and of American **vaudeville**.

As separate sections, patters are found in such standard songs as "Swanee" (1919) and "Mountain Greenery" (1926); in the latter, it is designated as a "trio-patter" and segues to the **release** of the second chorus. Patter sections are also featured in "I Whistle a Happy Tune," from *The King and I* (1951), and in two music-hall type songs from *My Fair Lady* (1956): "Get Me to the Church on Time" and "With a Little Bit of Luck." Another patter-like passage was sung in **counterpoint** to the principal theme of "Mine," from *Let 'em Eat Cake* (1933).

The term "patter-song" refers to one that is sung very rapidly. A famous example is "Tschaikowsky," a **catalogue song** of classical composers that was sung at a furious pace by Danny Kaye in the 1941 musical *Lady in the Dark.*

See also: **Chorus; Vamp; Verse**

PEABODY

The Peabody, a very fast, gliding ballroom dance, evolved from the **one-step** around 1920. It became very popular during the **Roaring Twenties** and remained so into the early 1930s. With the advent of the **big bands**, however, its popularity slowly faded away.

Usually in 2/4 **meter**, the **tempo** of the Peabody was among the fastest in popular music: marked *presto* (approximately $\downarrow$ =132). At the height of its popularity, dancers glided across polished floors to the sounds of such songs as "Chinatown, My Chinatown" (1910), "The Sheik of Araby" (1921), and "China Boy" (1922).

See also: **Dance Crazes; Fox Trot**

PEDAL POINT

A pedal point is a note or group of notes that is sustained in the bass under changing harmonies; its name derives from the pedal keyboard of the organ. It is one of the oldest and most consistently used devices in music.

Pedal points are frequently found in popular song. They sometimes consist of alternating tonic and dominant tones in the lowest register extending over a number of bars, as in "My Funny Valentine" (1937), "Where or When" (1937), "That Old Black Magic" (1943), "Hello, Young Lovers" (1951), and "People" (1964). At other times, they consist of single notes, as in the pedal point of the "Theme From *Valley of the Dolls*" (1967), which extends over nineteen bars.

Several outstanding examples of pedal point emanate from Britain. For example, fifteen of the twenty-two measures that make up the 1960 song "A Taste of Honey" have a D pedal point, with a different harmony in each measure. But if a prize were given for unrelenting use of the device, it would probably go to Andrew Lloyd Webber. He makes prominent use of pedal point in the verse of "Don't Cry for Me Argentina," from *Evita* (1978), and again in "Love Changes Everything," from *Aspects of Love* (1989). In addition, almost the entire score of his *Phantom of the Opera* (1986) is awash in pedal point, in particular the songs "Think of Me," "All I Ask of You," and "The Point of No Return."

See also: **Bass Line; Boogie-Woogie**

PENTATONIC SCALE. SEE SCALE

PEOPLE

More popular songs have been written about people than about any other **subject** except **love**. Besides the countless songs based on people's **names**, there are numerous songs about **babies, boys, children, girls, ladies, women, men, mothers,** and **fathers**. In the broadest sense, almost all songs have to do with people in some way.

One of the best-known collective songs on the subject is entitled simply "People" (1964). Written by Bob Merrill and Jule Styne for the show *Funny Girl*, this impressive ballad ends with the words: "People who need people are the luckiest people in the world." Two other unforgettable songs about people are "People Will Say We're in Love," from *Oklahoma!* (1943), and "The Poor People of Paris," an import from France that is at once a "people" song and a "place" song.

The subject of two people in love has also produced its share of songs, among them "The Folks Who Live on the Hill" (1937), "Two Sleepy People" (1938), and "No Two People" (1952).

Additional Songs

Another Hundred People (1970)
Dear Hearts and Gentle People (1950)
Everyday People (1969)
Games People Play (1968)
People Are Strange (1967)
People Get Ready (1965)
People Got to Be Free (1968)
The Purple People Eater (1958)
Sergeant Pepper's Lonely Hearts Club Band (1967)
Shower the People (1975)
A Terrific Band and a Real Nice Crowd (1978)
Wake the Town and Tell the People (1954)

> *See also*: **Falling in Love; Friendship; Togetherness; World**

PERCUSSION

Percussion instruments may be divided into those of indefinite pitch and those of definite pitch; of these, the first category is by far the most important in popular music. At its simplest, percussion is usually represented by the drum set: bass drum, snare drum, tom-toms, hi-hat cymbals, and singly mounted cymbal. Many other percussive sounds can be produced by striking sticks, mallets, brushes, hands, and fingers on an almost infinite variety of surfaces, such as bongos, timbales, temple blocks, cowbells, and Indian tabla drums. An even greater variety of percussion instruments are used in Latin American music, including maracas, claves, bongos, and gourds.

An important unit in **jazz** ensembles and **big bands** is the rhythm section, consisting of varying combinations of keyboard, guitar, double or electric bass, and drums. The latter has graduated from being an instrument that merely beats out time to one with the status of a melody instrument, as played by virtuosos like Gene Krupa, Dave Tough, Art Blakey, Max Roach, and

Shelly Manne; Krupa's lengthy drum solo in "Sing, Sing, Sing, Sing" (1936) is a classic example. Other renowned drummers include Baby Dodds, Zutty Singleton, Ray Bauduc, George Wettling, Cozy Cole, Big Sid Catlett, Chico Hamilton, and Sunny Murray.

The vibraphone is the most prominent percussion instrument of definite pitch used in jazz. Its foremost exponents have been Lionel Hampton and Milt Jackson. Less commonly used instruments in this category include the xylophone, celesta, marimba, and Balinese gongs.

> *See also*: **Improvisation; Instrumentation**

PERFORMER-SONGWRITERS

Since the 1960s, the concept of the performing songwriter in popular music has taken root and flourished. But the idea is far from new. Singers of the **blues, folk song,** and **country and western** music have had a tradition of performing their own material since early in the century, often accompanying themselves on **guitar** or banjo. In addition, many pre-1960 songwriters of **Broadway** and **Tin Pan Alley** were known as talented performers: George M. Cohan and Johnny Mercer as **singers**; Noël Coward, Hoagy Carmichael, and Harold Arlen as singer-pianists; and George Gershwin and Michel Legrand as pianists—to mention but a few. At the other extreme are individuals who were primarily singers but also co-wrote successful songs on occasion, such as, for example, Mel Tormé ("The Christmas Song"; 1946) and Peggy Lee ("Mañana [Is Soon Enough for Me]"; 1948).

Nevertheless, it was only in the 1960s that performing songwriters came into their own. Inspired by the example of the Beatles—whose most successful songs, such as "Yesterday" (1965) and "Michelle" (1966), were written by two members of the group, John Lennon and Paul McCartney—many groups from **Britain** and America made frequent use of their own material. Coinciding with the emergence of rock and the renaissance of folk song, singer-songwriters such as Joni Mitchell, James Taylor, Carole King, Cat Stevens, Leonard Cohen, and Carly Simon came to the forefront (*See* Rock [VI]).

Performer-songwriters come in several varieties. Most abundant are the singer-guitarists, among them Bob Dylan ("Blowin' in the Wind"; 1962), Joni Mitchell ("Both Sides Now"; 1967), Leonard Cohen ("Bird on the Wire"; 1968), John Denver ("Leaving on a Jet Plane"; 1967), Paul Simon ("Bridge Over Troubled Water"; 1969), Paul Williams ("We've Only Just Begun"; 1970), Don McLean ("American Pie"; 1971), and Jim Croce ("Time in a Bottle"; 1971).

Other singer-songwriters customarily accompany themselves on the piano. These include Randy Newman ("I Think It's Going to Rain Today"; 1966), Laura Nyro

("Wedding Bell Blues"; 1966), Burt Bacharach ("Raindrops Keep Fallin' on My Head"; 1969), Stevie Wonder ("You Are the Sunshine of My Life"; 1972), Billy Joel ("Piano Man"; 1973), and Neil Sedaka ("Laughter in the Rain"; 1974).

Still other performer-songwriters are noted for their vocal talents are well as for their songwriting ability. These include Rod McKuen ("Jean"; 1969), James Taylor ("Fire and Rain"; 1969), Carole King ("You've Got a Friend"; 1971), and Carly Simon ("Anticipation"; 1971).

Like their counterparts, the troubadours and trouvères of the Middle Ages, performer-songwriters of the late twentieth century have been masters of social commentary—sometimes witty, sometimes ironic, sometimes revolutionary, but always in tune with their times.

> *See also*: **Collaboration; Composer-Lyricists; Composers; Instrumentation; Lyricists; Motown; Rhythm and Blues; Rock 'n' Roll; Soul; Women as Songwriters**

PIANO

In the 1890s, a piano was found in almost every living room. Its ubiquitousness contributed to the growing importance of **sheet music**. The piano became even more closely identified with popular music with the emergence of **ragtime**; essentially an instrumental genre for piano, its chief proponent was Scott Joplin. The piano, although not always used in the performance of **Dixieland**, maintained its importance as an essential instrument in the performance of **jazz**. At the same time, it remained the most important accompanying instrument for all types of popular music until it was superseded by the guitar in the 1950s.

Because of the versatile and many-layered nature of the instrument, pianists often doubled as **composers**. The most famous example of a piano-playing composer is George Gershwin. His skill as a pianist is revealed in his many piano rolls as well as in his transcriptions of his own songs for solo piano, including his famous arrangements of "I'll Build a Stairway to Paradise" (1922), "Somebody Loves Me" (1924), "Liza (All the Clouds'll Roll Away)" (1929), and "I Got Rhythm" (1930).

Many other pianist-composers could be cited. Edward "Zez" Confrey, a ragtime pianist, wrote such novelty numbers as "Kitten on the Keys" (1921) and "Stumbling" (1922). James P. Johnson, an early stride pianist, composed "Charleston" in 1923, thus initiating an early **dance craze**. Thomas "Fats" Waller was an impressive pianist and singer, as well as composer of such lasting songs as "Ain't Misbehavin'," "Honeysuckle Rose," and "I've Got a Feeling I'm Falling" (all 1929).

In the next decade, Earl "Fatha" Hines—known as "the Houdini of jazz piano"—composed the jazz standard "Rosetta" (1935). Rube Bloom, an accomplished

pianist, composed "Truckin'" (the title song of another dance craze) in 1935, as well as such standards as "Day In—Day Out" and "Don't Worry 'bout Me" (both 1939) and "Fools Rush In" (1940).

Edward Kennedy "Duke" Ellington was known for his three-fold talents as pianist, **big band** leader, and composer. He participated in the creation of dozens of hit songs, among them "Mood Indigo" (1931), "Sophisticated Lady" (1933), "Solitude" (1934), "I Got It Bad (And That Ain't Good)" (1941), "Do Nothin' Till You Hear From Me" (1943), "Don't Get Around Much Anymore" (1943), and "Satin Doll" (1958). William "Count" Basie, also triply-talented, composed, among other songs, "Jumpin' at the Woodside" and "One O'Clock Jump" (both in 1938).

Several renowned jazz pianists co-wrote hit songs in the 1950s: George Shearing, with "Lullaby of Birdland" in 1952; Erroll Garner, with "Misty" in 1954; and Eddie Heywood, Jr., with "Canadian Sunset" in 1956. Among the most prominent of other jazz pianists were Jelly Roll Morton, Willie "The Lion" Smith, Art Tatum, Jess Stacy, Teddy Wilson, Earl "Bud" Powell, Thelonious Monk, Dave Brubeck, Mary Lou Williams, Lenny Tristano, Horace Silver, Oscar Peterson, Ahmad Jamal, Bill Evans, Herbie Hancock, Chick Corea, Keith Jarrett, and Cecil Taylor.

A particular style of piano playing initiated by such performers as Clarence "Pine Top" Smith and Jimmy Yancey had a lasting impact as **boogie-woogie**. This lively, "eight-to-the-bar" style is epitomized in Meade "Lux" Lewis's "Honky Tonk Train" (1939) and was carried over into **rhythm and blues, rock 'n' roll,** and **rock**.

The piano has also exerted influence as a subject for popular song. Songs about the instrument range from Irving Berlin's "I Love a Piano" (1915) to "The Old Piano Roll Blues" (1949), "The Old Pi-anna Rag" (1955), and Billy Joel's 1973 lament, "Piano Man."

Bibliography

Taylor, Billy. *Jazz Piano: A Jazz History*. 1982.

> *See also*: **Improvisation; Instrumentation; Player-Piano**

PICKUP

The note or notes of a **melody** occurring before the first accented beat of a song are known individually or collectively as the pickup. Most American popular songs begin either directly on the beat, as in "All the Things You Are" (1939), or have but one pickup note, as in "As Time Goes By" (1931). There are, in addition, innumerable songs with pickups of two, three, or four notes. The 1975 song "You Needed Me," for example, has a three-note pickup of two repeated notes followed by the note an **octave** higher; the last note of the pickup is then repeated on the beat.

However, several songs stand out for the sheer number of notes in their pickups. Seven pickup notes are found in "Cocktails for Two" (1934), "Frenesi" (1939), and "Never on Sunday" (1960). The length of the seven-note pickup in the French import "Cherry Pink and Apple Blossom White" (1955) is further extended by the use of a fermata, or hold, on the fourth note.

Six notes constitute the pickups of Charles Gates Dawes's "It's All in the Game" (1951); Sigmund Romberg's "Marianne," from *The New Moon* (1928); Ernesto Lecuona's "Always in My Heart" (1942); and Michel Legrand's "What Are You Doing the Rest of Your Life" (1969).

Five-note pickups characterize a number of songs, including three from Latin America: "Green Eyes" (1929), "What a Diff'rence a Day Made" (1934), and "You Belong to My Heart" (1941), as well as two more recent American songs: "The Shadow of Your Smile" (1965) and "We've Only Just Begun" (1970).

In most of these pickups, melodic motion is by skip or step. George Gershwin's melody for "They Can't Take That Away From Me" (1937), on the other hand, uses five **repeated notes**. Repeated notes (either two or three) are also found in the pickups of a number of diverse songs, including "La Cucaracha" (1916), "Night and Day" (1932), "The Last Round-up" (1933), "Mama Yo Quiero (I Want My Mama)" (1940), "It's a Big Wide, Wonderful World" (1940), "You'll Never Walk Alone" (1945), "If I Were a Bell" (1950), and "I Get Ideas" (1951).

PLACES

Songs have been written about places near and far, real and imaginary, ordinary and exotic. Myriads of songs are on **subjects** as diverse as **cities, states, nations, streets, rivers, mountains,** or the **world**. Other places frequently covered in song are far more distant: the **moon, sun, stars, sky,** and **heaven.**

Songs have also been written about modes of **travel** used to reach these places, especially taking the **train** and **boating.** Among other favorite places expressed in song are **home,** the **ocean,** and the **waterfront.** Even the **cardinal points**—north, east, south, and west—are sung about.

There are, in addition, a number of songs about unspecified places, as exemplified in Rodgers and Hart's first published song, "Any Old Place With You" (1919), and John Lennon and Paul McCartney's "Here, There and Everywhere" (1966). Rodgers and Hart went on to write songs about other places, specific and nonspecific, such as "Manhattan" (1925), "Mountain Greenery" (1926), "On a Desert Island With Thee" (1927), and "There's a Small Hotel" (1936).

Several **catalogue songs** list places accessible only by rhyme. An example is the 1941 song "Let's Get Away From It All," which suggests the impossible: taking "a kayak from Quincy to Nyack." In a more general sense, distant places are also the subject of songs like "Long Ago (And Far Away)" (1944), "Far Away Places" (1948), and "From a Distance" (1987).

Places of the **imagination** are sometimes vividly portrayed in song, as in "Over the Rainbow," from *The Wizard of Oz* (1939)—which begins: "Somewhere over the rainbow"—or "Somewhere Out There" (1986). In a similar vein, "Somewhere," from *West Side Story* (1957), starts with Stephen Sondheim's memorable line: "There's a place for us, Somewhere a place for us."

Additional Songs

(There's No Place Like) Home for the Holidays (1954)
I Know a Place (1965)
A Place in the Sun (1966)
Right Place, Wrong Time (1973)
Somewhere a Voice Is Calling (1911)
Somewhere Along the Way (1952)
Somewhere My Love (Lara's Theme) (1966)
Theme From *A Summer Place* (1959)
There's a Star Spangled Banner Waving Somewhere (1942)
We Gotta Get Out of This Place (1965)

PLAGIARISM. *SEE* BORROWING

PLAYER PIANO

The player piano, a late nineteenth-century invention, enabled one and all to be the "life of the party." After simply inserting a piano roll into a specially equipped **piano,** a person could pump away on foot pedals and produce memorable music without touching the keys.

Early in the twentieth century, both Americans and Europeans fell in love with the instrument, which didn't take up much room and could be operated by children as well as adults. Sales and production boomed from 1910 to 1925 and did not decline until the **Depression years** of the 1930s, when the **radio** and phonograph took its place in many American homes. In the peak year of 1923, almost half the pianos built in the United States were of the player variety; by 1931, in contrast, the proportion had shrunk to only 4 percent. There was also a coin-operated variety, called the nickelodeon, which was the ancestor of the **jukebox.**

Two basic methods of reproduction were employed. The earliest was the Pianola, a patented device of the Aeolian Company of New York. It consisted of a mechanism that could be moved to any piano and included hammers striking only 65 notes of the 88-note piano keyboard. The Pianola was later superseded by the player piano proper, wherein the mechanism was incorporated within the piano cabinet, using the piano's own hammers and encompassing all 88 keys.

The music was reproduced on a piano roll, consisting of a perforated roll of paper passing over a bar and activated by air from a bellows motivated either mechanically, by foot pedals, or by electricity. Piano rolls were produced by the tens of thousands at the turn of the century and by the millions in the mid-1920s. From the late 1890s to about 1910, the 65-note roll dominated the home market, but it soon lost its position to the 88-note roll, which made use of all notes on the standard keyboard. By 1920, the 88-note roll had become the norm.

Many brands of player piano existed, among them the Duo-Art, Phonola, and Cecilian—the name of the last obviously derived from that of St. Cecilia, the patron saint of music.

In the earlier instruments, one could tell without looking whether or not a piano was a player—by its sound. Since the mechanism used the same amount of force to reproduce each note, every note sounded at the same volume, in contrast to the piano, in which unequal pressure is exerted on notes. Thus, the difference between the player and the real piano was readily discernible to the average listener.

This was later remedied by another invention, the reproducer: a more sophisticated mechanism that was installed in high-quality grand pianos. Reproducers were able to capture a musician's every nuance, including infinite shades of dynamics. Many pianists and composers recorded reproducing rolls for posterity, including Paderewski, Rachmaninoff, Rubinstein, Richard Strauss, Debussy, and George Gershwin.

A striking example of longevity in the piano-roll business is QRS Music Rolls, Incorporated. Founded in 1900, the firm reached its peak in 1926, when it sold an amazing ten million piano rolls. Although the Company fell on hard times in the Depression, it managed to hold on. Today, its catalogue contains several thousand selections, ranging from the 1920s to the 1990s.

Like the mail order catalogue and the dodo bird, the player piano never quite became obsolete. It is still with us in the 1990s, and now high technology is perpetuating its growth. Yamaha has produced a Disklavier, a player piano driven by a floppy disk—doing away with pumping pedals. Technicians have been able to transform piano rolls from the 1920s into computer information for use in the Disklavier. Two songs attest to the continuing popularity of mechanical instruments: "The Old Piano Roll Blues" (1949) and "Music! Music! Music!" (1950, about putting another nickel in the nickelodeon).

William D. Askin

Bibliography

Buchner, Alexander (translated by Iris Urwin). *Mechanical Musical Instruments*. N.d.
Fine, Larry. *The Piano Book*. 1987.
Reblitz, A. A., and Q. D. Bowers. *Treasures of Mechanical Music*. 1981.

POLKA

The polka is a moderately fast *dance* in 2/4 meter. Originating in Bohemia in the early nineteenth century, it became very popular throughout Europe largely through the efforts of Johann Strauss, father and son. It retained little of its popularity in twentieth-century America, except among people of Central and Eastern European background, for whom it was often performed by polka bands featuring the piano accordion and clarinet. Typically, a polka consists of three sections: two in the tonic key and the third—called the trio—in the dominant.

The dance joined the mainstream of music in the United States with the tremendously successful recording of "Beer Barrel Polka (Roll Out the Barrel)" by the Andrews Sisters in 1939. Quite appropriate to the dance's origin, this work was taken from a Czech song called "Skoda Lasky," or "Lost Love." This initial success inspired singing groups to introduce other polkas: "Pennsylvania Polka" (1942) and "Too Fat Polka (She's Too Fat for Me)" (1947), both sung by the Andrews Sisters; and "Strip Polka (Take It Off—Take It Off)," by the King Sisters. Also popular in the United States was the German "Liechtensteiner Polka," in 1957.

Several songs by Alan Jay Lerner and Frederick Loewe are in the spirit and tempo—if not the tripartite form—of the polka: "Get Me to the Church on Time," and "With a Little Bit of Luck," both from the musical play *My Fair Lady* (1956); and "The Night They Invented Champagne," from the musical film *Gigi* (1958).

See also: **Czechoslovakia**

POP

"Pop," an abbreviation of "popular," is an umbrella term denoting songs intended for the teenaged market and therefore of the highest commercial value. It came into use in mid-century, when it was applied to recordings by teenage idols such as the singers Frank Sinatra and Johnnie Ray. With the coming of rock 'n' roll, Elvis Presley became the first true pop star. He was followed by a host of others, including Bobby Darin, Frankie Avalon, Paul Anka, and Fabian.

The Beatles phenomenon of the 1960s led to a new world of pop, featuring the group rather than the individual and the performer-songwriter rather than the mere performer. Pop-rock came alive with groups like the Rolling Stones and Herman's Hermits. Another branch of pop featured folk song and was perpetuated by such singers as Bob Dylan, Judy Collins, and Joan Baez. Solidly in the pop mainstream were middle-of-the-road performer-songwriters like the Beach Boys,

Simon and Garfunkel, the Mamas and the Papas, Billy Joel, Carole King, and Neil Diamond.

See also: Awards; Popular Song; Rock; Top Forty

POPULAR SONG

The traditional definition of a popular song describes it as a short poem—or, more properly **lyrics**—intended for singing. Furthermore, it is distinguished from other poems in its "unbuttoned," or natural, quality: its freer rhyme and rhythmic association with the music. In addition, American popular song differs from classical song (lied) or operatic song (aria) in its temporality, its responsiveness to the spirit of the times. War songs such as George M. Cohan's "Over There," songs of the **Depression years** such as "Brother, Can You Spare a Dime?" as well as the ever-present romantic ballads, demonstrated the broad range of sentiment in this genre.

"Over There" was written in 1917 as the United States entered World War I. It appealed to pride of country and the belief that the Yanks could fix everything "over there." The Great Depression of the 1930s was expressed in song by E. Y. Harburg and Jay Gorney's "Brother, Can You Spare a Dime?" (1932); it tells of a man who has lost everything in the stock market crash of 1929 and is reduced to begging. The Beatles' nostalgic ballad of happier days, "Yesterday" (1965)—when "my love was here to stay"—describes the sadness of a lost love.

Only rarely is a song the work of one person. A team of **composer** and **lyricist** working together creates the song or, in the case of a musical show, collaborates on all the musical numbers. The names of George and Ira Gershwin, Richard Rodgers and Oscar Hammerstein II, Alan Jay Lerner and Frederick Loewe, and Leonard Bernstein and Stephen Sondheim are well known in musical theater. A few of these men of the musical stage have distinguished themselves by writing both words and music. Of these, Irving Berlin and Cole Porter are the most illustrious.

Before a song is published or recorded, a vast and influential enterprise is at work, one requiring that millions of dollars be spent to create a product that will sell. Composer, lyricist, arranger, vocalist(s), instrumentalists, director, producer, advertiser, and other support personnel become part of the team responsible for the product. In many cases, this complex production effort is centered around the charisma of the solo **singer**, all facets of his or her personality becoming a matter of public interest.

Through the years, singing stars have achieved notoriety as much for their lifestyles as for their artistic accomplishments. From the alcohol and drug problems of the late Judy Garland to the machismo of Mick Jagger's persona, private lives are put on display in this unreal world of superstardom. Accompanied by slick promotion, the product is bought by the public, and in the process, the public is furnished with much-needed heroes and antiheroes. Can all this adulation be due simply to the way these artists sing their songs? Is the ability to rouse feelings in millions of people created by some mysterious quality of the vocalist? How important to success is the timeliness of the lyrics, the beauty of the poem, the music itself? Whatever the answer, to these questions may be, it is quite obvious that popular song is a true indicator of the times.

I. Before Tin Pan Alley

Viewed from our vantage point in the last quarter of the twentieth century, popular song, as well as the entire field of popular music, seems to be a well-defined genre, easily distinguishable from classical music. Such, however, was not always the case. Only in the middle of the last century did such a distinction take root. Prior to that time, the singing and playing of all types of music in the home was commonplace. Sales of **sheet music**, along with vocal and piano collections, were the main source of revenue for the fledgling music publishing business.

Music making in the home by family members served as the chief source of entertainment well into the present century. Although Thomas Alva Edison patented the phonograph in 1877, it took another quarter of a century before marketable recorded music became available to the general public. **Radio** did not appear as a medium for widespread use until the 1920s. Collections of music for the home contained patriotic airs from the Revolutionary era; popular songs of the day by Americans Stephen Foster and Dan Emmett; and European waltzes, marches, polkas, and arias from operas by composers such as Mozart, Rossini, Bellini, Donizetti, and Verdi.

From the earliest days of the republic, songs reflecting the times were heard in public and private entertainments. "Yankee Doodle," first published in 1767 and sung by both English and American troops (albeit with different words), was to become the first truly American popular song. It was heard in theaters, in concerts, and at political gatherings throughout the thirteen colonies. The tune, with changed lyrics, was used in political campaigns of the nineteenth century as well. In 1904, George M. Cohan revitalized the theme by quoting it in his paraphrastic "The Yankee Doodle Boy."

In the first third of the nineteenth century, thousands of Irish immigrants brought their rich and varied musical heritage to our shores. Many of their songs became a permanent part of the American repertoire: "The Harp That Once Through Tara's Halls" (1807), "Believe Me If All Those Endearing Young Charms" (1807), "The Minstrel-Boy" (1813), and "Tis the Last

Rose of Summer" (1813). The poems were largely the creation of the Irishman Thomas Moore, while the music was written by various composers, among whom Sir Henry Bishop remains the best known. They are simple tunes that provide the singer with a lyrical melody for the projection of the poem. The themes reflect the sentimental, somewhat formalized style of the times, dealing mainly with romance and longing for the old country, all overlaid with a certain wistfulness.

Moore's *Irish Melodies* and Stephen Foster's songs were the two most popular collections in mid-century America. No music program, whether at home or in the theater, was complete without one of these sure-fire crowd pleasers. The high quality of the poetry and the suitability of the music to the lyrics guaranteed their popularity even to the present day.

America's leading songwriter of the nineteenth century, Stephen Foster (1826–1864), grew up in Pittsburgh in a home where music making was a regular event. At an early age Foster sang the Irish songs of Moore and melodies of other composers, both European and American. Even at the age of nine he was a performer in neighborhood productions which featured the then current "Ethiopian songs" popular in **minstrel shows**. Songs such as "Jim Crow" (1830) and "Old Zip Coon" (1834) influenced Foster's developing compositional style. His sympathetic feelings toward his black brethren were lovingly portrayed in songs which, in turn, reflected an experience that is wholly American. The unique blending of high spirits and jaunty rhythms in "Oh! Susanna" (1848), "De Camptown Races" (1850), "Hard Times Come Again No More" (1854), and "Some Folks" (1855) reveal an African-American amalgam in one of its early manifestations. This musical and cultural fusion became one of the hallmarks of American popular song.

The calamitous Civil War, in which the two key issues were slavery and states' rights versus federal jurisdiction, brought forth powerful internecine bitterness which continues in isolated communities, albeit diluted by the passage of time, to the present day. The high number of young American men and boys killed or maimed in this war and the ruination of vast stretches of the Southland characterized a confrontation which may be the greatest tragedy our nation has yet faced.

Civil War songs aroused the feelings of citizens in both Union and Confederate camps. Daniel Decatur Emmett's "Dixie" (1860), Julia Ward Howe's "Battle Hymn of the Republic" (1862), and numerous other stirring melodies served to marshal all elements of the population, North against South. George Frederick Root's inspiring "The Battle Cry of Freedom" (1863) was sung at numerous patriotic and political rallies and by Union troops going into battle.

After the Civil War, and for the remainder of the century, American popular song turned to hypersentimental and nostalgic themes with such tunes as "When You and I Were Young, Maggie" (1866), "Silver Threads Among the Gold" (1873), "Grandfather's Clock" (1876), and "I'll Take You Home Again Kathleen" (1876). These songs and countless others of their type used a standardized and predictable form consisting of verse and chorus. They, as well as novelty numbers like "The Daring Young Man (On the Flying Trapeze)" (1868), were sung in variety shows of the Reconstruction Period. At the same time, the minstrel show picked up where it had left off at the opening of hostilities. Numerous entertainments known as "extravaganzas" also appeared at this time, giving birth to a tradition that led eventually to the Broadway musical of the next century.

This postwar era was also a golden age of cowboy and western songs. "The Streets of Laredo" (c. 1860), "Home on the Range" (1873), "The Old Chisholm Trail" (c. 1880), and "The Red River Valley" (1896) express in sentimental lyrics the romanticized city-dweller's view of a cowboy's life in the Wild West.

II. Tin Pan Alley

By the turn of the century, **Tin Pan Alley** came to represent an area of **New York City** centering around 28th Street between Fifth Avenue and Broadway. It was here, starting in the 1890s, that most **publishers** of popular music had relocated.

Songwriter and music publisher Charles K. Harris, following his unparalleled financial success with "After the Ball" (1892), published a book called *How to Write a Popular Song*. As recounted by Ian Whitcomb, Harris advised the reader to "look at newspapers for your story-line, acquaint yourself with the style in vogue, avoid slang, and know the copyright laws." It is doubtful that any reader ever achieved more than modest success based on Harris's advice. His "words of wisdom," however, reflect the "made to order" approach to songwriting popular in the early days of commercialization in this field.

The popularity of "After the Ball" made Harris a rich man. This was the first American song to sell millions of copies of sheet music. It was translated into numerous languages and was widely distributed in Europe as well as at home. It even turned up in Jerome Kern's 1927 Broadway musical *Show Boat*. The song itself is like hundreds of other sentimental, story-telling **ballads** set to music. The usual verse and chorus sections are heard in serial fashion as the Victorian tale unfolds. A simple melody is used for the verse and a more lyrical one for the chorus, all in **waltz** time. When Harris advised his songwriting readers to "acquaint yourself with the style in vogue," he knew whereof he spoke. The most popular dance of his day was the *waltz*. It supplied a graceful and familiar design of rhythm to a simple, lilting melodic line. Over ten million copies of "After the Ball" were sold before 1910!

Although it would be pleasant to believe that fame and fortune came without effort to Harris and the other songwriters who achieved success at the turn of the century, the truth is somewhat different. Many young musicians got started as **song pluggers**, singing and/or playing the piano. The most famous of these was George Gershwin who, at sixteen years of age, became a plugger for Remick's publishing firm. It was here that he learned the song business in detail, training that was to prove useful in his future career as a composer for the musical stage.

Harris and Gershwin were extroverted, gregarious men, as were most of the song pluggers of the day. Of a contrasting temperament was Harris's contemporary Paul Dresser, whose most famous song, written in 1899, was "On the Banks of the Wabash Far Away," Although the song is sentimental, the nostalgic quality it evokes somehow squares more with real life than does "After the Ball." The evocation of a country scene has a firm footing in the popular tradition and rings true to our ears, even ninety years later. Stephen Foster's "Old Folks at Home (Way Down Upon the Swanee River)" (1857), Dan Emmett's "Dixie" (1860), Irving Caesar and George Gershwin's "Swanee" (1919), and Stuart Gorrell and Hoagy Carmichael's "Georgia on my Mind" (1930) all summon memories of some place near or distant, fondly remembered. This impossible desire for simpler times or a return to the past, a kind of bittersweet nostalgia, provided tunesmiths with a veritable lodestone, the mining of which continues unabated to the present day.

The Tin Pan Alley writers mentioned earlier—Charles K. Harris and Paul Dresser—represent the early years of the alley. The next era, from 1920 to 1950, produced songwriters who represent the maturity and peak of the American song, both in terms of the quality of musical and poetic conception and in its impact on American society. Among the most famous were George Gershwin, Irving Berlin, Harold Arlen, Jerome Kern, Cole Porter, Frank Loesser, Frederick Loewe, and Richard Rodgers. Along with these men, however, there were dozens of other composers who wrote beautiful and timely melodies that have been elevated to the status of standards or classics in the popular music field. Eubie Blake's "I'm Just Wild About Harry" (1921), Lou Silvers's "April Showers" (1921), Johnny Green's "Body and Soul" (1930), Peter DeRose's "Deep Purple" (1934), Hoagy Carmichael's "Star Dust" (1929), Victor Young's "I Don't Stand a Ghost of a Chance (With You)" (1932), Vernon Duke's "I Can't Get Started" (1935), Jimmy McHugh's "I'm in the Mood for Love" (1935), Johnny Mercer's "Dream" (1944), and Jule Styne's "It's Been a Long, Long Time" (1945) are only a few of the melodies written during this remarkable flowering of popular song.

The period from 1900 to 1950 has received detailed, insightful analysis and praise from a distinguished American composer, Alec Wilder. His book *American Popular Song: The Great Innovators, 1900–1950* pays tribute to the musical imagination in hundreds of these songs, some famous, some little-known today. One of the earliest, and to many minds the greatest, of the songwriters in this **golden age** was Irving Berlin. He had an unerring sense of timeliness and tunefulness. Thus his "White Christmas" of 1942 was one of the greatest hits of all time, expressing the yearning for home felt by thousands of American soldiers during **World War II**. His "God Bless America" (1939) became an unofficial national anthem; both Republicans and Democrats used it at their 1940 presidential conventions.

Berlin's first great success was "Alexander's Ragtime Band," written in 1911. The immense popularity and longevity of this piece is based, perhaps, on the snappy, jazzy rhythm and the happy times evoked by the **lyrics**. It is obvious that Berlin's poetry is hardly more than doggerel. In this regard, however, he improved considerably during ensuing years. The lyrics for many of his songs—for example, "The Girl That I Marry," "You Can't Get a Man With a Gun," "Doin' What Comes Natur'lly," and "I Got the Sun in the Morning" (all from his 1946 **musical comedy** *Annie Get Your Gun*)—demonstrate a rather good marriage of words and music.

"Alexander's Ragtime Band," like many American songs from the earliest times, uses the vernacular, the language of the common man. Catchy rhymes and topical allusions are tastefully sprinkled throughout the chorus. The interpolation of a pseudo-bugle call, coming just a decade after the Spanish-American War, may have resonated with the patriotic spirit of the times. And the cleverest stroke of all occurs with the **quotation** from the Stephen Foster original "Old Folks at Home" (1851); nostalgia was, and still is, a strong sentiment. The Swanee River seemed to be the most popular image to summon forth this feeling.

An amusing anecdote about "Alexander's Ragtime Band," apocryphal though it may be, has to do with Berlin's reply to a query about the lack of "ragtime" style in this song. His retort was that he never did know what ragtime really was! Regardless, he was able to capture the spirit of the times in a song that launched him on one of the most successful careers in American music.

III. World War I

As the United States entered the war that was supposed to "make the world safe for democracy," George M. Cohan penned a brilliant evocation of the "glamor of war." "Over There" quickened the heart of many "doughboys" who would never return from the battlefields of Europe. The lyrics seemed to say that we would finish the job and, in so doing, emerge victorious from "the war to end all wars." Unfortunately, this war neither made the world safe for democracy nor did it silence the guns of future wars. A quarter of a century later, however, Cohan received the Congressional Medal of Honor, awarded by President Franklin D. Roosevelt for his patriotic song.

Ever quick to catch the mood of the moment, Berlin also wrote several war songs as a result of his firsthand experience in the Army. While stationed at Camp Upton, New York, he wrote the music and lyrics for *Yip! Yip! Yaphank* (1918) and also choreographed, acted in, directed, and produced this wartime musical. The goal was to raise $35,000 for a Soldiers' Service Center. The immediate success of the show—with an all-soldier cast—resulted in raising more than five times the original goal. Two songs from the production, "Oh, How I Hate to Get Up in the Morning" and "Mandy," exceeded a million copies in sheet music sales; they also remained as standards.

In 1919 the young George Gershwin wrote the song that took him to the first echelon of Tin Pan Alley composers. "Swanee" was first heard and seen as a production dance number in a **vaudeville** show. The famous singer Al Jolson took a fancy to it and soon afterward interpolated it into an extravaganza called *Sinbad*. The immediate success of the song broke all previous records, for in less than a year it sold one million copies of sheet music and two million records.

IV. The Roaring Twenties

The era of the **Roaring Twenties** has been well documented in all popular forms of entertainment: fiction, movies, **recordings**, musical theater, and **revues**. Perhaps the combination of Prohibition, mass migration to the large industrialized cities of the North, rampant gangsterism, corrupt politicians and law-enforcement agencies, and the disillusionment felt by returning soldiers contributed to the changing way of life. Morals became looser than they had been in the preceding years, excesses of all types abounded, and speakeasies flaunted the law. Music, ever the handmaiden of popular trends, reflected these new attitudes. The bold, brassy flapper girl replaced the sedate, curvaceous Gibson girl of the prewar era. People smoked and drank (illegally) to excess. F. Scott Fitzgerald's novel *The Great Gatsby* paints a colorful yet grim picture of the smart set of the 1920s.

The Jazz Age emerged in full flower after the war. Hundreds of black musicians emigrated northward, especially from the environs of New Orleans, to settle in Chicago, Philadelphia, Pittsburgh, Detroit, New York, and other metropolitan areas. They found employment wherever they could, whether in speakeasies playing for white patrons, in their own neighborhoods, or in saloons or dance halls. These amazing, self-taught improvisers from the South had a profound influence

on the young white musicians of the North. The original New Orleans style was taken over by white **Dixieland** groups as the exciting new **jazz** sounds affected everyone.

These years also saw the first flowering of two distinctly American genres, **musical comedy** and revue, led by composers like Jerome Kern and Vincent Youmans and the songwriting teams of Richard Rodgers and Lorenz Hart and George and Ira Gershwin. Many songs from these theatrical productions—like Rodgers and Hart's "You Took Advantage of Me," from the musical comedy *Present Arms* (1928)—remained popular long after their shows had been forgotten.

V. The Great Depression

The collapse of the stock market in October 1929 signaled a depression which, for sheer damage to the American dream of individual wealth and financial security, has not been equaled in the more than two hundred years of our country's existence. The wanton, frivolous pursuits of the hedonists of the decade came to a grinding halt. Almost every family was hit with a significant tragedy; several tycoons committed suicide as their fortunes disappeared overnight because of bank failure and the collapse of the stock market. It is estimated that during the deepest part of the Depression, 1929–34, well over one-fourth of the nation's work force was jobless. Soup kitchens, hobo camps, streetcorner peddlers, and beggars were a common sight. Families dissolved as the husband or father wandered aimlessly, looking for nonexistent employment.

In 1932 Franklin D. Roosevelt was elected President on an election promise of a "New Deal" for the country. Gradually, by the middle of the decade, the gloom began to dissipate, due in part to the massive aid programs of the federal government and investors' renewed faith in the economy.

Popular song was important both as a weather vane of our feelings and as a harbinger of the changing times. No song caught the mood as well as Jay Gorney and E. Y. Harburg's Depression song "Brother, Can You Spare a Dime?" of 1932. Bing Crosby was the first singer to popularize this poignant ballad of a tycoon reduced to the role of a panhandler. The stanza beginning "Once in Khaki Suits" reminds one of the **Word War I** veterans who felt cheated on their return home. It became so bad that thousands of them, demanding promised bonus money, marched on Washington, D. C. They were turned back by armed government troops and, of necessity, joined the vast hordes of forlorn, unemployed men.

Not all, however, was gloom and misery during these days of intense economic hardship. Escape was important. In 1932, Duke Ellington composed a song that helped usher in the swing era: "It Don't Mean a Thing (If It Ain't Got That Swing)," With lighthearted lyrics by Irving Mills, this bouncy syncopated tune points up the primacy of dance music during the **big band** era by imitating muted brass instruments with doo-wahs in the lyrics.

Music was very often used as a morale booster during the years of Depression. One such tune is "Happy Days Are Here Again" (1929), which later served as a rallying call for the Democratic Party; it was the campaign song of Presidents Franklin D. Roosevelt, Harry S. Truman, and John F. Kennedy. The **film musical** was a vital escape in the Depression; *Top Hat* (1935) took place in a dream world, like a fairy tale.

As the catastrophic Depression began lifting in the mid-1930s, the emerging big bands filled a void in public entertainment. Most of the successful **singers** of the 1930s and the two following decades began their careers as vocalists with one or another of these large dance orchestras. Bing Crosby started in the late 1920s with the Paul Whiteman Orchestra; Ella Fitzgerald made her debut in 1934—at the age of sixteen—with Chick Webb's orchestra; Billie Holiday started with Count Basie in 1937; Peggy Lee sang with the "King of Swing," Benny Goodman; Doris Day launched her career with Les Brown.

VI. GIs and Bobby-Soxers

A song written in 1942 for the film *Holiday Inn*, starring Bing Crosby, became the piece most hummed, sung, and whistled by U.S. servicemen in **World War II**. Irving Berlin's "White Christmas," with its slowly rising, lyrical melody, was heard in every base and camp where the American military had a presence. The "Voice of America" radio broadcasts, visiting entertainment troupes (such as the Bob Hope group), and service bands stationed abroad sang and played this haunting melody. Credit for its success must be given to both Irving Berlin, the creator, and Bing Crosby, the interpreter. Crosby's rich, husky baritone voice and understated delivery were admirably suited to the piece. Irving Berlin's deceptively simple words brought back all their pleasant memories to these lonely GIs.

Some fifty years later, especially during the holiday season, one still cannot escape "White Christmas." It is blared over loudspeakers in plazas, malls, supermarkets, doctors' and dentists' offices, and even over the telephone. To survive such overuse, a piece of music must be both hearty and timeless. Of no song is this more true than of this perennial favorite, which has sold more records than any other song. Bing Crosby was a crooner with charisma who captivated audiences. His laidback California style and his mythic personality created by the entertainment industry—that of a pipe-smoking, kindly, all-American family man—launched a career that dominated the field for over four decades. The titles of his hits reflect his penchant for light lyrics and bland humor; he avoided the heavier, romantic

ballads. In addition to "White Christmas," there were "Too-ra-loo-ra-loo-ral, That's an Irish Lullaby" (1914), "Easter Parade" (1933), "You Are My Sunshine" (1940), "Deep in the Heart of Texas" (1941), and "Swinging on a Star" (1944).

The limitless topic of **love** had a very strong appeal during the years of America's involvement in World War II. This period produced beautiful and deeply moving ballads of unfulfilled love, bittersweet **romance**, and the aching heart of **loneliness**. Teenaged girls missed their youthful swains who had been drafted into the Army.

A dreamy-looking, youthful Frank Sinatra filled the holes in the hearts of millions of these American girls. Sinatra's singing style and personality differed markedly from that of his early idol, Bing Crosby; his quiet intensity, total immersion in a song, and velvety voice had immense appeal to the young set. A smooth, seemingly effortless delivery and an undercurrent of sensuality made him the ideal figure to be lionized by these lonely hearts.

In 1942 Columbia Records re-released "All or Nothing at All." It had been recorded in 1939 by the Harry James Orchestra, with the then relatively unknown Sinatra, but the song had had very little success and was withdrawn from the market. By 1942, however, "the Voice" had achieved quasi-stardom as the featured vocalist with the first-rate Tommy Dorsey Orchestra. When Sinatra sang this and other romantic ballads at New York's Paramount Theater in 1944, thousands of teenaged bobby-soxers swooned as he crooned personally (or so it seemed) to each and every one of them.

The long-lined, melancholy tune seemed to tell the youngsters to hold on to their dreams and to wait for their returning heroes. The words were sung with flawless diction, superb intonation, and satin smoothness. Sinatra changed the dimensions of popular song performance as he created a sound of palpable emotional expression. In 1941 the music magazine *Down Beat*, in a national poll, rated him the leading vocalist, edging out Bing Crosby, who had been voted Number One for the past four years. Half a century later, Sinatra's reputation as a singer and entertainer remained very high. He had achieved superstardom, with personal appearances throughout the world, hundreds of recordings, numerous movies, dozens of awards, and an international fan club.

VII. The Latin Connection

The United States has long been a haven for émigrés from all over the world. Over the past hundred years, vast numbers of Europeans have come to our shores seeking a better life for themselves and their children. After World War II, many new immigrants arrived from **Cuba, Mexico**, and other parts of **Latin America**. Puerto Ricans, who had become United States citizens in 1917, were now free to emigrate to the mainland. They, along with other Hispanics, tended to settle in large cities; many settled in a section of **New York City** known as El Barrio or Spanish Harlem. Their presence added greatly to America's unique ethnic diversity.

Besides such obvious contributions as the **tango**, **rumba**, and other dances, Hispanic culture provided fertile sources of new material for North American songwriters. In 1953, for example, Duke Ellington, Billy Strayhorn, and Johnny Mercer collaborated in a frivolous, light vein on a song of homage to the "hip" Hispanic-American female, "Satin Doll." This song catches the mood of the day with its insouciant lyrics in 1950s street-jive language: "Speaks Latin, that Satin Doll." In *West Side Story*, the sensitive musical of 1957 by Leonard Bernstein and Stephen Sondheim, the dislocation of Puerto Rican life in Manhattan was a major ingredient in the retelling of Shakespeare's immortal *Romeo and Juliet.*

VIII. Rock 'n' Roll: The Youth Revolution

Black music in America has had an illustrious presence despite, until the advent of **rock 'n' roll** in the mid-1950s, a somewhat separate existence from the music of white America. The same type of insularity is also true of southern rural music, sometimes referred to as **country and western** or just country music. Each had its own dynamic qualities and adherents; each was an accurate reflection of the people, times, and sentiments it expressed.

Many white musicians growing up in the South were influenced by the raw, emotional lyrics of the black man's **blues**. The citified, post–World War II blues, known as **rhythm and blues**, added a driving beat to the strong language of the earlier blues and appealed to young whites in northern cities as well.

A young rebel who came along at just the right time to fuse these two disparate styles was Elvis Presley. As a youth growing up in Memphis, he had heard and imitated black bluesmen like Arthur (Big Boy) Crudup; he also had a strong attachment to **gospel** music. Presley's guitar playing and singing style came out of the Jimmie Rodgers, Chet Atkins, and Hank Williams country tradition. All of this, coupled with his superb natural talent, sexy stage manner, and somewhat naughty, defiant facial expressions, heralded the age of rock 'n' roll. Presley was the giant figure of the 1950s, a lover in the imagination of untold millions of girls and a macho-figure to boys in their troubled teen years. His albums were immediate top sellers, earning millions of dollars for the sycophants connected with this most valuable "property." In 1969 he earned over $1 million for a four-week engagement in Las Vegas. His movies earned over $180 million for the studios. This kind of unbridled success often warps a personality and creates an unreal world for the star and his admirers. Unfortu-

nately, in Presley's case, it played a major role in his untimely death.

Willie Mae (Big Mama) Thornton, a black blues artist, recorded "Hound Dog" in 1952. This twelve-bar blues with the driving beat and wailing electric guitar of postwar rhythm and blues furnished Presley with a **cover** record that became an instantaneous hit. The original words convey the "double entendre" so prevalent in blues lyrics. Presley's version is "cleaned up," even though his singing tries to imitate the earthiness of the original by Thornton. He definitely comes off second best in this comparison, but it was of little consequence because, as noted above, everything Presley touched turned to gold or, even better, to platinum.

In 1955 Presley had his first Number One hit in the country music category with a cover version of Junior Parker's "Mystery Train." In 1956 he recorded a string of gold singles: "Heartbreak Hotel," "I Was the One," "I Want You, I Need You, I Love You," "Hound Dog," "Don't Be Cruel," "Love Me Tender," and "Any Way You Want Me (That's How I Will Be)."

By this time he had become the idol of millions of American teenagers, the intensity of whose feeling lavished on this cult figure was tantamount to fetishism. The anticipated backlash was unleashed by outraged citizens, parents, clergy, fellow musicians, and entertainers. His suggestive body movements (Elvis the Pelvis), as much as the content of the music, proved anathema to an older generation brought up on Bing Crosby, Doris Day, and Dinah Shore. This heated controversy was, of course, excellent for the music industry. It also fanned the fires of youthful rebellion as it widened the gulf between the generations.

Parents were still reeling from the Elvis phenomenon when a second one hit the youth market. The Beatles led the so-called British invasion and, in so doing, changed the course of popular music for all time. Mature **rock**, beginning in the early 1960s, became a vital cultural force, changing the way the Western world thinks and behaves. Never again would people's lives be the same; nor would Americans retain the insularity that had so characterized their past artistic expression.

The Beatles wrote most of their own pieces, both words and music, in a startling burst of fecundity during the decade of the 1960s. They produced album after album of very high quality music in an amazing variety of styles. Their songs had immediate success, crossing over from rock to **pop** to country with amazing frequency. They covered Chuck Berry's "Roll Over Beethoven" (1956), invoked the classical muse in "Yesterday" (1965), the folk aesthetic in "Love Me Do" (1962), and the sound of East Indian instrumentation in "Norwegian Wood" (1966).

One of the ways in which their material changed

the direction of popular music can be found in the song "Yesterday," written by John Lennon and Paul McCartney. Here they purposely avoid the trappings of rock, relying instead on the beauty of the poetry and the classical sonority of a string quartet. Following their lead, it gradually became acceptable to borrow, even to indulge in, the most eclectic of sources for lyrics, tone colors, and special effects. The progressive (art) rock movement certainly found more ready acceptance because of the Beatles' pioneering efforts.

"Yesterday" became one of the biggest-selling singles of all time and, subsequently, one of the most covered songs ever written. The loss of love, often for inexplicable reasons, leaves one in a distraught state; self-assurance is gone, one can't face the world, life is cloudy. What person hasn't experienced these feelings at least once in a lifetime? The folk-style singing of Paul McCartney is eloquent and perfectly suitable here. His vocalized understatement lends credence to the melancholy quality of the lyrics. There is no need for percussive sounds or strong rhythms in the accompaniment, nor for dramatic gestures in the vocals.

IX. Songs of Conscience: Folk Song Revival

In the 1960s, college-age youth sparked a **folk song** renaissance that had as its central theme disillusionment with the American political process that sent America's young men to Vietnam and denied equal opportunities to minorities, the poor, and the nation's downtrodden citizens. Who can forget the spirituality of Paul Simon's "Bridge Over Troubled Water" (1970), or Bob Dylan's "Blowin' in the Wind" (1963)? Joan Baez, Joni Mitchell, Judy Collins, John Denver, Pete Seeger, Simon and Garfunkel, Helen Reddy, the Kingston Trio, the New Christy Minstrels, and Peter, Paul and Mary all made deep inroads into the American psyche during this turbulent era.

Perhaps the person who stood out above all others as the voice of protest was Bob Dylan. Neither a brilliant vocalist nor instrumentalist, he was, nevertheless, a passionate and acerbic critic of the political/military/business establishment. His influence on fellow artists and future activists was as important as that of any person or group, including the Beatles.

Dylan had been inspired and given artistic direction by an older folk musician, Woody Guthrie. From Guthrie's Depression-era songs, he learned how to relate lyrics, music, and trouble to his own times. As an American troubadour of the twentieth century, he spoke as no one else, with force and eloquence. His songs, such as "The Times, They Are A-Changin'," "Blowin' in the Wind," "Hard Rain's A-Gonna Fall," and "Masters of War" (all of 1963), focus our attention on the perceived ills of American society.

X. Tailor-Made Songs in Mainstream Pop

While the folk revival and the rock revolution set the tone for the 1960s, more traditional and conservative audiences found sustenance and relaxation in the beautiful songs of composer Burt Bacharach and lyricist Hal David. This talented team had a fortuitous meeting with Dionne Warwick in the early years of the decade. They wrote music ideally suited to her considerable vocal talent. More than three dozen songs sung by her appeared on the charts, with several of them climbing to the Top Ten. Among the best remembered of these are "Walk On By" (1961), "Anyone Who Had a Heart" (1963), "I Say a Little Prayer" (1967), and "Do You Know the Way to San Jose?" (1967). "Promises, Promises" was the title song of a highly successful Broadway musical of 1968. In the same show, "I'll Never Fall in Love Again" reveals the considerable craft involved in joining together poetry and music. Unlike the songs of Elvis Presley, the Beatles, or the folk artists of the 1960s, this work is the product of two men who served their apprenticeship studying and absorbing the music of the best composers and lyricists of stage and screen. The lighthearted humor found here, as well as the masterful **rhyme** scheme with its flawless musical setting, pleased audiences in middle-class, middle-aged America. This tradition of light melody, pleasing consonant harmonies, and clear-cut structural relationships is typical of middle-of-the-road (MOR) songs in America.

XI. Country Music and Popular Song

Ray Charles was such a superb musician, with so much charisma, that he could do no wrong, musically speaking. Charles, more than any other black artist, opened the doors of the white-dominated entertainment industry. His raspy voice and pounding piano endeared him to large segments of the music-loving public. As a **crossover** artist, he was unmatched for sheer eclecticism. His most fascinating bit of musical legerdemain remains his performance of country music. His albums in this genre include *Modern Sounds in Country and Western Music*, with Volumes One and Two recorded in the early 1960s. Selections from these albums were joined with several other country and western songs on the 1981 album *The Legend Lives: Ray Charles*. His single "I Can't Stop Loving You," by Don Gibson, recorded in 1962, brought him a **Grammy Award** in the **country and western** division. He has won Grammys in at least six other areas as well, including **soul**, rhythm and blues, gospel, pop, **jazz**, and rock.

Charles's treatment of the country repertoire is unusual, to say the least. In addition to the use of his raspy voice, funky blue notes, and the rhythmic freedom of jazz, he employs a string section and a gospel choir. One cannot imagine the results being anything but a tasteless melange, cooked up for purely commercial gain; but, improbable as it may seem, the concoction does work.

No one can doubt the tremendous growth and popularity of country music in America. It became, in fact, the most popular form of music of the last half of the twentieth century. The names of country singers are well known: Willie Nelson, Kenny Rogers, Dolly Parton, Johnny Cash, Glen Campbell, Kris Kristofferson, Tammy Wynette, Loretta Lynn, Waylon Jennings, Charley Pride, Ronnie Milsap, Roy Clark, Alabama, The Charlie Daniels Band, and The Oak Ridge Boys. Many more could be mentioned, but this register should adequately demonstrate the viability of country music in the marketplace.

Country songs generally have a direct emotional appeal through the lyrics and melody, with little ambiguity and few explicit sexual references. The **Nashville** sound incorporates state-of-the-art technology and equipment, the highest-paid session men in the country, and well-trained, perceptive executives.

A hit record of this period that brought both the singer and the song instant notoriety was Glen Campbell's "Gentle on My Mind" (1967). The music and lyrics were written by Campbell's friend and fellow musician John Hartford. The song is simplicity itself: in four choruses it tells the story of a man—a drifter, if you will—who has fond memories of the girl he has left behind. He cannot be tied down, but he will be back because he knows that he is "not shackled by forgotten words and bonds." His memories are pleasant as he sings about the "back road" and "rivers of my memory." It is a tender piece, using lovely poetic metaphors to describe the singer's need for freedom and his wanderlust.

During the 1970s, the message of country music spread worldwide. Arrangers adopted the fuller backup sound used in recording studios in New York and Los Angeles. Although country singers retained most of the features—"straight" singing, clear diction, on-beat rhythms, and little or no improvisation—the instrumental support groups became larger and had a more prominent role than heretofore.

Outside the Nashville orbit, John Denver achieved remarkable success as a singer-songwriter crossing over between the pop, folk, and country fields. He recorded twenty-one albums between 1968 and 1983. Of these, all reached gold status, and four became platinum albums. His "Take Me Home, Country Roads" was an immense success in 1971. Denver represents a breed of modern musician coming out of the 1960s with a concern for the environment and man's threat to it. His concerns were shared by an ever-growing number of popular musicians, as we shall see when we explore the music of the 1980s.

XII. Motown: A Major Black Presence

Motown, a record company founded on a shoestring by Berry Gordy in Detroit in 1959, developed a type of vocal pop style that garnered a large segment of the lucrative record business. Gordy wrote songs and hired others to follow a plain, yet appealing, formula.

The names of the artists who recorded and toured worldwide under the Motown banner reads like a "Who's Who in Black Music": Diana Ross and the Supremes, Marvin Gaye, Smokey Robinson, Martha and the Vandellas, Gladys Knight and the Pips, the Temptations, Stevie Wonder, Junior Walker, the Isley Brothers, the Miracles, the Jackson 5, the Four Tops, and Lionel Richie. Motown, alive and well in the 1980s, released "Endless Love," a duet sung by Lionel Richie and Diana Ross. A sentimental **ballad** and the title song of a 1981 film, it went on to become the biggest-selling single of the year.

XIII. The 1970s: The Dominance of Dance

With the advent of studio-oriented rock, the music industry took advantage of sophisticated recording and production technology. Almost any kind of musical fabric could be fashioned, for technology permitted materials to be, among other things, altered, transformed, dubbed, echoed, and filtered. Still, the 1970s represented a low point in the history of popular song. Perhaps the Beatles, Bob Dylan, and other innovators set impossibly high standards for the next generation. Certainly **protest songs** were not in the mainstream of the 1970s. What emerged was a phenomenon that started with the discothèques of the 1960s and really came into its own with the **disco** craze of the 1970s.

The dance beat underlies much of American popular music. The steady four-beat pulse is never far from the surface of our songs and instrumental numbers. At certain times, however, dancing becomes a craze and music becomes glorified rhythm. Earlier in this century, the cakewalk, black bottom, **fox trot**, shimmy, one-step, two-step, Charleston, bunny hug, Lindy hop, jitterbug, and a host of Latin dance steps kept America on its feet (*see* Dance Crazes). With the advent of the 1960s, a new type of dance fever broke out, as the Twist set in motion a renewed desire for physical exhibitionism on the dance floor.

Disco dancing was done to recorded rather than live music. It emerged from a subculture of New York's young male community, but rapidly gained popularity with the jet set and other elements of "high society." **Disc jockeys**, in choosing records for their patrons, found most of their repertoire in the black pop library. In addition to choosing the music, the disc jockey also programmed a "light show" on the dance floor.

The Bee Gees' soundtrack for the film *Saturday Night Fever*, released in 1977, helped carry this movement forward. This double album was the biggest-selling popular record to date. Disco lounges sprang up everywhere and were the hottest thing in music and dance. The craze had begun in the preceding decade with

"The Twist" (1960), in which dancers needed no partner, instead, they did "their own thing" alone, or by simply facing another gyrating body. Chubby Checker took this song to the Top Ten for the years 1960 and 1962. It also had an unusually long run on the charts: forty-three weeks. There were no basic dance steps for the Twist, but the body rotated or twisted from side to side in time with the music. Although overshadowed by the earlier rock, disco finally became dominant in the 1970s, as rock's powerful grip loosened.

Donna Summer had a quick rise to fame as a disco singing star. Her recordings of "Bad Girls" and "Hot Stuff" in 1979 made the top of the charts in both the pop and rhythm and blues categories. Diana Ross released a disco hit in 1979; her version of Ashford and Simpson's "The Boss" reached the Top Twenty on both the pop and rhythm and blues charts.

Several of the dominant characteristics of 1960s rock carried over into disco: the tempo is moderate; the beat itself is overlaid with "bubbling," percussive rhythms; the vocal and instrumental tracks are recorded at the same level, thus making the words difficult to comprehend. As popular song of the 1970s became suffused with the beat and rhythm of rock and disco, it gave up the beautiful melodic line and sophisticated lyrics of the previous-century, the Tin Pan Alley epoch. Songs now were more declaratory in style, emphasizing short rhythmic motives, separated by instrumental answers. The lyric impulse was of secondary importance to the rhythmic vitality. Words were sometimes intelligible, sometimes not.

During this decade, in which rhythm was the rule, a few singers stood out for "swimming against the current"—adhering to the traditional repertoire of songs and to the concept of singing with beauty, clarity, and a wide range of musical expression. One of the best was Barbra Streisand, a singer whose long and distinguished career brought the older pop songs to a new, younger audience. In the 1970s she had two singles that were among Cash Box's "Top Ten of the Year" listings: "The Way We Were" in 1974 and "Evergreen" in 1977, both songs from films. Other outstanding vocalists who returned time and again to songs of an earlier day were Melissa Manchester and Linda Ronstadt.

XIV. Rock On

Bruce Springsteen stands out from the plethora of rock artists searching for a new voice: a pop/rock artist who received international acclaim not for innovative music per se, but rather for being a keeper of the flame. His album Born in the U.S.A. sold more than ten million copies from its release in mid-1984 to the end of 1985. It was the Number One album of 1985 on Billboard's year-end chart.

Musicians have often responded to worthy causes, such as people in need and natural disasters, by donating their services for fundraising programs. For example, in February 1968 the Beatles, Bee Gees, and other prominent musicians began a charitable project to aid the World Wildlife Fund by donating the proceeds of a concert as well as the income from an album, No One's Gonna Change Our World.

In 1971 George Harrison (of the Beatles) and friends organized a concert for the benefit of the victims of the wars and massive population dislocations in Bangladesh. This concert was held in Madison Square Garden, New York, and led the way to more aid programs in the 1980s. In July 1985 a giant twin concert—"Live Aid"—event was held simultaneously in Philadelphia and London to raise money for African famine relief. Over ninety million dollars was raised in a single day. Ninety thousand fans jammed the J. F. Kennedy Stadium in Philadelphia and an equal number assembled in London to take part in this marathon event. The prime mover was Irish rock musician Bob Geldof. As a result of this venture, a permanent organization, the U.S.A. for Africa Foundation, was founded with Lionel Richie, Jr. as one of its directors. The song "We Are the World," written by Richie and Michael Jackson, was featured at this concert and later issued as a recording, the royalties of which were to go to the foundation. Richie and Jackson received a Grammy for this song as the best pop composition of 1985. In addition to Richie and Jackson, other performers featured in the piece included Joan Baez, Phil Collins, Black Sabbath, Run-D.M.C., the Four Tops, and Judas Priest.

Turning their attention to the plight of the American farmer, some of the nation's leading country stars organized a "Farm Aid" concert in Illinois. The $10 million proceeds were used to rescue the farmers of America from imminent foreclosure and poverty. This concert, in September 1985, featured such artists as Willie Nelson, Waylon Jennings, Johnny Cash, John Cougar Mellencamp, Neil Young, John Conley, Billy Joel, Randy Newman, and The Charlie Daniels Band.

On another note, the album Sun City was released in 1985 by the "Artists United Against Apartheid," and involved a total of forty-nine artists of different musical traditions from all parts of the world. A partial list of the names familiar to American audiences includes Pat Benatar, Rubén Blades, Jackson Browne, Ron Carter, Jimmie Cliff, Miles Davis, Bob Geldof, Daryl Hall, Herbie Hancock, John Oates, Bonnie Raitt, Lou Reed, Bruce Springsteen, Ringo Starr, Pete Townshend, and Tony Williams. These humanitarian responses to people in great need belie the not uncommon opinion that the present-day musical artist is little more than a self-indulgent, pleasure-seeking creature, devoid of compassion for his less fortunate brethren. These genuine outpourings of compassion in 1985 perhaps demonstrate that popular musicians are, indeed, among the most empathic and caring of individuals appearing before today's public.

In this article we have seen how popular song expresses the wide range of human emotions, feelings, and sensitivities, ranging from love and escape to loneliness, yearning for the past, dislocation from home, patriotism, self-pity, and humor. Great songwriting teams and performers have joined up to capture the sometimes fickle and ephemeral tastes of the musical public. There have been strong influences at work in our society, all of which have been told in song. In this century alone we have been involved in two world wars, two Asian wars, a disastrous depression, a huge influx of immigrants, a massive civil rights movement, and radical changes in the way women perceive themselves, and in the way young people respond to the pressures of society, all reflected in song. Popular song has also reflected with startling intensity the frustrations and desires of the two largest minority populations, the Blacks and the Hispanic-Americans, most recently in **rap** and **reggae**. Songs of love and romance are woven into the fabric of this music as one of the most-needed elements in a fast-paced, sometimes frenzied world.

Allen Sigel

Bibliography

Booth, Mark W. *American Popular Music: A Reference Guide.* 1983.

Cohen-Stratyner, Barbara, ed. *Popular Music, 1900–1919.* 1986.

Ewen, David. *All the Years of American Music.* 1977.

Furia, Philip. *The Poets of Tin Pan Alley: A History of America's Great Lyricists.* 1990.

Gammond, Peter. *The Oxford Companion to Popular Music.* 1991.

Hamm, Charles. *Yesterdays: Popular Song in America.* 1979.

Iwashkin, Roman. *Popular Music: A Reference Guide.* 1986.

Kanter, Kenneth Aaron. *The Jews on Tin Pan Alley: The Jewish Contribution to American Popular Music, 1870–1940.* 1982.

Lax, Roger, and Frederick Smith. *The Great Song Thesaurus.* 1989.

Marcus, Greil. *Mystery Train.* 1975.

Mast, Gerald. *Can't Help Singin': The American Musical on Stage and Screen.* 1987.

Pareles, Jon, and Patricia Romanowski. *The Rolling Stone Encyclopedia of Rock and Roll.* 1983.

Shapiro, Nat, and Bruce Pollock, eds. *Popular Music, 1920–1979.* 1984.

Spaeth, Sigmund. *A History of Popular Music in America.* 1960.

Whitcomb, Ian. *After the Ball: Pop Music From Rag to Rock.* 1972.

Wilder, Alec. *American Popular Song: The Great Innovators, 1900–1950.* 1972.

See also: Collaboration; Composer-Lyricists; Landmarks of Stage and Screen; Women as Songwriters

PROTEST SONG

Protest music has its roots in the troubadours and minstrels of Elizabethan England, who sang songs of topical interest, and in the Scottish ballad tradition. In today's music culture, protest music refers to songs with a "message," as opposed to the thematic emphasis on **love** and sex in the overwhelming majority of pop music.

Protest songs tend to be simple in structure, for their purpose is to communicate a point of view and to effect solidarity rather than to impress listeners musically. Repetition of lyrics is characteristic, allowing for easy, perhaps spontaneous, participation by large groups of people. In the "talking blues" form usually employed for protest material, the singer virtually talks rather than sings, accompanied by a simple 4/4 background.

The protest song in the contemporary sense began in the industrial, democratic age, and attained its fullest importance during the political struggles of the 1930s. Fueled by the Great Depression, the labor movement, and the growth of the American New Left, or Communist Party—so crucial to the decade's history—labor songs of protest provided both ideological support through their lyrics and a feeling of solidarity in their group performance. These labor songs of protest were often parodies or adaptations of **gospel** hymns, their musical source further strengthening that communal sense which was their very *raison d'être*.

In a way, the **blues**, as a musical form, might be considered a genre of protest music. Blues songs (for example, Robert Johnson's "Crossroads," (published in 1968), frequently criticized the Jim Crow realities of black American life, while the dominant theme of the blues, sexual love, was itself a protest against the saccharine vision of romantic love characteristic of popular music. A similar argument can also be made for **reggae**; its lyrics, full of biblical references, metaphorically rail against the pernicious influence of Americanism ("Babylon") on indigenous Jamaican culture.

During the 1930s, dust bowl balladeer Woody Guthrie infused the protest song with leftist political significance, an approach maintained by such later protest singers as the Weavers in the 1950s and Pete Seeger in the 1960s. These last-mentioned singers came on the scene just as popular music experienced a folk music revival, along with a significant element of protest. In fact, protest and **freedom songs** written in the folk song style, such as "We Shall Overcome," became essential to the civil rights movement of the 1960s.

Popular folk artists include Leadbelly with "So Long (It's Been Good to Know Yuh)" (1939) and the Weavers with "Goodnight Irene," a Number One hit in 1950. The Kingston Trio made popular "Where Have All the Flowers Gone?"; they also had a Number One hit with their adaptation of a Civil War ballad, "Tom

Dooley," in 1958. Other groups soon followed, such as the Brothers Four ("Green Fields," 1960) and the Chad Mitchell Trio ("The Marvelous Toy," 1963). Peter, Paul and Mary had charted hits with recordings of "If I Had a Hammer" in 1962 and Bob Dylan's "Blowin' in the Wind" in 1963, among others.

Songs of protest clearly entered the mainstream in the "folk-rock" explosion of the mid-1960s. Phil Ochs, Tom Paxton, Donovan, and other singer-songwriters combined songs of protest and poetry. The movement was spearheaded by Dylan, previously a folk balladeer in the Guthrie tradition. At both the Newport Folk Festival and his concert in Forest Hills, New York, in 1965, Dylan stirred considerable controversy by switching from acoustic **guitar** (the preferred instrument of the folksinger) to electric guitar and **instrumentation** (the format of rock 'n' roll), welding pop and protest music in the process. Dylan was able to make an impact on the pop charts ("Subterranean Homesick Blues" and "Like a Rolling Stone," both 1965), as were several groups recording his material. In addition to Peter, Paul and Mary, the most significant of these were the Byrds ("Mr. Tambourine Man," 1965) and the Turtles ("It Ain't Me, Babe," 1965).

These recordings achieved considerable commercial success in the highly charged political climate of the Vietnam era. As a result, the pop charts of the time were filled with protest songs with a beat: Simon and Garfunkel's "The Sound of Silence" (1964); Barry McGuire's "Eve of Destruction" (1965); the Spokesmen's "answer record," "The Dawn of Correction" (1966); and Buffalo Springfield's "For What It's Worth" (1966) are four of the most important. Since then, songs of protest have been a consistent element of an otherwise largely apolitical popular music.

Barry Keith Grant

Bibliography

Denisoff, R. Serge. *Great Day Coming: Folk Music and the American Left*. 1971.

———. *Sing a Song of Social Significance*. 1972.

———. and Richard Peterson, eds. *Sounds of Social Change*. 1972.

De Turk, David A., and A. Poulin, Jr., eds. *The American Folk Scene: Dimensions of the Folksong Revival*. 1967.

Greenway, John. *American Folksongs of Protest*. 1953.

See also: Folk Song

PUNK ROCK

An offshoot of **rock**, punk rock developed principally in **Britain** during the mid-1970s as a form of teenage revolt. The musical style itself was a throwback to that of **rock 'n' roll** in the early 1960s; most groups consisted of a vocalist, accompanied by loudly amplified guitar, bass guitar, and drums. But the essence of the music was in its performance; groups stopped at nothing for shocking effect—bizarre dress and hairdos, outrageous behavior, belligerence, profanity—in order to demonstrate their frustration and rage against the establishment.

Although punk-rock groups existed in the United States in the late 1960s, the movement did not achieve real success until the appearance of the Sex Pistols, a British group, in 1976, with Johnny Rotten (John Lydon) as vocalist and, later, Sid Vicious (John Simon Ritchie) as bassist. The Pistols was soon followed by two other successful British groups: the Clash and the Damned. Another British rock singer, Elvis Costello (Declan McManus), with his group the Attractions, found early success in the United States on Stiff Records with his own song, "Alison" (1977), performed in punk-rock style. However, punk rock did not survive as a genre into the following decade, although many of its features were absorbed into the general rock culture of the 1980s.

Bibliography

Vermorel, Fred, and Judy Vermorel. *The Sex Pistols: The Inside Story*. 1981.

See also: Heavy Metal; Protest Song; Rap; Reggae

q

QUESTIONS

Songs that pose a question come in many varieties. Often the question is merely rhetorical. Answers are neither given nor expected in such songs as "Where's That Rainbow?" (1926), "Why Was I Born?" (1929), "Isn't It Romantic?" (1932), "Isn't This is a Lovely Day" (1935), "Wouldn't It Be Loverly?" (1956), and "Isn't She Lovely?" (1976).

Sometimes a question elicits an immediate reply. In Jerome Kern's first hit, "How'd You Like to Spoon With Me?" (1905), the question in the title is at first answered with the words "I'd like to" and later by "Well rather." In Kern's "D'Ye Love Me?" (1925), the question is answered each time it is posed by the presumably affirmative syllables "Um-hu!"

A common practice is to reserve the answer for the end of the song. This occurs in "Who?" (1925), which is belatedly answered by the words "No one but you." In "Why Do I Love You?" (1927), the reply is "Because you love me," while "Why (Is There a Rainbow in the Sky?)" (1929) is answered by "'Cause I love you that's why."

Sometimes a question may be posed by a worried lover, as in "Should I (Reveal?)" (1929), "What's New?" (1939), "How Did He Look?" (1940), "Is You Is or Is You Ain't (Ma' Baby)" (1943), "What Now My Love?" (1962), and "Who Can I Turn To?" (1964).

A question can be insouciant, as in George and Ira Gershwin's "Who Cares?" (1931); can demonstrate a willingness to give romance a try, as in Cole Porter's "Why Shouldn't I?" (1935); can reflect comparative values (with or without a question mark), as in "How Deep Is the Ocean?" (1932) and "How Deep Is Your Love" (1977); or can be a request to be good, as in Porter's "Why Can't You Behave?" (1948). A question can mirror the times, as in the Depression song "Who's Afraid of the Big Bad Wolf?" (1933) or the protest song "Where Have All the Flowers Gone?" (1961). Some songs, such as "Answer Me (My Love)" (1954) and "A Lover's Question" (1958), are directly concerned with questions and answers.

A question can also be used as a story-telling device, as in "Have You Met Miss Jones?" (1937), which is the story of a romance; or as in "Is That all There Is?" (1966), which, despite the philosophical implications of its title, is in reality an autobiographical narrative. Possibly the longest question used as a title of a popular song is that of an Alan Jay Lerner and Burton Lane song from the film *Royal Wedding* (1951): "How Could You Believe Me When I Said I Love You When You Know I've Been a Liar All My Life?"

QUOTATION

Deliberate quotation from earlier music goes back to the Middle Ages, when entire works were commonly built around Gregorian chant. In popular song, quotation is distinguishable from other forms of **borrowing** in its frank acknowledgment of the source. Quotation became a part of songwriting at the turn of the twentieth century.

Songs by George M. Cohan and Irving Berlin, especially those from their early years, exemplify the use of deliberate quotation of pre-existing materials. In "The Yankee Doodle Boy" (1904), Cohan quite appropriately quoted from the original "Yankee Doodle" (1767). In "You're a Grand Old Flag" (1906), he borrowed both the words and music of "Auld Lang Syne" (c. 1711): "Should old acquaintance be forgot." The verse of Cohan's most spectacular hit, "Over There" (1917), quotes the words and music of "Johnny Get Your Gun," written in 1886, while the melody of its chorus is given a fitting military flavor by being built around the broken chord of a bugle call.

Irving Berlin, not to be outdone, used double quotation in his first great hit, "Alexander's Ragtime Band" (1911), with each quotation signalled by the lyrics.

First, he paraphrased a bugle call, and then Stephen Foster's "Old Folks at Home" (1851), referring to "the Swanee River played in ragtime." In his 1918 song "Oh, How I Hate to Get Up in the Morning," popular in two world wars, Berlin quoted a musical phrase from the bugle call "Reveille" (c. 1836), each time adding to it the words: "You've got to get up."

Direct quotation continued in use throughout the century, both in jazz **improvisation** and in the songs themselves. An example is the verse of "Bidin' My Time" (1930), in which Ira Gershwin managed to quote eight earlier song titles, including "Swingin' Down the Lane" (1923), "Tip Toe Through The Tulips With Me" (1929), and Singin' in the Rain" (1929). Other examples are the release of "Ghost Riders in the Sky" (1949)—which quotes the Civil War song "When Johnny Comes Marching Home" (1863)—and the release of "Music! Music! Music!" (1950), which borrows the music of Franz Liszt's *Hungarian Rhapsody No. 2*. In the 1980s, some of **rap**'s most successful songs quoted passages from earlier hits in a process known as digital sampling.

***See also:* Classics**

r

RADIO

Paradoxically, the glory days of radio coincided with the gloomy days of the **Depression years**. In the 1930s, when people could scarcely afford to go to the theater or cinema, radio—which they *could* afford—became the most powerful medium of entertainment in the United States. By the mid-1930s it was attracting as many as thirty million listeners each evening.

Although radio had been invented by Guglielmo Marconi as far back as 1897, it was not until 1920 that regular broadcasting began, emanating from such stations as KDKA in Pittsburgh, WWJ in Detroit, and WJZ in New York.

Radio grew by leaps and bounds during the 1920s. The first network, the National Broadcasting Company, was founded in 1926. The first remote broadcast was made by Vincent Lopez and His Orchestra from the Hotel Pennsylvania in New York in 1921. Remote broadcasts became one of the main ways of hearing the **big bands** during the 1930s and 1940s. Bands, broadcasting from ballrooms and hotel restaurants throughout the land, became a regular feature of Saturday-night programming.

As radio's popularity increased, it became a prime venue for **singers** and a showcase for the songs they introduced and popularized. One of the most popular radio singers of the 1930s was Rudy Vallee, who successfully revived such college songs as "There Is a Tavern in the Town" (1883), the University of Maine's "Stein Song" (1910), and Yale University's "The Whiffenpoof Song" (1918). Leading his group, the Connecticut Yankees (originally known as the Yale Collegians), he popularized his theme song, "My Time Is Your Time" (1927), as well as such standards as "Sweet Lorraine" (1928) and "Good Night Sweetheart" (1931) on his prime-time radio show, *The Fleischmann Hour.*

Bing Crosby also found his initial popular acceptance on radio, both as a soloist and as a member of the Rhythm Boys. Among the songs he introduced on radio, in a style that came to be called "crooning," were "I Surrender, Dear" (1931), "Just One More Chance" (1931), and "How Deep Is the Ocean?" (1932). Beginning in 1936, Crosby popularized hundreds of songs on his weekly variety show, *The Kraft Music Hall,* and went on to even further success in film.

Another crooner, Russ Columbo, also achieved great popularity on radio in 1931, introducing the songs "Prisoner of Love" and "You Call It Madness," among others. But one of the most widely popular of all singers on radio was Kate Smith, whose theme song was "When the Moon Comes Over the Mountain" (1931). Best known for her revival of Irving Berlin's patriotic song "God Bless America"—originally written in 1918—as war clouds were darkening in the late 1930s, she was the hostess of a series of radio shows throughout the decade in which she popularized hundreds of songs. Among other popular radio singers were Maurice Chevalier ("Valentine," 1926); Morton Downey ("Carolina Moon," 1928); Arthur Tracy, known as "The Street Singer" ("Marta," 1931); Belle Baker ("All of Me," 1931); Lanny Ross ("That's My Desire," 1931); Hildegarde ("Darling Je Vous Aime Beaucoup," 1936); and Frances Langford ("Music, Maestro Please," 1938).

Several comedians on radio were also identified with popular song. Eddie Cantor's *Chase and Sanborn Hour* was a regular Sunday night recreation for millions. Among songs he introduced on radio, all in 1931, were his closing theme, "(I'd Love to Spend) One Hour With You"; the Depression anthem "(Potatoes Are Cheaper—Tomatoes Are Cheaper) Now's the Time to Fall in Love"; and the political satire "When I'm the President"—known for its repeated chant to the words: "We want Cantor, We want Cantor." He was also instrumental in starting the careers of such future stars as Deanna Durbin, Eddie Fisher, and Dinah Shore. Bob Hope hosted another regular radio variety show in the late 1930s, using as his closing theme the song "Thanks for the Memory" (1937). In still another weekly variety show, the popular comedy team of George Burns and Gracie Allen used as their theme the venerable song "The Love Nest," written in 1920.

The ambition of all songwriters was to have their songs appear on the Saturday night radio show *Your Hit Parade*—a show which, like most of the variety shows, moved to **television** in the 1950s. This ranking and performance of the most popular songs of the week was eagerly awaited throughout the land.

Another type of radio performance utilized the quasi-symphonic approach. Songs were popularized by full orchestras in lush **arrangements** featuring a full complement of strings. One of the first organizations of this kind was Paul Whiteman and His Orchestra, which introduced the song "Deep Purple" in 1934. Others soon followed: André Kostelanetz; Morton Gould; Percy Faith; Harold Barlow and the Voice of Firestone; the Longines Symphonette; and Phil Spitalny and His All-Girl Orchestra, with Evelyn and "her magic violin."

Although live performance was at the heart of early radio, by the mid-1930s **recordings** gradually began to take over the airwaves. With the rise of the **disc jockey**, radio became primarily a medium for the exploitation of records. Beginning in the 1950s, the advent of the **Top Forty** format saw a new type of radio programming, leading to so-called Contemporary Hit Radio in the 1980s.

Additional Songs

Auf Wiederseh'n, My Dear (1932), popularized on radio by Russ Columbo
Betty Co-ed (1930), by Rudy Vallee
Cecilia (1925), by Whispering Jack Smith
Dream a Little Dream of Me (1931), by Kate Smith
Honey (1928), by Rudy Vallee
I Kiss Your Hand, Madame (1929), by Bing Crosby
If You Were the Only Girl in the World (1916), by Rudy Vallee
It Ain't Gonna Rain No Mo' (1923), by Wendell Hall
Let's Put Out the Lights (And Go to Sleep) (1932), by Rudy Vallee
Marie (1928), by Rudy Vallee
Mexicali Rose (1926), by the Cliquot Club Eskimos
Paradise (1931), by Russ Columbo
Please Don't Talk About Me When I'm Gone (1930), by Kate Smith
Say It Isn't So (1932), by Rudy Vallee
S'posin' (1929), by Rudy Vallee
Wabash Moon (1931), by Morton Downey
When Your Hair Has Turned to Silver (I Will Love You Just the Same) (1930), by Rudy Vallee
You and the Night and the Music (1934), by Conrad Thibault

Bibliography

Ewen, David. *All the Years of American Popular Music: A Comprehensive History.* 1977.
Lewis, Tom. *Empire of the Air: The Men Who Made Radio.* 1991.

RAGTIME

The term "ragtime" can be taken in three different contexts: as an instrumental genre, a type of song, or a musical style. The first meaning is by far the best known, but all three are important in the development of American popular song. Common to all three contexts is the employment of **syncopation**. In fact, ragtime's most characteristic feature is a syncopated treble over a measured bass.

Ragtime began in the 1890s in the southern midsection of the United States. Early centers were New Orleans; St. Louis; Sedalia, Missouri; and Chicago. It flourished during the first decade of the twentieth century, but died out soon after **World War I** with the advent of **jazz**.

To many people, the term "ragtime" refers to a three- or four-part piece for piano solo with the sectional form of a **march**. This conception was strengthened in the 1970s, when there was a veritable renaissance of ragtime. Interest was raised in the piano rags of Scott Joplin (1869–1917), in particular by the successful revivals by William Bolcom, Joshua Rifkin, and others of such Joplin works as "Maple Leaf Rag" (1899) and "The Entertainer" (1903). The latter piece formed the basis for much of the score of the film *The Sting* (1973). Although Joplin was the leading composer of ragtime during its heyday, there were other prominent composers of the genre, among them James Scott and Joseph Lamb.

Less well known is the ragtime song, a term which at first was almost synonymous with the syncopated **coon song**. Songs in this category include "A Hot Time in the Old Town" (1896), "Hello! Ma Baby" (1899), "Under the Bamboo Tree" (1902), and "Waiting for the Robert E. Lee" (1912). Shortly after the turn of the century, the ragtime song lost much of its derogatory racial connotation. The relatively innocuous "Bill Bailey, Won't You Please Come Home?" was a favorite of 1902, and by 1910 any syncopated song came to be called ragtime.

Inspired by the phenomenal success of Irving Berlin's "Alexander's Ragtime Band" in 1911, the ragtime song flourished. Although "Alexander's" is not a prime example of the genre—due to the scarcity of syncopation in its chorus—it led to a veritable craze for ragtime. Berlin himself, the so-called King of Ragtime, wrote many ragtime songs, beginning in 1909 when he ragged Felix Mendelssohn's "Spring Song" in "That Mesmerizing Mendelssohn Tune." Among other Berlin ragtime songs are "Everybody's Doin' It Now" (1911), "Ragtime Violin" (1911), "That Mysterious Rag" (with Ted Snyder, 1911), "When the Midnight Choo-Choo Leaves for Alabam'" (1912), and "That International Rag" (1913).

Ragtime songs by other songwriters proliferated in the second decade of the century, with such hits as "Oh, You Beautiful Doll" (1911), "Ragtime Cowboy Joe" (1912), "Ballin' the Jack" (1913), "12th Street Rag" (1914), "Are You From Dixie, 'Cause I'm From Dixie

Too" (1915), "Ragging the Scale" (1915), "Bugle Call Rag" (1916), "Tiger Rag" (1917), "Darktown Strutters' Ball" (1917), and "Dardanella" (1917). The ragtime song even spilled over into the **Roaring Twenties** with Noble Sissle and Eubie Blake's "I'm Just Wild About Harry" (1921).

For the most part, however, World War I marked a watershed dividing ragtime—with its emphasis on syncopation—from jazz, which featured dotted notes with or without syncopation. Nevertheless, the style of ragtime was perpetuated in novelty piano works by Felix Arndt ("Nola," 1916) and Zez Confrey ("Kitten on the Keys," 1921, and "Stumbling," 1922). Ragtime itself, with its emphasis on **rhythm** and syncopation, lives on both as a genre and as a profound influence on American popular song.

Bibliography

Berlin, Edward A. *Ragtime: A Musical and Cultural History.* 1980.

Blesh, Rudi, and Harriet Janis. *They All Played Ragtime.* 1971.

Lomax, Alan. *Mister Jelly Roll: The Fortunes of Jelly Roll Morton, New Orleans Creole and "Inventor of Jazz."* 1973.

Schafer, William J., and Johannes Riedel. *The Art of Ragtime: Form and Meaning of an Original Black American Art.* 1973.

Waldo, Terry. *This Is Ragtime.* 1976.

See also: **Cakewalk; Dance Crazes; Gay Nineties**

RAILROADS. SEE TRAINS

RAIN. SEE WEATHER

RAINBOW

The most enduring song with "rainbow" in its title was written for the film *The Wizard of Oz* in 1939. E. Y. Harburg and Harold Arlen's enchanting "Over the Rainbow" has captivated the hearts of the public for over half a century. One of its many attractions is its plaintive opening leap of an **octave.**

But there were precedents. "I'm Always Chasing Rainbows," based on the middle section of Frédéric Chopin's *Fantaisie Impromptu in C-sharp minor*, was an extraordinary success in 1918 (*see* Classics). Lorenz Hart and Richard Rodgers raised the **question** "Where's That Rainbow?" in 1926, while another question was raised three years later: "Why (Is There a Rainbow in the Sky?)." Al Jolson strutted through "There's a Rainbow Round My Shoulder" in the first film with songs, *The Singing Fool* (1928). The passage "I can see a rainbow" enhances the lyrics of another Arlen song, "I've Got the World on a String" (1932).

In 1946, an entire **musical comedy** centered around a rainbow. *Finian's Rainbow* introduced, along with other fine songs, the waltz "Look to the Rainbow." In 1964,

the song "Sunshine, Lollipops and Rainbows" was one of composer Marvin Hamlisch's earliest successes. In 1979, a charming waltz called "The Rainbow Connection" was introduced by Jim Henson as the voice of Kermit the Frog in *The Muppet Movie*. It asks why so many songs heve been written about rainbows and "what's on the other side?"

See also: **Colors; Sky; Weather**

RANGE

Popular songs, by their very nature, are confined to the span of the human voice, which is generally less than two octaves. In practice, however, many songs barely exceed the range of an **octave.**

Some songs are even narrower in range. The chorus of "Show Me the Way to Go Home" (1925), for example, has a range that spans an **interval** of only a fourth. That of Rodgers and Hart's "Lover" (1933) has a range of a major sixth, as do the choruses of "I'll Be Yours" (1945), originally known as "J'Attendrai") and "Day by Day," from the 1971 musical *Godspell*. The Mexican import "Love Me With All Your Heart" (1964) is one of many songs with a range of a major seventh.

Ranges of an octave are commonplace, as for example in the choruses of "It Could Happen to You" (1944), "The Girl That I Marry" (1946), and "My Cherie Amour" (1968). Even more common are ranges of a ninth, as in "Tea for Two" (1924), "Dancing on the Ceiling" (1930), "How Deep Is the Ocean?" (1932), "I'm In the Mood for Love" (1935), "I'm Old Fashioned" (1942), and "Send in the Clowns" (1973).

Several Jerome Kern songs are among the many with ranges of a tenth: "Why Do I Love You?" (1927), "Yesterdays" (1933), "Lovely to Look At" (1935), and "The Way You Look Tonight" (1936). Songs with ranges of an octave and a fourth include "The More I See You" (1945), "Mr. Lucky" (1959), "We've Only Just Begun" (1970), "Evergreen (Love-Theme From *A Star Is Born)*" (1976), and "Memory" (1981).

Wider ranges are more difficult for the average person to sing, and thus are far less common. They tend to appear in more innovative songs or in songs written for special purposes. Thus ranges of an octave and a fifth are found in "Body and Soul" (1930), "Begin the Beguine" (1935), and "Easy to Love" (1936); while such songs as "Ol' Man River" and "The Way He Makes Me Feel" (1983) have ranges of an octave and a sixth. Perhaps the widest range of all is found in Hoagy Carmichael's "Hong Kong Blues" (1939), which spans an interval only a half step less than two octaves.

See also: **Scale**

RAP

Rap is a musical genre characterized by fast talking and predominant **percussion.** Derived from the chant-like speech, or "rap," used by **disc jockeys** when cuing records on **radio** or at parties, it developed during the 1970s in the Harlem and Bronx sections of New York City. There, along with breakdancing and graffiti, rap was a component of the "hiphop" culture of black and Hispanic youth. Later in that decade, it spread throughout urban centers across the United States. Its popularity widened considerably during the 1980s, when it became a major part of the music industry.

As rap grew in importance during the late 1970s, labels such as Sugarhill Records formed in order to produce it for mass audiences, and rappers like Afrika Bombaata emerged as stars. The success of the Sugarhill Gang's 1979 single "Rapper's Delight," based on Chic's recording of the 1979 song "Good Times," helped push rap into prominence on a national level.

During the mid-1980s, digital sampling made it easier to reproduce and edit prerecorded songs, a fact that sparked some controversy due to varying interpretations of existing **copyright** laws. From an aesthetic sense, however, the background use of previous hits was consistent with a music derived from disc-jockey style. Thus some of rap's greatest commercial successes featured passages from earlier songs. M.C. Hammer's recording of "U Can't Touch This" (1990) utilized the bass line of Rick James's "Super Freak" (1981), while The 2 Live Crew's "Banned in the U.S.A." (1990) reiterated the chorus of Bruce Springsteen's "Born in the U.S.A." (1984). Also popular were **cover** versions of earlier hits, such as Run-DMC's "Walk This Way" (1975), previously recorded by Aerosmith; and M.C. Hammer's "Have You Seen Her" (1971), previously recorded by the Chi-Lites.

By the time Blondie released "Rapture" in 1981, it was clear that rap was reaching an audience that was not solely black, Hispanic, or urban. The rap audience quickly grew during the late 1980s largely because of videos played on cable **television**. The appeal of these videos to a mass audience helped make such songs as Biz Markie's "Just a Friend" (1989) and Tone Lōc's "Wild Thing" (1988) popular to a more ethnically and geographically diverse audience.

Ehrick V. Long

Bibliography

Hager, Steven. *Hip Hop: The Illustrated History of Break Dancing.* 1984.

Shaw, Arnold. *Black Popular Music in America: From the Spirituals, Minstrels, and Ragtime to Soul, Disco, and Hip-Hop.* 1986.

Toop. David. *The Rap Attack: African Jive to New York Hip-Hop.* 1984.

See also: Quotation; Recording

RECORDING

Since the 1920s, when it began to be more important than **sheet music**, recording has been the primary performance medium of popular song. Increasingly since then, the popularity of a song has come to be judged by the number of records it has sold, and recording a song has become the best way for a songwriter to achieve popularity and financial reward. Songwriters and publishers have sought to have their songs immediately recorded by well-known artists and to have their sales forces actively market the recordings nationwide; not until a song is recorded and heard throughout the nation can it bring a writer or publisher the **"hit song"** status desired. The same need for exposure is prevalent among recording artists; each vocalist wants a recording contract with a major company.

Recordings are sold not only to individuals for use at home, but also to **radio** stations, with their insatiable need for recordings of all kinds for use by **disc jockeys** in daily airplay. **Jukeboxes**, situated in local hangouts, corner saloons, restaurants, and taverns, are further avenues of song dissemination, while recordings supplied by **Muzak** and other companies also provide background music in department stores, elevators, offices, and shopping malls.

In 1877, Thomas Alva Edison invented a machine that could capture and reproduce sound; he called it a phonograph. Although it was originally intended as a dictating machine for use by office secretaries, it soon became apparent that it had much greater potential value in the recording of music. Edison's first machine employed tinfoil-covered cylinders, which soon gave way to wax cylinders.

In 1887, Emile Berliner invented the flat disc, an enormous improvement which made records easier to reproduce. Between 1877, when Edison first said "Mary had a little lamb" into the horn of his hand-cranked invention, and 1912, when the external horn machine lost its popularity, the U.S. Patent Office granted over two thousand patents for inventions and more than seventy for designs to more than one thousand inventors in the sound recording field. The Victor Talking Machine Company was founded in 1898, followed by the Edison Record Company and the Columbia Phonograph Company. All these firms produced instrumental and vocal recordings in both jazz and the classics. As phonographs and recordings improved in quality, home entertainment took on a new dimension.

The enormous success of Enrico Caruso's recordings in the United States enticed many other **singers** to record their voices. Among early recordings in the popular field were the discs by Chauncey Olcott of "My Wild Irish Rose" (1899) and "When Irish Eyes Are Smiling" (1912), and Nora Bayes's rendition of "Some of These Days" (1910). Paul Whiteman's recordings of "The Japanese Sandman" and "Whispering" in 1920, and of "Three O'Clock in the Morning" in 1922, were other early successes.

With the emergence of radio and the coming of the

Depression in the late 1920s and early 1930s, sales of recordings dropped dramatically. By the late 1930s, however, they began to rise again, spurred by the advertising slogan "Music you want when you want it." Brunswick and Decca soon joined Victor and Columbia as the main recording companies. They retained such singers as Bing Crosby and Ella Fitzgerald, with "White Christmas" (1942) and "A Tisket-A-Tasket" (1938), and such **singing groups** as the Andrews Sisters and the Mills Brothers, with "Bei Mir Bist Du Schön (Means That You're Grand)" (1937) and "Paper Doll" (1915).

As flat discs grew in popularity, a challenge arose for both the recording artist and the consumer. At the rate of 78 revolutions per minute, the ten-inch disc had only about three minutes of playing time. This limited the performance to the point where the artist could not fully develop a selection. Composers and arrangers felt restricted and artists sometimes felt they were not given adequate time for improvisation. The development of extended-play recordings, beginning in 1948, removed these constraints. The vinyl long-playing record (LP), with 33 ⅓ revolutions per minute, replaced the shellac disc with 78, and soon became standard—despite the popularity around 1950 of the seven-inch disc with 45 revolutions per minute, which remained popular to a lesser extent for several decades.

Many new record companies sprang up in the 1950s, and many new recording stars joined the old ones. The chief singers of this period were Frank Sinatra, Bing Crosby, Perry Como, Nat "King" Cole, and Patti Page—identified, respectively, with the songs "All the Way" (1957), "True Love" (1956), "Magic Moments" (1957), "Unforgettable" (1951), and "Tennessee Waltz" (1948). In 1958 the National Academy of Recording Arts and Sciences began giving **awards,** called "Grammys," to the recording industry in such categories as **country and western, rhythm and blues,** and **rock.** Recordings were also of primary importance in the growth of **folk music, Motown, rock 'n' roll,** and **soul,** as well as many other genres of popular song. They also contributed substantially to the success of many **performer-songwriters.**

The popularity of the LP soared in the following years, reaching a zenith in 1977, when 344 million were sold. But as the recording industry grew, it continued to produce innovations in both recording techniques and marketable recordings, and before long the LP fell out of favor. Technology in recording and playback changed the predominant form of recording from the record to the audiotape and then to the compact disc (CD). By 1988, sales of new LPs fell to 11.7 million discs, as the polycarbonate-and-aluminum CD outsold vinyl, while the total sales of recordings rose from $4.1 billion in 1978 to $6.3 billion in 1988.

A comparison of the *Statistical Abstract of the United States for 1982–1983* with that of 1990 reveals the following recording media sales for 1978 and 1988:

	1978	**1988**
LPs	47%	9.5%
singles	26%	8.6%
total recordings	73%	18.1%
cassettes	18.5%	59%
singles	8.4%	3%
total tapes	26.9%	62%
CDs	0	20%

With the increased sophistication of recording and playback, the quality of sound was enormously enhanced. This was linked to both the development of electronic hardware (receivers, speakers, tape decks) and the versatility of recording techniques. At the same time, the hardware became smaller and more portable. Listening to recorded songs was no longer a living-room activity. Songs were heard in autos, on congested highways, on jogging trails, and at the beach. These innovations gave specific groups, like teenagers, increased access to recorded music. Indeed, teenagers became the major support of the recording industry, their tastes keeping apace with current trends and popular artists.

In the 1980s there was a movement afoot by young artists to return to the style of the pre-rock era. Leaders of this movement were the brothers Wynton and Branford Marsalis, whose recordings did quite well. Song stylists such as Natalie Cole and Whitney Houston were doing vocally what the Marsalises were doing instrumentally.

Otto Werner

Bibliography

Denisoff, R. Serge. *Solid Gold: The Popular Record Industry.* 1975.

Karshner, Roger. *The Music Machine.* 1971.

Marco, Guy, ed. *Encyclopedia of Recorded Sound in the United States.* 1992.

Sanjek, Russell, and David Sanjek. *American Popular Music Business in the Twentieth Century.* 1991.

Shemel, Sidney, and M. William Krasilovsky. *This Business of Music.* 1990.

See also: **Grammy Awards**

RED. SEE COLORS

REGGAE

Reggae is a music of social protest that originated in Jamaica in the mid-1960s. It contains elements of African folk music, North American **rhythm and blues,** and an earlier, faster but similar type of Jamaican music called "ska." The **rhythm** of reggae persistently stresses the afterbeat, while the **tempo** is moderately slow. The lyrics are often concerned with poverty and the Jamaican religious movement known as Rastafarianism.

Reggae reached the United States before 1970, in imported works of small recording studios by Lee Perry and others. Songwriter proponents of reggae in the United States include Jimmy Cliff, whose hits include "Wonderful World, Beautiful People" (1969), "You Can Get It If You Really Want" (1970), and "The Harder They Come" (1973), and Bob Marley, composer-lyricist of "Stir It Up" (1972), "I Shot the Sheriff" (1974), and "Lively Up Yourself" (1975). Stevie Wonder made gentle fun of the movement in his 1975 hit "Boogie on Reggae Woman."

Henry Kelly

See also: Africa; Disco; Rap; Religion

RELEASE

A release, also known as a bridge or channel, is any contrasting section of a popular song. Most commonly the term refers specifically to the B section in **AABA** form, although releases are found in other formal constellations as well, such as ABA or ABAC. While the vast majority of releases are related to the A sections, others offer contrast—most often carried out by rhythmic or harmonic change.

Rhythmic contrast can involve the introduction of eighth notes into the B section, in contrast to the prevailing long notes of the A section, as for example in songs like Duke Ellington's "Solitude" (1934) and Harold Arlen's "Stormy Weather" (1933) and "Over the Rainbow" (1939).

Harmonic contrast flourished during the **golden age** of popular song, when AABA **form** predominated. The release gave the composer an opportunity to veer away harmonically from the established **tonality** of the A section. Some composers took advantage of this liberty in unexpected ways. Jerome Kern, in particular, took some very interesting harmonic excursions in his middle sections. In "The Song Is You" (1932), the release begins in the **key** of the mediant (E in the key of C) and modulates through the **circle of fifths** (D-sharp, G-sharp, C-sharp, F-sharp) to a dominant seventh chord on B, which acts as a leading tone to the return of the principal theme. Other releases by other composers, like that of Ray Henderson's "Five Foot Two, Eyes of Blue; Has Anybody Seen My Girl?" (1925), are less complex, simply wandering through the circle of fifths.

In Kern's "Smoke Gets in Your Eyes" (1933), the release is in the key of the enharmonic equivalent of the flatted submediant (B in the key of E-flat). The release of "I Won't Dance" (1935) also begins with the flatted submediant (A-flat in the key of C), but moves enharmonically through some unusual harmonies partly involving the circle of fifths: D-flat, B seventh, C seventh, E seventh, A minor, D minor, G seventh. The

release of "The Way You Look Tonight" (1936) is in the key of the flatted mediant (G-flat in the key of E-flat), while that of "All the Things You Are" (1939) is in the key of the leading tone (G in the key of A-flat).

Similarly, the release of Ellington's "Sophisticated Lady" (1933) is in the key of the leading tone (G in the key of A-flat), while that of John Green's "Body and Soul" (1930) is in the key of the flatted supertonic (D in the key of D-flat). Extreme harmonic complexity is found in the release of Richard Rodgers's "Have You Met Miss Jones?" (1937), which starts in the subdominant (B-flat in the key of F) and modulates enharmonically through D-flat, G-flat, A, D, D-flat, and G-flat to the C dominant-seventh, before returning to the tonic. Other examples of tonal contrast are the use of the mediant in the release of "You're Driving Me Crazy" (1930)—A in the key of F—and the flatted submediant in the release of "Dream a Little Dream of Me" (1931)—D-flat in the key of F.

The diversity of ideas in middle sections is astonishing. Some, such as those of Kern's "Ol' Man River" (1927) and "I've Told Ev'ry Little Star" (1932, use melodic and harmonic material identical to that of the **verse**. Some releases are short (six bars, in Kern's "The Folks Who Live on the Hill," 1937), while others are long and meandering (thirteen bars, in "[Where Do I Begin] Love Story" 1970).

In light of all this seeming complexity, it is worthwhile to note that some of the most effective releases are characterized by rhythmic and harmonic simplicity. A case in point is Kurt Weill's evocative eight-bar release for "September Song" (1938).

See also: Chorus; Enharmonic Equivalence; Harmony; Interval; Melody; Modulation

RELIGION

Music has always played a significant role in the history of religion in America, especially in the realm of Christianity. Inside the church walls, music has served to convey doctrine, to inspire worship, and to offer spiritual solace. Outside, music has functioned as an extension of the evangelist's power. Designed to attract nonbelievers to the **gospel** message, it intentionally mirrors contemporary styles of popular song.

In the 1960s, the secular-styled religious song not only won new converts but also accompanied those converts into their respective congregations, be they Protestant or Roman Catholic, black or white. Thus the music of evangelism often became the music for services of worship. Nowhere was this more evident than in the Roman Catholic Church after sweeping liturgical reforms were enacted by Vatican II between 1962 and 1965. With the required replacement of Latin by the vernacular in the *Mass* and the encouraged participation by lay persons in the liturgy, the framework was in place for the introduction of guitar-accompanied folksong masses such as Ray Repp's *Mass for Young Americans* (1964) and the use of new songs by the congregations. Responding to this need for new music, groups such as the St. Louis Jesuits issued recordings of newly composed songs suitable for liturgical use. The Jesuits' *Earthen Vessels* (1975) sold well over a million copies.

A similar invasion of the secular into the sacred realm occurred in Protestant churches. Bob Dylan's "Blowin' in the Wind" (1962) and Pete Seeger's "Turn! Turn! Turn!" (1962), along with folk masses, were as commonplace as the traditional hymnody. Guitars and instrumental combos augmented or supplanted the king of instruments, the organ.

The decade of the 1950s saw religious music gain a permanent foothold in commercial markets. Many recordings were listed on *Billboard*'s pop charts, and several achieved gold status. Sometimes the best-sellers came directly from traditional church hymns and gospel songs; at other times, the music represented close paraphrases of church-accepted materials. Examples of both types of songs (along with the performing artists) which made the charts in the 1950s include "The Bible Tells Me So" (Don Cornell) in 1955, "Every Time (I Feel His Spirit)" (Patti Page) and "Give Us This Day" (Joni James) in 1956, "Peace in the Valley" (Elvis Presley) in 1957, "He's Got the Whole World in His Hands" (Laurie London) in 1958, and "When the Saints Go Marching In" (Fats Domino) in 1959.

Additional examples of hymns becoming best sellers are "Morning Has Broken" and "Amazing Grace," both with roots in English hymnody. Eleanor Farjeon wrote "Morning Has Broken" in 1931 and set the text to David Evans's harmonization of a Gaelic melody which had already appeared in print four years earlier. The hymn, designed to be sung in unison, is notated in 9/4 meter, thereby preserving the lilting quality of the original melody. Although the Farjeon-Evans hymn was included in several American mainline hymnals (such as *The Hymnbook* published for the Presbyterians in 1955), it was not well known until Cat Stevens popularized it in 1971.

"Amazing Grace" was penned in the 1770s by the English hymn writer, John Newton. Of all the different tunes to which the text has been paired, none has been a more suitable or powerful vehicle than that by an anonymous American folk hymn composer. This uniquely American version of "Amazing Grace" was published at least as early as 1854 in William Walker's *Southern Harmony*. Since that date, countless interpretations of the hymn have co-existed, both in the churches and shape-note soceites and in the commercial marketplace. Artists who have secured a place for "Amazing Grace" on the pop charts include Jean Ritchie, Judy Collins, Johnny Cash, Aretha Franklin, Marion Williams, and Jessie Norman.

One of the first singles to receive the RIAA award of a gold record was "He's Got the Whole World in His Hands" (1958). Over the next three years, Tennessee Ernie Ford released four gold albums: *Hymns* (1959), *Spirituals* (1961), *Nearer the Cross* (1962), and *Star Carol* (1962). The last-named album was one of more than fifteen Christmas albums that were gold records in the 1960s.

As Ford's album titles indicate, his material was derived from traditional church music. So, too, were the songs featured on two other gold albums: *The Lord's Prayer* (Mormon Tabernacle Choir) in 1963 and *How Great Thou Art* (Elvis Presley) in 1968. The title song of the Presley album was introduced to Americans at a 1954 Billy Graham Crusade by George Beverly Shea. This hymn, with its verse-refrain format, was composed in Sweden in 1885 by the Rev. Carl Robert. Almost a quarter of a century later, German and Russian translations of the hymn were published, followed by an English translation in 1948 by Stuart K. Hine, who also wrote an additional fourth stanza. It was the Hine version of "How Great Thou Art" that Shea sang at the 1954 Crusade and at many Graham crusades' thereafter. So popular was this hymn, heard by millions of Americans tuned in to the crusades via radio and television, that it quickly made its way into many Protestant hymnals. Presley further popularized the hymn with his gold album in 1968. "How Great Thou Art" continued to be a popular standard into the 1990s.

With the 1960s came an era of political activism tempered with spiritual ideals—an era that was indelibly marked by the Jesus Movement, which began in San Francisco's coffee houses in 1967, and an era in which ecumenism and the pluralism of the world's religions was experienced. A line from Bob Dylan's "Blowin' in the Wind" asks "How many roads must a man walk down?"—a very pertinent question for the 1960s, for the paths individuals traversed in their spiritual quest for the meaning of life and in their search for peace, truth, and love were as numerous as they were varied.

Dylan's own life traversed four religious paths—from Judaism to religious protest, from born-again Christian back to Judaism—and several musical paths—folk, rock, and gospel. Although "Blowin' in the Wind" will forever remain Dylan's signature piece, it is but one among many of his songs which are religiously oriented. "The Times They Are A-Changin'" (1964) and "Desolation Row" (1965) are two that incorporate biblical references to underscore Dylan's message of protest against American society. Both songs follow the same structural design: the words of their respective titles are repeated after each stanza.

That so many religious songs rose to the top of the charts is due in large measure to the talents of the recording artists. A case in point is Pete Seeger's "Turn! Turn! Turn!" with its lyrics paraphrased from a well-known passage from Ecclesiastes. Twice in the same year, 1965, this song made the charts, in recordings by the Byrds and Judy Collins. Recordings by Peter, Paul and Mary also were successful in bringing to the charts a number of important religious and social-activist songs: "If I Had a Hammer" in 1962, "Blowin' in the Wind" in 1963, and "Oh, Rock My Soul" and "Go Tell It on the Mountain" in 1964.

From the 1970s come two highly controversial yet successful musicals based upon the life of Jesus as revealed in the gospels: *Jesus Christ Superstar* (1970) by Andrew Lloyd Webber and Tim Rice and *Godspell* (1971) by Stephen Schwartz. *Jesus Christ Superstar* was first released as a recording (1970), then staged as a Broadway play (1971), and finally made into a film (1973), whose soundtrack album won a platinum award. This rock-styled musical (sometimes called a rock opera) caused problems theologically because the libretto cast Jesus not as half-mortal and half-divine, but simply as mortal: Jesus experiences death, but not resurrection. Of course, those who espoused the Jesus Movement, among others, were quite comfortable with the Webber-Rice portrayal of Jesus, for they envisioned Jesus as "a rebel," one involved with religion on the streets rather than in the churches. Hit songs from this work are "Superstar (Jesus Christ, Do You Think You're What They Say You Are?)" and "I Don't Know How to Love Him."

Godspell was presented first as a stage musical and then as a film. The latter was not as highly acclaimed as the stage version, mainly because *Godspell* depends upon physical interaction between actors and audience, achieved by use of the auditorium space and stage area by both groups. In this work, Jesus is cast as a gentle clown and his parables are set forth in slapstick comic style accompanied by songs that reverberate with American dance rhythms such as the cakewalk. The *Godspell* album was awarded gold status and one of its songs, "Day By Day," was a hit single. Also popular was the "Willow Song," a close paraphrase of the opening verses of Psalm 137, which begins with the words "By the water of Babylon."

Although the majority of religious songs that were popular hits, along with their respective performing artists, were associated in one way or another with mainline Christian traditions, there was a significant corpus of hit materials that represented other religious persuasions. For example, the Seals and Crofts album *Summer Breeze* (1972) contains songs in praise of nature, peace, and love—songs that expressed the Baha'i faith that James Seals and Dash Crofts embraced in the late 1960s. Two songs on this album make direct reference to the Baha'i scriptures: "Hummingbird" and "East of Ginger Trees." While some of their contemporaries were stressing war and drugs in their songs, Seals and Crofts emphasized the nonpolitical nature of religion. *Summer Breeze* was meant to signal a kind of "worship" in

which one "serves mankind and ministers to the needs of the people."

The beliefs of Rastafarians, a religious group indigenous to Jamaica, were brought into popular culture with the music of **reggae** artists Bob Marley and Peter Tosh. Reggae lyrics stress the messages of the faith and emphasize the Rastafarian concept of God as a living creature, one who is here on earth amidst his people. "Rivers of Babylon," made popular in the movie *The Harder They Come*, is a reggae song based upon Psalm 137 of the Hebrew scriptures. It uses a device favored in black spirituals, namely, assigning double meanings to the lyrics: "Babylon" is really Jamaica and "Zion" is Ethiopia, the promised land.

Additional Songs

All You Need Is Love (1967)
Dominique (1963)
Eve of Destruction (1965)
Oh Happy Day (1969)
He (1954)
I Believe (1952)
I'll Take You There (1972)
Joy (1972)
Michael (Row the Boat Ashore) (1960)
My Sweet Lord (1970)
Put Your Hand in the Hand (1971)
Spirit in the Sky (1969)
There's a Gold Mine in the Sky (1937)
You'll Never Walk Alone (1945)

Hermine W. Williams

See also Angels; Folk Song; Gospel; Heaven; Inspiration; Protest Song; Sky; Soul

REMEMBRANCE. SEE MEMORY

REPEATED NOTE

Repeated notes are very common in the **melodies** of popular songs; they are so common, in fact, that they may be said to represent an idiosyncratic style characteristic of the genre.

When used in **verses**, repeated notes are reminiscent of the role played by recitative in opera, where repetition of notes is commonly used for declamatory purposes. The verse of the 1944 song "The Boy Next Door," for example, is noted for its recitation of two neighboring addresses on Kensington Avenue in St. Louis, using twenty-four repeated notes. Similarly, the verse of "It Never Entered My Mind" (1940) starts with twenty-seven repeated notes, before repeating notes on other degrees of the scale. The verse of "Night and Day" (1932) has thirty-five consecutive B-flats at its beginning and eleven more at its end, accompanied by such alliterative words as "beat, beat, beat" and "tick, tick, tock." The verse of "I Could Write a Book" (1940) begins with thirteen repetitions of the note "G", reciting the letters "A, B, C, D, E, F, G," and concludes with fourteen more reciting the numbers "1, 2, 3, 4, 5, 6, 7."

Repeated notes are also common in **choruses**. Monotony, always a risk, is averted by the use of changing **harmonies** and moving **bass lines** beneath the identical notes of the melody. The opening note of Johnny Mercer and Harold Arlen's "Come Rain or Come Shine" (1946), for example, is repeated thirteen times to the lyrics "I'm gonna love you like nobody's loved you, come rain or come shine," but the declamatory nature of the words, the constantly changing harmonies, and the moving bass line prevent the listener's loss of interest. The opening note of "One Note Samba" (1961), as its title suggests, is repeated forty-seven times, but the song is rescued from boredom by its interesting bass line, descending chromatically.

Repeated notes are used extensively too in Irving Berlin's "I Got Lost in His Arms" (1946). The opening phrase (in the key of F) repeats the note "C" nine times and the note "D" ten times, before moving on. Then, just as the tension created by the repetition threatens to bring about a loss of interest, the melody drops in a lovely, falling motion and the listener breathes a sigh of relief.

Cole Porter was fond of repeated notes. In his ballad "Ev'ry Time We Say Goodbye," the opening "G" is sounded eight times before the melody moves up a half step. Repeated notes are also used in the choruses of Porter's "Night and Day" (1932), "Just One of Those Things" (1935), "It's D'Lovely" (1936), and "I Love Paris" (1953), among other songs.

Another interesting example of repeated notes lies in Rodgers and Hammerstein's "The Surrey With the Fringe on Top" (1943). The beginning note is repeated six times before the melody dips down a half step; it then returns to the repeated note and moves up a fourth. The insistent repetition of the first note gives the effect of the clip-clop sound of a horse-drawn surrey.

Repeated notes frequently enhance the **lyrics** of songs by George and Ira Gershwin. Few can forget their fortuitous use, accompanying such passages as "Come to Papa, come to Papa do," in "Embraceable You" (1930), and "The way you hold your hat," in "They Can't Take That Away From Me" (1937).

Many other examples could be given. In the French song "(All of a Sudden) My Heart Sings" (1941), the melody is simply a diatonic **scale**, moving upward and then downward, with each note repeated from eight to ten times. In the 1954 song "Shake, Rattle and Roll," repeated notes always appear along with the title, which itself is repeated over and over. Repeated notes bring character to the melodies of such diverse songs as "Dancing in the Dark" (1931), "That Old Black Magic" (1942), "The Trolley Song" (1943), and "Gentle on My Mind" (1967). Repeated notes are also sometimes found in the **releases** of otherwise conventional songs, as for

example in "Serenade in Blue" (1942) and "Moonlight in Vermont" (1944).

The 1950 song "Be Mine," recorded by Mindy Carson, probably breaks all records for repeated notes. It consists of one note, a "G," repeated 111 times. The harmony beneath this one-note melody moves about, alternating between the keys of C and E-flat. Despite its limitations, the song remains a standard, proving that repeated notes have earned a hallowed place in popular song.

Loonis McGlohon

REVUES

A revue is a theatrical production featuring songs and comic sketches which may or may not be related to one another by a theme or plot. Conceived in the 1890s, the genre developed out of **vaudeville** and reached its apogee in the United States during the 1920s and 1930s. By the 1950s it had all but disappeared, overwhelmed by the rival spectacles of **musical comedy**, **operetta**, and **film musicals**, although it survived into the 1990s in the form of the retrospective revue.

In its halcyon days, revues were a feast for the eyes, characterized by "glorified" girls, extravagant costumes, lavish sets, and hummable songs. Today, sadly, only the songs remain. Some of our most enduring standards were introduced in revues, presented both in theaters and nightclubs (*see* Table 14).

Six series of revues contributed the most to popular song: Florenz Ziegfeld, Jr.'s *Follies*, George White's *Scandals*, J. J. and Lee Shubert's various editions of *The Passing Show*, Sam H. Harris and Irving Berlin's *Music Box Revues*, Earl Carroll's *Vanities*, and various annual revues called *The Blackbirds*.

Among the many songs introduced in one or another of Ziegfeld's *Follies*, which ran intermittently from 1907 to 1957, were "Shine On, Harvest Moon" in 1908; "By the Light of the Silvery Moon" in 1909; "Row, Row, Row" in 1912; "A Pretty Girl Is Like a Melody" and "You'd Be Surprised" (both in 1919—the latter introduced by Eddie Cantor); "My Man" and "Second Hand Rose" (both introduced by Fanny Brice in 1921); "The Last Roundup," "Wagon Wheels," and "What Is There to Say?" in 1934; and "I Can't Get Started" in 1936.

George White's Scandals, running from 1919 to 1939, introduced two songs by a young composer named George Gershwin: "I'll Build a Stairway to Paradise" (1922) and "Somebody Loves Me" (1924). Other songs first performed in the series were "The Birth of the Blues," "Black Bottom," and "Lucky Day" in 1926; "Life Is Just a Bowl of Cherries," "That's Why Darkies Were Born," and "The Thrill Is Gone" in 1931; and "Are You Havin' Any Fun?" in 1939.

The Passing Shows, no relation to *The Passing Show* of 1894, ran from 1912 to 1924 and introduced such songs as "By the Beautiful Sea" and "The Trail of the Lonesome Pine" (1914), "Pretty Baby" (1916),

"Smiles" (1917), and "Carolina in the Morning" (1922).

The *Music Box Revues* appeared in only four editions, from 1921 to 1924. A showcase for Berlin's songs, they were presented in the exquisite Music Box Theatre, owned by Harris and Berlin. Songs introduced there included "Everybody Step" and "Say It With Music" (1921), "Lady of the Evening" and "What'll I Do?" (1923), and "All Alone" (1924).

Earl Carroll's Vanities, which ran from 1923 to 1940, resulted in only two standards: "Good Night Sweetheart" and "I Gotta Right to Sing the Blues," both from the 1932 edition. From the *Blackbirds*, running sporadically from 1928 to 1939, came "Diga Diga Doo" and "I Can't Give You Anything But Love," from the 1928 edition; and "Memories of You," from that of 1930.

There were, of course, other revue series as well as independent revues. From *The Greenwich Village Follies* of 1920 came Ted Lewis's theme song "When My Baby Smiles at Me," while "Three O'Clock in the Morning" (1921) and Cole Porter's "I'm in Love Again" (1924) were first presented in subsequent editions. There were two editions of *The Garrick Gaieties*. From the 1925 edition, the first real success of the songwriting team of Richard Rodgers and Lorenz Hart, came "Manhattan" and "Sentimental Me," while out of the 1926 revue came "Mountain Greenery." There were three editions of *The Little Show*, from 1929 to 1931. Out of the first came the songs "Can't We Be Friends?," "I Guess I'll Have to Change My Plan," and "Moanin' Low," while *The Third Little Show* introduced "Mad Dogs and Englishmen" and "When Yuba Plays the Rumba on the Tuba."

Several revues not appearing in series also stand out for their songs. From one of them, *Chauve-Souris* (1922)—an interesting theater piece featuring Russian émigrés—came the 1905 German song, "Parade of the Wooden Soldiers." Two outstanding standards were introduced in the 1930 revue *Three's a Crowd* (1930): "Body and Soul" and "Something to Remember You By." In the same year, *Lew Leslie's International Revue* introduced the perennial favorites "Exactly Like You" and "On the Sunny Side of the Street." From *The Band Wagon* (1931) came "Dancing in the Dark" and "I Love Louisa"; *Flying Colors*, produced a year later, introduced "Alone Together," "Louisiana Hayride," and "A Shine on Your Shoes." Still another revue of 1931 was *Crazy Quilt*, from which came "I Found a Million Dollar Baby (In a Five and Ten Cent Store)." Vernon Duke's immortal "April in Paris" was first presented in a revue called *Walk a Little Faster* (1934), while *The Show Is On*, a revue of 1936, introduced Ira and George Gershwin's "By Strauss" and Stanley Adams and Hoagy Carmichael's "Little Old Lady."

Two of Berlin's most successful revues were *As Thousands Cheer* (1933) and *This Is the Army* (1942). From the former came "Easter Parade," "Heat Wave," and "Not for All the Rice in China"; from the latter, "I Left My Heart at the Stage Door Canteen" and "This Is the Army Mister Jones," as well as reprises of Berlin's songs "Mandy" and "Oh, How I Hate to Get Up in the Morning," both originally presented in his revue *Yip! Yip! Yaphank* of 1918.

Lean years for the genre began during and after **World War II**. A few memorable songs appeared—"Ev'ry Time We Say Goodbye," from *Seven Lively Arts* (1944); "South America, Take It Away," from *Call Me Mister* (1946); "Rhode Island Is Famous for You," from *Inside U.S.A.* (1948); "Boston Beguine" and "Love Is a Simple Thing," from *New Faces of 1952*—but the rising tides of musical comedy, operetta, **radio, television,** and **film** contributed to the revue's downfall.

Beginning in the 1960s, revues turned from originality to retrospection. Songwriters were the first to be remembered: Cole Porter in *The Decline and Fall of the Entire World as Seen Through the Eyes of Cole Porter* (1965); Jacques Brel in *Jacques Brel Is Alive and Well and Living in Paris* (1968); Bert Williams, Shelton Brooks, Eubie Blake, Duke Ellington, and Thomas "Fats" Waller in *Bubbling Brown Sugar* (1976); Stephen Sondheim in *Side by Side by Sondheim* (1978); John Lennon and Paul McCartney in *Beatlemania* (1977); Thomas "Fats" Waller in *Ain't Misbehavin'* (1978); Eubie Blake in *Eubie* (1978); and Duke Ellington in *Sophisticated Ladies* (1982). Retrospective revues featuring veteran performers began with *Sugar Babies* (1979), featuring Ann Miller and Mickey Rooney, and continued with *Lena Horne: The Lady and Her Music* (1982).

In its heyday, the revue, so often topical, produced a number of standards that have endured far longer than their writers could have envisioned. Long gone are the tinsel and gold of such revues as the *Follies* and the *Scandals*, but their songs endure.

Bibliography

Baral, Robert. *Revue: A Nostalgic Reprise of the Great Broadway Period.* 1970.

Bordman, Gerald. *American Musical Revue: From the Passing Show to Sugar Babies.* 1985.

Ewen, David. *All the Years of American Popular Music: A Comprehensive History.* 1977.

See also: **Broadway; Cabaret**

TABLE 14
Songs Introduced in Revues

Americana (1932)
lyrics: E. Y. Harburg, music: Jay Gorney
Brother, Can You Spare a Dime?

As Thousands Cheer (1933)
lyrics and music: Irving Berlin
Easter Parade
Heat Wave
Not for All the Rice in China
Supper Time

The Band Wagon (1931)
lyrics: Howard Dietz, music: Arthur Schwartz
Dancing in the Dark
I Love Louisa

Blackbirds (of 1928)
lyrics: Dorothy Fields, music: Jimmy McHugh
Diga Diga Do
I Can't Give You Anything But Love

Blackbirds of 1930
lyrics: Andy Razaf, music: Eubie Blake
Memories of You

Call Me Mister (1946)
lyrics and music: Harold Rome
South America, Take It Away

Chauve-Souris (1922)
lyrics: Ballard MacDonald, lyrics: Leon Jessel
Parade of the Wooden Soldiers

Crazy Quilt (1931)
lyrics: Mort Dixon and Billy Rose, music: Harry Warren
I Found a Million Dollar Baby (In a Five and Ten Cent Store)

Earl Carroll's Vanities (1932)
lyrics and music: Ray Noble, Jimmy Campbell, and Reginald Connelly
Good Night Sweetheart
lyrics: Ted Koehler, music: Harold Arlen
I Gotta Right to Sing the Blues

Flying Colors (1932)
lyrics: Howard Dietz, music: Arthur Schwartz
Alone Together
Louisiana Hayride
A Shine on Your Shoes

Follies, *See:* **Ziegfeld Follies**

The Garrick Gaieties (First Edition, 1925)
lyrics: Lorenz Hart, music: Richard Rodgers
Manhattan
Sentimental Me

The Garrick Gaieties (Second Edition, 1926)
lyrics: Lorenz Hart, music: Richard Rodgers
Mountain Greenery

George White's Music Hall Varieties (1932)
lyrics and music: Herman Hupfeld
Let's Put Out the Lights (And Go to Sleep)

George White's Scandals of 1922
lyrics: Arthur Francis (pseud. Ira Gershwin), music:

George Gershwin
I'll Build a Stairway to Paradise

George White's Scandals of 1924
lyrics: B. G. DeSylva and Ballard MacDonald, music: George Gershwin
Somebody Loves Me

George White's Scandals of 1926
lyrics: B. G. DeSylva and Lew Brown, music: Ray Henderson
The Birth of the Blues
Black Bottom
Lucky Day

George White's Scandals of 1931
lyrics: Lew Brown, music: Ray Henderson
Life Is Just a Bowl of Cherries
lyrics: B. G. DeSylva and Lew Brown, music: Ray Henderson
That's Why Darkies Were Born
The Thrill Is Gone

George White's Scandals of 1939
lyrics: Jack Yellen, music: Sammy Fain
Are You Havin' Any Fun?

The Greenwich Village Follies, 1920
lyrics: Andrew B. Sterling and Ted Lewis, music: Bill Munro
When My Baby Smiles at Me

The Greenwich Village Follies of 1921
lyrics: Dorothy Terris, music: Julian Robeldo
Three O'Clock in the Morning

The Greenwich Village Follies of 1924
lyrics and music: Cole Porter
I'm in Love Again

Hot Chocolates (1929)
lyrics: Andy Razaf, music: Thomas "Fats" Waller and Harry Brooks
Ain't Misbehavin'

Inside U.S.A. (1948)
lyrics: Howard Dietz, music: Arthur Schwartz
Rhode Island Is Famous for You

Lew Leslie's International Revue (1930)
lyrics: Dorothy Fields, music: Jimmy McHugh
Exactly Like You
On the Sunny Side of the Street

The Little Show (1929)
lyrics: Paul James, music: Kay Swift
Can't We Be Friends?
lyrics: Howard Dietz, music: Arthur Schwartz
I Guess I'll Have to Change My Plan
lyrics: Howard Dietz, music: Ralph Rainger
Moanin' Low

The Little Show (1931)
lyrics and music: Noël Coward
Mad Dogs and Englishmen
lyrics and music: Herman Hupfeld
When Yuba Plays the Rumba on the Tuba

Load of Coal (1929)
 lyrics: Andy Razaf, music: Thomas "Fats" Waller
  Honeysuckle Rose

The Music Box Revue (1921)
 lyrics and music: Irving Berlin
  Everybody Step
  Say It With Music

The Music Box Revue of 1922
 lyrics and music: Irving Berlin
  Lady of the Evening

The Music Box Revue of 1923
 lyrics and music: Irving Berlin
  What'll I Do?

The Music Box Revue of 1924
 lyrics and music: Irving Berlin
  All Alone

New Faces of 1952
 lyrics: June Carroll, music: Arthur Siegel
  Boston Beguine
  Love Is a Simple Thing

The Passing Show of 1914
 lyrics: Harold R. Atteridge, music: Harry Carroll
  By the Beautiful Sea
 lyrics: Ballard MacDonald, music: Harry Carroll
  The Trail of the Lonesome Pine

The Passing Show of 1916
 lyrics: Gus Kahn, music: Egbert Van Alstyne
  Pretty Baby

The Passing Show of 1918
 lyrics: Will Callahan, music: Lee G. Roberts
  Smiles

The Passing Show of 1922
 lyrics: Gus Kahn, music: Walter Donaldson
  Carolina in the Morning

Scandals. *See:* **George White's Scandals**

Seven Lively Arts (1944)
 lyrics and music: Cole Porter
  Ev'ry Time We Say Goodbye

The Show Is On (1936)
 lyrics: Ira Gershwin, music: George Gershwin
  By Strauss
 lyrics: Stanley Adams, music: Hoagy Carmichael
  Little Old Lady

Shuffle Along (1921)
 lyrics: Noble Sissle, music: Eubie Blake
  I'm Just Wild About Harry

This Is the Army (1942)
 lyrics and music: Irving Berlin
  I Left My Heart at the Stage Door Canteen
  This Is the Army, Mr. Jones

Three's a Crowd (1930)
 lyrics: Edward Heyman, Robert Sour, and Frank Eyton, music: John Green
  Body and Soul
 lyrics: Howard Dietz, music: Arthur Schwartz
  Something to Remember You By

Thumbs Up! (1934)
 lyrics and music: Vernon Duke
  Autumn in New York

Vanities. *See:* **Earl Carroll's Vanities**

Walk a Little Faster (1934)
 lyrics: E. Y. Harburg, music: Vernon Duke
  April in Paris

Will o' the Whispers (1927)
 lyrics: George Whiting, music: Walter Donaldson
  My Blue Heaven

Ziegfeld Follies of 1908
 lyrics: Jack Norworth, music: Nora Bayes and Jack Norworth
  Shine On, Harvest Moon

Ziegfeld Follies of 1909
 lyrics: Edward Madden, music: Gus Edwards
  By the Light of the Silvery Moon

Ziegfeld Follies of 1912
 lyrics: William Jerome, music: James V. Monaco
  Row, Row, Row

Ziegfeld Follies of 1919
 lyrics and music: Irving Berlin
  Mandy
  A Pretty Girl Is Like a Melody
  You'd Be Surprised

Ziegfeld Follies of 1921
 lyrics: Channing Pollock, music: Maurice Yvain
  My Man
 lyrics: Grant Clarke, music: James F. Hanley
  Second Hand Rose

Ziegfeld Follies of 1934
 lyrics and music: William Hill
  The Last Round-Up
 lyrics: Billy Hill, music: Peter DeRose
  Wagon Wheels
 lyrics: E. Y. Harburg, music: Vernon Duke
  What Is There to Say?

Ziegfeld Follies of 1936
 lyrics: Ira Gershwin, music: Vernon Duke
  I Can't Get Started

RHYME

Rhyme, the echoing of similar sounds at the end of a line, is perhaps the most immediately recognizable element of a song's **lyrics**. As with many other aspects of popular song, the decade of the 1960s acted as a watershed between perfect rhyme (meet/street) and near rhyme (crime/wine).

In the first part of the twentieth century, perfect rhyme prevailed, inspired by the works of virtuoso **lyricist** W. S. Gilbert. Author (with Arthur Sullivan) of such international successes as *H.M.S. Pinafore* (1878) and *The Mikado* (1885), Gilbert could seemingly effortlessly rhyme "astronomical" with "comical" or "urbanity" with "insanity."

Rhyme comes in several varieties. The most common, masculine rhyme, involves the matching of only one syllable (e.g., true/blue). In feminine rhyme, on the other hand, two syllables agree (e.g., blameful/shameful), while triple rhyme matches three syllables, as in Ira Gershwin's unforgettable pairing of "embraceable" with "irreplaceable" in "Embraceable You" (1930).

Lorenz Hart was the acknowledged master of rhyme in all its varieties. His rhymes are seldom found in rhyming dictionaries. Sometimes they refer to celebrities: for example, the pairing of "Dietrich" with "sweet trick" in "the Most Beautiful Girl in the World" (1935). When necessary, Hart would invent a word, as he did with "laughable" and "unphotographable" in "My Funny Valentine" (1937). Another Hart specialty was internal rhyme—matching sounds within a sentence—as in "Sang out with gusto and just overloaded the place," in "Johnny One Note" (1937).

Gershwin, on the other hand, was not always a slave to rhyme. The chorus of "I Got Rhythm" (1930), for example, avoids it, relying instead on repetition of the phrase "Who could ask for anything more." Yet the verse of the same song compensates by supplying two rhymes for each line: rhyming "sunny" with "money," "sigh" with "buy," "tree sing" with "we sing," "song" with "along," "day" with "way," and "lot" with "got." Other songs, such as "Moonlight in Vermont" (1944) and "Annie's Song" (1974), stand on their own without any rhyme at all.

In the **golden age** of popular song, careful rhyming was the rule, carried out by such craftsmen and craftswomen as E. Y. "Yip" Harburg, Cole Porter, Johnny Mercer, and Dorothy Fields. But from the 1960s on, perfect rhyme fell out of fashion in much of popular song—along with such other pre-1960 manifestations as AABA **form** and nonelectric instruments. In its place came consonance (the matching of consonants), assonance (the matching of vowels), other forms of near rhyme, or the avoidance of rhyme altogether. In general, rhyming became less important to songwriters, who used such near rhymes as "mine/time" ("The First Time Ever I Saw Your Face," 1962) and "eyes/cry" ("After the Lovin'" 1974).

By the 1980s, near rhyme was the rule, in pairings like "down/around" and "radio/already know" ("Sad Songs [Say So Much]," 1984). But perfect rhyme never ceased. The traditions of rhyming established by Gilbert still held sway in the musical theater, as in "The Music of the Night," from *The Phantom of the Opera* (1986), which has such romantic couplings as "sensation/imagination," "caress you/possess you," and "sweet intoxication/savour each sensation."

Bibliography

Davis, Sheila. *The Craft of Lyric Writing*. 1985.

Furia, Philip. *The Poets of Tin Pan Alley: A History of America's Great Lyricists*. 1990.

Gershwin. Ira. *Lyrics on Special Occasions: A Selection of Stage and Screen Lyrics*. 1978.

Hart, Dorothy, ed. *Thou Swell, Thou Witty*. 1976.

See also: **Alliteration**

RHYTHM

In popular music, the term "rhythm" usually refers to the recurrence of regular patterns of strong and weak accents, commonly known as the "beat." This regularity of rhythmic accent is particularly characteristic of much music with African-American roots: for example, the **blues, boogie-woogie, gospel, ragtime, jazz, swing, rhythm and blues, Motown,** and **soul.** But in the sense of a steady and persistent pulse, rhythm is an integral part of virtually all music.

Other less-apparent aspects of rhythm have also been of importance in popular music. With the emergence of ragtime around the turn of the century, a craze for **syncopation** took hold. Although this fad lessened somewhat ins subsequent years, syncopation has remained an important component of popular music in both composition and performance through the years.

Polyrhythm, another rhythmic aspect with African roots (among others), has been of special importance in the performance of Latin American dances, such as the **bossa nova, cha cha cha, conga, guaracha, mambo, merengue, rumba, salsa,** and **samba.** In these dance genres, multiple rhythms juxtapose the simple with the complex, the loud with the soft, the regular with the irregular, the extended with the contracted, in a vivid conglomeration of sounds. Overlapping rhythmic elements are also prominent features in the performance of jazz and swing.

With the advent of **rock 'n' roll** in the 1950s and **rock** in the 1960s, even more emphasis was placed on persistent and loud rhythmic accent, now called the "big beat." This phenomenon was greatly magnified by the introduction of electronic instruments. In some genres, for example, **disco, heavy metal,** and **rap,** the beat, greatly amplified, *is* in fact the music.

Aspects of rhythm enter into the other elements of music as well: **melody, harmony** (as **harmonic rhythm**), **texture, form,** and **dynamics.** Many rhythmical elements are incorporated into the melodies of popular song. The rhythm of George Gershwin's melody (and Ira Gershwin's lyrics) for "Fascinating Rhythm" (1924) is particularly provocative and indeed fascinating:

Other unusual rhythmic patterns are found in the melodies of "Puttin' On the Ritz" (1929), "Lullaby of Broadway" (1935), and many other songs. "Tea for Two" (1924) is worthy of note for its persistent use of the simple rhythmic figure of a dotted quarter and eighth in all but the second section of its chorus, where it is slightly varied as follows:

The word "rhythm" also appears as part of the title of a number of songs, including "Crazy Rhythm" (1928), "I Got Rhythm" (1930), "Broadway Rhythm" (1935), "Lullaby in Rhythm" (1938), "Rhythm of the Rain" (1962), and "Walking in Rhythm" (1974).

See also: Africa; Dance Crazes; Meter; Tempo

RHYTHM AND BLUES

"Rhythm and blues" was a term applied in the mid-1940s to indicate musical **recordings** produced by blacks for a predominantly black audience. The term was standardized in 1949 by **Billboard** magazine, the bible of the music industry, when it was applied to their "race" recording chart, replacing such pre–World War II designations of the music as "ebony" or "sepia." As a term indicating black music, "rhythm and blues" has lasted into the 1990s, but its audience has changed from black to universal.

In the 1940s, rhythm and blues (sometimes abbreviated "R&B") was almost always a vocal music, and more often than not dance-oriented. Its songs were often written in **blues** or **AABA** form. It frequently used **boogie-woogie** rhythm and incorporated elements of the then-current **big band** sound. Such bands as those

of Lionel Hampton and Count Basie were very popular at that time, producing such early precursors of R&B as Hampton's "Flying Home" (1941), "Hey! Ba-Ba-Re-Bop" (1946), and "Blowtop Blues" (1947); and Basie's "Rusty Dusty Blues" (1943) and "Open the Door, Richard!" (1947). These bands could comfortably play for both listening and dancing audiences.

Meanwhile, other bands, like those of Lucky Millinder ("Who Threw the Whiskey in the Well?," 1945) and Buddy Johnson ("Since I Fell for You," 1948), geared their music more for dancing. At the same time, smaller combos arose, using simpler **instrumentation** that included electric guitar, drums, bass, piano, and a honking tenor saxophone. This style of rhythm and blues became known as "city blues," and under its rubric fell such subordinate genres as jump, boogie, and the group singing of ballads.

The most distinctive feature of city blues was its pervasive **rhythm,** either fast or slow. Many R&B singers, especially those of the jump and boogie idioms, almost shouted the lyrics. Most were also adept at accompanying themselves on piano, guitar, or saxophone.

The changes that were occurring in black music did not lead to an abandonment of the basic style of the blues. On the contrary, many urban black musicians made names for themselves by continuing to perform in a style that was primitive in regard to guitar accompaniment and raw vocalization. This type of music became known as "country blues." Among its practitioners were John Lee Hooker, Elmore James, and Muddy Waters.

Besides love and romance, other common themes of R&B songs of the 1940s were drinking, partying, sex, and virility. These subjects were augmented in the 1950s by fast cars, money problems, crime, punishment, and remorse.

One of the most successful rhythm-and-blues recording artists of the 1940s was Louis Jordan with his jump-blues combo called The Tympany Five. He appealed equally to black and white audiences with his witty songs, boogie-woogie rhythms, and proficiency on the alto sax. Among his long string of hit recordings, many of which were about having a good time, were "Is You Is or Is You Ain't (Ma' Baby?)" (1944), "Caldonia (What Makes Your Big Head So Hard?)" (1945), and the classic "Choo Choo Ch'Boogie" (1946).

Two other leading performers in jump-blues combo style were Roy Milton and Amos Milburn. Unlike Jordan, who had a very distinctive singing style, Milton and Milburn placed greater emphasis on the rhythmic accompaniment than on the vocal performance. They were among the first to feature boogie rhythms with a single **riff** repeated throughout a song, a technique later taken up in **rock 'n' roll.** Many popular songs of this time were about drinking, including Milburn's "Bad Bad Whiskey" (1950). A hit of the same year was "The

Honeydripper," played by Joe Liggins and His Honeydrippers. Based on a simple shuffle rhythm, it sold over a million records.

Rhythm and blues was a fertile field for vocalists as well. Wynonie Harris was a very exciting blues shouter who recorded fast-paced songs, many of them off-color. Roy Brown was another popular blues singer, but instead of shouting, he cried the blues. His intense, passionate style influenced many other singers, including James Brown, B. B. King, and Johnny Ray. Larry Darnell also had several hits in a style similar to Brown's, including "For You My Love" in 1949.

Another popular rhythm-and-blues singer of this period was Charles Brown, who was featured vocalist with Johnny Moore's Three Blazers. Brown inspired Ivory Joe Hunter, who also played the piano and sang sentimental, self-pitying songs. Among Hunter's hits were "Guess Who" (1949) and two country-flavored songs he wrote himself: "I Almost Lost My Mind" (1950) and "Since I Met You Baby" (1956). The blues shouter Bullmoose Jackson had an R&B **cover** hit with "Why Don't You Haul Off and Love Me?" in 1949. Other R&B vocalists who accompanied themselves on piano included Julia Lee, with her band, The Boyfriends, and Nellie Lutcher, famous for her frantic performance of "Fine Brown Frame" in 1948, a song originally introduced in 1944 by Buddy Johnson and His Orchestra with a vocal by Arthur Prysock.

The 1940s was also the period of the black vocal-group harmony known as **doo-wop**. Three leading groups of this genre were the Mills Brothers, the Ink Spots, and the Ravens, all based more on the traditions of mainstream popular music than on those of R&B. Nevertheless, elements of their style, especially the booming bass voice of Ravens member Jimmy Ricks, were influences on the sound of black group harmony in the 1950s. Among the Ravens' hits were their classic R&B versions of "Ol' Man River" (1927) and "White Christmas" (1942) in 1947 and 1948 and their recording of "Write Me a Letter" in 1947.

One of the seminal figures of rhythm and blues in the 1950s was Johnny Otis. Besides being an excellent vibraphone player and drummer, he led an ever-changing configuration of Los Angeles musicians in orchestras and combos. He was famous for his revues, featuring such previously undiscovered talents as the popular vocal group the Robins and one of the leading female stars of R&B, Little Esther Phillips. After Phillips left Otis, her career seemed to flounder, but in 1962 she scored a Number One hit with "Release Me," a cover of a 1954 country-and-western hit. Otis recorded and backed many other artists, including Willie Mae "Big Mama" Thornton in the original version of "Hound Dog" (1953).

The Robins (who eventually evolved into the Coasters in 1956) were among a plethora of rhythm-and-blues vocal groups named after **birds**. Apparently these groups felt that if it worked for the Ravens in the 1940s, it would work for them in the 1950s. They included the Swallows ("Beside You," 1947), the Crows ("Gee!," 1954), the Penguins ("Earth Angel [Will You Be Mine]" 1955), and the Cardinals ("The Door Is Still Open to My Heart," 1955), as well as such groups as the Wrens and the Meadowlarks. Even a part of a bird's anatomy became the name of a group called the Feathers. One bird group, the Orioles, led by the emotionally charged Sonny Til, was famous for its 1953 recording of "Crying in the Chapel," a song about religious redemption.

Two of the best-selling vocal groups, the Clovers and the Dominoes, were *not* named after birds. The Clovers, who were equally adept at jump tunes and ballads, recorded many hit records, including "Fool, Fool, Fool" (1951), "One Mint Julep" (1952) "Good Lovin'" (1953), "Lovely Dovey" (1954), "Devil or Angel" (1956), and "Love! Love! Love!" (1956). The Dominoes were fortunate in having two splendid lead vocalists—Clyde McPhatter and Jackie Wilson—both of whom went on to become influential solo stars. McPhatter had three records that reached Number One on the R&B charts: "Treasure of Love" (1956), "Long Lonely Nights" (1957), and "A Lover's Question" (1958). He later became the first of many lead singers for the Drifters, one of the leading singing groups in the formative years of **rock 'n' roll**. McPhatter and Wilson, along with James Brown and Ray Charles, were instrumental in bringing the **gospel** sound to rhythm and blues, and later to rock 'n' roll and **soul**.

Although the recordings made by Hank Ballard and the Midnighters were not as sophisticated as those of the Clovers and the Dominoes, they did have about them an infectious, joyous excitement. Even their song titles, like "Work With Me, Annie" (1954), spoke volumes. Ballard's most successful song, "The Twist" (1959), went unrecognized until 1962, when it was covered by Chubby Checker, initiating a new **dance craze**.

Among other illustrious singers of rhythm and blues in the 1950s were Ruth Brown and LaVern Baker, the first important female singers to record for Atlantic. Although their songs were recorded in city jump-blues style, they were essentially rock 'n' roll. Brown made a name for herself with "Teardrops From My Eyes" (1950), and Baker melded together blues, jazz, and pop in such recordings as "Jim Dandy" (1957) and "I Cried a Tear" (1958).

Although blues shouter Joe Turner had been recording in relative obscurity since the late 1930s, his fortunes changed for the better after he signed with Atlantic Records in 1950, with such hits as "Chains of Love" (1951) and the raucous "Shake, Rattle and Roll" (1954). By this time, rock 'n' roll had become a definitive musical style. At the advanced age of forty-three, "Big" Joe became a rock 'n' roll star with "Flip Flop and Fly" (1955). However, this fame was not to last; Turner's shouting style was not embraced by teenagers.

Ballad singing in R&B style was also very popular in the early 1950s. Percy Mayfield was a talented songwriter who sang in a gentle manner. His best-selling record was "Please Send Me Someone to Love" (1950), a song in which he expressed his understanding of and concern for world problems (the Korean War was going on at the time) but declared that he had problems of his own. With this song, Mayfield set a standard for other sentimental singers to follow.

Several vocalists followed in Mayfield's wake. Among them were Johnny Ace—whose hits included the moody R&B standard "Pledging My Love" (1955), backed by Johnny Otis—and Jesse Belvin, who was a pivotal force in the Los Angeles R&B music scene. Belvin wrote "Earth Angel (Will You Be Mine)" (1954) and, in addition, was half of the singing duo of Jesse and Marvin (Philips). Inheriting Ace's mantle, Belvin sang such songs as "Goodnight My Love" (Pleasant Dreams) (1956) in a sentimental style. Chuck Willis couched a simpler sentimentality in a melancholy blues style in songs like "I Feel So Bad" (1954) and "What Am I Living For?" (1958).

Perhaps the most famous American blues singer and guitarist of the last half of the twentieth century was B. B. King, whose recording career began in 1949. Unlike other country-blues performers of the 1940s and 1950s, his moving style of singing tended more to gospel-influenced ballads and to Roy Brown's "crying" style than to traditional hard blues. Between 1951 and 1969, King scored forty-one **Top Forty** hits, including his version of the 1931 standard "The Thrill Is Gone" in 1954; and of the 1952 song "Every Day I Have the Blues" in 1955.

Another R&B vocalist who started performing in the 1940s was Lloyd Price. He found stardom in 1952, with his recording of "Lawdy Miss Clawdy": a big hit that helped pave the way for a more raucous, New Orleans sound in rock 'n' roll. One of the most appealing elements of this arrangement was its slow boogie rhythm supplied by pianist Antoine "Fats" Domino (uncredited), whose own successful recording career began in 1949 with his recording of "The Fat Man." Other recordings by Price included "Just Because" (1957), "Stagger Lee" (1958), "Personality" (1959), and "I'm Gonna Get Married" (1959).

Among other exponents of New Orleans rhythm and blues was Smiley Lewis, who played piano in a style similar to Domino. However, his shouting style of singing in songs like "I Hear You Knocking" (1955) limited his success. Another famous act was Huey "Piano" Smith and the Clowns, best known for its delightful rendition of "Rockin' Pneumonia and the Boggie Woogie Flu" (1957).

Shirley Goodman and Leonard Lee, better known as Shirley and Lee, was a very popular singing duo from New Orleans. Their first R&B hit was the medium-tempo love song, "I'm Gone" (1952). But they are most famous for two exuberant recordings: "Let The Good Times Roll" (1956) and "Feel So Fine (Feel So Good) (1960). Among other duo recordings were those by

Marvin and Johnny ("Cherry Pie," (1954), Gene and Eunice ("Ko Ko Mo, I Love You So," 1955), Mickey and Sylvia ("Love Is Strange," 1956) and Johnny and Joe ("Over the Mountain Across the Sea," 1957).

During the 1960s, the lines that had been drawn between rhythm and blues and pop tended to disappear; leading black artists were selling almost as many records to white fans as to black. The most telling indication of this was the phenomenal success of **Motown** Records, the first major black-owned and operated record company. The trademark slogan of Motown was "the sound of young America"—not the sound of black or white America, but the sound of *young* America.

However, some acts still did much better with black audiences than with white. Among them were Bobby Bland and Ike and Tina Turner. Bland's records were a mixture of blues and jazz and seemed to appeal to a mature audience in such songs as "Call On Me" (1962). Ike Turner had been involved in music since he was eleven years old, when he accompanied famed bluesman Sonny Boy Williamson on the piano. In 1960, he teamed with his singer-dancer wife, Tina, to form a group called the Ike and Tina Turner Revue. In performance, Tina was filled with unbridled energy; she performed like a dynamo gone askew on such records as "A Fool in Love (Tell Me What's Wrong)" (1960) and "It's Gonna Work Out Fine" (1961).

By the mid-1950s, much of the hard edge of rhythm and blues had been absorbed into rock 'n' roll. Now that black music was being purchased by whites, a smoother type of singer, akin to Nat "King" Cole, emerged. Sam Cooke, an influential former gospel singer, went secular in 1957 with "You Send Me"—a hit that, by retaining an element of soulfulness in a pop format, set a pattern for other black artists to follow. Brook Benton was another artist who performed equally well in soul and pop. Among his hits were three of his own ballads: "It's Just a Matter of Time," "Endlessly," and "Thank You Pretty Baby" (all in 1959). In 1960, he performed a duet with Dinah Washington: "A Rockin' Good Way (To Mess Around and Fall in Love)."

Ben E. King, a former lead singer with the Drifters, brought his subdued gospel approach to his versions of "Spanish Harlem" (1961), "Stand by Me" (1961), "Don't Play That Song" (1962), and "I Who Have Nothing" (1963).

Dionne Warwick, originally a member of a gospel group, became one of the leading female vocalists in both rhythm and blues and pop during the 1960s. Her sound was a mixture of jazz and pop. Most of her hits were supplied by the songwriting team of Burt Bacharach and Hal David: "Walk On By" (1961), "Don't Make Me Over" (1962), "Message to Michael" (1963), and "Alfie" (1967). Warwick's main musical contribution was as a bridge between the rhythm and blues productions of the late 1950s and the smooth soul sound of the early 1970s.

By the mid-1960s, the predominant black musical style was **soul**; indeed, in 1969 *Billboard* magazine changed the name of its rhythm-and-blues chart to "Soul." The styles of **rock** and rhythm and blues tended to merge in the ensuing decades in such groups as the Rolling Stones. But R&B never really died; in 1990 *Billboard* brought back an old name for its black music chart: "rhythm and blues."

Additional Songs

Ain't Nobody Here But Us Chickens (1946)
Bewildered (1938)
Blue Light Boogie (1950)
Boogie Chillun (1949)
Drinkin' Wine, Spo-dee-o-dee (1949)
Five Guys Named Moe (1943)
Night Train (1952)
Saturday Night Fish Fry (1949)
Short Fat Fannie (1957)
Sixty Minute Man (1951)

Jeffrey Cahn

Bibliography

Berry, Jason. *Up From the Cradle of Jazz: New Orleans Rhythm and Blues, and Beyond.* 1984

Broven, John. *Walking to New Orleans: The Story of New Orleans Rhythm and Blues.* 1977.

Gillett, Charlie. *The Sound of the City: The Rise of Rock and Roll.* 1983.

Lydon, Michael. *Boogie Lightning.* 1980.

McCutcheon, Lynn Ellis. *Rhythm and Blues: An Experience and Adventure in Its Origin and Development.* 1971.

McGowan, James A. *Hear Today! Here to Stay! A Personal History of Rhythm and Blues.* 1983.

Propes, Steve. *Those Oldies But Goodies: A Guide to 50's Record Collecting.* 1973.

Redd. Lawrence N. *Rock Is Rhythm and Blues: The Impact of the Mass Media.* 1974.

Shaw, Arnold. *Honkers and Shouters: The Golden Years of Rhythm and Blues.* 1978.

Whitburn, Joel. *Joel Whitburn's Top R&B Singles: 1942–1988.* 1988.

See also: **Funk; Singing Groups**

RIFF

A riff is a brief melodic phrase that is repeated, usually over changing harmonies. Developing out of the tradition of **call and response**, it became a feature of **jazz** improvisation, and was later taken up by the **big bands** in their performance of **swing**.

Many songs are built on riffs. As early as 1925, the release of George Gershwin's "Sweet and Low-Down" consisted of a two-bar riff stated three times over three different harmonies. The idea of the riff was taken up with a vengeance during the swing era, when many instrumentals based on riffs were turned into songs.

Among songs based on literal phrase repetition over changing harmonies were "Stompin' at the Savoy" (1936), "The Dipsy Doodle" (1937), "One O'Clock Jump" (1938), "Flying Home" (1941), "In the Mood" (1939), "Undecided" (1939), "Tuxedo Junction" (1940) "A String of Pearls" (1941), and "Jersey Bounce" (1941). A number of other songs, like "Sentimental Journey" (1944) and "Satin Doll" (1958), although not based on literal repetition, are sufficiently riff-like in character to warrant inclusion here.

During the late 1940s and early 1950s, riffs played by alternating sections of big bands became a prominent feature in performance of the **mambo**. The device was also regularly used in **salsa** during the 1970s.

See also: **Brass; Improvisation; Instrumentation; Woodwinds**

RIVERS

Songs about rivers are prevalent in many cultures, and America is no exception. During the nineteenth century, some of the most popular songs were about rivers: "Shenandoah (Across the Wide Missouri)" (c.1826), Stephen Foster's "The Old Folks at Home (Way Down Upon the Swanee River)" (1851), "Down by the Riverside" (1865), "There's One Wide River to Cross (Noah's Ark)" (1865), and "The Red River Valley" (1896).

This tradition continued into the twentieth century, often with specific rivers in mind. Needless to say, the queen of American rivers plays a prominent role in popular song. It is spelled out in the song "M-I-S-S-I-S-S-I-P-P-I" (1916); glorified in Ferde Grofé's *Mississippi Suite* of 1926, from which the composer later extracted his song "Daybreak" (1942); made fun of in "Mississippi Mud" (1927); and immortalized in the magnificent "Ol' Man River," from *Show Boat* (1927), itself centering about a river. The film *Mississippi* of 1935 had several memorable songs, including one called "Down by the River." "Proud Mary," popularized by Creedence Clearwater Revival in 1968, is about a "riverboat queen . . . rollin on the river."

The Ohio River, an important tributary of the Mississippi has at least two songs to its credit: "Down by the O-Hi-O (O-My!-O!)" (1920) and "Beautiful Ohio" (1918). At least two other rivers have their place in American song. The Suwannee, flowing through Georgia and Florida into the Gulf of Mexico, was misspelled both in Foster's song, mentioned above, and in George Gershwin's first hit, "Swanee" (1919). The Rio Grande, which forms part of the border between Mexico and the United States, is the subject of two famous songs: "Rose of the Rio Grande" (1922) and "I'm an Old Cow Hand (From the Rio Grande)" (1936). The rivers in two other songs, "Riverboat Shuffle" (1925) and "Lazy River" (1931) are unspecified.

Rivers have also been used symbolically in songs; two examples are "Cry Me a River" (1953) and "Moon River" (1961), neither of which is about a river; rather, the songs are about **crying** and **friendship**, respectively. "River, Stay 'Way from My Door" (1931) functions on two levels: as a plea to keep the flood away, and—at the height of the Depression—as a prayer to keep the wolf away from the door.

Foreign rivers also have a place in American song. There is the Jordan ("Deep River," 1917), the Ganges ("Moonlight on the Ganges," 1926), the Kwai ("The River Kwai March," 1957), the Seine ("La Seine," 1949), and the Thames ("Cruising Down the River," 1945).

But a much smaller body of water is the subject of the barbershop favorite "Down by the Old Mill Stream" (1910).

Additional Songs

Allegheny Moon (1956)
Ferry 'Cross the Mersey (1964)
Island in the Stream (1983)
Let the River Run (1988)
Roll On, Mississippi, Roll On (1931)
Wabash Moon (1931)

> *See also*: Boating; Ocean; Waterfront

Roads. See Streets

Roaring Twenties

The decade of the 1920s, stereotyped by flappers and "jazz babies," has been called both the "Jazz Age" and the "Roaring Twenties." Actually, only a portion of this decade should be called "roaring," for the 1920s, like the 1950s, roared best in the latter half of the decade.

The stereotypical flapper and her beau did not really emerge until 1925, when skirts flapped around girls' knees and the "Charleston" (1923) became the most popular dance among professional entertainers and the general public. This was the age of college girls with bobbed hair, cloche hats, short skirts, pearls to twirl, and wonderful songs for singing and dancing. The "Roaring Twenties" is nostalgically remembered as a collage of speakeasies, gang wars, monkey trials, flagpole sitters, flaming youth, dance marathons, bathtub gin, Lucky Lindy, Stutz Bearcats, Rudolph Valentino, the Four Horsemen, and F. Scott Fitzgerald. The "Twenties" also served as an incubator for many enduring songs.

The flapper and her beau would supposedly do almost anything as long as it was fun: they kissed indiscriminately, wore provocative clothing, used profanity freely, drank plenty of liquor (legal or otherwise), laughed and giggled with abandon, danced whenever they had the chance, and sang their favorite songs with gusto. Suitable theme songs for this "lost generation," as it has been called, might include "Ain't We Got Fun?" (1921), "Runnin' Wild!" (1922), and "Let's Do It (Let's Fall in Love)" (1928). The "in" sayings or catch phrases included "the cat's pajamas," "the bee's knees,"

"twenty-three skiddoo," "Oh, you kid," and "stew in your own juice."

Whenever the United States is perceived to be prosperous and politically stable, this secure environment is mirrored in the lifestyle of its citizens, who appear happy and content. And when people are happy and successful, they express this in song and dance. Although life in the 1920s was not all smooth sailing, people sang and danced as if they had nothing more to worry about than having a good time. "Goin' to hell in a handbasket," a popular expression of the time, sums up that optimistic outlook.

At the beginning of the 1920s, **sheet music** sales provided the music industry with its main source of profit. By the middle of that decade, however, a second, very competitive source of profit came into being: **recording**. It had been technically possible to record music since as far back as the 1870s, but the phonograph disc had not advanced beyond the novelty stage even as late as the turn of the century. By the end of **World War I**, however, that situation changed dramatically. America's stage stars were becoming household names, entering the country's living rooms via records. By the mid-1920s, the recording industry was not just a reality; it was a major musical force, with more than 130 million records being sold annually.

At first, records—weighty ten- or twelve-inch discs—were played on gramophones at 78 or 80 revolutions per minute. The gramophones had to be wound up, and the needle had to be changed after each playing. By the end of the decade, electrically automated record-changers and long-lasting tungsten needles were available, and this made listening to records a much less toilsome affair.

Among memorable recordings of the decade, the following achieved the greatest success: Gene Austin's version of "My Blue Heaven" (1927), the runner-up as the most popular nonholiday recording of the pre-rock era; Ben Selvin and His Orchestra's rendition of "Dardanella" (1919), a syncopated ragtime ditty; Vernon Dalhart's 1925 recording of "The Prisoner's Song," a horribly corny tearjerker that became the best-selling disc of the pre-electrified era; Al Jolson's rendition of the sentimental "Sonny Boy" (1928) from *The Singing Fool*; Paul Whiteman and His Orchestra's recording of "Whispering" (1920); Jolson's "April Showers" (1921) from *Bombo*; the Whiteman Orchestra's "Valencia" (1926); Nick Lucas's recording of "Tip Toe Through the Tulips With Me" (1929); Jolson's rendition of Irving Caesar and George Gershwin's "Swanee" (1919), which was interpolated into a Sigmund Romberg show, *Sinbad*; and the Whiteman Orchestra's version of "Three O'Clock in the Morning" (1922).

Paul Whiteman not only produced some of the top recordings of the decade, as shown by the list above, he also had one of the most popular bands; it featured a symphonic string section, sweet and lush arrangements, and a danceable beat. He was called "The King of Jazz," a title that seems somewhat inappropriate today, for his music does not sound "jazzy" to modern ears. At the time, though, popular music was called "jazz," and Whiteman was certainly concerned with the genre. In fact, he commissioned George Gershwin to compose a jazz concerto to help prove that jazz was an idiom that commanded respect. Out of that commission came *Rhapsody in Blue* (1924). Even some members of Whiteman's orchestra went on to become jazz soloists: Bix Beiderbecke, the Dorsey Brothers, and Henry Busse.

Other top artists of the 1920s include Ben Selvin and His Orchestra (who produced over two thousand recordings, and featured several future bandleaders, most notably Benny Goodman); clarinetist-singer Ted Lewis and his band; Al Jolson, the self-styled "World's Greatest Entertainer"; soft-voiced Gene Austin, the most popular vocalist of the second half of the decade; bandleader-composer Isham Jones and His Orchestra, probably the best dance band of the pre-swing era; Nat Shilkret and the Victor Orchestra; Fred Waring's Pennsylvanians; Ruth Etting, the decade's most famous singer of **torch songs**; Fanny Brice, its favorite comedienne; and Marion Harris, who was featured in several Broadway musicals during the decade.

Above all else, the decade of the "Roaring Twenties" should be remembered for its music for the theater. While Victor Herbert was still around to take a few more bows and Cole Porter was just beginning his string of successful **musical comedies**, the majority of **composers** and **lyricists**—George and Ira Gershwin, Irving Berlin, Richard Rodgers, Jerome Kern, Lorenz Hart, Oscar Hammerstein II, Vincent Youmans, Rudolph Friml, Sigmund Romberg, Ray Henderson, and Walter Donaldson—were at or near their peak. The Broadway musicals of the decade yielded hundreds of marvelous show tunes, including some of the most beloved songs of the century.

When the decade opened, **operetta**, which had been looked upon as anti-American during World War I, found new life. Romberg's *Blossom Time* (1921) inspired a revival of interest in the genre. Throughout the decade, numerous operettas were produced, including Herbert's *Orange Blossoms* (1922), Friml's *Rose-Marie* (1924) and *The Vagabond King* (1925), and Romberg's *The Student Prince* (1924), *The Desert Song* (1926), and *New Moon* (1929).

Also popular in this decade were the "Cinderella" musicals, with their stories about waifs who were propelled to stardom on Broadway. *Irene* (1919) set the style, and several others followed the pattern; *Mary* (1920), *Sally* (1920), and *Sunny* (1926) are the most notable examples.

Of all these musicals, one in particular stands out. It was a product of a Kern and Hammerstein collaboration in which both composer and lyricist set out to write a musical that was not a synthetic product manufactured for specific stars and their specialties. To-

gether, in 1927, they remodeled Edna Ferber's novel *Show Boat* into one of the foremost classics of the Broadway stage, which, in turn, became the forerunner of a new genre, the **musical play**. The music was stunning, the lyrics were pertinent, and the story was touching. In short, the effect of the entire production was stupendous.

The posh Broadway **revue** was in its full glory in the 1920s. The *Ziegfeld Follies*, the yardstick by which revues were usually measured, was slightly past its heyday, but it remained one of the ultimate stage entertainments of the era. Other important revues included editions of George White's *Scandals*, the Theatre Guild Junior Players' *The Garrick Gaieties*, Irving Berlin's *Music Box Revues*, *The Passing Shows*, and other less well-known productions. White Broadway audiences first heard jazz in all-black revues like *Shuffle Along* (1921), *Runnin' Wild* (1923)—which introduced the "**Charleston**"—*Lew Leslie's Blackbirds* (1928), and *Hot Chocolates* (1929).

More than four hundred shows were produced on Broadway after World War I, providing, among others, these standards: "My Mammy" (1918), popularized by Al Jolson in the famous routine where he knelt down on one knee as if pleading with his "Mammy"; Alice Blue Gown" (1919), a song about the favorite color of Alice Roosevelt, daughter of President Theodore Roosevelt; Jerome Kern's "Look for the Silver Lining" (1921); "My Man" (1921), made famous by Fanny Brice's rendition in the 1921 *Ziegfeld Follies*; Al Jolson's interpolations into musicals, including "April Showers" (1921), "Toot, Toot, Tootsie" (Goo' Bye)" (1922), and "California, Here I Come" (1924); "Charleston" (1924), the **dance craze** of the decade; "Indian Love Call" (1924), an operetta excerpt that has remained popular through the years; Irving Berlin's "All Alone" (1924); "Tea for Two" (1925), the famous song about marital bliss from *No, No, Nanette*; "The Birth of the Blues" (1926), presented in George White's *Scandals* as part of a debate to prove that the blues are as "good" as classical music; Kern and Hammerstein's "Can't Help Lovin' Dat Man" (1927) and "Ol' Man River" (1927), from *Show Boat*; "Love Me or Leave Me" (1928), popularized by Ruth Etting; and the revivalistic title song from the musical *Great Day* (1929).

Although the scripts of most musicals were built around the songs, many were tailor-made to suit the personalities of certain top stars. Nowhere was this more true than in the case of Jolson, who seldom, if ever, sang a note from the score of the numerous musicals in which he appeared. Instead, at a particular moment during the evening, Jolson would simply step forward, get completely out of character, and sing whatever song or songs he chose to sing at that performance. He may have been an egotist, but audiences loved him. Jolson, always in blackface, introduced most of his hit songs of this decade as interpolations in the various musicals in which he appeared.

Due to his extraordinary popularity, Jolson had a

hand in the first motion picture in which characters actually spoke and sang. The film, *The Jazz Singer* (1927), was only partially a sound film, but in it Jolson performed six of his favorite songs. The phenomenal success of what was first considered a novelty launched both the sound age in film and a new genre, the **film musical**.

Jolson's next film, *The Singing Fool* (1928), became the most financially successful talking picture in Hollywood history, at least until the arrival of *Gone With the Wind* in 1939. It was followed by "All-Talking! All-Singing! All-Dancing!" films like the Oscar winner *Broadway Melody* and *The Hollywood Revue* (both 1929), whose arrival coincided with the close of the decade.

Wireless telegraphy had been around for years, but the miracle of having **radio** in one's own home came only with the 1920s. On November 2, 1920, station KDKA, installed at the Westinghouse plant in East Pittsburgh, went on the air with the news that Warren G. Harding had been elected President of the United States. Within a year there were eight more stations; within two years, there were 564. Radio, as entertainment, had arrived. Millions of Americans were making new friends with radio personalities.

In 1922, $60 million worth of radio sets were sold in the United States, but by 1929, $842 million had been sold. Radio quickly traveled from infancy to maturity. Many bands and singers of the decade owe their fame and fortune to radio. Paul Whiteman and His Orchestra appeared regularly on radio, as did Rudy Vallee and His Yale Collegians (or as they were renamed, Connecticut Yankees). Vaughn DeLeath was one of the first female singers to gain national attention on radio. Wendell Hall became the singing star of *The Eveready Hour*, one of radio's earliest variety programs. Others who owe a great deal of their stardom to radio include Little Jack Little, "Whispering" Jack Smith, Lanny Ross, Jessica Dragonette, Baby Rose Marie, and the "Sweethearts of the Air"—Peter DeRose and May Singhi Breen, the Ukulele Girl.

The radio microphone and perhaps the intimacy it afforded were uniquely suited to the birth of the crooning style of singing. Those **singers** who adapted their singing to the gentle, relaxed, soft, crooning style became the most successful on radio.

Never had popular music been so diverse and so lucrative; never had it had such national impact. The popular music of the decade included revivals of hits from the past ("Somebody Stole My Gal," written in 1918 but popularized in 1924); silly songs ("Barney Google," 1923); **name** songs ("Sweet Sue," 1928); **boy** songs ("Sonny Boy," 1928); **mother** songs ("My Mammy," 1921); **baby** songs ("Yes Sir, That's My Baby," 1925); and **blues** songs ("The Wang Wang Blues," 1921).

The "Roaring Twenties" was a rowdy, bawdy time in which many people seemed to be on one big bash that lasted for the entire decade. It was a nonsensical

time that questioned the mores of previous generations, a time for lilting laughter and pitching woo. It was also a decade when tunesmiths produced a plethora of memorable songs that still reflect the spirit of the times. Many of these melodies and lyrics have remained with us, and continue to speak to us.

Don Tyler

Bibliography

Ewen, David. *All The Years of American Popular Music.* 1977.
———. *American Popular Song.* 1966.
Shaw, Arnold. *The Jazz Age: Popular Music in the 1920s.* 1987.
Tyler, Don. *Hit Parade, 1920–1955.* 1985.
Whitburn, Joel. *Pop Memories 1890–1954.* 1986.

See also: **Tin Pan Alley**

ROCK

The term "rock" embraces a broad spectrum of popular music in the United States from the mid-1960s into the 1990s. Rock evolved out of **rock 'n' roll**, to which it is related. However it differs from the earlier genre in several respects: increased use of amplification and electronic instruments, **lyrics** often involving ambiguity and protest, more provocative dress and exaggerated performance, increased use of extended formal structures, and the growing importance of the **performer-songwriter**. Almost from its beginnings, rock was a joint British-American venture aimed at a predominantly young, white middle-class audience.

Politically, culturally, and socially the mid-1960s offered a much broader and more objective outlet for youthful discontent than had the 1950s, when the chief obstacles teenagers had to face were their own parents. Lyrics became intensely personal and political and often gained respect for their poetic style. At times songs were so draped in allegory that they were perfect aural stimuli for the commonly used hallucinogenic drugs of the day.

So intent was rock on expanding the boundaries of rock 'n' roll that musical experimentation became essential. Rock concerts became more than mere entertainment and offered a common ground where America's youth could attain a sense of their own community, a place where they could heed Harvard Professor Timothy Leary's dictum to "tune in, turn on, drop out!" At these gatherings, rock groups would play extended sets and jam sessions. As a consequence, rock **recordings** became longer in duration than those of their rock 'n' roll predecessors and many hit songs originally released on 45rpm records were given much longer versions on albums.

Experimentation led to greater use of the electric guitar and of amplification in general. The **guitar** no longer was confined to setting the lead or keeping the rhythm; it now helped fashion, shape, and even distort the entire context of the song. So wide was the scope of rock's experimentation that it crossed over to other musical genres and subgenres, leading to such hybrid forms as country rock, folk rock, jazz rock, and **rockabilly**.

The history of rock can best be outlined by discussing key performers and concepts: the Beach Boys, the Beatles, the British invasion, Bob Dylan, folk rock, the singer-songwriter, acid rock, the second British invasion, art rock, commercial rock, new wave, and music video.

I. The Beach Boys

Influenced by Chuck Berry's music and lyrics and by the production techniques of Phil Spector, the Beach Boys was a transitional group, straddling the line between the genres of rock 'n' roll and pure rock. With Brian Wilson as their leader, writer, and producer, they created some of the best-known and best-written songs of the day: "Be True to Your School," "Surfer Girl," and "Surfin' U.S.A.," in 1963; "Fun, Fun, Fun" and "I Get Around," in 1964; and "California Girls" and "Help Me Rhonda," in 1965. At first hearing, these songs seem to be about endless summers, chasing girls, racing cars, and hanging out with friends, but on closer examination the lyrics indicate something deeper and more meaningful. Songs like "In My Room", "Don't Worry Baby", and "When I Grow Up (To Be a Man)" (all 1964) express feelings of insecurity, worry, and the inability to cope—subjects that had previously rarely been addressed in popular song. At the same time, the Beach Boys were gaining complete control of the recording studio, a feat practically unheard of in rock 'n' roll.

The Beatles album *Rubber Soul*, released in 1965, was the first album that contained songs that were of equal importance—not just one or two hits, with the rest as filler. In his desire to compete with the Beatles, Wilson released an album called *Pet Sounds* in 1966. In this brilliant album, every song is a masterwork of lyrics, music, and sonority. The production was so complex that it virtually precluded live performance. Nevertheless, some of the songs on the album became hit singles, among them "Wouldn't It Be Nice?," backed up with "God Only Knows," and "Sloop John B"—the last based on a West Indian folk song of 1927. Later in 1966, the Beach Boys revolutionary recording of "Good Vibrations" was released; this psychedelic song was the most elaborate and expensive single produced in pop music up to that time. The Beach Boys had now reached their artistic peak and, in doing so, had assured themselves a position in the ranks of America's top rock groups.

II. The Beatles

One of the most important sociological and cultural phenomena in the history of popular music began with the Beatles' appearance on the nationally televised *Ed Sullivan Show* on February 9, 1964. In actuality, the Beatles—John Lennon, Paul McCartney, George Harrison, and Ringo Starr—had been recording rock 'n' roll songs almost exclusively in 1962 and 1963. Their repertoire included Little Richard and Chuck Berry classics along with rockabilly, **Motown** and **rhythm-and-blues** tunes. But they differed from other groups in the fact that many of their songs were written by two of their own members, Lennon and McCartney, and were of fine quality.

Their earliest hit singles in America were "I Want to Hold Your Hand," backed with "I Saw Her Standing There"; "Please Please Me"; "Can't Buy Me Love"; "Do You Want to Know a Secret?"; "Love Me Do"; and "She Loves You," famous for its exuberant "yeah, yeah, yeah" chorus. All of these 1964 releases hinted at harmonies and melodies more sophisticated than those of standard rock 'n' roll songs of the day, but most music critics still dismissed the Beatles as nothing more than the year's new fad. The first indication that they might be wrong came in August 1965 with the release of "Yesterday," the first true Beatles standard; by 1989, there were 2,500 recorded versions of this song.

The Beatles continued to improve on rock 'n' roll by developing new approaches to the music and lyrics. In such songs as "Help!" and "We Can Work It Out" (1965), the words became more personal, reflecting their experiences and feelings. In the same year (1965) they continued to push the boundaries of **pop** even further with the release of their breakthrough album *Rubber Soul*. It contained such wonderful songs as "Norwegian Wood," "Nowhere Man," and the tender ballad "Michelle," incorporating French lyrics. This album demonstrated that their music had become more inventive and their lyrics could be witty and ironic.

Further evolutionary growth was made by the Beatles in the following year (1966) with their next album, *Revolver*. Here their music took on an aura of mystery and Eastern mysticism, mainly through the addition of an Indian sitar. This exotic sound, combined with lyrics that were infused with many layers of meaning, made the record quite fascinating. Songs from this album include the surreal "Eleanor Rigby" and the charming novelty "Yellow Submarine."

The Beatles continued exploring and evolving as songwriters and musicians. Their imagination seemed unbridled; the recording studio became an instrument as important as the electric guitar. This creative process culminated in 1967 with their album *Sgt. Pepper's Lonely Hearts Club Band*, rock's first "concept" album, in which the individual songs were thematically connected. Widely considered one of the most important rock albums, it featured an entire canvas of musical influences and seemingly every form of **instrumentation**, including ragtime piano and harpsichord. Songs included "With a Little Help From My Friends," "Lucy in the Sky With Diamonds," "When I'm Sixty-Four," and "A Day in the Life." The last-named song appeared to be about a character whose depressing experience led to his death. With the Beatles' chanting "We love to turn you on," it seemed to be an endorsement of drug use. But it was more. It was actually a song about "turning on" to life, making it better for oneself and for others. The Beatles *were* involved with drug experimentation at the time and they did mean for the album to be mind-expanding. Because the album's overall feeling was psychedelic, much of it seems dated today; yet, due to its artistic integrity, it stands as a landmark in the history of pop and quite literally marks the moment when all the boundaries of pop came crashing down.

After this album, the Beatles began slowly to disintegrate. They could no longer tour because their recorded music could not be satisfactorily reproduced live, their manager had died suddenly, their use of drugs had increased, and their individual egos and aspirations took them in different directions. Even through all of this, they still were able to make marvelous music, including such hit songs as "Penny Lane," "Strawberry Fields Forever," and "All You Need Is Love" in 1967; "Lady Madonna," "Hey Jude," and "Revolution" in 1968; and "Come Together," "Give Peace a Chance," and George Harrison's "Something" in 1969. After their single hits of "Let It Be" and "The Long and Winding Road" in 1970, the Beatles' demise as a group was complete.

But each member of the Beatles went on to a solo career. John Lennon had hits in 1971 with the political songs "Power to the People" and the simple but eloquent "Imagine." Other hits followed until his untimely death, an assassination, occurred on December 8, 1980. Paul McCartney's songwriting credits as a Beatle and his subsequent solo work eventually elevated him into one of pop's top songwriters, but his immediate post-Beatles work is essentially fluff. His biggest hits—written in collaboration with his wife, Linda—were "Uncle Albert/Admiral Halsey" (1971), "My Love" (1973), "Band on the Run" (1974), "Listen to What the Man Said" (1975), and "Silly Love Songs" (1976).

George Harrison's early solo work was inspired by his interest in Eastern religion and philosophy; these hits included "My Sweet Lord" and "What Is Life?" (1970) and "Give Me Love (Give Me Peace on Earth)" (1973). In 1981 he had another hit with "All Those Years Ago," a song about the Beatles. Ringo Starr had several hits with **covers** of old rock 'n' roll songs and also performed new songs by Richard Starkey: "It Don't Come Easy" (1971) and "Back Off Boogaloo" (1972). Individually, none of the four members of the Beatles matched the level of artistic achievement gained by the group as a whole, although John Lennon came the closest to doing so.

The importance of the Beatles is incalculable. Not only did they make some of the best pop recordings of the last half of the twentieth century, but the songwriting team of Lennon and McCartney was by far rock's best; many of their compositions have become standards.

III. The British Invasion

Before the coming of the Beatles, British rock 'n' roll had not been popular in the United States; American teen-agers considered it too conservative for their tastes. This all changed in the wake of the Beatles. Now everything English invaded American airwaves and turntables. These "British Invasion" groups, usually from Liverpool or Manchester, offered listeners their "Mersey Beat," a lighthearted pop sound containing elements of the original American rock 'n' roll style.

One of the most popular of these groups was Herman's Hermits, with many hit records such as "Can't You Hear My Heartbeat?" (1965), "A Must to Avoid" (1966), "There's a Kind of Hush" (1966), and four songs recorded in 1965 in English music hall style: "Mrs. Brown, You've Got a Lovely Daughter," "I'm Henry VIII, I Am" (a song originally published in 1911), "Leaning on a Lamp-Post" (a revival of a 1937 song), and "Dandy." Another British group, Freddie and the Dreamers, had hits in 1965 with "I'm Telling You Now," "You Were Made for Me," and "Do the Freddie"; the last refers to a spastic dance they did while performing their songs. Peter and Gordon were a pleasant-sounding duo who had hits with "A World Without Love" (1964), especially written for them by Lennon and McCartney, and "I Go to Pieces" (1965), written for them by American rock 'n' roll star Del Shannon, who had his own success with "Runaway" in 1961. Gerry and the Pacemakers had two very sweet and sentimental ballads among their hits: "Don't Let the Sun Catch You Crying" and "Ferry 'Cross the Mersey" (both 1964).

Although some Mersey-beat songs could be dismissed as expendable pop with no lasting musical value, there were others from this school that were worthy of note. In 1965 the Mindbenders really shone with lead singer Wayne Fontana in their recording of "The Game of Love," a minor classic with its prominent bass guitar and Bo Diddley–style break. In the following year came the gentle ballad "A Groovy Kind of Love."

Other hits were recorded in 1964 by the Dave Clark Five, with Clark's ballad "Because" and the loud jackhammer sound of "Glad All Over" and "Bits and Pieces." Although this group's recording career was limited, two other English groups, the Kinks and the Who, achieved fame among rock's best with their hard-driving hits. The Kinks, with "All Day and All of the Night" and "You Really Got Me" (which had a guitar riff acquired from "Louie Louie," the rock 'n' roll standard made famous by the Kingsmen in 1963), had two raw 1964 hits that eventually inspired **heavy metal** and **punk rock**. In a short time, the Kinks shifted gears with songs of biting social commentary such as "A Well Respected Man" (1965) and "Dedicated Follower of Fashion" (1966) and "Lola," a clever song about transvestites (1970). Although hit singles stopped coming after this, the group continued to make ambitious albums throughout the 1970s.

The Who recorded brash and noisy numbers which usually showed disdain for the establishment. One of their first hits was the anarchistic "My Generation"

(1965). As their recording career progressed in songs such as "I Can See for Miles" (1967) and "Pinball Wizard" (1969), Peter Townshend's lyrics became more sardonic, while retaining their rock 'n' roll aggression. The Who also were responsible for one of the landmarks of rock music—*Tommy* (1969) the first rock opera.

Among other British rock bands to make lasting contributions were blues-revivalist groups that enlarged on the work of American blues artists like Muddy Waters, John Lee Hooker, and Howlin' Wolf. These groups included the Yardbirds, with songs such as "Heart Full of Soul" (1965). The Animals, with lead singer Eric Burdon, utilized both the folk and blues genres with their adaptations of a folk song in "The House of the Rising Sun" (1964), and a 1925 blues song in "See See Rider" (1966). They also introduced new songs by Tin Pan Alley songwriters, including "Don't Let Me Be Misunderstood" and "We Gotta Get Out of This Place," both in 1965.

Next to the Beatles, the most famous British rock group was the Rolling Stones. In their prime, they were considered the ultimate rock band. Their lead singer was Mick Jagger, backed by Keith Richards, Bill Wyman, Charlie Watts, and Brian Jones (replaced after his death by Mick Taylor and subsequently by Ron Wood). The only serious competition they ever had came from the Beatles, which may seem strange given that the Beatles were the direct antithesis of the Stones. Whereas the former were perceived as cute and charming, the latter were unattractive, dangerous, and menacing. The Beatles' musical scope was broad, tapping into many different styles, while the Rolling Stones adopted the black blues form and at times even borrowed its phrasing and enunciation. This is evident in the Stones' recordings, which have a dark, foreboding sound, almost primitive compared to the Beatles' crisp pop productions.

At first, the Stones did covers of blues and rhythm-and-blues songs, but in 1965 they broke away from this pattern, producing Mick Jagger and Keith Richards's "(I Can't Get No) Satisfaction," a true rock classic that captured the pent-up frustration of a generation. Subsequent recordings that reached the charts as single releases included "Get Off of My Cloud" (1965), and "As Tears Go By," "19th Nervous Breakdown," "Paint It Black," and "Mother's Little Helper" (a song about a parent's need for sedation), all from 1966. As the decade drew to a close, songs such as "Jumpin' Jack Flash" (1968) and "Honky Tonk Women" (1969) topped the charts. In the 1970s they continued their winning streak with "Brown Sugar" (a song about interracial love, 1971), "Tumbling Dice" (1972), "Angie" (1973), "Miss You" (1978), and "Beast of Burden" (1978). Their hits of the 1980s included "Emotional Rescue" (1980), "Start Me Up" (1981), "Undercover of the Night" (1983), and "Rock and a Hard Place" (1989). All of these songs were written by rock's second-greatest songwriting team, Mick Jagger and Keith Richards.

There are other British groups of this time worthy of mention. The Spencer Davis Group performed inspired songs in a dancelike rhythm-and-blues style, such as "Gimme Some Loving" (1966). The Zombies had three terrific pop-styled hits with "She's Not There" in 1964, "Tell Her No" in 1965, and "Time of the Season" in 1967. A group from Ireland, called Them, recorded two memorable songs, the blues ballad "Here Comes the Night" (1965) and "Gloria" (1966); the latter was not a hit at the time, but has since become a true rock standard. The lead singer of Them was Van Morrison, who became a legend in his own right. After leaving the group, he recorded several hits that were imbued with an uptempo joyous warmth, including "Brown Eyed Girl" (1967), "Domino" (1970), and "Wild Night" (1971). In 1968 Morrison recorded one of the most impressive rock albums, *Astral Weeks*.

IV. Bob Dylan

At the same time that the first wave of British rock groups was giving music its heartbeat, Bob Dylan, a young folk singer from Minnesota, was giving rock its poetic soul. In the early years of his performing career, Dylan mirrored the country folk style of Woody Guthrie. Although his singing style was unpolished and had a nasal quality, Dylan more than compensated for it in the creation of innovative and visionary songs. His early compositions showed him to be an astute commentator on social and political issues. Among these songs were "Blowin' in the Wind" (1962) "A Hard Rain's A-Gonna Fall," and "Master of War" (both 1963) and "The Times They Are A-Changing'," (1964). The last-named song gives a warning to parents: "Your sons and your daughters are beyond your command." With these songs Dylan became the leader of the folk-protest movement, but, like the Beatles, he was not content to rest on his laurels.

In 1965 Dylan recorded "Subterranean Homesick Blues." With its allusive, surreal lyrics combined with an amplified rhythm section, he was laying the foundation for the development of folk rock, a subgenre that reached its peak in three Dylan albums, all masterpieces of rock music: *Bringing It All Back Home* and *Highway 61 Revisited* (both 1965), and *Blonde on Blonde* (1966). Dylan had now exchanged his acoustic guitar for an electrified model. He had softened his overtly political tone and switched to more personal subjects. With his 1965 song "Like a Rolling Stone," Dylan had become a full-fledged rock star. This song was loud, cynical, and angry—a slap in the face to the establishment and adrenaline to the alienated and disillusioned youth of America. His "When You Ain't Got Nothin', You Got Nothin' to Lose" was as important to the rock generation as "Blue Suede Shoes" (1955) was to the previous generation.

Throughout the 1960s, Dylan continued to explore the parameters of pop music. On the one hand, in 1965 songs like "Desolation Row" and "Gates of Eden" ("He who is not busy being born is busy dying"), he showed an ability to fashion ideas containing stream-of-consciousness imagery while at the same time allowing these songs to be interpreted freely by those listening to them. On the other hand, in the ballads "She Belongs to Me" (1965), "Lay, Lady, Lay" (1969), and "If Not for You" (1970), and in the classic "Just Like a Woman" (1966) with lyrics such as "She aches just like a woman but she breaks just like a little girl," he showed he could masterfully construct songs of emotional simplicity. And then there were the songs in which he combined allusion with simple lyrics: "Maggie's Farm" and "Ballad of a Thin Man" ("Something is happening and you don't know what it is, do you, Mr. Jones?") from 1965, and "I Want You" from 1966.

In the 1970s and 1980s, Dylan continued to change his musical style and persona, but only sporadically did his creative output match his monumental work of the 1960s. Examples include "Watching the River Flow" and "George Jackson" (1971), "Knockin on Heaven's Door" (1973), "Tangled Up in Blue" (1974), "Hurricane" (1975), and "Gotta Serve Somebody" (1979). None of these songs made the Top Ten, but then, few of Dylan's songs ever did. Nevertheless, Bob Dylan left an indelible mark on pop music and influenced a legion of rock musicians.

V. Folk Rock

The first folk-rock group to be directly inspired by Bob Dylan was the Byrds. The inventiveness of this Los Angeles–based group enabled them to directly challenge the British domination of American pop charts, a feat somewhat ironic considering that the Byrds' sound showed influence from the Beatles. The Byrds achieved their first two hits with Dylan compositions written in 1964: "Mr. Tambourine Man" and "All I Really Want to Do." Another 1965 hit was "Turn! Turn! Turn!," with lyrics adapted in 1962 by folk singer Pete Seeger from the biblical Book of Ecclesiastes. In 1966, the Byrds recorded their own composition, "Eight Miles High," one of the first rock records to be banned by many radio stations for its alleged references to drugs. "So You Want to Be a Rock and Roll Star" was a 1967 hit, warning of the pitfalls of rock stardom. In the late 1960s, the Byrds' music took on a country-and-western feeling, helping to usher in the country-rock sound.

Three other famous acts influenced by Bob Dylan were the Turtles, the Band, and Donovan Leitch. In 1965 the Turtles catapulted to success with Dylan's "It Ain't Me Babe." They followed with several newly written folk-rock hits: "You Showed Me" (1965), "Happy Together" and "She'd Rather Be With Me" (1966), and "Elenore" (1968). The Band was known as the Hawks whenever they provided occasional back-up assistance for Dylan during the mid-1960s. On their own, the Band recorded the seminal rock album *Music From Big*

Pink (1968), which contained some new songs written by Dylan. However, its major hit, "The Weight," was written by the leader of the Band, Robbie Robertson. This song, along with "Up on Cripple Creek" (1969), which was also written by Robertson, preserved the lyrical content and force of the traditional folk classic. Donovan Leitch, who was billed simply as Donovan, had his first hit in 1965 with the self-composed ersatz Dylan song "Catch the Wind." He later proved himself a talent with the release of his original psychedelic folk singles "Sunshine Superman" and "Mellow Yellow" (1966), "Hurdy Gurdy Man" (1968), and "Atlantis" (1969).

The Lovin' Spoonful, led by John Sebastian, was a group that added jug-band instrumentation to folk rock, creating a delightful mixture of good-natured and friendly music. Their biggest hits included their 1965 paean to rock and roll, "Do You Believe in Magic?" ("the music that can set you free"); "You Didn't Have to Be So Nice" (1965); "Did You Ever Have to Make Up Your Mind?" and "Daydream" (1966); and "Summer in the City" (1967), which captured the feel of tough urban life.

Buffalo Springfield, a group that was not actually a folk-rock band, incorporated qualities of the genre into songs that featured melodic harmonies and poignant lyrics. Their outstanding recording was "For What It's Worth" in 1967. Written by Stephen Stills, it is a protest song reflecting on the battle lines then being drawn between the younger and older generations. Stills and Neil Young, another Buffalo member, went on to become leading figures in rock. Stills, along with David Crosby of the Byrds and Graham Nash of the Hollies, formed Crosby, Stills and Nash in 1968. This trio excelled in lovely acoustic music and sonorous harmony. Two 1969 hits were "Marrakesh Express" and "Suite: Judy Blue Eyes," written about folk singer Judy Collins. In 1970 Neil Young joined the group, which had hits that year with "Teach Your Children," "Our House," and "Ohio"—the last written by Young after four students at Kent State University were killed by the National Guard during an antiwar protest. Young is still recording, and over the years has released many respected albums; his only hit singles, however, were in the early 1970s, and include "Old Man" and "Heart of Gold" from 1972.

Simon and Garfunkel were a folk-rock duo, blending protest lyrics with Everly Brothers–style harmony to create some of the most sophisticated songs in rock history. Paul Simon wrote all of their original compositions, which were usually about the individual's place in society, while Art Garfunkel provided the sweet, close harmonies that helped the songs achieve their distinctive sounds. Their most popular songs were sung in a wistful melancholy mood: "I Am a Rock" and "The Sound of Silence" (both 1964), "Homeward Bound" (1966), "Scarborough Fair" (1968) and "The Boxer" (both 1968), and "Bridge Over Troubled Water"

(1969)—the last a song that has become a true standard in popular music. Because of the intentional or coincidental spirituality of its lyrics, the last-named song has also become a favorite with gospel singers.

Simon and Garfunkel were also adept at applying their mood-evoking sound to more upbeat rhythmic hits, including "A Hazy Shade of Winter" (1966), "Cecilia" (1970), and "Mrs. Robinson" (1968). This last was a song more about anxiety and despair than about a specific person, with its classic line, "Where have you gone Joe Di Maggio, A nation turns its lonely eyes to you."

The Simon and Garfunkel duo broke up in 1971, but Paul Simon continued on as a vital force in pop music throughout the 1980s. His hits as a solo artist include "Mother and Child Reunion" (1971), "Kodachrome" (1973), "Fifty Ways to Leave Your Lover" (1976), and "Slip Slidin' Away" (1977). In the late 1980s, Simon embraced music of different cultures, such as South Africa and Brazil, creating a unique pop sound.

VI. The Singer-Songwriter

Throughout the history of popular music, there have been songwriters who sang their own songs, but the singer-songwriter of rock was of a different breed, one who grew out of the introspective nature of folk rock. Through their songs, these performers shared their innermost confidences and fears, in an almost confessional manner. Their songs seemed to sum up their personality; this is what made them very attractive to their audiences.

Joni Mitchell was the most accomplished of these singer-songwriters. Her voice was majestically beautiful, and throughout most of her career she continued to progress artistically and technically. Before she became an established star, she wrote the classic "Both Sides Now" for Judy Collins in 1967 and "Woodstock" in 1969 for Crosby, Stills, Nash, and Young. The latter song was about the August 1969 rock festival held in New York State that attracted over half a million people—at the time, the largest audience ever assembled at an entertainment event. More than just a straightforward narration, this song immortalized the hippie ideals of peace, love, and brotherhood. Mitchell's own single hits were "You Turn Me On, I'm a Radio" in 1972; "Help Me" and "Free Man in Paris" in 1974; and "Big Yellow Taxi," a 1975 version of a song she originally recorded as an album cut in 1970.

James Taylor's songwriting skills were much simpler than Mitchell's. At times he seemed to be reluctant to make his life an open book, but apparently he relented when he recorded "Fire and Rain" in 1970 and sang about his time in a mental institution, his heroin addiction, and a friend's suicide. This was an evocative song, but Taylor generally chose to use his pleasant and melodic voice on songs with less harrowing subject matter, such as the laid-back and relaxed "Country Road" (1970), "Don't Let Me Be Lonely Tonight" (1972), "Shower the People" (1975), "Your Smiling Face" (1977), and his only Number One song, "You've Got a Friend" (1971), written by the great rock-'n'-roll era songwriter Carole King.

King became one of the leading singer-songwriters in the early 1970s; her 1971 album, *Tapestry*, was one of the biggest sellers in recording history. She combined her songwriting talent with the candor inherent in the genre on songs such as "It's Too Late," "I Feel the Earth Move," and "So Far Away" (all in 1971). "Sweet Seasons" (1971) was also a big hit.

Other leading singer-songwriters of the period included Cat Stevens, whose sensitive and straightforward writing made him very popular. Among his best songs are "Wild World," and "Moon Shadow" (1970), and "Peace Train" and "Morning Has Broken" (1971). Leonard Cohen was a brilliant Canadian poet whose somber singing style poignantly conveyed his songs about being a loser in love and about experiencing the psychic torment of relationships. Although "Suzanne" (1966) and "Bird on the Wire" (1969) were not commercial hits for Cohen, they remain some of the best songs of their kind. Carly Simon (at one time married to James Taylor) sang in a smoother and sexier style than most of the other singer-songwriters. Her hits included "That's the Way I've Always Heard It Should Be" (1971), "Anticipation" (1972), "You're So Vain" (1972), and "Haven't Got Time for the Pain" (1974).

VII. Acid Rock

During the mid-1960s, a great number of American youths experimented with drugs. San Francisco has traditionally been a city tolerant of alternative lifestyles and it was here that a society of stoned-out kids came together and created a form of rock music known as acid rock, or "the San Francisco sound."

The core of this sound was predicated on the fact that this was music on which to get high. It was very loud, featured furious vocal performances, and placed tremendous emphasis on amplification with deliberate feedback and distortion. The music relied heavily on the droning mystical qualities of Indian ragas, which were perfectly suited for the extended improvisations needed to sustain the psychedelic experience. Most of the recordings of this music were designed for albums, and thus only a few songs ever made the pop singles charts.

Many groups came out of the Bay Area, but the following are among the best known. The Jefferson Airplane was the finest of the San Francisco bands, taking elements of folk rock, such as protest, politics, allusion, and love, and mixing them with jazz, blues, and strange harmonies. Grace Slick was the explosive lead singer of the group; her unique voice was perfectly matched to the provocative and turbulent lyrics of the songs. Two of the Airplane's most famous songs were recorded in 1967: the drug-related "White Rabbit," which made an analogy between Alice in Wonderland and dropping acid, and "Somebody to Love." This latter was a song to which a generation of young people looking for meaning in life could relate: "When the truth is found to be lies and all the joy within you dies, don't you want somebody to love?" In 1975, after a series of personnel changes, the group was reorganized as Jefferson Starship and had a huge hit that same year with "Miracles."

The Grateful Dead was San Francisco's most beloved band. Their music, often performed while the group is under the influence of drugs, lends itself to lengthy and moody extemporization. The Dead are famous for rich, rocking songs in medium tempo and for leader Jerry Garcia's bluegrass-sounding guitar playing. In 1987, "Touch of Grey," a humorous song commenting on growing old in rock, was their first single ever to crack the Top Ten. No group in popular music has more loyal fans than they. Known as "dead heads," the fans follow the Dead as they tour the country.

Santana, a group led by lead guitarist Carlos Santana, brought Latin influences to the San Francisco sound. Although the group could improvise with the best of them, its music was much tighter than the acid rock of other bands. The two songs that made Santana famous are "Black Magic Woman" and "Evil Ways" (both recorded in 1970).

It is quite remarkable that out of the relatively small number of excellent groups in San Francisco, two of them, featuring the female voices of Grace Slick and Janis Joplin, would make lasting impressions in rock music. Joplin was lead singer with Big Brother and the Holding Company, but her star status quickly overshadowed the rest of the band. Her voice was rough and raw, and she sang in a very passionate, sexual style. No other white woman has been able to sing the blues like she did. Most of her songs were originally done by others, but her interpretations were so amazing that she made them her own. "Ball and Chain" and "Piece of My Heart" were two 1968 hits. Janis died of a heroin overdose on October 4, 1970; four months later her version of "Me and Bobby McGee" went to Number One on the pop charts.

Another well-known group from San Francisco was Country Joe and the Fish, with more theatrical music and stage presentation than those of the other bands.

Probably the two best-known acid-rock bands *not* originating in San Francisco were Iron Butterfly and Vanilla Fudge. These two groups became famous despite having only one hit each. Iron Butterfly recorded in 1968 a song called "In-a-gadda-da-vida." Not only was it over seventeen minutes long (it took up an entire side of an album), but legend has it that the actual name of the song was "In the Garden of Eden" and that the vocalist was allegedly so stoned that the title came out sounding the way it is now pronounced. Vanilla Fudge's

1967 hit was a remake of "You Keep Me Hangin' On" (originally done by the Supremes in 1966), with the overall psychedelic effect stemming from the pseudo-sitar-sounding guitar and the neoclassical organ melodramatics creating an exciting record.

Jimi Hendrix was an American guitarist who first became popular performing in England with his band, the Jimi Hendrix Experience. He was the first black man to become a rock star, and he totally redefined the way the electric guitar could be played. He did not have a strong singing voice, but his scintillating psychedelic blues was the ultimate in dope music and the heaviest that rock had been up to that point. Some of his most famous recordings were "Hey Joe" (1967, originally a hit the previous year by the Leaves) and several songs of his own mystical imagery: "Purple Haze," with explicit drug references; "The Wind Cries Mary"; and "Foxy Lady" (all 1967). His only charted Top Forty single was also from 1968: "All Along the Watchtower," written by Bob Dylan.

Hendrix was one of rock's greatest performers. On stage he exuded a magnetic charisma and theatricality, which included setting his guitar ablaze. At the Woodstock music festival of 1969, he performed his version of "The Star Spangled Banner," one that has since become part of the folklore of rock music. A year later he died of a drug overdose. Hendrix's musical anarchy helped pave the way for an overall harder rock sound that would soon come with the second great wave of British bands.

VIII. The Second British Invasion

One of the most important of these new groups from Britain was Cream, whose style combined explosive blues-based music with unusual transfixing lyrics. The group's popular songs were "Sunshine of Your Love" (1967), "White Room" (1968), and "Crossroads" (1969, originally recorded by blues legend Robert Johnson in 1936). Most of Cream's unique sound can be attributed to the lead guitarist, Eric Clapton, perhaps the most-imitated white blues guitarist in rock. He was so renowned in England that during the mid- to late 1960s it was not uncommon to see "Clapton is God" spray-painted on London walls.

Originally a member of the Yardbirds, Clapton played in many bands including John Mayall's Bluesbreakers, Cream, and Blind Faith. In 1970, with his group Derek and the Dominoes, Clapton recorded one of the most popular rock songs ever, the emotionally intoxicating "Layla." This song also featured famed guitarist Duane Allman, who with the Allman Brothers Band of Macon, Georgia, was the leading exponent of southern rock. As a solo artist, Eric Clapton had hits with "I Shot the Sheriff" (1974), written by **reggae** artist Bob Marley; "Lay Down Sally"; and "Wonderful Tonight" (both 1978).

One of the most prolific British groups of this

period was the Bee Gees, known for their romantic, ornate orchestrations. They had a great many hits with their own songs: "To Love Somebody," "New York Mining Disaster 1941," "Holiday," "Massachusetts" (all from 1967); "Words" (1968); "Lonely Days" (1970); and "How Can You Mend a Broken Heart" (1971). One of their most interesting songs was "I Started a Joke," a 1968 hit whose lyrics constituted an effective allegorical poem with a meaning open to various interpretations.

Another band, Procol Harum, recorded a song called "A Whiter Shade of Pale" (1967). It attracted attention for two reasons: its mesmerizing music borrowed from Bach and its cerebral lyrics, which, incidentally, have been printed in poetry books without any indication of their source.

Much of the music being made by these British groups was considered "progressive" and arty, classically inspired, and more serious than regular rock, implying that in some way this music was better. The Moody Blues was the biggest culprit. They even went so far as to record their 1968 album *Days of Future Passed* with the London Symphony Orchestra. This album contained the beautiful and mysterious "Nights in White Satin," a song that became a single hit four years later.

IX. Art Rock

As rock progressed further, attempts were made to turn it into an art form. This new eclecticism produced some new bands, including the Velvet Underground, from New York, and the Mothers of Invention, from Los Angeles. The Velvet Underground was one of the most influential bands in rock, although it was never commercially successful. Lou Reed, the lead singer and songwriter, infused his lyrics with documentary realism and, along with avant-garde musician John Cale on bass and viola, touched on subjects seldom explored in popular music before the 1970s: drug addiction and sadomasochism. The band broke up in 1970, but Lou Reed went on to a solo career and his first and only **Top Forty** hit, "Walk on the Wild Side" (1972), a song dealing with a veritable freak show of real characters living in New York City.

The Mothers of Invention was one of the first rock groups to stage mixed-media presentations. In its recordings, leader Frank Zappa had the group doing much the same thing by mixing together social satire, classical music, and **doo-wop**—all with a rock base. The group recorded a wide range of interesting and often brilliant albums, but was able to attain popularity only with rock's underground. The 1967 album *Freak Out* was once cited by Paul McCartney as an inspiration for the Beatles' *Sgt. Pepper's Lonely Hearts Club Band. We're Only in It for the Money* (1968) was in essence Zappa's sarcastic dig at the Beatles' *Sgt. Pepper's* album.

As the 1960s drew to a close, some of the most interesting and diverse sounds in rock came from a band called the Doors, from Los Angeles. Its keyboard player,

Ray Manzarek, was classically trained, while Jim Morrison, the sexy lead singer with the brooding voice, was one of the most erudite of rock stars. Two persons whose lives were an inspiration to Morrison were William Blake and Friedrich Nietzsche. Morrison's own poetic lyrics were very mystical and showed a preoccupation with sex and death. The result was powerful rock, with a very theatrical and erotic sound. The Doors' biggest hits included "Light My Fire" and "People Are Strange" in 1967, "Hello, I Love You" in 1968, "Touch Me" in 1969, and "Love Her Madly" and "Riders on the Storm" in 1971. Jim Morrison introduced a hypnotically sexual performance style that rock has never since experienced. He died of a heart attack, assumed to have been drug-induced, in 1971.

Sly Stone, the second black man to emerge as a rock star, led his interracial band, Sly and the Family Stone, in rousing songs that combined elements of soul, jazz, rhythm and blues, and acid rock. His biggest hits were moralistic. They focused on the ideas that each man should be respected as an individual and that all men can live peacefully as one. Among these hits were "Dance to the Music" (1968); "Everyday People," "Hot Fun in the Summertime," and "I Want to Take You Higher" (1969); "Thank You Falettin Me Be Mice Elf Again" and "Family Affair" (1971).

Creedence Clearwater Revival was an anomaly in this period of rock music. Its sound was deeply rooted in 1950s rockabilly and rhythm and blues. While everyone else in rock was interested in mind expansion, Creedence just wanted to rock 'n' roll. While most rock bands were releasing conceptual albums, Creedence was interested in making albums comprised of potential hit singles. But even though its songs were reminiscent of the original rock 'n' roll sound, Creedence *was* a rock band. Its songs, as much as anyone's, addressed the cultural, social, and political issues of the day. The message was even more effective because it was camouflaged with the good-time sound of rock 'n' roll. All of the songs were written by John Fogerty, who was also the distinctive, raspy-voiced lead singer. Creedence Clearwater Revival made some of the best singles ever to be found on the pop charts, yet none of them reached Number One. Among them were the southern-flavored "Proud Mary" (1968) and "Down on the Corner" (1969). "Fortunate Son" and the ominous "Bad Moon Rising" were also hits that year. "Who'll Stop the Rain?," "Up Around the Bend," "Lookin' Out My Back Door," and the Little Richard–sounding "Travelin' Band" were all hits in 1970. "Have You Ever Seen the Rain" (1970) was their final hit.

The 1960s ended with two jazz-oriented rock groups making a name for themselves. Blood, Sweat, and Tears was formed in 1968 by famed session musician Al Kooper, but he quit the band just before it recorded its biggest hits, featuring lead singer David Clayton Thomas: "And When I Die," "Spinning Wheel," and "You've Made Me So Very Happy" (all in 1969). In that same year, a band called Chicago Transit Authority recorded its first album, featuring the popular "Does Anybody Really Know What Time It Is?" In 1970, it shortened its name to Chicago, and the group remained phenomenally successful through the 1980s. Among its many hits were "Make Me Smile" and "25 or 6 to 4" in 1970; "Beginnings," backed with "Colour My World" in 1971; "Saturday in the Park" in 1972; If You Leave Me Now" in 1976; "Hard to Say I'm Sorry" in 1982; "You're the Inspiration" in 1984; and "Look Away" in 1988.

X. Commercial Rock

Rock was at its best in the 1960s when it was both a part of the counterculture and a world apart from mainstream entertainment. But in the 1970s, rock was accepted by the establishment, and the term "rock" became an umbrella term for most genres and subgenres of popular music. Now that rock music was everybody's music, it became a huge money-making machine. Gone from rock was its main ingredient, rebelliousness. Many rock acts struggled with their image as they tried to look antisocial without really being so. Selling records became so important that an act's status on the pop music charts was closely watched. Among the most successful acts of the 1970s were Rod Stewart, Elton John, the Eagles, and David Bowie.

Stewart sang like his vocal cords were scratched with sandpaper. He originally made a name for himself with a Second-Wave British band called the Faces. When the 1970s began, he was renowned for his ability to sing rhythm and blues, soul, folk, and rock excellently, sometimes blending them all together. Stewart was a marvelous stage performer and a songwriter who wrote with humor and humility. He could show small details of life that otherwise would have been missed and had a penchant for songs that told heartfelt stories. His hits were "Maggie May" (1971), a classic song about a schoolboy's liaison with a prostitute; "You Wear It Well" (1972); and "Tonight's the Night (It's Gonna Be Alright)" (1976). Around 1977, both Stewart's songwriting and choice of songs diminished in quality. Even his stage performance became self-parody, all posturing and teasing, an attitude that was emulated by many heavy metal singers.

Elton John was so popular in the 1970s that he became one of the most celebrated and highest-paid rock performers in history. He was also one of the most flamboyant, a kind of Liberace of rock music. John had an affable singing voice and was an accomplished piano player. Most of his hits were written in collaboration with lyricist Bernie Taupin. Sentimentality was the main attribute of their songs, and it was used by them in both ballads and rocking songs. Between 1970 and 1988, Elton John had forty-three Top Forty hits. Among them were "Your Song" (1969); "Rocket Man," "Crocodile Rock," and "Honky Cat" (1972); "Daniel" and "Goodbye Yellow Brick Road" (1973); "Bennie and the Jets," "Don't Let the Sun Go Down on Me," and "The Bitch Is Back" (1974); "Philadelphia Freedom," "Someone Saved My Life Tonight," and "Island Girl" (1975); "Sorry Seems to Be the Hardest Word" and a duet with Kiki Dee, "Don't Go Breaking My Heart" (1976); and "Mama Can't Buy You Love" (1979).

The Eagles were the most commercial American rock band of the 1970s. Their slick country-rock songs were very appealing to fans of mellower rock stylings. Songwriting credits varied, but the majority of their songs were written by group members Glenn Frey and Don Henley. They include "One of These Nights" and "Lyin' Eyes" (1975); "Take It to the Limit," "New Kid in Town," and "Hotel California" (1977); and "Heartache Tonight" (1979).

English-born David Bowie may not have been one of the biggest-selling artists in the 1970s but he was certainly one of the most interesting. By constantly changing his performance style and by cleverly manipulating the media, he became one of the most avantgarde rock stars. He was the first androgynous rock star, wearing decadent makeup and outlandish futuristic costumes. This look helped usher in the short-lived but influential "glam-rock" period. His performance style became pop theater, and with each image change he continued to examine the underside of rock. Bowie's most popular songs were "Space Oddity" (1969); "Fame" (1975); "Golden Years" (1976); and "Let's Dance," "China Girl," and "Modern Love" (1983). "Blue Jean" in 1984 was his last big hit, except for his duet with Mick Jagger in a revival of the 1964 Motown classic "Dancing in the Street," in 1985.

XI. New Wave

In the 1970s new forms of rock music began to emerge, including heavy metal, **punk rock**, and New Wave. New Wave artists grew tired of rock's rampant commercialism and of groups trying to out "art" each other. They wanted to return rock to its early high-velocity tempo and to the use of only necessary instruments. The New Wave artist was also less concerned with the audience as a rock community. Many New Wave records were released on small, independent labels.

As with most forms of renegade music, New Wave eventually became commercial, in the late 1970s and early 1980s. The first of these groups to have hit records was the Knack, with "My Sharona" (1978). Other popular groups were the B-52's and Devo, but the most successful was the Cars, whose hits included "Let's Go" (1979) and "You Might Think" and "Drive" (1984).

XII. Music Video

At the beginning of the 1980s, radio was no longer the only place where rock music was broadcast; the MTV cable television network started airing music videos around the clock. The audience not only heard the music, but saw it being performed, which generated new interest and excitement in rock music. Several new stars emerged who felt the need to go back to the basics. They revitalized the music by incorporating elements of 1960s rock.

One of these artists was Bruce Springsteen, whose input into rock's regeneration actually began in the 1970s, a full decade before he became a legend. The first album to establish Springsteen as a full-blown rock star was *Born to Run* (1975). The title song itself renewed rock with the original passion of rock 'n' roll: rebellion and restlessness. Springsteen sang this song with the histrionics of a Roy Orbison and the sensibilities of a Del Shannon, and the whole mood was set through a Phil Spector–like production. In subsequent albums, he showed his lyrical ingenuity by telling dramatic narrative tales about subjects that mattered to him: the need for freedom, making sense out of life's madness, loving commitments that would combat loneliness, and the hidden good in everyone. These ideas could be found in songs of jubilant energy or emotional ballads. His recording career climaxed with *Born in the U.S.A.*; this 1984 album was a triumph of the revival of consciousness in rock music. Thematically it was about a troubled American and the need for a sense of community. Springsteen also released several immensely popular singles during this decade: "Hungry Heart" (1980); "Dancing in the Dark," "Cover Me," and "Born in the U.S.A." (1984); "I'm on Fire," "Glory Days," "I'm Goin' Down," and "My Hometown" (1985); and "Brilliant Disguise" and "Tunnel of Love" (1987).

When Michael Jackson was racking up hits as part of his act with his brothers, the Jackson 5, in 1970 at the age of twelve, no one would have guessed that in 1982 he would release *Thriller*, the best-selling album of all time at this writing. Jackson's earlier album, *Off the Wall* (1979), showed that he was a talent to be reckoned with. He matured into a soulful tenor who definitely had his finger on the pulse of modern pop and dance music. Two big hits from this album were "Don't Stop 'Til You Get Enough" and "Rock With You." Nevertheless, except for fans of rhythm and blues, pop, and dance, the general public was still unaware of him. That all changed in May 1983 when he appeared on a televised salute to Motown's twenty-fifth anniversary. His performance of "Billie Jean" in 1983 generated almost as much excitement as when the Beatles first appeared on *The Ed Sullivan Show*. His body literally exploded into a dancing machine complete with kicks, spins, and a robotic "moonwalk." The song itself was perfectly mated with the dance. It had a prominent bass drum sound that seemed to make Michael's voice pulsate and quiver, spewing out the lines as if his life depended on it.

After that show, it seemed as if *Thriller* was purchased by everyone—black and white, young and old. It was the first album of the rock era to thoroughly unite America's fragmented audience. The album also broke another record by having seven of its songs go to the Top Ten as single hits: the aforementioned "Billie Jean," "Beat It," "Wanna Be Startin' Somethin'," "Human Nature," "P.Y.T. (Pretty Young Thing)," "Thriller," and his duet with Paul McCartney, "The Girl Is Mine." The video versions of these songs made Michael Jackson the first major video star.

The only rival to Michael Jackson's dominant position at this time was Prince (Prince Rogers Nelson). He had recorded his first album in 1980, but it was not until two years later that his breakthrough occurred with the album *1999*. The most successful singles to come from it were the title song and "Little Red Corvette," the most sexually explicit record ever to make its way into the Top Ten. Prince was one of rock's greatest innovators in the 1980s, mixing carnal pleasure, religion, and nuclear war in his lyrics. By creating an exhilarating pop and funk dance groove, he helped bridge the gap between black and white rock. With the release of his hit motion picture and soundtrack album, *Purple Rain*, in 1984, Prince proved to have enormous appeal, which further solidified the bonds with his audiences. His remarkable string of hits included "Delirious" (1983); "When Doves Cry," "Let's Go Crazy," and "I Would Die 4 U" (1984); "Raspberry Beret" and "Pop Life" (1985); "Kiss" (1986); and "Sign o' the Times" and "U Got the Look" (1987).

Madonna Louise Ciccone, better known simply as Madonna, was not only the top female rock star of the 1980s, but gave every indication that she would continue her reign into the twenty-first century. She was the perfect rock star for the times. Besides openly flaunting her hedonistic sexuality through the video medium, she kept changing her persona from single release to single release. At one time she was "Like a Virgin" (1984), the next time she was a "Material Girl" (1985). But whatever she may have been, she always had one asking "Who's That Girl?" (1987).

Madonna was not only the most accomplished manipulator of the media since David Bowie, she was also a fine ballad singer and a dance-hall diva. Her records are among the most dynamic dance recordings ever made, but many of them also contain pertinent messages. For example, the controversial "Papa Don't Preach" (1986)—which many people think is about teenage pregnancy—may simply be about a girl's reluctance to break up with her boyfriend. Not knowing the real meaning is part of Madonna's charm and her ability to sell a song. Some of her other hits include and "Crazy for You" (1983) and "Lucky Star" (1984). Two hits of 1986 were "Live to Tell," a song about child abuse, and "True Blue," with a 1960s girl-group sound.

As the 1980s ended and the 1990s began, rock musicians were still trying to consolidate the elements that had made rock a powerful force in previous years. The problem was that rock was now a billion-dollar industry, unwilling to take the chances it took in the 1960s when the industry and the music were young. Rock music will never die as long as it speaks for the youthful rebelliousness in all of us. Nevertheless, it will probably never again be as potent an influence as it was in the 1960s.

Additional Songs

Along Comes Mary (1965)
American Pie (1971)
Another Brick in the Wall, Part II (1979)
The Beat Goes On (1967)
Born to Be Wild (1968)
Brother Louie (1973)
Do It Again (1968)
Eli's Coming (1967)
Elusive Butterfly (1965)
Eve of Destruction (1965)
Go Your Own Way (1976)
Good Lovin' (1965)
He Ain't Heavy . . . He's My Brother (1969)
Heart of Glass (1978)
Hello, It's Me (1968)
I Fought the Law (1961)
The Joker (1973)
The Letter (1967)
Lies (Are Breakin' My Heart) (1965)
Lowdown (1976)
Mama Told Me (Not to Come) (1966)
96 Tears (1966)
Psychotic Reaction (1966)
Ramblin' Man (1973)
She's About a Mover (1965)
Society's Child (1966)
Suspicious Minds (1968)
Sweet Home Alabama (1974)
What a Fool Believes (1978)
Wild Thing (1965)
Wooly Bully (1964)

Jeffrey Cahn

Bibliography

Battcock, Gregory, ed. *Breaking the Sound Barrier: A Critical Anthology of the New Music.* 1981.

Belz, Carl. *The Story of Rock.* 1972.

Bronson, Fred. *The Billboard Book of Number One Hits.* 1988.

Hardy, Phil, and David Laing, eds. *The Encyclopedia of Rock.* 1976.

Logan, Nick, and Bob Wiffenden. *The Illustrated History of Rock.* 1976.

Marsh, Dave. *The Heart of Rock and Soul.* 1989.

Miller, Jim, ed. *The Rolling Stone Illustrated History of Rock and Roll.* 1980.

Noble, Peter. *Future Pop: Music for the Eighties.* 1983.

Podell, Janet, ed. *Rock Music in America.* 1987.

Pollock, Bruce. *When the Music Mattered: Rock in the 1960s.* 1984.

Propes, Steve. *Golden Oldies: A Guide to 60s Record Collecting.* 1974.

Schaffner, Nicholas. *The Beatles Forever.* 1977.

———. *The British Invasion.* 1982.

Shaw, Arnold. *A Dictionary of American Pop-Rock.* 1982.

———. *The Rock Revolution.* 1971.

Stambler, Irwin. *Encyclopedia of Pop, Rock, and Soul.* 1975.

Whitburn, Joel. *The Billboard Book of Top 40 Hits.* 1989

ROCK 'N' ROLL

Rock 'n' roll was the prevailing type of American popular music from 1954 until the Beatles' first appearance on American pop charts in 1964. The term subsequently became generic for many diverse styles of youth-oriented popular music of the late 1950s and early 1960s.

The origin of the term can be traced to Cleveland **disc jockey** Alan Freed, who introduced it in 1951 on his **radio** show, *Moondog's Rock 'n' Roll Party.* However, the individual words "rock" and "roll" could be found in blues records dating back as far as the 1920s. With the release of the film *Blackboard Jungle* in 1955, "(We're Gonna) Rock Around the Clock"—a song recorded the previous year by Bill Haley and his Comets—created a sensation. Teenagers connected the song, and the music it represented, with rebellion. They formulated the attitude that this music was their own, a musical territory that adults could not enter. Indeed, many adults believed that rock 'n' roll—with its fast tempo, loud, raucous vocals, and lyrics filled with sexual innuendo—would turn their children into juvenile delinquents and tear asunder the fabric of middle-class American family life.

The major complaint by the detractors of rock 'n' roll was that the words were unintelligible and sometimes nonsensical. Although this was true to some extent, the grievance's importance was overrided by the powerful stimulus of the driving beat, which made fans feel good, lose their inhibitions, and want to dance. This "beat" was the most important aspect of the music; it was emphasized on the first beat of each bar in 4/4 meter. The music itself was very often in twelve-bar **blues** form. The typical **instrumentation** of electric guitars, drums, saxophones, piano, and electric bass gave the music its drive and tension, perfectly complementing the energies of its youthful admirers.

The roots of rock 'n' roll can be found in the blues as well as in **country and western** music; mixed in are traces of **jazz, folk music, gospel,** and **Tin Pan Alley.** Rock 'n' roll was a direct outgrowth of **rhythm and blues**—which differed from it, however, by being created and performed by blacks for blacks.

In contrast, rock 'n' roll was a thoroughly integrated music designed for an interracial audience. This, however, presented a problem for marketing the new product. As late as the mid-1950s, many "white" radio stations still would not play records featuring black rhythm-and-blues artists. Instead, white singers were solicited by record companies to **cover** existing hits. For example, in 1954, Georgia Gibbs covered LaVern Baker's recording of "Tweedle Dee" and the Crew Cuts rerecorded the Chords' "Sh-Boom." Pat Boone's career consisted almost entirely of covers: like those of Fats Domino's "Ain't That a Shame" in 1955 and Little Richard's "Long Tall Sally" in 1956. This subterfuge worked for a while, but cover recordings faded away when teenagers were exposed to the almost always superior versions of the original black artists. From that time on, the history of rock 'n' roll is largely an account of its individual performers, vocal groups, teen idols, songwriters, and "girl-group" recordings.

I. Individual Performers

Little Richard Penniman, from Macon, Georgia, was the archetype of rock flamboyance and histrionics. He screamed and wailed the lyrics and assaulted the piano keyboard unmercifully in such rock 'n' roll classics as "Tutti-Frutti," "Rip It Up," and "Ready Teddy" (all 1956) and "Good Golly Miss Molly" (1958). More than any other performer, he incited critics of rock 'n' roll to call it "jungle music" and "the devil's music." Possibly Little Richard believed his own press, because in 1958, at the height of his popularity, he retired from the music business to the quiet life of a theology student, although he did resume his musical career in the 1960s.

Antoine "Fats" Domino brought the sound of his native New Orleans to rock 'n' roll. Rather than attempting to revolutionize music, he continued to play piano in the same fun-loving style he had used since the late 1940s. In songs he co-wrote with Dave Bartholomew—such as "I'm in Love Again" (1956) and "Blue Monday" (1957), "I'm Walkin'" (1957), and "Whole Lotta Loving" (1958)—he gave rock 'n' roll an appealing, good-time feeling.

Chuck Berry (Charles Edward Anderson), born in St. Louis, had his first hit in 1955 with "Maybelline," made for Chess Records; it was essentially a rhythm-and-blues song with country-and-western guitar playing. He soon shifted gears, however, to create the seminal rock 'n' roll sound. Berry was the genre's first musical poet. He had an amazing awareness of the American teenage market and wrote about things they cared about and with which they could identify. In "Roll Over Beethoven" (1956), he wrote about their rebellious attitude; in "Rock and Roll Music" (1957), he wrote about their love for the music; in "Sweet Little Sixteen" (1958), he tried to enter the mind

of a teenaged girl. The sum of Berry's contribution could be found in "Johnny B. Goode" (1958), a song that not only gave rock 'n' roll its first central character in a fully realized story line, but, in its opening chords, formed the bedrock for all subsequent rock 'n' roll guitar playing.

Elvis Aron Presley, Mississippi-born and Tennessee-raised, remains the preeminent **singer** of rock 'n' roll. His contribution was so large that it transcended the music he sang, little of which he wrote himself. His persona grew to such mythological proportions that he became more than a singer: he became the most potent symbol of this new music and its culture. He recorded only five singles for Sam Phillips's Sun Records. All ten sides were of songs that had previously been recorded by rhythm-and-blues and country-and-western artists, like "Blue Moon of Kentucky" (1947). Presley did more than cover these songs; he improved them. He was one of those rare artists whose remakes far surpass the originals.

In the 1960s Presley concentrated more on his film career than on making records. Despite this, he was able to chart an unparalleled fifty-one Top Forty hits during the decade. Among these recordings were two Number One hits of 1969 that were already well-known from previous years: "Are You Lonesome Tonight?", originally recorded in 1926, and "It's Now or Never" (1960), adapted from the Italian song "O Sole Mio" of 1898. As the decade drew to a close, Presley recorded some of the finest songs of his career, including "Suspicious Minds," in 1969 and two message songs: "If I Can Dream," in 1968, and "In the Ghetto" in 1969. On August 16, 1977, at the age of forty-two, Elvis Presley died at his Graceland estate in Memphis. To this day, he remains, of all solo artists, the largest seller of popular records.

Two other country-based artists who recorded for Sun Records were Jerry Lee Lewis and Carl Perkins. Lewis was as wild and flamboyant a performer as Little Richard, battering his piano with a honky-tonk style. Where Presley had the simultaneous appearance of a tiger and a teddy bear, Lewis appeared just plain dangerous. He was, in fact, known as "the killer." Among the songs he introduced, some of which he wrote himself, were "Whole Lot-ta Shakin' Goin' On" and "Great Balls of Fire" (both 1957) and "Breathless" and "High School Confidential" (both 1958).

Unlike Lewis, Carl Perkins's image was one of the perfect gentleman. Nonetheless, he was filled with the rock 'n' roll spirit. One day in 1955, he composed the ultimate song of rock 'n' roll rebellion, "Blue Suede Shoes." When it was released in early 1956, teenagers adopted this song as their battle cry in their conflict with the older generation. Its essence has permeated all of rock 'n' roll and the **rock** music that followed. Perkins was also one of the founders of the hybrid genre known as **rockabilly**.

Charles Hardin (Buddy) Holley (he later dropped the "e") was another country boy with a love for rhythm and blues. Holly created a body of music of understated brilliance, credited to him either as a solo artist or with his group, the Crickets. He was not averse to innovation, being the first rock 'n' roll star to play the Stratocaster guitar, which later became a staple. He was also one of the first to use the now-classic instrumentation of electric guitars, drums, and bass, with a songwriting lead singer. Holly died in the same plane crash that killed J. P. (The Big Bopper) Richardson,— composer of "Chantilly Lace" (1958), and Ritchie Valens, the first Latino rock 'n' roll star, whose hits included "Donna" and "La Bamba" (both 1958). Although Holly's career spanned only a few short years, his influence was felt throughout the 1980s.

The Everly Brothers, from Kentucky, also came from the country tradition. Phil and Don's voices were so close to each other in timbre that they sometimes sounded like one multitracked voice. They best expressed themselves in songs of teenage sorrow, loneliness, and loss. Many of their most famous songs were written by the songwriting team of Boudleaux and Felice Bryant or by Boudleaux Bryant alone. These included "Bye Bye Love" and "Wake Up Little Susie," (1957); "Bird Dog," "All I Have to Do Is Dream," and "Devoted to You" (1958); and "Love Hurts" (1960). They also sang songs of their own, which they wrote either singly or together, including "'Til I Kissed You" (1959)," When Will I Be Loved?" (1960), and "Cathy's Clown" (1960).

Three performers, James Brown, Sam Cooke, and Ray Charles, introduced gospel elements into rock 'n' roll and helped plant the seeds for the **soul** music to come. Brown's stylistic inventions continued through the 1980s, but in the early years of rock 'n' roll his singing was a mixture of gospel and rhythm and blues, as in the song "Think" (1957). He also reworked such standards as "Bewildered" (1938) and "Prisoner of Love" (1931) in his inimitable style. Cooke was a former gospel singer who effortlessly converted his sweet and sensual voice into rock 'n' roll, in such songs of his own as "Only Sixteen" (1959), "Cupid" (1961), "Twisting the Night Away" (1962), and "Another Saturday Night" (1963). Charles has become famous for his ability to sing and play piano effectively in almost any genre. His string of gospel- and blues-oriented hits included his own "Hallelujah I Love Her So" (1956), as well as songs by others, among them "Hit the Road, Jack" and "Unchain My Heart" (both recorded in 1961).

Bo Diddley (Elias Bates McDaniel) was one of the first rock 'n' roll artists to explore the electric guitar to its full potential. He relied heavily on the maracas, which, combined with his frenetic guitar playing, made for a hypnotic and powerfully charged sound, later to be known as the "Bo Diddley beat." His first recording was a double-sided hit of 1955: the autobiographical "Bo Diddley" and I'm a Man." Both songs acted as strong influences on Diddley's American contemporaries and, later, on the British rockers.

Eddie Cochran was another artist whose electric guitar sound endured. His career ended tragically in a 1960 auto crash. Songs such as "Summertime Blues" and "C'mon Everybody" (both 1958) were rockabilly-based, but the primordial hard-rock sound that Cochran lent to them was influential on **heavy metal** and **punk rock**.

Roy Orbison's career was launched in 1956, with a rockabilly song called "Ooby Dooby," but the style did not fit him well. His ethereal and haunting voice came into its own when he sang his own songs of sorrow, yearning, and unrequited love, such as "Only the Lonely (Know the Way I Feel)" and "Cryin'" (both in 1961), "Dream Baby, How Long Must I Dream?" (1962), and "In Dreams" (1963). In 1964 he was able to combat the British invasion with two hit songs: "It's Over" and "Oh, Pretty Woman."

Jackie Wilson was another singer who used his voice in an exciting and theatrical way. Coming out of rhythm and blues with the Dominoes, he began to solo in 1957 with the rhythmical and guttural "Reet Petite." One of his writers was Berry Gordy, Jr., who later became the founder of **Motown** Records. In songs like "That's Why" (1957), "Lonely Teardrops" (1958), and "I'll Be Satisfied" (1959), and "Doggin' Around" and "Alone at Last" (both 1960), he drove his audience into a frenzy with his vocal acrobatics.

II. Vocal Groups

The vocal-group sound of rock 'n' roll developed out of the **doo-wop** performance of rhythm and blues, in which songs were embellished with **nonsense** syllables like "sh-boom" or "sha-da-da." These doo-wop records of early rock 'n' roll were made by both black and white groups, as well as by integrated ensembles. Some of the songs they introduced are classics, including "Earth Angel (Will You Be Mine)" (1954), sung by the Penguins; "Speedoo," (1955), by the Cadillacs; "Why Do Fools Fall in Love?" (1956), by Frankie Lymon and the Teenagers; "Come Go With Me" and "Whispering Bells" (both 1957), by the Del Vikings; "Book of Love" (1958), by the Monotones; and "One Summer Night" (1958), by the Danleers. Two older songs were also brought back in doo-wop form: "I Only Have Eyes for You" (1934), sung by the Flamingos in 1959; and "In the Still of the Night" (1939), sung by the Five Satins in 1956.

Three vocal groups were consistent money makers: the Platters, the Drifters, and the Coasters. The Platters, with the lush leading voice of Tony Williams, was the most commercially successful. They recorded almost exclusively in an upbeat ballad style. Most of their hits were produced by Buck Ram, who also wrote their signature songs, "Only You" and "The Great Pretender" (both 1955). The Platters also revived some old standards, including "Smoke Gets in Your Eyes" (1933), "My Prayer" (1939), "Harbor Lights" (1940), and "Twilight Time" (1944).

The Drifters were a group that would not only change their sound—from rhythm and blues to gospel to Latin to pop—but also their personnel. They varied their lead singers. Clyde McPhatter was heard on "Money Honey" in 1953 and "Honey Love" in 1954; Bobby Hendricks on "Drip Drop" in 1958; and Ben E. King on "Dance With Me" and "There Goes My Baby" (both in 1959) and "This Magic Moment" and "Save the Last Dance for Me" (both in 1960). Rudy Lewis was the lead singer on "Some Kind-A Wonderful" (1961), "Up on the Roof" (1962), and "On Broadway" (1963); followed by Johnny Moore, the lead singer for "Saturday Night at the Movies" and "Under the Boardwalk" (both 1964).

The Coasters were the first vocal group to present rock 'n' roll with a comedic slant. All of their hits were written and produced by Jerry Leiber and Mike Stoller, who formed the Coasters from the remnants of the famous rhythm-and-blues group the Robins. Their repertoire included "Young Blood" (1957), a song about an obsessive girl-watcher; "Searchin'" (1957), a song about looking for the girl that got away; and "Yakety Yak" (1958), a song about the generation gap written a few years before that term was used. Like several other Coasters hits, this record featured King Curtis, rock 'n' roll's premier tenor saxophone soloist. Three hits of 1959 were "Charlie Brown," the tale of a typical class clown; "Along Came Jones," a song about heroes of television westerns; and "Poison Ivy," about a woman who is not what she appears to be.

Dion DiMucci was one of the most consistently imaginative performers to come out of doo-wop. With his group, Dion and the Belmonts, he recorded the contemporary songs "I Wonder Why" (1958) and "A Teenager in Love" (1959), and revived Rodgers and Hart's classic "Where or When?" (1937) in 1960. He also recorded some solo recordings embellished by finger-snapping and hand-clapping, including "The Wanderer" in 1960 and "Runaround Sue" (which he co-wrote) in 1961.

As the 1950s turned into the 1960s, doo-wop lost much of its luster and was soon replaced with the lighter sound of such groups as the Four Seasons. Their first major hit, "Sherry" (1962), established that group's unique style, which featured the manic falsetto of lead singer Frankie Valli. Over the next few years their distinctive and well-produced records included "Big Girls Don't Cry" (1962), "Walk Like a Man" (1963), "Candy Girl" (1963), "Dawn" (1964), and "Rag Doll" (1964).

III. Teen Idols

In the early 1960s, Dick Clark was broadcasting his daily television show, *American Bandstand*, from Philadelphia; it became the national showcase for rock 'n' roll. Record companies made a practice of sending singers there for possible exposure on *Bandstand*. These so-called Teen Idols were cute, charming, and geared to the daydreams of teenaged girls. Yet they appeared to be wholesome, and thus inspired parental support.

One of the best known of these idols was Fabiano Forte, simply called Fabian, whose hits included "Turn Me Loose" and "Tiger" (both 1959). Frankie Avalon scored with "Dede Dinah" (1958), in which he held his nose when he sang in order to affect a nasal sound. His normal voice wasn't much better in such hit records as "Bobby Sox to Stockings" and "Venus" (both 1959) and "Why" (1960). Bobby Rydell was a better singer and entertainer in such big sellers as "Kissin' Time" (1959), "Swingin' School" and "Wild One" (both 1960), and "Forget Him" (1963).

Hollywood was another major center for manufacturing teen idols. Any popular actor or actress with teen appeal, whether or not he or she could sing, was encouraged to make a record. The only Hollywood personality of lasting significance in this sense was Ricky Nelson, who gained national exposure on his parents' weekly television show, *The Adventures of Ozzie and Harriet*. In 1957, he sang a cover of Fats Domino's "I'm Walkin'" on the show. Thus began a run of thirty-five **Top Forty** hits, none of which he wrote, including "Stood Up" and "Waitin' in School" (both in 1957), "Lonesome Town" and "Poor Little Fool" (both in 1958), and "Hello, Mary Lou" and "Travelin' Man" (both in 1961). Nelson combined a laid-back singing style with rockabilly- and blues-based music. His band—featuring one of rock 'n' roll's leading guitar players, James Burton—also contributed to his success.

Although many teen idols were short on talent, several fine performers did emerge. One of them was a Canadian, Paul Anka, whose songwriting and performing skills sustained his career through the 1980s. Among his early hits were "Diana" (1957), "You Are My Destiny" (1958), "(I'm Just a) Lonely Boy" (1959), "Put Your Head on My Shoulder" (1959), and "Puppy Love" (1959).

Bobby Darin was another very talented all-around performer. He got his start co-writing and performing such teen-idol songs as "Splish Splash" and "Queen of the Hop" in 1958. "Dream Lover," which he wrote and recorded in 1959, became one of the most popular songs of the rock 'n' roll years. Later that same year, Darin recorded Kurt Weill's "Mack the Knife" (1952) in a swinging style akin to Frank Sinatra's. That marked his abandonment of rock 'n' roll.

There were also several female teen idols, most notably Brenda Lee and Connie Francis. Lee's basic style was pseudo-rockabilly. In 1959 she had her first major hit with "Sweet Nothin's"; her big voice and exciting performing style belied the fact that she was only fifteen at the time. In 1960 her releases included "I'm Sorry," "I Want to Be Wanted," and the rock-'n'-roll **Christmas** standard "Rockin' Around the Christmas Tree."

Francis's initial appeal was to teenagers, in such songs as "Stupid Cupid" (1958), "Lipstick on Your Collar" (1959), and "Where the Boys Are" (1960). But her mature contralto was also accepted by an adult record-buying audience on her versions of such Tin Pan Alley standards as "Who's Sorry Now?" (1923), "Among My Souvenirs" (1927), and "My Happiness" (1948).

IV. "Girl-Group" Recordings

Another phenomenon of the period involved songs that were sung from the girl's point of view. Known as "girl-group recordings," these songs were warm and affecting. Lyrically, almost all of them used simple end-rhymes, but this simplicity belied their inherent emotionalism. The songs, sung almost reverently, were usually about a teenaged girl's love. Many of them had a certain spiritual quality and conveyed a feeling of underlying sadness and quiet desperation. Commercially, these recordings filled a void when the spark of rock 'n' roll began to dim. In fact, girl-group rock 'n' roll was the closest thing to the genuine article until the Beatles rekindled the flame. In fact, some of the first Beatles records were covers of girl-group hits.

The first group to established the style was the Shirelles, with lead singer Shirley Alston. Among the songs they introduced were "Will You Love Me Tomorrow?" in 1960, "Baby, It's You" in 1961, and "Soldier Boy" in 1962.

The Chantels, with lead singer Arlene Smith, gave an impassioned vocal performance of "Maybe" in 1958. This song was actually closer to gospel then to the slickly harmonized arrangements that later became associated with girl groups.

The Orlons were influenced by the Shirelles, but had a more upbeat and danceable sound. Among their hits were "Don't Hang Up" in 1962 and "South Street" in 1963.

The Chiffons had an infectious hit with "He's So Fine" in 1963. The sound of little girls pretending to get married was heard in the Dixie Cups' major hit, "Chapel of Love", (1964). Its spoken-word introduction probably had an influence on "Leader of the Pack," sung and spoken by the Shangri-Las in 1964. One of the strangest songs in all of rock 'n' roll was recorded by the Jaynettes in 1963: "Sally Go 'Round the Roses" has an ominous air about it, with ambiguous and metaphorical lyrics.

The girl-group sound applied as well to such solo artists as Claudine Clark and Lesley Gore. Clark had only one national hit, "Party Lights," which she wrote, produced, and recorded in 1962. Gore was originally discovered by Quincy Jones, who produced all her hit records, including "It's My Party," "Judy's Turn to Cry," and "She's a Fool" (all 1963). He also produced "You Don't Own Me" in the same year—a song many critics feel to have been a harbinger of the woman's liberation movement. Gore also had two hits in 1964: "Look of Love" and "Maybe I Know."

Despite all this seeming activity, rock 'n' roll had lost much of its initial excitement and had ceased to be rebellious by the early 1960s. Many of its founding fathers were not to be found. Little Richard retired, Fats Domino was performing in Las Vegas, Jerry Lee Lewis had lost his audience after he married his thirteen-year-old cousin, Buddy Holly was dead, and Elvis Presley came out of his two-year hitch in the Army as a changed performer, appearing on television in a tuxedo and singing along with Frank Sinatra. The United States desperately needed something new in music. This came about in 1964, when four long-haired lads from Liverpool, called the Beatles, landed on our shores.

Additional Songs

Be-Bop-A-Lula (1956)
Be My Baby (1963)
Black Denim Trousers and Motorcycle Boots (1955)
Breaking Up Is Hard to Do (1962)
Calendar Girl (1961)
Da Doo Ron Ron (When He Walked Me Home) 1963
Daddy's Home (1961)
The Diary (1958)
Don't (1957)
Duke of Earl (1961)
Halfway to Paradise (1961)
Happy Birthday, Sweet Sixteen (1961)
Her Royal Majesty (1961)
He's a Rebel (1962)
He's Sure the Boy I Love (1962)
Hey, Girl (1963)
Hushabye (1959)
It Might as Well Rain Until September (1962)
Jailhouse Rock (1957)
Kansas City (1959)
Let the Good Times Roll (1956)
Little Devil (1961)
Little Sister (1961)
The Loco-Motion (1962)
Love Is Strange (1956)
Love Potion Number Nine (1959)
Lover, Please (1961)
Loving You (1957)
Lucky Lips (1957)
A Mess o' Blues (1960)
Mr. Lee (1957)
My Dad (1962)
Oh! Carol (1959)
One Fine Day (1963)

Pretty Little Angel Eyes (1961)
Quarter to Three (1961)
Rock and Roll Is Here to Stay (1958)
Runaway (1961)
Spanish Harlem (1961)
Stairway to Heaven (1960)
Stand by Me (1961)
Surfin' Bird (1964)
Surrender (1960)
Suspicion (1962)
Take Good Care of My Baby (1961)
To Know Him Is to Love Him (1958)
Treat Me Nice (1957)
Twist and Shout (1960)
Uptown (1962)
Walking in the Rain (1964)
Who Put the Bomp (In the Bomp, Ba Bomp, Ba Bomp) (1961)
You've Lost That Lovin' Feelin' (1964)

Jeffrey Cahn

Bibliography

Belz, Carl. *The Story of Rock.* 1972.

Escott, Colin, with Martin Hawkins. *Good Rockin' Tonight: Sun Records and the Birth of Rock 'n' Roll.* 1991.

Gillett, Charlie. *The Sound of the City—The Rise of Rock and Roll.* 1983

Hardy, Phil, and Dave Laing, eds. *The Encyclopedia of Rock.* 1976.

Jackson, John A. *Big Beat Heat: Alan Freed and the Early Years of Rock & Roll.* 1991.

Marcus, Greil. *Mystery Train—Images of America in Rock 'n' Roll Music.* 1982.

Nite, Norman N. *Rock On—The Illustrated Encyclopedia of Rock and Roll.* 1977.

Propes, Steve. *Those Oldies But Goodies—A Guide to 50's Record Collecting.* 1973.

Shaw, Arnold. *The Rockin' '50s.* 1975.

Stambler, Irwin. *Encyclopedia of Pop, Rock, and Soul.* 1975.

Whitburn, Joel. *Top Pop Artists and Singles, 1955–1978.* 1979.

See also: **Rock, Soul**

ROCKABILLY

The combined sounds of **country and western** and **rhythm and blues** came to be known as "rockabilly" style. They chiefly emanated from Sam Phillips's Sun Records studios in Memphis in the late 1950s, although Sun was not the sole purveyor of this music. Rockabilly had many of the earmarks of black rhythm and blues, but it was performed by white musicians. It was usually sung with a country twang, accompanied by guitar and string bass, but without drums.

Elvis Presley used the style in some of his early recordings, but its chief proponents were Carl Perkins, Roy Orbison, the Everly Brothers, Brenda Lee, and Conway Twitty, all of whom went on to perform in other styles. Among songs originally performed in rockabilly style were Perkins's "Blue Suede Shoes" (1955) and "Matchbox" (1957) and Orbison's "Ooby Dooby" (1956). By 1959, the relatively simple sounds of rockabilly had given way to the raucous sounds of early **rock 'n' roll**.

Bibliography

Guralnick, Peter. *Lost Highways: Journeys and Arrivals of American Musicians.* 1979.

See also: **Bluegrass**

ROMANCE

Songs about "romance" are scarcely distinguishable from those about "love." Nevertheless, a significant number of attractive songs have been written on the subject, most of them dating from the 1920s and 1930s.

Two songs are entitled simply "Romance." One was introduced by Vivienne Segal in the Otto Harbach-Oscar Hammerstein II-Sigmund Romberg operetta *The Desert Song* (1926); the other, written by Edgar Leslie and Walter Donaldson, was introduced (by J. Harold Murray in the 1929 film *Cameo Kirby.* Lorenz Hart and Richard Rodgers used variations on the theme in the titles of two beautiful ballads: "Isn't It Romantic?," introduced by Maurice Chevalier and Jeanette MacDonald in the film *Love Me Tonight* (1932), and "My Romance," introduced by Donald Novis and Gloria Grafton in the revue **Jumbo** (1935).

Fred Astaire first sang Dorothy Fields's ironic lyrics to "A Fine Romance" in the film *Swing Time* (1936), complaining to Ginger Rogers that she was "just as hard to land as the 'Ile de France.'" A year later, "I'll Take Romance," a lovely waltz by Oscar Hammerstein II and Ben Oakland, was introduced by Grace Moore in the film of the same name.

Judging from the song titles, the early years of the century were the more romantic ones; few songs about romance have been produced in the more pragmatic second half of the century.

ROSES. SEE FLOWERS

RUMBA

"Rumba" is a composite term embracing several varieties of Cuban dance and their accompanying music: the son, the rural rumba, the **bolero**, and the **guaracha**. Derived from African ceremonial dances, the music is usually in 4/4 meter and moderate to fast tempo and relies on percussion instruments such as bongos, claves, conga drums, maracas, sticks, and timbales.

The rumba was the second Latin American dance to become a craze in the United States. In 1930, twenty-six years after the Argentine **tango** captured New York City, the resounding success of "The Peanut Vendor," derived from the Cuban song "El Manicero," initiated a new craze that was to last for twenty years.

Other rumbas of Cuban origin also appeared: "Siboney" in 1929; "Jungle Drums" in 1930; "Adios," "Green Eyes (Aquellos Ojos Verdes), and "Mama Inez" in 1931; "Taboo" in 1934; "Say 'Si Si" in 1936; "Babalu" in 1939; and "The Breeze and I" in 1940. In addition, rumbas came from places as diverse as Mexico ("Frenesi" and "Perfidia," both 1939) and Greece ("Misirlou," 1941). Not to be outdone, people from the United States wrote rumbas as well, including songs like "When Yuba Plays the Rumba on His Tuba" (1931), "My Shawl" (1934), "The Lady in Red" (1935), "Miami Beach Rumba" (1946), and "Managua Nicaragua" (1946). Another rumba popular in 1947 was "Perhaps, Perhaps, Perhaps (Quizas, Quizas, Quizas)."

In the early 1950s, much of the excitement of the rumba was transferred to two new Cuban **dance crazes**: the **cha cha cha** and the **mambo**. Nevertheless, the rumba lived on as one of the most popular of ballroom dances.

Bibliography

Roberts, John Storm. *The Latin Tinge: The Impact of Latin American Music on the United States.* 1979.

RUSSIA

Russia's influence on American popular song lies principally in its being the birthplace of several outstanding songwriters, including the **composer-lyricist** Irving Berlin, the **lyricist** Lew Brown, and the **composer** Vernon Duke.

Berlin, according to official records, was born as Israel Baline in the town of Mohilev in White Russia on May 11, 1888—although his birthplace has long been erroneously given as Temun (Siberia), a place that does not exist. He came to the United States in 1893. Brown was born in Odessa in 1893 and came to the United States when he was five years old. Most of his lyrics were written in **collaboration** with B. G. DeSylva. Duke was born Vladimir Dukelsky in the village of Parpanovka on October 10, 1903. He composed both "serious" and popular music, using his given name for the former and his pen name for the latter. After the Russian Revolution of 1917, he lived in France and England before settling in the United States in 1929.

Many other songwriters can claim Russian ancestry, even though they were not born in Russia. George and Ira Gershwin's father, for example, was a Russian immigrant to Brooklyn, named Jacob Gershowitz, who later shortened his family name to Gershvin.

Few Russian songs reached the United States from the time of the Revolution until the end of the Cold War. The Russian gypsy waltz "Otchi Tchorniya" remained a standard after it was arranged, Anglicized, and performed on radio as "Dark Eyes" by Harry Horlick and the A&P Gypsies. "Meadowlands" (1939), the Soviet Army song, was briefly popular in the United States during World War II. "Midnight in Moscow," "(Moscovian Nights)," based on the Russian song "Padmoskoveeye Vietchera," was popularized in 1961 by its co-writer, Kenny Ball. Also, many themes from the Russian **classics** were converted into popular songs, in particular those by the composers Tchaikovsky, Borodin, and Rachmaninoff.

See also: **Foreign Influence**

S

SALSA

"Salsa" is the Spanish word for "sauce," and has the connotation of spiciness. It has accordingly been used since the late 1960s as an umbrella term for much Afro-Cuban and Puerto Rican dance music. It represents a fusion of **jazz** and the **mambo**, along with elements of the **boogaloo**. Salsa flourished during the 1970s in such urban centers as Miami and **New York City**, and was performed in ballrooms and on record albums by such bandleaders as Ray Barretto, Willie Colon, Johnny Pacheco, and Eddie Palmieri.

Most of salsa's songs are in the Spanish language. The innovations are in the **arrangements** and the instrumentation, which is often eclectic, using strings, flutes, and synthesizers. A San Francisco group led by Carlos Santana helped create a fusion between salsa and **rock** in the early 1970s. Salsa was in great demand as an ingredient of the **disco** dance craze of the 1970s.

Bibliography

Gerard, C., and M. Sheller. *Salsa! The Rhythm of Latin Music.* 1989.

Roberts, John Storm. *The Latin Tinge: The Impact of Latin American Music on the United States.* 1985.

See also: Cuba; Latin America

SAMBA

The samba was the first dance from **Brazil** to receive worldwide recognition. Although many varieties existed in different parts of Brazil, it was the urban dance established in Rio de Janeiro in the 1920s that became the international standard. To this day, at Carnival time in Rio, organizations known as *scolas da samba* compete as to styles of percussion and dancing. These competitions and their pervasive rhythmic accompaniment are admirably illustrated in the 1959 film *Black Orpheus*, which itself contains an enduring example of the genre: "Samba de Orfeu."

The dance and its music had their origins in the songs and dances of Brazilians of African descent, such as the batuque, and in European-derived urban genres like the maxixe. The dance is characterized by jaunty and uninhibited, body-swinging movements. The music is usually in 2/4 meter and moderate tempo. It is heavily percussive, with complex rhythms in layers of patterns like this:

The first samba to become popular in the United States was "Come to the Mardi Gras" (1937), originally "Nao Tenho Lagrimas." It was followed, two years later, by an outstanding success: the prototypical samba, "Aquarela do Brasil," retitled "Brazil." In 1944, two lasting sambas were introduced in musical films: "Tico Tico," in the cartoon feature *Saludos Amigos*, and "Baia," in *The Three*

Caballeros. Most other popular sambas of this period were non-Brazilian in origin. They include "Anna," the title song of the film of that name (1952), which starred Silvana Mangano; and several made-to-order sambas of North American origin: "I Yi Yi Yi Yi (I Like You Very Much)" (1941), "The Wedding Samba" (1947), "Mañana (Is Soon Enough for Me)" (1948), and "Enjoy Yourself (It's Later Than You Think)" (1948).

In the 1960s, the craze for the samba was largely replaced by one for a related Brazilian dance and song type, the **bossa nova.** The relationship of that dance to the samba is underscored by the title of one of its first successes, "One Note Samba," a bossa written by Antonio Carlos Jobim in 1961.

Additional Songs

Aurora (1941)
Chiu, Chiu (1942)
Cuanto le Gusta (1940)
Delicado (1952)
Good, Good, Good (That's You, That's You) (1944)
I Want My Mama (Mama Yo Quiero) (1940)

Bibliography

Roberts, John Storm. *The Latin Tinge: The Impact of Latin American Music on the United States.* 1979.

See also: **Dance Crazes**

SATURDAY. *See* DAYS OF THE WEEK

SAXOPHONE. *See* WOODWINDS

SCALE

Three scales are commonly used as building blocks in the **melodies** of popular song: the diatonic, the chromatic, and the pentatonic. Of these, the diatonic is by far the most prominent and, in its major form, is common is many songs. The scale is usually incomplete and is manifested by predominantly stepwise melodic motion in such songs as "It Had to Be You" (1924) and "S'posin'" (1929).

However, one composer, Richard Rodgers, made frequent use of substantial portions of the scale in his music. The seven-tone diatonic scale (which can be exemplified by the white notes from c to c' on the piano keyboard) is an integral part of many of the songs he wrote with Lorenz Hart, among them "Dancing on the Ceiling" (1930) and "My Romance" (1935). In songs like "Where or When?" (1937) and "Have You Met Miss Jones?" (1937), the scales are stated completely only in the closing A section, where both melodies rise in the diatonic scale over a **range** of more than an **octave.** Sometimes, as in such songs as "The Blue Room" (1926), "The Girl Friend " (1926), "My Heart Stood Still" (1927), and "Johnny One Note" (1937), there are

intervening notes between the pitches of a generally rising scale. Rodgers also made liberal use of the diatonic scale in several songs he wrote with Oscar Hammerstein II, for example, "Younger Than Springtime," from *South Pacific* (1949). But he brought his infatuation with the diatonic scale to its culmination in a song that is literally about the scale and solmization: "Do-Re-Mi," from *The Sound of Music* (1959).

Many other composers employed the diatonic major scale in their music. One song, above all, stands out for its unabashed use of this scale. "(All of a Sudden) My Heart Sings," a French song adapted by Harold Rome in 1941, makes complete statements of both the ascending and descending diatonic scale in a range of one octave and with liberal employment of **repeated notes** at each pitch. Monotony is avoided by the constantly changing harmonies, making the song surprisingly evocative. The diatonic scale is also prominent in the **release** of the 1928 song "(I Got a Woman Crazy for Me) She's Funny That Way," where it is stated twice in its ascending form.

The chromatic scale is much less common in popular song. This twelve-tone scale (which can be demonstrated by using both white and black notes on the piano keyboard from c to c') is perhaps expressed most completely in Cole Porter's 1934 song "All Through the Night," the melody of which descends in half steps (with some note repetition) over a range of a minor seventh. Other chromatic descents are more limited. The principal theme of Jerome Kern's "I Dream Too Much" (1935), for example, consists of three motives which descend sequentially and paraphrase the chromatic scale over a range of only a tritone. That of Rodgers's "Lover" (1933) descends chromatically (with repetitions and elaborations) for a total range of only a fourth in each A section, while Duke Ellington's "Prelude to a Kiss" (1938) spans only a third.

Probably the chief proponent of the pentatonic scale was Irving Berlin. This scale (which can be represented by playing only the black keys on the piano) was a favorite of the composer, who preferred to write his songs in the **key** of F-sharp, using a specially made transposing piano. In the 1925 song "Always," for example, the first six notes—c, d, f, g, a, c'—describe a perfect pentatonic scale. Many other Berlin melodies, such as that of "Remember" (1925), also use the scale. The pianist-composer Zez Confrey was another advocate of the pentatonic scale, using it in his 1926 song "Stumbling." George Gershwin also used it in such songs as "Clap Yo' Hands" (1926) and "They All Laughed" (1937).

See also: **Blue Note; Chromaticism; Gypsy Music; Interval; Modality; Mode; Sequence**

SCANDALS. *See* REVUES

SCAT SINGING

Scat singing is a vocal jazz style in which the singer imitates the phrasing of an instrument through the use of nonsense syllables. According to jazz lore, scatting began in 1926 when Louis Armstrong, while recording "Heebie Jeebies," dropped (or forgot, depending upon which version of the story one hears) his lyric sheet and so completed the chorus vocally with improvised nonsense syllables.

Since jazz developed in large part from blues, shouts, spirituals, and work songs, much of its phrasing was influenced by the voice. With scat singing the evolution comes full circle, as the voice now borrows its inflections from jazz instrumentation. One needs only to listen to Armstrong to hear how he brings the same stylistic approach to his vocals that he does to his trumpet-playing.

Scat singing is often used as an accompaniment to instrumental performance, as in the simultaneous bass-bowing and scatting of Slam Stewart, or in Mose Allison's occasional mumbling while playing the piano. Speed of execution seems particularly valued in scatting, as exemplified by the rapid-fire style of Joe Henricks. It was been argued that it is scat singing that separates the true jazz vocalists from those who sing with only a degree of jazz interest.

Duke Ellington used the female voice to provide texture for his sensitive orchestral palette as early as 1927, in his "Creole Love Call." In this recording, Adelaide Hall's vocal part clearly emulates the trombone, and so anticipates later, more assertive scat singing. Ella Fitzgerald displayed a polished scatting ability in some of her early recordings with the Chick Webb Orchestra in the late 1930s. She went on to use the device throughout her long career in such recordings as "If You Can't Sing It You'll Have to Swing It (Mister Paganini)" (1936), "It's All Right With Me" (1953), and "Teach Me Tonight," among others. Leo Watson had a humorous approach to scatting that owed as much to philology as to instrumental phrasing.

Scatting was a favorite device of bebop musicians in the 1940s and 1950s; the lack of true lyrics made the tunes more abstract and fitted in with the entire philosophy of the bop movement. Vocalists such as Joe Carroll, Kenneth "Pancho" Hagood, Earl Coleman, and, of course, bop co-founder Dizzy Gillespie himself, scatted through such compositions as "In the Land of Ooo-Bla-Dee" (1949).

Barry Keith Grant

Bibliography

Friedland, Will. *Jazz Singing: America's Great Voices From Bessie Smith to Bebop and Beyond*. 1990.

Gourse, Leslie. *Louis's Children: American Jazz Singers*. 1984.

See also: Improvisation; Vocalese

SCOTLAND. *SEE* BRITAIN

SEA. *SEE* OCEAN

SEASONS

Songs about the seasons show a strong preference for the warmer months of the year; more songs have been written about summer than about all other seasons combined. On the other hand, the cold months of winter are represented by relatively few standards, such as "Winter Wonderland" (1934), a perennial favorite during the Christmas season.

Spring, bearing its promise of more clement weather to come, boasts at least four charming songs: "Spring Is Here" (1938), "Spring Will Be a Little Late This Year" (1944), "It Might as Well Be Spring" (1946), and "Younger Than Springtime" (1949); it is interesting to note that Richard Rodgers wrote the music for all but the second of these.

Even songs about autumn seem to favor the earlier, more benign months of the season, judging from such titles as "Autumn Leaves" (1947) and "Early Autumn" (1949). Other songs about the season include "Autumn Nocturne" (1941) and Vernon Duke's haunting "Autumn in New York" (1934). Indian summer, a deceptively warm part of late autumn, is memorialized in Victor Herbert's "Indian Summer" (1919; lyrics added by Al Dubin only in 1939).

Summer songs go far back in time, as demonstrated by the mid-thirteenth-century round "Sumer Is Icumen In." In the present century, one of the earliest songs about summer, "In the Good Old Summertime," was composed in 1902 by one of the last minstrels, George Evans, after an excursion to New York's Brighton Beach. Two songs about summer are notable for their melodic and harmonic invention. George Gershwin's "Summertime" (with DuBose Heyward) was written as a lullaby for his opera *Porgy and Bess* (1935); Michel Legrand's "The Summer Knows" (with Alan and Marilyn Bergman) was taken from the theme of the film *Summer of '42* (1971).

Additional Songs

The Boys of Summer (1985)
Cruel Summer (1983)
The Green Leaves of Summer (1960)
Hot Fun in the Summertime (1969)
One Summer Night (1956)
Paris in the Spring (1935)
Seasons in the Sun (1964)
Soft Summer Breeze (1955)
Summer Breeze (1971)
Summer in the City (1966)
Theme From *A Summer Place* (1959)
Summer Wind (1965)
Summertime Blues (1958)

Summertime in Venice (1955)
Summertime, Summertime (1958)
Sweet Seasons (1971)
Those Lazy Hazy Crazy Days of Summer (1964)
Time of the Season (1967)
'Tis Autumn (1941)
When It's Springtime in the Rockies (1929)

See also: **Holidays**

SEEING

Songs on the subject of seeing can be conveniently divided into those that deal with the past, the present, and the future. Songs in the first category include the tongue-in-cheek novelty song "I Saw Mommy Kissing Santa Claus" (1952), the wistful "I Saw Her Again Last Night" (1966), the rap song "Have You Seen Her" (1971), and the romantic ballad "The First Time Ever I Saw Your Face" (1962). Among songs about the present are "I See Your Face Before Me" (1937), "On a Clear Day You Can See Forever" (1966), "I Can See for Miles" (1967), and "I Can See Clearly Now" (1972).

Songs about the future include four striking ballads: "I'll See You in My Dreams" (1924), "I'll See You Again" (1929), "I'll Be Seeing You" (1938) and "See You in September" (1959). Also in that category are the novelties "The Boys in the Back Room" (better known by its first line: "See what the boys in the back room will have" and unforgettably sung by Marlene Dietrich in the film *Destry Rides Again*, 1939) and "See You Later, Alligator," performed by Bill Haley and the Comets in the film *Rock Around the Clock* (1955)

There are also several songs about vision disorders, among them "I Used to Be Color Blind" (1938), "Sweet Blindness" (1967), and "Blinded by the Light" (1972).

See also: **Anatomy; Beauty**

SENTIMENT

The adjective "sentimental" appears in the titles of several well-known songs from the era of the **big bands**. The appeal of the word to songwriters is twofold: the inner rhyme of the word itself and the emotionalism it conveys. Two big band themes use the word: Tommy Dorsey's "I'm Gettin' Sentimental Over You" (1932) and Les Brown's "Sentimental Journey" (1944). Another big band leader, Duke Ellington, was co-writer of the expressive ballad "In a Sentimental Mood" (1935).

Among other "sentimental" songs are two that are entitled "Sentimental Me": one written by Rodgers and Hart in 1925 for the first edition of the revue *The Garrick Gaieties*, and the second popularized by the Ames Brothers in 1950; and "(I Love You) For Sentimental Reasons," a ballad popularized by Nat "King" Cole in 1947.

See also: **Feeling; Love; Moods; Romance; Tenderness**

SEQUENCE

Sequence, the repetition of a phrase or progression at different pitch levels, can be either melodic or harmonic in nature. Both types occur in popular song, although melodic sequence is far more common than harmonic. Very often both types are intermingled, as in Rodgers and Hart's "Lover" (1933). There, the A section is built on a descending chromatic progression of both **melody** and **harmony**, moving downward six half steps from C' to G.

Music originating in **France** is frequently characterized by downward melodic sequence, sometimes giving the melody a melancholy aspect. Examples of this tendency are "Autumn Leaves" (1947), "I Wish You Love" (1963), "The Windmills of Your Mind" (1968), and "(Where Do I Begin), Love Story" the theme from the film *Love Story* (1970).

Of all American composers, Jerome Kern used sequence the most tellingly. A prime example is the A section of "All the Things You Are" (1939) with its descending melodic sequence in both whole and half steps. The charming melodies of "Smoke Gets in Your Eyes" (1933) and "A Fine Romance" incorporate both upward and downward melodic sequence.

Upward melodic sequence is found in several songs. Perhaps the best-known instance is in the 1931 song "As Time Goes By," in which the opening motive ascends first a whole step, then a fourth, and then another whole step. In another song, "It's the Talk of the Town" (1933), the three-note motive ascends over four whole steps. These passages barely escape the banality of "rosalia": a term indicating relentless upward sequence in whole steps.

See also: **Interval; Repeated Note**

SHEET MUSIC

The printing of music on unbound sheets of paper began in the United States in 1788. From then until the 1920s—when it was overtaken by the phonograph record as the primary means of song dissemination—sheet music was the music publisher's largest source of revenue. Although the status of sheet music decreased measurably in the ensuing years, it remained the most important single printed source of popular music into the 1990s.

When sheet music was in its heyday around the turn of the century, almost every home had a **piano**, and amateur pianists and singers abounded. Sheet music sales burgeoned, spurred on by the unprecedented success of Charles K. Harris's "After the Ball" in 1892, with sales of $5 million. The publishers and **song pluggers** of **Tin Pan Alley** brought a new dimension to salesmanship in the promotion of their very profitable wares.

The publications themselves consisted of simple **arrangements**, initially for voice and piano. By the 1920s, diagrams were often added, depicting the four strings of the ukulele or banjulele banjo. Many of these ukulele arrangements were made by May Singhi Breen, "The Ukulele Lady," as seen in the 1930 song "When Your Hair Has Turned to Silver (I Will Love You Just the Same)." In that publication, as well as in many later ones, the ukulele diagrams are often supplemented by such harmonic symbols as G mi., A 7, and A aug. 5. Harmonic symbols remained an essential part of sheet music arrangements thereafter. Sometimes they appeared alone ("On Green Dolphin Street," 1947) and sometimes they were placed in a square box ("Close as Pages in a Book," 1944). But from the 1950s on, the symbols were placed most often over diagrams for six-string guitar ("All I Have to Do Is Dream," 1958).

The size of sheet music has varied somewhat through the years. Before World War I, folio or large size (11" by 14") was the preferred dimension, as in "My Hero" (1908) and "Missouri Waltz" (1914). Because of the shortage of paper during the war, many songs were published in octavo, or small size (7" by 10"). After the war, folio size made a brief reappearance for about a year, but soon quarto or medium size (9" by 12") became the standard, and has remained so. Nevertheless, exceptions such as "Proud Mary" (1965) (which is 8" by 11") have appeared through the years.

The price of sheet music has remained remarkably stable considering the extent of inflation over the last hundred years. In the 1890s, 40 cents or 50 cents was the norm. By 1914, the "Missouri Waltz" was 60 cents. In 1955, the sheet music of "Love Is a Many-Splendored Thing" still fetched only 50 cents. But by the 1960s, the most common price was $1.50 ("The 59th Street Bridge Song—Feelin' Groovy," 1966). In the early 1970s, it was $1.95 ("Laughter in the Rain," 1974). Around 1980, prices ranged from $2.50 ("Lady," 1980) to $2.95 ("Saving All My Love for You," 1978). Almost ten years later, $3.50 was the norm ("Under the Sea," 1988).

During the nineteenth century, sheet music covers were often lavishly illustrated by artwork. A height of elegance in this regard was the beautiful portrayal of a gala ball gracing the cover of "After the Ball" (1892). Often, as on the cover of "I Don't Care" (1905), a portrait of the artist who introduced the song appears—in this case, Eva Tanguay. Occasionally, a cover contains an advertisement. For example, the cover for "Ta-Ra-Ra-Boom-De-Ay!" (1891) reads: "Bromo-Seltzer cures all Headaches and Neuralgia/Trial Bottles 10 cents—sold Everywhere." Until the 1950s, the back cover was often used to advertise other songs from the publisher's portfolio.

Although artwork continued on covers throughout the century (the wartime song "Till We Meet Again" [1918] has an idealized picture of a soldier and his sweetheart), it was most often associated with songs from the musical theater and cinema, where it usually copied the poster artwork of the show or film. Examples include the songs from *Show Boat* (1927) and *Carousel* (1945). The cover of "Love Is a Many-Splendored Thing" is a romantic representation of William Holden and Jennifer Jones, the stars of the film of the same name.

From the 1950s on, it became customary to include on the cover a photograph of the recording artist or artists who introduced the subject song. Most covers since then have adhered to that formula: "All I Have to Do Is Dream" (1958) features the Everly Brothers, "Proud Mary" (1968) shows Creedence Clearwater Revival, "I Won't Last a Day Without You" (1972) has a portrait of the Carpenters, "Lady" (1980) depicts Kenny Rogers.

The nostalgia associated with sheet music and the colorfulness of its covers have attracted legions of collectors. Public and private collections of sheet music abound. The largest collections are those of the Library of Congress and the New York Public Library's Music Division. Another significant collection, that of the Archive of Popular American Music at the University of California, Los Angeles, had as its nucleus the private collection of composer-lyricist Meredith Willson.

Bibliography

Dichter, Harry. *Handbook of American Sheet Music: A Catalog of Sheet Music for Sale by the Compiler and Publishers.* 1953.

———, and Elliott Shapiro. *Handbook of Early American Sheet Music, 1768–1889.* 1977.

Fuld, James J. *The Book of World-Famous Music: Classical, Popular and Folk.* 1985.

Klamkin, Marian. *Old Sheet Music.* 1975.

Priest, Daniel B. *American Sheet Music: A Guide to Collecting Sheet Music, From 1775 to 1975.* 1978.

Wilk, Max, ed. *Memory Lane, 1890 to 1925: Ragtime, Jazz, Foxtrot, and Other Popular Music and Music Covers.* 1976.

See also: Lead Sheet; Recording

SHOW TUNE

The term "show tune," in its most literal sense, applies to any song that was first performed in a **Broadway** show. In recent years, however, the term has been broadened to include any song of quality, whether it is introduced in a **film musical** ("Love Is Here to Stay," 1938), in a dramatic film ("How Little We Know," 1947), or in no show at all ("It's All in the Game," 1951). As far as **tempo** and **meter** are concerned, a show tune may be a **ballad** ("All the Things You Are," 1939), a **waltz** ("It's a Big Wide, Wonderful World," 1940), or an uptempo song ("From This Moment On," 1950).

Many previously obscure show tunes have been rescued from oblivion by **cabaret** performers like Mabel Mercer, Hugh Shannon, and Bobby Short; such entertainers regularly included in their repertoires such gems as "Little Girl Blue" (1935), "My Funny Valentine" (1937), and "Wait Till You See Her" (1942). Show tunes have also long been favored by dance bands such as those of Lester Lanin and Peter Duchin, where they are frequently played in society tempo.

See also: Musical Comedy; Musical Plays; Operetta; Revues; Vaudeville

SINGER-SONGWRITERS. *SEE PERFORMER-SONGWRITERS*

SINGERS

The singer has long been a fundamental force in bringing a song's message to the public. In the late nineteenth century, individual performers as well as singing groups introduced and popularized songs in minstrel shows and music halls. By the turn of the century, singers were largely transferring their attentions to vaudeville and taking advantage of new technological advances. Recording soon became their primary means of transmission and remained so throughout the century, often aided and abetted by radio, and—to a lesser extent—film musicals and television.

Hundreds of singers have contributed to the popularity of American songs over the past hundred years; the list seems endless (*see* Table 15). There were, for instance, Irish tenors (John McCormack), torch singers (Helen Morgan, Ruth Etting), crooners (Rudy Vallee, Russ Columbo), jazz singers (Bessie Smith, Dinah Washington), big band singers (Helen O'Connell, Anita O'Day), film singers (Dick Powell, Alice Faye), pop singers (Patti Page, Teresa Brewer), show business legends (Ethel Merman, Liza Minnelli), patriotic singers (Kate Smith), and a myriad of others too numerous to mention.

But amid this plethora of vocalists, four performers stand out for their enormous contribution to popular song: Bing Crosby, Frank Sinatra, Nat "King" Cole, and Elvis Presley. Among other influential singers of the century were Al Jolson, Mabel Mercer, Louis Armstrong, Billie Holiday, Ella Fitzgerald, Peggy Lee, Judy Garland, and Barbra Streisand.

Bing Crosby (1903–1977) possessed a light and mellow baritone voice and a style that was casual and conversational. He enjoyed a long career in radio and film and sold more records than any other singer, exclusive of rock performers. His most popular recorded song, "White Christmas" (1942), has sold more copies than any other individual song. Among his other most successful recordings were "Just One More Chance" in 1931, "Love in Bloom" and "June in January" in 1934, and "Pennies From Heaven" in 1936.

Frank Sinatra (b. 1915) is a legendary star. Perhaps the most celebrated singer of the century, he is frequently referred to as "The Voice." His career began with the Tommy Dorsey band in 1940; his legato, "instrumental" phrasing reflected that training. Sinatra knew early on how to exploit the microphone as an instrument while still maintaining an intimate style. His most popular recordings over the years included "All or Nothing at All" (1940) in 1943, "Young at Heart" (1954), "Strangers in the Night" (1966), "My Way" (1967), and "(Theme From) New York, New York" (1977) in 1980.

Nat "King" Cole (1917–1965) had a warm, resonant voice characterized by careful phrasing and clear articulation. He was an accomplished pianist as well as a singer. His career reached a peak in the late 1940s and 1950s, when he dominated the charts with such hits as "Nature Boy" (1946), "Mona Lisa" (1949), and "Too Young" and "Unforgettable" (both 1951).

Elvis Presley (1935–1977) had a background in blues and gospel as well as in country and western music, but became famous as the "King" of rock 'n' roll. Elevated to the rank of pop idol in the 1950s, he was famous for his gestures and mannered performance (which reflected the burgeoning rebellion of youth) more than for his singing. His career peaked in 1956 with his recordings of "Heartbreak Hotel," "Don't Be Cruel," and "Love Me Tender."

Al Jolson (1886–1950) was a very different sort of singer. He was the embodiment of show business in the Roaring Twenties: alternately brash and sentimental. Jolson was a seminal influence on other singers, popularizing such lasting songs as "You Made Me Love You (I Didn't Want to Do It)" (1913), "Rock-A-Bye Your Baby With a Dixie Melody" (1918), and "Toot Toot Tootsie (Goo' Bye)" (1922). Jolson also helped initiate a new genre for introducing a song, the film musical, when he sang "Sonny Boy" in *The Singing Fool* (1928). In addition, he is credited as co-writer of a number of songs, including "Avalon" (1920), "California, Here I Come" (1924), "Me and My Shadow" (1927), "Back in Your Own Back Yard" (1928), "There's a Rainbow Round My Shoulder" (1928), "Sonny Boy" (1928), and "Anniversary Song" (1946).

Mabel Mercer (1900–1984) was known as a "singer's singer." She was a prime influence on virtually every other vocalist of the century, noted for her careful enunciation and *parlando* style. Her singing emphasized the lyrics, but never at the expense of the music, which she glorified with her phrasing. She searched out little-known songs of quality for her appearances at cabarets—songs like "Little Girl Blue" (1935), "Glad to Be Unhappy" (1936), and "While We're Young" (1943).

Louis Armstrong (1901–1971) was a consummate instrumentalist as well as singer. Whether playing trumpet or singing, he had his own unique intonation, with a gravelly voice that was the essence of jazz. His most successful recordings were of the songs "Mack the Knife" (1952), "All of Me" (1931), and "Hello Dolly"

(1964). Armstrong also had a hand in writing several songs: "I Wish I Could Shimmy Like My Sister Kate" (1919), "Struttin' With Some Barbecue" (with his wife, Lil Hardin, in 1927), and "Ol' Man Mose" (1938).

Billie Holiday (1915–1959) was a singer of great emotional intensity. Her soulful recordings of show tunes like "The Man I Love" (1924), "Body and Soul" (1930), and "Summertime" (1935) brought her a cult following. She also co-wrote several songs, including "God Bless the Child" (1941).

Ella Fitzgerald (b. 1918; known as the First Lady of American Song") has a remarkably versatile voice with a range of two-and-a-half octaves. She has often used it as an instrument in the form of scat singing, notably in her recordings in 1947 of "Oh, Lady Be Good" (1924) and "How High the Moon" (1940). She has also brought her superb phrasing to a host of show tunes as well as to pop songs like "A-Tisket A-Tasket," of which she was co-adapter in 1938.

Peggy Lee (b. 1920) is an important songwriter as well as singer. Her singing is often understated but always characterized by impeccable phrasing. She began with Will Osborne's big band, but her first hit, "Why Don't You Do Right?" (1942), was with Benny Goodman's. She soon branched out on her own and as a soloist brought her own special verve to Rodgers and Hart's "Lover" (1933) in 1952, and to contemporary song, "Fever," in 1958. She also co-wrote a number of songs with her husband, Dave Barbour, including "It's a Good Day" (1946) and "Mañana (Is Soon Enough for Me)" (1948).

Judy Garland (1922–1969) was a show business legend, in a class by herself. Her resonant voice always carried with it a tinge of fragility, but she could belt out a song with the best of them. Her first success was as Dorothy, singing "Over the Rainbow" in the film *The Wizard of Oz* (1939). She appeared in many film musicals thereafter, introducing such songs as "The Boy Next Door" and "The Trolley Song" (from *Meet Me in St. Louis*, 1944), "On the Atchison, Topeka and the Santa Fe" (from *The Harvey Girls*, 1946), and "Be a Clown" (from *The Pirate*, 1948). She went on to make a series of outstanding recordings in the 1950s, including those of Harold Arlen's "Come Rain or Come Shine" (written in 1946, with Johnny Mercer) and "The Man That Got Away" (written in 1954, with Ira Gershwin).

Barbra Streisand (b. 1942) is a multitalented personality: singer, songwriter, actress, director, and producer. Her singing, like her other activities, is characterized by individuality. She introduced the songs "Don't Rain on My Parade" and "People" in the 1964 show *Funny Girl*, in which she portrayed Fanny Brice. Streisand had many other recording hits over the years. She herself was composer of one of the most successful: "Evergreen," the love theme from *A Star Is Born*, with lyrics by Paul Williams (1977).

Even with so brief a summary, it is clear that the singer's effect on American popular song has been enormous. In addition, especially since the 1960s, a new type of singer has come to the forefront, one who acts as accompanist and often helps write the songs. The performer-songwriter became the mainstay of rock, as exemplified in such individuals as Billy Joel, Paul Simon, Stevie Wonder, and Ray Charles.

Bibliography

Friedwald, Will. *Jazz Singing: America's Great Voices From Bessie Smith to Bebop and Beyond*. 1990.

Harris, Sheldon. *Blues Who's Who: A Biographical Dictionary of Blues Singers*. 1981.

Hemming, Ray, and David Hajdu. *Discovering Great Singers of Classic Pop*. 1991.

Lawless, Ray McKinley. *Folksingers and Folk Songs in America: A Handbook of Biography, Bibliography, and Discography*. 1981.

Pleasants, Henry. *The Great American Popular Singers*. 1974.

See also: Folk Song; Motown; Rhythm and Blues; Rock 'n' Roll; Soul; Torch Song; Women as Songwriters

TABLE 15

Mainstream Singers and Their Signature Songs

Not included in this list are many singers primarily identified with country and western music, folk song, gospel, Motown, rhythm and blues, rock 'n' roll, rock, and soul. Dates are of the songs themselves, not the performances. For additional singers, see also Table 10: Grammy Awards, and the following articles: Performer-Songwriters; Protest Song; Singing Groups; and Women as Songwriters.

Louis Armstrong
All of Me (1931)
Hello Dolly (1964)

Fred Astaire
Cheek to Cheek (1935)
Night and Day (1932)
The Way You Look Tonight (1936)

Gene Austin
My Blue Heaven (1927)
Ramona (1927)

Frankie Avalon
Venus (1959)
Why (1960)

Mildred Bailey
(Ol') Rockin' Chair (1930)

Harry Belafonte
The Banana Boat Song (Day-O) (1957)

Tony Bennett
Because of You (1940)
Cold, Cold Heart (1951)
The Good Life (1963)
I Left My Heart in San Francisco (1954)
I Wanna Be Around (1959)
Rags to Riches (1953)
This Is All I Ask (Beautiful Girls Walk a Little Slower) (1958)

Debby Boone
You Light Up My Life (1976)

Pat Boone
Ain't That a Shame (1955)
April Love (1957)
Love Letters in the Sand (1931)

Connee Boswell
Sand in My Shoes (1941)

Teresa Brewer
Music! Music! Music! (1950)
Till I Waltz Again With You (1952)

Henry Burr
In the Shade of the Old Apple Tree (1905)
Meet Me Tonight in Dreamland (1910)

Glen Campbell
By the Time I Get to Phoenix (1967)
Galveston (1969)
Gentle on My Mind (1967)
Wichita Lineman (1968)

Johnny Cash
A Boy Named Sue (1969)

Ray Charles
Georgia on My Mind (1930)
Hit the Road, Jack (1961)
I Can't Stop Loving You (1958)

Cher
Gypsies, Tramps and Thieves (1971)

Petula Clark
Downtown (1964)

Rosemary Clooney
Botch-A-Me (1952)
Come On-a My House (1950)
Hey There (1954)
This Ole House (1954)

Nat "King" Cole
The Christmas Song (1946)
Mona Lisa (1949)
Nature Boy (1946)
Straighten Up and Fly Right (1944)
Too Young (1951)
Unforgettable (1951)

Arthur Collins
Bill Bailey, Won't You Please Come Home? (1902)
Under the Bamboo Tree (1902)

Judy Collins
Amazing Grace (c. 1800)
Both Sides Now (1967)
Send in the Clowns (1973)

Phil Collins
Against All Odds (Take a Look at Me Now) (1984)

Russ Columbo
Prisoner of Love (1931)
You Call It Madness (Ah, But I Call It Love) (1931)

Perry Como
Don't Let the Stars Get in Your Eyes (1953)
If (1934)
If I Loved You (1945)
It's Impossible (1970)
Long Ago (And Far Away) (1944)
Till the End of Time (1945)

Bing Crosby
June in January (1934)
Just One More Chance (1931)
Love in Bloom (1934)
Only Forever (1940)
Pennies From Heaven (1936)
Sunday, Monday or Always (1943)
Sweet Leilani (1937)
White Christmas (1942)

Vic Damone
I Have But One Heart (1945)
On the Street Where You Live (1956)
You're Breaking My Heart (1948)

Bobby Darin
Mack the Knife (1952)
Splish Splash (1958)

Sammy Davis, Jr.
The Candy Man (1970)
What Kind of Fool Am I? (1961)

Doris Day
Whatever Will Be, Will Be (Que Sera, Sera) (1955)
Secret Love (1954)
Sentimental Journey (1944)

John Denver
Leaving on a Jet Plane (1967)
Rocky Mountain High (1972)
Thank God I'm a Country Boy (1974)

Bob Dylan
Blowin' in the Wind (1962)
Hard Rain's A-Gonna Fall (1963)
The Times They Are A-Changin'' (1963)

Ruth Etting
Love Me or Leave Me (1928)
Mean to Me (1929)
More Than You Know (1929)
Ten Cents a Dance (1930)

Eddie Fisher
Oh My Papa (1953)

Ella Fitzgerald
A-Tisket A-Tasket (1938)
How High the Moon (1940)
Oh, Lady Be Good (1924)

Roberta Flack
The First Time Ever I Saw Your Face (1972)
Killing Me Softly With His Song (1972)

"Tennessee" Ernie Ford
Sixteen Tons (1955)

Helen Forrest
I Cried for You (1923)
I Don't Want to Walk Without You (1941)
I Had the Craziest Dream (1943)
I've Heard That Song Before (1942)

Connie Francis
Lipstick on Your Collar (1959)
Stupid Cupid (1958)
Where the Boys Are (1960)

Aretha Franklin
Chain of Fools (1967)
Freeway of Love (1985)
(You Make Me Feel Like) A Natural Woman (1967)
Respect (1965)

Judy Garland
Be a Clown (1948)
The Boy Next Door (1943)
Come Rain or Come Shine (1946)
The Man That Got Away (1954)
On the Atchison, Topeka and the Santa Fe (1945)
Over the Rainbow (1939)
The Trolley Song (1943)

George G. Gaskin
My Wild Irish Rose (1899)
Oh Promise Me (1893)
On the Banks of the Wabash, Far Away (1899)

Eydie Gormé
Blame It on the Bossa Nova (1962)
If He Walked Into My Life (1966)

Gogi Grant
The Wayward Wind (1956)

Byron G. Harlan
My Gal Sal (1905)
Tell Me, Pretty Maiden (1900)

Dick Haymes
I'll Get By (As Long As I Have You) (1928)
Little White Lies (1930)
Mam'selle (1947)
You'll Never Know (1943)

Billie Holiday
Body and Soul (1930)
God Bless the Child (1941)
The Man I Love (1924)
Summertime (1935)

Lena Horne
Stormy Weather (1933)

Whitney Houston
The Greatest Love of All (1977)
How Will I Know (1985)
Saving All My Love for You (1978)
Where Do Broken Hearts Go? (1985)

Michael Jackson
The Way You Make Me Feel (1987)

Billy Joel
Just the Way You Are (1978)
New York State of Mind (1975)
Piano Man (1973)

Al Jolson
April Showers (1921)
Avalon (1920)
Back in Your Own Back Yard (1928)
California, Here I Come (1924)
Rock-a-Bye Your Baby with a Dixie Melody (1918)
Swanee (1919)
Toot Toot Tootsie (Goo' Bye) (1922)
You Made Me Love You (I Didn't Want to Do It) (1913)

Ada Jones
By the Beautiful Sea (1914)
I've Got Rings on My Fingers (1909)

Jack Jones
Lollipops and Roses (1960)
(Hey, Little Girl) Wives and Lovers (1963)

Tom Jones
The Green, Green Grass of Home (1965)
It's Not Unusual (1965)

Frankie Laine
I Believe (1952)
Mule Train (1949)
That Lucky Old Sun (1949)

Frances Langford
I Feel a Song Comin' On (1935)
I'm in the Mood for Love (1935)

Mario Lanza
Be My Love (1950)

Steve Lawrence
Go Away, Little Girl (1962)

Peggy Lee
Fever (1956)
Is That All There Is? (1966)
It's a Good Day (1946)
Lover (1933)
Mañana (Is Soon Enough for Me) (1948)
Why Don't You Do Right? (1942)

Harry MacDonough
Down by the Old Mill Stream (1910)
Shine On, Harvest Moon (1908)

Madonna
Crazy for You (1983)
Like a Virgin (1984)
Papa Don't Preach (1986)

Barry Manilow
Copacabana (At the Copa) (1977)
I Write the Songs (1974)
Looks Like We Made It (1976)
Mandy (1971)

Dean Martin
Everybody Loves Somebody (1948)
Memories Are Made of This (1955)
That's Amore (1956)

Johnny Mathis
Chances Are (1957)
It's Not for Me to Say (1957)
Wonderful, Wonderful (1957)

John McCormack
All Alone (1924)
I'm Falling in Love With Someone (1910)
It's a Long Way to Tipperary (1912)
Mother Machree (1910)

Mabel Mercer
Glad to Be Unhappy (1936)
Little Girl Blue (1935)
My Funny Valentine (1937)
While We're Young (1943)

Ethel Merman
Everything's Coming Up Roses (1959)
I Got Rhythm (1930)
There's No Business Like Show Business (1946)

Bette Midler
From a Distance (1987)
The Rose (1977)
The Wind Beneath My Wings (1982)

Liza Minnelli
Cabaret (1967)
Maybe This Time (1966)
(Theme From) New York, New York (1977)

Vaughn Monroe
Ballerina (1947)
(Ghost) Riders in the Sky (A Cowboy Legend) (1949)

Helen Morgan
Bill (1927)
Cant' Help Lovin' Dat Man (1927)
Don't Ever Leave Me (1929)
Why Was I Born? (1929)

Billy Murray
Harrigan (1908)
Take Me Out to the Ball Game (1908)

Ricky Nelson
Poor Little Fool (1958)
Travelin' Man (1960)

Willie Nelson
Always on My Mind (1971)
Blue Eyes Crying in the Rain (1945)
Crazy (1961)
Georgia on My Mind (1930)

Olivia Newton-John
Hopelessly Devoted to You (1978)
I Honestly Love You (1974)
Magic (1980)
Physical (1981)

Patti Page
Allegheny Moon (1956)
(How Much Is That) Doggie in the Window? (1953)
Tennessee Waltz (1948)

Elvis Presley
Blue Suede Shoes (1955)
Don't Be Cruel (1956)
Heartbreak Hotel (1956)
Hound Dog (1956)
It's Now or Never (1960)
Love Me Tender (1956)

Johnny Ray
Cry (1951)
The Little White Cloud That Cried (1951)

Helen Reddy
Delta Dawn (1973)
I Am Woman (1971)

Kenny Rogers
Lady (1980)
She Believes in Me (1977)
Through the Years (1980)
You Decorated My Life (1978)

Linda Ronstadt
Blue Bayou (1963)
I Never Will Marry (1958)
You're No Good (1963)

Diana Ross
Ain't No Mountain High Enough (1970)
Love Hangover (1976)
Theme From *Mahogany* (Do You Know Where You're Going To?) (1973)
Touch Me in the Morning (1972)

Dinah Shore
Buttons and Bows (1948)
Dear Hearts and Gentle People (1950)
The Gypsy (1946)
I'll Walk Alone (1944)
Yes My Darling Daughter (1939)

Frank Sinatra
All or Nothing at All (1943)
My Way (1967)
(Theme From) New York, New York (1977)
Oh! What It Seemed to Be (1945)
Strangers in the Night (1966)
Young at Heart (1954)

Bessie Smith
Down Hearted Blues (1923)

Kate Smith
God Bless America (1939)
When the Moon Comes Over the Mountain (1931)

Len Spencer
Hello! Ma Baby (1899)
A Hot Time in the Old Town (1896)
Ta-Ra-Ra Boom-De-Ay! (1891)

Bruce Springsteen
Born in the U.S.A. (1965)
Dancing in the Dark (1984)
Glory Days (1984)

Jo Stafford
Candy (1944)
Make Love to Me (1953)
Shrimp Boats (1951)
You Belong to Me (1952)

Frank Stanton
Blue Bell (1904)
Tramp! Tramp! Tramp! Along the Highway (1910)

Barbara Streisand
Don't Rain on My Parade (1963)
Evergreen (Love Theme From *A Star Is Born*) (1977)
Memory (1981)
My Heart Belongs to Me (1977)
People (1964)
The Way We Were (1973)
Woman in Love (1980)
You Don't Bring Me Flowers (1978)

Mel Tormé
The Christmas Song (1946)

Rudy Vallee
I'm Just a Vagabond Lover (1929)
My Time Is Your Time (1924)

Bobby Vinton
Blue Velvet (1951)
My Melody of Love (1973)
There! I've Said It Again (1941)

Dionne Warwick
Do You Know the Way to San Jose? (1967)
Don't Make Me Over (1962)
I'll Never Fall in Love Again (1968)
That's What Friends Are For (1985)
Then Came You (1974)
What the World Needs Now Is Love (1965)

Dinah Washington
Blowtop Blues (1945)
Evil Gal Blues (1944)
What a Diff'rence a Day Made (1934)

Ethel Waters
Cabin in the Sky (1940)
Happiness Is a Thing Called Joe (1942)
Taking a Chance on Love (1940)

Margaret Whiting
It Might as Well Be Spring (1945)
Moonlight in Vermont (1944)
My Ideal (1930)
That Old Black Magic (1942)

Lee Wiley
It's Only a Paper Moon (1933)
Time on My Hands (1930)

Andy Williams
Canadian Sunset (1956)
(Where Do I Begin) Love Story (1970)
Moon River (1961)

Stevie Wonder
I Just Called to Say I Love You (1984)
My Cherie Amour (1968)
You Are the Sunshine of My Life (1972)

SINGING GROUPS

Singing groups have long been a staple of American popular music. Most early performances by vocal groups were in one of three styles: that of the **minstrel show, barbershop** harmony, or European-influenced singing. Three of the major turn-of-the-century vocal groups were the Haydn, American, and Peerless Quartets, the members of which were all male.

In 1898, the Haydn Quartet (then known as the Edison Quartet because they recorded on phonograph cylinders for Thomas Alva Edison's company) released the first recorded version of Stephen Collins Foster's "My Old Kentucky Home," originally written in 1853. The Haydn Quartet went on to have other hits, including "In the Good Old Summertime" in 1903 and "Toyland," with music by Victor Herbert, in 1904. In 1908, their recording of "Take Me Out to the Ball Game" was released: the most popular version of that song ever made. In 1910 they had a hit with "By the Light of the Silv'ry Moon." Also in 1910, the American Quartet premiered the classic "Casey Jones." Among their other successes were "Chinatown, My Chinatown" (1910), "Oh, You Beautiful Doll" (1911), and "(On) Moonlight Bay" (1912).

Unlike the singing groups of later years, both the Haydn and American Quartets shared a common lead singer on many of their records: tenor Billy Murray, who, when recording as a soloist, was the most prolific star of the pre-1920 recording business. Murray also fronted another singing group, the Heidelberg Quintet. Two of its big hits were "Waiting for the Robert E. Lee" (1912) and "By the Beautiful Sea" (1914). It was during these years that the flat phonograph disc replaced the cylinder as the most popular way to listen to recorded music and that a more natural and casual style of singing evolved.

The Peerless Quartet was the most popular and long-lived of these early vocal groups. Although its repertoire included more songs than other groups, Peerless introduced only a few songs that would become standards, including "Let Me Call You Sweetheart" in 1911 and "Way Down Yonder in New Orleans" in 1922. There is a certain controversy as to which group first recorded "You're the Flower of My Heart, Sweet Adeline"; both the Peerless and Haydn Quartets recorded the song in late 1904.

The only vocal group to rival the Peerless Quartet in popularity during the 1920s was the Revelers. Among their many recorded hits were versions of "Dinah," "The Birth of the Blues," and "Blue Room" in 1926 and "Among My Souvenirs" in 1928.

Although the Boswell Sisters were the most popular vocal group of the 1930s, they were not the first all-female group to make **recordings**; that distinction belongs to the "That Girl" Quartet, which had a hit with "Put Your Arms Around Me, Honey" (1911). New

Orleans-born Martha, Helvetia, and Connee Boswell were frequently accompanied by some of the top **jazz** musicians on their famous recordings of "When I Take My Sugar to Tea," "Roll On, Mississippi, Roll On," "I Found a Million Dollar Baby (In a Five and Ten Cent Store)," and "It's the Girl"; all in 1931. Other hits for the Boswell Sisters were their recordings of "The Object of My Affection," "Alexander's Ragtime Band" (first recorded in 1911), and "I'm Gonna Sit Right Down and Write Myself a Letter," all recorded in 1935. Connee Boswell also recorded as a solo singer and had chart hits from 1932 through 1954.

The 1930s also marked the beginning of the long-running career of the Mills Brothers—a black group that would have chart hits into the 1970s. Donald, Herbert, and Harry Mills were born in Piqua, Ohio. With their older brother, John, supplying them with their only instrumental accompaniment, the guitar, they perfected a smooth-as-silk sound first heard in their recordings, of "Tiger Rag" in (1931), "Rockin' Chair" in 1932, and "Sleepy Head" in (1934). John died in late 1935 and was replaced by their father, John, Sr., who stayed with his sons until his retirement in 1956. In 1942, the Mills Brothers had the biggest nonholiday hit of the decade, "Paper Doll," which sold six million records on its initial release. Other hits followed, notably "You Always Hurt the One You Love" and "Till Then" (both 1944). In the 1950s the Mills Brothers augmented their traditional guitar accompaniment with other instruments. In 1952, with the help of an arrangement by Sy Oliver, they scored a hit with "The Glow-Worm," an adaptation of a song first heard in the 1902 German operetta *Lysistrata*; the new English lyrics were supplied by Johnny Mercer. The Mills Brothers had their last chart success with "Cab Driver" in 1968.

Another tremendously popular black group of the 1940s was the Ink Spots, who had a direct influence on **rhythm and blues** and **rock 'n' roll**. Their personnel changed through the years, but they were best known for the falsetto lead of Bill Kenny and the spoken interludes of bass Orville "Hoppy" Jones and, later, Herb Kenny. Among their most memorable records were their versions of "If I Didn't Care" and "My Prayer" in 1930, "We Three (My Echo, My Shadow and Me)" and "Java Jive" in 1940, "I'm Making Believe" and "Into Each Life Some Rain Must Fall" in 1944, and "The Gypsy" and "To Each His Own" in 1946.

Three sisters from Minneapolis—Patti, Maxene, and LaVerne Andrews—started their recording career in 1938 with "Bei Mir Bist Du Schön (Means That You're Grand)," from the 1933 Yiddish musical *I Would If I Could.* They went on to become the most popular female vocal group of the pre–rock 'n' roll era, which began in 1954. Their songbook included many hits: "Hold Tight, Hold Tight (Want Some Sea Food Mama)" and "Beer Barrel Polka (Roll Out the Barrel)" in 1939,

"Ferry Boat Serenade" and "Beat Me Daddy, Eight to the Bar" in 1940, "Aurora" and "I'll Be With You in Apple Blossom Time" in 1941, "Rum and Coca-Cola" in 1945, and "I Can Dream, Can't I?" in 1949. The Andrews Sisters also produced many records with Bing Crosby, not as background voices but rather as co-vocalists with shared billing. Their biggest hits with Crosby were "Pistol Packin' Mama" (1943), "Don't Fence Me In" (1944), and "South America, Take It Away" (1946).

Several groups who rose to fame performing with the **big bands** struck out on their own to make hit records. Two of the more popular ones were the Pied Pipers and the Modernaires. The first group, which originally sang with the Tommy Dorsey band, had hits with "The Trolley Song" in 1944 and "Dream" in 1945. The Modernaires, with lead singer Paula Kelly, became famous singing with the Glenn Miller band, but had hits on their own with "To Each His Own" in 1946 and "Zip-A-Dee-Doo-Dah" in 1947.

Popular music of the early and mid-1950s was essentially bland, emphasizing sentimentality, romance, and homely virtues. Commercially speaking, it was a cornucopia of show tunes, novelties, and foreign-flavored songs from **Italy**, Jamaica and **Latin America**. The "big beat" of **rock 'n' roll** was destined to break through in 1954–55, but this early 1950s brand of pop lasted as late as 1958.

Singing groups popular at this time included the Ames Brothers, the Gaylords, the Four Lads, and the Four Aces. The Ames Brothers had hits with "Rag Mop" and "Sentimental Me" in 1950, "Undecided" in 1951, "You You You" in 1953, and "The Naughty Lady of Shady Lane" in 1954. Ed Ames went on to a solo career in the 1960s. The Gaylords were a Detroit trio that had hits with "Tell Me You're Mine" in 1953 (based on a 1939 Italian song, "Per un Bacio d'Amore") and "The Little Shoemaker" in 1954. The Four Lads originally accompanied Johnny Ray on his 1951 chart-topper, "Cry," but went on to have several hits of their own, such as "Istanbul, Not Constantinople" in 1953; "Skokiaan," a South African song, in 1954; "Moments to Remember" in 1955; and "Standing on the Corner" in 1956. The Four Aces, with lead singer Al Alberts, had hits with "Tell Me Why" (1951), "Three Coins in the Fountain" (1954), and "Melody of Love" and "Love Is a Many-Splendored Thing" (both 1955).

The late 1940s witnessed a **folk song** revival; several groups aligned with this type of music produced hit recordings. Among the first to push folk music into pop consciousness was the group called the Weavers. This historic group, which included Pete Seeger, along with others formerly involved with the Almanac Hootenannies, recorded a number of hits: Woody Guthrie's "So Long (It's Been Good to Know Yuh)" of 1939, John Lomax and Huddy Ledbetter's 1936 song "Goodnight Irene" (which sold over two million copies), and "On

Top of Old Smokey" (a 1951 adaptation of a traditional folk song from the southern Highlands).

One of the most popular singing groups of this time was the Kingston Trio. Songs they introduced included "The M.T.A." (for Metropolitan Transit Authority) in 1956, a revival of a traditional American folk song of 1866 under the title "Tom Dooley" in 1958, and "The Tijuana Jail" in 1959.

Still other singing groups made careers of covering hit **rhythm and blues** songs that were not played on white-owned radio stations. Among these were the watered-down **covers** of the Charms' "Heart of Stone" (1964) by the Fontana Sisters, the Chords' "Sh-Boom" (1954) by the Crewcuts, and the Moonglows' "Sincerely" (1954) by the McGuire Sisters. These performances enticed listeners to buy the covered versions, even though the original versions were far superior. In addition, the McGuire Sisters achieved success on their own in 1958, with "Sugartime."

Among other singing groups of the 1950s were the Tarriers, with "Cindy, Oh Cindy" and "The Banana Boat Song" (1956); the Four Preps, with "Twenty-Six Miles (Catalina)" and "Big Man" (both 1958); the Chordettes, with "Lollipop" (1958); and the Poni Tails, with "Born Too Late" (1958).

In the ten-year period from 1945 to 1955, audiences geared to rhythm and blues had been entertained by a mere handful of vocal groups. Over the course of the following ten years, when rock 'n' roll came into its own, audiences experienced a wealth of new talent, and the number of singing groups on the entertainment circuit reached its peak. What is more, the make-up of the audiences exposed to the vibrant sounds of these singing groups changed considerably, becoming a much more representative cross-section of the American public.

Three of the most prolific of these new groups were the Drifters, the Platters, and the Coasters. Others included the Turbans, with "When You Dance" (1955); the Channels, with "The Closer You Are" (1956); the Dubs, with "Could This Be Magic" (1957); and the Tune Weavers, with "Happy, Happy Birthday Baby" (1957). In 1958 one could hear the mood-inspiring "One Summer Night," sung by the Dandleers, and the Elegants' "Little Star," based on the nursery rhyme. In 1959, it was the Falcons' recording of "You're So Fine." The sound being produced by these groups came to be known as "**doo-wop**," a designation derived from the use of nonsense syllables by back-up vocalists.

As the 1950s passed into the 1960s, the rhythm and blues feeling of these songs was gradually replaced by a lighter pop sound with greater emphasis on the production. A transitional group representing this change was Little Anthony and the Imperials. Their first hits, "Tears on My Pillow" in 1958 and "Shimmy, Shimmy, Ko-Ko-Bop" in 1960, were definitely within the doo-wop tradition, but by the time they had their last successful recordings, "Goin' Out of My Head" in 1964 and "Hurt So Bad" in 1965, they were part of the newer sound of rock.

Two of the most successful groups practicing this "rock" style were Jay and the Americans and the Four Seasons. The first group had hits with "She Cried" in 1962, "Only in America" in 1963, "Let's Lock the Door (And Throw Away the Key) in 1964, and "Cara Mia" in 1965 (originally a 1954 hit for English singer David Whitfield). The Four Seasons continued their chart success with "Ronnie" and "Bye Bye Baby (Baby Goodbye)," in 1964, and "Let's Hang On (To What We've Got)" in 1965.

Other hits by vocal groups at this time included the Skyliners' "Since I Don't Have You" and the Tempos' "See You in September" (both in 1959). The Fleetwoods, a trio comprised of two women and a man, had a unique singing style, almost akin to a whisper; among their hits were "Come Softly to Me" and "Mr. Blue" (both in 1959). "The Lion Sleeps Tonight," based on a South African Zulu song originally released in 1951 as "Wimoweh," was popularized by the Tokens in 1961. The Lettermen, a group that updated the early 1950s vocal-group sound of close harmony, had big sellers in 1961, with the 1951 ballad "When I Fall in Love," and in 1965, with the 1959 song "Theme From *A Summer Place*." In the same year, the Ad Libs introduced the joyous song "The Boy From New York City."

Female vocal groups, whose popularity had peaked in the rock 'n' roll years of the late 1950s, continued to enjoy success into the 1960s. Representative of the songs introduced by these groups were the Paris Sisters' "I Love How You Love Me" (produced by Phil Spector in 1961), the Exciters' "Tell Him" (1963), the Murmaids' "Popsicles and Icicles" (1963), and the Cookies' "Don't Say Nothin' Bad (About My Baby)" (1963). The Jelly Beans had a 1964 hit with "I Wanna Love Him So Bad" and the Toys had a hit in 1965 with "A Lover's Concerto," based on Beethoven's *Minuet in G.*

The folk influence was still felt in the early 1960s in such hits as "Michael (Row the Boat Ashore)" by the Highwaymen in 1961 (a faithful rendition of a traditional nineteenth-century folk song) and "Walk Right In," a 1930 song revived in 1963 by the Rooftop Singers. The most popular folk-singing group of this time was Peter, Paul and Mary. Their thought-provoking singing of "If I Had a Hammer" (1962) and Bob Dylan's "Don't Think Twice, It's All Right" and "Blowin' in the Wind" (both 1963) helped ignite the spark of the **folk-rock** revolution to come.

The folk influence also extended to **lyrics.** Songs were no longer exclusively about "moon," "June," and "spoon"; now they were setting forth a "message." This style of song was better suited to a solo voice or to a group that not only sang but also provided its own instrumental accompaniment (hence the rise of the **performer-songwriter**).

Some transitional groups recorded in a variety of styles. Thus in 1965 the Vogues sang "You're the One" in the style of the early 1960s, "Five O'Clock World" in a style that foretold what was to come, and "You Were on My Mind" in a combination of both styles.

Two singing groups, the Mamas and the Papas and the Fifth Dimension, were the most successful in combining vocal-group harmony with rock sensibility. The Mamas and the Papas had three hits in 1966: "California Dreaming," "Monday, Monday," and "I Saw Her Again Last Night." In 1967 they had two more: "Creeque Alley" and "Twelve Thirty (Young Girls Are Comin' to the Canyon)." The Fifth Dimension had a string of big sellers starting in 1967 and continuing into the early 1970s. These included "Up, Up and Away" (1967), "Stoned Soul Picnic" and "Sweet Blindness" (both 1968), and "Wedding Bell Blues" (1969). In the same year they recorded "Aquarius/Let the Sunshine In," from the Broadway rock musical *Hair,* followed by "One Less Bell to Answer" (1970) and "Last Night I Didn't Get to Sleep at All" (1971).

By the 1970s, rhythm and blues and **soul** were among the few genres in which singing groups could still meet with success. Subjects such as romance, dancing, and civil rights were still acceptable if they came from vocal groups. "Cool Jerk," recorded by the Capitols in 1966, was about a hip fool. A 1967 hit by the Esquires was the morale-building "Get On Up." Three songs about romance recorded in 1968 were the Delfonics' "La La La (Means I Love You)," the Intruders' "Cowboys to Girls," and the O'Kaysions' "Girl Watcher." "Choice of Colors" was a fantastic civil rights message song recorded in 1969 by the Impressions. Three songs were about love gone awry: the plaintive "Give Me Just a Little More Time" (1970) by the Chairmen of the Board; "Have You Seen Her" by the Chi-Lites in 1971; and "Everybody Plays the Fool," a 1972 hit by the Main Ingredient.

The preeminent singing group of the 1970s was Dawn, later to be renamed Tony Orlando and Dawn, with fourteen **Top Forty** hits including three which reached Number One on the charts: "Knock Three Times" (1970), "He Don't Love You (Like I Love You)" (1975), and "Tie a Yellow Ribbon Round the Ole Oak Tree": a 1972 song which inspired a new-found American custom of welcoming back soldiers and hostages. Another singing group, Manhattan Transfer, made its presence known in nightclubs and on television but was not successful on the pop charts. That versatile quartet had a hit with "Operator," a jazzy **gospel** song in 1975. The Hillside Singers was a nine-member vocal group assembled in 1971 to take advantage of a popular Coca-Cola jingle, "I'd Like to Teach the World to Sing (In Perfect Harmony)."

In the 1980s, the only singing groups worthy of mention were the Oak Ridge Boys, a country-pop group that had a hit with "Elvira" in 1981 and Bananarama, a female trio from London that had three hits: "Cruel Summer" in 1984; "Venus," a 1986 remake of 1970 hit by the Dutch rock group Shocking Blue; and "I Heard a Rumour" in 1987. By the end of this decade, it had become apparent that with few exceptions, such as the **Motown** family of singing groups, vocal-group recording was no longer commercially successful.

Additional Songs

Candida (1970), by Dawn
Daddy's Little Girl (1949), by the Mills Brothers
I Wonder What She's Doing Tonight? (1967), by Tommy Boyce and Bobby Heart
A Little Bit of Soap (1961), by the Jarmels
Man With the Banjo (1953), by the Ames Brothers
My True Story (1961), by the Jive Five and Joe Rene
Puff (The Magic Dragon) (1963), by Peter, Paul and Mary
Ruby Baby (1955), by the Drifters
So Much in Love (1963), by the Tymes
Step by Step (1960), by the Crests
Sweet Inspirations (1967), by the Sweet Inspirations
Turn Around, Look at Me (1961), by the Vogues
Where Have All the Flowers Gone? (1961), by the Kingston Trio
Working My Way Back to You (1965), by the Four Seasons

Jeffrey Cahn

Bibliography

Whitburn, Joel. *The Billboard Book of Top 40 Hits.* 1989.
———. *Pop Memories 1890–1954.* 1986.

SKY

There are several types of songs about the sky. Some are related to **color**, as exemplified in such songs as "From the Land of the Sky Blue Water" (1909), "Blue Skies" (1927), "Beyond the Blue Horizon" (1930), and "Ole Buttermilk Sky" (1946). Others—"There's a Gold Mine in the Sky" (1937), "Cabin in the Sky" (1940), and "(Ghost) Riders in the Sky (A Cowboy Legend)" (1949)—are more concerned with **religion** or the **imagination**. Then there is "Lucy in the Sky With Diamonds," a 1969 Beatles song whose title in initials has been said to allude to the hallucinatory drug LSD.

There are also a number of songs about clouds, but they seldom make reference to the sky. In these songs, clouds are most often used as metaphors for the temporary interruption of happiness. Examples are "Till the Clouds Roll By" (1917), "Look for the Silver Lining" (1920), "Liza (All the Clouds'll Roll Away)" (1929), and "Both Sides Now" (1967)—which is also known as "Clouds." One song about a single cloud, Johnny Ray's "The Little White Cloud That Cried," sold over two million records in 1951 (with the song "Cry" on its flip side).

Additional Songs

Get Off My Cloud (1965)
A Melody From the Sky (1935)
Sky High (1975)
Skylark (1942)
Skyliner (1944)
Under Paris Skies (1953)
Why (Is There a Rainbow in the Sky?) (1929)

See also: **Heaven; Moon; Rainbow; Stars; Sun**

SLANG

Popular song would hardly be worthy of its name if it disdained the vernacular. For that reason, many songs contain nonstandard language. For example, "Mister Johnson, Turn Me Loose" (1896) used the then-current colloquialism for policeman, while "Oh by Jingo, Oh by Gee, You're the Only Girl for Me" (1919) was written in the lingo of its day.

Irving Berlin, always fond of catch-phrases, used slang titles throughout his career, among them "Puttin' On the Ritz" (1929), "Not for All the Rice in China" (1933), "I'm Putting All My Eggs in One Basket" (1936), "A Couple of Swells" (1947), "Steppin' Out With My Baby" (1947), and 'The Hostess With the Mostes' on the Ball" (1950). Cole Porter, another outstanding **composer-lyricist**, was found of such slang titles as "You've Got That Thing" (1929), "I Get a Kick Out of You" (1934), "Just One of Those Things" (1935), "I've Got You Under My Skin" and "Ridin' High" (both 1936), "Let's Be Buddies" (1940), and "Don't Fence Me In" (1944). Porter also frequently used slang expressions in his **lyrics**, as in his 1936 song "It's D'Lovely": "What a swell night this is for romance."

Several **lyricists** had a special penchant for slang. Johnny Mercer, for instance, used the word "peepers"—slang for eyes—and the phrase "Gosh all git up" in his 1938 song "Jeepers Creepers"; his 1941 song "Blues in the Night" is replete with such colloquialisms as "big eye," "sweet talk," and "two-face."

Two popular songs of 1928, "Diga Diga Doo" and "Makin' Whoopee—with lyrics by Dorothy Fields and Gus Kahn, respectively, used slang expressions for sex that were then in vogue. Fields used slang in many of her songs. Her other hit of 1928, "I Can't Give You Anything But Love," includes words such as "swell" and "baby," while her 1938 song "You Couldn't Be Cuter" contains such expressions as "I'm hooked! The well-known goose is cooked," and "You look so fresh from the cleaner." E. Y. Harburg's lyrics for "Old Devil Moon," from *Finian's Rainbow* (1947), are full of slang expressions as well: "can't hold a candle," "too hot to handle," "wanna laugh like a loon."

In true gangland fashion, Stephen Sondheim's lyrics for "Cool," from *West Side Story* (1957), are almost entirely in New York gang jargon, from "Got a rocket in your pocket" to "Easy does it" to "Turn off the juice, boy."

That "groovy" was a "hip" expression in 1966 is evidenced in songs like "Feelin' Groovy" (the subtitle of Paul Simon's "The 59th Street Bridge Song") and "A Groovy Kind of Love." But very soon, "groovy" became antiquated: an example of the transitory nature of many slang expressions.

Bibliography

Davis, Sheila. *The Craft of Lyric Writing*. 1985.

Furia, Philip. *The Poets of Tin Pan Alley: A History of America's Great Lyricists*. 1990.

See also: **Contractions; Dialect; Foreign Influence**

SLEEP

Songs on the subject of sleep fall into several categories. There are the true lullabies, such as "Too-ra-loo-ra-loo-ral, That's an Irish Lullaby" (1914) and "Russian Lullaby" (1927), as well as the ironic ones, like "Lullaby of Broadway" (1935) and "Lullaby of Birdland" (1952). Then there are songs about the legendary sandman, who puts children to sleep by sprinkling sand in their eyes, represented by "The Japanese Sandman" (1920) and "Mister Sandman" (1954).

Insomnia, often a result of unrequited love, is the subject of "I Couldn't Sleep a Wink Last Night" (1943), "Tossin' and Turnin'" (1961), and "(Last Night) I Didn't Get to Sleep at All" (1971). Sleep itself is the subject of the 1923 song "Sleep," which was the theme song of Fred Waring's Pennsylvanians, while the British import "Don't Sleep in the Subway" (1967) is more a catalogue song about taking good care of oneself, including the words: "Don't walk in the pouring rain." "Gypsy Love Song" (1898) begins with the lyrics "Slumber on, my little Gypsy sweetheart." On the other hand, in the famous bass aria "Asleep in the Deep" (1897), sleep is used as a metaphor for death.

Being tired is the subject of two Depression songs, "Let's Put Out the Lights (And Go to Sleep)" (1932) and "Two Sleepy People" (1938). Other songs use the word "sleepy" as a synonym for "inactive." They include "Sleepy Time Gal" (1924), "(By the) Sleepy Lagoon" (1930), "When It's Sleepy Time Down South" (1931), "Sleepy Serenade" (1941), and "Sleepy Shores" (1972).

See also: **Dreams; Farewells**

SMILING

In the 1917 song "Smiles," several types of smiles are described. There are "smiles that make you happy"—found in such songs as "When Irish Eyes Are Smiling" (1912), "The Sunshine of Your Smile" (1915), "When My Baby Smiles at Me" (1920), "Let a Smile Be Your Umbrella (On a Rainy Day)" (1927), and "When You're

Smiling" (1928). Then there are "smiles that make you blue," as in The Shadow of Your Smile" (1965).

Yet there are other types of smiles in popular song. There are smiles in the face of adversity, exemplified by the **World War I** songs "Pack Up Your Troubles in Your Old Kit Bag and Smile, Smile, Smile" (1915) and "Smilin' Through" (1919), and by Charles Chaplin's "Smile," from his 1954 film *Modern Times*. There are other exhortations to smile (even if one doesn't feel like it), as in such songs as "Smile, Darn Ya, Smile" (1931) and "Put On a Happy Face" (1960). There are also songs about unrequited **love**, telling of the impossibility of smiling in the absence of one's beloved: "I'll Never Smile Again" (1939) and "Can't Smile Without You" (1978).

See also: **Anatomy; Happiness**

SOCIETY TEMPO

"Society tempo, also known as the "businessman's bounce," refers to a musical **tempo** that is characteristically fast (Presto) and in cut time. It is often favored for dance music at coming-out parties, charity balls, country clubs, and other social functions of the well-to-do. Uptempo medleys were initiated during the 1940s by bandleader Meyer Davis, and later by Lester Lanin, Peter Duchin, and other "society" bandleaders.

Typically, a series of songs is played in medleys that may last as long as half an hour. Although almost any song is adaptable to this tempo, in practice **show tunes** are most often used, in particular those originally written in moderate or fast tempo. Many songs by Cole Porter—himself an icon of society—are amenable to society tempo, among them "Let's Do It, (Let's Fall in Love)" (1928); "Love for Sale" (1930); "Anything Goes," "I Get a Kick Out of You," and "You're the Top" (all 1934); "Just One of Those Things" (1935); "It's D' Lovely" (1936); "From This Moment On" (1950); and "It's All Right With Me" (1953).

Among the hundreds of other songs often performed in society tempo are "'S Wonderful" (1927); "I Got Rhythm" (1930); "The Continental" (1934); "Cheek to Cheek," "Lullaby of Broadway," and "Top Hat, White Tie and Tails" (all 1935); "The Lady Is a Tramp," (1937); and "Change Partners" (1938).

See also: **Dance Crazes; Meter; Rhythm**

SOFTNESS. SEE TENDERNESS

SONG PLUGGERS

Song pluggers were individuals hired by music publishers to persuade performers to play and sing their songs. Most active from the **Gay Nineties** to the **Roaring Twenties**, they often resorted to subtle or not-so-subtle forms of bribery. In the early days they went to music halls, beer gardens, and to music and department stores, where they played and sang the latest **sheet music**. They also used their considerable powers of persuasion on **vaudeville** performers.

Many early song pluggers, such as Fred Fisher, Ernest Ball, Jerome Kern, Jean Schwartz, and George Gershwin, went on to become songwriters themselves. By the mid-1930s, much of the activity of these promoters moved to the **recording** studio and the **radio** station. In this era of technology, the **disc jockey**—with his relentlessly repetitive programming—and the **Top Forty** format have largely replaced the song plugger.

Bibliography

Marks, Edward B. *They All Sang: From Tony Pastor to Rudy Vallee.* As told to Abbott J. Liebling. 1934.

SONGS. *SEE* MUSIC

SONGWRITERS. *SEE* COMPOSER-LYRICISTS; COMPOSERS; LYRICISTS; PERFORMER-SONGWRITERS; WOMEN AS SONGWRITERS

SOUL

"Soul" refers to a type of black popular music that flourished in the 1960s and 1970s before merging with the popular mainstream. Its genesis could be found both in the black church and with secular performers of **rhythm and blues**, who borrowed heavily from **gospel** singing. Emotion and its effect on the voice were of paramount importance in performance. At various times, singing would vary from controlled to improvised; passionate voices sometimes emitted moans, shouts, cries, and shrieks. It was akin to a musical exorcism that sprang from the deepest well of black cultural experience.

Most gospel-style songs recorded before 1961 were pop in orientation but gospel in approach. Among the first rhythm and blues singers to utilize soul in a pop context were Fay Adams, with "Shake a Hand" (1953); Ray Charles, with "I Got a Woman" (1954); and James Brown in two recordings: "Please Please Please" (1956) and "Try Me" (1958). Other songs of this nature include Roy Hamilton's "Don't Let Go" (1957) and Ray Charles's "What'd I Say?" (1959); a **call-and-response** structure was inherent to both of these songs. The early **rock 'n' roll** songwriting team of Jerry Leiber and Mike Stoller fashioned the sound of a revival meeting in their song "Saved" (1960), which was recorded by LaVern Baker.

Other revivalist-type recordings, such as Jackie Wilson's "Lonely Teardrops" (1958) and the Isley Brothers' "Shout" (1959), emanated the excitement of unabated emotional performance. Both "You Send Me" (1957)—Sam Cooke's first secular hit after leaving the gospel group the Soul Stirrers—and "For Your Precious Love" (1958)—recorded by Jerry Butler and the Impressions—evoked deep feelings of religious devotion. In fact, the depth of emotion in both songs was so great that one could have imagined the lyrics being centered on the love of God instead of on the love of a woman.

Although a majority of soul singers came from the South, some notable artists arose in other parts of the country. Cooke, an outstanding soul singer, was born in Chicago. With his perfection of articulation and phrasing, it is not surprising that he acted as an inspirational force in the burgeoning soul movement. His "Bring It On Home to Me" (1962) and "That's Where It's At" (1964) helped define the soul experience. His posthumous hit of 1965, "A Change Is Gonna Come," helped usher in the period when soul music reflected black pride and civil rights activism.

It was not until Solomon Burke's recordings that soul music became a genuine movement; his impassioned singing style was all soul. In 1963 Burke recorded his version of "If You Need Me"; with its gospel harmonies, fervent message, and spoken interludes, the song became a soul classic.

Wilson Pickett also recorded "If You Need Me." Known as "The Wicked Pickett," he proved to be a very exciting, high-voltage performer of soul. Many of Pickett's recordings were among the most commercially successful of the genre. They include "Don't Fight It" (1965), "Mustang Sally" (1966), the fervently sung "I'm in Love" (1967), and "In the Midnight Hour" (1965)—a masterpiece of soul.

The soul singer and songwriter Joe Tex introduced elements of worldliness, wit, and heartfelt sermonizing to his songs. Among his hits were the comic "Skinny Legs and All" (1967) and two morality lessons: "Hold What You've Got" (1964) and "The Love You Save" (1970).

The first soul song to reach Number One on the Pop music charts was "When a Man Loves a Woman," recorded by Percy Sledge in 1966. The song—with its reverent feeling, its impassioned lyrics, and its Bach-inspired organ accompaniment—became a soul standard. Sam and Dave, a singing duo, brought the excitement of soul music to ensemble singing. Their aggressive vocals and gospel shouts are the main virtues of two recordings: "Hold On (I'm Coming)" (1966) and "Soul Man" (1967). Both songs are characterized by catchy titles and hard-driving horn lines. These songs and many others mentioned above were recorded either in Memphis, in nearby Muscle Shoals (Alabama), or in New Orleans. Although the performers were black, the music was played, written, and produced by both blacks and whites.

But the South was not the sole purveyor of soul

music. Chicago, Philadelphia, and Detroit's **Motown** also contributed mightily. The Chicago sound was more refined and restrained than the southern variety, but at its core, it retained the gospel feel. The Impressions, led by Curtis Mayfield, gave soul some "message" songs, including "Keep On Pushing" (1964), "We're a Winner" (1967), and "People Get Ready" (1965): the last was inspired by the Civil Rights Act, which had been passed a year earlier.

Jerry Butler, later called the "Iceman," was the original lead singer of the Impressions. His deeply rich, cool, sophisticated sound was perfectly suited to such a solo **recording** as "Make It Easy on Yourself" (1962). Other Chicago soul recordings were Major Lance's of "The Monkey Time" (1963); Pontella Bass's of "Rescue Me" (1965); Billy Stewart's of "I Do Love You" (1965); and Stewart's reworking of the naturally soulful "Summertime," from *Porgy and Bess* (1935). The Dells also reworked a song in 1969: "Oh, What a Night," a **doo-wop** hit they had first recorded in 1956. Two other notable Chicago recordings of soul were Tyrone Davis's "Turn Back the Hands of Time" (1970) and the Chi-Lites' "Have You Seen Her" (1971).

In Philadelphia, soul went through further refinement. Here the sound was sweeter, contrasting dry and restrained voices with full, lush arrangements. Examples are the Intruders' recording of "Cowboys to Girls" (1968), Barbara Acklin's of "Love Makes a Woman" (1968), and Eddie Holman's of "Hey There Lonely Girl"—originally "Hey There Lonely Boy" (1962). Two proponents of other types of soul music adapted the Philadelphia sound: Butler, in his recording of "Only the Strong Survive" (1969) and Pickett, in "Don't Let the Green Grass Fool You" (1971).

Four singers stand above all others in the history of soul: Otis Redding, Aretha Franklin, James Brown, and Al Green. The Georgia-born Redding was an artist of primitive intensity who sang uptempo soul as well as slow ballads. His voice was raw; his renderings of songs unique. Among his most successful recordings were "Pain in My Heart" (1963) and three songs from 1965: "I've Been Loving You Too Long," "I Can't Turn You Loose," and "Respect." Just as he was beginning to gain the acceptance of the general public, he died in a 1967 plane crash. He never lived to see his soul classic, "(Sittin' on the) Dock of the Bay," become Number One on the pop charts of 1968.

One of the songs associated with Franklin is her 1967 **cover** of Redding's "Respect". This association was not by mere chance; Franklin has a talent for reinterpreting songs and giving them new moods and meanings. Often, her recordings become the definitive versions. Franklin—who was dubbed "Lady Soul" or the "Queen of Soul"—was the daughter of the Reverend C. L. Franklin, a Baptist preacher. She grew up with gospel songs and began singing in her father's church in

Detroit. As in the case of Redding, some of her best recordings were made in Memphis. Among them were the emotionally charged "I Never Loved a Man (The Way I Love You)," "Chain of Fools," and "(You Make Me Feel Like) A Natural Woman"—all of 1967. The following year saw the releases of "Since You've Been Gone (Sweet, Sweet Baby)" and "I Say a Little Prayer." The latter, a cover of Dionne Warwick's pop recording of Hal David and Burt Bacharach's song of 1967, marked Franklin's move away from soul in the direction of lighter and more pop-based material.

James Brown was idolized by other soul singers. Known as the "Godfather of Soul" and "Soul Brother Number One," his voice was harsh and frayed, but charged with emotional tension and excitement. Brown brought with him a greater emphasis on hard rhythms and instrumental backing. He could dance as well as sing, adding to a thrilling performance. After several rhythm-and-blues hits in 1956, he burst into superstardom in 1964, with "Papa's Got a Brand New Bag" and "I Got You (I Feel Good)" in 1965, "It's a Man's, Man's World (But It Wouldn't Be Nothing Without a Woman)" in 1966, and "Cold Sweat" in 1967. Of all southern soul singers (he was born in Georgia), Brown's recordings retain the strongest link to southern gospel and rhythm and blues. He wrote and produced virtually all his own music. Brown's experimentation with jazz and African rhythms in the early 1970s influenced the coming of **funk** and moved him away from soul.

Al Green, the last of the innovators of soul, was born in Arkansas but raised in Michigan. He first sang gospel with three older brothers. Going solo in 1969, he combined cool Chicago soul with the gritty sound of Memphis. Green had the ability to control the timbre of his voice and to make original use of phrasing and inflection. He combined all these elements in his romantic recordings of soul—using many songs which he wrote or co-wrote. Among his hits were "Tired of Being Along" and "Let's Stay Together" in 1971 and "I'm Still in Love With You" and "You Oughta Be With Me" in 1972. Green eventually abandoned soul music and returned to gospel singing in 1980.

With the passing of Redding and the moving on of Franklin, Brown, and Green to other musical styles, soul ceased to exist as a distinctive musical genre. After 1972, many of its characteristics became part of the popular mainstream. But soul still lives in the energy and emotionalism of many performers of today.

Additional Songs

B-A-B-Y (1966)
Back Stabbers (1972)
Clean Up Woman (1971)
Cry Baby (1963)
Expressway to Your Heart (1967)
Girl Watcher (1968)
(Your Love Has Lifted Me) Higher and Higher (1967)

I'll Be Around (1972)
Knock on Wood (1966)
Me and Mrs. Jones (1972)
Mr. Big Stuff (1971)
Power of Love (1971)
Respect Yourself (1971)
Ride Your Pony (1965)
Slip Away (1968)
Superfly (1972)
Sweet Inspirations (1967)
Sweet Soul Music (1967)
Tell It Like It Is (1966)
Tell Mama (1968)
Time Is on My Side (1963)
Walking the Dog (1963)
Who's Making Love? (1968)

Jeffrey Cahn

Bibliography

Cummings, Tony. *The Sound of Philadelphia.* 1975.

Garland, Phyl. *The Sound of Soul: The Story of Black Music.* 1971.

Gilett, Charlie. "Are We Together? Soul Music." In *The Sound of the City.* 1983.

Guralnick, Peter. "Soul." In *The Rolling Stone Illustrated History of Rock and Roll.* 1980.

Haralambos, Michael. *Right On: From Blues to Soul in Black America.* 1979.

Hirshey, Gerri. *Nowhere to Run: The Story of Soul Music.* 1984.

Larkin, Rochelle. *Soul Music! The Sound, the Stars, the Story.* 1970.

Shaw, Arnold. *The World of Soul: Black America's Contribution to the Pop Music Scene.* 1971.

> See also: Africa; Popular Song; Religion; Singing Groups

STANDARD

In the world of popular music, a standard is a song that has endured. Since neither the criteria to determine this endurance nor the number of years necessary are specified, the word has an elusive quality; one person's standard may not necessarily be another's. No one would doubt that "My Melancholy Baby" (1912), "Always" (1925), "Star Dust" (1929), and "As Time Goes By" (1931) are standards; they have stood the test on time. Whether or not more recent songs will become standards is, of course, open to question.

The term, firmly entrenched in popular song vocabulary, often appears with qualifying words, such as **country-and-western** standard, **rhythm-and-blues** standard, **rock 'n' roll** standard, **rock** standard, **soul** standard, or **waltz** standard. One of the more clearly defined of these hybrid terms is "jazz standard," applied by jazz musicians to songs they frequently perform. Among the many songs in this category are "Body and Soul" (1930), "Georgia on My Mind" (1930), "All of

Me" (1931), and "When Sunny Gets Blue" (1956).

> *See also:* Show Tune

STARS

Songs about the stars are legion and universal—including such worldwide favorites as the French-English "Twinkle, Twinkle, Little Star" (1806) and the Mexican "Estrellita (Little Star)" (1914).

In America, some songs, such as "Stars Fell on Alabama" (1934), "Stairway to the Stars" (1939), "The Story of a Starry Night" (1941), and "Stella by Starlight" (1946), use the stars as a backdrop for romance. Other songs, like "Stars in My Eyes" (1936), "Star Eyes" (1943), "Don't Let the Stars Get in Your Eyes" (1953), and "Stars Shine in Your Eyes" (1956), seem to have an affinity for the eyes. As symbols of love, the stars shine brightly in "I've Told Ev'ry Little Star" (1932), "You are My Lucky Star" (1935), and "You're the Only Star in My Blue Heaven" (1938). Stars are also good for wishing upon, as in "When You Wish Upon a Star" (1940) and "Catch a Falling Star" (1957), or even for swinging upon, as in "Swinging On a Star" (1949).

But two melodious "star" songs are not really about the stars at all. Mitchell Parish and Hoagy Carmichael's "Star Dust" (1929)—probably the most famous star song of all—is a lament for a lost love. Maxwell Anderson and Kurt Weill's "Lost in the Stars" (1946) is a call for human dignity.

Additional Songs

Blue Star (1955)
Good Morning Starshine (1969)
I Speak to the Stars (1954)
Little Star (1959)
Lucky Star (1984)
Shining Star (1975)

> *See also:* Heaven; Moon; Sky; Sun

STARTING. SEE BEGINNING

STATES

It is sometimes difficult to determine whether a given song is about a state, a **city**, a **river**, or a college. Is "New York State of Mind" (1977) about the city or the state? Is "Missouri Waltz" (1914) concerned with the river or the state? (Both are, in fact, state songs.) "Beautiful Ohio" (1918), on the other hand, refers to the river, while "On Wisconsin" (1909) alludes to the university. Usually, however, the author's intention seems clear.

More songs have been written about the states of the South than about those of any other region of the United States. Alabama appears in at least four: "Alabamy Bound" (1925, actually a **train** song), "Alabama-Song," or "Moon of Alabama" (written by Bertolt Brecht and Kurt Weill in 1928), "Stars Fell on Alabama" (best known of the four, written in 1934), and "Sweet Home Alabama" (1974). The states of North Carolina and South Carolina must share the credit for both "Carolina in the Morning" (1922) and "Carolina Moon" (1928), but South Carolina is the obvious location of "Just a Little Bit South of North Carolina" (1940). The protagonist of "Sweet Georgia Brown" (1925) may or may not come from Georgia, but Hoagy Carmichael's immortal "Georgia on My Mind" (1930) clearly has the state in mind, as does the 1979 song "The Devil Went Down to Georgia." Other states of the South immortalized in song include Kentucky and Tennessee: in Bill Monroe's **bluegrass** song "Blue Moon of Kentucky" (1947) and in the country **crossover** hit "Tennessee Waltz" (1948); and Louisiana in "Louisiana Hayride" (1932).

Turning to the Southwest, a landmark musical play was written about one of the states of that region; its rousing title song, "Oklahoma" (1943), is a perennial favorite. Texas is represented by a number of songs: "The Eyes of Texas Are Upon You" (1903), "Deep in the Heart of Texas" (1941), "T for Texas," or "Blue Yodel No. 1" (1953), and "The Yellow Rose of Texas"— adapted in 1955 from a song originally written in 1858.

Songs about New England include "My Old New Hampshire Home" (1898—Harry Von Tilzer's first hit), "Moonlight in Vermont" (a jazz classic written in 1944), "Rhode Island Is Famous for You" (from the revue *Inside USA*, 1948), and the Bee Gee's "(The Lights Went Out in) Massachusetts" (1967).

The Northeast is represented in song by "Jersey Bounce," a big band favorite of 1941; "Pennsylvania Polka" (1942), a lively dance tune written in the same year; and Billy Joel's "New York State of Mind" (1975).

Several songs have the Midwest in mind. One of the earliest and most enduring state songs was President Harry Truman's favorite: "The Missouri Waltz." "Indiana (Back Home Again in Indiana) (1917) is another lasting song about the region. Two songs are entitled "Ohio": one, from *Wonderful Town* (1953), begins: "Why-oh-why-oh-why-oh, Why did I ever leave Ohio?"; the other was popularized by Crosby, Stills, Nash, and Young in 1970.

As for the West, there is California, whose numerous songs include "California, Here I Come" (1924), "California Dreaming" (1965), "It Never Rains in Southern California" (1972), and "Hotel California" (1977); and Hawaii, with "The Hawaiian Wedding Song (Ke Kali Nei Au)" (1926), "Hawaiian War Chant" (1936), "Blue Hawaii" (1937), and "Hawaii Five O" (1969).

Certain states are conspicuous by their absence; no lasting songs have been written about Alaska, Nebraska, or the Dakotas. Perhaps songwriters prefer gentler climates.

See also: **Patriotism; Places**

STOPPING. SEE ENDING

STREETS

Three types of street songs can be distinguished: the general, the specific, and the metaphoric. In the first category are songs about unnamed thoroughfares; of these, "On the Sunny Side of the Street" (1930) and "On the Street Where You Live" (1956) are probably best known. Other songs in this category are "Italian Street Song" (1910), "When My Sugar Walks Down the Street, All the Birdies Go Tweet, Tweet, Tweet" (1924), and "A Little Street Where Old Friends Meet" (1932). "Standing on the Corner," from *The Most Happy Fella* (1956), could apply to the junction of any two streets where one could watch "the girls go by."

Specific streets are most often located in **New York City**; songs about its principal thoroughfare, **Broadway**, are in a category of their own. "Forty-second Street" (1932), the most important crosstown street in Manhattan, is also the title song of one of the earliest **film musicals** and of a 1980 musical comedy derived from it. Another Manhattan cross street is named in Paul Simon's "The 59th Street Bridge Song (Feelin' Groovy)" (1966). Irving Berlin's "Easter Parade" (1933) takes place, of course, on New York's Fifth Avenue. The 1894 favorite "The Sidewalks of New York," or "East Side, West Side," would seem to encompass all the streets of Manhattan, as does "In Old New York," or "The Streets of New York," from Victor Herbert's *The Red Mill* of 1906.

Other **cities** represented in song by specific streets are New Orleans ("Basin Street Blues," 1928; "South Rampart Street Parade," 1938), Kansas City ("12th Street Rag," 1914), Memphis ("Beale Street Blues," 1916), Philadelphia ("Between 18th and 19th on Chestnut Street," 1939), Atlantic City ("On the Boardwalk in Atlantic City," 1946), Liverpool ("Penny Lane," 1967) London ("A Nightingale Sang in Berkeley Square," 1940; "Baker Street," 1978), and Paris ("Pigalle," 1949). The location of "On Green Dolphin Street" (1947) is uncertain, but the song—which comes from the soundtrack of the film of the same name—remains a jazz classic.

There are also a number of songs about roads, some of which go to specific destinations: "On the Road to Mandalay" (1907), "The Road to Morocco" (1942), "(Get Your Kicks on) Route 66" (1946), "Take Me Home, Country Roads" (1971), and "On the Road Again" (1979). "King of the Road," (1964), in contrast, is a **train** song.

Songs about metaphorical thoroughfares include "The Lonesome Road" (1927), "(On the) Street of Dreams" (1932), "The Boulevard of Broken Dreams" (1933), "Easy Street" (1941), "Hit the Road to Dreamland" (1942), "Dead End Street" (1967), and "The Long and Winding Road" (1970).

Additional Songs

Caminito (Little Road) (1936)
Country Road (1970)
Dancing in the Street (1964)
Ease on Down the Road (1974)
Freeway of Love (1985)
Goodbye Yellow Brick Road (1973)
Hit the Road, Jack (1961)
The Naughty Lady of Shady Lane (1954)
One for My Baby (And One More for the Road) (1943)
Tramp! Tramp! Tramp! Along the Highway (1910)
Two for the Road (1967)
Under the Boardwalk (1964)

See also: **Places; Travel**

STRINGS

Three types of stringed instruments are used in the performance of popular music: those that are plucked, those that are struck, and those that are bowed. The plucked instruments include not only the **guitar**, but also the banjo, mandolin, Appalachian dulcimer, ukulele, harp, and double bass. The banjo, originally brought to the United States from **Africa**, became a staple of the **minstrel show** and was used as **accompaniment** in the performance of **blues** and **bluegrass**. The mandolin has also been used in bluegrass, while the Appalachian dulcimer, with three or four strings, is widely used to accompany **folk song**. The ukulele is a simple Hawaiian instrument that became popular with amateurs during the periods of the two world wars. The harp has been used to a much lesser extent in popular music, for the most part as a component of large orchestras.

The double bass, also known as the "bass fiddle," has become of abiding importance in **jazz**, where it replaced the tuba, which had been used in **Dixieland**. Although almost always plucked, the double bass is sometimes bowed for solos (the bassist "Slam" Stewart also hummed along with his **improvisations** at the octave). Other jazz bassists include Jimmy Blanton, Oscar Pettiford, Ray Brown, Charlie Mingus, Chubby Jackson, Ron Carter, Bob Haggart, Ed Safranski, and Milt Hinton. Since the 1960s, the double bass has been largely superseded by the electronic bass guitar.

The foremost example of a stringed instrument that is struck is the **piano**, which is activated by hammers. The Hungarian *cimbalom*—often used in the performance of **gypsy music**—also falls into this category.

As for the bowed instruments (the traditional violin, viola, and cello), they are of much less importance in the performance of popular music than they are in classical music—usually used in ensemble playing and functioning as accompaniment. The violin has also been used to some extent in jazz improvisation, notably by Eddie South, Joe Venuti, and Stuff Smith.

Songs about strings include "Fit as a Fiddle" (1932),

"Play, Fiddle, Play" (1932), "When a Gypsy Makes His Violin Cry" (1935), "Slap That Bass" (1937), and "Love Is Like a Violin" (1945).

See also: **Arrangement; Instrumentation**

SUBJECTS

The subjects of popular song are legion, embracing virtually every aspect of the life experience. But one subject, romantic **love**, has predominated through the years—especially during the second quarter of the twentieth century, when songs like "I Wanna Be Loved by You" (1928) and "So in Love" (1949) permeated the airwaves. Songs about **people**—with or without names—and **places** are a distant second, but still very much in evidence; "Daisy Bell" (1892) and "The Sidewalks of New York" (1894) were as popular in the late nineteenth century as were "Rosanna" (1982) and "(Theme From) New York, New York" (1977) in the late twentieth. Many other subjects have occupied songwriters through the years, particularly parts of the body (*see* Anatomy), **colors**, saying goodbye (*see* Farewells), **loneliness**, the **moon**, the **stars**, the **day**, the **night**, the **seasons**, and the **weather**.

With the revival of **folk song** in mid-century, the spectrum of song subjects broadened considerably. Songs increasingly carried messages relating to social and political causes as well as to personal problems. After the successes of songs like "If I Had a Hammer" and "Blowin' in the Wind" (both 1962), the era of the **protest song** was at hand. But through it all—from "Little Annie Rooney" (1890) to "Love Changes Everything" (1989)—the subject of love has reigned supreme.

See also: **Classified Guide to the Articles**

SUN

The sun has offered less inspiration to songwriters than the **moon**, possibly because it lacks the latter's traditional association with love and romance. Songs about the sun tend to be more pragmatic, in the line of "Wait 'Til the Sun Shines, Nelly" (1905), "I Got the Sun in the Morning" (1946), and "Seasons in the Sun" (1964). Significantly, one of the few romantic ballads to refer to the sun, "East of the Sun (And West of the Moon)" (1934), also cites the moon.

Sunshine has had a long association with **happiness**, dating back at least to the 1915 song "The Sunshine of Your Smile." In the same tradition are the standards "You are My Sunshine" (1940), "Let the Sunshine In" (1969), and "You Are the Sunshine of My Life" (1972).

The word "sunny," as a synonym for "cheerful," is found in two jaunty uptempo songs, "Sunny Side Up" (1929) and "On the Sunny Side of the Street" (1930), as well as in two **"name"** songs entitled "Sunny," from 1925 and 1966. The sun also gets passing mention in a number of **time-of-day** songs, including "The World Is Waiting for the Sunrise" (1919), "At Sundown" (1927), "Softly, as in a Morning Sunrise" (1928), "Red Sails in the Sunset" (1935), "Sunrise Serenade" (1938), "Canadian Sunset" (1956), and "Sunrise, Sunset" (1964).

Additional Songs

Ain't No Sunshine (1971)
Don't Let the Sun Go Down on Me (1974)
Here Comes the Sun (1969)
Midnight Sun (1947)
New Sun in the Sky (1931)
Please Mister Sun (1951)
Powder Your Face With Sunshine (1948)
Sunshine, Lollipops and Rainbows (1964)
Sunshine of Your Love (1967)
Sunshine on My Shoulders (1971)
That Lucky Old Sun (1949)
We'll Sing in the Sunshine (1963)
When the Sun Comes Out (1940)

See also: **Heaven; Sky**

SUPERLATIVES

While "more" is the **comparative** of choice in popular song, the most frequently used superlative is "best." The roster of hits bearing that word includes such songs as "The Best Thing for You" (1950), "The Best Is Yet to Come" (1959), and "The Best of Times" (1981), as well as two songs with seemingly contradictory philosophies: "The Best Things in Life Are Free" (1927) and "Diamonds Are a Girl's Best Friend" (1949).

Other superlatives found in popular song titles include "most" and "sweetest," as in "The Most Beautiful Girl in the World" (1936) and "The Sweetest Sounds" (1962). But one of the most comprehensive collections of superlatives is found in Cole Porter's "You're the Top" (1934). In that **catalogue song,** people and objects supposedly of the highest caliber are listed, rhyming the "Colosseum" with the "Louvre Museum," "Mahatma Gandhi" with "Napoleon brandy," and a "Waldorf salad" with a "Berlin ballad."

Additional Songs

Arthur's Theme (Best That You Can Do) (1981)
Best of My Love (1974)
Best of My Love (1977)
(You're the) Best Thing That Ever Happened to Me (1972)
Giving You the Best That I Got (1988)
Last Night on the Back Porch, I Love Her Best of All (1923)
The Most Beautiful Girl (1973)
The Most Happy Fella (1956)
The Sweetest Music This Side of Heaven (1934)

SWEETNESS

Sweetness serves several functions in popular song. It is, first of all, often used as a term of **endearment,** such as "sweetheart," "sweetie," "sugar," or "honey." It is also employed as an adjective describing a person, thing, or concept. More literally, there are songs about sweet-tasting **food and drink.**

As a term of endearment, "sweetheart" was consistently used until the 1950s, in such songs as "My Sweetheart's the Man in the Moon" (1892), "Let Me Call You Sweetheart" (1910), "The Sweetheart of Sigma Chi" (1912), "Nobody's Sweetheart Now" (1924), "Good Night, Sweetheart" (1931), and "Auf Wiederseh'n Sweetheart" (1952). *Sweethearts* was also the name of a Victor Herbert operetta of 1913 and of its title song. In contrast to this abundance, the last half of the twentieth century has seen few "sweetheart" songs.

The term "sugar" has a long history, stretching from "When My Sugar Walks Down the Street All the Birdies Go Tweet Tweet Tweet" (1924) to "I Lost My Sugar in Salt Lake City" (1942) and "Sugar, Sugar" (1969). The same holds true for "honey," which appears in two songs named "Honey" (one from 1928, the other 1968) as well as in "Honey Bun" (1949) and "A Taste of Honey" (1960). The last song supplements the title with the words: "A taste much sweeter than wine." Furthermore, part of the charm of the jazz standard "Honeysuckle Rose" (1929) surely derives from its association with sweetness.

As an adjective, "sweet" describes a remarkable gallery of ladies specifically by **name:** "Sweet Rosie O'Grady" (1898), "Ida, Sweet as Apple Cider" (1902), "You're the Flower of My Heart, Sweet Adeline" (1903), "Sweet Georgia Brown" (1925), "Sweet Lorraine" (1928), "Sweet Sue" (1928), "Sweet Leilani" (1937), and "Say Has Anybody Seen My Sweet Gypsy Rose" (1973). Several other songs are about unnamed sweet persons: "Ain't She Sweet?" (1927), "Sweet and Lovely" (1931), and "Stay as Sweet as You Are" (1934).

Also described as sweet in various songs are **life** ("Ah! Sweet Mystery of Life," 1910), **love** ("Love Is the Sweetest Thing," 1933), **kisses** ("Kisses Sweeter Than Wine," 1951), **clothing** ("Alice Blue Gown," 1919), sounds ("The Sweetest Sounds," 1962), and **music** ("Love's Own Sweet Song," 1914; "Sweet and Low-Down," 1925; "Sweet Soul Music," 1967).

In the 1945 song "Candy," the title is quite obviously a term of endearment: "I call my sugar 'candy.'" More literal are the sweets in "On the Good Ship Lollipop" (1934), "Lollipops and Roses" (1960), "Sunshine, Lollipops and Rainbows" (1964), and "The Candy Man" (1970).

Additional Songs

Candy Girl (1963)
Honey Love (1954)

Honeycomb (1954)
How Sweet It Is (To Be Loved by You) (1964)
How Sweet You Are (1943)
I Love You, Sweetheart of All My Dreams (1928)
Lollipop (1958)
Money Honey (1953)
My Sweet Lord (1970)
Since You've Been Gone (Sweet, Sweet Baby) (1968)
A Spoonful of Sugar (1963)
Sugar (1927)
Sugar Blues (1923)
Sugar Shack (1962)
Sugartime (1956)
Sweet Blindness (1968)
Sweet Inspirations (1967)
Sweet Love (1986)
Sweet Madness (1933)
Sweet Nothin's (1960)
Sweet Seasons (1971)
Sweet September (1962)
The Sweetest Music This Side of Heaven (1934)
To You Sweetheart, Aloha (1936)
When I Take My Sugar to Tea (1931)
When You Were Sweet Sixteen (1898)
Will You Remember (Sweetheart) (1917)
You're a Sweet Little Headache (1938)
You're a Sweetheart (1937)

See also: **Enduring Love; Falling in Love; Kissing; Marriage; Romance; Togetherness**

SWING

Swing is an almost indefinable style of playing or singing, characterized by a flowing, rhythmic pulse. It formed a large part of the repertoire of the **big bands** of the 1930s and 1940s. Its origins can be traced both to **jazz** and to the sweet bands of the 1920s. In the 1930s, true jazz, as the black bands played it, was kept alive by aficionados but was little known by the general public. Sweet music was the dominant style on **radio** and in **recording**. The swing style was a direct result of Benny Goodman's (and other white bandleaders') imitation of black bands by using the **arrangements** of Fletcher Henderson, Don Redman, Jimmy Mundy, and other black arrangers. Goodman introduced the sound of swing to a broad audience through radio, recordings, and engagements at hotels and ballrooms. He became the "King of Swing," and danceable jazz became the music of the day.

The swing era virtually coexisted with the era of the big bands; it has been variously dated from 1935 to 1945 and from 1939 to 1949. Although it is impossible to say precisely when swing began, Goodman's engagement at the Palomar Ballroom in Los Angeles in August 1935 was one of the early indications that a change was in the wind. Goodman decided to feature his swing repertoire rather than the sweet, "society" style of dance music that had previously been popular. The

audience, particularly its younger members, gave enthusiastic approval.

Swing was the music of youth, just as rock 'n' roll was to be in the 1950s. But there was a difference. In the swing era, the adults, not the youngsters, made the hits. Young people did not yet have enough buying power to make their favorites the top hits on the charts. Swing had to make inroads into the establishment before it could produce hits.

By the mid-1930s the United States had recovered from the worst of the Depression, but only a few years of relative calm lay between the economic debacle of the early 1930s and the upheaval of **World War II**. By 1937 Hitler was in power in Germany, Mussolini had brought fascism to Italy, the Spanish republic was under attack by Francisco Franco, and Japan had begun systematic attacks upon China. The United States was being inexorably drawn into another major war. As America began to recover from the Depression, people had more money in their pockets. They could afford entertainment and their musical tastes began to change.

Black musicians were the innovators who brought the hot sounds of swing into the dance bands, but the white bands made most of the money. As grossly unfair as this seems today, given the state of race relations in the late 1930s and early 1940s, most of the nation would not have accepted swing had not white (or at least interracial) bands begun to feature the sound. Goodman was primarily responsible for breaking the color barrier in bands, by being one of the first leaders to feature whites and blacks playing together in the same band.

Besides Goodman's, many other bands were organized around 1935; they were usually called "orchestras." The Dorsey Brothers—Jimmy and Tommy—formed theirs in 1934. Tommy withdrew in 1935 to lead his own group. Clarinetist Artie Shaw formed an orchestra with strings in 1936, but abandoned it in the face of Goodman's success and formed instead what he called the "loudest band in the world" in 1937—featuring swing. Similarly, Woody Herman took over and reworked the sweet sound of the Isham Jones aggregation in 1936.

The *Billboard* college survey of favorite bands between 1938 and 1943 included Benny Goodman (1938), Artie Shaw (1939), Glenn Miller (1940, 1941, 1942), and Harry James (1943)—all of whom emphasized swing. Black groups were not among the favorites, but they certainly made important contributions to the style. Some of the most influential black bands included those of Count Basie, Duke Ellington, Erskine Hawkins, Fletcher Henderson, Earl Hines, and Chick Webb.

Several of the big bands also featured small combos that played more authentic jazz with superb **improvisation**. For example, Benny Goodman at various times had a trio, quartet, and quintet; Tommy Dorsey had his

Clambake Seven; and Artie Shaw had his Gramercy Five.

By the end of the 1930s, a trend toward less boisterous music had become evident. Perhaps the nation anticipated difficult times as United States involvement in World War II appeared imminent. The popularity of Glenn Miller's soft, sweet sound in the early 1940s was an indication that people wanted to dance to dreamy music. The swing hysteria was passing. For several years, swing and sweet music flourished side by side; almost all bands played sweet music as part of their repertoire, at least occasionally.

The first peacetime military draft in United States history was instituted in 1940. The draft caused the bands to juggle their personnel and to look for replacements. Keeping together a band that could play complex swing arrangements became increasingly more difficult.

A trend toward the featuring of a **singer** or **singing group** within the band began in the early 1940s. Although the bands had always had vocalists, they were considered of secondary importance. By the early 1940s, however, vocalists were taking more of the spotlight, until by the middle of the decade, the singers had become the stars.

Wartime shortages, particularly of gasoline, also caused problems for the bands; neither they nor their fans could travel. In addition, a levied amusement tax made it very expensive for people to go out. These and other factors contributed to the demise of the big bands and the birth of a new era, featuring the vocalists.

The riots set off by Frank Sinatra's performances in the early 1940s clearly signalled the end of the swing era. The drawing power of the swing bands had declined. The next several years were dominated by the singers. But swing lived on into the 1990s, both as a style of performance and in the presence of bands like Harry Connick, Jr.'s, which brought back its sounds.

Additional Songs

A-Tisket A-Tasket (1938)
And the Angels Sing (1939)
Artistry in Rhythm (1941)
Caravan (1937)
Chattanooga Choo Choo (1941)
Cherokee (1938)
Ciribiribin (1898)
The Dipsy Doodle (1937)
Don't Be That Way (1938)
Don't Sit Under the Apple Tree (With Anyone Else but Me) (1942)
Frenesi (1939)
Green Eyes (1929)
I Let a Song Go Out of My Heart (1938)
In the Mood (1939)
It Don't Mean a Thing If It Ain't Got That Swing (1932)
I've Heard That Song Before (1942)
One O'Clock Jump (1938)

Sentimental Journey (1944)
Sing, Sing, Sing, Sing (1936)
Song of India (1897)
A String of Pearls (1941)
Swinging on a Star (1944)
Take the 'A' Train (1941)
Tangerine (1942)
Tuxedo Junction (1940)
Undecided (1939)

Don Tyler

Bibliography

Collier, James Lincoln. *Benny Goodman and the Swing Era.* 1989.

McCarthy, Albert. *Big Band Jazz.* 1974.

Schuller, Gunther. *The Swing Era: The Development of Jazz, 1930–1945.* 1989.

Simon, George T. *The Big Bands.* 1981.

———. *Simon Says: The Sights and Sounds of the Swing Era: 1935–1955.* 1971.

Tyler, Don. *Hit Parade: 1920–1955.* 1985.

Whitburn, Joel. *Pop Memories: 1890–1954.* 1986.

See also: **Dance Crazes; Depression Years**

SYNCOPATION

Syncopation refers to a temporary shift of accent in a musical passage; it is created by stressing a beat that is normally weak. Syncopation has appeared in many and diverse types of musical expression, from fourteenth-century European art music to traditional African folk music. Yet it has seldom been used as persistently as it was in the **ragtime** movement that developed in the United States in the 1890s. Its employment in the treble over a steady rhythmic accompaniment presented a provocative contradiction to the prevailing regularity of the **rhythm**. Syncopation created a sensation, so much so that writers of the period often equated it with ragtime.

Two types of syncopation are encountered in ragtime: the tied and the untied (examples a and b), although the types are frequently intermingled. "Hello! Ma Baby" (1902) illustrates the first, untied variety, while "Oh, You Beautiful Doll" (1911) is an example of the later, tied type of syncopation.

(a)

(b)

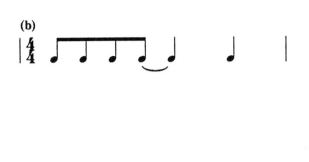

Ragtime brought syncopation to the forefront of popular music, and it has remained a prominent component ever since. It figures very strongly in music with a black heritage, such as **blues, jazz, rhythm and blues, rock 'n' roll, rock, Motown, and soul.** But it is also found in show tunes, such as two composed by Jerome Kern: "Ol' Man River" (1927)—an example of untied syncopation—and "Don't Ever Leave Me" (1929)—an example of tied.

Syncopation is also part and parcel of jazz performance whether or not it is written out. It figures in the anticipation of beats and in attacks between beats, rather than directly upon them. With the Brazilian and British invasions of the 1960s, syncopation became even more prominent; the **bossa nova**, in particular, is noted for its playful use of syncopation.

Beginning in the 1970s it became customary to write out the syncopation in virtually all popular songs, rather than leave it to the performer's discretion. Syncopation has become the essence of many pop hits and is quite complex in such songs as "You Are the Sunshine of My Life" and "This Masquerade" (both 1972). Rhythmic passages like this are common in late-century songs:

However, whether written out or realized in performance, syncopation remains an integral element of American popular song.

Bibliography

Berlin, Edward A. *Ragtime: A Musical and Cultural History*. 1980.

See also: **Melody**

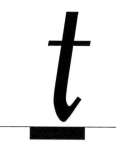

Talking

Songs on the subject of talking include four that are really about unrequited **love**: "Please Don't Talk About Me When I'm Gone" (1930), "Can't We Talk It Over?" (1931), "It's the Talk of the Town" (1933), and "I Talk to the Trees" (1951).

Other songs, such as "Happy Talk" (1949), "Yakety Yak" (1958), and "Jive Talkin'" (1975), delve into different styles of talking. Talking *sotto voce* is the subject of songs like "Whispering" (1920), "Whispers in the Dark (1937), and "Careless Whisper" (1984). Two famous songs about talking first appeared in two different films of 1967: "Everybody's Talkin'," in *Midnight Cowboy;* and "Talk to the Animals" in *Dr. Dolittle.*

In the 1980s, the act of talking, as practiced by **disc jockeys,** inspired a new genre of popular song called **rap,** a genre that is, essentially, talking to rhythmical accompaniment.

Additional Songs

Don't Talk to Strangers (1965)
I Heard It Through the Grape Vine (1966)
Our Language of Love (1956)
Talk to Me (1985)
Talk to Me (1987)
You Talk Too Much (1960)

    See also: **Dialect;** **Telephones**

Tango

The tango is both a dance and a type of music. It originated in **Argentina** in the late nineteenth century, created a sensation in Europe by 1907, and reached North America in 1913. Popularized by the dance team of Vernon and Irene Castle, the tango largely replaced the **waltz** as the foremost **dance craze** of pre-World War I society.

Both the dance and the music are dramatic. The dance features sudden movements and close embraces, while the music, in 4/4 **meter,** is characterized by a persistent, strongly accented rhythm with occasional alternating patterns of **syncopation:**

Each piece usually consists of two or three discrete sections, at least one of which is in the minor mode. Sudden changes of dynamics are common. Also common is use of the half **cadence** at the end of a piece.

Traditionally, the tango was performed by a string ensemble featuring the bandoneon, a form of accordion. By 1914 tea-dances had become fashionable in the cafés and hotel restaurants of New York City. One of the first tangos to be popularized in this manner was the Argentinian "El Choclo" (1913), sung in its original Spanish; it was given English lyrics only in 1952, when its first two sections were set to English words as "Kiss of Fire."

The tango became such a rage in the United States around 1914 that it infiltrated such native genres as **ragtime** and the **blues.** Although a number of "ragtime tangos" were written, none have endured as popular songs. However, that is not the case with the blues; one of the most famous blues songs of all, "St. Louis Blues" (1914), has a tango in the minor mode as its first section.

Several Argentinian tangos retained their popularity for dancing into the 1990s, using their original

Spanish words; these include "La Cumparsita" (1916) and "Caminito" (1936). The first section of a famous tango, "Adios Muchachos" (1929), was given English lyrics in 1951 as "I Get Ideas."

Many European tangos were written between the wars, and some reached these shores. One of the most famous was "Jalousie," written by the Danish composer Jacob Gade and given English lyrics in 1925. Several tangos from Austria, Germany, and other European countries were given English words and became popular in America; they include "I Kiss Your Hand, Madame" (1929), "Take Me in Your Arms" (1932), and "Love—What Are You Doing to My Heart?" (1933).

American composers took up the challenge of writing tangos as well. Two of the most successful were Sigmund Romberg—who wrote "Softly as in a Morning Sunrise" for his operetta *The New Moon* (1928)—and Vincent Youmans, whose "Orchids in the Moonlight," from the musical film *Flying Down to Rio* (1933), has an authentic Argentinian sound (even though the film was set in Brazil). Other popular American-made tangos of the 1930s were "Temptation" (1933), "You and the Night and the Music" (1934), and "The Moon Was Yellow" (1934).

It also became quite common to insert at least one tango into a musical play. Examples of this practice are "Hernando's Hideaway," from *The Pajama Game* (1954); "Whatever Lola Wants," from *Damn Yankees* (1955); and "The Rain in Spain," from *My Fair Lady* (1956). The 1977 musical *Evita*, which is about the Argentinian populist first lady Eva Perón, appropriately contains two tangos: "Don't Cry for Me, Argentina" and "On This Night of a Thousand Stars."

Bibliography

Roberts, John Storm. *The Latin Tinge: The Impact of Latin American Music on the United States.* 1985.

See also: Cuba; Latin America; Mexico; Rumba

TEARS. SEE CRYING

TELEPHONES

Alexander Graham Bell's invention of 1876 has inspired hundreds of songwriters for over one hundred years. Songs have been written about the telephone almost from the day of its invention and have continued to be written into the 1990s. Two of the most popular songs about the instrument (in two different centuries) were Ida Emerson and Joseph E. Howard's **ragtime** song "Hello! Ma Baby" (1899)—which features a picture of an antique mouthpiece and receiver on the cover of its sheet music—and Stevie Wonder's pop-rock hit "I Just Called to Say I Love You" (1984).

Charles K. Harris's "Hello, Central, Give Me Heaven" (1901) was a sentimental piece inspired by a newspaper report about a little girl who had lost her mother and called the telephone operator to speak to her mother in heaven. Like many other famous songs of its day, it had a sequel during World War I: "Hello, Central, Give Me No Man's Land" (1918).

The titles of several songs are actual telephone numbers. "Pennsylvania 6-5000," for example, was the number of the Hotel Pennsylvania in New York City. (It remained the telephone number of all other hotels at that site through the years.) The song was introduced in 1940 by Glenn Miller and His Orchestra, with its title sung in unison by the band members. Another telephone number, "Beechwood 4-5789," is the title of a song featured by the Marvelettes in 1962.

The telephone is also widely used in lyrics. The protagonist of Irving Berlin's "All Alone" (1924) is not only "all alone," but also "by the telephone." A British import of 1935, "These Foolish Things (Remind Me of You)," contains the memorable line: "A telephone that rings, but who's to answer?"

Among other songs about the telephone are at least a dozen entitled simply "Call Me." Of these, perhaps the most popular was British, written by Tony Hatch in 1965. It was subsequently used in Bell Telephone Systems radio and television commercials.

Additional Songs

Call Me (1980)
Don't Hang Up (1963)
Hello Frisco Hello (1915)
Hot Line (1977)
Operator (1975)
Telephone Line (1976)

See also: Farewells; Greetings; Talking

TELEVISION

Although invented during the 1920s, television did not become commercially available until shortly after World War II. Its initial success prompted a shift in many aspects of the entertainment industry. Popular music, long an important part of **radio**, played a key role in the new medium. By featuring the latest songs and performers, television became an important means of promotion. At the same time, songs associated with specific television shows received enough attention to become successful in their own right.

That early television patterned itself after radio is not surprising when one considers that the companies responsible for programming (NBC, CBS, and ABC) also developed television programming. Previously successful radio shows such as *Your Hit Parade* and radio formats like the fifteen-minute musical interlude (e.g., *Music Hall*, hosted by Patti Page) were adapted to television. Also popular were musical variety shows, hosted by such **singers** as Frank Sinatra, Nat "King"

Cole, and Judy Garland, who often appeared on television during the late 1950s and early 1960s.

While *Your Hit Parade* featured the top hits of the day, it was geared toward a general audience. On the other hand, *Paul Whiteman's Teen Club* aimed for a younger crowd. But it was only later in the 1950s that such shows as Alan Freed's *The Big Beat* and Dick Clark's *American Bandstand* capitalized on rock 'n' roll's emerging popularity and acceptance. Rock's influence within the entertainment industry had grown considerably by the time *Shindig* and *Hullabaloo*, two shows featuring such contemporary performers as Herman's Hermits and the Righteous Brothers, debuted in 1964. During the 1970s, rock programming continued in the form of *The Midnight Special*, hosted by Wolfman Jack (Robert Smith), and *Don Kirshner Presents*.

Television often popularized songs closely linked to specific programs. During the early 1960s, the teen-aged actors of several sitcoms had commercially successful songs that were helped by their television exposure. Shelley Fabares (*The Donna Reed Show*) had a hit with "Johnny Angel" in 1962, while Ricky Nelson (*The Adventures of Ozzie and Harriet*) had one with "Hello, Mary Lou" (1961). Later in the 1960s, Don Kirshner further exploited the youth-oriented music market with the creation of two television shows: *The Monkees*, which generated many Top Forty records including "Last Train to Clarksville" and "I'm a Believer" (both 1966), and *The Archies*, an animated cartoon series revolving around the activities of a fictitious band, which had a Number One song titled "Sugar, Sugar" (1969). Following the success of these made-for-TV groups, *The Partridge Family*, a situation comedy about a family that becomes a successful rock 'n' roll act, featured many songs, including the hit "I Think I Love You" (1970).

Sometimes the theme song of a program was as popular as the show it introduced. While some, such as "The Fishin' Hole" (the theme from *The Andy Griffith Show* [1961]), received only a high degree of recognition, others entered the pop charts. Indeed, many of the industry's top songwriters have written television themes. Lalo Schifrin won a Grammy Award for his "Mission: Impossible" theme (1966). Mort Stevens' "Hawaii Five O" was a Top Forty hit in 1969, as was Leon Gamble and Kenny Huff's "T.S.O.P. (The Sound of Philadelphia)," from *Soul Train* (1973). Norman Gimbel and Charles Fox wrote a variety of recognizable themes, including "Making Our Dreams Come True" from *Laverne and Shirley* (1976), "Different Worlds," from *Angie* (1979), and "Happy Days" (1974). Mike Post performed many of the themes he wrote or co-wrote including "Believe It or Not," from *The Greatest American Hero* (1981); "The Rockford Files" (1974); and the "Theme From *Hill Street Blues*" (1980). Other popular songs from television include "Song From M*A*S*H* (Suicide Is Painless)" (1970, originally written for the

film) and "Those Were the Days," or "Theme From *All in the Family*" (1971).

Television advertisements also featured popular songs and "jingles": "Chiquita Banana" (1946) was a well-known radio advertisement that was later used on television. Another song, "I'd Like to Teach the World to Sing" (1971), was a chart hit for both the New Seekers and the Hillside Singers. It too started out as a jingle: "(I'd Like to Buy the World a Coke)," also performed by the Hillside Singers.

Other television ads used songs that were already popular. Sometimes, as in Carly Simon's "Anticipation" (used for a catsup commercial in 1971), the advertiser sought a more contemporary sound. Other times, a more nostalgic image was fostered by the utilization of an older song. For example, one soft drink company featured the 1937 song "Bei Mir Bist du Schön (Means That You're Grand)" in an ad campaign that ran during the 1970s. Also, the Beatles' "Help!" of 1965 was used to sell automobiles during the mid-1980s, when the pace of using older songs for advertising purposes accelerated.

As cable television became more available during the late 1970s, many new networks were formed in order to cater to specific viewer tastes. One such network, Nickelodeon, was designed to appeal to young children. With the help of Michael Nesmith, president of the Pacific Arts Corporation, John Lack and Robert Pittman, the executives in charge of Nickelodeon, developed a series of "videos" (visual depictions of popular songs) for a show titled *Pop Clips*. The success of this show prompted Lack and Pittman to expand this concept into a separate network, MTV, which first aired in 1981.

MTV's subsequent success ushered in a new generation of popular music. Many performers took advantage of the new venue by creating songs that were not only aurally, but also visually captivating. The characteristically fast-paced, nonlinear collage of images associated with MTV video was notably used by such performers as Toni Basil, in "Mickey" (1979), the Vapors in "Turning Japanese" (1979), and Duran Duran in "Hungry Like the Wolf" (1983). Songs such as Michael Jackson's "Billie Jean" (1982) and Paula Abdul's "Straight Up" (1988), both of which had videos featuring spectacular dancing, were ideally suited for this medium. Other performers used a more provocative approach in the visual depiction of their songs. Madonna's "Express Yourself" (1989) and "Justify My Love" (1990) received much attention due to their depictions of sexuality.

Since 1981, other networks have aired shows that feature music videos—NBC's *Friday Night Videos* is one example—but no one else has dominated the video phenomenon like MTV, which eventually expanded into a separate network, VH-1, in 1985. Although the musical variety shows that promoted popular songs virtually disappeared, shows such as *American Bandstand* and *Soul Train* were still broadcast throughout the 1980s. Songs associated with some shows, such as Jan Hammer's "Miami Vice Theme" (1984), continued to reach the pop charts; other songs, like *Married With Children*'s "Love and Marriage" (1955), had become popular long before the show's run.

Ehrick V. Long

Bibliography

Brooks, Tim, and Earle Marsh. *The Complete Directory to Prime Time Network TV Shows 1946—Present*, 4th ed. 1989.

Denisoff, R. Serge. *Inside MTV*. 1988.

Kaplan, E. Ann. *Rocking Around the Clock: Music Television, Postmodernism, and Consumer Culture*. 1989.

Shore, Michael. *The Rolling Stone Book of Rock Video*. 1984.

TEMPO

In popular song, speeds of performance cover a broad spectrum from very slow (Largo) to very fast (Presto). Tempos are seldom fixed and vary according to the performer's interpretation. Very often, songs are played or sung in tempos far removed from those originally conceived by their creators. This is especially true in **jazz** performance, where slow **ballads** like "Out of Nowhere" (1931) and "The Song Is You" (1932) are often performed in fast tempo. Many originally slow or moderate songs are also often played for dancing in **society tempo**.

Four general classes of tempo can be distinguished in popular music: slow, moderately slow, uptempo, and very fast; but within these classes there are an infinite number of gradations. Slow ballads are usually marked "Slowly," sometimes with a qualifier such as "with expression" or "with sentiment"—examples are "Moonglow" (1934), "Here's That Rainy Day" (1953), and "I Left My Heart in San Francisco" (1954).

Moderately slow songs are often captioned "Moderately," as in "One Morning in May" (1933). However, that marking can apply equally well to uptempo songs (see below). Jerome Kern, who was fond of the traditional Italian tempo markings, used "Andantino semplice" and "Andante quasi allegretto" for his moderately slow songs "The Song Is You" (1932) and "Yesterdays" (1933). Kern combined two languages in his tempo marking for "Can't Help Lovin' Dat Man" (1927): "Tempo di Blues (slowly)." One of the few accurately marked songs in this tempo is Stuart Gorrell and Hoagy Carmichael's "Georgia on My Mind," which is marked "Moderately Slow."

"Uptempo" is a rather vague term used almost exclusively in popular performance to designate a tempo other than very slow or very fast. It roughly covers the entire range of moderato, allegretto, and allegro. Examples are "Baby, Won't You Please Come Home" (1923), which is marked "Medium Bounce"; Kern's "I've Told Ev'ry Little Star" (1932), marked "Allegretto grazioso"; and the 1942 big band song "I've Got a Gal in Kalamazoo," marked "Moderate Swing." Uptempo songs were often not written as such. Rodgers and Hart's "Mimi" (1932), usually played molto allegro, is marked "very gaily, but in moderate tempo"; while their "The Lady Is a Tramp" (1937)—almost always performed "allegro"—is marked "gaily, but not fast." Many of Rodgers and Hart's tempo markings, in fact, give little indication of the desired tempo: "The Girl Friend" (1926) bears the caption "Joyously"; "Thou Swell" (1927) is marked "Calmly"; and "You Took Advantage of Me" (1928), "Gracefully."

Very fast tempo is reserved for certain dances, including the **Peabody,** the **polka,** the **merengue,** and a variety of **disco** and **rock** numbers.

Many pieces have no tempo markings of any kind. At the other extreme are songs with specific metronome markings. These were exceedingly rare until the late 1970s. They appear in such songs as "It Might Be You," the theme from the film *Tootsie* (1982)—which is marked: "Slowly ♩ = 92"; and "Against All Odds." from the film of the same name (1984), marked "Slow Rock ♩ = 56."

Apart from the nonexistent and the specific there are an almost infinite number of verbal tempo markings in popular song, including "Expressively," "With Feeling," "Mournfully," "Medium Beat (4)," "Molto Moderato," "Brightly," "Lively," "Fast Fox Trot," and "Fast Rock." All should be taken with caution.

See also: Fox Trot; Meter

TENDERNESS

One of the earliest songs on the subject of tenderness, the 1932 ballad "Try a Little Tenderness," is characterized by a slowly rising and falling melody evocative of gentleness. The song has been revived several times over the years: in 1967 by Otis Redding and, appropriately enough, in a 1980 advertising campaign for Perdue Chicken. The song "Tenderly," notable for the jagged contour of its melody, originated as a waltz in 1946. It remains a hardy perennial as both waltz and fox trot.

The 1955 song "The Tender Trap," from the film of the same name, refers of course to **love**. Squarely in the tradition of swing, it was greatly popularized by Frank Sinatra. A year later, another singer, Elvis Presley, introduced the ballad "Love Me Tender" in the film of the same name. Presley and co-writer Vera Matson adapted it from the 1861 Civil War song "Aura Lee."

Similar ideas are expressed in song using the words "softly" and "gentle." Two Italian-American songs employ the former: "Softly as I Leave You" (1962) and "Speak Softly Love," the latter song adapted from the theme of the 1972 film *The Godfather*. Another example is "Killing Me Softly With His Song," introduced by Roberta Flack in 1973. Perhaps the best-known song using the word "gentle" is the 1967 country hit "Gentle on My Mind."

Additional Songs

Break It to Me Gently (1961)
Come Softly to Me (1959)
Dear Hearts and Gentle People (1950)
Rock Me Gently (1974)
Soft Lights and Sweet Music (1932)
Soft Summer Breeze (1955)
Soft, as in a Morning Sunrise (1928)
Speak Low (1943)
Sweet and Gentle (1955)
While My Guitar Gently Weeps (1968)

See also: **Feeling; Moods; Romance; Sentiment**

TEXTURE

The various combinations of voice and instrument used in the performance of popular song are collectively known as texture. Although virtually all songs are written on lead sheets and arranged in sheet music as melody with accompaniment (a type of homophonic texture), many other textures exist in actual performance.

There is, for example, the polyphony of **Dixieland**—with simultaneous melodic lines played in **improvisation** by cornet or trumpet, clarinet, trombone, and other instruments. Then there is heterophony, where two or more versions of the same melody are given simultaneously. This textural style is widespread in all types of popular music from **jazz** to **rock**, especially where the melody is sung and, at the same time, played in an ornamental version by accompanying instruments. A third but rarer type of texture, used to some extent in stage musicals, is **counterpoint** (used in the narrower sense of the term), where two or more melodic lines are sung simultaneously.

In general over the last half century, the musical fabric has tended to broaden in popular song. Sometimes many varieties of texture occur in a single piece. There has also been a notable increase in melody-bass polarization, aided by the growth of electronics and amplification. At the other extreme, in songs like "Nadia's Theme (The Young and the Restless)" (1976) and "The Rose" (1977) the texture is very thin, supporting the melody with the barest minimum of an accompaniment.

In short, all varieties of texture, from monophony (unaccompanied melody) to the densest forms of polyphony, are found in the performance of popular song, a genre which in its written form consists primarily of melody and accompaniment.

See also: **Countermelody; Dynamics; Harmony; Instrumentation; Range; Rhythm**

THINKING

The majority of songs on the subject of thinking have some connection with **love** or **romance**, as demonstrated in titles such as "I May Be Wrong (But I Think You're Wonderful)" (1929), "The Very Thought of You" (1934), "I Concentrate on You" (1939), and "I Think I Love You" (1970). Still deeper thoughts are expressed in songs like "My Reverie" (1938) and "Meditation" (1963).

At the other extreme of thinking are such lighthearted songs as "If I Only Had a Brain" and "Scatterbrain" (both 1939). But the message of one song, written in 1949, is more to the point: "Enjoy Yourself (It's Later Than You Think)."

Additional Songs

Don't Think Twice, It's All Right (1963)
I Still Get a Thrill (Thinking of You) (1930)
I Think of You (1941)
Losing My Mind (1971)
She Is Not Thinking of Me (Waltz at Maxim's) (1958)
Stop and Think It Over (1964)
Think (1957)
Think About Me (1979)
Think of Laura (1984)
Thinking of You (1927)

See also: **Dreams; Madness; Memory; Mind**

TIME

Songs on the subject of time number in the hundreds and include many important **standards**. Perhaps best known is "As Time Goes By" (1931), which is essentially a message song, saying that "the fundamental things apply." Other lasting songs about time include: "Any Time" (1921), "Time on My Hands" (1930), "Bidin' My Time" (1930), "I Didn't Know What Time It Was" (1939), "Till the End of Time" (1945), "Time After Time" (1947), "Just in Time" (1956), "A Time for Us"—the love theme from the film *Romeo and Juliet* (1969)—and "Time in a Bottle" (1971).

There are, of course, many songs about specific times, whether they be a **time of day** ("Three O'Clock in the Morning," 1921), a **season** ("Summertime," 1935), or a special moment ("The First Time Ever I Saw Your Face," 1972). There are nostalgic songs as well. Although many of them refer to time in the plural—as in "Seems Like Old Times" (1946), "For the Good Times" (1968), and "Times of Your Life" (1974)—some, like "Time Was" (1941), make reference in the singular.

There are, in addition, songs about hours ("My Shining Hour," 1943), minutes ("Minute by Minute," 1978), moments ("From This Moment On," 1950), and special times of the **day** ("Twilight Time," 1944).

Additional Songs

After All This Time (1988)
By the Time I Get to Phoenix (1967)
Crying Time (1964)
Ev'ry Time We Say Goodbye (1944)
Five Minutes More (1946)
Get Me to the Church on Time (1956)
Give Me Just a Little More Time (1970)
Green-Up Time (1948)
A Hot Time in the Old Town (1896)
If I Could Be With You One Hour To-Night (1926)
I'll Be With You in Apple Blossom Time (1910)
It's Been a Long, Long Time (1945)
It's Too Late (1971)
Jeannine, I Dream of Lilac Time (1928)
The Last Time I Saw Paris (1940)
Let the Good Times Roll (1946)
Long Ago (And Far Away) (1944)
Magic Moments (1958)
Maybe This Time (1966)
Moments to Remember (1955)
My Time Is Your Time (1924)
Nick of Time (1989)
Now Is the Hour (1948)
(Potatoes Are Cheaper, Tomatoes Are Cheaper) Now's the
    Time to Fall in Love (1931)
Once in a Lifetime (1961)
Once in a While (1937)
Once Upon a Time (1962)
(I'd Love to Spend) One Hour With You (1932)
One Moment Alone (1931)
One Moment in Time (1987)
The Second Time Around (1960)
Sometimes I'm Happy (1927)
Soon (1929)
Soon (Maybe Not Tomorrow) (1935)
Soon It's Gonna Rain (1960)
Sooner or Later (I Always Get My Man) (1990)
This Magic Moment (1960)
Time Is on My Side (1963)
(I've Had) The Time of My Life (1987)
The Times They Are A-Changin' (1963)
Turn Back the Hands of Time (1970)
When It's Sleepy Time Down South (1931)
Younger Than Springtime (1949)

See also: **Days of the Week; Months; Night**

TIME OF DAY

The morning hours are the favorite times of day re-
ferred to in popular song. This preference goes back a
long way; "Happy Birthday to You," after all, was
originally written in 1892 as "Good Morning to All."
Among other songs having to do with the morning are
"At Dawning" (1906), "Oh How I Hate to Get Up in the
Morning" (1918), "Carolina in the Morning" (1922),
"Softly, as in a Morning Sunrise" (1918), "Oh What a
Beautiful Mornin'" (1943), "Come Saturday Morning"
(1969), "Morning Has Broken" (1971), and "September

Morn" (1978).

Specific times of the morning, especially the very
early hours, appear in song as well. In this category are
Count Basie's "One O'Clock Jump" (1938), the waltz
"Three O'Clock in the Morning" (1921), and Johnny
Mercer and Harold Arlen's "One for My Baby (And
One More for the Road)" (1943), which begins with the
words: "It's quarter to three." "(In the) Wee Small Hours
(Of the Morning)," popularized by Frank Sinatra in
1955, nicely sums up this tendency.

The afternoon, by contrast, can claim relatively few
songs, among them the 1902 waltz "On a Sunday
Afternoon," the theme from the film *High Noon* (1952),
also known as "Do Not Forsake Me" and the languid
ballad "Lazy Afternoon" (1954). Late afternoon, in
particular, is represented by several songs, including
"At Sundown" (1927), "Red Sails in the Sunset" (1935),
"Twilight Time" (1944), and "Canadian Sunset" (1956).

One song, "Sunrise, Sunset" (1964), neatly defines
the beginning and ending times of the **day**. Dolly
Parton's hit "9 to 5," from the 1981 film of the same
name, delineates a typical working day, the end of
which is signalled by the device mentioned in a 1940
song: "The Five O'Clock Whistle."

Songs about the evening and the **night** form a
category of their own. One special time of evening,
which used to be the traditional starting time for a
Broadway show, is the subject of "About a Quarter to
Nine," a song introduced by Al Jolson in the 1935 film
Casino de Paree. Another specific time of night, midnight,
is the subject of a number of songs, including "Midnight
in Moscow" (1961), "Midnight Cowboy" (1969), and
"Midnight Train to Georgia" (1971).

There is, in addition, one song which literally
encompasses all hours of the day (and night): "(We're
Gonna) Rock Around the Clock," performed by Bill
Haley and the Comets in the 1955 film *The Blackboard
Jungle,* begins with the words: "One, two, three o'clock,
four o'clock rock," and goes on from there.

Additional Songs

Angel of the Morning (1967)
A Beautiful Morning (1968)
Dawn (Go Away) (1964)
Daybreak (1942)
Delta Dawn (1973)
Does Anybody Really Know What Time It Is? (1969)
Early in the Morning (1969)
Five O'Clock World (1965)
Good Morning, Good Morning (1967)
Good Morning Heartache (1946)
Good Morning, Starshine (1969)
I Got the Sun in the Morning (1946)
In the Midnight Hour (1966)
Midnight Blue (1974)
Midnight Sun (1947)
Mornin' (1983)
The Morning After (1973)

Morning Train (Nine to Five) (1981)
One Morning in May (1933)
Quarter to Three (1961)
'Round Midnight (1944)
Sunday Mornin' (1967)
Sunrise Serenade (1938)
Touch Me in the Morning (1972)
Twelve Thirty (Young Girls Are Comin' to the Canyon) (1967)
Twilight on the Trail (1936)
When the Midnight Choo-Choo Leaves for Alabam' (1912)
The World Is Waiting for the Sunrise (1919)

See also: Days of the Week; Time

TIN PAN ALLEY

The term "Tin Pan Alley" has come to represent the popular music business in general. More specifically, however, it refers to various centers of the music publishing industry that sprang up in New York City from the 1890s through the 1950s. These locations tended gradually to move northward, along with the growth of the city. In the 1890s, publishers' offices centered about Union Square, at 14th Street. Around 1900 they moved to the block of West 28th Street between Broadway and Sixth Avenue. Beginning in the 1920s, most publishers' offices were gathered around Times Square, on Broadway and its surrounding streets between 42nd and 50th Streets. By the mid-1940s the heaviest concentration of publishers was in the Brill Building, at Broadway and 49th Street.

The name itself has an interesting origin. It was coined by songwriter Monroe H. Rosenfeld, who in 1900 was asked to write an article for the New York Herald about the publishers and songwriters then congregating on West 28th Street. Hearing the cacophonous sound of the many upright pianos emanating from the buildings—made tinnier by strips of newspaper used to muffle the strings—Rosenfeld likened it to the clatter of tin pans.

The somewhat frivolous name, however, masked serious commercial endeavor; the purpose of Tin Pan Alley was to make money. Music publishers, many of whom started out as salesmen in other fields, concentrated on marketing their wares—in this case, sheet music—in innovative ways. They hired song pluggers to demonstrate new songs to the public as well as to professional entertainers in vaudeville and other types of musical theater. Many songwriters, including Irving Berlin, Jerome Kern, and George Gershwin, began their musical careers as song pluggers. Publishers also resorted to subtle and not-so-subtle forms of bribery in order to get songs performed, long before the practice was called "payola."

Even before it had a name, Tin Pan Alley produced many hits. One of the first, Charles K. Harris's "After the Ball," sold $5 million worth of sheet music in 1892.

Like many other songs of its day, it tells a melodramatic tale of misunderstanding in a series of verses, each followed by a reiterated chorus, or refrain. Among early Alley hits were other waltzes like "The Bowery" (1892), "Daisy Bell" (1892), and "The Sidewalks of New York" (1894). Also popular were so-called coon songs, like "A Hot Time in the Old Town" (1896), "Bill Bailey, Won't You Please Come Home?," and "Under the Bamboo Tree" (1902).

In the first decade of the new century, George M. Cohan brought new life to Tin Pan Alley in his use of the vernacular. His songs "Give My Regards to Broadway" (1904), "The Yankee Doodle Boy" (1904), "Mary's a Grand Old Name" (1905), and "You're a Grand Old Flag" (1906) were hits of the day. Other songwriters, such as Shelton Brooks in "Some of These Days" (1910) and Joseph McCarthy and James V. Monaco in "You Made Me Love You" (1913), managed to combine the coon song with the sentimental ballad. The success of Irving Berlin's "Alexander's Ragtime Band" in 1911 led to a vogue for ragtime songs. Songwriters, including Berlin himself, wrote them by the hundreds. Shortly thereafter it was the turn of the blues, brought to the Alley by W. C. Handy in two famous songs: "The Memphis Blues" (1912) and "St. Louis Blues" (1914).

With the success of Jerome Kern's landmark ballad "They Didn't Believe Me" (with lyrics by Herbert Reynolds) in 1914, the main product of Tin Pan Alley became standardized: a thirty-two-bar ballad on the subject of love. This formula, most often in AABA or some related form, became the norm through the 1950s. Many of America's most innovative and enduring standards were written in the face of these seeming constraints.

The golden age of Tin Pan Alley lasted from about 1924 to 1945, coinciding with the Roaring Twenties, the Depression Years, and World War II. A roll call of those years might include the following songs: "Tea for Two" (1924), "Always" (1925), "Tiptoe Through the Tulips" (1926), "My Blue Heaven" (1927), "If I Had You" (1928), "Star Dust" (1929), "Tip Toe Through The Tulips With Me" (1929), "Body and Soul" (1930), "As Time Goes By" (1931), "How Deep Is the Ocean?" (1932), "Don't Blame Me" (1933), "Blue Moon" (1934), "Pennies From Heaven" (1936), "Once in a While" (1937), "I'll Be Seeing You" (1938), "What's New?" (1939), "How High the Moon" (1940), "I Understand" (1941), "You'll Never Know" (1943), and "The More I See You" (1945). Although some of these songs were introduced in the musical theater or in film musicals, most of them were published on Tin Pan Alley, and all adhere to the Alley formula.

As radio and recording became more important than sheet music in the dissemination of popular song, Tin Pan Alley began to disintegrate. Many publishers became parts of large conglomerates, active in recording or film production. The growth of **rock 'n' roll** and **country and western** music led to new methods of music publication and distribution. Such far-flung cities as Nashville, Detroit, and Los Angeles became publishing centers. Although some music publishers stayed in New York City, the glorious days of Tin Pan Alley were gone. Only the songs remain.

Bibliography

Ewen, David. *The Life and Death of Tin Pan Alley: The Golden Age of American Popular Music.* 1964.

Furia, Philip. *Poets of Tin Pan Alley: A History of America's Greatest Lyricists.* 1990.

Goldberg, Isaac. *Tin Pan Alley: A Chronicle of American Popular Music.* 1961.

Hamm, Charles E. *Yesterdays: Popular Song in America.* 1979.

Marks, Edward Bennet. *They All Sang: From Tony Pastor to Rudy Vallee.* 1934.

Shepherd, John. *Tin Pan Alley.* 1982.

Spaeth, Sigmund Gottfried. *A History of Popular Music in America.* 1948.

Whitcomb, Ian. *After the Ball: Pop Music From Rag to Rock.* 1974.

TOGETHERNESS

At least two distinct types of togetherness are celebrated in popular song: **friendship and love.** That "good fellows" getting together was a common activity around the turn of the century and shortly thereafter is attested to in several famous songs: "It's Always Fair Weather When Good Fellows Get Together" (also known as "A Stein Song"), written in 1898; "Hail, Hail, the Gang's All Here" (1917); "That Old Gang of Mine" (1923); and its sequel, "Wedding Bells Are Breaking Up That Old Gang of Mine" (1929). Of similar nature is the 1933 song "Marching Along Together," made famous by Kate Smith. Later songs about companionship are somewhat more sinister, including "Chain Gang" (1960) and "Leader of the Pack" (1964).

Far more prevalent, however, are songs about **lovers** getting together. One of the best known is the 1928 waltz entitled simply "Together." Another is "Alone Together," a striking song in the minor mode from the 1932 revue *Flying Colors*. Other memorable songs on the subject are the 1940 ballad "We Could Make Such Beautiful Music (Together)"; Frankie Laine's theme song of 1945, "We'll Be Together Again"; and "Love Will Keep Us Together," popularized in 1975 by the Captain and Tennille.

Additional Songs

Cocktails for Two (1934)
Come Together (1969)
A Couple of Swells (1947)
The Folks Who Live on the Hill (1937)
Get Together (1963)
Just the Two of Us (1981)
Let's Stay Together (1972)
The Little Things You Do Together (1970)
No Two People (1951)
The Odd Couple (1968)
Sharing the Night Together (1978)
Side by Side (1927)
Side by Side by Side (1970)
Takes Two to Tango (1952)
Tea for Two (1924)
Together Wherever We Go (1959)
Togetherness (1960)
Two Cigarettes in the Dark (1934)
(Theme From) Two for the Road (1967)
Two Hearts in Three Quarter Time (1930)
Two Sleepy People (1938)

See also: **Enduring Love; Falling in Love; Marriage; Romance**

TOMORROW. SEE DAY

TONALITY

In the first half of the twentieth century, the vast majority of popular songs had definite tonal centers, revolving around the tonic and its closest relatives, the dominant and subdominant. Such seeming diversions of tonality as did occur could be ascribed to the adventuresome **modulations** of composers like Jerome Kern and Richard Rodgers.

A general loosening of tonal parameters began in the 1950s. For example, the song "Unforgettable," immortalized by Nat "King" Cole in 1951, starts in the **key** of G major and, with a key signature of one sharp, seems to be rooted in that tonality. Nevertheless, it ends solidly (and logically) in the key of C major.

The 1960s saw an acceleration of this tendency. John Lennon and Paul McCartney's "Michelle" (1966) has a key signature of one flat (D minor), but is in the tonality of D major throughout; it ends with a half **cadence** on A major. Jim Webb's "By the Time I Get to Phoenix" (1967), in the key of D major, ends with a B major chord. George Harrison's "Something" (1969) has a bipolar tonality, vacillating between B-flat and G major.

No tonal center at all can be found in Webb's "Up, Up and Away," of 1967. The song passes through a remarkable succession of keys—G major, B-flat major, D-flat major, A major—and ends somewhat ambiguously by fading away with chords alternating between A major and F major. The same writer's "MacArthur Park," of 1968, also passes through a series of unrelated keys.

In the "Theme From Mahogany (Do You Know Where You're Going To?)," written in 1973, there are two main tonal centers, C major and E-flat major. However, the piece as a whole modulates through many keys: G-flat major, E-flat major, C major, E-flat major, C major, E-flat major, C major, A major, G-flat major, before ending on E-flat major.

A common device in **arrangements** of popular songs is to raise the key of the final chorus (the so-called sock chorus in the days of the big bands). This effective modulation is often carried over to the songs themselves. In Harold Arlen's "One for My Baby (And One More for the Road)" (1943), for example, the first A section is in the key of E-flat major, while the following sections are all in G major.

Effective key changes became a hallmark of many songs to follow. Jacques Brel's "Marieke" (1968) moves up a half step from A major to B-flat major; "Mandy" (1971) ascends from B-flat major to C major; "After the Lovin'" (1974), from C major to D-flat major; "I Write the Songs" (1974), from F major to A major. In the 1974 song "My Eyes Adored You," the tonality is raised three times: from A major to B-flat major, and then again to B major and C major.

Rising tonalities are something of a mannerism in many songs composed by Andrew Lloyd Webber, including "Memory," from *Cats* (1981); "The Point of No Return" and "Think of Me," from *The Phantom of the Opera* (1986); and "Anything But Lonely" and "Love Changes Everything," from *Aspects of Love* (1989).

See also: Harmony; Interval; Scale

TOP FORTY

The term "Top Forty" is used to describe most commercial formats in **radio** music programming since the 1950s. Devised by Todd Storz in 1953 and modified by Bill Drake in 1965, the innovative Top Forty approach to radio music became a quick success. Once the format of AM radio only, various versions of Top Forty programming came to dominate airplay on both AM and FM.

The "philosophy" of Top Forty is that listeners prefer to hear both current hits and familiar music, and that the medium of music radio is necessarily organized demographically. Hence, the format consists of a relatively small playlist. In actuality, the "forty" in Top Forty is an approximation, a guideline, not a strict limit, primarily featuring currently charted songs. Within this restricted rotation, the few top songs of the day are played even more frequently, thus assuring listeners frequent play of the hottest hits, sprinkled with the powerful appeal of nostalgia by the inclusion of an occasional classic oldie. As Top Forty came to mean **rock 'n' roll** rather than pop, the playlist was heard within a frenzied mixture of fast-talking **disc jockeys**, publicity stunts, identification jingles, and advertisements.

In the medium's early history, stations programmed a broad variety of shows, aimed at the widest spectrum of listeners. Some material was supplied to affiliates by the network; other shows originated locally. A station's regular programming usually included live music of several types (e.g., classical, swing, country), as well as live drama, news, and comedy. In short, variety was the common theme.

But with the introduction of commercial **television** in the early 1950s, radio formats shifted away from spoken entertainment, which the new visual medium could exploit much more successfully. Yet live music performed by in-studio bands was expensive, and of course this was one of the reasons why the **big bands** began to fold in the postwar era. Record companies, initially thinking that consumers would be less inclined to buy records if they heard them on the radio, had by this time altered that view. Radio and the **recording** industry discovered a convenient reciprocity: the former received free programming from record companies; the latter, free advertising for their new products.

When rock 'n' roll developed in the mid-1950s, Top Forty conveniently provided a contemporaneous development that proved perfectly suited to the music and its new demographic audience of teenagers. Having more leisure time in the affluent Eisenhower decade than ever before, this age group frequently determined what stations the family radio would be tuned to. Moreover, the development of the transistor radio in the same period meant that young people could take their music with them outside the home or the car. So AM stations battled intensely with each other from the late 1950s through the mid-1960s, sponsoring contests and promotional stunts, even experimenting with a somewhat expanded playlist in the hope of creating regional hits.

However, the format proved relatively restrictive, attempting to appeal to the largest possible audience of record buyers even as the music itself was separating into radically distinct styles and accompanying subcultures. Thus Top Forty prompted an inevitable negative reaction from the growing number of more discerning listeners.

This reaction was prompted by dramatic developments in **rock** music in the mid-1960s, beginning with the "British invasion" by bands like the Beatles and the Rolling Stones, and then the San Francisco psychedelic sound promulgated by artists like the Jefferson Airplane and the Grateful Dead. Even the Beach Boys, emblematic of an earlier and simpler, more pastoral period of rock, moved from surf music to sophisticated electronic experimentation, as in "Good Vibrations" (1966). The ambitions of many of these musicians was signalled by their foray into extended composition; both the Stones, on their 1966 long-playing record (LP) *Aftermath*, and the Doors, on their eponymous 1967 debut album, included songs that were over eleven minutes in length. Other bands, such as the Mothers of Invention, Iron Butterfly, and Vanilla Fudge, regularly included songs on their LPs that exceeded the conventional three-minute limit of the pop 45rpm record.

Previously, the LP had been conceived largely as a follow-up to a hit single, a way of selling more product by the artist of a charted song. Hence albums frequently tended to be comprised largely of "filler." With the Beatles' *Sgt. Pepper's Lonely Hearts Club Band* in June 1967, the concept album and the idea of rock as art was emphatically established.

Top Forty stations, steadfastly maintaining their format, included in their playlist some of this material—if, of course, it was charted. But because of their restrictive philosophy and the limited length of the 45rpm single, most of these songs could not be played in their entirety. Thus, for example, Dylan's "Like a Rolling Stone" (1965) was divided into two parts on the 45 release version, Top Forty stations playing only Part One, which ended with an awkward fade; other songs, such as Cream's "Sunshine of Your Love" and the Doors' "Light My Fire" (both 1967), were crammed onto 45s by lifting out the instrumental solos and leaving only the vocal choruses. If one wanted to hear the song in its entirety, one had to buy the LP or turn to the more experimental, less restrictive programming beginning to find its way onto the FM band.

This problem was alleviated to some extent by the extended play (EP) 45rpm record, which ran to five minutes and twenty seconds, as against the LP's three minutes and could thus provide either more songs or longer songs. Hundreds of millions of these records sold in the early 1950s, particularly those of Frank Sinatra.

In the major metropolitan areas, FM owners picked up on the growing disparity between rock music and the Top Forty format and the consequent dissatisfaction of many AM listeners, and responded with more eclectic and experimental programming. Not only rock, but also folk, fusion, **jazz**, and **blues** were played, and disc jockeys became more muted, emphasizing the music rather than their own manic patter. Since songs were played in their entirety, and the playlist was not restricted to the current hits, the LP rather than the 45 record became the standard for these FM stations. Moreover, FM's stereo signal allowed for more faithful reproduction of the elaborate production values that were now becoming standard in rock recording. Thus album-oriented rock (AOR) was born, in stark opposition to Top Forty. Eventually, however, Top Forty responded by switching from the AM to the FM band.

By the mid-1960s, rock music consisted of an amazing variety of genres: **Motown**, **rhythm and blues**, pop ballads, **folk rock**, psychedelic rock, **novelty songs**, and hard rock all appeared together on the charts and thus in Top Forty playlists. But by the 1970s, the audience for popular music had become fragmented into smaller, more clearly defined segments: **heavy metal**, **country and western**, easy listening, **soul**, and so on. "Narrow-casting" developed as an attempt to attract these clearly defined groups of listeners. Furthermore, as rock's early listeners were aging, they were finding it harder to relate to some of the newer musical forms such as **disco** and **punk**. Consequently, hits of the past—always mixed lightly into the Top Forty playlist—became more important, and many stations switched formats, concentrating exclusively on the nostalgia value of "oldies."

Yet Top Forty has survived—albeit with a more acceptable designation, Contemporary Hit Radio—finding its niche amidst keen competition and a multiplicity of "narrow-casting" formats. However, whether the approach represents the commercialization of music radio in an extreme form—a rigid formula that shapes consumer desire, aesthetic sensibility, and purchasing choices—or provides a democratic forum whereby listeners determine the **hits**—in a sense, a paradigm of capitalist business practices, where the fittest survive—remains a matter of debate.

Barry Keith Grant

Bibliography

Barnes, Ken. "Top 40 Radio: A Fragment of the Imagination." In *Facing the Music*, ed. Simon Frith. 1988.

See also: **Tin Pan Alley; Your Hit Parade**

TORCH SONG

A torch song is an emotional **ballad** about a **love** that is usually unreciprocated. When Helen Morgan perched atop a piano, and in a tear-stained voice sang "He's just my Bill, an ordinary boy," she was singing a torch song: "Bill," from Oscar Hammerstein II and Jerome Kern's *Show Boat* of 1927. Those who have heard one of the few available copies of this classic recording are often surprised that instead of the expected low, throaty contralto register, Morgan had a rather thin soprano voice. Yet she managed to project the image of one person carrying a mighty torch for another.

The song "My Man," performed by Fanny Brice in the *Ziegfeld Follies of 1921*, became a model for the kind of tragic, self-pitying piece that came to represent the torch song. Frequently, these songs told the story of a woman "done wrong," sometimes even abused, by her man. (In "My Man," the woman confesses: "He beats me, too.") Seldom did there seem to be the possibility of a happy ending. One of the best-known songs of this type, "Moanin' Low," was introduced by Libby Holman in the first edition of the revue *The Little Show* (1929). It became her theme song thereafter. Ruth Etting was another preeminent torch singer of the time, featuring such songs as "Love Me or Leave Me" (1928) and "Ten Cents a Dance" (1930).

By the early 1930s the label "torch song" began to

appear in song titles, such as "The Torch Song" (1931) and "I've Got to Sing a Torch Song" (1933). "Why Was I Born?," another plaintive example of the genre, was first heard in Hammerstein and Kern's *Sweet Adeline* (1929). "Sentimental and Melancholy," still another example, was specially written for Wini Shaw to sing in the 1937 film *Ready, Willing and Able*. (Shaw had previously introduced the production number "Lullaby of Broadway" in the film *Gold Diggers of Broadway*, 1935.)

One of the most popular of all torch songs, "Stormy Weather," was written by Ted Koehler and Harold Arlen in 1933. This blues-oriented lament has been performed by virtually every female singer; Lena Horne, Ella Fitzgerald, Judy Garland, and Eileen Farrell are among those who have put their personal stamp on the song. In 1941 Arlen, along with Johnny Mercer, wrote another song that became a vehicle for torch singers, "Blues in the Night." Although the male lyrics are better known, Mercer also wrote a female version for long-suffering women to sing, thus carrying on the torch song tradition. In the same year Duke Ellington introduced the torch song "I Got It Bad (And That Ain't Good)," which he had written with Paul Francis Webster. In this plaintive song, the protagonist complains that her man never treats her "sweet and gentle, the way he should."

During the 1930s and 1940s, Billie Holiday co-authored and performed some notable torch songs. In the blues song "Fine and Mellow" (1939), she complains: "My man treats me awful mean." In an autobiographical song of 1946, "Don't Explain" (written with Arthur Herzog, Jr.), she tells her lover not to explain the lipstick on his collar. Another song popularized by Holiday in 1946, "Good Morning Heartache," is a fine example of the brooding loneliness of a mistreated woman; Holiday's version of this song is the definitive one. Although she preferred to be called a jazz singer, Holiday evoked all the emotions of the torch song when she sang such laments as "Lover Man (Oh Where Can You Be?)" in 1942 and "The End of a Love Affair" in 1950.

A torch song classic was written by Ira Gershwin and Harold Arlen for the 1954 film *A Star Is Born*. The song, "The Man That Got Away," was a perfect vehicle for Judy Garland, who was able to wring every bit of sadness out of the piece. Audiences demanded it for the rest of her life. The song soars, fades away, and then explodes. It is no wonder that it has been performed so often. According to Eileen Farrell, "The Man That Got Away" is the song most often performed by students auditioning for her master classes.

Although male singers of torch songs are not unknown, the classic torch song still belongs to the woman who has been wronged or deserted. No one can remain unmoved upon hearing a Cleo Laine or an Eileen Farrell lamenting a lost love in so emotional a

song as DuBose Heyward and George Gershwin's "My Man's Gone Now," from *Porgy and Bess* (1935).

Loonis McGlohon

See also: Crying; Loneliness; Sentiment

TOWNS. *SEE* CITIES

TRAINS

Trains have inspired songs since the first railroad tracks were laid in the early nineteenth century. There have been songs about trackworkers ("I've Been Working on the Railroad," c. 1880), heroic engineers ("Casey Jones," 1909), and disasters ("The Wreck of the Southern Old '97," 1924).

Many train songs try to imitate the clacking of the rails and the whistling of the locomotives by using shuffling **accompaniment** and whistle-like vocal and instrumental passages. Examples are Irving Berlin's "When the Midnight Choo-Choo Leaves for Alabam'" (1912), one of his earliest hits, and Al Dubin and Harry Warren's "Shuffle Off to Buffalo" from the 1932 film *Forty-Second Street*, which glamorized the sleeping car in the first film production number to be set on a train.

Several train songs were popularized by the **big bands** in the early 1940s, including "Tuxedo Junction" (1940), "Chattanooga Choo Choo" (1941), and "On the Atchison, Topeka, and the Santa Fe" (1945). Two slow **blues** songs, "Blues in the Night" (1941) and "Night Train" (1959), correlate lonely train rides with lost loves; both imitate train whistles. The protagonist of the 1964 song "King of the Road" is a hobo who takes the "third box car" on the "midnight train; destination Bangor, Maine." Other songs having to do with trains include "Trains and Boats and Planes" (1964), "Last Train to Clarksville" (1966), "Midnight Train to Georgia" (1971) and "Love Train" (1972).

Two related types of transportation are treated in Billy Strayhorn's "Take the 'A' Train" (1941), about the New York subway, and Hugh Martin and Ralph Blane's "The Trolley Song" (1943), about the St. Louis trolley. Another subway song, "Don't Sleep in the Subway," imported from Britain in 1967, was written with the London subway in mind, but it has enjoyed a universal appeal.

See also: Boating; Travel

TRAVEL

Numerous modes of travel have been the subjects of popular song. They range from **walking** to **boating**, from taking a **train**, subway, or trolley to riding on "a bicycle built for two" with "Daisy Bell" (1892), and even to an outing in "The Surrey With the Fringe on Top" somewhere in the state of *Oklahoma!* (1943). Nor have other forms of transportation—the automobile, the airplane, the balloon—been neglected.

One of the earliest "automobile" songs, the waltz "In My Merry Oldsmobile" (1905), carries a brand name. So does "See the U.S.A. in Your Chevrolet" (1948), which began life as an advertising jingle on Dinah Shore's television show *The Chevrolet Hour*. More generic are the cars used in songs of the open road, like "(Get Your Kicks) On Route 66" (1946) and "Take Me Home Country Roads" (1971).

Airplane songs also go back a long way, at least to 1910, when "Come, Josephine, in My Flying Machine" was an invitation to go "Up she goes" in the newfangled invention. John Denver's 1967 song "Leaving on a Jet Plane," on the other hand, is a song about parting; the singer does not know when he or she will be back again.

Two songs have been written about balloon rides. The waltz "Around the World" taken from the soundtrack of the 1956 film *Around the World in Eighty Days*, is about a fictional trip around the world, partly in a balloon. The lyrics of Jim Webb's "Up, Up and Away" (1967), rhapsodize about floating in a balloon "among the stars together, you and I, For we can fly!"

Additional Songs

Big Yellow Taxi (1975)
Ease On Down the Road (1974)
Fast Car (1988)
He'd Have to Get Under, Get Out and Get Under, to Fix Up His Automobile (1913)
Hit the Road, Jack (1961)
Little Red Corvette (1982)
The Long and Winding Road (1970)
On the Road Again (1979)
The Road to Morocco (1942)
Trains and Boats and Planes (1964)
Travelin' Man (1960)

TREES

Songs about trees form an illustrious company: spanning half a century, from "Trees" (1922) to "Tie a Yellow Ribbon Round the Ole Oak Tree" (1972). The former is a setting of Joyce Kilmer's famous poem, inspired by an oak tree in New Brunswick, New Jersey; the latter, written as a love song about a returning convict, led to the practice—widespread in the 1980s— of tying yellow ribbons around trees until the return of prisoners of war, hostages, or military servicemen.

Songs about trees in general include Rodgers and Hart's "Mountain Greenery" (1926), Lerner and Loewe's "I Talk to the Trees" (1951), and Horst Jankowski's "A Walk in the Black Forest" (1965). As for individual species, apple trees have attracted more than their share of songs, including the 1905 waltz "In the Shade of the Old Apple Tree," the World War II novelty "Don't Sit Under the Apple Tree (With Anyone Else but Me)" (1942), and the English version of the French

waltz "When the World Was Young" (1952)—which begins with Johnny Mercer's unforgettable words: "Ah, the apple trees."

A tropical species is referred to in the 1902 ragtime song "Under the Bamboo Tree," while trees of more temperate climes are the subjects of "The Trail of the Lonesome Pine" (1913) and "Willow Weep for Me" (1932). In 1936, another tropical tree was commemorated in the bolero "Poinciana."

There have also been several songs about leaves. Perhaps the most famous, "Autumn Leaves," was adapted in 1947 from the French song "Les Feuilles Mortes." Among other songs about leaves are "I'm Looking Over a Four Leaf Clover" (1927), "Lullaby of the Leaves" (1932), and "The Green Leaves of Summer" (1960).

Additional Songs

Down Among the Sheltering Palms (1914)
A Tree in the Meadow (1948)
Woodman, Woodman, Spare That Tree (1911)
   See also: **Flowers; Food and Drink**

TRIPLET

A triplet consists of three notes of equal value performed in the time ordinarily allotted to two. The most common varieties found in popular song are based on the half note, quarter note, and eighth note, and are written as follows:

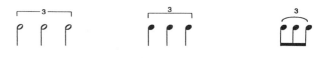

Triplets are especially prevalent in the **melodies** of Cole Porter. For instance, half-note triplets are abundant throughout the chorus of "I Get a Kick Out of You" (1934) at such verbal passages as "flying too high" and "guy in the sky." Another example is the primary motive of "Begin the Beguine" (1935), which consists of a quarter-note triplet followed by a sustained note. The triplets in "I've Got You Under My Skin" (1936) are often accompanied by **repeated notes**, emphasizing the lyrics most appropriately at the words: "Repeats and repeats in my ear."

Of course, other composers have used triplets as important ingredients for their melodies as well. Most common are quarter-note triplets, found in such songs as "Out of Nowhere" (1931) and "What a Diff'rence a Day Made" (1934). In "You Go To My Head" (1938), triplets are used both with repeated notes (in the **release**) and **broken chords** (in the **coda**).

Hoagy Carmichael was among the few composers to favor eighth-note triplets. They are found in two of his "bird" songs: "Skylark" and "Baltimore Oriole" both (1942). Both eighth- and quarter-note triplets are used as building blocks in the latter song, the melody of which is built almost entirely upon triplets.

With the increasing use of compound **meters** after the 1960s, triplets fell somewhat out of use. Songs written in 9/8 meter ("The Impossible Dream," 1965) or 12/8 ("Colour My World," 1972; "Send in the Clowns," 1973; or "Memory," 1981) clearly obviate the need for triplets.

Additional Songs

After the Lovin' (1974)
Don't Worry 'Bout Me (1939)
East of the Sun (And West of the Moon) (1934)
The Good Life (1962)
If We Only Have Love (1968)
Love Me With All Your Heart (1961)

Magic Moments (1957)
Maybe This Time (1966)
Misty (1954)
Penthouse Serenade (When We're Alone) (1931)
What Now My Love? (1962)

TROMBONE, TRUMPET. *SEE* BRASS

TWO-STEP

Next to the **waltz**, the two-step was the most popular social dance of the **Gay Nineties**. It remained so through the first decade of the new century and until around 1913, when it was succeeded by a similar dance called the **fox trot**. It was in duple **meter** and moderate-to-fast **tempo**. At first the two-step was danced to **marches** and **ragtime** songs. However, as the century progressed, it was increasingly danced to such uptempo popular songs as "Bill Bailey, Won't You Please Come Home?" (1902), "You're a Grand Old Flag" (1906), and "Alexander's Ragtime Band" (1911).

See also: **Dance Crazes; Cakewalk; One-Step**

$\mathcal{U}$

UPTEMPO. *SEE* **SOCIETY TEMPO**

$\mathcal{V}$

Vamp

A vamp is a type of **accompaniment**, usually simple, that begins, accompanies, or ends a song. It is very often played by a solo instrument capable of producing chords, such as the **guitar**, banjo, or **piano**, but can also be performed by larger aggregates, even a full orchestra. On the piano, in 4/4 meter, a typical vamp consists of bass notes in octaves on the first and third beats played with the left hand and chords on the second and fourth beats played with the right, in this fashion:

In performance, vamps are traditionally used as introductions to rhythmic ballads and uptempo songs, as opposed to **arpeggios**, which are often used to introduce slow ballads. In **vaudeville**, vamps were often repeated indefinitely until the performer was ready to begin—hence the expression: "Vamp till ready."

In early sheet music, it became the custom to write out vamp-like passages to be repeated by the accompanist until the singer was ready to begin the verse. Very often these are harmonic or melodic paraphrases of the opening material, with such markings as "Vamp" or "Till ready." Such passages are found in "Peg o' My Heart" (1913), "When You Wore a Tulip and I Wore a Big Red Rose" (1914), "Remember" (1925), "M-I-S-S-I-S-S-I-P-P-I" (1916), "At Sundown" (1927), "A Cottage for Sale" (1930), and innumerable other songs. In addition, the vamp is an essential element in much **gospel** music.

Vamps also function as integral parts of many songs, such as "Get Happy" (1930) and "Make Someone Happy" (1960); in the latter song, the vamp also acts as **countermelody**. One famous vamp is the four-bar chromatic passage that introduces "The Continental" (1934), at the words: "Beautiful music! . . . dangerous rhythm!" Another vamp, somewhat offbeat, introduces the chorus of "Lullaby of Broadway" (1935). The famous vamp for "Begin the Beguine" (1935) uses the rhythmic pattern of the **beguine**. Similar vamps are found in many other songs, for example, "Tonight," from *West Side Story* (1957). The insistent vamp of "Something's Coming," also from *West Side Story*, underlies the entire piece, and at the words "Could it be?, Yes it could," it is incorporated into the melody.

John Lennon and Paul McCartney were fond of vamps as well. The four-bar vamp of "And I Love Her" (1964) repeats an introductory four-note motive with chordal accompaniment. "Hey Jude" (1968) ends and fades out with a vamp-like passage sung to the syllables "Da da da—da da da da—da da da da—Hey Jude." A similar device is found in a Stevie Wonder song of the same year, "My Cherie Amour," to the syllables: La la la la la la, La la la la la la."

More elaborate vamps are featured in several songs of the 1970s. The major and minor seventh chords of "One," from *A Chorus Line* (1975), function both as introduction and **fade-out**. Other vamps that are integral parts of their songs include the melodic introduction to "Evergreen" (Love Theme From *A Star Is Born*) (1976) and the repeated triads of the "(Theme From) New York, New York" (1977).

Much simpler vamps, consisting of unaccompanied treble chords, are also found in several songs, like "Nadia's Theme" (1971) and "The Rose" (1977). The latter vamp, the essence of simplicity, consists of only two notes, the tonic (c") and dominant (g"), struck simultaneously. It acts effectively throughout the piece: first as introduction, then as accompaniment, and finally as the song's ending.

See also: Patter

VAUDEVILLE

Vaudeville (the name may have been derived from the French "voix de ville") is a collective term for the variety shows that proliferated all over the United States during the first decades of this century, becoming the prime medium for introducing and popularizing songs.

Vaudeville consisted of a string of specialty acts involving acrobats, animals, dancers, comedians, jugglers, singers, and the like. These acts traveled throughout the country in circuits, the most prominent of which were those of Marcus Loew and Keith-Albee (which later became the United Booking Office). Since acts, once formed, usually remained stabilized throughout each tour, singers and other entertainers became prime targets for aspiring songwriters and song pluggers. It became quite common for the latter to offer monetary and other inducements to stars in return for singing their current songs on the circuit. Indeed, vaudeville, during its heyday, was the most effective method of making a song a hit by constant exposure throughout the land.

Vaudeville grew out of the music hall and the minstrel show in the 1880s and 1890s, largely through the efforts of such entrepreneurs as Tony Pastor, John Koster, and Rudolf Bial, who had emporiums at various locations in New York City. Thousands of songs were either first heard or popularized at these and other establishments, among them "Little Annie Rooney" (1890), "Ta-Ra-Ra-Boom-De-Ay!" (1891), "A Bird in a Gilded Cage" (1900), "Bill Bailey, Won't You Please Come Home?" (1902), "In the Good Old Summertime" (1902), and "You're the Flower of My Heart, Sweet Adeline" (1903). Janet Allen created a sensation in 1905 with "Will You Love Me in December as You Do in May," which was equalled by Blanche Ring in 1909 with "I've Got Rings on My Fingers."

Other famous early vaudeville acts were those of Harrigan and Hart, Weber and Fields, the Four Cohans, Eddie Foy and the Seven Little Foys, and Clayton, Jackson and Durante. The singers May Irwin, Lillian Russell, Belle Baker, Elsie Janis, Blossom Seeley, and Fanny Brice got their starts in vaudeville. So did such future stalwarts of radio and film as Mae West, Ed Wynn, Eddie Cantor, Fred Allen, Milton Berle, the Marx Brothers, W. C. Fields, Jack Benny, and George Burns.

Many vaudeville entertainers became identified with special songs: Emma Caras with "Take Back Your Gold" (1897), Nora Bayes (later known as the Empress of Vaudeville) with "Down Where the Würzburger Flows" (1902), Bert Williams with "Nobody" (1905), Eva Tanguay with "I Don't Care" (1905), and, above all, Sophie Tucker with her immortal theme song "Some of These Days" (1910), written by Shelton Brooks.

One of the most influential personages of vaudeville was the multitalented Gus Edwards: adept as writer, composer, producer, and entertainer. He wrote a series of acts revolving around young boys and girls. In their performance, he discovered such juvenile talents as Ray Bolger, Eddie Cantor, Georgie Jessel, and Groucho Marx. Edwards himself, with several different lyricists, composed many songs for vaudeville, including "In My Merry Oldsmobile" (1905), "School Days (When We Were a Couple of Kids)" (1906), and "By the Light of the Silvery Moon" (1909).

Soon after 1913, when the Palace Theatre was built by Martin Beck on Broadway in New York, it became the leading vaudeville house in the United States. Throughout the 1920s the goal of every performer was to play the Palace. But the combined effects of talking pictures and radio (each of which had its own kind of variety show) led to vaudeville's demise. By 1932, the Palace Theatre had become a palace of film. Vaudeville was no more, except for a brief and unsuccessful revival in the 1950s. Only its songs remain.

Additional Songs

The Aba Daba Honeymoon (1914)
Alexander's Ragtime Band (1911)
The Darktown Strutters' Ball (1917)
Down by the Old Mill Stream (1910)
He'd Have to Get Under, Get Out and Get Under, to Fix Up
  His Automobile (1913)
Heaven Will Protect the Working Girl (1909)
I Don't Want to Play in Your Yard (1894)
I'll Be With You in Apple Blossom Time (1920)
In the Shade of the Old Apple Tree (1905)
The Japanese Sandman (1920)
Let Me Call You Sweetheart (1910)
Mother Machree (1910)
My Melancholy Baby (1912)
My Wild Irish Rose (1899)
Playmates (1889)
Sweet Rosie O'Grady (1896)
Take Me Out to the Ball Game (1908)
Tammany (1905)
Waiting for the Robert E. Lee (1912)
When You Were Sweet Sixteen (1898)
Where Did You Get That Hat? (1888)
You Made Me Love You (I Didn't Want to Do It) 1913

Bibliography

DiMeglio, John E. *Vaudeville, U.S.A.* 1973.
Gilbert, Douglas. *American Vaudeville: Its Life and Times.* 1983.

Keegan, Marcia. *We Can Still Hear Them Clapping*. 1975.

Laurie, Joe, Jr. *Vaudeville: From the Honky-Tonks to the Palace.* 1972

McClean, Albert F. *American Vaudeville as Ritual.* 1965.

Samuels, Charles, and Louise Samuels. *Once Upon a Stage: The Merry World of Vaudeville.* 1974.

Short, Ernest Henry. *Fifty Years of Vaudeville.* 1978.

Slide, Anthony. *The Vaudevillians.* 1981.

Smith, Bill. *Two a Day: The World of Vaudeville.* 1976.

Stein, Charles W., ed. *American Vaudeville as Seen by Its Contemporaries.* 1984.

See also: Musical Comedy; Revues, Tin Pan Alley

VERSE

The verse is traditionally that part of a popular song preceding the **chorus**. In practice, however, the term can apply to a subsidiary part of a song wherever it appears. Over the years, verses have varied in size and importance, at times virtually disappearing, only to rebound again.

In the 1890s verses tended to be lengthy and, like the recitative in opera, carried forth the story line. To this end, many verses consisted of three or more sets of lyrics. "After the Ball" (1892), for example, has three verses, each of sixty-four measures, narrating a tale of mistaken identity, each followed by the famous thirty-two-bar chorus. Sometimes—as in "Little Annie Rooney" (1890), "A Bird in a Gilded Cage" (1900), and "The Curse of an Aching Heart" (1913)—the music of the verse offers little contrast to that of the chorus. Other songs, like "A Hot Time in the Old Town" (1896), offer considerable contrast between dotted notes (verse) and long notes (chorus).

Two famous verses are those of "Alexander's Ragtime Band" (1911)—which is in the dominant key and contains the only true "ragtime" in the piece—and "Swanee" (1919), which is in the parallel minor key (F minor) of the chorus in F major.

Verses were still lengthy in the 1920s, but they were often reduced to only two sets of lyrics, as in "I'm Sitting on Top of the World" and "Remember" (both 1925). A particularly long and evocative verse, but with only one set of lyrics, is that of Noël Coward's "I'll See You Again," from the operetta *Bitter Sweet* (1929): sixty measures as against the thirty-two-bar chorus.

In the 1930s verses began to lose some of their glory. Indeed, many songs lacked them entirely, among them "Smoke Gets in Your Eyes" (1933), "I Got Plenty o' Nuttin'" (1935), and "I've Got You Under My Skin" (1936). Even if a song contained a verse, it was more often than not ignored by both performers and the public. More and more, a song came to be identified by its chorus alone.

Nevertheless, verses survived and frequently constitute integral parts of their songs. Indeed, the verses of Oscar Hammerstein II and Jerome Kern's "Ol' Man River" (1927) and "I've Told Ev'ry Little Star" (1932) are constructed of the same musical material as each song's **release**. The verse of their "Make Believe" (1927), on the other hand, has an enchanting lyrical quality all its own. Other verses, such as the famous one written for "Star Dust" (1929), could stand on their own as complete songs. Traditionally, in most **tangos**, the verses are of equal importance to the chorus, as exemplified in "Orchids in the Moonlight" (1933) and "Don't Cry for Me, Argentina" (1977).

Other verses are in striking contrast to their choruses. For instance, the **key** of the verse of the 1939 song "All the Things You Are" (G major) seems far removed from the key of the refrain (A-flat major). Nevertheless, a graceful **modulation** is accomplished through the intervention of the C dominant seventh, leading to the opening chord of the refrain: F minor.

Verses retain their importance in much folk-oriented music, like "Oh What a Beautiful Mornin'," from *Oklahoma!* (1943). Verse/chorus **form** is also employed in much **country and western** music; for example, John Denver's "Leaving on a Jet Plane" (1967) has a verse with three sets of lyrics. There are distinctive verses in all kinds of songs, from "Proud Mary" (1968) to "Tie a Yellow Ribbon Round the Ole Oak Tree" (1972) and "You Light Up My Life" (1976). Sometimes, as in "Both Sides Now" (1968) and "Bridge Over Troubled Water" (1969), sections of songs are, in fact, verses, even though they are not so designated.

Occasionally, the verse appears after the chorus, rather than before it. An early example is Rodgers and Hart's "Little Girl Blue" (1935), which has a verse in waltz tempo, described in the sheet music as a "Trio," which appears after the chorus (in common time) and is followed by a repetition of the chorus. The verse of "The End of a Love Affair" (1950) also appears after the chorus, and also leads into a second chorus. Similarly placed, and with three sets of lyrics, is the verse of Paul Simon's "Mrs. Robinson" (1968).

See also: Patter

VOCAL GROUPS. SEE SINGING GROUPS

VOCALESE

The term "vocalese," in popular music, denotes a particular type of **jazz** singing that involves taking instrumental jazz **recordings** and substituting **lyrics** for each note. As in **scat singing**, the voice is made to imitate instruments, although in this case specific performances serve as the models for the vocals. Vocalese thus depends upon the recording medium for its very existence, since it reproduces exactly what the instrument has already done.

That is not to say, however, that vocalese versions simply duplicate, for the words provide additional or entirely new implications to the original instrumental phrasing. Eddie Jefferson, the originator of vocalese and singer for many years with James Moody's band, once said that he imagined great jazz performances as stories. His lyrics often literalize this idea, giving the listener the same musical phrases while commenting on the musicians themselves. More generally, though, the concrete, denotative power of language provides handles for listeners that help make the instrumental versions more accessible, as jazz critic Gary Giddens has noted.

The style has its roots in the imaginative and humorous **bebop** vocals of such singers as Leo Watson, whose associative approach to lyrics dates back to the 1930s. But vocalese as such actually began with Jefferson, originally an instrumentalist and dancer, who made it a practice while on tour to sit in his hotel room and listen to his favorite jazz recordings, memorizing the solos and substituting lyrics for each note.

In 1951, King Pleasure (Clarence Beeks) heard Jefferson's lyrics for Moody's **improvisation** on "I'm in the Mood for Love" (1935). He then sang the tune, known as "Moody's Mood," at an amateur hour performance at Harlem's Apollo Theatre and, as a result, received a recording contract with Prestige Records (as Jefferson himself did later). In 1953, both Pleasure's "Moody's Mood" and Annie Ross's "Twisted" (with amusing lyrics about neurosis set to a tenor saxophone improvisation by Wardell Gray) proved extremely popular and familiarized audiences with the vocalese style. In 1958, Ross joined with Dave Lambert and Jon Hendricks in a recording of vocalese versions of Count Basie compositions called "Sing a Song of Basie." Through overdubbing, the trio sang the parts of all sections of the Basie band, including the solos, and so extended the potential of vocalese to the limits of recording technology at that time.

Although contemporary jazz singers have neither the artistry nor humor of these pioneers, vocalese survived into the 1990s, with such practitioners as Mark Murphy, Joni Mitchell, and Manhattan Transfer. Even pop star Barry Manilow forayed into vocalese with a recording of Lambert, Hendricks, and Ross's version of Basie's "Avenue C."

Barry Keith Grant

Bibliography

Friedwald, Will. *Jazz Singing: America's Great Voices From Bessie Smith to Bebop and Beyond.* 1990.

Gourse, Leslie. *Louis's Children: American Jazz Singers.* 1984.

See also: Brass; Woodwinds

W

WAITING

Many objects of waiting are expressed in song. They are as diverse as fair weather ("Wait 'till the Sun Shines, Nellie," 1905), a steamboat ("Waiting for the Robert E. Lee," 1912), daybreak ("The World Is Waiting for the Sunrise," 1919), and a new girlfriend ("Wait Till You See Her," 1942).

Sometimes waiting borders on lethargy, as in "Bidin' My Time" (1930): "I'll just keep on nappin'." At other times, waiting is only one aspect of **enduring love,** as in the haunting theme from the 1965 film *The Umbrellas of Cherbourg,* "(If it takes forever) I Will Wait for You."

Additional Songs

Anticipation (1971)
Heaven Can Wait (1930)
I Knew You Were Waiting (For Me) (1987)
Just You Wait (1956)
Love Won't Let Me Wait (1974)
Waitin' in School (1957)
Waiting for the Girls Upstairs (1971)

WALKING

Songs about walking come in several varieties. There are, first of all, songs about the act of walking per se, such as "Tramp! Tramp! Tramp! Along the Highway" (1910), "A Walk in the Black Forest" (1965), and "These Boots Are Made for Walking" (1966). Then there are songs about walking *with* someone; "Walkin' My Baby Back Home" (1930), "Would You Like to Take a Walk?" (1930), and "Let's Take an Old-Fashioned Walk" (1948) are examples. At the opposite extreme are songs about walking alone, like "I Don't Want to Walk Without You" (1941) and "I'll Walk Alone" (1944); these were understandably popular during **World War II.**

Songs of admiration form another category, as in "When My Sugar Walks Down the Street, All the Birdies Go Tweet, Tweet, Tweet" (1924), "Did You Ever See a Dream Walking" (1933), and "Love Walked

In" (1938). Several dances have been called "walks" as well, notably the "Lambeth Walk," from *Me and My Girl* (1937). But perhaps the best-known song on the subject is Oscar Hammerstein II and Richard Rodgers's heartfelt song of **inspiration** "You'll Never Walk Alone," from *Carousel* (1945).

Additional Songs

Da Doo Ron Ron (When He Walked Me Home) (1963)
If He Walked Into My Life (1966)
I'm Walkin' (1957)
I'm Walking Behind You (1953)
Just Walking in the Rain (1953)
On the Boardwalk in Atlantic City (1946)
On the Trail (1933)
Struttin' With Some Barbecue (1927)
The Trail of the Lonesome Pine (1913)
Truckin' (1935)
Walk Like a Man (1963)
Walk On By (1966)
Walk on the Wild Side (1972)
Walk Right In (1930)
Walk This Way (1975)
Walking in Rhythm (1974)
Walking in the Rain (1964)
Walking the Floor Over You (1941)

See also: **Dance Crazes; Dancing**

WALTZ

The most enduring modern dance, the waltz, has profoundly affected popular music in America for well over one hundred years. That effect was readily apparent in the 1890s, when many popular songs were written in 3/4 **meter;** it became much less so in the latter half of the twentieth century, despite the fact that waltzes were still being written.

Three varieties can be distinguished, largely on the basis of **tempo:** the slow, or Boston, waltz; the moderate waltz, related to the Austrian and German country dances known as Ländler; and the faster song, related to the Viennese waltz. Around the turn of the century, the second (moderate) variety was predominant, as exemplified in such lively songs as "After the Ball," "The Bowery," and "Daisy Bell" (all 1892); "The Sidewalks of New York" (1894); "The Band Played On" (1895); "In the Good Old Summertime" and "On a Sunday Afternoon" (both 1902); "Meet Me in St. Louis, Louis" (1904); "In My Merry Oldsmobile" (1905); "School Days" (1907); and "Take Me Out to the Ball Game" (1908).

The slow variety came to the forefront around 1910, coinciding with increased interest in **dancing** in general, and in ballroom dancing in particular. Some of the most enduring waltz **ballads** are of this variety: "Let Me Call You Sweetheart" and "I'm Falling in Love With Someone" (both 1910); "When Irish Eyes Are Smiling" (1912); "If I Had My Way" (1913); "Will You Remember?" (1917); "Beautiful Ohio" (1918); and "Alice Blue Gown" (1919). Irving Berlin carried on the tradition for several more decades with his waltz ballads "All Alone" (1924), "Always" (1925), "Remember" (1925), "The Girl That I Marry" (1946), and Let's Take an Old-Fashioned Walk" (1948).

The third, or faster, type of waltz was resurrected almost single-handedly by composer Richard Rodgers, who, along with his lyricists Lorenz Hart and Oscar Hammerstein II, gave it a distinctive American flavor despite its Viennese origin. Among their innovative songs in this faster tempo are "Lover" (1933), "The Most Beautiful Girl in the World" (1935), "Falling in Love With Love" (1938), "It's a Grand Night for Singing" (1945), "A Wonderful Guy" (1949), and "My Favorite Things" (1959). Rodgers also wrote a slower, more tender, variety of waltz, found in the verse of "Little Girl Blue" (1935) and in the choruses of "Wait Till You See Her" (1942), "Oh What a Beautiful Mornin'" and "Out of My Dreams" (both 1943), "This Nearly Was Mine" (1949), and "Hello Young Lovers" (1951).

Other composers were not as adept with the waltz. Jerome Kern wrote few of them. Two moderate waltzes, "The Touch of Your Hand" (1933) and "I Dream Too Much" (1935), are replete with chromaticism, in the European late-Romantic tradition. Two brighter ones, "The Waltz in Swing Time" (1936) and "Can't Help Singing" (1944), are somewhat self-consciously labored. George Gershwin was even less at ease in his spoof of the Viennese waltz, "By Strauss" (1936). Cole Porter also made fun of the waltz in two persiflages, "Wunderbar" (1948) and "True Love" (1956).

Many waltzes have originated in the musical theater, especially from **operetta** and the **musical play**. From the former have come such standards as "The Merry Widow Waltz" (1907), "My Hero" (1909), "Sweethearts" (1913), "Will You Remember?" (1917), and "I'll See You Again" (1929); the latter venue has produced a multitude of fine waltzes, including "When I'm Not Near the Girl I Love" (1947), "I Feel Pretty" (1957), "Try to Remember" (1960), and "Sunrise Sunset" (1964). At one time there was, in fact, a tradition to include at least one waltz in every musical. This tendency was carried to extremes in Stephen Sondheim's score for A Little Night Music (1973); the work is almost entirely in waltz time, with the notable exception of its principal song, "Send In the Clowns," which is predominantly in 6/8 meter.

The cinema has given us more than its share of waltzes as well, either in songs derived from movie themes, such as "Around the World" (1956), "Moon River" (1961), and "Charade" (1963), or in songs first performed in **film musicals**, like "Stars in My Eyes" (1936), "Some Day My Prince Will Come" (1937), and "The Boy Next Door" (1943).

Among the hundreds of waltzes in the **folk music** and **country-and-western** tradition are "The Missouri Waltz" (1914), "Goodnight Irene" (1936), "Tennessee Waltz" (1948), "Time in a Bottle" (1971) and "Annie's Song" (1974). Other waltzes have come from **France, Italy, Austria, Germany,** and elsewhere. Indeed, it can be said that the indestructible waltz has permeated all aspects of popular music in this century and continues to do so.

See also: **Dance Crazes; Part II: Catalogue Of Songs**

WATERFRONT

The meeting place of land and water has always borne an aura of romance, reflected in such songs as "Ebb Tide" (1953), "Stranger on the Shore" (1961), and "Sleepy Shores" (1971). In addition, the waterfront serves other functions in popular song: in "I Cover the Waterfront" (1933), it is a place to search for one's love; in "(Sittin' on the) Dock of the Bay" (1968), it is a place to relax and watch "the tide roll away."

Whether it be alongside a **river**, as in "On the Banks of the Wabash Far Away" (1899); a bay, as in "Harbor Lights" (1937); or the **ocean**, as in "Under the Boardwalk" (1964), the waterfront has been a continual source of inspiration to songwriters for well over one hundred years.

Additional Songs

Love Letters in the Sand (1931)
Miami Beach Rumba (1946)
On the Boardwalk in Atlantic City (1946)
Sand in My Shoes (1941)
She Sells Sea Shells (On the Seashore) (1908)
(By the) Sleepy Lagoon (1930)

See also: **Boating**

WEATHER

It is interesting to observe that more songs have been written about the rain than about all other kinds of weather combined. There are several reasons for this. First, there is the traditional association of rain with the **blues**; rain often serves as a metaphor for a feeling of depression. A prime example of this is "Stormy Weather" (1933), in which the torch singer complains that since her man has left, it "keeps rainin' all the time."

A second reason is rain's transitoriness, illustrated in the lyrics of "April Showers" (1932), where the showers of April will "bring the flowers that bloom in May." Third, rain is romantic, provided it doesn't fall too heavily. There is something decidedly romantic about singing in the rain, as Fred Astaire does in the film musical *Top Hat* (1935) when he sings "Isn't This a Lovely Day" to Ginger Rogers. Other songs of this nature are "A Garden in the Rain" (1928), "September in the Rain" (1937), "Just Walking in the Rain" (1953), and "Walking in the Rain" (1964).

Finally, raindrops can be easily simulated in music by the judicious use of **repeated notes** and staccato passages. In the classical tradition, repeated notes suggest raindrops in Chopin's fifteenth prelude, in D-flat major, which has been dubbed the *Raindrop Prelude* because of its repeated A-flats and G-sharps. Examples of melodic repetition suggesting raindrops in popular song include "Come Rain or Come Shine" (1946), "Soon It's Gonna Rain" (1960), and "Raindrops Keep Fallin' on My Head" (1969). Among songs with persistent staccato passages are "Rain" (1927), "Singin' in the Rain" (1929), "Rain on the Roof" (1932), and "Laughter in the Rain" (1974).

Fog, like the rain, has romantic connotations, as demonstrated in the music and lyrics of "Lost in a Fog" (1934) and "A Foggy Day" (1937). Cloudiness too can be transitory, as in two early songs with music by Jerome Kern: "Till the Clouds Roll By" (1917) and "Look for the Silver Lining" (1920)

Other types of weather memorialized in song sometimes go to extremes. Either it's too hot, as in "Heat Wave" (1933), "Too Darn Hot" (1948), and "(Love Is Like a) Heat Wave" (1963), or too cold, as in "I've Got My Love to Keep Me Warm" (1937) and "Baby, It's Cold Outside" (1948).

Snow, too, has its songs, usually associated with **Christmas**: "Winter Wonderland" (1934), "Let It Snow! Let It Snow! Let It Snow!" (1945), and "Frosty the Snowman" (1946). Another feature of the weather, the wind, is found in "Breezing Along with the Breeze" (1926), "The Breeze and I" (1940), and "High on a Windy Hill" (1940).

Few songs have been written about fair weather. One might mention the **barbershop** song "It's Always Fair Weather When Good Fellows Get Together" (1898) or "Let the Sunshine In," from *Hair* (1969). But the quintessential fair weather song is "On a Clear Day (You Can See Forever)" (1966), a versatile ballad often performed as jazz classic.

Additional Songs

Baby, the Rain Must Fall (1964)
Blue Eyes Crying in the Rain (1945)
Both Sides Now, or Clouds (1967)
Come In From the Rain (1975)
The Day the Rains Came (1957)
Don't Rain on My Parade (1963)
Dust in the Wind (1977)
Fire and Rain (1970)
Hard Rain's A-Gonna Fall (1963)
Have You Ever Seen the Rain (1970)
Here's That Rainy Day (1953)
I Can See Clearly Now (1972)
I Found You in the Rain (1941)
I Get the Blues When It Rains (1928)
I Love a Rainy Night (1980)
Into Each Life Some Rain Must Fall (1944)
It Ain't Gonna Rain No Mo' (1923)
It Looks Like Rain in Cherry Blossom Lane (1937)
It Might as Well Rain Until September (1962)
It Never Rains in Southern California (1972)
Let a Smile Be Your Umbrella (On a Rainy Day) (1927)
LiLacs in the Rain (1939)
The Little White Cloud That Cried (1951)
Liza (All the Clouds'll Roll Away) (1929)
The Rain in Spain (1956)
Rainy Days and Mondays (1970)
Rainy Night in Rio (1946)
Rhythm of the Rain (1962)
Right as the Rain (1944)
Save It for a Rainy Day (1977)
Snowbird (1970)
Soft Summer Breeze (1955)
They Call the Wind Maria (1951)
Those Lazy Hazy Crazy Days of Summer (1964)
The Wayward Wind (1956)
Windy (1967)
With the Wind and the Rain in Your Hair (1930)
Who'll Stop the Rain? (1970)

See also: **Moon; Rainbow; Seasons; Sky; Stars; Sun**

WEDDINGS. SEE MARRIAGE

WISHING

Wishing, like many other concepts of popular song, often involves some aspect of **love**. Songs such as "That's My Desire" (1931), "I Wish I Were in Love Again" (1937), "Wish You Were Here" (1952), and "I Wish You Love" (1963) demonstrate this tendency. There are also numerous love songs in which the singer "wants" something, including "I Want a Girl Just Like the Girl That Married Dear Old Dad" (1911), "I Want to Be Happy" (1924), "I Wanna Get Married" (1944), "I

Want to Hold Your Hand" (1963), and "I Just Want to Be Your Everything" (1977).

At other times a wish can be a supplication, as illustrated in several songs from Disney animated films: "I'm Wishing" and "Some Day My Prince Will Come," from *Snow White and the Seven Dwarfs* (1937); "When You Wish Upon a Star," from *Pinocchio* (1940); and "A Dream Is a Wish Your Heart Makes," from *Cinderella* (1949).

Wishing can sometimes imply superstition, as in the 1954 song "Three Coins in the Fountain," referring to the legendary fountains of Rome. In the 1939 song "Wishing (Will Make It So)," one is given the assurance that wishing "hard enough" and "long enough" will make one's **dream** a reality.

Additional Songs

High Hopes (1959)
I Wanna Be Around (1959)
I Wanna Be Loved by You (1928)
I Want to Be Wanted (1960)
I Want What I Want When I Want It (1905)
I Want You Back (1969)
I Wish (1977)
I Wish I Could Shimmy Like My Sister Kate (1919)
I Wished on the Moon (1935)
Wishin' and Hopin' (1963)

WOMAN

With the exception of **love**, more popular songs have been written about women than about any other **subject**. Relatively few of these, however, actually have the word "woman" in the title or lyrics, preferring such designations as **girl, lady, doll,** and **baby.**

A sampling of song titles illustrates the great strides women have taken during this century, from "(I Got a Woman Crazy for Me) She's Funny That Way" (1928) and "Bess You Is My Woman" (1935), to "How to Handle a Woman" (1960), and finally to "I Am Woman" (1971). The last is almost an emancipation proclamation for women, declaring: "Hear me roar in numbers too big to ignore."

Two striking songs are about women in love: "A Woman in Love," written specially for the film *Guys and Dolls* (1955); and "Woman in Love," popularized in 1980 by Barbra Streisand. Another outstanding song, "A Man and a Woman" (1966), from the French film of the same name, is about a love affair.

There are also a number of variations on the theme of womanhood, using such appellations as maiden, siren, madame, mademoiselle, belle, and dame. These include "Tell Me Pretty Maiden (Are There Any More At Home Like You?)," from *Floradora* (1900); "The Siren's Song," from *Leave It to Jane* (1917); a German import, "I Kiss Your Hand, Madame" (1929); the American song "Mam'selle" (1947); a French import, "Mademoiselle de Paree" (1948); Leroy Anderson's sweeping

waltz, "Belle of the Ball" (1953); and a song from *South Pacific* noted for its impertinence: "There Is Nothin' Like a Dame" (1949).

Additional Songs

Boogie On Reggae Woman (1974)
Honky Tonk Women (1969)
I Got a Woman (1954)
Just Like a Woman (1966)
Love Makes a Woman (1968)
More Than a Woman (1977)
(You Make Me Feel Like) A Natural Woman (1967)
Oh Pretty Woman (1964)
Pretty Women (1978)
When a Man Loves a Woman (1966)
A Woman Is a Sometime Thing (1935)
You Are Woman (I Am Man) (1964)

See also: **Beauty; Man**

WOMEN AS SONGWRITERS

Women associated with the history of American popular song have been noted far more frequently for their performances as vocalists, instrumentalists, and actresses than for their creativity as **lyricists** and **composers**. Yet ever since the 1880s, women as songwriters have contributed significantly to the development of American music. What follows is a chronological survey of representative songwriters, many of whose songs have remained standards for more than fifty years.

Pre-1900

One of the first women to attract attention in the field of popular song was Jennie Lindsay, a songwriter and singer whose "Always Take Mother's Advice" (1884) was successfully marketed by the publisher T. B. Harms. Another was Effie I. Canning, an actress whose "Rock-a-bye Baby" (1884) earned her a sizeable sum of money during the first few months of sales. Canning wrote both the music and lyrics, the latter adapted from *Mother Goose's Melodies* (1765). Another lullaby by Canning is "Safely Rocked in Mother's Arms" (1887).

The composer-lyricist Hattie Starr was among the first women to invade **Tin Pan Alley**. She came to New York City from the southern part of the country, determined to market her cache of songs. That she achieved her goal in a relatively short time may be credited to the singer Josephine Sable, who introduced Starr's songs to the public, beginning with "Somebody Loves Me" (1893)—not to be confused with a later song of the same title. Starr also wrote, among others, "Little Alabama Coon" (1893), a type of Negro song known as a "**coon song**" which was popular in the theaters during the 1890s. Coon songs involved a particular performance style that was somewhat akin to a "gospel shout." The singer and comedienne May Irwin was noted for her "coon" and ragtime-styled performances, many of which included her own songs, such as "Mamie, Come Kiss Your Honey," heard in the 1893 musical *A Country Spirit.*

The year 1893 saw at least two other standards come into being: "Happy Birthday to You" and "America, the Beautiful." Patty and Mildred Hill, sisters and kindergarten teachers, can take credit for the first of these two songs even though the title and opening lyrics of their creation originally read "Good Morning to All." In this form, the song was published in *Song Stories for Children*, but sometime before 1910, Patty Hill's lyrics were anonymously transformed into "Happy Birthday to You."

The lyrics for "America, the Beautiful" come from a poem written in 1893 by Katherine Lee Bates and published in a Boston magazine in 1895. This poem, inspired by the beauty and grandeur of Pike's Peak in Colorado, was thought by Thomas B. Aldrich, to be material worthy of the country's national anthem, and thus Aldrich suggested it be set to suitable music. Who actually wed the Bates poem with Samuel Augustus Ward's tune "Materna" (published in *The Parish Choir*, 1888)—an inseparable marriage to this day—remains a mystery.

Songwriters active at the turn of the century include Ida Emerson, Maude Nugent, and Anita Owen. Emerson and her songwriting partner, Joseph Howard, wrote "Hello! Ma Baby," "My Georgia Lady Love," and "Queen of Charcoal Alley"—all published by T. B. Harms in 1899. Nugent, a noted jazz musician, contributed "Sweet Rosie O'Grady" (1896), an Irish waltz which became a hit, thanks to Nugent's plugging her own songs in performances at the Madison Square Roof Garden and Tony Pastor's Theater. A bit of the Irish also appears in her "Mamie Reilly" (1897) and "Down at Rosie Riley's Flat" (1902). Owen focused on flowers, especially daisies, for some of her best-known songs: "Sweet Bunch of Daisies" (1894), a waltz song with refrain; "Daisies Won't Tell" (1908); and "Just a Chain of Daisies" (1911). Perhaps her interest in daisies stemmed (no pun intended) from that other well-known 1890s hit by Harry Dacre, "Daisy Bell (A Bicycle Built for Two)."

1900–29

One of the best ways to market a song was to have it performed in a theater, either as a spur-of-the-moment interpolation or as an integral part of a musical or vaudeville show. Sometimes the song, show, and performance were the creative responsibility of one and the same person. Such was the case with the career of Nora Bayes (born Dora Goldberg). Bayes was not only a star in the *Ziegfeld Follies* and her one-woman shows, but also a composer, lyricist, and co-songwriter for many vaudeville shows and musicals staged in New York City between 1908 and 1920.

Songs most often associated with Bayes are either those she promoted as a singer ("Down Where the Würzburger Flows" by Harry von Tilzer) or those she created with Jack Norworth, the second of her five husbands. One in the latter category is "Shine On Harvest Moon," used in the *Follies of 1908* and the 1908 musical *Miss Innocence.* Among other Bayes and Norworth songs are "Blarney," "Falling Star," "I'm Glad I'm a Boy/ I'm Glad I'm a Girl," and "I'm Learning Something Every Day"—all from 1909. This songwriting team also worked together on the score for the 1911 Broadway musical *Little Miss Fix-It.*

Bayes did not limit her collaborative efforts exclusively to Norworth. She co-authored a number of hits with other men, providing either the lyrics ("Without You," 1918) or the music ("Prohibition Blues," 1918). This last-named song appeared in *Ladies First* (1918), a "suffragist" musical by Bayes in which she introduced not only her own songs but also George and Ira Gershwin's "The Real American Folk Song."

Because so many of Bayes's songs involved a co-author, it is easy to overlook the number of hits she composed by herself. Two representative examples are "I Wonder If They're True to Me" (1908) and "When Jack Comes Sailing Home Again" (1918).

Unlike Bayes, Clare Kummer (born Clare Rodman Beecher) was involved with the theater behind the scenes. She wrote plays (*Good Gracious, Annabelle*, 1916) and librettos (*Ninety in the Shade*, 1915), collaborated with Jerome Kern and Sigmund Romberg on Broadway productions, and composed the lyrics and music for a significant number of songs. A sample of her songwriting efforts includes "June" (1903), "Dearie" (1905), "In My Dreams of You" (1910), "Other Eyes" (1916), and "Bluebird" (1916). With few exceptions, Kummer's songs were incorporated into theatrical productions.

Two other women collaborated as lyricists with Sigmund Romberg and Jerome Kern. Dorothy Donnelly worked with Romberg, and her lyrics live on in some of that composer's most memorable songs. They include "Three Little Maids" and "Song of Love" from *Blossom Time* (1921); "Deep in My Heart, Dear," "Drinking Song," "Golden Days," and "Serenade" from *The Student Prince* (1924); and "Silver Moon" from *Maryland* (1927). Anne Caldwell wrote for Kern between 1920 and 1926, creating important songs for Broadway musicals. The popularity of the blues in the 1920s is reflected in two of the Caldwell-Kern songs: "Let Alone Blues" (1920) and "Blue Danube Blues" (1922). Other songs from this songwriting duo include "Once in a Blue Moon" and "Raggedy Ann" for the musical *Stepping Stones* (1923). Caldwell also wrote "I Know That You Know" (1926) with Vincent Youmans.

In the 1920s, three black women—Mamie Smith, Gertrude "Ma" Rainey, and Bessie Smith—gained national recognition as singers of the classic blues. All three made recordings that not only brought the blues to the widest possible audience but also influenced significantly the world of jazz. Of the three, Bessie Smith was undoubtedly the most famous, and this fame translated into opportunities to have her own songs popularized, among them "Reckless Blues," "Dixie Flyer Blues," and "Young Woman's Blues"—all recorded in 1924 and 1925.

Another talented blues singer whose career bridges the decades of the 1920s and 1930s is Ethel Waters. Although known principally as an actress-singer in vaudeville and Broadway productions, Waters was also adept at writing songs. Among the works that she recorded in the late 1920s are two songs she co-wrote with Sydney Easton: Waters wrote the lyrics for "Maybe Not at All" (1925) and the music for "Go Back Where You Stayed Last Night" (1926).

If success in the songwriting business can be equated with money earned, then Blanche Merrill was surely one of the more successful women. Some measure of her success can be gleaned from a 1917 article on women as songwriters, which reports that she earned "$20,000 a year writing popular hits." For many of these hits Merrill wrote both lyrics and music. Her songs range from the comic "Give an Imitation of Me" (used in a vaudeville act, 1910) and "I Got a Rock" (incorporating Italian dialect, 1911) to the patriotic "We Take Our Hats Off to You, Mr. Wilson" (1914)—a tribute to President Woodrow Wilson. Lengthy titles seem to be Merrill's trademark even when her contribution to the song is limited to the lyrics: "We've Had a Lovely Time, So Long, Good Bye" (1912), "If You Want a Little Doggie, Whistle and I'll Come to You" (interpolated by Nora Bayes into Maid in America, 1915), and "Oh God! Let My Dream Come True" (1916).

Not all of the women writing songs had their attention focused on the commercial markets. Caro Roma, for instance, was well versed in the classical musical tradition. She was a famous opera singer, a conductor, a composer, and even a director of an opera company. In addition, she wrote over two thousand poems. How then did her songs become part of the popular music scene? Quite simply, her art songs were so well liked that they became commercial successes. Some songs display the full extent of Roma's talent; among them are "Thinking of Thee" (1906), "Faded Rose" (1908), and "My Jean" (1920). Others have either her lyrics ("In the Garden of My Heart," 1908) or her music ("Can't Yo' Hear Me Callin', Caroline," 1914; "Bamboo Baby," 1920).

Carrie Jacobs-Bond (whose last name appears in song indices with and without a hyphen) was both a writer of art songs that enjoyed widespread popularity and a singer whose excellence was admired by Presidents Theodore Roosevelt and Warren G. Harding, both of whom invited her to perform at the White House. From her publication Seven Songs come the standards "Just A-Wearying for You" and "I Love You Truly," both written in 1901 and the latter popularized by a best-selling 1934 recording by Bing Crosby. Perhaps her biggest hit was "A Perfect Day" (1910). It was an art song that was equally at home in the church or barroom, for it was used regularly for weddings and funerals as well as for Army camp sing-a-longs. Other songs for which Jacobs-Bond was the composer-lyricist include "Over Hills and Fields of Daisies," "A Little Pink Rose," and "Through the Years"—all from 1906.

Elsa Maxwell responded to the social and political events of her generation by addressing current issues in her songs. Two examples are "I Have Never Seen the Russian Ballet" (1916) and "My Star" (1918). The first is a comic song, written for an operetta, Melinda and Her Sisters, which was staged as a benefit for the suffragist campaign. The "Russian Ballet" is none other than Sergey Diaghilev's Ballet Russe, on tour in the United States in 1916–17. The second song was more in the nature of a hymn, the "star" referring to service star flags for men killed in World War I. "My Star" was popularized by the glee clubs of Yale, Princeton, and Harvard in their war-related benefit concerts. Among other songs by Maxwell are "Please Keep Out of My Dreams" (1915), a ballad recorded by Nora Bayes, and "The Sum of Life" (1909), an art song heard in concert halls and vaudeville shows.

Women sometimes adopted pseudonyms for their songwriting credits to avoid having songs judged on sex rather than merit. This happened even when a songwriting duo involved a married couple, as exemplified by the lyricist Theodora Morse, wife of composer-publisher Theodore Morse. Mrs. Morse used not one but two pseudonyms: D. A. Esrom and Dorothy Terriss. Under the Esrom name, she wrote the lyrics for many of her husband's songs, including "Another Rag" (1911) and "When Jose Plays a Ragtime on His Banjo" (1912). Under the Terriss name, she and the composer Julian Robeldo brought forth one of the all-time waltz hits, "Three O'Clock in the Morning." This song was featured in the Greenwich Village Follies of 1921, and the following year it was recorded by Paul Whiteman and His Orchestra, selling more than a million copies. Helen Guy used the pseudonym Guy d'Hardelot when she composed the wedding song "Because" (1902).

In the waning years of the 1920s, the American labor movement moved to center stage, creating an environment ripe for pro-union and labor-activist songs written in the folksong tradition. Although this material sprang up in very localized areas, it was quickly disseminated throughout the nation by way of published song collections such as the Red Song Book (1932) and New Workers' Song Book (1933).

Women were not shy about getting involved in the labor movement, and a few, such as Ella Mae Wiggins, paid the ultimate price with their lives. Their support manifested itself in songs expressing the feelings of the blue-collar workers, especially those laboring in the disastrous conditions of Kentucky's coal mines. Aunt Molly Jackson was among those whose songwriting focused on the need for unionization to alleviate unfair labor conditions. Her songs range from those which describe the plight of coal miners in her native Kentucky, to "I Am a Union Woman" (1931), which signaled her unfailing faith in the labor movement. Wiggins tied her lyrics to well-known southern folk tunes, thereby increasing the ease with which her songs might be learned. The courage displayed by women backing the workers who tried to unionize, especially women like Jackson and Wiggins, did not go unnoticed by other songwriters. "Union Maid" (1940) is Woody Guthrie's tribute to that courage.

1930–49

With the coming of the 1930s, women acquired yet another avenue through which they could market their songwriting talents: Hollywood films. One of the first women to compose and conduct for Hollywood was Ann Ronell. Her film credits include scores for *Algiers*, (1938) *The Story of G.I. Joe*, (1945) and *The Three Little Pigs*, (1933) a Walt Disney cartoon. This last-named film featured the song most frequently associated with Ronell and lyricist Frank Churchill, "Who's Afraid of the Big Bad Wolf?," in which the wolf is equated with the Depression. Songs representing Ronell as a composer-lyricist include "Rain on the Roof" (1932) and "Willow Weep for Me" (1932).

The lyricist Dorothy Fields was also involved with Hollywood films, but the focus of her career was decidedly centered on Broadway (*see* Lyricists). To her credit are more than eighty-five hit songs, many of them created with her first songwriting partner, Jimmy McHugh. For ten years, the fruits of their combined talents were savored in New York City and Hollywood. They began by writing the score for *Lew Leslie's Blackbirds of 1928*, a revue which contained, among others, "I Can't Give You Anything But Love" (heard again in three films: *Bringing Up Baby*, 1938; *True to the Army*, 1942; and *Stormy Weather*, 1943) and "Diga, Diga, Doo" (also in *Stormy Weather*). This pattern of creating songs for Broadway revues and musicals that would reappear in films remained fairly constant throughout Field's career. What is more, the Fields-McHugh songs were so representative of the 1930s that they were sought after in later decades to evoke that era. A case in point is "On the Sunny Side of the Street" (1930). Created originally for *Lew Leslie's International Review*, it found its way not only into five Hollywood films made between 1943 and 1959 (including one bearing the song's title) but also into the 1973 film *The Way We Were*, where the song is used to recall the Depression years.

Field's uncanny ability to create material that would prove successful on the Broadway stage may be due in part to her family background. Her father, Lew, was part of the famous burlesque extravaganza duo of Weber and Fields, whose comedy routines were performed in their own theater off Broadway near 29th Street. Her brothers, Joseph and Herbert, were well-known librettists. For whatever reason, Dorothy Field's lyrics were marketable and in great demand.

Even while still writing with McHugh, Fields started to work with other musicians, all of whom are now numbered among the best composers of American musicals. In the 1930s, she wrote lyrics for four screen musicals by Jerome Kern. One of the Fields-Kern standards from this partnership was "The Way You Look Tonight," from *Swing Time* (1936), winner of an **Academy Award** for best song. In the 1940s, she and Sigmund Romberg created four key songs for the musical *Up in Central Park* (1945): "April Snow," "Close as Pages in a Book," "Carrousel in the Park," and "It Doesn't Cost You Anything to Dream." In the 1950s, her lyrics were set to the music of Arthur Schwartz for the musical comedies *A Tree Grows in Brooklyn* (1951) and *By the Beautiful Sea* (1954), and to that of Albert Hague for *Redhead* (1959). In the 1960s and 1970s, Fields and Cy Coleman produced *Sweet Charity* (1966), with hits such as "If My Friends Could See Me Now," and *Seesaw* (1973), with "Nobody Does It Like Me." *Seesaw* was her final Broadway musical. Fields died in 1974.

In contrast to the corpus of hit songs created by Dorothy Fields, some songwriters have made their mark on the industry with but a single entry. The English lyricist Eleanor Farjeon falls into this category, but in her case, her song was never intended to be represented in the popular music category. In fact, no one would have been more surprised than Farjeon to learn that her folk hymn, "Morning Has Broken" (1931), set to David Evan's 1927 harmonization of a Gaelic tune, had moved from church hymnal to the popular charts; yet that is exactly what happened. The Farjeon-Evans folk hymn was readily accessible in hymnals, such as *The Hymnbook* (1955), of the Presbyterian and Reformed Churches in America, but it had engendered little interest among congregations. That all changed when Cat Stevens picked up "Morning Has Broken" and pushed it to the top of the charts in 1971. Its popularity caught the attention of those involved with folk music in the churches, and it was reintroduced into its sacred setting where it continues to be sung, especially by the young people for whom Farjeon originally wrote the song.

Beginning in the 1920s, **radio** featured popular song programs performed solely by instrumentalists. For example, André Kostelanetz's orchestral arrangements of songs became as popular as any vocal renditions and they were broadcast regularly on the CBS network. In the 1930s, radio carried the *Music by Gershwin* program on which George Gershwin, at the piano, played not only his own music but also that of other popular music composers, especially works by those just starting to climb the ladder of success. One of these composers was Dana Suesse. Her "Jazz Nocturne" (1931)—a strictly instrumental work, which remains a standard into the 1990s—was adapted by the composer and lyricist Edward Heyman for "My Silent Love" (1932). Other Heyman-Suesse songs are "Ho Hum" (1931), sung in the film *Monkey Business*, and "You Oughta Be in Pictures" (1934), heard first in the *Ziegfeld Follies of 1934* and later sung in the 1951 film *Starlift*. Suesse's "Yours for a Song" (1939) was introduced at the New York World's Fair in *Billy Rose's Aquacade*.

Three more composers whose musical settings of other people's lyrics made notable contributions to the songs of this era are Kay Swift, Maria Grever, and Margarita Lecuona. Swift had the good fortune to have her music placed before the public night after night (331 nights, to be exact) in the *Little Show* of 1929, a revue that included her song "Can't We Be Friends?" Other Swift songs include "Fine and Dandy" and "Can This Be Love?" (both 1930). Grever is perhaps best known for "What a Diff'rence a Day Made," because her 1934 song was popularized by Dinah Washington's acclaimed rhythm-and-blues recording of 1959. She also wrote "Magic Is the Moonlight" (1930) and "Ti-Pi-Tin" (1938). "Taboo" (1934) and "Babalu" (1939) are songs by Margarita Lecuona.

A new institution took root in the mid-1930s that would have an important role to play in the history of popular song. *Your Lucky Strike Hit Parade* broadcast its first show on April 20, 1935, and the Number One song on that initial program was the Fields-Kern "Lovely to Look At." *Your Hit Parade* became a measuring rod for judging success in the music industry, and over the years, songs written by women found a well-deserved place there.

Ruth Lowe was represented on the show more than once with her songwriting. Frank Sinatra's recording with Tommy Dorsey and His Orchestra of her song "I'll Never Smile Again" (1939) not only made the *Hit Parade*, it also became his best-selling record of 1940. For his 1945–47 radio shows, Sinatra adopted as his "signature" music a song with lyrics by Lowe, "Put Your Dreams Away" (1942). In 1940, she composed the music for "Too Beautiful to Last" and in 1943 the lyrics and music for "More Than Anything in the World."

Joan Whitney and Alex Kramer, songwriting partners, were no strangers to the *Hit Parade*. In 1949 they garnered the top spot with "Far Away Places." Between 1940 and the end of the decade, Whitney and Kramer composed a dozen or more songs, most of them producing best-selling records by musicians such as the Andrews Sisters and Jimmy Dorsey and His Orchestra.

"High on a Windy Hill" (1940), "Money Is the Root of All Evil" (1945), and "Love Somebody" (1947) are representative songs. Occasionally Whitney and Kramer were joined by one or two other people in the creation of a song: "Comme Ci, Comme Ça" (1949, with Bruno Coquatrix) is one such example.

Billie Holiday and Ella Fitzgerald, two top-ranked jazz singers, are so frequently lauded for their vocal artistry that their songwriting talents are either minimized or forgotten altogether. Holiday was vocalist with several well-known bands, Count Basie's in 1937 and Artie Shaw's in 1938, to name but two. In this role, she could easily take her own songs to the public by way of the various road trips and recordings as well as with her performances to overflow crowds in Carnegie Hall (1948) and in a Broadway **revue**, *Holiday on Broadway*. Her gift of melodic improvisation was matched by that of songwriting. Especially noteworthy are the songs in which she unleashes pent-up frustrations with life and career: "Billie's Blues" (1936), "Fine and Mellow" (1939), "God Bless the Child" (1941), and "Don't Explain" (1946). So powerful was the effect of this singer and songwriter upon popular music that long after her death in 1959, Holiday was honored first by a 1972 film based upon her autobiography, *Lady Sings the Blues*, and then by a 1974 Alvin Ailey ballet, *Portrait of Billie*, which uses music drawn from Holiday's recordings.

Ella Fitzgerald, chosen "woman of the year" in 1967 by the National Association of Television and Radio Announcers, earned honor after honor for her career as a singer of other people's songs. However, she herself co-authored several songs including "A-Tisket, A-Tasket" (1938 with Al Feldman), adapted from an 1879 nursery song, and "Oh, But I Do" (1945 with Kenneth Watts). Fitzgerald introduced "A-Tisket, A-Tasket" with a recording backed by Chick Webb and his orchestra; later, she sang it in the film *Ride 'Em Cowboy* (1942). Her career was rocketed to new heights with this song, which, of course, became a standard.

Songwriters who are also singers are certainly at an advantage when it comes to promoting their songs. Peggy Lee, a singer with Benny Goodman in the early 1940s before she embarked upon a solo career, had no trouble bringing to public attention the songs she and her husband, composer Dave Barbour, wrote. "It's a Good Day" (1946) and "Mañana (Is Soon Enough for Me)" (1948) are two of their best-known works from among at least a dozen songs.

Country music songwriter Jenny Lou Carson, who has more than twelve songs to her credit, relied upon Grand Ole Opry stars—Tex Ritter and Ernest Tubb, among others—to popularize her material: "Jealous Heart" (1944), "You Two-Timed Me Once Too Often" (1945), and "Don't Rob Another Man's Castle" (1949). Her 1953 song "Let Me Go Devil!" was revised with lyrics by Al Hill for a television show in 1954; it was released under the title "Let Me Go Lover."

Lyricist Sylvia Dee, with songwriting partner Sidney Lippmann, created most of her hit songs in the 1940s: "Chickery Chick" (1945), "My Sugar is So Refined" (1946, made into a best-selling record by Johnny Mercer), and "Who Do You Think You Are?" (1947). There were, however, a few later hits. For instance, the one song that is associated with Dee and Lippmann more than any other is "Too Young" (1951). Nat "King" Cole recorded this song in 1951, and it made Number One on *Your Hit Parade* for several weeks that year. Dee was still producing hits into the 1960s, as "The End of the World" (1962), with music by Arthur Kent, indicates.

1950–75

More than this twenty-five-year period is needed to adequately encompass the contributions of Betty Comden and Adolph Green to popular music. This most talented duo did not set out to make their living as librettists, lyricists, or film screen writers. Acting, not writing, was the career to which both had aspired in the late 1930s, but when theatrical roles did not materialize for them, Comden and Green, along with three other aspiring actors, founded The Revuers. They determined to make a place for themselves in the theater, and to that end, The Revuers wrote, produced, and acted in their own shows, starting with *Where to Go in New York* (1938). This venture revealed the ability of Comden and Green to work as co-writers, a cooperative arrangement that has lasted into the 1990s.

The first Broadway show for which Comden and Green supplied both text and lyrics was Leonard Bernstein's *On the Town* (1944). They followed this production with film scripts (*Take Me Out to the Ball Game*, 1949; *Singin' in the Rain*, 1952; *It's Always Fair Weather*, 1955), a second musical with Bernstein (*Wonderful Town*, 1953), and a series of shows with Jule Styne, spanning the years 1951–72. In the course of their many years as co-writers, Comden and Green amassed an impressive list of songs, many of which became standards. To celebrate their achievements, they staged *A Party With Betty Comden and Adolph Green* (1958), in which they performed some of their most popular material. The show opened off Broadway, then was taken on tour, and finally was televised in a revised format in 1977. A sampling of the songs for which Comden and Green are justly famous includes "Lucky to Be Me" and "New York, New York" (1944), "Give a Little, Get a Little Love" (1951), "It's Love" and "A Quiet Girl" (1953), "I Like Myself" (1954), "Long Before I Knew You" (1956), "Make Someone Happy" (1960), and "I Won't Let You Get Away" (1973).

Before Carolyn Leigh was invited by Cy Coleman in 1957 to be his songwriting partner, she had already achieved considerable success as a lyricist. For example, nine of her songs were included in the musical

Peter Pan (1954), among them "I Won't Grow Up" and "I'm Flying." Leigh's first standard, however, was "Young at Heart" (1954, with Johnny Richards), and the song, as recorded by Sinatra, not only made the *Hit Parade* numerous times in 1954 but also was used as the theme for a 1955 film of the same title. During the five years she worked with Coleman, Leigh wrote the scores for two musicals and several films, but these enterprises did not match the quality and popularity of their individual songs. "Witchcraft" (1957), "Firefly" (1958), "Hey, Look Me Over" (1960), and "Little Me" (1962) are but a few of the more than forty songs that carry Leigh's lyrics.

Alan and Marilyn Bergman are among the most celebrated lyricists to write for stage and screen. Before they were married, each had already taken the first steps toward songwriting. But when the two talents became one, the flow of top-quality lyrics, molded to accommodate each person and situation, was seemingly endless.

Their first major work can be found in the lyrics of "Yellow Bird" (1957), set to Norman Luboff's arrangement of a West Indian **folk song**. From this initial success, they moved quickly into the limelight, writing lyrics for more than a dozen composers who, over the next two decades, won Oscars, Grammys, and every other kind of award for songs that involved the Bergmans. With Michel Legrand, for example, they won their first Oscar in 1968 for "The Windmills of Your Mind" and received Oscar nominations for "What Are You Doing the Rest of Your Life?" (1969) and "Pieces of Dreams" (1970). With Marvin Hamlisch, they earned two awards for "The Way We Were" (1973), one of the songs for which the Bergmans are justly famous: an Oscar for "best song" in 1973 and a Grammy for "song of the year" in 1974.

After a quarter of a century of co-producing lyrics, one would have thought the Bergmans' well of creativity would run dry. That it did not is indicated by the combined efforts of the Bergmans and Legrand in writing all the songs for *Yentl* (1983), which was directed by Barbra Streisand. Two of these songs are "Papa, Can You Hear Me" and "The Way He Makes Me Feel." Other songs by the Bergmans include "Make Me Rainbows" (1967), "All His Children" (1971); "Marmalade, Molasses, and Honey" (1972), "I Love to Dance" (1978), "If We Were in Love" (1981), "It Might Be You" (1982), "Leave It All to Me" (1987), and "Alone in the World" (1990, for the film *The Russia House*).

As mentioned above, Barbra Streisand sometimes filled the role of director, but for the most part her career has been, and continues to be, devoted to acting and singing on stage and screen. Her performances are legendary. Streisand, however, can also add songwriting to her list of credits, essentially for one song that not only won an Academy Award in 1976 and a Grammy in 1977 but also became a favorite for weddings during the late 1970s and 1980s. That song was "Evergreen" (1976), with lyrics by Paul Williams, and it was heard in the film *A Star Is Born* (1976).

"Come Saturday Morning" (1969), popularized in the film *The Sterile Cuckoo*, is among Dory Previn's best-known songs. It was co-written with Fred Karlin during a period in Previn's life when she had rediscovered the art of songwriting, without the benefit of her ex-husband's partnership. André Previn had drawn Dory into his well-established profession as composer for film and stage, and together they had created hits such as those heard in the film *Valley of the Dolls* (1967): "Theme From *Valley of the Dolls*," "I'll Plant My Own Tree," and "It's Impossible."

When the Previn marriage ended in divorce in the late 1960s, Dory set out to carve a distinctive niche for herself in the music industry. Initially, she wed her lyrics to music by other composers. The Karlin song cited above is one example; another is "Daddy's Gone a-Hunting" (1971), with music by John Williams. By the mid-1970s, Dory asserted her independence, establishing her solo career as singer-songwriter with the release of two albums—*Dory Previn* and *Phone Calls*—and the writing of a show, *The Flight of the Groovy Bird*, and a screenplay plus music for a TV movie, *Third Girl From the Left*.

Another important and prolific songwriting partnership is that of Cynthia Weil and Barry Mann, one of several "teams" initially anchored at the Brill Building in New York City. Although some encyclopedic works on popular song list Weil solely under the entry for Barry Mann, she is by no means a mere secondary or incidental component of the songwriting process. Nor does she restrict her lyrics to Mann's music, as "He's So Shy" (1980, with Tom Snow) and "Running With the Night" (1983, with Lionel Richie, Jr.) demonstrate.

Weil was trained as an actress and dancer, and early in her career she wrote lyrics for Frank Loesser. The stage, however, was not to be her locus of activity. In 1961, Weil's marriage to Barry Mann brought the talents of lyricist and composer into a union that produced a wide variety of songs. In the 1960s, they wrote what might be called "urban" protest songs, in which the lyrics describe how falling in love is an escape for young people from the tribulations of city living: "He's Sure the Boy I Love" and "Uptown" (1962), and "Magic Town" (1965).

Among the Weil-Mann hits from the 1960s are "Don't Be Afraid Little Darlin'" (1963) and "You've Lost That Lovin' Feeling" (1964, revived in 1969). Those from the 1970s and 1980s include "New World Coming" (1970), "Here You Come Again" (1977), "Never Gonna Let You Go" (1981), and "Somewhere Out There" (1986, with James Horner).

The dominance of show tunes in the commercial market began to weaken in the late 1950s, and in its place came a plethora of musical styles, each seemingly directed toward a particular segment of society. What follows is a look at some of these styles through the compositions of women who contributed substantially to all but hard or acid rock. Some attempt has been made to group the songwriters within a specific style, but such grouping should be viewed as mere convenience, since most of the women cited explored more than one musical style in the course of their careers.

In the 1950s, Nashville was home to country musicians, most of whom were both performers and songwriters. The Bryants were an exception. Boudleaux Bryant and his wife, Felice, were simply songwriters, hired by the country music publishers of Nashville as staff writers. Although the Bryants had experienced success in the songwriting business before moving to Nashville in the late 1950s, they nonetheless found that their new position gave them access to **rock 'n' roll** groups such as the Everly Brothers, who turned the Bryants' songs into gold records. Examples are "Bye Bye Love" (1957) and "Wake Up Little Susie" (1957, revived in 1982).

Country and western music, along with rhythm and blues, provided the fertile ground upon which rock 'n' roll was nurtured before it burst upon the music world with full force in 1957. Elvis Presley was a product of this emerging style, and was strongly influenced by the sounds of the South, including gospel and black urban folk music. His performances dominated the airwaves, films, and concert halls, and the songs he chose obviously became well publicized.

Benefiting from Presley's fame were Ruth Batchelor and Joy Byers, whose songs Presley performed during the 1960s. For example, he introduced two songs with lyrics by Batchelor into films of 1962: "Where Do You Come From" and "King of the Whole Wide World"—both with music by Bob Roberts. Presley also recorded at least seven songs by Byers, including "Stop, Look, Listen" (1964), "So Close, Yet So Far" (1965), and "Please Don't Stop Loving Me" (1966).

When the Country Music Association instituted annual awards in 1967, two women were among the first recipients: Loretta Lynn and Dolly Parton. Along with Tammy Wynette, Donna Fargo, and Bobbie Gentry, they went on to win additional awards, not only as performers but also as songwriters.

Loretta Lynn was based in Nashville, home of the Grand Ole Opry. "Coal Miner's Daughter" (1969) is surely one of her best-known songs; it is autobiographical and refers to her childhood years in Kentucky where her father did indeed work in the mines. Other songs by Lynn include "You Ain't Woman Enough" and "Dear Uncle Sam" (1965), and "I Wanna Be Free" (1970).

Some of Wynette's songs were also autobiographical. In describing relationships between a man and a woman, Wynette was actually describing her own relationship with her husband, from whom she was divorced in 1975. Examples of her standards are "Stand by Your Man" (1968) and "We Sure Can Love Each Other" (1971), both with music by Billy Sherrill, and "The Ways to Love a Man" (1969), for which she wrote lyrics and music.

Dolly Parton's popularity as a singer-songwriter in the 1970s continued unabated into the 1980s, as the list of her songs indicates. Parton's song "9 to 5" (1980), which she introduced in the film of the same title, won an Academy Award for Best Song. She followed this film hit with "Appalachian Memories" (1983) and "Tennessee Homesick Blues" (1984). Representative songs of Donna Fargo are "Funny Face" (1967), "Happiest Girl in the Whole U.S.A." (1971), and "That Was Yesterday" (1976, one of her best-selling records).

One recording was all Bobbie Gentry needed to transform herself into a star. For the 1967 recording of her ballad "Ode to Billie Joe," this singer-guitarist was awarded three Grammys and became an overnight celebrity. Gentry built upon this initial success, garnering additional awards for her songwriting: "Fancy" (1969), for example, won the ASCAP Country Music Award in 1970. Gentry was based in California, but her songs and style of performance never lost the flavor of her native Mississippi, as "Mississippi Delta" and "Mean Stepmama Blues" (both 1967) demonstrate.

San Francisco was an important locus of **rock** music activity in the 1960s and saw the birth of several groups destined to challenge the seemingly insurmountable domination of those from England, such as the Beatles and Rolling Stones. One of these was Jefferson Airplane, a group that made its debut in 1965 with Grace Slick, lead vocalist and bass/guitar player. The songs which Slick sang spoke to the drug culture surrounding rock musicians and their audiences, and they included some of the singer's own compositions. For example, she wrote "White Rabbit" (1967), a song in the "acid" or hard rock style that is concerned with drug-related experiences. "White Rabbit" was a hit, both as a single and as part of the group's first album, which has gold status.

Another group out of San Francisco was Big Brother and the Holding Company, with Janis Joplin as lead vocalist from 1966 to 1968. Joplin knew relatively little about singing in the rock style before joining Big Brother, but she quickly transformed her blues style into the new medium. An appearance at the 1967 Monterey International Pop Festival was a turning point in Joplin's career. Recording contracts for the group followed this event, and before long Joplin was being heard coast to coast, gaining recognition both as a singer and as a songwriter. Songs for which she wrote lyrics and music are "Down on Me" (1967) and "Move Over" (1970); those for which she supplied only the lyrics are "I Need a Man to Love" (1968) and "Mercedes Benz" (1970), which she recorded with just tambourine accompaniment.

Drugs once again figured into the lyrics of these songs, but, in Joplin's case, they also accounted for her untimely death at age twenty-seven. Just how powerful a figure Janis Joplin had been in the music world can be measured in part by the number of items marketed after 1970 (the year of her death) that pay tribute to her life: the song "Janis," written in her memory; a documentary film, Janis; several published biographies; and two albums, one a retrospective of her live concerts and the other a collection of her greatest hits.

Laura Nyro grew up in the Bronx, and her music reflects the sights and sounds of urban life. As a singer, songwriter, and pianist, she explored many different musical styles such as blues, jazz, rock, and even that of show tunes. Nyro appeared at the same Monterey Pop Festival (1967) that launched Janis Joplin's career, but with a far different outcome. Joplin was part of the acid rock culture; Nyro was not, and hence her music was not considered newsworthy. Nevertheless, established groups—the Mamas and the Papas, Three Dog Night, and Blood, Sweat, and Tears—took some of her songs and pushed them to the top of the charts: "Wedding Bell Blues" (1966), "Stoned Soul Picnic" and "Eli's Coming" (1967), and "Save the Country" (1968).

Nyro recorded her own songs, but unlike the albums she made of other people's songs, those devoted to her own material were seldom as successful as the albums of her songs made by her peers. Nyro's live concerts, however, drew large crowds, and like Joan Baez and Judy Collins, she became idolized as a performer. Her music, along with that of Carole King, provided a viable alternative to hard rock.

Carole King has been writing songs since she was in high school; her earliest works were fashioned in the rhythm-and-blues style. She left college to marry another songwriter, Gerry Goffin, and together they pooled their talents to produce a number of hit songs: "Will You Love Me Tomorrow?" (1960), "Happy Days Are Here Again" (1961, with Cynthia Weil), and "Go Away, Little Girl" (1962), among many others. King did sing some of her own compositions, making at least one recording that was a hit on both sides of the Atlantic, but in this first phase of her career, she preferred to let recognized artists do the recordings.

The period from 1968 to 1970 was anything but happy for Goffin and King. Their particular style of songwriting was being pushed into a secondary position by the more aggressive rock sounds of groups like the Beatles, and within a very short time the Goffin-King songs lost their market. With this loss came another: their marriage ended in divorce.

The second phase of King's career began with her acknowledgement that she was both a composer and a performer. In celebration of this new image of independence, King made a solo appearance as singer-songwriter-pianist in a program of her own songs at

Carnegie Hall in 1971. That year, King achieved another milestone: she released *Tapestry*, an album of her songs which sold more than 13 million copies—a record for the industry to that date. In addition to the title song, this album included, among others, "You've Got a Friend" and "So Far Away."

Although King found it possible and even desirable to write her own material, she did not abandon the partnership idea of songwriting. For example, King's lyrics appear in "It's Too Late" (1971), with music by Toni Sterns, and in "Simple Things Mean a Lot to Me" (1977), with music by Richard Evers, her third husband.

After *Tapestry*, King released a number of albums containing hits such as "You Light Up My Life" (1976) and "Believe in Humanity (1973)," each of which received either a Grammy or gold record. She also expanded her sphere of activity, composing music to Maurice Sendak's lyrics for *Really Rosiee* (1975), a television cartoon that was adapted into an off Broadway show in 1980. King was not an activist to the extent that some of her peers were, but she did feel strongly about endorsing a lifestyle that avoided the use of drugs and fostered racial and sexual equality. Songs speaking to these themes can be found on her album *Fantasy*.

One of the stars of soft rock in the 1970s was singer-songwriter Carly Simon. Her first hit was "That's the Way I've Always Heard It Should Be" (1971), with music composed to Jacob Brackman's lyrics. Also in 1971, she performed her own songs, such as "Anticipation," "Legend in Your Own Time," and "Three Days," on a best-selling album. "Anticipation" was later used in a Heinz catsup commercial. These 1971 songs, along with "Right Thing to Do" and "You're So Vain" (1972) and "Mockingbird" (1975), reinforce Simon's motto: "I write songs for myself." Underlying her easily remembered melodies are lyrics that probe deeply into the concerns of Simon and her audiences.

In the next decade, Simon released albums that moved in the direction from soft to hard rock and incorporated the rhythms of **reggae**. From this era come "Jesse" (1982), a gold single; music for the theme song in the film *Torchlight* (1984); "Let the River Run" (1988), which was in the film *Working Girl* and won the 1988 Academy Award for Best Song; and "Better Not Tell Her" (1990).

The 1960s saw folk music, in its various guises, move into the forefront of American popular music. Mary Travers, for example, reintroduced indigenous folk songs to the public by way of her skillful arrangements and adaptations. So, too, did Jean Ritchie, but she also wrote and performed original songs such as "Black Waters" (1967).

Others, like Buffy Sainte-Marie and Judy Collins, introduced folk-styled music—often referred to as urban folk music—as a means to convey a "message"

about political and social injustices in American society. War, peace, racial inequality, women's rights—these were some of the subjects woven into the folksong fabric displayed at Woodstock and the Newport Folk Festivals, in coffee houses and on college campuses. The "message" was frequently delivered by a singer-guitarist who was, with few exceptions, the songwriter.

Joan Baez was, for the most part, one of those exceptions. Her concerts and albums (released at the rate of one a year between 1961 and 1972) kept Baez and the message of nonviolence, which she embraced wholeheartedly, before the public. Yet the songs she performed were usually not of her own creation: she was first and foremost a folksinger. In fact, not until the 1970s, when the fever of antiwar activism cooled, did Baez come forth with a significant number of her own songs, including two from 1975: "Winds of the Old Days" and "Diamonds and Rust."

For Buffy Sainte-Marie, a Cree Indian, the "message" varied from song to song. In some she protested against war ("Universal Soldier," 1963); in others she deplored discrimination against Native Americans ("My Country 'Tis of Thy People You're Dying," c. 1965). She did not, however, restrict her songwriting and performances to protest material. In fact, the subjects explored in her lyrics are as varied as the styles in her music. Songs for which she is best known include "It's My Way" (1964), "When the Buffalo's Gone" and "Until It's Time for You to Go" (1965), and "A Man" (1974).

Singer-songwriter Malvina Reynolds set aside plans for a career as a college teacher (she held a doctorate in medieval literature) and embarked upon a musical journey that would give voice to her political and social concerns. With guitar in hand, she delivered her messages in song. "What Have They Done to the Rain?" (1962) conveys her antinuclear message and "Little Boxes" (1964) is her protest against conformity; the "boxes" refer to row upon row of look-alike housing in suburbia. In other songs she deplored environmental pollution, condemned American involvement in Vietnam, and supported the rights of blacks and women. Reynolds recorded her songs and published them in folksong collections.

Helen Reddy, from Australia, had a message of a different sort. Hers was focused on the feminist movement. She wrote the lyrics for "I Am Woman" (1971), a song adopted by the National Organization for Women because it expressed the ideals of the group. Reddy also recorded "I Am Woman" in 1972. It sold two million copies and in 1973 earned her a Grammy as "best female rock-pop-folk vocal performance." Although she supplied the lyrics for other songs, nothing else Reddy wrote ever matched the success of this one song.

Janis Ian was only sixteen when, in 1967, she recorded "Society's Child" (1966), a biting commentary on problems faced by teenagers growing up in New

York City. The positive response to this song from the public paved the way for Ian to perform her songs with similar messages in concert halls and on television. Although her popularity waned considerably in the early 1970s, her determination to be a performer-songwriter never faltered. By the mid-1970s, she was once again front-page news, winning awards for albums that included "At Seventeen," "In the Winter," and "Watercolors"—all from 1975.

Joni Mitchell, a Canadian, proved to be one of the outstanding folk songwriters of the 1970s. According to an interview Mitchell gave *Rolling Stone* in 1979, the spark that ignited the music within her came from Bob Dylan's "poetic songs." When she realized that serious poetry could be sung in a popular musical style, her career as a singer-songwriter moved into realms that were distinctly her own. Mitchell's musical palette embraces, folk, rock, jazz, country, and even classical styles, but what she hoped to achieve was a synthesis of styles that would be labeled "American."

The albums *Joni Mitchell* (1968) and *Clouds* (1969) contain so many notable songs, that the general public often considers these songs to represent the composer's entire career. "Song to a Seagull," "Chelsea Morning," "Michael From Mountains," "Woodstock," and "Both Sides Now"—these became hit songs not only for Mitchell herself but also for peers such as Judy Collins, who cut a best-selling record of "Chelsea Morning" in 1969.

Having gained a pillar of security with her first album, Mitchell dared to follow her creative instincts in subsequent releases. *Blue* (1970) is a pivotal album. It includes ten of Mitchell's own songs: some are in the style of the earlier albums; others explore rhythms and sounds suggestive of rock.

Two albums appeared in 1972, but they are as different as dream is from reality. *For the Roses* is experimental. Here the boundaries of "popular" are stretched to the limit, not by the poetry but by the negation of anticipated patterns of melody, rhythm, and harmony. "Lesson in Survival" is perhaps the most experimental song on the album. *Court and Spark* shares none of the introspective qualities of *For the Roses*. One of its songs, "Help Me," was released as a single and became a Top Forty hit.

Mitchell continued to release albums into the 1980s, each of which became an instant best-seller or won an award. Representative songs from these albums include "My Secret Place" (1987), with words and music by Mitchell; and "Lakota" (1985) and "The Tea Leaf Prophecy (Lay Down Your Arms)" (1988), with music by Larry Klein.

Judy Collins spent her early years preparing to be a concert pianist, and she did appear with several orchestras before the age of sixteen. By the time she entered college, however, she had developed other musical talents, namely those of singing and songwriting.

In several aspects, the careers of Judy Collins and Joan Baez show interesting parallels. Collins came to the folk repertoire, as did Baez, by way of the Anglo-American ballad, and her recording of "Amazing Grace," which achieved gold status in 1971, remains one of the treasured interpretations of that standard to this day. When the civil rights movement shifted into high gear in the 1960s, Collins did more than lend her music to the cause: she actually helped blacks in Mississippi with voter registration. "Action with song" seemed to be the Collins philosophy as she joined Baez in rallies against the Vietnam War. She also assisted Baez and other activists in cutting an album to support the Woman's Strike for Peace and in raising funds for the Baez Institute for the Study of Nonviolence.

Collins brought her **folk song** performances to the Newport Folk Festival in 1963, to concert halls such as Town Hall and Carnegie Hall in New York City in 1964 and 1965, respectively, and to foreign countries (Japan, New Zealand, Poland) in overseas tours in 1966 and 1967. Since most of the repertoire for these programs was taken from music composed by her peers, her own compositions have often remained in the shadows. A few that deserve to be mentioned are "Albatross" (1967, used in the film *The Subject Was Roses*), "My Father" (1968), "Sweet Gardens" (1972), and "Born to the Breed" (1975).

So much attention has been focused on white songwriters involved with protest movements that it is easy to lose sight of black women who lent their skills to these same causes. Bringing the "message" through song was not new to the black community. Dorothy Love Coates, called by some *the* message singer, had communicated the **gospel** message in the lyrics of her songs—"He's Right on Time" and "You Must Be Born Again"—throughout the 1950s. What was new was the challenge presented to black women to address social and political issues.

In the mid-1960s, events relating to civil rights had become so violent that blacks such as Ella Fitzgerald and Nina Simone felt the need to channel the community's outrage into song. Fitzgerald wrote "It's Up to You and Me," dedicated to Martin Luther King, Jr. Simone responded to events in Mississippi and Alabama with "Mississippi Goddam!" (1964) and "Four Women" (1966).

Simone has been lauded as "high priestess of soul," the title of one of her albums. She shares this accolade with a younger soul singer, Aretha Franklin. Franklin grew up learning firsthand about soul and gospel because James Cleveland, "king of soul," lived with the Franklin family. Her rise to stardom as a leading female vocalist and recording artist earned her a number of Grammys; some of her own songs also became hit singles. Songs she co-authored with Ted White include "Dr. Feelgood" (1967) and "Since You've Been Gone" and "Think" (both 1968). Other songs solely of her own creation are "Call Me" and "Spirit in the Dark" (both 1970), "Rock Steady" (1971), and "Day Dreaming" (1972).

1975–90

A prolific contributor to popular song in this fifteen-year period has been pop lyricist-singer Carole Bayer Sager. In 1970, at age twenty-three, Sager became the youngest lyricist to write a Broadway musical. Although *Georgy* lasted but five nights, it brought Sager invaluable experience for her songwriting career. Sager's collaboration with singer-songwriter Melissa Manchester produced a number of hits. One of their most successful was "Midnight Blue" (1974); Manchester's recording brought it to the Top Ten in 1975. Other songs co-written by Sager and Manchester are "Just You and I" (1975), and "Come In From the Rain" (1975) and "Better Days" (1976). Manchester wrote a few songs with collaborators other than Sager ("Just Too Many People," 1975, and "Whenever I Call You 'Friend,'" 1978), but for the most part she concentrated upon singing rather than songwriting.

In 1977, Sager entered into a very successful songwriting partnership with Marvin Hamlisch. Together they wrote, among others, "Nobody Does It Better" (1977), sung by Carly Simon for the film *The Spy Who Loved Me*; "Theme from *Ice Castles* (Through the Eyes of Love)" (1978), sung by Melissa Manchester for the film *Ice Castles*; songs for Neil Simon's musical *They're Playing Our Song* (1979); and "One Hello" (1982) for the film *I Oughta Be in Pictures*.

Sager married composer Burt Bacharach in 1982, and thereafter the majority of her songs were written with her husband. One of their first collaborations produced "That's What Friends Are For" (1982)—heard in the film *Nightshift* and on *Friends*, an album released in 1985 to benefit AIDS research. Other Sager-Bacharach songs are "On My Own (1986) and "Love Power" (1987).

Sometimes Sager's songwriting credits are listed simply as co-writer rather than as lyricist. Such is the case with "Under Your Spell" (1986), which she wrote with Bob Dylan, who later introduced the song on his album *Knocked Out Loaded*.

The 1970s and 1980s had a number of successful songwriting partnerships: Bonnie Bramlett and Eric Clapton ("Lovin' You Lovin' Me," 1970), Deborah Harry and Chris Stein ("Pretty Baby," 1978), Sandy Linzer and Denny Randell ("You Keep Me Dancing," 1977), Catherine and Dan Peek ("Lonely People," 1974), Adrienne Anderson and Barry Manilow ("Some Kind of Friend," 1982), and Judy Hart Angelo and Gary Portnoy ("Every Time I Turn Around," 1984). In each of these partnerships women are paired with men. Far fewer examples can be found of women paired with other women. One has already been discussed, that of Carole Bayer Sager and Melissa Manchester. Another is that of

Ann and Nancy Wilson, who co-authored "Crazy on You" (with Roger Fisher), "Dreamboat Annie," and "Magic Man" in 1976 and "Heartless" in 1977.

The late 1970s saw a continuation of the soft rock sound in songs and performances by Karla Bonoff. "Lose Again" (1975), "Someone to Lay Down Beside Me" and "Falling Star" (both 1976), and "Restless Nights" (1979) are representative of Bonoff's songs, many of which she and Linda Ronstadt released on albums such as *Hasten Down the Wind* (1976).

The New Wave singer-songwriter Patti Smith also arrived on the music scene in the late 1970s. Her poetry and lyrics mirror the enduring legacy of Bob Dylan. Occasionally Smith wrote both lyrics and music, as in "Frederick" (1979). More often she confined her role in the songwriting process to the lyrics: "Ask the Angels" (1976, with Ivan Kral) and "Because the Night" (1978, with Bruce Springsteen). Patti married Fred Smith in 1979; shortly thereafter, she retired from writing and performing songs until 1988, when she and her husband produced the album *Dream of Life*. Among their songs on this album are "People Have Power" and "Where Duty Calls," this last a reflection on life in war-ravaged Beirut.

Songs focused on social issues appear in full force in the mid-1980s. For example, in 1986 Madonna addressed problems of teenage sex in "Papa Don't Preach"; Marie Burns (with Ron Riddle) wrote "I Wonder Who's Out Tonight," the theme song for, *After the Sexual Revolution* a TV documentary on women; and Joni Mitchell introduced her "Number One" at an Amnesty International Conspiracy of Hope Concert in New Jersey. In 1987, Natalie Merchant and Suzanne Vega spoke to the problems of child abuse with "What's the Matter Here?" and "Luka," respectively, while Julie Gold expressed antiwar sentiments in "From a Distance," a ballad revived in 1990 by Bette Midler on *Some People's Lives* to coincide with troops leaving for duty in the Persian Gulf war.

Debbie Gibson, who in 1991–92 appeared for a time on Broadway in *Les Misérables*, is one of popular music's true prodigies. At age sixteen, she reportedly was one of the youngest artists ever to write, produce, and sing a Number One hit. That first hit was "Only in My Dreams" (1987). She followed it with "Out of the Blues" and "Electric Youth" (both 1988) and "No More Rhyme" (1989), along with many others released on her albums.

Suzanne Vega—singer, songwriter, and guitarist—was nurtured within the folk music environment before she was launched into the realm of the avant-garde with Philip Glass. One of her most influential songs was "Luka," cited above, but songs written in a style not unlike that of the later works of Dory Previn and Laura Nyro include "Marlene on the Wall," "Knight Moves," and "Freeze Tag"—all from 1985. In 1986, she entered into a theatrical performance conceived by Philip Glass and executed with the help of Linda Ronstadt and the Glass ensemble. *Songs From Liquid Days* merges the distinctive musical style of Glass with the writing skills of several lyricists. Vega's contribution to this event was "Freezing." To date, "Luka" has proven to be one of Vega's most successful creations, earning Grammy nominations in 1987 for best song and best record.

One songwriter of the last two decades does not fit the mold of most other women discussed in this survey. Laurie Anderson was first and foremost a painter and sculptor, who, upon graduation from college, used her newly acquired knowledge to teach art history. Ever restless to explore the unknown and experiment with the untried (such as her construction of a violin with internal speakers), she exchanged a somewhat predictable path in the academic world for an unpredictable one in the musical and theatrical worlds. She was fully equipped for this challenge, for in addition to her art credentials she was a violinist, composer, singer, and, ultimately, a performance artist. Mixed-media performances fascinated her and, beginning in 1973, she created several for the Brooklyn Academy of Music. Her songs play an integral part in these performances and have appeal for progressive rock fans. *Mr. Heartbreak*, both a film and an album (1983), offers a sampling of songs: "Gravity's Angel," "Sharkey's Day," and "Sharkey's Night." Other songs include "O Superman" (1981), which made the pop charts in Britain, and "Beautiful Red Dress" (1989).

As a performance artist, Anderson joins the ranks of others like Ana Mendietta and Betsy Damon, who seek to express individuality through the collective consciousness of the feminist movement.

Bonnie Raitt, a blues singer, wrote and performed a number of hits prior to 1986, and during this same period lent her support to the antinuclear movement. Personal problems caused a brief hiatus in her career, but in 1989 she released *Nick of Time*, an album that won four Grammy Awards. She followed it with *Luck of the Draw* in 1991, also a Grammy winner. The pervading theme of the 1991 album is that success in career and relationships often defies logic; it is more often than not attributable simply to luck. The album shows the diversity of Raitt's songwriting ability. Those solely from her pen include "Tangled and Dark" and "Come to Me." "One Part Be My Lover" was co-written with her husband, Michael O'Keefe, and "Papa Come Quick," was written with Billy Vera. Raitt's commitment to the blues never wavers, but influences from country and reggae music filter into her musical palette.

Women's success in the songwriting business may at times appear to be "the luck of the draw," but overall it comes from innate talents and skills which have contributed substantially to the repertoire of American popular music over the past hundred years.

Hermine W. Williams

Bibliography

Block, Adrienne Fried, and Carol Neal-Bates, comps. *Women in American Music: A Bibliography of Music and Literature.* 1979.

Bloom, Ken, *American Song.* 1985.

Booth, Mark. *American Popular Music: A Reference Guide.* 1983,

Chapple, Steve, and Reebee Garolfalo. *Rock 'n' Roll Is Here to Pay: The History and Politics of the Music Industry.* 1977.

Clarke, Donald, ed. *The Penguin Encyclopedia of Popular Music,* 1989.

Cohen-Stratyner, Barbara. *Popular Music 1900–1919.* 1988.

Ewen, David. *All the Years of American Popular Music.* 1977.

———. *American Songwriters.* 1987.

Gargan, William, and Sue Shama. *Find That Tune: An Index to Rock, Folk-Rock, Disco, and Soul.* 1984.

Jacobs, Dick. *Who Wrote That Song?* 1988.

Lax, Roger, and Frederick Smith. *The Great Song Thesaurus.* 1989.

The New Grove Dictionary of American Music, 1984.

Orloff, Katherine. *Rock 'n' Roll Woman.* 1974.

Shapiro, Nat, and Bruce Pollock. *Popular Music 1920–1979.* 3 vols. 1985.

Skowronski, Jo Ann. *Women in American Music.* 1978.

Stambler, Irwin. *The Encyclopedia of Pop, Rock, and Soul,* 1989.

———, and Grelun Landon. *The Encyclopedia of Folk, Country, and Western Music.* 1982.

Wenner, Hilda E., and Elizabeth Freilicher. *Here's to the Women.* 1987.

WONDER

The adjective "wonderful," like its cousin "beautiful," is a three-syllable expression of admiration that lends itself well to popular song. Several important waltzes incorporate the word in their titles: "(My) Wonderful One" (1922), "It's a Big Wide, Wonderful World" (1940), "A Wonderful Guy" (1949), "Wonderful Copenhagen" (1952), and (in German) "Wunderbar" (1948). The word is equally at home in duple meter, as in "'S Wonderful" (1927), "They Say It's Wonderful" (1946), "Mister Wonderful" (1956), "(On) A Wonderful Day Like Today" (1964), and "What a Wonderful World" (1967).

Another type of wonder, more akin to puzzlement than to admiration, occurs in several older songs, "I Wonder Who's Kissing Her Now?" (1909) and "I Wonder What's Become of Sally?" (1924). The famous holiday song "Winter Wonderland" (1934) expresses a feeling of awe, while the song "What's the Use of Wond'rin'," from *Carousel* (1945), questions whether wondering is worthwhile when one is in love. The musical *Small Wonder* was produced on Broadway in 1948.

Additional Songs

Alice in Wonderland (1951)

I May Be Wrong (But I Think You're Wonderful) (1929)
It's a Wonderful World (1939)
Some Kind-A-Wonderful (1961)
Wonderful, Wonderful (1957)
(What a) Wonderful World (1959)
Wonderland by Night (1961)
You (Gee But You're Wonderful) (1936)

See also: Beauty

WOODWINDS

Perhaps no family of instruments has been more closely identifed with popular music than that of the woodwinds. Of these, the clarinet and saxophone reign supreme, bringing their idiosyncratic timbers to **jazz** and **swing**. Used to a much lesser extent as solo instruments are the other major members of the woodwind family: the flute and piccolo—increasingly used in jazz and Latin American music—and the oboe, bassoon, and English horn.

The clarinet was among the first instruments to be used in **Dixieland** jazz, where it contrapuntally filled in the improvisational space between trumpet and trombone. When jazz migrated to Chicago, the clarinet became essential in small jazz ensembles, where it was used in both its chalumeau (lower) and upper registers. It became customary for saxophonists to double on clarinet in the **big bands**, three of whose most celebrated leaders—Benny Goodman, Artie Shaw, and Woody Herman—were accomplished clarinetists. Other jazz and swing clarinetists included Johnny Dodds, Jimmie Noone, Sidney Bechet, Barney Bigard, Leon Rappolo, Pee Wee Russell, Pete Fountain, Edmond Hall, and Jimmy Giuffre. The bass clarinet, sounding an octave lower than the regular clarinet, has been used to a lesser extent by Eric Dolphy and others.

Adolphe Sax's invention of 1841, the saxophone, has always been used much more extensively in military bands and popular music than in traditional orchestral or chamber music. Perhaps this is because the saxophone combines expression and mobility with a special kind of earthiness. Certainly, the instrument reached its top potential in popular music. Five varieties of saxophone are used: soprano, alto, tenor, baritone, and bass. Of these, the tenor in B-flat has been by far the favorite through the years, its only challengers being the alto and soprano saxophones in E-flat. The saxophone came to jazz later than the clarinet, but was commonly used from the 1930s on, when the saxophone section of five or more players—most of them doubling on other woodwinds—became a staple of the big band.

The tenor saxophone has survived through jazz, swing, rhythm and blues, rock 'n' roll, soul, Motown, and rock. Among its most outstanding performers through the years have been Coleman Hawkins, Lester Young, Chu Berry, Herschel Evans, Ben Websters, Bud Freeman, Zoot Sims, Al Cohn, and Sonny Rollins. The instrument received fresh recognition as played by Stan Getz in the "cool" tradition of West Coast jazz, with the coming of the **bossa nova** to the United States in the 1960s. Among memorable tenor sax solos were those recorded by Berry, of "I Don't Stand a Ghost of a Chance With You" (1932), and Evans, of "Blue and Sentimental" (1939).

As for the alto sax, one name towers above all others, that of Charlie Parker, one of the founders of **bebop**. Other notable players have included Johnny Hodges, long a staple of the Duke Ellington Orchestra; Benny Carter; Willie Smith; Lee Konitz; Paul Desmond; and Ornette Coleman. Jimmy Dorsey was perhaps the most famous alto saxophonist who was also a bandleader.

The soprano saxophone in E-flat has been used in jazz most notably by Sidney Bechet, John Coltrane, Steve Lacy, Wayne Shorter, and Paul Winter. Two jazz classics recorded on the instrument are Coltrane's expressive solo rendition of "My Favorite Things" (1959) and Shorter's of the Brazilian song "Dindi" (1965).

The E-flat baritone sax has been principally promoted in jazz by Gerry Mulligan, Harry Carney, and Serge Chaloff, and the bass saxophone in B-flat by Adrian Rollini. The jazz performer Branford Marsalis brought renewed interest to the saxophone in the 1980s.

Songs about woodwinds include "Clarinet Marmalade" (1918), first performed in 1918 by the Original Dixieland Jazz band, and the tongue-in-cheek "I'm Looking for a Guy Who Plays Alto and Baritone and Doubles on a Clarinet and Wears a Size Thirty-seven Suit," introduced by Ozzie Nelson and His Orchestra in 1940.

See also: Brass; Improvisation; Instrumentation

WORLD

The waltz "Around the World", derived from the soundtrack of the 1956 film *Around The World in Eighty Days*, is one of the few songs that refers to the world as a planet. Virtually all other songs treat the world in its collective sense, embracing all of humanity. Examples are "The World Is Waiting for the Sunrise" (1919); "When You're Smiling (The Whole World Smiles With You)" (1928); "Dear World" (1969); the Coca-Cola song, "I'd Like to Teach the World to Sing" (1971); and Michael Jackson and Lionel Richie's "We Are the World" (1985).

Some songs about the world tend to go to extremes, for example, "Small World" (1959) can be arrayed against "It's a Big Wide, Wonderful World" (1940); "It's a Wonderful World" (1939) against "It's a Mad, Mad, Mad, Mad World" (1963); "I'm Sitting on Top of the World" (1925) against "It's a Blue World" (1939); and "Joy to the World; (1970) against "The End of the World" (1962).

As with so many other topics, **love** often enters the picture, as exemplified in the romantic songs "If You Were the Only Girl in the World" (1916), "Let the Rest of the World Go By" (1919), "I've Got the World on a String" (1932), "I Don't Want to Set the World on Fire" (1941), "Love Makes the World Go Round" (1961), and "You and Me Against the World" (1974).

Still other songs bear messages, such as the World War II ballad "When the Lights Go On Again (All Over the World)" (1942); the spiritual revival "He's Got the Whole World in His Hands" (1927); the civil rights song "What the World Needs Now Is Love" (1965); and the call for peace and justice, looking at the world from afar: "From a Distance" (1987).

Additional Songs

All Over the World (1963)
Clear Out of This World (1940)
Color My World (1966)
Different Worlds (1979)
Love Me and the World Is Mine (1906)
Make the World Go Away (1963)
The Most Beautiful Girl in the World (1935)
The Most Beautiful Girl (1973)
Two Different Worlds (1956)
Welcome to My World (1961)
What a Wonderful World (1967)
When the World Was Young (1952)
Wild World (1971)
(What a) Wonderful World (1959)
The World Is Mine (Tonight) (1935)
The World We Knew (1967)
A World Without Love (1964)

WORLD WAR I

Songs inspired by war are effective on several levels: as propaganda, as a unifying force for **patriotism**, and as a source of comfort for the soldiers and for the families left behind. During the years of World War I, 1914 through 1918, **Tin Pan Alley** poured out songs for singing, playing, and dancing. **Pianos** and **player pianos** became enormously popular in homes that could afford them, and most families either owned or had access to a recent invention, the phonograph.

In 1914, when war broke out in Europe, the attitude of President Woodrow Wilson was for America to remain neutral. Tin Pan Alley, in its never-ending search for commercial inspiration, immediately seized upon this opportunity and produced "We Take Our Hats Off to You, Mr. Wilson" (1914) and, shortly after, "I Didn't Raise My Boy to Be a Soldier" (1915).

The American political tide soon changed; on April 6, 1917, President Wilson declared war on Germany. Now it was the job of the Alleymen to inspire Americans to go to war. "Let's All Be Americans Now" (1917), written by Irving Berlin in collaboration with Edgar Leslie and George W. Meyer, was a direct appeal to European immigrants and their children who could not

entirely forget old loyalties, relatives, and friends now regarded as enemies. In the same year, Berlin's "For Your Country and My Country" assured us that if George Washington were alive, he would be in the thick of it, while "Send Me Away With a Smile" encouraged every red-blooded American boy to run to the nearest recruiting station. One song, "Good Luck and God Be With You, Laddie Boy" (1917), used the time-honored device of having women indirectly serve the country by urging their men to fight. Other popular songs of 1917 were "Where Do We Go From Here?," a comic novelty; and the haunting "There's a Long, Long Trail," originally written in 1914.

The most famous song of World War I was George M. Cohan's "Over There." Written the day after America declared war on Germany, it immediately became a song of and for the people, sung by soldiers and civilians alike. The melody was actually based on a simple bugle call and the song used only four chords. Interestingly, it was not recorded by Cohan, but sold millions of records for Nora Bayes. The celebrated Enrico Caruso, singing the song in broken English, had a major hit recording of it in 1918. As a testament to the song's enduring quality, "Over There" was also extremely popular during **World War II** .

Once the United States was fully involved with the war, songs dealt less with propaganda and more with the ordinary soldier. Irving Berlin wrote a lament of the newly inducted private in "Oh! How I Hate to Get Up in the Morning," from the revue *Yip! Yip! Yaphank* (1918). "K-K-K-Katy," the stuttering novelty, was another soldier favorite. "Indianola" (1918) was a comic analogy of the war made famous by Billy Murray, a major **recording** star of the time.

As the war progressed, Americans began to realize the toll it was taking on their sons. Out of the five million men in service, 100,000 lost their lives: 50,000 in battle and most of the others from pneumonia and influenza. The wounded numbered 200,000. Songs became more somber in tone: "Hello Central! Give Me No Man's Land," and a standard that would be revived again during World War II, "Till We Meet Again" (both from 1918).

Three songs of British origin that were cherished by American soldiers were actually written before our involvement with the war. "It's a Long Way From Tipperary" was written in 1912 as a music hall tune with no thought of eventually using it as a war song. Soldiers adopted the song because it had a merry rhythm and was good for marching. It also contained jolly lyrics about an Irishman in London who pined for his sweetheart back home in Tipperary; soldiers overseas could surely identify with this. "Pack Up Your Troubles in Your Old Kit Bag" (1915) lent itself well to being sung in rousing gaiety. American soldiers, moved by the lyrics' urgency to "smile, smile, smile," accepted the song gladly. "Keep the Home Fires Burning," written in

1915, was the number one homefront song of the war. With a melancholy melody and heartrending lyrics, its appeal was very strong. The version recorded by the Irish tenor John McCormack, was a resounding success in 1917.

Immediately following the war, several songs with war-related themes became popular. Irving Berlin's "I've Got My Captain Working for Me Now" was popularized in 1919 by Broadway's biggest star of the time, Al Jolson. It was a clever song about the joy an ex-soldier has in employing his former military superior. "How Ya Gonna Keep 'Em Down on the Farm After They've Seen Paris?," also from 1919, implied that the returning soldier might be bored with his social life at home after his experiences in France. "Roses of Picardy," originally written in 1916, was a beautiful ballad of a love left behind, set in a region of France that was the site of the battle that led to the defeat of the German army.

During the 1920s, the war was not forgotten. Many new recordings were made of old favorites, and new songs written that hinted of a lost loved one or comrade. One of the best songs of this type was Walter Donaldson and Gus Kahn's "My Buddy" (1922). Although the song did not directly refer to the war, most people could not separate the war from it. A song that did not hide the fact that it was about World War I was "My Dream of the Big Parade," written in 1926 by Jimmy McHugh and Al Dubin, a touching reminder of "the war to end all wars."

Additional Songs

Goodbye Broadway, Hello France (1917)
Hinky Dinky Parlay Voo (Mad'moiselle From Armentieres) (1918)
'Til the Clouds Roll By (1917)
The U.S. Field Artillery March (The Caissons Go Rolling Along) (1918)
When the Boys Come Home (1917)

Jeffrey Cahn

Bibliography

Browne, C. A. *The Story of Our National Ballads*. 1960.
Whitcomb, Ian. *After the Ball: Pop Music From Rag to Rock*. 1972.

See also: Roaring Twenties

WORLD WAR II

Unlike the majority of songs born of World War I, few songs written during World War II dealt with propaganda, **patriotism**, and morale; songs written during this war were more about sentiment than strength. One of the few overtly patriotic songs was "He's 1-A in the Army and He's A-1 in My Heart," recorded seven weeks prior to December 8, 1941, the date the United States entered the war. The song's romantic patriotism was deeply felt as America's sons received their draft no-

tices. Other songs from 1941 that accurately reflected the first surge of patriotism were "We Did It Before and We Can Do It Again" and "Goodbye, Mama, I'm Off to Yokohama."

The first outright "war" song to reach the top of the pop charts was Frank Loesser's "Praise the Lord and Pass the Ammunition" (1942). The song's catchy melody and its assumption that God was on America's side were factors in its appeal. Two other war-related songs appeared in 1942: "There's a Star-Spangled Banner Waving Somewhere" and "When the Lights Go On Again (All Over the World)."

Many songs written during the war years did not refer directly to the conflict; the years from 1941 to 1945 saw some of the most touching and emotional songs ever written. When one drapes them in the context of war, the songs become even more heartfelt. One song that did refer to the war, "(There'll Be Bluebirds Over) The White Cliffs of Dover" (1941), contained moving and sentimental lyrics of simple eloquence about "love and laughter . . . . Tomorrow, when the world is free." Other hits from 1941 included the rumba "Yours" (originally written four years earlier) and "Boogie Woogie Bugle Boy," introduced by the Andrews Sisters, a singing trio whose unmistakable sound helped to define the wartime era.

The biggest novelty hit of the war was "Der Fuehrer's Face" (1942), recorded by Spike Jones & His City Slickers; the song's melody is a parody of a Nazi anthem, "Horst Wessell Lied." When this song became popular, the enormity of Nazi inhumanity was not yet known. Hitler was merely the enemy, a fact that made it easy for American humorists to poke fun at him.

Among songs from 1942 that have endured are "I Don't Want to Walk Without You," written by Frank Loesser and Jule Styne the year before; and "There Are Such Things," recorded by Tommy Dorsey and His Orchestra with a vocal by a young man who would become an icon of popular song in the twentieth century, Frank Sinatra. Two other songs of the year had been written in the previous decade: "I'm Thinking Tonight of My Blue Eyes" (1930) and "As Time Goes By" (1931)—a song with special meaning for separated lovers that was performed by pianist Dooley Wilson in the film *Casablanca*. "Lover Man (Oh, Where Can You Be?)," performed by Billie Holiday, struck a chord with many of the women left behind. "Don't Sit Under the Apple Tree (With Anyone Else but Me)" and "I Had the Craziest Dream" were two other great successes of 1942. Of all the standards to come out of that fateful year, one became the best-selling record of all time: "White Christmas," written by Irving Berlin and performed by Bing Crosby. It too held special meaning for separated loved ones.

Due to a royalty dispute, the American Federation of Musicians banned all **recording** by its members from August 1942 to November 1944. At first, singers were only allowed to record without instrumental accompaniment. Recorded in 1943 in this *a cappella* style were "You'll Never Know," sung by Dick Haymes, and "Comin' In on a Wing and a Prayer," sung by the Song Spinners. When Decca Records signed a new contract with the union late in 1943, instrumental accompaniment returned. "No Love, No Nothin'," "Vict'ry Polka," and "Shoo-Shoo-Baby" were three of the earliest hits Decca had after the settlement with the musicians' union. Capitol Records soon followed suit, and in December 1943, Johnny Mercer's "G.I. Jive" was released. Mercer, who founded Capitol Records, was one of the most prolific **lyricists** in history. In 1944, he contributed his morale-building standard, "Ac-cent-tchu-ate the Positive," with music by Harold Arlen.

During the final phase of World War II, the increased longing for loved ones fighting overseas found expression in several songs. Among them were Ira Gershwin and Jerome Kern's "Long Ago (And Far Away)" (1944), Sammy Cahn and Jule Styne's "I'll Walk Alone" (1944), and a revival of Irving Kahal and Sammy Fain's 1938 classic, "I'll Be Seeing You." "Lili Marleen," a German song, the words of which were originally written in 1915, gained tremendous popularity with American soldiers when Tommie Connor gave it English lyrics in 1940. A moving song of separation and longing was "I Wonder" (1944), a record whose label listed the artist as "Private Cecil Gant, the G.I. Singsation."

When the war ended on August 14, 1945, the feeling of joy felt throughout the nation was expressed in such songs as "My Guy's Come Back" (1945). When the initial euphoria died down, America had to face the toll the war had taken. There were 300,000 dead from the Army and Air Force. Naval fatalities numbered almost 90,000, while 250,000 servicemen had sustained injuries. As a result, most songs of this time did not convey a sense of joy or glee but rather reflected a bittersweet happiness, as in the songs "My Dreams Are Getting Better All the Time" (1944), "Sentimental Journey" (1944), "It's Been a Long, Long Time" (1945), and the 1946 ballad "Seems Like Old Times."

During World War II, **radios**, record players, and **jukeboxes** made music more available than ever before. Almost everyone in America and Europe could hear popular music. Because of the technological advances, the music of World War II did more to build the fighting man's morale than at any previous time, aided by a woman named Tokyo Rose, broadcasting from Japan, who played current American hits for servicemen in the Pacific. Her program was one of the most listened-to radio shows in the world and gave American soldiers access to the latest music.

Additional Songs

He Wears a Pair of Silver Wings (1941)

I Left My Heart at the Stage Door Canteen (1942)
I'll Be Home for Christmas (1943)
The Last Time I Saw Paris (1940)
Rosie the Riveter (1942)
Say a Prayer for the Boys Over There (1943)
Till the End of Time (1945)
Till Then (1944)
Time Waits for No One (1944)
Waitin' for the Train to Come In (1945)
Wonder When My Baby's Coming Home (1943)

Jeffrey Cahn

Bibliography

Browne, C. A. *The Story of Our National Ballads*. 1960.

WRITING

Popular songs on the subject of writing are almost equally divided in number between those about writing letters and those about writing books.

With a few exceptions, such as the 1974 ballad, "I Write the Songs," virtually all songs about writing are concerned with some aspect of **love** or **romance**. For example, in "I'm Gonna Sit Write Down and Write Myself a Letter"—one of the most famous "letter" songs—the singer is going to "make believe" the letter comes from his or her beloved. Other romantic songs about letters include the imaginary "Love Letters in the Sand" (1931) and the more realistic "Love Letters" (1945); presumably, both of them would be "Sealed With a Kiss" (1962). Postcripts are also available in at least two songs called "P.S. I Love You": one introduced by Rudy Vallee in 1934, the other by the Beatles in 1962.

Songs about books also serve romance. For instance, in Rodgers and Hart's "I Could Write a Book" from *Pal Joey* (1940), the "simple secret of the plot" is revealed to be "that I love you a lot." Books are also frequently used as metaphors in the pursuit of romance, as in the songs "Close as Pages in a Book" (1944), "Book of Love" (1957), "My Heart Is an Open Book" (1957), and "My Coloring Book" (1962). One famous line from the 1937 song "Too Marvelous for Words" even carries its own bibliographic citation, rhyming "very very" with "Webster's Dictionary."

Additional Songs

The Diary (1958)
It's in the Book (1952)
The Letter (1967)
Paperback Writer (1966)
Please Mister Postman (1961)
Return to Sender (1962)
Strawberry Letter 23 (1971)
Take a Letter, Maria (1969)
Write Me a Letter (1947)

Y

YESTERDAY. *SEE* DAY

YOUR HIT PARADE

An important musical event occurred on the night of April 20, 1935: the broadcast of the first program of a weekly network **radio** show called *Lucky Strike Hit Parade*, airing the top songs of the week. This new program, heard almost exclusively on Saturday night (except for its last season, when it was broadcast on Friday night) ran for twenty-three years, until June 7, 1958. The program was briefly revived later in 1958—lasting until April 1959—and then again in 1974, when it presented the top hits from *Billboard*'s chart.

When the show moved to **television** in 1950, it was given the name *Your Hit Parade* and presented the songs of the week in various settings and costumes, sung by such performers as Dorothy Collins, Snooky Lanson, Gisele MacKenzie, and Russell Arms. During its first years on television, the program was presented in simulcast, i.e., with the television soundtrack broadcast simultaneously over the radio.

America's Saturday-night obsession during the show's best years was to guess which song would be Number One for the week; wagers were often made on the outcome. During its early years, the program served as a valuable measure of a song's success. However, with the emergence of the *Billboard, Variety,* and *Cash Box* Top 10, 40, and 100 lists, it no longer remained the sole barometer of a song's popularity. Still, it was at all times an important and prestigious vehicle for determining the nation's top hits.

The Hit Parade survey was conducted by the advertising agency of Batton, Barton, Durstine, and Osburn. The exact system that was used to determine each week's winners was as secret as the U.S. government's classified information files. Each Friday before the broadcast, a Brink's armored truck collected information from various unidentified sources—carefully screened music shops, key radio stations, music machine (**jukebox**) operators, and selected bandleaders—regarding the frequency of sales, performances, and requests. This information was collated by the show's producers in order to determine the ranking of songs for each weekly broadcast. The exact order of the songs surveyed was kept secret until the last possible moment.

In its twenty-three-year history, *Your Hit Parade* aired over 1,275 songs; of that number, 350 reached Number One. "White Christmas" (1942) held first position longer than any other song, appearing 38 times as Number One, during various Christmas seasons. As for the longest consecutive run on the show, "People Will Say We're in Love," from *Oklahoma!* (1943), holds the record, with 38 appearances between June 1943 and January 1944. During that period, however, it attained Number One for only three weeks. "Too Young" (1951) holds the record for top position in a single run, appearing in first place for 12 consecutive weeks. One of the most ephemeral songs was "I Saw Mommy Kissing Santa Claus" (1952), which appeared on only one show, albeit in first place. Similarly, "Peter Cottontail" (1950) achieved second place in its only appearance.

Perhaps *Your Hit Parade* died of old age, but there may have been other reasons for its demise. In its early years, the public tended to like a song, rather than a specific performer's performance of it. With the advent of rock 'n' roll, however, the public wanted to hear the song performed by the person or group that made it popular. *Your Hit Parade* had an ensemble cast that performed the songs each week. The public did not want to hear Snooky Lanson sing Elvis Presley's hits or Gisele MacKenzie sing the Everly Brothers' songs. Perhaps this emphasis on performance over composition was the primary reason for the program's death. Other possibilities are the rise of the radio **disc jockey** and the ascendancy of the charts, especially *Billboard*'s *Hot 100*.

Additional Songs

Because of You (1940)
Buttons and Bows (1948)
The Gypsy (1948)
Hey There (1954)
If (1934)
I'll Be Seeing You (1943)
I'll Walk Alone (1944)
My Foolish Heart (1949)
My Heart Tells Me (1943)
Now Is the Hour (1948)
Peg o' My Heart (1913)
Some Enchanted Evening (1949)

The Song From Moulin Rouge (Where Is Your Heart?) (1953)
A Tree in the Meadow (1948)
You'll Never Know (1943)

Don Tyler

Bibliography

Ewen, David. *All the Years of American Popular Music.* 1977.
Tyler, Don. *Hit Parade, 1920–55.* 1985.
Williams, John R. *This Was Your Hit Parade.* 1973.

See also: **Awards; Grammy Awards; Top Forty**

YOUTH. SEE AGE

Z

ZYDECO

Zydeco is a hybrid genre, combining elements of **blues, country and western**, Caribbean music, **rhythm and blues**, and **rock 'n' roll** into a music of its own. It originated among the blacks of southwest Louisiana; the parallel music of white Louisianans is called "Cajun." The term itself is said to be a corruption of the French "les haricots" (beans), popularized in a song of that name. Among zydeco's foremost performers are Fernest Arceneaux and Clifton Chenier.

Perhaps the most striking difference between Zydeco and the music of its surroundings lies in its **instrumentation**. Zydeco ensembles are typically led by a piano-accordionist and consist of washboard, electric guitar, bass, and drums. Violin and saxophone are sometimes used as melody instruments.

Bibliography

Ancelot, Barry J. *The Makers of Cajun Music.* 1984.

Daigle, Pierre V. *Tears, Love, and Laughter: The Story of the Acadians.* 1972.

Sheet music cover: "Ta-Ra-Ra-Boom-De-Ay!," 1891.

Sheet music cover: "Daisy Bell (A Bicycle Made For Two)," 1892.

Sheet music cover: "Hello! Ma Baby," 1899.

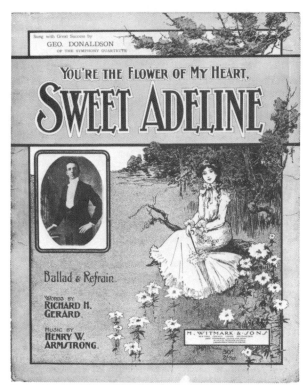

Sheet music cover: "In the Good Old Summer Time," 1902.

Sheet music cover: "You're the Flower of My Heart, Sweet Adeline (Sweet Adeline)," 1903.

Sheet music cover: "My Hero," 1909.

Sheet music cover: "The Missouri Waltz (Hush-a-bye Ma Baby)," 1914.

Cover of dance album and instruction manual, 1914.

Sheet music cover: "Over There," 1917.

Sheet music cover: "Charleston," 1923.

Sheet music cover: "Five Foot Two, Eyes of Blue: Has Anybody Seen My Girl?" 1925.

Sheet music cover: "Charmaine," 1926.

Sheet music cover: "Lover Come Back To Me!" 1928.

Sheet music cover: "I Found A Million Dollar Baby (In A Five and Ten Cent Store)," 1931.

Sheet music cover: "My Man's Gone Now," 1935.

Sheet music cover: "Moon River," 1961.

Music Box Theater, New York City: Irving Berlin's showcase, built in 1920. (Marvin E. Paymer)

Apollo Theater, New York City: Harlem center of rhythm and blues, gospel, and soul since 1934. (Marvin E. Paymer)

Entrance to the Brill Building, New York City: last outpost of Tin Pan Alley. (Marvin E. Paymer)

Downstairs lobby of the Brill Building, New York City: longtime songwriters' mecca. (Marvin E. Paymer)

*St. James Theater, New York City: site of the opening of "Oklahoma!",
March 31, 1943. (Marvin E. Paymer)*

Cole Porter. (The Jeff Cahn Collection)

Irving Berlin. (The Jeff Cahn Collection)

Hoagy Carmichael. (The Jeff Cahn Collection)

Johnny Mercer. (The Jeff Cahn Collection)

The Andrew Sisters, early 1940's. Left to right: Maxene, Patty, and LaVerne. (The Jeff Cahn Collection)

Frank Sinatra, 1955. (The Jeff Cahn Collection)

Nat "King" Cole. (The Jeff Cahn Collection)

Bing Crosby. Left, circa 1930's: right, circa 1960's. (The Jeff Cahn Collection)

Harry James, 1950. (The Jeff Cahn Collection)

Glenn Miller, 1940. (The Jeff Cahn Collection)

Al Jolson, in blackface. (The Jeff Cahn Collection)

The Ink Spots. (The Jeff Cahn Collection)

Rudy Vallee. (The Jeff Cahn Collection)

Peggy Lee and Woody Herman. (The Jeff Cahn Collection)

Little Richard, 1956. (The Jeff Cahn Collection)

Chuck Berry. (The Jeff Cahn Collection)

Willie Nelson and Ray Charles. (The Jeff Cahn Collection)

Elvis Presley, 1957. (The Jeff Cahn Collection)

Stevie Wonder. (The Jeff Cahn Collection)

Aretha Franklin. (The Jeff Cahn Collection)

The Beatles, 1964. Left to right: Paul, Ringo, George, and John. (The Jeff Cahn Collection)

Janis Joplin. (The Jeff Cahn Collection)

Michael Jackson, 1987. (The Jeff Cahn Collection)

Madonna. (The Jeff Cahn Collection)

Part II

Catalogue of Songs

Catalogue of Songs

The following catalogue lists some 4,400 songs mentioned in the articles. Each entry includes the title, year, songwriter(s), and the articles in which the song is discussed. Spelling and punctuation of song titles corresponds to that of the published edition, with alternative titles shown in parentheses. Dating is in accordance with the earliest copyright or publication in the English language and does not always coincide with that of the medium of introduction (play, film, recording) or type of award (Academy, BMI, Grammy).

Writers credited solely with lyrics or music are set down in that order and separated by a slash: e.g.,

Oscar Hammerstein II/Jerome Kern. The presence of a comma indicates that the writers are jointly credited with the lyrics, the music, or the song. A single name indicates that the writer is credited with both words and music, unless the name is preceded by the abbreviation "m.," for music only, or "w.," for words only. When songs have been translated from other languages, only the English lyricist is shown. Alphabetization ignores initial phrases in parentheses. For example, "(Hey Won't You Play) Another Somebody Done Somebody Wrong Song?" is alphabetized under A, not H.

"A-Tisket A-Tasket," 1938
Ella Fitzgerald, Al Feldman
JUKEBOX, NOVELTY SONG, RECORDING, SINGERS, TABLE 15, SWING, WOMEN AS SONGWRITERS

"The Aba Daba Honeymoon," 1914
Arthur Fields, Walter Donovan
ANIMALS, NONSENSE, VAUDEVILLE

"ABC," 1970
Deke Richards, Berry Gordy, Jr., Frederick Perren, Alphonso Mizell
MOTOWN

"About a Quarter to Nine," 1935
Al Dubin/Harry Warren
TABLE 9, TIME OF DAY

"Abraham, Martin and John," 1968
Dick Holler
NAMES

"Ac-cent-tchu-ate the Positive," 1944
Johnny Mercer/Harold Arlen
TABLE 9, INSPIRATION, LYRICISTS, WORLD WAR II

"Acercate Mas," see "Come Closer to Me"

"Across the Wide Missouri," see "Shenandoah"

"Act Naturally," 1963
Vonie Morrison/Johnny Russell
COUNTRY AND WESTERN

"Addicted to Love," 1986
Robert Palmer
TABLE 10-j

"Addictive Love," 1991
BeBe Winans, CeCe Winans
GOSPEL

"ADDIO, ADDIO," 1961
Carl Sigman (Eng.)/Domenico Modugno
FAREWELLS, FOREIGN LANGUAGE, ITALY

"ADELAIDE'S LAMENT," 1950
Frank Loesser
HUMOR

"ADESTE FIDELES," *SEE* "O COME ALL YE FAITHFUL"

"ADIOS," 1931
Eddie Woods (Eng.)/Enric Madriguera
FAREWELLS, FOREIGN LANGUAGE, RUMBA

"ADIOS MUCHACHOS," 1929; *SEE ALSO* "I GET IDEAS"
Cesar F. Vedani (Span.)/Julio Cesar A. Sanders
ARGENTINA, BORROWING, BOY, FAREWELLS, TANGO

"AN AFFAIR TO REMEMBER," 1957
Harold Adamson, Leo McCarey/Harry Warren
TABLE 8

"AFTER ALL THIS TIME," 1988
Rodney Crowell
TABLE 10-w, TIME

"AFTER THE BALL," 1892
Charles K. Harris
BALLAD, BARBERSHOP, BROKEN CHORD, DANCE CRAZES, DANCING, FORM, GAY NINETIES, HARMONIC RHYTHM, HIT SONG, KEY, LYRICS, MUSICAL COMEDY, TABLE 11, POPULAR SONG-ii, SHEET MUSIC, VERSE, WALTZ

"AFTER THE LOVE HAS GONE," 1979
David Foster, Jay Graydon, William Champlin
TABLE 10-p, TABLE 10-q, LOVE

"AFTER THE LOVIN'," 1974
Alan Bernstein, Ritchie Adams
TABLE 4-d, LOVE, RHYME, TONALITY, TRIPLET

"AFTER YOU'VE GONE," 1918
Henry Creamer, Turner Layton
BEBOP, TABLE 3, BREAK, HARMONIC RHYTHM, KEY, LENGTH

"AGAINST ALL ODDS (TAKE A LOOK AT ME NOW)," 1984
Phil Collins
BRITAIN, TABLE 8, TABLE 10-g, TABLE 15, TEMPO

"AGAINST THE WIND," 1980
Bob Seger
TABLE 10-l

"AH, SWEET MYSTERY OF LIFE," 1910
Rida Johnson Young/Victor Herbert
ART SONG, OPERETTA, TABLE 13, SWEETNESS

"AIN'T IT A SHAME?," 1922
W. A. Hann, Joseph Simms, Al W. Brown
DIALECT

"AIN'T MISBEHAVIN'," 1929
Andy Razaf/Thomas "Fats" Waller, Harry Brooks
BALLAD, DIALECT, GOLDEN AGE, PIANO, TABLE 14

"AIN'T NO MOUNTAIN HIGH ENOUGH," 1967
Nickolas Ashford, Valerie Simpson
DIALECT, HEIGHT, MOUNTAINS, TABLE 15

"AIN'T NO STOPPIN' US NOW," 1979
Jerry Cohen, Gene McFadden, John Whitehead
DIALECT

"AIN'T NO SUNSHINE," 1971
Bill Withers
TABLE 10-q, SUN

"AIN'T NO WAY TO TREAT A LADY," 1974
Harriet Schock
DIALECT

"AIN'T NOBODY," 1983
David Wolinski
TABLE 10-p

"AIN'T NOBODY HERE BUT US CHICKENS," 1946
Alex Kramer, Joan Whitney
BIRDS, RHYTHM AND BLUES

"AIN'T NOTHING LIKE THE REAL THING," 1974
Nickolas Ashford, Valerie Simpson
TABLE 10-n

"AIN'T SHE SWEET?," 1927
Jack Yellen/Milton Ager
BREAK, SWEETNESS

"AIN'T THAT A SHAME," 1955
Antoine "Fats" Domino, Dave Bartholomew
COVER, ROCK 'N' ROLL, TABLE 15

"AIN'T WE GOT FUN?," 1921
Gus Kahn, Raymond B. Egan/Richard A. Whiting
LYRICISTS, ROARING TWENTIES

"ALABAMA-SONG (MOON OF ALABAMA)," 1928
Bertolt Brecht/Kurt Weill
MOON, STATES

"ALABAMY BOUND," 1925
B. G. DeSylva, Bud Green/Ray Henderson
STATES

"ALBATROSS," 1967
Judy Collins
BIRDS, FOLK SONG, WOMEN AS
SONGWRITERS

"ALEXANDER'S RAGTIME BAND," 1911
Irving Berlin
COMPOSER-LYRICISTS, CONTRACTIONS, KEY,
LYRICISTS, NAMES, NOVELTY SONG, POPU-
LAR SONG-ii, QUOTATION, RAGTIME, SING-
ING GROUPS, TIN PAN ALLEY, TWO-STEP,
VAUDEVILLE, VERSE

"ALFIE," 1966
Hal David/Burt Bacharach
CADENCE, COLLABORATION, COMPOSERS,
TABLE 8, LYRICISTS, NAMES, RHYTHM AND
BLUES

"ALICE BLUE GOWN," 1919
Joseph McCarthy/Harry Tierney
CLOTHING, COLORS, TABLE 7, DANCE
CRAZES, TABLE 11, NAMES, SWEETNESS,
WALTZ

"ALICE IN WONDERLAND," 1951
Bob Hilliard/Sammy Fain
WONDER

"ALICE'S RESTAURANT," 1966
Arlo Guthrie
FOLK SONG, FOOD AND DRINK, LYRICS

"ALISON," 1977
Elvis Costello
PUNK ROCK

"ALL ALONE," 1924
Irving Berlin
LONELINESS, NEW YORK CITY, REVUES,
TABLE 14, ROARING TWENTIES, TABLE 15,
TELEPHONES, WALTZ

"ALL ALONG THE WATCHTOWER," 1968
Bob Dylan
ROCK-vii

"ALL COONS LOOK ALIKE TO ME," 1896
Ernest Hogan
COON SONG

"ALL DAY AND ALL OF THE NIGHT," 1964
Ray Davies
DAY, ROCK-iii

"ALL HIS CHILDREN," 1971
Alan Bergman, Marilyn Bergman/Henry Mancini
WOMEN AS SONGWRITERS

"ALL I ASK OF YOU," 1986
Charles Hart, Richard Stilgoe/Andrew Lloyd Webber
BRITAIN, TABLE 12, PEDAL POINT

"ALL I DO IS DREAM OF YOU," 1934
Arthur Freed/Nacio Herb Brown
DREAM, TABLE 8

"ALL I HAVE TO DO IS DREAM," 1958
Boudleaux Bryant
TABLE 4-c, ROCK 'N' ROLL-i, SHEET MUSIC

"ALL I NEED IS THE GIRL," 1959
Stephen Sondheim/Jule Styne
GIRL, TABLE 11

"ALL I NEED TO KNOW (DON'T KNOW
MUCH)," 1980
Cynthia Weil, Tom Snow/Barry Mann, Tom Snow
TABLE 10-h

"ALL I REALLY WANT TO DO," 1964
Bob Dylan
ROCK-v

"ALL I WANT FOR CHRISTMAS (IS MY TWO FRONT TEETH)," 1950
Donald Yetter Gardner
CHRISTMAS

"ALL MY LIFE," 1989
Karla Bonoff
TABLE 10-h

"ALL MY LOVE," 1947
Al Jolson, Saul Chaplin, Harry Akst
CLASSICS, TABLE 6

"ALL MY LOVE (BOLÉRO)," 1950
Mitchell Parish/Paul Durand
BOLERO

"ALL MY LOVING," 1963
John Lennon, Paul McCartney
BRITAIN

"ALL OF ME," 1931
Seymour Simons, Gerald Marks
ANATOMY, BALLAD, BROKEN CHORD, CIRCLE OF FIFTHS, GOLDEN AGE, RADIO, SINGERS, TABLE 15, STANDARD

"ALL OF YOU," 1954
Cole Porter
ANATOMY, CARDINAL POINTS, IMPROVISATION, TABLE 11

"ALL OR NOTHING AT ALL," 1940
Jack Lawrence, Arthur Altman
TABLE 3, POPULAR SONG-vi, SINGERS, TABLE 15

"ALL OVER THE WORLD," 1963
Charles Tobias/Al Frisch
WORLD

"ALL SHOOK UP," 1957
Otis Blackwell, Elvis Presley
BMI

"ALL THE THINGS YOU ARE," 1939
Oscar Hammerstein II/Jerome Kern
ART SONG, BALLAD, COMPOSERS, ENHARMONIC EQUIVALENCE, GOLDEN AGE,

INTERVAL, KEY, LANDMARKS OF STAGE AND SCREEN, LYRICISTS, MELODY, MODULATION, TABLE 11, PICKUP, RELEASE, SEQUENCE, SHOW TUNE, VERSE

"ALL THE WAY," 1957
Sammy Cahn/James Van Heusen
TABLE 1, TABLE 8, LYRICISTS, RECORDING

"ALL THOSE YEARS AGO," 1981
George Harrison
ROCK-ii

"ALL THROUGH THE DAY," 1946
Oscar Hammerstein II/Jerome Kern
DAY, MODULATION, TABLE 9

"ALL THROUGH THE NIGHT," 1934
Cole Porter
CHROMATICISM, TABLE 11, NIGHT, SCALE

"ALL YOU NEED IS LOVE," 1967
John Lennon, Paul McCartney
RELIGION, ROCK-ii

"ALLEGHENY MOON," 1956
Al Hoffman, Dick Manning
MOON, RIVER, TABLE 15

"ALLEY CAT," 1962
Jack Harlen, pseud, Britt Simonson (Eng.)/Frank Bjorn
ANIMALS, DENMARK, TABLE 10-e

"ALLEY OOP," 1960
Dallas Frazier
NONSENSE

"ALLEZ-VOUS EN, GO AWAY," 1953
Cole Porter
FOREIGN LANGUAGE, TABLE 11

"ALMOST LIKE BEING IN LOVE," 1947
Alan Jay Lerner/Frederick Loewe
AABA, LYRICISTS, TABLE 12

"ALMOST PERSUADED," 1966
Billy Sherrill, Glenn Sutton
TABLE 10-s, TABLE 10-u, TABLE 10-w

"ALOHA OE," 1878
Queen Liliuokalani
FAREWELLS, GREETINGS

"ALONE," 1935
Arthur Freed/Nacio Herb Brown
COMPOSERS, TABLE 9, INTERVAL, LONELI-
NESS

"ALONE AGAIN (NATURALLY)," 1972
Raymond O'Sullivan
TABLE 4-d, LONELINESS

"ALONE AT LAST," 1960
Johnny Lehmann
CLASSICS, TABLE 6, LONELINESS, ROCK 'N'
ROLL-i

"ALONE IN THE WORLD," 1990
Alan Bergman, Marilyn Bergman/Jerry Goldsmith
WOMEN AS SONGWRITERS

"ALONE TOGETHER," 1932
Howard Dietz/Arthur Schwartz
COLLABORATION, COMPOSERS, KEY, LONE-
LINESS, LYRICISTS, MODE, REVUES, TABLE 14,
TOGETHERNESS

"ALONG CAME JONES," 1959
Jerry Leiber, Mike Stoller
ROCK 'N' ROLL-ii

"ALONG COMES MARY," 1965
Tandyn Almer
NAMES, ROCK

"ALONG THE SANTA FE TRAIL," 1940
Al Dubin, Edwina Coolidge/Will Grosz
TABLE 8

"ALOUETTE," 1879
traditional French-Canadian song
CANADA

"ALWAYS," 1925
Irving Berlin
BALLAD, COMPOSER-LYRICISTS, ENDURING
LOVE, GOLDEN AGE, SCALE, STANDARD, TIN
PAN ALLEY, WALTZ

"ALWAYS IN MY HEART (SIEMPRE EN MI
CORAZON)," 1942
Kim Gannon (Eng.)/Ernesto Lecuona
TABLE 2, BOLERO, CUBA, ENDURING LOVE,
TABLE 9, PICKUP

"ALWAYS ON MY MIND," 1971
Wayne Thompson, Mark James, Johnny Christopher
TABLE 4-d, COUNTRY AND WESTERN, TABLE
10-b, TABLE 10-u, TABLE 10-w, MIND, TABLE 15

"ALWAYS TAKE MOTHER'S ADVICE," 1884
Jennie Lindsay
WOMEN AS SONGWRITERS

"ALWAYS TRUE TO YOU (IN MY FASHION),"
1948
Cole Porter
CATALOGUE SONG, ENDURING LOVE,
HUMOR, TABLE 11

"AM I BLUE?," 1929
Grant Clarke/Harry Akst
BLUE NOTE, BLUES, COLORS, TABLE 7, TABLE
9

"AMAPOLA (PRETTY LITTLE POPPY)," 1924
Joseph M. Lacalle (Eng.)/Joseph M. Lacalle
TABLE 3

"AMAZING GRACE," 1779
John Newton/anon. c. 1850
FOLK SONG, GOSPEL, RELIGION, TABLE 15,
WOMEN AS SONGWRITERS

"L'ÂME DES POÈTES," SEE "AT LAST! AT
LAST!," "THE POET'S DREAM"

"AMERICA (MY COUNTRY 'TIS OF THEE),"
1832
Samuel Francis Smith/unknown
PATRIOTISM

"AMERICA," 1957
Stephen Sondheim/Leonard Bernstein
METER, TABLE 12, NATIONS, PATRIOTISM

"AMERICA," 1980
Neil Diamond
PATRIOTISM

"AMERICA, I LOVE YOU," 1915
Edgar Leslie/Archie Gottler
NATIONS, PATRIOTISM

"AMERICA THE BEAUTIFUL," 1895
Katherine Lee Bates/Samuel Augustus Ward
BEAUTY, GAY NINETIES, NATIONS, PATRIO-
TISM, WOMEN AS SONGWRITERS

"AN AMERICAN IN PARIS," 1929
M. George Gershwin
COMPOSERS

**"AMERICAN PATROL," 1885; SEE ALSO "WE
MUST BE VIGILANT"**
M. F. W. Meacham
ADAPTATION, PATRIOTISM

"AMERICAN PIE," 1971
Don McLean
FOOD AND DRINK, NATIONS, PATRIOTISM,
PERFORMER-SONGWRITERS, ROCK

"AMONG MY SOUVENIRS," 1927
Edgar Leslie/Horatio Nicholls (pseud. Lawrence
Wright)
MEMORY, ROCK 'N' ROLL-ii, SINGING GROUPS

"AMOR," 1941
Norman Newell (Eng.)/Gabriel Ruiz
BOLERO, BROKEN CHORD, FOREIGN LAN-
GUAGE, LOVE, MEXICO

"L'AMOUR EST BLEU," SEE "LOVE IS BLUE"

"L'AMOUR TOUJOURS L'AMOUR," 1922
Catherine Chisholm Cushing/Rudolf Friml
CZECHOSLOVAKIA, FOREIGN LANGUAGE,
LOVE

"ANASTASIA," 1956
Paul Francis Webster/Alfred Newman
TABLE 8, NAMES

"ANCHORS AWEIGH," 1907
Capt. Alfred Hart Miles/Charles A. Zimmerman,
George D. Lottman
BOATING, MARCH, OCEAN, PATRIOTISM

"AND HER TEARS FLOWED LIKE WINE," 1943
Joe Greene/Stan Kenton, Charles Lawrence
TABLE 3, CRYING, FOOD AND DRINK

**"AND I AM TELLING YOU I'M NOT GOING,"
1981**
Tom Eyen/Henry Krieger
TABLE 10-n

"AND I LOVE HER," 1964
John Lennon, Paul McCartney
TABLE 4-d, BRITAIN, COLLABORATION,
MODE, VAMP

"AND I LOVE YOU SO," 1970
Don McLean
TABLE 4-d

"AND THE ANGELS SING," 1939
Johnny Mercer/Ziggy Elman
ANGELS, DISC JOCKEY, SWING

"AND THIS IS MY BELOVED," 1953
Robert Wright, George Forrest
CLASSICS, TABLE 6, MUSICAL PLAYS, TABLE 12

"AND WHEN I DIE," 1969
Laura Nyro
ROCK-ix

"ANEMA E CORE," 1954
Mann Curtis, Harry Akst/Salve d'Esposito
TABLE 2, FOREIGN LANGUAGE, ITALY

"ANGEL," 1984
Madonna, Steve Bray
ANGELS

"ANGEL EYES," 1953
Earl Brent/Matt Davis
ANGELS

"THE ANGEL IN YOUR ARMS," 1976
Clayton Ivey, Terry Woodford, Tom Brasfield
ANGELS

"ANGEL OF THE MORNING," 1967
Chip Taylor
ANGELS, TABLE 4-c, TIME OF DAY

"Angela Mia (My Angel)," 1928
Lew Pollack/Erno Rapee
ANGELS

"Angie," 1973
Mick Jagger, Keith Richards
ROCK-iii

"Anna," 1952
William Engvick (Eng.)/R. Vatro
TABLE 8, NAMES, SAMBA

"L'Année Passée," 1906; SEE ALSO "Rum and Coca-Cola"
M. Lionel Belasco
BORROWING

"Annie Laurie," 1838
William Douglas/Lady John Scott (Alicia Ann Spottiswoode)
FILM MUSIC, NAMES

"Annie's Song," 1974
John Denver
NAMES, RHYME, WALTZ

"Anniversary Song," 1946
Al Jolson, Saul Chaplin
CLASSICS, TABLE 6, MARRIAGE, MODE, OCCASIONAL SONG, SINGERS

"The Anniversary Waltz," 1941
Dave Franklin, Al Dubin
MARRIAGE, OCCASIONAL SONG

"Another Brick in the Wall, Part II," 1979
Roger Waters
ROCK

"Another Day in Paradise," 1989
Phil Collins
TABLE 10-a

"Another Hundred People," 1970
Stephen Sondheim
TABLE 11, PEOPLE

"Another Op'nin', Another Show," 1948
Cole Porter
BROADWAY, TABLE 11

"Another Rag," 1911
D. A. Esrom (pseud. Theodora Morse)/Theodore Morse
WOMEN AS SONGWRITERS

"Another Saturday Night," 1963
Sam Cooke
DAYS OF THE WEEK, ROCK 'N' ROLL-i

"(Hey Won't You Play) Another Somebody Done Somebody Wrong Song?," 1975
Larry Butler, Chips Moman
TABLE 4-d, MUSIC, TABLE 10-w

"Answer Me, My Love," 1954
Carl Sigman (Eng.)/Gerhard Winkler, Fred Rauch
GERMANY, QUESTIONS

"Anticipation," 1971
Carly Simon
FOLK ROCK, PERFORMER-SONGWRITERS, ROCK-vi, TELEVISION, WAITING, WOMEN AS SONGWRITERS

"Any Old Place With You," 1919
Lorenz Hart/Richard Rodgers
CATALOGUE SONG, PLACES

"Any Time," 1921
Herbert Happy Lawson
COUNTRY AND WESTERN, TIME

"Any Way You Want Me (That's How I Will Be)," 1956
Aaron Schroeder, Cliff Owens
POPULAR SONG-viii

"Anyone Can Move a Mountain," 1966
Johnny Marks
INSPIRATION, MOUNTAINS

"Anyone Who Had a Heart," 1963
Hal David/Burt Bacharach
POPULAR SONG-x

"ANYTHING BUT LONELY," 1988
Don Black, Charles Hart/Andrew Lloyd Webber
LONELINESS, TABLE 12, TONALITY

"ANYTHING GOES," 1934
Cole Porter
CATALOGUE SONG, COMPOSER-LYRICISTS,
TABLE 11, SOCIETY TEMPO

"ANYTHING YOU CAN DO," 1946
Irving Berlin
COMPARATIVES

"ANYWHERE I WANDER," 1952
Frank Loesser
TABLE 9

"APPALACHIAN MEMORIES," 1983
Dolly Parton
WOMEN AS SONGWRITERS

"THE APRIL FOOLS," 1969
Hal David/Burt Bacharach
FOOLS, MONTHS

"APRIL IN PARIS," 1932
E. Y. Harburg/Vernon Duke
ARRANGEMENT, CITIES, TABLE 5, CODA,
COMPOSERS, GOLDEN AGE, LYRICISTS,
MONTHS, REVUES, TABLE 14

"APRIL IN PORTUGAL," 1953
Jimmy Kennedy (Eng.)/Raul Ferrão
MODE, MONTHS

"APRIL LOVE," 1957
Paul Francis Webster/Sammy Fain
AGE, TABLE 9, LOVE, MONTHS, TABLE 15

"APRIL SHOWERS," 1921
B. G. DeSylva/Louis Silvers
AABA, FORM, LYRICISTS, MONTHS, POPULAR
SONG-ii, ROARING TWENTIES, TABLE 15,
WEATHER

"APRIL SNOW," 1944
Dorothy Fields/Sigmund Romberg
WOMEN AS SONGWRITERS

"AQUARELA DO BRASIL," SEE "BRAZIL"

"AQUARIUS," 1967; SEE ALSO "LET THE SUN-
SHINE IN"
Gerome Ragni, James Rado/Galt MacDermot
TABLE 10-a, TABLE 10-h, HARMONIC RHYTHM,
MAGIC, TABLE 11, OPERA, SINGING GROUPS

"AQUELLOS OJOS VERDES," SEE "GREEN EYES"

"ARE YOU FROM DIXIE, 'CAUSE I'M FROM
DIXIE TOO," 1915
Jack Yellen, George L. Cobb
NOVELTY SONG, RAGTIME

"ARE YOU HAVIN' ANY FUN?," 1939
Jack Yellen/Sammy Fain
REVUES, TABLE 14

"ARE YOU LONESOME TONIGHT?," 1926
Roy Turk, Lou Handman
LONELINESS, ROCK 'N' ROLL-i

"ARE YOU MAKIN' ANY MONEY?," 1933
Herman Hupfeld
DEPRESSION YEARS, MONEY

"ARE YOU SURE HANK DONE IT THIS WAY?,"
1975
Waylon Jennings
COUNTRY AND WESTERN

"AREN'T YOU GLAD YOU'RE YOU?," 1945
Johnny Burke/James Van Heusen
HAPPINESS

"THE ARMY AIR CORPS," 1939
Robert Crawford
MARCH, METER, PATRIOTISM

"AROUND THE PIANO," SEE "ALLEY CAT"

"AROUND THE WORLD," 1956
Harold Adamson/Victor Young
FILM MUSIC, TABLE 8, TRAVEL, WALTZ,
WORLD

"ARRIVEDERCI ROMA," 1954
Carl Sigman (Eng.)/Renato Rascel (pseud. Renato Ranucci)
BOLERO, TABLE 5, FAREWELLS, TABLE 9, FOREIGN LANGUAGE, ITALY

"ARTHUR MURRAY TAUGHT ME DANCING IN A HURRY," 1942
Johnny Mercer/Victor Schertzinger
DANCING, TABLE 9

"ARTHUR'S THEME (BEST THAT YOU CAN DO)," 1981
Carole Bayer Sager, Christopher Cross, Peter Allen, Burt Bacharach
TABLE 1, CIRCLE OF FIFTHS, TABLE 8, SUPER-LATIVES

"ARTISTRY IN RHYTHM," 1941
m. Stan Kenton
SWING

"AS LONG AS HE NEEDS ME," 1960
Lionel Bart
BRITAIN, ENDURING LOVE

"AS LONG AS I LIVE," 1934
Ted Koehler/Harold Arlen
ENDURING LOVE, HARLEM

"AS TEARS GO BY," 1964
Mick Jagger, Andrew Oldham, Keith Richards
ROCK-iii

"AS TIME GOES BY," 1931
Herman Hupfeld
AABA, COMPOSER-LYRICISTS, FILM MUSIC, GOLDEN AGE, LANDMARKS OF STAGE AND SCREEN, MELODY, PICKUP, SEQUENCE, STANDARD, TIME, TIN PAN ALLEY, WORLD WAR II

"AS YEARS GO BY," 1947
Charles Tobias, Peter De Rose
TABLE 6

"ASK THE ANGELS," 1976
Patti Smith, Ivan Krull
WOMEN AS SONGWRITERS

"ASLEEP IN THE DEEP," 1897
Arthur J. Lamb/Henry W. Petrie
DEPTH, GAY NINETIES, SLEEP

"AT A GEORGIA CAMP MEETING," 1897
Kerry Mills
COON SONG, MEETING

"AT DAWNING," 1906
Nelle Richmond Eberhart/Charles Wakefield Cadman
TIME OF DAY

"AT LAST," 1942
Mack Gordon/Harry Warren
TABLE 3, BLUE NOTE

"AT LAST! AT LAST! (L'ÂME DES POÈTES)," 1951
Florence Miles (Eng.)/Charles Trenet
FRANCE

"AT LONG LAST LOVE," 1938
Cole Porter
CATALOGUE SONG, LOVE, TABLE 11

"AT SEVENTEEN," 1974
Janis Ian
AGE, TABLE 10-f, WOMEN AS SONGWRITERS

"AT SUNDOWN," 1927
Walter Donaldson
TABLE 9, SUN, TIME OF DAY, VAMP

"AT THE BALALAIKA," 1939
Eric Maschwitz, Bob Wright, Chet Forrest/George Posford, Herbert Stothart
BRITAIN

"AT THE COPA," SEE "COPACABANA"

"AT THE CROSSROADS," 1942
Bob Russell (Eng.)/Ernesto Lecuona
ADAPTATION, TABLE 6, CUBA

"AT THE JAZZ BAND BALL," 1918
Edwin B. Edwards, James La Rocca, Anthony Sbarbaro, Larry Shields
DIXIELAND

"ATLANTIS," 1968
Donovan Leitch
ROCK-v

"AU REVOIR, PLEASANT DREAMS," 1930
Jack Meskill/Jean Schwartz
FAREWELLS, FOREIGN LANGUAGE, HUNGARY

"AUF WIEDERSEH'N," 1915
Herbert Reynolds/Sigmund Romberg
FAREWELLS, FOREIGN LANGUAGE

"AUF WIEDERSEH'N, MY DEAR," 1932
Al Hoffman, Ed. G. Nelson, Al Goodhart, Milton
Ager
FAREWELLS, FOREIGN LANGUAGE, RADIO

"AUF WIEDERSEH'N, SWEETHEART," 1952
John Sexton, John Turner (Eng.)/Eberhard Storch
FAREWELLS, FOREIGN LANGUAGE, GERMANY,
SWEETNESS

"AULD LANG SYNE," 1711
Robert Burns/traditional Scottish Song
TABLE 3, GAY NINETIES, HOLIDAYS, PATRIO-
TISM, QUOTATION

"AUNT HAGAR'S BLUES," 1920
J. Tim Brymn/W. C. Handy
BLUES

**"AURA LEE," 1861; SEE ALSO "LOVE ME
TENDER"**
W. W. Fosdick/George R. Poulton
BORROWING, TENDERNESS

"AURORA," 1941
Harold Adamson (Eng.)/Mario Lago, Roberto Roberti
SAMBA, SINGING GROUPS

"AUTUMN CONCERTO," 1956
Paul Siegel (Eng.)/Camillo Bargoni
ITALY

"AUTUMN IN NEW YORK," 1934
Vernon Duke
TABLE 5, COMPOSERS, GOLDEN AGE, HAR-
MONY, TABLE 14, SEASONS

**"AUTUMN LEAVES (LES FEUILLES MORTES),"
1947**
Johnny Mercer (Eng.)/Joseph Kosma
BOLERO, FRANCE, LYRICISTS, MODE, SEA-
SONS, SEQUENCE, TREES

"AUTUMN NOCTURNE," 1941
Kim Gannon/Josef Myrow
SEASONS

"AUTUMN SERENADE," 1945
Sammy Gallop/Peter De Rose
MUSIC

"AVALON," 1920
Al Jolson, Vincent Rose
TABLE 5, CLASSICS, TABLE 6, ITALY, LYRI-
CISTS, OPERA, SINGERS, TABLE 15

"AVANT DE MOURIR," SEE "MY PRAYER"

"AVENUE C," 1958
m. Count Basie
VOCALESE

"B-A-B-Y," 1966
David Porter, Isaac Hayes
BABY, SOUL

"BA-BA-BACIAMI PICCINA," SEE "BOTCH-A-ME"

"BABALU," 1939
S. K. Russell (Eng.)/Margarita Lecuona
RUMBA, WOMEN AS SONGWRITERS

"BABY DON'T GET HOOKED ON ME," 1972
Mac Davis
BABY, TABLE 4-d

"BABY FACE," 1926
Benny Davis, Harry Akst
TABLE 2, BABY, DISCO

"BABY, IT'S COLD OUTSIDE," 1948
Frank Loesser
TABLE 1, BABY, COMPOSER-LYRICISTS,
WEATHER

"BABY, IT'S YOU," 1961
Mack David, Burt Bacharach, Barney Williams
BABY, ROCK 'N' ROLL-iv

"BABY LOVE," 1964
Brian Holland, Lamont Dozier, Eddie Holland
BABY, MOTOWN

"BABY MINE," 1878
Charles Mackay/Archibald Johnston
BABY

"BABY, THE RAIN MUST FALL," 1964
Ernie Sheldon/Elmer Bernstein
WEATHER

**"BABY, WON'T YOU PLEASE COME HOME?"
1923**
Charles Warfield/Clarence Williams
BABY, HOME, TEMPO

"BABY, YOU'RE A RICH MAN," 1967
John Lennon, Paul McCartney
BABY, MONEY

"BACK IN MY ARMS AGAIN," 1965
Eddie Holland, Brian Holland, Lamont Dozier
MOTOWN

"BACK IN YOUR OWN BACK YARD," 1928
Al Jolson, Billy Rose, Dave Dreyer
SINGERS, TABLE 15

"BACK OFF BOOGALOO," 1972
Richard Starkey
ROCK-ii

"BACK STABBERS," 1972
Leon Huff, Gene McFadden, John Whitehead
SOUL

"BACK TO LIFE," 1989
Simon Laws, Caron Wheeler, Nelle Hooper, Bereford Romeo
TABLE 10-p, LIFE

"BACK TRACK! (PASSE TON CHEMIN)," 1954
Lee Wilson, Lynn Russell (Eng.)/Gilbert Becaud
FRANCE

"BACK WHERE YOU STARTED," 1986
Bryan Adams, Jim Vallance
TABLE 10-i

**"THE BAD AND THE BEAUTIFUL (LOVE IS FOR
THE VERY YOUNG)," 1953**
Dory Langdon/David Raksin
BEAUTY, TABLE 8

"BAD, BAD LEROY BROWN," 1972
Jim Croce
NAMES

"BAD, BAD WHISKEY," 1950
Thomas Maxwell Davis
FOOD AND DRINK

"BAD GIRLS," 1978
Donna Summer/Bruce Sudano, Joe Esposito, Eddie Hokenson
GIRL, POPULAR SONG-xiii

"THE BAD IN EVERY MAN," SEE **"BLUE MOON"**

"BAD LOVE," 1990
Eric Clapton, Mick Jones
TABLE 10-j

"BAD MOON RISING," 1969
John C. Fogerty
MOON, ROCK-ix

"BADGE," 1969
Eric Clapton, George Harrison
HEAVY METAL

"BAIA," 1944
Ray Gilbert (Eng.)/Ary Barroso
BRAZIL, TABLE 5, TABLE 9, SAMBA

"BAKER STREET," 1978
Gerry Rafferty
STREETS

"BALI HA'I," 1949
Oscar Hammerstein II/Richard Rodgers
MOUNTAINS, MUSICAL PLAYS, TABLE 12

"BALL AND CHAIN," 1968
  Willie Mae Thornton
  ROCK-vii

"BALLAD FOR AMERICANS," 1940
  John Latouche/Earl Robinson
  BALLAD

"BALLAD OF A THIN MAN," 1965
  Bob Dylan
  ROCK-iv

"THE BALLAD OF BONNIE AND CLYDE," 1967
  Mitch Murray, Peter Callander
  BALLAD, FILM MUSIC, TABLE 8, NAMES

"THE BALLAD OF DAVY CROCKETT," 1955
  Tom Blackburn/George Bruns
  BALLAD, TABLE 8, NAMES

"BALLAD OF JED CLAMPETT," 1962
  Paul Henning
  BLUEGRASS

"THE BALLAD OF SWEENEY TODD," 1979
  Stephen Sondheim
  BALLAD

"THE BALLAD OF THE GREEN BERETS," 1966
  Barry Sadler, Robin Moore
  BALLAD, CLOTHING, TABLE 7

"BALLERINA," 1947
  Bob Russell, Carl Sigman
  TABLE 15

"BALLIN' THE JACK," 1913
  James Henry Burris/Chris Smith
  CIRCLE OF FIFTHS, DANCE CRAZES, OPERA,
  RAGTIME

"BALTIMORE ORIOLE," 1942
  Paul Francis Webster/Hoagy Carmichael
  BIRDS, TRIPLET

"LA BAMBA," 1958
  William Clauson
  MEXICO, ROCK 'N' ROLL-i

"BAMBOO BABY," 1920
  Caro Roma
  WOMEN AS SONGWRITERS

"THE BANANA BOAT SONG (DAY-O)," 1956
  Erik Darling, Bob Carey, Alan Arkin
  BOATING, CALYPSO, FOOD AND DRINK,
  TABLE 15, SINGING GROUPS

"BAND ON THE RUN," 1974
  Paul McCartney, Linda McCartney
  TABLE 10-h, ROCK-ii

"THE BAND PLAYED ON," 1895
  John E. Palmer/Charles B. Ward
  HARMONIC RHYTHM, HARMONY, MUSIC,
  WALTZ

"BANG BANG (MY BABY SHOT ME DOWN),"
  1966
  Sonny Bono
  BOOGALOO

"BANNED IN THE U.S.A.," 1990
  Bruce Springsteen and Featuring the 2 Live Crew
  Luke
  RAP

"BARNEY GOOGLE," 1923
  Billy Rose, Con Conrad
  NAMES, NOVELTY SONG, ROARING TWEN-
  TIES

"BASIN STREET BLUES," 1928
  Spencer Williams
  BLUES, STREETS

"THE BATTLE CRY OF FREEDOM," 1863
  George Frederick Root
  POPULAR SONG-i

"BATTLE HYMN OF THE REPUBLIC," 1862
  Julia Ward Howe
  POPULAR SONG-i

"THE BATTLE OF NEW ORLEANS," 1957
  Jimmy Driftwood
  TABLE 5, COUNTRY AND WESTERN, TABLE 10-
  b, TABLE 10-s

"Baubles, Bangles, and Beads," 1953
Robert Wright, George Forrest
CLASSICS, TABLE 6, JEWELRY, MUSICAL PLAYS,
TABLE 12

"Be a Clown," 1948
Cole Porter
CIRCUS, TABLE 9, SINGERS, TABLE 15

"Be-Baba-Luba," 1945
Helen Humes
BEBOP

"Be-Bop," 1944
Dizzy Gillespie
BEBOP

"Be-Bop-A-Lula," 1956
Gene Vincent, Tex Davis
NONSENSE, ROCK 'N' ROLL

"Be Careful, It's My Heart," 1942
Irving Berlin
TABLE 9, HOLIDAYS

"Be Mine," 1950
Jack Elliott/Harold Spina
REPEATED NOTE

"Be My Baby," 1963
Phil Spector, Ellie Greenwich, Jeff Barry
BABY, ROCK 'N' ROLL

"Be My Love," 1949
Sammy Cahn/Nicholas Brodszky
TABLE 9, TABLE 15

"Be True to Your School," 1963
Brian Wilson
ROCK-i

"Beale Street Blues," 1916
W. C. Handy
BLUES, STREETS

"Beast of Burden," 1978
Mick Jagger, Keith Richards
ROCK-iii

"The Beat Goes On," 1966
Sonny Bono
ROCK

"Beat It," 1982
Michael Jackson
TABLE 10-a, TABLE 10-j, ROCK-xii

"Beat Me Daddy, Eight to the Bar," 1940
Hughie Prince, Don Raye, Eleanor Sheehy
BOOGIE-WOOGIE, FATHERS, MUSIC, SINGING
GROUPS

"A Beautiful Friendship," 1956
Stanley Styne/Donald Cahn
BEAUTY, FRIENDSHIP

"A Beautiful Lady in Blue," 1935
Sam H. Lewis/J. Fred Coots
BEAUTY

"Beautiful Love," 1931
Haven Gillespie/Victor Young, Wayne King, Egbert
van Alstyne
BEAUTY

"A Beautiful Morning," 1968
Edward Brigati, Jr., Felix Cavaliere
TIME OF DAY

"Beautiful Ohio," 1918
Ballard MacDonald/Mary Earl
RIVERS, STATES, WALTZ

"Beautiful Red Dress," 1959
Laurie Anderson
WOMEN AS SONGWRITERS

"Beauty and the Beast," 1991
Howard Ashman/Alan Menken
TABLE 1, TABLE 9

"Because," 1902
Edward Teschemacher (Eng.)/Guy d'Hardelot (pseud.
Mrs. W. I. Rhodes, Helen Guy)
ART SONG, FRANCE, MARRIAGE

"Because," 1964
Dave Clark
ROCK-iii

"BECAUSE HE LIVES," 1971
Bill Gaither
GOSPEL

"BECAUSE OF YOU," 1940
Arthur Hammerstein, Dudley Wilkinson
TABLE 15, *YOUR HIT PARADE*

"BECAUSE THE NIGHT," 1978
Patti Smith, Bruce Springsteen
WOMEN AS SONGWRITERS

"BECAUSE YOU'RE YOU," 1906
Henry Blossom/Victor Herbert
TABLE 11

"BEECHWOOD 4-5789," 1962
William Stevenson, George Gordy, Marvin Gaye
MOTOWN, TELEPHONES

"BEER BARREL POLKA (ROLL OUT THE BARREL)," 1939
Lew Brown (Eng.)/Jaromir Vejvoda
CZECHOSLOVAKIA, DANCE CRAZES, FOOD AND DRINK, JUKEBOX, LYRICISTS, NOVELTY SONG, POLKA, SINGING GROUPS

"BEFORE THE NEXT TEARDROP FALLS," 1967
Vivian Keith, Ben Peters
COUNTRY AND WESTERN, CRYING

"BEGIN THE BEGUINE," 1935
Cole Porter
ALLITERATION, ARRANGEMENT, BEGINNING, BEGUINE, BIG BANDS, TABLE 3, CODA, COMPOSER-LYRICISTS, DYNAMICS, GOLDEN AGE, HIT SONG, LANDMARKS OF STAGE AND SCREEN, LENGTH, MUSICAL COMEDY, TABLE 11, RANGE, TRIPLET, VAMP

"(I'VE GOT) BEGINNER'S LUCK," 1937
Ira Gershwin/George Gershwin
BEGINNING, TABLE 9, LUCK

"BEGINNINGS," 1969
Robert Lamm
BEGINNING, ROCK-ix

"BEHIND CLOSED DOORS," 1973
Kenny O'Dell (pseud, Kenneth Gist, Jr.)
TABLE 4-d, COUNTRY AND WESTERN, TABLE 10-u, 10-w

"BEI MIR BIST DU SCHÖN (MEANS THAT YOU'RE GRAND)," 1933
Sammy Cahn, Saul Chaplin (Eng.)/Sholom Secunda
FOREIGN LANGUAGE, JUKEBOX, MODE, NOVELTY SONG, RECORDING, SINGING GROUPS, TELEVISION

"BELIEVE IN HUMANITY," 1973
Carole King
WOMEN AS SONGWRITERS

"BELIEVE IT OR NOT (THE THEME FROM *THE GREATEST AMERICAN HERO*)," 1981
Stephen Geyer/Mike Post
TELEVISION

"BELIEVE ME IF ALL THOSE ENDEARING YOUNG CHARMS," 1807
Thomas Moore/unknown
POPULAR SONG-i

"BELLE OF THE BALL," 1953
Mitchell Parish/Leroy Anderson
WOMAN

"THE BELLS," 1963
Edgar Allan Poe/Phil Ochs
FOLK SONG

"BEN," 1971
Don Black/Walter Scharf
ANIMALS, TABLE 8

"BENNIE AND THE JETS," 1973
Elton John, Bernie Taupin
ROCK-x

"BERNIE'S TUNE," 1953
Bernie Miller, Mike Stoller, Jerry Leiber
MELODY

"BESAME MUCHO," 1941
Sunny Skylar (Eng.)/Consuelo Velasquez
BOLERO, TABLE 6, FOREIGN LANGUAGE, KISSING, MEXICO, MODE

"BESIDE YOU," 1947
Jay Livingston, Ray Evans
CLOSENESS, RHYTHM AND BLUES

"BESS, YOU IS MY WOMAN," 1935
DuBose Heyward, Ira Gershwin/George Gershwin
ACCOMPANIMENT, BLUE NOTE, DIALECT, LANDMARKS OF STAGE AND SCREEN, NAMES, OPERA, WOMAN

"THE BEST IS YET TO COME," 1959
Carolyn Leigh/Cy Coleman
SUPERLATIVES

"BEST OF MY LOVE," 1974
Glenn Frey, Don Henley, John David Souther
SUPERLATIVES

"BEST OF MY LOVE," 1977
Maurice White, Albert McKay
TABLE 10-p, LOVE, SUPERLATIVES

"THE BEST OF TIMES," 1981
Jerry Herman
TABLE 11, SUPERLATIVES

"BEST THAT YOU CAN DO," SEE **"ARTHUR'S SONG"**

"THE BEST THING FOR YOU," 1950
Irving Berlin
SUPERLATIVES

"(YOU'RE THE) BEST THING THAT EVER HAPPENED TO ME," 1972
Jim Weatherly
SUPERLATIVES

"THE BEST THINGS IN LIFE ARE FREE," 1927
B. G. DeSylva, Lew Brown, Ray Henderson
COMPOSERS, LYRICISTS, MONEY, TABLE 11, SUPERLATIVES

"BETTE DAVIS EYES," 1975
Donna Weiss/Jackie DeShannon
TABLE 2, TABLE 10-a, TABLE 10-b

"BETTER BE GOOD TO ME," 1984
Holly Knight, Mike Chapman, Nicky Chinn
TABLE 10-i

"BETTER DAYS," 1976
Carole Bayer Sager, Melissa Manchester
WOMEN AS SONGWRITERS

"BETTER NOT TELL HER," 1990
Carly Simon
WOMEN AS SONGWRITERS

"BETTY CO-ED," 1930
J. Paul Fogarty, Rudy Vallee
NAMES, RADIO

"BETWEEN 18TH AND 19TH ON CHESTNUT STREET," 1939
Dick Rogers, Will Osborne
STREETS

"BETWEEN THE DEVIL AND THE DEEP BLUE SEA," 1931
Ted Koehler/Harold Arlen
TABLE 7, DEPTH MAGIC, OCEAN

"BEWILDERED," 1938
Leonard Whitcup/Teddy Powell
RHYTHM AND BLUES, ROCK 'N' ROLL-i

"BEWITCHED," 1941
Lorenz Hart/Richard Rodgers
ALLITERATION, CATALOGUE SONG, GOLDEN AGE, LYRICISTS, MAGIC, MUSICAL COMEDY, TABLE 11

"BEYOND THE BLUE HORIZON," 1930
Leo Robin/Richard A. Whiting, W. Franke Harling
TABLE 7, TABLE 9, LYRICISTS, SKY

"BEYOND THE SEA (LA MER)," 1947
Jack Lawrence (Eng.)/Charles Trenet
FRANCE, OCEAN

"BIBBIDI-BOBBIDI-BOO," 1948
Mack David, Al Hoffman, Jerry Livingston
NONSENSE

"THE BIBLE TELLS ME SO," 1955
Dale Evans
RELIGION

"A BICYCLE MADE FOR TWO," *SEE* "DAISY BELL"

"BIDIN' MY TIME," 1930
Ira Gershwin/George Gershwin
CONTRACTIONS, FORM, MUSICAL COMEDY, TABLE 11, QUOTATION, TIME, WAITING

"BIG BAD JOHN," 1961
Jimmy Dean
COUNTRY AND WESTERN, NAMES, TABLE 10-s

"BIG D," 1956
Frank Loesser
TABLE 5, TABLE 12

"BIG GIRLS DON'T CRY," 1962
Bob Crewe, Bob Gaudio
CRYING, GIRL, ROCK 'N' ROLL-ii

"BIG MAN," 1958
Glen Larson, Bruce Belland
MAN, SINGING GROUPS

"BIG NOISE FROM WINNETKA," 1940
Gil Rodin, Bob Crosby/Bob Haggart, Ray Bauduc
TABLE 3, TABLE 5

"THE BIG ROCK CANDY MOUNTAIN," 1895
traditional song
FOLK SONG

"BIG SPENDER," 1965
Dorothy Fields/Cy Coleman
MONEY

"BIG YELLOW TAXI," 1970
Joni Mitchell
TABLE 7, ROCK-vi, TRAVEL

"THE BILBAO SONG," 1961
Johnny Mercer (Eng.)/Kurt Weill
GERMANY, OPERA

"BILL," 1927
P. G. Wodehouse, Oscar Hammerstein II/Jerome Kern
MUSICAL PLAYS, TABLE 12, TABLE 15, TORCH SONG

"BILL BAILEY, WON'T YOU PLEASE COME HOME?," 1902
Hughie Cannon
COON SONG, DIALECT, HARMONIC RHYTHM, HOME, LYRICS, NAMES, NOVELTY SONG, RAGTIME, TABLE 15, TIN PAN ALLEY, TWO-STEP, VAUDEVILLE

"BILLIE JEAN," 1982
Michael Jackson
TABLE 10-o, TABLE 10-q, NAMES, ROCK-xii, TELEVISION

"BILLIE'S BLUES," 1936
Billie Holiday
WOMEN AS SONGWRITERS

"BILLY BOY," 1824
traditional English song
FOLK SONG

"BIM BAM BOOM," 1941
Harold Adamson, Noro Morales, John A. Camacho
NONSENSE

"BIRD DOG," 1958
Boudleaux Bryant
ANIMALS, ROCK 'N' ROLL-i

"A BIRD IN A GILDED CAGE," 1899
Arthur J. Lamb/Harry Von Tilzer
BIRDS, GAY NINETIES, VAUDEVILLE, VERSE

"BIRD ON THE WIRE," 1968
Leonard Cohen
BIRDS, PERFORMER-SONGWRITERS, ROCK-vi

"BIRMINGHAM JAIL," *SEE* "DOWN IN THE VALLEY"

"THE BIRTH OF THE BLUES," 1926
B. G. DeSylva, Lew Brown/Ray Henderson
ALLITERATION, BIRTH, BLUES, COLLABORATION, COMPOSERS, LYRICISTS, REVUES, TABLE 14, ROARING TWENTIES, SINGING GROUPS

"THE BITCH IS BACK," 1974
Elton John, Bernie Taupin
ROCK-x

"BITS AND PIECES," 1963
Dave Clark, Mike Smith
ROCK-iii

"BLACK & WHITE," 1956
David Arkin/Earl Robinson
TABLE 7

"BLACK BOTTOM," 1926
B. G. DeSylva, Lew Brown/Ray Henderson
ALLITERATION, TABLE 7, DANCE CRAZES,
REVUES, TABLE 14

"BLACK DENIM TROUSERS AND MOTORCYCLE
BOOTS," 1955
Mike Stoller/Jerry Leiber
CLOTHING, TABLE 7, ROCK 'N' ROLL

"BLACK DOG," 1972
Jimmy Page, Robert Plant, John Paul Jones
ANIMALS, HEAVY METAL

"BLACK IS THE COLOR OF MY TRUE LOVE'S
HAIR," c. 1875
traditional American song
FOLK SONG

"BLACK MAGIC WOMAN," 1968
Peter Green
MAGIC, ROCK-vii

"BLACK VELVET," 1990
David Tyson, Christopher Ward
TABLE 10-i

"BLACK WATERS," 1967
Jean Ritchie
WOMEN AS SONGWRITERS

"BLAME IT ON THE BOSSA NOVA," 1963
Barry Mann, Cynthia Weil
BOSSA NOVA, TABLE 15

"BLARNEY," 1909
Nora Bayes, Jack Norworth
WOMEN AS SONGWRITERS

"BLESS THIS HOUSE," 1927
Helen Taylor/Mary H. Brahe
BRITAIN

"BLINDED BY THE LIGHT," 1972
Bruce Springsteen
SEEING

"BLOW, GABRIEL, BLOW," 1934
Cole Porter
LENGTH, TABLE 11, NAMES

"BLOW THE MAN DOWN," 1880
traditional English folk song
FOLK SONG

"BLOWIN' IN THE WIND," 1962
Bob Dylan
FOLK SONG, HARMONY, PERFORMER-
SONGWRITERS, POPULAR SONG-ix, PROTEST
SONG, RELIGION, ROCK-iv, TABLE 15, SING-
ING GROUPS, SUBJECTS

"BLOWTOP BLUES," 1945
Leonard Feather, Jane Feather
BLUES, RHYTHM AND BLUES, TABLE 15

"BLUE AND BROKEN HEARTED," 1922
Grant Clarke, Edgar Leslie/Lou Handman
BLUES

"BLUE AND SENTIMENTAL," 1939
Count Basie, Jerry Livingston, Mack David
WOODWINDS

"BLUE BAYOU," 1963
Roy Orbison, Joe Melson
TABLE 4-d, TABLE 7, TABLE 15

"BLUE BELL," 1904
Edward Madden, Dolly Morse, Theodore F. Morse
TABLE 15

"BLUE CHAMPAGNE," 1941
Frank Ryerson, Grady Watts
TABLE 7, FOOD AND DRINK

"THE BLUE DANUBE," SEE "ON THE BEAUTIFUL
BLUE DANUBE"

"BLUE DANUBE BLUES," 1922
Anne Caldwell/Jerome Kern
WOMEN AS SONGWRITERS

"BLUE EYES CRYING IN THE RAIN," 1945
Fred Rose
TABLE 2, COUNTRY AND WESTERN, CRYING,
TABLE 10-u, TABLE 15, WEATHER

"BLUE HAWAII," 1937
Leo Robin, Ralph Rainger
TABLE 7, TABLE 9, STATES

"BLUE JEAN," 1984
David Bowie
ROCK-x

"BLUE LIGHT BOOGIE," 1950
Jessie May Robinson, Louis Jordan
BOOGIE-WOOGIE, RHYTHM AND BLUES

"BLUE MONDAY," 1957
Dave Bartholomew, Antoine "Fats" Domino
DAYS OF THE WEEK, ROCK 'N' ROLL-i, TABLE
7

"BLUE MOON," 1934
Lorenz Hart/Richard Rodgers
ADAPTATION, BORROWING, COLORS, TABLE
7, CROSSOVER, DOO-WOP, GOLDEN AGE,
LYRICISTS, MOON, TIN PAN ALLEY

"BLUE MOON OF KENTUCKY," 1947
Bill Monroe
BLUEGRASS, MOON, ROCK 'N' ROLL-i, STATES

"BLUE ORCHIDS," 1939
Hoagy Carmichael
TABLE 7, FLOWERS

"BLUE ROOM," 1926
Lorenz Hart/Richard Rodgers
COLORS, TABLE 7, GOLDEN AGE, INTERVAL,
TABLE 11, SCALE, SINGING GROUPS

"BLUE SKIES," 1927
Irving Berlin
TABLE 3, COLORS, TABLE 7, FILM MUSICALS,
GOLDEN AGE, MODE, SKY

"BLUE STAR," 1955
Edward Heyman/Victor Young
STARS

"BLUE SUEDE SHOES," 1955
Carl Lee Perkins
CLOTHING, TABLE 7, ROCK-iv, ROCK 'N'
ROLL-i, ROCKABILLY, TABLE 15

"THE BLUE TAIL FLY," SEE "JIM CRACK CORN"

"BLUE VELVET," 1951
Bernie Wayne, Lee Morris
TABLE 4-d, TABLE 7, TABLE 15

"BLUE YODEL NO. 1," SEE "T FOR TEXAS"

"BLUE YODEL NO. 8," SEE "MULE SKINNER BLUES"

"BLUEBERRY HILL" 1940
Al Lewis, Larry Stock, Vincent Rose
TABLE 7, TABLE 9, MOUNTAINS

"BLUEBIRD," 1916
Clare Kummer (pseud. Clare Rodman Beecher)
WOMEN AS SONGWRITERS

"BLUEBIRD OF HAPPINESS," 1934
Edward Heyman, Harry Parr Davies/Sandor Harmati
BIRDS, HAPPINESS

"BLUES IN THE NIGHT," 1941
Johnny Mercer/Harold Arlen
BLUES, CITIES, COMPOSERS, TABLE 9,
GOLDEN AGE, LENGTH, LYRICISTS, NIGHT,
SLANG, TORCH SONG, TRAINS

"BLUIN' THE BLUES," 1919
Sidney D. Mitchell/H. W. Ragas
BLUES

"BO DIDDLEY," 1955
E. McDaniels
NAMES, ROCK 'N' ROLL-i

"BOBBY SOX TO STOCKINGS" 1959
Russell Faith, Clarence Way Kehner, R. di Cicco
CLOTHING, ROCK 'N' ROLL-iii

"BODY AND SOUL," 1930
Edward Heyman, Robert Sour, Frank Eyton/John Green
ANATOMY, TABLE 2, TABLE, 3, COMPOSERS, DEPRESSION YEARS, GOLDEN AGE, HARMONY, IMPROVISATION, KEY, POPULAR SONG-ii, RANGE, RELEASE, REVUES, TABLE 14, SINGERS, TABLE 15, STANDARD, TIN PAN ALLEY

"BOJANGLES OF HARLEM," 1936
Dorothy Fields/Jerome Kern
HARLEM

"BOLÉRO," SEE "ALL MY LOVE"

"BOO-HOO!," 1937
Edward Heyman/John Jacob Loeb, Carmen Lombardo
TABLE 3, CANADA, CRYING

"BOOGALOO DOWN BROADWAY," 1967
Jesse James
BOOGALOO, BROADWAY

"BOOGIE CHILLUN," 1949
John Lee Hooker
BOOGIE-WOOGIE, RHYTHM AND BLUES

"BOOGIE DOWN," 1973
Anita Poree, Frank Wilson, Leonard Caston
BOOGIE-WOOGIE

"BOOGIE FEVER," 1976
Frederick J. Perren, Kenny St. Louis
BOOGIE-WOOGIE

"BOOGIE ON REGGAE WOMAN," 1974
Stevie Wonder
BLUE NOTE, BOOGIE-WOOGIE, TABLE 10-o, REGGAE, WOMAN

"BOOGIE OOGIE OOGIE," 1978
Janice Johnson, Perry Kibble
BOOGIE-WOOGIE, DISCO

"BOOGIE WOOGIE," 1929
m. Clarence "Pinetop" Smith
BOOGIE-WOOGIE, HIT SONG

"BOOGIE-WOOGIE BUGLE BOY," 1941
Hughie Prince, Don Raye
ALLITERATION, BOOGIE-WOOGIE, BOY, BRASS, HIT SONG, HUMOR, NOVELTY SONG, WORLD WAR II

"BOOK OF LOVE," 1957
Warren Davis, George Malone, Charles Patrick
DOO-WOP, ROCK 'N' ROLL-ii, WRITING

"BOOLA BOOLA," 1898
unknown
BORROWING, NONSENSE

"BOOMPS-A-DAISY," 1939
Annette Mills
DANCE CRAZES, NONSENSE

"BORN FREE," 1966
Don Black/John Barry
TABLE 1, ANIMALS, BIRTH, TABLE 4-d, TABLE 8

"BORN IN THE U.S.A.," 1984
Bruce Springsteen
BIRTH, NATIONS, PATRIOTISM, RAP, ROCK-xii, TABLE 15

"BORN TO BE WILD," 1968
Mars Bonfire
BIRTH, HEAVY METAL, ROCK

"BORN TO LOSE," 1943
Frankie Brown
BIRTH, COUNTRY AND WESTERN

"BORN TO THE BREED," 1975
Judy Collins
BIRTH, FOLK SONG, WOMEN AS SONGWRITERS

"BORN TOO LATE," 1958
Fred Tobias/Charles Strouse
BIRTH, SINGING GROUPS

"THE BOSS," 1979
Nickolas Ashford, Valerie Simpson
POPULAR SONG-xiii

"BOSTON BEGUINE," 1952
Sheldon M. Harnick
TABLE 5, HUMOR, REVUES, TABLE 14

"BOTCH-A-ME (BA-BA-BACIAMI PICCINA),"
1957
Eddie Y. Stanley (Eng.)/R. Morbelli, L. Astore
FOREIGN LANGUAGE, ITALY, KISSING, NOV-
ELTY SONG, TABLE 15

"BOTH SIDES NOW (CLOUDS)," 1967
Joni Mitchell
TABLE 4-c, CANADA, FADE-OUT, FOLK SONG,
HARMONY, PERFORMER-SONGWRITERS,
ROCK-vi, TABLE 15, SKY, VERSE, WEATHER,
WOMEN AS SONGWRITERS

"BOTTLE OF WINE," 1963
Tom Paxton
FOLK SONG

"THE BOULEVARD OF BROKEN DREAMS," 1933
Al Dubin/Harry Warren
DREAMS, LYRICISTS, MODE, STREETS

"BOUND FOR GLORY," 1963
Phil Ochs
FOLK SONG

"BOUQUET OF ROSES," 1948
Steve Nelson, Bob Hilliard
COUNTRY AND WESTERN, FLOWERS

"THE BOWERY," 1892
Charles H. Hoyt/Percy Gaunt
BARBERSHOP, BRITAIN, GAY NINETIES, ITALY,
KEY, LENGTH, MUSICAL COMEDY, TABLE 11,
TIN PAN ALLEY, WALTZ

"THE BOXER," 1968
Paul Simon
ROCK-v

"THE BOY FROM . . .," 1966
Stephen Sondheim
BOY

"THE BOY FROM NEW YORK CITY," 1964
John Taylor
TABLE 5, TABLE 10-h, SINGING GROUPS

"A BOY LIKE THAT," 1957
Stephen Sondheim/Leonard Bernstein
BOY

"A BOY NAMED SUE," 1969
Shel Silverstein
BOY, TABLE 10-u, TABLE 10-w, NAMES, TABLE
15

"THE BOY NEXT DOOR," 1943
Hugh Martin, Ralph Blane
BOY, CHILDHOOD, TABLE 9, HARMONY,
REPEATED NOTE, SINGERS, TABLE 15, WALTZ

"THE BOYS IN THE BACK ROOM," 1939
Frank Loesser/Frederick Hollander
TABLE 8, SEEING

"THE BOYS OF SUMMER," 1985
Don Henley, Mike Campbell
TABLE 10-j, SEASONS

"BRAZIL," 1939
S. K. Russell (Eng.)/Ary Barroso
TABLE 4-d, BRAZIL, DISCO, TABLE 9, NATIONS,
SAMBA

"BREAK IT TO ME GENTLY," 1961
Diane Lampert, Joe Seneca
TABLE 10-t, TENDERNESS

"BREAK THE NEWS TO MOTHER," 1897
Charles K. Harris
GAY NINETIES, MOTHERS

"BREAKING UP IS HARD TO DO," 1962
Neil Sedaka, Howard Greenfield
TABLE 4-c, BRILL BUILDING, ENDING, ROCK
'N' ROLL

"BREATHLESS," 1958
Otis Blackwell
ROCK 'N' ROLL-i

"THE BREEZE AND I," 1940
Al Stillman (Eng.)/Ernesto Lecuona, T. Camarata
ADAPTATION, TABLE 4-d, TABLE 6, CUBA,
RUMBA, WEATHER

"Breezin' Along With the Breeze," 1926
Haven Gillespie, Seymour Simons, Richard A.
Whiting
WEATHER

"Brian's Song," 1972
Alan Bergman, Marilyn Bergman/Michel Legrand
COLLABORATION, FRANCE, MUSIC

"Bridge Over Troubled Water," 1969
Paul Simon
TABLE 4-b, CADENCE, FOLK ROCK, FRIEND-
SHIP, TABLE 10-a, TABLE 10-b, TABLE 10-n,
PERFORMER-SONGWRITERS, POPULAR SONG-
ix, ROCK-v, VERSE

"Brilliant Disguise," 1987
Bruce Springsteen
ROCK-xii

"Bring Him Home," 1985
Herbert Kretzmer (Eng.)/Claude-Michel Schönberg
TABLE 12

"Bring It On Home to Me," 1962
Sam Cooke
HOME, SOUL

"The Broadway Melody," 1929
Arthur Freed/Nacio Herb Brown
BROADWAY, MELODY

"Broadway Rhythm," 1935
Arthur Freed/Nacio Herb Brown
BROADWAY, TABLE 9, RHYTHM

"Broken Lady," 1975
Larry Gatlin
TABLE 10-w

"Brother, Can You Spare a Dime?," 1932
E. Y. Harburg/Jay Gorney
DEPRESSION YEARS, LYRICISTS, MONEY,
POPULAR SONG, POPULAR SONG-v, TABLE 14

"Brother Louie," 1973
Errol Brown, Anthony Wilson
ROCK

"Brown Eyed Girl," 1967
Van Morrison
TABLE 2, ROCK-iii

"Brown Sugar," 1971
Mick Jagger, Keith Richards
ROCK-iii

"Brush Up Your Shakespeare," 1948
Cole Porter
CATALOGUE SONG, TABLE 11

"Buckle Down, Winsockie," 1941
Hugh Martin, Ralph Blane
MARCH

**"Buffalo Gals (Won't You Come Out
Tonight?)," or "Lubly Fan," 1844; SEE
ALSO "Dance With a Dolly"**
Cool White (John Hodges)
BORROWING, DOLL, FOLK SONG

"Bugle Call Rag," 1923
Jack Pettis, Billy Meyers, Elmer Schoebel
BRASS, DIXIELAND, RAGTIME

**"Bulldog! Bulldog! Bow, Wow, Wow,"
1911**
Cole Porter
ANIMALS

"The Bunny Hop," 1952
Ray Anthony, Leonard Auletti
ANIMALS, DANCE CRAZES

"Burning Love," 1972
Dennis Linde
FIRE

"A Bushel and a Peck," 1950
Frank Loesser
TABLE 11

"Busted," 1962
Harlan Howard
TABLE 10-m

"But Beautiful," 1947
Johnny Burke/James Van Heusen
BEAUTY, COLLABORATION, TABLE 9

"But Not for Me," 1930
Ira Gershwin/George Gershwin
COLLABORATION, TABLE 10-c, HUMOR,
MUSICAL COMEDY, TABLE 11

"The Butcher Boy," SEE **"Oh Mama"**

"Button Up Your Overcoat!," 1928
B.G. DeSylva, Lew Brown, Ray Henderson
CLOTHING, COLLABORATION

"Buttons and Bows," 1948
Jay Livingston, Ray Evans
TABLE 1, CARDINAL POINTS, TABLE 8, TABLE
15, YOUR HIT PARADE

"By a Waterfall," 1933
Irving Kahal/Sammy Fain
TABLE 9

"By Myself," 1937
Howard Dietz/Arthur Schwartz
COLLABORATION, FILM MUSICALS, LONELI-
NESS, LYRICISTS, TABLE 11

"By Strauss," 1936
Ira Gershwin/George Gershwin
REVUES, TABLE 14, WALTZ

"By the Beautiful Sea," 1914
Harold R. Atteridge/Harry Carroll
BARBERSHOP, OCEAN, REVUES, TABLE 14,
TABLE 15, SINGING GROUPS

"By the Light of the Silvery Moon," 1909
Edward Madden, Gus Edwards
BARBERSHOP, TABLE 7, MOON, REVUES,
TABLE 14, SINGING GROUPS, VAUDEVILLE

"By the Time I Get to Phoenix," 1967
Jim Webb
TABLE 4-b, CITIES, TABLE 5, COMPOSER-
LYRICISTS, COUNTRY AND WESTERN, FORM,
TABLE 10-d, TABLE 10-g, TABLE 15, TIME,
TONALITY

"Bye Bye Baby," 1949
Leo Rubin/Jule Styne
BABY, FAREWELLS

"Bye Bye Baby (Baby Goodbye)," 1964
Bob Gaudio, Bob Crewe
BABY, FAREWELLS, SINGING GROUPS

"Bye Bye Blackbird," 1926
Mort Dixon/Ray Henderson
BIRDS, TABLE 7, COMPOSERS, FAREWELLS

"Bye Bye Blues," 1930
Fred Hamm, Dave Bennett, Bert Lown, Chauncey
Gray
BLUES, BORROWING, FAREWELLS

"Bye Bye Love," 1957
Felice Bryant, Boudleaux Bryant
FAREWELLS, LOVE, ROCK 'N' ROLL-i, WOMEN
AS SONGWRITERS

"Ça, C'Est l'Amour," 1957
Cole Porter
FOREIGN LANGUAGE

"Cab Driver," 1963
Carson Parks
SINGING GROUPS

"Cabaret," 1966
Fred Ebb/John Kander
AABA, TABLE 4-d, CABARET, CODA, LIFE,
TABLE 15

"Cabin in the Sky," 1940
John Latouche/Vernon Duke
TABLE 11, TABLE 15, SKY

"Cachita," 1936
Bernardo C. Sancristobal (Span.)/Rafael Hernandez
GUARACHA

"Cactus Tree," 1968
Joni Mitchell
FOLK SONG

"THE CAISSONS GO ROLLING ALONG," *SEE* "THE U.S. FIELD ARTILLERY MARCH"

"CALDONIA (WHAT MAKES YOUR BIG HEAD SO HARD?)," 1945
Fleecie Moore
TABLE 2, TABLE 9, RHYTHM AND BLUES

"CALENDAR GIRL," 1961
Howard Greenfield, Neil Sedaka
ROCK 'N' ROLL

"CALIFORNIA DREAMING," 1965
John Phillips, Michele Gilliam Phillips
DREAMS, SINGING GROUPS, STATES

"CALIFORNIA GIRLS," 1965
Brian Wilson
ROCK-i

"CALIFORNIA, HERE I COME," 1924
Al Jolson, B. G. DeSylva, Joseph Meyer
BREAK, LYRICISTS, TABLE 11, ROARING TWENTIES, SINGERS, TABLE 15, STATES

"CALL ME," 1965
Tony Hatch
TABLE 4-d, BRITAIN

"CALL ME," 1970
Aretha Franklin
WOMEN AS SONGWRITERS

"CALL ME," 1980
Giorgio Moroder, Debbie Harry (Eng.)
TELEPHONES

"CALL ME IRRESPONSIBLE," 1962
Sammy Cahn/James Van Heusen
TABLE 1, CHROMATICISM, COMPOSERS, TABLE 8, FOX TROT, LYRICISTS

"THE CALL OF THE FAR-AWAY HILL," 1952
Mack David, Victor Young
TABLE 8, MOUNTAINS

"CALL ON ME," 1962
Deadric Malone
RHYTHM AND BLUES

"CALYPSO," 1975
John Denver
CALYPSO

"CAMELOT," 1960
Alan Jay Lerner/Frederick Loewe
MUSICAL PLAYS, TABLE 12, OCTAVE

"CAMINITO (LITTLE ROAD)," 1936
Penaloza Gabin Coria, Juan de Dios Filiberto
ARGENTINA, STREETS, TANGO

"DE CAMPTOWN RACES (G'WINE TO RUN ALL NIGHT)," 1850
Stephen Collins Foster
FOLK SONG, POPULAR SONG-i

"CAN I FORGET YOU?," 1937
Oscar Hammerstein II/Jerome Kern
TABLE 9, FORGETTING

"CAN THAT BOY FOX TROT!," 1971
Stephen Sondheim
HUMOR

"CAN THIS BE LOVE?," 1930
Paul James/Kay Swift
WOMEN AS SONGWRITERS

"CAN YOU READ MY MIND? (LOVE THEME FROM SUPERMAN)," 1978
Leslie Bricusse/John Williams
BRITAIN, TABLE 8, MIND

"CANADIAN CAPERS," 1915
Gus Chandler, Bert White, Henry Cohen
NATIONS

"CANADIAN SUNSET," 1956
Norman Gimbel/Eddie Heywood
TABLE 4-b, NATIONS, PIANO, TABLE 15, SUN, TIME OF DAY

"CANDIDA," 1970
Toni Wine, Irwin Levine
SINGING GROUPS

"CANDY," 1944
Mack David, Joan Whitney, Alex Kramer
TABLE 15, NAMES, SWEETNESS

"CANDY GIRL," 1963
Larry Santos
GIRL, ROCK 'N' ROLL-ii, SWEETNESS

"THE CANDY MAN," 1970
Leslie Bricusse, Anthony Newley
BRITAIN, FADE-OUT, TABLE 8, FOOD AND
DRINK, MAN, TABLE 15, SWEETNESS

"CAN'T BUY ME LOVE," 1964
John Lennon, Paul McCartney
COLLABORATION, MONEY, ROCK-ii

"CAN'T GET OUT OF THIS MOOD," 1942
Frank Loesser/Jimmy McHugh
MOODS

"CAN'T HELP FALLING IN LOVE," 1961
George Weiss, Luigi Creatore, Hugo Peretti
CLASSICS, TABLE 6, FALLING IN LOVE, LOVE,
TABLE 9

"CAN'T HELP LOVIN' DAT MAN," 1927
Oscar Hammerstein II/Jerome Kern
ANIMALS, BALLAD, COMPOSERS, DIALECT,
LANDMARKS OF STAGE AND SCREEN, LOVE,
MAN, MUSICAL PLAYS, TABLE 12, ROARING
TWENTIES, TABLE 15, TEMPO

"CAN'T HELP SINGING," 1944
E. Y. Harburg/Jerome Kern
TABLE 9, WALTZ

"CAN'T SMILE WITHOUT YOU," 1975
Geoff Morrow, Chris Arnold, David Martin
BRITAIN, SMILING

"CAN'T TAKE MY EYES OFF YOU," 1967
Bob Crewe, Bob Gaudio
ANATOMY, TABLE 2, TABLE 4-c

"CAN'T WE BE FRIENDS?," 1929
Paul James (pseud. James Warburg)/Kay Swift
FRIENDSHIP, REVUES, TABLE 14, WOMEN AS
SONGWRITERS

"CAN'T WE TALK IT OVER?," 1931
Ned Washington/Victor Young
TALKING

**"CAN'T YO' HEAH ME CALLIN', CAROLINE?,"
1914**
William H. Gardner, Caro Roma
DIALECT, WOMEN AS SONGWRITERS

"CAN'T YOU HEAR MY HEART BEAT?," 1965
Carter-Lewis (pseud. John Shakespeare, Kenneth
Hawker)
ROCK-iii

"CANTO D'AMORE," 1962
Deni' (Ital.)/Carlo Rustichelli
FOREIGN LANGUAGE, ITALY

"CARA MIA," 1954
Tulio Tranpani, Lee Lange
ENDEARMENT, FOREIGN LANGUAGE, SING-
ING GROUPS

"CARAVAN," 1937
Irving Mills/Duke Ellington, Juan Tizol
BRASS, SWING

"CARELESS WHISPER," 1984
George Michael, Andrew Ridgely
TALKING

**"CARIBBEAN QUEEN (NO MORE LOVE ON THE
RUN)," 1984**
Keith Diamond, Billy Ocean
TABLE 10-o

"CARIOCA," 1933
Gus Kahn, Edward Eliscu/Vincent Youmans
BRAZIL, DANCE CRAZES, TABLE 9

"CAROLINA IN THE MORNING," 1922
Gus Kahn/Walter Donaldson
INTERVAL, LYRICISTS, REVUES, TABLE 14,
STATES, TIME OF DAY

"CAROLINA MOON," 1928
Benny Davis, Joe Burke
MOON, RADIO, STATES

"CAROUSEL," 1959
Eric Blau (Eng.)/Jacques Brel
BELGIUM, CABARET, CIRCUS

"CARROUSEL IN THE PARK," 1944
Dorothy Fields/Sigmund Romberg
WOMEN AS SONGWRITERS

"CARRY ME BACK TO OLD VIRGINNY," 1878
James A. Bland
FOLK SONG

"CASEY JONES," 1909
T. Lawrence Seibert/Eddie Newton
FOLK SONG, SINGING GROUPS, TRAINS

"CASTLE ON A CLOUD," 1985
Herbert Kretzmer (Eng.)/Claude-Michel Schönberg
FRANCE

"CATCH A FALLING STAR," 1957
Paul Vance, Lee Pockriss
TABLE 10-d, STARS

"CATCH THE WIND," 1965
Donovan Leitch
ROCK-v

"CATHY'S CLOWN," 1960
Don Everly, Phil Everly
CIRCUS, NAMES, ROCK 'N' ROLL-i

"THE CATTLE CALL," 1934
Tex Owens
ANIMALS, COUNTRY AND WESTERN

"CECILIA," 1925
Herman Ruby/Dave Dreyer
MOTHERS, NAMES, RADIO

"CECILIA," 1969
Paul Simon
FOLK ROCK, NAMES, ROCK-v

"CERAZO ROSA," SEE "CHERRY PINK AND APPLE
BLOSSOM WHITE"

"A CERTAIN SMILE," 1958
Paul Francis Webster/Sammy Fain
TABLE 8

"C'EST MAGNIFIQUE," 1953
Cole Porter
FOREIGN LANGUAGE, TABLE II

"C'EST SI BON," 1950
Jerry Seelen (Eng.)/Henri Betti
FOREIGN LANGUAGE, FRANCE

"CHAIN GANG," 1956
Sol Quasha, Herb Yakus
TOGETHERNESS

"CHAIN OF FOOLS," 1967
Don Covay
FOOLS, TABLE 10-n, TABLE 15, SOUL

"CHAINS OF LOVE," 1951
Ahmet Ertegun/Van Walls
RHYTHM AND BLUES

"THE CHAMPAGNE WALTZ," 1934
Milton Drake, Ben Oakland, Con Conrad
FOOD AND DRINK

"CHANCES ARE," 1957
Al Stillman/Robert Allen
LUCK, TABLE 15

"A CHANGE IS GONNA COME," 1964
Sam Cooke
SOUL

"CHANGE PARTNERS," 1938
Irving Berlin
COMPOSER-LYRICISTS, DANCING, TABLE 9,
SOCIETY TEMPO

"CHANSON," "CHANSONETTE"; SEE "THE DON-
KEY SERENADE"

"CHANSON D'AMOUR," 1958
Wayne Shanklin
FOREIGN LANGUAGE

"CHANSON DU COEUR BRISÉ," SEE "THE SONG
OF SONGS"

"CHANTEZ-CHANTEZ," 1957
Albert Gamse/Irving Fields
FOREIGN LANGUAGE

"CHANTILLY LACE," 1958
J. P. Richardson
ROCK 'N' ROLL-i

"Chapel of Love," 1964
Jeff Barry, Ellie Greenwich, Phil Spector
ROCK 'N' ROLL-iv

"Charade," 1963
Johnny Mercer/Henry Mancini
COMPOSERS, TABLE 8, MODE, WALTZ

"Charleston," 1923
Cecil Mack (pseud. Richard C. McPherson), James P. Johnson
CHARLESTON, CITIES, TABLE 5, DANCE CRAZES, NOVELTY SONG, PIANO, ROARING TWENTIES

"Charley, My Boy," 1924
Gus Kahn, Ted Fiorito
BOY, NAMES

"Charlie Brown," 1959
Jerry Leiber, Mike Stoller
NAMES, ROCK 'N' ROLL-ii

"Charmaine," 1926
Erno Rapee, Lew Pollack
FILM MUSIC, TABLE 8, NAMES

"Chattanooga Choo Choo," 1941
Mack Gordon/Harry Warren
ALLITERATION, TABLE 3, TABLE 5, COLLABORATION, LYRICISTS, NOVELTY SONG, SWING, TRAINS

"Chattanooga Shoe Shine Boy," 1950
Harry Stone, Jack Stapp
TABLE 5

"Cheek to Cheek," 1935
Irving Berlin
ANATOMY, TABLE 2, COMPOSER-LYRICISTS, DANCING, FILM MUSICALS, TABLE 9, GOLDEN AGE, HEAVEN, LENGTH, TABLE 15, SOCIETY TEMPO

"Cheerful Little Earful," 1930
Ira Gershwin, Billy Rose/Harry Warren
TABLE 2

"Chelsea Morning," 1967
Joni Mitchell
CANADA, FOLK SONG, WOMEN AS SONGWRITERS

"Cherie," 1921
Leo Wood/Irving Bibo
ENDEARMENT

"Cherish," 1965
Terry Kirkman
TABLE 4-c

"Cherokee," 1938
Ray Noble
ARRANGEMENT, BEBOP, TABLE 3, BRITAIN, SWING

"Cherry Pie," 1954
Joe Josea, Marvin Phillips
FOOD AND DRINK, RHYTHM AND BLUES

"Cherry Pies Ought to Be You," 1950
Cole Porter
FOOD AND DRINK

"Cherry Pink and Apple Blossom White," 1955
Mack David (Eng.)/Louiquy
CHA CHA CHA, TABLE 7, CUBA, TABLE 8, FRANCE, PICKUP

"Chestnuts Roasting on an Open Fire," SEE **"The Christmas Song"**

"Chica Chica Boom Chic," 1941
Mack Gordon/Harry Warren
BRAZIL, TABLE 9, NONSENSE

"Chicago (That Toddling Town)," 1922
Fred Fisher
CITIES, TABLE 5

"Chickery Chick," 1945
Sylvia Dee/Sidney Lippman
WOMEN AS SONGWRITERS

"The Children's Marching Song (This Old Man)," 1958
Malcolm Arnold
TABLE 8, MAN

"Chim Chim Cher-ee," 1963
Richard M. Sherman, Robert B. Sherman
ACADEMY AWARDS, TABLE 1, TABLE 9, NONSENSE

"China Boy," 1922
Dick Winfree, Phil Boutelje
BOY, NATIONS, PEABODY

"China Girl," 1977
Iggy Pop, David Bowie
ROCK-x

"Chinatown, My Chinatown," 1910
William Jerome/Jean Schwartz
TABLE 5, HUNGARY, NATIONS, ONE-STEP,
PEABODY, SINGING GROUPS

"The Chipmunk Song (Christmas Don't be Late)," 1958
Ross Bagdasarian
ANIMALS, CHRISTMAS

"Chiquita Banana," 1946
Leonard MacKenzie, Garth Montgomery, William
Wirges
TELEVISION

"Chitty Chitty Bang Bang," 1968
Richard M. Sherman, Robert B. Sherman
NONSENSE

"Chiu, Chiu," 1942
Alan Surgal (Eng.)/Nicanor Molinare
SAMBA

"Chloe," 1927
Gus Kahn/Neil Moret (pseud. Charles N. Daniels)
HUMOR

"El Choclo," 1913; SEE ALSO "Kiss of Fire"
m. Angel G. Villoldo
ARGENTINA, BORROWING, DANCE CRAZES,
FIRE, KISSING

"Choice of Colors," 1969
Curtis Mayfield
SINGING GROUPS

"The Chokin' Kind," 1967
Harlan Howard
TABLE 10-o

"Choo Choo Ch'Boogie," 1945
Vaughn Horton, Denver Darling, Milton Gabler
BOOGIE-WOOGIE, RHYTHM AND BLUES

"Christmas Don't Be Late," SEE "The Chipmunk Song"

"The Christmas Song (Chestnuts Roasting on an Open Fire)," 1946
Robert Wells, Mel Tormé
CHRISTMAS, FIRE, PERFORMER-
SONGWRITERS, TABLE 15

"Christopher Columbus," 1936
Andy Razaf/Leon Berry
NAMES

"Church Bells May Ring," 1956
Morty and the Willows Craft
COVER

"Ciao, Ciao, Bambina," 1959
Mitchell Parish (Eng.)/Domenico Modugno
BABY, BOLERO, FAREWELLS, FOREIGN LAN-
GUAGE, ITALY

"Cielito Lindo (Ay, Ay, Ay)," 1919
Quirino Mendoza y Cortez
MEXICO

"Cindy, Oh Cindy," 1956
Bob Barron, Burt Long
SINGING GROUPS

"Circus," 1949
Bob Russell/Louis Alter
CIRCUS

"Ciribiribin," 1898
Rudolf Thaler/Alberto Pestalozza
BIG BANDS, TABLE 3, FOREIGN LANGUAGE,
ITALY, SWING

"The City of New Orleans," 1970
Steve Goodman
TABLE 5, TABLE 10-w

"Clap Yo' Hands," 1926
Ira Gershwin/George Gershwin
ANATOMY, TABLE 2, CHARLESTON, CON-
TRACTIONS, MUSICAL COMEDY, TABLE 11,
SCALE

"Clarinet Marmalade," 1918
Edwin B. Edwards, D. James La Rocca, Anthony
Sbarbaro, Larry Shields
WOODWINDS

"Class of '57," 1972
Harold Reid, Don Reid
TABLE 10-v

"Classical Gas," 1967
m. Mason Williams
TABLE 4-d

"Clean Up Woman," 1971
Clarence Reid, Willie Clarke
SOUL

"Clear Out of This World," 1940
Al Dubin/Jimmy McHugh
WORLD

"Climb Ev'ry Mountain," 1959
Oscar Hammerstein II/Richard Rodgers
INSPIRATION, MODULATION, MOUNTAINS,
MUSICAL PLAYS, TABLE 12

"Clopin-Clopant," *see* **"Comme Ci, Comme Ça"**

"Close as Pages in a Book," 1944
Dorothy Fields/Sigmund Romberg
CLOSENESS, HUNGARY, SHEET MUSIC,
WOMEN AS SONGWRITERS, WRITING

"(They Long to Be) Close to You," 1963
Hal David/Burt Bacharach
CLOSENESS, CODA, COLLABORATION,
COMPOSERS, FADE-OUT, TABLE 10-h, LYRI-
CISTS

"The Closer You Are," 1956
Earle Lewis, Morgan C. Robinson
CLOSENESS, SINGING GROUPS

"Cloud Nine," 1968
Barrett Strong, Norman Whitfield
TABLE 10-p

"Clouds," *see* **"Both Sides Now"**

"C'mon Everybody," 1958
Eddie Cochran, Jerry Capehart
ROCK 'N' ROLL-i

"Coal Miner's Daughter," 1969
Loretta Lynn
COUNTRY AND WESTERN, WOMEN AS
SONGWRITERS

"Coat of Many Colors," 1969
Dolly Parton
CLOTHING, TABLE 7, COUNTRY AND WEST-
ERN

"A Cock-Eyed Optimist," 1949
Oscar Hammerstein II/Richard Rodgers
TABLE 12

"Cocktails for Two," 1934
Arthur Johnston, Sam Coslow
TABLE 9, FOOD AND DRINK, HUMOR,
PICKUP, TELEPHONES, TOGETHERNESS

"Cod'ine," 1964
Buffy Sainte-Marie
FOLK SONG

"The Coffee Song (They've Got an Awful Lot of Coffee in Brazil)," 1946
Bob Hilliard, Dick Miles
FOOD AND DRINK, NATIONS

"Cold, Cold Heart," 1951
Hank Williams
TABLE 2, TABLE 4-d, COUNTRY AND WEST-
ERN, COVER, TABLE 15

"Cold Sweat," 1967
James Brown, Alfred Ellis
SOUL

"Color Him Father," 1969
Richard Spencer
FATHERS, TABLE 10-q

"Color My World," 1966
Jackie Trent, Tony Hatch
BRITAIN, TABLE 7, WORLD

"COLOUR MY WORLD," 1970
James Pankow
TABLE 7, METER, ROCK-ix

"COME BACK TO ME," 1965
Alan Jay Lerner/Burton Lane
HUMOR

"COME BACK TO SORRENTO (TORNA A SURRIENTO)," 1904; *SEE ALSO* "SURRENDER"
Ernesto de Curtis, Claude Aveling
TABLE 5

"COME CLOSER TO ME (ACERCATE MAS)," 1940
Al Stewart (Eng.)/Osvaldo Farres
BOLERO, CLOSENESS, COMPARATIVES, MEXICO

"COME DANCE WITH ME," 1959
George Blake, Richard Leibert
DANCING

"COME GO WITH ME," 1957
C. E. Quick
ROCK 'N' ROLL-ii

"COME IN FROM THE RAIN," 1975
Melissa Manchester, Carole Bayer Sager
WEATHER, WOMEN AS SONGWRITERS

"COME JOSEPHINE IN MY FLYING MACHINE," 1910
Alfred Bryan/Fred Fisher
TRAVEL

"COME ON-A-MY HOUSE," 1950
Ross Bagdasarian, William Saroyan
HOME, NOVELTY SONG, TABLE 15

"COME ON AND PET ME," *SEE* "SOMETIMES I'M HAPPY"

"COME RAIN OR COME SHINE," 1946
Johnny Mercer/Harold Arlen
REPEATED NOTE, SINGERS, TABLE 15, WEATHER

"COME SATURDAY MORNING," 1969
Dory Previn/Fred Karlin
DAYS OF THE WEEK, FADE-OUT, TABLE 8, TIME OF DAY, WOMEN AS SONGWRITERS

"COME SEE ABOUT ME," 1964
Brian Holland, Eddie Holland, Lamont Dozier
MOTOWN

"COME SOFTLY TO ME," 1959
Gary Troxel, Gretchen Christopher, Barbara Ellis
SINGING GROUPS, TENDERNESS

"COME TO ME, BEND TO ME," 1947
Alan Jay Lerner/Frederick Loewe
COLLABORATION, MUSICAL PLAYS

"COME TO THE MARDI GRAS," 1937
Ervin Drake, Jimmy Shirl/Max Bulhoes, Milton de Oliveira
BRAZIL, TABLE 5, SAMBA

"COME TOGETHER," 1969
John Lennon, Paul McCartney
ROCK-ii, TOGETHERNESS

"COMEDY TONIGHT," 1962
Stephen Sondheim
TABLE 11

"COMIN' IN ON A WING AND A PRAYER," 1943
Harold Adamson/Jimmy McHugh
PATRIOTISM, WORLD WAR II

"COMME CI, COMME ÇA (CLOPIN-CLOPANT)," 1949
Joan Whitney, Alex Cramer (Eng.)/Bruno Coquatrix
FOREIGN LANGUAGE, FRANCE, WOMEN AS SONGWRITERS

"COMPADRE PEDRO JUAN," 1955
Luis Alberti
MERENGUE

"COMRADES," 1894
Felix McGlennon
GAY NINETIES

"Concerto in F," 1925
m. George Gershwin
COMPOSERS

"El Condor Pasa," 1970
David Robles, Paul Simon
TABLE 4-d

"La Conga," 1938
Eliseo Grenet
CONGA

"Conga," 1985
Enrique Garcia
CONGA

"Consider Yourself," 1960
Lionel Bart
BRITAIN

"The Continental," 1934
Herb Magidson/Con Conrad
ACADEMY AWARDS, TABLE 1, DANCE CRAZES,
FILM MUSICALS, TABLE 9, LENGTH, SOCIETY
TEMPO, VAMP

"Cool," 1957
Stephen Sondheim/Leonard Bernstein
SLANG

"Cool Jerk," 1966
Donald Storball
SINGING GROUPS

"Cool Water," 1936
Bob Nolan
COUNTRY AND WESTERN

"Copacabana (At the Copa)," 1977
Barry Manilow, Bruce Sussman, Jack Feldman/Barry
Manilow
TABLE 10-g, TABLE 15

"Coquette," 1928
Gus Kahn/Carmen Lombardo, John W. Green
TABLE 3, CANADA

"Corcovado," SEE **"Quiet Nights of Quiet
Stars"**

"A Cottage for Sale," 1930
Larry Conley/Willard Robison
DEPRESSION YEARS, HOME, VAMP

"Could I Have This Dance," 1980
Wayland Holyfield, Bob House
DANCING, TABLE 10-t

"Could This Be Magic," 1957
Hiram Johnson, Richard Blandon
MAGIC, SINGING GROUPS

"Country Road," 1970
James Taylor
FOLK ROCK, ROCK-vi, STREETS

"A Couple of Swells," 1947
Irving Berlin
TABLE 9, SLANG, TOGETHERNESS

"Cover Me," 1984
Bruce Springsteen
ROCK-xii

**"Cow-Cow Boogie (Cuma-Ti-Yi-Yi-Ay),"
1941**
Benny Carter, Don Raye, Gene de Paul
BOOGIE-WOOGIE

"A Cowboy Legend," SEE **"(Ghost) Riders in
the Sky"**

"The Cowboy Tune," SEE **"The End Is Not
in Sight"**

"Cowboys to Girls," 1968
Kenny Gamble, Leon Huff
GIRL, SINGING GROUPS, SOUL

"Cracklin' Rosie," 1970
Neil Diamond
NAMES

"Crazy," 1961
Willie Nelson
BMI, COUNTRY AND WESTERN, MADNESS,
TABLE 15

"CRAZY ARMS," 1956
Chuck Seals, Ralph Mooney
TABLE 2, COUNTRY AND WESTERN, MADNESS

"CRAZY FOR YOU," 1983
John Betts/Jon Lind
MADNESS, ROCK-xii, TABLE 15

"CRAZY LOVE," 1978
Russell Young
MADNESS

"CRAZY ON YOU," 1976
Ann Wilson, Nancy Wilson, Roger Fisher
WOMEN AS SONGWRITERS

"THE CRAZY OTTO RAG," 1955
Edward R. White, Mack Wilson, Hugo Peretti, Luigi
Creatore
MADNESS

"CRAZY RHYTHM," 1928
Irving Caesar/Joseph Meyer, Roger Wolfe Kahn
CHARLESTON, MADNESS, NOVELTY SONG,
RHYTHM

"CREEQUE ALLEY," 1967
John Phillips, Michelle Gilliam
SINGING GROUPS

"CREOLE LOVE CALL," 1927
Duke Ellington
SCAT SINGING

"CROCODILE ROCK," 1972
Elton John, Bernie Taupin
ANIMALS, ROCK-x

"CROSSROADS," 1968
Robert Johnson
PROTEST SONG

"CRUEL SUMMER," 1983
Tony Swain, Steve Jolley
SEASONS, SINGING GROUPS

**"CRUISING DOWN THE RIVER (ON A SUNDAY
AFTERNOON)," 1945**
Eily Beadell, Nell Tollerton
BOATING, BRITAIN, RIVERS

"CRY," 1951
Churchill Kohlman
CRYING, TABLE 15, SINGING GROUPS, SKY

"CRY BABY," 1963
Bert Russell, Norman Meade
BABY, CRYING, SOUL

"CRY LIKE A BABY," 1968
Dan Penn (pseud. Wallace Daniel Pennington),
Spooner Oldham (pseud. Dewey Lindon Oldham, Jr.)
CRYING

"CRY ME A RIVER," 1953
Arthur Hamilton
CRYING, MODE, RIVERS

"CRYING," 1961
Roy Orbison, Joe Melson
BMI, CRYING, TABLE 4-d, ROCK 'N' ROLL-i

"CRYING IN THE CHAPEL," 1953
Artie Glenn
CRYING, DOO-WOP, RHYTHM AND BLUES

"CRYING TIME," 1964
Buck Owens
CRYING, TABLE 10-m, TABLE 10-o, TIME

"CUANDO CALIENTE EL SOL," SEE **"LOVE ME
WITH ALL YOUR HEART"**

"CUANDO VUELVA A TU LADO," SEE **"WHAT A
DIFF'RENCE A DAY MADE"**

"CUANTO LE GUSTA," 1940
Ray Gilbert (Eng.)/Gabriel Ruiz
GUARACHA, MEXICO, SAMBA

"CUBAN LOVE SONG," 1931
Herbert Stothart, Jimmy McHugh, Dorothy Fields
TABLE 9, NATIONS

"CUBAN MAMBO," 1950
Jack Wiseman/Xavier Cugat, Rafael Angulo
CUBA, MAMBO

"CUBAN PETE," 1936
Jose Norman (pseud. Norman Henderson)
NATIONS

"LA CUCARACHA (THE COCKROACH)," C.1916
traditional Mexican song
ANIMALS, BORROWING, MEXICO, PICKUP

"CUDDLE UP A LITTLE CLOSER, LOVEY MINE," 1908
Otto Harbach/Karl Hoschna
AUSTRIA, CLOSENESS

"EL CUMBANCHERO," 1943
Rafael Hernandez
GUARACHA, MEXICO

"LA CUMPARSITA," 1916
Carol Raven (Eng.)/G. H. Matos Rodriguez
ARGENTINA, DANCE CRAZES, TANGO

"CUPID," 1961
Sam Cooke
TABLE 4-d, ROCK 'N' ROLL-i

"THE CURSE OF AN ACHING HEART," 1913
Henry Fink/Al Piantadosi
VERSE

"THE CURSE OF THE DREAMER," 1899
Paul Dresser
GAY NINETIES

"DA DOO RON RON (WHEN HE WALKED ME HOME)," 1963
Jeff Barry, Ellie Greenwich, Phil Spector
NONSENSE, ROCK 'N' ROLL, WALKING

"DADDY," 1941
Bob Troup
FATHERS

"DADDY WOULDN'T BUY ME A BOW-WOW," 1892
Joseph Tabrar
FATHERS

"DADDY'S GONE A-HUNTING," 1971
Dory Previn/John Williams
WOMEN AS SONGWRITERS

"DADDY'S HOME," 1961
James Sheppard, William Miller
FATHERS, ROCK 'N' ROLL

"DADDY'S LITTLE GIRL," 1905
Edward Madden/Theodore F. Morse
FATHERS, GIRL, SINGING GROUPS

"DADDY'S LITTLE GIRL," 1949
Bobby Burke, Horace Gerlach
FATHERS, GIRL

"DAISIES WON'T TELL," 1908
Anita Owen
WOMEN AS SONGWRITERS

"DAISY BELL (A BICYCLE MADE FOR TWO)," 1892
Harry Dacre
BARBERSHOP, BRITAIN, BROKEN CHORD, GAY NINETIES, MELODY, NAMES, SUBJECTS, TIN PAN ALLEY, TRAVEL, WALTZ

"DALLAS BLUES," 1912
Lloyd Garrett/Hart A. Wand
BLUES, TABLE 5

"DANCE TO THE MUSIC," 1968
Sylvester Stewart
ROCK-ix

"DANCE WITH A DOLLY (WITH A HOLE IN HER STOCKIN')," 1940
Terry Shand, Jimmy Eaton, Mickey Leader
BORROWING, DANCING, DOLL

"DANCE WITH ME," 1959
Louis Lebish, George Treadwell, Irv Nahan, Elmo Glick (pseud. Jerry Leiber, Mike Stoller)
DANCING, ROCK 'N' ROLL-ii

"DANCE WITH ME HENRY (THE WALL-FLOWER)," 1955
Johnny Otis, Hank Ballard, Etta James
DANCING, NAMES

"DANCING IN THE DARK," 1931
Howard Dietz/Arthur Schwartz
ALLITERATION, DANCING, DEPRESSION YEARS, GOLDEN AGE, INTERVAL, LYRICISTS, NEW YORK CITY, NIGHT, REPEATED NOTE, REVUES, TABLE 14

"Dancing in the Dark," 1984
Bruce Springsteen
DANCING, TABLE 10-j, ROCK-xii, TABLE 15

"Dancing in the Street," 1964
William Stevenson, Marvin Gaye, Ivy Hunter
DANCING, MOTOWN, ROCK-x, STREETS

"Dancing Machine," 1973
Hal Davis, Don Fletcher, Weldon Dean Parks
DANCING

"Dancing on the Ceiling," 1930
Lorenz Hart/Richard Rodgers
DANCING, LYRICISTS, TABLE 11, RANGE,
SCALE

"Dancing Queen," 1976
Benny Andersson, Björn Ulvaeus, Stig Anderson
DANCING, DISCO

"Dancing With Tears in My Eyes," 1930
Al Dubin/Joe Burke
CRYING, DANCING

"Dandy," 1966
Ray Davies
ROCK-iii

"Dang Me," 1964
Roger Miller
TABLE 10-r, TABLE 10-u, TABLE 10-w

"The Dangling Conversation," 1966
Paul Simon
FOLK ROCK

"Daniel," 1973
Elton John, Bernie Taupin
TABLE 4-d, NAMES, ROCK-x

"Danke Schoen," 1963
Kurt Schwabach, Milt Gabler (Eng.)/Bert Kaempfert
FOREIGN LANGUAGE, GERMANY

"Danny Boy," 1913
Fred Weatherly
BORROWING, BOY, IRELAND, NAMES

"Dardanella," 1919
Fred Fisher/Felix Bernard, Johnny S. Black
BOOGIE-WOOGIE, RAGTIME, ROARING
TWENTIES

**"The Daring Young Man (On the Flying
Trapeze)," 1868; *see also* "The Man on
the Flying Trapeze"**
George Leybourne/Alfred Lee
CIRCUS, MAN, POPULAR SONG-i

"Dark Eyes," 1926
traditional Russian Gypsy song; arr. Harry Horlick
TABLE 2, BORROWING, GYPSY MUSIC, RUSSIA

"The Darktown Strutters' Ball," 1917
Shelton Brooks
BREAK, BROKEN CHORD, CANADA, TABLE 5,
DANCING, JAZZ, NOVELTY SONG, RAGTIME,
VAUDEVILLE

"Darling, Je Vous Aime Beaucoup," 1935
Anna Sosenko
ENDEARMENT, FOREIGN LANGUAGE, RADIO

"Darn That Dream," 1939
Eddie De Lange/James Van Heusen
BALLAD, CHROMATICISM, DREAMS

"Dat's Love," 1943
Oscar Hammerstein II/Georges Bizet
OPERA

"The Daughter of Rosie O'Grady," 1918
Monty C. Brice/Walter Donaldson
IRELAND

"Dawn (Go Away)," 1963
Bob Gaudio, Sandy Linzer
ROCK 'N' ROLL-ii, TIME OF DAY

"Dawn of Correction," 1965
John Madara, David White, Raymond Gilmore
PROTEST SONG

"Day by Day," 1945
Sammy Cahn, Axel Stordahl, Paul Weston
DAY, INTERVAL

"Day by Day,"1971
John-Michael Tebelak/Stephen Schwartz
DAY, METER, RANGE, RELIGION

"Day Dreaming," 1972
Aretha Franklin
WOMEN AS SONGWRITERS

"Day In—Day Out," 1939
Johnny Mercer/Rube Bloom
DAY, INTERVAL, PIANO

"A Day in the Life," 1967
John Lennon, Paul McCartney
DAY, LIFE, ROCK-ii

"A Day in the Life of a Fool," 1966
Carl Sigman (Eng.)/Luis Bonfa
DAY, FOOLS

"The Day the Rains Came," 1957
Carl Sigman (Eng.)/Gilbert Becaud
WEATHER

"Day Tripper," 1965
John Lennon, Paul McCartney
BRAZIL

"Daybreak," 1942
Harold Adamson/Ferde Grofé
ADAPTATION, DAY, RIVERS, TIME OF DAY

"Daydream," 1966
John B. Sebastian
DAY, ROCK-v

"Daydream Believer," 1967
John Stewart
TABLE 4-d, DAY

"Days of Wine and Roses," 1962
Johnny Mercer/Henry Mancini
COMPOSERS, DAY, FILM MUSIC, TABLE 8,
FLOWERS, FOOD AND DRINK, TABLE 10-a,
TABLE 10-b

"Dead End Street," 1967
Ben Raleigh/David Axelrod
TABLE 10-o, STREETS

"Dear Heart," 1964
Jay Livingston, Ray Evans/Henry Mancini
TABLE 2, ENDEARMENT, TABLE 8

"Dear Hearts and Gentle People," 1949
Bob Hilliard/Sammy Fain
ENDEARMENT, PEOPLE, TABLE 15, TENDER-
NESS

"Dear Little Boy of Mine," 1918
J. Keirn Brennan/Ernest R. Ball
BOY

"Dear Old Girl," 1903
Richard Henry Buck/Theodore F. Morse
ENDEARMENT, GIRL

"Dear Uncle Sam," 1965
Loretta Lynn
WOMEN AS SONGWRITERS

"Dear World," 1969
Jerry Herman
WORLD

"Dearie," 1905
Clare Kummer (pseud. Clare Rodman Beecher)
WOMEN AS SONGWRITERS

"Dearie," 1950
Bob Hilliard, Dave Mann
ENDEARMENT

"Dearly Beloved," 1942
Johnny Mercer/Jerome Kern
BEGUINE, ENDEARMENT, TABLE 9, LOVE

**"December 1963 (Oh What a Night),"
1975**
Bob Gaudio, Judy Parker/Bob Gaudio
MONTHS

**"Deck the Halls With Boughs of Holly,"
1784**
anon./traditional Welsh air
CHRISTMAS

"Dede Dinah," 1958
Bob Marcucci/Peter De Angelis
ROCK 'N' ROLL-iii

"DEDICATED FOLLOWER OF FASHION," 1966
Ray Davies
ROCK-iii

"DEEP IN A DREAM," 1938
Eddie De Lange/James Van Heusen
DEPTH, DREAMS

"DEEP IN MY HEART, DEAR," 1924
Dorothy Donnelly/Sigmund Romberg
TABLE 2, DEPTH, ENDEARMENT, HUNGARY,
TABLE 13, WOMEN AS SONGWRITERS

"DEEP IN THE HEART OF TEXAS," 1941
June Hershey/Don Swander
BROKEN CHORD, DEPTH, TABLE 9, HAR-
MONIC RHYTHM, POPULAR SONG-vi, STATES

"DEEP NIGHT," 1929
Rudy Vallee/Charlie Henderson
NIGHT

"DEEP PURPLE," 1939
Mitchell Parish/Peter De Rose
ADAPTATION, TABLE 3, COLORS, TABLE 7,
DEPTH, GOLDEN AGE, TABLE 10-e, OCTAVE,
POPULAR SONG-ii, RADIO

"DEEP RIVER," 1913
H. T. Burleigh
DEPTH, RIVERS

"DEIN IST MEIN GANZES HERZ," SEE "YOURS IS
MY HEART ALONE"

"DEJA VU," 1978
Adrienne Anderson/Isaac Hayes
TABLE 10-n

"DELICADO," 1952
Jack Lawrence/Waldyr Azevedo
SAMBA

"DELILAH," 1968
Les Reed, Barry Mason
NAMES

"DELIRIOUS," 1982
Prince Rogers Nelson
ROCK-xii

"DELTA DAWN," 1972
Alex Harvey, Larry Collins
NAMES, TABLE 15, TIME OF DAY

"DEPEND ON YOU," 1991
BeBe Winans, CeCe Winans
GOSPEL

"DESAFINADO (SLIGHTLY OUT OF TUNE),"
1962
Jon Hendricks, Jesse Cavanaugh (pseud. Howard S.
Richmond) (Eng.)/Antonio Carlos Jobim
BOSSA NOVA, BRAZIL

"THE DESERT SONG," 1926
Otto Harbach, Oscar Hammerstein II/Sigmund
Romberg
HUNGARY, MODE, TABLE 13

"DESIRE," 1988
Bono/U2
TABLE 10-l

"DESOLATION ROW," 1965
Bob Dylan
ROCK-iv

"DETROIT CITY," 1963
Mel Tillis, Danny Dill
TABLE 5, COUNTRY AND WESTERN

"DEVIL OR ANGEL," 1955
Blanche Carter
ANGELS, RHYTHM AND BLUES

"THE DEVIL WENT DOWN TO GEORGIA," 1979
Tom Crain, Taz DiGregorio, Fred Edwards, Jim
Marshall, Charles Hayward, Charlie Daniels
TABLE 10-v, MAGIC, STATES

"DEVOTED TO YOU," 1958
Boudleaux Bryant
ROCK 'N' ROLL-i

"DIAMONDS AND RUST," 1975
Joan Baez
FOLK SONG, WOMEN AS SONGWRITERS

"DIAMONDS ARE A GIRL'S BEST FRIEND," 1949
Leo Robin/Jule Styne
BROKEN CHORD, COMPOSERS, FRIENDSHIP,
GIRL, JEWELRY, TABLE 11, SUPERLATIVES

"DIANA," 1957
Paul Anka
NAMES, ROCK 'N' ROLL-iii

"(I'M IN HEAVEN WHEN I SEE YOU SMILE) DIANE," 1927
Erno Rapee, Lew Pollack
FILM MUSIC, TABLE 8, NAMES

"THE DIARY," 1958
Howard Greenfield/Neil Sedaka
ROCK 'N' ROLL, WRITING

"DID YOU EVER HAVE TO MAKE UP YOUR MIND?," 1965
John B. Sebastian
MIND

"DID YOU EVER SEE A DREAM WALKING?," 1933
Mack Gordon/Harry Revel
DREAMS, TABLE 9, LYRICISTS, WALKING

"DID YOU EVER THINK AS THE HEARSE ROLLS BY (THE WORMS CRAWL IN, THE WORMS CRAWL OUT)," 1923
traditional British Song
ANIMALS

"DID YOU SEE MY SAVIOR?," C. 1930
Thomas A. Dorsey
GOSPEL

"DID YOUR MOTHER COME FROM IRELAND?," 1936
Jimmy Kennedy, Michael Carr
IRELAND, MOTHERS, NATIONS

"DIDN'T I (BLOW YOUR MIND THIS TIME?)," 1970
Thom Bell, William Hart/Thom Bell
TABLE 10-p

"DIFFERENT WORLDS," 1979
Norman Gimbel/Charles Fox
TELEVISION, WORLD

"DIGA DIGA DOO," 1928
Dorothy Fields/Jimmy McHugh
NONSENSE, REVUE, TABLE 14, SLANG, WOMEN AS SONGWRITERS

"¿DIME?," SEE "FEELINGS"

"DINAH," 1925
Sam M. Lewis, Joe Young/Harry Akst
SINGING GROUPS

"DINDI," 1965
Ray Gilbert (Eng.)/Antonio Carlos Jobim
WOODWINDS

"DING-DONG! THE WITCH IS DEAD," 1939
E. Y. Harburg/Harold Arlen
TABLE 9, MAGIC

"DINNER FOR ONE PLEASE, JAMES," 1935
Michael Carr
BRITAIN, FOOD AND DRINK

"THE DIPSY DOODLE," 1937
Larry Clinton
ALLITERATION, TABLE 3, NONSENSE, RIFF, SWING

"DISCO INFERNO," 1977
Leroy Green, Ron Kersey
DISCO

"DISCO LADY," 1976
Don Davis, Harvet Scales, Albert Vance
DISCO

"DITES-MOI," 1949
Oscar Hammerstein II/Richard Rodgers
FOREIGN LANGUAGE, TABLE 12

"DIXIE," 1860
Daniel Decatur Emmett
POPULAR SONG-i, POPULAR SONG-ii

"DIXIE FLYER BLUES," 1925
Bessie Smith
WOMEN AS SONGWRITERS

"DIXIELAND BAND," 1935
Johnny Mercer/Bernard Hanighen
DIXIELAND

"DO DO DO," 1926
Ira Gershwin/George Gershwin
TABLE 11

"Do I Hear a Waltz?," 1965
Stephen Sondheim/Richard Rodgers
LYRICISTS

"Do I Love You?," 1939
Cole Porter
LOVE, TABLE 11

"Do I Love You Because You're Beautiful?," 1957
Oscar Hammerstein II/Richard Rodgers
BEAUTY

"Do It Again," 1968
Brian Wilson, Mike Love
ROCK

"Do Not Forsake Me," SEE "High Noon"

"Do Nothin' Till You Hear From Me," 1943
Bob Russell/Duke Ellington
TABLE 3, PIANO

"Do-Re-Mi," 1959
Oscar Hammerstein II/Richard Rodgers
CHILDHOOD, MUSIC, TABLE 12, SCALE

"Do the Freddie," 1965
Lou Courtney, Dennis Lambert
ROCK-iii

"Do They Know It's Christmas," 1984
Bob Geldof, Midge Ure
CHRISTMAS

"Do Wah Diddy Diddy," 1963
Jeff Barry, Ellie Greenwich
NONSENSE

"Do You Believe in Magic?," 1965
John Sebastian
MAGIC, ROCK-v

"Do You Know the Way to San Jose?," 1967
Hal David/Burt Bacharach
TABLE 5, COLLABORATION, TABLE 10-f, POPULAR SONG-x, TABLE 15

"Do You Know Where You're Going To?," SEE "Theme From Mahogany"

"Do You Love Me?," 1962
Berry Gordy, Jr.
MOTOWN

"Do You Think I'm Sexy?," 1979
Carmone Appice, Jr., Rod Stewart
DISCO

"Do You Want to Know a Secret?," 1963
John Lennon, Paul McCartney
ROCK-ii

"Doan Ye Cry Mah Honey," 1899
Albert W. Noll
GAY NINETIES

"(Sittin' on the) Dock of the Bay," 1968
Steve Cropper, Otis Redding
TABLE 4-c, TABLE 10-o, SOUL, WATERFRONT

"Doctor Feelgood," 1967
Aretha Franklin, Ted White
WOMEN AS SONGWRITERS

"Doctor's Orders," 1974
Roger Cook, Roger Greenaway, Geoff Stephens
DISCO

"Does Anybody Really Know What Time It Is?," 1969
Robert Lamm
ROCK-ix, TIME OF DAY

"Does the Spearmint Lose Its Flavor on the Bedpost Over Night?,"1924
Billy Rose, Marty Bloom/Ernest Breuer
NOVELTY SONG

"Does Your Heart Beat for Me?," 1936
Mitchell Parish/Russ Morgan, Arnold Johnson
TABLE 3

"(How Much Is That) Doggie in the Window?," 1953
Bob Merrill
ANIMALS, NOVELTY SONG, TABLE 15

"DOGGIN' AROUND," 1960
Lena Agree
ROCK 'N' ROLL-i

"DOIN' WHAT COMES NATUR'LLY," 1946
Irving Berlin
CONTRACTIONS, TABLE 11, POPULAR SONG-ii

"DOMANI (TOMORROW)," 1955
Tony Velona/Ulpio Minucci
DAY, ITALY

"DOMINIQUE," 1963
Noel Regney (Eng.)/Soeur Sourire, O.P.
BELGIUM, TABLE 8, RELIGION

"DOMINO," 1950
Don Raye (Eng.)/Louis Ferrari
FRANCE, MODE

"DOMINO," 1970
Van Morrison
ROCK-iii

"THE DONKEY SERENADE," 1937
Bob Wright, George Forrest/Rudolf Friml, Herbert Stothart
ADAPTATION, CZECHOSLOVAKIA, MUSIC

"DONNA," 1958
Ritchie Valens
ROCK 'N' ROLL-i

"DON'T," 1957
Jerry Leiber, Mike Stoller
ROCK 'N' ROLL

"DON'T BE AFRAID, LITTLE DARLIN'," 1963
Cynthia Weil, Barry Mann
WOMEN AS SONGWRITERS

"DON'T BE ANGRY," 1955
Napoleon Brown, Fred Madison, Rose Marie McCoy
COVER

"DON'T BE CRUEL (TO A HEART THAT'S TRUE)," 1956
Otis Blackwell, Elvis Presley
BMI, TABLE 4-d, POPULAR SONG-viii, SINGERS, TABLE 15

"DON'T BE THAT WAY," 1938
Mitchell Parish/Benny Goodman, Edgar Sampson
TABLE 3, SWING

"DON'T BLAME ME," 1933
Dorothy Fields/Jimmy McHugh
BEBOP, COLLABORATION, FORGETTING, LYRICISTS, TIN PAN ALLEY

"DON'T CRY FOR ME, ARGENTINA," 1976
Tim Rice/Andrew Lloyd Webber
ARGENTINA, BRITAIN, CHORUS, CRYING, TABLE 12, NATIONS, PEDAL POINT, TANGO, VERSE

"DON'T CRY OUT LOUD," 1976
Peter Allen, Carole Bayer Sager
CRYING, FORM

"DON'T EVER LEAVE ME," 1929
Oscar Hammerstein II/Jerome Kern
SYNCOPATION

"DON'T EXPLAIN," 1946
Arthur Herzog, Jr./Billie Holiday
TORCH SONG, WOMEN AS SONGWRITERS

"DON'T FENCE ME IN," 1944
Cole Porter
COMPOSER-LYRICISTS, TABLE 9, INTERVAL, SINGING GROUPS, SLANG

"DON'T GET AROUND MUCH ANYMORE," 1942
Bob Russell/Duke Ellington
TABLE 3, COMPOSERS, DAYS OF THE WEEK, PIANO

"DON'T GIVE UP THE SHIP," 1935
Al Dubin/Harry Warren
TABLE 9

"DON'T GO BREAKING MY HEART," 1976
Elton John, Bernie Taupin
ROCK-x

"DON'T HANG UP," 1963
Kal Mann/Dave Appell
ROCK 'N' ROLL-iv, TELEPHONES

**"Don't It Make My Brown Eyes Blue,"
1977**
Richard Leigh
TABLE 2, COUNTRY AND WESTERN, TABLE 10-t, TABLE 10-w

"Don't Know Much," *see* **"All I Need to Know (Don't Know Much)"**

"Don't Leave Me This Way," 1977
Kenny Gamble, Leon Huff, Cary Gilbert
TABLE 10-n

"Don't Let Go," 1957
Jesse Stone
SOUL

"Don't Let Me Be Lonely Tonight," 1972
James Taylor
LONELINESS, ROCK-vi

"Don't Let Me Be Misunderstood," 1964
Bennie Benjamin, Sol Marcus, Gloria Caldwell
ROCK-iii

**"Don't Let the Green Grass Fool You,"
1970**
Jerry Akines, Johnnie Bellmon, Victor Drayton, Reginald Turner
SOUL

**"Don't Let the Stars Get in Your Eyes,"
1953**
Slim Willet, Cactus Pryor, Barbara Trammel
TABLE 2, TABLE 15, STARS

**"Don't Let the Sun Catch You Crying,"
1964**
Gerrard Marsden
CRYING, ROCK-iii

**"Don't Let the Sun Go Down on Me,"
1974**
Elton John, Bernie Taupin
ROCK-x, SUN

"Don't Make Me Over," 1962
Hal David/Burt Bacharach
RHYTHM AND BLUES, TABLE 15

"Don't Play That Song (You Lied)," 1962
Ahmet M. Ertegun, Betty Nelson
TABLE 10-n, MUSIC, RHYTHM AND BLUES

"Don't Pull Your Love," 1970
Dennis Lambert, Brian Potter
TABLE 4-d

"Don't Rain on My Parade," 1963
Bob Merrill/Jule Styne
TABLE 11, TABLE 15, WEATHER

"Don't Rob Another Man's Castle," 1949
Jenny Lou Carson
WOMEN AS SONGWRITERS

**"Don't Say Nothin' Bad (About My Baby),"
1963**
Gerry Goffin, Carole King
BABY, SINGING GROUPS

**"Don't Sit Under the Apple Tree (With
Anyone Else But Me)," 1942**
Lew Brown, Charles Tobias, Sam H. Stept
BORROWING, TABLE 9, SWING, TREES,
WORLD WAR II

"Don't Sleep in the Subway," 1967
Tony Hatch, Jackie Trent
BRITAIN, SLEEP, TRAINS

"Don't Stand So Close to Me," 1980
Sting (pseud. Gordon Sumner)
CLOSENESS, TABLE 10-l

"Don't Stop 'Til You Get Enough," 1978
Michael Jackson
ENDING, TABLE 10-o

"Don't Talk to Strangers," 1965
Bob Durand/Ron Elliott
TALKING

"Don't Think Twice, It's All Right," 1963
Bob Dylan
SINGING GROUPS, THINKING

"Don't Touch Me," 1966
Hank Cochran
TABLE 10-t

"DON'T WORRY BABY," 1964
Brian Wilson, Roger Christian
BABY, ROCK-i

"DON'T WORRY, BE HAPPY," 1988
Bobby McFerrin
TABLE 10-a, TABLE 10-b, TABLE 10-g

"DON'T WORRY 'BOUT ME," 1939
Ted Koehler/Rube Bloom
PIANO, TRIPLET

"DON'T YOU CRY MY HONEY," *SEE* **"DOAN YE CRY MAH HONEY"**

"DON'T YOU KNOW?" 1959
Bobby Worth
TABLE 6, OPERA

"THE DOOR IS STILL OPEN TO MY HEART," 1955
Chuck Willis
TABLE 2, RHYTHM AND BLUES

"DOWN AMONG THE SHELTERING PALMS," 1914
James Brockman/Abe Olman
TREES

"DOWN ARGENTINA WAY," 1940
Mack Gordon/Harry Warren
NATIONS

"DOWN AT ROSIE RILEY'S FLAT," 1902
Maude Nugent
WOMEN AS SONGWRITERS

"DOWN AT THE TWIST AND SHOUT," 1991
Mary-Chapin Carpenter
TABLE 10-t

"DOWN BY THE O-HI-O(O-MY!-O!)," 1920
Jack Yellen/Abe Olman
RIVERS

"DOWN BY THE OLD MILL STREAM," 1910
Tell Taylor
BARBERSHOP, KEY, RIVERS, TABLE 15, VAUDEVILLE

"DOWN BY THE RIVER," 1934
Lorenz Hart, Richard Rodgers
RIVERS

"DOWN BY THE RIVERSIDE," C. **1865**
traditional African-American spiritual
RIVERS

"DOWN HEARTED BLUES," 1923
Alberta Hunter/Lovie Austin
BLUES, TABLE 15

"DOWN HOME IN NEW ENGLAND," *SEE* **"YOU'RE THE FLOWER OF MY HEART, SWEET ADELINE"**

"DOWN IN THE DEPTHS, ON THE NINETIETH FLOOR," 1936
Cole Porter
CABARET, DEPTH, TABLE 11

"DOWN IN THE VALLEY (BIRMINGHAM JAIL)," C. 1845, PUB. 1917
traditional American folk song
TABLE 5, COUNTRY AND WESTERN

"DOWN ON ME," 1967
Janis Joplin
WOMEN AS SONGWRITERS

"DOWN ON THE CORNER," 1969
John C. Fogerty
ROCK-ix

"DOWN WHERE THE WURZBURGER FLOWS," 1902
Vincent P. Bryan/Harry Von Tilzer
FOOD AND DRINK, VAUDEVILLE, WOMEN AS SONGWRITERS

"DOWNTOWN," 1964
Tony Hatch
BRITAIN, TABLE 5, FADE-OUT, TABLE 10-e, TABLE 15

"DREAM," 1944
Johnny Mercer
COMPOSER-LYRICISTS, DREAMS, FAREWELLS, FEELING, POPULAR SONG-ii, SINGING GROUPS

"Dream a Little Dream of Me," 1931
Gus Kahn/Wilbur Schandt, Fabian Andre
DREAMS, RADIO, RELEASE

"Dream Baby, How Long Must I Dream?," 1962
Cindy Walker
BABY, DREAMS, ROCK 'N' ROLL-i

"A Dream Is a Wish Your Heart Makes," 1948
Mack David, Al Hoffman, Jerry Livingston
TABLE 9, WISHING

"Dream Lover," 1959
Bobby Darin
DREAMS, LOVER, ROCK 'N' ROLL-iii

"The Dream of Olwen," 1947
Winifred May/Charles Williams
DREAMS

"Dreamboat Annie," 1976
Ann Wilson, Nancy Wilson
WOMEN AS SONGWRITERS

"Dreams," 1977
Stephanie Nicks
TABLE 4-d, DREAMS

"Drifting and Dreaming," 1925
Haven Gillespie/Egbert Van Alstyne, Erwin R. Schmidt, Loyal Curtis
DREAMS

"Drinkin' Wine, Spo-dee-o-dee," 1949
Granville "Stick" McGhee, J. Mayo Williams
RHYTHM AND BLUES

"Drinking Song," 1924
Dorothy Donnelly/Sigmund Romberg
FOOD AND DRINK, TABLE 13, WOMEN AS SONGWRITERS

"Drip Drop," 1954
Jerry Leiber, Mike Stoller
ROCK 'N' ROLL-ii

"Drive," 1984
Ric Ocasek
ROCK-xi

"Dueling Banjos," 1972
m. Arthur Smith
BLUEGRASS, TABLE 8

"Duerme," see "Time Was"

"Duke of Earl," 1961
Earl Edwards, Bernie Williams, Eugene Dixon
ROCK 'N' ROLL

"Dulcinea," 1965
Joe Darion/Mitch Leigh
TABLE 12

"Dust in the Wind," 1977
Kerry Livgren
TABLE 4-d, WEATHER

"D'Ye Love Me?," 1925
Otto Harbach, Oscar Hammerstein II/Jerome Kern
QUESTIONS

"D'Yer Maker," 1973
John Bonham, John Baldwin, Robert Plant
HEAVY METAL

"Eadie Was a Lady," 1932
B. G. DeSylva/Nacio Herb Brown, Richard A. Whiting
NAMES

"The Eagle and Me," 1944
E. Y. Harburg/Harold Arlen
BIRDS

"Early Autumn," 1949
Johnny Mercer/Ralph Burns, Woody Herman
IMPROVISATION, SEASONS

"Early in the Morning," 1969
Mike Leander, Eddie Seago
TIME OF DAY

"Earth Angel (Will You Be Mine)," 1954
Jesse Belvin
ANGELS, COVER, DOO-WOP, RHYTHM AND BLUES, ROCK 'N' ROLL-ii

"Ease On Down the Road," 1974
Charlie Smalls
STREETS, TRAVEL

"EAST OF GINGER TREES," 1972
James Seals, Darrell Crofts
RELIGION

"EAST OF THE SUN (AND WEST OF THE
MOON)," 1934
Brooks Bowman
TABLE 3,CARDINAL POINTS, MOON, SUN,
TRIPLET

"EAST SIDE, WEST SIDE," SEE "THE SIDEWALKS
OF NEW YORK"

"EASTER PARADE," 1933
Irving Berlin
ADAPTATION, CITIES, CLOTHING, COM-
POSER-LYRICISTS, GOLDEN AGE, HOLIDAYS,
POPULAR SONG-vi, REVUES, TABLE 14,
STREETS

"EASY STREET," 1941
Alan Rankin Jones
STREETS

"EASY TO LOVE," 1936
Cole Porter
BEGUINE, CONTRACTIONS, TABLE 9, RANGE

"EBB TIDE," 1953
Carl Sigman/Robert Maxwell
TABLE 8, OCEAN, WATERFRONT

"EDELWEISS," 1959
Oscar Hammerstein II/Richard Rodgers
MUSICAL PLAYS, TABLE 12

"EH CUMPARI!," 1953
Julius La Rosa, Archie Bleyer (Eng.)
BORROWING, ITALY

"EIGHT DAYS A WEEK," 1964
John Lennon, Paul McCartney
DAYS OF THE WEEK

"EIGHT MILES HIGH," 1966
Gene Clark (pseud. Harold E. Clark), David Crosby,
Jim McGuinn
HEIGHT, ROCK-v

"80'S LADIES," 1987
K. T. Oslin
TABLE 10-t

"EILEEN," 1917
Henry Blossom/Victor Herbert
IRELAND

"EL PASO," 1959
Marty Robbins
TABLE 4-d, TABLE 5, COUNTRY AND WEST-
ERN, TABLE 10-s

"ELEANOR RIGBY," 1966
John Lennon, Paul McCartney
TABLE 4-d, TABLE 10-g, HARMONIC RHYTHM,
LONELINESS, MODE, NAMES

"ELECTRIC YOUTH," 1988
Deborah Gibson
WOMEN AS SONGWRITERS

"ELENORE," 1968
Howard Kaylan, Mark Volman, Jim Pons, Al Nichol,
John Barbata
NAMES, ROCK-v

"ELI'S COMING," 1967
Laura Nyro
NAMES, ROCK

"ELMER'S TUNE," 1941
Sammy Gallop, Dick Jurgens, Elmer Albrecht
MELODY, NAMES

"ELSIE FROM CHELSEA," 1896
Harry Dacre
GAY NINETIES

"ELUSIVE BUTTERFLY," 1965
Bob Lind
ROCK

"ELVIRA," 1965
Dallas Frazier
TABLE 10-v, NAMES

"EMBRACEABLE YOU," 1930
Ira Gershwin/George Gershwin
BEBOP, TABLE 3, COMPOSERS, FORM,
GOLDEN AGE, GYPSY MUSIC, LYRICISTS,
MUSICAL COMEDY, TABLE 11, REPEATED
NOTE, RHYME

"EMOTION," 1977
Barry Gibb, Robin Gibb
TABLE 4-d

"EMOTIONAL RESCUE," 1980
Mick Jagger, Keith Richards
ROCK-iii

"THE END IS NOT IN SIGHT (THE COWBOY TUNE)," 1976
H. Russell Smith
TABLE 10-v

"THE END OF A LOVE AFFAIR," 1950
Edward C. Redding
CABARET, ENDING, LOVE, TORCH SONG, VERSE

"THE END OF THE WORLD" 1962
Sylvia Dee/Arthur Kent
WOMEN AS SONGWRITERS, WORLD

"ENDLESS LOVE," 1981
Lionel Richie, Jr.
ENDING, ENDURING LOVE, TABLE 8, POPULAR SONG-xii

"ENDLESSLY," 1959
Clyde Otis, Brook Benton
ENDING, ENDURING LOVE, RHYTHM AND BLUES

"ENJOY YOURSELF (IT'S LATER THAN YOU THINK)," 1948
Herb Magidson/Carl Sigman
SAMBA, THINKING

"THE ENTERTAINER," 1903
m. Scott Joplin
RAGTIME

"ESTRELLITA (LITTLE STAR)," 1914
m. Manuel M. Ponce
STARS

"ET MAINTENANT," SEE "WHAT NOW MY LOVE?"

"ETERNALLY (LIMELIGHT, THE TERRY THEME)," 1953
Geoffrey Parsons/Charles Chaplin
ENDURING LOVE, TABLE 8

"EVE OF DESTRUCTION," 1965
Phil F. Sloan/Steve Barri
PROTEST SONG, RELIGION, ROCK

"EVERGREEN (LOVE THEME FROM A STAR IS BORN)," 1976
Paul Williams/Barbra Streisand
TABLE 1, COLORS, TABLE 7, TABLE 8, TABLE 10-b, TABLE 10-f, KEY, LENGTH, MARRIAGE, POPULAR SONG-xiii, RANGE, SINGERS, TABLE 15, VAMP, WOMEN AS SONGWRITERS

"EVERLASTING LOVE," 1967
James Cason, Mac Grayden
DISCO, ENDURING LOVE

"EVERY BREATH YOU TAKE," 1983
Sting (pseud. Gordon Sumner)
TABLE 10-b, TABLE 10-h

"EVERY DAY I HAVE THE BLUES," 1952
Peter Chatman
BLUES, RHYTHM AND BLUES

"EVERY DAY IS LADIES' DAY WITH ME," 1906
Henry Blossom/Victor Herbert
DAY, LADY, TABLE 11

"EVERY LITTLE MOVEMENT," 1910
Otto Harbach/Karl Hoschna
AUSTRIA, LENGTH, TABLE 11

"EVERY LITTLE STEP," 1988
L. A. Reid (pseud. Antonio Reid), Babyface (pseud. Kenny Edmunds)
TABLE 10-o

"EVERY TIME (I FEEL HIS SPIRIT)," 1956
paraphrase of traditional American spiritual, arr. Patti Page
RELIGION

"EVERY TIME I TURN AROUND," 1984
Judy Hart Angelo, Gary Portnoy
WOMEN AS SONGWRITERS

"EVERYBODY LOVES A LOVER," 1958
Richard Adler/Robert Allen
LOVERS

"EVERYBODY LOVES SOMEBODY," 1948
Irving Taylor/Ken Lane
TABLE 15

"EVERYBODY PLAYS THE FOOL," 1971
Kenneth Williams, Rudy Clark, Jim Bailey
FOOLS

"Falling in Love With Love," 1938
Lorenz Hart/Richard Rodgers
FALLING IN LOVE, MUSICAL COMEDY, TABLE 11, WALTZ

"Falling Star," 1976
Karla Bonoff
WOMEN AS SONGWRITERS

"Fame," 1980
Dean Pitchford/Michael Gore
TABLE 1, ROCK-x

"Family Affair," 1971
Sylvester Stewart
ROCK-ix

"Fancy," 1969
Bobbie Gentry
WOMEN AS SONGWRITERS

"Fanny," 1954
Harold Rome
TABLE 12, NAMES

"Far Away Places," 1948
Joan Whitney, Alex Kramer
PLACES, WOMEN AS SONGWRITERS

"Farewell Blues," 1923
Elmer Schoebel, Paul Mares, Leon Rappolo
DIXIELAND, FAREWELLS

"The Farmer in the Dell," 1883
traditional German song
MARRIAGE

"Fascinating Rhythm," 1924
Ira Gershwin/George Gershwin
BLUE NOTE, MUSIC, MUSICAL COMEDY, TABLE 11, RHYTHM

"Fascination," 1932; newly adapted in 1957
Dick Manning (Eng.)/F. D. Marchetti
ADAPTATION, FRANCE, GYPSY MUSIC

"Fast Car," 1988
Tracy Chapman
TABLE 10-f, TRAVEL

"The Fat Man," 1950
Antoine "Fats" Domino/Dave Bartholomew
MAN, RHYTHM AND BLUES

"Feel Like Makin' Love," 1973
Gene McDaniels
FEELING, TABLE 4-d, LOVE

"Feel So Fine (Feel So Good)," 1960
Leonard Lee
RHYTHM AND BLUES

"Feelin' Groovy," SEE "The 59th Street Bridge Song"

"Feelings (¿Dime?)," 1974
Morris Albert (Eng.)/Morris Albert
FADE-OUT, FEELING, MELODY

"Feels So Good," 1977
Chuck Mangione
FEELING, TABLE 4-d

"A Fellow Needs a Girl," 1947
Oscar Hammerstein II/Richard Rodgers
GIRL, MAN, TABLE 12

"Ferry-Boat Serenade," 1940
Harold Adamson (Eng.)/Eldo di Lazzaro
BOATING, SINGING GROUPS

"Ferry 'Cross the Mersey," 1964
Gerrard Marsden
RIVERS, ROCK-iii

"Les Feuilles Mortes," SEE "Autumn Leaves"

"Fever," 1956
Eddie Cooley, John R. Davenport
TABLE 4-d, SINGERS, TABLE 15

"A Fifth of Beethoven," 1976
M. Walter Murphy
TABLE 6

"The 59th Street Bridge Song (Feelin' Groovy)," 1966
Paul Simon
TABLE 4-d, FEELING, FOLK ROCK, SHEET MUSIC, SLANG, STREETS

"Fifty Ways to Leave Your Lover," 1975
Paul Simon
LOVER, ROCK-v

"Fine and Dandy," 1930
Paul James/Kay Swift
WOMEN AS SONGWRITERS

"Fine and Mellow," 1939
Billie Holiday
TORCH SONG, WOMEN AS SONGWRITERS

"Fine Brown Frame," 1944
Guadalupe Cartiero, J. Mayo Williams
TABLE 7, RHYTHM AND BLUES

"A Fine Romance," 1936
Dorothy Fields/Jerome Kern
CATALOGUE SONG, CHORUS, COMPOSERS, FILM MUSICALS, TABLE 9, ROMANCE SEQUENCE

"Fire and Ice," 1981
Pat Benatar, Scott Sheets, Tom Kelly
TABLE 10-i

"Fire and Rain," 1969
James Taylor
TABLE 4-d, PERFORMER-SONGWRITERS, ROCK-vi, WEATHER

"Firefly," 1958
Carolyn Leigh/Cy Coleman
WOMEN AS SONGWRITERS

"The First Noël," 1833
traditional English carol
CHRISTMAS

"The First Time Ever I Saw Your Face," 1962
Ewan MacColl
ANATOMY, TABLE 2, TABLE 4-d, TABLE 10-a, TABLE 10-b, RHYME, SEEING, TABLE 15, TIME

"The Fishin' Hole (Theme From The Andy Griffith Show)," 1961
Everett Sloane/Earle Hagen, Herb Spencer
TELEVISION

"Fit as a Fiddle," 1932
Arthur Freed, Al Hoffman, Al Goodhart
STRINGS

"Five Foot Two, Eyes of Blue; Has Anybody Seen My Girl," 1925
Sam M. Lewis, Joe Young/Ray Henderson
AABA, TABLE 2, CHARLESTON, CIRCLE OF FIFTHS, COLORS, TABLE 7, COMPOSERS, GIRL, RELEASE

"Five Guys Named Moe," 1941
Larry Wynn/Jerry Bresler
NAMES, RHYTHM AND BLUES

"Five Minutes More," 1946
Sammy Cahn/Jule Styne
TIME

"The Five O'Clock Whistle," 1940
Kim Gannon, Gene Irwin, Josef Myrow
TIME OF DAY

"Five O'Clock World," 1965
Allen Reynolds
SINGING GROUPS, TIME OF DAY

"Flamingo," 1941
Edmund Anderson/Ted Grouya
BIRDS

"Flashdance . . . What a Feeling," 1983
Keith Forsey, Irene Cara/Giorgio Moroder
TABLE 1, DANCING, TABLE 9, TABLE 10-f

"Flat Foot Floogie," 1938
Slim Gaillard, Slam Stewart, Bud Green
NONSENSE

"Flip Flop and Fly," 1955
Charles Calhoun, Lou Willie Turner
RHYTHM AND BLUES

"Flowers on the Wall," 1965
Lewis DeWitt
FLOWERS, TABLE 10-h

"Fly Me to the Moon," or "In Other Words," 1954
Bart Howard
BALLAD, BORROWING, MOON

"Fly, Robin, Fly," 1975
Sylvester Levay, Stephen Prager (Eng.)
DISCO

"Flying Down to Rio," 1933
Gus Kahn, Edward Eliscu/Vincent Youmans
TABLE 9

"Flying Home," 1941
Sid Robin/Benny Goodman, Lionel Hampton
HOME, RHYTHM AND BLUES, RIFF

"A Foggy Day," 1937
Ira Gershwin/George Gershwin
CITIES, TABLE 5, COMPOSERS, DAY, FILM
MUSICALS, TABLE 9, GOLDEN AGE, WEATHER

"Foggy Mountain Breakdown," 1950
Earl Scruggs
BLUEGRASS, MOUNTAINS

"The Folks Who Live on the Hill," 1937
Oscar Hammerstein II/Jerome Kern
CABARET, MOUNTAINS, PEOPLE, RELEASE,
TOGETHERNESS

"Follow Me," 1960
Alan Jay Lerner/Frederick Loewe
TABLE 12

"Folsom Prison Blues," 1956
Johnny Cash
TABLE 10-u

"Food, Glorious Food," 1960
Lionel Bart
FOOD AND DRINK

"Fool, Fool, Fool," 1951
Ahmet Ertegun
FOOD, RHYTHM AND BLUES

"A Fool in Love (Tell Me What's Wrong)," 1960
Ike Turner
FOOL, RHYTHM AND BLUES

"The Fool on the Hill," 1967
John Lennon, Paul McCartney
BRITAIN, FOOLS, METER, MOUNTAINS

"Fools Rush In," 1940
Johnny Mercer/Rube Bloom
FOOLS, INTERVAL, PIANO

"For All We Know," 1970
Robb Roger, James Griffin/Fred Karlin
TABLE 1, TABLE 4-c, TABLE 8

"For Just a Moment," see "Love Theme From St. Elmo's Fire"

"For Me and My Gal," 1917
Edgar Leslie, E. Ray Goetz/George W. Meyer
GIRL

"(I Love You) For Sentimental Reasons," 1945
Deek Watson/William Best
SENTIMENT

"For the Good Times," 1968
Kris Kristofferson
ANATOMY, TABLE 4-c, COUNTRY AND WEST-
ERN, TABLE 10-u, TIME

"For What It's Worth," 1966
Stephen Sills
PROTEST SONG, ROCK-v

"For You," 1930
Al Dubin/Joe Burke
BALLAD, TABLE 3

"For You, for Me, for Evermore," 1946
Ira Gershwin/George Gershwin
ENDURING LOVE, TABLE 9

"For You My Love," 1949
Paul Gayten
RHYTHM AND BLUES

"For Your Country and My Country," 1917
Irving Berlin
WORLD WAR I

"For Your Precious Love," 1958
Arthur Brooks, Richard Brooks, Jerry Butler
SOUL

"FOREVER AND EVER, AMEN," 1987
Paul Overstreet, Don Schlitz
TABLE 10-w

"FOREVER YOUNG," 1973
Bob Dylan
AGE, ROCK-iv

"FORGET DOMANI," 1975
Norman Newell/Riz Ortolani
FORGETTING

"FORGET HIM," 1963
Mark Anthony (pseud. Tony Hatch)
FORGETTING, ROCK 'N' ROLL-iii

"FORGOTTEN," 1894
Flora Wulschner/Eugene Cowles
GAY NINETIES

"FORTUNATE SON," 1969
John C. Fogerty
ROCK-ix

"FORTY-FIVE MINUTES FROM BROADWAY," 1906
George M. Cohan
BROADWAY, TABLE 11

"FORTY-SECOND STREET," 1932
Al Dubin/Harry Warren
BROKEN CHORD, TABLE 9, LYRICISTS, MODE, STREETS

"FOUR WOMEN," 1966
Nina Simone
WOMEN AS SONGWRITERS

"FOXY LADY," 1967
Jimi Hendrix
LADY, ROCK-vii

"FRANKIE AND JOHNNY," C. 1870, PUB. 1912
traditional American folk ballad
NAMES

"FRASQUITA SERENADE," SEE "MY LITTLE NEST OF HEAVENLY BLUE"

"FREDERICK," 1979
Patti Smith
WOMEN AS SONGWRITERS

"FREE MAN IN PARIS," 1973
Joni Mitchell
TABLE 5, ROCK-vi

"FREEWAY OF LOVE," 1985
Jeffrey Cohen, Narada Michael Walden
TABLE 10-n, TABLE 10-q, LOVE, TABLE 15, STREETS

"FREEZE TAG," 1985
Suzanne Vega
WOMEN AS SONGWRITERS

"FREEZING," 1986
Suzanne Vega/Philip Glass
WOMEN AS SONGWRITERS

"FRENESI," 1939
Ray Charles, S. K. Russell (Eng.)/Alberto Dominguez
TABLE 3, MEXICO, PICKUP, RUMBA, SWING

"FRIENDLY PERSUASION," 1956
Paul Francis Webster/Dimitri Tiomkin
TABLE 8, FRIENDSHIP

"FRIENDSHIP," 1939
Cole Porter
FRIENDSHIP, TABLE 11

"FROM A DISTANCE," 1987
Julie Gold
TABLE 10-b, PLACES, TABLE 15, WORLD

"FROM HERE TO ETERNITY," 1953
Bob Wells/Fred Karger
ENDURING LOVE, TABLE 8

"FROM NOW ON," 1938
Cole Porter
TABLE 11

"FROM RUSSIA WITH LOVE," 1963
Lionel Bart
TABLE 8

"FROM THE BOTTLE TO THE BOTTOM," 1973
Kris Kristofferson
TABLE 10-v

"FROM THE HALLS OF MONTEZUMA TO THE
SHORES OF TRIPOLI," SEE "THE MARINE'S
HYMN"

"FROM THE LAND OF THE SKY BLUE WATER,"
1909
Nelle Richmond Eberhart/Charles Wakefield Cadman
ART SONG, SKY

"FROM THIS MOMENT ON," 1950
Cole Porter
COMPOSERS, MODE, TABLE 11, SHOW TUNE,
SOCIETY TEMPO, TIME

"FROSTY THE SNOWMAN," 1950
Steve Nelson, Jack Rollins
CHRISTMAS, WEATHER

"DER FUEHRER'S FACE," 1942
Oliver Wallace
HUMOR, WORLD WAR II

"FUGUE FOR TINHORNS," 1950
Frank Loesser
BRASS, COUNTERPOINT, TABLE 11

"FULL MOON AND EMPTY ARMS," 1946
Buddy Kaye, Ted Mossman
TABLE 6, MOON

"FUN, FUN, FUN," 1964
Brian Wilson
ROCK-i

"FUNKY BROADWAY," 1966
Arlester Christian
FUNK

"FUNKYTOWN," 1979
Steve Greenberg
FUNK

"FUNNY FACE," 1927
Ira Gershwin/George Gershwin
TABLE 11

"FUNNY FACE," 1967
Donna Fargo
WOMEN AS SONGWRITERS

"FUNNY HOW TIME SLIPS AWAY," 1961
Willie Nelson
COUNTRY AND WESTERN

"FUNNY WAY OF LAUGHIN'," 1962
Hank Cochran
TABLE 10-s

"G.I. JIVE," 1943
Johnny Mercer
WORLD WAR II

"A GAL IN CALICO," 1946
Leo Robin/Arthur Schwartz
TABLE 9

"GALVESTON," 1968
Jim Webb
TABLE 5, COMPOSER-LYRICISTS, TABLE 15

"THE GAMBLER," 1978
Don Schlitz
TABLE 10-u, TABLE 10-w

"THE GAME OF LOVE," 1964
Clint Ballard
ROCK-iii

"GAMES PEOPLE PLAY," 1968
Joe South
TABLE 4-d, TABLE 10-b, PEOPLE

"THE GANG THAT SANG HEART OF MY
HEART," SEE "HEART OF MY HEART"

"A GARDEN IN THE RAIN," 1929
James Dyrenforth/Carroll Gibbons
BRITAIN, WEATHER

"GARY, INDIANA," 1957
Meredith Willson
TABLE 5

"GATES OF EDEN," 1965
Bob Dylan
ROCK-iv

"A Gay Ranchero," 1936
Abe Tuvim, Francia Lubin/J. J. Espinosa
MEXICO

"Gee!," 1953
Viola Watkins, Daniel Norton, William Davis
RHYTHM AND BLUES

"Gee, But It's Great to Meet a Friend From Your Old Home Town," 1910
William Tracey/James McGavisk
TABLE 5, FRIENDSHIP, MEETING

"Gentle on My Mind," 1967
John Hartford
TABLE 4-b, COUNTRY AND WESTERN, TABLE 10-v, TABLE 10-w, HARMONIC RHYTHM, HARMONY, MIND, POPULAR SONG-xi, REPEATED NOTE, TABLE 15, TENDERNESS

"The Gentleman Is a Dope," 1947
Oscar Hammerstein II/Richard Rodgers
TABLE 12

"George Jackson," 1971
Bob Dylan
ROCK-iv

"Georgia on My Mind," 1930
Stuart Gorrell/Hoagy Carmichael
TABLE 4-b, COMPOSERS, FORM, GOLDEN AGE, TABLE 10-d, TABLE 10-e, TABLE 10-u, MIND, POPULAR SONG-ii, TABLE 15, STANDARD, STATES, TEMPO

"Georgy Girl," 1966
Jim Dale/Tom Springfield
TABLE 8, GIRL, HARMONIC RHYTHM, MODALITY, NAMES

"Get a Job," 1957
Earl T. Beal, Raymond W. Edwards, William F. Horton, Richard A. Lewis (The Silhouettes)
DOO-WOP

"Get Down Tonight," 1975
Harry Casey, Richard Finch
DISCO

"Get Happy," 1930
Ted Koehler/Harold Arlen
HAPPINESS, VAMP

"Get Me to the Church on Time," 1956
Alan Jay Lerner/Frederick Loewe
MARRIAGE, MUSICAL PLAYS, TABLE 12, PATTER, POLKA, TIME

"Get Off My Cloud," 1965
Mick Jagger, Keith Richards
ROCK-iii, SKY

"Get Out of Town," 1938
Cole Porter
TABLE 5, COMPOSER-LYRICISTS, DYNAMICS, MODE

"Get Together," 1963
Chester Powers
TOGETHERNESS

"Get Up and Boogie," 1976
Sylvester Levay, Stephen Prager
BOOGIE-WOOGIE

"Get Your Kicks on Route 66!," SEE **"Route 66!"**

"Getting to Know You," 1951
Oscar Hammerstein II/Richard Rodgers
COLLABORATION, MUSICAL PLAYS, TABLE 12

"Ghost Riders in the Sky," SEE **Riders in the Sky"**

"Gianina Mia," 1912
Otto Harbach/Rudolf Friml
CZECHOSLOVAKIA, TABLE 13

"Gigi," 1958
Alan Jay Lerner/Frederick Loewe
TABLE 1, TABLE 9, NAMES

"Gimme a Little Kiss, Will Ya Huh?," 1926
Roy Turk, Jack Smith, Maceo Pinkard
TABLE 3, KISSING

"Gimme Some Loving," 1966
Steve Winwood, Muff Winwood, Spencer Davis
ROCK-iii

"The Girl Friend," 1926
Lorenz Hart/Richard Rodgers
BASS LINE, CHARLESTON, FRIENDSHIP, GIRL,
TABLE 11, SCALE, TEMPO

"The Girl From Ipanema," 1963
Norman Gimbel (Eng.)/Antonio Carlos Jobim
TABLE 4-c, BOSSA NOVA, BRAZIL, GIRL, TABLE
10-a, GUITAR, HARMONY

"The Girl Is Mine," 1982
Michael Jackson
GIRL, ROCK-xii

"Girl of My Dreams," 1927
Sunny Clapp
DREAMS, GIRL, KEY

"The Girl That I Marry," 1946
Irving Berlin
BROKEN CHORD, GIRL, MARRIAGE, TABLE 11,
POPULAR SONG-ii, RANGE, WALTZ

"Girl Watcher," 1968
Buck Trail (pseud. Ronald B. Killette)
GIRL, SINGING GROUPS, SOUL

"Girls, Girls, Girls," 1907
Adrian Ross (Eng.)/Franz Lehár
AUSTRIA, GIRL, OPERETTA, TABLE 13

"(Whoopie Ti Yi Yo) Git Along Little Dogies," c. 1880
traditional American folk song
FOLK SONG, NONSENSE

"Give a Little, Get a Little Love," 1951
Betty Comden, Adolph Green/Jule Styne
WOMEN AS SONGWRITERS

"Give an Imitation of Me," 1910
Blanche Merrill
WOMEN AS SONGWRITERS

"Give Me Just a Little More Time," 1970
Brian Holland, Edythe Wayne
SINGING GROUPS, TIME

"Give Me Love (Give Me Peace on Earth)," 1973
George Harrison
ROCK-ii

"Give Me the Night," 1980
Rod Temperton
NIGHT

"Give My Regards to Broadway," 1904
George M. Cohan
COMPOSER-LYRICISTS, FORM, MUSICAL
COMEDY, TABLE 11, TIN PAN ALLEY

"Give Peace a Chance," 1969
John Lennon, Paul McCartney
ROCK-ii

"Give Us This Day," 1956
Buddy Kaye/Bobby Day
RELIGION

"Giving You the Best That I Got," 1988
Anita Baker, Skip Scarborough, Randy Holland
TABLE 10-n, TABLE 10-q, SUPERLATIVES

"Glad All Over," 1964
Dave Clark, Mike Smith
ROCK-iii

"Glad to Be Unhappy," 1936
Lorenz Hart/Richard Rodgers
HAPPINESS, TABLE 11, SINGERS, TABLE 15

"Gloria," 1965
Van Morrison
NAMES, ROCK-iii

"Glory Days," 1984
Bruce Springsteen
ROCK-xii, TABLE 15

"The Glory of Love," 1936
Billy Hill
LOVE

"THE GLOW-WORM," 1907
Lilla Cayley Robinson (Eng.)/Paul Lincke
ANIMALS, SINGING GROUPS

"GLÜHWÜRMCHEN," SEE **"THE GLOW-WORM"**

"GO AWAY, LITTLE GIRL," 1962
Gerry Goffin, Carole King
TABLE 4-d, BRILL BUILDING, GIRL, TABLE 15,
WOMEN AS SONGWRITERS

"GO BACK WHERE YOU STAYED LAST NIGHT," 1926
Sydney Easton, Ethel Waters
WOMEN AS SONGWRITERS

"GO DOWN, MOSES (LET MY PEOPLE GO)," 1917
traditional American spiritual
FOLK SONG

"GO, LITTLE BOAT," 1917
P. G. Wodehouse/Jerome Kern
BOATING

"GO TELL IT ON THE MOUNTAIN," 1865
John W. Work III (1940)/African-American spiritual
RELIGION

"GO YOUR OWN WAY," 1976
Lindsay Buckingham
ROCK

"GOD BE WITH YOU," 1947
Thomas A. Dorsey
GOSPEL

"GOD BLESS AMERICA," 1939
Irving Berlin
COMPOSERS, COMPOSER-LYRICISTS, HIT
SONG, PATRIOTISM, POPULAR SONG-ii,
RADIO, TABLE 15

"GOD BLESS THE CHILD," 1941
Arthur Herzog, Jr./Billie Holiday
CHILDHOOD, SINGERS, TABLE 15, WOMEN AS
SONGWRITERS

"GOD ONLY KNOWS," 1966
Tony Asher, Brian Wilson/Brian Wilson
ROCK-i

"GOD REST YE MERRY GENTLEMEN," 1827
traditional English carol
CHRISTMAS

"GOD SAVE THE KING," 1744
Henry Carey
PATRIOTISM

"GOD SHALL WIPE ALL TEARS AWAY," 1937
Antonio Haskell
GOSPEL

"THE GODFATHER," SEE **"SPEAK SOFTLY LOVE"**

"GOD'S GONNA SEPARATE THE WHEAT FROM THE TARES," 1937
Mahalia Jackson
GOSPEL

"GOIN' HOME," 1922
William Arms Fisher/Antonin Dvořák
CLASSICS, HOME

"GOIN' OUT OF MY HEAD," 1964
Teddy Randazzo, Bobby Weinstein
ANATOMY, TABLE 2, TABLE 4-c, FADE-OUT,
HARMONY, MODALITY, SINGING GROUPS

"THE GOLD DIGGERS' SONG," SEE **"WE'RE IN THE MONEY"**

"GOLDEN DAYS," 1924
Dorothy Donnelly/Sigmund Romberg
DAY, TABLE 13, WOMEN AS SONGWRITERS

"GOLDEN EARRINGS," 1946
Jay Livingston, Ray Evans/Victor Young
TABLE 8

"(OH DEM) GOLDEN SLIPPERS," 1879
James A. Bland
FOLK SONG

"GOLDEN YEARS," 1976
David Bowie
ROCK-x

"GOLDFINGER," 1964
Leslie Bricusse, Anthony Newley/John Barry
BRITAIN, TABLE 8

"Gonna Build a Mountain," 1961
Leslie Bricusse, Anthony Newley
BRITAIN, INSPIRATION, MOUNTAINS

"Gonna Fly Now (Theme From Rocky)," 1976
Ayn Robbins, Carol Connors/Bill Conti
TABLE 8

"Good-bye," 1935
Gordon Jenkins
BIG BANDS, TABLE 3, FAREWELLS

"Good Bye My Lady Love," 1904
Joseph E. Howard
FAREWELLS, LADY

"Good Golly Miss Molly," 1958
Robert Blackwell, John Marascalco
NAMES, ROCK 'N' ROLL -i

"Good, Good, Good (That's You, That's You)," 1944
Allan Roberts, Doris Fisher
SAMBA

"Good King Wenceslas," c. 1860
John Mason Neale/anon. Swedish
CHRISTMAS

"The Good Life," 1963
Jack Reardon (Eng.)/Sacha Distel
FRANCE, LIFE, TABLE 15, TRIPLET

"Good Lovin'," 1953
Leroy Kirkland, Danny Taylor, Ahmet Ertegun, Jesse Stone
RHYTHM AND BLUES

"Good Lovin'," 1965
Rudy Clark, Arthur Resnick
ROCK

"Good Luck and God Be With You, Laddie Boy," 1917
Will D. Cobb/Gus Edwards
WORLD WAR I

"Good Luck Charm," 1962
Wally Gold, Aaron Schroeder
LUCK

"Good Man, Good Woman," 1991
C. Womack, L. Womack
TABLE 10-l

"A Good Man Is Hard to Find," 1918
Eddie Green
MAN

"Good Morning, Good Morning," 1967
John Lennon, Paul McCartney
TIME OF DAY

"Good Morning Heartache," 1946
Irene Higginbotham, Ervin Drake, Dan Fisher
TABLE 2, TIME OF DAY, TORCH SONG

"Good Morning Starshine," 1967
Gerome Ragni, James Rado/Galt MacDermot
TABLE 11, STARS, TIME OF DAY

"Good Morning to All," SEE "Happy Birthday to You"

"Good Night," 1968
John Lennon, Paul McCartney
FAREWELLS

"Good Night Ladies (Merrily We Roll Along)," 1847
E. P. Christy/traditional American melody
FAREWELLS

"Good Night Sweetheart," 1931
Ray Noble, Jimmy Campbell, Reginald Connelly; American version by Rudy Vallee
TABLE 3, BRITAIN, TABLE 6, FAREWELLS, NIGHT, RADIO, REVUES, TABLE 14, SWEETNESS

"The Good, the Bad and the Ugly," 1967
Ennio Morricone
TABLE 8

"Good Times," 1979
Bernard Edwards, Nile Rodgers
RAP

"Good Vibrations," 1966
Brian Wilson, Mike Love/Brian Wilson
TOP FORTY

"**Goodbye Broadway, Hello France**," 1917
C. Francis Reisner, Benny Davis/Billy Baskette
FAREWELLS, GREETINGS, WORLD WAR I

"**Goodbye, Mama, I'm Off to Yokohama**," 1941
J. Fred Coots
WORLD WAR II

"**Goodbye Yellow Brick Road**," 1973
Elton John, Bernie Taupin
FAREWELLS, ROCK-x, STREETS

"**Goodnight Irene**," 1936
Huddie Ledbetter, John Lomax
BMI, FAREWELLS, FOLK SONG, GUITAR,
NAMES, PROTEST SONG, SINGING GROUPS,
WALTZ

"**Goodnight, My Love**," 1936
Mack Gordon/Harry Revel
FAREWELLS

"**Goodnight My Love (Pleasant Dreams)**," 1956
George Motola, John Manascalco
RHYTHM AND BLUES

"**Goodnight My Someone**," 1957
Meredith Willson
FAREWELLS, TABLE 11

"**Goodnight Tonight**," 1979
Paul McCartney
FAREWELLS

"**Goodnight, Well It's Time to Go**," 1954
Calvin Carter, James Hudson
FAREWELLS

"**Got a Date With an Angel**," 1931
Clifford Grey, Sonny Miller/Jack Waller, Joseph
Tunbridge
ANGELS, TABLE 3, BRITAIN

"**Got the Jitters**," 1934
Billy Rose, Paul Francis Webster/John Jacob Loeb
DEPRESSION YEARS

"**Gotta Serve Somebody**," 1979
Bob Dylan
TABLE 10-j, ROCK-iv

"**La Goulant du Pauvre Jean**," *see* "**The Poor People of Paris**"

"**Graceland**," 1986
Paul Simon
TABLE 10-a, HOME

"**Granada**," 1932
Dorothy Dodd (Eng.)/Augustin Lara
CITIES, TABLE 5, MEXICO

"**The Grand Tour**," 1974
Carmol Taylor, George Richie, Norro Wilson
COUNTRY AND WESTERN

"**Grandfather's Clock**," 1876
Henry Clay Work
POPULAR SONG-i

"**Grandpa (Tell Me 'Bout the Good Old Days)**," 1986
Jamie O'Hara
TABLE 10-v, TABLE 10-w

"**Gravity's Angel**," 1984
Laurie Anderson
WOMEN AS SONGWRITERS

"**Great Balls of Fire**," 1957
Jack Hammer, Otis Blackwell
FIRE, ROCK 'N' ROLL-i

"**Great Day!**," 1929
Billy Rose, Edward Eliscu/Vincent Youmans
DAY, ROARING TWENTIES

"**The Great Pretender**," 1955
Buck Ram
ROCK 'N' ROLL-ii

"**The Great Speckled Bird**," 1937
Rev. Guy Smith
BIRDS, COUNTRY AND WESTERN

"The Greatest Love of All," 1977
Linda Creed/Michael Masser
LOVE, TABLE 15

"Green Dolphin Street," see "On Green Dolphin Street"

"Green Eyes (Aquellos Ojos Verdes)," 1929
E. Rivera, Eddie Woods (Eng.)/Nilo Menendez
TABLE 2, ARRANGEMENT, TABLE 3, COLORS, TABLE 7, CUBA, PICKUP, RUMBA, SWING

"Green Fields," 1960
Terry Gilkyson, Richard Dehr, Frank Miller
PROTEST SONG

"The Green, Green Grass of Home," 1965
Curly Putman
TABLE 4-d, TABLE 7, COUNTRY AND WESTERN, HOME, TABLE 15

"The Green Leaves of Summer," 1960
Paul Francis Webster/Dimitri Tiomkin
TABLE 7, TABLE 8, SEASONS, TREES

"Green-Up Time," 1948
Alan Jay Lerner/Kurt Weill
TABLE 7, TABLE II, TIME

"Greensleeves," c. 1580; see also "What Child Is This?"
traditional English song
CHRISTMAS

"A Groovy Kind of Love," 1966
Toni Wine, Carole Bayer
ROCK-iii, SLANG

"Guantanamera," 1963
Bernard Gasso (Eng., 1966)/Pete Seeger, Hector Angulo
CUBA, FOLK SONG

"Guess Who," 1949
Beatrice Hunter
RHYTHM AND BLUES

"Guilty," 1931
Gus Kahn, Harry Akst, Richard A. Whiting
FORGIVENESS

"Guilty," 1980
Barry Gibb, Robin Gibb, Maurice Gibb
TABLE 10-h

"A Guy Is a Guy," 1951
Oscar Brand
FOLK SONG

"Guys and Dolls," 1950
Frank Loesser
MAN, TABLE 11

"Gypsies, Tramps and Thieves, " 1971
Robert Stone
GYPSY MUSIC, TABLE 15

"The Gypsy," 1945
Billy Reid
GYPSY MUSIC, TABLE 15, SINGING GROUPS, YOUR HIT PARADE

"The Gypsy in Me," 1934
Cole Porter
GYPSY MUSIC

"The Gypsy in My Soul," 1937
Moe Jaffe/Clay Boland
GYPSY MUSIC

"Gypsy Love Song," 1898
Harry B. Smith/Victor Herbert
ART SONG, CLASSICS, TABLE 6, GAY NINETIES, GYPSY MUSIC, MODE, OPERETTA, TABLE 13, SLEEP

"Gypsy Maiden," 1912
Adrian Ross (Eng.)/Franz Lehár
GYPSY MUSIC

"Hail, Hail, the Gang's All Here," 1917
D. A. Esrom (pseud. Theodora Morse)/Theodore Morse
CLASSICS, TABLE 6, FRIENDSHIP, OPERA TOGETHERNESS

"Half as Much," 1951
Curley Williams
COUNTRY AND WESTERN

"The Half of It Dearie Blues," 1924
Ira Gershwin/George Gershwin
BLUES

"Halfway to Paradise," 1961
Gerry Goffin, Carole King
ROCK 'N' ROLL

"Hallelujah!," 1927
Clifford Grey, Leo Robin/Vincent Youmans
LYRICISTS, MUSICAL COMEDY, TABLE 11

"Hallelujah I Love Her So," 1956
Ray Charles
ROCK 'N' ROLL-i

"Hands Across the Table," 1934
Mitchell Parish/Jean Delettre
TABLE 2, TABLE 3

"Handy Man," 1959
Otis Blackwell, Jimmy Jones
TABLE 4-d, TABLE 10-g, MAN

"Happiest Girl in the Whole U.S.A.," 1971
Donna Fargo
GIRL, TABLE 10-t, HAPPINESS

"Happiness Is a Thing Called Joe," 1942
E. Y. Harburg/Harold Arlen
HAPPINESS, NAMES, TABLE 15

"Happy (Love Theme From Lady Sings the Blues)," 1972
William "Smokey" Robinson/Michel Legrand
TABLE 9, HAPPINESS

"Happy Birthday, Sweet Sixteen," 1961
Neil Sedaka, Howard Greenfield
AGE, OCCASIONAL SONG, ROCK 'N' ROLL

"Happy Birthday to You," 1893
Patty Smith Hill/Mildred J. Hill
BIRTH, HAPPINESS, LENGTH, OCCASIONAL SONG, TIME OF DAY, WOMEN AS SONGWRITERS

"(O) Happy Day," 1855
Rev. Philip Doddridge/Attrib. Edward F. Rimbault
BORROWING

"Happy Days," 1974
Norman Gimbel/Charles Fox
HAPPINESS, TELEVISION

"Happy Days Are Here Again," 1929
Jack Yellen/Milton Ager
TABLE 3, BROKEN CHORD, DAY, DEPRESSION YEARS, HAPPINESS, POPULAR SONG-v

"Happy Days Are Here Again," 1961
Carole King, Cynthia Weil
WOMEN AS SONGWRITERS

"Happy, Happy Birthday Baby," 1957
Margo Sylvia, Gilbert Lopez
OCCASIONAL SONG, SINGING GROUPS

"Happy Holiday," 1942
Irving Berlin
TABLE 9, HAPPINESS, HOLIDAYS

"Happy Talk," 1949
Oscar Hammerstein II/Richard Rodgers
HAPPINESS, TABLE 12, TALKING

"Happy Together," 1966
Garry Bonner, Alan Lee Gordon
TABLE 4-d, HAPPINESS, ROCK-v

"The Happy Wanderer (Val-de-Ri Val-de Ra)," 1954
Antonia Ridge (Eng.)/Friedrich Wilhelm Moeller
HAPPINESS

"Harbor Lights," 1937
Jimmy Kennedy/Hugh Williams (pseud. Will Grosz)
TABLE 3, BRITAIN, DISC JOCKEY, OCEAN ROCK 'N' ROLL-ii, WATERFRONT

"A Hard Day's Night," 1964
John Lennon, Paul McCartney
DAY, TABLE 9

"Hard Hearted Hannah, the Vamp of Savannah," 1924
Jack Yellen, Bob Bigelow, Charles Bates
NAMES

"HARD RAIN'S A-GONNA FALL," 1963
Bob Dylan
FOLK SONG, POPULAR SONG-ix, ROCK-iv,
TABLE 15, WEATHER

"HARD TIMES COME AGAIN NO MORE," 1854
Stephen Collins Foster
POPULAR SONG-i

"HARD TO SAY I'M SORRY," 1982
Peter Cetera, David Foster
ROCK-ix

"THE HARDER THEY COME," 1973
Jimmy Cliff
REGGAE

"HARK THE HERALD ANGELS SING," 1855
Charles Wesley/Felix Mendelssohn
CHRISTMAS

"HARLEM NOCTURNE," 1940
Dick Rogers/Earl Hagen
TABLE 5, HARLEM

"THE HARP THAT ONCE THROUGH TARA'S HALLS," 1807
Thomas Moore/traditional Irish melody
POPULAR SONG-i

"THE HARPER VALLEY P.T.A.," 1967
Tom T. Hall
COUNTRY AND WESTERN, TABLE 10-t

"HARRIGAN," 1908
George M. Cohan
COMPOSER-LYRICISTS, IRELAND, TABLE 15

"HAVA NAGILA," 1963
traditional Israeli dance
MODALITY

"HAVE I TOLD YOU LATELY THAT I LOVE YOU," 1945
Scott Wiseman
CROSSOVER

"HAVE YOU EVER BEEN LONELY (HAVE YOU EVER BEEN BLUE?)," 1933
Billy Hill/Peter De Rose
TABLE 7, LONELINESS

"HAVE YOU EVER SEEN THE RAIN," 1970
John C. Fogerty
ROCK-ix, WEATHER

"HAVE YOU MET MISS JONES?," 1937
Lorenz Hart/Richard Rodgers
HARMONIC RHYTHM, MEETING, MODULA-
TION, TABLE 11, NAMES, QUESTIONS, RE-
LEASE, SCALE

"HAVE YOU NEVER BEEN MELLOW," 1974
John Farrar
TABLE 4-d

"HAVE YOU SEEN HER," 1971
Eugene Record, Barbara Acklin
RAP, SEEING, SINGING GROUPS, SOUL

"HAVE YOURSELF A MERRY LITTLE CHRISTMAS," 1943
Hugh Martin, Ralph Blane
BROKEN CHORD, CHRISTMAS, TABLE 9

"HAVEN'T GOT TIME FOR THE PAIN," 1974
Jacob Brackman, Carly Simon
ROCK-vi

"(YOU'RE) HAVING MY BABY," 1974
Paul Anka
TABLE 4-d

"HAWAII FIVE-O," 1969
Mort Stevens
STATES, TELEVISION

"HAWAIIAN WAR CHANT," 1936
Ralph Freed (Eng.)/John Noble, Lelieohaku
BORROWING, HUMOR, STATES

"THE HAWAIIAN WEDDING SONG (KE KALI NEI AU)," 1926 (HAWAIIAN); 1958 (ENG.)
Al Hoffman, Dick Manning (Eng.)/Charles E. King
MARRIAGE, STATES

"A Hazy Shade of Winter," 1966
Paul Simon
ROCK-v

"He," 1954
Richard Mullan/Jack Richards
RELIGION

**"He Ain't Heavy . . . He's My Brother,"
1969**
Bob Russell, Bobby Scott
ROCK

**"He Don't Love You (Like I Love You),"
1975**
Curtis Mayfield, Calvin Carter
SINGING GROUPS

"He Loves and She Loves," 1927
Ira Gershwin/George Gershwin
COLLABORATION, MUSICAL COMEDY, TABLE
11

"He Stopped Loving Her Today," 1978
Bobby Bradock, Curley Putman
TABLE 10-u

"He Wears a Pair of Silver Wings," 1941
Eric Maschwitz/Michael Carr
WORLD WAR II

"Hear My Song, Violetta," 1938
Buddy Bernier, Bob Emmerich (Eng.)/Rudolf
Luckesch, Othmar Klose
AUSTRIA

"Hearere Ra," SEE **"Now Is the Hour"**

"Heart," 1955
Richard Adler, Jerry Ross
TABLE 11

"Heart and Soul," 1939
Frank Loesser/Hoagy Carmichael
TABLE 2

"Heart Full of Soul," 1965
Graham Gouldman
ROCK-iii

"Heart of Glass," 1978
Deborah Harry, Christopher Stein
ROCK

"Heart of Gold," 1971
Neil Young
ROCK-v

"Heart of My Heart," SEE **"The Story of
the Rose"**

**"(The Gang That Sang) Heart of My
Heart," 1926**
Ben Ryan
FRIENDSHIP

"Heart of Stone," 1964
Mick Jagger, Keith Richards
SINGING GROUPS

"Heartache Tonight," 1979
Bob Segar, Don Henley, John David Souther, Glenn
Frey
TABLE 10-l, ROCK-x

"Heartaches," 1931
John Klenner/Al Hoffman
TABLE 2, TABLE 3

"Heartbreak Hotel," 1956
Mae Boren Axton, Tommy Durden, Elvis Presley
TABLE 2, POPULAR SONG-viii, SINGERS, TABLE
15

"Hearts and Flowers," 1899
Mary D. Brine/Theodore Moses-Tobani
TABLE 2, TABLE 6, FLOWERS, GAY NINETIES

"Heat Wave," 1933
Irving Berlin
REVUES, TABLE 14, WEATHER

"(Love Is Like a) Heat Wave," 1963
Eddie Holland, Lamont Dozier, Brian Holland
MOTOWN, WEATHER

"The Heather on the Hill," 1947
Alan Jay Lerner/Frederick Loewe
MOUNTAINS, TABLE 12

"HEAVEN CAN WAIT," 1939
Edgar De Lange/James Van Heusen
HEAVEN, WAITING

"HEAVEN HELP US ALL," 1970
Ronald Miller
HEAVEN

"HEAVEN IS A PLACE ON EARTH," 1987
Rick Nowels, Ellen Shipley
HEAVEN

"HEAVEN KNOWS," 1978
Peter Bellotte, Giorgio Moroder, Donna Summer,
Gregg Mathieson
HEAVEN

"HEAVEN MUST BE MISSING AN ANGEL," 1976
Kenny St. Lewis, Frederick Perren
HEAVEN

"HEAVEN MUST HAVE SENT YOU," 1966
Lamont Dozier, Brian Holland, Eddie Holland
HEAVEN

"HEAVEN ON THE SEVENTH FLOOR," 1977
Dominique Bugatti, Frank Musker
HEAVEN

"HEAVEN WILL PROTECT THE WORKING GIRL," 1909
Edgar Smith/A. Baldwin Sloane
GIRL, HEAVEN, VAUDEVILLE

"HEAVEN'S JUST A SIN AWAY," 1977
Jerry Gillespie
TABLE 10-v

"HE'D HAVE TO GET UNDER, GET OUT AND GET UNDER, TO FIX UP HIS AUTOMOBILE," 1913
Grant Clarke, Edgar Leslie/Maurice Abrahams
TRAVEL, VAUDEVILLE

"HEEBIE JEEBIES," 1926
Boyd Atkins
SCAT SINGING

"HEIGH-HO," 1938
Larry Morey/Frank Churchill
TABLE 9, NONSENSE

"HE'LL HAVE TO GO," 1959
Joe Allison, Audrey Allison
COUNTRY AND WESTERN

"HELLO," 1983
Lionel Richie
GREETINGS

"HELLO CENTRAL, GIVE ME HEAVEN," 1901
Charles K. Harris
GREETINGS, HEAVEN, TELEPHONES

"HELLO CENTRAL, GIVE ME NO MAN'S LAND," 1918
Sam M. Lewis, Joe Young/Jean Schwartz
TELEPHONES, WORLD WAR I

"HELLO DARLIN'," 1969
Conway Twitty
COUNTRY AND WESTERN

"HELLO, DOLLY!," 1963
Jerry Herman
BORROWING, BROKEN CHORD, COMPOSER-
LYRICISTS, TABLE, 10-b, TABLE 10-d, GREET-
INGS, TABLE 11, NAMES, SINGERS, TABLE 15

"HELLO FRISCO HELLO," 1925
Gene Buck/Louis A. Hirsch
TABLE 5, GREETINGS, TELEPHONES

"HELLO, GOODBYE," 1967
John Lennon, Paul McCartney
GREETINGS

"HELLO, I LOVE YOU," 1968
John Densmore, Robert Krieger, Raymond Manzarek,
James Morrison (The Doors)
GREETINGS, ROCK-ix

"HELLO, IT'S ME," 1968
Todd Rundgren
GREETINGS, ROCK

"HELLO LITTLE GIRL," 1963
John Lennon, Paul McCartney
GREETINGS

"HELLO! MA BABY," 1899
Ida Emerson, Joseph E. Howard
BABY, CAKEWALK, COON SONG, DANCE
CRAZES, GAY NINETIES, GREETINGS, TABLE
15, SYNCOPATION, WOMEN AS
SONGWRITERS

"HELLO, MARY LOU," 1961
Gene Pitney
NAMES, ROCK 'N' ROLL-iii, TELEVISION

"HELLO MUDDAH, HELLO FADDUH," 1963
Alan Sherman/Lou Busch
TABLE 6, FATHERS, GREETINGS, HUMOR,
MOTHERS

"HELLO, MY LOVER, GOODBYE," 1931
Edward Heyman/John Green
FAREWELLS, GREETINGS

"HELLO, YOUNG LOVERS," 1951
Oscar Hammerstein II/Richard Rodgers
AGE, CHILDREN, GREETINGS, LOVERS, LYRI-
CISTS, MUSICAL PLAYS, TABLE 12, WALTZ

"HELP!," 1965
John Lennon, Paul McCartney
ROCK-ii, TELEVISION

"HELP ME," 1972
Joni Mitchell
FOLK SONG, ROCK-vi, WOMEN AS
SONGWRITERS

**"HELP ME MAKE IT THROUGH THE NIGHT,"
1970**
Kris Kristofferson
TABLE 4-c, COUNTRY AND WESTERN, TABLE
10-t, TABLE 10-w, NIGHT

"HELP ME RHONDA," 1965
Brian Wilson
NAMES, ROCK-i

"HELTER SKELTER," 1968
John Lennon, Paul McCartney
NONSENSE

"HER ROYAL MAJESTY," 1961
Gerry Goffin, Carole King
ROCK 'N' ROLL

"HERE," 1954
Dorcas Cochran, Harold Grant
OPERA

"HERE AND NOW," 1989
Terry Steele, David L. Elliott
TABLE 10-o

"HERE COMES MY BABY BACK AGAIN," 1964
Dottie West, Bill West
TABLE 10-t

"HERE COMES THE NIGHT," 1965
Bert Berns
NIGHT, ROCK-iii

"HERE COMES THE SHOW BOAT," 1927
Billy Rose/Maceo Pinkard
BOATING

"HERE COMES THE SUN," 1969
George Harrison
TABLE 4-d, SUN

"HERE I'LL STAY," 1948
Alan Jay Lerner/Kurt Weill
ENDURING LOVE, TABLE 11

"HERE IN MY ARMS," 1925
Lorenz Hart/Richard Rodgers
TABLE 11

"HERE, THERE AND EVERYWHERE," 1966
John Lennon, Paul McCartney
TABLE 4-d, BRITAIN, COLLABORATION,
PLACES

""HERE YOU COME AGAIN," 1977
Barry Mann, Cynthia Weil
TABLE 4-d, WOMEN AS SONGWRITERS

"HERE'S THAT RAINY DAY," 1953
Johnny Burke/James Van Heusen
COMPOSERS, DAY, HARMONY, JAZZ, LYRI-
CISTS, TEMPO, WEATHER

"HERNANDO'S HIDEAWAY," 1954
Richard Adler, Jerry Ross
TABLE 11, TANGO

"HE'S A REBEL," 1962
Gene Pitney
ROCK 'N' ROLL

"HE'S GOT THE WHOLE WORLD IN
HIS HANDS," 1924
traditional American gospel song; adapted 1957 by
Geoff Love
BORROWING, RELIGION, WORLD

"HE'S 1-A IN THE ARMY AND HE'S A-1
IN MY HEART," 1941
Redd Evans
WORLD WAR II

"HE'S RIGHT ON TIME," c. 1955
Dorothy Love Coates
WOMEN AS SONGWRITERS

"HE'S SO FINE," 1962
Ronald Mack
ROCK 'N' ROLL-iv

"HE'S SO SHY," 1980
Cynthia Weil/Tom Snow
WOMEN AS SONGWRITERS

"HE'S SURE THE BOY I LOVE," 1962
Barry Mann, Cynthia Weil
BOY, ROCK 'N' ROLL, WOMEN AS
SONGWRITERS

"HEY! BA-BA-RE-BOP," 1945
Lionel Hampton, Curley Hamner
BEBOP, GREETINGS, NONSENSE, RHYTHM
AND BLUES

"HEY, BABY," 1961
Margaret Cobb, Bruce Channel
BABY, GREETINGS

"HEY BIG SPENDER," SEE "BIG SPENDER"

"HEY, GIRL," 1963
Gerry Goffin, Carole King
GIRL, GREETINGS, ROCK 'N' ROLL

"HEY GOOD LOOKIN'," 1951
Hank Williams
BEAUTY, COUNTRY AND WESTERN, GREET-
INGS

"HEY! JEALOUS LOVER," 1956
Sammy Cahn, Kay Twomey, Bee Walker
GREETINGS, LOVERS

"HEY JOE," 1965
Dino Valenti
NAMES, ROCK-vii

"HEY JUDE," 1968
John Lennon, Paul McCartney
BASS LINE, TABLE 4-d, BRITAIN, COLLABORA-
TION, FADE-OUT, GREETINGS, ROCK-ii, VAMP

"HEY, LITTLE GIRL," SEE "WIVES AND LOVERS"

"HEY, LOOK ME OVER," 1960
Carolyn Leigh/Cy Coleman
GREETINGS, MARCH, TABLE 11, WOMEN AS
SONGWRITERS

"HEY, MR. BANJO," 1955
Freddy Morgan, Norman Malkin
GREETINGS

"HEY, PAULA," 1963
Ray Hildebrand
GREETINGS

"HEY THERE," 1954
Richard Adler, Jerry Ross
GREETINGS, TABLE 11, TABLE 15, YOUR HIT
PARADE

"HEY THERE, GOOD TIMES," 1977
Michael Stewart/Cy Coleman
GREETINGS

"HEY THERE LONELY GIRL/HEY THERE LONELY
BOY," 1962
Earl Shuman/Leon Carr
BOY, GIRL, GREETINGS, SOUL

"HEY WON'T YOU PLAY ANOTHER SOMEBODY DONE SOMEBODY WRONG SONG?," *SEE* "ANOTHER SOMEBODY DONE SOMEBODY WRONG SONG"

"HI-DIDDLE-DEE-DEE (AN ACTOR'S LIFE FOR ME)," 1940
Ned Washington, Leigh Harline
NONSENSE

"HI-LILI, HI-LO," 1952
Helen Deutsch/Bronislaw Kaper
TABLE 6, GREETINGS, NONSENSE

"HI, NEIGHBOR," 1941
Jack Owens
GREETINGS

"HIER ENCORE," *SEE* "YESTERDAY, WHEN I WAS YOUNG"

"THE HIGH AND THE MIGHTY," 1954
Ned Washington/Dimitri Tiomkin
TABLE 8, HEIGHT

"HIGH HOPES," 1959
Sammy Cahn/James Van Heusen
TABLE 1, HEIGHT, INSPIRATION, WISHING

"HIGH NOON (DO NOT FORSAKE ME)," 1952
Ned Washington/Dimitri Tiomkin
TABLE 1, TABLE 8, TIME OF DAY

"HIGH ON A WINDY HILL," 1940
Alex C. Kramer, Joan Whitney
HEIGHT, MOUNTAINS, WEATHER, WOMEN AS SONGWRITERS

"HIGH SCHOOL CONFIDENTIAL," 1958
Ron Hargrave, Jerry Lee Lewis
ROCK 'N' ROLL-i

"(YOUR LOVE HAS LIFTED ME) HIGHER AND HIGHER," 1967
Gary Jackson, Carl William Smith, Raynard Miner
TABLE 4-d, HEIGHT, SOUL

"HIGHER LOVE," 1986
Will Jennings/Steve Winwood
TABLE 10-a, TABLE 10-g

"THE HILL STREET BLUES THEME," 1980
m. Mike Post
TELEVISION

"HINKY DINKY PARLAY VOO (MAD 'MOISELLE FROM ARMENTIÈRES)," 1918
anonymous
NONSENSE, WORLD WAR I

"HIT THE ROAD, JACK," 1961
Percy Mayfield
TABLE 10-m, ROCK 'N' ROLL-i, TABLE 15, STREETS, TRAVEL

"HIT THE ROAD TO DREAMLAND," 1942
Johnny Mercer/Harold Arlen
DREAMS, STREETS

"HO HUM," 1931
Edward Heyman/Dana Suesse
WOMEN AS SONGWRITERS

"HOLD IT RIGHT THERE," 1966
Eddie "Mr Cleanhead" Vinson
TABLE 10-p

"HOLD ME," 1987
K.T. Oslin
TABLE 10-t, TABLE 10-w

"HOLD MY HAND," 1950
Jack Lawrence, Richard Meyers
TABLE 2

"HOLD ON (I'M COMING)," 1966
David Porter, Isaac Hayes
TABLE 10-n, SOUL

"HOLD TIGHT—HOLD TIGHT (WANT SOME SEA FOOD, MAMA)," 1939
Leonard Ware, Leonard Kent, Jerry Brandow, Edward Robinson, Willie Spottswood
SINGING GROUPS

"HOLD WHAT YOU'VE GOT," 1964
Joe Tex
SOUL

"HOLDING HANDS (J'AI TA MAIN)," 1945
Harold Rome (Eng.)/Charles Trenet
FRANCE

"HOLIDAY," 1967
Barry Gibb, Robin Gibb, Maurice Gibb
HOLIDAYS, ROCK-viii

"HOLLYWOOD SWINGING," 1973
Ricky West, Claydes Smith, George Brown, Ronald
Bell, Robert Bell, Robert Mickens, Dennis Thomas
FUNK

"HOME (WHEN SHADOWS FALL)," 1931
Harry Clarkson, Peter Van Steeden, Jeff Clarkson
HOME

"HOME AGAIN BLUES," 1920
Harry Akst, Irving Berlin
BLUES

"(THERE'S NO PLACE LIKE) HOME FOR THE
HOLIDAYS," 1955
Al Stillman/Robert Allen
HOLIDAYS, HOME, PLACES

"HOME ON THE RANGE," 1873
Brewster M. Higley/Daniel E. Kelley
HOME, POPULAR SONG-i

"HOME SWEET HEAVEN," 1964
Hugh Martin, Timothy Gray
HEAVEN

"HOME! SWEET HOME!," 1823
John Howard Payne/Henry R. Bishop
HOME

"HOMEWARD BOUND," 1966
Paul Simon
ROCK-v

"HONEY BUN," 1949
Oscar Hammerstein II/Richard Rodgers
TABLE 12, SWEETNESS

"HONEY LOVE," 1954
Clyde McPhatter, J. Gerald
ROCK 'N' ROLL-ii, SWEETNESS

"HONEYCOMB," 1954
Bob Merrill
SWEETNESS

"THE HONEYDRIPPER," 1945
Joe Liggins
RHYTHM AND BLUES

"HONEYSUCKLE ROSE," 1929
Andy Razaf/Thomas "Fats" Waller
BEBOP, FLOWERS, TABLE 14, SWEETNESS

"HONG KONG BLUES," 1939
Hoagy Carmichael
TABLE 5, RANGE

"HONKY CAT," 1972
Elton John, Bernie Taupin
ANIMALS

"HONKY TONK TRAIN," 1939
m. Meade "Lux" Lewis
PIANO

"HONKY TONK WOMEN," 1969
Mick Jagger, Keith Richards
FADE-OUT, ROCK-iii, WOMAN

"HOOKED ON A FEELING," 1968
Mark James (pseud. Francis Rodney Zambon)
TABLE 4-d, FEELING

"LA HOOLA BOOLA," SEE "BOOLA BOOLA"

"HOORAY FOR HAZEL," 1966
Tommy Roe
NAMES

"HOORAY FOR HOLLYWOOD," 1937
Johnny Mercer/Richard A. Whiting
TABLE 5, TABLE 9

"HOPELESSLY DEVOTED TO YOU," 1978
John Farrar
METER, TABLE 15

"HORST WESSELL LIED," SEE "DER FUEHRER'S
FACE"

"How Dry I Am," 1921
Will B. Johnstone/Tom A. Johnstone
BORROWING, FOOD AND DRINK

"(You Don't Know) How Glad I Am," 1975
Jimmy Williams, Larry Harrison
TABLE 10-m, HAPPINESS

"How Great Thou Art," 1885
Stuart K. Hine (Eng.)/Rev. Carl Robert
RELIGION

"How High the Moon," 1940
Nancy Hamilton/Morgan Lewis
BEBOP, TABLE 3, GOLDEN AGE, HARMONY, HEIGHT, IMPROVISATION, MOON, SINGERS, TABLE 15, TIN PAN ALLEY

"How I Got Over," c. 1948
W. Herbert Brewster
GOSPEL

"How Insensitive," 1963
Norman Gimbel (Eng.)/Antonio Carlos Jobim
BOSSA NOVA, BRAZIL, CHROMATICISM

"How Long Has This Been Going On?," 1927
Ira Gershwin/George Gershwin
COLLABORATION

"How Long, How Long Blues," 1929
Ann Engberg/Leroy Carr
BLUES

"How Lucky Can You Get," 1975
John Kander, Fred Ebb
LUCK

"How Much I Really Cared," *see* **"I Didn't Raise My Boy to Be a Soldier"**

"How Sweet It Is (To Be Loved by You)," 1964
Brian Holland, Lamont Dozier, Eddie Holland
TABLE 4-d, SWEETNESS

"How Sweet You Are," 1943
Frank Loesser/Arthur Schwartz
SWEETNESS

"How to Handle a Woman," 1960
Alan Jay Lerner/Frederick Loewe
COLLABORATION, TABLE 12, WOMAN

"How Will I Know," 1985
Gary Merrill, Shannon Rubicam, Narada Michael Walden
TABLE 15

"How Ya Gonna Keep 'Em Down on the Farm After They've Seen Paris?," 1919
Sam M. Lewis, Joe Young/Walter Donaldson
TABLE 5, WORLD WAR I

"How'd You Like to Spoon With Me?," 1905
Edward Laska/Jerome Kern
QUESTIONS

"Human Nature," 1982
John Bettis/Jeff Porcaro
ROCK-xii

"Hummingbird," 1972
James Seals, Darrell Crofts
RELIGION

"Hungry Eyes," 1969
Merle Haggard
COUNTRY AND WESTERN

"Hungry Heart," 1980
Bruce Springsteen
ROCK-xii

"Hungry Like the Wolf," 1983
Duran Duran
ANIMALS, TELEVISION

"Hurdy Gurdy Man," 1968
Donovan Leitch
ROCK-v

"Hurricane (Part I)," 1977
Bob Dylan
ROCK-iv

"Hurt So Bad," 1965
Bobby Hart, Teddy Randazzo, Bobby Wilding
TABLE 4-d, SINGING GROUPS

"Hurt So Good," 1982
John Cougar Mellencamp, George Michael Green
TABLE 10-j

"Hushabye," 1959
Doc Pomus, Mort Shuman
ROCK 'N' ROLL

"Hush-a-bye Ma Baby," *see* **"The Missouri Waltz"**

"The Hustle," 1975
Van McCoy
DANCE CRAZES, DISCO

"Hut Sut Song," 1939
Leo Killion, Ted McMichael, Jack Owens
TABLE 9, NONSENSE

"Hymne à l'Amour," *see* **"If You Love Me, Really Love Me"**

"I.O.U.," 1983
Kerry Chater, Austin Roberts
TABLE 10-u

"I Ain't Gonna Give Nobody None o' This Jelly Roll," 1919
Clarence Williams, Spencer Williams
DIXIELAND

"I Ain't Got Nobody," 1916
Roger Graham/Spencer Williams
DIALECT

"I Almost Lost My Mind," 1950
Ivory Joe Hunter
MIND, RHYTHM AND BLUES

"I Am a Rock," 1964
Paul Simon
FOLK ROCK, ROCK-v

"I Am a Union Woman," 1931 (copyrighted 1966)
Aunt Molly Jackson/Baptist hymn-tune, "Lay the Lily Low"
WOMEN AS SONGWRITERS

"I Am What I Am," 1983
Jerry Herman
TABLE 11

"I Am Woman," 1971
Helen Reddy/Ray Burton
TABLE 10-f, TABLE 15, WOMAN, WOMEN AS SONGWRITERS

"I Apologize," 1931
Al Hoffman, Al Goodhart, Ed Nelson
FORGIVENESS

"I Believe," 1952
Ervin Drake, Irvin Graham, Jimmy Shirl, Al Stillman
RELIGION, TABLE 15

"I Believe in You," 1961
Frank Loesser
HUMOR, TABLE 11

"I Cain't Say No," 1943
Oscar Hammerstein II/Richard Rodgers
DIALECT, HUMOR, TABLE 12

"I Can Dream, Can't I?," 1937
Irving Kahal/Sammy Fain
DREAMS, SINGING GROUPS

"I Can See Clearly Now," 1972
Johnny Nash
MODALITY, SEEING, WEATHER

"I Can See for Miles," 1967
Peter Townshend
ROCK-iii, SEEING

"I Can't Begin to Tell You," 1945
Mack Gordon/James V. Monaco
BEGINNING, BORROWING

"I Can't Get Next to You," 1969
Barrett Strong, Norman Whitfield
MOTOWN

"I Can't Get No Satisfaction," *see* **"Satisfaction"**

"I Can't Get Started," 1935
Ira Gershwin/Vernon Duke
BEGINNING, BIG BANDS, TABLE 3, BORROW-
ING, CATALOGUE SONG, COMPOSERS,
GOLDEN AGE, HARMONIC RHYTHM, LYRI-
CISTS, POPULAR SONG-ii, REVUES, TABLE 14

"I Can't Give You Anything But Love," 1928
Dorothy Fields/Jimmy McHugh
COLLABORATION, COMPOSERS, GOLDEN
AGE, LYRICISTS, MONEY, REVUES, TABLE 14,
SLANG, WOMEN AS SONGWRITERS

"I Can't Help It (If I'm Still in Love With You)," 1951
Hank Williams
COUNTRY AND WESTERN, TABLE 10-t

"I Can't Help Myself," 1965
Eddie Holland, Brian Holland, Lamont Dozier
MOTOWN

"I Can't Stop Loving You," 1958
Don Gibson
TABLE 4-b, COUNTRY AND WESTERN, END-
ING, TABLE 10-m, LOVE, POPULAR SONG-xi,
TABLE 15

"I Can't Turn You Loose," 1965
Otis Redding
SOUL

"I Concentrate on You," 1939
Cole Porter
BEGUINE, CHROMATICISM, COMPOSERS,
COMPOSER-LYRICISTS, THINKING

"I Could Have Danced All Night," 1956
Alan Jay Lerner/Frederick Loewe
DANCING, MELODY, MUSICAL PLAYS, TABLE
12, NIGHT

"I Could Write a Book," 1940
Lorenz Hart/Richard Rodgers
MUSICAL COMEDY, TABLE 11, REPEATED
NOTE, WRITING

"I Couldn't Sleep a Wink Last Night," 1943
Harold Adamson/Jimmy McHugh
NIGHT, SLEEP

"I Cover the Waterfront," 1933
Edward Heyman/John Green
COMPOSERS, FILM MUSIC, TABLE 8, INTER-
VAL, WATERFRONT

"I Cried a Tear," 1958
Al Julia, Fred Jay
CRYING, RHYTHM AND BLUES

"I Cried for You," 1923
Arthur Freed, Gus Arnheim, Abe Lyman
TABLE 3, CRYING, MELODY, TABLE 15

"(Last Night) I Didn't Get to Sleep at All," 1972
Tony Macaulay
SINGING GROUPS, SLEEP

"I Didn't Know What Time It Was," 1939
Lorenz Hart/Richard Rodgers
BEGUINE, TABLE 11, TIME

"I Didn't Raise My Boy to Be a Soldier," 1915
Alfred Bryan/Al Piantadosi
BORROWING, BOY, WORLD WAR I

"I Do Love You," 1965
Billy Stewart
SOUL

"I Don't Care," 1905
Jean Lenox/Harry O. Sutton
SHEET MUSIC, VAUDEVILLE

"I Don't Know How to Love Him," 1970
Tim Rice/Andrew Lloyd Webber
BRITAIN, CLASSICS, TABLE 6, KEY, RELIGION

"I Don't Know Why (I Just Do)," 1931
Roy Turk/Fred E. Ahlert
BALLAD, FOX TROT

"I Don't Know Why You Don't Want Me," 1985
Rosanne Cash, Rodney Crowell
TABLE 10-t

"I Don't Stand a Ghost of a Chance With You," 1932
Bing Crosby, Ned Washington/Victor Young
TABLE 3, GOLDEN AGE, LUCK, POPULAR SONG-ii, WOODWINDS

"I Don't Wanna Play House," 1967
Glenn Sutton, Billy Sherrill
TABLE 10-t

"I Don't Want to Play in Your Yard," 1894
Phipil Wingate/H. W. Petrie
GAY NINETIES, VAUDEVILLE

"I Don't Want to Set the World on Fire," 1941
Eddie Seiler, Sol Marcus, Bennie Benjamin, Eddie Durham
FIRE, WORLD

"I Don't Want to Walk Without You," 1941
Frank Loesser/Jule Styne
BABY, TABLE 3, COMPOSERS, TABLE 9, TABLE 15, WALKING, WORLD WAR II

"I Dream Too Much," 1935
Dorothy Fields/Jerome Kern
ART SONG, DREAMS, TABLE 9, SCALE, WALTZ

"I Dreamed a Dream," 1985
Herbert Kretzmer (Eng.)/Claude-Michel Schönberg
FRANCE, TABLE 12

"I Enjoy Being a Girl," 1958
Oscar Hammerstein II/Richard Rodgers
GIRL

"I Fall in Love Too Easily," 1944
Sammy Cahn/Jule Styne
FALLING IN LOVE, TABLE 9

"I Fall to Pieces," 1960
Hank Cochran/Harlan Howard
COUNTRY AND WESTERN

"I Feel a Song Comin' On," 1935
Dorothy Fields, George Oppenheimer, Jimmy McHugh
FEELING, TABLE 9, TABLE 15

"I Feel Fine," 1964
John Lennon, Paul McCartney
FEELING

"I Feel for You," 1979
Prince Rogers Nelson
FEELING, TABLE 10-n, TABLE 10-q

"I Feel Love," 1977
Donna Summer, Giorgio Moroder, Peter Bellotte
DISCO, FEELING

"I Feel Pretty," 1957
Stephen Sondheim/Leonard Bernstein
BEAUTY, FEELING, MUSICAL PLAYS, TABLE 12, OPERA, WALTZ

"I Feel So Bad," 1954
Chuck Willis
RHYTHM AND BLUES

"I Feel the Earth Move," 1971
Carole King
FEELING, ROCK-vi

"I Fought the Law," 1961
Sonny Curtis
ROCK

"I Found a Million Dollar Baby (In a Five and Ten Cent Store)," 1931
Mort Dixon, Billy Rose/Harry Warren
BABY, MONEY, REVUES, TABLE 14, SINGING GROUPS

"I Found a New Baby," 1925
Jack Palmer, Spencer Williams
BABY

"I Found You in the Rain," 1941
H. Barlow
WEATHER

"I Gave My Love a Cherry (The Riddle Song)," c. 1850
traditional American folk song
FOLK SONG

"I Get a Kick Out of You," 1934
Cole Porter
COMPOSER-LYRICISTS, FOOD AND DRINK, MUSICAL COMEDY, TABLE 11, SLANG, SOCIETY TEMPO, TRIPLET

"I Get Around," 1964
Brian Wilson
ROCK-i

"I Get Ideas," 1951; see also "Adios Muchachos"
Dorcas Cochran/Julio Sanders
ARGENTINA, BORROWING, PICKUP, TANGO

"I Get the Blues When It Rains," 1928
Marcy Klauber/Harry Stoddard
WEATHER

"I Go to Pieces," 1964
Del Shannon
ROCK-iii

"I Got a Rock," 1911
Blanche Merrill
WOMEN AS SONGWRITERS

"I Got a Woman," 1954
Ray Charles, Renald J. Richard
SOUL, WOMAN

"I Got a Woman Crazy for Me," see "She's Funny That Way"

"I Got It Bad (And That Ain't Good)," 1941
Paul Francis Webster/Duke Ellington
TABLE 3, PIANO, TORCH SONG

"I Got Plenty o'Nuttin'," 1935
Ira Gershwin, DuBose Heyward/George Gershwin
ACCOMPANIMENT, COMPOSERS, DIALECT, LANDMARKS OF STAGE AND SCREEN, MONEY, OPERA, VERSE

"I Got Rhythm," 1930
Ira Gershwin/George Gershwin
BEBOP, CIRCLE OF FIFTHS, COMPOSERS, LYRICS, MUSICAL COMEDY, TABLE 11, PIANO, RHYME, RHYTHM, TABLE 15, SOCIETY TEMPO

"I Got the Sun in The Morning," 1946
Irving Berlin
MONEY, TABLE 11, POPULAR SONG-ii, SUN, TIME OF DAY

"I Got You (I Feel Good)," 1966
James Brown
FEELING, SOUL

"I Got You Babe," 1965
Sonny Bono
BABY

"I Gotta Right to Sing the Blues," 1932
Ted Koehler/Harold Arlen
DIALECT, REVUES, TABLE 14

"I Guess I'll Have to Change My Plan," 1929
Howard Dietz/Arthur Schwartz
BORROWING, CLOTHING, COLLABORATION, LENGTH, LYRICISTS, REVUES, TABLE 14

"I Had the Craziest Dream," 1942
Mack Gordon/Harry Warren
COLLABORATION, DREAMS, TABLE 9, LYRICISTS, MADNESS, TABLE 15, WORLD WAR II

"I Hadn't Anyone Till You," 1938
Ray Noble
BRITAIN

"I Hate Men," 1949
Cole Porter
MAN, TABLE 11

"I Have But One Heart," 1945
Johnny Farrow, Marty Symes/Johnny Farrow
TABLE 2, TABLE 15

"I Have Dreamed," 1951
Oscar Hammerstein II/Richard Rodgers
COLLABORATION, DREAMS, MODULATION,
TABLE 12

"I Have Never Seen the Russian Ballet," 1916
Elsa Maxwell
WOMEN AS SONGWRITERS

"I Have to Tell You," 1954
Harold Rome
TABLE 12

"I Hear a Symphony," 1965
Brian Holland, Lamont Dozier, Eddie Holland
MOTOWN, MUSIC

"I Hear Music," 1940
Frank Loesser/Burton Lane
MUSIC

"I Hear You Knocking," 1955
Dave Bartholomew, Pearl King
COVER, RHYTHM AND BLUES

"I Heard a Rumour," 1987
Sarah Dallin, Siobhan Fahey, Keren Woodward, Mike
Stock, Matt Aitker, Pete Waterman (Bananarama)
SINGING GROUPS

"I Heard It Through the Grapevine," 1966
Norman Whitfield, Barrett Strong
MOTOWN, TALKING

"I Honestly Love You," 1974
Peter Allen, Jeff Barry
TABLE 4-c, TABLE 10-a, TABLE 10-f, TABLE 15

"I Just Called to Say I Love You," 1984
Stevie Wonder
TABLE 1, LOVE, TABLE 15, TELEPHONES

"I Just Fall in Love Again," 1977
Stephen H. Dorff, Larry Herbstritt, Harry Lloyd,
Gloria Sklerov
FALLING IN LOVE

"I Just Want to Be Your Everything," 1977
Barry Gibb
DISCO, WISHING

"I Kiss Your Hand, Madame," 1929
Samuel Lewis, Joseph Young (Eng.)/Ralph Erwin
TABLE 2, GERMANY, KISSING, RADIO, TANGO,
WOMAN

"I Knew You Were Waiting (For Me)," 1987
Simon Climie, Dennis Morgan
TABLE 10-p, WAITING

"I Know a Place," 1965
Tony Hatch
TABLE 10-f, PLACES

"I Know That You Know," 1926
Anne Caldwell/Vincent Youmans
WOMEN AS SONGWRITERS

"I Left My Heart at the Stage Door Canteen," 1942
Irving Berlin
TABLE 2, BROADWAY, PATRIOTISM, REVUES,
TABLE 14, WORLD WAR II

"I Left My Heart in San Francisco," 1954
Douglass Cross/George Cory
TABLE 2, CITIES, TABLE 5, TABLE 10-a, TABLE
10-d, METER, TABLE 15, TEMPO

"I Let a Song Go Out of My Heart," 1938
Irving Mills, Henry Nemo, John Redmond/Duke
Ellington
TABLE 2, TABLE 3, MUSIC, SWING

"I Like It Like That," 1961
Chris Kenner, Allen Toussaint
BOOGALOO

"I Like Mountain Music," 1933
James Cavanaugh/Frank Weldon
MOUNTAINS

"I Like Myself," 1954
Betty Comden, Adolph Green/André Previn
WOMEN AS SONGWRITERS

"I LIKE TO RECOGNIZE THE TUNE," 1939
Lorenz Hart/Richard Rodgers
MELODY

"I LOST MY SUGAR IN SALT LAKE CITY," 1942
Leon Rene, Johnny Lange
TABLE 5, SWEETNESS

"I LOVE A PARADE," 1931
Ted Koehler/Harold Arlen
TABLE 9, MARCH

"I LOVE A PIANO," 1915
Irving Berlin
PIANO

"I LOVE A RAINY NIGHT," 1980
David Malloy, Eddie Rabbitt, Even Stevens
TABLE 4-d, NIGHT, WEATHER

"I LOVE COFFEE, I LOVE TEA," 1915
anonymous
FOOD AND DRINK

"I LOVE HOW YOU LOVE ME," 1961
Larry Kolber, Barry Mann
TABLE 4-d, SINGING GROUPS

"I LOVE LOUISA," 1931
Howard Dietz/Arthur Schwartz
REVUES, TABLE 14

"I LOVE PARIS," 1953
Cole Porter
CITIES, TABLE 5, MODE, TABLE 11

"I LOVE THE NIGHTLIFE," 1977
Alicia Bridges, Susan Hutcheson
DISCO

"I LOVE TO DANCE," 1978
Alan Bergman, Marilyn Bergman/Billy Goldenberg
WOMEN AS SONGWRITERS

"I LOVE TO LIE AWAKE IN BED," SEE **"I GUESS I'LL HAVE TO CHANGE MY PLAN"**

"I LOVE YOU," 1923
Harlan Thompson/Harry Archer
LOVE, TABLE 11

"I LOVE YOU," 1943
Cole Porter
COMPOSER-LYRICISTS, INTERVAL, LOVE, TABLE 11

"I LOVE YOU," 1944
Robert Wright, George Forrest
TABLE 12

"I LOVE YOU A THOUSAND WAYS," 1951
Lefty Frizzell, Jim Beck
COUNTRY AND WESTERN

"I LOVE YOU BECAUSE," 1949
Leon Payne
COUNTRY AND WESTERN

"I LOVE YOU FOR SENTIMENTAL REASONS," SEE **"FOR SENTIMENTAL REASONS"**

"I LOVE YOU SO," SEE **"THE MERRY WIDOW WALTZ"**

"I LOVE YOU, SWEETHEART OF ALL MY DREAMS," 1928
Art Fitch, Kay Fitch, Bert Lowe
LOVE, SWEETNESS

"I LOVE YOU TRULY," 1901
Carrie Jacobs-Bond
ART SONG, LOVE, MARRIAGE, WOMEN AS SONGWRITERS

"I LOVED YOU ONCE IN SILENCE," 1960
Alan Jay Lerner/Frederick Loewe
TABLE 12

"I LOVES YOU PORGY," 1935
DuBose Heyward, Ira Gershwin/George Gershwin
DIALECT

"I MARRIED AN ANGEL," 1938
Lorenz Hart/Richard Rodgers
ANGELS, MARRIAGE, TABLE 11

"I MAY BE WRONG (BUT I THINK YOU'RE WONDERFUL)," 1929
Harry Ruskin/Henry Sullivan
THINKING, WONDER

"I Need a Man to Love," 1968
Janis Joplin/Sam Andrew
WOMEN AS SONGWRITERS

I Never Loved a Man (The Way I Love You)," 1966
Ronnie Shannon
MAN, SOUL

"I Never Promised You a Rose Garden," SEE "Rose Garden"

"I Never Will Marry," 1958
Fred Hellerman
MARRIAGE, TABLE 15

"I Only Have Eyes for You," 1934
Al Dubin/Harry Warren
ANATOMY, TABLE 2, COLLABORATION, COMPOSERS, CROSSOVER, TABLE 9, LYRICISTS, ROCK 'N' ROLL-ii

"I Remember It Well," 1958
Alan Jay Lerner/Frederick Loewe
TABLE 9, MEMORY

"I Remember You," 1942
Johnny Mercer, Victor Schertzinger
TABLE 9, MEMORY

"I Saw Her Again Last Night," 1966
John Phillips, Dennis Doherty
SEEING, SINGING GROUPS

"I Saw Her Standing There," 1963
John Lennon, Paul McCartney
ROCK-ii

"I Saw Mommy Kissing Santa Claus," 1952
Tommie Connor
CHRISTMAS, KISSING, MOTHER, SEEING, YOUR HIT PARADE

"I Say a Little Prayer," 1967
Hal David/Burt Bacharach
COLLABORATION, POPULAR SONG-x, SOUL

"I See Your Face Before Me," 1937
Howard Dietz/Arthur Schwartz
TABLE 2, COLLABORATION, TABLE 11, SEEING

"I Shall Be Released," 1967
Bob Dylan
FOLK SONG

"I Shot the Sheriff," 1974
Bob Marley
REGGAE, ROCK-viii

"I Should Care," 1945
Sammy Cahn, Axel Stordahl, Paul Weston
TABLE 9

"I Speak to the Stars," 1954
Paul Francis Webster/Sammy Fain
STARS

"I Started a Joke," 1968
Barry Gibb, Robin Gibb, Maurice Gibb
ROCK-viii

"I Still Get a Thrill (Thinking of You)," 1930
Benny Davis/J. Fred Coots
THINKING

"I Surrender, Dear," 1931
Gordon Clifford/Harry Barris
TABLE 3, MODE, RADIO

"I Talk to the Trees," 1951
Alan Jay Lerner/Frederick Loewe
TABLE 12, TALKING, TREE

"I Think I Love You," 1970
Tony Romeo
TELEVISION, THINKING

"I Think It's Going to Rain Today," 1966
Randy Newman
PERFORMER-SONGWRITERS

"I Think of You," 1941
Jack Elliot, Don Marcotte
THINKING

"I Threw a Kiss in the Ocean," 1942
Irving Berlin
OCEAN

"I UNDERSTAND," 1941
Kim Gannon/Mabel Wayne
TABLE 3, FORGIVENESS, TIN PAN ALLEY

"I USED TO BE COLOR BLIND," 1938
Irving Berlin
SEEING

"I WALK THE LINE," 1956
Johnny Cash
COUNTRY AND WESTERN

"I WANNA BE AROUND," 1959
Johnny Mercer, Sadie Vimmerstedt
TABLE 15, WISHING

"I WANNA BE LOVED BY YOU," 1928
Bert Kalmar/Herbert Stothart, Harry Ruby
SUBJECT, WISHING

"I WANNA DANCE WITH SOMEBODY (WHO LOVES ME)," 1986
George Merrill, Shannon Rubicam
TABLE 10-f

"I WANNA GET MARRIED," 1944
Dan Shapiro, Milton Pascal/Phil Charig
MARRIAGE, TABLE 11, WISHING

"I WANNA LOVE HIM SO BAD," 1964
Jeff Barry, Ellie Greenwich
SINGING GROUPS

"I WANT A GIRL JUST LIKE THE GIRL THAT MARRIED DEAR OLD DAD," 1911
William Dillon/Harry Von Tilzer
FATHERS, GIRL, MARRIAGE, MOTHERS, WISHING

"I WANT MY MAMA," SEE **"MAMA YO QUIERO"**

"I WANT TO BE A COWBOY'S SWEETHEART," 1936
Patsy Montana
COUNTRY AND WESTERN

"I WANT TO BE HAPPY," 1924
Irving Caesar/Vincent Youmans
HAPPINESS, MUSICAL COMEDY, TABLE 11, WISHING

"I WANT TO HOLD YOUR HAND," 1963
John Lennon, Paul McCartney
ANATOMY, TABLE 2, ROCK-ii, WISHING

"I WANT TO TAKE YOU HIGHER," 1968
Sylvester Stewart
HEIGHT, ROCK-ix

"I WANT WHAT I WANT WHEN I WANT IT," 1905
Henry Blossom/Victor Herbert
WISHING

"I WANT YOU," 1966
Bob Dylan
ROCK-iv

"I WANT YOU BACK," 1969
Berry Gordy, Jr., Alphonso J. Mizell, Frederick J. Perren, Deke Richards
MOTOWN, WISHING

"I WANT YOU, I NEED YOU, I LOVE YOU," 1956
Maurice Mysels/Ira Kosloff
POPULAR SONG-viii

"I WAS THE ONE," 1956
Aaron Schroeder, Claude De Metruis, Hal Blair, Bill Peppers
POPULAR SONG-viii

"I WENT TO YOUR WEDDING," 1952
Jessie Mae Robinson
MARRIAGE

"I WHISTLE A HAPPY TUNE," 1951
Oscar Hammerstein II/Richard Rodgers
CHILDREN, HAPPINESS, MELODY, MUSIC, MUSICAL PLAYS, TABLE 12, PATTER

"I WHO HAVE NOTHING," 1961
Jerry Leiber, Mike Stoller (Eng.)/Carlo Donida
RHYTHM AND BLUES

"I WILL WAIT FOR YOU," 1964
Norman Gimbel (Eng.)/Michel Legrand
TABLE 4-d, ENDURING LOVE, TABLE 8, FRANCE, MODE, WAITING

**"I'D REALLY LOVE TO SEE YOU TONIGHT,"
1975**
Parker McGee
TABLE 4-d

"IDA, SWEET AS APPLE CIDER," 1903
Eddie Leonard/Eddie Munson
MINSTREL SHOW, NAMES, SWEETNESS

"IF," 1934
Robert Hargreaves, Stanley J. Damerell/Tolchard
Evans
TABLE 15, *YOUR HIT PARADE*

"IF EVER I WOULD LEAVE YOU," 1960
Alan Jay Lerner/Frederick Loewe
COLLABORATION, LYRICISTS, MUSICAL
PLAYS, TABLE 12

"IF HE WALKED INTO MY LIFE," 1966
Jerry Herman
TABLE 10-c, LIFE, TABLE 11, TABLE 15, WALK-
ING

"IF I CAN DREAM," 1968
W. Earl Brown
ROCK 'N' ROLL-i

"IF I CAN'T HAVE YOU," 1977
Barry Gibb, Maurice Gibb, Robin Gibb
DISCO

**"IF I COULD BE WITH YOU ONE HOUR TO-
NIGHT," 1926**
Henry Creamer, Jimmy P. Johnson
TIME

"IF I DIDN'T CARE," 1939
Jack Lawrence
BALLAD, SINGING GROUPS

"IF I GIVE MY HEART TO YOU," 1954
Jimmy Crane, Al Jacobs, Jimmy Brewster
TABLE 2

"IF I HAD A HAMMER," 1958
Lee Hays, Peter Seeger
FOLK SONG, PROTEST SONG, RELIGION,
SINGING GROUPS, SUBJECTS

"IF I HAD A TALKING PICTURE OF YOU," 1929
B. G. DeSylva, Lew Brown, Ray Henderson
TABLE 9

"IF I HAD MY WAY," 1913
Lou Klein/James Kendis
WALTZ

**"IF I HAD THE WINGS OF AN ANGEL," SEE "THE
PRISONER'S SONG"**

"IF I HAD YOU," 1928
Ted Shapiro, Jimmy Campbell, Reginald Connelly
TABLE 9, GOLDEN AGE, TIN PAN ALLEY

**"IF I KNEW YOU WERE COMIN' I'D'VE BAKED A
CAKE," 1950**
Al Hoffman, Robert Merrill, Clem Watts
FOOD AND DRINK

"IF I LOVED YOU," 1945
Oscar Hammerstein II/Richard Rodgers
COLLABORATION, GOLDEN AGE, LOVE,
MUSICAL PLAYS, TABLE 12, TABLE 15

"IF I ONLY HAD A BRAIN," 1939
E. Y. Harburg/Harold Arlen
TABLE 2, TABLE 9, THINKING

"IF I WERE A BELL," 1950
Frank Loesser
LYRICS, TABLE 11, PICKUP

"IF I WERE A CARPENTER," 1966
Tim Hardin
TABLE 4-d, TABLE 10-v

"IF I WERE A RICH MAN," 1964
Sheldon Harnick/Jerry Bock
MONEY, TABLE 12

**"IF JACK WERE ONLY HERE," SEE "MOTHER
WAS A LADY"**

"IF MOMMA WAS MARRIED," 1959
Stephen Sondheim/Jule Styne
MARRIAGE

"IF MY FRIENDS COULD SEE ME NOW," 1965
Dorothy Fields/Cy Coleman
WOMEN AS SONGWRITERS

"IF NOT FOR YOU," 1970
Bob Dylan
ROCK-iv

"IF THERE IS SOMEONE LOVELIER THAN YOU," 1934
Howard Dietz/Arthur Schwartz
BEAUTY, TABLE 11

"IF THIS ISN'T LOVE," 1946
E. Y. Harburg/Burton Lane
TABLE 11

"IF WE ONLY HAVE LOVE (QUAND ON N'A QUE L'AMOUR)," 1968
Mort Shuman, Eric Blau/Jacques Brel
BELGIUM, CABARET, TRIPLET

"IF WE WERE IN LOVE," 1981
Alan Bergman, Marilyn Bergman/John Williams
WOMEN AS SONGWRITERS

"IF YOU ARE BUT A DREAM," 1941
Moe Jaffe, Jack Fulton, Nat Bonx
TABLE 6, DREAMS

"IF YOU CAN'T SING IT YOU'LL HAVE TO SWING IT (MISTER PAGANINI)," 1936
Sam Coslow
SCAT SINGING

"IF YOU COULD READ MY MIND," 1969
Gordon Lightfoot
MIND

"IF YOU DON'T KNOW ME BY NOW," 1972
Kenny Gamble, Leon Huff
TABLE 10-q

"IF YOU KNEW SUSIE LIKE I KNOW SUSIE," 1925
B. G. DeSylva, Joseph Meyer
TABLE 11, NAMES

"IF YOU LEAVE ME NOW," 1976
Peter Cetera
TABLE 10-h, ROCK-ix

"IF YOU LOVE ME (LET ME KNOW)," 1974
John Rostill
TABLE 4-d

"IF YOU LOVE ME, REALLY LOVE ME (HYMNE À L'AMOUR)," 1953
Geoffrey Parsons (Eng.)/Marguerite Monnot
FRANCE

"IF YOU NEED ME," 1963
Wilson Pickett, Robert Bateman, Sonny Sanders
SOUL

"IF YOU SEE MY SAVIOR, TELL HIM THAT YOU SAW ME," 1928
Thomas A. Dorsey
GOSPEL

"IF YOU WANNA BE HAPPY," 1962
Frank J. Guida, Carmela Guida, Joseph Royster
HAPPINESS

"IF YOU WANT A LITTLE DOGGIE, WHISTLE AND I'LL COME TO YOU," 1915
Blanche Merrill/Leo Edwards
WOMEN AS SONGWRITERS

"IF YOU WERE THE ONLY GIRL IN THE WORLD," 1916
Clifford Grey/Nat D. Ayer
BRITAIN, GIRL, RADIO, WORLD

"IF YOU'VE GOT THE MONEY, I'VE GOT THE TIME," 1950
Letty Frizzell, Jim Beck
COUNTRY AND WESTERN

"I'LL ALWAYS BE IN LOVE WITH YOU," 1929
Bud Green, Herman Ruby, Sam H. Stept
TABLE 9

"I'LL ALWAYS LOVE YOU," 1987
Jimmy George
ENDURING LOVE

"I'LL BE AROUND," 1972
Earl Randle
SOUL

"I'LL BE GOOD TO YOU," 1976
Louis Johnson, George Johnson, Senora Sam
TABLE 10-p

"I'LL BE HOME," 1956
Ferdinand Washington, Stan Lewis
COVER

"I'LL BE HOME FOR CHRISTMAS," 1943
Kim Gannon, Walter Kent, Buck Ram
CHRISTMAS, HOME, WORLD WAR II

"I'LL BE SATISFIED," 1959
Berry Gordy, Jr., Gwen Gordy, Tyran Carlo
ROCK 'N' ROLL-i

"I'LL BE SEEING YOU," 1938
Irving Kahal/Sammy Fain
DISC JOCKEY, FAREWELLS, SEEING, TIN PAN ALLEY, WORLD WAR II, *YOUR HIT PARADE*

"I'LL BE THERE," 1970
Bob West, Hal Davis, Willie Hutch, Berry Gordy, Jr.
MOTOWN

"I'LL BE WITH YOU IN APPLE BLOSSOM TIME," 1920
Nevil Fleeson/Albert Von Tilzer
FLOWERS, SINGING GROUPS, TIME, VAUDE-VILLE

"I'LL BE YOURS (J'ATTENDRAI)," 1945
Anna Sosenko (Eng.)/Dino Olivieri
FRANCE, RANGE

"I'LL BUILD A STAIRWAY TO PARADISE," 1922
B. G. DeSylva, Arthur Francis (pseud. Ira Gershwin)/George Gershwin
HEAVEN, IMAGINATION, INTERVAL, LYRI-CISTS, PIANO, REVUES, TABLE 14

"I'LL DANCE AT YOUR WEDDING," 1947
Herb Magidson/Ben Oakland
DANCING, MARRIAGE

"I'LL FOLLOW MY SECRET HEART," 1934
Noël Coward
TABLE 2, BRITAIN, COMPOSER-LYRICISTS

"I'LL GET BY (AS LONG AS I HAVE YOU)," 1928
Roy Turk/Fred E. Ahlert
TABLE 3, TABLE 15

"I'LL HOLD YOU IN MY HEART (TILL I CAN HOLD YOU IN MY ARMS)," 1947
Eddy Arnold, Hal Horton, Tommy Dilbeck
TABLE 2, COUNTRY AND WESTERN

"I'LL KNOW," 1950
Frank Loesser
TABLE 11

"I'LL NEVER FALL IN LOVE AGAIN," 1968
Hal David/Burt Bacharach
COLLABORATION, COMPOSERS, FALLING IN LOVE, TABLE 10-f, LYRICISTS, POPULAR SONG-x, TABLE 15

"I'LL NEVER LOVE THIS WAY AGAIN," 1977
Richard Kerr, Will Jennings
TABLE 10-f

"I'LL NEVER SMILE AGAIN," 1939
Ruth Lowe
BIG BANDS, TABLE 3, SMILING, WOMEN AS SONGWRITERS

"I'LL OVERCOME SOMEDAY," 1901; *SEE ALSO* **"WE SHALL OVERCOME"**
Charles A. Tindley
GOSPEL

"I'LL PLANT MY OWN TREE," 1967
Dory Previn/André Previn
WOMEN AS SONGWRITERS

"I'LL REMEMBER APRIL," 1941
Don Raye, Gene DePaul, Patricia Johnston
TABLE 9, FORM, MEMORY, MONTHS

"I'LL SEE YOU AGAIN," 1929
Noël Coward
BALLAD, BRITAIN, COMPOSER-LYRICISTS, FAREWELLS, TABLE 13, SEEING, VERSE, WALTZ

"I'll See You in My Dreams," 1924
Gus Kahn/Isham Jones
TABLE 3, DREAMS, FAREWELLS, LYRICISTS,
SEEING

"I'll String Along With You," 1934
Al Dubin/Harry Warren
ANGELS, TABLE 9

"I'll Take Romance," 1937
Oscar Hammerstein II/Ben Oakland
TABLE 9, ROMANCE

**"I'll Take You Home Again Kathleen,"
1876**
Thomas P. Westendorf
HOME, POPULAR SONG-i

"I'll Take You There," 1972
Alvertis Isbell
GOSPEL, RELIGION

"I'll Walk Alone," 1944
Sammy Cahn/Jule Styne
LONELINESS, LYRICISTS, TABLE 15, WALKING,
WORLD WAR II, YOUR HIT PARADE

"I'm a Believer," 1966
Neil Diamond
TELEVISION

"I'm a Dreamer, Aren't We All?," 1929
B. G. DeSylva, Lew Brown, Ray Henderson
DREAMS

"I'm a Man," 1958
Doc Pomus, Mort Shuman
MAN, ROCK 'N' ROLL-i

"I'm a Stand by Your Woman Man," 1976
Kent Robbins, Billy Sherrill, Tammy Wynette
TABLE 10-u

**"I'm a Yankee Doodle Dandy," SEE "The
Yankee Doodle Boy"**

"I'm Always Chasing Rainbows," 1918
Joseph McCarthy/Harry Carroll
CLASSICS, TABLE 6, RAINBOW

**"I'm Always True to You (In My Fashion),"
SEE "Always True To You (In My Fashion)"**

**"I'm an Old Cow Hand (From the Rio
Grande)," 1936**
Johnny Mercer
COMPOSER-LYRICISTS, TABLE 9, RIVERS

"I'm an Ordinary Man," 1956
Alan Jay Lerner/Frederick Loewe
MAN, TABLE 12

"I'm Beginning to See the Light," 1944
Harry James, Duke Ellington, Johnny Hodges, Don
George
BEGINNING, TABLE 3

"I'm Easy," 1975
Keith Carradine
TABLE 1

"Im Falling in Love With Some One," 1910
Rida Johnson Young/Victor Herbert
FALLING IN LOVE, OPERETTA, TABLE 13,
TABLE 15, WALTZ

"I'm Flying," 1954
Carolyn Leigh/Mark Charlap
WOMEN AS SONGWRITERS

"I'm Gettin' Sentimental Over You," 1932
Ned Washington/George Bassman
BIG BANDS, TABLE 3, BRASS, SENTIMENT

**"I'm Glad I'm a Boy/I'm Glad I'm a Girl,"
1909**
Nora Bayes (pseud. Dora Goldberg), Jack Norworth
WOMEN AS SONGWRITERS

**"I'm Glad I'm Not Young Any More,"
1958**
Alan Jay Lerner/Frederick Loewe
AGE, COLLABORATION, TABLE 9

"I'm Glad There Is You," 1941
Paul Madeira, Jimmy Dorsey
HAPPINESS

"I'M GOIN' DOWN," 1984
Bruce Springsteen
ROCK-xii

"I'M GONE," 1952
Leonard Lee, Dave Bartholomew
RHYTHM AND BLUES

"I'M GONNA GET MARRIED," 1959
Lloyd Price, Harold Logan
MARRIAGE, RHYTHM AND BLUES

"I'M GONNA LIVE THE LIFE I SING ABOUT IN MY SONG," C. 1940
Thomas A. Dorsey
GOSPEL

"I'M GONNA LIVE TILL I DIE," 1950
Walter Kent, Mann Curtis, Al Hoffman
LIFE

"I'M GONNA SIT RIGHT DOWN AND WRITE MYSELF A LETTER," 1935
Joe Young/Fred E. Ahlert
SINGING GROUPS, WRITING

"I'M GONNA WASH THAT MAN RIGHT OUTA MY HAIR," 1949
Oscar Hammerstein II/Richard Rodgers
TABLE 2, MAN, MUSICAL PLAYS, TABLE 12

"I'M HENRY VIII, I AM," 1911
R. P. Weston, Fred Murray
ROCK-iii

"I'M IN A DANCING MOOD," 1936
Maurice Sigler, Al Goodhart, Al Hoffman
DANCING

"I'M IN LOVE AGAIN," 1925
Cole Porter
CABARET, REVUES, TABLE 14

"I'M IN LOVE AGAIN," 1956
Antoine "Fats" Domino, Dave Bartholomew
ROCK 'N' ROLL-i

"I'M IN LOVE WITH A WONDERFUL GUY," SEE "A WONDERFUL GUY"

"I'M IN LOVE WITH MISS LOGAN," 1952
Ronny Graham
CHILDHOOD

"I'M IN THE MOOD FOR LOVE," 1935
Jimmy McHugh, Dorothy Fields
COMPOSERS, FILM MUSIC, TABLE 9, LOVE, LYRICISTS, MOOD, POPULAR SONG-ii, RANGE, TABLE 15, VOCALESE

"I'M JUST A LUCKY SO-AND-SO," 1945
Mack David/Duke Ellington
LUCK

"I'M JUST A VAGABOND LOVER," 1929
Rudy Vallee, Leon Zimmerman
LOVERS, TABLE 15

"I'M JUST WILD ABOUT HARRY," 1921
Noble Sissle, Eubie Blake
NAMES, POPULAR SONG-ii, RAGTIME, TABLE 14

"I'M LEARNING SOMETHING EVERY DAY," 1909
Nora Bayes (pseud. Dora Goldberg), Jack Norworth
WOMEN AS SONGWRITERS

"I'M LOOKING FOR A GUY WHO PLAYS ALTO AND BARITONE AND DOUBLES ON THE CLARINET AND WEARS A SIZE THIRTY-SEVEN SUIT," 1940
Ozzie Nelson
HUMOR, WOODWINDS

"I'M LOOKING OVER A FOUR LEAF CLOVER," 1927
Mort Dixon/Harry Woods
TREES

"I'M MAKING BELIEVE," 1944
Mack Gordon/James V. Monaco
SINGING GROUPS

"I'M MOVIN' ON," 1950
Hank Snow
TABLE 4-d, COUNTRY AND WESTERN

"I'M NOBODY'S BABY," 1921
Benny Davis, Milton Ager, Lester Santly
BABY

"I'M OLD FASHIONED," 1942
Johnny Mercer/Jerome Kern
BEGUINE, TABLE 9, FORM, RANGE

"I'M ON FIRE," 1984
Bruce Springsteen
FIRE, ROCK-xii

**"I'M PUTTING ALL MY EGGS IN ONE BASKET,"
1936**
Irving Berlin
TABLE 9, SLANG

"I'M SHOOTING HIGH," 1935
Ted Koehler/Jimmy McHugh
TABLE 9, HEIGHT

"I'M SITTING ON TOP OF THE WORLD," 1925
Sam M. Lewis, Joe Young/Ray Henderson
VERSE, WORLD

"I'M SO LONESOME I COULD CRY," 1949
Hank Williams
TABLE 4-d, COUNTRY AND WESTERN, CRY-ING, LONELINESS

"I'M SORRY," 1960
Ronnie Self, Dub Allbritten
FORGIVENESS, ROCK 'N' ROLL-iii

"I'M SORRY," 1975
John Denver
FORGIVENESS

"I'M STEPPING OUT WITH A MEMORY TO-NIGHT," 1940
Herb Magidson/Allie Wrubel
MEMORY

"I'M STILL HERE," 1971
Stephen Sondheim
CATALOGUE SONG, CIRCLE OF FIFTHS, ENHARMONIC EQUIVALENCE, INTERVAL, TABLE 11

"I'M STILL IN LOVE WITH YOU," 1972
Al Green, Willie Mitchell, Al Jackson
ENDURING LOVE, SOUL

"I'M TELLING YOU NOW," 1963
Freddie Garrity, Mitch Murray
ROCK-iii

"I'M THE LONESOMEST GAL IN TOWN," 1912
Lew Brown/Albert Van Tilzer
TABLE 5, LONELINESS

**"I'M THINKING TONIGHT OF MY BLUE EYES,"
1930**
A. P. Carter; revived in 1942 with additional lyrics by Don Marcotte
WORLD WAR II

"I'M THRU WITH LOVE," 1931
Gus Kahn/Matt Malneck, Fud Livingston
LOVE

"I'M WALKIN'," 1957
Antoine "Fats" Domino, Dave Bartholomew
ROCK 'N' ROLL-iii, WALKING

"I'M WALKING BEHIND YOU," 1953
Billy Reid
WALKING

"I'M WISHING," 1937
Larry Morey/Frank Churchill
WISHING

"I'M YOUR BOOGIE MAN," 1977
Harry Casey, Richard Finch
BOOGIE-WOOGIE, DISCO, MAN

"I'M YOURS," 1930
E. Y. Harburg/John W. Green
COMPOSERS

"IMAGINARY LOVER," 1978
Buddy Buie, Robert Nix, Dean Daughtry
IMAGINATION, LOVERS

"IMAGINATION," 1940
Johnny Burke/James Van Heusen
COLLABORATION, IMAGINATION, LYRICISTS

"IMAGINE," 1971
John Lennon
TABLE 4-d, ROCK-ii

"Immigrant Song," 1970
Robert Plant, Jimmy Page
HEAVY METAL

"The Impossible Dream (The Quest)," 1965
Joe Darion/Mitch Leigh
DREAMS, HIT SONG, INSPIRATION, METER,
TABLE 12, TRIPLET

"In-a-gadda-da-vida," 1968
Doug Ingle
HEAVY METAL, NONSENSE, ROCK-vii

"In a Little Spanish Town," 1926
Sam M. Lewis, Joe Young/Mabel Wayne
TABLE 5, NATIONS

"In a Persian Market," 1920
m. Albert W. Ketèlbey (pseud. William Aston)
NATIONS

"In a Sentimental Mood," 1935
Duke Ellington, Irving Mills, Manny Kurtz
TABLE 3, CHROMATICISM, MOOD, SENTI-
MENT

"In a Shanty in Old Shanty Town," SEE
"(In) A Shanty in Old Shanty Town"

**"In an Eighteenth-Century Drawing
Room," 1939**
Jack Lawrence/Raymond Scott
TABLE 6

"In Dreams," 1963
Roy Orbison
DREAMS, ROCK 'N' ROLL-i

"In Love in Vain," 1946
Leo Robin/Jerome Kern
TABLE 9, LOVE

"In My Dreams," 1984
Paul Kennerley
DREAMS, TABLE 10-t

"In My Dreams of You," 1910
Clare Kummer (pseud. Clare Rodman Beecher)
WOMEN AS SONGWRITERS

"In My Little Tin Box," SEE **"(In My) Little
Tin Box"**

"In My Merry Oldsmobile," 1905
Vincent P. Bryan/Gus Edwards
KEY, TRAVEL, VAUDEVILLE, WALTZ

"In My Room," 1964
Brian Wilson, Gary Usher
ROCK-i

"In Old Lisbon," SEE **"Lisbon Antigua"**

"In Old New York," SEE **"The Streets of
New York"**

"In Other Words," SEE **"Fly Me to the
Moon"**

"In the Blue of Evening," 1942
Thomas Adair/Alfred A. D'Artega
NIGHT

"In the Chapel in the Moonlight," 1936
Billy Hill
MOON

**"In the Cool, Cool, Cool of the Evening,"
1951**
Johnny Mercer/Hoagy Carmichael
TABLE 1, NIGHT

"In the Garden of Eden," SEE **"In-a-gadda-
da-vida"**

"In the Garden of My Heart," 1908
Caro Roma
WOMEN AS SONGWRITERS

**"In the Ghetto (The Vicious Circle),"
1969**
Mac Davis
ROCK 'N' ROLL-i

"In the Good Old Summer Time," 1902
Ren Shields/George Evans
BARBERSHOP, KEY, MINSTREL SHOW, SEA-
SONS, SINGING GROUPS, VAUDEVILLE,
WALTZ

"IN THE LAND OF OO-BLA-DEE," 1949
Mary Lou Williams, Milton Orent
SCAT SINGING

"IN THE MIDNIGHT HOUR," 1966
Wilson Pickett, Steve Cropper
SOUL, TIME OF DAY

"IN THE MOOD," 1939
Andy Razaf/Joseph Garland
BIG BANDS, TABLE 3, BROKEN CHORD, CODA,
HARMONIC RHYTHM, MOOD, RIFF, SWING

"IN THE NAVY," 1979
Henri Belolo, Victor Willis (Eng.)/Jacques Morali
DISCO

"IN THE SHADE OF THE OLD APPLE TREE," 1905
Harry H. Williams/Egbert van Alstyne
BARBERSHOP, LYRICS, TABLE 15, TREES,
VAUDEVILLE

"IN THE STILL OF THE NIGHT," 1937
Cole Porter
BEGUINE, COMPOSER-LYRICISTS, DOO-WOP,
DYNAMICS, NIGHT, ROCK 'N' ROLL-ii

"IN THE WEE SMALL HOURS OF THE MORNING,"
SEE **"WEE SMALL HOURS (OF THE MORN-
ING)"**

"IN THE WINTER," 1975
Janice Ian
WOMEN AS SONGWRITERS

"INDIAN LOVE CALL," 1924
Otto Harbach, Oscar Hammerstein II/Rudolf Friml
TABLE 3, CZECHOSLOVAKIA, LYRICISTS,
OPERETTA, TABLE 13, ROARING TWENTIES

"INDIAN SUMMER," 1939
Al Dubin/Victor Herbert
SEASONS

"INDIANA (BACK HOME AGAIN IN INDIANA)," 1917
Ballard MacDonald/James F. Hanley
BEBOP, HOME, JAZZ, STATES

"INDIANOLA," 1918
Frank Warren (Eng.)/S. R. Henry, D. Onivas (pseud. Domenico Savino)
WORLD WAR I

"INKA DINKA DOO," 1933
Ben Ryan/Jimmy Durante
NONSENSE

"INTERMEZZO (A LOVE STORY)," 1940
Robert Henning (Eng.)/Heinz Provost
TABLE 3, TABLE 8

"INTO EACH LIFE SOME RAIN MUST FALL," 1944
Allan Roberts, Doris Fisher
LIFE, SINGING GROUPS, WEATHER

"INVITATION," 1952
Paul Francis Webster (1956)/Bronislaw Kaper
TABLE 8

"IRELAND MUST BE HEAVEN FOR MY MOTHER CAME FROM THERE," 1916
Joseph McCarthy, Howard Johnson, Fred Fisher
MOTHERS

"IRENE," 1919
Joseph McCarthy/Harry Tierney
TABLE 11, NAMES

"IRISH WASHERWOMAN," c. 1790
traditional Irish dance
IRELAND

"IS THAT ALL THERE IS?," 1966
Jerry Leiber, Mike Stoller
TABLE 10-f, METER, QUESTIONS, TABLE 15

"IS YOU IS, OR IS YOU AIN'T (MA' BABY)," 1943
Billy Austin, Louis Jordan
BABY, CONTRACTIONS, DIALECT, TABLE 9,
MODE, QUESTIONS, RHYTHM AND BLUES

"ISLAND GIRL," 1975
Elton John, Bernie Taupin
GIRL, ROCK-x

"ISLANDS IN THE STREAM," 1983
Barry Gibb, Robin Gibb, Maurice Gibb
TABLE 4-d, RIVERS

"ISLE OF CAPRI," 1934
Jimmy Kennedy/Will Grosz
BRITAIN, TABLE 5

"ISN'T IT ROMANTIC?," 1932
Lorenz Hart, Richard Rodgers
CATALOGUE SONG, TABLE 9, QUESTIONS,
ROMANCE

"ISN'T SHE LOVELY," 1976
Stevie Wonder
QUESTIONS

"ISN'T THIS A LOVELY DAY," 1935
Irving Berlin
BEAUTY, CONTRACTIONS, DAY, TABLE 9,
QUESTIONS, WEATHER

"ISTANBUL, NOT CONSTANTINOPLE," 1953
Jimmy Kennedy/Nat Simon
TABLE 5, SINGING GROUPS

"IT AIN'T GONNA RAIN NO MO'," 1923
Wendell Hall
DIALECT, RADIO, WEATHER

"IT AIN'T ME, BABE," 1964
Bob Dylan
BABY, PROTEST SONG, ROCK-v

"IT AIN'T NECESSARILY SO," 1935
Ira Gershwin/George Gershwin
ACCOMPANIMENT, CONTRACTIONS, DIA-
LECT, DUMMY LYRICS, LANDMARKS OF
STAGE AND SCREEN, MODE, OCTAVE, OPERA

"IT ALL DEPENDS ON YOU," 1926
B. G. DeSylva, Lew Brown/Ray Henderson
COMPOSERS

"IT CAME UPON A MIDNIGHT CLEAR," 1850
Edmund Hamilton Sears/Richard Storrs Willis
CHRISTMAS

"IT COULD HAPPEN TO YOU," 1944
Johnny Burke/James Van Heusen
CHROMATICISM, COLLABORATION, COM-
POSERS, TABLE 9, GOLDEN AGE, LYRICISTS,
RANGE

**"IT DOESN'T COST ANYTHING TO DREAM,"
1945**
Dorothy Fields/Sigmund Romberg
WOMEN AS SONGWRITERS

"IT DON'T COME EASY," 1971
Richard Starkey
ROCK-ii

**"IT DON'T MEAN A THING (IF IT AIN'T GOT
THAT SWING)," 1932**
Irving Mills, Duke Ellington
MUSIC, POPULAR SONG-v, SWING

"IT GOES LIKE IT GOES," 1979
Norman Gimbel/David Shire
TABLE 1

"IT HAD TO BE YOU," 1924
Gus Kahn/Isham Jones
TABLE 3, LYRICISTS, SCALE

"IT HAPPENED IN MONTEREY," 1930
Billy Rose/Mabel Wayne
TABLE 5, TABLE 9

"IT ISN'T FAIR," 1933
Richard Himber/Richard Himber, Frank Warshauer,
Sylvester Sprigato
TABLE 3

**"IT LOOKS LIKE RAIN IN CHERRY BLOSSOM
LANE," 1937**
Edgar Leslie, Joseph Burke
FLOWERS, WEATHER

"IT MIGHT AS WELL BE SPRING," 1945
Oscar Hammerstein II/Richard Rodgers
TABLE 1, CHILDREN, COLLABORATION,
TABLE 9, LYRICS, SEASONS, TABLE 15

"It Might as Well Rain Until September,"
1962
Gerry Goffin, Carole King
MONTHS, ROCK 'N' ROLL, WEATHER

"It Might Be You (Theme From Tootsie),"
1982
Alan Bergman, Marilyn Bergman/Dave Grusin
TEMPO, WOMEN AS SONGWRITERS

"It Never Entered My Mind," 1940
Lorenz Hart/Richard Rodgers
CABARET, MIND, REPEATED NOTE

"It Never Rains in Southern California,"
1972
Albert Hammond, Mike Hazelwood
STATES, WEATHER

"It Only Happens When I Dance With
You," 1947
Irving Berlin
DANCING, TABLE 9

"It Was a Very Good Year," 1961
Ervin Drake
AGE, TABLE 10-d

"It Wasn't God Who Made Honky Tonk
Angels," 1952
J.D. Miller
COUNTRY AND WESTERN

"Italian Street Song," 1910
Rida Johnson Young/Victor Herbert
ART SONG, STREETS

"It's a Big, Wide, Wonderful World,"
1940
John Rox
CABARET, PICKUP, SHOW TUNE, WONDER,
WORLD

"It's a Blue World," 1939
Robert Wright, Chet Forrest
TABLE 7, WORLD

"It's a Good Day," 1946
Peggy Lee, Dave Barbour
DAY, SINGERS, TABLE 15, WOMEN AS
SONGWRITERS

"It's a Grand Night for Singing," 1945
Oscar Hammerstein II/Richard Rodgers
TABLE 9, NIGHT, OCTAVE, WALTZ

"It's a Great Day for the Irish," 1940
Roger Edens
DAY, IRELAND, NATIONS

"It's Hap-Hap-Happy Day," 1939
Sammy Timberg, Winston Sharples, Al Neiburg
HAPPINESS

"It's a Long Way to Tipperary," 1912
Jack Judge, Harry H. Williams
MARCH, TABLE 15, WORLD WAR I

"It's a Lovely Day Today," 1950
Irving Berlin
BEAUTY, DAY, TABLE 11

"It's a Lovely Day Tomorrow," 1939
Irving Berlin
BEAUTY, DAY

"It's a Mad, Mad, Mad, Mad World,"
1963
Mack David/Ernest Gold
MADNESS, WORLD

"It's a Man's, Man's World (But It
Wouldn't Be Nothing Without a
Woman) . . .," 1966
James Brown, Betty Jean Newsome
MAN, SOUL

"It's a Most Unusual Day," 1948
Harold Adamson/Jimmy McHugh
DAY, TABLE 9

"It's a Pity to Say Goodnight," 1946
Billy Reid
FAREWELLS

"It's a Wonderful World," 1939
Harold Adamson/Jan Savitt, Johnny Watson
WONDER, WORLD

"It's All in the Game," 1951
Carl Sigman/Charles Gates Dawes
ADAPTATION, PICKUP, SHOW TUNE

"It's Not Unusual," 1965
Gordon Mills, Les Reed
TABLE 15

"It's Now or Never," 1960
Aaron Schroeder, Wally Gold
ITALY, ROCK 'N' ROLL-i, TABLE 15

"It's Only a Paper Moon," 1933
E. Y. Harburg, Billy Rose/Harold Arlen
CIRCUS, COMPOSERS, DEPRESSION YEARS,
GOLDEN AGE, LYRICISTS, MOON, OCTAVE,
TABLE 15

"It's Only Make Believe," 1958
Jack Nance, Conway Twitty
TABLE 4-d, COUNTRY AND WESTERN, IMAGI-
NATION

"It's Over," 1964
Roy Orbison, Bill Dees
ENDING, ROCK 'N' ROLL-i

"It's So Nice to Have a Man Around the House," 1950
Jack Elliott/Harold Spina
HOME, MAN

"It's the Girl," 1931
Dave Oppenheim/Abel Baer
SINGING GROUPS

"It's the Same Old Shillelagh," 1940
Pat White
NATIONS

"It's the Same Old Song," 1965
Eddie Holland, Lamont Dozier, Brian Holland
MOTOWN, MUSIC

"It's the Talk of the Town," 1933
Marty Symes, Al J. Neiberg/Jerry Livingston
TABLE 3, TABLE 5, SEQUENCE, TALKING

"It's Too Late," 1971
Toni Stern/Carole King
TABLE 10-a, ROCK-vi, TIME, WOMEN AS
SONGWRITERS

"It's Up to You and Me," c. 1963
Ella Fitzgerald
WOMEN AS SONGWRITERS

"It's Your Thing," 1969
Rudolph Isley, Ronald Isley, O'Kelly Isley
TABLE 10-p

"Itsy Bitsy Teenie Weenie Yellow Polkadot Bikini," 1960
Paul J. Vance, Lee Pockriss
NOVELTY SONG

"I've Already Loved You in My Mind," 1977
Conway Twitty
COUNTRY AND WESTERN

"I've Been Loving You Too Long," 1965
Otis Redding, Jerry Butler
SOUL

"I've Been Working on the Railroad," 1894
traditional American folk song
BORROWING, FOLK SONG, GAY NINETIES,
TRAINS

"I've Got a Crush on You," 1928
Ira Gershwin/George Gershwin
CABARET, COLLABORATION, CONTRAC-
TIONS, INTERVAL, LYRICISTS, MUSICAL
PLAYS, TABLE 12, FALLING IN LOVE, FEELING,
PIANO

"I've Got a Feelin' You're Foolin'," 1935
Arthur Freed/Nacio Herb Brown
TABLE 9, FOOLS

"I've Got a Feeling I'm Falling," 1929
Billy Rose/Harry Link, Thomas "Fats" Waller
FALLING IN LOVE, FEELING, PIANO

"I've Got a Gal in Kalamazoo," 1942
Mack Gordon/Harry Warren
TABLE 3, TABLE 5, COLLABORATION, TABLE 9,
GIRL, TEMPO

"THE JAPANESE SANDMAN," 1920
Raymond B. Egan/Richard A. Whiting
NATIONS, RECORDING, SLEEP, VAUDEVILLE

"J'ATTENDRAI," SEE "I'LL BE YOURS"

"JAVA JIVE," 1940
Milton Drake/Ben Oakland
SINGING GROUPS

"THE JAZZ ME BLUES," 1921
Tom Delaney
DIXIELAND

"JAZZ NOCTURNE," 1931
m. Dana Suisse
WOMEN AS SONGWRITERS

"JE T'APPARTIENS," SEE "LET IT BE ME"

"JEALOUSY (JALOUSIE)," 1925
Vera Bloom (Eng.)/Jacob Gade
DENMARK, GYPSY MUSIC

"JEAN," 1969
Rod McKuen
TABLE 8, NAMES, PERFORMER-SONGWRITERS

"JEANIE WITH THE LIGHT BROWN HAIR," 1854
Stephen Collins Foster
ANATOMY, ASCAP, BMI, NAMES

"JEANNINE, I DREAM OF LILAC TIME," 1928
L. Wolfe Gilbert/Nathaniel Shilkret
DREAMS, FILM MUSIC, TABLE 8, FLOWERS,
NAMES, TIME

"JEEPERS CREEPERS," 1938
Johnny Mercer/Harry Warren
ANATOMY, TABLE 9, NONSENSE, SLANG

"JENNY," 1941
Ira Gershwin/Kurt Weill
TABLE 11

"JERSEY BOUNCE," 1941
Robert B. Wright/Bobby Plater, Tiny Bradshaw,
Edward Johnson
RIFF, STATES

"JESSE," 1972
Janis Ian
WOMEN AS SONGWRITERS

"JESSE'S GIRL," 1981
Rick Springfield
TABLE 10-j

"JESUS CHRIST, DO YOU THINK YOU'RE WHAT
THEY SAY YOU ARE," SEE "SUPERSTAR"

"JET SONG," 1957
Stephen Sondheim/Leonard Bernstein
TABLE 12

"JIM CRACK CORN," OR "THE BLUE TAIL FLY,"
1846
attributed to Daniel Decatur Emmett
FOLK SONG

"JIM CROW," 1830
anonymous minstrel song
POPULAR SONG-i

"JIM DANDY," 1957
Lincoln Chase
RHYTHM AND BLUES

"JINGLE-BELL ROCK," 1957
Joseph Carleton Beal, James Ross Boothe
CHRISTMAS, COUNTRY AND WESTERN

"JINGLE BELLS," OR "THE ONE HORSE OPEN
SLEIGH," 1857
James S. Pierpont
CHRISTMAS

"JINGLE, JANGLE, JINGLE," 1942
Frank Loesser/Joseph J. Lilley
ALLITERATION, TABLE 8

"JIVE TALKIN'," 1975
Barry Gibb, Robin Gibb, Maurice Gibb
TALKING

"JOE HILL," 1938
Alfred Hayes/Earl Robinson
OPERA

"JOE HILL," 1966
Phil Ochs
OPERA

"JOHN HENRY," 1873
traditional American folk song
FOLK SONG

"THE JOHN HENRY BLUES," 1922
William C. Handy
BLUES

"JOHNNY ANGEL," 1960
Lyn Duddy/Lee Pockriss
TELEVISION

"JOHNNY B. GOODE," 1958
Chuck Berry
BMI, NAMES, ROCK 'N' ROLL-i

"JOHNNY GET YOUR GUN," 1886
Monroe Rosenfeld
PATRIOTISM, QUOTATION

"JOHNNY ONE NOTE," 1937
Lorenz Hart/Richard Rodgers
HUMOR, MUSIC, NOVELTY SONG, RHYME,
SCALE

"THE JOKER," 1973
Eddie Curtis, Steve Miller
ROCK

"JOLTIN' JOE DI MAGGIO," 1941
Alan Courtney, Ben Homer
NAMES

"JOY," 1972
Ross Parker (Eng.)/Ludwig van Beethoven
TABLE 6, RELIGION

"THE JOY OF LOVE," SEE "CAN'T HELP FALLING
IN LOVE"

"JOY TO THE WORLD," 1970
Hoyt Axton
WORLD

"JUDY'S TURN TO CRY," 1963
Edna Lewis/Beverly Ross
CRYING, ROCK 'N' ROLL-iv

"JUMP (FOR MY LOVE)," 1983
Marti Sharron, Steve Mitchell, Gary Skardina
TABLE 10-h

"JUMPIN' AT THE WOODSIDE," 1938
m. William "Count" Basie
PIANO

"JUMPIN' JACK FLASH," 1968
Mick Jagger, Keith Richards
ROCK-iii

"JUNE," 1903
Clare Kummer (pseud. Clare Rodman Beecher)
WOMEN AS SONGWRITERS

"JUNE IN JANUARY," 1934
Leo Robin, Ralph Rainger
DEPRESSION YEARS, TABLE 9, MONTHS,
SINGERS, TABLE 15

"JUNE IS BUSTIN' OUT ALL OVER," 1945
Oscar Hammerstein II/Richard Rodgers
DIALECT, MONTHS, TABLE 12

"JUNE NIGHT," SEE "JUST GIVE ME A JUNE
NIGHT, THE MOONLIGHT, AND YOU"

"JUNGLE BOOGIE," 1973
Ronald Bell,. Robert Bell, George M. Brown, Richard
Westfield, Claydes Smith, Robert Mickens, Donald
Boyce, Dennis Thomas (Kool & the Gang)
BOOGIE-WOOGIE, FUNK

"JUNGLE DRUMS (CANTO KARABALI)," 1930
Carmen Lombardo, Charles O'Flynn (Eng.)/Ernesto
Lecuona
CANADA, CUBA

"JUST A CHAIN OF DAISIES," 1911
Anita Owen
WOMEN AS SONGWRITERS

"JUST A FRIEND," 1989
Biz Markie
FRIENDSHIP, RAP

"Just a Gigolo," 1929
Irving Caesar (Eng.)/Leonello Casucci
AUSTRIA, DEPRESSION YEARS

"Just a Girl That Men Forget," 1923
Al Dubin, Fred Rath, Joe Garren
GIRL

"Just a Little Bit South of North Carolina," 1940
Sunny Skylar, Bette Cannon, Arthur Shaftel
CARDINAL POINTS, STATES

"Just a Little Lovin' (Will Go a Long Way)," 1948
Zeke Clements, Eddy Arnold
COUNTRY AND WESTERN

"Just a Memory," 1927
B. G. DeSylva, Lew Brown, Ray Henderson
MEMORY

"Just A-Wearying for You," 1901
Frank L. Stanton/Carrie Jacobs-Bond
DIALECT, WOMEN AS SONGWRITERS

"Just Because," 1957
Lloyd Price
RHYTHM AND BLUES

"Just Friends," 1931
Sam M. Lewis/John Klenner
FRIENDSHIP

"Just Give Me a June Night, the Moonlight, and You," 1924
Cliff Friend/Abel Baer
MONTHS, NIGHT

"Just Imagine," 1927
B. G. DeSylva, Lew Brown, Ray Henderson
IMAGINATION

"Just in Time," 1956
Betty Comden, Adolph Green/Jule Styne
COLLABORATION, COMPOSERS, LYRICISTS

"Just Like a Woman," 1966
Bob Dylan
ROCK-iv, WOMAN

"Just My Imagination (Running Away With Me)," 1970
Norman Whitfield, Barrett Strong
MOTOWN

"Just One More Chance," 1931
Sam Coslow, Arthur Johnston
DEPRESSION YEARS, LUCK, RADIO, SINGERS, TABLE 15

"Just One of Those Things," 1935
Cole Porter
CHROMATICISM, COMPOSER-LYRICISTS, LANDMARKS OF STAGE AND SCREEN, MODE, TABLE 11, OCTAVE, SLANG, SOCIETY TEMPO

"Just Over the Hill," c. 1948
W. Herbert Brewster
GOSPEL

"Just the Two of Us," 1981
Ralph MacDonald, William Salter, Bill Withers
TABLE 10-q, TOGETHERNESS

"Just the Way You Are," 1977
Billy Joel
BALLAD, TABLE 10-a, TABLE 10-b, LENGTH, TABLE 15

"Just to See Her," 1987
Lou Pardini, Jimmy George
TABLE 10-o

"Just Too Many People," 1975
Melissa Manchester, Vini Poncia
WOMEN AS SONGWRITERS

"Just Walking in the Rain," 1953
Johnny Bragg, Robert S. Riley
WALKING, WEATHER

"Just You and I," 1975
Carole Bayer Sager, Melissa Manchester
WOMEN AS SONGWRITERS

"Just You Wait," 1956
Alan Jay Lerner/Frederick Loewe
HUMOR, WAITING

"Justify My Love," 1990
Lenny Kravitz, Madonna Ciccone
TELEVISION

"K-K-K-Katy," 1918
Geoffrey O'Hara
ALLITERATION, HUMOR, NAMES

"K-ra-zy for You," 1928
Ira Gershwin/George Gershwin
MADNESS

"Ka-lu-a," 1921
Anne Caldwell/Jerome Kern
BOOGIE-WOOGIE

"Kansas City," 1943
Oscar Hammerstein II/Richard Rodgers
TABLE 5

"Kansas City," 1959
Mike Stoller, Jerry Leiber
TABLE 5, ROCK 'N' ROLL

"Kaw-Liga," 1952
Fred Rose, Hank Williams
COUNTRY AND WESTERN

"Keep On Pushing," 1964
Curtis Mayfield
SOUL

"Keep On Truckin'," 1973
Frank Wilson, Anita Poree, Leonard Caston
DANCING

"Keep the Home Fires Burning," 1915
Lena Guilbert Ford/Ivor Novello
BOY, BRITAIN, FIRE, HOME, WORLD WARD I

"Keep Your Sunny Side Up," SEE **"Sunny Side Up"**

"Kentucky Babe," 1896
Richard Buck/Adam Geibel
GAY NINETIES

"Kids," 1960
Lee Adams/Charles Strouse
CHILDHOOD

"Killing Me Softly With His Song," 1972
Norman Gimbel, Charles Fox
TABLE 4-c, TABLE 10-a, TABLE 10-b, TABLE 10-e,
HARMONY, MUSIC, TABLE 15, TENDERNESS

"King of the Road," 1964
Roger Miller
TABLE 4-d, COUNTRY AND WESTERN, TABLE
10-e, TABLE 10-g, TABLE 10-r, TABLE 10-u
TABLE 10-w, STREETS, TRAINS

"King of the Whole Wide World," 1962
Ruth Batchelor, Bob Roberts
WOMEN AS SONGWRITERS

"King Porter Stomp," 1924
m. Ferdinand "Jelly Roll" Morton
DIXIELAND

"Der Kirmessbauer," SEE **"The Farmer in the Dell"**

"Kiss," 1986
Prince Rogers Nelson
TABLE 10-p, KISSING, ROCK-xii

"Kiss an Angel Good Morning," 1971
Ben Peters
ANGELS, COUNTRY AND WESTERN, TABLE
10-w

"Kiss and Say Goodbye," 1976
Winfred Lovett
FAREWELLS, KISSING

"A Kiss in the Dark," 1922
B. G. DeSylva/Victor Herbert
KISSING, LYRICISTS, NIGHT

"Kiss Me Again," 1905
Henry Blossom/Victor Herbert
KISSING

"Kiss of Fire," 1952
Lester Allen, Robert B. Hill (Eng.)/Angel G. Villoldo
BORROWING, FIRE, KISSING, TANGO

"A KISS TO BUILD A DREAM ON," 1935
Bert Kalmar, Harry Ruby, Oscar Hammerstein II
DREAMS, KISSING

"KISS YOU ALL OVER," 1978
Mike Chapman, Nicky Chinn
KISSING

"KISSES SWEETER THAN WINE," 1951
Paul Campbell (pseud. the Weavers)/Joel Newman
(pseud. Huddie Ledbetter)
COMPARATIVES, FOLK SONG, KISSING,
SWEETNESS

"KISSIN' TIME," 1959
Leonard Frazier, James Frazier
KISSING, ROCK 'N' ROLL-iii

"KITTEN ON THE KEYS," 1921
m. Zez Confrey
PIANO, RAGTIME

"KNIGHT MOVES," 1985
Suzanne Vega
WOMEN AS SONGWRITERS

"KNOCK ON WOOD," 1966
Eddie Floyd, Steve Cropper
DISCO, SOUL

"KNOCK THREE TIMES," 1970
Irwin Levine, L. Russell Brown
SINGING GROUPS

"KNOCKIN' ON HEAVEN'S DOOR," 1973
Bob Dylan
ROCK-iv

"KO KO MO, I LOVE YOU SO," 1955
Jake Porter, Eunice Levy, Forest Wilson
RHYTHM AND BLUES

"KODACHROME," 1973
Paul Simon
ROCK-v

"LA LA LA (MEANS I LOVE YOU)," 1968
William Hart/Thomas Bell
SINGING GROUPS

"LADY," 1980
Lionel Richie, Jr.
LADY, SHEET MUSIC, TABLE 15

"LADY BE GOOD," SEE **"OH, LADY BE GOOD"**

"THE LADY IN RED," 1935
Mort Dixon/Allie Wrubel
TABLE 7, RUMBA

"THE LADY IS A TRAMP," 1937
Lorenz Hart/Richard Rodgers
CATALOGUE SONG, FOX TROT, LADY, TABLE
11, SOCIETY TEMPO

"LADY MADONNA," 1968
John Lennon, Paul McCartney
LADY, ROCK-ii

"LADY MARMALADE," 1974
Kenny Nolan Helfman, Bob Crewe
LADY

"LADY OF SPAIN," 1931
Robert Hargreaves, Tolchard Evans, Stanley J.
Damerell, Henry B. Tisley
LADY, NATIONS

"LADY OF THE EVENING," 1922
Irving Berlin
LADY, REVUES, TABLE 14

"LADY, PLAY YOUR MANDOLIN," 1930
Irving Caesar/Oscar Levant
LADY

"THE LADY'S IN LOVE WITH YOU," 1939
Frank Loesser/Burton Lane
LADY

"LAKOTA," 1985
Joni Mitchell/Larry Klein
WOMEN AS SONGWRITERS

"LAMBETH WALK," 1937
Douglas Furber/Noel Gay (pseud. Reginald M.
Armitage)
BRITAIN, CITIES, TABLE 5, DANCE CRAZES,
TABLE 11, WALKING

"THE LAMP IS LOW," 1939
Mitchell Parish/Peter De Rose, Bert Shefter
CLASSICS, TABLE 6, FRANCE

"LARA'S THEME," SEE "SOMEWHERE MY LOVE"

"LAST DANCE," 1977
Paul Jabara
TABLE 1, DANCING, DISCO, TABLE 10-n, 10-q

"LAST DATE," 1960
Floyd Cramer
TABLE 4-d

"LAST NIGHT," 1961
The Mar-Keys
NIGHT

"LAST NIGHT I DIDN'T GET TO SLEEP AT ALL,"
SEE "I DIDN'T GET TO SLEEP AT ALL"

"LAST NIGHT ON THE BACK PORCH, I LOVED
HER BEST OF ALL," 1923
Lew Brown, Carl Schraubstader
NIGHT, SUPERLATIVES

"LAST NIGHT WHEN WE WERE YOUNG," 1936
E. Y. Harburg/Harold Arlen
AGE, NIGHT

"THE LAST ROUND-UP," 1933
Billy Hill
PICKUP, REVUES, TABLE 14

"THE LAST TIME I SAW PARIS," 1940
Oscar Hammerstein II/Jerome Kern
TABLE 1, CITIES, TABLE 5, LYRICISTS, TIME,
WORLD WAR II

"LAST TRAIN TO CLARKSVILLE," 1966
Tommy Boyce, Bobby Hart
TELEVISION, TRAINS

"LAUGH! CLOWN! LAUGH!," 1928
Sam M. Lewis, Joe Young/Ted Fiorito
CIRCUS

"LAUGHTER IN THE RAIN," 1974

Neil Sedaka, Phil Cody
TABLE 4-d, PERFORMER-SONGWRITERS,
SHEET MUSIC, WEATHER

"LAURA," 1945
Johnny Mercer/David Raksin
FILM MUSIC, TABLE 8, GOLDEN AGE, INTER-
VAL, LYRICISTS, NAMES

"LAWD, YOU MADE THE NIGHT TOO LONG,"
1932
Sam L. Lewis/Victor Young
HUMOR

"LAWDY MISS CLAWDY," 1952
Lloyd Price
NAMES, RHYTHM AND BLUES

"LAY DOWN SALLY," 1977
Eric Clapton, Marcy Levy, George Terry
ROCK-viii

"LAY DOWN YOUR ARMS," SEE "THE TEA LEAF
PROPHECY"

"LAY, LADY, LAY," 1969
Bob Dylan
ROCK-iv

"LAYLA," 1970
Eric Clapton, James Beck Gordon
ROCK-viii

"LAZY AFTERNOON," 1954
John Latouche/Jerome Moross
TIME OF DAY

"LAZY BONES," 1933
Johnny Mercer/Hoagy Carmichael
TABLE 3, CHILDHOOD

"LAZY RIVER," 1931
Hoagy Carmichael, Sidney Arodin
RIVERS

"LEADER OF THE PACK," 1964
Ellie Greenwich, Jeff Barry, George Morton
FRIENDSHIP, ROCK 'N' ROLL-iv, TOGETHER-
NESS

"LEAN ON ME," 1972
Bill Withers
TABLE 10-q

"LEANING ON A LAMP-POST," 1937
Noel Gay (pseud. Reginald M. Armitago)
ROCK-iii

"LEAVE IT ALL TO ME," 1987
Paul Anka, Alan Bergman, Marilyn Bergman
WOMEN AS SONGWRITERS

"LEAVE IT THERE," 1910
Charles A. Tindley
GOSPEL

"LEAVING ON A JET PLANE," 1967
John Denver (pseud. H. J. Deutschendorf, Jr.)
FADE-OUT, PERFORMER-SONGWRITERS,
TABLE 15, TRAVEL, VERSE

"LEGEND IN YOUR OWN TIME," 1971
Carly Simon
WOMEN AS SONGWRITERS

"LESSON IN SURVIVAL," 1972
Joni Mitchell
WOMEN AS SONGWRITERS

"LET A SMILE BE YOUR UMBRELLA (ON A RAINY DAY)," 1927
Irving Kahal, Francis Wheeler/Sammy Fain
DAY, SMILING, WEATHER

"LET ALONE BLUES," 1920
Anne Caldwell/Jerome Kern
WOMEN AS SONGWRITERS

"LET IT BE," 1970
John Lennon, Paul McCartney
TABLE 4-d, ROCK-ii

"LET IT BE ME," 1955
Mann Curtis (Eng.)/Gilbert Becaud
FRANCE

"LET IT SNOW! LET IT SNOW! LET IT SNOW!," 1945
Sammy Cahn/Jule Styne
CHRISTMAS, LYRICS, WEATHER

"LET IT WHIP," 1981
Leon Chancler, Reginald Andrews
TABLE 10-p

"LET ME BE THERE," 1973
John Rostill
TABLE 4-d, TABLE 10-t

"LET ME CALL YOU SWEETHEART (I'M IN LOVE WITH YOU)," 1910
Beth Slater Whitson/Leo Friedman
BARBERSHOP, DANCE CRAZES, SINGING
GROUPS, SWEETNESS, VAUDEVILLE, WALTZ

"LET ME ENTERTAIN YOU," 1959
Stephen Sondheim/Jule Styne
BROADWAY, LYRICISTS, TABLE 11

"LET ME GO DEVIL!," 1953
Jenny Lou Carson
WOMEN AS SONGWRITERS

"LET THE GOOD TIMES ROLL," 1946
Sam Theard, Fleecie Moore
TABLE 10-m, TIME

"LET THE GOOD TIMES ROLL," 1956
Leonard Lee
RHYTHM AND BLUES, ROCK 'N' ROLL

"LET THE REST OF THE WORLD GO BY," 1919
J. Keirn Brennan/Ernest R. Ball
WORLD

"LET THE RIVER RUN," 1988
Carly Simon
TABLE 1, RIVERS, WOMEN AS SONGWRITERS

"LET THE SUNSHINE IN," 1966
Gerome Ragni, James Rado/Galt MacDermot
TABLE 10-a, TABLE 10-h, OPERA, SINGING
GROUPS, WEATHER

"LET YOUR LOVE FLOW," 1976
Lawrence Williams
TABLE 4-d

"LET YOURSELF GO," 1936
Irving Berlin
TABLE 9

"LET'S ALL BE AMERICANS NOW," 1917
Irving Berlin
WORLD WAR I

"LET'S ALL SING LIKE THE BIRDIES SING," 1932
Robert Hargreaves, Stanley J. Damerell/Tolchard Evans
BIRDS

"LET'S BE BUDDIES," 1940
Cole Porter
FRIENDSHIP, TABLE 11, SLANG

"LET'S BEGIN," 1933
Otto Harbach/Jerome Kern
BEGINNING, TABLE 11

"LET'S CALL THE WHOLE THING OFF," 1937
Ira Gershwin/George Gershwin
TABLE 9, FOOD AND DRINK

"LET'S DANCE," 1935
Fanny Baldridge/Joseph Bonine, Gregory Stone
BIG BANDS, TABLE 3, DANCING, ROCK-x

"LET'S DO IT (LET'S FALL IN LOVE)," 1928
Cole Porter
ALLITERATION, ANIMALS, CATALOGUE SONG, CHROMATICISM, COMPOSER-LYRICISTS, CONTRACTIONS, FALLING IN LOVE, HUMOR, KEY, MUSICAL COMEDY, TABLE 11, ROARING TWENTIES, SOCIETY TEMPO

"LET'S FACE THE MUSIC AND DANCE," 1936
Irving Berlin
COMPOSER-LYRICISTS, CONTRACTIONS, DANCING, DEPRESSION YEARS, TABLE 9, MODE, MUSIC

"LET'S FALL IN LOVE," 1933
Ted Koehler/Harold Arlen
FALLING IN LOVE, TABLE 9

"LET'S GET AWAY FROM IT ALL," 1941
Thomas Adair/Matt Dennis
PLACES

"LET'S GO," 1979
Ric Ocasek
ROCK-xi

"LET'S GO CRAZY," 1984
Prince Rogers Nelson
ROCK-xii

"LET'S HANG ON (TO WHAT WE'VE GOT)," 1965
Bob Crewe, Sandy Linzer, Denny Randell
SINGING GROUPS

"LET'S HAVE ANOTHER CUP OF COFFEE," 1932
Irving Berlin
FOOD AND DRINK, TABLE 11

"LET'S LOCK THE DOOR (AND THROW AWAY THE KEY)," 1964
Roy Alfred, Wes Farrell
SINGING GROUPS

"LET'S PUT OUT THE LIGHTS (AND GO TO SLEEP)," 1932
Herman Hupfeld
DEPRESSION YEARS, RADIO, TABLE 14, SLEEP

"LET'S START THE NEW YEAR RIGHT," 1942
Irving Berlin
HOLIDAYS

"LET'S STAY TOGETHER," 1971
Willie Mitchell, Al Green, Al Jackson
SOUL, TOGETHERNESS

"LET'S TAKE AN OLD-FASHIONED WALK," 1948
Irving Berlin
WALKING, WALTZ

"LET'S TWIST AGAIN," 1961
Kal Mann, Dave Appell
DANCE CRAZES, TABLE 10-e

"THE LETTER," 1967
Wayne Carson Thompson
ROCK, WRITING

"LIDA ROSE," 1957
Meredith Willson
TABLE 11

"LIECHTENSTEINER POLKA," 1957
Edmund Kötscher, R. Lindt
POLKA

"LIES (ARE BREAKIN' MY HEART)," 1965
Buddy Randell, Beau Charles
ROCK

"LIFE IS JUST A BOWL OF CHERRIES," 1931
Lew Brown, Ray Henderson
DEPRESSION YEARS, FOOD AND DRINK, LIFE,
REVUES, TABLE 14

"LIFE, LOVE AND LAUGHTER," 1945
Ira Gershwin/Kurt Weill
LIFE

"LIGHT MY FIRE," 1967
John Densmore, Robert Krieger, Raymond Manzarek,
Jim Morrison (The Doors)
BASS LINE, FIRE, TABLE 10-g, ROCK-ix, TOP
FORTY

"LIKE A ROLLING STONE," 1965
Bob Dylan
PROTEST SONG, TOP FORTY

"LIKE A VIRGIN," 1984
Billy Steinberg, Tom Kelly
ROCK-xii, TABLE 15

"LIKE SOMEONE IN LOVE," 1944
Johnny Burke/James Van Heusen
LOVE

"LIKE YOUNG," 1958
Paul Francis Webster/André Previn
AGE

"LI'L DARLIN'," 1958
m. Neal Hefti
ARRANGEMENT

"LILACS IN THE RAIN," 1939
Mitchell Parish/Peter De Rose
ADAPTATION, FLOWERS, WEATHER

"LILI MARLEEN," 1940
Tommie Connor (Eng.)/Norbert Schultze
GERMANY, NAMES, WORLD WAR II

"LIMEHOUSE BLUES," 1922
Douglas Furber/Philip Braham
CITIES, TABLE 5

"LINDA," 1947
Ann Ronell
NAMES

**"THE LION SLEEPS TONIGHT," 1961; SEE ALSO
"WIMOWEH"**
Hugo Peretti, Luigi Creatore, George Weiss, Albert
Stanton
ANIMALS, BORROWING, SINGING GROUPS

"LIPSTICK ON YOUR COLLAR," 1959
Edna Lewis/George Goehring
CLOTHING, ROCK 'N' ROLL-iii, TABLE 15

"LISBON ANTIGUA (IN OLD LISBON)," 1954
Harry Dupree (Eng.)/Raul Portela
TABLE 5

"LISTEN TO WHAT THE MAN SAID," 1975
Paul McCartney, Linda McCartney
ROCK-ii

"LITTLE ALABAMA COON," 1893
Hattie Starr
WOMEN AS SONGWRITERS

"LITTLE ANNIE ROONEY," 1890
Michael Nolan
BRITAIN, GAY NINETIES, NAMES, SUBJECTS,
VAUDEVILLE, VERSE

**"A LITTLE BIT OF HEAVEN, SHURE THEY CALL
IT IRELAND," 1914**
J. Keirn Brennan/Ernest R. Ball
HEAVEN, IRELAND, NATIONS

"A LITTLE BIT OF LUCK," 1957
Alan Jay Lerner/Frederick Loewe
TABLE 12

"A LITTLE BIT OF SOAP," 1961
Bert Russell
SINGING GROUPS

"LITTLE DARLIN'," 1957
Maurice Williams
COVER, ENDEARMENT

"LITTLE DEVIL," 1961
Neil Sedaka, Howard Greenfield
ROCK 'N' ROLL

"THE LITTLE DRUMMER BOY," 1958
Harry Simeone, Henry Onorati, Katherine Davis
BOY, CHRISTMAS

"LITTLE GIRL BLUE," 1935
Lorenz Hart/Richard Rodgers
COLLABORATION, TABLE 7, GIRL, METER,
TABLE 11, SHOW TUNE, SINGERS, TABLE 15,
VERSE, WALTZ

"A LITTLE GOOD NEWS," 1983
Charlie Black, Rory Bourke, Thomas Rocco
TABLE 10-t

"LITTLE GREEN APPLES," 1968
Bobby Russell
TABLE 7, FOOD AND DRINK, TABLE 10-b,
TABLE 10-w

"LITTLE GREY HOME IN THE WEST," 1911
D. Eardley-Wilmot/Hermann Löhr
HOME

"THE LITTLE LOST CHILD," 1894
Edward B. Marks/Joseph W. Stern
GAY NINETIES

"(JUST) A LITTLE LOVE, A LITTLE KISS," 1912
Adrian Ross (Eng.)/Lao Silesu
KISSING

"LITTLE ME," 1962
Carolyn Leigh/Cy Coleman
WOMEN AS SONGWRITERS

"LITTLE OLD LADY," 1936
Stanley Adams/Hoagy Carmichael
LADY, TABLE 14

"A LITTLE ON THE LONELY SIDE," 1944
Dick Robertson, James Cavanaugh, Frank Weldon
LONELINESS

"A LITTLE PINK ROSE," 1906
Carrie Jacobs-Bond
WOMEN AS SONGWRITERS

"LITTLE RED CORVETTE," 1982
Prince Rogers Nelson
TRAVEL

"THE LITTLE SHOEMAKER," 1954
Geoffrey Parsons, John Turner (Eng.)/Rudi Revil
SINGING GROUPS

"LITTLE SISTER," 1961
Doc Pomus, Mort Shuman
ROCK 'N' ROLL

"LITTLE STAR," SEE "ESTRELLITA"

"LITTLE STAR," 1958
Arthur Venosa, Vito Picone
BORROWING, SINGING GROUPS

"A LITTLE STREET WHERE OLD FRIENDS MEET," 1932
Gus Kahn, Harry M. Woods
STREETS

"THE LITTLE THINGS YOU DO TOGETHER," 1970
Stephen Sondheim
TOGETHERNESS

"(IN MY) LITTLE TIN BOX," 1959
Sheldon Harnick/Jerry Bock
HUMOR

"THE LITTLE WHITE CLOUD THAT CRIED," 1951
Johnnie Ray
TABLE 7, CRYING, TABLE 15, SKY, WEATHER

"THE LITTLE WHITE DUCK," 1950
Walt Barroes, Bernard Zaritsky
BIRDS

"LITTLE WHITE LIES," 1930
Walter Donaldson
TABLE 3, TABLE 7, TABLE 15

"LIVE AND LET DIE," 1973
Paul McCartney, Linda McCartney
LIFE

"LIVE FOR LIFE," 1967
Norman Gimbell (Eng.)/Francis Lai
LIFE

"LIVE TO TELL," 1986
Madonna Ciccone, Pat Leonard
ROCK-xii

"LIVELY UP YOURSELF," 1975
Bob Marley
REGGAE

"LIVERY STABLE BLUES," 1916
Marvin Lee, Ray Lopez, Alcide Nunez
DIXIELAND

"LIVING FOR THE CITY," 1973
Stevie Wonder
TABLE 5, TABLE 10-o TABLE 10-q, LIFE

"LIVING IN AMERICA," 1985
Don Hartman, Charlie Midnight
TABLE 10-o, LIFE, NATIONS

**"LIZA (ALL THE CLOUDS'LL ROLL AWAY),"
1929**
Ira Gershwin, Gus Kahn/George Gershwin
CONTRACTIONS, NAMES, PIANO, SKY,
WEATHER

"THE LOCO-MOTION," 1962
Gerry Goffin, Carole King
ROCK 'N' ROLL

"LOLA," 1970
Ray Davies
NAMES, ROCK-iii

"LOLLIPOP," 1958
Julius Dixon, Beverly Ross
SINGING GROUPS, SWEETNESS

"LOLLIPOPS AND ROSES," 1960
Tony Velona
FLOWERS, FOOD AND DRINK, TABLE 10-d,
TABLE 15, SWEETNESS

"LONDON PRIDE," 1941
Noël Coward
TABLE 5, COMPOSER-LYRICISTS

"LONDONDERRY AIR," SEE "DANNY BOY"

"THE LONE FISH BALL," SEE "ONE MEAT BALL"

"(I'M JUST A) LONELY BOY," 1958
Paul Anka
BOY, LONELINESS, ROCK 'N' ROLL-iii

"LONELY BOY," 1977
Andrew Gold
BOY

"THE LONELY BULL," 1962
m. Sol Lake
BOLERO

"LONELY DAYS," 1970
Barry Gibb, Maurice Gibb, Robin Gibb
LONELINESS, ROCK-viii

"LONELY HOUSE," 1946
Langston Hughes/Kurt Weill
LONELINESS

"LONELY PEOPLE," 1974
Catherine Peek, Dan Peek
WOMEN AS SONGWRITERS

"LONELY TEARDROPS," 1958
Berry Gordy, Jr., Gwen Gordy, Tyran Carlo
CRYING, LONELINESS, MOTOWN, ROCK 'N'
ROLL-i, SOUL

"LONELY TOWN," 1945
Betty Comden, Adolph Green/Leonard Bernstein
LONELINESS, TABLE 11

"THE LONESOME ROAD," 1927
Gene Austin/Nathaniel Shilkret
STREETS

"LONESOME TOWN," 1958
Baker Knight
LONELINESS, ROCK 'N' ROLL-iii

"LONG AGO (AND FAR AWAY)," 1944
Ira Gershwin/Jerome Kern
COMPOSERS, TABLE 9, LYRICISTS, PLACES,
TABLE 15, TIME, WORLD WAR II

"The Long and Winding Road," 1970
John Lennon, Paul McCartney
TABLE 4-d, KEY, ROCK-ii, STREETS, TRAVEL

"Long Before I Knew You," 1956
Betty Comden, Adolph Green/Jule Styne
WOMEN AS SONGWRITERS

"Long Black Veil," 1959
Marijohn Wilkin, Danny Dill
COUNTRY AND WESTERN

"Long Lonely Nights," 1957
Lee Andrews, Bernice Davis, Douglas Henderson,
Mimi Uniman
LONELINESS, RHYTHM AND BLUES

"Long, Long Ago," 1833
Thomas Haynes Bayly
BORROWING

"Long Tall Sally," 1956
Enotris Johnson, Richard Penniman, Robert Blackwell
HEIGHT, NAMES, ROCK 'N' ROLL

"Look Away," 1988
Diane Warren
ROCK-ix

"Look Down, Look Down That Lonesome
Road," 1865
traditional American spiritual
FOLK SONG

"Look for the Silver Lining," 1920
B. G. DeSylva/Jerome Kern
TABLE 7, INSPIRATION, LYRICISTS, MUSICAL
COMEDY, TABLE 11, ROARING TWENTIES,
SKY, WEATHER

"Look of Love," 1964
Jeff Barry, Elie Greenwich
ROCK-iv

"The Look of Love," 1965
Hal David/Burt Bacharach
BOSSA NOVA, BRAZIL, COMPOSERS, TABLE 8,
LOVE, LYRICISTS

"Look to the Rainbow," 1947
E. Y. Harburg/Burton Lane
TABLE 11, RAINBOW

"Look What They've Done to My Song,
Ma," 1970
Melanie Safka
MOTHERS

"Lookin' Out My Back Door," 1970
John C. Fogerty
ROCK-ix

"Looking for a Boy," 1925
Ira Gershwin/George Gershwin
BOY

"Looks Like We Made It," 1976
Will Jennings/Richard Kerr
TABLE 15

"Lose Again," 1975
Karla Bonoff
WOMEN AS SONGWRITERS

"Losing My Mind," 1971
Stephen Sondheim
MADNESS, MIND, TABLE 11, THINKING

"Losing My Religion," 1991
Bill Berry, Peter Buck, Mike Mills, Michael Stipe
TABLE 10-h

"Lost in a Fog," 1934
Dorothy Fields/Jimmy McHugh
WEATHER

"Lost in the Fifties Tonight (In the Still
of the Night)," 1985
Troy Seals, Mike Reid, Frederick Parris
TABLE 10-u

"Lost in the Stars," 1946
Maxwell Anderson/Kurt Weill
STARS

"Lost Love," SEE "Beer Barrel Polka"

"A LOT OF LIVIN' TO DO," 1960
Lee Adams/Charles Strouse
LIFE, TABLE 11

"LOUIE LOUIE," 1963
Richard Berry
NAMES, ROCK-iii

"LOUISE," 1929
Leo Robin/Richard A. Whiting
LYRICISTS, NAMES

"LOUISIANA HAYRIDE," 1932
Howard Dietz/Arthur Schwartz
REVUES, TABLE 14, STATES

"LOVE," 1945
Hugh Martin, Ralph Blane
LOVE

"LOVE AND MARRIAGE," 1955
Sammy Cahn/James Van Heusen
LOVE, MARRIAGE, OCCASIONAL SONG,
TELEVISION

"THE LOVE BOAT," 1977
Paul Williams/Charles Fox
BOATING

"LOVE CAN BUILD A BRIDGE," 1991
Naomi Judd, John Jarvis, Paul Overstreet
TABLE 10-v, TABLE 10-w

"LOVE CAN MAKE YOU HAPPY," 1969
Jack Sigler, Jr.
HAPPINESS

"LOVE CHANGES EVERYTHING," 1988
Don Black, Charles Hart/Andrew Lloyd Webber
BRITAIN, LOVE, TABLE 12, PEDAL POINT,
TONALITY

"LOVE CHILD," 1968
Frank E. Wilson, Deke Richards, Pam Sawyer, R.
Dean Taylor
MOTOWN

"LOVE FOR SALE," 1930
Cole Porter
DEPRESSION YEARS, LOVE, MODE, TABLE 11,
SOCIETY TEMPO

"LOVE HANGOVER," 1976
Marilyn McLeod, Pamela Joan Sawyer
TABLE 15

"LOVE HER MADLY," 1971
Robert Krieger, Ray Manzarek, John Densmore
ROCK-ix

"LOVE HURTS," 1960
Boudleaux Bryant
ROCK 'N' ROLL-i

"LOVE IN BLOOM," 1934
Leo Robin, Ralph Rainger
TABLE 9, FLOWERS, LOVE, LYRICISTS, SING-
ERS, TABLE 15

"LOVE IS A BATTLEFIELD," 1983
Mike Chapman, Holly Knight
TABLE 10-i

"LOVE IS A HURTIN' THING," 1966
Ben Raleigh, Dave Linden
LOVE

"LOVE IS A MANY-SPLENDORED THING," 1955
Paul Francis Webster/Sammy Fain
TABLE 1, *BILLBOARD*, CLASSICS, TABLE 6,
TABLE 8, LOVE, SHEET MUSIC, TABLE 15

"LOVE IS A SIMPLE THING," 1952
June Carroll/Arthur Siegel
LOVE, REVUES, TABLE 14

"LOVE IS BLUE (L'AMOUR EST BLEU)," 1968
Bryan Blackburn (Eng.)/André Popp, Pierre Cour
TABLE 7, FRANCE, LOVE

"LOVE IS FOR THE VERY YOUNG," SEE **"THE BAD AND THE BEAUTIFUL"**

"LOVE IS HERE TO STAY," 1938
Ira Gershwin/George Gershwin
COMPOSERS, ENDURING LOVE, LOVE,
LYRICISTS, MOUNTAINS, SHOW TUNE

"LOVE IS JUST AROUND THE CORNER," 1934
Leo Robin, Lewis E. Gensler
TABLE 9, LOVE

"LOVE IS LIKE A FIREFLY," 1912
Otto Harbach/Rudolf Friml
LOVE, TABLE 13

"LOVE IS LIKE A VIOLIN," 1945
Miarka Laparcerie, Jimmy Kennedy
LOVE, STRINGS

"LOVE IS STRANGE," 1956
Mickey Baker, Ethel Smith
RHYTHM AND BLUES, ROCK 'N' ROLL

"LOVE IS SWEEPING THE COUNTRY," 1931
Ira Gershwin/George Gershwin
LOVE, MUSICAL PLAYS, TABLE 12

"LOVE IS THE SWEETEST THING," 1933
Ray Noble
TABLE 3, BRITAIN, TABLE 9, LOVE, SWEETNESS

"LOVE IS WHERE YOU FIND IT," 1948
Earl Brent/Nacio Herb Brown
TABLE 9, LOVE

"LOVE LETTERS," 1945
Edward Heyman, Victor Young
TABLE 8, LOVE, WRITING

"LOVE LETTERS IN THE SAND," 1931
Nick Kenny, Charles Kenny/J. Fred Coots
BORROWING, LOVE, TABLE 15, WRITING

"LOVE, LOOK AWAY," 1958
Oscar Hammerstein II/Richard Rodgers
LOVE

"LOVE! LOVE! LOVE!," 1956
Teddy McRae, Sid Syche, Sunny David (The Clovers)
RHYTHM AND BLUES

"LOVE MAKES A WOMAN," 1968
Eugene Record, William Sanders, Carl Davis
SOUL

"LOVE MAKES THE WORLD GO 'ROUND (THEME FROM CARNIVAL!)," 1961
Bob Merrill
CIRCUS, LOVE, TABLE 11, WORLD

"LOVE ME DO," 1962
John Lennon, Paul McCartney
LOVE, POPULAR SONG-viii, ROCK-ii

"LOVE ME OR LEAVE ME," 1928
Gus Kahn/Walter Donaldson
ALLITERATION, LOVE, TABLE 11, ROARING TWENTIES, TABLE 15, TORCH SONG

"LOVE ME TENDER," 1956
Vera Matson, Elvis Presley
TABLE 4-d, BORROWING, TABLE 8, KEY, LOVE, POPULAR SONG-viii, SINGERS, TABLE 15, TENDERNESS

"LOVE ME WITH ALL YOUR HEART (CUANDO CALIENTE EL SOL)," 1961
Michael Vaughn (Eng.)/Carlos Rigual
TABLE 2, BOLERO, LOVE, MEXICO, RANGE

"THE LOVE NEST," 1920
Otto Harbach/Louis A. Hirsch
LOVE, TABLE 11, RADIO

"LOVE ON THE ROCKS," 1980
Neil Diamond, Gilbert Becaud
LOVE

"LOVE OVERBOARD," 1987
Reggie Calloway
TABLE 10-p

"LOVE POTION NUMBER NINE," 1959
Mike Stoller, Jerry Leiber
ROCK 'N' ROLL

"LOVE POWER," 1987
Carole Bayer Sager/Burt Bacharach
WOMEN AS SONGWRITERS

"LOVE SOMEBODY," 1947
Joan Whitney, Alex Kramer
WOMEN AS SONGWRITERS

"(WHERE DO I BEGIN) LOVE STORY," 1970
Carl Sigman/Francis Lai
BEGINNING, TABLE 8, INTERVAL, RELEASE, SEQUENCE, TABLE 15

"LOVE THEME FROM *THE GODFATHER*," SEE
"SPEAK SOFTLY LOVE"

"LOVE THEME FROM *LADY SINGS THE BLUES*,"
SEE "HAPPY"

"LOVE THEME FROM *ROMEO AND JULIET*," SEE
"A TIME FOR US"

"LOVE THEME FROM *ST. ELMO'S FIRE* (FOR
JUST A MOMENT)," 1985
Cynthia Weil/David Foster
TABLE 8

"LOVE THEME FROM *A STAR IS BORN*," SEE
"EVERGREEN"

"LOVE THEME FROM *SUPERMAN*," SEE "CAN
YOU READ MY MIND?"

"LOVE THEME FROM *TOP GUN*," SEE "TAKE
MY BREATH AWAY"

"LOVE THY NEIGHBOR," 1934
Mack Gordon/Harry Revel
LOVE

"LOVE TO LOVE YOU BABY," 1976
Peter Bellotte, Donna Summer, Giorgio Moroder
BABY, DISCO, LOVE

"LOVE TRAIN," 1972
Kenny Gamble, Leon Huff
LOVE, TRAINS

"LOVE WALKED IN," 1938
Ira Gershwin/George Gershwin
BROKEN CHORD, COMPOSERS, LOVE, WALK-
ING

"LOVE—WHAT ARE YOU DOING TO MY
HEART?," 1933
Tibor Barczi, Samuel M. Lewis
TABLE 2, LOVE, TANGO

"LOVE WILL KEEP US TOGETHER," 1975
Howard Greenfield, Neil Sedaka
TABLE 4-d, TABLE 10-a, LOVE, TOGETHERNESS

"LOVE WON'T LET ME WAIT," 1974
Vinnie Barrett, Bobby Eli
WAITING

"THE LOVE YOU SAVE," 1970
Berry Gordy, Jr., Fonce Mizell, Deke Richards,
Freddie Perren
MOTOWN, SOUL

"LOVE, YOUR MAGIC SPELL IS EVERYWHERE,"
1929
Elsie Janis/Edmund Goulding
TABLE 8, LOVE, MAGIC

"THE LOVELIEST NIGHT OF THE YEAR," 1950
Paul Francis Webster/Irving Aaronson
BEAUTY, TABLE 6, TABLE 9, MEXICO, NIGHT

"LOVELY LADY," 1935
Ted Koehler/Jimmy McHugh
BEAUTY, TABLE 9, LADY

"LOVELY TO LOOK AT," 1935
Dorothy Fields, Jimmy McHugh/Jerome Kern
ALLITERATION, BEAUTY, LENGTH, TABLE 11,
RANGE, WOMEN AS SONGWRITERS

"A LOVELY WAY TO SPEND AN EVENING,"
1943
Harold Adamson/Jimmy McHugh
BEAUTY

"LOVER" 1933
Lorenz Hart/Richard Rodgers
CHROMATICISM, TABLE 9, GOLDEN AGE,
LOVER, RANGE, SCALE, SINGERS, TABLE 15,
WALTZ

"LOVER, COME BACK TO ME!," 1928
Oscar Hammerstein II/Sigmund Romberg
TABLE 3, TABLE 6, HUNGARY, LOVER, OPER-
ETTA, TABLE 13

"LOVER MAN (OH WHERE CAN YOU BE?),"
1942
Jimmy Davis, Roger "Ram" Ramirez, Jimmy Sherman
BEBOP, CROSSOVER, LOVER, MAN, TORCH
SONG, WORLD WAR II

"LOVER, PLEASE," 1961
Billy Swan
TABLE 10-v, LOVER, ROCK 'N' ROLL

"A LOVER'S CONCERTO," 1965
Denny Randell, Sandy Linzer
TABLE 6, LOVER, MUSIC, SINGING GROUPS

"A LOVER'S QUESTION," 1958
Brook Benton, Jimmy Williams
QUESTIONS, RHYTHM AND BLUES

"LOVE'S OWN SWEET SONG (SARI WALTZ)," 1914
C. C. S. Cushing, E. P. Heath (Eng.)/Emmerich Kalmán
AUSTRIA, TABLE 13, SWEETNESS

"LOVE'S ROUNDELAY," 1908
Joseph W. Herbert (Eng.)/Oscar Straus
TABLE 13

"LOVE'S THEME," 1973
Barry White
TABLE 4-d

"LOVEY DOVEY," 1954
Ahmet Ertegun, Memphis Curtis
RHYTHM AND BLUES

"LOVIN' YOU LOVIN' ME," 1970
Bonnie Bramlett, Eric Clapton
WOMEN AS SONGWRITERS

"LOVING HER WAS EASIER (THAN ANYTHING I'LL EVER DO AGAIN)," 1970
Kris Kristofferson
COUNTRY AND WESTERN

"LOVING YOU," 1957
Jerry Leiber, Mike Stoller
ROCK 'N' ROLL

"LOWDOWN," 1976
Boz Scaggs, David Paich
TABLE 10-q, ROCK

"LUBLY FAN," SEE "BUFFALO GALS (WON'T YOU COME OUT TONIGHT?)"

"LUCILLE," 1976
Roger Bowling, Hal Bynum
TABLE 4-d, TABLE 10-u, NAMES

"LUCK BE A LADY," 1950
Frank Loesser
LADY, LUCK, TABLE 11

"LUCKY DAY," 1926
B. G. DeSylva, Lew Brown/Ray Henderson
DAY, LUCK, REVUE, TABLE 14

"LUCKY LIPS," 1957
Jerry Leiber, Mike Stoller
TABLE 2, LUCK, ROCK 'N' ROLL

"LUCKY STAR," 1983
Madonna Ciccone
LUCK, ROCK-xii

"LUCKY TO BE ME," 1944
Betty Comden, Adolph Green/Leonard Bernstein
CABARET, COLLABORATION, LUCK, LYRICISTS, TABLE 11, WOMEN AS SONGWRITERS

"LUCY IN THE SKY WITH DIAMONDS," 1967
John Lennon, Paul McCartney
JEWELRY, NAMES, ROCK-ii, SKY

"LUKA," 1987
Suzanne Vega
WOMEN AS SONGWRITERS

"LULLABY IN RHYTHM," 1938
Walter Hirsch/Benny Goodman, Edgar Sampson, Clarence Profit
RHYTHM

"LULLABY OF BIRDLAND," 1952
George Shearing, George Weiss
BIRDS, TABLE 4-d, CROSSOVER, NEW YORK CITY, PIANO, SLEEP

"LULLABY OF BROADWAY," 1935
Al Dubin/Harry Warren
TABLE 1, BROADWAY, COLLABORATION, COMPOSERS, TABLE 9, LENGTH, LYRICISTS, RHYTHM, SLEEP, SOCIETY TEMPO, TORCH SONG, VAMP

"Lullaby of the Leaves," 1932
Joe Young/Bernice Petkere
MODE, TREES

"Lulu's Back in Town," 1935
Al Dubin/Harry Warren
NAMES

"Lyin' Eyes," 1975
Don Henley, Glenn Frey
TABLE 2, TABLE 10-h, ROCK-x

"M*A*S*H," see "Song From M*A*S*H"

"M-I-S-S-I-S-S-I-P-P-I," 1916
Bert Hanlon, Ben Ryan/Harry Tierney
RIVERS, VAMP

"M-O-T-H-E-R (A Word That Means the World to Me)," 1915
Howard Johnson/Theodore F. Morse
MOTHERS

"Ma! (He's Making Eyes at Me)," 1921
Sidney Clare/Con Conrad
TABLE 2, MOTHERS

"MacArthur Park," 1968
Jim Webb
TABLE 5, COMPOSER-LYRICISTS, TABLE 10-v, LENGTH, TONALITY

"Macho Man" 1978
Henri Belolo, Victor Willis, Peter Whitehead (Eng.)/Jacques Morali
DISCO, MAN

"Mack the Knife (Moritat), (Theme From The Threepenny Opera)," 1928 (Ger.), 1952 (Eng.)
Marc Blitzstein (Eng.)/Kurt Weill
COMPOSERS, GERMANY, TABLE 10-a, TABLE 10-c, INTERVAL, MONEY, OPERA, ROCK 'N' ROLL-iii, SINGERS, TABLE 15

"MacNamara's Band," 1914
John J. Stamford/Shaumus O'Connor
IRELAND

"Mad About the Boy," 1935
Noël Coward
BOY, COMPOSER-LYRICISTS, MADNESS, MODE

"Mad Dogs and Englishmen," 1931
Noël Coward
ANIMALS, COMPOSER-LYRICISTS, HUMOR, MADNESS, NATIONS, REVUES, TABLE 14

"Madelon," 1918
Alfred Bryan (Eng.)/Camille Robert
FRANCE

"Mademoiselle de Paree," 1948
Mitchell Parish (Eng.)/Paul Durang
TABLE 5, FRANCE, WOMAN

"Mad'moiselle From Armentières," see "Hinky Dinky Parlay Voo"

"Maggie May," 1971
Rod Stewart, Martin Quittenton
ROCK-x

"Maggie's Farm," 1965
Bob Dylan
NAMES, ROCK-iv

"Magic," 1980
John Farrar
MAGIC, TABLE 15

"Magic Is the Moonlight," 1930
Charles Pasquale (Eng.)/Maria Grever
ALLITERATION, BOLERO, MAGIC, MEXICO, MOON, WOMEN AS SONGWRITERS

"Magic Man," 1976
Ann Wilson, Nancy Wilson
WOMEN AS SONGWRITERS

"Magic Moments," 1957
Hal David, Burt F. Bacharach
MAGIC, RECORDING, TIME, TRIPLET

"Magic Town," 1965
Barry Mann, Cynthia Weil
WOMEN AS SONGWRITERS

"MAHOGANY," SEE "THEME FROM MAHOGANY"

"MAIRZY DOATS," 1943
Milton Drake, Al Hoffman, Jerry Livingston
ANIMALS, NONSENSE, NOVELTY SONG

"MAKE BELIEVE," 1927
Oscar Hammerstein II/Jerome Kern
COMPOSERS, DIALECT, IMAGINATION,
LANDMARKS OF STAGE AND SCREEN, MUSI-
CAL PLAYS, TABLE 12, OPERA, VERSE

"MAKE IT ANOTHER OLD-FASHIONED, PLEASE,"
1940
Cole Porter
FOOD AND DRINK

"MAKE IT EASY ON YOURSELF," 1962
Hal David/Burt F. Bacharach
SOUL

"MAKE LOVE TO ME," 1953
Bill Norvas, Allan Copeland/Leon Rappolo, Paul
Mares, Benny Pollack, George Brunies, Mel Stitzel,
Walter Melrose
TABLE 15

"MAKE ME A STAR," SEE "BLUE MOON"

"MAKE ME RAINBOWS," 1967
Alan Bergman, Marilyn Bergman/John Williams
WOMEN AS SONGWRITERS

"MAKE ME SMILE," 1969
James Pankow
ROCK-ix

"MAKE SOMEONE HAPPY," 1960
Betty Comden, Adolph Green/Jule Styne
COLLABORATION, COUNTERMELODY,
LYRICISTS, TABLE 11, VAMP, WOMEN AS
SONGWRITERS

"MAKE THE WORLD GO AWAY," 1963
Hank Cochran
TABLE 4-d, COUNTRY AND WESTERN, WORLD

"MAKIN' WHOOPEE," 1928
Gus Kahn/Walter Donaldson
CONTRACTIONS, KEY, LYRICISTS, TABLE 11,
SLANG

"MAKING OUR DREAMS COME TRUE," 1976
Norman Gimbel/Charles Fox
DREAMS, TELEVISION

"MAMA," 1946
Harold Barlow, Phil Brito (Eng)/C. A. Bixio
MOTHERS

"MAMA CAN'T BUY YOU LOVE," 1977
Leroy Bell, Casey James
MOTHER, ROCK-x

"MAMA HE'S CRAZY," 1983
Kenny O'Dell
TABLE 10-v

"MAMA INEZ," 1931
L. Wolfe Gilbert (Eng.)/Eliseo Grenet
CUBA, MOTHERS, RUMBA

"MAMA TOLD ME (NOT TO COME)," 1966
Randy Newman
MOTHERS, ROCK

"MAMA TRIED," 1968
Merle Haggard
COUNTRY AND WESTERN, MOTHERS

"MAMA YO QUIERO (I WANT MY MAMA),"
1940
Al Stillman (Eng.)/Jararaca Paiva, Vincente Paiva
BROKEN CHORD, MOTHERS, PICKUP

"MAMBO ITALIANO," 1954
Bob Merrill
MAMBO

"MAMBO JAMBO," 1950
Raymond Karl, Charlie Towne (Eng.)/Perez Prado
CUBA, MAMBO

"MAME," 1966
Jerry Herman
TABLE 11, NAMES

"MAMIE, COME KISS YOUR HONEY," 1893
May Irwin
WOMEN AS SONGWRITERS

"MAMIE REILLY," 1897
Maude Nugent
WOMEN AS SONGWRITERS

"MAMMAS DON'T LET YOUR BABIES GROW UP
TO BE COWBOYS," 1975
Ed Bruce, Patsy Bruce
TABLE 10-v

"MAM'SELLE," 1947
Mack Gordon/Edmund Goulding
TABLE 8, FOREIGN LANGUAGE, TABLE 15,
WOMAN

"A MAN," 1974
Buffy Sainte-Marie
WOMEN AS SONGWRITERS

"A MAN AND A WOMAN," 1966
Jerry Keller (Eng.)/Francis Lai
BOSSA NOVA, CHROMATICISM, CODA, TABLE
8, INTERNAL, MAN, METER, WOMAN

"THE MAN I LOVE," 1924
Ira Gershwin/George Gershwin
BLUE NOTE, COMPOSERS, DAYS OF THE
WEEK, INTERVAL, LOVE, LYRICISTS, MAN,
MELODY, SINGERS, TABLE 15

"MAN OF LA MANCHA," 1965
Joe Darion/Mitch Leigh
TABLE 12

"THE MAN ON THE FLYING TRAPEZE," 1933;
SEE ALSO "THE DARING YOUNG MAN (ON
THE FLYING TRAPEZE)"
Walter O'Keefe
CIRCUS

"THE MAN THAT GOT AWAY," 1954
Ira Gershwin/Harold Arlen
COMPOSERS, LYRICISTS, MAN, SINGERS,
TABLE 15, TORCH SONG

"THE MAN WHO BROKE THE BANK AT MONTE
CARLO," 1892
Fred Gilbert
MAN

"MAN WITH THE BANJO," 1953
Robert Mellin (Eng.)/Fritz Schulz
MAN, SINGING GROUPS

"A MAN WITHOUT LOVE," 1968
Barry Mason (Eng.)/R. Livraghi, D. Pace, M. Panzeri
ITALY, MAN

"MANAGUA NICARAGUA," 1946
Albert Gamse/Irving Fields
TABLE 5, RUMBA

"MAÑANA (IS SOON ENOUGH FOR ME)," 1948
Peggy Lee, David Barbour
DAY, PERFORMER-SONGWRITERS, SAMBA,
SINGERS, TABLE 15, WOMEN AS
SONGWRITERS

"MANDY," 1919
Irving Berlin
LENGTH, NAMES, POPULAR SONG-iii, TABLE
14

"MANDY," 1971
Scott English, Richard Kerr
TABLE 4-d, NAMES, TABLE 15, TONALITY

"MANDY LEE," 1899
Thurland Chattaway
GAY NINETIES

"MANHA DE CARNAVAL," SEE "A DAY IN THE
LIFE OF A FOOL"

"MANHATTAN," 1925
Lorenz Hart/Richard Rodgers
TABLE 5, GOLDEN AGE, PLACES, REVUES,
TABLE 14

"MANHATTAN MELODRAMA," SEE "BLUE MOON"

"MANHATTAN SERENADE," 1928
Harold Adamson/Louis Alter
TABLE 5, MUSIC

"EL MANICERO," SEE "THE PEANUT VENDOR"

"MANY A NEW DAY," 1943
Oscar Hammerstein II/Richard Rodgers
DAY

"Maple Leaf Rag," 1899
m. Scott Joplin
RAGTIME

"March of the Musketeers," 1928
P. G. Wodehouse, Cliford Grey/Rudolf Friml
MARCH, TABLE 13

"The March of the Toys," 1903
Glen MacDonough/Victor Herbert
MARCH

"Marcheta," 1913
Victor Schertzinger
TABLE 6, OPERA

"Marching Along Together," 1933
Mort Dixon, Edward Pola, Franz K. W. Steininger
BRITAIN, MARCH, TOGETHERNESS

"Margaritaville," 1977
Jimmy Buffett
TABLE 4-d

"Margie," 1920
Benny Davis/Con Conrad, J. Russel Robinson
NAMES

"Maria," 1957
Stephen Sondheim/Leonard Bernstein
LANDMARKS OF STAGE AND SCREEN, LYRI-
CISTS, MUSICAL PLAYS, TABLE 12, OPERA

"Maria Elena," 1933
S. K. Russell (Eng.)/Lorenzo Barcelata
TABLE 3, TABLE 4-d, TABLE 8, MEXICO, NAMES

"Marianne," 1928
Oscar Hammerstein II/Sigmund Romberg
NAMES, TABLE 13, PICKUP

"Marianne," 1955
Richard Dehr, Frank Miller, Terry Gilkyson
CALYPSO, NAMES

"Marie," 1928
Irving Berlin
TABLE 3, NAMES, RADIO

"Marie From Sunny Italy," 1907
Irving Berlin/Nick Nicholson
COMPOSER-LYRICISTS

"Marieke," 1968
Eric Blau (Eng.)/Jacques Brel, Gerard Jouannest
BELGIUM, CABARET, FOREIGN LANGUAGE,
METER, TONALITY

"The Marine's Hymn," 1919
attributed to L.Z. Phillips/Jacques Offenbach (1868)
CLASSICS, TABLE 6, OPERA, PATRIOTISM

"Marlene on the Wall," 1985
Suzanne Vega
WOMEN AS SONGWRITERS

"Marmalade, Molasses and Honey," 1972
Alan Bergman, Marilyn Bergman/Maurice Jarre
WOMEN AS SONGWRITERS

"Marrakesh Express," 1969
Graham Nash
TABLE 5, ROCK-v

"Married I Can Always Get," 1956
Gordon Jenkins
MARRIAGE

"Marrying for Love," 1950
Irving Berlin
MARRIAGE

"Marta," 1931
L. Wolfe Gilbert (Eng.)/Moises Simon
RADIO

"The Marvelous Toy," 1961
Tom Paxton
PROTEST SONG

"Mary's a Grand Old Name," 1905
George M. Cohan
AABA, BROKEN CHORD, COMPOSER-LYRI-
CISTS, FORM, MUSICAL COMEDY, TABLE 11,
NAMES

"(The Lights Went Out in) Massachusetts," 1967

Barry Gibb, Robin Gibb, Maurice Gibb
ROCK-viii, STATES

"MASTER OF EYES," 1973
Bernie Hart, Aretha Franklin
TABLE 10-n

"MASTER OF THE HOUSE," 1985
Herbert Kretzmer (Eng.)/Claude-Michel Schönberg
FRANCE

"MASTERS OF WAR," 1963
Bob Dylan
FOLK SONG

"MATCHBOX," 1957
Carl Perkins
ROCKABILLY

"MATCHMAKER, MATCHMAKER," 1964
Sheldon Harnick/Jerry Bock
MARRIAGE, TABLE 12

"MATERIAL GIRL," 1984
Peter Brown, Robert Rans
GIRL, ROCK-xii

"MATERNA," SEE "AMERICA THE BEAUTIFUL"

"MATILDA, MATILDA," 1953
Harry Thomas
CALYPSO, NAMES

"MAXIM'S," 1907
Adrian Ross (Eng.)/Franz Lehár
AUSTRIA, OPERETTA, TABLE 13

"MAYBE," 1926
Ira Gershwin/George Gershwin
TABLE 11

"MAYBE," 1958
George Goldner
ROCK-iv

"MAYBE I KNOW," 1964
Ellie Greenwich, Jeff Barry
ROCK 'N' ROLL-iv

"MAYBE NOT AT ALL," 1925
Ethel Waters/Sydney Easton
WOMEN AS SONGWRITERS

"MAYBE THIS TIME," 1966
Fred Ebb/John Kander
TABLE 15, TIME, TRIPLET

"MAYBELLINE," 1955
Chuck Berry, Russel D. Frato, Alan Freed
BMI, NAMES, ROCK 'N' ROLL-i

"ME AND BOBBY MCGEE," 1969
Kris Kristofferson, Fred L. Foster
COUNTRY AND WESTERN, NAMES, ROCK-vi

"ME AND MARIE," 1935
Cole Porter
BILLBOARD

"ME AND MRS. JONES," 1972
Kenny Gamble, Leon Huff, Cary Gilbert
TABLE 10-o, NAMES, SOUL

"ME AND MY GIRL," 1937
Douglas Furber/Noel Gay
BRITAIN, GIRL, TABLE 11

"ME AND MY SHADOW," 1927
Billy Rose/Al Jolson, Dave Dreyer
SINGERS

"ME LO DIJO ADELA," SEE "SWEET AND GENTLE"

"MEADOWLANDS," 1939
Olga Paul (Eng.)/Lev Knipper
RUSSIA

"MEAN STEPMAMA BLUES," 1967
Bobbie Gentry
c.WOMEN AS SONGWRITERS

"MEAN TO ME," 1929
Roy Turk, Fred E. Ahlert
TABLE 15

"MEDITATION (MEDITACÁO)," 1962
Norman Gimbel (Eng.)/Antonio Carlos Jobim, Newton Mendonca
BOSSA NOVA, BRAZIL, THINKING

"Meet Me in St. Louis, Louis," 1904
Andrew B. Sterling/Kerry Mills
CITIES, TABLE 5, FORM, MEETING, WALTZ

"Meet Me Tonight in Dreamland," 1909
Beth Slater Whitson/Leo Friedman
DREAMS, MEETING, TABLE 15

"Melancholy," SEE "My Melancholy Baby"

"Mellow Yellow," 1966
Donovan Leitch
TABLE 7, ROCK-v

"Melodie d'Amour," 1957
Leo Johns (Eng.)/Henri Salvador
CALYPSO, FOREIGN LANGUAGE, MELODY

"Melody," SEE "It's All in the Game"

"A Melody From the Sky," 1935
Sidney D. Mitchell, Louis Alter
TABLE 8, MELODY, SKY

"Melody of Love," 1954
Tom Glazer/H. Engelmann
SINGING GROUPS

"Memories," 1915
Gus Kahn/Egbert Van Alstyne
LYRICISTS, MEMORY

"Memories Are Made of This," 1955
Terry Gilkyson, Richard Dehr, Frank Miller
TABLE 4-d, TABLE 9, MEMORY, TABLE 15

"Memories of You," 1930
Andy Razaf/Eubie Blake
MEMORY, REVUE, TABLE 14

"Memory," 1981
Trevor Nunn after T. S. Eliot/Andrew Lloyd Webber
AABA, DYNAMICS, MEMORY, METER, TABLE 12, RANGE, TABLE 15, TONALITY, TRIPLET

"The Memphis Blues," 1912
George A. Norton/William Christopher Handy
BLUES, TABLE 15, TIN PAN ALLEY

"La Mer," SEE "Beyond the Sea"

"Mercedes Benz," 1970
Janis Joplin/Michael McClure
WOMEN AS SONGWRITERS

"Merrily We Roll Along," SEE "Good Night Ladies"

"The Merry-Go-Round Broke Down," 1937
Cliff Friend, Dave Franklin
CIRCUS

"The Merry Widow Waltz (I Love You So)," 1907
Adrian Ross (Eng.)/Franz Lehár
ART SONG, AUSTRIA, DANCE CRAZES, HUNGARY, OPERETTA, TABLE 13, WALTZ

"A Mess o' Blues," 1960
Doc Pomus, Mort Shuman
ROCK 'N' ROLL

"Message to Michael," 1963
Hal David/Burt F. Bacharach
NAMES, RHYTHM AND BLUES

"Mexicali Rose," 1923
Helen Stone/Jack B. Tenny
TABLE 5, RADIO

"Mexican Hat Dance (Popular Jarabe Tapatio)," 1919
m. arr. F. A. Partichela
MEXICO

"Mexican Joe," 1953
Mitchell Torok
NATIONS

"(My Heart's in) Mexico," 1961
Boudleaux Bryant, Felice Bryant/Boudleaux Bryant
NATIONS

"Miami Beach Rumba," 1946
Albert Gamse (Eng.)/Irving Fields
TABLE 5, RUMBA, WATERFRONT

"MIAMI VICE THEME," 1984
m. Jan Hammer
TABLE 5, TELEVISION

"MICHAEL FROM MOUNTAINS," 1967
Joni Mitchell
WOMEN AS SONGWRITERS

"MICHAEL (ROW THE BOAT ASHORE)," 1960
Dave Fisher
BOATING, FOLK SONG, RELIGION, SINGING
GROUPS

"MICHELLE," 1966
John Lennon, Paul McCartney
TABLE 4-b, BRITAIN, COLLABORATION,
FOREIGN LANGUAGE, TABLE 10-b, NAMES,
PERFORMER-SONGWRITERS, ROCK-ii, TONAL-
ITY

"MICKEY," 1979
Nicky Chinn, Mike Chapman
TELEVISION

"MIDNIGHT BLUE," 1974
Melissa Manchester, Carole Bayer Sager/Melissa
Manchester
TABLE 4-d, TABLE 7, TIME OF DAY, WOMEN AS
SONGWRITERS

"MIDNIGHT COWBOY," 1969
Jacob Gold/John Barry
TABLE 8, TIME OF DAY

"MIDNIGHT FLYER," 1959
Mayme Watts, Robert Mosley
TABLE 10-e

**"MIDNIGHT IN MOSCOW (MOSCOVIAN
NIGHTS)," 1961**
Kenny Ball, Jan Burgers
BORROWING, TABLE 5, RUSSIA, TIME OF DAY

"MIDNIGHT SUN," 1947
Johnny Mercer/Sonny Burke, Lionel Hampton
LYRICISTS, SUN, TIME OF DAY

**"MIDNIGHT TRAIN TO GEORGIA (MIDNIGHT
PLANE TO HOUSTON)," 1971**
Jim Weatherly
TABLE 10-p, TIME OF DAY, TRAINS

"MIGHTY LAK' A ROSE," 1901
Frank L. Stanton/Ethelbert Nevin
ART SONG, BARBERSHOP, DIALECT, FLOWERS

"MILENBERG JOYS," 1925
Walter Melrose/Leon Rappolo, Paul Mares, Ferdinand
"Jelly Roll" Morton
DIXIELAND

"MIMI," 1932
Lorenz Hart/Richard Rodgers
TABLE 9, TEMPO

"MINE," 1933
Ira Gershwin/George Gershwin
COUNTERPOINT, INTERVAL

"MINNIE THE MOOCHER," 1931
Cab Calloway, Irving Mills, Clarence Gaskill
BORROWING, MONEY, NAMES

"THE MINSTREL-BOY," 1813
Thomas Moore/based on "The Moreen"
POPULAR SONG-i

"MINUTE BY MINUTE," 1978
Lester Abrams/Lester Abrams, Michael McDonald
TABLE 10-h, TIME

"MIRACLES," 1975
Marty Balin (pseud. Martyn Buchwald)
ROCK-vi

"MISIRLOU," 1941
Milton Leeds, S. K. Russell, Fred Wise/R. N.
Roubanis
BOLERO, GREECE, MODALITY, RUMBA

**"MISS OTIS REGRETS (SHE'S UNABLE TO LUNCH
TODAY)," 1934**
Cole Porter
CABARET, NAMES

"MISS YOU," 1978
Mick Jagger, Keith Richards
ROCK-iii

"MISSION: IMPOSSIBLE," 1966
m. Lalo Shifrin
TELEVISION

"MISSIONARY MAN," 1986
Annie Lennox, Dave Stewart
TABLE 10-l

"MISSISSIPPI DELTA," 1967
Bobbie Gentry
WOMEN AS SONGWRITERS

"MISSISSIPPI GODDAM!," 1964
Nina Simone
WOMEN AS SONGWRITERS

"MISSISSIPPI MUD," 1927
Harry Barris, James Cavanaugh
RIVERS

"THE MISSOURI WALTZ (HUSH-A-BYE MA
BABY)," 1914
James Royce Shannon/John Valentine Eppel, arranged
by Frederick Knight Logan
SHEET MUSIC, STATES, WALTZ

"MRS. BROWN, YOU'VE GOT A LOVELY
DAUGHTER," 1964
Trevor Peacock
ROCK-iii

"MRS. ROBINSON," 1968
Paul Simon
TABLE 4-b, FILM MUSIC, TABLE 8, FOLK ROCK,
TABLE 10-a, TABLE 10-h, NAMES, ROCK-v,
VERSE

"MR. BIG STUFF," 1971
Joseph Broussard, Ralph G. Williams, Carrol Washington
SOUL

"MR. BLUE," 1959
DeWayne Blackwell
TABLE 7, SINGING GROUPS

"MR. BOJANGLES," 1968
Jerry Jeff Walker
TABLE 4-d, NAMES, NOVELTY SONG

"MISTER JOHNSON, TURN ME LOOSE," 1896
Ben R. Harney
COON SONG, SLANG

"MR. LEE," 1957
Heather Dixon, Helen Gathers, Emma Ruth Pought,
Laura Webb, Jannie Pought
ROCK 'N' ROLL

"MR. LUCKY," 1959
Jay Livingston, Ray Evans/Henry Mancini
INTERVAL, LUCK, RANGE

"MISTER PAGANINI," SEE "IF YOU CAN'T SING
IT YOU'LL HAVE TO SWING IT"

"MISTER SANDMAN," 1954
Pat Ballard
SLEEP

"MR. TAMBOURINE MAN," 1964
Bob Dylan
FOLK SONG, PROTEST SONG, ROCK-v

"MR. WONDERFUL," 1956
Jerry Bock, Larry Holofcener, George Weiss
TABLE 11, WONDER

"MISTY," 1954
Johnny Burke/Erroll Garner
CROSSOVER, CRYING, FILM MUSIC, JAZZ,
LYRICISTS, PIANO, TRIPLET

"MISTY BLUE," 1965
Bob Montgomery
TABLE 4-d, TABLE 7

"MOANIN' LOW," 1929
Howard Dietz/Ralph Rainger
CRYING, DEPRESSION YEARS, REVUES, TABLE
14, TORCH SONG

"MOCKING BIRD HILL," 1949
Vaughn Horton
MOUNTAINS

"MOCKINGBIRD," 1963
Charlie Foxx, Inez Foxx
WOMEN AS SONGWRITERS

"MODERN LOVE," 1983
David Bowie
ROCK-x

"MOMENTS TO REMEMBER," 1955
Al Stillman/Robert Allen
MEMORY, SINGING GROUPS, TIME

"MON HABITUDE," SEE "MY WAY"

"MON HOMME," SEE "MY MAN"

"MONA LISA," 1949
Jay Livingston, Ray Evans
TABLE 8, NAMES, SINGERS, TABLE 15

"MONDAY, MONDAY," 1966
John E. A. Phillips
DAYS OF THE WEEK, FADE-OUT, TABLE 10-h,
SINGING GROUPS

"MONEY (THAT'S WHAT I WANT)," 1959
Berry Gordy, Janie Bradford
MONEY, MOTOWN

"MONEY FOR NOTHING," 1985
Sting (pseud. Gordon Sumner), Mark Knopfler
TABLE 10-l

"MONEY HONEY," 1953
Jesse Stone
MONEY, ROCK 'N' ROLL-ii, SWEETNESS

"MONEY IS THE ROOT OF ALL EVIL," 1945
Joan Whitney, Alex Kramer
WOMEN AS SONGWRITERS

"THE MONEY SONG," 1966
Fred Ebb/John Kander
MONEY

"THE MONEY TREE," 1956
Cliff Ferre/Mark McIntyre
MONEY

"THE MONKEY TIME," 1963
Curtis Mayfield
SOUL

"MOOD INDIGO," 1931
Duke Ellington, Irving Mills, Albany Bigard
TABLE 3, COLORS, TABLE 7, GOLDEN AGE,
MOODS, PIANO

"MOODY'S MOOD," 1951
King Pleasure (pseud. Clarence Beeks)/James Moody
VOCALESE

"MOON LOVE," 1939
Mack David, Mack Davis, André Kostelanetz
CLASSICS, TABLE 6, LOVE, MOON

"THE MOON OF MANAKOORA," 1937
Frank Loesser/Alfred Newman
TABLE 8, MOON

"MOON OVER MIAMI," 1935
Edgar Leslie/Joe Burke
TABLE 5, MOON

"MOON RIVER," 1961
Johnny Mercer/Henry Mancini
TABLE 1, COMPOSERS, FILM MUSIC, TABLE 8,
FRIENDSHIP, TABLE 10-a, TABLE 10-b, HAR-
MONIC RHYTHM, LYRICISTS, MOON, RIVERS,
TABLE 15, WALTZ

"MOON SHADOW," 1970
Cat Stevens
MOON, ROCK-vi

"THE MOON WAS YELLOW," 1934
Edgar Leslie/Fred E. Ahlert
TABLE 7, MOON, TANGO

"MOONGLOW," 1934
Will Hudson, Eddie Delange, Irving Mills
MOON, TEMPO

"MOONLIGHT AND ROSES (BRING MEM'RIES OF
YOU)," 1925
Ben Black, Neil Moret
TABLE 6, FILM MUSIC, FLOWERS, MOON

"(ON) MOONLIGHT BAY," 1912
Edward Madden/Percy Wenrich
BARBERSHOP, BOATING, MOON, SINGING
GROUPS

"MOONLIGHT BECOMES YOU," 1942
Johnny Burke/James Van Heusen
TABLE 9, MOON

"MOONLIGHT COCKTAIL," 1941
Kim Gannon/C. Luckeyth Roberts
BORROWING, TABLE 9, MOON

"MOONLIGHT IN VERMONT," 1944
John Blackburn/Karl Suessdorf
AABA, CODA, HARMONY, MOON, REPEATED
NOTE, RHYME, TABLE 15, STATES

"MOONLIGHT MASQUERADE," 1941
Jack Lawrence/Toots Camarata
TABLE 6, MOON

"MOONLIGHT ON THE GANGES," 1926
Chester Wallace/Sherman Myers
BRITAIN, MOON, RIVERS

"MOONLIGHT SERENADE," 1939
Mitchell Parish/Glenn Miller
TABLE 3, MOON

"MORE (THEME FROM MONDO CANE)," 1963
Norman Newell (Eng.)/Nino Oliviero, Riz Ortolani
TABLE 4-b, COMPARATIVES, TABLE 8

"MORE AND MORE," 1944
E. Y. Harburg/Jerome Kern
COMPARATIVES

"MORE I CANNOT WISH YOU," 1950
Frank Loesser
COMPARATIVES, METER

"THE MORE I SEE YOU," 1945
Mack Gordon/Harry Warren
COMPARATIVES, FILM MUSICALS, TABLE 9,
LYRICISTS, RANGE, TIN PAN ALLEY

"MORE THAN A FEELING," 1976
Tom Scholz
FEELING

"MORE THAN A WOMAN," 1977
Barry Gibb, Robin Gibb, Maurice Gibb
COMPARATIVES, TABLE 9, WOMAN

"MORE THAN ANYTHING IN THE WORLD," 1943
Ruth Lowe
WOMEN AS SONGWRITERS

"MORE THAN YOU KNOW," 1929
Billy Rose, Edward Eliscu/Vincent Youmans
COMPARATIVES, COMPOSERS, GOLDEN AGE,
TABLE 15

"MORITAT," SEE "MACK THE KNIFE"

"MORNIN'," 1983
Al Jarreau, Jay Graydon, David Foster
TIME OF DAY

"THE MORNING AFTER," 1972
Al Kasha, Joel Hirschhorn
TABLE 1, BOATING, TABLE 8, TIME OF DAY

"MORNING HAS BROKEN," 1971
Eleanor Farjeon/David Evans (adapted by Cat
Stevens)
RELIGION, ROCK-vi, TIME OF DAY, WOMEN
AS SONGWRITERS

"MORNING TRAIN (NINE TO FIVE)," 1981
Florrie Palmer
TIME OF DAY

"MOSCOVIAN NIGHTS," SEE "MIDNIGHT IN MOSCOW"

"THE MOST BEAUTIFUL GIRL," 1973
Rory Bourke, Billy Sherrill, Norris Wilson
BEAUTY, TABLE 4-c, FADE-OUT, GIRL, SUPER-
LATIVES, WORLD

"THE MOST BEAUTIFUL GIRL IN THE WORLD," 1935
Lorenz Hart/Richard Rodgers
BEAUTY, GIRL, TABLE 11, RHYME, WALTZ,
WORLD

"THE MOST HAPPY FELLA," 1956
Frank Loesser
DIALECT, HAPPINESS, MAN, TABLE 12, SUPER-
LATIVES

"MOTHER AND CHILD REUNION," 1971
Paul Simon
ROCK-v

"MOTHER-IN-LAW," 1961
Allen Toussaint
MOTHERS

"MOTHER MACHREE," 1910
Rida Johnson Young/Ernest R. Ball, Chauncey Olcott
IRELAND, MOTHERS, TABLE 15, VAUDEVILLE

"MOTHER WAS A LADY," OR "IF JACK WERE ONLY HERE," 1896
Edward B. Marks/Joseph W. Stern
GAY NINETIES, LADY, MOTHERS

"MOTHER'S LITTLE HELPER," 1966
Mick Jagger, Keith Richards
MOTHERS

"MOULIN ROUGE," SEE "THE SONG FROM MOULIN ROUGE"

"MOUNTAIN GREENERY," 1926
Lorenz Hart/Richard Rodgers
CATALOGUE SONG, COLORS, TABLE 7, KEY, MOUNTAINS, TABLE 11, PATTER, PLACES, REVUES, TABLE 14, TREES

"THE MOUNTAINS HIGH," 1961
Dick Gosting
HEIGHT, MOUNTAINS

"MOVE ON UP A LITTLE HIGHER," 1946
W. Herbert Brewster
GOSPEL

"MOVE OVER," 1970
Janis Joplin
WOMEN AS SONGWRITERS

"THE M.T.A.," 1956
Jaqueline Steiner, Bess Hawes
SINGING GROUPS

"MULE SKINNER BLUES," 1931
Jimmy Rodgers, George Vaughn
BLUES, COUNTRY AND WESTERN, GUITAR

"MULE TRAIN," 1949
Johnny Lange, Hy Heath, Fred Glickman
ANIMALS, TABLE 15

"THE MUSIC GOES 'ROUND AND 'ROUND," 1935
"Red" Hodgson/Edward Farley, Michael Riley
TABLE 6, JUKEBOX, MUSIC, NOVELTY SONG

"MUSIC, MAESTRO, PLEASE," 1938
Herb Magidson/Allie Wrubel
MUSIC, RADIO

"MUSIC! MUSIC! MUSIC!," 1950
Stephen Weiss, Bernie Baum
TABLE 6, MUSIC, NOVELTY SONG, PLAYER PIANO, QUOTATION, TABLE 15

"THE MUSIC OF THE NIGHT," 1986
Charles Hart, Richard Stilgoe/Andrew Lloyd Webber
ENHARMONIC EQUIVALENCE, MUSIC, TABLE 12, RHYME

"MUSIC TO WATCH GIRLS BY," 1966
Tony Velona/Sid Ramin
GIRL, MUSIC

"MUSKRAT RAMBLE," 1926
Ray Gilbert (1950)/Edward Ory
ANIMALS, TABLE 3, DIXIELAND

"A MUST TO AVOID," 1966
F. Sloan, Steve Barry
ROCK-iii

"MUSTANG SALLY," 1965
Bonny Rice
SOUL

"MY BABY JUST CARES FOR ME," 1930
Gus Kahn/Walter Donaldson
BABY

"MY BLUE HEAVEN," 1927
George Whiting/Walter Donaldson
COLORS, TABLE 7, GOLDEN AGE, HEAVEN, TABLE 14, TABLE 15, TIN PAN ALLEY

"MY BONNIE LIES OVER THE OCEAN," 1881
traditional Scottish song
OCEAN

"MY BUDDY," 1922
Gus Kahn/Walter Donaldson
FRIENDSHIP, INTERVAL, WORLD WAR I

"MY CHERIE AMOUR," 1968
Stevie Wonder, Henry Cosby, Sylvia Moy
TABLE 4-c, ENDEARMENT, FADE-OUT, FOREIGN LANGUAGE, RANGE, TABLE 15, VAMP

"My Coloring Book," 1962
Fred Ebb/John Kander
TABLE 7, WRITING

"My Country 'Tis of Thy People You're Dying," c. 1965
Buffy Sainte-Marie
WOMEN AS SONGWRITERS

"My Dad," 1962
Barry Mann, Cynthia Weil
FATHERS, ROCK 'N' ROLL

"My Darling," 1932
Edward Heyman/Richard Myers
ENDEARMENT

"My Darling, My Darling," 1948
Frank Loesser
ENDEARMENT, TABLE 1

"My Dream of the Big Parade," 1926
Al Dubin/Jimmy McHugh
WORLD WAR I

"My Dreams Are Getting Better All the Time," 1944
Vic Mizzy, Mann Curtis
WORLD WAR II

"My Eyes Adored You," 1974
Bob Crewe, Kenny Nolan Helfman
TABLE 2, TABLE 4-d, TONALITY

"My Father," 1968
Judy Collins
WOMEN AS SONGWRITERS

"My Favorite Things," 1959
Oscar Hammerstein II/Richard Rodgers
CATALOGUE SONG, CHILDHOOD, IMPROVI-SATION, MUSICAL PLAYS, TABLE 12, WALTZ, WOODWINDS

"My Foolish Heat," 1949
Ned Washington/Victor Young
TABLE 2, TABLE 8, FOOLS, *YOUR HIT PARADE*

"My Funny Valentine," 1937
Lorenz Hart/Richard Rodgers
CABARET, COLLABORATION, GOLDEN AGE, HIT SONG, HOLIDAYS, LYRICISTS, MODE, TABLE 11, PEDAL POINT, RHYME, SHOW TUNE, TABLE 15

"My Gal Is a High Born Lady," 1896
Barney Fagan
COON SONG, GAY NINETIES

"My Gal Sal," 1905
Paul Dresser
GIRL, NAMES, TABLE 15

"My Generation," 1965
Peter Townshend
AGE, ROCK-iii

"My Georgia Lady Love," 1899
Ida Emerson, Joseph Howard
WOMEN AS SONGWRITERS

"My Girl," 1964
William Robinson, Ronald White
MOTOWN

"My Girl Bill," 1974
Jim Stafford
NAMES

"My Guy," 1964
William "Smokey" Robinson, Jr.
MOTOWN

"My Guy's Come Back," 1945
Ray McKinley/Mel Powell
WORLD WAR II

"My Happiness," 1933
Betty Peterson/Borney Bergantine
HAPPINESS, ROCK 'N' ROLL-iii

"My Heart Belongs to Daddy," 1938
Cole Porter
ALLITERATION, TABLE 2, FATHERS, MODE, TABLE 11

"My Heart Belongs to Me," 1977
Alan Gordon
TABLE 15

"My Heart Cries for You," 1950
Percy Faith, Carl Sigman
TABLE 2, CRYING

"My Heart Has a Mind of Its Own," 1960
Howard Greenfield/Jack Keller
MIND

"My Heart Is an Open Book," 1957
Hal David/Lee Pockriss
WRITING

"(All of a Sudden) My Heart Sings," 1941
Harold Rome (Eng.)/Henri Herpin
ANATOMY, TABLE 2, COMPOSER-LYRICISTS,
FRANCE, REPEATED NOTE, SCALE

"My Heart Stood Still," 1927
Lorenz Hart/Richard Rodgers
ANATOMY, TABLE 2, MELODY, MUSICAL
COMEDY, TABLE 11, SCALE

"My Heart Tells Me," 1943
Mack Gordon/Harry Warren
YOUR HIT PARADE

"My Hero," 1909
Stanislaus Stange/Oscar Straus
AUSTRIA, OCTAVE, TABLE 13, SHEET MUSIC,
WALTZ

"My Hometown," 1984
Bruce Springsteen
ROCK-xii

"My Ideal," 1930
Leo Robin/Richard A. Whiting, Newell Chase
TABLE 9, TABLE 15

"My Jean," 1920
Caro Roma
WOMEN AS SONGWRITERS

"My Kind of Town," 1964
Sammy Cahn/James Van Heusen
CITIES, TABLE 5

"My Lily of the Lamplight," see **"Lili
Marleen"**

**"My Little Grass Shack in Kealakekua,
Hawaii," 1933**
John Avery Noble, Thomas J. Harrison
NOVELTY SONG

**"My Little Nest of Heavenly Blue
(Frasquita Serenade)," 1926**
Sigmund Spaeth (Eng.)/Franz Lehár
AUSTRIA, HEAVEN

"My Love," 1973
Paul McCartney, Linda McCartney
ROCK-ii

"My Mammy," 1918
Sam M. Lewis, Joe Young/Walter Donaldson
FILM MUSIC, FILM MUSICALS, MOTHERS,
ROARING TWENTIES

"My Man," 1921
Channing Pollock (Eng.)/Maurice Yvain
FRANCE, MAN, REVUES, TABLE 14, ROARING
TWENTIES, TORCH SONG

"My Man's Gone Now," 1935
DuBose Heyward/George Gershwin
TABLE 1, DIALECT, MAN, TORCH SONG

"My Melancholy Baby," 1912
George A. Norton/Ernie Burnett
AABA, BABY, STANDARD, VAUDEVILLE

"My Melody of Love," 1973
Bobby Vinton/Henry Mayer
MELODY, MUSIC, TABLE 15

"My Moonlight Madonna," 1933
Paul Francis Webster/William Scotti
TABLE 6, MOON

"My Mother's Eyes," 1928
L. Wolfe Gilbert/Abel Baer
MOTHER

"MY OLD FLAME," 1934
Arthur Johnston, Sam Coslow
TABLE 9, FIRE

"MY OLD KENTUCKY HOME," 1853
Stephen Collins Foster
HOME, SINGING GROUPS

"MY OLD NEW HAMPSHIRE HOME," 1898
Andrew B. Sterling/Harry Von Tilzer
GAY NINETIES, HOME, STATES

"MY ONE AND ONLY," 1927
Ira Gershwin/George Gershwin
BLUE NOTE, TABLE 11

"MY ONE AND ONLY HEART," 1953
Al Stillman/Robert Allen
TABLE 2

"MY OWN TRUE LOVE," SEE "TARA THEME"

"MY PONY BOY," 1909
Bobby Heath/Charles O'Donnell
ANIMALS, BOY, ONE-STEP

"MY PRAYER," 1939
Jimmy Kennedy/Jimmy Kennedy, Georges Boulanger
ADAPTATION, TABLE 6, FRANCE, ROCK 'N'
ROLL-ii, SINGING GROUPS

"MY REVERIE," 1938
Larry Clinton
TABLE 3, CLASSICS, TABLE 6, DREAMS,
FRANCE, THINKING

"MY ROMANCE," 1935
Lorenz Hart/Richard Rodgers
CABARET, CATALOGUE SONG, COLLABORA-
TION, KEY, TABLE 11, ROMANCE, SCALE

"MY SECRET PLACE," 1987
Joni Mitchell
WOMEN AS SONGWRITERS

"MY SHARONA," 1978
Berton Averre, Douglas Fieger
ROCK-xi

"MY SHAWL," 1934
Stanley Adams (Eng.)/Xavier Cugat
TABLE 3, RUMBA

"MY SHINING HOUR," 1943
Johnny Mercer/Harold Arlen
TABLE 9, TIME

"MY SHIP," 1941
Ira Gershwin/Kurt Weill
BOATING, CADENCE, LYRICISTS, TABLE 11

"MY SILENT LOVE," 1932
Edward Heyman/Dana Suesse
KEY, LOVE, WOMEN AS SONGWRITERS

"MY SPECIAL ANGEL," 1957
Jimmy Duncan
ANGELS, TABLE 4-d, COUNTRY AND WESTERN

"MY STAR," 1918
Elsa Maxwell
WOMEN AS SONGWRITERS

"MY SUGAR IS SO REFINED," 1946
Sylvia Dee, Josephine Proffitt/Sidney Lippman
WOMEN AS SONGWRITERS

**"MY SWEET GYPSY ROSE," SEE "SAY, HAS
ANYBODY SEEN MY SWEET GYPSY ROSE"**

"MY SWEET LORD," 1970
George Harrison
TABLE 4-d, RELIGION, ROCK-ii, SWEETNESS

**"MY SWEETHEART'S THE MAN IN THE MOON,"
1892**
James Thornton
BARBERSHOP, GAY NINETIES, MAN, MOON,
SWEETNESS

"MY TIME IS YOUR TIME," 1927
Eric Little (pseud. R. S. Hooper), Leo Dance (pseud.
H. M. Tennant)
RADIO, TABLE 15, TIME

"MY TRUE STORY," 1961
Eugene Pitt, Oscar Waltzer
SINGING GROUPS

"MY TWILIGHT DREAM," 1939
Lew Sherwood, Eddy Duchin
TABLE 6

"MY WAY," 1967
Paul Anka (Eng.)/Claude François, Jacques Revaux
TABLE 4-c, CANADA, FRANCE, HARMONIC
RHYTHM, INTERVAL, SINGERS, TABLE 15

"MY WILD IRISH ROSE," 1899
Chauncey Olcott
GAY NINETIES, IRELAND, NATIONS, RECORD-
ING, TABLE 15, VAUDEVILLE

"MY WOMAN, MY WOMAN, MY WIFE," 1969
Marty Robbins
TABLE 10-w, MARRIAGE

**"MY WONDERFUL ONE," SEE "(MY) WONDER-
FUL ONE"**

"MY YIDDISHE MOMME," 1925
Jack Yellen/Jack Yellen, Lew Pollack
DIALECT, MOTHER

"MYSTERY TRAIN," 1953
Sam C. Phillips, Junior Parker
POPULAR SONG-viii

**"NADIA'S THEME (THE YOUNG AND THE REST-
LESS)," 1976**
Perry Botkin, Jr., Barry DeVorzon
TEXTURE, TRIPLET

"NAGASAKI," 1928
Mort Dixon/Harry Warren
TABLE 5

**"NANA, HEY, HEY, KISS HIM GOODBYE,"
1969**
Gary De Carlo, Paul Leka, Dale Frashuer
NONSENSE

"NANCY (WITH THE LAUGHING FACE)," 1944
Phil Silvers/James Van Heusen
CHILDHOOD, TABLE 2, NAMES

**"NÃO TENHO LAGRIMAS," SEE "COME TO THE
MARDI GRAS"**

"NATIONAL EMBLEM," 1906
m. E. E. Bagley
ANIMALS, CIRCUS

"A NATURAL MAN," 1970
Bobby Hebb, Sandy Baron
TABLE 10-o, MAN

**"(YOU MAKE ME FEEL LIKE) A NATURAL
WOMAN," 1967**
Carole King, Jerry Wexler, Gerry Goffin
TABLE 15, SOUL

"NATURE BOY," 1946
Eden Ahbez
BOY, DISC JOCKEY, MODE, SINGERS, TABLE 15

"THE NAUGHTY LADY OF SHADY LANE," 1954
Sid Tepper, Roy C. Bennett
LADY, SINGING GROUPS, STREETS

"NEAPOLITAN NIGHTS," 1925
Harry D. Kerr/J. S. Zamecnik
TABLE 5

"NEAR YOU," 1947
Kermit Goell/Francis Craig
CLOSENESS, DISC JOCKEY

"THE NEARNESS OF YOU," 1937
Ned Washington/Hoagy Carmichael
CLOSENESS, COMPOSERS

"NEITHER ONE OF US," 1971
Jim Weatherly
TABLE 10-h

"NEL BLU, DIPINTO DI BLU," SEE "VOLARE"

"NEVER CAN SAY GOODBYE," 1970
Clifton Davis
TABLE 4-d, DISCO, FAREWELLS

"NEVER GONNA LET YOU GO," 1981
Cynthia Weil/Barry Mann
WOMEN AS SONGWRITERS

"NEVER KNEW LOVE LIKE THIS BEFORE," 1979
Reginald Lucas, James Mtume
TABLE 10-q

"NEVER MY LOVE," 1967
Don Addrisi, Dick Addrisi
TABLE 4-b, LOVE

"NEVER NEVER LAND," 1954
Betty Comden, Adolph Green/Jule Styne
COLLABORATION

"NEVER ON SUNDAY," 1960
Billy Towne (Eng.)/Manos Hadjidakis
TABLE 1, TABLE 4-c, CHA CHA CHA, CUBA,
DAYS OF THE WEEK, TABLE 8, GREECE,
PICKUP

"NEW KID IN TOWN," 1977
Glenn Frey, Don Henley, John David Souther
ROCK-x

"NEW SUN IN THE SKY," 1931
Howard Dietz/Arthur Schwartz
SUN

"NEW WORLD COMING," 1970
Cynthia Weil/Barry Mann
WOMEN AS SONGWRITERS

"NEW YORK MINING DISASTER 1941," 1967
Barry Gibb, Maurice Gibb, Robin Gibb
ROCK-viii

"NEW YORK, NEW YORK," 1944
Betty Comden, Adolph Green/Leonard Bernstein
CITIES, TABLE 5, TABLE 11, WOMEN AS
SONGWRITERS

**"(THEME FROM) NEW YORK, NEW YORK,"
1977**
Fred Ebb, John Kander
TABLE 5, TABLE 8, SINGERS, TABLE 15, SUB-
JECTS, VAMP

"NEW YORK STATE OF MIND," 1975
Billy Joel
TABLE 15, STATES

"NICE WORK IF YOU CAN GET IT," 1937
Ira Gershwin/George Gershwin
CIRCLE OF FIFTHS

"NICK OF TIME," 1989
Bonnie Raitt
TIME

"NIGHT AND DAY," 1932
Cole Porter
ALLITERATION, DAY, DEPRESSION YEARS,
FORM, LENGTH, MELODY, MUSICAL COM-
EDY, TABLE 11, NIGHT, PICKUP, REPEATED
NOTE, TABLE 15

"THE NIGHT CHICAGO DIED," 1974
Lionel Stitcher, Peter Callender
NIGHT

"NIGHT FEVER," 1977
Barry Gibb, Maurice Gibb, Robin Gibb
DISCO, NIGHT

"THE NIGHT HAS A THOUSAND EYES," 1948
Buddy Bernier/Jerry Brainin
NIGHT

"NIGHT ON DISCO MOUNTAIN," 1977
m. David Shire
TABLE 6, MOUNTAINS

**"THE NIGHT THE LIGHTS WENT OUT IN GEOR-
GIA," 1972**
Bobby Russell
NIGHT

**"THE NIGHT THEY INVENTED CHAMPAGNE,"
1958**
Alan Jay Lerner/Frederick Loewe
TABLE 9, FOOD AND DRINK, NIGHT, POLKA

"NIGHT TRAIN," 1952
Oscar Washington, Lewis C. Simpkins/Jimmy Forrest
TABLE 4-d, NIGHT, RHYTHM AND BLUES,
TRAINS

"THE NIGHT WAS MADE FOR LOVE," 1931
Otto Harbach/Jerome Kern
NIGHT

"NIGHTINGALE," 1942
Fred Wise (Eng.)/Xavier Cugat, George Rosner
BIRDS

"A NIGHTINGALE SANG IN BERKELEY SQUARE," 1940
Eric Maschwitz/Manning Sherwin
BIRDS, BRITAIN, CITIES, TABLE 5, STREETS

"NIGHTS IN WHITE SATIN," 1967
Justin Hayward
NIGHT, ROCK-viii

"NIGHTSHIFT," 1984
Walter Orange, Dennis Lambert, Frannie Golde
TABLE 10-p

"NINA," 1948
Cole Porter
FILM MUSICALS

"9 TO 5," 1980
Dolly Parton
TABLE 4-d, TABLE 10-t, TABLE 10-w, TIME OF DAY, WOMEN AS SONGWRITERS

"19TH NERVOUS BREAKDOWN," 1966
Mick Jagger, Keith Richards
ROCK-iii

"96 TEARS," 1966
Rudy Martinez
CRYING, ROCK

"NO GETTIN' OVER ME," 1981
Tom Brasfield, Walt Aldredge
TABLE 10-u

"NO LOVE, NO NOTHIN'," 1943
Leo Robin/Harry Warren
WORLD WAR II

"NO MOON AT ALL," 1949
Redd Evans/Dave Mann
MOON

"NO MORE RHYME," 1989
Debbie Gibson
WOMEN AS SONGWRITERS

"NO OTHER LOVE," 1950
Oscar Hammerstein II/Richard Rodgers
TABLE 11

"NO STRINGS," 1935
Irving Berlin
FILM MUSICALS

"NO STRINGS," 1962
Richard Rodgers
COMPOSER-LYRICISTS, TABLE 11

"NO TWO PEOPLE," 1951
Frank Loesser
TABLE 9, PEOPLE TOGETHERNESS

"NOAH'S ARK" SEE "THERE'S ONE WIDE RIVER TO CROSS"

"NOBODY," 1905
Alex Rogers/Bert A. Williams
VAUDEVILLE

"NOBODY DOES IT BETTER," 1977
Carole Bayer Sager/Marvin Hamlisch
TABLE 4-d, COMPARATIVES, FORM, WOMEN AS SONGWRITERS

"NOBODY DOES IT LIKE ME," 1973
Dorothy Fields/Cy Coleman
WOMEN AS SONGWRITERS

"NOBODY ELSE BUT ME," 1946
Oscar Hammerstein II/Jerome Kern
INTERVAL

"NOBODY KNOWS DE TROUBLE I'VE SEEN," 1867
traditional African-American spiritual
FOLK SONG

"NOBODY KNOWS YOU WHEN YOU'RE DOWN AND OUT," 1923
James Cox
DEPRESSION YEARS

"NOBODY'S SWEETHEART NOW," 1924
Gus Kahn, Ernie Erdman, Billy Meyers, Elmer Schoebel
SWEETNESS

"Non Dimenticar (Don't Forget)," 1953
Shelley Dobbins (Eng.)/P. G. Redi
FOREIGN LANGUAGE

"Norwegian Wood," 1966
John Lennon, Paul McCartney
COLLABORATION, NATIONS, POPULAR
SONG-viii, ROCK-ii

"Not for All the Rice in China," 1933
Irving Berlin
REVUES, TABLE 14, SLANG

"Not While I'm Around," 1979
Stephen Sondheim
OPERA

"Now Is the Hour," 1948
Dorothy Stewart, Maewa Kaihau, Clement Scott
TIME, *YOUR HIT PARADE*

"Now May There Be a Blessing," 1939
Stephen Vincent Benét/Douglas Moore
MARRIAGE, OPERA

"Nowhere Man," 1965
John Lennon, Paul McCartney
MAN, ROCK-ii

"(Potatoes Are Cheaper—Tomatoes Are Cheaper) Now's the Time to Fall in Love," 1931
Al Lewis/Al Sherman
DEPRESSION YEARS, FALLING IN LOVE, FOOD
AND DRINK, TIME

"Number One," 1986
Joni Mitchell
WOMEN AS SONGWRITERS

"A Nuptial Blessing," see **"Now May There Be a Blessing"**

"O Come All Ye Faithful (Adeste Fedeles)," 1782
John Francis Wade (Eng.)/John Francis Wade
CHRISTMAS

"O Happy Day," see **"(O) Happy Day"**

"O Holy Night," also known as "Christmas Song," 1858
John Sullivan Dwight/Adolphe Adam
CHRISTMAS

"O Little Town of Bethlehem," 1868
Phillips Brooks/Lewis H. Redner
CHRISTMAS

"O Mein Papa," see **"Oh! My Pa-pa"**

"O Mother Dear, Jerusalem," 1888
Samuel A. Ward
GAY NINETIES

"'O Sole Mio," 1898
Giovanni Capurro/Eduardo di Capua
ITALY, ROCK 'N' ROLL-i

"O Superman," 1981
Laurie Anderson
WOMEN AS SONGWRITERS

"Ob-La-Di Ob-La-Da," 1968
John Lennon, Paul McCartney
NONSENSE

"The Object of My Affection," 1934
Pinky Tomlin, Coy Poe, Jimmy Grier
SINGING GROUPS

"The Odd Couple," 1968
Sammy Cahn/Neal Hefti
TABLE 8, TOGETHERNESS

"Ode to Billy Joe," 1967
Bobbie Gentry
COUNTRY AND WESTERN, TABLE 10-c, TABLE
10-f, NAMES

"Of Thee I Sing," 1931
Ira Gershwin/George Gershwin
MUSICAL PLAYS, TABLE 12

"Oh, But I Do," 1945
Ella Fitzgerald, Kenneth Watts
WOMEN AS SONGWRITERS

"OH BY JINGO, OH BY GEE, YOU'RE THE ONLY GIRL FOR ME," 1919
Lew Brown/Albert von Tilzer
SLANG

"OH! CAROL," 1959
Howard Greenfield/Neil Sedaka
NAMES, ROCK 'N' ROLL

"OH DEM GOLDEN SLIPPERS," *SEE* **"(OH DEM) GOLDEN SLIPPERS"**

"OH GOD! LET MY DREAM COME TRUE!," 1916
Blanche Merrill/Al Piantadosi
WOMEN AS SONGWRITERS

"OH HAPPY DAY," 1969
traditional Baptist hymn, arr. by Edwin Hawkins
GOSPEL, RELIGION

"OH HOW I HATE TO GET UP IN THE MORNING," 1918
Irving Berlin
BROKEN CHORD, PATRIOTISM, POPULAR SONG-iii, QUOTATION, REVUES, TIME OF DAY, WORLD WAR I

"OH JOHNNY, OH JOHNNY, OH!," 1917
Ed Rose/Abe Olman
NAMES

"OH, LADY BE GOOD," 1924
Ira Gershwin/George Gershwin
BEBOP, BROKEN CHORD, COMPOSERS, LADY, MUSICAL COMEDY, TABLE 11, SINGERS, TABLE 15

"OH, LONESOME ME," 1958
Don Gibson
TABLE 4-d, LONELINESS

"OH! LOOK AT ME NOW!," 1941
John DeVries/Joe Bushkin
TABLE 3

"OH MAMA (THE BUTCHER BOY)," 1938
Lev Brown, Rudy Vallee (Eng.)/Paolo Citorello
BOY, ITALY, MOTHERS

"OH! MY PA-PA (O MEIN PAPA)," 1953
John Turner, Geoffrey Parsons/Paul Burkhard
FATHERS, TABLE 8, TABLE 15

"OH, PRETTY WOMAN," 1964
Roy Orbison, Bill Dees
BEAUTY, TABLE 10-g, ROCK 'N' ROLL-i, WOMAN

"OH PROMISE ME," 1887
Clement Scott/Reginald De Koven
ART SONG, GAY NINETIES, MARRIAGE, OPERA, TABLE 13, TABLE 15

"OH, ROCK MY SOUL," ALSO KNOWN AS **"OH, ROCK-A MY SOUL," 1964**
traditional folk song, recorded by Peter, Paul and Mary
RELIGION

"OH! SUSANNA," 1848
Stephen Collins Foster
NAMES, POPULAR SONG-i

"OH, WHAT A BEAUTIFUL MORNIN'," 1943
Oscar Hammerstein II/Richard Rodgers
BEAUTY, DIALECT, GOLDEN AGE, HARMONY, LANDMARKS, LENGTH, LYRICISTS, MUSICAL PLAYS, TABLE 12, TIME OF DAY, VERSE, WALTZ

"OH, WHAT A NIGHT," 1956
Marvin Junior, John Funches
NIGHT, SOUL

"OH! WHAT A PAL WAS MARY," 1919
Edgar Leslie, Bert Kalmar/Peter Wendling
FRIENDSHIP

"OH! WHAT IT SEEMED TO BE," 1945
Bennie Benjamin, George Weiss, Frankie Carle
TABLE 15

"OH, YOU BEAUTIFUL DOLL," 1911
Seymour Brown/Nat D. Ayer
DOLL, RAGTIME, SINGING GROUPS, SYNCOPATION

"OHIO," 1953
Betty Comden, Adolph Green/Leonard Bernstein
TABLE 11, STATES

"OHIO," 1970
Neil Young
ROCK-v, STATES

"OKLAHOMA!," 1943
Oscar Hammerstein II/Richard Rodgers
TABLE 12, PEOPLE

"OL' MAN MOSE," 1938
Louis Armstrong, Zilner Randolph
SINGERS

"OL' MAN RIVER," 1927
Oscar Hammerstein II/Jerome Kern
ART SONG, COMPOSERS, DIALECT, FORM,
LANDMARKS OF STAGE AND SCREEN, LYRI-
CISTS, MAN, MUSICAL PLAYS, TABLE 12,
OPERA, RANGE, RELEASE, RHYTHM AND
BLUES, RIVERS, ROARING TWENTIES, SYNCO-
PATION, VERSE

"OL' ROCKIN' CHAIR," SEE **"ROCKIN' CHAIR"**

"OLD BLACK JOE," 1860
Stephen Collins Foster
FOLK SONG

"THE OLD CHISHOLM TRAIL," C. **1880**
Anonymous
POPULAR SONG-i

"OLD DEVIL MOON," 1946
E. Y. Harburg/Burton Lane
BREAK, MODALITY, MOON, TABLE 11

**"THE OLD FASHIONED WAY (LES PLAISIRS
DÉMODÉS)," 1972**
Al Kasha, Joel Hirschhom (Eng.)/Georges Garvarentz
FRANCE

"OLD FOLKS AT HOME," 1851
Stephen Collins Foster
ARRANGEMENT, FOLK SONG, HOME, POPU-
LAR SONG-ii, QUOTATION, RIVERS

**"THE OLD GREY MARE (SHE AIN'T WHAT SHE
USED TO BE)," 1917**
traditional nineteenth-century American song, arr. by
Frank Panella
ANIMALS, TABLE 7

"OLD MAN," 1969
Neil Young
MAN, ROCK-v

"THE OLD PI-ANNA RAG," 1955
Don Phillips
PIANO

"THE OLD PIANO ROLL BLUES," 1949
Cy Coben
PIANO, PLAYER PIANO

"THE OLD REFRAIN," 1915
Fritz Kreisler (Eng.)/Fritz Kreisler
BORROWING, MUSIC

"THE OLD SOFT SHOE," 1951
Nancy Hamilton/Morgan Lewis
CLOTHING

"OLD TIME RELIGION," C. **1955**
African-American spiritual, arr. by James Cleveland
GOSPEL

"OLD ZIP COON," 1834
Anonymous Minstrel Song
POPULAR SONG-i

"OLE BUTTERMILK SKY," 1946
Hoagy Carmichael, Jack Brooks
TABLE 8, SKY

"OMKRING ET FLYGEL," SEE **"ALLEY CAT"**

**"ON A CLEAR DAY YOU CAN SEE FOREVER,"
1966**
Alan Jay Lerner/Burton Lane
COMPOSERS, DAY, HARMONY, INTERVAL,
LYRICISTS, SEEING, WEATHER

"ON A DESERT ISLAND WITH THEE," 1927
Lorenz Hart/Richard Rodgers
PLACES

"On a Slow Boat to China," 1948
Frank Loesser
COMPOSER-LYRICISTS, NATIONS

"On a Sunday Afternoon," 1902
Andrew B. Sterling/Harry von Tilzer
DAYS OF THE WEEK, MONTHS, TIME OF DAY,
WALTZ

"On a Wonderful Day Like Today," SEE "A WONDERFUL DAY LIKE TODAY"

"On and On," 1977
Stephen Bishop
TABLE 4-d

"On Broadway," 1962
Jerry Leiber, Barry Mann, Mike Stoller, Cynthia Weil
TABLE 4-d, BROADWAY, TABLE 10-o, ROCK 'N'
ROLL-ii

"On Green Dolphin Street," 1947
Ned Washington/Bronislau Kaper
COLORS, TABLE 7, TABLE 8, SHEET MUSIC,
STREETS

"On Moonlight Bay," SEE "MOONLIGHT BAY"

"On My Own," 1985
Herbert Kretzmer, John Caird, Trevor Nunn (Eng.)/
Claude-Michel Schönberg
FRANCE, TABLE 12

"On My Own," 1986
Carole Bayer Sager/Burt Bacharach
WOMEN AS SONGWRITERS

"On the Alamo," 1922
Gus Kahn, Joe Lyons/Isham Jones
TABLE 3, CITIES, TABLE 5

"On the Atchison, Topeka, and the Santa Fe," 1945
Johnny Mercer/Harry Warren
TABLE 1, TABLE 9, NOVELTY SONG, SINGERS,
TABLE 15, TRAINS

"On the Banks of the Wabash, Far Away," 1899
Paul Dresser
BARBERSHOP, GAY NINETIES, POPULAR
SONG-ii, TABLE 15

"On the Beautiful Blue Danube" 1867
m. Johann Strauss, Jr.
BROKEN CHORD

"On the Boardwalk in Atlantic City," 1946
Mack Gordon/Josef Myrow
TABLE 5, TABLE 9, OCEAN, STREETS, WALK-
ING, WATERFRONT

"On the Good Ship Lollipop," 1934
Sidney Clare, Richard A. Whiting
BOATING, SWEETNESS

"On the Isle of May," 1940
Mack David/André Kostelanetz
TABLE 6

"On the Road Again," 1979
Willie Nelson
TABLE 10-w, STREETS, TRAVEL

"On the Road to Mandalay," 1907
Rudyard Kipling/Oley Speaks
BRITAIN, CITIES, TABLE 5, STREETS

"On the Street of Dreams," SEE "(On the) STREET OF DREAMS"

"On the Street Where You Live," 1956
Alan Jay Lerner/Frederick Loewe
LYRICISTS, MUSICAL PLAYS, TABLE 12, TABLE
15, STREETS

"On the Sunny Side of the Street," 1930
Dorothy Fields/Jimmy McHugh
TABLE 3, COLLABORATION, COMPOSERS,
LYRICISTS, LYRICS, REVUES, TABLE 14,
STREETS, SUN, WOMEN AS SONGWRITERS

"On the Trail," 1933
Harold Adamson/Ferde Grofé
WALKING

"ON THE WILLOWS," 1971
Stephen Schwartz
RELIGION

"ON THIS NIGHT OF A THOUSAND STARS," 1976
Tim Rice/Andrew Lloyd Webber
TANGO

"ON TOP OF OLD SMOKEY," 1951
Pete Seeger
FOLK SONG, MOUNTAINS, SINGING GROUPS

"ON WISCONSIN," 1909
Carl Beck/W. T. Purdy
MARCH, STATES

"ONCE IN A BLUE MOON," 1923
Anne Caldwell/Jerome Kern
WOMEN AS SONGWRITERS

"ONCE IN A LIFETIME," 1961
Leslie Bricusse, Anthony Newley
BRITAIN, TIME

"ONCE IN A WHILE," 1937
Bud Green/Michael Edwards
TABLE 3, TIME, TIN PAN ALLEY

"ONCE IN LOVE WITH AMY," 1948
Frank Loesser
TABLE 11, NAMES

"ONCE UPON A TIME," 1962
Lee Adams/Charles Strouse
TIME

"ONE," 1975
Edward Kleban/Marvin Hamlisch
COMPOSERS, COUNTERPOINT FADE-OUT, INTERVAL, TABLE 11, VAMP

"ONE ALONE," 1926
Otto Harbach, Oscar Hammerstein II/Sigmund Romberg
HUNGARY, TABLE 13

"ONE FINE DAY," 1963
Gerry Goffin, Carole King
DAY, ROCK 'N' ROLL

"ONE FOR MY BABY (AND ONE MORE FOR THE ROAD)," 1943
Johnny Mercer/Harold Arlen
TABLE 9, FOOD AND DRINK, STREETS, TIME OF DAY, TONALITY

"ONE HAND, ONE HEART," 1957
Stephen Sondheim/Leonard Bernstein
ANATOMY, TABLE 2, TABLE 12

"ONE HELLO," 1982
Carole Bayer Sager/Marvin Hamlisch
WOMEN AS SONGWRITERS

"THE ONE HORSE OPEN SLEIGH," SEE "JINGLE BELLS"

"(I'D LOVE TO SPEND) ONE HOUR WITH YOU," 1932
Leo Robin/Richard A. Whiting
RADIO, TIME

"ONE HUNDRED WAYS," 1981
Tony Coleman, Benjamin Wright, Kathy Wakefield
TABLE 10-o

"THE ONE I LOVE BELONGS TO SOMEBODY ELSE," 1924
Gus Kahn/Isham Jones
TABLE 3

"ONE KISS," 1928
Oscar Hammerstein II/Sigmund Romberg
HUNGARY, KISSING, TABLE 13

"ONE LESS BELL TO ANSWER," 1967
Hal David/Burt Bacharach
SINGING GROUPS

"ONE MEAT BALL," 1944
Hy Zaret, Lou Singer
BORROWING

"ONE MINT JULEP," 1952
Rudolph Toombs
FOOD AND DRINK, RHYTHM AND BLUES

"ONE MOMENT ALONE," 1931
Otto Harbach/Jerome Kern
TIME

"ONE MOMENT IN TIME," 1987
Albert Hammond, John Bettis
TIME

"ONE MORNING IN MAY," 1933
Mitchell Parish/Hoagy Carmichael
MONTHS, TEMPO, TIME OF DAY

"ONE NIGHT OF LOVE," 1934
Gus Kahn/Victor Schertzinger
TABLE 9, NIGHT

"ONE NOTE SAMBA," 1961
Jon Hendricks (Eng.)/Antonio Carlos Jobim, N.
Mendonca
BASS LINE, BASSA NOVA, BRAZIL, CHROMATI-
CISM, REPEATED NOTE, SAMBA

"ONE O'CLOCK JUMP," 1938
William "Count" Basie
TABLE 3, PIANO, RIFF, SWING, TIME OF DAY

"ONE OF THE LIVING," 1985
Holly Knight
TABLE 10-i

"ONE OF THESE NIGHTS," 1975
Glenn Frey, Don Henley
NIGHT, ROCK-x

"ONE PART BE MY LOVER," 1991
Bonnie Raitt, Michael O'Keefe
WOMEN AS SONGWRITERS

"THE ONE ROSE THAT'S LEFT IN MY HEART,"
1929
Del Lyon, Lani McIntire
TABLE 2, FLOWERS

"ONE SUMMER NIGHT," 1958
Danny Webb
NIGHT, ROCK 'N' ROLL-ii, SINGING GROUPS

"ONLY A ROSE," 1925
Brian Hooker, Rudolf Friml
CZECHOSLOVAKIA, TABLE 13

"ONLY FOREVER," 1940
Johnny Burke/James V. Monaco
ENDURING LOVE, TABLE 9, TABLE 15

"ONLY IN AMERICA," 1963
Jerry Leiber, Cynthia Weil, Mike Stoller, Barry Mann
NATIONS, SINGING GROUPS

"ONLY IN MY DREAMS," 1987
Debbie Gibson
WOMEN AS SONGWRITERS

"ONLY LOVE CAN BREAK A HEART," 1962
Hal David/Burt Bacharach
LOVE

"ONLY SIXTEEN," 1959
Sam Cooke
AGE, ROCK 'N' ROLL-i

"ONLY THE LONELY (KNOW THE WAY I FEEL),"
1960
Roy Orbison, Joe Melson
FEELING, LONELINESS, ROCK 'N' ROLL-i

"ONLY THE STRONG SURVIVE," 1968
Kenny Gamble, Leon Huff, Jerry Butler
SOUL

"ONLY YOU (AND YOU ALONE)," 1955
Ande Rand, Buck Ram
TABLE 4-c, ROCK 'N' ROLL-ii

"OOBY DOOBY," 1956
Wade Moore, Dick Penner
NONSENSE, ROCK 'N' ROLL-i, ROCKABILLY

"OOH THAT KISS," 1931
Mort Dixon, Joe Young/Harry Warren
KISSING

"OPEN THE DOOR, RICHARD," 1947
"Dusty" Fletcher, John Mason/Jack McVea
NAMES, RHYTHM AND BLUES

"OPERATOR," 1975
William Spivey
SINGING GROUPS, TELEPHONES

"Opus (Number) One," 1944
Sid Garris/Sy Oliver
BMI, TABLE 4-d

"Orange Blossom Special," 1938
Ervin T. Rouse
COUNTRY AND WESTERN, FLOWERS

"Orange Colored Sky," 1950
Milton De Lugg, Willie Stein
TABLE 7

"Orchids in the Moonlight," 1933
Gus Kahn/Vincent Youmans
BRAZIL, TABLE 9, FLOWERS, MOON, TANGO, VERSE

"Original Dixieland One-Step," 1918
Joe Jordan, James D. La Rocca, J. Russel Robinson
DIXIELAND

"Ostrich Walk," 1918
Edwin B. Edwards, James D. La Rocca, Anthony Sbarbaro, Larry Shields
ANIMALS, DIXIELAND

"Otchi Tchorniya," SEE "Dark Eyes"

"Other Eyes," 1916
Clare Kummer
WOMEN AS SONGWRITERS

"Our House," 1970
Graham Nash
ROCK-v

"Our Language of Love," 1956
Julian More, David Heneker, Monty Norman (Eng.)/ Marguerite Monnot
TALKING

"Our Love," 1939
Larry Clinton, Buddy Bernier, Bob Emmerich
CLASSICS, TABLE 6, LOVE

"Our Love Is Here to Stay," SEE "Love Is Here to Stay"

"Our Song," 1937
Dorothy Fields/Jerome Kern
MUSIC

"Out of My Dreams," 1943
Oscar Hammerstein II/Richard Rodgers
DREAMS, TABLE 12, WALTZ

"Out of Nowhere," 1931
Edward Heyman/John Green
TABLE 8, HARMONY, TEMPO, TRIPLET

"Out of the Blues," 1988
Debbie Gibson
WOMEN AS SONGWRITERS

"Over Hills and Fields of Daisies," 1906
Carrie Jacobs-Bond
WOMEN AS SONGWRITERS

"Over the Mountain Across the Sea," 1957
Rex Garvin
MOUNTAINS, RHYTHM AND BLUES

"Over the Rainbow," 1939
E. Y. Harburg/Harold Arlen
ACADEMY AWARDS, TABLE 1, BALLAD, CODA, COMPOSERS, DEPRESSION YEARS, FILM MUSICALS, TABLE 9, GOLDEN AGE, IMAGINATION, LANDMARKS OF STAGE AND SCREEN, LYRICISTS, MAGIC, OCTAVE, PLACES, RELEASE, SINGERS, TABLE 15

"Over the Waves (Sobre los Olas)"; SEE ALSO "The Loveliest Night of the Year"
m. Juventino Rosas
MEXICO, OCEAN

"Over There," 1917
George M. Cohan
BROKEN CHORD, COMPOSER-LYRICISTS, MARCH, PATRIOTISM, POPULAR SONG, QUOTATION, RAINBOW, WORLD WAR I

"Pack Up Your Troubles in Your Old Kit Bag and Smile, Smile, Smile," 1915
George Asaf/Felix Powell
BRITAIN, SMILING, WORLD WAR II

"Paddlin' Madelin' Home," 1925
Harry Woods
BOATING, HOME

"PADMOSKOVEEYE VIETCHERA," SEE "MIDNIGHT IN MOSCOW"

"PAGAN LOVE SONG," 1929
Arthur Freed/Nacio Herb Brown
FILM MUSIC, TABLE 8

"PAIN IN MY HEART," 1963
Otis Redding
SOUL

"PAINT IT BLACK," 1966
Mick Jagger, Keith Richards
ROCK-iii

"PAPA, CAN YOU HEAR ME," 1983
Marilyn Bergman, Alan Bergman/Michel Legrand
WOMEN AS SONGWRITERS

"PAPA COME QUICK," 1991
Bonnie Raitt, Billy Vera
WOMEN AS SONGWRITERS

"PAPA DON'T PREACH," 1986
Brian Elliot, Madonna
FATHERS, ROCK-xii, TABLE 15, WOMEN AS SONGWRITERS

"PAPA LOVES MAMBO," 1954
Al Hoffman, Dick Manning, Bix Reichner
FATHERS, MAMBO

"PAPA WAS A ROLLIN' STONE," 1972
Barrett Strong, Norman Whitfield
FATHERS, TABLE 10-p, TABLE 10-q, MOTOWN

"PAPA, WON'T YOU DANCE WITH ME?," 1947
Sammy Cahn/Jule Styne
DANCING, FATHERS

"PAPA'S GOT A BRAND NEW BAG," 1965
James Brown
FATHERS, TABLE 10-m, SOUL

"PAPER DOLL," 1915
Johnny S. Black
DOLL, RECORDING, SINGING GROUPS

"PAPERBACK WRITER," 1966
John Lennon, Paul McCartney
WRITING

"PARADE OF THE WOODEN SOLDIERS," 1905
Ballard Macdonald (Eng.)/Leon Jessel
GERMANY, MARCH, REVUES, TABLE 14

"PARADISE," 1931
Nacio Herb Brown, Gordon Clifford/Nacio Herb Brown
TABLE 8, HEAVEN, RADIO

"PARIS IN THE SPRING," 1935
Mack Gordon/Harry Revel
TABLE 5, SEASONS

"PARLEZ-MOI D'AMOUR," SEE "SPEAK TO ME OF LOVE"

"PARTY LIGHTS," 1962
Claudine Clark
ROCK 'N' ROLL-iv

"THE PARTY'S OVER," 1956
Betty Comden, Adolph Green/Jule Styne
COLLABORATION, FAREWELLS, LYRICISTS

"PASS ME BY," 1964
Carolyn Leigh/Cy Coleman
TABLE 8

"PASSE TON CHEMIN," SEE "BACK TRACK!"

"PASSING BY," 1947
Jack Lawrence (Eng.)/John Hess, Paul Misraki
FRANCE

"PATCHES," 1970
Ronald Dunbar, General Johnson
TABLE 10-q

"PEACE BE STILL," c.1960
eighteenth-century song, arr. by James Cleveland
GOSPEL

"PEACE IN THE VALLEY," 1939
Thomas A. Dorsey
GOSPEL, RELIGION

"Peace Train," 1971
Cat Stevens
ROCK-vi

"The Peanut Vendor (El Manicero)," 1930
Marion Sunshine, L. Wolfe Gilbert/Moises Simons
CUBA, DANCE CRAZES, RUMBA

"Peckin'," 1937
Ben Pollack, Harry James
DANCE CRAZES

"Peg o' My Heart," 1913
Alfred Bryan/Fred Fischer
TABLE 2, *BILLBOARD*, VAMP, *YOUR HIT PARADE*

"Peggy Sue," 1958
Jerry Allison, Norman Petty, Buddy Holly
NAMES

"Pennies From Heaven," 1936
John Burke/Arthur Johnston
BRILL BUILDING, DEPRESSION YEARS, TABLE 9, GOLDEN AGE, HEAVEN, LYRICISTS, MONEY, SINGERS, TABLE 15, TIN PAN ALLEY

"Pennsylvania Polka," 1942
Lester Lee, Zeke Manners
TABLE 9, POLKA, STATES

"Pennsylvania 6-5000," 1940
Carl Sigman/Jerry Gray
TABLE 3, TELEPHONES

"Penny Lane," 1967
John Lennon, Paul McCartney
MONEY, ROCK-ii, STREETS

"Penthouse Serenade (When We're Alone)," 1931
Will Jason, Val Burton
CITIES, TABLE 5, HOME, LONELINESS, MUSIC, TRIPLET

"People," 1964
Bob Merrill/Jule Styne
COMPOSERS, TABLE 10-c, MELODY, TABLE 11, PEDAL POINT, PEOPLE, TABLE 15

"People Are Strange," 1967
Robert Krieger, James Morrison, John Densmore, Raymond Manzarek
PEOPLE, ROCK-ix

"People Get Ready," 1965
Curtis Mayfield
PEOPLE, SOUL

"People Got to Be Free," 1968
Edward Brigati, Jr., Felix Cavaliere
PEOPLE

"People Have Power," 1988
Patti Smith, Fred Smith
WOMEN AS SONGWRITERS

"People Will Say We're in Love," 1943
Oscar Hammerstein II/Richard Rodgers
LANDMARKS OF STAGE AND SCREEN, LOVE, LYRICISTS, MUSICAL PLAYS, TABLE 12, PEOPLE, *YOUR HIT PARADE*

"Per un Bacio d'Amore," *see* "Tell Me You're Mine"

"Perdido," 1942
H. J. Lengsfelder, Erwin Drake/Juan Trizol
TABLE 3, BRASS

"A Perfect Day," 1910
Carrie Jacobs-Bond
DAY, ENDING, WOMEN AS SONGWRITERS

"The Perfect Song," 1915
Clarence Lucas/Joseph Carl Briel
FILM MUSIC, TABLE 8

"Perfidia," 1939
Milton Leeds (Eng.)/Albert Dominguez
TABLE 4-d, BOLERO, MEXICO, RUMBA

"Perhaps, Perhaps, Perhaps (Quizas, Quizas, Quizas)," 1947
Joe Davis (Eng.)/Osvaldo Farres
CUBA, RUMBA

"PERSONALITY," 1945
Johnny Burke/James Van Heusen
TABLE 9, HUMOR, RHYTHM AND BLUES

"PETER COTTONTAIL," 1950
Steven Nelson, Jack Rollins
HOLIDAYS, *YOUR HIT PARADE*

"THE PHANTOM OF THE OPERA," 1986
Charles Hart, Richard Stilgoe, Mike Batt/Andrew
Lloyd Webber
KEY, TABLE 12

"PHILADELPHIA FREEDOM," 1974
Elton John, Bernie Taupin
TABLE 5, ROCK-x

"PHILADELPHIA, U.S.A.," 1958
Anthony Antonucci, Bill Borrelli, Jr.
TABLE 5

"PHYSICAL," 1981
Stephen Kipner, Terry Shaddick
TABLE 15

"PIANO MAN," 1973
Billy Joel
MAN, PERFORMER-SONGWRITERS, PIANO,
TABLE 15

"THE PICCOLINO," 1935
Irving Berlin
DANCE CRAZES, TABLE 9

"(THEME FROM) PICNIC," 1955
Steve Allen/George Duning
TABLE 8

"THE PICTURE THAT'S TURNED TOWARDS THE
WALL," 1891
Charles Graham
GAY NINETIES

"PIECE OF MY HEART," 1967
Bert Berns, Jerry Ragovoy
ROCK-vii

"PIECES OF DREAMS," 1970
Alan Bergman, Marilyn Bergman/Michel Legrand
TABLE 8, FRANCE, WOMEN AS SONGWRITERS

"PIGALLE," 1948
Charles Newman (Eng.)/Georges Ulmer
FRANCE, MODE

"PINBALL WIZARD," 1969
Peter Townshend
ROCK-iii

"PIRATE JENNY," 1928 (GER.), 1952 (ENG.)
Marc Blitzstein (Eng.)/Kurt Weill
GERMANY

"THE PIRATE'S CHORUS," 1879
Sir William Gilbert/Sir Arthur Sullivan
CLASSICS

"PISTOL PACKIN' MAMA," 1943
Al Dexter
COUNTRY AND WESTERN, MOTHERS, SING-
ING GROUPS

"A PLACE IN THE SUN," 1966
Ronald Miller/Bryan Wells
PLACES

"LES PLAISIRS DÉMODÉS," SEE "THE OLD
FASHIONED WAY"

"PLAY A SIMPLE MELODY," 1914
Irving Berlin
COUNTERPOINT, MELODY, MUSIC

"PLAY FIDDLE PLAY," 1932
Jack Lawrence/Emery Deutsch, Arthur Altman
GYPSY MUSIC, MODE, STRINGS

"PLAY GYPSIES—DANCE GYPSIES," 1926
Harry B. Smith (Eng.)/Emmerich Kalmán
AUSTRIA, DANCING, GYPSY MUSIC, HUN-
GARY, OPERETTA, TABLE 13

"PLAY THAT BARBERSHOP CHORD (MR.
JEFFERSON LORD)," 1910
Ballard MacDonald, William Tracey/Lewis F. Muir
BARBERSHOP, MUSIC

"PLAY THAT FUNKY MUSIC," 1976
Robert Parissi
FUNK

"Playground in My Mind," 1971
Paul Vance, Lee Pockriss
MIND

"Playmates," 1889
Harry Dacre
VAUDEVILLE

"Playmates," 1940
Saxie Dowell
FRIENDSHIP

"Please Don't Go," 1979
Harry Casey, Richard Finch
DISCO

"Please Don't Stop Loving Me," 1966
Joy Byers
WOMEN AS SONGWRITERS

"Please Don't Talk About Me When I'm Gone," 1930
Sidney Clare/Sam H. Stept
RADIO, TALKING

"Please Don't Tell Me How the Story Ends," 1971
Kris Kristofferson
TABLE 10-u

"Please Go 'Way and Let Me Sleep," SEE **"Somebody Else Is Taking My Place"**

"Please Keep Out of My Dreams," 1915
Elsa Maxwell
WOMEN AS SONGWRITERS

"Please Mister Postman," 1961
Brian Holland, Robert Bateman, Freddy Gorman, Georgia Dobbins, William Garrett
WRITING

"Please Mister Sun," 1951
Sid Frank/Ray Getzov
SUN

"Please Please Me," 1964
John Lennon, Paul McCartney
ROCK-ii

"Please Please Please," 1956
James Brown, Johnny Terry
SOUL

"Please Send Me Someone to Love," 1950
Percy Mayfield
RHYTHM AND BLUES

"Pledging My Love," 1954
Ferdinand Washington, Don D. Robey
RHYTHM AND BLUES

"Plenty to Be Thankful For," 1942
Irving Berlin
HOLIDAYS

"The Poet's Dream (L'Âme des Poètes)," 1959
Mel Peters (Eng.)/Charles Trenet
FRANCE

"Poinciana," 1936
Buddy Bernier (Eng.)/Nat Simon
BOLERO, TREES

"The Point of No Return," 1986
Charles Hart, Richard Stilgoe/Andrew Lloyd Webber
TABLE 12, PEDAL POINT, TONALITY

"Poison Ivy," 1959
Jerry Leiber, Mike Stoller
ROCK 'N' ROLL-ii

"Politics and Poker," 1959
Sheldon Harnick/Jerry Bock
HUMOR

"Polk Salad Annie," 1968
Tony Joe White
NAMES

"Polka Dots and Moonbeams," 1940
Johnny Burke/James Van Heusen
MOON

"Pomp and Circumstance," 1902
m. Sir Edward Edgar
MARCH

"POOR BUTTERFLY," 1916
John Golden/Raymond Hubbell
ANIMALS, KEY, OPERA

"POOR LITTLE BUTTERFLY IS A FLY GIRL NOW," 1919
Sam Lewis, Joe Young/M. K. Jerome
OPERA

"POOR LITTLE FOOL," 1958
Shari Sheeley
FOOLS, ROCK 'N' ROLL-iii, TABLE 15

"THE POOR PEOPLE OF PARIS," 1956
Jack Lawrence (Eng.)/Marguerite Monnot
ALLITERATION, TABLE 5, PEOPLE

"POOR SIDE OF TOWN," 1966
Johnny Rivers, Lou Adler
TABLE 5

"POP LIFE," 1985
Prince Rogers Nelson
ROCK-xii

"POPEYE THE SAILOR MAN," 1931
Sammy Lerner
MAN

"POPSICLES AND ICICLES," 1963
David Gates
SINGING GROUPS

"POPULAR JARABE TAPATIO," *SEE* **"MEXICAN HAT DANCE"**

"PORTRAIT OF MY LOVE," 1961
David West/Cyril Ornadel
BRITAIN

"POTATOES ARE CHEAPER—TOMATOES ARE CHEAPER NOW'S THE TIME TO FALL IN LOVE," *SEE* **"(POTATOES ARE CHEAPER—TOMATOES ARE CHEAPER) NOW'S THE TIME TO FALL IN LOVE"**

"POWDER YOUR FACE WITH SUNSHINE," 1948
Carmen Lombardo, Stanley Rochinski
SUN

"POWER OF LOVE," 1971
Kenny Gamble, Leon Huff, Joe Simon
SOUL

"POWER OF LOVE/LOVE POWER," 1991
Luther Vandross, Marcus Miller, Teddy Vann
TABLE 10-q

"POWER TO THE PEOPLE," 1971
John Lennon
ROCK-ii

"PRAISE THE LORD AND PASS THE AMMUNITION," 1942
Frank Loesser
TABLE 3, COMPOSER-LYRICISTS, PATRIOTISM, WORLD WAR II

"PRAYER," *SEE* **"BLUE MOON"**

"PRECIOUS LORD, TAKE MY HAND," 1932
Thomas A. Dorsey
GOSPEL

"PRELUDE TO A KISS," 1938
Irving Gordon, Irving Mills/Edward Kennedy "Duke" Ellington
TABLE 3, CHROMATICISM, CIRCLE OF FIFTHS, HARMONIC RHYTHM, HARMONY, KISSING, SCALE

"PRETEND," 1952
Lew Douglas, Cliff Parman, Frank Lavere
IMAGINATION

"PRETTY BABY," 1916
Gus Kahn, Tony Jackson, Egbert van Alstyne
BABY, REVUES, TABLE 14

"PRETTY BABY," 1978
Deborah Harry, Chris Stein
WOMEN AS SONGWRITERS

"A PRETTY GIRL IS LIKE A MELODY," 1919
Irving Berlin
BEAUTY, FOX TROT, GIRL, MELODY, MUSIC, REVUES

"PRETTY LADY," 1976
Stephen Sondheim
BEAUTY, LADY

"PRETTY LITTLE ANGEL EYES," 1961
Tommy Boyce, Curtis Lee
TABLE 2, ANGELS, ROCK 'N' ROLL

"PRETTY WOMEN," 1978
Stephen Sondheim
BEAUTY, OPERA, WOMAN

"PRIMA DONNA," 1986
Charles Hart, Richard Stilgoe/Andrew Lloyd Webber
TABLE 12

"PRISONER OF LOVE, 1931
Leo Robin/Russ Columbo, Clarence Gaskill
DEPRESSION YEARS, LOVE, LYRICISTS, RADIO,
ROCK 'N' ROLL-i, TABLE 15

"THE PRISONER'S SONG," 1924
Guy Massey
COUNTRY AND WESTERN, ROARING TWEN-
TIES

"PROHIBITION BLUES," 1918
Ring Lardner/Nora Bayes (pseud. Dora Goldberg)
WOMEN AS SONGWRITERS

"PROMISES, PROMISES," 1968
Hal David/Burt Bacharach
POPULAR SONG-x

"PROUD MARY," 1968
John C. Fogerty
TABLE 4-d, BOATING, FADE-OUT, TABLE 10-p,
NAMES, RIVERS, ROCK-ix, SHEET MUSIC,
VERSE

"P.S. I LOVE YOU," 1934
Johnny Mercer/Gordon Jenkins
LOVE, WRITING

"P.S. I LOVE YOU," 1962
John Lennon, Paul McCartney
LOVE, WRITING

"PSYCHOTIC REACTION," 1966
Ken Ellner, Roy Chaney, Craig Atkinson, John Byrne,
John Michalski
ROCK

"PUFF (THE MAGIC DRAGON)," 1963
Peter Yarrow, Leonard Lipton
FOLK SONG, MAGIC, SINGING GROUPS

"PUPPY LOVE," 1959
Paul Anka
AGE, LOVE, ROCK 'N' ROLL-iii

"PURPLE HAZE," 1967
Jimi Hendrix
TABLE 7, HEAVY METAL, ROCK-vii

"THE PURPLE PEOPLE EATER," 1958
Sheb Wooley
PEOPLE

"PUT A LITTLE LOVE IN YOUR HEART," 1969
Jackie DeShannon, Randy Myers, Jimmy Holiday
TABLE 4-d

"PUT ME OFF AT BUFFALO," 1895
Harry Dillon/John Dillon
GAY NINETIES

"PUT ON A HAPPY FACE," 1960
Lee Adams/Charles Strouse
ANATOMY, TABLE 2, HAPPINESS, TABLE 11,
SMILING

"PUT ON YOUR OLD GREY BONNET," 1909
Stanley Murphy/Percy Wenrich
CLOTHING, COLORS, TABLE 7, LENGTH

"PUT THE BLAME ON MAME," 1944
Allan Roberts, Doris Fisher
TABLE 9

"PUT YOUR ARMS AROUND ME HONEY," 1910
Junie McCree/Albert von Tilzer
ANATOMY, TABLE 2, BARBERSHOP, TABLE 11,
SINGING GROUPS

"PUT YOUR DREAMS AWAY," 1942
Ruth Lowe/Stephen Weiss, Paul Mann
WOMEN AS SONGWRITERS

"PUT YOUR HAND IN THE HAND," 1970
Gene Maclellan
RELIGION

"PUT YOUR HEAD ON MY SHOULDER," 1958
Paul Anka
ANATOMY, TABLE 2, CANADA, ROCK 'N'
ROLL-iii

"PUTTIN' ON THE RITZ," 1929
Irving Berlin
COMPOSERS, CONTRACTIONS, RHYTHM,
SLANG

"A PUZZLEMENT," 1951
Oscar Hammerstein II/Richard Rodgers
HUMOR

"P.Y.T. (PRETTY YOUNG THING)," 1984
James Ingram, Quincy Jones
ROCK-xii

"QUAND ON NÀ QUE L'AMOUR," SEE "IF WE ONLY HAVE LOVE"

"QUANDO, QUANDO, QUANDO (TELL ME WHEN)," 1962
Pat Boone (Eng.)/Tony Renis
ITALY

"QUARTER TO THREE," 1961
Frank Guida, Joe Royster, Gene Bargo, Gary Anderson
ROCK 'N' ROLL, TIME OF DAY

"QUE RESTE T'IL DE NOS AMOURS," SEE " I WISH YOU LOVE"

"QUE SERA, SERA," SEE "WHATEVER WILL BE, WILL BE,"

"QUEEN OF CHARCOAL ALLEY," 1899
Ida Emerson, Joseph Howard
WOMEN AS SONGWRITERS

"QUEEN OF THE HOP," 1958
Woody Harris, Bobby Darin
ROCK 'N' ROLL-iii

"QUEEN OF THE HOUSE," 1965; SEE ALSO "KING OF THE ROAD"
Mary Taylor/Roger Miller
TABLE 10-t

"THE QUEST," SEE "THE IMPOSSIBLE DREAM"

"QUIEN SERA," SEE "SWAY"

"QUIÉREME MUCHO," SEE "YOURS"

"QUIET NIGHTS OF QUIET STARS (CORCOVADO)," 1962
Gene Lees (Eng.)/Antonio Carlos Jobim
BASS LINE, BOSSA NOVA, BRAZIL, CHROMATICISM

"QUIZAS, QUIZAS, QUIZAS," SEE "PERHAPS, PERHAPS, PERHAPS"

"RACING WITH THE MOON," 1941
Vaughn Monroe, Pauline Pope/Johnny Watson
TABLE 3, MOON

"RAG DOLL," 1964
Bob Crewe, Bob Gaudio
DOLL, ROCK 'N' ROLL-ii

"RAG MOP," 1950
Johnnie Lee Wells, Deacon Anderson
SINGING GROUPS

"RAGGEDY ANN," 1923
Anne Caldwell/Jerome Kern
WOMEN AS SONGWRITERS

"RAGGING THE SCALE," 1915
Dave Ringle/Edward Claypoole
RAGTIME

"RAGS TO RICHES," 1953
Richard Adler, Jerry Ross
MONEY, TABLE 15

"RAGTIME COWBOY JOE," 1912
Grant Clarke/Lewis F. Muir, Maurice Abrahams
RAGTIME

"RAGTIME SEXTET," 1912
Irving Berlin
OPERA

"RAGTIME VIOLIN," 1911
Irving Berlin
RAGTIME

"The Rain in Spain," 1956
Alan Jay Lerner/Frederick Loewe
TABLE 12, NATIONS, TANGO, WEATHER

"Rain on the Roof," 1932
Ann Ronell
WEATHER, WOMEN AS SONGWRITERS

"The Rainbow Connection," 1979
Paul Williams, Kenny Ascher
RAINBOW

"Raindrops Keep Fallin' on My Head," 1969
Hal David/Burt Bacharach
TABLE 1, ANATOMY, TABLE 2, CODA, COL-
LABORATION, COMPOSERS, FILM MUSIC,
TABLE 8, LYRICISTS, PERFORMER-
SONGWRITERS, WEATHER

"Rainy Days and Mondays," 1970
Paul Williams, Roger Nichols
DAY, DAYS OF THE WEEK, WEATHER

"Rainy Night in Rio," 1946
Leo Robin/Arthur Schwartz
TABLE 5, TABLE 9, WEATHER

"Ramblin' Man," 1973
Richard Betts
MAN, ROCK

"Ramblin' Rose," 1962
Noel Sherman, Joe Sherman
NAMES

"Ramona," 1927
Wolfe Gilbert/Mabel Wayne
FILM MUSIC, TABLE 8, NAMES, TABLE 15

"The Rangers' Song," 1926
Joseph McCarthy/Harry Tierney
MARCH, TABLE 13

"Rapper's Delight," 1979
The Sugarhill Gang
RAP

"Rapture," 1980
Debbie Harry/Chris Stein
RAP

"Raspberry Beret," 1985
Prince Rogers Nelson
CLOTHING, TABLE 7, ROCK

"Reach Out I'll Be There," 1966
Brian Holland, Lamont Dozier, Eddie Holland
MOTOWN

"Ready Teddy," 1956
John Marascalco, Robert Blackwell
ROCK 'N' ROLL-i

"The Real American Folk Song (Is a Rag)," 1918
Ira Gershwin/George Gershwin
WOMEN AS SONGWRITERS

"Reckless Blues," 1925
Bessie Smith
WOMEN AS SONGWRITERS

"Red, Hot, and Blue," 1936
Cole Porter
MUSICAL COMEDY

"The Red River Valley," 1896
Anonymous
POPULAR SONG-i, RIVERS

"Red Roses for a Blue Lady," 1948
Sid Tepper, Roy Brodsky
COLORS, TABLE 7, LADY

"Red Sails in the Sunset," 1935
Jimmy Kennedy/Hugh Williams
BOATING, BRITAIN, TABLE 7, OCEAN, SUN,
TIME OF DAY

"Reet Petite," 1957
Berry Gordy, Jr., Tyran Carlo
MOTOWN, ROCK 'N' ROLL-i

"Reginella Campagnola," SEE "The Woodpecker Song"

"Release Me," 1954
Eddie Miller, W. S. Stevenson
TABLE 4-c, RHYTHM AND BLUES

"REMEMBER," 1925
Irving Berlin
BASS LINE, FORGETTING MEMORY, SCALE,
VAMP, VERSE, WALTZ

"REMEMBER ME," 1937
Al Dubin/Harry Warren
MEMORY

"REMEMBER MY FORGOTTEN MAN," 1933
Al Dubin/Harry Warren
DEPRESSION YEARS, FILM MUSICALS, TABLE 9

"REMEMBER PEARL HARBOR," 1941
Don Reid, Sammy Kaye
MEMORY

"REMINISCING," 1978
Graham Goble
TABLE 4-d

"RESCUE ME," 1965
Carl William Smith, Raynard Miner
SOUL

"RESPECT," 1965
Otis Redding
TABLE 10-m, TABLE 10-n, TABLE 15, SOUL

"RESPECT YOURSELF," 1971
Mack Rice, Luther Ingram
GOSPEL, SOUL

"RESTLESS HEART," 1954
Harold Rome
TABLE 12

"RESTLESS NIGHTS," 1979
Karla Bonoff
WOMEN AS SONGWRITERS

"RETREAT," DATE UNCERTAIN
m. anonymous bugle call
BROKEN CHORD

"RETURN TO SENDER," 1962
Otis Blackwell, Winfield Scott
WRITING

"REVEILLE," C. 1836
m. anonymous bugle call
BROKEN CHORD, QUOTATION

"REVOLUTION," 1968
John Lennon, Paul McCartney
ROCK-ii

"RHAPSODY IN BLUE," 1924
m. George Gershwin
BLUE NOTE, CITIES, COMPOSERS, ROARING
TWENTIES

"RHINESTONE COWBOY," 1973
Larry Weiss
JEWELRY

"RHODE ISLAND IS FAMOUS FOR YOU," 1948
Howard Dietz/Arthur Schwartz
REVUES, TABLE 14, STATES

"RHYTHM OF THE RAIN," 1962
John Gummoe
TABLE 4-d, RHYTHM, WEATHER

"RICH GIRL," 1976
Daryl Hall
MONEY

"THE RIDDLE SONG," ALSO KNOWN AS "I GAVE MY LOVE A CHERRY," C. 1850
Anonymous
FOLK SONG

"RIDE YOUR PONY," 1965
Naomi Neville
ANIMALS, SOUL

"(GHOST) RIDERS IN THE SKY (A COWBOY LEGEND)," 1949
Stan Jones
TABLE 3, TABLE 8, QUOTATION, TABLE 15,
SKY

"RIDERS ON THE STORM," 1971
John Densmore, Jim Morrison, Robert Krieger, Ray Manzarek (The Doors)
ROCK-ix

"RIDIN' HIGH," 1936
Cole Porter
HEIGHT

"THE RIFF SONG," 1926
Otto Harbach, Oscar Hammerstein II/Sigmund
Romberg
TABLE 13

"RIGHT AS THE RAIN," 1944
E. Y. Harburg/Harold Arlen
WEATHER

"RIGHT BACK WHERE WE STARTED FROM,"
1976
Pierre Tubbs, Vincent Edwards
BEGINNING, DISCO

"RIGHT PLACE, WRONG TIME," 1973
Mac Rebonnack
PLACES

"RIGHT THING TO DO," 1972
Carly Simon
WOMEN AS SONGWRITERS

"RIO RITA," 1926
Joseph McCarthy/Harry Tierney
ALLITERATION, TABLE 13

"RIP IT UP," 1956
Robert A. Blackwell, John Marascalco
ROCK 'N' ROLL-i

"RIPPLES OF THE NILE," SEE **"MOONLIGHT
COCKTAIL"**

"THE RIVER KWAI MARCH," 1957
Malcolm Arnold
TABLE 8, RIVERS

"THE RIVER SEINE," 1953
Allan Roberts, Alan Holt (Eng.)/Guy La Farge
FRANCE

"RIVER, STAY 'WAY FROM MY DOOR," 1931
Mort Dixon/Harry Woods
DEPRESSION YEARS, RIVERS

"RIVERBOAT SHUFFLE," 1925
Dick Voynow, Mitchell Parish, Irving Mills (1939)
Hoagy Carmichael
RIVERS

"THE ROAD TO MOROCCO," 1942
Johnny Burke/James Van Heusen
TABLE 9, NATIONS, STREETS, TRAVEL

"ROAMIN' IN THE GLOAMIN'," 1911
Harry Lauder
BRITAIN, DIALECT

"ROCK-A-BYE BABY," 1884
Effie I. Canning
WOMEN AS SONGWRITERS

**"ROCK-A-BYE YOUR BABY WITH A DIXIE
MELODY,"** 1918
Joe Young, Sam M. Lewis/Jean Schwartz
BABY, HUNGARY, MELODY, TABLE 11, SING-
ERS, TABLE 15

"ROCK AND A HARD PLACE," 1989
Mick Jagger, Keith Richards
ROCK-iii

"ROCK AND ROLL IS HERE TO STAY," 1958
Danny and the Juniors
ROCK 'N' ROLL

"ROCK AND ROLL MUSIC," 1957
Chuck Berry
MUSIC, ROCK 'N' ROLL-i

"(WE'RE GONNA) ROCK AROUND THE CLOCK,"
1953
Max C. Freedman, Jimmy De Knight
COUNTRY AND WESTERN, TABLE 8, ROCK 'N'
ROLL, TIME OF DAY

"ROCK ME GENTLY," 1974
Andy Kim
TENDERNESS

"ROCK STEADY," 1971
Aretha Franklin
WOMEN AS SONGWRITERS

"ROCK THE BOAT," 1973
Waldo Holmes
BOATING, DISCO

"ROCK WITH YOU," 1979
Rod Temperton
ROCK-xii

"ROCK YOUR BABY," 1974
Harry Casey, Richard Finch
BABY, DISCO

"ROCKET MAN," 1972
Elton John, Bernie Taupin
ROCK-x

"THE ROCKFORD FILES," 1974
m. Peter Carpenter, Mike Post
TELEVISION

"ROCKIN' AROUND THE CHRISTMAS TREE,"
1958
Johnny Marks
CHRISTMAS, ROCK 'N' ROLL-iii

"ROCKIN' CHAIR," 1930
Hoagy Carmichael
SINGING GROUPS

"A ROCKIN' GOOD WAY (TO MESS AROUND
AND FALL IN LOVE)," 1960
Brook Benton, Clyde Otis, Luchi De Jesus
FALLING IN LOVE, RHYTHM AND BLUES

"ROCKIN' PNEUMONIA AND THE BOOGIE
WOOGIE FLU," 1957
Huey P. Smith, Jôhn Vincent
BOOGIE-WOOGIE, RHYTHM AND BLUES

"ROCKIN' ROBIN," 1958
Jimmie Thomas
BILLBOARD, BIRDS, NAMES

"ROCKY MOUNTAIN HIGH," 1972
John Denver, Michael Taylor
HEIGHT, MOUNTAINS, TABLE 15

"ROLL ON, MISSISSIPPI, ROLL ON," 1931
Eugene West, James McCaffrey, Dave Ringle
RIVERS, SINGING GROUPS

"ROLL OUT THE BARREL," SEE "BEER BARREL
POLKA"

"ROLL OVER BEETHOVEN," 1956
Chuck Berry
POPULAR SONG -viii, ROCK 'N' ROLL-i

"ROMANCE," 1926
Otto Harbach, Oscar Hammerstein II/ Sigmund
Romberg
TABLE 13, ROMANCE

"ROMANCE," 1929
Edgar Leslie/Walter Donaldson
ROMANCE

"ROMANY LIFE," 1898
Harry Smith/Victor Herbert
ART SONG, TABLE 13

"A ROOM WITH A VIEW," 1928
Noël Coward
BRITAIN, COMPOSER-LYRICISTS

"ROSALIE," 1937
Cole Porter
NAMES

"ROSANNA," 1982
David Paich
TABLE 10-a, NAMES, SUBJECTS

"THE ROSE," 1977
Amanda McBroom
TABLE 4-d, TABLE 8, TABLE 10-f, TABLE 15,
TEXTURE

"(I NEVER PROMISED YOU A) ROSE GARDEN,"
1967
Joe South
TABLE 4-c, FLOWERS

"ROSE-MARIE," 1924
Otto Harbach, Oscar Hammerstein II/Rudolf Friml
NAMES, OPERETTA, TABLE 13, ROARING
TWENTIES

"ROSE OF THE RIO GRANDE," 1922
Edgar Leslie/Harry Warren, Ross Gorman
RIVERS

"THE ROSE OF TRALEE," 1912
Charles Glover, C. Mordaunt Spencer
IRELAND

"ROSE OF WASHINGTON SQUARE," 1919
Ballard MacDonald/James F. Hanley
NAMES

"ROSE ROOM," 1917
Harry Williams/Art Hickman
HARMONIC RHYTHM

"ROSES OF PICARDY," 1916
Fred E. Weatherly/Haydn Wood
FLOWERS, NATIONS, WORLD WAR I

"ROSETTA," 1935
Earl Hines, Henri Woode
PIANO

"ROSIE THE RIVETER," 1942
Redd Evans, John Jacob Loeb
WORLD WAR II

"(I'M COMIN' UP) THE ROUGH SIDE OF THE MOUNTAIN," 1984
F. C. Barnes, Janice Brown
GOSPEL

"'ROUND MIDNIGHT," 1944
Bernie Hanighen/Cootie Williams, Thelonious Monk
BEBOP, CROSSOVER, TIME OF DAY

"(GET YOUR KICKS ON) ROUTE 66!," 1946
Bob Troup
STREETS, TRAVEL

"ROW, ROW, ROW," 1912
William Jerome/James V. Monaco
BOATING, REVUES, TABLES 14

"ROYAL GARDEN BLUES," 1919
Clarence Williams, Spencer Williams
BLUES

"RUBY," 1953
Mitchell Parish/Heinz Roemheld
TABLE 8, NAMES

"RUBY BABY," 1955
Jerry Leiber, Mike Stoller
BABY, NAMES, SINGING GROUPS

"RUBY, DON'T TAKE YOUR LOVE TO TOWN," 1966
Mel Tillis
TABLE 4-d

"RUBY TUESDAY," 1967
Mick Jagger, Keith Richards
NAMES

"RUDOLPH THE RED-NOSED REINDEER," 1949
Johnny Marks
ANIMALS, CHRISTMAS, COLORS, TABLE 7

"RUM AND COCA-COLA," 1944; *SEE ALSO* **"L'ANNÉE PASSÉE," 1944**
Morey Amsterdam/Jeri Sullavan, Paul Baron
BORROWING, FOOD AND DRINK, SINGING GROUPS

"RUNAROUND SUE," 1961
Ernie Maresca, Dion Di Mucci
ROCK 'N' ROLL-ii

"RUNAWAY," 1961
Del Shannon/Max Crook, Del Shannon
ROCK-iii, ROCK 'N' ROLL

"RUNNIN' WILD," 1922
Joe Grey, Leo Wood/A. Harrington Gibbs
DEPRESSION YEARS, ROARING TWENTIES

"RUNNING WITH THE NIGHT," 1983
Cynthia Weil/Lionel Richie, Jr.
WOMEN AS SONGWRITERS

"RUSSIAN LULLABY," 1927
Irving Berlin
MODE, NATIONS, SLEEP

"RUSTY DUSTY BLUES," 1943
J. Mayo Williams
BLUES, RHYTHM AND BLUES

"'S WONDERFUL," 1927
Ira Gershwin/George Gershwin
AABA, COMPOSERS, CONTRACTIONS, LYRI-
CISTS, MUSICAL COMEDY, TABLE 11, SOCIETY
TEMPO, WONDER

"SAD SONGS (SAY SO MUCH)," 1984
Elton John, Bernie Taupin
RHYME

"SAFELY ROCKED IN MOTHER'S ARMS," 1887
Effie I. Canning
WOMEN AS SONGWRITERS

"SAIL ALONG, SILVERY MOON," 1937
Harry Tobias/Percy Wenrich
BOATING, MOON

"SAIL NAVY DOWN THE FIELD," *SEE* **"ANCHORS AWEIGH"**

"SAIL ON," 1979
Lionel B. Richie, Jr.
BOATING

"SAILBOAT IN THE MOONLIGHT," 1937
Carmen Lombardo, John Jacob Loeb
BOATING

"SAILING," 1979
Christopher Cross
BOATING, TABLE 10-a, TABLE 10-b

"ST. LOUIS BLUES," 1914
W. C. Handy
BLUES, TABLE 5, FORM, MODE, TANGO, TIN
PAN ALLEY

"SALLY GO 'ROUND THE ROSES," 1963
Lona Stevens (pseud. Lona Spector, Zell Sanders)
ROCK 'N' ROLL-iv

"SAM, YOU MADE THE PANTS TOO LONG," 1940; *SEE ALSO* **"LAWD, YOU MADE THE NIGHT TOO LONG"**
Sam Lewis, Victor Young, Milton Berle
HUMOR

"SAMBA DE ORFEU," 1959
Antonia Maria/Luis Bonfa
BRAZIL, SAMBA

"SAM'S SONG," 1950
Jack Elliott/Lew Quadling
NAMES

"SAN ANTONIO ROSE," 1940
Bob Wills
CITIES, TABLE 5, COUNTRY AND WESTERN,
TABLE 9

"SAN FERNANDO VALLEY," 1943
Gordon Jenkins
BORROWING, TABLE 5

"SAN FRANCISCO," 1936
Gus Kahn/Bronislaw Kaper, Walter Jurmann
CITIES, TABLE 5

"SAN FRANCISCO (BE SURE TO WEAR SOME FLOWERS IN YOUR HAIR)," 1967
John Phillips
CITIES, TABLE 5, FLOWERS

"SAND IN MY SHOES," 1941
Frank Loesser/Victor Schertzinger
CLOTHING, TABLE 9, TABLE 15, WATER-
FRONT

"SANTA CLAUS IS COMING TO TOWN," 1934
Haven Gillespie/J. Fred Coots
CHRISTMAS, TABLE 15

"SARI WALTZ," *SEE* **"LOVE'S OWN SWEET SONG"**

"SATIN DOLL," 1958
Johnny Mercer/Billy Strayhorn, Duke Ellington
AABA, TABLE 3, CLOTHING, DOLL, LYRICISTS,
PIANO, POPULAR SONG-vii, RIFF

"(I CAN'T GET NO) SATISFACTION," 1965
Mick Jagger, Keith Richards
ROCK-iii

"SATURDAY IN THE PARK," 1972
Robert Lamm
DAYS OF THE WEEK, ROCK-ix

"Saturday Night," 1976
Phil Coulter, Bill Martin
DAYS OF THE WEEK, NIGHT

"Saturday Night at the Movies," 1964
Barry Mann, Cynthia Weil
DAYS OF THE WEEK, ROCK 'N' ROCK-ii

"Saturday Night Fish Fry," 1949
Ellis Walsh, Louis Jordan
DAYS OF THE WEEK, RHYTHM AND BLUES

"Saturday Night (Is the Loneliest Night of the Week)," 1944
Sammy Cahn/Jule Styne
DAYS OF THE WEEK, LONELINESS, NIGHT

"Save It for a Rainy Day," 1977
Stephen Bishop
WEATHER

"Save the Country," 1968
Laura Nyro
WOMEN AS SONGWRITERS

"Save the Last Dance for Me," 1960
Jerome "Doc" Pomus, Mort Shuman
TABLE 4-d, DANCING, ROCK 'N' ROLL-ii

"Saved," 1960
Jerry Leiber, Mike Stoller
SOUL

"Saving All My Love for You," 1978
Gerry Goffin/Michael Masser
TABLE 10-f, METER, SHEET MUSIC, TABLE 15

"Say a Prayer for the Boys Over There," 1943
Herb Magidson/Jimmy McHugh
WORLD WAR II

"Say 'Au Revoir' But Not 'Goodbye,'" 1893
Harry Kennedy
FAREWELLS, FOREIGN LANGUAGE, GAY NINETIES

"Say, Has Anybody Seen My Sweet Gypsy Rose," 1973
Irwin Levine, L. Bussell Brown
GYPSY MUSIC, SWEETNESS

"Say It Isn't So," 1932
Irving Berlin
RADIO

"Say It With Music," 1921
Irving Berlin
MUSIC, NEW YORK CITY, REVUES, TABLE 14

"Say Not Love Is a Dream," 1912
Basil Hood (Eng.)/Franz Lehár
AUSTRIA, DREAM

"Say 'Si Si,'" 1936
Al Stillman (Eng.)/Ernesto Lecuona
CUBA, RUMBA

"Say You, Say Me" 1985
Lionel Richie
TABLE 1

"Scarborough Fair/Canticle," 1966
Paul Simon, Art Garfunkel
TABLE 4-c, TABLE 5, FOLK ROCK, ROCK-v

"Scarlet Ribbons (For Her Hair)," 1949
Jack Segal/Evelyn Danzig
TABLE 2, CLOTHING, COLORS, TABLE 7

"Scatter-brain," 1939
Johnny Burke/Frankie Masters, Kahn Keene, Carl Bean
TABLE 2, THINKING

"Schöner Gigolo," SEE "Just a Gigolo"

"School Days (When We Were a Couple of Kids)," 1906
Will D. Cobb/Gus Edwards
CHILDHOOD, DAY, VAUDEVILLE, WALTZ

"Scotch and Soda," 1959
Dave Guard
FOOD AND DRINK

"Serenade," 1921
Dorothy Donnelly/Sigmund Romberg, from Franz Schubert
TABLE 13

"Serenade," 1924
Dorothy Donnelly/Sigmund Romberg
HUNGARY, MUSIC, OPERETTA, TABLE 13, WOMEN AS SONGWRITERS

"Serenade in Blue," 1942
Mack Gordon/Harry Warren
TABLE 3, BLUE NOTE, COLLABORATION, COLORS, TABLE 7, TABLE 9, MUSIC, REPEATED NOTE

"Serenade in the Night," 1936
Jimmy Kennedy (Eng.)/Cesare A. Bixio, B. Cherubini
ADAPTATION, MUSIC, NIGHT

"Sergeant Pepper's Lonely Hearts Club Band," 1967
John Lennon, Paul McCartney
LONELINESS, PEOPLE

"Seventy-Six Trombones," 1957
Meredith Willson
BRASS, COMPOSER-LYRICISTS, TABLE 11

"Sexual Healing," 1982
Marvin Gaye
TABLE 10-o

"Sh-Boom," 1954
James Keyes, Claude Feaster, Carl Feaster, Floyd F. McRae, James Edwards
COVER, NONSENSE, ROCK 'N' ROLL, SINGING GROUPS

"Sha-La-La," 1964
Robert Mosley, Robert Taylor, Frances Hycock
DOO-WOP

"Shadow Dancing," 1978
Robin Gibb, Maurice Gibb, Barry Gibb, Andy Gibb
DANCING

"The Shadow of Your Smile," 1965
Paul Francis Webster/Johnny Mandel
TABLE 1, BOLERO, CIRCLE OF FIFTHS, TABLE 8, TABLE 10-b, MODE, PICKUP, SMILING

"Shadow Waltz," 1933
Al Dubin/Harry Warren
TABLE 9

"Shadows of the Night," 1980
David Leigh Byron
TABLE 10-i

"Shaft," see **"Theme From Shaft"**

"Shake a Hand," 1953
Joe Morris
TABLE 2, SOUL

"Shake, Rattle and Roll," 1954
Charles Calhoun
COVER, DANCING, NOVELTY SONG

"(Shake, Shake, Shake) Shake Your Booty," 1976
Harry Casey, Richard Finch
DISCO

"Shaking the Blues Away," 1927
Irving Berlin
BLUES

"Shall We Dance?," 1937
Ira Gershwin/George Gershwin
DANCING, TABLE 9

"Shall We Dance?," 1951
Oscar Hammerstein II/Richard Rodgers
DANCING, MUSICAL PLAYS, TABLE 12

"Shalom," 1961
Jerry Herman
GREETINGS

"Shame, Shame, Shame," 1974
Sylvia Robinson
DISCO

"Shanghai Lil," 1933
Al Dubin/Harry Warren
FILM MUSICALS

"Shangri-La," 1946
Carl Sigman/Matty Malneck, Robert Maxwell
HEAVEN

"(In) A Shanty in Old Shanty Town," 1932
Joe Young/Little Jack Little, John Siras
TABLE 3, TABLE 5, HOME

"Share Your Love With Me," 1963
Deadric Malone, Al Braggs
TABLE 10-n

"Sharing the Night Together," 1978
Ava Aldridge, Edward Struzick
TOGETHERNESS

"Sharkey's Day," 1983
Laurie Anderson
WOMEN AS SONGWRITERS

"Sharkey's Night," 1983
Laurie Anderson
WOMEN AS SONGWRITERS

"She Believes in Me," 1977
Steve Gibb
TABLE 15

"She Cried," 1962
Ted Daryll, Greg Richards
CRYING, SINGING GROUPS

"She Didn't Say `Yes'," 1931
Otto Harbach/Jerome Kern
INTERVAL, LENGTH

"She Is Not Thinking of Me (Waltz at Maxim's)," 1958
Alan Jay Lerner/Frederick Loewe
THINKING

"She Loves You," 1964
John Lennon, Paul McCartney
ROCK-ii

"She Sells Sea-Shells (On the Seashore)," 1908
Terry Sullivan/Harry Gifford
ALLITERATION, HUMOR, OCEAN, WATER-FRONT

"She Thinks I Still Care," 1962
Dickey Lee Lipscomb, Steve Duffy
COUNTRY AND WESTERN

"She Was Happy Till She Met You," 1899
Charles Graham/Monroe H. Rosenfeld
MEETING

"She'd Rather Be With Me," 1966
Garry Bonner, Alan Gordon
ROCK-v

"The Sheik of Araby," 1921
Harry B. Smith, Francis Wheeler/Ted Snyder
NATIONS, PEABODY

"She'll Be Comin' Round the Mountain," 1899
traditional African-American melody
FOLK SONG, MOUNTAINS

"Shenandoah (Across the Wide Missouri)," c. 1826
traditional American folk song
FOLK SONG, RIVERS

"Sherry," 1962
Bob Gaudio
ROCK 'N' ROLL-ii

"She's a Fool," 1963
Ben Raleigh, Mark Barkan
FOOLS, ROCK 'N' ROLL-iv

"She's a Lady," 1968
John B. Sebastian
LADY

"She's About a Mover," 1965
Doug Sahm
ROCK

"(I Got a Woman Crazy for Me) She's Funny That Way," 1928
Richard A. Whiting/Neil Moret
MADNESS, SCALE, WOMAN

"She's Leaving Home," 1967
John Lennon, Paul McCartney
HOME

"She's Not There," 1964
Rod Argent
ROCK-iii

"She's Out of My Life," 1979
Tom Bähler
LIFE

"She's the Daughter of Mother Machree," 1915
Jeff Nebarb (pseud. Jeff T. Branen)/Ernest R. Ball
IRELAND

"She's Too Fat for Me," *see* "Too Fat Polka"

"Shimmy, Shimmy, Ko-Ko-Bop," 1959
Bob Smith
NONSENSE, SINGING GROUPS

"Shine On, Harvest Moon," 1908
Jack Norworth/Nora Bayes (pseud. Dora Goldberg), Jack Norworth
BARBERSHOP, MOON, NEW YORK CITY, REVUES, TABLE 14, TABLE 15, WOMEN AS SONGWRITERS

"A Shine on Your Shoes," 1932
Howard Dietz/Arthur Schwartz
CLOTHING, FILM MUSICALS, REVUES, TABLE 14

"Shining Star," 1975
Maurice White, Philip Bailey, Larry Dunn
TABLE 10-p, STARS

"Shining Star," 1980
Lee Graham, Jr., Paul Richmond
TABLE 10-p

"A Ship Without a Sail," 1929
Lorenz Hart/Richard Rodgers
BOATING

"Shoo-Shoo Baby," 1943
Phil Moore
WORLD WAR II

"Shop Around," 1960
Berry Gordy, William "Smokey" Robinson, Jr.
MOTOWN

"Short Fat Fannie," 1957
Larry Williams
NAMES, RHYTHM AND BLUES

"Shortnin' Bread," 1925
Clement Wood, Jacques Wolfe
FOLK SONG

"Should I (Reveal?)," 1929
Arthur Freed/Nacio Herb Brown
QUESTIONS

"Shout," 1959
O'Kelly Isley, Ronald Isley, Rudolf Isley
SOUL

"Show Me," 1956
Alan Jay Lerner/Frederick Loewe
COLLABORATION, TABLE 12

"Show Me the Way to Go Home," 1925
Irving King (pseud. Reginald Connelly, Jimmy Campbell)
CANADA, HOME, RANGE

"Shower the People," 1975
James Taylor
PEOPLE, ROCK-vi

"Shrimp Boats," 1951
Paul Mason Howard, Paul Weston
BOATING, FOOD AND DRINK, TABLE 15

"Shuffle Off to Buffalo," 1932
Al Dubin/Harry Warren
TABLE 5, FILM MUSICALS, TABLE 9, TRAINS

"Siboney," 1929
Theodora Morse (Eng.)/Ernesto Lecuona
CUBA, RUMBA

"Side by Side by Side," 1970
Stephen Sondheim
TABLE 11, TOGETHERNESS

"The Sidewalks of New York" also known as "East Side, West Side," 1894
Charles B. Lawlor, James W. Blake
CARDINAL POINTS, CITIES, TABLE 5, GAY NINETIES, LENGTH, STREETS, SUBJECTS, TIN PAN ALLEY, WALTZ

"Siempre en Mi Corazon," see "Always in My Heart"

"Sign o' the Times," 1987
Prince Rogers Nelson
ROCK-xii

"Silent Night (Stille Nacht)," 1818
Anonymous (Eng.)/Franz Gruber
CHRISTMAS

"Silhouettes," 1957
Frank C. Slay, Jr., Bob Crewe
COVER

"Silly Love Songs," 1976
Paul McCartney, Linda McCartney
ROCK-ii

"Silver Bells," 1950
Jay Livingston, Ray Evans
CHRISTMAS, TABLE 8

"Silver Moon," 1927
Dorothy Donnelly/Sigmund Romberg
MOON, TABLE 13, WOMEN AS SONGWRITERS

"Silver Threads Among the Gold," 1873
Eben E. Rexford/H. P. Danks
POPULAR SONG-i

"Simple Things Mean a Lot to Me," 1977
Carole King/Richard Evers
WOMEN AS SONGWRITERS

"Simply Irresistible," 1988
Robert Palmer
TABLE 10-i

"Since I Don't Have You," 1958
James Beaumont, Janet Vogel, Joseph Verscharen, Walter Lester, John Taylor/Joseph Rock, Lennie Martin
DOO-WOP, SINGING GROUPS

"Since I Fell for You," 1948
Buddy Johnson
FALLING IN LOVE, RHYTHM AND BLUES

"Since I Met You Baby," 1956
Ivory Joe Hunter
BABY, RHYTHM AND BLUES

"Since You've Been Gone (Sweet, Sweet Baby)," 1968
Aretha Franklin, Ted White
SOUL, WOMEN AS SONGWRITERS

"Sincerely," 1954
Harvey Fuqua, Alan Freed
SINGING GROUPS

"Sing a Song of Basie," 1958
Annie Ross, Dave Lambert, Jon Hendricks
VOCALESE

"Sing for Your Supper," 1938
Lorenz Hart/Richard Rodgers
FOOD AND DRINK

"Sing, Sing, Sing, Sing," 1936
Louis Prima
TABLE 3, PERCUSSION, SWING

"Singin' in the Rain," 1929
Arthur Freed/Nacio Herb Brown
COMPOSERS, FILM MUSIC, TABLE 9, QUOTATION, WEATHER

"Singing the Blues," 1954
Melvin Endsley
BLUES, TABLE 4-d, COUNTRY AND WESTERN

"Sioux City Sue," 1945
Ray Freedman/Dick Thomas
TABLE 5, NAMES

"Sir Duke," 1976
Stevie Wonder
KEY

"The Siren's Song," 1917
P. G. Wodehouse/Jerome Kern
BROKEN CHORD, FRIENDSHIP, TABLE 11, WOMAN

"Sit Down Servant," c. 1955
James Cleveland
GOSPEL

"Sit Down, You're Rockin' the Boat," 1950
Frank Loesser
BOATING, TABLE 11

"Sit Down, You're Rocking the Boat,"
1913
William Jerome, Grant Clarke, Jean Schwartz
BOATING

"Sittin' on the Dock of the Bay," *SEE*
"Dock of the Bay"

"Six Days on the Road," 1963
Earl Green, Carl Montgomery
COUNTRY AND WESTERN

"Sixteen Candles," 1959
Luther Dixon, Allyson R. Khent
AGE

"Sixteen Going on Seventeen," 1959
Oscar Hammerstein II/Richard Rodgers
AGE, CHILDHOOD

"Sixteen Tons," 1947
Merle Travis
COUNTRY AND WESTERN, TABLE 15

"Sixty Minute Man," 1951
William Ward, Rose Marks
MAN, RHYTHM AND BLUES

"Sketches of Spain" 1959
m. Gil Evans, with Miles Davis
ARRANGEMENT

"Skinny Legs and All," 1967
Joe Tex
SOUL

"Skoda Lasky," *SEE* **"Beer Barrel Polka"**

"Skokiaan," 1954
Tom Glazer (Eng.)/August Msarurgwa
SINGING GROUPS

"Sky High," 1975
Clive Scott, Desmond Dyer
HEIGHT, SKY

"Skylark," 1942
Johnny Mercer/Hoagy Carmichael
TABLE 3, BIRDS, INTERVAL, SKY, TRIPLET

"Skyliner," 1944
m. Charlie Barnet
SKY

"Slap That Bass," 1937
Ira Gershwin/George Gershwin
TABLE 9, STRINGS

"Sleep," 1923
Earl Lebieg
SLEEP

"Sleepy Head," 1926
Benny Davis, Jesse Green
SINGING GROUPS

"(By the) Sleepy Lagoon," 1930
Jack Lawrence/Eric Coates
SLEEP, WATERFRONT

"Sleepy Serenade," 1941
Mort Green/Lou Singer
SLEEP

"Sleepy Shores," 1971
m. Johnny Pearson
BRITAIN, OCEAN, SLEEP, WATERFRONT

"Sleepy Time Gal," 1924
Joseph R. Alden, Raymond B. Egan/Angie Lorenzo,
Richard A. Whiting
GIRL, SLEEP

"Sleigh Ride," 1950
Mitchell Parish/Leroy Anderson
CHRISTMAS

"Slip Away," 1968
William Armstrong, Wilbur Terrell, Marcus Daniel
SOUL

"Slip Slidin' Away," 1977
Paul Simon
ROCK-v

"Slippin' Around," 1949
Floyd Tillman
COUNTRY AND WESTERN

"Sloop John B.," 1966
Brian Wilson, based on Bahamian folk song (1927)
BOATING, ROCK-i

"Slow Hand," 1980
John Bettis/Michael Clark
TABLE 4-d

"Small Fry," 1938
Frank Loesser, Hoagy Carmichael
CHILDHOOD

"Small World," 1959
Stephen Sondheim/Jule Styne
TABLE 11, WORLD

"Smile," 1954
John Turner, Geoffrey Parsons/Charles Chaplin
SMILING

"Smile and Show Your Dimple," *see* **"Easter Parade"**

"Smile, Darn Ya, Smile," 1931
Charles O'Flynn, Jack Meskill/Max Rice
SMILING

"Smiles," 1917
J. Will Callahan/Lee S. Roberts
REVUES, TABLE 14, SMILING

"Smilin' Through," 1919
Arthur A. Penn
SMILING

"Smoke Dreams," 1936
Arthur Freed/Nacio Herb Brown
DREAMS

"Smoke Gets in Your Eyes," 1933
Otto Harbach/Jerome Kern
ACCOMPANIMENT, ANATOMY, TABLE 2, ART SONG, CHORUS, COMPOSERS, COUNTERMELODY, ENHARMONIC EQUIVALENCE, GOLDEN AGE, KEY, MELODY, MUSICAL COMEDY, TABLE 11, RELEASE, ROCK 'N' ROLL-ii, SEQUENCE, VERSE

"Smoke Rings," 1933
Ned Washington/H. Eugene Gifford
TABLE 3

"Snowbird," 1970
Gene MacLellan
TABLE 4-c, CANADA, WEATHER

"So Close, Yet So Far," 1965
Joy Byers
WOMEN AS SONGWRITERS

"So Far," 1947
Oscar Hammerstein II/Richard Rodgers
TABLE 12

"So Far Away," 1971
Carole King
ROCK-vi, WOMEN AS SONGWRITERS

"So in Love," 1948
Cole Porter
BEGUINE, COMPOSER-LYRICISTS, INTERVAL, MODE, MUSICAL COMEDY, TABLE 11, SUBJECTS

"So Long (It's Been Good to Know Yuh)," 1939
Woody Guthrie
FAREWELLS, FOLK SONG, GUITAR, PROTEST SONG, SINGING GROUPS

"So Much in Love," 1963
Roy Straigis, William Jackson III, George Williams
SINGING GROUPS

"So Rare," 1937
Jack Sharpe/Jerry Herst
TABLE 3

"So You Want to Be a Rock and Roll Star," 1966
Jim McGuinn, Chris Hillman
ROCK-v

"Sobre los Olas," *see* **"Over the Waves"**

"Society's Child," 1966
Janis Ian
ROCK, WOMEN AS SONGWRITERS

"SOFT LIGHTS AND SWEET MUSIC," 1932
Irving Berlin
MUSIC, TABLE 11, TENDERNESS

"SOFT SUMMER BREEZE," 1955
Judy Spencer/Eddie Heywood
SEASONS, TENDERNESS, WEATHER

"SOFTLY AS I LEAVE YOU," 1960
Hal Shaper (Eng.)/A. De Vita
ITALY, TENDERNESS

"SOFTLY, AS IN A MORNING SUNRISE," 1928
Oscar Hammerstein II/Sigmund Romberg
HUNGARY, MODE, TABLE 13, SUN, TANGO,
TENDERNESS, TIME OF DAY

"SOLAMENTE UNA VEZ," SEE "YOU BELONG TO
MY HEART"

"SOLDIER BOY," 1961
Luther Dixon, Florence Green
BOY, ROCK 'N' ROLL-iv

"SOLILOQUY," 1945
Oscar Hammerstein II/Richard Rodgers
CHILDHOOD, FATHERS, GIRL, TABLE 12

"SOLITUDE," 1934
Eddie DeLange, Irving Mills/Duke Ellington
TABLE 3, COMPOSERS, LONELINESS, PIANO,
RELEASE

"SOME DAY I'LL FIND YOU," 1931
Noël Coward
BRITAIN, COMPOSER-LYRICISTS, DAY

"SOME DAY MY PRINCE WILL COME," 1937
Larry Morey/Frank Churchill
DAY, TABLE 9, HUMOR, WALTZ, WISHING

"SOME DAY WE'LL BE TOGETHER," 1970
Harvey Fuqua, Jackey Beavers, Johnny Bristol
DAY, MOTOWN

"SOME DAY YOU'LL WANT ME TO WANT
YOU," 1946
Jimmie Hodges
DAY

"SOME ENCHANTED EVENING," 1949
Oscar Hammerstein II/Richard Rodgers
CODA, LYRICISTS, MUSICAL PLAYS, TABLE 12,
YOUR HIT PARADE

"SOME FOLKS," 1855
Stephen Collins Foster
POPULAR SONG-i

"SOME KIND-A-WONDERFUL," 1961
Gerry Goffin, Carole King
ROCK 'N' ROLL-ii, WONDER

"SOME KIND OF FRIEND," 1982
Adrienne Anderson/Barry Manilow
WOMEN AS SONGWRITERS

"SOME OF THESE DAYS," 1910
Shelton Brooks
CANADA, COON SONG, DAY, FORM, RE-
CORDING, TIN PAN ALLEY, VAUDEVILLE

"SOMEBODY ELSE IS TAKING MY PLACE," 1937
Richard Howard, Bob Ellsworth, Russ Morgan
BORROWING

"SOMEBODY LOVES ME," 1893
Hattie Starr
WOMEN AS SONGWRITERS

"SOMEBODY LOVES ME," 1924
B. G. DeSylva, Ballard MacDonald/George Gershwin
AABA, BLUE NOTE, LOVE, PIANO, REVUES,
TABLE 14

"SOMEBODY, SOMEWHERE," 1956
Frank Loesser
OPERA

"SOMEBODY STOLE MY GAL," 1918
Leo Wood
GIRL

"SOMEBODY TO LOVE," 1967
Darby Slick
ROCK-vii

"SOMEDAY SOON," 1963
Ian Tyson
BOLERO

"SOMEONE SAVED MY LIFE TONIGHT," 1974
Elton John, Bernie Taupin
LIFE, ROCK-x

"SOMEONE TO LAY DOWN BESIDE ME," 1976
Karla Bonoff
WOMEN AS SONGWRITERS

"SOMEONE TO WATCH OVER ME," 1926
Ira Gershwin/George Gershwin
COLLABORATION, COMPOSERS, CONTRAC-
TIONS, FILM MUSIC, GOLDEN AGE, LYRI-
CISTS, MUSICAL COMEDY, TABLE 11

"SOMEONE'S ROCKING MY DREAMBOAT," 1941
Emerson Scott, Otis Rene, Leon Rene
BOATING, DREAMS

"SOMETHIN' STUPID," 1967
Carson C. Parks
TABLE 4-d

"SOMETHING," 1969
George Harrison
TABLE 4-b, ROCK-ii, TONALITY

"SOMETHING BLUE," 1960
m. Gil Evans, with Miles Davis
ARRANGEMENT

"SOMETHING TO REMEMBER YOU BY," 1930
Howard Dietz/Arthur Schwartz
COLLABORATION, COMPOSERS, LYRICISTS,
MEMORY, REVUES, TABLE 14

"SOMETHING WONDERFUL," 1951
Oscar Hammerstein II/Richard Rodgers
COLLABORATION, MUSICAL PLAYS, TABLE 12,
WONDER

"SOMETHING'S COMING," 1957
Stephen Sondheim/Leonard Bernstein
METER, TABLE 12, VAMP

"SOMETHING'S GOTTA GIVE," 1955
Johnny Mercer
COMPOSER-LYRICISTS

"SOMETIMES I FEEL LIKE A MOTHERLESS CHILD," 1899
traditional African-American spiritual
FEELINGS, MOTHERS

"SOMETIMES I'M HAPPY," 1927
Leo Robin, Clifford Grey/Vincent Youmans
ADAPTATION, TABLE 3, COMPOSERS, HAPPI-
NESS, MUSICAL COMEDY, TABLE 11, TIME

"SOMETIMES WHEN WE TOUCH," 1977
Dan Hill/Barry Mann
TABLE 4-d

"SOMEWHERE," 1957
Stephen Sondheim/Leonard Bernstein
ENHARMONIC EQUIVALENCE, LANDMARKS
OF STAGE AND SCREEN, MELODY, MODULA-
TION, MUSICAL PLAYS, TABLE 12, PLACES

"SOMEWHERE A VOICE IS CALLING," 1911
Eileen Newton/Arthur F. Tate
PLACES

"SOMEWHERE ALONG THE WAY," 1952
Sammy Gallop/Kurt Adams
PLACES

"SOMEWHERE MY LOVE (LARA'S THEME)," 1966
Paul Francis Webster/Maurice Jarre
FILM MUSIC, TABLE 8, PLACES

"SOMEWHERE OUT THERE," 1986
James Horner, Barry Mann, Cynthia Weil
BRITAIN, TABLE 9, TABLE 10-b, IMAGINATION,
LYRICS, PLACES, WOMEN AS SONGWRITERS

"SOMOS NOVOS," SEE "IT'S IMPOSSIBLE"

"SONG FROM M*A*S*H (SUICIDE IS PAIN-LESS)," 1970
Mike Altman, Johnny Mandel
TABLE 8, TELEVISION

"THE SONG FROM MOULIN ROUGE (WHERE IS YOUR HEART?)," 1953
William Engvick/Georges Auric
TABLE 2, TABLE 4-c, TABLE 8, FRANCE, YOUR
HIT PARADE

"The Song Is Ended But the Melody Lingers On," 1927
Irving Berlin
ENDING, MELODY, MUSIC

"The Song Is You," 1932
Oscar Hammerstein II/Jerome Kern
ACCOMPANIMENT, ART SONG, COMPOSERS,
COUNTERMELODY, GOLDEN AGE, LYRICISTS,
MUSIC, TABLE 11, RELEASE TEMPO

"Song of India," 1897
m. Nicolai Rimsky-Korsakov
SWING

"Song of Love," 1921
Dorothy Donnelly/Sigmund Romberg
AUSTRIA, CLASSICS, TABLE 6, HUNGARY,
MUSIC, TABLE 13, WOMEN AS SONGWRITERS

"The Song of Songs," 1914
Clarence Lucas (Eng.)/Moya (pseud. Harold Vicars)
ART SONG, MUSIC

"Song of the Islands," 1915
Charles E. King
IMPROVISATION

"Song of the Vagabonds," 1925
Brian Hooker/Rudolf Friml
TABLE 13

"Song Sung Blue," 1972
Neil Diamond
TABLE 7, MUSIC

"Song to a Seagull," 1967
Joni Mitchell
WOMEN AS SONGWRITERS

"Sonny Boy," 1928
Al Jolson, B. G. DeSylva, Lew Brown, Ray Henderson
AGE, BOY, CHILDHOOD, FILM MUSICALS,
TABLE 9, MODE, ROARING TWENTIES, SINGERS, TABLE 15

"Soon," 1929
Ira Gershwin/George Gershwin
BLUE NOTE, TABLE 12, TIME

"Soon (Maybe Not Tomorrow)," 1935
Lorenz Hart/Richard Rodgers
TIME

"Soon It's Gonna Rain," 1960
Tom Jones/Harvey Schmidt
TABLE 11, TIME, WEATHER

"Sooner or Later (I Always Get My Man)," 1990
Stephen Sondheim
TABLE 1, MAN, TIME

"Sophisticated Lady," 1933
Irving Mills, Mitchell Parish/Duke Ellington
BASS LINE, TABLE 3, CHROMATICISM, COMPOSERS, GOLDEN AGE, HARMONIC RHYTHM,
HARMONY, LADY, PIANO, RELEASE

"Sophisticated Lady (She's a Different Lady)," 1976
Marvin Yancy, Chuck Jackson, Jr., Natalie Cole
TABLE 10-n

"Sorry Seems to Be the Hardest Word," 1976
Elton John
ROCK-x

"Soul Man," 1967
David Porter, Isaac Hayes
TABLE 10-p, SOUL

"The Sound of Music," 1959
Oscar Hammerstein II/Richard Rodgers
LYRICISTS, MUSIC, MUSICAL PLAYS, TABLE 12

"The Sound of Silence," 1964
Paul Simon
ALLITERATION, TABLE 4-c, CADENCE, FOLK
ROCK, LYRICS, MODALITY, PROTEST SONG,
ROCK-v

"Sous le Ciel de Paris," see **"Under Paris Skies"**

"Sous les Ponts de Paris," see **"Under the Bridges of Paris"**

"SOUTH AMERICA, TAKE IT AWAY," 1946
Harold Rome
NATIONS, REVUES, TABLE 14, SINGING
GROUPS

"SOUTH AMERICAN WAY," 1939
Al Dubin/Jimmy McHugh
NATIONS

"SOUTH OF THE BORDER (DOWN MEXICO WAY)," 1939
Jimmy Kennedy, Michael Carr
TABLE 3, CARDINAL POINTS, NATIONS

"SOUTH RAMPART STREET PARADE," 1938
Steve Allen/Ray Bauduc, Bob Haggart
TABLE 3, DIXIELAND, STREETS

"SOUTH STREET," 1963
Kal Mann/Dave Appell
ROCK 'N' ROLL-iv

"SOUTHERN NIGHTS," 1974
Allen Toussaint
TABLE 4-d, NIGHT

"SOUVENIR DE VIENNE," SEE "INTERMEZZO"

"SPACE ODDITY," 1969
David Bowie
ROCK-x

"LA SPAGNOLA," SEE "THE BOWERY"

"THE SPANISH CAVALIER," SEE "LOVE LETTERS IN THE SAND"

"SPANISH EYES," 1965
Eddie Snyder, Charles Singleton (Eng.)/Bert Kaempfert
ANATOMY, TABLE 2, TABLE 4-c, NATIONS

"SPANISH FLEA," 1965
m. Julius Wechter
ANIMALS, NATIONS

"SPANISH HARLEM," 1960
Phil Spector, Jerry Leiber
TABLE 4-d, TABLE 5, HARLEM, RHYTHM AND
BLUES, ROCK 'N' ROLL

"SPEAK LOW," 1943
Ogden Nash/Kurt Weill
BEGUINE, COMPOSERS, TABLE 11, TENDER-
NESS

"SPEAK SOFTLY LOVE (LOVE THEME FROM THE GODFATHER)," 1972
Larry Kusik/Nino Rota
BROKEN CHORD, FILM MUSIC, TABLE 8,
ITALY, MODE, TENDERNESS

"SPEAK TO ME OF LOVE," 1932
Bruce Sievier (Eng.)/Jean Lenoir
FRANCE, LOVE

"SPEEDOO," 1955
Esther Navarro
ROCK 'N' ROLL-ii

"SPINNING WHEEL," 1968
David Clayton Thomas
TABLE 4-d, FADE-OUT, ROCK-ix

"SPIRIT IN THE DARK," 1970
Aretha Franklin
WOMEN AS SONGWRITERS

"SPIRIT IN THE SKY," 1969
Norman Greenbaum
RELIGION

"SPLISH SPLASH," 1958
Bobby Darin, Jean Murray
ROCK 'N' ROLL-iii, TABLE 15

"A SPOONFUL OF SUGAR," 1963
Richard M. Sherman, Robert B. Sherman
TABLE 9, SWEETNESS

"S'POSIN," 1929
Andy Razaf/Paul Denniker
IMAGINATION, RADIO, SCALE

"SPRING IS HERE," 1938
Lorenz Hart, Richard Rodgers
TABLE 11, SEASONS

"SPRING WILL BE A LITTLE LATE THIS YEAR," 1944
Frank Loesser
COMPOSER-LYRICISTS, SEASONS

"STAGGER LEE," 1958
 Harold Logan, Lloyd Price
 NAMES, RHYTHM AND BLUES

"STAIRWAY TO HEAVEN," 1960
 Howard Greenfield/Neil Sedaka
 HEAVEN, ROCK 'N' ROLL

"STAIRWAY TO HEAVEN," 1972
 Jimmy Page, Robert Plant
 HEAVY METAL

"STAIRWAY TO THE STARS," 1939
 Mitchell Parish/Matt Malneck, Frank Signorelli
 IMAGINATION, STARS

"STAN' UP AND FIGHT," 1943
 Oscar Hammerstein II/Georges Bizet
 OPERA

"STAND BY ME," 1905
 Charles A. Tindley
 GOSPEL

"STAND BY ME," C. 1955
 James Cleveland
 GOSPEL

"STAND BY ME," 1961
 Ben E. King, Jerry Leiber, Mike Stoller
 TABLE 4-c, RHYTHM AND BLUES, ROCK 'N'
 ROLL

"STAND BY YOUR MAN," 1968
 Tammy Wynette, Billy Sherrill
 COUNTRY AND WESTERN, MAN, WOMEN AS
 SONGWRITERS

"STANDING ON THE CORNER," 1956
 Frank Loesser
 TABLE 12, OPERA, SINGING GROUPS, STREETS

"THE STAR," SEE "BYE BYE BLUES"

"STAR DUST," 1929
 Mitchell Parish/Hoagy Carmichael
 ADAPTATION, TABLE 3, COMPOSERS, CROSS-
 OVER, GOLDEN AGE, HIT SONG, KEY, POPU-
 LAR SONG-ii, STANDARD, STARS, TIN PAN
 ALLEY, VERSE

"STAR EYES," 1943
 Don Raye, Gene De Paul
 TABLE 2, STARS

"THE STAR-SPANGLED BANNER," 1814
 Francis Scott Key/John Stafford Smith
 BROKEN CHORD, PATRIOTISM, ROCK-vii

"THE STARS AND STRIPES FOREVER," 1897
 John Philip Sousa
 GAY NINETIES, PATRIOTISM

"STARS FELL ON ALABAMA," 1934
 Mitchell Parish/Frank Perkins
 STARS, STATES

"STARS IN MY EYES," 1936
 Dorothy Fields/Fritz Kreisler
 TABLE 2, AUSTRIA, TABLE 9, STARS, WALTZ

"STARS SHINE IN YOUR EYES (THEME FROM LA
 STRADA)," 1956
 John Turner, Geoffrey Parsons/Nino Rota
 ITALY, STARS

"START ME UP," 1981
 Mick Jagger, Keith Richards
 ROCK-iii

"STAY AS SWEET AS YOU ARE," 1934
 Mack Gordon/Harry Revel
 TABLE 9, SWEETNESS

"STAYIN' ALIVE," 1977
 Barry Gibb, Robin Gibb, Maurice Gibb
 TABLE 9

"STEAM HEAT," 1954
 Richard Adler, Jerry Ross
 TABLE 11

"STEEL GUITAR RAG," 1941
 Merle Travis, Cliff Stone/Leon McAuliffe
 COUNTRY AND WESTERN

"A STEIN SONG," SEE "IT'S ALWAYS FAIR
 WEATHER WHEN GOOD FELLOWS GET
 TOGETHER"

"STEIN SONG (UNIVERSITY OF MAINE)," 1910
Lincoln Colcord/E. A. Fenstad
MARCH, RADIO

"STELLA BY STARLIGHT," 1946
Ned Washington/Victor Young
FILM MUSIC, TABLE 8, INTERVAL, NAMES,
STARS

"STEP BY STEP," 1960
Ollie Jones, Billy Dawn Smith
SINGING GROUPS

"STEPPIN' OUT WITH MY BABY," 1947
Irving Berlin
BABY, CONTRACTIONS, TABLE 9, SLANG

"STILLE NACHT," *SEE* **"SILENT NIGHT"**

"STIR IT UP," 1972
Bob Marley
REGGAE

"STOMPIN' AT THE SAVOY," 1934
Andy Razaf/Benny Goodman, Edgar Sampson, Chick
Webb
DANCING, HARLEM, RIFF

"STONED SOUL PICNIC," 1967
Laura Nyro
SINGING GROUPS, WOMEN AS SONGWRITERS

"STOOD UP," 1957
Dub Dickerson, Erma Herrold
ROCK 'N' ROLL-iii

"STOP AND THINK IT OVER," 1964
Jake Graffagnino
ENDING, THINKING

"STOP! IN THE NAME OF LOVE," 1965
Eddie Holland, Brian Holland, Lamont Dozier
ENDING, LOVE, MOTOWN

"STOP, LOOK, LISTEN," 1964
Joy Byers
WOMEN AS SONGWRITERS

"STORMY WEATHER," 1933
Ted Koehler/Harold Arlen
COMPOSERS, DEPRESSION YEARS, HARLEM,
LENGTH, RELEASE, TABLE 15, TORCH SONG,
WEATHER

"THE STORY OF A STARRY NIGHT," 1941
Jerry Livingston, Al Hoffman, Mann Curtis
TABLE 6, NIGHT, STARS

**"THE STORY OF THE ROSE (HEART OF MY
HEART),"** 1899
"Alice"/Andrew Mack
TABLE 2, BARBERSHOP

"A STORY UNTOLD," 1955
LeRoy Griffin, Marty Wilson
COVER

"STOUTHEARTED MEN," 1928
Oscar Hammerstein II/Sigmund Romberg
TABLE 2, HUNGARY, MAN, TABLE 13

"STRAIGHT UP," 1988
Elliott Wolf
TELEVISION

"STRAIGHTEN UP AND FLY RIGHT," 1944
Irving Mills, Nat "King" Cole
TABLE 15

"STRANGE MUSIC," 1944
Robert Wright, George Forrest
CLASSICS, TABLE 6, MUSICAL PLAYS, TABLE 12

"STRANGER IN MY HOUSE," 1983
Mike Reid
TABLE 10-w

"STRANGER IN PARADISE," 1953
Robert Wright, George Forrest
CLASSICS, TABLE 6, MUSICAL PLAYS, TABLE
12, OPERA

"STRANGER ON THE SHORE," 1961
Robert Mellin/Acker Bilk
TABLE 4-d, BRITAIN, OCEAN, WATERFRONT

"Strangers in the Night," 1966
Eddie Snyder, Charles Singleton/Bert Kaempfert
TABLE 4-b, TABLE 8, GERMANY, TABLE 10-a,
TABLE 10-d, HARMONIC RHYTHM, NIGHT,
SINGERS, TABLE 15

"Strawberry Fields Forever," 1967
John Lennon, Paul McCartney
BRITAIN, ROCK-ii

"Strawberry Letter 23," 1971
Shuggie Otis
WRITING

"(On the) Street of Dreams," 1932
Samuel M. Lewis/Victor Young
DREAMS, STREETS

"The Streets of Laredo," c. 1860
traditional Irish melody
POPULAR SONG-i

"The Streets of New York (In Old New York)," 1906
Henry Blossom/Victor Herbert
CITIES, TABLE 5, TABLE 11

"Strike Up the Band," 1927
Ira Gershwin/George Gershwin
MARCH, TABLE 12

"A String of Pearls," 1941
Eddie De Lange/Jerry Gray
ARRANGEMENT, JAZZ, JEWELRY, RIFF, SWING

"Strip Polka (Take It Off—Take It Off)," 1942
Johnny Mercer
POLKA

"The Stripper," 1961
m. David Rose
TABLE 8

"Struttin' With Some Barbecue," 1927
Louis Armstrong, Lil Hardin
FOOD AND DRINK, SINGERS, WALKING

"Stumbling," 1922
Zez Confrey
PIANO, RAGTIME, SCALE

"Stupid Cupid," 1958
Howard Greenfield/Neil Sedaka
ROCK 'N' ROLL-iii, TABLE 15

"Subterranean Homesick Blues," 1965
Bob Dylan
BLUES, PROTEST SONG, ROCK-iv

"Sugar," 1927
Sidney Mitchell, Edna Alexander/Maceo Pinkard
SWEETNESS

"Sugar Blues," 1923
Lucy Fletcher/Clarence Williams
BLUES, SWEETNESS

"Sugar Foot Stomp," 1926
Walter Melrose/Joseph "King" Oliver
DIXIELAND

"Sugar Shack," 1962
Keith McCormack, Faye Voss
SWEETNESS

"Sugar Sugar," 1969
Jeff Barry, Andy Kim
SWEETNESS, TELEVISION

"Sugartime," 1956
Charlie Phillips, Odis Echols
SINGING GROUPS, SWEETNESS

"Suicide Is Painless," *see* **"Song From M*A*S*H"**

"Suite: Judy Blue Eyes," 1969
Stephen Sills
ROCK-v

"Sukiyaki," 1963
Tom Leslie, Buzz Cason (Eng.)/Ei Rokusuke,
Hachidai Nakamura
TABLE 4-d

"The Sum of Life," 1909
Elsa Maxwell
WOMEN AS SONGWRITERS

"Sumer is Icumin In," c. 1250
traditional English round
SEASONS

"SUMMER BREEZE," 1971
James Seals/Darrell Crofts
TABLE 4-d, SEASONS

"SUMMER IN THE CITY," 1966
John B. Sebastian, Mark Sebastian, Steve Boone
TABLE 5, ROCK-v, SEASONS

"THE SUMMER KNOWS (THEME FROM *SUMMER OF '42*)," 1971
Alan Bergman, Marilyn Bergman/Michel Legrand
COLLABORATION, TABLE 8, FRANCE, SEASONS

"SUMMER NIGHT," 1936
Al Dubin/Harry Warren
NIGHT

"A SUMMER PLACE," SEE "THEME FROM A SUMMER PLACE"

"SUMMER WIND," 1965
Johnny Mercer (Eng.)/Henry Mayer
SEASONS

"SUMMERTIME," 1935
DuBose Heyward/George Gershwin
ACCOMPANIMENT, TABLE 3, COMPOSERS, COUNTERMELODY, HIT SONG, LANDMARKS OF STAGE AND SCREEN, MODE, OPERA, SEASONS, SINGERS, TABLE 15, SOUL, TIME

"SUMMERTIME BLUES," 1958
Eddie Cochran, Jerry Capeheart
BILLBOARD, ROCK 'N' ROLL-i, SEASONS

"SUMMERTIME IN VENICE," 1955
Carl Sigman (Eng.)/Icini
BOLERO, TABLE 5, ITALY, SEASONS

"SUMMERTIME, SUMMERTIME," 1958
Sherm Feller, Tom Jameson
SEASONS

"A SUNDAY KIND OF LOVE," 1946
Barbara Belle, Anita Leonard, Louis Prima, Stan Rhodes
DAYS OF THE WEEK

"SUNDAY, MONDAY OR ALWAYS," 1943
Johnny Mercer/James Van Heusen
DAYS OF THE WEEK, TABLE 9, TABLE 15

"SUNDAY MORNIN'," 1967
Margo Guryan
DAYS OF THE WEEK, TIME OF DAY

"SUNFLOWER," 1948
Mack David
BORROWING

"SUNNY," 1925
Otto Harbach, Oscar Hammerstein II/Jerome Kern
TABLE 11

"SUNNY," 1965
Bobby Hebb
TABLE 4-c, FADE-OUT

"SUNNY SIDE UP," 1929
B. G. DeSylva, Lew Brown/Ray Henderson
COLLABORATION, INSPIRATION, SUN

"SUNRISE SERENADE," 1938
Jack Lawrence/Frankie Carle
TABLE 3, MUSIC, SUN, TIME OF DAY

"SUNRISE, SUNSET," 1964
Sheldon Harnick/Jerry Bock
BROKEN CHORD, MARRIAGE, MODE, TABLE 12, OCCASIONAL SONG, SUN, TIME OF DAY, WALTZ

"SUNSHINE, LOLLIPOPS AND RAINBOWS," 1964
Howard Liebling/Marvin Hamlisch
RAINBOW, SUN, SWEETNESS

"SUNSHINE OF YOUR LOVE," 1968
Jack Bruce, Peter Brown, Eric Clapton
HEAVY METAL, ROCK-viii, SUN, TOP FORTY

"THE SUNSHINE OF YOUR SMILE," 1915
Leonard Cooke/Lillian Raye
SMILING, SUN

"SUNSHINE ON MY SHOULDERS," 1971
John Denver, Richard L. Kniss, Michael C. Taylor
SUN

"SUNSHINE SUPERMAN," 1966
Donovan Leitch
ROCK-v

"SUPER FREAK," 1981
Rick James
RAP

"SUPERCALIFRAGILISTICEXPIALIDOCIOUS," 1963
Richard M. Sherman, Robert B. Sherman
TABLE 9, HUMOR, NONSENSE

"SUPERFLY," 1972
Curtis Mayfield
SOUL

"SUPERSTAR (JESUS CHRIST, DO YOU THINK YOU'RE WHAT THEY SAY YOU ARE?)," 1970
Tim Rice/Andrew Lloyd Webber
RELIGION

"SUPERSTITION," 1972
Stevie Wonder
TABLE 10-o, TABLE 10-q

"SUPPER TIME," 1933
Irving Berlin
FOOD AND DRINK, TABLE 14

"SURELY GOD IS ABLE," 1949
W. Herbert Brewster
GOSPEL

"SURF CITY," 1963
Brian Wilson, Jan Berry
OCEAN

"SURFER GIRL," 1963
Brian Wilson
ROCK-i

"SURFIN' BIRD," 1964
Al Frazier, Carl White, John Earl Harris, Turner Wilson
ROCK 'N' ROLL

"SURFIN' SAFARI," 1962
Mike Love, Brian Wilson
OCEAN

"SURFIN' U.S.A.," 1963
Chuck Berry
OCEAN, ROCK-i

"SURRENDER," 1960; SEE ALSO "COME BACK TO SORRENTO"
Jerome "Doc" Pomus (Eng.)/Jerome "Doc" Pomus, Mort Shuman
ITALY, ROCK 'N' ROLL

"THE SURREY WITH THE FRINGE ON TOP," 1943
Oscar Hammerstein II/Richard Rodgers
LANDMARKS OF STAGE AND SCREEN, MUSICAL PLAYS, TABLE 12, TRAVEL

"SUSPICION," 1962
Jerome "Doc" Pomus, Mort Shuman
ROCK 'N' ROLL

"SUSPICIOUS MINDS," 1968
Fred Zambon
TABLE 4-d, MIND, ROCK, ROCK 'N' ROLL-i

"SUZANNE," 1967
Leonard Cohen
CANADA, ROCK-vi

"SWANEE," 1919
Irving Caesar/George Gershwin
COMPOSERS, FORM, MODE, TABLE 11, PATTER, POPULAR SONG-ii, POPULAR SONG-iii, RIVER, ROARING TWENTIES, TABLE 15, VERSE

"SWANEE RIVER," SEE "OLD FOLKS AT HOME"

"SWAY (QUIEN SERA)," 1953
Norman Gimbel (Eng.)/Pablo Beltran Ruiz
CUBA, MAMBO

"SWEET ADELINE," SEE "YOU'RE THE FLOWER OF MY HEART, SWEET ADELINE"

"SWEET AND GENTLE (ME LO DIJO ADELA)," 1955
George Thorn (Eng.)/Otilio Portal
CHA CHA CHA, CUBA, TENDERNESS

"SWEET AND HOT," SEE "SAN FERNANDO VALLEY"

"Sweet and Lovely," 1931
Gus Arnheim, Harry Tobias, Jules Lemare
SWEETNESS

"Sweet and Low-Down," 1925
Ira Gershwin/George Gershwin
DYNAMICS, RIFF, SWEETNESS

"Sweet Blindness," 1967
Laura Nyro
SEEING, SINGING GROUPS, SWEETNESS

"Sweet Bunch of Daisies," 1894
Anita Owen
WOMEN AS SONGWRITERS

"Sweet Gardens," 1972
Judy Collins
WOMEN AS SONGWRITERS

"Sweet Georgia Brown," 1925
Kenneth Casey, Maceo Pinkard, Ben Bernie
CHARLESTON, CIRCLE OF FIFTHS, NAMES, STATES, SWEETNESS

"Sweet Home Alabama," 1974
Ronnie Van Zant, Edward King, Gary Rossington
ROCK, STATES

"Sweet Inspirations," 1967
Dan Penn, Spooner Oldham
SINGING GROUPS, SOUL, SWEETNESS

"Sweet Leilani," 1937
Harry Owens
TABLE 1, TABLE 9, NAMES, TABLE 15, SWEETNESS

"Sweet Little Sixteen," 1958
Chuck Berry
AGE, ROCK 'N' ROLL-i

"Sweet Lorraine," 1928
Mitchell Parish/Clifford Burwell
NAMES, RADIO, SWEETNESS

"Sweet Love," 1986
Anita Baker, Louis A. Johnson, Gary Bias
TABLE 10-q, LOVE, SWEETNESS

"Sweet Madness," 1933
Ned Washington/Victor Young
MADNESS, SWEETNESS

"Sweet Nothin's," 1959
Ronnie Self
COUNTRY AND WESTERN, ROCK 'N' ROLL-iii, SWEETNESS

"Sweet Rosie O'Grady," 1896
Maude Nugent
IRELAND, NAMES, SWEETNESS, VAUDEVILLE, WOMEN AS SONGWRITERS

"Sweet Seasons," 1971
Carole King, Toni Stern
ROCK-vi, SEASONS, SWEETNESS

"Sweet September," 1962
Bill McGuffie, Lorraine Philips, Peter Stanley
MONTHS, SWEETNESS

"Sweet Soul Music," 1967
Sam Cooke, with Otis Redding, Jr., Arthur Conley
SOUL, SWEETNESS

"Sweet Sue," 1928
Will J. Harris/Victor Young
NAMES, ROARING TWENTIES, SWEETNESS

"Sweet Violets," 1882
Joseph Emmet
FLOWERS

"The Sweetest Music This Side of Heaven," 1934
Carmen Lombardo, Cliff Friend
HEAVEN, SUPERLATIVES, SWEETNESS

"The Sweetest Sounds," 1962
Richard Rodgers
COMPOSER-LYRICISTS, MUSIC, TABLE 11, SUPERLATIVES, SWEETNESS

"The Sweetheart of Sigma Chi," 1912
Byron D. Stokes/F. Dudlegh Vernor
SWEETNESS

"Sweethearts," 1913
Robert B. Smith/Victor Herbert
OPERETTA, TABLE 13, WALTZ

"Swingin' Down the Lane," 1923
Gus Kahn/Isham Jones
TABLE 3, QUOTATION

"Swingin' School," 1960
Dave Appell, Bernie Lowe, Kal Mann
ROCK 'N' ROLL-iii

"The Swingin' Shepherd Blues," 1958
Rhoda Roberts, Kenny Jacobson/Moe Kossman
CANADA

"Swinging on a Star," 1944
Johnny Burke/James Van Heusen
TABLE 1, ANIMALS, TABLE 9, LYRICISTS,
POPULAR SONG-vi, STARS, SWING

"Sympathy," 1912
Otto Harbach/Rudolf Friml
TABLE 13

"Symphony," 1945
Jack Lawrence (Eng.)/Alex Alstone
FRANCE, MUSIC

"T for Texas," 1927
Jimmie Rodgers
COUNTRY AND WESTERN, STATES

"T.S.O.P. (The Sound of Philadelphia),"
1973
Kenneth Gamble, Leon Huff
TELEVISION

"Ta-Ra-Ra-Boom-De-Ay!," 1891
Henry J. Sayers
BARBERSHOP, BRITAIN, GAY NINETIES, NON-
SENSE, SHEET MUSIC, TABLE 15, VAUDEVILLE

"Taboo," 1934
S. K. Russell (Eng.)/Margarita Lecuona
RUMBA, WOMEN AS SONGWRITERS

"Take a Letter, Maria," 1969
Sonny Childe (pseud. Ronald Bertram Greaves)
WRITING

"Take a Look at Me Now," SEE **"Against**
All Odds"

"Take Back Your Gold," 1897
Monroe H. Rosenfeld
VAUDEVILLE

"Take Good Care of My Baby," 1961
Gerry Goffin, Carole King
BABY, ROCK 'N' ROLL

"Take It Off—Take It Off," SEE **"Strip**
Polka"

"Take It to the Limit," 1976
Don Henley, Randy Meisner
ROCK-x

"Take Me Home," 1979
Michele Aller, Bob Esty
HOME

"Take Me Home, Country Roads," 1971
Bill Danoff, Taffy Danoff, John Denver
COUNTRY AND WESTERN, CROSSOVER,
HOME, POPULAR SONG-xi, STREETS, TRAVEL

"Take Me in Your Arms," 1932
Mitchell Parish (Eng.)/Fritz Rotter, Alfred Markush
TABLE 2, GERMANY, TANGO

"Take Me to Your Heart Again," SEE **"La**
Vie en Rose"

"Take Me Out to the Ball Game," 1908
Jack Norworth/Albert Von Tilzer
BARBERSHOP, DANCE CRAZES, KEY, OCTAVE,
TABLE 15, SINGING GROUPS, VAUDEVILLE,
WALTZ

"Take My Breath Away (Love Theme from
Top Gun)," 1986
Giorgio Moroder, Tom Whitlock
TABLE 1

"Take the 'A' Train," 1941
Billy Strayhorn
BIG BANDS, TABLE 3, BROKEN CHORD,
SWING, TRAINS

"Take These Chains From My Heart,"
1952
Fred Rose, Hy Heath
COUNTRY AND WESTERN

"Take This Job and Shove It," 1977
David Allen Coe
COUNTRY AND WESTERN

"Takes Two to Tango," 1952
Al Hoffman, Dick Manning
TOGETHERNESS

"Taking a Chance on Love," 1940
John Latouche, Ted Fetter/Vernon Duke
COMPOSERS, LUCK, TABLE 11, TABLE 15

"Talk to Me," 1985
Charles Sandford
TALKING

"Talk to Me," 1987
N. Mundy, F. Golde, P. Fox
TALKING

"Talk to the Animals," 1967
Leslie Bricusse
TABLE 1, ANIMALS, BRITAIN, TABLE 9, TALK-ING

"Tammany," 1905
Vincent P. Bryan/Gus Edwards
VAUDEVILLE

"Tammy," 1957
Jay Livingston, Ray Evans
NAMES

"Tangerine," 1942
Johnny Mercer/Victor Schertzinger
TABLE 3, DISCO, NAMES, SWING

"Tangled and Dark," 1991
Bonnie Raitt
WOMEN AS SONGWRITERS

"Tangled Up in Blue," 1974
Bob Dylan
ROCK-iv

"Taps," 1862
m. Daniel O. Butterfield
BROKEN CHORD

"Tara Theme (My Own True Love)," 1939
Mack David (1954)/Max Steiner
TABLE 8

"A Taste of Honey," 1960
Bobby Scott, Ric Marlow
AABA, TABLE 10-a, HARMONIC RHYTHM, LYRICS, METER, MODE, PEDAL POINT, SWEET-NESS

"Tea for Two," 1924
Irving Caesar/Vincent Youmans
COMPOSERS, DUMMY LYRICS, FOOD AND DRINK, IMAGINATION, MUSICAL COMEDY, TABLE 11, RANGE, RHYTHM, ROARING TWEN-TIES, TIN PAN ALLEY, TOGETHERNESS

"The Tea Leaf Prophecy (Lay Down Your Arms)," 1988
Joni Mitchell/Joni Mitchell, Larry Klein
WOMEN AS SONGWRITERS

"Teach Me Tonight," 1953
Sammy Cahn/Gene De Paul
ALLITERATION, LYRICISTS, SCAT SINGING

"Teach Your Children," 1970
Graham Nash
ROCK-v

"Teardrops From My Eyes," 1950
Rudolph Toombs
CRYING, RHYTHM AND BLUES

"Tears of a Clown," 1967
Henry Cosby, Stevie Wonder, William "Smokey" Robinson, Jr.
CIRCUS, CRYING

"Tears on My Pillow," 1958
Sylvester Bradford, Al Lewis
CRYING, SINGING GROUPS

"A Teenager in Love," 1959
Jerome "Doc" Pomus, Mort Shuman
AGE, ROCK 'N' ROLL-ii

"Telephone Line," 1976
Jeff Lynne
TELEPHONES

"TELL HER NO," 1964
Rod Argent
ROCK-iii

"TELL HIM," 1963
Bert Russell
SINGING GROUPS

"TELL IT LIKE IT IS," 1966
George Davis, Lee Diamond
SOUL

"TELL MAMA," 1968
Clarence Carter, Marcus Daniel, Wilbur Terrell
MOTHERS, SOUL

"TELL ME PRETTY MAIDEN (ARE THERE MANY MORE AT HOME LIKE YOU?)," 1900
Owen Hall/Leslie Stuart (pseud. Thomas A. Barrett)
BEAUTY, HOME, TABLE 15, WOMAN

"TELL ME SOMETHING GOOD," 1974
Stevie Wonder
TABLE 10-p

"TELL ME WHY," 1951
Al Alberts/Marty Gold
SINGING GROUPS

"TELL ME YOU LOVE ME," 1951
Sammy Kaye
OPERA

"TELL ME YOU'RE MINE," 1953
Ronnie Vincent (Eng.)/D. Ravasino
SINGING GROUPS

"TEMPTATION," 1933
Arthur Freed/Nacio Herb Brown
BOLERO, COMPOSERS, TABLE 9, TANGO

"TEN CENTS A DANCE," 1930
Lorenz Hart/Richard Rodgers
DANCING, DEPRESSION YEARS, TABLE 11, TABLE 15, TORCH SONG

"THE TENDER TRAP," 1955
Sammy Cahn/James Van Heusen
ALLITERATION, TABLE 8, TENDERNESS

"TENDERLY," 1946
Jack Lawrence/Walter Gross
TENDERNESS

"TENNESSEE HOMESICK BLUES," 1984
Dolly Parton
WOMEN AS SONGWRITERS

"TENNESSEE WALTZ," 1948
Pee Wee King, Redd Stewart
TABLE 4-c, COUNTRY AND WESTERN, RECORDING, TABLE 15, STATES, WALTZ

"TEQUILA," 1958
M. Chuck Rio
FOOD AND DRINK, TABLE 10-m

"A TERRIFIC BAND AND A REAL NICE CROWD," 1978
Alan Bergman, Marilyn Bergman/Billy Goldenberg
PEOPLE

"THANK GOD I'M A COUNTRY BOY," 1974
John Martin Sommers
BOY, COUNTRY AND WESTERN, TABLE 15

"THANK HEAVEN FOR LITTLE GIRLS," 1958
Alan Jay Lerner/Frederick Loewe
CHILDHOOD, GIRL, TABLE 9, HEAVEN, LYRICISTS

"THANK YOU FALETTIN ME BE MICE ELF AGAIN," 1970
Sylvester Stewart
ROCK-ix

"THANK YOU PRETTY BABY," 1958
Clyde Otis, Brook Benton
BABY, RHYTHM AND BLUES

"THANKS FOR THE MEMORY," 1937
Leo Robin/Ralph Rainger
TABLE 1, TABLE 9, MEMORY, RADIO

"THAT CERTAIN FEELING," 1925
Ira Gershwin/George Gershwin
FEELING

"THAT GIRL," 1981
Stevie Wonder
KEY

"THAT GREAT COME-AND-GET-IT DAY," 1946
E. Y. Harburg/Burton Lane
DAY, TABLE 11

"THAT INTERNATIONAL RAG," 1913
Irving Berlin
RAGTIME

"THAT LOVIN' YOU FEELIN' AGAIN," 1980
Roy Orbison, Chris Price
TABLE 10-v

"THAT LUCKY OLD SUN," 1949
Haven Gillespie/Beasley Smith
TABLE 15, SUN

"THAT MESMERIZING MENDELSSOHN TUNE,"
1909
Irving Berlin
TABLE 6, COMPOSER-LYRICISTS, MELODY,
RAGTIME

"THAT MYSTERIOUS RAG," 1911
Irving Berlin, Ted Snyder
RAGTIME

"THAT OLD BLACK MAGIC," 1942
Johnny Mercer/Harold Arlen
ANATOMY, CODA, COLORS, TABLE 7, COM-
POSERS, LENGTH, LYRICISTS, MAGIC, PEDAL
POINT, REPEATED NOTE, TABLE 15

"THAT OLD FEELING," 1937
Lew Brown/Sammy Fain
FEELING

"THAT OLD GANG OF MINE," 1923
Billy Rose, Mort Dixon/Ray Henderson
TOGETHERNESS

"THAT SILVER-HAIRED DADDY OF MINE,"
1932
Gene Autry, Jimmy Long
TABLE 7, COUNTRY AND WESTERN, FATHERS

"THAT WAS YESTERDAY," 1976
Donna Fargo
WOMEN AS SONGWRITERS

"THAT'LL BE THE DAY," 1957
Jerry Allison, Norman Petty, Buddy Holly
TABLE 4-d

"THAT'S A PLENTY," 1909
Henry Creamer/Bert A. Williams
DIXIELAND

"THAT'S ALL RIGHT," 1947
Arthur Crudup
COUNTRY AND WESTERN

"THAT'S AMORE," 1953
Jack Brooks, Harry Warren
TABLE 8, ITALY, LOVE, TABLE 15

"THAT'S ENTERTAINMENT," 1953
Howard Dietz/Arthur Schwartz
BROADWAY, COLLABORATION

"THAT'S FOR ME," 1945
Oscar Hammerstein II/Richard Rodgers
TABLE 9

"THAT'S LIFE," 1964
Dean Kay, Kelly Gordon
LIFE

"THAT'S MY DESIRE," 1931
Carroll Loveday/Helmy Kresa
RADIO, WISHING

"THAT'S THE WAY (I LIKE IT)," 1975
Harry Casey, Richard Finch
DISCO

"THAT'S THE WAY I'VE ALWAYS HEARD IT
SHOULD BE," 1971
Jacob Brackman/Carly Simon
ROCK-vi, WOMEN AS SONGWRITERS

"THAT'S THE WAY LOVE GOES," 1973
Whitey Shafer, Lefty Frizzell
TABLE 10-u

"THAT'S WHAT FRIENDS ARE FOR," 1982
Carole Bayer Sager, Burt Bacharach
FRIENDSHIP, TABLE 10-b, TABLE 10-h, TABLE
15, WOMEN AS SONGWRITERS

"THAT'S WHAT I LIKE ABOUT THE SOUTH,"
1944
Andy Razaf
CARDINAL POINTS

"THAT'S WHERE IT'S AT," 1964
Sam Cooke
SOUL

"THAT'S WHY," 1957
Berry Gordy, Jr., Gwendolyn Gordy, Tryan Carlo
ROCK 'N' ROLL-i

"THAT'S WHY DARKIES WERE BORN," 1931
B. G. DeSylva, Lew Brown/Ray Henderson
BIRTH, REVUES, TABLE 14

"THEM THERE EYES," 1930
Maceo Pinkard, Doris Tauber, William Tracey
TABLE 2

"THEME FROM ALL IN THE FAMILY," SEE
"THOSE WERE THE DAYS"

"THEME FROM THE ANDY GRIFFITH SHOW,"
SEE "THE FISHIN' HOLE"

"THEME FROM CARNIVAL," SEE "LOVE MAKES
THE WORLD GO 'ROUND"

"THEME FROM EXODUS," 1960
Pat Boone/Ernest Gold
TABLE 8, TABLE 10-b

"THEME FROM THE GREATEST AMERICAN
HERO," SEE "BELIEVE IT OR NOT"

"THEME FROM HILL STREET BLUES," 1980
m. Mike Post
TELEVISION

"THEME FROM ICE CASTLES (THROUGH THE
EYES OF LOVE)," 1978
Carole Bayer Sager/Marvin Hamlisch
TABLE 2, TABLE 8, WOMEN AS SONGWRITERS

"THEME FROM MAHOGANY (DO YOU KNOW
WHERE YOU'RE GOING TO?)," 1973
Gerry Goffin/Michael Masser
AABA, TABLE 4-d, TABLE 8, HARMONIC
RHYTHM, KEY, TABLE 15, TONALITY

"THEME FROM MONDO CANE," SEE "MORE"

"THEME FROM NEW YORK, NEW YORK," SEE
"(THEME FROM) NEW YORK, NEW YORK"

"THEME FROM SHAFT," 1971
Isaac Hayes
ACADEMY AWARDS, TABLE 1

"THEME FROM LA STRADA," SEE "STARS SHINE
IN YOUR EYES"

"THEME FROM SUMMER OF '42," SEE "THE
SUMMER KNOWS"

"THEME FROM A SUMMER PLACE," 1959
m. Max Steiner
TABLE 8, TABLE 10-a, PLACES, SEASONS,
SINGING GROUPS

"THEME FROM SUPERMAN," SEE "CAN YOU
READ MY MIND?"

"THEME FROM THE THOMAS CROWN AFFAIR,"
SEE "THE WINDMILLS OF YOUR MIND"

"THEME FROM THE THREEPENNY OPERA," SEE
"MACK THE KNIFE"

"THEME FROM VALLEY OF THE DOLLS," 1967
Dory Previn/André Previn
TABLE 5, DOLL, METER, WOMEN AS
SONGWRITERS

"THEME FROM ZORBA THE GREEK," 1965
m. Mikos Theodorakis
GREECE

"THEN CAME YOU," 1974
Sherman Marshall, Phillip Pugh
TABLE 15

"THEN I'LL BE TIRED OF YOU," 1934
E. Y. Harburg/Arthur Schwartz
CATALOGUE SONG

"THERE ARE SUCH THINGS," 1942
Stanley Adams, Abel Baer, George W. Meyer
WORLD WAR II

"THERE BUT FOR YOU GO I," 1947
Alan Jay Lerner/Frederick Loewe
TABLE 12

"THERE GOES MY BABY," 1959
Benjamin Nelson, Lover Patterson, George Treadwell
BABY, ROCK 'N' ROLL-ii

"THERE IS A LAND OF PURE DELIGHT," 1868
Isaac Watts/J. C. H. Rink
GOSPEL

"THERE IS A TAVERN IN THE TOWN," 1883
Anonymous
RADIO

"THERE IS LOVE," SEE "THE WEDDING SONG

"THERE IS NOTHIN' LIKE A DAME," 1949
Oscar Hammerstein II/Richard Rodgers
TABLE 12, WOMAN

"THERE! I'VE SAID IT AGAIN," 1941
Redd Evans, Dave Mann
TABLE 15

"THERE STANDS THE GLASS," 1951
Mary Jean Shurtz, Russ Hull, Audrey Grisham
COUNTRY AND WESTERN, FOOD AND DRINK

"THERE WILL NEVER BE ANOTHER YOU," 1942
Mack Gordon/Harry Warren
BEBOP, COLLABORATION, TABLE 9, LYRICISTS

"THERE'LL ALWAYS BE AN ENGLAND," 1939
Ross Parker, Hughie Charles
BRITAIN, NATIONS

"THERE'S A BOAT DAT'S LEAVIN' SOON FOR NEW YORK," 1935
Ira Gershwin/George Gershwin
BOATING, TABLE 5, DIALECT

"THERE'S A GOLD MINE IN THE SKY," 1937
Charles Kenny, Nick Kenny
RELIGION, SKY

"THERE'S A KIND OF HUSH," 1966
Geoff Stephens, Les Reed
ROCK-iii

"THERE'S A LONG, LONG TRAIL," 1913
Stoddard King/Zo Elliott
WORLD WAR I

"THERE'S A RAINBOW ROUND MY SHOULDER," 1928
Al Jolson, Billy Rose, Dave Dreyer
RAINBOW, SINGERS

"THERE'S A SMALL HOTEL," 1936
Lorenz Hart/Richard Rodgers
COLLABORATION, MUSICAL COMEDY, TABLE 11, PLACES

"THERE'S A STAR-SPANGLED BANNER WAVING SOMEWHERE," 1942
Paul Roberts, Shelby Darnell
COUNTRY AND WESTERN, PATRIOTISM, PLACES, WORLD WAR II

"THERE'S ALWAYS SOMETHING THERE TO REMIND ME," 1964
Hal David/Burt Bacharach
MEMORY

"THERE'S NO BUSINESS LIKE SHOW BUSINESS," 1946
Irving Berlin
BROADWAY, BROKEN CHORD, CONTRACTIONS, TABLE 11, OCTAVE, TABLE 15

"THERE'S NO TOMORROW," 1949
Al Hoffman, Leo Corday, Leon Carr
DAY, ITALY

"THERE'S ONE WIDE RIVER TO CROSS (NOAH'S ARK)," 1865
traditional African-American spiritual
RIVERS

"THERE'S YES YES IN YOUR EYES," 1924
Cliff Friend/Joseph H. Santley
TABLE 2, BORROWING

"THESE ARE THEY," C. 1948
W. Herbert Brewster
GOSPEL

"THESE BOOTS ARE MADE FOR WALKING," 1966
Lee Hazlewood
WALKING

"THESE FOOLISH THINGS (REMIND ME OF YOU),"
1935
Holt Marvell/Jack Strachey, Harry Link
BRITAIN, CATALOGUE SONG, FOOLS,
MEMORY, TELEPHONES

"THEY ALL LAUGHED," 1937
Ira Gershwin/George Gershwin
TABLE 9, SCALE

"THEY CALL THE WIND MARIA," 1951
Alan Jay Lerner/Frederick Loewe
TABLE 12, NAMES, WEATHER

"THEY CAN'T TAKE THAT AWAY FROM ME,"
1937
Ira Gershwin/George Gershwin
COMPOSERS, FILM MUSICALS, TABLE 9,
LYRICISTS, MELODY, PICKUP, REPEATED
NOTE

"THEY DIDN'T BELIEVE ME," 1914
Herbert Reynolds/Jerome Kern
COMPOSERS, LANDMARKS OF STAGE AND
SCREEN, MUSICAL COMEDY, TABLE 11, TIN
PAN ALLEY

"THEY JUST CAN'T STOP IT (THE GAMES PEOPLE
PLAY)," 1975
Joseph Jefferson, Bruce Hawes, Charles Simmons
ENDING

"THEY SAY IT'S WONDERFUL," 1946
Irving Berlin
TABLE 11, WONDER

"THEY WERE DOING THE MAMBO," 1954
Sonny Burke, Don Raye
MAMBO

"THEY WERE YOU," 1960
Tom Jones/Harvey Schmidt
TABLE 11

"THEY'RE EITHER TOO YOUNG OR TOO OLD,"
1943
Frank Loesser/Arthur Schwartz
AGE

"THEY'RE PLAYING OUR SONG," 1978
Carole Bayer Sager/Marvin Hamlisch
MUSIC

"THEY'VE GOT AN AWFUL LOT OF COFFEE IN
BRAZIL," SEE "THE COFFEE SONG"

"THINE ALONE," 1917
Henry Blossom/Victor Herbert
IRELAND

"THE THINGS I LOVE," 1941
Lew Harris, Harold Barlow
TABLE 6

"THINK," 1957
Lowman Pauling
ROCK 'N' ROLL-i, THINKING

"THINK," 1968
Aretha Franklin, Ted White
WOMEN AS SONGWRITERS

"THINK ABOUT ME," 1979
Christine McVie
THINKING

"THINK OF LAURA," 1984
Christopher Cross
NAMES, THINKING

"THINK OF ME," 1986
Charles Hart, Richard Stilgoe/Andrew Lloyd Webber
PEDAL POINT, TONALITY

"THINKING OF THEE," 1906
Caro Roma
WOMEN AS SONGWRITERS

"THINKING OF YOU," 1927
Bert Kalmar/Harry Ruby
THINKING

"THE THIRD MAN THEME," 1949
m. Anton Karas
FILM MUSIC

"THIS CAN'T BE LOVE," 1938
Lorenz Hart/Richard Rodgers
COLLABORATION, LOVE, MUSICAL COMEDY,
TABLE 11

"THIS COULD BE THE START OF SOMETHING
BIG," 1956
Steve Allen
BEGINNING

"THIS DIAMOND RING," 1964
Bob Brass, Irwin Levine, Al Kooper
JEWELRY, MARRIAGE

"THIS GUY'S IN LOVE WITH YOU," 1968
Hal David/Burt Bacharach
COLLABORATION, LOVE, MAN

"THIS HEART OF MINE," 1943
Arthur Freed/Harry Warren
TABLE 2

"THIS IS ALL I ASK (BEAUTIFUL GIRLS WALK A
LITTLE SLOWER)," 1958
Gordon Jenkins
BEAUTY, TABLE 15

"THIS IS IT," 1979
Kenny Loggins, Michael McDonald
TABLE 10-g

"THIS IS NEW," 1941
Ira Gershwin/Kurt Weill
TABLE 11

"THIS IS THE ARMY, MR. JONES," 1942
Irving Berlin
REVUES, TABLE 14

"THIS LAND IS YOUR LAND," 1956
Woody Guthrie
BMI, FOLK SONG, PATRIOTISM

"THIS LOVE OF MINE," 1941
Frank Sinatra/Sol Parker, Henry Sanicola
TABLE 3

"THIS MAGIC MOMENT," 1960
Jerome "Doc" Pomus, Mort Shuman
MAGIC, ROCK 'N' ROLL-ii, TIME

"THIS MASQUERADE," 1972
Leon Russell
TABLE 10-a, MODE, SYNCOPATION

"THIS NEARLY WAS MINE," 1949
Oscar Hammerstein II/Richard Rodgers
TABLE 12, WALTZ

"THIS OLD MAN," SEE "THE CHILDREN'S
MARCHING SONG"

"THIS OLE HOUSE," 1954
Stuart Hamblen
HOME, TABLE 15

"THIS WILL BE (AN EVERLASTING LOVE),"
1975
Marvin Yancy, Chuck Jackson
TABLE 10-n

"THIS YEAR'S KISSES," 1937
Irving Berlin
KISSING

"THOROUGHLY MODERN MILLIE," 1967
Sammy Cahn/James Van Heusen
TABLE 9, NAMES

"THOSE GOOD OLD DREAMS," 1981
John Bettis/Richard Carpenter
KEY

"THOSE LAZY HAZY CRAZY DAYS OF SUMMER,"
1964
Charles Tobias/Hans Carste
DAY, MADNESS, SEASONS, WEATHER

"THOSE WERE THE DAYS," 1962
Gene Raskin
BORROWING, DAY, MEMORY

"THOSE WERE THE DAYS (THEME FROM ALL IN THE FAMILY)," 1971
Charles Strouse, Lee Adams
TELEVISION

"THOU SWELL," 1927
Lorenz Hart/Richard Rodgers
MUSICAL COMEDY, TABLE 11, TEMPO

"THREE COINS IN THE FOUNTAIN," 1954
Sammy Cahn/Jule Styne
TABLE 1, TABLE 8, LUCK, LYRICISTS, MONEY,
SINGING GROUPS, WISHING

"THREE DAYS," 1971
Carly Simon
WOMEN AS SONGWRITERS

"THREE LITTLE FISHES," 1939
Saxie Dowell
ANIMALS, TABLE 3, JUKEBOX

"THREE LITTLE MAIDS," 1921
Dorothy Donnelly/Sigmund Romberg
WOMEN AS SONGWRITERS

"THREE LITTLE WORDS," 1930
Bert Kalmar/Harry Ruby
LOVE

"THREE O'CLOCK IN THE MORNING," 1921
Dorothy Terriss (pseud. Theodora Morse)/Julian
Robeldo
RECORDING, REVUES, TABLE 14, ROARING
TWENTIES, TIME, TIME OF DAY, WOMEN AS
SONGWRITERS

"THE THRILL IS GONE," 1931
B. G. DeSylva, Lew Brown/Ray Henderson
TABLE 10-o, MODE, REVUES, TABLE 14,
RHYTHM AND BLUES

"THRILLER," 1982
Rod Temperton
ROCK-xii

"THROUGH THE EYES OF LOVE," SEE **"THEME FROM ICE CASTLES"**

"THROUGH THE YEARS," 1906
Carrie Jacobs-Bond
WOMEN AS SONGWRITERS

"THROUGH THE YEARS," 1980
Steve Dorff, Marty Panzer
ENDURING LOVE, TABLE 15

"THROW ANOTHER LOG ON THE FIRE," 1933
Charles Tobias, Jack Scholl, Murray Mencher
FIRE

"TI-PI-TIN," 1938
Raymond Leveen (Eng.)/Maria Grever
MEXICO, NONSENSE, WOMEN AS
SONGWRITERS

"TICO TICO," 1943
Ervin Drake (Eng.)/Zequinha Abreu
BRAZIL, TABLE 9

"TIE A YELLOW RIBBON ROUND THE OLE OAK TREE," 1972
Irwin Levine, L. Russell Brown
TABLE 4-c, TABLE 7, SINGING GROUPS, TREES,
VERSE

"TIGER," 1959
Ollie Jones
ANIMALS, ROCK 'N' ROLL-iii

"TIGER RAG," 1917
Harry DeCosta/The Original Dixieland Jazz Band
ANIMALS, DIXIELAND, RAGTIME, SINGING
GROUPS

"THE TIJUANA JAIL," 1959
Denny Thompson
TABLE 5, FOLK ROCK, SINGING GROUPS

"TIJUANA TAXI," 1965
Ervan F. Coleman
TABLE 5

"'TIL I KISSED YOU," 1959
Don Everly
KISSING, ROCK 'N' ROLL-i

"Till I Waltz Again With You," 1952
Sidney Prosen
TABLE 15

"Till the Clouds Roll By," 1917
Jerome Kern, P. G. Wodehouse/Jerome Kern
COMPOSERS, MUSICAL COMEDY, TABLE 11,
SKY, WEATHER, WORLD WAR I

"Till the End of Time," 1945
Buddy Kaye, Ted Mossman
CLASSICS, TABLE 6, ENDURING LOVE, TABLE
8, TABLE 15, TIME, WORLD WAR II

"Till Then," 1944
Eddie Seiler, Sol Marcus, Guy Wood
SINGING GROUPS, WORLD WAR II

"Till There Was You," 1957
Meredith Willson
COMPOSER-LYRICISTS, TABLE 11

"Till Tomorrow," 1959
Sheldon Harnick/Jerry Bock
DAY

"Till We Meet Again," 1918
Raymond B. Egan/Richard A. Whiting
MEETING, SHEET MUSIC, WORLD WAR I

"Time After Time," 1947
Sammy Cahn/Jule Styne
LYRICISTS, TIME

"A Time For Us (Love Theme From Romeo and Juliet)," 1968
Larry Kusik, Eddie Snyder, Nino Rota
TABLE 8, ITALY, MODE, TIME

"Time in a Bottle," 1971
Jim Croce
MODE, PERFORMER-SONGWRITERS, TIME,
WALTZ

"Time Is on My Side," 1963
Jerry Ragovoy
SOUL, TIME

"(I've Had) The Time of My Life," 1987
Frankie Previte/Donald Markowitz, John DeNicola
TABLE 1, TABLE 10-h, TIME

"Time of the Season," 1967
Rod Argent
ROCK-iii, SEASONS

"Time on My Hands," 1930
Harold Adamson, Mack Gordon/Vincent Youmans
TABLE 2, COMPOSERS, LYRICISTS, TABLE 15,
TIME

"Time Waits for No One," 1944
Clifford Friend, Charles Tobias
WORLD WAR II

"Time was (Duerme)," 1941
S. K. Russell (Eng.)/Miguel Prado
TIME

"Times of Your Life," 1974
Bill Lane/Roger Nichols
TIME

"The Times, They Are A-Changin'," 1963
Bob Dylan
POPULAR SONG-ix, RELIGION, ROCK-iv,
TABLE 15, TIME

"Tin Roof Blues," 1923
Walter Melrose/Leon Rappolo, Paul Mares, Benny
Pollack, George Brunies, Mel Stitzel (New Orleans
Rhythm Kings)
DIXIELAND

"Tip Toe Through the Tulips With Me," 1929
Al Dubin/Joe Burke
ALLITERATION, FLOWERS, QUOTATION,
ROARING TWENTIES, TIN PAN ALLEY

"Tired of Being Alone," 1971
Al Green
LONELINESS, SOUL

"'Tis Autumn," 1941
Henry Nemo
TABLE 3, SEASONS

"'Tis the Last Rose of Summer," 1813
Thomas Moore/Richard Alfred Milliken
OPERA, POPULAR SONG-i

"Tishomingo Blues," 1917
Spencer Williams
BLUES

"To Anacreon in Heaven," *see* "The Star-Spangled Banner"

"To Each His Own," 1946
Jay Livingston, Ray Evans
TABLE 8, SINGING GROUPS

"To Know Him Is to Love Him," 1958
Phil Spector
ROCK 'N' ROLL

"To Life (L'Chaim)," 1964
Sheldon Harnick/Jerry Bock
LIFE, TABLE 12

"To Love Somebody," 1967
Barry Gibb, Robin Gibb, Maurice Gibb
ROCK-viii

"To You Sweetheart, Aloha," 1936
Harry Owens
FAREWELLS, GREETINGS, SWEETNESS

"Together," 1928
B. G. DeSylva, Lew Brown/Ray Henderson
TOGETHERNESS

"Together Wherever We Go," 1959
Stephen Sondheim/Jule Styne
TOGETHERNESS

"Togetherness," 1960
Russell Faith
TOGETHERNESS

"Tom Dooley," 1958
traditional American folk song, adapted by Alan
Lomax, Frank Warner
FOLK ROCK, TABLE 10-s, NAMES, PROTEST
SONG, SINGING GROUPS

"Tomorrow," 1977
Martin Charnin/Charles Strouse
DAY, TABLE 11

"Tonight," 1957
Stephen Sondheim/Leonard Bernstein
BEGUINE, DOO-WOP, LANDMARKS OF STAGE
AND SCREEN, LYRICISTS, MUSICAL PLAYS,
TABLE 12, NIGHT OPERA, VAMP

"Tonight We Love," 1941
Bobby Worth/Ray Austin, Freddy Martin
TABLE 3, CLASSICS, TABLE 6, NIGHT

"Tonight's the Night (It's Gonna Be
Alright)," 1976
Rod Stewart
NIGHT, ROCK-x

"Too Beautiful to Last," 1940
Marty Symes/Ruth Lowe
WOMEN AS SONGWRITERS

"Too Close for Comfort," 1956
Jerry Bock, Larry Holofcener, George Weiss
CLOSENESS, TABLE 11

"Too Darn Hot," 1948
Cole Porter
WEATHER

"Too Fat Polka (She's Too Fat for Me),"
1947
Ross Mac Lean, Arthur Richardson
POLKA

"Too Late Now," 1950
Alan Jay Lerner/Burton Lane
TABLE 9

"Too Many Rings Around Rosie," 1924
Otto Harbach, Irving Caesar/Vincent Youmans
JEWELRY

"Too Marvelous for Words," 1937
Johnny Mercer/Richard A. Whiting
TABLE 9, LYRICISTS, WRITING

"TOO-RA-LOO-RA-LOO-RAL, THAT'S AN IRISH LULLABY," 1914
James R. Shannon
FOREIGN LANGUAGE, IRELAND, NATIONS, POPULAR SONG-vi, SLEEP

"TOO YOUNG," 1951
Sylvia Dee/Sidney Lippman
AGE, CHILDHOOD, SINGERS, TABLE 15, WOMEN AS SONGWRITERS

"TOOT TOOT TOOTSIE (GOO'BYE)," 1922
Gus Kahn, Ernie Erdman, Ted Fiorito, Robert A. King
ALLITERATION, FAREWELLS, FILM MUSICALS, LYRICISTS, ROARING TWENTIES, SINGERS, TABLE 15

"TOP HAT, WHITE TIE AND TAILS," 1935
Irving Berlin
CLOTHING, TABLE 7, COMPOSER-LYRICISTS, TABLE 9, SOCIETY TEMPO

"THE TORCH SONG," 1931
Joe Young, Mort Dixon/Harry Warren
TORCH SONG

"TORN BETWEEN TWO LOVERS," 1976
Phil Jarrell, Peter Yarrow
TABLE 4-d, LOVERS

"TORNA A SURRIENTO," SEE "COME BACK TO SORRENTO," "SURRENDER"

"TOSSIN' AND TURNIN'," 1961
Malou Rene, Ritchie Adams
SLEEP

"TOUCH ME," 1968
James Morrison, John Densmore, Robert Krieger, Raymond Manzarek (The Doors)
ROCK-ix

"TOUCH ME IN THE MORNING," 1972
Ron Miller/Michael Masser
TABLE 15, TIME OF DAY

"TOUCH OF GREY," 1987
Robert Hunter/Jerry Garcia
TABLE 7, ROCK-vii

"THE TOUCH OF YOUR HAND," 1933
Otto Harbach/Jerome Kern
ANATOMY, TABLE 2, ART SONG, HARMONIC RHYTHM, MUSICAL COMEDY, TABLE 11, WALTZ

"THE TOUCH OF YOUR LIPS," 1936
Ray Noble
TABLE 2, TABLE 3, BRITAIN

"THE TOY TRUMPET," 1938
Sidney Mitchell, Lew Pollack/Raymond Scott
BRASS

"TOYLAND," 1903
Glen MacDonough/Victor Herbert
SINGING GROUPS

"TRACES," 1969
Buddy Buie, James Cobb, Emory Gordy
TABLE 4-c

"THE TRAIL OF THE LONESOME PINE," 1913
Ballard MacDonald/Harry Carroll
MOUNTAINS, REVUES, TABLE 14, TREES, WALKING

"TRAINS AND BOATS AND PLANES," 1964
Hal David/Burt Bacharach
BOATING, TRAINS, TRAVEL

"TRAMP! TRAMP! TRAMP! ALONG THE HIGHWAY," 1910
Rida Johnson Young/Victor Herbert
MARCH, TABLE 13, TABLE 15, STREETS, WALKING

"TRAVELIN' BAND," 1970
John C. Fogerty
ROCK-ix

"TRAVELIN' MAN," 1960
Jerry Fuller
MAN, ROCK 'N' ROLL-iii, TABLE 15, TRAVEL

"TREASURE OF LOVE," 1956
J. Shapiro, Lou Stallman
RHYTHM AND BLUES

"Treat Me Nice," 1957
Mike Stoller, Jerry Leiber
ROCK 'N' ROLL

"A Tree in the Meadow," 1948
Billy Reid
TREES, *YOUR HIT PARADE*

"Trees," 1922
Joyce Kilmer/Oscar Rasbach
TREES

"The Trolley Song," 1943
Hugh Martin/Ralph Blane
TABLE 9, INTERVAL, LENGTH, REPEATED
NOTE, SINGERS, TABLE 15, SINGING GROUPS,
TRAINS

"Trouble in My Way," c. 1953
Ira Tucker and the Dixie Hummingbirds
GOSPEL

"Truckin'," 1935
Ted Koehler/Rube Bloom
DANCE CRAZES, PIANO, WALKING

"True Blue," 1986
Madonna, Steve Bray
TABLE 7, ROCK-xii

"True Love," 1956
Cole Porter
TABLE 9, LOVE, LYRICISTS, RECORDING,
WALTZ

"Truly," 1982
Lionel Richie, Jr.
TABLE 10-g

"Trust in Me," 1934
Ned Wever/Jean Schwartz, Milton Ager
HUNGARY

"Try a Little Tenderness," 1932
Harry Woods, Jimmy Campbell, Reginald Connelly
TENDERNESS

"Try Me," 1958
James Brown
SOUL

"Try to Remember," 1960
Tom Jones/Harvey Schmidt
MEMORY, MONTHS, TABLE II, WALTZ

"Tschaikowsky," 1941
Ira Gershwin/Kurt Weill
CATALOGUE SONG, PATTER

"Tubby the Tuba," 1948
George Kleinsinger, Paul Tripp
BRASS

"Tumbling Dice," 1972
Mick Jagger, Keith Richards
ROCK-iii

"Tumbling Tumbleweeds," 1934
Bob Nolan
ALLITERATION, COUNTRY AND WESTERN

"Tunnel of Love," 1987
Bruce Springsteen
ROCK-xii

"Turkish Tom Toms," *see* "Dardanella"

"Turn Around, Look at Me," 1961
Jerry Câpehart
SINGING GROUPS

"Turn Back the Hands of Time," 1970
Jack Daniels, Bonnie Thompson
SOUL, TIME

"Turn Me Loose," 1959
Jerome "Doc" Pomus, Mort Shuman
ROCK 'N' ROLL-iii

"Turn! Turn! Turn!," 1962
Pete Seeger
FOLK SONG, RELIGION, ROCK-v

"Turn Your Love Around," 1981
Jay Graydon, Steve Lukather, Bill Champlin
TABLE 10-q

"Turning Japanese," 1979
David Fenton
TELEVISION

"Tutti-Frutti," 1955
Richard Penniman, D. La Bostrie, Joe Lubin
COVER, ROCK 'N' ROLL-i

"Tuxedo Junction," 1940
Buddy Feyne/William Johnson, Erskine Hawkins,
Julian Dash
TABLE 3, CODA, HIT SONG, RIFF, SWING,
TRAINS

"Tweedle Dee," 1954
Winfield Scott
ROCK 'N' ROLL

"12th Street Rag," 1914
James S. Sumner (1919)/Euday L. Bowman
DIXIELAND, RAGTIME, STREETS

"The Twelve Days of Christmas," c. 1700
traditional English carol
CHRISTMAS

"Twelve Thirty (Young Girls Are Comin'
to the Canyon)," 1967
John Phillips
SINGING GROUPS, TIME OF DAY

"25 or 6 to 4," 1969
Robert Lamm
ROCK-ix

"Twenty-Six Miles (Catalina)," 1958
Glenn Larson, Bruce Belland
SINGING GROUPS

"Twilight on the Trail," 1936
Sidney D. Mitchell/Louis Alter
TABLE 8, NIGHT, TIME OF DAY

"Twilight Time," 1944
Buck Ram/Marty Nevins, Al Nevins, Artie Donn
TABLE 4-c, NIGHT, ROCK 'N' ROLL-ii, TIME,
TIME OF DAY

"Twinkle, Twinkle, Little Star (Ah! Vous
Dirais-Je Maman)," 1761; SEE ALSO
"Little Star"
Jane Taylor (Eng., 1806)/traditional French song
STARS

"The Twist," 1959
Hank Ballard
COVER, DANCE CRAZES, POPULAR SONG-xiii,
RHYTHM AND BLUES

"Twist and Shout," 1960
Bert Russell, Philip Medley
DANCE CRAZES, ROCK 'N' ROLL

"Twisted," 1953
Annie Ross/Wardell Gray
VOCALESE

"Twistin' U.S.A.," 1960
Kal Mann
DANCE CRAZES

"Twisting the Night Away," 1962
Sam Cooke
BMI, DANCE CRAZES, DANCING, NIGHT,
ROCK 'N' ROLL-i

"Two Cigarettes in the Dark," 1934
Paul Francis Webster/Lew Pollack
TABLE 8, TOGETHERNESS

"Two Different Worlds," 1956
Sid Wayne/Al Frisch
WORLD

"Two for the Road," 1967
Leslie Bricusse/Henry Mancini
STREETS, TOGETHERNESS

"Two Hearts in Three Quarter Time,"
1930
Joe Young (Eng.)/Robert Stolz
TABLE 2, MUSIC, TOGETHERNESS

"Two Hearts That Pass in the Night,"
1941
Forman Brown (Eng.)/Ernesto Lecuona
CUBA

"Two Loves Have I," 1931
J. P. Murray, Barry Trivers (Eng.)/Vincent Scotto
OCTAVE

"TWO SLEEPY PEOPLE," 1938
Frank Loesser/Hoagy Carmichael
FILM MUSIC, PEDAL POINT, PEOPLE, SLEEP,
TOGETHERNESS

"TZENA, TZENA, TZENA," 1950
Mitchell Parish (Eng.)/Julius Grossman, Issachar
Miron
BORROWING

"U CAN'T TOUCH THIS," 1990
Rick James, Alonzo Miller, M. C. Hammer
TABLE 10-q, RAP

"U GOT THE LOOK," 1987
Prince Rogers Nelson
ROCK-xii

"UNCHAIN MY HEART," 1960
Agnes Jones, Freddy James
ROCK 'N' ROLL-i

"UNCHAINED MELODY," 1955
Hy Zaret/Álex North
TABLE 8

"UNCLE ALBERT/ADMIRAL HALSEY," 1971
Paul McCartney, Linda McCartney
ROCK-ii

"UNCLE PEN," 1951
Bill Monroe
BLUEGRASS

"UNDECIDED," 1939
Sid Robin/Charles Shavers
RIFF, SINGING GROUPS, SWING

"UNDER A BLANKET OF BLUE," 1933
Marty Symes, Al J. Neuberg/Jerry Livingston
TABLE 3, TABLE 7

"UNDER A ROOF IN PAREE," 1931
Irving Caesar (Eng.)/Raoul Moretti
TABLE 5, FRANCE

"UNDER MY THUMB," 1966
Mick Jagger, Keith Richards
TABLE 2

"UNDER PARIS SKIES," 1953
Kim Gannon (Eng.)/Hubert Giraud
TABLE 5, FRANCE, MODE, SKY

"UNDER THE BAMBOO TREE," 1902
Robert Cole, J. Rosamond Johnson
CAKEWALK, COON SONG, DIALECT, RAG-
TIME, TABLE 15, TIN PAN ALLEY, TREES

"UNDER THE BOARDWALK," 1964
Artie Rosnick, Kenny Young
OCEAN, ROCK 'N' ROLL-ii, STREETS, WATER-
FRONT

"UNDER THE BRIDGES OF PARIS," 1953
Dorcas Cochran (Eng.)/Vincent Scotto
FRANCE

"UNDER THE SEA," 1988
Howard Ashman/Alan Menken
TABLE 1, CALYPSO, TABLE 9, OCEAN, SHEET
MUSIC

"UNDER YOUR SPELL," 1986
Carole Bayer Sager, Bob Dylan
WOMEN AS SONGWRITERS

"UNDERCOVER OF THE NIGHT," 1983
Mick Jagger, Keith Richards
ROCK-iii

"UNFORGETTABLE," 1951
Irving Gordon
FORGETTING, TABLE 10-a, TABLE 10-b, RE-
CORDING, SHOW TUNE, SINGERS, TABLE 15,
TONALITY

"UNION MAID," 1940
Woody Guthrie
WOMEN AS SONGWRITERS

"THE UNIVERSAL SOLDIER," 1964
Buffy Sainte-Marie
FOLK SONG, WOMEN AS SONGWRITERS

"UNTIL IT'S TIME FOR YOU TO GO," 1965
Buffy Sainte-Marie
FOLK SONG

"VILIA," 1907
Adrian Ross/Franz Lehár
ART SONG, AUSTRIA, NEW YORK CITY, TABLE 13

"VINCENT (STARRY, STARRY NIGHT)," 1971
Don McLean
NAMES

"VISION OF LOVE," 1990
Mariah Carey, Ben Margulies
TABLE 10-f

"VOLARE (NEL BLU, DIPINTO DI BLU)," 1958
Mitchell Parish (Eng.)/Domenico Modugno
FOREIGN LANGUAGE, GRAMMY AWARDS, TABLE 10-a, TABLE 10-b, ITALY

"VOUS QUI PASSEZ SANS ME VOIR," SEE "PASSING BY"

"WABASH CANNONBALL," 1940
A. F. Carter
FOLK SONG

"WABASH MOON," 1931
Dave Dreyer, Morton Downes, Billy McKenny
MOON, RADIO, RIVERS

"WAGON WHEELS," 1933
Billy Hill/Peter De Rose
REVUES, TABLE 14

"WAIT TILL THE SUN SHINES, NELLIE," 1905
Andrew B. Sterling/Harry Von Tilzer
NAMES, SUN, WAITING

"WAIT TILL YOU SEE HER," 1942
Lorenz Hart/Richard Rodgers
CABARET, TABLE 11, SHOW TUNE, WAITING, WALTZ

"WAITIN' FOR THE TRAIN TO COME IN," 1945
Sunny Skylar, Martin Block
WORLD WAR II

"WAITIN' IN SCHOOL," 1957
Johnny Burnette, Dorsey Burnette
ROCK 'N' ROLL-iii, WAITING

"WAITING FOR THE GIRLS UPSTAIRS," 1971
Stephen Sondheim
WAITING

"WAITING FOR THE ROBERT E. LEE," 1912
L. Wolfe Gilbert/Lewis F. Muir
BOATING, COON SONG, RAGTIME, SINGING GROUPS, VAUDEVILLE, WAITING

"WAKE THE TOWN AND TELL THE PEOPLE," 1954
Sammy Gallop/Sammy Gallop, Jerry Livingston
TABLE 5, PEOPLE

"WAKE UP LITTLE SUSIE," 1957
Boudleaux Bryant, Felice Bryant
NAMES, ROCK 'N' ROLL-i, WOMEN AS SONGWRITERS

"A WALK IN THE BLACK FOREST (EINE SCHWARZWALDFAHRT)," 1962
Anonymous/Horst Jankowski
GERMANY, TREES, WALKING

"WALK LIKE A MAN," 1963
Bob Crewe, Bob Gaudio
MAN, ROCK 'N' ROLL-ii

"WALK ON BY," 1961
Hal David/Burt Bacharach
POPULAR SONG-xi, RHYTHM AND BLUES

"WALK ON THE WILD SIDE," 1972
Lou Reed
ROCK-ix, WALKING

"WALK RIGHT IN," 1930
Gus Cannon, H. Woods
SINGING GROUPS, WALKING

"WALK THIS WAY," 1975
Joe Perry, Steven Tyler
RAP, WALKING

"WALKIN' MY BABY BACK HOME," 1930
Roy Turk, Fred E. Ahlert
BABY, HOME, WALKING

"WALKING IN RHYTHM," 1974
Barney Perry
RHYTHM, WALKING

"Walking in the Rain," 1964
Barry Mann, Cynthia Weil, Phil Spector
BRILL BUILDING, ROCK 'N' ROLL, WALKING, WEATHER

"Walking the Dog," 1963
Rufus Thomas
ANIMALS, SOUL

"Walking the Floor Over You," 1941
Ernest Tubb
COUNTRY AND WESTERN, WALKING

"Waltz at Maxim's," *see* **"She Is Not Thinking of Me"**

"A Waltz Dream," 1907
Adrian Ross, Oscar Straus
DREAMS

"The Waltz in Swing Time," 1936
Dorothy Fields/Jerome Kern
WALTZ

"Waltz Theme From The Godfather," 1972
Billy Meshel, Larry Kusik/Nino Rota
ITALY

"The Waltz You Saved for Me," 1930
Gus Kahn/Emil Flindt, Wayne King
TABLE 3

"The Wanderer," 1960
Ernest Maresca
ROCK 'N' ROLL-ii

"The Wang Wang Blues," 1921
Leo Wood/Gus Muller, "Buster" Johnson, Henry Busse
BLUES, ROARING TWENTIES

"Wanna Be Startin' Somethin'," 1982
Michael Jackson
BEGINNING, ROCK-xii

"Wanna Be With You," 1982
Maurice White, Wayne Vaughn
TABLE 10-p

"Wanting You," 1928
Oscar Hammerstein II/Sigmund Romberg
TABLE 13

"Wasted Days Wasted Nights," 1975
Freddy Fender, Wayne Duncan
COUNTRY AND WESTERN, DAY

"Watch What Happens," 1964
Norman Gimbel (Eng.)/Michel Legrand
TABLE 4-d, CHROMATICISM, TABLE 8, FRANCE

"Watching the River Flow," 1971
Bob Dylan
ROCK-iv

"Watercolors," 1975
Janis Ian
WOMEN AS SONGWRITERS

"Wave," 1967
Antonio Carlos Jobim
BOSSA NOVA, BRAZIL

"Waves of the Danube," *see* **"Anniversary Song"**

"Way Down Yonder in New Orleans," 1922
Henry Creamer, Turner Layton
TABLE 5, DIXIELAND, SINGING GROUPS

"The Way He Makes Me Feel," 1983
Alan Bergman, Marilyn Bergman/Michel Legrand
TABLE 8, FRANCE, RANGE, WOMEN AS SONGWRITERS

"The Way We Were," 1973
Alan Bergman, Marilyn Bergman/Marvin Hamlisch
TABLE 1, BALLAD, CODA, COLLABORATION, COMPOSERS, FILM MUSIC, TABLE 8, FORM, TABLE 10-b, POPULAR SONG-xiii, TABLE 15, WOMEN AS SONGWRITERS

"The Way You Look Tonight," 1936
Dorothy Fields/Jerome Kern
TABLE 1, ACCOMPANIMENT, BEAUTY, CHORUS, CODA, COMPOSERS, COUNTERMELODY, FILM MUSIC, FILM MUSICALS, TABLE 9, GOLDEN AGE, LYRICISTS, RANGE, RELEASE, TABLE 15, WOMEN AS SONGWRITERS

"The Way You Make Me Feel," 1987
Michael Jackson
FEELING, TABLE 15

"The Ways to Love a Man," 1969
Billy Sherrill, Glenn Sutton, Tammy Wynette
WOMEN AS SONGWRITERS

"The Wayward Wind," 1956
Stan Lebowsky, Herb Newman
BOLERO, WEATHER

"We Are the World," 1985
Michael Jackson, Lionel Richie, Jr.
TABLE 10-a, TABLE 10-b, TABLE 10-h, POPULAR
SONG-xiv, WORLD

"We Can Work It Out," 1965
John Lennon, Paul McCartney
ROCK-ii

"We Could Make Such Beautiful Music
(Together)," 1940
Robert Sour/Henry Manners
BEAUTY, MUSIC, TOGETHERNESS

"We Did It Before and We Can Do It
Again," 1941
Cliff Friend, Charles Tobias
WORLD WAR II

"We Gotta Get Out of This Place," 1965
Barry Mann, Cynthia Weil
PLACES, ROCK-iii

"We Kiss in a Shadow," 1951
Oscar Hammerstein II/Richard Rodgers
KISSING, MUSICAL PLAYS, TABLE 12

"We May Never Love Like This Again,"
1974
Joel Hirschhorn, Al Kasha
TABLE 1

"We Must Be Vigilant," 1942; SEE ALSO
"American Patrol"
Edgar Leslie/Joe Burke
ADAPTATION, PATRIOTISM

"We Saw the Sea," 1936
Irving Berlin
OCEAN

"We Shall Overcome," 1960
Zilphia Horton, Frank Hamilton, Guy Carawan, Pete
Seeger
BORROWING, FORM, FREEDOM SONG,
GOSPEL, PROTEST SONG

"We Sure Can Love Each Other," 1971
Billy Sherrill, Tammy Wynette
WOMEN AS SONGWRITERS

"We Sure Do Need Him Now," c. 1935
Thomas A. Dorsey
GOSPEL

"We Take Our Hats Off to You, Mr.
Wilson," 1914
Blanche Merrill
WOMEN AS SONGWRITERS, WORLD WAR I

"We Three (My Echo, My Shadow, and
Me)," 1940
Dick Robertson, Nelson Cogane, Sammy Mysels
SINGING GROUPS

"Wedding Bell Blues," 1966
Laura Nyro
TABLE 4-d, MARRIAGE, PERFORMER-
SONGWRITERS, SINGING GROUPS, WOMEN
AS SONGWRITERS

"Wedding Bells Are Breaking Up That Old
Gang of Mine," 1929
Irving Kahal, Willie Raskin/Sammy Fain
MARRIAGE, TOGETHERNESS

"The Wedding of the Painted Doll," 1929
Arthur Freed/Nacio Herb Brown
DOLL, TABLE 9, LENGTH, MARRIAGE

"The Wedding Samba," 1947
Abraham Ellstein, Allan Small, Joseph Liebowitz
SAMBA

"The Wedding Song (There Is Love),"
1971
Anonymous
MARRIAGE

"WEDNESDAY'S CHILD," 1967
Mack David
DAYS OF THE WEEK

"A WEE DEOCH-AN-DORIS," 1911
Gerald Grafton, Harry Lauder
DIALECT

"(IN THE) WEE SMALL HOURS (OF THE MORN-
ING)," 1955
Bob Hilliard/David Mann
TIME OF DAY

"WEEKEND IN NEW ENGLAND," 1975
Randy Edelman
TABLE 4-d

"WEIGHT," 1968
Jaime Robbie Robertson
ROCK-v

"WELCOME BACK," 1976
John Sebastian
GREETINGS

"WELCOME TO MY WORLD," 1961
Ray Winkler, John Hathcock
COUNTRY AND WESTERN, WORLD

"WE'LL BE TOGETHER AGAIN," 1945
Frankie Lane, Carl Fischer
TOGETHERNESS

"WE'LL MEET AGAIN," 1939
Ross Parker, Hughie Charles
MEETING

"A WELL RESPECTED MAN," 1965
Ray Davies
MAN, ROCK-iii

"WE'LL SING IN THE SUNSHINE," 1963
Gale Garnett
SUN

"WE'RE A WINNER," 1967
Curtis Mayfield
SOUL

"WE'RE AN AMERICAN BAND," 1973
Don Brewer
HEAVY METAL

"WE'RE GONNA ROCK AROUND THE CLOCK,"
SEE "(WE'RE GONNA) ROCK AROUND THE
CLOCK"

"WE'RE IN THE MONEY," ALSO KNOWN AS "THE
GOLD DIGGERS' SONG," 1933
Al Dubin/Harry Warren
DEPRESSION YEARS, FILM MUSICALS, TABLE 9,
LYRICISTS, MONEY

"WE'RE OFF TO SEE THE WIZARD," 1939
E. Y. Harburg/Harold Arlen
TABLE 9, MAGIC, MARCH

"WERE THINE THAT SPECIAL FACE," 1948
Cole Porter
TABLE 2

"WE'VE HAD A LOVELY TIME, SO LONG, GOOD
BYE," 1912
Blanche Merrill/Leo Edwards
WOMEN AS SONGWRITERS

"WE'VE ONLY JUST BEGUN," 1970
Paul Williams/Roger Nichols
BALLAD, BEGINNING, TABLE 4-c, PERFORMER-
SONGWRITERS, PICKUP, RANGE

"WHAT A DIFF'RENCE A DAY MADE," ALSO
KNOWN AS "WHAT A DIFFERENCE A DAY
MAKES," 1934
Stanley Adams (Eng.)/Maria Grever
TABLE 4-d, BOLERO, DAY, DISCO, TABLE 10-m,
MEXICO, PICKUP, TABLE 15, TRIPLET, WOMEN
AS SONGWRITERS

"WHAT A FOOL BELIEVES," 1978
Kenny Loggins/Michael McDonald
FOOLS, TABLE 10-a, TABLE 10-b, ROCK

"WHAT A WONDERFUL WORLD," 1967
George David Weiss, George Douglas
WONDER, WORLD

"**WHAT A WONDERFUL WORLD**," *SEE* "**WONDERFUL WORLD**"

"**WHAT AM I LIVING FOR?**," **1958**
Fred Jay, Art Harris
RHYTHM AND BLUES

"**WHAT ARE YOU DOING THE REST OF YOUR LIFE?**," **1969**
Alan Bergman, Marilyn Bergman/Michel Legrand
CARDINAL POINTS, CHROMATICISM, COLLABORATION, TABLE 8, FRANCE, MODE, PICKUP, WOMEN AS SONGWRITERS

"**WHAT CAN I SAY AFTER I SAY I'M SORRY?**," **1926**
Walter Donaldson, Abe Lyman
TABLE 3, FORGIVENESS, INTERVAL

"**WHAT CHILD IS THIS?**," **1861;** *SEE ALSO* "**GREENSLEEVES**"
William Chatterton Dix/traditional English melody
CHRISTMAS

"**WHAT DID YOU LEARN IN SCHOOL TODAY?**," **1962**
Tom Paxton
FOLK SONG

"**WHAT HAVE THEY DONE TO THE RAIN?**," **1962**
Malvina Reynolds
WOMEN AS SONGWRITERS

"**WHAT I DID FOR LOVE**," **1975**
Edward Kleban/Marvin Hamlisch
AABA, BALLAD, COMPOSERS, LOVE, MELODY, TABLE 11

"**WHAT IS LIFE?**," **1970**
George Harrison
ROCK-ii

"**WHAT IS THERE TO SAY?**," **1933**
E. Y. Harburg/Vernon Duke
REVUES, TABLE 14

"**WHAT IS THIS THING CALLED LOVE?**," **1929**
Cole Porter
BEBOP, COMPOSER-LYRICISTS, INTERVAL, LOVE, TABLE 11

"**WHAT KIND OF FOOL AM I?**," **1961**
Leslie Bricusse/Anthony Newley
BRITAIN, FOOLS, TABLE 10-b, TABLE 15

"**WHAT NOW MY LOVE?**," **1962**
Carl Sigman (Eng.)/Gilbert Becaud
BOLERO, FRANCE, LOVE, QUESTIONS, TRIPLET

"**WHAT THE WORLD NEEDS NOW IS LOVE**," **1965**
Hal David/Burt Bacharach
LOVE, LYRICISTS, TABLE 15, WORLD

"**WHAT'D I SAY?**," **1959**
Ray Charles
SOUL

"**WHATEVER GETS YOU THROUGH THE NIGHT**," **1974**
John Lennon
NIGHT

"**WHATEVER LOLA WANTS**," **1955**
Richard Adler, Jerry Ross
TABLE 11, NAMES, TANGO

"**WHATEVER WILL BE, WILL BE (QUE SERA, SERA)**," **1955**
Jay Livingston, Ray Evans
TABLE 1, TABLE 8, FOREIGN LANGUAGE, TABLE 15

"**WHAT'LL I DO?**," **1923**
Irving Berlin
COMPOSER-LYRICISTS, LYRICISTS, NEW YORK CITY, REVUES, TABLE 14

"**WHAT'S LOVE GOT TO DO WITH IT?**," **1984**
Terry Britten/Graham Lyle
TABLE 10-a, TABLE 10-b, TABLE 10-f

"**WHAT'S NEW?**," **1939**
Johnny Burke/Bob Haggart
BALLAD, TABLE 3, QUESTIONS, TIN PAN ALLEY

"**WHAT'S NEW PUSSYCAT?**," **1965**
Hal David/Burt Bacharach
ANIMALS, TABLE 8

"WHAT'S THE MATTER HERE?," 1987
Natalie Merchant, Suzanne Vega
WOMEN AS SONGWRITERS

"WHAT'S THE MATTER WITH FATHER?," 1910
Harry H. Williams/Egbert van Alstyne
FATHERS

"WHAT'S THE USE OF WOND'RIN?," 1945
Oscar Hammerstein II/Richard Rodgers
DIALECT, TABLE 12, WONDER

"WHAT'S YOUR NAME?," 1961
Claude Johnson
NAMES

"THE WHEEL OF FORTUNE," 1952
Bennie Benjamin, George Weiss
LUCK

"WHEN A GYPSY MAKES HIS VIOLIN CRY,"
1935
Dick Smith, Frank Winegar, Jimmy Rogan/Emery
Deutsch
CRYING, GYPSY MUSIC, STRINGS

"WHEN A MAN LOVES A WOMAN," 1966
Calvin H. Lewis, Andrew Wright
TABLE 10-g, MAN, SOUL, WOMAN

"WHEN DAY IS DONE," 1926
B. G. DeSylva/Robert Katscher
DAY, ENDING, FRANCE

"WHEN DID YOU LEAVE HEAVEN?," 1936
Walter Bullock/Richard A. Whiting
HEAVEN

"WHEN DOVES CRY," 1984
Prince Rogers Nelson
BIRDS, CRYING, ROCK-xii

"WHEN FRANCIS DANCES WITH ME," 1921
Benny Ryan/Sol Violinsky [Ginsberg]
DANCING

"WHEN I CALL YOUR NAME," 1990
Vince Gill, Tim Dubois
TABLE 10-u

"WHEN I FALL IN LOVE," 1951
Edward Heyman/Victor Young
FALLING IN LOVE, TABLE 8, MELODY, SING-
ING GROUPS

"WHEN I GROW TOO OLD TO DREAM," 1934
Oscar Hammerstein II/Sigmund Romberg
AGE, DREAMS, TABLE 9

"WHEN I GROW UP (TO BE A MAN)," 1964
Brian Wilson
AGE, ROCK-i

"WHEN I MARRY MISTER SNOW," 1945
Oscar Hammerstein II/Richard Rodgers
MARRIAGE, TABLE 12

"WHEN I NEED YOU," 1977
Carole Bayer Sager/Albert Hammond
TABLE 4-d

"WHEN I READ MY TITLE CLEAR," 1854
Isaac Watts, J.A. Wade, J.F. Wade/J.A. Wade, J.F.
Wade
GOSPEL

"WHEN I TAKE MY SUGAR TO TEA," 1931
Sammy Fain, Irving Kahal, Pierre Norman
FOOD AND DRINK, SINGING GROUPS,
SWEETNESS

"WHEN I'M NOT NEAR THE GIRL I LOVE,"
1946
E. Y. Harburg/Burton Lane
CLOSENESS, GIRL, HUMOR, TABLE 11, WALTZ

"WHEN I'M SIXTY-FOUR," 1967
John Lennon, Paul McCartney
AGE, ROCK-ii

"WHEN I'M THE PRESIDENT," 1931
Al Lewis, Al Sherman
RADIO

"WHEN IRISH EYES ARE SMILING," 1912
Chauncey Olcott/Ernest R. Ball, George Grarff, Jr.
ANATOMY, TABLE 2, IRELAND, NATIONS,
RECORDING, SMILING, WALTZ

"WHEN IT'S SLEEPY TIME DOWN SOUTH,"
1931
Leon Rene, Otis Rene, Clarence Muse
CARDINAL POINTS, SLEEP, TIME

"WHEN IT'S SPRINGTIME IN THE ROCKIES,"
1929
Mary Hale Woolsey/Robert Sauer
MOUNTAINS, SEASONS

"WHEN JACK COMES SAILING HOME AGAIN,"
1918
Nora Bayes
WOMEN AS SONGWRITERS

"WHEN JOHNNY COMES MARCHING HOME,"
1863
Patrick Sarsfield Gilmore
HOME, QUOTATION

"WHEN JOSE PLAYS A RAGTIME ON HIS BANJO,"
1912
D.A. Esrom (pseud. Theodora Morse)/Theodore
Morse
WOMEN AS SONGWRITERS

"WHEN LOVE IS YOUNG IN SPRINGTIME," SEE "I
CAN'T BEGIN TO TELL YOU"

"WHEN MY BABY SMILES AT ME," 1920
Andrew Sterling, Ted Lewis/Bill Munro
BABY, REVUE'S, TABLE 14, SMILING

"WHEN MY BLUE MOON TURNS TO GOLD
AGAIN," 1941
Wiley Walker, Gene Sullivan
TABLE 7, COUNTRY AND WESTERN

"WHEN MY SHIP COMES IN," 1934
Gus Kahn/Walter Donaldson
DEPRESSION YEARS

"WHEN MY SUGAR WALKS DOWN THE STREET,
ALL THE BIRDIES GO TWEET-TWEET-TWEET,"
1924
Gene Austin, Jimmy McHugh, Irving Mills
BIRDS, STREETS, SWEETNESS, WALKING

"WHEN SHADOWS FALL," SEE "HOME"

"WHEN SHALL I AGAIN SEE IRELAND?," 1917
Henry Blossom/Victor Herbert
IRELAND

"WHEN SUNNY GETS BLUE," 1956
Jack Segal/Marvin Fisher
COLORS, TABLE 7, STANDARD

"WHEN THE BOYS COME HOME," 1917
John Hay/Oley Speaks
WORLD WAR I

"WHEN THE BUFFALO'S GONE," 1965
Buffy Sainte-Marie
WOMEN AS SONGWRITERS

"WHEN THE CHARIOT COMES," SEE "SHE'LL BE
COMIN' ROUND THE MOUNTAIN"

"WHEN THE IDLE POOR BECOME THE IDLE
RICH," 1946
E. Y. Harburg/Burton Lane
HUMOR, MONEY

"WHEN THE LIGHTS GO ON AGAIN (ALL OVER
THE WORLD)," 1942
Eddie Seiler, Sol Marcus, Bennie Benjamin
TABLE 6, TABLE 8, WORLD, WORLD WAR II

"WHEN THE MIDNIGHT CHOO-CHOO LEAVES
FOR ALABAM'," 1912
Irving Berlin
RAGTIME, TIME OF DAY, TRAINS

"WHEN THE MOON COMES OVER THE MOUN-
TAIN," 1931
Kate Smith, Harry Woods, Harold Johnson
DEPRESSION YEARS, MOON, MOUNTAINS,
RADIO, TABLE 15

"WHEN THE RED, RED, ROBIN COMES BOB,
BOB, BOBBIN' ALONG," 1926
Harry Woods
BIRDS, COLORS, TABLE 7, NOVELTY SONG

"WHEN THE SAINTS GO MARCHING IN," 1896
Katherine E. Purvis/James M. Black
DIXIELAND, HARMONIC RHYTHM, RELIGION

"WHEN THE SUN COMES OUT," 1940
Ted Koehler/Harold Arlen
SUN

"WHEN THE SWALLOWS COME BACK TO
CAPISTRANO," 1940
Leon Rene
BIRDS

"WHEN THE WORLD WAS YOUNG," 1952
Johnny Mercer (Eng.)/Philippe Gerald Block
AGE, CHILDHOOD, TREES, WORLD

"WHEN WE'RE ALONE," *SEE* "PENTHOUSE
SERENADE"

"WHEN WILL I BE LOVED?," 1960
Phil Everly
TABLE 4-d, ROCK 'N' ROLL-i

"WHEN YOU AIN'T GOT NOTHIN', YOU GOT
NOTHIN' TO LOSE," 1965
Bob Dylan
ROCK-iv

"WHEN YOU AND I WERE YOUNG, MAGGIE,"
1866
George W. Johnson/James Austin Butterfield
POPULAR SONG-i

"WHEN YOU DANCE," 1955
Andrew Jones, L. Kirkland
DANCING, SINGING GROUPS

"WHEN YOU WERE SWEET SIXTEEN," 1898
James Thornton
AGE, BARBERSHOP, GAY NINETIES, SWEET-
NESS, VAUDEVILLE

"WHEN YOU WISH UPON A STAR," 1940
Ned Washington/Leigh Harline
TABLE 1, TABLE 9, OCTAVE, STARS, WISHING

"WHEN YOU WORE A TULIP AND I WORE A BIG
RED ROSE," 1914
Jack Mahoney/Percy Wenrich
COLORS, TABLE 7, FLOWERS, VAMP

"WHEN YOUR HAIR HAS TURNED TO SILVER (I
WILL LOVE YOU JUST THE SAME)," 1930
Charles Tobias/Peter De Rose
AGE, TABLE 2, TABLE 7, RADIO, SHEET MUSIC

"WHEN YOUR LOVER HAS GONE," 1931
E. A. Swan
TABLE 9, LOVE

"WHEN YOUR OLD WEDDING RING WAS
NEW," 1935
Charles McCarthy, Joe Solieri/Bert Douglas
JEWELRY, MARRIAGE

"WHEN YOU'RE HOT, YOU'RE HOT," 1971
Jerry Reed
TABLE 10-u

"WHEN YOU'RE SMILING (THE WHOLE WORLD
SMILES WITH YOU)," 1928
Mark Fisher, Joe Goodwin, Larry Shay
SMILING, WORLD

"WHEN YUBA PLAYS THE RUMBA ON HIS
TUBA," 1931
Herman Hupfeld
BRASS, REVUES, TABLE 14, RUMBA

"WHENEVER I CALL YOU 'FRIEND,'" 1978
Melissa Manchester, Kenny Loggins
WOMEN AS SONGWRITERS

"WHERE DID YOU GET THAT HAT?," 1888
Joseph J. Sullivan
OPERA, VAUDEVILLE

"WHERE DO BROKEN HEARTS GO?," 1985
Frank Wildhorn, Chuck Jackson
TABLE 15

"WHERE DO I BEGIN," *SEE* "LOVE STORY"

"WHERE DO WE GO FROM HERE?," 1917
Howard Johnson, Percy Wenrich
WORLD WAR I

"WHERE DO YOU COME FROM," 1962
Ruth Batchelor, Bob Roberts
WOMEN AS SONGWRITERS

"WHERE DO YOU WORK-A-JOHN?," 1926
Mortimer Weinberg, Charley Marks, Harry Warren
DIALECT, FOLK SONG, NOVELTY SONG

"WHERE DUTY CALLS," 1987
Patti Smith, Fred Smith
WOMEN AS SONGWRITERS

"WHERE HAVE ALL THE FLOWERS GONE?," 1961
Pete Seeger
AABA, FLOWERS, FOLK SONG, FORM, PRO-
TEST SONG, QUESTIONS, SINGING GROUPS

"WHERE IS LOVE?," 1963
Lionel Bart
CHILDHOOD

"WHERE IS THE LOVE?," 1971
Ralph McDonald, William Salter
TABLE 10-h

"WHERE IS THE LOVE?," 1975
Harry Wayne Casey, Richard Finch, Willie Clark,
Betty Wright
TABLE 10-h, TABLE 10-q

"WHERE IS YOUR HEART?," SEE "THE SONG FROM MOULIN ROUGE"

"WHERE OR WHEN?" 1937
Lorenz Hart/Richard Rodgers

ALLITERATION, COLLABORATION, KEY,
LYRICISTS, MELODY, TABLE 11, PEDAL POINT,
ROCK 'N' ROLL-ii, SCALE

"WHERE THE BLUE OF THE NIGHT MEETS THE GOLD OF THE DAY," 1931
Roy Turk, Bing Crosby, Fred E. Ahlert

TABLE 7, DAY, DEPRESSION YEARS, TABLE 9,
NIGHT

"WHERE THE BOYS ARE," 1960
Howard Greenfield/Neil Sedaka

BOY, ROCK 'N' ROLL-iii, TABLE 15

"WHERE THE RIVER SHANNON FLOWS," ALSO KNOWN AS "THE IRISH SHANNON RIVER," 1905
James T. Russell
IRELAND

"WHERE'S THAT RAINBOW?," 1926
Lorenz Hart/Richard Rodgers
QUESTIONS, RAINBOW

"WHERE'VE YOU BEEN," 1988
Don Henry, Jon Vezner
TABLE 10-t, TABLE 10-w

"THE WHIFFENPOOF SONG," 1918
Meade Minnigerode, George S. Pomeroy/Tob B.
Galloway
RADIO

"WHILE MY GUITAR GENTLY WEEPS," 1968
George Harrison
TENDERNESS

"WHILE WE'RE YOUNG," 1943
Bill Engvick/Alec Wilder, Morty Palitz
AGE, CABARET, CHILDHOOD, SHOW TUNE,
SINGERS, TABLE 15

"WHISPERING," 1920
John Schonberger, Richard Coburn, Vincent Rose
RECORDING, ROARING TWENTIES, TALKING

"WHISPERING BELLS," 1957
C. E. Quick
ROCK 'N' ROLL-ii

"WHISPERS IN THE DARK," 1937
Leo Robin/Frederick Hollander
TALKING

"WHISTLE WHILE YOU WORK," 1937
Larry Morey/Frank Churchill
TABLE 9

"WITCH DOCTOR," 1958
Ross Bagdasarian
MAGIC

"WHO'LL STOP THE RAIN," 1970
John C. Fogerty
ENDING, ROCK-ix, WEATHER

"WHOOPEE TI YI YO GIT ALONG LITTLE DOGIES," *SEE* **"(WHOOPEE TI YI YO) GIT ALONG LITTLE DOGIES"**

"WHO'S AFRAID OF THE BIG BAD WOLF?," 1933
Ann Ronell, Frank E. Churchill/Frank E. Churchill
ANIMALS, TABLE 9, QUESTIONS, WOMEN AS SONGWRITERS

"WHO'S MAKING LOVE?," 1968
Homer Banks, Bettye Crutcher, Don Davis, Raymond Jackson
SOUL

"WHO'S SORRY NOW?," 1923
Bert Kalmar, Harry Ruby/Ted Snyder
BROKEN CHORD, ROCK 'N' ROLL-iii

"WHO'S THAT GIRL?," 1987
Madonna, Patrick Leonard
GIRL, ROCK-xii

"WHY (IS THERE A RAINBOW IN THE SKY?)," 1929
Arthur Swanstrom, Benny Davis/J. Fred Coots
QUESTIONS, RAINBOW, SKY

"WHY," 1960
Bob Marcucci, Peter De Angelis
ROCK 'N' ROLL-iii, TABLE 15

"WHY CAN'T THE ENGLISH?," 1956
Alan Jay Lerner/Frederick Loewe
HUMOR, NATIONS

"WHY CAN'T YOU BEHAVE?," 1948
Cole Porter
QUESTIONS

"WHY DO FOOLS FALL IN LOVE?," 1956
Frank Lymon, George Goldner
COVER, FALLING IN LOVE, FOOLS, LOVE ROCK 'N' ROLL-ii

"WHY DO I LOVE YOU?," 1927
Oscar Hammerstein II/Jerome Kern
COMPOSERS, DIALECT, KEY, LANDMARKS OF STAGE AND SCREEN, LOVE, LYRICISTS, MUSICAL PLAYS, TABLE 12, OPERA, QUESTIONS, RANGE

"WHY DON'T YOU DO RIGHT?," 1942
Joe McCoy
SINGERS, TABLE 15

"WHY DON'T YOU HAUL OFF AND LOVE ME?," 1949
Wayne Raney, Lonnie Glosson
RHYTHM AND BLUES

"WHY SHOULDN'T I?," 1935
Cole Porter
CABARET, CONTRACTION, QUESTIONS

"WHY WAS I BORN?," 1929
Oscar Hammerstein II/Jerome Kern
BIRTH, DEPRESSION YEARS, QUESTIONS, TABLE 15, TORCH SONG

"WICHITA LINEMAN," 1968
Jim Webb
TABLE 5, COMPOSER-LYRICISTS, MAN, TABLE 15

"WIEN DU STADT MEINER TRÄUME," *SEE* **"VIENNA, MY CITY OF DREAMS"**

"WILD HORSES," 1970
Mick Jagger, Keith Richards
ANIMALS, TABLE 5

"WILD NIGHT," 1971
Van Morrison
NIGHT, ROCK-iii

"WILD ONE," 1960
Dave Appell, Bernie Lowe, Kal Mann
ROCK 'N' ROLL-iii

"THE WILD SIDE OF LIFE," 1952
W. Warren, A. A. Carter
COUNTRY AND WESTERN, LIFE

"WILD THING," 1965
Chip Taylor
ROCK

"WILD THING," 1988
Marvin Young, Tony Smith, Matt Dike, Michael Ross
RAP

"WILD WORLD," 1970
Cat Stevens
ROCK-vi, WORLD

"WILDFIRE," 1975
Larry Cansler, Michael Murphey
TABLE 4-d, FIRE

"WILDWOOD FLOWER," 1928
Hank Thompson
COUNTRY AND WESTERN, FLOWERS

"WILL YOU LOVE ME IN DECEMBER AS YOU DO IN MAY?," 1905
James J. Walker/Ernest R. Ball
BARBERSHOP, MONTHS, VAUDEVILLE

"WILL YOU LOVE ME TOMORROW?," 1960
Gerry Goffin/Carole King
ROCK 'N' ROLL-iv, WOMEN AS SONGWRITERS

"WILL YOU REMEMBER (SWEETHEART)," 1917
Rida Johnson Young/Sigmund Romberg
HUNGARY, MEMORY, OPERETTA, TABLE 13, SWEETNESS, WALTZ

"WILLKOMMEN," 1966
Fred Ebb/John Kander
CABARET, GREETINGS

"WILLOW SONG," 1971
Stephen Schwartz
RELIGION

"WILLOW WEEP FOR ME," 1932
Ann Ronnell
ALLITERATION, CRYING, TREES, WOMEN AS SONGWRITERS

"WIMOWEH," 1951; SEE ALSO "THE LION SLEEPS TONIGHT"
Roy Ilene (Eng.), Paul Campbell (pseud. the Weavers)/Paul Campbell
BORROWING, SINGING GROUPS

"WINCHESTER CATHEDRAL," 1966
Geoff Stevens
TABLE 5, TABLE 10-e, NOVELTY SONG

"THE WIND BENEATH MY WINGS," 1982
Larry Henley, Jeff Silbar
CODA, TABLE 8, FRIENDSHIP, TABLE 10-a TABLE 10-b, TABLE 15

"THE WIND CRIES MARY," 1967
Jimi Hendrix
NAMES, ROCK-vii

"THE WINDMILLS OF YOUR MIND (THEME FROM THE THOMAS CROWN AFFAIR)," 1968
Alan Bergman, Marilyn Bergman/Michel Legrand
TABLE 1, TABLE 8, FRANCE, MIND, MODE, SEQUENCE, WOMEN AS SONGWRITERS

"WINDS OF THE OLD DAYS," 1975
Joan Baez
WOMEN AS SONGWRITERS

"WINDY," 1967
Ruthann Friedman
TABLE 4-d, WEATHER

"WINTER WONDERLAND," 1934
Richard B. Smith/Felix Bernard
CHRISTMAS, SEASONS, WEATHER, WONDER

"WINTERGREEN FOR PRESIDENT," 1931
Ira Gershwin/George Gershwin
HUMOR, MARCH

"WIPE OUT," 1963
m. Robert Berryhill, Patrick Connolly, James Fuller, Ron Wilson
ENDING

"WISH YOU WERE HERE," 1952
Harold Rome
TABLE 11, WISHING

"Wishin' and Hopin'," 1963
Hal David/Burt Bacharach
WISHING

"Wishing (Will Make It So)," 1939
B. G. DeSylva
TABLE 8, WISHING

"Witch Doctor," 1958
Ross Bagdasarian
MAGIC

"Witchcraft," 1957
Dave Bartholomew, Pearl King
MAGIC, WOMEN AS SONGWRITERS

"With a Little Bit of Luck," 1956
Alan Jay Lerner/Frederick Loewe
LUCK, PATTER, POLKA

"With a Little Help From My Friends," 1967
John Lennon, Paul McCartney
FRIENDSHIP, ROCK-ii

"With a Song in My Heart," 1929
Lorenz Hart/Richard Rodgers
TABLE 2, MUSIC

"With My Eyes Wide Open, I'm Dreaming," 1934
Mack Gordon, Harry Revel
TABLE 2, DREAMS, TABLE 9

"With Plenty of Money and You," 1936
Al Dubin/Harry Warren
DEPRESSION YEARS, TABLE 9, MONEY

"With the Wind and the Rain in Your Hair," 1930
Clara Edwards, Jack Lawrence
TABLE 2, WEATHER

"With You I'm Born Again," 1979
Carol Connors/David Shire
BIRTH

"Without a Song," 1929
Billy Rose, Edward Eliscu, Vincent Youmans
ART SONG, MUSIC

"Without You," 1918
Nora Bayes/Irving Fisher
WOMEN AS SONGWRITERS

"Without You," 1970
Thomas Evans, William Peter Ham
TABLE 10-g

"Without You the World Doesn't Seem the Same," *see* **"There's Yes Yes in Your Eyes"**

"(Hey, Little Girl) Wives and Lovers," 1963
Hal David/Burt Bacharach
TABLE 8, TABLE 10-d, LOVERS, MARRIAGE, TABLE 15

"A Woman in Love," 1955
Frank Loesser
LOVE, WOMAN

"Woman in Love," 1980
Barry Gibb, Robin Gibb
KEY, LOVE, TABLE 15, WOMAN

"A Woman Is a Sometime Thing," 1935
DuBose Heyward/George Gershwin
DIALECT, WOMAN

"Wonder When My Baby's Coming Home," 1943
Kermit Goell, Arthur Kent
WORLD WAR II

"Wonderful Copenhagen," 1952
Frank Loesser
TABLE 5, TABLE 9

"(On) A Wonderful Day Like Today," 1964
Leslie Bricusse, Anthony Newley
BRITAIN, DAY, WONDER

"A Wonderful Guy," 1949
Oscar Hammerstein II/Richard Rodgers
MAN, MUSICAL PLAYS, TABLE 12, WALTZ, WONDER

"(MY) WONDERFUL ONE," 1922
Dorothy Terriss/Paul Whiteman, Ferde Grofé
WONDER

"WONDERFUL TONIGHT," 1977
Eric Clapton
ROCK-viii

"WONDERFUL, WONDERFUL," 1957
Ben Raleigh/Sherman Edwards
TABLE 15, WONDER

"(WHAT A) WONDERFUL WORLD," 1959
Sam Cooke, Lou Adler, Herb Alpert
TABLE 4-d, WONDER, WORLD

"WONDERFUL WORLD, BEAUTIFUL PEOPLE," 1969
Jimmy Cliff
REGGAE

"WONDERLAND BY NIGHT," 1961
Lincoln Chase/Klaus Gunter Neumann
WONDER

"WOODMAN, WOODMAN, SPARE THAT TREE," 1911
Irving Berlin, Vincent Bryant
TREES

"THE WOODPECKER SONG," 1940
Harold Adamson (Eng.)/Eldo di Lazzaro
BIRDS, TABLE 9

"WOODSTOCK," 1969
Joni Mitchell
FOLK SONG, ROCK-vi, WOMEN AS SONGWRITERS

"WOOLY BULLY," 1964
Domingo Samudio
ROCK

"WORK WITH ME, ANNIE," 1954
Henry Ballard
RHYTHM AND BLUES

"WORKING MY WAY BACK TO YOU," 1965
Sandy Linzer, Denny Randell
SINGING GROUPS

"THE WORLD IS MINE (TONIGHT)," 1935
Holt Marvell/George Posford
WORLD

"THE WORLD IS WAITING FOR THE SUNRISE," 1919
Eugene Lockhart/Ernest Seitz
ONE-STEP, SUN, TIME OF DAY, WAITING, WORLD

"THE WORLD WE KNEW," 1967
Carl Sigman (Eng.)/Bert Kaempfert, Herbert Rehbein
WORLD

"A WORLD WITHOUT LOVE," 1964
John Lennon, Paul McCartney
LOVE, ROCK-iii, WORLD

"THE WORMS CRAWL IN, THE WORMS CRAWL OUT," SEE "DID YOU EVER THINK AS THE HEARSE ROLLS BY"

"WOULD YOU LIKE TO TAKE A WALK?," 1930
Mort Dixon, Billy Rose/Harry Warren
WALKING

"WOULDN'T IT BE LOVERLY?," 1956
Alan Jay Lerner/Frederick Loewe
BEAUTY, DIALECT, TABLE 12, QUESTIONS

"WOULDN'T IT BE NICE?," 1966
Tony Asher, Brian Wilson/Brian Wilson
ROCK-i

"WRAP YOUR TROUBLES IN DREAMS (AND DREAM YOUR TROUBLES AWAY)," 1931
Ted Koehler, Billy Moll/Harry Barris
DEPRESSION YEARS, DREAMS

"THE WRECK OF THE SOUTHERN OLD 97," 1924
Charles W. Noell, Fred J. Lewey, Henry Whitter
COUNTRY AND WESTERN, TRAINS

"WRITE ME A LETTER," 1947
Howard Biggs
RHYTHM AND BLUES, WRITING

"WUNDERBAR," 1948
Cole Porter
MUSICAL COMEDY, TABLE 11, WALTZ, WON-DER

"Y.M.C.A.," 1978
J. Morali, H. Belolo, V. Willis
DISCO

"YAH MO B THERE," 1983
James Ingram, Michael McDonald, Rod Temperton, Quincy Jones
TABLE 10-p

"YAKETY YAK," 1958
Jerry Leiber, Mike Stoller
NONSENSE, ROCK 'N' ROLL-ii, TALKING

"YANKEE DOODLE," 1767
Anonymous
PATRIOTISM, POPULAR SONG-i, QUOTATION

"THE YANKEE DOODLE BLUES," 1922
Irving Caesar, B. G. DeSylva/George Gershwin
BLUES

"THE YANKEE DOODLE BOY," ALSO KNOWN AS "I'M A YANKEE DOODLE DANDY," 1904
George M. Cohan
BOY, COMPOSER-LYRICISTS, MARCH, MUSI-CAL COMEDY, TABLE 11, PATRIOTISM, POPU-LAR SONG-i, QUOTATION, TIN PAN ALLEY

"YELLOW BIRD," 1957
Norman Luboff, Marilyn Keith, Alan Bergman
BIRDS, CALYPSO, COLLABORATION, TABLE 7, WOMEN AS SONGWRITERS

"YELLOW DOG BLUES," 1928
W. C. Handy
ANIMALS, BLUES

"THE YELLOW ROSE OF TEXAS," 1955
Don George
TABLE 7, STATES

"YELLOW SUBMARINE," 1966
John Lennon, Paul McCartney
BOATING, TABLE 7, ROCK-ii

"YES MY DARLING DAUGHTER," 1939
Jack Lawrence
TABLE 15

"YES, SIR, THAT'S MY BABY," 1925
Gus Kahn/Walter Donaldson
BABY, CHARLESTON, LYRICISTS, ROARING TWENTIES

"YES! WE HAVE NO BANANAS," 1923
Frank Silver, Irving Cohn
FOOD AND DRINK, HUMOR, NOVELTY SONG

"YESTERDAY," 1965
John Lennon, Paul McCartney
AABA, BMI, TABLE 4-a, BRITAIN, COLLABORA-TION, CROSSOVER, DAY, HARMONIC RHYTHM, MEMORY, PERFORMER-SONGWRITERS, POPULAR SONG, POPULAR SONG-viii, ROCK-ii

"YESTERDAY ONCE MORE," 1973
John Bettis, Richard Carpenter
MEMORY

"YESTERDAY, WHEN I WAS YOUNG (HIER ENCORE)," 1965
Herbert Kretzmer (Eng.)/Charles Aznavour
DAY, MEMORY

"YESTERDAYS," 1933
Otto Harbach/Jerome Kern
DAY, FORM, GOLDEN AGE, MEMORY, MODE, TABLE 11, RANGE, TEMPO

"YIP-I-ADDY-I-AY," 1908
Will D. Cobb/John H. Flynn
NONSENSE

"YOU (GEE BUT YOU'RE WONDERFUL)," 1936
Harold Adamson/Walter Donaldson
TABLE 9, WONDER

"YOU AIN'T SEEN NOTHIN' YET," 1974
Randy Bachman
DIALECT

"YOU AIN'T WOMAN ENOUGH," 1965
Loretta Lynn
WOMEN AS SONGWRITERS

**"You Always Hurt the One You Love,"
1944**
Allan Roberts, Doris Fisher
HUMOR, SINGING GROUPS

"You and Me Against the World," 1974
Paul Williams, Ken Ascher
WORLD

"You and the Night and the Music," 1934
Howard Dietz/Arthur Schwartz
ALLITERATION, COLLABORATION, KEY,
LYRICISTS, MODE, MUSIC, TABLE 11, NIGHT,
RADIO, TANGO

"You Are Always in My Heart," SEE "Always in My Heart"

"You Are Free," 1919
William Le Baron/Victor Jacobi
TABLE 13

"You Are Love," 1927
Oscar Hammerstein II/Jerome Kern
ART SONG, DIALECT, LOVE, TABLE 12

"You Are My Darling," 1958
Paul Anka
ROCK 'N' ROLL-iii

"You Are My Destiny," 1958
Paul Anka
ROCK 'N' ROLL-iii

"You Are My Lucky Star," 1935
Arthur Freed/Nacio Herb Brown
OCTAVE, STARS

"You Are My Sunshine," 1940
Jimmie Davis, Charles Mitchell
TABLE 4-d, COUNTRY AND WESTERN, JUKE-
BOX, POPULAR SONG, SUN

"You Are Never Away," 1947
Oscar Hammerstein II/Richard Rodgers
TABLE 12

"You Are So Beautiful," 1973
Billy Preston, Bruce Fisher
TABLE 4-d

"You Are the Sunshine of My Life," 1972
Stevie Wonder
FORM, TABLE 10-g, LYRICS, PERFORMER-
SONGWRITERS, TABLE 15, SUN, SYNCOPA-
TION

"You Are Too Beautiful," 1932
Lorenz Hart/Richard Rodgers
BEAUTY, TABLE 9

"You Are Woman (I Am Man)," 1964
Bob Merrill/Jule Styne
MAN, TABLE 11, WOMAN

"You Belong to Me," 1952
Pee Wee King, Chilton Price, Redd Stewart
TABLE 4-d, TABLE 15

"You Belong to My Heart (Solamente una Vez)," 1941
Ray Gilbert (Eng.)/Agustin Lara
TABLE 2, BOLERO, ENDURING LOVE, TABLE 9,
MEXICO, PICKUP

"You Brought a New Kind of Love to Me," 1930
Sammy Fain, Irving Kahal, Pierre Norman
TABLE 9

"You Better Go Now," 1936
Irvin Graham, Bix Reichner
FAREWELLS

"You Call Everybody Darling," 1946
Sam Martin, Ben Trace, Clem Watts
ENDEARMENT

"You Call It Madness (Ah, But I Call It Love)," 1931
Gladys Du Bois, Paul Gregory, Con Conrad, Russ
Columbo
MADNESS, RADIO, TABLE 15

"You Came a Long Way From St. Louis," 1948
Bob Russell, John Benson Brooks
CITIES, TABLE 5

"You Came Along From Out of Nowhere,"
SEE "Out of Nowhere"

"You Can Get It If You Really Want,"
1970
Jimmy Cliff
REGGAE

"You Can't Get a Man With A Gun,"
1946
Irving Berlin
MAN, POPULAR SONG-ii

"You Can't Hurry Love," 1965
Lamont Dozier, Brian Holland, Eddie Holland
TABLE 4-d, MOTOWN

"You Could Drive a Person Crazy," 1970
Stephen Sondheim
MADNESS

"You Couldn't Be Cuter," 1938
Dorothy Field/Jerome Kern
BEAUTY, SLANG

"You Decorated My Life," 1978
Deborah Kap Hupp, Robert Morrison
TABLE 10-w, LIFE, TABLE 15

"You Didn't Have to Be So Nice," 1965
John Sebastian, Steve Boone
ROCK-v

"You Do Something to Me," 1929
Cole Porter
CONTRACTIONS, MAGIC, TABLE 11

"You Don't Bring Me Flowers," 1977
Neil Diamond, Marilyn Bergman, Alan Bergman/Neil
Diamond
FLOWERS, LENGTH, TABLE 15

"You Don't Have to Be a Star (To Be in
My Show)," 1976
James Dean, John Henry Glover, Jr.
TABLE 10-p

"You Don't Know How Glad I Am," SEE
"(You Don't Know) How Glad I Am"

"You Don't Know Me," 1955
Cindy Walker, Eddy Arnold
TABLE 4-d

"You Don't Own Me," 1963
John Madara, David White
ROCK 'N' ROLL-iv

"You Forgot Your Gloves," 1931
Edward Eliscu/Ned Lehac
CLOTHING, FORGETTING

"You Go to My Head," 1938
Haven Gillespie/J. Fred Coots
ANATOMY, TABLE 2, TABLE 3, CODA, TRIPLET

"You Keep Me Dancing," 1977
Sandy Linzer, Denny Randell
WOMEN AS SONGWRITERS

"You Keep Me Hangin' On," 1966
Eddie Holland, Lamont Dozier, Brian Holland
MOTOWN, ROCK-vii

"You Light Up My Life," 1976
Joe Brooks
TABLE 1, CHORUS, TABLE 8, LIFE, TABLE 15,
VERSE, WOMEN AS SONGWRITERS

"You Made Me Love You (I Didn't Want
to Do It)," 1913
Joseph McCarthy/James V. Monaco
BIG BANDS, TABLE 2, BRASS, COON SONG,
SHOW TUNE, SINGERS, TABLE 15, TIN PAN
ALLEY, VAUDEVILLE

"You Make Me Feel Brand New," 1974
Linda Creed, Thom Bell
FEELING

"You Make Me Feel Like A Natural
Woman," SEE "A Natural Woman"

"You Make Me Feel Like Dancing," 1976
Leo Sayer, Vini Poncia
DANCING, DISCO, FEELING, TABLE 10-q

"You Make Me Feel So Young," 1946
Mack Gordon/Josef Myrow
AGE, BREAK, FEELING, TABLE 9

"You May Not Be an Angel, But I'll String Along With You," *see* "I'll String Along With You"

"You Might Think," 1984
Ric Ocasek
ROCK-xi

"You Must Be Born Again," c. 1955
Dorothy Love Coates
WOMEN AS SONGWRITERS

"You Must Have Been a Beautiful Baby," 1938
Johnny Mercer/Harry Warren
BABY, BEAUTY, CHILDHOOD, LYRICISTS

"You Needed Me," 1975
Randy Goodrum
TABLE 10-f, PICKUP

"(Theme From) You Only Live Twice," 1967
Leslie Bricusse, John Barry
TABLE 8

"You Oughta Be in Pictures," 1934
Edward Heyman/Dana Suesse
WOMEN AS SONGWRITERS

"You Oughta Be With Me," 1972
Al Green, Willie Mitchell, Al Jackson
SOUL

"You Really Got Me," 1964
Ray Davies
ROCK-iii

"You Remind Me of My Mother," 1922
George M. Cohan
MOTHERS

"You Send Me," 1957
Sam Cooke
TABLE 4-d, RHYTHM AND BLUES, SOUL

"You Should Be Dancing," 1976
Barry Gibb, Maurice Gibb, Robin Gibb
DANCING

"You Should Hear How She Talks About You," 1981
Tom Snow, Dean Pitchford
TABLE 10-f

"You Showed Me," 1965
Gene Clark, Jim McGuinn
ROCK-v

"You Stepped Out of a Dream," 1940
Gus Kahn/Nacio Herb Brown
COMPOSERS, DREAMS, TABLE 9

"You Talk Too Much," 1960
Joe Jones, Reginald Hall
TALKING

"You Tell Me Your Dream, I'll Tell You Mine," 1908
Charles N. Daniels, Jay Blackton, Albert H. Brown, Seymour Rice
DREAMS, GAY NINETIES

"You Took Advantage of Me," 1928
Lorenz Hart/Richard Rodgers
ALLITERATION, POPULAR SONG-iv, TEMPO

"You Turn Me On, I'm a Radio," 1972
Joni Mitchell
ROCK-vi

"You Turned the Tables on Me," 1936
Sidney D. Mitchell/Louis Alter
BEBOP

"You Two-Timed Me Once Too Often," 1945
Jenny Lou Carson
WOMEN AS SONGWRITERS

"You Wear It Well," 1972
Rod Stewart, Martin Quittenton
ROCK-x

"You Were Made for Me," 1963
Mitch Murray
ROCK-iii

"You Were Meant for Me," 1929
Arthur Freed/Nacio Herb Brown
TABLE 9

"YOU'RE THE TOP," 1934
Cole Porter
TABLE 3, CATALOGUE SONG, COMPOSER-
LYRICISTS, CONTRACTIONS, GOLDEN AGE,
LYRICISTS, MUSICAL COMEDY, TABLE 11,
SUPERLATIVES

"YOU'RE TOO DANGEROUS, CHERIE," SEE "LA
VIE EN ROSE"

"YOURS (QUIÉREME MUCHO)," 1937
Jack Sherr, Albert Gamse (Eng.)/Gonzalo Roig
TABLE 3, TABLE 4-d, BOLERO, WORLD WAR II

"YOURS FOR A SONG," 1939
Billy Rose, Ted Fetter, Dana Suesse
WOMEN AS SONGWRITERS

"YOURS IS MY HEART ALONE (DEIN IST MEIN
GANZES HERZ)," 1931
Harry Bache Smith (Eng.)/Franz Lehár
TABLE 2, AUSTRIA, HUNGARY

"YOU'VE GOT A FRIEND," 1971
Carole King
FOLK ROCK, FRIENDSHIP, TABLE 10-b, TABLE
10-g, PERFORMER-SONGWRITERS, ROCK-vi,
WOMEN AS SONGWRITERS

"YOU'VE GOT ME CRYING AGAIN," 1933
Charles Newman/Isham Jones
CRYING

"YOU'VE GOT THAT THING," 1929
Cole Porter
TABLE 11, SLANG

"YOU'VE LOST THAT LOVIN' FEELIN'," 1964
Barry Mann, Phil Spector, Cynthia Weil
TABLE 4-c, FEELING, LOVE, ROCK 'N' ROLL,
WOMEN AS SONGWRITERS

"YOU'VE MADE ME SO VERY HAPPY," 1967
Brenda Holloway, Patrice Holloway, Frank Wilson,
Berry Gordy, Jr.
TABLE 4-d, HAPPINESS, ROCK-ix

"ZIGEUNER," 1929
Noël Coward
COMPOSER LYRICISTS, GYPSY MUSIC, TABLE
13

"ZING WENT THE STRINGS OF MY HEART,"
1935
James Hanley
TABLE 2

"ZIP-A-DEE-DOO-DAH," 1945
Ray Gilbert/Allie Wrubel
TABLE 1, TABLE 9, NONSENSE, SINGING
GROUPS

"ZORBA THE GREEK," SEE "THEME FROM ZORBA
THE GREEK"

Index

Page numbers of principal entries (which appear in small caps) are in boldface. In general, page numbers refer only to items substantially covered in the articles. For song titles, see "Catalogue of Songs," pp. 351–545.

About the General Editor

Marvin E. Paymer is a pianist, composer, and musicologist. He received his Ph.D. in Music from the City University of New York and has taught at York and Hunter Colleges. He is an internationally recognized authority on the authenticity of the hundreds of musical works attributed to the eighteenth-century Neapolitan composer Giovanni Battista Pergolesi, the vast majority of which, according to Paymer, are false. He is author or co-author of numerous articles and several books on the subject, including *Pergolesi: A Guide to Research* (Garland, 1989). He has received fellowships from the Andrew Mellon Foundation and the National Endowment for the Humanities and is co-founder of the Pergolesi Research Center and of the new Pergolesi *Complete Works*.

In addition to his research activities, Paymer has had an active career as pianist and music director, largely in the field of American popular music. His familiarity with many of the songs of the past hundred years encouraged him to undertake this project, in which he considers a much-neglected and seldom analyzed American art form which is as popular with today's public as the arias of Italian opera were two centuries ago.